Environmental Law and Policy

FOURTH EDITION

William A Tilleman

Alastair R Lucas

Sara L Bagg

Patricia Galvão Ferreira

Toronto, Canada
2020

Emond Montgomery Publications Limited
1 Eglinton Ave E, Suite 600
Toronto ON M4P 3A1

Printed in Canada.

We acknowledge the financial support of the Government of Canada and the assistance of the Government of Ontario.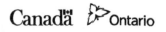

Emond Publishing has no responsibility for the persistence or accuracy of URLs for external or third-party Internet websites referred to in this publication, and does not guarantee that any content on such websites is, or will remain, accurate or appropriate.

Vice president, publishing: Anthony Rezek
Publisher: Danann Hawes
Director, development and production: Kelly Dickson
Production manager: Laura Bast
Production editor: Natalie Berchem
Copy editor: Rose Knecht
Permissions editor: Nadine Bachan
Typesetter: Amnet
Proofreader: Judy Hemming

Library and Archives Canada Cataloguing in Publication

Title: Environmental law and policy / William A. Tilleman, Alastair R. Lucas, Sara L. Bagg, Patricia Galvão Ferreira.

Names: Tilleman, William Arthur, II, 1955- editor. | Lucas, Alastair R., editor. | Bagg, Sara L., editor. | Galvão Ferreira, Patricia, editor.

Description: Fourth edition. | Previously published: Toronto: Emond Montgomery Publications, 2003.

Identifiers: Canadiana 20190135506 | ISBN 9781772555585 (hardcover)

Subjects: LCSH: Environmental law—Canada.

Classification: LCC KE3619 .E585 2019 | LCC KF3775.ZA2 E58 2019 kfmod | DDC 344.7104/6—dc23

To my 91-year-old mother, Jean Tilleman, who continues to provide life's stable navigation beacon to me, my family, and collectively to her 21 grandkids and 41 great-grandkids.

—William Tilleman

For Sandy.

—Alastair Lucas

For Esmé, Charlotte, Oliver, and Stella and their right to a healthy environment. For nature, with thanks.

—Sara Bagg

To Dirceu, my father, in memoriam.

—Patricia Galvão Ferreira

FOREWORD

Preparing and publishing a successful casebook in an area of law that is both highly specialized and very broad is no mean feat. Students require a resource that provides them with a comprehensive understanding of the law and the polices that provide the underpinning for this important field of study and practice. But that is just the starting point. Equally important is the need to provide students with a framework or the tools to make sense of such a complex, multifaceted, and dynamic field of law. Hardly a day goes by without another, often contradictory, scientific or political development that impacts environmental law. How to build a teaching and learning resource that is comprehensive, forward looking, and optimistic in the face of so many dire environmental events around the world today? This is indeed a challenge.

What, then, should the ultimate goal of the fourth edition of the *Environmental Law* casebook be? To describe the law as it is, knowing that what is, is soon likely to change? As the law might be, given the current political and scientific thinking, and knowing that what is needed and promised today may be difficult to achieve? As the law should be, knowing that the prospect of agreement on any "should" is highly elusive? Settling on any one of these approaches requires first that the authors agree on a specific body of law that they can confidently assert makes up the basis of a fine environmental law casebook. Domestic law clearly deserves a central place in the book. But what of international environmental law, trans-border issues, Indigenous environmental law, and citizen rights and standing? And finally, for those who believe that this is not simply an academic exercise, what can society expect in terms of a better environment from the teaching, scholarship, and, most importantly, practice of environmental law that the fourth edition of the casebook supports?

With many of these questions on their minds, a group of environmental scholars and practitioners met in 2008 (D Paul Emond, "'Are We There Yet?' Reflections on the Success of the Environmental Law Movement in Ontario" (2008) 46:2 Osgoode Hall LJ 219) in round table format to ask, "Are we there yet?" What, if anything, have we achieved of the "promise" of environmental law? The question invited participants to reflect on what the teaching academy had accomplished over the last 40-plus years and what remained to be done and to debate the prospects for the future. The question is somewhat reminiscent of one that is often asked on a long trip, especially by those who are not directing the trip. And the answer? For the optimist it is, "We're almost there. It is just around the next corner." For the pessimist, "No; don't keep asking. Can't you see how difficult this journey is?" And for the realist, "No. Be patient; we are doing the best we can. Soon, I hope, but who knows what lies around the next corner?" And so it is with environmental protection, conservation, and resource management. We are not there, but we are working on it. And the current work is being led by the outstanding authorial team behind this casebook.

At the 2008 round table, the participants all confessed to early optimism with the passage of key legislation in the 1970s and noted that some progress had been made; that slippage had occurred in certain areas; and, yes, that there is still much—no, a great deal—more work to do on the laws and policies, but especially on imbuing society with a culture of respect and care for the natural environment and our place in it. Until that happened, the short answer to the question, "Are we there yet?" is a resounding "No." I might add that recent events seem to have pushed the prospect of achieving the early promise of environmental law somewhat further into the future.

This led the round table to ask, "Who is most likely to bring about the much-needed changes, knowing that our needs will certainly change but that more positive action is a must?" Who are the pioneers of the next environmental law movement? The near unanimous answer was that change would come from the next generation of environmental law and environmental studies students. The future lay in the hands of successive generations of students committed to improving the environment. From the vantage point of summer 2019, one must also add, change must also come from the next generation of politicians because some current leaders seem intent on undoing much of what has been done over the last 40 years.

For students to assume this important role, they need three things. First, inspired teachers. Second, a passion to make a positive difference. This is something that many environmental law and environmental studies students have in spades. In some cases, it is what attracted them to study environmental law and policy. For those who didn't start their environmental law and studies courses with passion, they are often infected by the passion of their classmates and instructor. Finally, students need very good learning resources. This is where *Environmental Law and Policy*, Fourth Edition comes in. Twenty-five years in the making, each edition of the casebook has been a substantial improvement over earlier editions. Al Lucas and Bill Tilleman, who have been a part of each edition, have been joined by Sara Bagg and Patricia Galvão Ferreira, and together these four general editors have assembled a much expanded, more diverse, and very strong group of contributors. I have said before that the authorship of this casebook is a veritable who's who of environmental law scholarship and practice. That tradition has grown with the fourth edition. Twenty-four chapters authored by 30 editors/contributors from eleven law faculties speaks to the breadth of experience and perspective of those who are participating in this grand project to "get us there."

The fourth edition features the obvious—much increased coverage of the topic from an increased number of contributors; a focus on emerging areas of the field, including Indigenous environmental law and the now well-established duty to consult; the role of global environmental law and the tools it offers in responding to both domestic as well as international environmental challenges; and the central place of environmental ethics and the duties it imposes. The book also offers a very thoughtful chapter on ecological principles by two senior scholars, and, of course, a concluding chapter on the future of environmental law and its role in "getting us there." Woven throughout the book is a focus that moves from substantive law to process and back again. Obligations and duties to protect the environment are an essential first step, but the process by which these ends are achieved is equally important. The result is a new chapter on implementing sustainability and an expanded and deeper dive into administrative law principles and strategies.

All authors, contributors, and, especially, publishers struggle with the questions of what and how much to include in their casebooks. Too much and the book will be accused of lacking focus; too little and it will frustrate those who want a comprehensive work on the subject that can be used for future research. My preference has always been in favour of more. The faculty will decide what to teach and how to teach it. The students will see the value of a resource that offers more than just enough for their course. It is a reference work for further research; a guide for future practice. And, as for buying material that won't be used in class, don't worry. The additional cost of the expanded and better version of the casebook is really very little.

The fourth edition of *Environmental Law and Policy* is, in my view, very close to the ideal. Its goal, simply put, is to make a lasting contribution to the study and practice of environmental law and policy. And that is what it has done and will continue to do.

D Paul Emond
January 2020

PREFACE

Publishing a textbook in a specialized area of law involves authors and editors embracing the responsibility to provide students with a comprehensive understanding of the relevant case law, as well as the rules, regulations, and policy considerations required to practise in that area. When the first edition of *Environmental Law and Policy* was published in 1993, accomplishing this goal involved collecting cases piecemeal in an attempt to pull together, for the first time, the environmental laws of Canada. First edition editors Elaine Hughes, William Tilleman, and Alastair Lucas faced a sparse environmental law landscape. The preface to this first edition spoke to societal concerns about the environment and the necessity of creating a reference which would assist teachers and students alike in understanding environmental law and its relationship to science, politics, economics, and philosophy.

A distinctly weighty obligation rested on the editors of this 2020 edition given the wide range of challenges to the environment—including pollution, species elimination, habitat destruction, dwindling resources, and climate change—which are increasingly affecting humans and other living beings in Canada and beyond. This obligation—and this opportunity—was to enlist a large group of authors working on the leading edge of environmental law and policy scholarship and practice to facilitate professors, practitioners, and students of environmental law reflecting on the current state of our environment and on the role of law in addressing complex environmental problems. This resulting volume covers a broad range of environmental topics and perspectives in 24 chapters (expanded from the 16 chapters of the third edition). The textbook addresses not only basic environmental law concepts and themes, but also current shifts and trends in our understanding of the global and national environment and consequent legal developments. This new edition of *Environmental Law and Policy* could hardly be more opportune or more necessary.

In May of 2019, the Intergovernmental Science-Policy Platform on Biodiversity and Ecosystem Services (IPBES) assessed changes to our global environment over the past five decades and published a shocking report concerning the current state of nature, providing a comprehensive picture of the relationship between economic development and its impact.[1] The report, compiled by 145 expert authors from 50 countries over the past three years, makes the following findings:

- Three-quarters of the land-based environment and about 66% of the marine environment have been significantly altered by human actions. On average these trends have been less severe or avoided in areas held or managed by Indigenous Peoples and Local Communities.
- More than a third of the world's land surface and nearly 75% of freshwater resources are now devoted to crop or livestock production.
- The value of agricultural crop production has increased by about 300% since 1970, raw timber harvest has risen by 45% and approximately 60 billion tons of renewable and nonrenewable resources are now extracted globally every year—having nearly doubled since 1980.
- Land degradation has reduced the productivity of 23% of the global land surface, up to US$577 billion in annual global crops are at risk from pollinator loss and 100-300

---

1   IPBES, *The Global Assessment Report on Biodiversity and Ecosystem Services: Summary for Policymakers* (2019), online (pdf): <https://zenodo.org/record/3553579/files/ipbes_global_assessment_report_summary_for_policymakers.pdf>

million people are at increased risk of floods and hurricanes because of loss of coastal habitats and protection.

- In 2015, 33% of marine fish stocks were being harvested at unsustainable levels; 60% were maximally sustainably fished, with just 7% harvested at levels lower than what can be sustainably fished.
- Urban areas have more than doubled since 1992.
- Plastic pollution has increased tenfold since 1980, 300–400 million tons of heavy metals, solvents, toxic sludge and other wastes from industrial facilities are dumped annually into the world's waters, and fertilizers entering coastal ecosystems have produced more than 400 ocean "dead zones," totalling more than 245,000 km2 ... a combined area greater than that of the United Kingdom.
- Negative trends in nature will continue to 2050 and beyond in all of the policy scenarios explored in the Report, except those that include transformative change—due to the projected impacts of increasing land-use change, exploitation of organisms and climate change, although with significant differences between regions.[2]

The IPBES report adds to the series of three special reports the Intergovernmental Panel on Climate Change (IPCC) has released in 2018 and 2019: The *Special Report on Global Warming of 1.5°C*, the *Special Report on Climate and Land* and the *Special Report on Ocean and Cryosphere*.[3] Together, these three reports unequivocally demonstrate the need to strengthen the global response to climate change in order to promote the major and immediate transformation we need to avoid the devastating consequences allowing global warming to reach 2° or higher would have in our health, livelihoods, food security, water supply, human security, and long-term economic growth. The IPCC reports make it clear that we have the technical and the economic capacity to address climate change. The major obstacle is mastering the political will, and much depends on what countries such as Canada—which ranks among the ten largest greenhouse gas emitters in absolute terms and one of the top emitters *per capita*—will prove able to do.

Similar concerns arise with endangered species. Almost 50 years ago, the *Endangered Species Act* (USA 1973) passed and became a necessary and effective tool to protect endangered species and their habitat. Canada's *Species at Risk Act* dates from 2002. Some of the early concerns, including dates, were: 1914, the passenger pigeon became extinct; 1944, the whooping crane population reached its lowest level ever, with only 21 birds remaining. A minor victory came in 1972, when the USEPA outlawed DDT as a pesticide for its harmful effects on humans and wildlife, including bald eagles and peregrine falcons. Canada followed suit in the same year. There has also been some species recovery success: 1994, eastern north pacific gray whales were delisted due to recovery; 1994, the Arctic peregrine falcon was delisted due to recovery; 1999, the American peregrine falcon was delisted due to recovery; and 2007, the bald eagle was delisted following its recovery. These facts show how powerful and effective endangered species legislation can be. According to Ray Johnson, a prominent US fish and wildlife biologist, species can recover, but we need to have a plan and to act before they become threatened or endangered. He also says that we as humans are part of the ecosystem, our continued existence is dependent on how well we keep that ecosystem intact, and it would be a travesty if we lost a species that might help us survive.

---

2   IPBES, Press Release, "Nature's Dangerous Decline 'Unprecedented' Species Extinction Rates 'Accelerating'" (6 May 2019), online: *UNEP—UN Environment Program* <https://www.unenvironment.org/news-and-stories/press-release/natures-dangerous-decline-unprecedented-species-extinction-rates>

3   IPCC, *Special Report on Global warming of 1.5°C (SR 1.5)* (2018); IPCC, *Special Report on Climate Change and Land (SRCCL)* (2019); IPCC, *Special Report on the Ocean and Cryosphere in a Changing Climate* (2019); all available online: *IPCC* <https://www.ipcc.ch/about>

This book begins with an introduction to global environmental issues, as well as fundamental ecological, ethical, and legal thinking around such issues. It then moves to core legal issues and concepts, including international influences, common law principles, and remedies. From there, it moves on to constitutional jurisdiction and provincial versus federal regulatory regimes. The book examines emerging municipal and Indigenous jurisdictions and the development of environmental law in the Canadian Arctic. It also examines legal approaches ranging from command and control to risk-centred, market-based systems and environmental rights. A series of chapters present various preventative and remedial approaches to environmental issues, including protection of spaces and species, pollution prevention and contaminated site remediation, and enforcement and compliance. Some chapters concern new perspectives on law and policy strategies to engage current environmental problems. The book concludes with a chapter focusing on the future of environmental law.

Due to the global nature of our environmental challenges, this book gives greater attention than previous editions to international environmental law and its growing influence on Canadian law and policy. The integrity of global ecosystems, particularly centred on the idea of sustainability, is a recurring theme in the chapters to follow. The particularly urgent need for effective legal and policy responses to the threat presented by climate change is included mainly in the chapter on climate change, but it also permeates the chapters on international and domestic legal instruments and environmental rights. These chapters reveal the fundamental conflicts—between citizens and governments, between federal and provincial governments, and between provincial governments—that are emerging with unprecedented intensity concerning how to address global climate change. The legal issues surrounding interjurisdictional pipelines, as well as oil well abandonment and remediation, have produced judicial decisions pushing Canadian federalism's traditional boundaries.

This fourth edition contains comprehensive treatment of ecology and issues in environmental ethics. The insightful and impactful 1994 essay William Rees wrote for the first edition is revised for the new 2020 context. Additional chapters on ethics, sustainability, and environmental justice provide insights and working materials on the legal concepts and strategies essential for coming to grips with today's environmental issues in a social and political context. In this volume, readers will learn the fast-developing relationship between Canadian environmental law and Aboriginal rights and title concepts—as increasingly these concepts are being deployed to challenge the adequacy of Crown consultation in the regulatory processes designed to evaluate the legitimacy of major natural resource development projects.

Please enjoy this book.

ABOUT THE AUTHORS

Presently, **Sara L Bagg** is a justice of the peace of the provincial court of Alberta. Prior to this, she was engaged mainly in legal analysis and writing, specializing in the areas of administrative, environmental and regulatory law. Dr Bagg was a member of the Nunavut Bar and advised regulatory boards in the North on responsible resource development in accordance with the Nunavut Agreement. As a PhD (Philosophy), Dr. Bagg has thought deeply about the relationship between our moral obligations, our failure to recognize such obligations, and the current state of the environmental laws of Canada as a result.

Patricia Galvão Ferreira is an assistant professor of transnational law at the University of Windsor Faculty of Law. Besides teaching international environmental law and environmental law, she directs the Transnational Environmental Law and Policy Clinic. Her scholarship encompasses international, national, and sub-national dimensions of environmental law and policy, with a current focus on climate change. Dr Galvão-Ferreira holds a BA from UFBA (Brazil), an LLM from the Notre Dame University Faculty of Law (USA), and an SJD from the University of Toronto Faculty of Law, which she earned concurrently with a PhD on Dynamics of Global Change from the Munk School of Global Affairs.

Alastair R Lucas, QC is a professor emeritus and the associate director at the Canadian Institute of Resources Law (CIRL), University of Calgary Faculty of Law. He is a former dean of law at Calgary and has served as an acting member of Alberta's Energy Resources Conservation Board, a policy advisor at Environment Canada, and the director of the Sustainable Energy Development (SEDV) Interdisciplinary MSc Program at the University of Calgary. His research interests focus on energy and environmental regulation.

William Tilleman has been a justice with the Court of Queen's Bench since 2009. He was Alberta's first chair of the Environmental Appeals Board and later chaired Alberta's Energy and Utilities Board. Tilleman graduated from Columbia University School of Law and was adjunct full professor of law at the University of Calgary.

Nigel Bankes is a professor of law and holder of the Chair of Natural Resources Law at the University of Calgary. He was an adjunct professor of law with the KG Jebsen Centre for the Law of the Sea, at UiT (the University of Tromsø), the Arctic University of Norway from 2012 to August 2019. He posts on developments in Canadian oil and gas and energy law at ABlawg: <http://ablawg.ca>.

Brett Carlson is an associate in Borden Ladner Gervais' Commercial Litigation and Public Policy and Government Relations groups. Brett maintains a general litigation practice with experience in energy-related disputes and regulatory proceedings, as well as public, administrative law, and appellate matters. Prior to entering the legal profession, Brett worked as a policy advisor to the federal minister of environment.

Joseph F Castrilli is counsel with the Canadian Environmental Law Association (CELA) in Toronto. He is a member of the Ontario and British Columbia bars and is certified as a specialist in environmental law by the Law Society of Ontario. He has appeared before all levels of court, including the Supreme Court of Canada; taught environmental law at several Ontario law schools; and authored numerous articles, book chapters, and texts on the subject.

Nathalie Chalifour is an associate professor with the Centre for Environmental Law and Global Sustainability at the University of Ottawa, where she researches and teaches about environmental law and justice, climate change and the Constitution, and sustainability. She obtained her PhD in law from Stanford University and is elected to the Royal Society of Canada's College of New Scholars.

Géraud de Lassus St-Geniès, LLD is lecturer at the Laval University Faculty of Law, where he teaches environmental law, climate law, and international law.

Georgios Dimitropoulos is an associate professor at Hamad Bin Khalifa University College of Law (HBKU Law). Georgios studied law at the University of Athens and holds an LLM from Yale Law School and a PhD *summa cum laude* from the University of Heidelberg. Before joining HBKU Law, he was a senior research fellow at the Max Planck Institute Luxembourg and a Hauser Research Scholar at New York University (NYU) School of Law.

Stewart Elgie is a professor of law at the University of Ottawa. He is the founder and chair of the Smart Prosperity, a national environment–economy research institute, and the co-founder of Canada's Ecofiscal Commission, which advances market-based approaches to protect the environment. Previously, he was the founder of Ecojustice, Canada's largest environmental litigation organization and led the seven-year campaign to create Canada's *Species at Risk Act*.

Heather Fast, BA, JD, LLM is a PhD student at the Natural Resources Institute at the University of Manitoba. She is also a lawyer and a sessional professor at the Robson Hall Faculty of Law who specializes in the area of environmental governance. Heather's legal experience and graduate studies have been focused on the issues of public participation, law reform, and access to environmental justice.

Shaun Fluker is an associate professor at the University of Calgary Faculty of Law. He has published on a variety of topics related to environmental law, and he practises in public interest environmental litigation with the Public Interest Law Clinic at the University of Calgary.

Brenda L Gunn, BA, JD, LLM is an associate professor at the University of Manitoba Faculty of Law. As a proud Métis woman, she continues to combine her academic research with her activism pushing for greater recognition of Indigenous peoples' inherent rights as determined by Indigenous peoples' own legal traditions. Her current research focuses on promoting greater conformity between international law on the rights of Indigenous peoples and domestic law.

Paule Halley, LLD is a professor of law and holder of the Canada Research Chair in Environmental Law at the Université Laval Faculty of Law and a member of the Québec Bar. Halley has published a number of articles, papers, and books in the field of environmental law and sustainable development. Her work has been recognized at the national and international level (Prix Michel-Jurdant en sciences de l'environnement by the Association francophone pour le savoir [ACFAS, 2015], Prix scientifique de la Francophonie by the Conseil scientifique de l'Agence Universitaire de la Francophonie [AUF, 2005], and first prize for best monograph by the Québec Bar Foundation [2003]).

Allan Ingelson is the executive director of the Canadian Institute of Resources Law and a professor in the University of Calgary Faculty of Law who has published numerous articles in Canadian and international scholarly energy and environmental law journals on the regulation of hydraulic fracturing, produced water disposal and liability for induced seismicity.

Cameron SG Jefferies is an associate professor with the University of Alberta Faculty of Law. Dr. Jefferies's work focuses on matters of international and domestic environmental law, oceans law and policy, wildlife conservation, and tort law.

Arlene J Kwasniak, BSc (Eastern Michigan University), MA (Wayne State University), LLB (University of Alberta), LLM (Lewis and Clark, Northwestern School of Law) is, at the University of Calgary, professor emerita of law, Faculty of Law; adjunct professor, Faculty of Environmental Design; and senior research fellow, Canadian Institute of Resources Law. Arlene has been a member of the Alberta Law Society since 1981, has served on numerous policy/resource management committees, and has written several books.

Sharon Mascher is a professor at the University of Calgary and an honorary fellow at the University of Western Australia. Sharon teaches and researches in the area of climate change law with a focus on liability and responsibly and carbon pricing.

Karin Mickelson is an associate professor at the Allard School of Law, University of British Columbia.

Walters Nsoh, PhD (Law, University of Surrey), LLM (Distinction) (Environmental Law & Policy, University of Kent), and BSc (Hons) (Environmental Science, University of Buea, Cameroon) is a lecturer in law in the Birmingham Law School. His research and teaching interests relate primarily to the intersection between environmental and property (land) law and the regulation and governance of natural resources. Dr Nsoh has published in leading peer-reviewed journals and edited collections in the UK and internationally, and is the co-author of *The Privatisation of Biodiversity? New Approaches to Conservation Law* (Edward Elgar, 2016).

Damilola S Olawuyi, LLM (Calgary), LLM (Harvard), DPhil (Oxford) is an associate professor of law at Hamad Bin Khalifa University Law School, Qatar and Chancellor's Fellow and director at the Institute for Oil, Gas, Energy, Environment and Sustainable Development, Afe Babalola University, Nigeria. Email: dolawuyi@hbku.edu.qa.

Martin Olszynski is an associate professor at the University of Calgary Faculty of Law and a research fellow with the Canadian Institute of Resources Law. He obtained his BSc and LLB degrees from the University of Saskatchewan and an LLM from the University of California at Berkeley, and he is currently pursuing a PhD in regional land-use planning at the University of British Columbia's Institute for Resources, Environment and Sustainability.

William E Rees, PhD, FRSC is a human ecologist, ecological economist, professor emeritus and former director of UBC's School of Community and Regional Planning. The originator and co-developer of ecological footprint analysis, Rees has published hundreds of peer reviewed and popular articles on (un)sustainability. His work is globally recognized and frequently awarded.

Dayna Nadine Scott is an associate professor at Osgoode Hall Law School and the Faculty of Environmental Studies at York University. In 2018, she was appointed York University research chair in Environmental Law and Justice in the Green Economy.

Katie Sykes is associate professor at the Thompson Rivers University Faculty of Law. Her main area of research is animals and the law. She is the co-editor (with Peter Sankoff and Vaughan Black) of *Canadian Perspectives on Animals and the Law* (Irwin Law, 2015) and has published numerous articles on Canadian and international law concerning animal protection.

Chidinma B Thompson, PhD, FCIArb is a lawyer, trained arbitrator, and a partner at Borden Ladner Gervais LLP, Calgary. She practises law in the area of disputes, focusing on environmental, energy, and natural resources law. Chidinma has taught law courses, contributed book chapters, and worked as a legal researcher in various institutions. She frequently publishes articles and blogs and speaks at law conferences, and she has been honoured with awards including the Women in Law Leadership Award and the Young Women in Energy inaugural award.

Marcia Valiante is professor emerita in the University of Windsor Faculty of Law and has served as vice-chair of the Environmental Review Tribunal and Member of the Local Planning Appeal Tribunal and the Conservation Review Board in Ontario.

Kristen van de Biezenbos is an assistant professor at the University of Calgary Faculty of Law and Haskayne School of Business. She teaches and writes on the intersections of energy regulation, communities, access, and justice.

David V Wright is an assistant professor and a member of the Natural Resources, Energy and Environmental Law Research group at the University of Calgary Faculty of Law. He teaches in the areas of environmental and natural resources law.

SUMMARY TABLE OF CONTENTS

DETAILED TABLE OF CONTENTS

Chapter Nine   Environmental and Toxic Torts: Legal Realities and

TABLE OF CASES

This table includes cases referred to by the authors. It does not include cases cited within the reproduced texts and reports. A bold-face page number indicates that a (partial) report of the case is reproduced in the text.

ACKNOWLEDGMENTS

This book, like others of its nature, contains extracts from published materials. We have attempted to request permission from and to acknowledge in the text all sources of such material. We wish to make specific reference here to the authors, publishers, journals, and institutions that have been generous in giving their permission to reproduce works in this text. If we have inadvertently overlooked any acknowledgment, we offer our sincere apologies and undertake to rectify the omission in any further editions.

Agreement between the Government of Canada and the Government of the United States of America on the Conservation of the Porcupine Caribou Herd, Can TS 1987 No 31 (entered into force 17 July 1987). Reproduced with permission of Global Affairs Canada, Ottawa, 2019.

Agreement on the Conservation of Polar Bears, (15 November 1973) © 1973 United Nations. Reprinted with the permission of the United Nations.

Ambec, Stefan et al, "The Porter Hypothesis at 20: Can Environmental Regulation Enhance Innovation and Competitiveness?" (2013) 7:1 Rev Envtl Econ & Policy 2 at 2, 5, 13. Reproduced by permission of Oxford University Press on behalf of the Association of Environmental and Resource Economists.

Anand, R & IG Scott, QC, "Financing Public Participation in Environmental Decision Making" (1982) 60:1 Can Bar Rev 81 at 87-94 [footnotes omitted]. Copyright © 1982 Can Bar Rev by R Anand and IG Scott.

Barral, Virginie, "Sustainable Development in International Law: Nature and Operation of an Evolutive Legal Norm" (2012) 23:2 EJIL 377 at 383-85. Reprinted by permission of Oxford University Press on behalf of EJIL Ltd.

Berger, Thomas R, Northern Frontier, *Northern Homeland: The Report on the Mackenzie Valley Pipeline Inquiry,* vol 1 (Ottawa: Minister of Supply and Services Canada, 1977). Permission granted by the Privy Council Office. © Her Majesty the Queen in Right of Canada (2019)

Bosselmann, Klaus, "The Meaning of Sustainability" in *The Principle of Sustainability: Transforming Law and Governance,* 2nd ed (Florence: Taylor and Francis, 2016) ch 1 at 8-15 [footnotes omitted]. Copyright © 2017 Klaus Bosselmann and Routledge, reproduced by permission of Taylor & Francis Books UK.

Boyd, David R, *Cleaner, Greener, Healthier* (Vancouver: UBC Press, 2015) at 25, 139. Reprinted with permission of the Publisher. © University of British Columbia Press 2015. All rights reserved by the publisher.

Boyd, David R, *The Right to a Healthy Environment: Revitalizing Canada's Constitution* (Vancouver: UBC Press, 2012) at 6. Reprinted with permission of the Publisher. © University of British Columbia Press 2012. All rights reserved by the publisher.

Boyd, David R, *The Rights of Nature: A Legal Revolution that Could Save the World* (Toronto: ECW Press, 2017) at 230-31.

Brown, Katrina, "Global Environmental Change I: A Social Turn for Resilience?" (2014) 38:1 Progress in Human Geography 107 at 109, 114. Copyright © 2014 by SAGE Publications. Reprinted by Permission of SAGE Publications, Ltd.

Bruch, Carl et al, *Environmental Rule of Law: First Global Report* (United Nations Environmental Programme, 2019). © 2019 United Nations. Reprinted with the permission of the United Nations.

Canada, "Follow-Up Report to the House of Commons Standing Committee on Environment and Sustainable Development on the Canadian Environmental Protection Act, 1999," submitted by the Minister of Environment and Climate Change and the Minister of Health to the House of Commons Standing Committee on Environment and Sustainable Development on June 29, 2018. Courtesy of Environment and Climate Change Canada (ECCC).

Canada, *Pan-Canadian Framework on Clean Growth and Climate Change* (Gatineau, Qc: Environment and Climate Change Canada, 2016). Courtesy of Environment and Climate Change Canada (ECCC).

Canada, Commissioner of the Environment and Sustainable Development, *2016 Fall Reports of the Commissioner of the Environment and Sustainable Development, Report 4* (Ottawa: Government of Canada, 2016). Office of the Auditor General of Canada. Reproduced with the permissions of Her Majesty the Queen in Right of Canada, as represented by the Auditor General of Canada, 2020.

Canada, Environment and Climate Change Canada, "Maps of Subpopulations of Polar Bears and Protected Areas: Circumpolar Polar Bear Subpopulation and Status Map 2018" (last modified 6 June 2018). © IUCN/Polar Bear Specialist Group

Canadian Environmental Assessment Agency, *Report of the Federal Review Panel—New Prosperity Gold-Copper Mine Project* (31 October 2013) at 21. Reproduced with the permission of the Impact Assessment Agency of Canada.

Council of Canadian Academies, "Relative Densities (Low to High) of Human Access in Canada" from *Greater Than the Sum of Its Parts: Toward Integrated Natural Resource Management in Canada* (Ottawa: The Expert Panel on the State of Knowledge and Practice of Integrated Approaches to Natural Resource Management in Canada).

Craig, Robin Kundis & Melinda Harm Benson, "Replacing Sustainability" (2013) 46 Akron L Rev 841 at 847-49, 850, 858-60, 862, 865-66 [footnotes omitted].

Driedger, EA, "Statutes: Retroactive Retrospective Reflections" (1978) 56 Can Bar Rev 264 at 268-69. Copyright © 1978 Can Bar Rev by EA Driedger.

Eisen, Jessica, "Beyond Rights and Welfare: Democracy, Dialogue, and the Animal Welfare Act" (2018) 51:3 U Mich JL Ref 494 at 469-547.

Field, BC & ND Olewiler, *Environmental Economics*, 1st ed (Cdn) (Toronto: McGraw-Hill Ryerson, 1995) at 69-78. Reproduced with permission of McGraw-Hill Ryerson Ltd.

Forest Practices Board v Ministry of Forests and Riverside Forest Products Ltd (11 June 1996), Decision No 95/01(a) (BC Forest Appeals Commission), online: <https://www.fac.gov.bc.ca/forestPracCode/95-01a.pdf>. British Columbia Forest Appeals Commission. Copyright © 2019, Province of British Columbia

French, Duncan & Louis J Kotzé, "Introduction" in Duncan French & Louis J Kotzé, eds, *Sustainable Development Goals: Law, Theory and Implementation* (Northampton:

Edward Elgar, 2018) at 1-2 and 3-5. © The Editors and Contributing Authors. Reproduced with permission of the Licensor through PLSclear.

Gunn, Brenda L, "Beyond Van der Peet: Bringing Together International, Indigenous and Constitutional Law", 29-37, in *UNDRIP Implementation: Braiding International, Domestic and Indigenous Laws* (Waterloo, Ont: Centre for International Governance Innovation, 2017) 29. © 2017 Centre for International Governance Innovation. Reproduced by permission.

Hale, Benjamin, "Private Property and Environmental Ethics: Some New Directions" (2008) 39:3 Metaphilosophy 402 at 406. DOI: <10.1111/j.1467-9973.2008.00550.x> © 2008 The Author. Journal compilation © 2008 Metaphilosophy LLC and Blackwell Publishing Ltd.

Hardin, G, "The Tragedy of the Commons" (1968) 162 Science 1243 at 1244. Reprinted with permission from AAAS.

Impact Assessment Agency of Canada, *Federal Assessments in Progress* (July 2019). Reproduced with the permission of the Impact Assessment Agency of Canada. Please note there is a potential variation in projects from day to day.

Kimmel Jr, JP, "Disclosing the Environmental Impact of Human Activities: How a Federal Pollution Control Program Based on Individual Decision Making and Consumer Demand Might Accomplish the Environmental Goals of the 1970s in the 1990s" (1989) 138 U of Pa L Rev 505 at 526, 527-29 [footnotes omitted]. Republished with permission of University of Pennsylvania, Law School. © 1989; permission conveyed through Copyright Clearance Center, Inc.

Kotzé, Louis J, "Rethinking Global Environmental Law and Governance in the Anthropocene," (2014) 32:2 J Energy & Nat'l Res L 121 at 136-37. Reprinted by permission of the publisher (Taylor & Francis Ltd, <https://www.tandfonline.com>).

Leopold, Aldo, *A Sand County Almanac* (New York: Oxford University Press, 1949). © Oxford Publishing Limited Academic, 1949. Reproduced with permission of the Licensor through PLSclear.

Maitre-Ekern, Eléonore & Carl Dalhammar, "Regulating Planned Obsolescence: A Review of Legal Approaches to Increase Product Durability and Reparability in Europe" (2016) 25:3 RECIEL 378 at 378, 379, 379-380, 381, 387 and 387-388. Reprinted from Review of European, Comparative & International Environmental Law (RECIEL). Copyright by John Wiley & Sons, Inc.

Mascher, Sharon. "Striving for equivalency across the Alberta, British Columbia, Ontario and Québec carbon pricing systems: the Pan-Canadian carbon pricing benchmark," (2018) 18:8 Climate Policy at 1012-1027. <https://www.tandfonline.com>.

McCulloch, Paul & Danielle Meuleman, "Strategic Decisions in Environmental Prosecutions" in Allan Ingelson, ed, *Environment in the Courtroom* (Calgary: University of Calgary Press, 2019) ch 15 (endnotes omitted). Used with permission.

Muldoon, P & B Rutherford, "Environment and the Constitution: Submission to the House of Commons Standing Committee on Environment" (Toronto: Canadian Environmental Law Association and Pollution Probe, 1991), appendix E (edited).

Odum, William E, "Environmental Degradation and the Tyranny of Small Decisions" (1982) 32:9 Bioscience 728 at 728-29. Reproduced by permission of Oxford University Press on behalf of the American Institute of Biological Sciences.

Pellow, David N, "Critical Environmental Justice Studies: Black Lives Matter as an Environmental Justice Challenge" (2016) 13:2 Du Bois Rev 22 at 223. Justice Challenge-Corrigendum. Du Bois Review: Social Science Research on Race, reproduced with permission.

Philip, Christopher, CEAA Assessments Concluding Significant Adverse Environmental Effects Likely (1993–2016). The author of the chapter is grateful to Christopher Philip, UCalgary Law JD 2016, for permission to use this graph.

Polinsky, AM, *An Introduction to Law and Economics*, 2nd ed (Toronto: Little, Brown & Co, 1989) at 11-14. Reproduced with the permission of CCH Incorporated (ISBN 9780316712781).

Public Caribou Management Board, Porcupine Caribou Core Range and Protected Areas. Published by permission of the Porcupine Caribou Management Board, <https://www.pcmb.ca>.

Roberge, David E, "Nuisance Law in Quebec (Article 976 C.C.Q.): 10 Years After Ciment du Saint-Laurent, Where Do We Stand?" (2017) 76 R du B 321 at 336-37, 340 [footnotes omitted].

Rodríguez-Garavito, César, "A Human Right to a Healthy Environment? Moral, Legal and Empirical Considerations" in John H Knox & Ramin Pejan, eds, *The Human Right to a Healthy Environment* (Cambridge: Cambridge University Press, 2018) 155 at 157-58 (internal citations omitted). © Cambridge University Press. Reproduced with permission of the Licensor through PLSclear.

Sands, Philippe & Jacqueline Peel, "Principles of international environmental law" (Cambridge University Press, 2018) ch 1. © Phillipe Sands. Reproduced with permission of the Licensor through PLSclear.

Scott, Dayna Nadine, "Environmental Justice and the Hesitant Embrace of Human Rights" in James R May and Erin Daly, *Human Rights and the Environment: Legality, Indivisibility, Dignity and Geography*, Elgar Encyclopedia of Environmental Law (Cheltenham: Edward Elgar Press and the IUCN Academy of Environmental Law, 2019) at 453-55. © The editors and contributing authors. Reproduced with permission of the Licensor through PLSclear.

Shepheard, Mark L, "Farming, Good Neighbours, and Protecting the General Interest in Water Resources: How Effective Is the Promise of Sustainable Watershed Management in Quebec?" (2017) 13:2 McGill J of Sustainable Development L 271 at 280-82, 297-98 [footnotes omitted]. This research was undertaken with a Banting Postdoctoral Fellowship at McGill University's Faculty of Law. The author acknowledges the Social Sciences and Humanities Research Council of Canada for this award.

Teisl, MF, B Roe & RL Hicks, "Can Eco-Labels Tune a Market? Evidence from Dolphin-Safe Labeling" (2002) 43:3 J Envtl Econ & Mgmt 339 at 339-41 [footnotes omitted]. © 2002, with permission from Elsevier.

Thaler, Richard & Cass R Sunstein, *Nudge: Improving Decisions about Health, Wealth, and Happiness* (New Haven: Yale University Press, 2008) at 5-6 (endnotes omitted). © Yale University Press.

Tribe, Laurence H, "Ways Not to Think about Plastic Trees: New Foundations for Environmental Law" (1974) 83:7 Yale LJ 1315. Republished with permission of Yale Law

Journal Company, Inc., © 1974; permission conveyed through Copyright Clearance Center, Inc.

United Nations General Assembly, *The Future We Want*, UN General Assembly Resolution 88/288 of 27 July 2012, 66th Sess, UN Doc A/RES/66/288, Annex (11 September 2012). From "Outcome Document" by United Nations General Assembly, © 2012 United Nations. Reprinted with the permission of the United Nations.

United Nations General Assembly, Human Rights Council, *Report of the Special Rapporteur on the Issue of Human Rights Obligations Relating to the Enjoyment of a Safe, Clean, Healthy and Sustainable Environment*, UNAGOR, 31st Sess, UN Doc A/HRC/31/52 (1 February 2016) at paras 24-30. © 2016 United Nations. Reprinted with the permission of the United Nations.

United Nations Human Rights Council, *Final Report of the Study on Indigenous Peoples and the Right to Participate in Decision-Making: Expert Mechanism on the Rights of Indigenous Peoples*, UNHRC, 18th Sess, UN Doc A/HRC/18/42, 17 (2011). © 2011 United Nations. Reprinted with the permission of the United Nations.

United Nations Human Rights Council, *Free, Prior and Informed Consent: A Human Rights-Based Approach: Study of the Expert Mechanism on the Rights of Indigenous Peoples*, UNHRC, 39th Sess, UN Doc A/HR C/39/62 (2018). © 2018 United Nations. Reprinted with the permission of the United Nations.

US Environmental Protection Agency, US ENERGY STAR program. <www.energystar.gov>

Van De Biezenbos, Kristen, "The Rebirth of Social Licence" (2019) 14:2 MJSDL 153 at 162-65 [footnotes omitted].

Vasil, Adria, "What Canada's climate coalition looks like," *NOW Magazine*, July 8, 2015. Quoted material from Graham Reeder, "The next steps towards a new kind of climate movement" (July 18, 2015).

Victoria, City of, Minutes—Victoria City Council (17 January 2019) at 22. Office of the Mayor. © City of Victoria.

Waldron, Ingrid RG, *There's Something in the Water: Environmental Racism in Indigenous and Black Communities* (Halifax: Fernwood, 2018) at 2, 45, 84, 132, 44 (citations omitted).

Wood, Mary Christina, *Nature's Trust: Environmental Law for a New Ecological Age* (Cambridge: Cambridge University Press, 2013) ch 15 at 344-346, 349 and 350-351. © Mary Christina Wood. Reproduced with permission of the Licensor through PLSclear.

Wood, Patricia K & Liette Gilbert, "Multiculturalism in Canada: Accidental Discourse, Alternative Vision, Urban Practice" (2005) 29:3 Intl J Urban & Regional Research 679 at 682-83. DOI: <10.1111/j.1468-2427.2005.00612.x>

Wood, Stepan, Georgia Tanner & Benjamin J Richardson, "What Ever Happened to Canadian Environmental Law?" (2010) 37 Ecology LQ 981-1040 at 993-995, 1006-7, 1038-40 [footnotes omitted]. © 2010 by the Regents of the University of California by permission of the Regents of the University of California.

Wright, David V, "Federal Linear Energy Infrastructure Projects and the Rights of Indigenous Peoples: Current Legal Landscape and Emerging Developments" (2018) 23:1 Rev Const Stud 175 [footnotes omitted]. Originally published in (2018) 23:1 Review of Constitutional Studies.

CHAPTER ONE

THE ENVIRONMENT: ECOLOGICAL AND ETHICAL DIMENSIONS

William Rees and Karin Mickelson

I. INTRODUCTION

A. "ENVIRONMENTAL" LAW: SOCIAL MYTH OR ECOLOGICAL REALITY?

How any society relates to biophysical reality is profoundly affected by an elaborate set of accepted "facts," unquestioned assumptions, and entrenched beliefs about the world that are derived from the historical and cultural experience of its people. It is a culture's "story" about reality that provides the "context in which life [can] function in a meaningful manner and pro-foundly affects how [its people] act in the world."[1] In short, every culture expresses a world view or narrative that shapes its social relationships, its political institutions, and the nature of its economic enterprise.

We raise this fact to acknowledge that there can be as many world views as there are cul-tures and that each such narrative only more or less coincides with reality. Thus, our most sacred beliefs, however well sustained by the evidence to date, may simply be wrong. The important point is that while we may think we are acting from fact, much individual activity and government policy is undertaken on the basis of unsubstantiated *belief*. We will argue below that much of contemporary environmental law derives from erroneous perceptions and, thus, remains ecologically naïve. Indeed, much of our contemporary cultural narrative is little more than socially constructed myths, a collection of "shared illusions."[2]

B. SUSTAINABLE DEVELOPMENT AS A CONTEXT FOR CHANGE

The need to revisit the historic underpinnings of "environmental law" arises in the context of society's continuing efforts to shift to a more sustainable development path.[3] The potentially revolutionary quest for sustainability was stimulated by the publication of *Our Common Future*, the 1987 report of the World Commission on Environment and Development (the Brundtland commission).[4]

The Brundtland commission defined sustainable development as "development that meets the needs of the present without compromising the ability of future generations to meet their own needs"[5] but was curiously ambiguous in elaborating on its own definition. Emphasizing the role of poverty in the ecological degradation of less-developed countries (with less emphasis on the role of wealth and consumption in the North), the commission equated sustainable development with "more rapid economic growth in both industrial and developing countries" on grounds that "economic growth and diversification ... will help developing coun-tries mitigate the strains on the rural environment."[6] Consistent with this interpretation is the commission's observation that "a five- to tenfold increase in world industrial output can be anticipated by the time world population stabilizes sometime in the next century."[7] This

---

1 Thomas Berry, *The Dream of the Earth* (San Francisco: Sierra Club Books, 1988) at 123.

2 See Stafford Beer, "I Said, You Are Gods" (1981) 15:3 Teilhard Rev 1 at 5-8.

3 Part of this section is revised from William E Rees, "Defining 'Sustainable Development,'" CHS Research Bulletin, Bul 89-1 (Vancouver: UBC Centre for Human Settlements, 1989); William E Rees, "Sustainable Development and the Biosphere: Concepts and Principles," Teilhard Studies No 23 (Chambersburg, Pa: American Teilhard Association, 1990); and William E Rees, "The Ecology of Sustainable Development" (1990) 20:1 The Ecologist 18 at 18-23.

4 (Oxford: Oxford University Press, 1987) [Brundtland commission report].

5 *Ibid* at 43.

6 *Ibid* at 89.

7 *Ibid* at 213. This pace may seem extraordinary, but the economy has ballooned hundredfold in real terms just since the early 19th century: Max Roser, "Economic Growth" (last visited 30 July 2019), online: *Our World in Data* <https://ourworldindata.org/economic-growth#gdp-growth-since-1950>.

reflection of the prevailing expansionist world view guaranteed an enthusiastic reception of the commission's report in corporate boardrooms and by conservative governments everywhere.

At the same time, in recognition of the additional stress that such growth implies for the environment, the commission cast sustainable development in terms of more material- and energy-efficient resource use; new, ecologically benign technologies; and "a production system that respects the obligation to preserve the ecological base for development"[8] while guaranteeing "the sustainability of ecosystems on which the global economy depends."[9] Such environmental caveats seemed sufficient to capture the imagination of mainstream environmentalism and ensured nearly universal acceptance of the commission's report. In their initial enthusiasm, hardly anyone seemed to notice the commission's failure to analyze either the structural roots of poverty in our present economic system or whether the prescribed scale of material growth is biophysically possible under any conceivable production system.

Not surprisingly, following the Brundtland commission report, most mainstream prescriptions for sustainability required little more than modest adjustments to the status quo.[10] By contrast, in this chapter, we argue that sustainable development implies a fundamental shift in social attitudes and material expectations and a reconceptualization of the industrial economy. Many scientists believe that accelerating rates of resource depletion, gross pollution, and systems destabilization (including climate change) represent serious threats to critical life-support functions of the ecosphere. These negative trends cannot be corrected through improvements in material efficiency, so-called green technologies, and better waste treatment alone. Stabilizing and reversing global ecological decline requires that we revisit our growth-based cultural narrative, repurpose much economic activity, and restructure relevant sociopolitical institutions.

Our starting premise is that our present economic, legal, and institutional framework is unequal to this challenge. If the dominant social paradigm is fundamentally flawed, incremental changes in existing legal instruments would be counterproductive. Any major shift in societal values, objectives, and goals will require parallel changes in governance structures, including the regulatory environment. In short, rather than adjusting existing humankind–environment relationships, environmental law for sustainable development should help advance and entrench changes in the nature of those same relationships.

C. OUR PREVAILING CULTURAL MYTH

The modern or "scientific" world view is framed by French philosopher René Descartes's mechanical view of the universe as "a vast machine, wound up by God to tick forever."[11] Descartes extended his mechanistic model to include living organisms; he even saw human thought as an iterative mechanical process by which the mind confronts the world as a separate object. Descartes's separation of the observer from the observed and his reductionist approach provided the methodological framework for subsequent scientific enquiry and helped formalize the notion of objective knowledge.

In important ways, Sir Isaac Newton succeeded in validating the Cartesian world view. His 1687 *Principia* gave us apparently universal laws of mass and motion that describe the universe as a mechanical machine of unlimited dimensions behaving according to strict mathematical rules. For the first time, humankind had a body of science that satisfied Descartes's

8 Brundtland commission report, *supra* note 4 at 89.

9 *Ibid* at 67.

10 See Canadian Council of Resource and Environment Ministers (CCREM), *Report of the National Task Force on Environment and Economy* (Ottawa: CCREM, 1987) for a well-known Canadian example.

11 Morris Berman, *The Reenchantment of the World* (New York: Bantam, 1984) at 21.

mechanistic vision, including deterministic predictability, and promised humans the ability to manipulate nature indefinitely toward their own ends.

By the end of the 17th century, the mechanistic science had abolished the ancient perception of the Earth as a living entity. Religious superstition was in retreat and spiritual life much diminished. Scientific materialism provided the technical foundation of industrial society, the philosophical basis of market economics, and helped entrench a new myth of human dominance over the natural world. To be sure, postmodern philosophers have rejected the simplistic determinism of "normal" (Cartesian) science, and complex systems theory is beginning to undermine our confidence that nature is knowable and can be bent predictably to serve human purposes (discussed below). However, as we approach the third decade of the 21st century, industrial society still operates primarily from the belief that "nothing in nature can resist the human will." In effect, human beings "through technological advance [will seek] to simulate and redesign to our liking all biological processes, so that we may achieve ever more control over the conditions of life."[12] The arrogance of this anthropocentric utilitarian narrative permeates every aspect of modern life—our social relationships, the structure of our economic systems, the legal/institutional framework erected to support it, and the ethical framing from which we regulate our relationship to the natural world.

II. ECOLOGICAL PRINCIPLES

A. PURPOSE AND INTRODUCTION

The growth-oriented economics of techno-industrial global society pays little heed to the biological, chemical, and physical principles that ultimately govern real-world material and energy transformations. Existing environmental law reflects the prevailing bias. By contrast, in this section, we argue that certain immutable biophysical laws should shape the core of humanity's relationship with nature.

B. ECONOMICS AS HUMAN ECOLOGY?

For present purposes, ecology might be defined as the scientific study of the cooperative and competitive relationships that have evolved among organisms in natural ecosystems and how these relationships serve to determine the flows of vital energy and material resources among constituent species. Similarly, economics is defined as the scientific study of means for the efficient allocation of scarce resources among competing users in human society. Thus, ecology and economics share not only the same semantic roots, but also much of the same substantive focus. It could even be argued that economics is a branch of human ecology.

Or rather, it should be—the theoretical foundations of these sister disciplines have diverged significantly since their founding in the late 19th century. As already implied, contemporary neoclassical/neoliberal economics—which has enjoyed a remarkably uncritical sweep through the modern world over the past half century—finds its deepest roots in the concepts and methods of Newtonian analytic mechanics. By contrast, systems ecology draws on modern biology, chemistry, physics, complex systems theory, and the thermodynamic laws that regulate energy and material transformations in the natural world.

We are, therefore, confronted with a double irony in coping with problems of human economies and ecosystems. Ecologists, who possess appropriate theory, have mostly studied

---

12   William Leiss, "Instrumental Rationality, the Domination of Nature and Why We Do Not Need an Environmental Ethic" in Philip P Hanson, ed, *Environmental Ethics: Philosophical and Policy Perspectives* (Burnaby, BC: Institute for the Humanities, Simon Fraser University Publications, 1986) 175 at 178-79.

non-human species and have only recently begun to perceive *Homo sapiens* as an ecological entity. Meanwhile, mainstream economists, who deal with humans exclusively, treat people as mechanical automatons, devoid of family or community and isolated entirely from nature. This explains why, until recently, neither discipline has opened much of a window on the global human ecological crisis. We explore this conundrum below.

C. ECONOMY AS MECHANISM

Inspired by Newtonian physics, neoclassical economics was conceived as a sister science, "the mechanics of utility and self-interest."[13] Its founders abstracted the economic process from nature, viewing it as an independent and "self-sustaining circular flow between production and consumption," in which "complete reversibility is the general rule, just as in mechanics."[14] But there is a problem. Seeing the economy in terms of a self-generating circular flow without considering the unidirectional throughput of energy/material is akin to studying physiology as a circulatory system with no reference to the digestive track. One might as well ask engineering students to fathom how "a car can run on its own exhaust" or biology students to accept that "an organism can metabolize its own excretia."[15] Indeed, prevailing economic theory "lacks any [physical] representation of the materials, energy sources, physical structures, and time-dependent processes that are basic to an ecological approach."[16] It relies on analytic models based on reductionist assumptions about resources, people, firms, and technology that bear little relationship to their counterparts in the real world.

A major tenet of the neoclassical school is the belief that resources are more the product of human ingenuity than they are of nature. According to economic theory, rising market prices for scarce materials encourage conservation on the one hand and stimulate technological substitution on the other (for example, solar electricity for fossil fuel generation). It is part of the conventional wisdom of mainstream economists that market factors have been more than sufficient to overcome emerging resource scarcities.[17] Standard neoclassical texts, therefore, conclude that "exhaustible resources do not pose a fundamental problem."[18] Neoliberal economists have even dropped land/resources from their production functions—that is, nature's contribution to economic growth is negligible.[19]

Neither do we perceive pollution as a serious constraint on the human enterprise. Society accepts the degradation of ecosystems as a necessary trade-off against economic growth. We pollute in exchange for jobs or income and see the point at which to stop largely as a matter

---

13 William Jevons, *The Theory of Political Economy*, 5th ed (New York: Augustus M Kelley, 1965) at 21.

14 Nicholas Georgescu-Roegen, "Energy and Economic Myths" (1975) 41:3 South Econ J 347 at 348. In the circular flows model, firms pay wages/salaries to households in exchange for labour (national income); households use the money to purchase goods and services from firms (national product), enabling the cycle to repeat itself.

15 Herman E Daly, "The Circular Flow of Exchange Value and the Linear Throughput of Matter-Energy: A Case of Misplaced Concreteness" in *Steady-State Economics*, 2nd ed (Washington, DC: Island Press, 1991) ch 10 at 197.

16 Paul Christenson, "Driving Forces, Increasing Returns and Ecological Sustainability" in Robert Costanza, ed, *Ecological Economics: The Science and Management of Sustainability* (New York: Columbia University Press, 1991) 75 at 76.

17 Peter A Victor, "Indicators of Sustainable Development: Some Lessons from Capital Theory" (1991) 4:3 Ecol Econ 191.

18 Partha Dasgupta & Geoffrey Heal, *Economic Theory and Exhaustible Resources* (London: Cambridge University Press, 1979) at 205.

19 Martin Wolf, "Why Were Resources Expunged from Economics?" (12 July 2010), *Wolfexchange*, online (blog): *Financial Times* <http://blogs.ft.com/martin-wolf-exchange/2010/07/12/why-were-resources-expunged-from-neo-classical-economics>.

of negotiated public choice (that is, there are no systemic thresholds or other "fatal" repercussions along the way). Economists define the unaccounted damage costs of pollution as "externalities"—market imperfections—that we can "internalize" through investment in improved technology, better regulation, or pollution charges (for example, carbon taxes), if society chooses to get the prices right.

In summary, the neoclassical perspective sees the natural environment as little more than an aesthetic static backdrop to human affairs. Unburdened by any sense of significant environment–economy connectedness, mainstream analysts and politicians readily associate "sustainable development" with sustained economic growth abetted by technological progress. Governments acknowledge "environmental" concerns but as only one of many sets of competing values and interests. The presumption is that within a broadly anthropocentric, utilitarian framework, society will ultimately arrive at a politically "practical" interpretation of sustainable development through power-brokering, negotiation, and compromise. Biophysical absolutes have no seat at the bargaining table.

D. IN CONTRAST, ECOLOGICAL REALITY

The ecological world view holds that, despite our technological wizardry and purported mastery over the natural environment, humans are fundamentally similar to the millions of other species with which we share the planet. Like all other organisms, we survive and grow by extracting energy and materials from the ecosystems of which we are a part; like all other organisms, we "consume" these resources before returning them in altered form to those ecosystems. From this perspective, far from existing in splendid isolation, the human economy is and always has been an inextricably integrated, completely contained, and wholly dependent subset of the ecosphere.[20]

There are, of course, differences of degree and kind between humans and other organisms. For example, the Scientific/Industrial Revolution has (temporarily) freed *Homo sapiens* from various "negative feedbacks" (disease, starvation, resource scarcity, etc.) that normally hold population growth in check—and to spectacular effect. It took all of previous human history— 200,000 years—for our population to reach one billion in the early 1800s, but only 200 years— 1/1000th as much time!—to hit 7.6 billion in 2018. Meanwhile, the economy has ballooned hundredfold. (Ironically, this growth spurt, which people today take to be the norm, is actually the *single most anomalous period in history* and will almost certainly be reversed this century.)

The resultant surge in economic throughput is both imposing ever-mounting demands on biocapacity and permanently altering the chemistry of the ecosphere. Human-dominated ecosystems must cope not only with the natural metabolites of our bodies but also with thousands of industrial metabolites, the synthetic by-products of economic activity. While organic metabolites are readily assimilated and recycled, there is often no assimilative capacity for synthetics. Indeed, many industrial chemicals are dangerously toxic. These realities demand reanalysis of human–environment linkages.

1. Obligate Dependence

From a strictly anthropocentric perspective, the ecosphere provides three types of critical functions that sustain humankind. First, the ecosphere is the source of all material economic resources (increasingly referred to as "natural capital"). Some resources, such as air, water, and

---

20 Herman E Daly, "Uneconomic Growth in Theory and in Fact" (The First Annual Feasta Lecture, delivered at Trinity College, Dublin, 26 April 1999), (2001) Feasta Review No 1, online: *Feasta* <http://www.feasta .org/documents/feastareview/daly.htm>.

food, we consume directly. Others serve as raw material inputs to the production of economic goods and services. There are several categories of resources:

- non-renewable resources, such as petroleum, of which there are finite exhaustible stocks;
- renewable or self-producing resources, such as plants, animals, and entire ecosystems that are capable of regeneration;
- replenishable resources, including clean air, water, and soil, various components of which (for example, oxygen) are the products of biological processes and involved in continuous recycling (we all have carbon and other atoms that were once in dinosaurs);
- continuing resources such as solar radiation, wind, and tides that are limited in local availability or rate of supply but are essentially inexhaustible.

The second function of the ecosphere is waste assimilation. "Waste" includes the organic excretia and dead bodies of plants and animals, as well as industrial metabolites and the "dead bodies" of worn out manufactured products themselves. Natural organic matter and nutrients can be processed and recycled repeatedly through the ecosphere—this is essential to systems continuity (and explains why there is no real waste in nature). Industrial metabolites and products are more problematic. Some synthetics are non-reactive (biologically inert); others are toxic or otherwise harmful to life. Because of bioaccumulation, the environment may be said to have a near-zero tolerance for highly active toxins such as chemical carcinogens and radionuclides.

Third, the ecosphere provides certain "services" to humankind. These include aesthetic amenities such as ski slopes, beaches, and spectacular views. More important, however, are various life-support functions *essential to life as we know it*, including photosynthesizing food and fibre, maintaining atmospheric composition, stabilizing the climate, restoring the ozone layer, and assimilating carbon in vegetation and soils. While it is theoretically and practically impossible to price such services accurately,[21] they clearly have a great positive economic value. A pioneering 1997 study of the economic contribution of just 17 ecosystem services in 16 ecological regions estimated their worth at US$16-54 trillion per year (averaging $33 trillion) compared to a then total gross global product of US$18 trillion.[22]

2. The New Science: A World of Chaos

In recent decades, the world has seen the consolidation of a second scientific revolution. The seeds were planted with the development of Einsteinian relativity and quantum mechanics but have flowered with new mathematical tools and the astonishing number-crunching capacity of modern computers. Our mechanical paradigm is beginning to give way to a view of nature that, while still deterministic at its roots, is relentlessly non-linear. Terms such as "complexity theory," "deterministic chaos," and "non-linear dynamics" capture the flavour of the paradigm shift fairly well.

This new science of complex systems has serious implications for the assumptions regarding prediction and standards of proof that underlie environmental law.

Both theoretical and empirical studies reinforce the idea that the interaction of the simple laws of physics and chemistry can produce systems behaviour of extraordinary complexity. Conversely, systems of inordinate complexity are able to generate patterns of beautiful simplicity. Perhaps most important is the recognition that the interplay of even strictly deterministic

---

21 William E Rees, "Why Conventional Economic Logic Won't Protect Biodiversity" in DM Lavigne, ed, *Gaining Ground: In Pursuit of Ecological Sustainability* (Guelph, Ont: International Fund for Animal Welfare, 2006) 207, online (pdf): <https://s3.amazonaws.com/ifaw-pantheon/sites/default/files/legacy/gaining-ground/ifaw-gaining-ground-chapter-14.pdf>.

22 Robert Costanza et al, "The Value of the World's Ecosystem Services and Natural Capital" (1997) 387 Nature 253.

rules can quickly generate patterns of systems behaviour that are inherently unpredictable even if we possess near-perfect knowledge of the initial state of the system. To the extent that such counterintuitive behaviour is characteristic of real-world ecosystems, economic systems, and social systems, it requires a serious re-evaluation of dominant decision models and the prevailing approach to development and the environment.

Two classes of phenomena are particularly relevant to this issue. The first is the apparent "chaos" that can emerge from even the simplest dynamical system. In simplest terms, a dynamical system is one governed by strict rules such that the state of the system at any point in time unambiguously determines the future state of the system. In theory, then, if we know how the system is behaving now, we can predict what it will look like at any point in the future. In a model system, this requires simply performing an iterative sequence of calculations. The outcome of any calculation in the sequence both determines the next state of the system and provides the starting values for the subsequent iteration (that is, the model system's behaviour is governed by internal feedback).

This seems the very essence of predictable order, of Newtonian mechanism: simply determine the rules governing the behaviour of the system and insert the starting values, and the future will unfold without any surprises. However, when we attempt to model many real world phenomena, the state of the model *after just a few iterations* bears no evident relationship to its corresponding reality. The problem often lies in small measurement errors (or seemingly negligible differences in starting conditions). The internal dynamics of the model are such that these errors are fed back and amplified with each iteration. Given sufficient time, any inaccuracy will derail the model. Better measurement does not help, at least not for long. The bottom line is this: the tiniest, unavoidable, measurement error can render even a perfect model useless in predicting real-world systems behaviour very far in advance.

The general problem is called "sensitive dependence on initial conditions,"[23] and the behaviour it produces in mathematical models and real systems—even simple ones—is called chaos. Chaotic behaviour has always existed, but generally went unnoticed in our dedication to normal (Cartesian) science. If actually encountered, it was ignored because the math was too difficult. Now that computers are up to the task, "the dreadful truth has become inescapable: Chaos is everywhere. It is just as common as the nice simple behavior so valued by traditional physics."[24] Chaos explains why even the best computer models cannot predict the weather next week with complete confidence.

The second phenomenon is the unexpected, dramatic (that is, "catastrophic") change that can occur in previously stable systems under stress. Key variables of complex systems, including ecosystems, may range considerably within broad domains of stability. We have learned that, within these domains, all points tend to converge toward a centre of gravity called an "attractor."[25] Traditional dynamical models used in forecasting are characterized by a single equilibrium (a point attractor) or a repeating cycle of values (a periodic attractor). Chaotic systems, by contrast, trace a complex, often elegant, highly organized pattern of *individually unpredictable paths* that collectively define a "strange attractor" within the stable domain as internal feedback continually changes the system's dynamics. In any iteration, the system will retain its familiar overall character and behaviour *as long as key variables remain under the influence of their customary attractors*.

---

23 Sometimes called the butterfly effect—the flap of a butterfly's wing in New Guinea sets off a tornado in Texas the following week.

24 Jack Cohen & Ian Stewart, *The Collapse of Chaos* (New York: Penguin Books, 1994) at 190.

25 James J Kay in "A Nonequilibrium Thermodynamic Framework for Discussing Ecosystem Integrity" ((1991) 15:4 Environ Manage 483) refers to the stable domain and its attractor as the "thermodynamic branch" and "optimum operating point," respectively.

Although not evident from historical observations, dynamical systems may have several attractors separated by unstable "ridges" or bifurcations (picture a terrain of watersheds each isolated from the others by irregular hills and ridges). "Catastrophe" occurs when a key systems variable, perhaps driven by some persistent change in an important control factor, is displaced far from its usual attractor. If the variable reaches a bifurcation or tipping point (the top of a ridge), it may be captured by an adjacent attractor (valley) instead of returning to its accustomed domain. Suddenly, the quality of the system changes dramatically. Indeed, "catastrophe" is characterized by large discontinuous breaks in systems characteristics and behaviour resulting from incrementally small changes in key variables. If there is a final marginal change in temperature, pressure, or population, the whole system will flip into a new stability domain controlled by a different attractor.

If the new domain is part of a previously natural, human-managed system, it may now be hostile to human purposes, and there is *no guarantee that the system will ever return to its former state*. Complex systems ranging from commercial fisheries, malaria control, and acid-sensitive lakes to the Gulf stream, global climate, and the economy are prone to catastrophic behaviour. Ominously, James Kay has been "unable to find a single example of an ecosystem flipping back after undergoing such a dramatic reorganization."[26]

There are further worrisome complications. First, neither the existence nor the nature of multiple attractor(s), simple or chaotic, is knowable before the fact. Second, the very act of exploiting or otherwise manipulating the system changes its internal dynamics and shifts the location of both its attractor(s) and the bifurcations between them. Third, a customary attractor may shrink or disappear under stress, and new ones may emerge spontaneously.

All of this increases the probability of human-caused catastrophe. Politicians and policymakers must now be aware that any persistent incremental stress may increase the probability of dramatic qualitative and quantitative changes in the future state of critical systems, both the nature and magnitude of these changes are inherently unpredictable, and natural systems may become less resilient and more brittle the more humans exploit them.

It is precisely these concerns that stimulated climate scientists to warn that "even if the Paris Accord target of a 1.5°C to 2.0°C rise in temperature is met, we cannot exclude the risk that a cascade of feedbacks could push the Earth System irreversibly onto a 'Hothouse Earth' pathway."[27] Similar grave concerns were evident in the special report of the Intergovernmental Panel on Climate Change (IPCC) on the consequences of 1.5°C mean global warning (which is now virtually inevitable).[28] We ignore such findings at considerable risk to the human enterprise. Humans have become the dominant force in global ecological change, and there is every reason to believe that we are driving essential biophysical variables toward multiple unknown strange attractors.

3. The "Environmental" Crisis: Human Ecological Dysfunction

A continuous, adequate, and reliable supply of the three ecosphere functions described earlier is a necessary precondition for civilized existence. The functional integrity of the ecosphere is not something that can be indefinitely bargained away or "traded off" against other economic benefits. Ominously, the cumulative impact of precisely such trade-offs, in the form of thousands of individually insignificant decisions, has become the defining characteristic of the eco-crisis. By 2016, the human ecological footprint—the area of productive ecosystems required to produce the bio-resources used by people and to assimilate humanity's carbon

---

26 *Ibid* at 487.

27 Will Steffen et al, "Trajectories of the Earth System in the Anthropocene" (2018) 115:33 PNAS 8252, DOI: <https://doi.org/10.1073/pnas.1810141115>.

28 "Summary for Policymakers" in *Special Report: Global Warming of 1.5 °C* (2018), online: *IPCC* <https:// www.ipcc.ch/sr15/chapter/spm/>.

wastes—had reached about 20.5 billion hectares compared to the approximately 12.2 billion adequately productive hectares on Earth.[29] This shows that the human enterprise is in "overshoot" by approximately 69 percent—human consumption and waste production vastly exceed the regenerative and assimilative capacities of ecosystems.

Humanity can live in overshoot for a limited period because of the vast accumulations of natural capital in nature (for example, forests, fish stocks, soil, groundwater, and the atmosphere). However, we must recognize that, at present, population and economic growth are being "funded" by the liquidation of essential natural capital and the destruction of vital life-support functions. Consider the accelerating loss of biodiversity caused by the human competitive displacement of other life forms from their habitats and energy supplies (that is, food). From a fraction of 1 percent in Paleolithic times, *Homo sapiens* now comprises 36 percent, and farm animals another 60 percent, of the world's total mammalian biomass. Wild mammals cling to the edge with only 4 percent. (Humans plus livestock actually outweigh all other vertebrates combined [excluding fish].)[30] Other negative trends from contaminant accumulation to climate change similarly put other plant and animal groups at risk—even insects are experiencing "Armageddon" (and insect-dependent birds are not far behind).[31] We have yet to contemplate the ethical and legal implications of this human-induced "sixth extinction."

Clearly, the environmental crisis is one of human ecological dysfunction, not of ecosystems failure. It complicates matters that, as the economy expands, the human enterprise is likely pressing key biophysical variables ever closer to catastrophic tipping points. In short, there is a finite possibility that for all the *apparent* success of technology in freeing us from the whims of nature, we could actually be "on the verge of extinction, blissfully unaware that a mathematical fiction in the space of the possible is about to become reality. And the really nasty feature is that it may take only the tiniest of changes to trigger the switch."[32]

4. More Bad News: The Economy as Consumption

Economists' failure to appreciate the biophysical basis of the economic process is a crucial disciplinary shortcoming. Contrary to the assumptions of neoclassical economics, the ecologically relevant flows through the economy are not circular money flows but, rather, one-way energy and matter flows. This is because thermodynamic law, not static mechanics, regulates all energy and material transformations in all subsystems of the ecosphere, including the human enterprise.

Of particular relevance is the second law of thermodynamics (the entropy law): in every material transformation, useful (high-grade) energy/matter is irreversibly degraded to a more disordered, less useful state.[33] Thus, the economic process invariably feeds on useful

29 William E Rees, "Ecological Footprint, Concept of" in SA Levin, ed, *Encyclopedia of Biodiversity*, 2nd ed, vol 2 (Waltham, Mass: Academic Press, 2013) 701; most recent (2016) data from Global Footprint Network, "Country Trends" (last visited 20 August 2019), online: <http://data.footprintnetwork.org/#/countryTrends?cn=5001&type=BCtot,EFCtot>.

30 Yinon M Bar-On, Rob Phillips & Ron Milo, "The Biomass Distribution on Earth" (2018) 115:25 PNAS 6506, DOI: <https://doi.org/10.1073/pnas.1711842115>.

31 Caspar A Hallmann et al, "More Than 75 Percent Decline over 27 Years in Total Flying Insect Biomass in Protected Areas" (2017) 12(10):e0185809 PLOS ONE, DOI: <https://doi.org/10.1371/journal.pone.0185809>; see also Damian Carrington, "Insect Collapse: 'We Are Destroying Our Life Support Systems,'" *The Guardian* (15 January 2019), online: <https://www.theguardian.com/environment/2019/jan/15/insect-collapse-we-are-destroying-our-life-support-systems>.

32 Cohen & Stewart, *supra* note 24 at 212.

33 For example, gasoline is transformed into heat energy (which performs work) plus waste carbon dioxide and water. See Georgescu-Roegen, *supra* note 14 and "The Steady State and Ecological Salvation: A Thermodynamic Analysis" (1977) 27:4 BioScience 266.

high-grade energy/matter first produced by nature and returns it to the ecosphere as low-grade waste.[34] Most of the latter returns almost immediately, but even finished products eventually wear out and join the waste stream. In effect, the second law dictates that the material economy necessarily increases global net entropy (disorder) and, thus, frames the human enterprise as a massive "dissipative structure."[35] Without reference to this one-way entropic throughput, "it is impossible to relate the economy to the environment," yet the concept is "virtually absent from economics today."[36]

Perhaps the most ecologically relevant insight from this is recognition that all stages of economic "production" require consumption. Since the scale of the human enterprise is increasing, and the ecosystems upon which it depends is not, consumption virtually everywhere exceeds sustainable rates of bioproduction even as the resultant pollution undermines remaining productive capacity. Much of today's wealth, therefore, is an illusion, derived from the irreversible conversion of natural capital into perishable manufactured capital on the one hand and the dissipation of often toxic waste throughout the ecosphere on the other.

World economic output increased twelvefold between 1950 and 2015 alone[37] and is now generating havoc at the level of the ecosphere itself. Persistent deterioration of key environmental variables is no mere "externality" but, rather, symptomatic of severe ecological dysfunction. (William E Rees argues that evident unsustainability is an inevitable "emergent property" of the interaction of techno-industrial society, as presently configured, and the ecosphere.[38])

Prevailing confidence in markets and technological innovation to resolve this conundrum is misplaced. Prices, costs, and profits, which are the primary scarcity indicators offered by the neoclassical school, fail utterly when the assumptions upon which they are based do not apply.[39] For example, while scarcity-induced high prices may stimulate the search for substitutes in the case of non-renewable market commodities such as lithium, they are silent when it comes to valuing the essential non-market ("free") goods and services provided by nature.[40] The industrialized world is currently basking in the apparent triumph of capitalism and the prospect of vigorous material growth to support as many as 11 billion people (compare with 7.7 billion in 2019), yet even current rates of consumption and pollution are rapidly eroding essential life support, and we cannot depend on market signals to sound the alarm.

As noted, the real-world connectedness of the economy and the ecosphere generates biophysical forces and trends that may not be reversible if pressed beyond unseen tipping points. Unlike mainstream economics, ecological economics, therefore, argues that "public choice" respecting environmental quality is seriously constrained. Indeed, on one level, we have no choice. Humanity depends utterly on the integrity of the ecosphere; maintaining life

---

34 Material recycling may seem to contradict this principle. However, recycling is never 100 percent efficient and always involves the dissipation of *additional* energy and matter.

35 As defined by Ilya Prigogine (with Isabelle Stengers), *The End of Certainty* (New York: The Free Press, 1997). For example, a new automobile represents only a fraction of the energy and material that has been permanently "dissipated" as pollution in the manufacturing process (typically 25 metric tonnes per tonne of finished vehicle).

36 Herman E Daly, "Sustainable Development: From Concept and Theory Toward Operational Principles" in *Steady-State Economics*, 2nd ed, *supra* note 15, ch 13 at 241 [Daly, "Sustainable Development: From Concept and Theory"].

37 Roser, *supra* note 7.

38 "Globalization and Sustainability: Conflict or Convergence?" (2002) 22:4 Bull Sci Technol Soc 249.

39 Victor, *supra* note 17.

40 The ozone layer is a compelling example. It went from worthless to priceless as soon as its function was recognized and threatened.

support is an absolute condition for stable economies and long-term survival. To meet this condition requires acknowledgment of the biophysical constraints on economic activity, a near-complete rewrite of economic theory and corresponding adjustments to our growth-based sociocultural narrative.[41] How might environmental law reflect this biophysical imperative?

5. Some Good News: The Self-Producing Ecosphere

Fortunately, the ecosphere has the capacity to recover from human abuse—*ecosystems are inherently self-producing and self-sustaining*. The ecosphere, therefore, appears to defy the entropy law: it "is in many respects self-generating—its productivity and stability determined largely through its internal interactions."[42]

The capacity to self-produce—autopoiesis—is a key organizational property of living systems that emerges from the co-evolution of complex, interdependent relationships (energy, material, and information flows) linking the system's major components. The structural integrity of these relationships is essential not only to the functioning of the whole, *but also for the production and maintenance of the participating components themselves*[43] (for example, no major organ of the human body can survive absent the healthy functioning of all the others).

Ecosystems are autopoietic. They are able to produce and maintain themselves in a highly ordered "far-from-equilibrium"[44] state while continuously transforming and recycling the material basis of life. The "producer" components of ecosystems (green plants) self-produce using photosynthesis to "feed" on an extra-planetary source of high-grade energy—the sun.[45] They use this energy to reassemble carbon dioxide, water, and a few mineral nutrients into energy-rich plant biomass. Other ecosystem components (animal "consumers" and bacterial/fungal "decomposers") self-produce by feeding on plant biomass or on each other, dead or alive. Bacterial decomposition returns simple organic molecules and nutrients to the soil whence they can again be assimilated by plants to repeat the cycle. While matter recycles, degraded energy dissipates off the planet (for example, body heat), increasing the entropy of the universe.

Economies are also autopoietic but with an important difference. Economies are fully contained by, and self-produce by feeding on, the ecosphere. In industrial societies, the exploitation process is accelerated by the use of stored solar energy—fossil fuels. Thus, modern societies elevate themselves to a highly ordered far-from-equilibrium state by consuming energy/matter extracted from their supportive ecosystems and dissipating their waste energy/matter back into them. This increases the entropy (degradation) of the ecosphere.

Any civilization that dissipates and pollutes its host ecosystems faster than they can regenerate/assimilate is inherently self-destructive. Regrettably, the human enterprise, as currently configured, has become dangerously parasitic on the Earth. Over-exploitation and pollution destroy ecological integrity and are on the way to undermining the ability of the ecosphere to produce the type of environment necessary for civilized existence.

---

41 William E Rees, "End Game: The Economy as Eco-Catastrophe and What Needs to Change" (2019) 87 real-world economics review 132, online (pdf): <http://www.paecon.net/PAEReview/issue87/Rees87.pdf>.

42 David A Perry et al, "Bootstrapping in Ecosystems" (1989) 39:4 BioScience 230 at 230.

43 Humberto Maturana & Francisco Varela, *The Tree of Knowledge* (Boston: New Science Library, 1988) at 43.

44 Thermodynamic equilibrium implies total depletion, a fully disordered state in which nothing further can happen. Thus, "distance from equilibrium" is a distinguishing feature of life much as temperature is in classical thermodynamics. See Prigogine, *supra* note 35.

45 Photosynthesis is the thermodynamic engine of life, the most important productive process on Earth and the ultimate source of all bio-resources used by the human economy.

E. MAINTAINING NATURAL CAPITAL: A NECESSARY CONDITION FOR SUSTAINABILITY

Sustainability will not come from policies and practices that maintain current living standards by depleting productive assets and natural resources, or otherwise "leave future generations with poorer prospects and greater risks than our own."[46]

Awareness of the need to protect the integrity of the ecosphere has recently forced eco-logical economists to begin treating biophysical resources and processes as unique forms of productive capital. This convergence of ecological and economic thinking has resulted in vari-ous interpretations of a "constant capital stock" criterion for sustainability.[47] In essence, this criterion requires that each generation leave the next an undiminished stock of productive assets. There are two interpretations of the constant capital stock idea:[48]

1. Each generation should inherit an aggregate stock *per capita* of manufactured and natural capital at least equivalent *in value* to the stock inherited by the previous gen-eration. This corresponds to Herman Daly's condition for "weak sustainability."
2. Each generation should inherit *physical* stocks of natural capital *per capita* at least equivalent to the stocks of such assets inherited by the previous generation.[49] This is a version of "strong sustainability" as defined by Daly.[50]

The first interpretation reflects the neoclassical assumption that human-made and natural capital are substitutes and that biological assets (for example, forests) can rationally be liquid-ated through "development" as long as subsequent investment in manufactured capital (for example, machinery) provides an endowment of equivalent dollar value to the next generation.[51]

The second interpretation better reflects the ecological principles favoured here. In particu-lar, maintaining physical stocks of at least critical natural capital recognizes the multifunctional-ity of ecological resources, "including their role as life support systems."[52] In this respect, "strong sustainability" recognizes that manufactured and natural capital "are really not substitutes but

---

46 Robert Repetto, *World Enough and Time: Successful Strategies for Resource Management* (New Haven, Conn: Yale University Press, 1986) at 15.

47 See Daly, "Sustainable Development: From Concept and Theory," *supra* note 36; David Pearce, Anil Mar-kandya & Edward Barbier, *Blueprint for a Green Economy* (London: Earthscan, 1989) [Pearce, Markandya & Barbier, *Blueprint for a Green Economy*]; David Pearce, Edward Barbier & Anil Markandya, *Sustainable Development: Economics and Environment in the Third World* (Hants, UK: Edward Elgar, 1990) [Pearce, Barbier & Markandya, *Sustainable Development: Economics and Environment*]; Paul Ekins et al, "A Frame-work for the Practical Application of the Concepts of Critical Natural Capital and Strong Sustainability" (2003) 44:2-3 Ecol Econ 165; Simon Dietz & Eric Neumayer, "Weak and Strong Sustainability in the SEEA: Concepts and Measurement" (2007) 61:4 Ecol Econ 617.

48 Adapted from Pearce, Markandya & Barbier, *Blueprint for a Green Economy, supra* note 47. Both inter-pretations assume that existing stocks are adequate. If populations are growing or material standards increasing, the stock of productive capital will have to be increased to satisfy the sustainability criterion.

49 "Natural capital" encompasses not only material resources (for example, petroleum, forests, and soils) but also process resources (for example, waste assimilation, photosynthesis, and soils formation). For ecological reasons, our primary interest is in maintaining physical stocks of self-producing natural cap-ital. (The depletion of non-renewables could be compensated by investment in renewables.)

50 Daly, "Sustainable Development: From Concept and Theory," *supra* note 36.

51 "Equivalent endowment" would be defined in terms of monetary value, wealth-generating potential, jobs, and similar economic criteria. (It is worth noting that humankind has regrettably failed to achieve even the modest objectives of "weak sustainability" in much of the world.)

52 Pearce, Barbier & Markandya, *Sustainable Development: Economics and Environment, supra* note 47 at 7.

complements in most production functions."[53] (Indeed, since manufactured capital is made from natural capital, the latter is *prerequisite* for the former.)

Conventional economic analysis does suggest a theoretically simple method to identify the appropriate (optimal) level of natural capital and, therefore, the optimal scale of the economy: development of the "environment" should proceed only to the point at which the rising marginal costs of natural capital depletion (particularly reduced ecological services) just equal the falling marginal benefits (jobs and income from exploitation).[54] Beyond this point, growth of the material economy is anti-economic growth that ultimately makes us poorer rather than richer (costs > benefits).[55] However, there is a practical problem. It is relatively easy to estimate the money value derived from developing natural capital. However, scientific uncertainty and poor data make it virtually impossible to cost out (quantify and price) the loss of ecological services resulting from natural capital depletion. Theory succumbs to reality.

In the circumstances, Pearce, Barbier, and Markandya observe that further reductions of natural capital may impose significant risks on society, "even in countries where it might appear we can afford to [reduce stocks]."[56] These risks reside in our imperfect knowledge: the fact that loss of eco-functions may be irreversible and our inability to substitute for those functions once lost. In short, "[i]n the face of uncertainty and irreversibility, conserving what there is could be a sound risk-averse strategy."[57] No-growth economics, anyone?

F. IMPLICATIONS FOR ENVIRONMENTAL LAW

We have made the case that even the present world population, at current average material standards, using existing technologies, exceeds the long-term carrying capacity of Earth—the human enterprise is in overshoot. Fixing this problem means shifting our economic emphasis from the accumulation of financial and manufactured capital to the rehabilitation of natural capital. For the first time since the beginning of the Industrial Revolution, the environment should be treated as the independent variable and the economy the dependent one in the development equation. Environmental law must rise to the corresponding challenge of ensuring the restoration of essential natural capital and of protecting the common rights of all to the ecological services essential for civilized existence.

Unfortunately, current developmental trends such as urbanization, globalization, and freer trade create an increasingly competitive global environment and expose remaining pockets of natural capital to a growing, ever-wealthier global market. This militates against the constant natural capital stock criterion. Commodity price competition in the absence of legally enforceable ecological constraints may reduce prices and the economic surpluses exporters need to maintain productive forests, agricultural soils, fishery stocks, etc. If resource owners are forced to liquidate stocks to survive (or to provide investment capital for investment in some more lucrative alternative), they undermine life-support functions upon which we all depend. To address the domestic and international legal problems associated with such emergent problems requires a revolutionary extension of the bounds of environmental law.

---

53 Daly, "Sustainable Development: From Concept and Theory," *supra* note 36 at 250.

54 Marginal and cost–benefit analyses may be conceptually elegant but are fraught with serious theoretical problems and data limitations that limit their practical value. See Lester Lave & Howard Gruenspecht, "Increasing the Efficiency and Effectiveness of Environmental Decisions: Benefit–Cost Analysis and Effluent Fees—A Critical Review" (1991) 41 J Air Waste Manage Assn 680.

55 Herman E Daly, "Boundless Bull" (Summer 1990) Gannett Center J 113.

56 *Sustainable Development: Economics and Environment, supra* note 47 at 7.

57 *Ibid.*

III. ON ENVIRONMENTAL RACISM AND "ECO-APARTHEID"

The world must also confront unprecedented social conundrums on the way to a just and equitable shift to sustainability. Indeed, ecological problems remain inseparable from "social injustices such as poverty, racism, sexism, unemployment, urban deterioration, and the diminishing quality of life" resulting from both growing income inequality and errant corporate activity.[58] Environmental justice requires the meaningful engagement of all parties affected by resource development in decision-making and the enforcement of environmental laws and regulation, regardless of race, nationality, income, or social status.

It is well known that the relatively impoverished have always suffered the greatest consequences of local environmental decay. Certainly since the beginning of the Industrial Revolution, the urban poor, particularly racial and ethnic minorities, have borne the greatest ecological costs of economic activity and growth. However, a quarter century ago, Robert Bullard emphasized that the correlation between chronic exposure to ecological hazards and race is much stronger than that between exposure and poverty.[59]

There is little question that the environmental racism implicit in Bullard's assertion constitutes one of the most pressing moral and legal conundrums associated with achieving sustainability.[60] William Rees and Laura Westra argue that the problem is increasingly a global one—that unnecessary consumption by the wealthy is now indirectly visiting violence and even death on the poor and otherwise marginalized, particularly in developing countries—and that it is time for the international community to address the problem.[61] The potential destruction of small island states by a rise in sea level induced by global warming is a pressing example.

Toward this end, consider the five basic principles originally proposed by Bullard as the basis for a *national* legal framework for environmental justice:[62]

- The right to protection—no individual should need to fear exposure to personal risk from human-induced environmental degradation.
- A strategy of prevention—governments should aim for the elimination of risk before harm occurs.
- Shifting the burden of proof—entities applying for operating permits or undertaking activities potentially damaging to public health and property should be required to prove the safety of their operations.
- Obviating proof of intent—the law should allow statistical evidence of differential impact (on the poor or minorities) to infer discrimination "because proving intentional or purposeful discrimination [in court] is next to impossible."[63] Surely actions that manifest gross negligence with regard to the poor or minority races constitute de facto eco-injustice (or eco-racism).
- Redressing existing inequities—resources should be made available to mitigate ecological damage and compensate individuals for related health problems.

---

58 Richard Hofrichter, *Toxic Struggles: The Theory and Practice of Environmental Justice* (Gabriola Island, BC: New Society Publishers, 1993) at 3.

59 "Decision Making" in Laura Westra & Bill E Lawson, eds, *Faces of Environmental Racism: Confronting Issues of Global Justice*, 2nd ed (Lanham, Md: Rowman and Littlefield, 2001).

60 Laura Westra, "Institutionalized Environmental Violence and Human Rights" in David Pimentel, Laura Westra & Reed Noss, eds, *Ecological Integrity: Integrating Environment, Conservation and Health* (Washington, DC: Island Press, 2000) 279.

61 "When Consumption Does Violence: Can There Be Sustainability and Environmental Justice in a Resource-Limited World?" in Julian Agyeman, ed, *Just Sustainabilities: Development in an Unequal World* (London: Earthscan, 2002).

62 Bullard, *supra* note 59.

63 *Ibid* at 18.

Since eco-justice for all is also a desirable goal of international development, these principles could help frame international law governing relationships among countries and the behaviour of transnational corporations. The latter are increasingly being granted the rights of persons in international trade deals such as the *North American Free Trade Agreement* (NAFTA) and its successor, the *Canada–United States–Mexico Agreement* (CUSMA),[64] and should similarly be required to assume moral responsibility for their actions.

The formal logic of common law throws additional useful light on the subject. In Canada, for example, the most important common law tort action today, both in terms of the number of claims made and its theoretical importance, is the negligence cause of action (see the discussion in Chapter 9 of this book).

Negligence law focuses on compensation for losses caused by unreasonable conduct that harms legally protected interests. Unreasonable (negligent) conduct is taken to mean omitting to do something that a reasonable, prudent person would do in the same circumstances, or doing something that a prudent, reasonable person would not do in those circumstances. Here is clear recognition that fault may be found even in the case of unintended harm if the latter results from careless or unreasonable conduct. A negligence action may be launched in Canada in the event of environmental assault. The plaintiff must establish on balance five key elements of the tort—legal duty, breach of the standard of care, cause in fact, proximate cause, and damage to the plaintiff. How might this work in the international arena? There is no doubt that eco-violence—from oil spills to chemical sterilization—damages the plaintiff. The causal links between careless consumption/disposal and eco-violence are also becoming better established. In this light, failure to act responsibly on the part of liable or offending nations would seem to breach a reasonable standard of care. What is missing in international law is acknowledgment of the offence and the capacity to create and enforce a legal duty to act.[65]

Significantly, s 219 of Canada's *Criminal Code*,[66] as amended, states that lack of intent to harm is no defence if damage results from willing acts performed carelessly: "Every one is criminally negligent who (a) in doing anything, or (b) in omitting to do anything that it is his duty to do, shows wanton or reckless disregard for the lives or safety of other persons" (where "duty" means a duty imposed by law). Section 222(5)(b) of the Code states that a person commits culpable homicide (murder or manslaughter or infanticide) when, directly or indirectly, by any means, he or she causes the death of a human being by criminal negligence. Every person who causes the death of another person through criminal negligence is guilty of an indictable offence and liable to imprisonment for life.

There is no *prima facie* moral reason why the behavioural standards imposed by international law should not be as rigorous as those required by domestic law. For example, if human-induced climate change can be shown to be a cause of death and destruction, then are not high-emissions countries like Canada and the United States guilty of "wanton or reckless disregard for the lives or safety of other persons" if they fail to act decisively to reduce profligate fossil fuel consumption, particularly given the range of options for conservation and the increasing availability of alternative energy?

The overall point here is that if the world is to achieve global sustainability, it will require an unprecedented level of international cooperation both to acknowledge the existence of such problems and to create the international institutional and legal regime necessary to ensure the environmental safety and security of all persons. In particular, no resident of the global village

---

64 This often occurs at the expense of national sovereignty, democracy, and, possibly, eco-justice. For example, in August 2000, a NAFTA tribunal ordered Mexico to pay California-based Metalclad Corporation US$16.7 million as compensation for a Mexican municipality's refusal to allow the company to run a hazardous waste dump in the community.

65 Note, however, that there is no such reluctance to act in the case of alleged breaches of trade agreements.

66 RSC 1985, c C-46.

should be exposed to environmental hazards as the result of the negligent behaviour of persons, corporations, or governments, even if the causative act occurs in another nation.

IV. ENVIRONMENTAL ETHICS

A. INTRODUCTION: THE RELEVANCE OF ETHICAL CONSIDERATIONS

However radical they may appear, the advances in ecological economics noted above remain relentlessly anthropocentric in tone. Even environmental science is generally advanced on grounds that we should protect "the environment" to protect ourselves. This section carries the debate further, to a consideration of the ethical dimensions of humankind–ecosphere relationships. Such ethical considerations are highly relevant to the study of environmental law. It is true that in a discipline deeply influenced by positivism, any inquiry into the moral underpinnings of a field of law tends to be regarded with no small degree of suspicion. Nevertheless, an awareness of the ethical dimensions of environmental law is essential to an understanding of the field itself, its evolution into its present form, and its possible future development.

We proceed on the assumption that law generally, and environmental law in particular, embodies certain presuppositions regarding "nature" or "the environment." Traditionally, the environment has been regarded as a resource trove for human exploitation; to the extent that law has dealt with environmental issues, it has tended to do so with a view to safeguarding human interests in these resources. Environmental degradation or pollution are usually understood, if not defined, in terms of harm to humans or impairment of human interests; thus, even the assimilative capacity of ecosystems is treated as yet another resource for the benefit of humans. Consider the following definition of "pollution" in the British Columbia *Environmental Management Act*: "the presence in the environment of substances or contaminants that substantially alter or impair the *usefulness* of the environment."[67] While "environment" in the same Act is defined as "the air, land, water and all other external conditions or influences under which humans, animals and plants live or are developed" (s 1(1)), and it might, therefore, be argued that "usefulness" must be broadly understood to include usefulness to all species, there is no doubt that environmental protection is understood in instrumental terms as serving some purpose other than simply protecting ecosystems for their own sake. This position is not at all atypical; indeed, it can be said to characterize most current environmental law and policy.

There has long been an undercurrent of philosophical and legal opinion that has looked beyond these assumptions and attempted to construct alternative ways of conceptualizing the relationship between humans and the natural world. In the concluding paragraph to *Silent Spring*, the work widely credited with launching the modern environmental movement in North America, Rachel Carson asserted, "the 'control of nature' is a phrase conceived in arrogance, born of the Neanderthal age of biology and philosophy, when it was supposed that nature exists for the convenience of man."[68] Over the past half century, Carson's perspective has become widespread, challenging the legal system and its participants to confront the ethical dimensions of the broader legal framework within which we make decisions that affect the ecosphere. The fundamental implication is that environmental law already makes implicit assumptions about the ethical status (or lack of status) of the environment; a management framework or individual decision that treats the ecosphere as a store of resources for human use and enjoyment is not ethically value neutral.

---

67 SBC 2003, c 53, s 1(1).

68 (Boston: Houghton Mifflin, 1962) at 297.

In this section, we discuss alternative ethical perspectives on the environment. We do not attempt a comprehensive account of environmental ethics but, rather, highlight some of the most significant points of debate. We then consider some of the ways in which legal scholars have assessed and rethought the ethical dimensions of existing environmental law and policy.

B. APPROACHES TO ENVIRONMENTAL ETHICS

1. Introduction and Overview

The field of "environmental ethics" has become vast and complicated, with numerous points of consensus and controversy.[69] Of the latter, one of the most significant is whether environmental ethics ought to be utilitarian and instrumental (that is, derived from or contributing to human interests) or, instead, flow from the recognition that nature possesses "inherent" or "intrinsic" value, which should be respected (even at the cost of sacrificing certain human interests).

Environmental philosopher John Rodman identifies four "currents of thought" in modern environmentalism: resource conservationism, wilderness preservationism, moral extensionism, and ecological sensibility.[70] The first two schools, characteristic of the early environmental movement, are still very much a part of the current debate. Resource conservationism is primarily concerned with the development of "wise" resource use practices that take into account the interests of society as a whole and also incorporate notions of sustainability.[71] Wilderness preservationism focuses on the value of nature as a sanctuary, on nature's beauty and inspirational worth to humans. Historically, these two perspectives have occupied opposing camps; however, both view nature in essentially instrumental terms. Thus, Rodman characterizes the differences between them as "a family quarrel between advocates of two different forms of human use—economic and religio-esthetic."[72]

While these two approaches have clear ethical dimensions, such as the problem of how to account for the interests of future generations, they tend to leave the existing ethical framework essentially untouched—human interests remain the touchstone.[73] Rodman's third and

---

69 There are a number of journals devoted exclusively to the subject: for example, *Environmental Ethics*, *Environmental Values*, *Ethics and the Environment*, and *The Trumpeter: Journal of Ecosophy*. This is in addition to articles dealing with various aspects of environmental ethics published in other journals, as well as a growing number of anthologies and treatises. See, for example, Joseph R Des Jardins, *Environmental Ethics: An Introduction to Environmental Philosophy*, 2nd ed (Belmont, Cal: Wadsworth, 1997); Roderick F Nash, *The Rights of Nature* (Madison, Wis: University of Wisconsin Press, 1989); Andrew Light & Holmes Rolston III, eds, *Environmental Ethics: An Anthology* (Oxford: Blackwell, 2003); Clare Palmer, *Environmental Ethics* (Santa Barbara, Cal: ABC-CLIO, 1997); Christine Pierce & Donald VanDeVeer, eds, *People, Penguins and Plastic Trees: Basic Issues in Environmental Ethics*, 2nd ed (Belmont, Cal: Wadsworth, 1995); Louis Pojman, ed, *Environmental Ethics: Readings in Theory and Application*, 2nd ed (Belmont, Cal: Wadsworth, 1998); Alex Wellington, Allen Greenbaum & Wesley Cragg, eds, *Canadian Issues in Environmental Ethics* (Peterborough, Ont: Broadview Press, 1997). A useful concise survey of the field can be found in Clare Palmer, "An Overview of Environmental Ethics" in Light & Rolston III, eds, 15.

70 John Rodman, "Four Forms of Ecological Consciousness Reconsidered" in Donald Scherer & Thomas Attig, eds, *Ethics and the Environment* (Englewood Cliffs, NJ: Prentice Hall, 1983) 82.

71 *Ibid* at 82.

72 *Ibid* at 85.

73 Rodman acknowledges that some of the historical figures he places in the "preservationist" category do have some sense of the value of nature apart from human interests so his categorization may be an oversimplification. For present purposes, however, it has the merit of providing an analytical framework for a very complex field. The less anthropocentric aspects of wilderness preservationism are dealt with in the following discussion of extensionism and ecological sensibility.

fourth categories, however, pose significant challenges to traditional thinking by positing some notion of inherent or intrinsic value in nature. We focus on these visions for the remainder of this section.

2. Extending the Boundaries

The "extensionist" approach would extend ethical and moral consideration to entities that conventionally lie outside the moral community. This perspective results from the growing realization that these entities are "like us" in some morally relevant way: for example, they are sentient and may be capable of feeling pain. This approach has been pioneered in the literature on animal rights.[74] The most significant controversy in extensionism is that of "moral eligibility": whether a given entity ought to be included in humanity's moral community and, if so, where the ethical "cutoff line" should be drawn.[75] Aldo Leopold's famous "land ethic" represents the view that moral boundaries have to extend beyond living beings to reflect the interconnectedness of ecosystems:

> All ethics so far evolved rest upon a single premise: that the individual is a member of a community of interdependent parts. ... The land ethic simply enlarges the boundaries of the community to include soils, waters, plants and animals, or collectively: the land. ... [A] land ethic changes the role of *Homo sapiens* from conqueror of the land-community to mere member and citizen of it. It implies respect for his fellow-members and also respect for the community as such.[76]

An excellent example of extensionist thought is found in the work of Christopher Stone, discussed below, in Section IV.C.

3. "Re-visioning" the Framework

While extensionism stretches the boundaries of the existing ethical framework, Rodman's fourth stream, "ecological sensibility," calls for a re-visioning of the framework. Re-visionists agree with extensionists' criticisms of existing structures but remain skeptical that these structures can be reframed to accommodate radically different ways of thinking. They seek alternatives, focusing on the realization that we are all part of one moral and ecological community. Rather than merely extending to "others" the same consideration we expect for ourselves, many writers in this camp call for a reconceptualization of self to encompass notions of interconnectedness and interdependence. This is not so much reform as revolution; it questions the unexamined subtext of our individual and collective world views.

Deep ecology is one perspective that deliberately sets itself apart from more traditional approaches. The term "deep ecology" was first used by the Norwegian philosopher Arne Naess in 1972 to describe a way of relating to the natural world that would stand in stark contrast to the anthropocentric bias of "shallow ecology," a term under which Naess lumped most of the environmental and conservation movement.[77] As its name suggests, deep ecology goes

---

74 The animal rights or animal liberation literature is quite extensive. A classic articulation of the arguments can be found in Peter Singer, *Animal Liberation* (New York: Avon Books, 1975). For a treatment from a legal perspective, see David Hoch, "Environmental Ethics and Nonhuman Interests: A Challenge to Anthropocentric License" (1987-88) 23:2 Gonz L Rev 331. Over the years, there has been considerable debate about the connection between animal liberation and environmental ethics. See Dale Jamieson, "Animal Liberation Is an Environmental Ethic" (1998) 7:1 Envtl Values 41. See also the discussion in Chapter 20 of this book.

75 See the discussion in Nash, *supra* note 69 at 3-12.

76 Aldo Leopold, "The Land Ethic" in Light & Rolston III, eds, *supra* note 69, 38 at 39.

77 Arne Naess, "The Shallow and the Deep, Long-Range Ecology Movements: A Summary" (1973) 16 Inquiry 95.

beyond surface criticism to dissect the fundamental assumptions of the prevailing techno-industrial world view.[78]

Deep ecology sees the dominant world view as incorporating two conceptual flaws: first, and most important, anthropocentrism, the notion that humans are the most important of all entities and that they exercise dominion over the natural world; and, second, faith in "progress," growth, and the endless possibility of technological advancement. This narrative views the relationship between humanity and nature as hierarchical, with humanity firmly on top; the environment is not considered in any balance-of-interests test unless to do so would benefit humans. At the same time, faith in progress supports the conviction that environmental problems are temporary by-products of inferior technology that can be overcome through better science and more advanced technologies.

The dominant world view is reflected in contemporary consumption patterns, particularly the failure to distinguish between "vital" or basic needs and "peripheral" wants or desires. Humans are reduced to selfish consumers, and "the environment" becomes that which is consumed. Society's attitude toward the natural world is framed by the question: how can nature best be exploited to fulfill human needs and wants?

By contrast, deep ecology proposes an ethic grounded in two norms: self-realization and biocentric equality.[79] The notion of "self-realization" involves a concept of selfhood radically different from the current norm. It incorporates a sense of "organic wholeness"[80] or connectedness to a reality outside the boundaries of individual experience. In fact, deep ecologists question the reality of boundaries and argue that we are all part of an all-encompassing "self." Biocentric equality is the premise that "all things in the biosphere have an equal right to live and blossom and to reach their own individual form of unfolding and self-realization within the larger self-realization ... all organisms and entities in the ecosphere, as parts of the interrelated whole, are equal in intrinsic worth."[81] Thus, deep ecology adopts a holistic world view that accounts for the interconnectedness of all components of the ecosphere.

Obviously, these norms have far-reaching implications. The shift from anthropocentrism to biocentrism, for example, would abandon utilitarian rationales for environmental protection in favour of recognizing the intrinsic value of natural entities. This "life-centered" world view would require that we view ourselves, individually and collectively, as part of nature rather than above it. At the personal level, biocentrism would require accepting responsibility for our impacts on nature and recognizing the need to minimize our individual ecological footprints through voluntary limitations on damaging behaviour (for example, air travel) and material consumption. At the societal level, such a shift would have obvious implications for the cherished notion of infinite growth through endless progress. Indeed, mere growth (getting quantitatively bigger) would have to give way to genuine development (getting qualitatively better) before society could advance in ecologically sustainable and ethically justifiable ways.

Deep ecologists generalize about humanity's relationship to the rest of nature but save their most scathing criticism for modern industrialized society. By contrast, other environmental

---

78 For a general overview of deep ecology, see Bill Devall & George Sessions, *Deep Ecology, Living as if Nature Mattered* (Salt Lake City: Peregrine Smith, 1985); and Arne Naess, *Ecology, Community and Lifestyle: Outline of an Ecosophy*, trans and ed by David Rothenberg (Cambridge: Cambridge University Press, 1989). See also B Devall, *Simple in Means, Rich in Ends: Practicing Deep Ecology* (Salt Lake City: Peregrine Smith, 1988); Alan Drengson & Yuichi Inoue, eds, *The Deep Ecology Movement: An Introductory Anthology* (Berkeley, Cal: North Atlantic Books, 1995). For a recent concise survey by one of the leading figures in the movement, see Bill Devall, "The Deep, Long-Range Ecology Movement 1960-2000—A Review" (2001) 6 Ethics & the Environ 18.

79 See Devall & Sessions, *supra* note 78 at 66-69.

80 *Ibid* at 67.

81 *Ibid*.

ethicists extend their analyses of domination and hierarchy to consider how these perceived orderings are reproduced in a variety of human societies and relationships.

Social ecologists, for example, are reluctant to treat human domination of nature as conceptually monolithic; instead, their analysis considers how the hierarchy of humans over nature is reproduced in various other forms of hierarchy within society. Murray Bookchin, perhaps the best known among social ecologists, sums up their basic position as follows: "Social ecology has made the understanding of hierarchy—its rise, scope, and impact—the centerpiece of its message of a liberating, rational, and ecological society."[82] Bookchin and other social ecologists are suspicious of analyses of the environmental crisis that do not consider the varying degrees of responsibility of the players involved and, thus, lump together the powerful and the powerless. The latter, from this perspective, are more the victims of environmental degradation than its perpetrators.[83]

Similarly, ecofeminists have taken issue with deep ecologists' emphasis on "anthropocentrism" as a cause of environmental problems. Instead, they speak of "androcentrism" and wonder whether human domination of nature does not translate into male domination of nature.[84] The ecofeminist perspective postulates that the domination of nature by humans, of the poor by the rich, and of women by men are three facets of the same problem interconnected at the conceptual level.[85]

It may be slightly misleading to classify ecofeminism as one environmental perspective rather than a variety of related perspectives sensitive to this conceptual connection.[86] The point of agreement is that overcoming the "ideology of domination" requires an analysis of both feminist and ecological concerns; to ignore or downplay one form of hierarchy is to lose sight of the fact that the various forms reinforce each other and may be difficult to separate.[87]

---

82 *Remaking Society: Pathways to a Green Future* (Boston: South End Press, 1990) at 61 [Bookchin, *Remaking Society*]. See also Murray Bookchin, *The Philosophy of Social Ecology*, 2nd ed (Montreal: Black Rose, 1995); Janet Biehl & Murray Bookchin, *The Politics of Social Ecology* (Montreal: Black Rose, 1998); Janet Biehl, ed, *The Murray Bookchin Reader* (Montreal: Black Rose, 1999). A recent anthology that includes critical evaluations of social ecology is Andrew Light, ed, *Social Ecology After Bookchin* (New York: Guilford Press, 1998).

83 Social ecologists are also unwilling to name "rationality" per se as one of the sources of environmental problems. Bookchin states this position in no uncertain terms: "To sidestep the social basis of our ecological problems, to obscure it with primitivistic cobwebs spun by self-indulgent mystics and anti-rationalists, is to literally turn back the clock of ecological thinking to an atavistic level of trite sentiment that can be used for utterly reactionary purposes" (*Remaking Society*, supra note 82 at 43).

84 Anthologies that provide good introductions to ecofeminism are Irene Diamond & Gloria Orenstein, eds, *Reweaving the World: the Emergence of Ecofeminism* (San Francisco: Sierra Club Books, 1990); Judith Plant, ed, *Healing the Wounds: The Promise of Ecofeminism* (Toronto: Between the Lines, 1989); and Karen J Warren, ed, *Ecological Feminism* (London: Routledge, 1994). A recent work that examines the connection of ecofeminism to environmental politics is Chris Cuomo, *Feminism and Communities: An Ethic of Flourishing* (London: Routledge, 1998).

85 See Judith Plant, "Searching for Common Ground: Ecofeminism and Bioregionalism" in Diamond & Orenstein, eds, *supra* note 84 at 155 [Plant, "Searching for Common Ground"].

86 Some ecofeminist writers trace the connection between the types of dominance to the Scientific Revolution; others take the analysis further back. See e.g. Carolyn Merchant, *The Death of Nature: Women, Ecology and the Scientific Revolution* (San Francisco: Harper & Row, 1980). Ecofeminists also differ in the emphasis placed on the "bond" between women and nature. Some argue that this connection is "natural" and common to almost all cultural traditions; hence, its use (or misuse) by patriarchy should not be a reason to abandon or deny it. Others express concern about taking for granted some of the assumptions that have been used as justifications to subjugate and control both women and the natural world. For a discussion of this and other aspects of ecofeminism from a social ecologist perspective, see Janet Biehl, *Finding Our Way: Rethinking Ecofeminist Politics* (Montreal: Black Rose Books, 1991).

87 See Karen J Warren, "The Power and the Promise of Ecological Feminism" (1990) 12:2 Envtl Ethics 125.

Like deep ecologists, many ecofeminists seek to reconceptualize notions of selfhood, and derive ethics from the fact that "we are all part of one another."[88] In practical terms, ecofeminists seek to develop strategies to resist hierarchy and create alternatives to current eco-destructive practices. Thus, ecofeminism offers empowering visions of the role of individuals in bringing about change: "ecofeminism is concerned not only with preserving our planet, but with teaching us how to respect all cycles of life, how to celebrate all forms of diversity, and how to enrich the quality of our own lives and the lives that touch ours."[89]

The three perspectives outlined above grow out of Western tradition but are to varying degrees reactions against it. While fundamentally they are forms of secular philosophy, they express concepts that are sometimes articulated in religious or spiritual terms.

The notion that there is a spiritual dimension underlying human–nature relations is not a new one, but it is one that is gaining momentum as various religious groups come to realize the magnitude of environmental problems.[90] In particular, there has been strong interest in non-Western religious and cultural traditions that embody possibly more harmonious or at least less destructive ways of relating to the natural world.[91]

Jainism is one example. An ancient Jain aphorism states: "All life is bound together by mutual support and interdependence." Consistent with this belief, Jainism, best known for the concept of harm avoidance, extends this consideration to the natural world. Jain ethics, which include non-acquisitiveness and the avoidance of waste, place prime importance on non-violence in thought, speech, and action.[92] The focus is not merely on avoiding harm but on incorporating respect for life into one's everyday activities. These ethics are reflected in the practical rule that Jains are to have limited or no involvement in "industries which require raw materials from the plant and animal kingdoms or those which poison the air, earth, rivers and sea with harmful effluents."[93] This clearly separates Jainism from modern industrial society.

Jainism also downplays hierarchy, the importance of "progress," and material accumulation, which are ethical positions it shares with other traditions, including various land-based and Indigenous peoples.[94] For example, a comparison of attitudes relevant to law and environment among Hopi Indians in the modern United States shows that the Hopi value stability, balance, and harmony over growth, expansion, and progress.[95]

Marie Wilson, a spokesperson for the Gitskan Wet'suwet'en Tribal Council in northwestern British Columbia, articulates the similar Gitskan perspective:

> I believe all people started out connected to the land. People like the Gitskan copied nature because they were surrounded by it, not protected from it as we are. They saw the cycle of life, from the very smallest to the very largest, all connected, and saw that the system itself

---

88 Plant, "Searching for Common Ground," *supra* note 85 at 156.

89 Anne E Simon, "Ecofeminism: Information and Activism" (1991) 13:1 Women's Rts L Rep 35 at 35.

90 See Harold Coward & Daniel Maguire, *Visions of a New Earth: Religious Perspectives on Population, Consumption, and Ecology* (Albany, NY: SUNY Press, 2000).

91 There have, of course, also been a number of attempts to develop or rediscover this type of perspective from within the Judaeo–Christian–Islamic tradition of revealed monotheistic religion. See the chapter "The Greening of Religion" in Nash, *supra* note 69 at 87.

92 "A Five Point Plan for Jain Ecology" (1991) 18:1 Jain Digest 22.

93 *Ibid.*

94 For a useful, concise discussion, see Laurelyn Whitt et al, "Indigenous Perspectives" in Dale Jamieson, ed, *A Companion to Environmental Philosophy* (Oxford: Blackwell Publishers, 2001) 3. See also John A Grim, ed, *Indigenous Traditions and Ecology: The Interbeing of Cosmology and Community* (Cambridge, Mass: Harvard University Press, 2001).

95 John Ragsdale, "Law and Environment in Modern America and Among the Hopi Indians: A Comparison of Values" (1986) 10:2 Harv Envtl L Rev 417 at 456.

punished any breaking of the cycle. ... The people saw and understood the checks and balances that were exhibited by the cycle and chose to base their fundamental truths and authority and responsibility on something that has worked for millions of years. They fitted themselves to the cycle of life.[96]

Without taking anything away from contemporary Indigenous world views, we should note that even for pre-agricultural humans, learning to "[fit] themselves to the cycle of life" in new habitats may have been a hard lesson. The recent paleoecological, anthropological, and archeological literature tells a convincing story of the extinctions of large mammals and birds when human beings came into first contact with and settled in their habitats.[97] It may have been centuries before various groups of prehistoric hunter–gatherers came to live in more or less stable dynamic equilibrium—or steady state—within their human-altered ecosystems. (This is a lesson that modern humans will almost certainly be forced to relearn.)

The important point is that once people have adapted to their ecosystems and developed a sense of engaged consciousness with nature, they do not get to impose arbitrary environmental "law" on nature. Instead, ecologically ethical behaviour is shaped by biophysical realities and the natural laws (for example, the entropy law) governing all ecosystems, including their human elements. This is a radically different twist on the phrase "law of the land."

Some writers have raised the possibility of turning to the traditional wisdom of Indigenous peoples to find solutions to current environmental problems,[98] but this raises the issue of cultural appropriation.[99] Moreover, Indigenous views of a "proper" relationship to the environment may not necessarily coincide with environmentalist concerns. Wilson warns:

> At the risk of sounding scornful or derogatory, I have to say that the Indian attitude toward the natural world is different from the environmentalists'. I have had the awful feeling that when we are finished dealing with the courts and our land claims, we will then have to battle the environmentalists and they will not understand why. I feel quite sick at this prospect because the environmentalists want these beautiful places kept in a state of perfection: to not touch them, rather to keep them pure. So that we can leave our jobs and for two weeks we can venture into the wilderness and enjoy this ship in a bottle. In a way this is like denying that life is happening constantly in these wild places, that change is always occurring. Human life must be there too. Humans have requirements and they are going to have to use some of the life in these places. I do believe that life does not need humans but, rather, humans do need the rest of life. We are very small within the structure.[100]

---

96 "Wings of the Eagle" in Judith Plant & Christopher Plant, eds, *Turtle Talk* (Philadelphia: New Society Publishers, 1990) 76 at 79.

97 Jared Diamond, *The Third Chimpanzee* (New York: HarperCollins, 1992); Tim Flannery, *The Future Eaters: An Ecological History of the Australasian Lands and Peoples* (Chatsworth, NSW: Reed Books, 1994).

98 See e.g. Annie Booth & Harvey Jacobs, "Ties That Bind: Native American Beliefs as a Foundation for Environmental Consciousness" (1990) 12:1 Environ Ethics 27 [Booth & Jacobs, "Ties That Bind"]. Booth and Jacobs also prepared *Environmental Consciousness: Native American Worldviews and Sustainable Natural Resource Management—An Annotated Bibliography* (Chicago: Council of Planning Librarians, 1988).

99 Booth & Jacobs, "Ties That Bind," *supra* note 98 at 42-43, acknowledge that there is "a delicate line between respectful learning and intellectual plundering," but they are confident that "[a]n open hearted and respectful investigation of Native American cultures, particularly when members of these cultures voluntarily share with us their understandings and perceptions, can help us discover new directions in which to travel to realize our own potentials."

100 Wilson, *supra* note 96 at 82-83.

Society needs to balance interest in Indigenous perspectives against respect for the uniqueness of the cultural context in which those perspectives evolved. There are no "ready-made" answers, no set of solutions that we will be able to adopt wholesale from other cultures. While we may have to fashion our own solutions, the existence of alternative models reminds us of forgotten truths: there is nothing preordained about our present destructive path; there are alternative growth-bound definitions of "development"; and there may be many ways of relating sustainably to the ecosphere.

It is an awareness of choice that informs "bioregionalism," a life philosophy based on practical applications of ethical environmental thinking.[101] In some ways, bioregionalism could be characterized as a synthesis of ideas in environmental ethics with the sense of place common to land-based cultures. Bioregionalists seek "to become dwellers in the land ... to come to know the [E]arth fully and honestly, the crucial and perhaps only and all-encompassing task is to understand *place*, the immediate specific place where we live."[102] The bioregionalist perspective incorporates the analysis of hierarchy and domination and attempts to visualize alternative means of social organization that would lead to a more balanced relationship with the natural world. The human community would live "in place" as citizens of the land, taking no more than regional ecosystems could sustainably produce while retaining functional integrity.

C. ENVIRONMENTAL ETHICS: IMPLICATIONS FOR LAW

The preceding discussion has examined a number of perspectives that critique existing assumptions about the environment and propose alternatives. What are the implications for environmental law and policy?

Law and legal academics were affected by the increased awareness of environmental concerns in the early 1970s. As the philosophical debates about the ethical status (or non-status) of the environment grew more heated, corresponding debates among legal scholars increased. Two articles written at that time by legal academics are still considered important landmarks in the literature dealing with the extension of some form of ethical consideration to nature.

An early treatment of the subject, now a classic in the legal literature dealing with the environment, is the 1972 article "Should Trees Have Standing? Towards Legal Rights for Natural Objects," by Christopher Stone.[103] Stone, a law professor at the University of Southern California, proposed that legal consideration in the form of rights be extended "to forests, oceans, rivers and other so-called 'natural objects' in the environment—indeed to the natural environment as a whole."[104] This notion that the environment could have "rights" was greeted with considerable skepticism by the legal community, despite the fact that Stone was careful to fit his proposals within the existing legal framework, thus leaving its underlying assumptions more or less untouched.[105]

---

101 See e.g. Kirkpatrick Sale, *Dwellers in the Land* (San Francisco: Sierra Club Books, 1985); Van Andruss et al, eds, *Home! A Bioregional Reader* (Gabriola Island, BC: New Society, 1990).

102 Sale, *supra* note 101 at 42.

103 (1972) 45:2 S Cal L Rev 450 [Stone, "Should Trees Have Standing?" (1972)] (reprinted as *Should Trees Have Standing?—Towards Legal Rights for Natural Objects* (Los Altos, Cal: William Kaufman, 1974)) [Stone, *Should Trees Have Standing?* (1974)].

104 Stone, "Should Trees Have Standing?" (1972), *supra* note 103 at 456.

105 In fact, toward the end of the article, Stone does discuss the need for a fundamental transformation in our attitude toward the environment: *ibid* at 499–501. This perspective is developed in his more recent book, *Earth and Other Ethics: The Case for Moral Pluralism* (New York: Harper & Row, 1987) [Stone, *Earth and Other Ethics*]. Today, 30 years after the publication of the original article, one suspects that many if not most lawyers would still find his ideas not so much revolutionary as bizarre. This is either a tribute to Stone's farsightedness or a commentary on the slowness of change within the legal system; probably both. See also Chapter 20 of this book.

Stone was interested in what he termed the "interplay between law and the development of social awareness."[106] As a legal philosopher, he was intrigued by the ways in which law reflects societal understandings of ethical problems:

> Societies, like human beings, progress through different stages of sensitiveness, and ... in our progress through these stages the law ... has a role to play, dramatizing and summoning into the open the changes that are taking place within us.[107]

Stone's work in this area was motivated at least in part by longstanding theoretical interests; it is worth noting, however, that his decision to publish the "Standing" piece was a direct response to a concrete set of circumstances. The US Forest Service had granted a permit to Walt Disney Enterprises to develop Mineral King Valley, a wilderness area in the Sierra Nevada Mountains.[108] The Sierra Club brought suit for an injunction, arguing that the project would adversely affect the area's aesthetic and ecological balance. The Federal District Court granted a preliminary injunction; the Court of Appeals for the Ninth Circuit reversed the decision on the grounds that Sierra Club had no "standing" to bring the question to the courts.[109]

The case revolved around the question of standing: whether the Sierra Club was the proper party and whether it had a legally protectable and tangible interest at stake in the litigation. The irony of the situation was obvious to Stone; clearly, the entity that had a tangible interest at stake in the litigation was the valley itself. Thus, the basic thrust of his argument developed in response to the Mineral King situation: why should the valley itself not be granted some form of legal recognition? The Sierra Club was merely using whatever legal tactics it could to stop the development project. What was required was a conceptual framing that would eliminate the need for such legal gymnastics; Stone set out to develop such a framework.

Not at all unaware of the controversial nature of his proposals, Stone begins his argument with a discussion of "the unthinkable":

> Throughout legal history, each successive extension of rights to some new entity has been, theretofore, a bit unthinkable. We are inclined to suppose the rightlessness of rightless "things" to be a decree of nature, not a legal convention acting in support of some status quo. It is thus that we defer considering the choices involved in all their moral, social, and economic dimensions.[110]

Thus, the idea of extending rights to any entity "is bound to sound odd or frightening or laughable ... partly because until the rightless thing receives its rights, we cannot see it as anything but a *thing* for the use of 'us'—those who are holding rights at the time."[111]

Stone goes on to describe the "rightlessness" of natural objects at common law.[112] He uses the example of pollution of a stream to illustrate how a common law understanding of "environmental harm" focuses exclusively on the interests of any humans involved. The stream itself would be "rightless" in the sense that

1. it would not have standing to initiate proceedings;

---

106 Garrett Hardin, foreword to Stone, *Should Trees Have Standing?* (1974), *supra* note 103, ix at xii (quoting a conversation with Stone).

107 *Ibid* at xii–xiii.

108 The development was to consist of a $35 million complex of motels and recreational facilities.

109 *Sierra Club v Hickel*, 433 F.2d 24 (9th Cir 1970).

110 Stone, "Should Trees Have Standing?" (1972), *supra* note 103 at 453.

111 *Ibid* at 455.

112 *Ibid* at 459–63.

2. only damage to the interests of humans would be taken into account in determining the granting of legal relief (the notion of "damage to the stream" would be meaningless unless it were put in the context of damage to human interests); and

3. if there were a favourable judgment, it would be based on what it would take to compensate the human litigant and would run to his or her benefit.

The third aspect of the stream's "rightlessness" would be particularly important from an environmental standpoint, given that the amount needed to compensate the plaintiff would probably be far less than that needed to remedy the damage to the stream and that it would almost certainly be insufficient to force the polluter to stop polluting.[113]

Stone shows that bringing the environment into the existing framework can have considerable instrumental value. For example, he argues that the legal recognition of injuries should extend to accounting for the full cost to the environment; that is, make the quantum of damages correspond to the full extent of injury to the natural object in question.[114] From a wholly anthropocentric perspective, this would be one way—perhaps the only way—of taking the full costs of pollution into account; the natural object could be viewed as "the guardian of unborn generations as well as of otherwise unrepresented but distantly injured contemporary humans."[115]

However, Stone maintains that he is going beyond anthropocentricity in advocating the consideration of injuries that are presently not taken into account. These costs, such as those relating to the loss of commercially valueless species or the disappearance of wilderness areas, are not economically measurable and, thus, could not be assessed in the form of damages.[116] Moreover, Stone recognizes the limitations of "homocentricity," and, toward the end of his article, he discusses the need for a "radical new conception of man's relationship to the rest of nature."[117] He asks:

> What is it within us that gives us this need not just to satisfy basic biological wants, but to extend our wills over things, to objectify them, to make them ours, to manipulate them, to keep them at a psychic distance? Can it all be explained on "rational" bases? Should we not be suspect of such needs within us, cautious as to why we wish to gratify them?[118]

The actual proposals embodied in Stone's 1972 piece were overtaken by liberalization of standing requirements and statutory developments in US environmental law.[119] Nevertheless, the piece remains notable for its attempt to incorporate alternative ways of thinking about the environment into law.

Laurence Tribe's article "Ways Not To Think About Plastic Trees: New Foundations for Environmental Law" is another significant entry in the early legal literature on the environment.[120] Tribe goes further than Stone in attempting to move beyond anthropocentricity; his position can be seen as falling somewhere between a straight extensionist and a re-visionist approach.

Analyzing the newly emerging field of environmental law, Tribe describes the "basic platform" of the field as one of "analytic sophistication in the service of human need."[121] Tribe

---

113 *Ibid* at 462.

114 *Ibid* at 473-79.

115 *Ibid* at 475.

116 *Ibid*. In order to address the third aspect of "rightlessness," the problem of the potential beneficiary of the judgment, Stone advocates making the environment a beneficiary in its own right, through setting up a mechanism such as a trust fund, to be administered by the guardian in the interests of the natural object: *ibid* at 480-81.

117 *Ibid* at 495.

118 *Ibid* at 465-66.

119 See "Preface" in Stone, *Earth and Other Ethics*, *supra* note 105 at 3.

120 (1974) 83:7 Yale LJ 1315.

121 *Ibid* at 1317.

reviews the supposed obstacles to "good" environmental policy and finds none so trouble-some as the problem of "ideological boundaries." The tradition within which environmental planners operate "regards the satisfaction of individual human wants as the only defensible measure of the good" and "perceives the only legitimate task of reason to be that of con-sistently identifying and then serving individual appetite, preference, or desire."[122]

Tribe recognizes that environmentalists often make arguments on the basis of human inter-est out of a perfectly understandable desire to conform to the "demands of legal doctrine and the exigencies of political reality."[123] However, he regards this as self-defeating and proposes an alternative approach that would recognize value in nature quite apart from its instrumental value and would ground environmental policy in a sense of obligation toward the natural world. He expresses the following concern:

> What the environmentalist may not perceive is that, by couching his claims in terms of human self-interest—by articulating environmental goals wholly in terms of human needs and preferences—he may be helping to legitimate a system of discourse which so structures human thought and feeling as to erode, over the long run, the very sense of obligation which provided the initial impetus for his own protective efforts.[124]

Tribe further argues that if environmental concerns are couched in terms of human interests, there will be few obstacles to throwing those interests into the balance along with more con-ventional human values such as those associated with resource development:

> [O]nce obligation has been transformed into a mere matter of personal preference, the tendency is inevitable to compare the value of wilderness with the value of strip mined coal in terms of self-interest. From there, it is but a short step to an even more blatantly reduc-tionist approach: In order to insure that the comparison is "rational," the two values will almost certainly be translated into smoothly exchangeable units of satisfaction, such as dollars. While certain discontinuities may still be recognized—destruction of *all* wilderness areas may not be deemed worth even an infinite supply of coal—they will tend to be gradu-ally eroded by the pressure toward analytic conformity.[125]

As theoretical grounding for an alternative approach, Tribe proposes a "synthesis of imma-nence with transcendence," an approach that would combine respect for what exists now with an appreciation for the ongoing process of change in nature and of humanity as a part of nature. He describes this approach in the following terms:

> Such a synthesis requires the sanctification neither of the present nor of progress but of *evolving processes of interaction and change*—processes of action and choice that are val-ued for themselves, for the conceptions of being that they embody, at the same time that they are valued as means to the progressive evolution of the conceptions, experiences, and ends that characterize the human community in nature at any given point in its history.[126]

However, when Tribe attempts to address concrete proposals for incorporating such a synthesis into environmental law and policy, he retreats to extensionism. He falls back on vague notions of granting "rights" to natural objects and suggestions that environmental legis-lation incorporate language referring to obligations toward nature.[127] Tribe appears to be groping for a radically different approach but in the end relies on standard legal language and

---

122 *Ibid* at 1325.

123 *Ibid* at 1330.

124 *Ibid* at 1330-31.

125 *Ibid* at 1331-32.

126 *Ibid* at 1338.

127 *Ibid* at 1341.

mechanisms without really explaining how they could be adapted to new ways of thinking; thus, he fails to demonstrate how a "synthesis of immanence and transcendence" would translate into actual law and policy.[128]

Both Stone and Tribe view law as being adaptable to changing perceptions of the ethical status of the environment. Thus, after analyzing the treatment of the environment within the existing legal framework, Stone offers a concrete set of proposals to address its inadequacies. He argues that extending legal consideration to natural objects can be accomplished within existing legal traditions. On the question of standing, for example, he suggests that the legal problems of natural objects be handled through the appointment of a guardian—that is, in the same way as we handle those of human beings who are legally incompetent.[129] Tribe similarly visualizes reforms in environmental law and policy to reflect his proposed "new foundation," for example, requiring environmental impact statements to incorporate "explicit references to obligations felt towards nature."[130]

The pioneering approaches by Stone and Tribe have certainly not been uncontroversial. They have been broadly criticized from (at least) two sides: by writers who do not see the point of moving "beyond anthropocentrism" and by those who reject all variations of anthropocentric models, accusing Stone and Tribe of perpetuating the very bias they are supposedly trying to overcome.

A representative critic of the first school is Philip S Elder, whose basic point is that Stone and the deep ecologists, whom he lumps together, "do not take us anywhere in solving environmental disputes, that conventional ethics and law do not already go."[131] He argues that natural objects lack the characteristics upon which persons' claims to moral considerateness are based: "awareness, self-consciousness, the ability to formulate goals, act to attain them and to appreciate their attainment."[132] Elder continues:

> It is, therefore, a distortion of our concepts to claim that plants or non-living natural objects can "want" to survive or remain undisturbed. There is "nobody home" who could care, or who could suffer. And if they do not care, why should we?[133]

Elder goes on to critique what he sees as the implicit—and unavoidable—anthropocentrism of both Stone's proposals and the deep ecology perspective. In a nutshell, he is critical of any approach that presumes that humans can "speak for the environment." Given that we cannot avoid anthropocentricity, he seems to be saying, let us at least be upfront about it, and let us not "distort" our existing legal framework.

Attacking from the other direction, John Livingston points out that the power to "confer" rights implies control, and the conferral of rights is highly problematic when examined from

---

128 D Paul Emond points this out in "Co-operation in Nature: A New Foundation for Environmental Law" (1984) 22:2 Osgoode Hall LJ 323 at 325-26.

129 Stone, "Should Trees Have Standing?," *supra* note 103 at 464-73. The guardian would presumably be an environmental group, of which, as Stone points out, there are an increasing number with the requisite expertise and resources to enable them to function in this manner. The passage of time and corresponding mushrooming of environmental groups would only seem to strengthen Stone's argument on this point. Stone anticipates what is possibly the most significant objection to his proposal: it would be difficult if not impossible for the guardian to judge the needs of the natural object in its charge. He counters by arguing that in fact we judge the interests of "abstract" entities such as corporations all the time, and, if anything, it would probably be easier to determine or judge the needs of a natural object, where certain criteria of "wellness" are beyond dispute (at 471).

130 Tribe, *supra* note 119 at 1341.

131 "Legal Rights for Nature: The Wrong Answer to the Right(s) Question" (1984) 22:2 Osgoode Hall LJ 285 at 285.

132 *Ibid* at 288.

133 *Ibid*.

the perspective of concern about human domination of the natural world.[134] Livingston claims that advocates of rights for the environment have to address the "ultimate question ... whether *all* of non-human nature ought to move into the control of the human relationship."[135] He elaborates:

> Taken to its extreme, the result of the extension of rights would be to "humanize," or domesticate the entire planet. All life would be a human farm.[136]

Livingston's attitude toward environmental rights is essentially a reflection of his general skepticism as to whether modification of existing legal provisions can in fact deal with the "real" problem: "the *a priori* assumption that all non-human life is dedicated to human service."[137] He continues, "[t]he law cannot deal with this obstacle because it is neither a moral nor a statutory issue. It is a cultural predisposition."[138] Livingston does, however, find some "residual merit" in the debate over environmental rights, "if only for having shown that environmental despoliation, degradation and the barbarous interspecies behaviour of humankind may have no remedies within the Western cultural tradition."[139] He concludes:

> The need is not to invest endless time, energy and creativity in futile attempts to rationalize rights for non-humans within the existing belief structure, but rather to systematically address, with every intellectual tool at our disposal, the pathological species-chauvinist belief structure itself.[140]

In "Law Reform or World Re-form: The Problem of Environmental Rights,"[141] Cynthia Giagnocavo and Howard Goldstein are similarly skeptical about the effectiveness of mere reform. Arguing from a deep ecology perspective, these authors attack "neo-rights" theory, and particularly Stone and Tribe. To them, legal reform is mere tinkering at the margins:

> The legally trained will ask of deep ecology, "What are you offering lawyers?"; lawyers need to feel that there is something for them to do. Our response is that deep ecology offers lawyers, as "lawyers," precious little. Conservative jurisprudence, which sees law as being both the most appropriate and most effective instrument of social change, is in need of rethinking. Ecological disasters such as [climate change and plummeting biodiversity] provide ample evidence of how inadequate the legal framework is for dealing with deep-rooted cultural problems [not the least of which is] destruction of the [ecosphere].[142]

These authors go on to argue that legal reform is not only useless, but potentially dangerous in that it diverts attention from the need for real change: "Environmental rights might at best save a forest here or a river there, but in enriching and legitimating the very institution which contributes to the reification of trees and water as 'property,' they may be harming the world more than healing it."[143] They conclude that the changes required for a real and lasting solution to our environmental problems "can only be brought about by a re-writing of our metaphysic."[144]

---

134 John Livingston, "Rightness or Rights?" (1984) 22:2 Osgoode Hall LJ 309 at 309.

135 *Ibid* at 320.

136 *Ibid*.

137 *Ibid* at 314.

138 *Ibid*.

139 *Ibid*.

140 *Ibid* at 321.

141 (1990) 35:2 McGill LJ 345.

142 *Ibid* at 347.

143 *Ibid* at 384-85.

144 *Ibid* at 386.

Elaine Hughes takes a very different approach in "Fishwives and Other Tails: Ecofeminism and Environmental Law."[145] She argues, again, that fundamental changes are required in order to address environmental problems and that ecofeminism offers "a rich source of ideas about how one might 're-vision' the entire framework of environmental law."[146] Hughes acknowledges the potential danger of co-opting ecofeminism by attempting to incorporate its insights into a critique and reconstruction of environmental law; however, "a transition must begin somewhere."[147] Without trivializing the risk of co-option,[148] she sees that a failure to engage with the law has its own dangers.

Hughes sets out to analyze pollution control legislation, the most common type of which is the regulatory statute aimed at controlling the level of pollutant discharge into the ambient environment. She specifically focuses on water pollution provisions in the federal *Fisheries Act*.[149] Having set out the basic model for such legislation, Hughes evaluates it from a radical feminist perspective:

> [T]he entire approach is based upon setting up a hierarchy of degradation of (violence against) nature. We do not seek to protect nature from all harm, because of its inherent value. Instead, we seek to regulate how much harm is done, stopping short only when we might harm our own self-interest. As a result, some damage is simply allowed, such as pollution caused by an unregulated substance, or any pollution that falls within the regulatory standards or the permit terms and conditions. Other harm is deemed to be unacceptable, but in practice is condoned; pollution in contravention of the statute or permit is illegal, but the response is usually to allow such conduct to continue under the auspices of a compliance agreement. Even when formal sanctions, such as criminal prosecution, are used, the response is unlikely to require the polluter's activities to cease permanently. Instead, the best result expected from the application of formal sanctions is statutory compliance; the offender is reduced to an acceptable level of environmental harm.[150]

Hughes observes that there are parallels between the law's treatment of ecological damage and legal approaches to violence against, and degradation of, women. She notes that, in the regulation of pornography, the definition of what is "obscene" is to a large extent based on "the degree of societal harm that may flow from exposure to the material"[151] rather than on the "actual harm done to the women who must pose for the camera."[152] She concludes that "our laws regulate, rather than prohibit, this environmental damage, just as they engage in the social regulation (not prohibition) of the degree of violence against women."[153]

Hughes argues that the challenge is one of replacing a system based on domination with a system based on equality and that ecofeminism "suggests a number of different principles upon which human relationships with the environment could be based."[154] She explores the

---

145 (1995) 8:2 CJWL 502.

146 *Ibid* at 511.

147 *Ibid.*

148 In fact, she is quite upfront about the personal nature of her engagement with this issue and the need to think critically about her own position as an environmental lawyer: *ibid* at 510-11. For a commentary on the dangers of legal co-option in the context of the environmental justice movement, see Luke W Cole, "Foreword: A Jeremiad on Environmental Justice and the Law" (1995) 14:1 Stan Envtl LJ ix.

149 RSC 1985, c F-14.

150 Hughes, *supra* note 144 at 514.

151 *Ibid* at 515.

152 *Ibid.*

153 *Ibid* at 516.

154 *Ibid* at 517.

principles of "kinship, interconnection, cyclic patterns, use of emotion, and responsibility,"[155] before turning to a consideration of how they might be built into a "re-visioned" *Fisheries Act*:

> My approach has been to try to imagine a law in which nature is of central importance. ... I have tried to put fish into a social position of substantive equality, where their interests are accorded no less importance than human interests (while recognizing that their well-being is in our best interests). While there is a danger of anthropomorphism here, I have tried to avoid this by framing the law on the basis of human responsibility to nature, not by looking at nature's "rights." In other words, I have tried to draft a model law in which we are required to realize that fish do count, and which makes people both individually and collectively responsible for behaviour that treats fish as a "lesser other."[156]

Hughes's version of the *Fisheries Act* takes up less than four pages of text but provides a fascinating example of a fundamentally different legal framework that is, nonetheless, recognizable from the perspective of traditional environmental regulation.[157] Her approach exemplifies an attitude toward environmental protection that avoids the polar extremes of naïve optimism about the capacity of the legal system as it presently exists to address environmental problems and unrelieved cynicism about the capacity of law to do anything at all. However, as Hughes acknowledges, the most significant obstacle to implementing her approach is "the political and cultural acceptability of the underlying notion that nature should be treated with equality and respect."[158] She notes that "[u]nless our dominant cultural attitude toward nature changes, there can be no political will to even examine ecofeminist proposals."[159]

Thus, Hughes seems to leave us with the same question asked by the other scholars who have tackled the interface between environmental ethics and environmental law: can any species of legal mechanism or legal reform address problems the roots of which lie deep within our "cultural myths"?

V. CONCLUSION

> [The] extension of ethics, so far studied only by philosophers, is actually a process in ecological evolution. Its sequences may be described in ecological as well as in philosophical terms. An ethic, ecologically, is a limitation on freedom of action in the struggle for existence. An ethic, philosophically, is a differentiation of social from antisocial conduct. These are two definitions of one thing.[160]

This chapter has provided an overview of our evolving understanding of the relationship between humans and the ecosphere. The first substantive section contrasted prevailing economic rationality with basic ecological principles, including complexity theory and the implications of the second law of thermodynamics, and revealed that contemporary

---

155 *Ibid* at 526.

156 *Ibid* at 525.

157 Hughes points out that her attempt to incorporate ecofeminist principles led her to build on many of the same policies that "reform environmentalism has been working towards for years." She mentions participatory democracy, risk-averseness, environmental reclamation, and accountability. However, she insists, "[w]here ecofeminism takes the proposal beyond reform environmentalism is: first, in the requirement that decision-makers take into account the real dangers that lie in our current tendency to treat nature as 'something apart,' rather than our home; and second, in the notion that *no* level of harm is acceptable." *Ibid* at 526 (emphasis in original).

158 *Ibid* at 530.

159 *Ibid*.

160 Leopold, *supra* note 76 at 38.

mechanistic utilitarian economic models are dangerously inadequate in their treatment of biophysical reality. The chapter then provided a brief review of elements of ecological racism and their similarly inadequate treatment in theory and law. The final major section, on environmental ethics in law, showed that, compared to various Indigenous practices, current environmental law shares much with economic theory; in particular, the underlying premises of both treat the ecosphere merely as a treasure trove of resources for human use and enjoyment.

The analysis illustrates that the way modern culture—indeed, any culture—relates to the ecosphere, as revealed by its economic practices, management institutions, and environmental law, is invariably a reflection of that culture's dominant world view. Techno-industrial society's approach to "the environment" springs from an attitude of exploitive utilitarianism and dominance. In many respects, contemporary society's treatment of its visible minorities runs parallel to its treatment of the environment.

Any world view can be only a partial representation of reality and, therefore, should constantly evolve as knowledge improves and circumstances require. The important point is that environmental law derives not from nature but, rather, from human *perceptions* of nature. Existing environmental law in Canada embodies the dominant scientific and ethical perspective of industrial cultures everywhere, but there is nothing natural, preordained, or inevitable about that perspective. On the contrary, it is only one severely flawed variant among an indeterminate number of possible alternatives.

On an infinite planet, it might matter little how far human perceptions of nature departed from the "true" nature of biophysical reality. However, as the scale of the human enterprise converges with that of the ecosphere, it is essential that the structure, complexity, and behaviour of our management models reflect the corresponding characteristics of the natural world. Accelerating global change raises serious questions about the validity of contemporary framing of human–environment relationships. Indeed, since the human enterprise has significantly overshot long-term carrying capacity, the international community must abandon its prevailing myth of perpetual growth with decoupling. Instead, we should be developing a global plan aimed at controlled contraction with greater equity. Learning to live more fairly within the biophysical means of nature is an essential prerequisite for the sustainability of civilization beyond the 21st century.

Consider a precedent for such a dramatic, culture-wide paradigm shift: for most of recorded history, the Ptolemaic model, "Earth at the centre of the universe," served as an adequate first approximation of reality. In fact, even today, most people could live their entire lives, without penalty, acting as if this shared illusion were true. It became necessary to incorporate Copernicus's heliocentric view of the solar system into the European world view only with the need for accurate navigation that accompanied the expansion of trade during the Scientific/Industrial Revolution. Today, it is necessary to adopt a more holistic perspective on humans-in-the-ecosphere if we wish to avoid crashing the entire system, including the human enterprise. It will not be easy. Dramatic shifts in world view are stiffly resisted by established interests and painfully slow to triumph—only in 1992 did the Catholic Church admit its error in persecuting Galileo for his confirmation of Copernican reality over 300 years earlier.

Traditional land-based cultures live in immediate contact with their natural surroundings, often very aware of the limitations and the fragility of the ecosystems that sustain them. They have developed practices, sometimes over millennia, that enable them to survive and thrive as part of nature. These practices represent an understanding of, and adaptation to, the particular environment in which a culture has evolved (albeit sometimes after having significantly altered the habitat and driven easily hunted mammals and birds to extinction). The perceived role of humanity may vary considerably among differing traditional world views, from that of "one creature among many" to that of "steward of the whole," but often converges on recognition that humans actually have limited sway over the natural world.

We, too, must come to acknowledge the limitations of our scientific, economic, political, and legal paradigms. Human understanding is ever-evolving and forever partial. Newtonian science and derivative economic models see humanity as separate from and dominant over natural process, but contemporary science argues for holism and greater humility. As we embrace our new-found dependence on non-human nature, we must be open to novel ethical questions raised by that dependence.

Whether philosophical or scientific, new or ancient, the ways of thinking about the natural world and our place within it have profound implications for law. Certainly, accelerating global change is compelling evidence that the time has come for legal scholars and practitioners to abandon their prevailing "flat Earth" approach to the environment. This is a significant challenge. While law can sometimes be adapted to meet changing social perceptions, it tends to follow rather than to lead any transition. Those skeptical about the possibility of using law to alter our environmental practices, therefore, have a point. However, they do lose sight of one important consideration: while it may not create new realities, the law can mediate between those satisfied with the status quo and those striving to visualize and practise alternatives. In that sense, it has a crucial role to play.

QUESTIONS

1. Complexity theory, particularly in relation to ecosystem behaviour, shows the world to be a far less predictable place than implied by the "normal" (Newtonian) science upon which most environmental law is premised. For example, environmental impact assessment generally assumes smooth change and predictable outcomes. How should our emerging understanding of complex systems characterized by lags, thresholds, and other forms of discontinuous behaviour affect the structuring of legal responses to environmental protection?

2. Following the prevailing reductionist and mechanistic interpretation of nature, traditional property law assumes that the environment can be divided up into marketable commodities and harvested for private profit. At present, there is growing support for the privatization of "natural capital" stocks (for example, fish stocks and forests) on the assumption that private ownership will better ensure resource conservation. However, market and related economic conditions may encourage stock liquidation. This is problematic because we now recognize that these same stocks provide a wide range of common pool life-support functions in addition to being marketable goods. This means that the exploitation of a particular stock for private gain (for example, a forest for lumber) may destroy a greater value of biophysical services upon which all life depends (for example, carbon sink, biodiversity, and climate stabilization functions). How, in your opinion, should the common or public values associated with privately owned resource stocks be treated by society and in law?

3. Should human interests be the determinative factor in decision-making regarding environmental protection or resource exploitation? Do you agree with Stone that granting "rights" to the environment, or to particular natural objects, could offer a useful tool for balancing human and non-human interests? What are the conceptual and practical difficulties with Stone's proposal? What are the advantages of his proposal, both from an anthropocentric and from a non-anthropocentric perspective? Does Hughes's proposal, based on the notion of human responsibility toward nature, represent a better alternative?

4. Many now argue that far-reaching changes in societal values are going to be necessary in order to address the environmental problems that we currently face. Consider the following statement:

> When most people see a large automobile and think first of the air pollution it causes, rather than the social status it conveys, environmental ethics will have arrived. In a fragile biosphere, the ultimate fate of humanity may depend on whether we can cultivate deeper sources of fulfillment, founded on a widespread ethic of limiting consumption and finding

non-material enrichment. An ethic becomes widespread enough to restrain antisocial behaviour effectively, moreover, only when it is encoded in culture, in society's collective memory, experience, and wisdom.[161]

In your opinion, what role, if any, does law have to play in developing, promoting, or "encoding" such an ethic? How could it best do so?

5. What is our moral obligation to future generations?[162]

6. To what extent should questions of eco-justice and transboundary environmental impacts influence private consumption decisions? Could such considerations be incorporated into domestic laws?

FURTHER READINGS

Palmer, Clare, "An Overview of Environmental Ethics" in A Light & H Rolston III, eds, *Environmental Ethics: An Anthology* (Oxford: Blackwell, 2003) 15.

Rees, William E, "Avoiding Collapse: An Agenda for Sustainable Degrowth and Relocalizing the Economy," Climate Justice Project (BC) (2014), online (pdf): *Canadian Centre for Policy Alternatives* <https://www.policyalternatives.ca/sites/default/files/uploads/publications/BC%20Office/2014/06/ccpa-bc_AvoidingCollapse_Rees.pdf>.

Rees, William E, "Cities as Dissipative Structures: Global Change and the Vulnerability of Urban Civilization" in MP Weinstein & RE Turner, eds, *Sustainability Science: The Emerging Paradigm and the Urban Environment* (New York: Springer, 2012).

Rees, William E, "What's Blocking Sustainability? Human Nature, Cognition and Denial" (2010) 6:2 SSPP 13, online (pdf): *Texas A&M AgriLife* <https://agrilifecdn.tamu.edu/wefnexus/files/2017/01/WhatsBlockingSustainabilityRees2010_033015.pdf>.

World Commission on Environment and Development, *Our Common Future* (Oxford: Oxford University Press, 1987).

---

161 Alan Durning, "Asking How Much Is Enough" in LR Brown, S Postel, C Flavin, eds, *State of the World 1991: A Worldwatch Institute Report on Progress Toward a Sustainable Society* (New York and London: WW Norton, 1991) 153 at 165-66.

162 See J Gaba, "Environmental Ethics and Our Moral Relationship to Future Generations: Future Rights and Present Virtue" (1999) 24 Colum J Envtl L 249.

CHAPTER TWO

ETHICAL DIMENSIONS OF ENVIRONMENTAL LAW

Sara Bagg

I. ETHICS AND ITS RELATIONSHIP TO LAW

Generally speaking, the relationship between ethics and the law is complex and much debated.[1] Thus, in order to properly understand the relationship between environmental ethics and environmental law, we must begin with a discussion of the nature of this relationship more generally. A legal system in a democratic society is a tool to establish explicit rules of acceptable conduct, including prescribed sanctions in cases of rule violations and installing designated officials who are enabled to write, interpret, and enforce the rules. While ethical norms

---

1 For the reader's understanding, the terms "ethics" and "morality" are used basically interchangeably in this chapter (with ethics generally used in reference to moral values and principles at work in an applied context). These terms are technical terms defined variously by different authors in different contexts. The work these terms do here is ultimately clarified within these pages.

are action *guiding*, the law is a means of managing and controlling human interactions and relationships.

The law in Canada and other democracies is designed to protect citizens from harm and maintain well-ordered relations between the government and citizens, between organizations and citizens, and among citizens themselves. A legal system, on the whole, is made up of rules of conduct (sometimes called primary rules), which are recognizable; applicable; and understood by reference to their relationship with other, secondary rules (which establish how the rules of conduct can be ascertained, introduced, changed, or eliminated).[2] In Canada, the secondary rules include the Constitution, encompassing the *Canadian Charter of Rights and Freedoms*;[3] the "unwritten" constitutional principles; and laws of legal interpretation, including judicial interpretation and precedent.[4] A critical concept defining a legal system in a democracy is the rule of law. Mentioned in the preamble to our Charter, the rule of law is the idea that no person is above the law/every person is subject to the law—including lawmakers, law enforcers, and judges.

Whereas a valid law is one that is backed by an effective legal system, foundational ethical principles are deemed reliable when they are proven to be reliable beyond a given situation or context. Although there are likely no ethical principles that are held by all moral agents, neither are these principles simply personal or culturally relative. For the present purposes, we will suggest that the "universality" of basic ethical principles is secured through the meta-ethical ideals of integrity (that people ought to do what they say they will do), reciprocity (that equitable exchanges between people are vital), and the fact that it is wrong to harm innocent people (the principle of harm).

Opinions about the relationship between the law and morality vary widely, with theorists famously debating about whether morality is a necessary condition of a valid legal system (which means an unjust legal system is therefore not law) or whether the two concepts overlap in a manner that is inessential.[5] The separation thesis is the idea that legal and ethical norms each exist in their own sphere, and that the validity of a law depends only on how it is made.[6] An example of a Canadian law lacking moral content is the traffic law that establishes whether people are to drive on the right-hand side of the road (as in Canada or the United States) or the left-hand side (as in the United Kingdom, Australia, or Japan).

Despite this example, clearly many Canadian laws are rooted in moral principles.[7] The Charter is a part of the constitutional framework in accordance with which all Canadian public laws are written, and it guarantees that laws governing the relationship between citizens and the state do not infringe citizens' right to think and hold beliefs according to their own conscience, to be treated equally, to be secure, and to be free. Where a law conflicts with these legal rights, which are also moral principles, it is unconstitutional.[8] If the law cannot be properly amended, it will be found invalid (see, for example, the *Reference re Same-Sex*

---

2   HLA Hart, *The Concept of Law* (Oxford: Oxford University Press, 1961) [Hart, *The Concept of Law*].

3   Part I of the *Constitution Act, 1982*, being Schedule B to the *Canada Act 1982* (UK), 1982, c 11.

4   *The Constitution Act, 1982*, being Schedule B to the *Canada Act 1982* (UK), 1982, c 11; Owen Minns, "Hart's Rule of Recognition, in Canada?" (7 May 2007), online (pdf): *Minns.ca* <https://minns.ca/owen/image/portfolio/rule-of-recognition-in-canada-20070507r2.pdf>.

5   HLA Hart, "Positivism and the Separation of Law and Morals" (1957) 71 Harv L Rev 593; LL Fuller, "Positivism and Fidelity to Law—A Reply to Professor Hart" (1958) 71:4 Harv L Rev 630.

6   Hart, *The Concept of Law, supra* note 2.

7   Wilfrid J Waluchow, *A Common Law Theory of Judicial Review* (Cambridge: Cambridge University Press, 2007).

8   Wilfrid J Waluchow, "Constitutional Morality and Bills of Rights" in Grant Huscroft, ed, *Expounding the Constitution: Essays in Constitutional Theory* (Cambridge: Cambridge University Press, 2008).

Marriage).[9] Further instances of Canadian laws rooted in moral concepts or principles are not hard to find. See, for example, our criminal law, its purpose being to safeguard public peace, order, security, and health[10] with punishment that is ethical;[11] Canadian contract laws, which rely on the idea that a promisor has, by his or her promise, created a reasonable expectation that it will be kept;[12] and, finally, Canadian tort law, which has been conceived as a form of corrective justice concerned with restoring equality between a doer and a sufferer of harm.[13]

So, although Canada does have on the books laws that are morally neutral, and there exist examples of Canadian laws that at one time were applicable before they were found to breach Charter rights, there is an intuitive resonance to the idea that "the reasons we have for establishing, maintaining and reforming law include moral reasons."[14] Broadly speaking, we can say or hope that legislators and legal actors in Canada's legal system are striving, in their drafting and application of the law, to represent Canadians' ideas about what is good, right, virtuous, fair, and just—though our understanding of these concepts is extremely tenuous and ever-evolving, and consensus is difficult or impossible. At times, the public conversation about a legal issue will provoke a moral debate among citizens, deliberating as a society over appropriate ethical and legal responses to the issue. The result of this conversation may be an affirmation of the law, continued resistance to the law's validity in the form of social movements, or an evolution in the law to properly reflect an expression of Canadians' values at the time. A fitting example of this type of public conversation and the law's responsiveness to society's shifting values is the Supreme Court of Canada's decisions considering the morality and legality of medically assisted death: see *Rodriguez v British Columbia (Attorney General)*[15] and then, much later, *Carter v Canada (Attorney General)*.[16] In 2015, the Supreme Court recognized a shift in the social and factual landscape in the 22 years between the two cases and overturned its previous decision to uphold the law criminalizing medically assisted death.

II. MORAL ROOTS AND LEGAL RULES

The value of possessing a basic understanding of the moral principles upon which our environmental laws are founded can be usefully compared with the value of possessing a basic understanding of the importance of keeping promises to one's ability to interpret and apply contract law. Though commercial contract law can be incredibly complex, and result in years-long legal battles with multimillion-dollar judgments and hundred-page long judicial decisions, underpinning the law and arguments in these cases are certain basic principles and values we begin to absorb around kindergarten: say what you mean, tell the truth, ask questions if you do not understand, stick with what you choose, make good on your promises, and ask permission if you are not sure. While, of course, things become much more complicated, and

---

9   2004 SCC 79, [2004] 3 SCR 698.

10 *Reference re Validity of Section 5(a) of the Dairy Industry Act*, [1949] SCR 1, 1948 CanLII 2.

11 *Criminal Code*, RSC 1985, c C-46, s 718.

12 Sir David Hughes Parry, "The Sanctity of Contracts in English Law," *The Hamlyn Lectures*, Tenth Series (London: Steven & Sons, 1959).

13 Ernest Weinrib, "The Special Morality of Tort Law" (1989) 34 McGill LJ 3.

14 John Finnis, "The Truth in Legal Positivism" in Robert P George, ed, *The Autonomy of Law* (Oxford: Clarendon Press) at 204.

15 [1993] 3 SCR 519, 1993 CanLII 75.

16 2015 SCC 5, [2015] 1 SCR 331.

nuances and exceptions to the kindergarten rules (which are simply stated moral principles) abound, our grasp of these basic notions of fairness, equity, and consent allows us to comprehend the fundamentals of contract law. Our interpretations and applications of the law reflect this basic understanding. Also informing our understanding of contract law, at arguably the most basic level, is the underlying value we place on our ability to get along with others, which gives the kindergarten rules their shape and meaning. Human relationships tend to require some degree of predictability, trust, and fulfillment of obligations to one another if the relationships are to function well (whether we see this functioning well as a matter of maximizing well-being, a categorical imperative, or something else). While the associations made here are surely grossly oversimplified, they highlight a connection (perhaps necessary but certainly not sufficient) between the value we humans place on reliability in our relationships, the moral principles that direct us to fulfill our commitments to one another, and the laws of contract.

As we explore the relationship between environmental ethics and environmental law, we will find that things are much less obvious or intuitive, and much more complicated. As a starting place, there is no doubt that for most of us the values and morals informing our human relationships are more easily understood and articulated than our values and morals concerning our relationship to nature.

At the beginning of his famous paper, "Should Trees Have Standing? Towards Legal Rights for Natural Objects," Christopher Stone cites Charles Darwin's observation that

> the history of a man's moral development has been a continual extension in the objects of his "social instincts and sympathies." Originally each man had regard only for himself and those of a very narrow circle about him; later, he came to regard more and more "not only the welfare, but the happiness of all his fellow-men"; then "his sympathies became more tender and widely diffused, extending to men of all races."[17]

Stone's point, and Darwin's before him, is that we humans end up caring for those we can relate to. The suggestion is that our morals tend to arise out of our ability to sympathize with or at least comprehend the object of our attention. Following this idea, our environmental ethics are an extension of our ability to understand and relate to nature (for example, if or how we value nature, and our understanding of what is required for nature to thrive).

How do these possible ways of thinking about environmental ethics relate to our environmental laws? See, for example, the preamble to the *Canadian Environmental Protection Act, 1999*,[18] which reads like a moral treatise in its reference to environmental ethics concepts,

---

17 (1972) 45 S Cal L Rev 450 at 450.

18 SC 1999, c 33 [CEPA]. The preamble reads:
     Whereas the Government of Canada seeks to achieve sustainable development that is based on an ecologically efficient use of natural, social and economic resources and acknowledges the need to integrate environmental, economic and social factors in the making of all decisions by government and private entities;
     Whereas the Government of Canada is committed to implementing pollution prevention as a national goal and as the priority approach to environmental protection;
     Whereas the Government of Canada acknowledges the need to virtually eliminate the most persistent and bioaccumulative toxic substances and the need to control and manage pollutants and wastes if their release into the environment cannot be prevented;
     Whereas the Government of Canada recognizes the importance of an ecosystem approach;
     Whereas the Government of Canada will continue to demonstrate national leadership in establishing environmental standards, ecosystem objectives and environmental quality guidelines and codes of practice;
     Whereas the Government of Canada is committed to implementing the precautionary principle that, where there are threats of serious or irreversible damage, lack of full scientific certainty shall not be used as a reason for postponing cost-effective measures to prevent environmental degradation;

including sustainable development, pollution prevention, ecosystem approach, the pre-cautionary principle, environmental quality, and biological diversity. As the language of the preamble, these terms are meant to aid in interpreting the Act.[19] While in the contracts example we can logically connect the legal requirement to honour a contract with the moral requirement to keep our word, we lack a comparable comprehension of what "sustainable development" means or requires, or what is really at stake if we fail. The concept is abstract and not within the control of any identifiable member of the moral community. Outside of CEPA, we have heard references to these terms in various contexts in relation to caring for the environment: in lessons at school, in advertisements, in corporate mission statements, in pol-itical speeches, and by those who believe passionately about protecting and preserving nature. Though these concepts find their meaning within the context of environmental ethics, most Canadians cannot speak in a thoughtful or informed way about the values they protect and, as such, they are vacuous as moral concepts. Further, there is no meaningful connection to be drawn between such terms and a well-informed understanding of the fundamental purpose of CEPA and its regulations, which set out the rules for the manufacture, importation, process-ing, transport, sale, use, discard, or release of toxic substances into the environment. There is little evidence that CEPA's preamble has greatly affected the manner the Act has been inter-preted, enforced, or applied.[20]

Whereas the Government of Canada recognizes that all governments in Canada have authority that enables them to protect the environment and recognizes that all governments face environmental problems that can benefit from cooperative resolution;

Whereas the Government of Canada recognizes the importance of endeavouring, in cooperation with provinces, territories and aboriginal peoples, to achieve the highest level of environmental quality for all Canadians and ultimately contribute to sustainable development;

Whereas the Government of Canada recognizes that the risk of toxic substances in the environment is a matter of national concern and that toxic substances, once introduced into the environment, can-not always be contained within geographic boundaries;

Whereas the Government of Canada recognizes the integral role of science, as well as the role of traditional aboriginal knowledge, in the process of making decisions relating to the protection of the environment and human health and that environmental or health risks and social, economic and tech-nical matters are to be considered in that process;

Whereas the Government of Canada recognizes the responsibility of users and producers in relation to toxic substances and pollutants and wastes, and has adopted the "polluter pays" principle;

Whereas the Government of Canada is committed to ensuring that its operations and activities on federal and aboriginal lands are carried out in a manner that is consistent with the principles of pollution prevention and the protection of the environment and human health;

Whereas the Government of Canada will endeavour to remove threats to biological diversity through pollution prevention, the control and management of the risk of any adverse effects of the use and release of toxic substances, pollutants and wastes, and the virtual elimination of persistent and bioaccumulative toxic substances;

Whereas the Government of Canada recognizes the need to protect the environment, including its biological diversity, and human health, by ensuring the safe and effective use of biotechnology;

And whereas the Government of Canada must be able to fulfil its international obligations in respect of the environment.

19 In the House of Commons debates, when Bill C-74 (CEPA) was introduced, the proposed preamble was described by the Opposition as "elegant prose ... which really has no legal status at all." See *House of Commons Debates*, 33-2, vol 8 (25 September 1987) at 9325 (Hon W Rompkey).

20 According to Boyd, there is a wide gap between Canada's regulation of chemical contaminants relative to the standards and guidelines in other industrialized nations. Boyd provides that

[b]illions of kilograms of toxic chemicals—including known carcinogens, endocrine disruptors, and chemicals that harm respiratory health, cardiovascular health, and neurological development—are discharged into Canadian air, water, and land by industry each and every year. Industrial chemicals

In consideration of the above, this chapter will attempt to give the reader some understanding of the complicated relationship (or lack thereof) between environmental ethics and environmental law. It will address the reality that this relationship is tenuous and poorly developed and will explore the reasons why this is harmful. The case summaries and questions for discussion at the end of the chapter are designed to encourage the reader to analyze the law and legal issues from an ethical perspective, consider some examples where legal decision-makers have been influenced by moral values or principles, and, finally, recognize and consider certain long-held assumptions in the Western philosophical tradition that create barriers in terms of our ability to ground our thinking about the environment in a respect for nature.

III. WHAT IS ENVIRONMENTAL ETHICS?

Environmental ethics is an area of applied ethics—branching off from moral philosophy—that is concerned with putting moral concepts (such as obligation and responsibility, good and bad, right and wrong, virtue and vice) to work in the context of environmental decision-making. Very generally, moral theories evaluate and take a stance on the human motives, actions, or dispositions best able to reduce harm or bring about happiness or well-being. Applied ethics, to some extent, relies on the work done by moral theorists to attempt to find answers to ethical problems in a given context. The field of environmental ethics specifically tackles ethical problems related to our relationship to nature; our degree of accountability for the health of the planet; our responsibility to preserve and protect nature, its resources, and inhabitants; and the extent to which we ought to alter our current choices to protect and preserve our natural environment in the present and for the future.

A. APPROACHES TO ENVIRONMENTAL ETHICS

> [See the Notes and Questions section at the end of this chapter to gain a better understanding of the moral theories being referenced below and their application.]

To answer the ethical problems previously identified, we must consider who is accountable and to whom; what value we place upon animals, who cannot themselves be held morally accountable; and whether we believe nature has a value beyond its resources or is for our enjoyment. As we sort out our position on these questions, we need to know not just who or what we value, but also why we hold this point of view. We may focus on the idea that we have a duty to one another, based upon our intrinsic value or human dignity, and so make decisions that are consistent with preserving and protecting this value/dignity. Based on this idea, moral actions require morally defensible motives, regardless of the outcome in a particular case.

In the alternative, our ethical questions may be answered with a special interest in the consequences of our actions, and in consideration of making choices that maximize the current and future well-being of our moral community, as we have defined it. These ethical questions may relate to how we travel, source our food, or heat our homes. They may include where we work, what we work at, or who we vote for. Environmental decision-making occurs at the level of the individual, the family, community, municipality, province, nation, and internationally.

---

spewed into the Canadian environment in large quantities include arsenic, cadmium, formaldehyde, toluene, and xylene.

See David R Boyd, *Cleaner, Greener, Healthier* (Vancouver: UBC Press, 2015) at 139 and then at 25 [Boyd, *Cleaner, Greener, Healthier*], referencing "About the National Pollutant Release Inventory" (6 December 2018), online: *Government of Canada* <https://www.canada.ca/en/environment-climate-change/services/national-pollutant-release-inventory/about-national-pollutant-release-inventory.html>.

Weighing the relevant consequences of our decisions requires considering how our choices contribute to or mitigate problems on a global scale, with an awareness of environmental as well as socio-economic impacts, and considering the reality that some people may be affected disproportionately and so unfairly, with a sense of how these problems may evolve or compound over time.

As a virtuous or caring person is arguably the one best able to make choices that are environmentally just, we may approach ethical issues with a focus on our moral character, and the value in cultivating a love and respect for our natural environment. We may abandon the notion of objectivity and instead recognize that relationships of humans to the non-human environment are, in part, constitutive of what it is to be human.[21] In this vein, a question about whether to eat meat versus become vegetarian, for example, yields an answer not based upon a sense of obligation or cost-benefit analysis, but rather upon a deep understanding about the intrinsic value of all sentient beings and the survival of the Earth.

We may further choose to turn our focus more directly and immediately on the environmental problems we humans are facing, worrying less about what to value or why and attempting to be pragmatic about building consensus and getting things done. Globally, environmental problems relate to air and water pollution; water scarcity; deforestation and a loss of biodiversity; species and ecosystem extinction; waste disposal and plastics; climate change; and environmental justice issues (*intergenerational justice*: the rights of future generations; *intragenerational justice*: the idea that environmental harms and goods should be equitably and not unfairly affected by race, gender, or socio-economic status; and *inter-species justice*: the idea our human-centred laws are a form of discrimination). In Canada more specifically, the central problems of environmental ethics could include the oil sands; pipeline development; coal exports; mining; deforestation; fisheries; and Aboriginal rights issues (for example, the traditional or cultural value of exploited land, or access to clean drinking water on remote reserves). Law and policy implications will differ depending on whether or how we answer these questions, and ultimately which theory best explains our environmental decision-making.

IV. THE CURRENT STATE OF OUR ENVIRONMENT

[See the Notes and Questions section at the end of this chapter to learn how Canada is reacting to the United Nations position and policy on climate change.]

Whatever approach one takes to answer the central problems within the field of environmental ethics, there is no question that we are, at this time, in need of some greater understanding of how to minimize the effects of pollution, environmental degradation, and environmental disasters. We need to get a grip on the irreconcilable relationship between our economic reliance on nature's resources to maintain our way of life, and science's reality that such a way of life must be altered in order to avoid human suffering. In order to do this, we may need to explore our most basic assumptions about our relationship to nature or nature's *purpose*, and also accept the strong relationship between prudent environmental decision-making and relevant scientific considerations (including taking a precautionary approach where scientific evidence is indeterminate).

At an international level, we humans are undeniably failing each other in terms of our ability to understand how to care for one another where environmental welfare is concerned. A 2016 United Nations report on the issue of human rights and obligations relating to the enjoyment of a safe, clean, healthy, and sustainable environment provides a poignant sense of the

---

21 Karen J Warren, "The Power and the Promise of Ecological Feminism" in Byron Willison, ed, *Environmental Ethics for Canadians* (Oxford: Oxford University Press, 2012) at 167.

weightiness of our place in history, in terms of the extreme nature of the effects of humans' environmental decision-making to this point, and the hyper-importance of our environmental choices to address these consequences, going forward:

> As average global temperatures rise, deaths, injuries and displacement of persons from climate-related disasters such as tropical cyclones increase, as do mortality and illness from heat waves, drought, disease and malnutrition. In general, the greater the increase in average temperature, the greater the effects on the rights to life and health as well as other human rights. The foreseeable consequences of even a 2°C rise in average global temperature are dramatic. ...
>
> Climate change will compound the problem of access to safe drinking water, currently denied to about 1.1 billion people. It has been estimated that about 8 per cent of the global population will see a severe reduction in water resources with a 1°C rise in the global mean temperature, rising to 14 per cent at 2°C. ...
>
> With respect to the right to food, climate change is already impairing the ability of some communities to feed themselves, and the number affected will grow as temperatures rise. The Intergovernmental Panel on Climate Change states that "all aspects of food security are potentially affected by climate change, including food access, utilization, and price stability." ...
>
> As the Human Rights Council has recognized, the worst effects of climate change are felt by those who are already vulnerable because of factors such as geography, poverty, gender, age, indigenous or minority status, national or social origin, birth or other status and disability. In the words of the Intergovernmental Panel on Climate Change, "People who are socially, economically, culturally, politically, institutionally or otherwise marginalized are especially vulnerable to climate change and also to some adaptation and mitigation responses."
>
> • • •
>
> Climate change also threatens to devastate the other forms of life that share this planet with us. As the world warms, increasingly disastrous consequences will ensue. One study has found that if global temperatures increase by more than 2 to 3°C, 20 to 30 per cent of the assessed plant and animal species are likely to be at a high risk of extinction. The decimation of other species will harm the human species too.[22]

These harms and threats to human life and well-being caused by climate change (as above, relating to environmental disasters, the scarcity of food and water, social injustices, and endangered species), and similarly the harms and threats to human life and well-being caused by pollution and resource depletion, are the consequences of our modern industrial society. This includes resource extraction—its methods and consumption, using the environment as a vehicle for waste disposal, creating imbalances in the chemistry and biochemistry of the Earth, and the like. To the extent that the law is one of the most practical and powerful tools to offer protection, it is critical that the law's authors, interpreters, and implementers understand the current state of environmental problems and their effect on the people whom the law is designed to protect.

On the best evidence available (given the predicted trajectory of environmental degradation, pollution, and climate change), our environmental laws are not doing enough. According to Canadian David Boyd, the United Nations' special rapporteur on human rights and the environment:

---

22 United Nations General Assembly, Human Rights Council, *Report of the Special Rapporteur on the Issue of Human Rights Obligations Relating to the Enjoyment of a Safe, Clean, Healthy and Sustainable Environment*, UNGAOR, 31st Sess, UN Doc A/HRC/31/52 (1 February 2016) at paras 24-30.

Contrary to the myth of a pristine green country providing environmental leadership to the world, a huge pile of studies proves beyond a reasonable doubt that Canada lags behind other nations in terms of environmental performance. According to researchers at Simon Fraser University, Canada's environmental performance ranks twenty-fourth out of the twenty-five wealthiest nations in the Organisation for Economic Co-operation and Development (OECD). The OECD has published blistering criticisms of Canada's weak laws and policies, perverse subsidies for unsustainable industries, and poor environmental performance.[23]

Boyd further observes that

this conclusion holds true across the entire spectrum of environmental issues, including air quality, drinking water, food safety, toxic substances, climate change and biodiversity. The consequences of these weak environmental laws and policies include thousands of premature deaths, millions of preventable diseases, billions of wasted dollars, and troubling injustices in the distribution of negative health outcomes.[24]

Based on Environment and Climate Change Canada's 2019 report,

Canada's climate has warmed and will warm further in the future, driven by human influence. Both past and future warming in Canada is, on average, about double the magnitude of global warming. Northern Canada has warmed and will continue to warm at even more than double the global rate.

• • •

The effects of widespread warming are evident in many parts of Canada and are projected to intensify in the future. The rate and magnitude of climate change under high versus low emission scenarios project two very different futures for Canada. Scenarios with large and rapid warming illustrate the profound effects on Canadian climate of continued growth in greenhouse gas emissions. Scenarios with limited warming will only occur if Canada and the rest of the world reduce carbon emissions to near zero early in the second half of the century and reduce emissions of other greenhouse gases substantially.

Beyond the next few decades, the largest uncertainty about the magnitude of future climate change is rooted in uncertainty about human behaviour, that is, whether the world will follow a pathway of low, medium, or high emissions. Given this uncertainty, projections based on a range of emission scenarios are needed to inform impact assessment, climate risk management, and policy development.[25]

A. THE CURRENT STATE OF OUR ENVIRONMENTAL LAW

In *Cleaner, Greener, Healthier*, Boyd explains how environmental laws, regulations, and policies, intended to protect human health from environmental hazards but watered down by economic and political factors, are failing Canadians.[26] Boyd argues that because our environmental laws

23 David R Boyd, *The Right to a Healthy Environment: Revitalizing Canada's Constitution* (Vancouver: UBC Press, 2012) at 6.

24 Boyd, *Cleaner, Greener, Healthier, supra* note 20 at 199.

25 Canada, Environment and Climate Change Canada, *Canada's Changing Climate Report—Executive Summary* (2019) at 5, 16, online (pdf): <https://changingclimate.ca/site/assets/uploads/sites/2/2019/03/CCCR_ExecSummary.pdf> (internal references omitted).

26 For more information, see Chapter 20 of this text; Boyd, *Cleaner, Greener, Healthier, supra* note 20; or Stepan Wood, Georgia Tanner & Benjamin Richardson, "What Ever Happened to Canadian Environmental Law?" (2010) 37 Ecology LQ 981, online: <http://digitalcommons.osgoode.yorku.ca/scholarly_works/1>.

are not written, interpreted, enforced, or applied in consideration of Canadians' right to a healthy environment, they are weak, easily changed, and poorly enforced. Boyd's arguments support the more general claim made at the beginning of the chapter that Canadian environmental law lacks a moral foundation.

According to Boyd, there are certain "fundamental constraints" that limit the effectiveness of environmental law and that can be applied at a global level. These constraints are as follows:

1. Environmental laws generally ignore the laws of nature, by ignoring the reality that the Earth and its resources are finite.
2. Environmental laws are made and then enforced by governments who are reliant on the revenue generated by the ecologically destructive activities they regulate.
3. Environmental laws exist within a context that tends to value and thus prioritize limitless growth, consumerism, the primacy of property rights over the public good, and the domination of transnational corporations.[27]

Boyd further argues that Canada's environmental laws, in comparison to those of other UN nations, stand out as particularly weak, and there are further economic, political, and legal factors that uniquely explain this vulnerability. These are as follows:

1. The false idea that Canada's economy depends on the extraction and export of natural resources (with industry holding the power to influence the government to delay, weaken, or reverse the impact of environmental laws).
2. The basic functioning of our first-past-the-post political system (leaving the smaller political parties with less populist priorities—such as the Green Party—at a substantial disadvantage in terms of their ability to influence policy or law-making.
3. The silence of our Constitution on the question of who, between Parliament and the provinces, holds law-making authority over the environment (leaving both the federal and provincial governments hesitant to create and enforce environmental laws, with governments either passing the buck or resisting enforcement by the other level of government). This problem is then further exacerbated by the lack of a constitutionally protected right to a healthy environment.[28]

In her essay "Complexities and Uncertainties in Matters of Human Rights and the Environment: Identifying the Judicial Role," Dinah Shelton discusses the elements required for a state to ensure a clean and healthy environment consistent with the enjoyment of human rights. These include the following: (1) the state should adopt laws and regulations to control pollution and limit the unsustainable exploitation of natural resources, (2) these environmental laws and regulations should be based on agreed-upon and scientific definitions of what constitutes "pollution" and "unsustainable" exploitation, (3) the state should have relevant agencies or other governing bodies applying the law and evaluating proposed projects or activities within their jurisdiction to assess possible impacts on the environment and persons who may be negatively affected, and, finally, (4) the public and all those involved in the approval process should be fully informed of the risks and harm and be able to make their voices heard before a decision is made.[29] In her assessment of contexts in which these requirements may not be

---

27 Boyd, *Cleaner, Greener, Healthier, supra* note 20 at 200-1.

28 *Ibid* at 201-18.

29 Dinah Shelton, "Complexities and Uncertainties in Matters of Human Rights and the Environment: Identifying the Judicial Role" in John H Knox & Ramin Pejan, eds, *The Human Right to a Healthy Environment* (Cambridge: Cambridge University Press, 2018) 97 at 97. Note that a similar position was set out over 20 years ago by WA Tilleman in "Public Participation in the Environmental Assessment Process: A Comparative Study of Impact Assessment in Canada, the United States, and the European Community" (1995) 33 Colum J of Transnat'l L 337 at 339.

met, Shelton suggests this may be due to states lacking the proper constitutional framework to prevent environmental harm that can infringe human rights or inadequacies in environmental laws or their enforcement (as suggested by Boyd). Shelton finds that the response in many countries to such failures of the law is litigation, with cases being brought forward to prevent projects, to challenge project approvals, to obtain redress when harm has occurred or is imminent, or to challenge the validity of inadequate laws for violating basic rights.[30]

B. UNARTICULATED VALUES

Without disagreeing with Shelton's suggestion about the potential role of the courts in ensuring environmental rights and health, Shelton's analysis of the necessary conditions for a robust environmental law that protects human rights ignores the role of moral values and principles in our ability to comprehend, or our willingness to enforce or uphold the law. In *Environmental Ethics*, Joseph R Desjardins writes:

> The tendency in our culture is to treat such issues as simply scientific, technological, or political problems. But they are much more than that. These environmental and ecological controversies raise fundamental questions about what we as human beings value, about the kind of beings we are, the kinds of lives we should live, our place in nature, and the kind of world in which we might flourish.[31]

Analysis of environmental law often focuses on the scientific, technological, economic, or political dimensions. Furthermore, a moral perspective is often perceived as facing off against these other lenses through which we view the law. Because of the idea that moral principles are in conflict with certain aspects of the law's purpose as opposed to being at the very heart of the law's purpose, we lack a shared understanding about why the law matters and what would be lost without it.

V. ENVIRONMENTAL ETHICS AND ENVIRONMENTAL LAW

In her paper "In Search of an Environmental Ethic," Alyson Flournoy argues that a robust environmental ethics is critical to the sound development of environmental law and policy.[32] Flournoy further argues that a better translation of our laws into a "language of ethics" is needed to facilitate this process.[33] Flournoy supports the earlier contention that to understand the ethic underlying our laws "we must uncover not just the objects of concern but the bases for our concern. ... [T]he continued maturation of a body of law appropriate to our society's needs and values depends on greater awareness of the values and ethics we currently embrace through our laws."[34]

In her work, Flournoy discusses how our ethical attunement influences the law in reference to our identification and analysis of the moral basis for punishment in the criminal law context (which in Canada is grounded in utilitarian and retributive justifications for punishment):

---

30 Shelton, *supra* note 29 at 98.

31 *Environmental Ethics: An Introduction to Environmental Philosophy*, 5th ed (Boston: Wadsworth Cengage Learning, 2013) at xii.

32 Alyson C Flournoy, "In Search of an Environmental Ethic" (2003) 28:1 Colum J of Envtl L 63.

33 *Ibid* at 69.

34 *Ibid* at 68 and 118.

These competing ethics and the values they advance are often discussed not just by philosophers but also by legal scholars and policymakers. In criminal law scholarship, it is not
uncommon for the ethical justification for a particular rule or decision to be addressed by a
scholar as part of legal analysis; it is part of the mainstream of criminal legal scholarship.
Because the debate is grounded in traditional philosophies long identified as the core ethical
force in this field, scholars are well versed in the subject. Either despite the fact that the
paths for arguing these issues are fairly well trod—or because they are—discourse about the
ethical theories that justify a given law, sentencing approach or reform proposal is quite
common to mainstream criminal law scholarship.[35]

As in the case of Canada's decriminalization of physician-assisted suicide more than 20
years after this was first considered by the Supreme Court, the law's failure to properly represent our moral values becomes a means for criticizing the law or bringing about the evolution
of the law. Furthermore, our understanding at the most basic level of why we have the rules
we do, why they matter, what harm they prevent, and what is lost if the rule is ignored in a
given instance grounds our ability to think critically and creatively about what the law should
say and how it should be interpreted, applied, and potentially amended.

In contrast to the contracts example, where the connection between the law, our moral
principles, and our values is easily traced, Flournoy states:

> The language of the law and the substance of public debate over environmental law both
> reveal scant attention to its ethical content. Our environmental laws remain politically con-
> troversial and subject to continuous debate over directions for reform. Yet there is only
> superficial discourse about the complex mix of values at stake. This limited discourse does
> not reflect the richness of the possibilities in this area. ...[36]
>
> Clearly, environmental laws and policies reflect normative or value judgments. As a
> society, we are making decisions about right and wrong, about priorities and imperatives,
> when we adopt policies and rules. If neither the public nor the decisionmakers articulate the
> ethical issues involved, we cannot ultimately know whether our laws and policies are con-
> sistent with our ethics. Just as in archery one learns from seeing where the last arrow struck
> and adjusts one's aim, we need to know what the bulls-eye is for environmental law, or else
> we're simply launching arrow after arrow with only random improvement. ...
>
> A more open process of identifying and debating the values at stake may allow a fuller
> development of the public's values. Ethics can broaden our ability to see and define the
> problem, by focusing us on what we care about. Also, there may be a risk that environmental
> values will not remain protected if they are poorly understood and articulated. Essential to
> long-term environmental protection is a clear understanding of the values that the laws
> serve. These values are and will continue to be in conflict with other values. If they are
> poorly articulated and understood, they can be too easily trumped.[37]

Flournoy highlights the problem:

> One possible explanation for why little attention has been paid to the ethical content of
> environmental law is that these ethics are inchoate. Articulating an ethic in this area is rela-
> tively challenging, involving—as environmental protection decisions do—complex technical
> decisions, significant uncertainty, a focus on the impacts of human actions on non-humans
> who may or may not be valued, and issues that may have long-term effects that extend far
> beyond a human lifetime. The complexity of environmental issues makes determining the
> values served by any given law or regulatory decision extremely difficult in many cases. Our

---

35 *Ibid* at 113.

36 *Ibid* at 109.

37 *Ibid* at 115-16.

limited understanding of the natural processes we continually affect makes uncertainty an unavoidable aspect of environmental decisions.[38]

VI. JUDICIAL INTERPRETATION OF ENVIRONMENTAL LAWS

The remainder of this chapter is designed to encourage conversation about the nature of environmental law in Canada, its moral foundation (or lack thereof), the question of whether or how Canadians value nature, and what this means for our choices (political, economic, moral, practical, and legal).

A. TO PUNISH VERSUS PROTECT

R v Hydro-Québec[39] is a leading case on constitutional law division of powers and a course-altering decision in the common law interpretation of Canada's environmental law. Hydro-Québec was charged with discharging polychlorinated biphenyls (PCBs) into the St Maurice River in Quebec in contravention of an order made under CEPA. Hydro-Québec challenged the constitutionality of the order. In its decision, the Supreme Court grounded Parliament's jurisdiction to govern a variety of environmental matters, including air and water pollution, waste management, and toxic substances, under its criminal law power under s 91(27) of the *Constitution Act, 1867*.[40] While the legislative scheme of CEPA clearly looks nothing like a standard criminal law prohibition, for constitutional purposes the courts have defined "criminal law" very broadly, requiring (1) a prohibition, (2) a penalty, and (3) a typically criminal purpose. While four out of nine members of the Supreme Court did not agree that CEPA fit within the criminal law framework, a five-member majority held that, because CEPA's administrative processes culminated in a prohibition enforced by a penalty, the scheme was sufficiently prohibitory to count as criminal law. The case is described above as "course-altering" because the Supreme Court could have considered an alternative to grounding Parliament's power to protect the environment in the criminal power, but chose not to do so in this case. With the benefit of hindsight, and in consideration of the current state of the global environmental crisis, the court might have found Parliament's jurisdiction over the environment to be a matter affecting the peace, order, and good government (POGG) of Canadians under s 91 of the *Constitution Act, 1867*. Ten years earlier in *R v Crown Zellerbach Canada Ltd*,[41] the Supreme Court upheld the validity of the *Ocean Dumping Act*[42] on the basis that all matters related to polluting the ocean were within the exclusive jurisdiction of the federal government, owing to the national concern branch of POGG. In *Crown Zellerbach*, the court explained the relevance of the national concern doctrine under POGG to matters touching all Canadians:

> [T]he true test must be found in the real subject matter of the legislation: if it is such that it goes beyond local or provincial concern or interests and must from its inherent nature be the concern of the Dominion as a whole ... then it will fall within the competence of the Dominion Parliament as a matter affecting the peace, order and good government of Canada, though it may in another aspect touch on matters specially reserved to the

---

38 *Ibid* at 110.

39 [1997] 3 SCR 213, 1997 CanLII 318.

40 (UK), 30 & 31 Vict, c 3, s 91.

41 [1988] 1 SCR 401, 1988 CanLII 63 [*Crown Zellerbach* cited to SCR].

42 SC 1974-75-76, c 55.

provincial legislatures. War and pestilence, no doubt, are instances; so, too, may be the drink or drug traffic, or the carrying of arms. In *Russell v. The Queen* [[(1882), 7 App Cas 829 (JCPC)]], Sir Montague Smith gave as an instance of valid Dominion legislation a law which prohibited or restricted the sale or exposure of cattle having a contagious disease. Nor is the validity of the legislation, when due to its inherent nature, affected because there may still be room for enactments by a provincial legislature dealing with an aspect of the same subject in so far as it specially affects that province.[43]

Bolstering the possibility that Canada's environmental law may have been more fittingly identified in reference to Parliament's powers under POGG, Jocelyn Stacey has argued that "the best way to understand the challenge that environmental issues pose for law is through the lens of an ongoing emergency. Like emergencies, environmental issues require decisions to be taken under conditions of deep uncertainty where the possibility of a catastrophe cannot be reliably eliminated in advance."[44]

In *Hydro-Québec* the Supreme Court failed to grapple with policy arguments that were introduced by Environment Canada and the Law Reform Commission concerning the necessity of a healthy environment to Canadians' health and well-being. Additionally the court failed to grapple with its own previous reasoning in *Ontario v Canadian Pacific Ltd* and *114957 Canada Ltée (Spraytech, Société d'arrosage) v Hudson (Town)*, where the court referred to "the right to a safe environment"; the importance of a "healthy environment"; and recognized that "[e]veryone is aware that individually and collectively, we are responsible for preserving the natural environment ... environmental protection [has] emerged as a fundamental value in Canadian society."[45] Failing to further entrench such values into Canada's environmental law jurisprudence, *Hydro-Québec* marked Canada's environmental law as punitive at its core, undervalued the role of environmental law to protect Canadians' health, and ignored the reality that protecting the environment is essential to this role.

B. EXISTENCE AND INHERENT VALUE

In order to calculate the damages owed to the province as a result of a forest fire caused by Canadian Forest Products Ltd, the Supreme Court in *British Columbia v Canadian Forest Products Ltd* examined various approaches to assessing the value of the forest:

> "Use value" includes the services provided by the ecosystem to human beings, including food sources, water quality and recreational opportunities. Even if the public are not charged for these services, it may be possible to quantify them economically by observing what the public pays for comparable services on the market.

• • •

> "Passive use" or "existence" value recognizes that a member of the public may be prepared to pay something for the protection of a natural resource, even if he or she never directly uses it. It includes both the psychological benefit to the public of knowing that the resource is protected, and the option value of being able to use it in the future. The branch of economics

---

43 *Crown Zellerbach, supra* note 41 at 423-24, quoting *Attorney-General for Ontario v Canada Temperance Federation*, 1946 CanLII 351, [1946] AC 193 at 205-6.

44 See Jocelyn Stacey, *The Constitution of the Environmental Emergency* (Oxford: Hart, 2018) at 1, noting however that Stacey does not address Parliament's powers under POGG but takes a completely different line of argument.

45 *Ontario v Canadian Pacific Ltd*, [1995] 2 SCR 1031 at para 55, 1995 CanLII 112; *114957 Canada Ltée (Spraytech, Société d'arrosage) v Hudson (Town)*, 2001 SCC 40 at para 1, [2001] 2 SCR 241.

known as *"contingent valuation"* uses survey techniques to attempt to quantify what the public would be prepared to pay to maintain these benefits. [Emphasis in original.]

• • •

Finally, an ecosystem may be said to have an "inherent value" beyond its usefulness to humans. Those who invoke inherent value argue that ecosystems should be preserved not just for their utility to humans, but because they are important in and of themselves. ... [T]o the extent humans recognize this inherent value, and are willing to forego income or wealth for it, it becomes a part of passive use value and becomes compensable.[46]

Though the court in this case did not award damages based on the "existence" or "inherent" value of the environment, the court stated that this was because of narrowly and commercially focused pleadings. Though the court was not given the tools to assess "ecological" or "environmental" losses in this case, it advised that it would have considered these things with the proper evidence.

C. CULTURAL VALUE

The court in *Platinex Inc v Kitchenuhmaykoosib Inninuwug First Nation*[47] introduced this case as one that highlighted the clash of "the desire for the economic development of the rich resources located on a vast tract of pristine land in a remote portion of Northwestern Ontario" and "an Aboriginal community fighting to safeguard and preserve its traditional land, culture, way of life and core beliefs."[48] Analyzing the potential harm that could result if an injunction to halt exploratory mining were not granted to the Kitchenuhmaykoosib Inninuwug First Nation, the court found:

It is critical to consider the nature of the potential loss from an Aboriginal perspective. From that perspective, the relationship that Aboriginal peoples have with the land cannot be understated. The land is the very essence of their being. It is their very heart and soul. No amount of money can compensate for its loss. Aboriginal identity, spirituality, laws, traditions, culture, and rights are connected to and arise from this relationship to the land. This is a perspective that is foreign to and often difficult to understand from a non-Aboriginal viewpoint.[49]

By granting the injunction, the Superior Court of Ontario arguably recognized the foundational relationship between Indigenous peoples' moral values and principles and the law (akin to the earlier discussion of the fundamental understanding of the importance of promise-keeping to contract law).[50]

---

46 2004 SCC 38 at para 138, [2004] 2 SCR 74.

47 2006 CanLII 26171, 272 DLR (4th) 727 (Ont Sup Ct J).

48 *Ibid* at para 1.

49 *Ibid* at para 80.

50 While there is no room in this chapter to explore the manner in which Indigenous peoples' relationship to nature may provide a valuable reference point to Canadians seeking some moral grounding for Canadian environmental law, a helpful reference is David Suzuki, "Indigenous People Are Fighting for Us All" (2 February 2017), online: <https://davidsuzuki.org/story/indigenous-people-are-fighting-for-us-all/>; and F Kohler et al, "Embracing Diverse Worldviews to Share Planet Earth" (2019) Conservation Biology, DOI: <https://doi.org/10.1111/cobi.13304>.

D. VALUING BIOLOGICAL DIVERSITY

In *Groupe Maison Candiac Inc v Canada (Attorney General)*,[51] the Federal Court upheld an emergency protection order issued by the governor in council under the *Species at Risk Act*[52] preventing the residential development of a Montreal suburb to protect the threatened western chorus frog. The protection order prohibited any removal of soil, alteration of surface water flows, draining of wetlands, or construction of infrastructure in portions of the region that constituted habitat for the western chorus frog, and the effect was that development could not proceed.[53]

In its decision the court referred to the following:

> The Earth Summit, held in Rio de Janeiro, Brazil, in June 1992 under the auspices of the United Nations, led to the signing of an important international agreement, the *United Nations Convention on Biological Diversity* [5 June 1992, 1760 UNTS 79, 31 ILM 818 (entered into force 29 December 1993) (the Convention on Biodiversity)]. This convention, which was ratified by 196 countries, is founded on a certain consensus, with the Contracting Parties stating, in particular, that they are:
>
> > a. conscious of "the intrinsic value of biological diversity and of the ecological, genetic, social, economic, scientific, educational, cultural, recreational and aesthetic values of biological diversity" and of "the importance of biological diversity for evolution and for maintaining life sustaining systems of the biosphere."[54]

E. RULE OF LAW (ACCOUNTABILITY TO LEGISLATIVE INTENT/ CONSTITUTIONAL RIGHTS AND COMMON LAW INTERPRETATIONS)

In *Tsleil-Waututh Nation v Canada (Attorney General)*,[55] the court unanimously quashed an order in council approving the Kinder Morgan pipeline project, holding the National Energy Board to a strict interpretation of the requirements set out in legislation and case law for assessing and approving pipeline projects.

First, the court found that the National Energy Board had scoped the project too narrowly in its assessment, ignoring the environmental effects of increased marine tanker traffic on endangered southern resident orcas. The court also found that Canada had failed to discharge its constitutionally rooted duty to consult and accommodate affected Indigenous peoples.

The scoping of the project subject to an environmental assessment was a threshold issue under the *Canadian Environmental Assessment Act, 2012*.[56] Because the National Energy Board found the regulation of marine shipping to be beyond its jurisdiction, the board scoped the project in a manner that found marine shipping to be an effect of the project as opposed to a central element. As a result, the board concluded that the pipeline project was not likely to cause significant adverse environmental effects to the orcas. This finding was notwithstanding the fact that the National Energy Board had concluded that project-related marine shipping was likely to result in significant adverse effects to endangered orcas and would further contribute to cumulative effects that are already jeopardizing the survival and recovery of the orcas. The board had found that the project would affect numerous individuals of the orca

---

51 2018 FC 643.

52 SC 2002, c 29 [SARA].

53 For more information, see Shaun Fluker, "More Justice for the Western Chorus Frog" (12 September 2018), online (blog) (pdf): *ABLawg.ca* <http://ablawg.ca/wp-content/uploads/2018/09/Blog_SF_Groupe Candiac_Sept2018.pdf>.

54 *Groupe Maison, supra* note 51 at para 10.

55 2018 FCA 153.

56 SC 2012, c 19, s 52.

population in their habitat, which was was identified as critical to the orcas' recovery. Further, the project would result in vessel noise that would threaten the acoustic integrity of this habitat. The board further found that the project-related death of an individual orca could result in population level impacts that could jeopardize the entire population.

Because the Federal Court of Appeal disagreed with the board and found that the shipping of oil from Canada to its offshore markets was a central element of the Kinder Morgan project, the court concluded that the National Energy Board had failed to comply with its obligations under s 79(2) of SARA to ensure that if the project was carried out, measures would be≈taken to avoid or lessen effects on the orcas, and, further, that those measures would be monitored.

On the issue of whether the government had adequately discharged its duty to consult, the Federal Court of Appeal applied established legal principles underpinning the duty to consult Indigenous peoples and First Nations to find that Canada had failed to engage, dialogue, and grapple with the concerns expressed by all of the applicant/appellant First Nations in good faith. The court found that the Crown had simply reiterated the National Energy Board findings and conditions, without meaningfully engaging with the concerns that had been raised. The Crown consultation team construed its mandate in a way that was too limited, involving little more than note-taking, with no real and sustained effort to pursue a meaningful two-way dialogue.[57]

F. POLLUTER PAYS

In *Orphan Well Association v Grant Thornton Ltd*,[58] Redwater was an Alberta oil and gas company that owned over a hundred wells, pipelines, and facilities. In 2015, when most of its wells were dry, Redwater went bankrupt, and Grant Thornton became its trustee. In order to avoid properly dismantling and restoring its well sites at the time of bankruptcy, Grant Thornton attempted to, in essence, disown its useless wells and sell productive sites to pay creditors. The Alberta Energy Regulator ordered Grant Thornton to dismantle the disowned sites. The case involved an arguable conflict between federal bankruptcy laws and Alberta environmental laws requiring oil and gas companies to properly abandon wells, pipelines, and facilities, and to reclaim licensed land.[59]

The court found that Alberta's regulatory regime aligned with the "polluter pays" principle: "assign[ing] polluters the responsibility for remedying environmental damage for which they are responsible, thereby incentivizing companies to pay attention to the environment in the course of their economic activities."[60] The court further found that the regulator's abandonment orders had been issued in the public interest and for the public good.[61]

---

57 In response to the Court overturning the original authorization of the pipeline in this case, the Canadian government re-initiated its consultations with Indigenous and First Nations groups. Following this, on June 18, 2019, the Governor in Council approved the Trans Mountain pipeline expansion. On September 4, 2019, however, the Federal Court of Appeal again granted Indigenous and First Nations leave to appeal the June 19, 2019 Order in Council on the basis that the duty to consult remained unsatisfied. See *Raincoast Conservation Foundation v Canada (Attorney General)*, 2019 FCA 224.

58 2019 SCC 5.

59 *Oil and Gas Conservation Act*, RSA 2000, c O-6 s 1(1)(cc); *Environmental Protection and Enhancement Act*, RSA 2000, c E-12, s 134(b)(vi); and *Pipeline Act*, RSA 2000, c P-15, s 1(1)(n).

60 *Orphan Well Association, supra* note 57 at para 29.

61 To consider the regulator's need to seek court orders to force companies to comply with its health or safety orders, see *Alberta Energy Regulator v Lexin Resources Ltd*, 2017 ABQB 219. Here Tilleman JA found that the regulator's governing legislation explicitly provides for the development of Alberta's energy resources only if this development is environmentally responsible.

G. ENVIRONMENTAL RIGHTS AND FUTURE GENERATIONS

In November 2018, ENvironnement JEUnesse (ENJEU), an environmental non-profit in Quebec, applied to bring a class action lawsuit against the Government of Canada on behalf of Quebec citizens aged 35 and under.[62] The claim alleged that the government failed to take sufficient action to reduce greenhouse gas emissions in the face of climate change and therefore failed to protect the fundamental rights of Quebec youth under both the Charter and Quebec's *Charter of Human Rights and Freedoms*.[63] If permitted to proceed, the claim seeks various declaratory orders and punitive damages. Similar cases have succeeded in the Netherlands (*Urgenda Foundation v The State of the Netherlands*),[64] Pakistan (*Leghari v Federation of Pakistan*),[65] and Colombia (*Decision C-035/16 of February 8, 2016*).[66] The Sabin Center for Climate Change Law at Columbia Law School estimates that more than 1,000 climate cases have now been commenced worldwide.[67]

NOTES AND QUESTIONS[68]

1. The various moral theories underlying the approaches set out in the chapter are, in order, deontological, utilitarian, virtue based, eco-feminist, and pragmatist, any of which could be explored further in Byron Williston, ed, *Environmental Ethics for Canadians*.[69]

   a. Imagine Jim, Gerry, and Jill, each of whom holds a different view about whether a company ought to be allowed to develop a ski resort on a piece of privately owned but environmentally sensitive land. Jim owns the land and wants to lease it to the company, Jill is an environmental activist, and Gerry is a municipal official in the town where the proposed development is to take place. Jim wants the development to go forward on a large scale. Gerry is cautiously supportive of development but wants it to proceed on a scale that is more limited than what Jim is proposing. Jill thinks that valuable and sensitive ecosystems will be damaged with any development and so opposes the project on any scale.[70]

---

62 *Environnement Jeunesse c Procureur général du Canada*, 2019 QCCS 2885; Ingrid Peritz, "Quebec Group Sues Federal Government over Climate Change," *The Globe and Mail* (26 November 2018), online: <https://www.theglobeandmail.com/canada/article-quebec-group-sues-federal-government-over-climate-change/>. On July 11, 2019, the Superior Court of Quebec refused the class action suit. Relatedly, however, on October 25, 2019, fifteen young Canadians filed a statement of claim in Canada's Federal Court asking the Canadian government to develop a climate recovery plan using the best available science. The claim relies upon Charter ss 7 and 15(1). The likelihood of the claim's success is indirectly considered in Chapter 20 of this book.

63 CQLR c C-12.

64 HAZA C/09/00456689 (24 June 2015) (Hague Dist Ct), aff'd HAZA C/09/456689 13-1396 (9 October 2018) (Hague CA).

65 (2015) WP No 25501/2015 (Lahore HC).

66 Constitutional Court, Feb 8, 2016, Decision C-035/16. See United Nations Environment Programme, *The Status of Climate Change Litigation: A Global Review* (May 2017) at 15-19, online (pdf): <http://columbiaclimatelaw.com/files/2017/05/Burger-Gundlach-2017-05-UN-Envt-CC-Litigation.pdf>.

67 United Nations Environment Programme, *supra* note 66 at 10-11.

68 Thank you to Bruce Morito for his conversation and draft ideas, which led to the formulation of several of these questions and discussion topics.

69 (Oxford: Oxford University Press, 2012).

70 *Ibid* at 145.

   i. Discuss the moral theories that could be used to defend these points of view.

   ii. Paul Thompson[71] claims that participants of such disputes are more likely to reach a workable solution by refraining from theoretical arguments from a particular moral point of view, because moral justifications for differing positions will lead to incompatibility. Do you agree? If yes, what is the best way to reach consensus on a solution?

   b. The question of what and if there is a moral foundation to our environmental laws in North America can be traced back to a debate in the late 1800s between John Muir and Gifford Pinchot (the first Chief of the Forest Service in the United States), with both men attempting to influence President Theodore Roosevelt in the writing of the United States' National Park policy. Muir pushed for a policy for United States wilderness parks that was rooted in the principle of preservation, based upon respect for the intrinsic value of nature and a duty to protect wilderness for its own sake. Pinchot lobbied for conservationism, based on the principle of the greatest good for the greatest number, recognizing the multiple values of the environment and arguing that the park system should allow multiple uses, including the exploitation of resources (in particular, forestry and mining). Arguably, the resource orientation of the United States' environmental law shows that Pinchot's conservation ethic won in the eyes of the US Park Service (though the US Forest Service claims that the two have been harmonized).[72] This debate between competing ethical frameworks continues today. Which of the ethical frameworks alluded to above are at play in this debate?

   c. The *Canada National Parks Act*[73] provides:

   4(1) The national parks of Canada are hereby dedicated to the people of Canada for their benefit, education and enjoyment, subject to this Act and the regulations, and the parks shall be maintained and made use of so as to leave them unimpaired for the enjoyment of future generations.

   The Act also states:

   8(2) Maintenance or restoration of ecological integrity, through the protection of natural resources and natural processes, shall be the first priority of the Minister when considering all aspects of the management of parks.

"Ecological integrity" is defined in s 2(1) of the Act as "a condition that is determined to be characteristic of its natural region and likely to persist, including abiotic components and the composition and abundance of native species and biological communities, rates of change and supporting processes." Based on these sections of the legislation, is Canada taking a conservation, preservation, or harmonized approach to managing its national parks?

   d. Pick an environmental issue discussed in class or in the media and attempt to frame it from various environmental ethical perspectives. Is there an ethical approach to the problem that you see as preferable? If yes, what is the reason you prefer it? Is the preference contextual (based on the particular question you have asked) or do you think that the approach which works best in this case would be preferable in other contexts? Think about the economic/political/scientific considerations that may be relevant to the selected issue. How do relevant ethical considerations bear up against these additional factors? Do you see values that ground your ethical approach to the issue at hand? Are these values or the ethical

---

71 Paul B Thompson, "The Case of Water" in Andrew Light & Eric Katz, eds, *Environmental Pragmatism* (London, UK: Routledge, 1996) at 187.

72 See Robert Hudson Westover, "Conservation Versus Preservation?" (22 March 2016), online (blog): *US Forest Service* <https://www.fs.fed.us/blogs/conservation-versus-preservation>.

73 SC 2000, c 32.

considerations recognized at all by the legal paradigm in which the environmental issue arises? If not, is this problematic?

2. According to Boyd, one of the "fundamental constraints" inhibiting the effectiveness of environmental law is our human ignorance of the reality that the Earth and its resources are finite. Boyd argues that our environmental law is limited to mitigating the worst effects of the dominant model of economic development, as opposed to challenging or transforming that model.[74] Today, many theorists, environmentalists, academics, and lawyers are arguing that in order to transform the model upon which our environmental laws are based, we must first recognize the flawed assumptions upon which the current model relies. In this vein, consider the following philosophical theories and how they may contribute to or correct errors in our reasoning.

a. Philosopher René Descartes (1596–1650) viewed the human self (the mind) as fundamentally separate and different in kind from bodily existence (the body). Given this distinction, persons were free and independent of the machine-like mechanisms of nature. Human beings (divine-like in their reasoning capacities) had a special place in creation, as right-bearing agents who could use nature as they pleased, just as they could use machines as they pleased. In relation to developments in neurophysiology[75] and now-standard approaches to teaching in the philosophy of mind,[76] rationally, it has become next to impossible to hold to the traditional Cartesian concept of the mind and person. Hence, the factual supports that have given us confidence in traditional normative beliefs, especially those asserting that we have some divinely sponsored right to exploit the Earth, have eroded.

b. According to philosopher John Locke (1632–1704), human beings create value in a world that would otherwise remain valueless. Value is conferred on nature through the acts of human beings, who mix with it their labour to produce useful commodities. The results of such labour then become the property of the labourer:

> [I]f I hammer a bundle of logs and boards together and fashion a table, I can rightly call this table my own. I can do so because I have transformed an otherwise worthless pile of logs and boards into something of value, by using my own hard work and sweat. Once I have established that I am the owner of the table, I can then do with it as I wish. I can use it, I can sell it, or I can burn it. Prior to my ownership of the table, the bundle of logs and boards was just wood, belonging to nobody. It is my intervention, my creation, my labor, that gives the table its value and gives me the right to call the table my own.[77]

In this, not only do humans stand apart from nature, they give nature its value. Consider whether capturing or conquering the property of something wild can take away its real (or inherent) value.[78]

c. In 1973, Arne Naess introduced the term "deep ecology" into environmental ethics. Deep ecology asserts that a redesign of our entire system of values and methods is necessary in order to recognize human beings as only one among the many inherently valuable beings formed of ecosystem processes.[79] Compare the Deep Ecology Platform outlined below with the ideas of Descartes and Locke:

---

74 Boyd, *Cleaner, Greener, Healthier, supra* note 20, chs 8, 9.

75 See Daniel C Dennett, *Consciousness Explained* (Boston: Little, Brown and Co, 1991).

76 See, for example, Brian Cooney, *The Place of Mind* (Belmont, Cal: Wadsworth Thomson Learning, 2000).

77 Benjamin Hale, "Private Property and Environmental Ethics: Some New Directions" (2008) 39:3 Metaphilosophy 402 at 406.

78 See *Pierson v Post*, 3 Cai R 175 (NY Sup Ct 1805).

79 Arne Naess & George Sessions, "The Deep Ecology Platform" (1984), online: *Foundation for Deep Ecology* <http://www.deepecology.org/platform.htm>.

1. The well-being and flourishing of human and nonhuman life on Earth have value in themselves ... independent of the usefulness of the nonhuman world for human purposes.
2. Richness and diversity of life forms contribute to the realization of these values and are also values in themselves.
3. Humans have no right to reduce this richness and diversity except to satisfy vital needs.
4. Present human interference with the nonhuman world is excessive, and the situation is rapidly worsening.
5. The flourishing of human life and cultures is compatible with a substantial decrease of the human population. The flourishing of nonhuman life requires such a decrease.
6. Policies must therefore be changed. The changes in policies affect basic economic, technological, and ideological structures. The resulting state of affairs will be deeply different from the present.
7. The ideological change is mainly that of appreciating life quality ... rather than adhering to an increasingly higher standard of living. ...
8. Those who subscribe to the foregoing points have an obligation directly or indirectly to participate in the attempt to implement the necessary changes.

Do you think our environmental attitudes, practices, and laws would be different if Naess's views had been introduced into Western philosophical thinking in place of those of Descartes and Locke?

d. In her 1993 book *Feminism and the Mastery of Nature*,[80] Val Plumwood introduced a theory of ecological feminism in which she tackled the dualism of Descartes and Locke, and also the failure of deep ecology to acknowledge difference. According to Plumwood, Western culture has adopted a "complex cultural identity of the master formed in the context of class, race, species and gender,"[81] which dominates our conception of reason and results in our inability to recognize humans' dependency on nature. Plumwood contrasts the concept of reason and the concept of nature, arguing that reason in the Western world has been constructed as the privileged domain of the master, with nature being conceived as the subordinate, or slave. Plumwood's work explores the category of nature as a field of exclusion and control.

3. Chapter 20 considers Canada's moral and legal obligations at a national and international level to mitigate climate change and other negative impacts as a result of environmental degradation. Considering Section IV of this chapter, how would you frame these obligations? Consider the environmental ethical frameworks and philosophical theories introduced above. Consider the following additional government actions, including argument(s) in *favour* of them. Identify whether these arguments are political, economic, ethical, or legal (or some combination). Can the argument(s) in favour be reconciled with the concerns with regard to environmental degradation/pollution/climate change raised in the chapter?

a. In 2002, Canada ratified the *Kyoto Protocol,* (adopted in 1997), implementing the objective of the *Kyoto Protocol,* to reduce the onset of global warming by reducing greenhouse gas concentrations in the atmosphere to "a level that would prevent dangerous anthropogenic interference with the climate system."[82] Canada's *Kyoto Protocol Implementation Act*[83] was assented to in 2007; however, Canada failed to meet its commitments under the protocol, and the Implementation Act was repealed in 2012 by Bill C-38, the

---

80 (New York: Routledge, 1993).

81 *Ibid* at v.

82 *United Nations Framework Convention on Climate Change*, 9 May 1992, 1771 UNTS 107 (entered into force 21 March 1994), art 2, online (pdf): *United Nations* <https://unfccc.int/resource/docs/convkp/conveng.pdf>.

83 SC 2007, c 30.

Jobs, Growth and Long-term Prosperity Act.[84] While this legislation was self-described as "an Act to implement certain provisions of the budget tabled in Parliament," it made broad and significant changes to many of Canada's federal environmental laws, including repealing and replacing the 1992 *Canadian Environmental Assessment Act*[85] with a completely new Act (*Canadian Environmental Assessment Act, 2012*), with a more limited focus on the environmental effects of projects, weakened powers of the Canadian Environmental Assessment Agency, and expanded powers for the minister. Other federal environmental legislation was also all amended and weakened. These changes were described by the Canadian government as consistent with "Responsible Resource Development, which seeks to modernize Canada's regulatory system for major projects."[86]

b. In 2015, Canada and 195 other countries signed the *Paris Agreement.*[87] The specific aim of this international climate change agreement is to limit global warming to 1.5-2°C above pre-industrial levels to prevent further or worse impacts as a result of climate change. Under the *Paris Agreement*, every country's commitment to reduce its emissions is measured according to NDCs (or nationally determined contributors), and each country is required to prepare, communicate, and maintain the NDCs it intends to achieve. According to the independent climate analytics of the website *Climate Action Tracker*, Canada's commitments to reducing carbon emissions, based on Canada's *Pan-Canadian Framework on Clean Growth and Climate*, are rated:

Highly Insufficient

[N]ot at all consistent with holding warming to below 2°C let alone with the Paris Agreement's stronger 1.5°C limit. If all government targets were in this range, warming would reach between 3°C and 4°C.[88]

4. In *Tsleil-Waututh Nation*,[89] the National Energy Board assessed the adverse effects of the Kinder Morgan pipeline project. In its assessment, the board framed project-related marine shipping as an effect of the project as opposed to as a central element. As a result of this, the board's findings concerning the effect of the project on endangered orcas did not heavily influence the final outcome of its assessment.

a. Use the environment ethical frameworks and philosophical theories introduced above to assess the conclusion of the National Energy Board that the effects of marine shipping were not a central element of the project.

b. The preamble to SARA, which goes to the interpretation of the legislation but is not legally binding, states:

Canada's natural heritage is an integral part of our national identity and history, wildlife, in all its forms, has value in and of itself and is valued by Canadians for aesthetic, cultural, spiritual, recreational, educational, historical, economic, medical, ecological and scientific reasons,

Canadian wildlife species and ecosystems are also part of the world's heritage and the Government of Canada has ratified the United Nations Convention on the Conservation of Biological Diversity.

---

84 SC 2012, c 19.

85 SC 1992, c 37.

86 J Oliver, *2011-2012 Departmental Performance Report* at 57, online (pdf): *Natural Resources Canada* <https://www.nrcan.gc.ca/sites/www.nrcan.gc.ca/files/performancereports/files/DPR%20-%20Final%20 ENG.pdf>.

87 12 December 2015, UN Doc FCCC/CP/2015/10/Add.1 (entered into force 4 November 2016).

88 "Canada" (30 November 2018), online: *Climate Action Tracker* <https://climateactiontracker.org/ countries/canada/>.

89 *Supra* note 55.

Do you think that these ethical principles, articulated in SARA, are relevant?

c. In its decision, the Federal Court of Appeal recognized "the cultural importance of the killer whale to certain Indigenous groups."[90] What is the underlying moral value articulated in this finding? Compare this to the preamble to SARA.

5. In *Tsleil-Waututh Nation*, the Federal Court of Appeal found that the Crown had failed to discharge its duty to consult Indigenous peoples pursuant to s 35 of the *Constitution Act, 1982*.[91] The Federal Court of Appeal noted that the consultation process in this case was an opportunity for Canada to apply the court's directions from the 2016 decision in *Gitxaala Nation v Canada*,[92] which came out five months before the governor in council approved the Kinder Morgan project. The court found that although Phase III of the consultation process had been the first opportunity for Indigenous applicants to dialogue directly with Canada about matters of substance as opposed to process, the Crown failed to "engage, dialogue meaningfully and grapple with the concerns expressed to it in good faith by the Indigenous applicants so as to explore possible accommodation of these concerns."[93]

a. What is the moral grounding beneath the Crown's duty to consult? Can this moral grounding, which relates to land use, be understood in terms of environmental ethics?

b. While there is now significant Supreme and Federal Court jurisprudence that fleshes out the content of the duty to consult, in your view, what is the effect of this duty being rooted in the Constitution?

c. What moral theory works best for understanding and articulating the value of land for cultural or traditional reasons? In answering this question, consider the case summary above for *Platinex Inc v Kitchenuhmaykoosib Inninuwug First Nation*.[94]

FURTHER READINGS

Callicott, J Baird & Michael P Nelson, *American Indian Environmental Ethics: An Ojibwa Case Study* (Indiana: Prentice Hall, 2004).

Carson, Rachel L, *Silent Spring* (New York: First Mariner Books, 1963).

Leopold, Aldo, *A Sand County Almanac* (Oxford: Oxford University Press, 1949).

Norton, Bryan G, *Toward Unity Among Environmentalists* (New York: Oxford University Press, 1991).

Taylor, Paul W, *Respect for Nature: A Theory of Environmental Ethics* (New Jersey: Princeton University Press, 1986).

World Commission on Environment and Development (Brundtland Commission), *Our Common Future* (Oxford: Oxford University Press, 1987).

---

90 *Ibid* at para 426.

91 In *R v Sparrow*, [1990] 1 SCR 1075, 1990 CanLII 104, the court provided a map for interpreting s 35 and found that "existing aboriginal and treaty rights" under s 35 included any right that had not been clearly and plainly extinguished before 1982. In *Sparrow*, the court also confirmed the Crown's constitutional duty to provide certain guarantees to Indigenous peoples (the Crown's fiduciary duty). In *Haida Nation v British Columbia (Minister of Forests)*, 2004 SCC 73, the Supreme Court then found that, in accordance with this fiduciary duty, the Crown was required to consult and accommodate Indigenous peoples prior to exploiting land to which they have or may have a valid claim.

92 2016 FCA 187.

93 *Tsleil-Waututh Nation, supra* note 55 at para 754.

94 *Supra* note 47.

CHAPTER THREE

ENVIRONMENTAL JUSTICE

Nathalie J Chalifour and Dayna N Scott[1]

"I wish to stress that since I was the one who took these [air quality] samples, the contaminants found were not just numbers in a lab result but [were] part of the air I was breathing on [those] days."
—Ada Lockridge, in her affidavit filed in the Aamjiwnaang Charter challenge (2011) at para 65.[2]

I. WHAT IS ENVIRONMENTAL JUSTICE?

The term "environmental justice" is used to describe a rapidly evolving set of ideas, theories, debates, and principles that examine and critique the connection between environmental burdens

1   The authors wish to thank Taylor Wormington, JD candidate at uOttawa, for his excellent research assistance and to acknowledge research support from the Social Sciences and Humanities Research Council.

2   See Dayna N Scott, "Environmental Justice and the Hesitant Embrace of Rights" in James R May & Erin Daly, eds, *Human Rights and the Environment: Indivisibility, Dignity, and Legality*, Encyclopedia of Environmental Law (Cheltenham: Edward Elgar Press and the IUCN Academy of Environmental Law, 2019) [Scott, "The Hesitant Embrace of Rights"], which is excerpted in Section V.A. of this chapter.

and identity factors such as race, gender, and socioeconomic status. It is as much a grassroots movement for change as it is a framework through which to understand the distribution of environmental harms and benefits among different groups and individuals, and the processes, biases, and structures that lead to distributional inequities. It is a critical study of the hegemonies and colonialist power structures that enable environmental discrimination, as well as a push for change.

Developed largely by people of colour, environmental justice is a discourse "framed around concepts like autonomy, self-determination, access to resources, fairness and justice, and civil and human rights," issues that are often absent from mainstream environmental movements.[3] As Dayna N Scott elaborates:

> The environmental justice movement distinguishes itself from the mainstream environmental movement by making grassroots political organizing its central priority. Where environmentalists over the past three decades have invested heavily in legal strategies as a means to achieve social change, the environmental justice movement, in contrast, explicitly calls this focus on law reform into question by noting how it continues to privilege elites at the expense of people working on the ground to improve their communities. Similarly, the environmental justice movement has focused on the health and wellbeing of people, rather than on the need to protect "the environment" conceptualized as wilderness spaces, endangered species or national parks, with the latter sometimes dismissed as "playgrounds for the rich." Thus, activists in the environmental justice movement are increasingly turning their attention to environmental harms derived not only from air, water or soil contamination, but from toxic workplaces, urban planning and transit decisions, conditions in public housing projects (such as lead paint or mould), water and sanitation services on native reserves, urban "food deserts" etc.[4]

The concept of environmental justice is such a diverse and richly nuanced idea that care must be taken when attempting to define it.[5] In describing their groundbreaking new volume on the topic of environmental justice in Canada, *Speaking for Ourselves: Environmental Justice in Canada*, in 2009, Julian Agyeman et al note that

> [n]o collection can be *the* definitive statement on the relationships between land, resources, nature, history, power relations, society, peoples, inequity, and all our (human and other-than-human) relations. ...
>
> Unwittingly or deliberately, academic scholarship subverts the very justice sought by so-called liberal societies, especially if elite and powerful actors within the mainstream are inconvenienced or discounted by it.[6]

The environmental justice movement is often said to have been born in the early 1980s in Warren County, North Carolina, when protesters contested the siting of a hazardous waste facility in a neighbourhood that was predominantly Black and low income.[7] The demonstrations

---

3   Julian Agyeman et al, "Trends and Directions in Environmental Justice: From Inequity to Everyday Life" (2016) 41 Annual Rev Environ & Resources 321 at 325 [Agyeman et al, "Trends and Directions"], citing Dorceta E Taylor, "The Rise of the Environmental Justice Paradigm: Injustice Framing and the Social Construction of Environmental Discourses" (2000) 43:4 American Behavioral Scientist 508 at 534.

4   Dayna N Scott, "What Is Environmental Justice?" (2014) 10:16 Osgoode Legal Studies Research Paper Series, Research Paper No 72 at 5, online: <http://digitalcommons.osgoode.yorku.ca/olsrps/4> [Scott, "What Is Environmental Justice?"].

5   Nathalie J Chalifour, "Environmental Justice and the Charter: Do Environmental Injustices Infringe Sections 7 and 15 of the Charter?" (2015) 28:1 J Envtl L & Prac 89 at 95 [Chalifour, "Environmental Justice and the Charter"].

6   (Vancouver: UBC Press, 2009) at 3-4 [Agyeman et al, *Speaking for Ourselves*].

7   Other roots of the movement can be found in the resistance by Indigenous peoples to the dispossession of their lands by colonial settlers and the connections between workers' rights and environmental health put forward by migrant farm workers led by César Chávez in California in the 1960s.

led to the United States government analyzing the correlation between race, socioeconomic status, and the location of toxic waste sites.[8] The resulting report, which provided empirical analysis of the correlation and aptly characterized it as an "[i]nsidious form of racism," empowered the environmental justice movement to advocate for change.[9] It also opened up a space for a broader conversation about the way in which racialized and poor communities bear a disproportionate burden of environmental harm, laying the groundwork for activism and further research to document the discrimination. As Andil Gosine and Cheryl Teelucksingh elaborate in their seminal 2008 book *Environmental Justice and Racism in Canada: An Introduction*:

> In the United States, the first notions of *environmental justice* were tied to struggles over the location of toxic waste sites and articulated as claims for "equal treatment" of differentially racialized communities. Environmental justice was viewed as a state in which social conditions were absent of structured, racialized, and class inequalities. By the late 1980s, however, a much broader understanding of the term and its implications became widely accepted. In 1991, a gathering of delegates at the First National People of Color Environmental Leadership Summit held in Washington, D.C., drafted and adopted 17 Principles of Environmental Justice that have since served as a defining advocacy and policy document.[10]

Although drafted in 1991, the *Principles of Environmental Justice* (reproduced below) remain a relevant foundation for the environmental justice movement even as it has evolved in scale and scope.

PRINCIPLES OF ENVIRONMENTAL JUSTICE
Drafted and adapted at the First National People of Color Environmental Leadership Summit held on 24-27 October 1991 in Washington, DC

PREAMBLE

WE, THE PEOPLE OF COLOR, gathered together at this multinational People of Color Environmental Leadership Summit, to begin to build a national and international movement of all peoples of color to fight the destruction and taking of our lands and communities, do hereby re-establish our spiritual interdependence to the sacredness of our Mother Earth; to respect and celebrate each of our cultures, languages and beliefs about the natural world and our roles in healing ourselves; to ensure environmental justice; to promote economic alternatives which would contribute to the development of environmentally safe livelihoods; and, to secure our political, economic and cultural liberation that has been denied for over 500 years of colonization and oppression, resulting in the poisoning of our communities and land and the genocide of our peoples, do affirm and adopt these Principles of Environmental Justice:

1) **Environmental Justice** affirms the sacredness of Mother Earth, ecological unity and the interdependence of all species, and the right to be free from ecological destruction.

---

8   US, General Accounting Office, *Siting of Hazardous Waste Landfills and Their Correlation with Racial and Economic Status of Surrounding Communities*, RCED-83-168 (Washington, DC: US Government Printing Office, 1983).

9   United Church of Christ, Commission for Racial Justice, *Toxic Wastes and Race in the United States—A National Report on the Racial and Socio-Economic Characteristics of Communities with Hazardous Waste Sites* (1987).

10 (Toronto: Emond Montgomery, 2008) at 9.

2) **Environmental Justice** demands that public policy be based on mutual respect and justice for all peoples, free from any form of discrimination or bias.

3) **Environmental Justice** mandates the right to ethical, balanced and responsible uses of land and renewable resources in the interest of a sustainable planet for humans and other living things.

4) **Environmental Justice** calls for universal protection from nuclear testing, extraction, production and disposal of toxic/hazardous wastes and poisons and nuclear testing that threaten the fundamental right to clean air, land, water, and food.

5) **Environmental Justice** affirms the fundamental right to political, economic, cultural and environmental self-determination of all peoples.

6) **Environmental Justice** demands the cessation of the production of all toxins, hazardous wastes, and radioactive materials, and that all past and current producers be held strictly accountable to the people for detoxification and the containment at the point of production.

7) **Environmental Justice** demands the right to participate as equal partners at every level of decision-making, including needs assessment, planning, implementation, enforcement and evaluation.

8) **Environmental Justice** affirms the right of all workers to a safe and healthy work environment without being forced to choose between an unsafe livelihood and unemployment. It also affirms the right of those who work at home to be free from environmental hazards.

9) **Environmental Justice** protects the right of victims of environmental injustice to receive full compensation and reparations for damages as well as quality health care.

10) **Environmental Justice** considers governmental acts of environmental injustice a violation of international law, the Universal Declaration On Human Rights, and the United Nations Convention on Genocide.

11) **Environmental Justice** must recognize a special legal and natural relationship of Native Peoples to the U.S. government through treaties, agreements, compacts, and covenants affirming sovereignty and self-determination.

12) **Environmental Justice** affirms the need for urban and rural ecological policies to clean up and rebuild our cities and rural areas in balance with nature, honoring the cultural integrity of all our communities, and provided fair access for all to the full range of resources.

13) **Environmental Justice** calls for the strict enforcement of principles of informed consent, and a halt to the testing of experimental reproductive and medical procedures and vaccinations on people of color.

14) **Environmental Justice** opposes the destructive operations of multi-national corporations.

15) **Environmental Justice** opposes military occupation, repression and exploitation of lands, peoples and cultures, and other life forms.

16) **Environmental Justice** calls for the education of present and future generations which emphasizes social and environmental issues, based on our experience and an appreciation of our diverse cultural perspectives.

17) **Environmental Justice** requires that we, as individuals, make personal and consumer choices to consume as little of Mother Earth's resources and to produce as little waste as possible; and make the conscious decision to challenge and reprioritize our lifestyles to ensure the health of the natural world for present and future generations.

As a result of its roots in the US civil rights movement, environmental justice is closely related to a number of other discourses, including environmental racism:

> Benjamin Chavis is frequently cited as having coined the term *environmental racism*, which has been in use since at least 1981. The term was elaborated on in the 1987 report *Toxic Waste and Race in the United States,* which Chavis co-authored as head of the United Church of Christ's Commission for Racial Justice. The commission found racial identity to be the strongest variable in predicting where landfills were located in the United States, and thus defined the term *environmental racism* as the intentional siting of hazardous waste sites, landfills, incinerators and polluting industries in areas inhabited mainly by Blacks, Latinos, Indigenous peoples, Asians, migrant farm workers and low-income peoples (in the United States). Environmental racism, the report's authors further concluded, was an extension of the institutional racism many had encountered in the past, including discrimination in housing, employment, education, municipal services, and law enforcement.
>
> Echoing this position, Bullard (1996) [Robert D Bullard, "Environmental Justice: It's More Than Waste Facility Siting" (1996) 77:3 Social Science Quarterly 493] defined *environmental racism* as "any policy, practice or directive that differentially affects or disadvantages (whether intended or unintended) individuals, groups or communities based on race or colour." (p 497).[11]

While the environmental justice movement initially focused on the disparities in environmental burdens between differently situated communities, the analytical frameworks of environmental justice have evolved to consider disparities flowing from power relations *within* communities as well. Scott illustrates this latter dynamic, using the example of gender:

> It is now well-documented that racialized and marginalized communities, including and perhaps especially Indigenous communities, in many parts of the world bear much more than their "fair share" of environmental burdens; it is also becoming increasingly clear that disadvantaged and historically oppressed peoples within those communities will often be disproportionately harmed, often along familiar social gradients of gender, class, sexuality, caste, (dis)ability etc. With respect to gender, it is worth noting that at the second People of Colour Environmental Leadership Summit in 2002, Peggy Shepard of West Harlem Environmental Action argued that women on-the-ground [sic] are driving this movement, despite the fact that they remain underrepresented in leadership roles. And as Barbara Rahder has demonstrated, there are structural and spatial inequities in production and reproduction inherent to the neoliberal political economy that serve to perpetuate this reality. Deficiencies in childcare and eldercare regimes, and the persistently uneven and gendered division of domestic work, exacerbate the problem. Debates persist over whether the central role of women in this movement is an expression of an inherent ethic or politics of care, or, as Sherilyn MacGregor has put forward, a form of politicized ecological citizenship.[12]

II. ENVIRONMENTAL JUSTICE RESEARCH AND THEORETICAL APPROACH

Environmental justice scholarship has evolved considerably over the last several decades. The first generation of environmental justice research was characterized largely by efforts to define and understand environmental justice, supported by the development of an empirical base of

---

11 *Ibid* at 4.

12 Scott, "What Is Environmental Justice?," *supra* note 3 at 8-9.

evidence employing largely spatial analytical models.[13] David Pellow describes this first genera-tion of environmental justice scholarship as research "focused primarily on documenting environmental inequality through the lens of race and class."[14] While quantitative research aimed at documenting distributional inequities has persisted, in the mid-1990s, environmental justice research broadened considerably, and included more qualitative approaches and a diversification and proliferation of methodologies, disciplines, and approaches.[15] Both within the environmental justice movement and in research, attention expanded to include not only pollution and contamination but various aspects of the built environment, such as green space and housing, worker health and safety, and pollution. Pellow describes this second generation of environmental justice research as extending "beyond questions of distribution to incorpor-ate a deeper consideration of theory and the ways that gender, sexuality, and other categories of difference shape EJ [environmental justice] struggles."[16]

Environmental justice has been theorized in a number of ways, but the most common framework used to analyze environmental injustices addresses three dimensions:

> The first dimension is the one that is most often identified and discussed in the literature. Sometimes called distributive or substantive justice, it focuses on inequities in the distribu-tion of environmental outcomes and consequences among different social groups. It draws upon various theories of distributive rights, which in the context of the environment speaks to how the environmental pie is divided up among members of society. Who bears which environmental risks (e.g. in whose backyard are the toxic waste sites located and who suffers most from air pollution?), and who receives which environmental benefits (e.g. in which urban neighbourhoods are the best greenspaces, and where is pollution best controlled?)? It also questions what is being distributed (which part of the environmental pie?) and on what basis this distribution is made (is it the market economy at work, are there redistributive policies in place?).
>
> The second dimension focuses on procedural justice, referring in part to unequal partici-pation in decision-making processes due to factors such as limited access to information or flawed consultation processes. This dimension leads us to question the institutional settings in which decisions are made, and how people access those institutions. It encompasses con-sideration of the "roll out of state functions under neoliberalism to non-state actors, including the private sector, public-private partnerships and third sector organizations." It also consid-ers who has (and who does not have) access to justice through the courts and other means.
>
> The third dimension, which [David] Schlosberg and others have characterized as recog-nition, relates to the unbalanced power relations embedded in colonialism, in the market, and other spheres of domination and oppression. These structural and systemic issues can determine, for instance, which types of knowledge "count" and which types are marginal-ized in environmental decision-making; who can speak, how, and when; and, ultimately, how environmental burdens and benefits are distributed.
>
> Several writers, including Schlosberg, Agyeman et al. and [Gordon] Walker, emphasize the interlocking nature of these dimensions, suggesting that one cannot speak of a single dimension without it leading to another.[17]

---

13 Agyeman et al, "Trends and Directions," *supra* note 2 at 326.

14 David N Pellow, "Critical Environmental Justice Studies: Black Lives Matter as an Environmental Justice Challenge" (2016) 13:2 Du Bois Rev 221 at 223.

15 Agyeman et al, "Trends and Directions," *supra* note 2 at 326.

16 Pellow, *supra* note 13 at 223; for a discussion of the environmental justice dimensions of pollution regulation and extraction employing feminist theory of the body, see Dayna N Scott, "'We Are the Monitors Now': Experiential Knowledge, Transcorporeality and Environmental Justice" (2016) 25:3 Soc & Leg Stud 261.

17 Chalifour, "Environmental Justice and the Charter," *supra* note 4 at 95-97 [endnotes omitted].

While environmental justice research was initially criticized for being mostly reactive, it has evolved to include proactive analyses examining land-use planning, sustainable communities, public transit, and more.[18] It has also expanded to include a global scope, including issues such as climate justice and trade and investment agreements, and to include a broad range of issues, such as consumption, resource extraction, energy production, food justice, and more.[19] The term "critical environmental justice studies" has been offered by scholars David Pellow and Robert Brulle to capture scholarship that examines "how multiple social categories of difference are entangled in the production of environmental injustice,"[20] among other critical interventions. It engages critically with environmental justice research to address some of its limitations and tensions, including, as Pellow describes:

(1) questions concerning the degree to which scholars should place emphasis on one or more social categories of difference (e.g., race, class, gender, sexuality, species, etc.) versus a focus on multiple forms of inequality; (2) the extent to which scholars studying [environmental justice] EJ issues should focus on single-scale versus multi-scalar analyses of the causes, consequences, and possible resolutions of EJ struggles; (3) the degree to which various forms of social inequality and power—including state power—are viewed as entrenched and embedded in society; and (4) the largely unexamined question of the *expendability* of human and non-human populations facing socioecological threats from states, industries, and other political economic forces.[21]

Today, the environmental justice movement is a pluralist one that "links the environment to race, class, gender, and social justice, effectively reframing environmental issues as injustice issues."[22] As Scott explains:

Jonathan London and Julie Sze have conceptualized environmental justice as praxis, noting that it draws from and integrates theory and practice into a mutually informing dialogue. Framing environmental justice in this way provides the flexibility needed to allow it to encompass the wide variety of dynamics that are brought forward by many different populations, problems and places.[23]

Agyeman et al add that "the movement has been pluralist in its concepts, foci, strategies, and actions from the beginning ... resonat[ing] with a wide range of new constituencies, including people of color and working- and middle-class whites."[24] For example, an idea that links with environmental justice is that of "just sustainabilities." This idea is the "infusion of ideas of equity and justice into a discourse whose sole focus at that time was on environmental sustainability."[25]

Finally, while the environmental justice movement has focused primarily on intragenerational justice, the inquiry can be broadened to include intergenerational and interspecies

---

18 Agyeman et al, "Trends and Directions," *supra* note 2 at 328.

19 *Ibid*.

20 See David Naguib Pellow & Robert J Brulle, "Power, Justice, and the Environment: Toward Critical Environmental Justice Studies" in David Naguib Pellow & Robert J Brulle, eds, *Power, Justice, and the Environment: A Critical Appraisal of the Environmental Justice Movement* (Cambridge, Mass: MIT Press, 2005) 1; and Pellow, *supra* note 13 at 223. For a Canadian application considering the dynamics of the emerging green energy economy, see Dayna N Scott & Adrian A Smith, "Sacrifice Zones in the Green Energy Economy: Towards an Environmental Justice Framework" (2017) 62:3 McGill LJ 1.

21 Pellow, *supra* note 13 at 223.

22 Agyeman et al, "Trends and Directions," *supra* note 2 at 326.

23 Scott, "What Is Environmental Justice?," *supra* note 3 at 4.

24 Agyeman et al, "Trends and Directions," *supra* note 2 at 326.

25 *Ibid* at 326.

justice.[26] This wider scope brings future generations into the analysis and requires consideration of the relationship between humans and the non-human world in which we live and upon which we rely for subsistence.[27] This approach draws upon intersecting spheres of literature, such as the rapidly evolving literature on the rights of nature, climate justice, and Indigenous legal traditions.[28]

NOTES AND QUESTIONS

1. We have described environmental justice in many different ways, including as a movement, paradigm, idea, critical framework, and discourse, and explained that it intersects with many other approaches, such as critical race and gender studies, settler colonial studies, and just sustainabilities. Why is it challenging to articulate one definition of environmental justice? What are the repercussions, if any, of this fluidity? Should there be one definition? If so, what would it be? If not, why not?

2. Do the 17 *Principles of Environmental Justice* still have relevance today? Are they specific to the US, or do they have broader geographical application? Should they be the basis upon which progress on environmental justice is measured? Do any of the principles need to be adapted?

3. Is the integration of environmental justice into some mainstream discourses, such as environmental law and sustainable development, problematic? If so, how? What are the advantages and disadvantages of the mainstream environmental movement advocating for environmental justice?

4. What is the relationship between environmental justice and environmental racism? Do they need to be linked, or can they persist as separate, but related, discourses?

5. What is the impact of including intergenerational justice within the environmental justice framework? What about intraspecies justice? It is possible to reconcile the distributional goals of intragenerational environmental justice with interspecies justice?

III. APPLYING THE ENVIRONMENTAL JUSTICE FRAMEWORK IN CANADA

"Environmental justice is not an American invention."
—Andil Gosine & Cheryl Teelucksingh, *supra* note 9 at 1.

If environmental justice as a movement or a framework has its roots in the US civil rights context, the broader struggles that underlie the concept—that of people standing up for their communities, defending their ways of life, and exercising their authority to decide based on their vast experience and knowledge of the interconnections between lands and bodies—have a long history in the lands we now call Canada.[29] Indigenous resistance to colonial occupations,

---

26 See e.g. Heather McLeod-Kilmurray, "Does Preserving the Environment Advance or Conflict with Social Justice and Human Rights?" in Sanda Rodgers & Sheila McIntyre, eds, *The Supreme Court of Canada and Social Justice: Commitment, Retrenchment or Retreat* (Toronto: LexisNexis, 2010) 465; Jessica Eisen, Roxanne Mykitiuk & Dayna N Scott, "Constituting Bodies into the Future: Intergenerational Harm, Toxics and Relational Theory" (2018) 51:1 UBC L Rev 1.

27 See Klaus Bosselmann, "Ecological Justice" in *The Principle of Sustainability: Transforming Law and Governance*, 2nd ed (London: Routledge, 2017) ch 3.

28 See David R Boyd, *The Rights of Nature: A Legal Revolution That Could Save the World* (Toronto: ECW Press, 2017); Sheila Watt-Cloutier, *The Right to Be Cold: One Woman's Story of Protecting Her Culture, the Arctic and the Whole Planet* (Toronto: Allen Lane, 2015); John Borrows, *Canada's Indigenous Constitution* (Toronto: University of Toronto Press, 2010), respectively.

29 Randolph Haluza-DeLay et al, "Introduction: Speaking for Ourselves, Speaking Together: Environmental Justice in Canada" in Agyeman et al, *Speaking for Ourselves*, *supra* note 5 at 2.

land theft, and various industrial incursions is well documented and continues today.[30] Similarly, racialized communities such as the displaced and dispossessed Black Loyalists of Africville, Nova Scotia, have left a powerful legacy of environmental justice struggle. In other words, environmental justice and environmental racism are highly relevant in the Canadian context.

Deborah McGregor, Canada Research Chair in Indigenous Environmental Justice, reminds us that the environmental justice framework emerges from Western worldviews and requires a rethinking of colonial power structures.[31] In the following excerpt, she writes from her own perspective, "as an Anishnaabe woman from Wiigwaaskinga (Birch Island, Ontario)."[32]

DEBORAH MCGREGOR, "HONOURING OUR RELATIONS: AN ANISHNAABE PERSPECTIVE ON ENVIRONMENTAL JUSTICE"
in Agyeman et al, *Speaking for Ourselves: Environmental Justice in Canada* (Vancouver: UBC Press, 2009) at 27, 30

As I learn more teachings about water and the concept of "all our relations" I have come to understand that relationships based on environmental justice are not limited to relations between people but consist of those among all beings of Creation. From the perspective of the world view within which I am embedded, environmental justice is most certainly about power relationships among people and between people and various institutions of colonization. It concerns issues of cultural dominance, of environmental destruction, and of inequity in terms of how certain groups of people are impacted differently by environmental destruction from others, sometimes by design. But environmental justice from an Aboriginal perspective is more than all of these. It is about justice for all beings of Creation, not only because threats to their existence threaten ours but because from an Aboriginal perspective justice among beings of Creation is life-affirming. Aboriginal authors such as Anishnaabe environmental activist Winona LaDuke refer to this as "natural law" (LaDuke, 1994). While people certainly have a responsibility for justice, so do other beings (e.g., water and medicinal plants).

• • •

ENVIRONMENTAL JUSTICE AND THE ANISHNAABE

Environmental justice is not a new concept in Anishnaabe culture. Natural laws have existed for generations that ensure justice for "all our relations." In contrast to perhaps more mainstream writings of environmental justice, all beings of Creation will be described in this chapter as having agency and entitlement, according to Anishnaabe tradition. As well, the ancestors of current beings and those yet to come (at least as far ahead as seven generations from now) also have entitlement to environmental justice. From an Anishnaabe perspective, the spirit world and all beings of Creation, including people, have relationships and responsibilities. Anishinaabe [*sic*] legal scholar Darlene Johnston (2006) states: "In Anishnaabeg culture, there is an ongoing relationship between the Dead and the Living; between Ancestors and Descendants" (p. 17). Anishnaabeg have to routinely consider questions such as,

---

30 See "Indigenous Environmental Justice Project" (last visited 7 May 2019), online: *York University* <http://iejproject.info.yorku.ca>.

31 See Deborah McGregor, "Honouring Our Relations: An Anishnaabe Perspective on Environmental Justice" in Agyeman et al, *Speaking for Ourselves, supra* note 5.

32 *Ibid* at 27.

What is our relationship with our ancestors? Are we honouring our relationships with our ancestors? Are we doing justice to our ancestors and to those yet to come?

In their influential text, Gosine and Teelucksingh lay out "three challenges to naming and framing environmental justice in the Canadian context."[33] They are (1) the idea that "racism did not happen here"; (2) Canada's official multiculturalism policy and the myth of the "Canadian mosaic"; and (3) the distinct spatial organization of race in Canadian cities. We address these in turn.

A. RACISM HAPPENED (AND HAPPENS) HERE

As Dalhousie University professor Ingrid Waldron says, "Canada was founded on enslavement and dispossession."[34] Thus, her work foregrounds the importance of an intersectional analysis of environmental justice that includes race as a fundamental component:

[R]ace must be a fundamental analytical entry point in the struggle for environmental justice in Nova Scotia and Canada, ... one cannot fully understand how environmental racism manifests within structures, policies and practices ... without an appreciation for how race intersects with and interprets other social identities.

• • •

The meaning of race, gender, class, and other social identities only becomes clear when we understand the historical and site-specific ways in which they converge to position people in different and ever-changing positions of power, privilege and disadvantage.

• • •

[E]nvironmental racism is similar to other structurally induced racial and gendered forms of state violence that result in high rates of underemployment and unemployment, income insecurity and poverty, low educational attainment, high rates of incarceration, and other harms common in Indigenous and Black communities.[35]

Importantly, Waldron argues that engagement with environmental racism in Canada[36] suffers from a kind of "strategic inadvertence" that mutes the specificity of Indigenous and Black experiences of racism and environmental hazards by obscuring it within discussions about class.

INGRID RG WALDRON, THERE'S SOMETHING IN THE WATER: ENVIRONMENTAL RACISM IN INDIGENOUS AND BLACK COMMUNITIES
(Halifax: Fernwood, 2018) at 2, 84, 132 [in-text citations omitted]

For those who argue that environmental racism is an issue of class and not race, I maintain [following Michael Eric Dyson] that "race makes class hurt more." In other

---

33 Gosine & Teelucksingh, *supra* note 9 at 34.

34 Ingrid RG Waldron, "Re-Thinking Waste: Mapping Racial Geographies of Violence on the Colonial Landscape" (2018) 4:1 Environmental Sociology 36 at 39.

35 Ingrid RG Waldron, *There's Something in the Water: Environmental Racism in Indigenous and Black Communities* (Halifax: Fernwood, 2018) at 4-5 [Waldron, *Something in the Water*].

36 Although her research is focused primarily on Nova Scotia, Waldron's ideas are essential to understanding environmental racism and environmental justice in Canada.

words, for non-white or racialized peoples, the added burden of racism deepens existing inequalities and disadvantages they are already experiencing related to class, such as unemployment, low income, poverty, food insecurity, and residence in under-resourced neighborhoods.

Perhaps the inability of many people to acknowledge race as a defining factor in social relations and policymaking [in Canada] can be attributed to narrow conceptualizations of racism that focus on individual, malicious acts—the acknowledgement of which requires "evidence" and "proof"—rather than subtler or systemic forms of racism that are entrenched within institutions and decision making (citing Pulido 2000).

• • •

THE INJUSTICE OF AFRICVILLE

Perhaps no other African Nova Scotian community has served as more of a classic example and symbol of segregation, racism, inequality, profits at all costs, and environmental racism than Africville. The community was located just north of Halifax on the shore of the Bedford Basin and was first settled in the mid-1800s by Black refugees who came to Nova Scotia following the War of 1812. Some Africville residents ran fishing businesses and farms and owned small stores towards the end of the nineteenth century.

The community was subjected to injustice on many levels. For example, although the City of Halifax collected taxes in Africville, they did not provide the community with basic utilities and infrastructure offered to other parts of the city, such as paved roads, sanitary water, sewage, public transportation, garbage collection, recreational facilities, fire protection, street lights, and adequate police protection.

As early as 1912, the City had decided to use Africville's land for industrial development, and in 1947 it rezoned Africville as industrial land. By 1965 the City had embarked on an urban renewal campaign, resulting in the expropriation of and bulldozing of homes and the forcible displacement of Africville residents. Some residents were moved to derelict housing or rented public housing. The final property was expropriated and demolished in 1969, when the last of Africville's four hundred residents left. One resident, Eddie Carvery, remains in Africville after returning to the site in 1970 and pitching a tent in protest.

Africville became host to a number of environmental hazards, including a fertilizer plant, a slaughter house, a tar factory, a stone and coal crushing plant, a cotton factory, a prison, two infectious disease hospitals, and three systems of railway tracks. In the 1950s, the City built an open-pit dump in Africville, which many considered to be a health menace.

In 2010, some former Africville residents reached a multi-million dollar settlement with the City. While no individual compensation was paid out, the settlement included an apology, a hectare of land on the former site to rebuild the Seaview African United Baptist Church, and $3 million to help build it. African Nova Scotian Affairs was also established by the municipality. In November 2016, up to three hundred former residents of Africville and their descendants joined a lawsuit against the City of Halifax over the loss of their land four decades ago, if the Supreme Court of Nova Scotia certified the case as a class-action lawsuit for former residents of Africville.

[Waldron argues convincingly for an anti-racism analysis in environmental justice frameworks:]

It is important that policymakers, environmental organizations, activists, and others involved in environmental and social justice struggles acknowledge the central role that racism plays through the enduring impacts of colonialism and capitalism on the cultures, lands, and bodies of Indigenous and Black communities. A race analysis must be explicit in analyses of environmental concerns affecting these communities, as well as in decision, policies, and strategies developed to promote more equitable distribution of industry. Reducing inequitable siting of polluting industries can't be achieved unless deliberate attention is paid to educating environmentalists and others about the systemic ways in which racist ideologies get written into environmental decision-making and policy. In other words, antiracism initiatives must be connected to anticapitalist struggles in the pursuit of a social system premised on equality and cooperation, rather than competition and hierarchical relationships based on race, colour, gender, and other social identities (Leong 2013).

Environmental racism, therefore, is as much an integral and intersecting component of environmental justice in Canada as it is anywhere.

B. MULTICULTURALISM AND THE MYTH OF THE "CANADIAN MOSAIC"

Canada's distinct history of immigration and settlement gives rise to distinct spatial dynamics, as well as different politics, compared to that of the US. The country's embrace of an ideal of multiculturalism and the so-called "Canadian mosaic" is thought to have created barriers to accepting the idea of "environmental racism" as it was emerging in the US.[37] Consider how Patricia K Wood and Liette Gilbert describe multiculturalism in Canada:

Multiculturalism is commonly understood as three different yet related notions: as a specific governmental policy of political pluralism, as a social reality of a demographically diverse society, and as a political ideology advocating cultural pluralism. According to [Audrey] Kobayashi (1993), the Canadian policy of multiculturalism has occurred in three different stages: demographic, symbolic and structural. When adopted in 1971, the policy was first based on the demographic recognition and symbolic celebration of different cultural heritages as part of the Canadian heritage. Criticized for its symbolic intervention, the main interest of the policy went from reproducing cultural traditions to emphasizing structural reform and legislation for equal opportunity and equal protection of all groups. The revised law of 1988 includes both the recognition and development of cultural heritage, and the legislative shift to promote equality, political participation and institutional reform. Despite its best attempt to promote an understanding of people from all cultures, more particularly those who were not part of Canada's "two solitudes" [French and English], multiculturalism was predominantly a way to deal with the "immigrant issue."[38]

Although perhaps less glaring outside the context of Indigenous peoples living on reserve, other patterns of environmental racism exist in the Canadian context as well. As J David Hulchanski's influential analysis in "The Three Cities Within Toronto: Income Polarization Among Toronto's Neighbourhoods, 1970–2005"[39] vividly demonstrates, the patterns of segregation within cities are always changing. Looking at spatial organization by income, Hulchanski documented how Toronto's lowest-income communities had moved, over a 30- or 40-year period,

---

37 Gosine & Teelucksingh, *supra* note 9 at 46.

38 "Multiculturalism in Canada: Accidental Discourse, Alternative Vision, Urban Practice" (2005) 29:3 Intl J Urban & Regional Research 679 at 682-83.

39 (2010), online (pdf): *University of Toronto* <http://www.urbancentre.utoronto.ca/pdfs/curp/tnrn/Three-Cities-Within-Toronto-2010-Final.pdf>.

from the city's inner core to its outer suburbs. Toronto became known, over a similar period, as one of the most "multicultural" cities in the world. But the inner city, where incomes were the highest, was becoming whiter, while racialized communities and newcomers were largely concentrated in the city's outer suburbs.[40]

Gosine and Teelucksingh highlight a number of grassroots initiatives led by a variety of urban environmental justice advocates in Canada. For example, Karen Okamoto has been a food activist promoting food justice within the Jane and Finch region of Toronto. Beenash Jafri has engaged in anti-racism youth activism in Toronto for many years, and she has helped bring an environmental justice lens to her work, evolving the Anti-Racism Committee at York University into the Anti-Racist Environmental Coalition.[41] Climate justice movements, in recent years, have been comprised of an increasingly diverse mix of racialized peoples and Indigenous peoples as well as faith-based groups, spanning urban–rural divides and generations. Adria Vasil, writing in *NOW Magazine* in 2015, described "What Canada's Climate Coalition Looks Like":

> For a group long accused of being mostly white, upper-middle-class and male-led, it's a massive shift. [According to] 350.org's Canadian media coordinator, Graham Reeder ... "It's no secret that the traditional environmental movement has long-standing tensions around the world with Indigenous, racial justice, labour and feminist movements (and many others). We had to build grassroots power to win ... [and] start healing old wounds between those who are our best allies, those who coincidentally are at the greatest risk from climate catastrophe."[42]

C. THE SPATIAL ORGANIZATION OF ENVIRONMENTAL RACISM IN CANADA

Canada's unique history and geography has given way to a distinct spatiality in relation to environmental justice struggles. Where racial segregation along Black/white lines characterizes the dominant US narrative of environmental justice, in Canada the state policy of establishing reserves for Indigenous peoples throughout the process of colonial settlement in the 19th century presents the most dominant and enduring form of spatial segregation. Thus, in the Canadian context, the precise contours of the relationship between race and space is distinct, but the broader trends hold. As Waldron explains, Canada's history was built on racial capitalism:

> Canada was founded on enslavement and dispossession. Canada in the eighteenth and nineteenth centuries was characterized by assimilationist ideologies, practices, and policies; displacement, discrimination, subjugation, and oppression of Indigenous and Black peoples and cultures by Europeans; and the expropriation of Indigenous lands. In Canada, "the primitive accumulation of capital through the colonial theft of land is foundational to both current capitalist wealth and to state jurisdiction."
>
> Racism drives and sustains capitalism, which is a racial, gendered, and patriarchal regime. Racial capitalism describes the commodification of racialized peoples for the purposes of acquiring social and economic value that benefits white people and white institutions .... Ultimately, racial capitalism harms racialized peoples through the reinforcement of social and economic inequalities that have the most disadvantageous impacts on racialized peoples whose economic well-being is determined by their market value. Capitalism is preserved through the ongoing salience and resilience of racism and substandard wages provided to racialized peoples, immigrants, and women. It relies on the position of Indigenous land, the

---

40 *Ibid* at 11.

41 Gosine & Teelucksingh, *supra* note 9 at 130-41.

42 (8 July 2015), online: <https://nowtoronto.com/news/what-canada-s-climate-coalition-looks-like/>.

perceived expendability of Indigenous peoples, and the perceived value of gendered and racialized labour.[43]

Because the environmental justice framework invites a spatial analysis, it is important to consider theories on the relationship between race, space, and segregation. For example, Sherene H Razack states that

> our focus on racial formations is automatically a focus on class and gender hierarchies as well. Racial hierarchies come into existence through patriarchy and capitalism, each system of domination mutually constituting the other. The lure of a spatial approach is precisely the possibility of charting the simultaneous operation of multiple systems of domination.
>
> • • •
>
> To denaturalize or unmap spaces, then, we begin by exploring space as a social product, uncovering how bodies are produced in spaces and how spaces produce bodies.[44]

The Native Youth Sexual Health Network, in collaboration with the Women's Earth Alliance, produced an influential report in 2016 that made very clear the connection between environmental contamination and pollution, and people's health. The report states:

> For Indigenous communities … the links between land and body create a powerful intersection—one that, when overlooked or discounted, can threaten their very existence. Extractive industries have drilled, mined, and fracked on lands on or near resource-rich Indigenous territories for decades. Although the economic gains have been a boon to transnational corporations and the economies of the U.S. and Canada, they come at a significant cost to Indigenous communities, particularly women and young people.
>
> Many of these communities are sites of chemical manufacturing and waste dumping, while others have seen an introduction of large encampments of men ("man camps") to work for the gas and oil industry. The devastating impacts of the environmental violence this causes ranges from sexual and domestic violence, drugs and alcohol, murders and disappearances, reproductive illnesses and toxic exposure, threats to culture and Indigenous lifeways, crime, and other social stressors.[45]

Another way in which environmental injustice and racism manifests itself in Canada is through the clustering of industry around certain communities. For example, the Aamjiwnaang First Nation and residents of Sarnia are surrounded by one of the most concentrated clusters of chemical refineries in North America; it affects their health and well-being and, in the case of the former, their culture and rights to self-determination. The lands, waters, and peoples in the Athabasca region have been polluted and harmed by the ongoing exploitation of oil in the region, considered the largest industrial project on Earth. The Athabasca Chipewyan First Nations, for example, have been raising concerns about the devastating impacts of the extractive industry on water quality, biodiversity, including caribou and moose populations, and the health of the people for decades.[46]

In other words, while the patterns of environmental injustices in Canada are different from those in the US, they are no less pervasive.

---

43 Waldron, *Something in the Water*, *supra* note 34 at 44 [citations omitted].

44 "When Place Becomes Race" in Tania Das Gupta et al, eds, *Race and Racialization*, 2nd ed (Toronto: Canadian Scholars' Press, 2018) at 117, 125.

45 Woman's Earth Alliance & Native Youth Sexual Health Network, *Violence on the Land, Violence on our Bodies: Building an Indigenous Response to Environmental Violence* (2016) at 2 [endnote omitted], online (pdf): *Land Body Defense* <http://landbodydefense.org/uploads/files/VLVBReportToolkit2016.pdf>.

46 "Tar Sands" (last visited 8 May 2019), online: *Indigenous Environmental Network* <https://ienearth.org/what-we-do/tar-sands>.

DRINKING WATER ON FIRST NATIONS' RESERVES

The issue of drinking water on First Nations' reserves provides a shameful example of systemic environmental racism in Canada. According to Ecojustice, approximately two-thirds of Indigenous communities in Canada have faced at least one boil-water advisory in the last ten years.[47] In 2019, over 100 First Nations' reserves are subject to boil-water advisories, many that are long-term. For example, the Shoal Lake 40 First Nation, which straddles the Ontario – Manitoba border, has had a boil-water advisory for 22 years. The Neskantaga First Nation in the far north of Ontario has had one for 24 years. The fact that these communities do not have access to safe water is discriminatory and inexcusable and contributes to ongoing health problems that exacerbate the hardships and disadvantages already faced by Indigenous communities. While efforts to address the problem have ramped up since the Trudeau government came into office in 2015 with a promise to end the problem, and there are certainly complex factors involved in providing clean water in remote areas, sometimes fly-in only, there is no excuse for failing to provide a basic human right for so many Indigenous peoples in Canada. It is virtually certain that the resolve and resources required to address the problems, no matter how complex, would be quickly found if this were happening in privileged, non-Indigenous communities.

IV. SHIFTS AND TRENDS IN THE APPLICATION OF THE ENVIRONMENTAL JUSTICE FRAMEWORK IN CANADA

More and more, social movements in Canada employ the language of "environmental justice" rather than environmental protection; advocates are also mobilizing the language of "climate justice" to force attention to the critical distributional concerns associated with a changing climate.

CLIMATE JUSTICE AND THE NORTH

Indigenous communities around the world are disproportionately affected by climate change, in part because of their close ties to the land and waters upon which they subsist and thrive. With temperatures in the Arctic rising faster than anywhere else in the world,[48] the Inuit and other Indigenous communities living in the North are especially affected. Warming in the North is melting glaciers, thinning ice and snow, thawing permafrost, eroding coastlines, and changing habitats for populations of polar bears, seals, walruses, and other Arctic wildlife. This rapid warming has grave implications for the Inuit and Indigenous peoples who live there, jeopardizing their culture and very survival. Additionally, the potential opening of the Northwest Passage may bring more resource extraction and pollution to the North. In 2005, Sheila Watt-Cloutier (Inuk woman, former chair of the Inuit Circumpolar Conference and

---

47 Kaitlyn Mitchell, "World Water Day: The State of Drinking Water in Indigenous Communities" (22 March 2018), online: *Ecojustice* <http://www.ecojustice.ca/world-water-day-the-state-of-drinking-water-in-indigenous-communities>.

48 Myles Allen et al, *Global Warming of 1.5°C: An IPCC Special Report on the Impacts of Global Warming of 1.5°C Above Pre-industrial Levels and Related Global Greenhouse Gas Emission Pathways, in the Context of Strengthening the Global Response to the Threat of Climate Change, Sustainable Development, and Efforts to Eradicate Poverty* (2018), online: *IPCC* <https://www.ipcc.ch/sr15>.

author of *The Right to Be Cold: One Woman's Story of Protecting Her Culture, the Arctic and the Whole Planet*[49]) presented a petition to the Inter-American Commission on Human Rights (IACHR), framing the ongoing greenhouse gas emissions of the US as a human rights violation of Inuit populations. The IACHR dismissed the groundbreaking petition, but the effort focused global attention on the impacts of climate change in the Arctic on the Inuit and framed the issue as a matter of human rights.

Today, the experience of Indigenous communities in the North, including the Inuit, can be framed as an issue of climate injustice. It can also be framed as another example of environmental racism in Canada since, although the Indigenous and Inuit communities are facing some of the most glaring, rapid changes caused by climate change, the government response (in terms of speeding up mitigation efforts as well as supporting adaptation and resilience in these communities) is slow and inadequate.

Similar to the changing language around environmental justice, over the past decade, we have witnessed a shift in language used to describe Indigenous peoples taking direct action to protect valued ecosystems or to object to legislative rollbacks in relation to the environment, from environmental justice "activists" or "protesters" to people describing themselves as "land defenders" and "water defenders." This is in line with ongoing attempts to foster synergies between movements for environmental justice and Indigenous self-determination. Clayton Thomas-Mueller of the Indigenous Environmental Network called Aboriginal rights "Our Last Best Hope to Save Our Water, Air and Earth" in 2013.[50] The effort to align environmental and Indigenous goals has come together perhaps most prominently in the new "pipeline wars" in Canada.

TRANS MOUNTAIN PIPELINE EXPANSION

Pipeline projects have a history of being divisive in Canada, and the Trans Mountain Pipeline Expansion project is no exception. In 2013, Kinder Morgan applied to the National Energy Board (NEB) to expand the capacity of the existing pipeline, which runs from Strathcona, Alberta, to Burnaby, British Columbia, through Treaty 6, Treaty 8, and Métis territory. The expansion would almost triple the capacity of the existing pipeline, from 300,000 to 890,000 barrels per day. After a review and assessment of the project, the NEB concluded that the project was in the public interest and recommended that it proceed, subject to 157 conditions. The federal government approved the project in November 2016.

The proposal, however, was strongly opposed by many stakeholders, including environmental groups and Indigenous communities who had raised a number of concerns during the assessment process. Many of the approximately 120 Indigenous communities along the route felt that they had not been adequately consulted on the project or accommodated. Environmentally, many expressed concern about the increased risks of a spill in Burrard Inlet due to a significant increase in tanker traffic (for example, from five per month to one per day). The inlet is home to a population

---

49 (Toronto: Allen Lane, 2015).

50 "The Rise of the Native Rights-Based Strategic Framework: Our Last Best Hope to Save Our Water, Air and Earth" (23 May 2013), online: *Canadian Dimension* <https://canadiandimension.com/articles/view/the-rise-of-the-native-rights-based-strategic-framework>.

of endangered southern killer whales. The risks of a spill are exacerbated by the fact that the oil being transported is diluted bitumen, which is heavier than conventional oil. This means that it sinks to the ocean floor and mixes with sediment, making cleanup more difficult.

Nearly two dozen lawsuits seeking judicial review of the decision to approve the expansion were filed. The Federal Court of Appeal combined the lawsuits into one challenge and unanimously decided to overturn the approval in August 2018 on two bases.[51] First, the court held that the NEB had erred in failing to include marine traffic in the scope of its review. This meant that it had failed to consider the implications of the approval for the resident whale population. Second, the court held that the government had not adequately consulted and accommodated Indigenous peoples, such as the Tsleil-Waututh and Squamish First Nations, who were among the challengers.

The Federal Court ordered the federal government to mandate the NEB to consider the impact of increased tanker traffic on the southern resident killer whale population and to undertake proper consultations with Indigenous groups. The NEB completed the review of tanker traffic and recommended approval of the project with 156 conditions, plus an additional 16 non-binding recommendations. Meanwhile, the federal government made additional efforts to consult and accommodate Indigenous groups by increasing the number and capacity of Crown consultants, as well as authorizing them to engage constructively and offer accommodations. The federal government also purchased the pipeline from Kinder Morgan in August 2018. On June 18, 2019, Prime Minister Justin Trudeau and his cabinet approved the pipeline expansion.

The environmental justice implications of the pipeline project are numerous, interrelated, and complex. In addition to the risk of spills along the route and in Burrard Inlet, environmentalists point to the upstream greenhouse gas emissions that the pipeline will generate (an estimated 13 to 15 metric tonnes of CO_2 equivalent annually).[52] As already discussed, climate change has major environmental justice implications in that it disproportionately affects certain groups. Many Indigenous groups are concerned about the impacts of the pipeline expansion on their inherent and constitutionally protected rights. Opposition to the pipeline is not monolithic, however, with some Indigenous communities supporting the pipeline expansion. For instance, some First Nations, such as the Mikisew Cree, have pointed to the fact that the resource is being extracted from Indigenous territory and that it only makes sense that Indigenous groups own part of the pipeline. They have signed benefit agreements with the government relating to the expansion and are negotiating partial ownership.[53] According to the chief executive of the Indian Resource Council, who has been in discussions with government officials about having an ownership stake in the pipeline expansion, Indigenous groups are interested in the economic development and job opportunities tied to the project.[54]

Expanding a fossil fuel pipeline at a time when we must urgently and rapidly reduce greenhouse gas emissions makes little sense Yet, the fact that the project is

---

51 *Tsleil-Waututh Nation v Canada (Attorney General)*, 2018 FCA 153.

52 Environment and Climate Change Canada, *Trans Mountain Pipeline ULC – Trans Mountain Expansion Project: Review of Related Upstream Greenhouse Gas Emissions Estimates* (2016), online (pdf): *Canadian Environmental Assessment Agency* <https://ceaa-acee.gc.ca/050/documents/p80061/116524E.pdf>.

53 Kyle Bakx & Geneviève Normand, "More Than 100 First Nations Could Purchase the Trans Mountain Expansion Pipeline" *CBC News* (25 January 2019), online: <https://www.cbc.ca/news/business/tmx-irc-indigenous-1.4975243>.

54 *Ibid*.

tied to job opportunities and economic development for communities, Indigenous and non-Indigenous, adds a level of complexity to the issue. Bringing an environmental justice lens to the project requires unpacking the issues, seeing them from multiple perspectives, and getting at the heart of what is at stake.

To summarize, environmental justice manifests differently in Canada than it does in the US, where the concept was initially articulated and written about by non-governmental organizations, academic scholars and activists. However, the difference does not undermine its presence in Canada. In fact, the less obvious but more insidious legacy of colonialism may make the issues more challenging to identify and address. In Section V of this chapter, we consider how advocacy groups are using legal tools to attempt to remedy environmental injustices in Canada.

QUESTIONS FOR SECTIONS III AND IV

1. Consider Teelucksingh's comment in light of your own experiences of Canadian cities: "Although Toronto may not exhibit the racial and spatial vestiges of American inner-city-style ghettos, nonetheless, Toronto is not free of racialization. Again, normalized racialized spaces may not be readily apparent," but they do exist.[55] How do you think Canadians' embrace of multiculturalism influences our conceptions of environmental justice?

2. What is the significance of saying one is fighting for "climate justice" versus fighting "climate change"? Are they mutually exclusive? Reinforcing? Does it matter whether the issue is considered at a global versus regional or local scale?

3. What makes it more difficult, from a legal perspective, to justify the issuance of an injunction to remove "land defenders" participating in a blockade, as an example, than one to remove "environmental activists"?

4. Consider the extent to which Thomas-Mueller's framing mitigates or exacerbates the historical tension between "environmentalists" and Indigenous activists that in some way the environmental justice movement aims to overcome. Are environmentalists "jumping on the bandwagon" of Aboriginal rights in order to advance conservation or environmental protection goals, or are they genuinely interested in Indigenous self-determination? Does it matter? Do you agree with Thomas-Mueller that Aboriginal rights and environmental protection are mutually supportive? What about environmental justice?

V. ENVIRONMENTAL JUSTICE IN LAW

Environmental justice intersects with law in multiple ways. In some cases, inadequate laws, in substance and operationalization, and governance mechanisms are the agents of environmental injustices, as illustrated by the case of the mercury poisoning of the Grassy Narrows community.[56] In other cases, legal strategies may offer opportunities for redress or compensation, as illustrated by arguments that the environmental injustices experienced by the Aamjiwnaang First Nation violate s 7 of the *Canadian Charter of Rights and Freedoms*,[57] or that systemic problems with the quality of drinking water on reserves violate s 15 equality rights.[58]

55 Cheryl Teelucksingh, *In Somebody's Backyard: Racialized Space and Environmental Justice in Toronto (Canada)* (PhD Dissertation, York University Faculty of Sociology, 2001) at 36.

56 See Grassy Narrows First Nation, "Grassy Narrows Sues Ontario over Mercury Health Threat from Clearcut Logging" (14 September 2015), online: *Free Grassy Narrows* <http://freegrassy.net/2015/09/14/grassy-narrows-sues-ontario-over-mercury-health-threat-from-clearcut-logging>.

57 Part I of the *Constitution Act, 1982*, being Schedule B to the *Canada Act 1982* (UK), 1982, c 11 [Charter].

58 See e.g. Nathalie J Chalifour "Environmental Discrimination and the Charter's Equality Guarantee: The Case of Drinking Water for First Nations Living on Reserves" (2013) 43 RGD 183 [Chalifour, "Environmental Discrimination"] and Scott, "The Hesitant Embrace of Rights," *supra* note 1 at 447-59.

The petition by the Inuit for redress within the Inter-American Court of Human Rights offers another example of seeking redress through legal mechanisms.[59]

Thus far, there is no jurisprudence in Canada that has directly engaged with the idea or principles of environmental justice per se. In this section, however, we include excerpts from cases that have attempted to bring an environmental justice perspective to the courts, and cases that have tangentially addressed questions we would characterize as engaging environmental justice. From there, we consider the law reform efforts of environmental justice advocates, as illustrated by a private member's bill on environmental racism in Nova Scotia and the recommendations made in the context of the recent Parliamentary review of the *Canadian Environmental Protection Act, 1999.*[60]

The following example details how some environmental justice activists in Canada approached strategic litigation in an attempt to deploy environmental rights as a defence to the chronic pollution burdens facing Indigenous communities. The attempt ultimately failed, but further efforts are still underway, and we have much to learn from looking closely at this experience.

A. CHEMICAL VALLEY CHARTER CHALLENGE

In the following excerpt, Scott describes the first legal challenge in Canada that was explicitly brought in the language of "environmental justice."

DAYNA N SCOTT, "ENVIRONMENTAL JUSTICE AND THE HESITANT EMBRACE OF HUMAN RIGHTS"
in James R May & Erin Daly, eds, *Human Rights and the Environment: Indivisibility, Dignity, and Legality*, Elgar Encyclopedia of Environmental Law (Cheltenham: Edward Elgar Press and the IUCN Academy of Environmental Law, 2019) at 453–55

[The case, *Lockridge v Ontario (Director, Ministry of the Environment)*, 2012 ONSC 2316 (Div Ct), or the "Chemical Valley Charter challenge," was a 2010 judicial review application brought in Ontario as a challenge to the local air pollution regime. "Chemical Valley" in Sarnia, Ontario, is "a major pollution hotspot that disproportionately affects" the neighbouring Anishinaabe community at Aamjiwnaang First Nation. The application "was withdrawn in 2016 to the great disappointment of many across the country." (See Kaitlyn Mitchell et al, "Defending the Rights of Chemical Valley Residents—Charter Challenge" (last visited 8 May 2019), online: *Ecojustice* <http://www.ecojustice.ca/case/defending-the-rights-of-chemical-valley-residents-charter-challenge>; Margot Venton et al, "Changing Course in Chemical Valley" (last updated 26 July 2016), online: *Ecojustice* <http://www.ecojustice.ca/changing-course-chemical-valley>.)]

This innovative [case], which was explicitly oriented against the environmental racism that perpetuates the chronic releases of toxic air pollution in the region, had promised to provide Canada's courts with an opportunity to declare that all

59 See Sheila Watt-Cloutier, "Petition to the Inter-American Commission on Human Rights Seeking Relief from Violations Resulting from Global Warming Caused by Acts and Omissions of the United States" (2005), online: *Climate Case Chart* <http://climatecasechart.com/non-us-case/petition-to-the-inter-american-commission-on-human-rights-seeking-relief-from-violations-resulting-from-global-warming-caused-by-acts-and-omissions-of-the-united-states/?cn-reloaded=1>.

60 SC 1999, c 33 [CEPA].

Canadians have a "right to a healthy environment," despite one not being provided for in the [Charter] or elsewhere in the … Constitution.

The claim, filed by two members of the Aamjiwnaang First Nation … , questioned the constitutionality of permits granted to Suncor Inc., a major multinational oil company which operates a refinery in the massive petrochemical cluster near Sarnia, Ontario. Industrial emissions from Sarnia's Chemical Valley—consisting of several refineries and heavy industries accounting for approximately 40 per cent of Canada's chemical production—flow downwind towards the Aamjiwnaang First Nation reserve. The high air pollution burden in Aamjiwnaang and the devastating environmental health impacts, including higher than expected rates of cancer and miscarriage, respiratory illness and developmental disorders in the community, have been well documented. [See Elaine MacDonald & Sarah Rang, "Exposing Canada's Chemical Valley: An Investigation of Cumulative Air Pollution Emissions in the Sarnia, Ontario Area" (October 2007), online: *Ecojustice* <http://www.ecojustice.ca/case/defending-the-rights-of-chemical-valley-residents-charter-challenge/>; Constanze A Mac-kenzie, Ada Lockridge & Margaret Keith, "Declining Sex Ratio in a First Nation Community" (2005) 113:10 Environmental Health Perspectives 1295; Environmental Commissioner of Ontario, "MOE Continues to Fail the Aamjiwnaang First Nation" in Environmental Commissioner of Ontario, ed, *Managing New Challenges: Annual Report 2013/2014* (Toronto: Environmental Commissioner of Ontario, 2014) 114.]

[The applicants] contended that the decision by Ontario's Ministry of Environment ("MOE") to allow Suncor to increase its emissions to air, without proper consideration for the cumulative effects from all industrial emissions in the area, violated their [Charter rights]. [See *Lockridge v Ontario (Director, Ministry of the Environment)*, 2012 ONSC 2316 at para 1.] The applicants argued that the decisions and practices of the MOE contributed to exceedingly high levels of emissions that threaten their health and force them to confront risks and trade-offs that non-Indigenous Canadians do not face, engaging the Charter's equality guarantee. This reasoning was also in line with persuasive accounts by leading Canadian environmental law scholars who argue that [s 7 of the Charter]—which guarantees the right to life, liberty, and security of the person—is "available to strike down laws that allow pollution at levels that interfere with human health and well-being." [See Chalifour, "Environmental Justice and the Charter," *supra* note 4 at 103, citing Lynda Collins, "An Ecologically Literate Reading of the Canadian Charter of Rights and Freedoms" (2009) 26 Windsor Rev Legal Soc Issues 7; see also David R Boyd, *The Environmental Rights Revolution: A Global Study of Constitutions, Human Rights, and the Environment* (Vancouver: UBC Press, 2012); David Wu, "Embedding Environmental Rights in Section 7 of the Canadian Charter: Resolving the Tension Between the Need for Precaution and the Need for Harm" (2015) 33 NJCL 191.] But despite the Supreme Court of Canada's emphasis on environmental protection as a central value in Canadian society and expansive jurisprudence interpreting section 7, this case was withdrawn and will not be heard, at least in part because the applicants lost some critical preliminary motions, including the motion for a protective costs order, and thus faced the prospect of paying Suncor's "considerable" legal bill at the end of a protracted litigation heavy on expert evidence.

The company's lawyers brought several preliminary challenges to the application: a collateral attack motion, which the applicants won, and a motion to strike much of the affidavit evidence filed by the applicants. The company argued that the residents' knowledge about the "health effects allegedly flowing from [the] emissions … is irrelevant," and that their affidavits contained "improper opinion evidence, inadmissible hearsay, argument or speculation." [See *Lockridge v Ontario (Director, Ministry of the Environment)*, 2012 ONSC 2316 at para 4.] These motions consumed the majority of four days of oral argument. The Court agreed that some portions of the evidence should be struck, but [left most of the evidence in]. Even though [it was] not successful in all of the preliminary motions, the company ... certainly succeeded in delaying the ultimate hearing of the application and ratcheting up the time and financial resources necessary to proceed with the suit. To use that strategy to maximum effect, the company's lawyers also successfully opposed the applicants' motion for a "protective costs order," which would have insulated the residents, absent improper conduct, from adverse costs if the application was ultimately unsuccessful. Worse, in the course of deciding the matter of the protective costs order, the company managed to convince the Court that the scope of the judicial review application was very narrow. The Court stated that all that was at stake was the quashing of one specific regulatory approval; the decision "would not affect general emissions from the refinery, and could not generally impose a cumulative effects assessment into the regulatory process." [See *Lockridge v Ontario (Director, Ministry of the Environment)*, 2012 ONSC 2316 at para 162.] All of the meaning that the local activists and their *pro bono* lawyers tried to pour into the case—the environmental racism, the disproportionate burdens, the right to breathe clean air—drained out as the shape of the air-tight legal compartments solidified through the preliminary motions.

This case illustrates the potential utility of fundamental rights and freedoms recognized by scholars in the environmental justice movement—many young activists were inspired, politicized, and became engaged in the fight for environmental justice through this community's ongoing struggle—but it also exemplifies why many in the movement feel a real scepticism towards legal strategies and litigation for achieving change. [Of course, winning in court is not always the driving purpose of bringing forward strategic litigation. See Jacqueline Peel & Hari M Osofsky, "A Rights Turn in Climate Change Legislation?" (2018) 7:1 Transnat'l Envtl L 37 at 67 ("[e]ven 'losing' cases can have important flow-on effects through the ways in which they shape public dialogue, business attitudes and government action"). In the final analysis, as the authors point out in relation to climate change litigation more specifically, "the strongest benefit from a turn towards rights arguments" lies in these more "informal effects."] Many deserving claims are blocked from even being heard by procedural and logistical barriers, such as standing or costs rules, and are denied the opportunity to be examined on their merits, thus sapping energy and resources from the communities mobilizing against environmental injustice. Here, as in many other cases, affected marginalized people are silenced, despite the best efforts of their lawyers to engage and involve them; to give them voice through the process. This is because the very structure of the enterprise, in this case a judicial review raising Charter issues, requires the "repackaging of client grievances in a form the court [can] understand." [See Lucie E White, "Mobilization on the Margins of the Lawsuit: Making Space for Clients to Speak" (1987-88) 16:4 NYU Rev L & Soc Change 535 at 543-44.]

B. GRASSY NARROWS

A second Charter challenge employing the same s 7 and s 15 formula was brought in 2015, when Grassy Narrows First Nation launched a constitutional claim against the Government of Ontario, alleging that the province's decision to allow clear-cut logging of forests around the community would release mercury into the local waterways.[61] Two years later, the environmental commissioner of Ontario published a report naming the Grassy Narrows community

---

61 "Grassy Narrows alleges that the logging plan will prolong and deepen the ongoing tragedy of mercury poisoning in their community and therefore violates their Charter rights to security and freedom from discrimination." See Grassy Narrows First Nation, *supra* note 55.

as only one example of environmental injustice perpetuated against Indigenous communities in that province, and calling out the Ontario government for allowing it to persist:

> Indigenous people and communities are disproportionately affected by environmental problems, due to a long and shameful history of mistreatment by all levels of government. Indigenous people have often been subjected to environmental decisions made without consideration of their interests, let alone their participation. Many of these decisions have caused profound harm that carries on to today. Even the locations of some First Nation reserves were chosen because the lands were viewed as worthless to white settlers. Today, many First Nations are engaged in legal battles for more control over how and what activities will be permitted on their traditional lands.

> • • •

> For almost 60 years, mercury contamination has severely damaged the Wabigoon-English River ecosystem. This contamination has stripped the people of Wabaseemoong and Grassy Narrows of important facets of their cultural practices, livelihoods and health. The company that profited from the pollution sold the property, settled legal claims, and moved on 30 years ago. The government long ago abandoned the communities to bear the consequences, and has only very recently begun to take the first steps towards remediating the river system, as well as the government's relationship with the affected communities.

> • • •

> After accepting financial responsibility for the mercury contamination, the Ontario government declined to take action for decades, largely ignoring the suffering of the Grassy Narrows First Nation and Wabaseemoong peoples. Over and over, the Ontario government chose to do nothing. It chose *not* to remove the sediment, *not* to investigate in more detail, *not* to monitor whether mercury levels were indeed declining. In other words, it chose to allow the ongoing poisoning of the communities.

> • • •

> The [Environmental Commissioner of Ontario] recommends that the Government of Ontario incorporate environmental justice as part of its commitment to reconciliation with Indigenous people and communities.[62]

At the time of writing this chapter, the Grassy Narrows claim is awaiting trial.

C. PROCEDURAL JUSTICE

Pursuing environmental justice through litigation is costly and time-consuming, and potential claimants face numerous procedural barriers. Class actions offer one method for claimants to pool resources and efforts, but they have proven difficult to pursue in Canada. As Heather McLeod-Kilmurray has noted, the unique features of environmental claims hamper the prospects of class actions as a tool of environmental justice: "If procedures such as class actions are to have a significant and useful role, they must be interpreted according to the unique properties of the substantive area of law they are called upon to serve."[63] To date, only one environmental class action in Canada, outside of Quebec, has been argued on its

---

62 Dianne Saxe, "Environmental Injustice: Pollution and Indigenous Communities" in Dianne Saxe, ed, *Good Choices, Bad Choices: Environmental Rights and Environmental Protection in Ontario*, 2017 Environmental Protection Report (Toronto: Environmental Commissioner for Ontario, 2017) ch 3 at 100, 111, 142 [endnote omitted], online (pdf): *Environmental Commissioner for Ontario* <https://docs.assets.eco.on.ca/reports/environmental-protection/2017/Good-Choices-Bad-Choices.pdf>.

63 "Hollick and Environmental Class Actions: Putting the Substance into Class Action Procedure" (2003) 34:2 Ottawa L Rev 263 at 306.

merits: *Smith v Inco Ltd*.[64] In that case, a class action on behalf of 7,000 residents of Port Colborne, Ontario claimed that the high concentrations of nickel in the soil caused by Inco's refinery operations over many decades qualified as a nuisance affecting their property values. While the case succeeded at trial, the Ontario Court of Appeal overturned the decision. The plaintiffs' loss was doubled when the corporate defendant was awarded $1.7 million in costs.[65]

In Quebec, a class action lawsuit by neighbours of a cement factory seeking compensation for adverse effects related to noise, dust, and odour eventually succeeded at the Supreme Court of Canada in 2008.[66] In another case, the organization ENvironnement JEUnesse (ENJEU) has filed a class action on behalf of Quebec youth for inaction on climate change.[67]

To date, class actions in Canada offer little hope for victims of environmental racism or environmental injustice. This may start to shift if the ENJEU class action is certified, but it would only be a small step forward.

Another barrier that individuals or groups aiming to seek environmental justice in the courts or other administrative proceedings face is the potential for a SLAPP. SLAPP stands for "Strategic Lawsuits Against Public Participation" and refers to a lawsuit aimed at intimidating or silencing critics or opposition to a project. These actions are usually brought by actors with ample financial resources and can be a significant barrier to those seeking legal remedies for environmental justice. Some jurisdictions, including Ontario, Quebec, and British Columbia, have enacted legislation aimed at providing safeguards against the growing number of SLAPP suits.[68] Once the target of a SLAPP establishes that its proceeding relates to a matter of genuine public interest, the entity bringing the SLAPP must establish that the lawsuit is merit based and not just an effort at intimidation or otherwise silencing activists pursuing a legitimate objective. Anti-SLAPP legislation is one way to protect activists seeking environmental justice against intimidation.

EXERCISE—CLAIMING THAT THE LACK OF SAFE DRINKING WATER ON FIRST NATIONS RESERVES VIOLATES THE CHARTER'S EQUALITY GUARANTEE

As discussed earlier, substandard quality of drinking water on First Nations reserves is a historical problem that has not significantly improved with time. Some scholars and activists have argued that this qualifies as environmental discrimination and could form the basis of a claim under s 15 of the Charter.[69] Section 15 of the Charter states, "Every individual is equal before and under the law and has the right to the equal protection and equal benefit of the law without discrimination and, in particular, without discrimination based on race, national or ethnic origin, colour, religion, sex, age or mental or physical disability."

How would you go about framing a claim under s 15 of the Charter? Would it be better to build the case for one First Nations community that has had long-term boil-water advisories, or frame it as a class action on behalf of all communities that have lacked clean drinking water for a particular length of time? What government conduct would you challenge? Would you

---

64 2011 ONCA 628.

65 *Smith v Inco Ltd*, 2013 ONCA 724.

66 *St Lawrence Cement Inc v Barrette*, 2008 SCC 64, [2008] 3 SCR 392.

67 "Youth vs Canada" (last visited 6 June 2019), online: *Environnement Jeunesse* <http://enjeu.qc.ca/justice-eng/>.

68 See e.g. the *Protection of Public Participation Act, 2015*, SO 2015, c 23.

69 See e.g. Chalifour, "Environmental Discrimination", *supra* note 57; David R Boyd, "No Taps, No Toilets: First Nations and the Constitutional Right to Water in Canada" (2011) 57:1 McGill LJ 81; Constance MacIntosh, "Public Health Protection and Drinking Water Quality on First Nation Reserves: Considering the New Federal Regulatory Proposal" (2009) 18:1 Health L Rev 5.

instead try to argue that the government has an obligation under s 15 to provide clean drinking water to your client? If so, under what basis would you make this argument? Does it matter that there is no self-standing right to clean water in our Charter? How would you respond to arguments that the Charter does not create positive obligations for governments to provide particular services? What remedy would you seek?

D. LAW REFORM

1. Environmental Racism Prevention Act

In a bold effort to make race explicit, in 2015, Waldron worked with Lenore Zann, NDP member of the legislative assembly in Nova Scotia, to introduce a private member's bill on environmental racism—namely Bill 111.[70] The Act did not make it beyond first reading, but the Bill has been reintroduced most recently on September 13, 2018 as Bill 31, *An Act to Redressing Environmental Racism*. If it succeeds, the Bill will represent the first explicit incorporation of the term "environmental racism" into the Canadian legislative landscape.

> ### BILL 31, AN ACT TO REDRESS ENVIRONMENTAL RACISM
> 2nd Sess, 63rd Leg, Nova Scotia, 2018 (first reading 13 September 2018)
>
> WHEREAS a recent report from a working group of the United Nations Human Rights Council has noted the legacy of anti-black racism in Canada;
> THEREFORE be it enacted by the Governor and Assembly as follows:
> 1 This Act may be cited as the Redressing Environmental Racism Act.
> 2 In this Act,
>   (a) "Ministers" means the Minister of Environment and the Minister responsible for the Human Rights Act;
>   (b) "panel" means the panel established pursuant to this Act.
> 3(1) The Ministers shall establish a panel, as set out in this Section, to examine the issue of environmental racism in the Province, and provide recommendations to address it.
>   (2) The panel is to be composed of
>   (a) three members chosen by the Minister of Environment from among the members of the Round Table established pursuant to the Environment Act;
>   (b) two members chosen by the Minister responsible for the Human Rights Act from among the members of the Nova Scotia Human Rights Commission; and
>   (c) three members chosen by the Minister responsible for the Human Rights Act, of whom there must be one member from each of
>   (i) the African Nova Scotian community,
>   (ii) the First Nations community, and
>   (iii) the Acadian community.
>   (3) Her Majesty in right of the Province shall, subject to Section 6, pay the members of the panel such remuneration as is determined by the Ministers, together with the members' reasonable expenses.
>   4(1) Within one year of the coming into force of this Act, the panel shall consult the public, on a Province-wide basis, about the issue of environmental racism, with

---

70 *Environmental Racism Prevention Act*, 2nd Sess, 62nd Leg, Nova Scotia, 2015 (first reading 29 April 2015).

special emphasis given to consultation with the African Nova Scotian, First Nations and Acadian communities, and provide a report to the Ministers that sets out its findings and recommendations.

(2) Subject to Section 6, the panel may provide funding for participation in the consultation referred to in subsection (1), and may, in its sole discretion, determine

(a) the recipients of funding; and

(b) the amount of funding to be provided to a particular recipient.

(3) The report referred to in subsection (1) must include

(a) an investigation into the causes and rates of cancer or any other negative health outcomes, including mental health outcomes, in communities that may have been negatively affected by environmental racism;

(b) an investigation into the effect of environmental racism on property values; and

(c) recommendations for addressing environmental racism including

(i) compensation for individuals or communities,

(ii) ongoing funding for community groups in affected communities, and

(iii) specific steps to ensure affected communities have access to clean air and water.

5 The Ministers shall, within 10 days of receiving the report referred to in Section 4, table the report in the Assembly if the Assembly is then sitting or, where it is not then sitting, file the report with the Clerk of the Assembly.

6 The money required for the purpose of this Act must be paid out of money appropriated for that purpose by the Legislature.

2. CEPA Review

Section 343 of CEPA states that there must be a review of the Act and its administration by a parliamentary committee every five years after the Act comes into force. As a result of its first review of the Act, the House of Commons Standing Committee on Environment and Sustainable Development released a report in 2007 making several important recommendations that were largely ignored.[71] In the next review, not conducted until 2016, a key element of the committee's recommendations to the government included the introduction of the concepts of "environmental justice" and a "right to a healthy environment" into Canadian environmental law.[72] While the government has declined to implement those recommendations in the present Parliament, the committee's report is comprehensive, and it is hoped that it will inform future legislative directions in Canada.[73]

---

71 House of Commons, Standing Committee on Environment and Sustainable Development, *The Canadian Environmental Protection Act, 1999—Five-Year Review: Closing the Gaps* (April 2007).

72 House of Commons, Standing Committee on Environment and Sustainable Development, *Report 8— Healthy Environment, Healthy Canadians, Healthy Economy: Strengthening the Canadian Environmental Protection Act, 1999—Report of the Standing Committee on Environment and Sustainable Development* (June 2017) (Chair: Deborah Schulte) (presented to the House 15 June 2017), online (pdf): *House of Commons* <https://www.ourcommons.ca/Content/Committee/421/ENVI/Reports/RP9037962/envirp08/envirp08-e.pdf> [Standing Committee on Environment and Sustainable Development, *Report 8*].

73 Environment and Climate Change Canada, Government Response to the Eighth Report of the Standing Committee on Environment and Sustainable Development (presented to the House 6 October 2017), online (pdf): *House of Commons* <https://www.ourcommons.ca/content/Committee/421/ENVI/GovResponse/RP9148698/421_ENVI_Rpt08_GR/421_ENVI_Rpt08_GR-e.pdf>. This was not the first time that the government has failed to implement reforms suggested by the standing committee.

Consider the following excerpt from the committee's report:

The obligation of non-discrimination in environmental protection, known more commonly as "environmental justice," is a means of addressing the inequitable distribution of the environmental burden of toxic exposure in Canada. Discussion on the strengths and weaknesses of implementing various aspects of environmental justice were largely initiated by interveners calling on the Committee to recommend that the government better take into account vulnerable populations and windows of vulnerability in the assessment and management of toxic substances. Calls for binding, national standards for drinking water and air quality, as discussed in more detail in this report, could also be described as submissions related to environmental justice, as could calls for enhanced analysis of cumulative effects in assessment and management of toxic substances.[74]

And now consider the response of the Government of Canada, below.[75]

FOLLOW-UP REPORT TO THE HOUSE OF COMMONS STANDING COMMITTEE ON ENVIRONMENT AND SUSTAINABLE DEVELOPMENT ON THE CANADIAN ENVIRONMENTAL PROTECTION ACT, 1999

Environment and Climate Change Canada & Health Canada (29 June 2018) at 5, 13-15, 33, 39-40, online (pdf): *House of Commons* <https://www.ourcommons.ca/content/Committee/421/ENVI/WebDoc/WD10002919/421_ENVI_reldoc12_PDF/DeptOfTheEnvironment-e.pdf>

The Committee's recommendations related to codifying a right to a clean environment raise some fundamental issues regarding the role of laws in expressing social values, and the degree to which general statements of values can, or should [*sic*] guide and constrain ongoing legislative, regulatory and policy decisions. The Committee characterized environmental rights as having three dimensions ... The Committee's report provides a helpful starting point for continued discussions on these topics, which will contribute to the Government's commitment to update CEPA in future Parliamentary sessions.

• • •

3.4.3 VULNERABLE POPULATIONS, CUMULATIVE EFFECTS AND MONITORING

The Committee's report placed a large focus on strengthening protections for vulnerable populations and ensuring that the cumulative impacts of certain chemicals are considered. The Committee recommended that "[...] the preamble of CEPA be amended [...] to mention the importance of considering vulnerable populations in risk assessments [...]" (Recommendation 3, sub-bullet 2). ... The Committee also recommended amending section 3 of CEPA "[...] to include a broad definition of the

---

74 Standing Committee on Environment and Sustainable Development, *Report 8*, *supra* note 71 at 6 [footnotes omitted].

75 Environment and Climate Change Canada & Health Canada, *Follow-Up Report to the House of Commons Standing Committee on Environment and Sustainable Development on the Canadian Environmental Protection Act, 1999* (29 June 2018) at 5, 33, 39-40, 13-15, online (pdf): *House of Commons* <https://www.ourcommons.ca/content/Committee/421/ENVI/WebDoc/WD10002919/421_ENVI_reldoc12_PDF/DeptOfTheEnvironment-e.pdf> [Environment and Climate Change Canada & Health Canada, *Follow-Up Report*].

term 'vulnerable populations'" (Recommendation 42), that CEPA be amended "[...] to require that the Ministers or their delegates, when determining if a substance is toxic, assess exposures of vulnerable populations and marginalized communities, including exposures during critical windows of vulnerability, with appropriate use of safety factors and that this section clarify that, for some substances, there may be no safe exposure thresholds" (Recommendation 43), and that CEPA be amended to "[...] require investigation of the effects of any proposed or final regulation or instrument on vulnerable populations and marginalized communities [...and...] aggregate exposures, and cumulative and synergistic effects, in determining how to regulate a toxic substance" (Recommendation 56). The Government supports the intent of these recommendations and will consider them as part of its work to reform CEPA.

The Committee also recommended that [Environment and Climate Change Canada] "[...] undertake, in consultation with the provinces, territories, Indigenous communities and the public, an assessment of potential hot spots or areas of potential intensified or cumulative emissions of toxins to ensure protection for vulnerable persons" (Recommendation 45). ... The Government commits to further consider the Committee's recommendations as part of its stakeholder engagement on these issues through the CMP [Chemicals Management Plan] Post-2020 Process, which will inform how CEPA is reformed ... .

In the interim, the Government will continue to consider available information on vulnerable populations when conducting risk assessments. Further, the Government is committed to continuously improving the consideration of vulnerable populations in the assessment and management of chemicals. As part of this broad commitment, the Government also commits to develop, engage on, and publish under CEPA a policy on vulnerable populations, which will include a definition of vulnerable populations and the objectives of the program, including the framework for how the Government considers vulnerable populations as part of risk assessments.

[With respect to vulnerable populations and marginalized communities that may face disproportionate toxic burdens, the government states:]

Some Canadians, due to greater susceptibility (such as pregnant women and children) or greater exposure (such as those Canadians living in the vicinity of an industrial facility), may be at greater risk than the general population. The CMP routinely considers these risks both in conducting risk assessments and in designing risk management measures. This includes specific consideration of the developing fetus, infants, children, pregnant women, individuals living in the vicinity of industrial or commercial facilities, and First Nations and Inuit populations (Recommendation 43). Where assessments identify risks in specific populations, targeted risk management approaches are developed to reduce the risks for that group (Recommendation 56).

• • •

When information is limited, risk assessors under CEPA apply conservative assumptions to ensure protection of human health, including the health of vulnerable populations. In accordance with precautionary assessment protocols, assessors may apply additional safety factors or make "worst case" assumptions regarding exposure.

• • •

5.1 A SUBSTANTIVE RIGHT TO ENVIRONMENTAL QUALITY

The Committee recommended that the preamble of CEPA be amended to explicitly "[...] recognize the right to a healthy environment" ..., and that the "[...] Government consider amending CEPA to include the right to a healthy environment [...]" in a number of specific sections of CEPA (Recommendation 4). However, the Committee did not define what such a right would mean. The Committee recognized that the environmental protections provided in CEPA already establish substantive protections for environmental quality. The Government commits to further study and stakeholder engagement on the implications of these recommendations.

5.2 PROCEDURAL ENVIRONMENTAL RIGHTS

As noted by the Committee, procedural rights are already strongly represented in CEPA, including access to information, public participation and access to justice (e.g., codified consultation and public comment periods; requirements to publish information and maintain the CEPA online registry; the ability of the public to bring civil actions against alleged offenders, and to request reviews of existing laws and policies and whistle-blower protections). ...

• • •

5.4 ENVIRONMENTAL JUSTICE

Environmental Justice, or the obligation of non-discrimination in environmental protection, relates to addressing the unequal burden of exposure of certain groups of the population to environmental impacts. For example, environmental exposure to certain substances may pose greater health risks for certain more vulnerable members of society, such as children, expectant mothers, and elderly persons, than for the general population, owing to physiological differences such as body size, weight, metabolism and growth rate. It is also important that risk management decisions provide protection to all Canadians, and avoid situations where low income or other groups of people are exposed to higher risks than others. The Committee made several recommendations relating to vulnerable populations and "hot spots" designed to help improve environmental justice under CEPA.

QUESTIONS

1. What are the operative provisions in Bill 31, *Redressing Environmental Racism Act*? Do you believe that legislation like this, if enacted, would be effective? What about small everyday "acts" of preventing or confronting environmental racism? Can you think of some that would be more effective?

2. According to Scott's submission to the committee,

[w]omen, infants and children, and members of low-income, racialized and Indigenous communities, are often more highly exposed to toxic substances, and they experience unequal effects of these exposures. Further, the burden of managing exposures falls disproportionately on women. For these reasons, the failure of Part 5 to prevent pollution has had disproportionate and inequitable impacts.[76]

---

76 Dayna N Scott, "Reforming the Canadian Environmental Protection Act: The Assessment and Regulation of Toxic Substances Should Be Equitable, Precautionary, and Evidence-Based," Brief to the Standing Committee on Environment and Sustainable Development (3 June 2016) at 3-4 [footnotes omitted], online (pdf): *House of Commons* <https://www.ourcommons.ca/Content/Committee/421/ENVI/Brief/BR8384458/br-external/ScottDayna-e.pdf>. See also Dayna N Scott & Sarah Lewis, "Sex and Gender in Canada's Chemicals Management Plan" in Dayna N Scott, ed, *Our Chemical Selves: Gender, Toxics and Environmental Health* (Vancouver: UBC Press, 2015).

How do you think women come to experience higher toxic exposures? Why would these exposures have different impacts according to sex? Gender? How do you think gender influences the burdens of managing exposures?

3. According to its proponents, the environmental monitoring of ambient conditions is crucial for environmental law:

> It can provide essential information to regulators, legislators, industry, and the public about the cleanliness of our air and water and about the conditions of the ecosystems that human life depends upon. This is information that legislators use to hold regulators accountable, that regulators use to improve regulatory programs, and that the public uses to make decisions about the environmental risks of everyday activities.[77]

> But critics argue that governments often invest in environmental monitoring, including biomonitoring of humans, instead of measures that would actually prevent the pollution— that is, they are more interested in measuring it than stopping it.

Consider what the government's response said about biomonitoring:

> The Committee emphasized the importance of biomonitoring and environmental monitoring as an important source of information, particularly with respect to vulnerable populations and geographic "hot spots." The Government agrees with the Committee that biomonitoring data are [sic] an important source of information on levels of exposure to vulnerable populations, as well as on combined exposures to multiple chemicals, and we are placing a high priority on monitoring. The Government also commits to continuously improve biomonitoring in support of protecting vulnerable populations ... .

> For instance, the Government is committed to continuing to use and improve sources such as the Canadian Health Measures Survey (CHMS), the Maternal-Infant Research on Environmental Chemicals (MIREC) Research Platform and the First Nations Biomonitoring Initiative (FNBI) and Northern Contaminants Program (NCP). In the spirit of the Committee's recommendations, in December 2017 the Government signed a memorandum of understanding with the Government of Alberta formalizing responsibilities to continue a long-term environmental monitoring program in the Athabasca River basin region, and to include greater Indigenous involvement in establishing monitoring priorities. This will improve understanding of the long-term cumulative effects of oil sands development.[78]

A further critique of biomonitoring points out that, because of long latency periods for environmental health effects to manifest, waiting for results from biomonitoring studies before acting to regulate exposures will fail to prevent adverse effects. Take the MIREC program as an example. This program collects data on pregnant women and their children in a longitudinal study in an attempt to understand the fetal origins of chronic diseases such as obesity or Alzheimer's in adults. For infants whose prenatal exposures are measured today, how long will we need to wait before we start making correlations to the incidence of these diseases later in their lives? Is this information useful from a regulatory perspective? Does it implement the precautionary principle? Can it further environmental justice?

VI. CONCLUSION

To summarize, environmental justice and environmental racism are vast concepts that transcend any particular discipline or analytical approach. They teach us to take great care when we examine environmental issues to ensure we do so with full recognition of our own biases and experiences, and that we recognize the diversity of ways in which power, capitalism, and hegemonic institutions reproduce injustices experienced through the environment.

---

77 Eric Biber, "The Problem of Environmental Monitoring" (2011) 83:1 Colo L Rev 1 at 5.

78 Environment and Climate Change Canada & Health Canada, Follow-Up Report, *supra* note 74 at 15.

While environmental justice is experienced differently in Canada, it is no less a phenomenon here than in the US or elsewhere. In fact, the experience of many Indigenous peoples in Canada who have been, and continue to be, harmed by environmental degradation is a shameful example of systemic environmental racism.

Environmental justice advocates in Canada are employing a diversity of strategies aimed at redressing existing harms and creating more just decision-making systems, including strategic litigation and efforts at law reform. Because the voices of those most affected by environmental injustices are often unheard, communities across the country use direct action to generate law reform; see, for example, the protests by the Elsipogtog First Nation advocating for a moratorium on fracking in New Brunswick and the protests by Indigenous communities on Wet'suwet'en against TransCanada Pipelines Ltd.

CHAPTER FOUR

IMPLEMENTING SUSTAINABILITY

Géraud de Lassus St-Geniès and Paule Halley

I. INTRODUCTION

Since the publication of the Brundtland Report[1] in 1987, the concept of sustainability has elicited considerable interest from political scientists, economists, legal scholars, and lawyers. Because this interest has never really diminished over time, an extensive literature on the concept, which has been the subject of countless definitions, theories, and even explanatory diagrams (for example, Venn diagrams and continuous triangular and concentric diagrams), has been developed.[2] As a result, the legal discourse on sustainability is both heterogenous and inconsistent. The concept is sometimes presented as a guiding principle, with legal meaning and practical implications, and sometimes merely regarded as a goal for mankind or a value that remains outside the realm of law. Some commentators focus on the place the concept of sustainability occupies under the law, while others prefer to use sustainability as a framework for assessing whether existing laws adequately address the current environmental challenges. Some experts are interested in understanding and categorizing the different meanings of sustainability (weak versus strong; ecocentric versus anthropocentric), while others prefer to

---

1   World Commission on Environment and Development, *Our Common Future* (Oxford: Oxford University Press, 1987).

2   See Kathryn Davidson, "A Typology to Categorize the Ideologies of Actors in the Sustainable Development Debate" (2014) 22:1 Sustainable Development 1; Arnaud Z Dragicevic, "Deconstructing Sustainability" (2018) 26:6 Sustainable Development 525; Walter A Salas-Zapata & Sara Ortiz-Muñoz, "Analysis of Meanings of the Concept of Sustainability" (2019) 27:1 Sustainable Development 153.

focus on the conceptual relationship between sustainability and sustainable development (to ensure that the two concepts are aligned). Some consider that sustainability is a goal that can be achieved through sustainable development, while others see sustainable development as a goal that can be achieved only once the process of sustainability is implemented.

This diversity of definitions and approaches represents the first significant challenge when it comes to implementing sustainability. There is broad consensus on the need to implement sustainability. But opinion on the understanding of the concept and on how to move toward a more sustainable society is divided.

The goal of this chapter is not to engage in a theoretical debate on the meaning of sustainability or on the conceptual issues surrounding this notion. For the purpose of this chapter, suffice it to say that sustainability is often associated with sustainable development, a concept usually defined as "a development that meets the needs of the present without compromising the ability of future generations to meet their own needs"[3] and is generally used to express the necessity to balance economic development, social development, and environmental protection.

The objectives of this chapter, rather, are to give an account of how the law can be mobilized to implement sustainability and to discuss the limits of this tool in that respect. To that end, the chapter highlights the basic legal questions regarding sustainability—including why sustainability should be implemented—and presents some of the legal tools that can contribute to the achievement of sustainable outcomes. A final section examines the relevance of initiatives by non-state actors to implementing sustainability.

II. WHY IMPLEMENT SUSTAINABILITY?

Despite its popularity (or more likely because of it), the concept of sustainability is often criticized. As one author argues, "[s]ustainability for ecological debates is now being used, and perhaps abused, in webs of questions and answers to refocus national economic prosperity as well as reposition present-day cultural identity in a corporate material culture of more efficient, but still unsustainable, consumption."[4] Another author offers a similar criticism, affirming that "the idea of sustainable development is a fine phrase without much meaning,"[5] and that sustainability is a concept characterized by "weakness"[6] and lacking an "operational definition."[7] This section counters the critiques by first recalling the relevance of the concept of sustainability and by subsequently inviting the reader to reflect on why sustainability should be implemented.

The extracts from the following three texts address the concepts of sustainability and sustainable development, each from a different perspective. Klaus Bosselmann adopts an ethical and ecological approach to highlight the need to view sustainability as a fundamental societal value. According to this expert, the survival of any community depends on whether development is carried out within the limits imposed by ecological processes, which is why implementing sustainability is crucial. Virginie Barral and Natasha Affolder also discuss the notions of sustainability and sustainable development but through a more legal and formalist lens. They explain that those concepts are now an integral part of international and Canadian law, that they have a legal meaning, and that their formal recognition entails legal consequences.

---

3   World Commission on Environment and Development, *supra* note 1 at 43.

4   Timothy W Luke, "Neither Sustainable nor Development: Reconsidering Sustainability in Development" (2005) 13:4 Sustainable Development 228 at 228.

5   Michael McCloskey, "The Emperor Has No Clothes: The Conundrum of Sustainable Development" (Spring 1999) Duke Envtl L & Policy Forum 153 at 157.

6   *Ibid* at 158.

7   *Ibid* at 159.

KLAUS BOSSELMANN, "THE MEANING OF SUSTAINABILITY"
in *The Principle of Sustainability: Transforming Law and Governance*, 2nd
ed (London, UK: Routledge, 2017) ch 1 at 8-15 [footnotes omitted]

WHAT IS SUSTAINABILITY?

Sustainability is both simple and complex. Herein it is similar to the idea of justice. Most of us intuitively know when something is not "just" or "fair." Similarly, most of us are fully aware of unsustainable things: waste, fossil fuels, polluting cars, unhealthy food and so on. We can also assume that many people have a clear sense of justice and sustainability. For example, they feel that a just, sustainable world is desperately needed no matter how distant an ideal it may be.

In its most elementary form sustainability reflects pure necessity. The air that we breathe, the water that we drink, the soils where our food comes from are essential to our survival. The basic rule of human existence is to sustain the conditions life depends on. To this end, the idea of sustainability is simple.

But sustainability is also complex, again like justice. It is difficult to categorically say what justice is. There is no uniformly accepted definition. Justice cannot be defined without further reflection on its guiding criteria, values and principles. Such reflection is subjective by nature and open to debate. The same is true for sustainability. It cannot be defined without further reflection on values and principles. Thus, any discourse about sustainability is essentially an ethical discourse.

The term sustainability triggers a similar response as the term justice. Everybody agrees with it, but nobody seems to know much about it. We have only a vague idea what sustainability involves or how it could be achieved. We may be able to *imagine* a sustainable society, but probably not how to get there. On the other hand, a "just society" reflects an ideal which may never be fully achieved. Ideals such as justice, peace and sustainability are fundamental to any society. We cannot do without them.

Sustainability and justice evoke similar sentiments. In some ways, however, sustainability appears more distant than justice. There are several reasons for that. First, many of today's societies can be described as just, at least, in a sense of providing the means for peaceful conflict resolution. By contrast, none of today's societies are sustainable. They are too deeply enmeshed in wasteful production and consumption to realize their unsustainable character. Second, the absence of justice is harder to bear than the absence of sustainability. Persist[ent] unjust treatment of people by political regimes, for example, will not be tolerated for long. Either internal or external forces will revolt against it. Unsustainable treatment of the environment, on the other hand, is more likely to be tolerated. The reason is that people are less immediately affected by its impacts. The distance in space (global environment) and time (future generations) prevent us from acting with urgency.

Yet, perceiving sustainability with a similar immediacy as we perceive justice is entirely appropriate, precisely because the distances are vanishing. The world has become a small place and the future is already here. Climate change is an example in case. For a long time, the impacts of climate change appeared as distant possibilities. This is no longer the case. Now, climate change makes headlines on a daily basis. Since Al Gore's "Inconvenient Truth," Nicholas Stern's report on the economic costs of global warming, and George Bush's acceptance of climate change as a "serious problem," the media have firmly embraced climate change as the most pressing issue of our time.

As we realize the impacts of climate change, we begin to feel its morality as possibly the biggest challenge. How can we justify the fact that our actions today will almost certainly threaten the planet's future? We are failing to meet the most basic obligation of each generation, i.e. to provide for the future of our children. This raises a moral question typical for sustainability *and* justice. How can we organize a fair distribution of goods and burdens throughout the generations?

It is hard to avoid the conclusion that sustainability fundamentally poses a challenge to the idea of justice. If a person lives at the expense of others, we consider this to be "unfair." If rich societies live at the expense of poor societies, we consider this also to be "unfair." Why then should it be acceptable to live at the expense of future generations and the natural environment? Whether or not sustainability requires, in fact, a rethinking of the idea of justice needs further consideration. However, realizing the linkages between the two concepts also helps us to access the meaning of sustainability. It is an idea that refers to the continuity of human societies and nature.

Going back into history, we find that continuity of cultures and societies could only be ensured if ecological systems were sustained. Jared Diamond identified five factors contributing to the collapse of civilizations: climate change, hostile neighbours, trade partners, environmental problems and, finally, society's response to its environmental problems. The first four may or may not prove crucial for the demise of society, Diamond claims, but the fifth always does. The salient point, of course, is that a society's response to environmental problems is completely within its control, which is not always true of the other factors. In other words, as his subtitle puts it, a society can "*choose* to fail." The fact that choice is at the heart of continuity makes sustainability a matter of ethics. A society can choose to incorporate or to ignore the need to live within the boundaries of ecological sustainability.

It is at the level of basic values, therefore, where sustainability—like justice—needs to be conceived in the first place. For this reason, the vision of a "just and sustainable society" is not a distant dream, but conditional to any civilized society.

History gives us a clue why sustainability has always been a concern of society. The modern sustainability debate is by no means new, it only adopted the new focus on "sustainable development." Whether or not this focus has helped to understand the principle of sustainability or deviate from it is the big question.

The answer that will be offered in this chapter is that the concept of sustainable development is only meaningful if related to the core idea of ecological sustainability. We will see that sustainable development needs to be understood as an application of the principle of sustainability, not the other way round. The vision of a "sustainable society" is another, broader application of the same idea. Other applications can be seen in the terms "sustainable growth," "sustainable economy," "sustainable production," "sustainable trade" and so on. No matter how clear or confusing such terminological combinations are, they all employ a basic idea of sustainability. ...

Sustainable development does not call for a balancing act between the needs of people living today and the needs of people living in the future, nor for a balancing act between economic, social and environmental needs. The notion of sustainable development, if words and their history have any meaning, is quite clear. It calls for development based on ecological sustainability in order to meet the needs of people living today and in the future. Understood in this way, the concept provides content and direction. It can be used in society and enforced through law. ...

· · ·

A SHORT HISTORY OF SUSTAINABILITY

· · ·

THE TERM

Even more clearly than the underlying idea, the term sustainability reveals its message for today: if you want long-term economic prosperity, look after the environment first!

VIRGINIE BARRAL, "SUSTAINABLE DEVELOPMENT IN INTERNATIONAL LAW: NATURE AND OPERATION OF AN EVOLUTIVE LEGAL NORM"

(2012) 23:2 EJIL 377 at 383-85 [footnotes omitted]

Sustainable development has, over the last 30 years, received wide support in a vast array of non-binding international legal documents. It finds expression in countless Declarations of states, resolutions of international organizations, programmes of action, and codes of conduct. To the extent that these various instruments are not recognized as among the formal sources of international law, they are incapable, in and of themselves, of giving rise to a valid legal rule relating to sustainable development, irrespective of the legal strength of their formulation. But sustainable development also finds expression in a far from negligible number of international treaties. It is included in over 300 conventions, and a brief survey of these is revealing from the point of view of the categories of conventions at stake, the location of the proposition relating to sustainable development, and the function attributed to it. References to sustainable development can indeed be found in 112 multilateral treaties, roughly 30 of which are aimed at universal participation. This points to a certain level of consensus among the international community concerning the relevance of sustainable development for international law. But what is particularly significant about the inclusion of sustainable development in conventional law is the location of this inclusion. A common impression among international lawyers is that even though sustainable development receives recognition in a great number of treaties, this recognition is of little legal significance since such references are mainly confined to the preamble, which is not binding. However an empirical analysis shows that 207 of these references are to be found in the operative part of the conventions which is technically binding on the parties. Closer study further reveals that for the most part sustainable development is referred to as an objective that contracting parties must strive to achieve, occasionally with an indication of the types of measures to be undertaken to that effect.

Clearly, then, sustainable development has widely penetrated treaty law. However, unlike in non-binding instruments such as the Rio Declaration [*Rio Declaration on Environment and Development*, UNGA, UN Doc No A/CONF.151/26/Rev.1 (Vol 1), annex I (1992)], the formulation of provisions relating to sustainable development in formally binding international treaties can be rather flexible. The wording can be vague and imprecise, characterized by the use of the conditional, and the provisions are often closer to setting out an incentive than purporting to be strictly constraining. ... Certainly, in most cases conventional provisions relating to sustainable development are too soft to impose an obligation on states to develop sustainably. But they may still impose an obligation on states to "strive to achieve" or "promote" sustainable development. Such an obligation, an obligation of means, far from being deprived of normative character, is just a norm with a different object: not one that requests a result to be achieved, but only means to be put in place to try to achieve that result.

NATASHA AFFOLDER, "THE LEGAL CONCEPT OF SUSTAINABILITY"
(Paper delivered at A Symposium on Environment in the Courtroom: Key
Environmental Concepts and the Unique Nature of Environmental Damage,
University of Calgary, 23-24 March 2012) at 9-10 [footnotes omitted]

While judicial consideration of Canadian statutory provisions on sustainability is
not extensive, the ecological core of sustainability has been identified and affirmed
by Canadian judges. The importance of ecological integrity as a "fundamental value
in Canadian society" has been affirmed by the Supreme Court of Canada in a series of judgments. Justice Binnie, writing for the majority in *British Columbia v.
Canadian Forest Products* [2004 SCC 38, [2004] 2 SCR 74], summarized this judicial
history:

> As the Court observed in *R. v. Hydro-Québec*, [1977] 3 S.C.R. 213, at para. 85, legal
> measures to protect the environment "related to a public purpose of superordinate
> importance." In *Friends of the Oldman River Society v. Canada (Minister of
> Transport)*, [1992] 1 S.C.R. 3, the Court declared at 16 that "[t]he protection of the
> environment has become one of the major challenges of our time." In *Ontario v.
> Canadian Pacific Ltd.*, [1995] 2 S.C.R. 1031, "stewardship of the natural environment"
> was described as a fundamental value (para. 55; italics in original). Still more
> recently, in *114957 Canada Ltée (Spraytech Société d'arrosage) v. Spraytech
> (Town)*, [2001] 2 S.C.R. 241, 2001 SCC 40, the Court reiterated at para. 1: "... our com-
> mon future, that of every Canadian community, depends on a healthy environ-
> ment ... This Court has recognized that '[e]veryone is aware that individually
> and collectively, we are responsible for preserving the natural environment . ...
> Environmental protection [has] emerged as a fundamental value in Canadian
> society.'"

• • •

Importantly, Canadian judges and administrative decision makers have also
rejected an approach to sustainable development that frames this concept as simply
a balancing of competing pressures. The appellant in *Re Ainsworth Lumber Co.*
[[2000] AEABD No 33] argued that the principle of sustainable development requires
that environmental protection measures be weighed against economic factors. In
this case, that would mean an abandonment of the requirement of best available
technology as there were economic arguments to favour a lower cost approach. The
Alberta Environmental Appeal Board firmly concluded that sustainable development
did not support the use of the lowest cost emissions control alternative by the appellant. In so doing, the Board affirmed that the core of sustainable development
requires "that resources should be developed in a manner that is sustainable for the
use by future generations."

The legal concepts of sustainability and sustainable development have not been
introduced in a mere handful of Canadian statutes over the past two decades. They
have been inserted into over 85 pieces of legislation. The cumulative impact of this
re-writing of Canadian law to respect the concept of sustainability signals something
greater than a requirement that competing interests be balanced. Rather, the density
of references in Canadian legislation to sustainability and sustainable development
suggests that legally significant expectations are crystallizing around these
concepts.

QUESTIONS

1. What differences do you see between the concepts of sustainability and sustainable development? Do you think the two notions should be distinguished, and why? Would you say that sustainability is a concept that is too vague to be implemented?

2. Do the laws of your province refer to sustainability and/or sustainable development? Have these concepts been used in a judicial context? If so, how and with what outcome?

3. What are the reasons that can be put forward to justify the implementation of sustainability?

III. THE ROLE OF LAW IN IMPLEMENTING SUSTAINABILITY

Law can be a powerful tool for reform in society. It can be used to regulate and influence individual behaviours and also to guide and frame governmental action. Accordingly, law is often portrayed as an essential instrument in the movement toward more sustainable patterns of production and consumption. This was already the case with the Brundtland Report, which contained many recommendations for institutional and legal changes. However, as the following text shows, the role that law can play in implementing sustainability is, in reality, more complex than what might appear at first glance.

DUNCAN FRENCH & LOUIS J KOTZÉ, "INTRODUCTION"
in Duncan French & Louis J Kotzé, eds, *Sustainable Development Goals: Law, Theory and Implementation* (Northampton, Mass: Edward Elgar, 2018) at 1-2 and 3-5 [footnotes omitted]

The negotiation, and adoption in September 2015, of the Sustainable Development Goals (SDGs) within the framework of the United Nations (UN) has been heralded as a notable step in the international community's ongoing, if uneven, commitment to global development. More than just a continuation of the Millennium Development Goals (MDGs), which ran from 2000 to 2015, the SDGs—more rhetorically known as the "Global Goals"—seek to encapsulate and promote global aspirations across a wide array of topic areas broadly associated with sustainable development.

First proposed at the 2012 UN Conference on Sustainable Development (the "Rio +20" Summit), the Global Goals were finally reduced through intergovernmental negotiation, following more open-ended dialogues with civil society, interest groups, business and others, to 17 Goals, though within that reflecting 169 targets and many more indicators. Unlike the MDGs, which were numerically limited to eight goals, the Global Goals ultimately adopted contain a plurality of objectives. The 2015 UN General Assembly document, *Transforming Our World: the 2030 Agenda for Sustainable Development* [UNGAOR, 70th Sess, UN Doc A/Res/70/1 (21 October 2015)], which adopted the Global Goals, sets out very much in the usual way of UN documents high rhetoric around international cooperation, development and the onward progression of humanity. Nevertheless, within such rhetoric, there is also a level, if not quite precision, of detail around what the international community should strive to achieve over the next 15 years. Noticeably less on how, and by what means.

The Goals included range from those rather similar in overview (if differing in quite a lot of respects as regards content and detail) from those set out in the MDGs, such as SDG 1 on the eradication of poverty, SDG 2 on zero hunger and SDG 4 on education, to those much newer to the SDGs, including SDG 11 on sustainable cities and SDG 16 focusing on access to justice and the rule of law. Of particular note is the inclusion of numerous "green" Goals, namely on climate (SDG 13), life below water (SDG 14) and life on land (SDG 15). This is in contrast to the rather more summary, vague—and indeed cursory—MDG 7 on environmental sustainability.

Also notable is the inclusion of what might be termed overtly polycentric issues, such as good health and well-being (SDG 3), gender equality (SDG 5) and decent work (SDG 8). Such Goals—like the environmental cluster—are polycentric not simply because they require a complex mix of policy actions (which might be said to be a hallmark of all the Goals), but because they cannot be achieved, whether directly or indirectly, by simple improvements in economic growth and industrialisation. Indeed, unlike the MDGs, which were purposely directed at "supporting" the Global South, the SDGs are targeted at all States, including more developed Northern States. Perhaps this is the reason why there are multiple tensions at the heart of the Goals; progress towards some risks jeopardising, at least without the imposition of appropriate measures and integrated planning, progress on others. The promotion of sustainable industry and infrastructure (SDG 9) sits uneasily against not only the environmental Goals, but also sustainable consumption and production targets (SDG 12); or, at least, might do. To that extent, the Global Goals present a complex and problematic agenda of transformative social change.

• • •

Second, [sic] is the question of the role (or absence) of law in the implementation of the Global Goals. The Goals are, by their nature, policy objectives, but within them they contain measures that can either very specifically or more obliquely be promoted (or harmful activity proscribed) by the adoption of laws and regulations. Within this, of course, is a multitude of possibilities, encompassing both public law and administration, rights-based approaches and the encouragement of contractual and other private forms of law-making. In this context, law is easily reduced to an instrumental form, merely seeing it as a question as to how it can assist in the achievement of the Goals. Putting to one side the alternative—the capacity of law to inhibit the Goals (which is considered below) —there are nevertheless other, pertinent issues around law and implementation. One is existential and conceptual; the very function of law in the achievement of sustainable development. That has been widely debated, perhaps too much so. There is a general consensus—at least among lawyers—that law can play a pivotal role in improving development. And when the Global Goals are placed within their proper context of sustainable development, law has been central to its progress since it was first endorsed internationally in 1987. While the debate continues as to what are essential and what are contextual factors to ensure successful legal implementation in the matter of development, there is nevertheless a general sense that law, if properly devised, can be an instrument of change.

A further, positive, analysis—building on this understanding—would be to affirm the constitutive role of law in the achievement of the Goals. Law as a social construction provides one, and by no means the most effective, form of political action and social mobilisation. Nevertheless, because of the authority in which it is held, measures taken by accepted means of legality often have a definitive quality to them. Though this is a quality often surpassing their actual capacity to achieve the level of societal change desired, the fact that such change is enshrined in law has a catalysing impact, beyond its immediate effect. The promotion of gender equality and eradication of racism are perhaps good examples of such a positive role for law. It is incapable of achieving fully the objective itself, but beyond its pure instrumentalism it has a constitutive effect in changing social understandings and challenging previous assumptions. To that extent, law in this area can be both instrumental and constitutive.

Nevertheless, there are more critical questions around the implementation of the Goals through law. Law has its own culture, its own way of seeing things—beyond the aspiration of human rights, regulatory law is often narrow and constrained. Private law more so. To say that law can implement the Goals says little about the relative power, and conflicting and diverse interests of the rule- and decision-makers. Even more than that, law can be a hindrance to the achievement of development, and there is often little movement against the most entrenched political and economic interests. The Goals themselves say little about tax evasion, the regulation of multinational corporations or the prohibition of those activities truly destructive of global Earth system integrity [sic]. Law as a means of implementation of the Goals should be neither preferred nor unquestioned. Moreover, as an instrument of political choices, it must equally be acknowledged that law may be used as much as to deny progress on the Goals as to promote them.

NOTES AND QUESTIONS

The text concludes by suggesting that law can be used both to implement and to hinder sustainability. In the latter case, a distinction should probably be established between laws that allow or encourage unsustainable activities or practices and rules that can make achieving sustainable outcomes more difficult but do not per se promote unsustainable activities or practices. For example, the division of powers between the federal government and the provinces established by the Canadian constitution, the fundamental rights and freedoms protected by the Canadian Charter (think of the freedom of opinion and expression in the case of climate deniers), and the provincial statues that lay down the municipal powers all represent legal constraints that rule-makers have to navigate when drafting robust environmental legislation or promoting sustainability. The achievement of sustainability, however essential it may be, cannot enable rule-makers to override existing laws. It should be recalled that this powerful tool for the implementation of sustainability operates within an existing framework and that the law can be used to achieve multiple purposes, many of which are inimical to sustainability. Law, per se, is just a means to formalize the political will of policy-makers, and whether or not law is used to promote sustainability ultimately depends on policy-makers' commitment to that cause.

1. Can you think of specific cases where the law is used to promote unsustainable activities and/or practices? How do those laws fit with legislation that seeks to implement sustainability? How do judges manage the tensions that can arise between "sustainability laws" and laws that disfavour sustainability?

2. In your opinion, what are the major limitations of using law as a tool to promote sustainability?

3. Apart from the law, which mechanisms or approaches could be used to implement sustainability?

IV. IS ENVIRONMENTAL AND NATURAL RESOURCES LAW ENOUGH TO IMPLEMENT SUSTAINABILITY?

Legal reflection on sustainability often focuses on environmental law and natural resources law. This is understandable, since unsustainable ways of life usually lead to environmental degradation and overexploitation of natural resources. Furthermore, the notions of sustainability and sustainable development are mentioned in many statutes that deal with environmental protection and natural resources management. For example, the preamble to the *Canadian Environmental Protection Act, 1999* states that "the protection of the environment is essential to the well-being of Canadians and that the primary purpose of this Act is to contribute to sustainable development through pollution prevention."[8] It also asserts that the "Government of Canada seeks to achieve sustainable development that is based on an ecologically efficient use of natural, social and economic resources and acknowledges the need to integrate environmental, economic and social factors in the making of all decisions by government and private entities." Similarly, the Quebec *Sustainable Forest Development Act* establishes a forest regime that is "designed to ... implement sustainable forest development, in particular through ecosystem-based development,"[9] and, in Manitoba, the *Water Resources Management Act* implements a water resource management scheme that is "based on the precautionary principle and on sustainable water resource management practices."[10] In the light of these examples, one might imagine that implementing sustainability is essentially a task that falls to environmental law and natural resources law. However, such a simplistic approach risks jeopardizing the implementation of sustainability. As Bosselmann points out:

> [E]nvironmental law is hampered by a reductionist approach to its subject, *i.e.*, the environment or more precisely, the human-nature relationship. This relationship is misconceived because of the domination of certain philosophical and cultural traditions in European history. As a consequence, modern legislation to protect the natural environment has developed in a compartmentalized, fragmented, economistic, and anthropocentric manner. For environmental legislation to become effective, broader coverage and better enforcement are not enough. The inherent design flaw in these laws is the absence of a fundamental rule prohibiting harm to the integrity of ecosystems. Such a rule requires the acceptance of sustainability as an overarching ethical and legal principle.[11]

Some 40 years after the adoption of the first environmental laws, the general state of the Earth's health as well as our patterns of production and consumption are still far from satisfactory. Moreover, implementing sustainability requires radical and profound changes in society that cannot be achieved solely through environmental law and natural resources law. Expressions such as "sustainable consumption," "sustainable growth," "sustainable tourism," and "sustainable agriculture" speak to the global nature of the problem and the need to mobilize all the branches of law. Implementing sustainability is, therefore, a goal that should activate all aspects of law:

> To achieve sustainability, we also need to recognize that, while environmental law is a key to achieving sustainability, it is only part of the necessary legal framework. Other needed legal involve a wide range of other laws, including land use and property laws, tax laws, laws involving our governmental structure, and the like.[12]

QUESTIONS

1. The last excerpt emphasizes the need to mobilize a wide range of other laws to achieve sustainability. In addition to those mentioned by the author, can you identify other fields of law that could play an important role in achieving sustainable outcomes?

---

8   SC 1999, c 33.

9   CQLR c A-18.1, s 1.

10 CCSM c W72, preamble.

11 Klaus Bosselmann, "Losing the Forest for the Trees: Environmental Reductionsim in the Law" (2010) 2:8 Sustainability 2424 at 25.

12 John C Dernach & Joel A Mintz, "Environmental Laws and Sustainability: An Introduction" (2011) 3:3 Sustainability 531 at 532.

2. Can you suggest specific legislative or regulatory changes that should be made to non-environmental laws in order to promote sustainability?

V. LEGAL TOOLS TO ACHIEVE SUSTAINABILITY

Sustainability can be achieved through a wide range of legal tools, implementable at different levels of governance (global, national, and local). Because of this diversity, the aim here is not to give an exhaustive and methodical analysis of all the legal means through which sustainability can be implemented, but rather to discuss three of the more common such methods.

A. STRATEGIC PLANNING

In 1992, UN member states were urged under s 8.7 of the *Agenda 21*[13] action plan to "adopt a national strategy for sustainable development." The goal of those strategies "should be to ensure socially responsible economic development while protecting the resource base and the environment for the benefit of future generations." *Agenda 21* also recommended that governments develop their own strategies "through the widest possible participation" and on the basis of a "thorough assessment of the current situation and initiatives." This strategic planning approach led governments at national and sub-national levels to put in place strategies for sustainable development.

In 2008, the Canadian federal Parliament passed the *Federal Sustainable Development Act*. The Act defines "sustainable development" as "development that meets the needs of the present without compromising the ability of future generations to meet their own needs" and defines "sustainability" as "the capacity of a thing, action, activity, or process to be maintained indefinitely."[14] Pursuant to the Act, the government is required to prepare every three years a federal sustainable development strategy that sets out the federal sustainable development goals and targets. The Act also establishes mechanisms to ensure adequate accountability and control.

DAVID POND, "THE ROLE OF PARLIAMENTARY OFFICERS: A CASE STUDY OF TWO OFFICERS"
(2010) 33:4 Can Par Rev 19 at 19-22 [endnotes omitted]

Under the Liberal government's amendments to the *Auditor General Act* [RSC 1985, c A-17] (C-83 [*An Act to amend the Auditor General Act*, SC 1995, c 43]), the Auditor General appoints the Commissioner of the Environment and Sustainable Development [CESD]. The Commissioner monitors how government departments are implementing their sustainable development strategies. The first generation of these strategies had to be tabled in the House of Commons within two years, with regular updates every three years thereafter. ...

Departments paid attention when they were selected for an audit by the OAG [Office of the Auditor General]. They would now also have to answer to an external commissioner on whether they were meeting their environmental commitments. The Liberal Minister of the Environment, Sheila Copps, acknowledged that the CESD/OAG would be empowered to embarrass the government over its alleged lack of

---

13 United Nations Conference on Environment & Development, Rio de Janeiro, Brazil, 3-14 June 1992, online (pdf): *United Nations Sustainable Development* <https://sustainabledevelopment.un.org/content/documents/Agenda21.pdf>.

14 *Federal Sustainable Development Act*, SC 2008, c 33, s 2.

progress on the environmental file, just as the Auditor General routinely did in other areas of public administration. But this trade-off was more attractive to the government than the Standing Committee's proposal for a high profile parliamentary officer with a mandate to challenge ministers over their reluctance to embrace the sustainable development paradigm.

THE AUDITOR GENERAL ON THE ROLE OF THE CESD

• • •

C-83 did not provide for the CESD to be a policy advocate, "because this role would require the commissioner to actively advance the principles of sustainable development, while auditors would generally limit themselves to pointing out instances of non-compliance with these principles." Leadership in formulating departmental sustainable development plans, as well as the management systems for monitoring progress in achieving the plans, had to be the responsibility of government departments. ...

• • •

CRISIS

After Johanne Gélinas became Commissioner in 2001 the obvious failure of the sustainable development program became a regular complaint in the CESD's annual reports. The 2002 report began with a reminder that Canada had committed itself to a broad sustainable development agenda at the 1992 Rio Summit and the follow-up 2002 Johannesburg Summit. The lack of progress on a variety of high-profile environmental issues in the years since Rio was pointedly linked to Canada's global reputation for delivering on it commitments. The 2003 report warned that the inability of the federal government to close the gap between its commitments and its actions would pass an increasing burden on to future generations. ...

The Commissioner's 2006 report on climate change policy was similarly framed in apocalyptic language. She began:

> Climate change is a global problem with global consequences: The implications are profound ... I am more troubled than ever by the federal government's long-standing failure to confront one of the greatest challenges of our time. Our future is at stake.

• • •

Climate change failure reflected the broader unwillingness of the Canadian government to embrace the substance of the sustainable development discourse.

• • •

In January 2007 Auditor General Fraser dismissed Commissioner Gélinas. Mr. Fraser framed this decision in terms of the 1995 debate over the creation of the CESD. Responsible government imposed limits on what the OAG/CESD could offer parliamentarians. The credibility of the audit function depended on the refusal of the auditor to engage in policy advocacy. There was always pressure from MPs and the environmental community to cross the line, but to do so would violate the 1995 agreement under which the OAG accepted responsibility for the CESD.

• • •

RENEWAL

The minority Conservative government now found itself in much the same position as its Liberal predecessor in 1994-95. The government had committed itself to a revival of the sustainable development initiative when the fourth round of departmental sustainable development strategies was tabled in December 2006. Yet at the same time the Conservatives had no intention of permitting this paradigm to drive their own agenda. So the government was receptive when Liberal MP John Godfrey offered a Private Members' Public Bill, C-474, which appeared to reconstitute the sustainable development initiative in terms acceptable to the opposition.

Bill C-474, the *Federal Sustainable Development Act*, was passed by Parliament in June 2008. The cabinet is now required to develop an over-arching sustainable development strategy setting out the terms and conditions for the departmental strategies. A new cabinet committee must oversee the development of this comprehensive strategy. Implementation is to be monitored by a Sustainable Development Office within the Ministry of the Environment. A draft of the strategy must be submitted for comments to an advisory council of stakeholders. Civil servants' performance-based contracts must contain provisions for meeting the targets set out in the federal strategy and departmental strategies.

The *Federal Sustainable Development Act* renews the 1995 settlement between the executive and the OAG/CESD. The Act affirms the symbolic commitment of the federal government to the sustainable development paradigm. For the first time the obligation to plan for sustainable development is formally fixed at the cabinet level. Nevertheless the new Act does not impede the PMO's control over the decision-making process. Direct responsibility for formulating the new federal strategy is assigned to the Minister of the Environment, not a central agency. The Act sets the table for the Ministry of the Environment to become an important central agency but that decision will still be up to the PMO.

At the same time the OAG retains the tools it needs to protect the institutional autonomy of the audit. Its status as the guardian of the CESD's independence is confirmed. The Auditor General will continue to appoint the Commissioner, not Parliament. The CESD will monitor how departments are meeting the targets set out in their own plans, and as well how the departments are contributing to the targets set out in the Federal Strategy. The new Act does not affect the CESD's existing authority to select departmental programs for auditing—affirming the legitimacy of this process and the role of the CESD as Parliament's environmental auditor.

REPORT 4—REVIEW OF THE 2015 PROGRESS REPORT OF THE FEDERAL SUSTAINABLE DEVELOPMENT STRATEGY

Canada, Commissioner of the Environment and Sustainable Development, 2016 Fall Reports of the Commissioner of the Environment and Sustainable Development (2016), online: *Office of the Auditor General of Canada* <http://www.oag-bvg.gc.ca/internet/English/parl_cesd_201610_04_e_41674.html>

INTRODUCTION

BACKGROUND INFORMATION

4.1 The *Federal Sustainable Development Act* requires the Minister of the Environment (renamed Environment and Climate Change) to develop a Federal Sustainable Development Strategy (FSDS). The Minister is required to report to

Parliament at least once every three years on the federal government's progress in implementing the FSDS. The Department, Environment and Climate Change Canada, is responsible for preparing this report. The Commissioner of the Environment and Sustainable Development must examine each FSDS progress report to assess the fairness of the information presented on the federal government's progress in implementing the FSDS.

4.2 The Minister has issued three progress reports to date. The most recent is the 2015 Progress Report of the Federal Sustainable Development Strategy (released in February 2016), which relates to the 2013–2016 FSDS. The four themes of the 2013–2016 FSDS are

- addressing climate change and air quality,
- maintaining water quality and availability,
- protecting nature and Canadians, and
- shrinking the environmental footprint—beginning with government.

These themes had 8 goals, which were supported by 34 targets and 225 implementation strategies. The 2015 Progress Report provided performance information about the 8 goals and 34 targets.

• • •

FINDINGS, RECOMMENDATIONS, AND RESPONSES

ASSESSING THE 2015 PROGRESS REPORT OF THE FEDERAL SUSTAINABLE DEVELOPMENT STRATEGY

4.9 Overall, we found that the information in the 2015 Progress Report of the Federal Sustainable Development Strategy provided a fair presentation of the government's progress in implementing the 2013–2016 Federal Sustainable Development Strategy. It conveyed a general sense of progress made and also included specific information regarding progress on many of the 34 targets. However, the Progress Report did not always explain why progress had been slow in some areas. In addition, the Progress Report did not present information on how sustainable development had been considered in decision making.

4.10 This finding is important because sustainable development strategies allow the federal government to advance sustainable development and make decision making more transparent and accountable to Parliament. Periodic reports that present a fair picture of progress are fundamental to both the credibility and the impact of the strategies.

• • •

The 2015 Progress Report was missing important information on integrating sustainable development into government decision making

4.57 We found that, in contrast to the information provided in 2012, the 2015 Progress Report of the Federal Sustainable Development Strategy (FSDS) did not discuss either progress on integrating sustainability into government decision making or the results relating to the government's commitment to strategic environmental assessments.

• • •

4.66 **Recommendation.** Environment and Climate Change Canada should ensure that future progress reports contain information on progress related to integrating sustainable development into decision making, using tools such as strategic environmental assessments.

The Department's response. Agreed. Environment and Climate Change Canada will explore ways to report on how sustainable development is being integrated into decision making.

C SCOTT FINDLAY ET AL, "SUSTAINABILITY LOST: COMMENTS ON 'PLANNING FOR A SUSTAINABLE FUTURE: A FEDERAL SUSTAINABLE DEVELOPMENT STRATEGY FOR CANADA,'" CASE COMMENT
(2010) 22:1 J Envtl L & Prac 77 at 79 [footnotes omitted]

Within Canada, several provincial jurisdictions have also directly addressed the challenges of governing sustainably within the scope of their responsibilities. Nova Scotia, Quebec and Manitoba are prominent examples. The latter province has one of the oldest sustainability statutes in Canada whose wide-ranging purpose is stated to be "to create a framework through which sustainable development will be implemented in the provincial public sector and promoted in private industry and in society generally." Principles and guidelines are set out in detail, including a commitment to integrated decision-making and planning described as "encouraging and facilitating decision making and planning processes that are efficient, timely, accountable and cross-sectoral and which incorporate an inter-generational perspective of future needs and consequences." A more recent legislative measure from Quebec [*Sustainable Development Act*, CQLR c D-8.1.1, s 1] adopts an extensive set of sustainability principles to be applied in pursuit of a forcefully stated objective:

> The measures introduced by this Act are intended ... to bring about the necessary change within society with respect to non-viable development methods by further integrating the pursuit of sustainable development into the policies, programs and actions of the Administration, at all levels and in all areas of intervention. They are designed to ensure that government actions in the area of sustainable development are coherent and to enhance the accountability of the Administration in that area, in particular through the controls exercised by the Sustainable Development Commissioner under the *Auditor General Act* [CQLR c V-5.01].

B. DIRECT REGULATION

The establishment of clear command-and-control rules mandating specific conduct may seem like the most efficient way to achieve sustainable development outcomes. However, as illustrated by the following text on the experience in the European Union, direct regulation based on command-and-control approaches can face serious implementation challenges.[15]

---

15 For an overview of these challenges in the context of local action, see Melissa Gorrie, "Addressing the Elephant in the Climate Change Room: Using the Law to Reduce Individual and Household Consumption" (2018) 31:2 J Envtl L & Prac 137.

ELÉONORE MAITRE-EKERN & CARL DALHAMMAR, "REGULATING PLANNED OBSOLESCENCE: A REVIEW OF LEGAL APPROACHES TO INCREASE PRODUCT DURABILITY AND REPARABILITY IN EUROPE"

(2016) 25:3 RECIEL 378 at 378, 379, 379-80, 381, 387, 387-88 [footnotes omitted]

INTRODUCTION

There is a growing political consensus in the European Union (EU) that we have to move away from our current linear economic system to one that is based on closing material loops, a circular economy. This implies that we need to move up the waste management hierarchy; while material recycling and incineration with energy recovery are better options than land filling, there is a need to consider how we can promote waste prevention through designing more durable products, and how we can stimulate re-use, repair, remanufacturing and refurbishment of products.

The design of more durable products can save resources by keeping products in use longer, while also saving money for consumers that do not have to replace their products as often. The term "durability" is often used interchangeably with "product lifetime." While there is no legal definition of durability, the following definition has been proposed:

> Durability is the ability of a product to perform its function at the anticipated per-formance level over a given period (number of cycles/uses/hours in use), under the expected conditions of use and under foreseeable actions. Performing the recom-mended regular servicing, maintenance, and replacement activities as specified by the manufacturer will help to ensure that a product achieves its intended lifetime.

• • •

While designing products that last longer is not optimal from an environmental perspective in all cases, it is desirable for most product groups both due to environ-mental benefits and in order to save money for consumers. However, making products durable is not always in the best interest of industry. There are several reasons for why manufacturers may not design durable products. In some cases they may even intentionally plan the obsolescence of products, artificially reducing the lifespan to stimulate repetitive consumption. Intention on the part of producers is often hard to establish, however, even for experts. Moreover, it must be acknowl-edged that some cases of obsolescence may not be intentional.

If manufacturers have limited incentives to design durable products, and there is great difficulty for consumers to promote change through consumer choices, legislation seems necessary.

• • •

PRODUCT DURABILITY AND PLANNED OBSOLESCENCE

PLANNING FOR PREMATURE FAILURE

According to Oxford Dictionaries, planned obsolescence is "a policy of producing consumer goods that rapidly become obsolete and so require replacing, achieved by frequent changes in design, termination of the supply of spare parts, and the use of non-durable materials." This definition highlights three important ways to stimu-late repetitive consumption: the limitation of material durability, the lack of reparabil-ity and the psychological element of design.

Planned obsolescence *per se* [*sic*] is characterized by the deliberate planning and design of obsolescence in products to make them fail before the "normal" end of life. This is the most severe case of planned obsolescence, as it means that producers intentionally introduce a failure that will unduly limit a product's life.

• • •

A recurring argument from producers accused of planned obsolescence is that they did not intend to reduce the lifespan of products, but that obsolescence may be a side effect from efforts to improve user-friendliness, lower prices or develop new technologies. Beyond discussions about the true intention of producers, what such claims reveal is that the focus of many producers is not on durability, and that the intervention of legislators might be necessary.

Obviously, there is a variety of ways in which a producer can plan for the obsolescence of its product. The policy solutions have to be diverse as well. Whether a product is meant to fail prematurely or whether its reparation is made economically unattractive, both circumstances will limit the durability of that product, but the manner in which to address these issues must be different.

• • •

THE FRENCH APPROACH: CRIMINALIZING INTENTIONAL BEHAVIOUR AND IMPROVING REPARABILITY

CRIMINALIZING PLANNED OBSOLESCENCE

France is the first country to adopt a law that expressly refers to planned obsolescence and defines it. Article L. 213-4-1 of the *Consumer Code* [Law n°2014-344 of 17 March 2014, published in JORF n°0065 of 18 March 2014, p 5400, n°1] now reads: "Planned obsolescence is defined by all the techniques by which a person that places goods on the market seeks to deliberately reduce the lifespan of a product to increase the substitution rate." ...

France is also a pioneer in the fight against planned obsolescence because the behaviour is now criminalized. Indeed, the new Article L. 213-4-1 of the Consumer Code introduces planned obsolescence as an infraction that can be punished by up to two years in prison and a fine of €300,000, which can be increased by up to 5% of the average annual revenue calculated on the basis of the three previous known annual turnovers. The amount should be in proportion with the benefits gained from the breach of the law.

Notwithstanding the rather wide definition of planned obsolescence in the law, convicting a producer of infraction will not be easy. Consumer and environmental associations heavily criticized the use of the word "deliberately," which requires a proof of intention from the side of the producer. Yet, apart from a few blatant cases such as the light bulb affair, in most cases producers can argue that there was no intentional design choice: the battery of the iPhone was sealed for aesthetical purposes (the iPhone chassis has no gaps), to make the equipment as thin and light as possible, and to reduce the chances of moisture and dirt getting inside; the chip of the printer cartridge stops functioning at 25% capacity because from that point on there is a high risk of the ink being paler or uneven on the page; incompatibilities with older versions of a same product result from an unexpected but fundamental technology innovation. The possibility for producers to demonstrate their good intentions is undeniably great and their rationale not always inaccurate, though it may cover less worthy objectives.

In addition, the plaintiff must prove that the defendant has reduced the lifespan of a product for the purpose of increasing its substitution. We have mentioned in the previous section a number of examples of planned obsolescence that appear quite obvious. However, bringing proof that the lifespan of a product has been reduced, in particular in a deliberate manner, so that a judge can deliver a judgment is another matter, and leads to a number of important yet arduous questions: How does one establish the theoretical lifespan of a product? When does a product have a short lifespan and when does it have a reduced lifespan? How do you unveil the intention of the producer? This may require access to internal documents of the incriminated firm. Also, how does one prove that the reduced lifespan was intending to boost sales and not to reduce production costs?

C. INFORMATION-BASED INSTRUMENTS

Regulation by disclosure is another legal technique that governments can use to encourage citizens to adopt behaviour patterns that are more respectful of the environment. It entails the disclosure of information to third parties (such as employees or consumers) or to the general public regarding environmental operations or performance with a view to supplementing traditional regulatory strategies with economic markets and public opinion. The objective is to enable citizens to make responsible choices.

> ### RÓNÁN KENNEDY, "RETHINKING REFLEXIVE LAW FOR THE INFORMATION AGE: HYBRID AND FLEXIBLE REGULATION BY DISCLOSURE"
> (2016) 7:2 Geo Wash J Energy & Envtl L 124 at 124, 128, 130, 132, 133, 135-36 [footnotes omitted]

Although it has its defenders, command-and-control environmental regulation has been criticised for being economically inefficient and for relying on the effectiveness of the regulator and its staff. Scholars have claimed that traditional command-and-control methods of dealing with pollution, involving the use of uniform technology standards, operate in a fragmented manner with the inefficiency of a large central bureaucracy and without coordination. Unresponsive to new information, these methods do not always properly balance the costs and benefits of regulation and do not encourage continual reductions in pollution. These arguments have led to the development of a "second generation" of regulatory instruments: market-based, further upstream, more flexible, built on public transparency, integrated into business planning, and focusing on incentives rather than punishment. These new instruments may operate in a flexible, modular way.

Disclosure-based regulation is one of the responses to the perceived inefficiency and ineffectiveness of traditional command-and-control regulation. While disclosure-based regulation has a history that stretches back to U.S. federal securities laws in the 1930s, it has become a significant feature of environmental regulation since the 1960s. Much of the promise of the application of information and communications technology ("ICT") to environmental regulation relies on the power of information to change behaviour, whether individual or organizational. ...

• • •

II. REFLEXIVE REGULATION: THE THIRD GENERATION OF ENVIRONMENTAL LAW

What is sometimes called the third generation of environmental law is characterised by the use of "collaborative and participatory processes, outcomes-based instrument choice, reflexive law principles, distributive justice concerns, sustainable development principles, and adaptive ecosystem management." The adoption of these so-called new environmental policy instruments ("NEPIs") is driven largely by economic factors—the cost of "traditional" regulation to regulators and regulated entities; a perception that NEPIs were more efficient; a shift from models of government to lighter-touch governance approaches; ...

• • •

B. REFLEXIVE AND INFORMATIONAL REGULATION

• • •

Informational approaches, which require only that firms provide information about their products and services to the public, have also been receiving attention in recent years. "Informational regulation" is a prominent example of the direct application of reflexive law principles through disclosure requirements and is defined as "rules requiring mandatory disclosure of information on environmental operations or performance of regulated entities to third parties, such as workers, consumers, shareholders, or the public in general." One example of reflexive environmental informational regulation is honesty in environmental advertising and labelling. The application of informational regulation can be broadly categorised as "descriptive" or "persuasive," depending on whether information is simply disclosed or is framed in such a way as to encourage individuals to change the behaviour. It can take negative or positive forms, be aimed at consumers or businesses, and be simple or complex. Examples include warnings on cigarette packets, environmental impact statements, and eco-labels.

• • •

III. CRITIQUING DISCLOSURE AS A REGULATORY TOOL

• • •

A. DEVELOPMENT OF DISCLOSURE

Informational regulation is not new. Railway regulation has used it since the 1860s, financial regulation has used it since the 1930s, and informational regulation was a significant part of the development of environmental and health and safety law in the 1960s and 1970s. In the United States, informational disclosure developed as a middle ground between the competing priorities of the Republican and Democratic Parties, who favoured less government and more risk-based regulation respectively. ...

The practical development of these styles of regulation have [sic] been driven by several critiques of conventional command-and-control regulation—many major pollution problems have been identified and dealt with to the extent that is economically feasible, and the significant problems that remain are generally non-point sources, such as water pollution, which are much less amenable to centralised solutions. They are also connected to the increasing availability of ICT, which provide new capabilities to access, integrate, and select information. From an academic perspective, the conceptual development of reflexive law can be traced back to Gunther Teubner's work from the 1980s on, in which he argued that law goes through three phases of development, from "formal law" (basic rules) to "substantive law" (administrative procedures) to "reflexive law" (indirect, abstract, rational).

• • •

B. RATIONALES FOR REGULATION BY DISCLOSURE

• • •

Regulation by disclosure has been labelled "populist maxi-min regulation," which can be thought of simply as a kind of environmental blacklisting. The requirement that information on environmental performance be disclosed may drive behaviour change in a number of ways. It can focus the minds of senior management on a problem that has hitherto been hidden, or unnoticed. For commercial firms, the incentive may be the impact on financial performance—the stock market seems to read new information on pollution emissions as indicative of future performance and future costs, something which can directly impact on share prices. Requiring firms to provide information to the public reduces the transaction costs incurred by individuals in gathering information on pollution, thus mitigating or eliminating the information asymmetry that would otherwise exist between the citizen and the corporation. The social impact of being explicitly highlighted for bad performance in a "name and shame" campaign may serve as a form of punishment. It can also serve to alert consumers to a problem, thus motivating them to put pressure elsewhere in the regulatory structure in order to bring about change. Finally, firms come under significant external pressure to act in line with an implicit social contract which constrains their behaviour in ways that go beyond the strict legal requirement but may be a rational response to an expectation of further [regulation] in the future; the use of disclosure requirements to highlight transgressions of these unspoken rules may incentivise higher levels of compliance.

• • •

C. APPLICATIONS OF REGULATION BY DISCLOSURE

Perhaps the best-known example of the application of information disclosure in environmental regulation, developed as a response to a catastrophic leak of toxic chemicals at the Union Carbide plant in Bhopal India, is the U.S. Toxics Release Inventory ("TRI"), required under section 313 of the Emergency Planning and Community Right-To-Know Act [*Emergency Planning and Community Right-to-Know Act of 1986*, Pub L No 99-499, 100 Stat 1728 (codified as amended at 42 USC §§ 11001–11050 (2012))]. This requires regulated firms to submit annual data to the EPA on the volumes of certain toxic chemicals released into the air, water, land or transferred off-site. This information is made publicly accessible through an online database and otherwise. Data is reported and commented upon by the media and environmental NGOs. It seems to have reduced the release of chemicals subject to reporting requirements by as much as forty percent or perhaps even sixty-one percent and as much as eighty-two percent in some locations. There may be other reasons for this reduction, such as other regulations, changes in production levels and improvements in technology, but it seems clear that TRI was a success and brought about significant voluntary reductions in chemical releases. Similar programmes have been applied successfully at the state level in the United States.

• • •

E. DIFFICULTIES WITH DISCLOSURE

• • •

Overall, the impact of regulation through disclosure is still not adequately studied or properly understood. Its results may be limited, it does not always achieve the desired results, and the response from practitioners is not always positive.

More information is not necessarily better but may instead cause overload and poorer decisionmaking. Simply disclosing raw data may not have a significant impact on emissions reduction; further processing to make the information useful and relevant to end users increases the possibility that the overall policy goal will be achieved. There are also social and environmental justice issues, as not all individuals and groups have the same capability to analyse and use the information. Seeming reductions in emissions may actually be the result of underreporting rather than better environmental management. Reclassification of activities can remove reporting requirements and there may be little reduction in use of toxic chemicals at source. In addition, polluters may respond strategically to the thresholds in a reporting program. A study of the Massachusetts Toxics Use Reduction Act [Lori Snyder Bennear, "Strategic Response to Regulatory Thresholds: Evidence From the Massachusetts Toxics Use Reduction Act," (27 June 2005) (unpublished manuscript, Duke University Nicholas School of the Environment), online: <https://papers.ssrn.com/sol3/papers.cfm?abstract_id=776504>] reveals that there was "a significant behavioral response to regulatory thresholds ... [and] up to [forty] percent of the observed decrease in releases in Massachusetts may be artificial declines created by strategic behavior around the reporting thresholds." Finally, implementation is very context-specific; if the political, legal, and market conditions are not suitable, it may only achieve limited results.

QUESTIONS

1. Do you think that strategic planning is an important tool for implementing sustainability? If so, why? What are the main issues that should inform the development of sustainable development strategies?

2. What are the benefits of using direct regulation to achieve sustainability? Why can the implementation of direct regulation based on command-and-control approaches be challenging?

3. How can regulation by disclosure encourage citizens to improve their environmental performance? What are the safeguards that should be implemented to ensure that regulation by disclosure leads to tangible outcomes?

4. Could the three legal tools presented in this section be used simultaneously? Do you think this kind of policy mix is desirable? If so, explain how these legal tools can be complementary and mutually reinforcing.

VI. THE RELEVANCE OF THE NON-STATE ACTORS IN IMPLEMENTING SUSTAINABILITY

Implementing sustainability requires governments to behave as strategists to define long-term policies and objectives, and to establish the necessary legal frameworks to pursue these objectives. However, sustainability is a shared concern, and many non-state stakeholders (such as private corporations and civil society organizations) also have a role to play in transforming the current patterns of production and consumption.

A. THE PRIVATE SECTOR

Integrated and sustainable decision-making is the "keystone" of the legal principles of corporate social responsibility (CSR), which requires directors of corporations to take account of environmental, social, and economic issues in their decision-making. Although legal literature has shown that voluntary principles may have a regulatory impact, the effectiveness of voluntary principles of integrated decision-making in furthering environmental, social, and economic issues is not a given.[16]

EVGUENIA PARAMONOVA, "STEERING TOWARD TRUE NORTH: CANADIAN CORPORATE LAW, CORPORATE SOCIAL RESPONSIBILITY, AND CREATING SHARED VALUE"
(2016) 12:1 McGill Int'l J Sust Dev L & Pol'y 25 at 29-30, 31-34, 37, 41-42, 48
[footnotes omitted]

1. INTRODUCTION

Corporate social responsibility (CSR) among traditional corporations is evolving. It appears to be transforming from a cosmetic side-project to an entrenched priority in corporate boardrooms around the world. The question is no longer whether, but rather how companies demonstrate that they are promoting the public good. Business scholars generally agree that CSR should become a dimension of a company's core business strategy and operations. Academics see CSR as an opportunity to gain a competitive advantage in the market, while simultaneously contributing to sustainable development. A particularly resonant variant of this school of thought is entitled Creating Shared Value (CSV). CSV does not represent a radical departure from the latest wave of strategic CSR mentioned above. Rather, it is a manifestation of an existing theory that has been particularly well-received [sic] by both scholars and the industry. Developed by [Michael E] Porter and [Mark R] Kramer at Harvard Business School, the CSV approach encourages managers to focus on intersection points between business needs and social problems, leveraging both for mutual gain, or "shared value," between the firm and its stakeholders. ["Strategy & Society: the Link Between Competitive Advantage and Corporate Social Responsibility," *Harvard Business Review* (December 2006) 78.] At the heart of the CSV approach is the principle that a corporation's true purpose should be to maximize "shared value" rather than shareholder value. This is what is referred to as the CSV norm. While the operationalization of CSV is still in its early stages, evidence from academic publications, policymaking bodies, and business decision-makers suggests that it is shaping "big brand" company behaviour in Canada and around the world.

• • •

2. THE EVOLUTION OF CSR AND THE EMERGING CSV NORM

CSV must be understood against the backdrop of an evolving attitude towards corporate social and environmental engagement, and an evolving understanding of the corporation's purpose in society. CSR emerged in the 1980s amid a series of industrial disasters which dealt serious blows to certain industries' reputations as well as anti-apartheid campaigns which pressured corporations operating in South Africa to adopt voluntary codes of conduct. This trend accelerated in the early to mid-2000s as more "big brand" corporations responded to mounting stakeholder pressure to be socially accountable for their global operations. ...

The next wave of CSR was born out of this growing dissatisfaction and the desire to procure deeper commitments to sustainability from mainstream companies.

---

16 See Michael Kerr, Richard Janda & Chip Pitts, *Corporate Social Responsibility: A Legal Analysis* (Toronto: LexisNexis, 2009).

Working in parallel, a number of scholars reconceptualised corporate engagement as a business opportunity, rather than an added expense or damage control. If CSR were integrated into a firm's core strategy and operational process, it could be a driver of innovation, competitive advantage, and growth for the firm, while simultaneously creating lasting social impact. The appeal of this "strategic CSR" was its pragmatic harnessing of corporate self-interest: "If a business benefits from a CSR initiative, it is more likely to last, and its involvement may be more dynamic and innovative too." Scholars who have analyzed levels of CSR involvement by firms situate strategic CSR near the highest possible level of engagement.

Within this broader school of thought, Porter and Kramer's CSV approach has served not only as an umbrella for related theories, but also as a more fundamental reflection on the corporation's place in society. Their enlightened vision of the corporation is what gives CSV its normative pull and potential for cross-disciplinary uptake by law. They argue that earlier waves of CSR fell short because of a narrow, outdated interpretation of capitalism—the understanding that corporations benefit the public solely by maximizing shareholder value, to the exclusion of broader social considerations. ...

In contrast, CSV is rooted in an acknowledged interdependence of firms and society. Companies need healthy communities for quality inputs, use of public assets, social licenses, and sustained demand. Society needs businesses for jobs, innovation, and improved living standards. CSV identifies and leverages these connections to generate shared value. ...

• • •

3. THE RELATIONSHIP BETWEEN LAW AND CSR

• • •

[A] growing number of countries and international bodies are promulgating formal laws of an instrumental nature that are meant to encourage, monitor, and enforce CSR. Regulators are effectively transforming a voluntary endeavour into a mandatory one. For example, [Carol] Liao predicts that "the next significant stage in the CSR movement will be in the reformation and creation of corporate legal models that not only enable, but require, CSR concepts to be embodied within corporate governance practices." ...

• • •

5. CANADIAN CORPORATE LAW AND THE FIDUCIARY DUTY IN PRACTICE

Canada's federal corporate statute [*Canada Business Corporations Act*, RSC 1985, c C-44, s 122(1)] contains a broadly-phrased fiduciary duty: "Every director and officer of a corporation in exercising their powers and discharging their duties shall ... act honestly and in good faith with a view to the best interests of the corporation." The legislation does not define "the best interests of the corporation" and is silent as far as stakeholder[s] are concerned; these aspects have been left to judicial elaboration.

Historically, Canadian common law has embraced a shareholder-centric fiduciary duty. However, the recent Supreme Court of Canada (SCC) case *BCE Inc v 1976 Debentureholders* [2008 SCC 69, [2008] 3 SCR 560] has overtly departed from shareholder primacy and arguably embraced elements of stakeholder theory, even if the Court did not explicitly refer to the theory in the decision. *BCE* affirms and builds on an earlier case, *Peoples Department Stores Inc (Trustee of) v Wise* [2004 SCC 68, [2004] 3 SCR 461]. ...

While *BCE* was decided in the particular context of a change-of-control trans-action, the ruling has general relevance for directors' accountability and fiduciary duties to stakeholders. The case involved a plan of arrangement contested by a group of debentureholders on the grounds that it was oppressive and in breach of manage-ment's fiduciary duty to them. The SCC explained that the fiduciary duty is a "broad, contextual concept. It is not confined to short term profit or share value. Where the corporation is an ongoing concern, it looks to the long-term interests of the corpor-ation." The Court added, "In considering what is in the best interests of the corpor-ation, directors may look to the interests of, *inter alia*, shareholders, employees, creditors, consumers, governments, and the environment to inform their decision." Lastly, the SCC implied that corporations may have a socially-oriented component when it described directors as acting in the best interests of the corporation as a "good corporate citizen" or "responsible corporate citizen"—language not previously used by the Court to describe corporations.

It is not clear to what extent the SCC had CSR, stakeholder theory, or CSV in mind when handing down its decision. Scholars can only speculate. However, the practical result of *BCE* is that it has revealed cracks in the notion of shareholder primacy. By recognizing emerging notions and interests beyond shareholder primacy, the SCC reinforced CSR implementation in Canada, whether intentionally or not. It chal-lenged the perception that directors ought to focus exclusively on shareholder interests and financial returns, freeing management to pursue CSV more rigorously. Furthermore, the *BCE* language of "good corporate citizenship" acknowledged emerging social attitudes about the public embeddedness of corporations—the underlying premise of CSV. Some scholars propose that Canada is on the cusp of a fundamental transformation: "The indications from the SCC suggest that Canada is poised to transform its corporate law to embrace a stakeholder approach to govern-ance that may permit, [*sic*] and one day even require some form of CSR."

• • •

7. CONCLUSION

• • •

The migration of CSV towards law is part of a broader feedback loop: business giving rise to influential norms that invigorate the law so that the law can serve as a stronger framework for business. Corporations, policymakers, and business academics are recognizing shared value generation as a marker of "true North" for sustainable twenty-first century businesses, where corporations should orient their operations toward shared value creation. The operationalization of this norm would benefit from a supportive legal regime. This paper suggests that Canada's legal regime can become more supportive by internalizing the very phenomenon it seeks to regulate: CSV.

Some wonder if the CSR evolution actually needs law in order to continue. If companies are already forging ahead with voluntary CSV initiatives, what need is there for formal regulation? The response depends on our faith in law's instrumental capacity. Law can facilitate and even accelerate change; it can play a transformational role in corporate social responsibility. Kent Greenfield has said in a seminal article, "It is foolish and inefficient as a matter of public policy to leave corporate law as an untapped resource." Business leaders already recognize the potential of law to help them achieve sustainability goals. It is time that law realized its own potential.

B. THE CIVIL SOCIETY

In order to promote long-term sustainability, the United Nations encourage participation by the public so that citizens may become aware of the interaction between the economic, social, and environmental spheres and see the impact of their everyday behaviour. By mobilizing around global or local environmental issues, associations, NGOs, and citizens interact with their governments to help steer development or seek to find solutions to the problems identified themselves.

MARY CHRISTINA WOOD, NATURE'S TRUST: ENVIRONMENTAL LAW FOR A NEW ECOLOGICAL AGE
(Cambridge: Cambridge University Press, 2013) ch 15 at 344-46, 349, 350-51 [endnotes omitted]

Transformative societal change rarely happens, however, without strong pressure also arising from outside government institutions. Changing the frame often means turning civic energy away from the processes fixed in place by the old frame. As Professor Francis Fox Piven, a scholar of social movements, writes, "[A] movement must use its distinctive repertoire of drama and disturbance, of crowds and marches and banners and chants, to raise the issues that are being papered over by normal politics, for the obvious reason that normal politics is inevitably dominated by money and propaganda." When an environmental regulatory agency or a legislature becomes fully captive to industry, avenues of paper democracy (such as letters to Congressmen and comments on proposed agency rule-makings) lose much of their former effectiveness. Piven attributes history-changing movements partly to their exertion of the "kind of power that results from refusing co-operation in the routines that institutionalized social life requires." She elaborates: "That is the power that workers wield when they walk off the job, or that students muster when they refuse to go to class, or that tenants have when [they] refuse to pay the rent, or that urban crowds exert when they block streets and highways."

Peaceful public demonstration remains one of the most highly cherished and fundamental forms of expression. It stays effective precisely because it puts faces on the issue and puts the issue in the faces of elected officials. When conventional processes of citizen democracy become rigged and ineffectual, citizens inevitably turn to street democracy through public protest. Throughout history, major movements have gained unstoppable momentum at this stage. Mahatma Gandhi's famous salt march to the sea, for example, epitomized the populist assertion of public trust rights through civil disobedience. The British government had essentially alienated an asset in the public trust corpus by imposing a heavy tax on salt to benefit corporate interests, thereby preventing the commoners in India from collecting a resource vital for their needs. A nonviolent march led by Gandhi proclaiming public rights to salt grew into a cause joined by thousands. The masses of arrested people ultimately overwhelmed the jails and forced the British government to concede the people's ancient right.

Today, the environmental movement shows clear signs of shifting out of the political frame as climate protests mount worldwide. In the largest climate protest in U.S. history, more than 35,000 citizens marched in the streets of Washington, D.C. on February 17, 2013 to condemn the proposed Keystone XL Pipeline project. Global protests also rise over predatory capitalism and government corruption, both systemic forces behind environmental eradication. The 2011 Occupy protests occurring throughout the United States and other countries took the torch to some of industrial society's "deep institutional lacunae and inconsistencies," as Piven notes. [Burns H] Weston and [David] Bollier observe: "What united the wildly diverse [Occupy] protesters is precisely the conviction that *the system itself is the problem*." These sweeping insurrections stand poised to force transformative societal change.

To save the planet, an idea must catch this current of social change and spread virally across the globe through all possible forums, both within and outside of existing legal processes. Nature is not a commodity; it comprises a trust endowment to support the survival of present and future generations, and government remains duty-bound to protect and restore it. The public trust embraces an idea whose time, once again, has come.

MODELING INDIVIDUAL LIFESTYLE CHANGE

[T]he necessary frame change must extend to the individual level. It will do little good to insist on fiduciary performance by government in protecting climate and ecology if adults continue to overconsume resources and devour the assets of their children's natural trust. ...

• • •

Terry Tempest Williams writes: "The eyes of the future are looking back at us and they are praying for us to see beyond our own lifetime." Climate crisis calls forth the basic parental responsibility to secure a safe future for our collective children. Human beings have always had the instinct to protect their young. Urgent, singular dangers to children tend to provoke immediate and heroic responses, even from strangers. But reacting to universal climate change and environmental collapse is not as clear as, say, grabbing a toddler before she runs into a busy street or falls into a swift river. The sheer enormity of the challenge can make one feel as if personal actions rank insignificant, even infinitesimal. Looming climate tipping points cause some to think the task impossible.

• • •

Our actions in these next few years will determine the future for our children, their children, and innumerable generations to come. We, the living generation, once had a dependent position in the great wheel of life—not yet born, but with primal expectations nonetheless vested in the hearts of our ancestors, our interests clearly at stake in their decisions. Rather than living life according to Jefferson's great rule that all generations come equally, a generational power now reins in tyranny over the planet and its people. It is a power held in fortune and corruption, exercised through laws at every level that allow the devastation of society's survival resources: the air, the oceans, the forests, the fisheries, the wildlife, the rivers, the aquifers, and the lands.

Humanity's timeless covenant running through the generations finds its highest legal expression in the principled essence of the public trust. We must wake it, teach it, preach it, plant it, enforce it, write it, till it, build it, and all live it now. This fleeting time on Earth calls forth all cultures, peoples, and nations across the world to carry out the sacred promise that has sustained civilization since the dawn of time. Together we hold not the *power* of life, but the *trust* of life.

QUESTIONS

1. What differences do you see between the concept of "shareholder value" and that of "shared value"? Would you say that shared value is too vague a concept to be implemented?

2. How could CSR be incorporated into Canadian law and be made enforceable against commercial undertakings? What can be achieved through CSR that might not otherwise be achieved with traditional regulation?

3. In your opinion, what reasons can be put forward to justify the participation of civil society and citizens in the implementation of sustainability? Do you find the existing public participation mechanisms appropriate? What would you improve?

4. To what extent do you think legal tools can bring effective changes at the individual level?

FURTHER READINGS

Agyeman, Julian, Robert D Bullard & Bob Evans, "Exploring the Nexus: Bringing Together Sustainability, Environmental Justice and Equity" (2002) 6:1 Space & Polity 77.

Benidickson, Jamie, et al, eds, *Environmental Law and Sustainability after Rio* (Cheltenham, UK: Edward Elgar, 2011).

Bosselmann, Klaus, *The Principle of Sustainability: Transforming Law and Governance*, 2nd ed (London, UK: Routledge, 2017).

French, Duncan & Louis J Kotzé, *Sustainable Development Goals: Law, Theory and Implementation* (Northampton: Edward Elgar, 2018).

Gehring, Markus W, "Legal Transition to the Green Economy" (2016) 12:2 McGill Int'l J Sust Dev L & Pol'y 135.

Guèvremont, Véronique, "Integrating Culture in Sustainable Development: Quebec's Agenda 21 for Culture, a Model for the Implementation of Article 13" in Lilian Richieri Hanania, ed, *Effectiveness and Normativity of the 2005 UNESCO Convention on the Diversity of Cultural Expressions* (London, UK: Routledge, 2014) 265.

Kennedy, Amanda L, "Using Community-Based Social Marketing Techniques to Enhance Environmental Regulation" (2010) 2:4 Sustainability 1138.

Richardson, Benjamin J & Stepan Wood, *Environmental Law for Sustainability: A Reader* (Oxford: Hart, 2006).

CHAPTER FIVE

INTERNATIONAL LAW INFLUENCES

Patricia Galvão Ferreira

I. INTRODUCTION

International law has significantly influenced the design and the application of domestic environmental law in Canada in two main ways. First, as some environmental challenges affecting the country transcend national frontiers, Canadian laws to address these challenges have been shaped through international legal cooperation. By signing onto bilateral legal agreements to address environmental problems with a transboundary nature (for example, the Canada–US *Boundary Waters Treaty*, 11 January 1909, 36 US Stat 2448 (entered into force 1910), as well as multilateral treaties to confront global challenges like climate change (for example, the *Paris Agreement*, 12 December 2015, UN Doc FCCC/CP/2015/10/Add.1 (entered into force 4 November 2016)), Canada has devised national laws and policies to comply with the international obligations to which it agrees before other nations. Second, as the relatively new area of Canadian environmental law has developed concurrently with the body of public international law to protect the environment, it has been greatly affected by international environmental law (IEL) principles, norms, and institutions.

This chapter examines the various ways in which IEL has helped to shape the design and the application of Canadian domestic environmental law. It first provides an overview of the importance and the evolution of international law responses to current and emerging environmental challenges before reviewing concrete cases in which Canadian environmental norms and principles can be directly linked to IEL. Finally, it reviews how Canadian courts are engaging with international environmental law principles. Note that this chapter does not purport to address or to summarize the important elements of IEL as a branch of international law. To learn about characteristics of IEL when compared with other areas of international law, sources of IEL, and actors engaged in the making of IEL, or for a full history of the discipline, see the list of further readings at the end of this chapter. The goal here is to emphasize that the broader international context in which Canada's environmental laws are embedded helps to illuminate how environmental regulations came to be and how they continue to be designed and interpreted today. Other examples of how international law has influenced Canadian environmental law can be found throughout the chapters in this book.

II. THE IMPORTANCE AND THE EVOLUTION OF IEL

The excerpt below, from Philippe Sands and Jacqueline Peel, discusses the reasons behind the existence of a substantial and growing body of international norms, principles, and institutions to protect the environment, and describes how those principles and norms have evolved in the last 50 years. Sands and Peel also discuss how IEL has been an important driver for national states creating domestic environmental laws. This discussion is followed by an excerpt from a 2018 report by the United Nations Environmental Programme (UNEP) on environmental rule of law. The UNEP report recognizes that despite the dramatic expansion in the number of international and national environmental laws since the 1970s, the world remains far from adequately responding to long-standing environmental problems like air pollution and water contamination. Meanwhile, our societies now face new environmental challenges, such as climate change, which puts our legal systems even more to the test. The UNEP report suggests that there is a considerable gap between existing environmental laws and their implementation and enforcement, emphasizing the importance of taking environmental justice into account in domestic systems in order to protect the environment.

PHILIPPE SANDS & JACQUELINE PEEL, "THE ENVIRONMENT AND INTERNATIONAL SOCIETY: ISSUES, CONCEPTS AND DEFINITIONS"
in *Principles of International Environmental Law*, 4th ed (Cambridge: Cambridge University Press, 2018) ch 1 [footnotes omitted]

INTRODUCTION: THE ENVIRONMENTAL CHALLENGE

It is widely recognised that the planet faces serious environmental challenges that can only be addressed through international cooperation. Climate change and ozone depletion, loss of biodiversity, toxic and hazardous pollution of air and sea, pollution of rivers and depletion of freshwater resources are among the issues that international law is called upon to address. ... [E]nvironmental threats are accompanied by a recognition that ecological interdependence does not respect national boundaries and that issues once considered to be matters of national concern have international implications—at the bilateral, subregional, regional or global levels— that can often only be addressed by international cooperation, including by law and regulation.

• • •

THE INTERNATIONAL LEGAL ORDER

Environmental issues pose significant challenges for the traditional international legal order, in at least three ways. They pose challenges, first, for the legislative, administrative and adjudicative functions of international law; second, for the manner in which international legal arrangements are organised (i.e. along territorial lines); and, third, for the various actors who are considered to be members of the international community and participants in the various processes and practices of the international legal order. ...

• • •

The international legal order regulates the activities of an international community comprising states, international organisations and non-state actors. States have the primary role in the international legal order, as both international lawmakers and holders of international rights and obligations. Under international law, states are sovereign and have equal rights and duties as members of the international community, notwithstanding differences of an economic, social, political or other nature. ...

The sovereignty and exclusive jurisdiction ... over their territory means, in principle, that [states] alone have the competence to develop policies and laws in respect of the natural resources and the environment of their territory, which comprises:

(1) the land within its boundaries, including the subsoil;
(2) internal waters, such as lakes, rivers and canals;
(3) the territorial sea, which is adjacent to the coast, including its seabed, subsoil and the resources thereof; and
(4) the airspace above its land, internal waters and territorial sea, up to the point at which the legal regime of outer space begins.

Additionally, states have limited sovereign rights and jurisdiction over other areas, including: a contiguous zone adjacent to the territorial seas; the resources of the continental shelf, its seabed and subsoil; certain fishing zones; and the exclusive economic zone. It follows that certain areas fall outside the territory of any state, and in respect of these no state has exclusive jurisdiction. These areas, which are sometimes referred to as the "global commons," include the high seas and its seabed and subsoil, outer space and, according to a majority of states, the Antarctic. The atmosphere is also sometimes considered to be part of the global commons. This apparently straightforward international legal order worked satisfactorily as an organising structure until technological developments permeated national boundaries. This structure does not, however, coexist comfortably with an environmental order that consists of a biosphere of interdependent ecosystems, which do not respect artificial national territorial boundaries. Many natural resources and their environmental components are ecologically shared. The use by one state of natural resources within its territory will invariably have consequences for the use of natural resources and their environmental components in another state. This is evident where a river runs through two or more countries, or where living resources migrate between two or more sovereign territories. Even apparently innocent activities in one country, such as the release of greenhouse gases or (possibly) genetically modified organisms, can have significant effects upon the environment of other states or in areas beyond national jurisdiction. Ecological interdependence poses a fundamental challenge for international law, and explains why international cooperation and the development of international environmental standards are indispensable: the challenge for international law in the world of sovereign states remains to reconcile the fundamental independence of each state with the inherent and fundamental interdependence of the environment.

PHILIPPE SANDS & JACQUELINE PEEL, "HISTORY"
in *Principles of International Environmental Law* (Cambridge: Cambridge University Press, 2018) ch 2 [footnotes omitted]

International environmental law has evolved over four distinct periods, reflecting developments in scientific knowledge, the application of new technologies and an understanding of their impacts, changes in political consciousness and the changing structure of the international legal order and institutions.

A first period began with bilateral fisheries treaties in the nineteenth century, and concluded with the creation of the new international organisations in 1945. During this period, peoples and nations began to understand that the process of industrialisation and development required limitations on the exploitation of certain natural resources (flora and fauna) and the adoption of appropriate legal instruments. The second period commenced with the creation of the UN and culminated with the UN Conference on the Human Environment, held in Stockholm in June 1972. Over this period, a range of international organisations with competence in environmental matters was created, and legal instruments were adopted, at both the regional and the global levels, which addressed particular sources of pollution and the conservation of general and particular environmental resources, such as oil pollution, nuclear testing, wetlands, the marine environment and its living resources, the quality of freshwaters and the dumping of waste at sea. The third period ran from the 1972 Stockholm Conference and concluded with the UN Conference on Environment and Development (UNCED) in June 1992. During this period, the UN tried to put in place a system for coordinating responses to international environmental issues, regional and global conventions were adopted, and for the first time the production, consumption and international trade in certain products were banned at the global level. The fourth period was set in motion by UNCED, and may be characterised as a period of integration: when environmental concerns should, as a matter of international law and policy, be integrated into all activities and into the broader development agenda concerned with poverty eradication and improving human health. This has also been the period in which increased attention has been paid to compliance with international environmental obligations, with the result that there is now a well-developed body of international jurisprudence.

• • •

UNCED

• • •

UNCED was held in Rio de Janeiro, Brazil, on 3-14 June 1992, and was attended by 176 states, more than fifty intergovernmental organisations, and several thousand corporations and non-governmental organisations. ...

UNCED's contribution to international law includes the Commission on Sustainable Development ... , the endorsement of a new topic area known as the "international law of sustainable development" ... , a number of the Rio Declaration Principles [*Rio Declaration on Environment and Development*, UNGA, UN Doc No A/CONF.151/26/Rev.1 (Vol 1), annex I (1992)], and the framework established by Agenda 21 [United Nations Conference on Environment & Development, Rio de Janeiro, Brazil, 3-14 June 1992]. At the time of UNCED, it was suggested that its endorsement of sustainable development might undermine "the autonomy of environmental law as a body of rules and standards designed to restrain and prevent the environmentally destructive effects of certain kinds of economic activity," and there might be some reason to fear that the Rio Conference constituted "the beginning of the decline of international environmental law as an autonomous branch of international law." This has not occurred; international environmental law has continued to develop and expand since 1992. Nonetheless, UNCED's concern with the balance between environmental protection and economic development has necessitated a reorientation of international environmental regulation [so that environmental concerns would be] integrated into economic and development activities. The challenge for international environmental law has been to facilitate this interlinkage without environmental protection objectives being overwhelmed by the more powerful rules of international economic cooperation.

THE RIO DECLARATION

The Rio Declaration represented a series of compromises between developed and developing countries and a balance between the objectives of environmental protection and economic development. ... The Declaration comprises twenty-seven Principles, which set out the basis upon which states and people are to cooperate and further develop "international law in the field of sustainable development" (Principle 27). Although it is non-binding, some provisions reflect rules of customary law, others reflect emerging rules, and yet others provide guidance as to future legal developments. A number of the principles—for example, in relation to precaution—have been frequently referred to by national and international courts. ...

• • •

The heart of the Rio Declaration is in Principles 3 and 4, which should be read together to understand the political context and the trade-off they represent. Both Principles were initially controversial. Principle 3 provides that "[t]he right to development must be fulfilled so as to equitably meet developmental and environmental needs of present and future generations." It represents something of a victory for developing countries and the Group of 77, being the first time that the "right to development" was affirmed in an international instrument adopted by consensus. In return for Principle 3, the developed countries extracted Principle 4, which provides that "[i] n order to achieve sustainable development, environmental protection shall constitute an integral part of the development process and cannot be considered in isolation from it." This reflects a commitment to moving environmental considerations and objectives from the periphery of international relations to its economic core. ...

The Rio Declaration recognised a new principle of "common but differentiated responsibility." Principle 7 notes the different contributions of countries to regional and global environmental degradation, and provides that:

[i]n view of the different contributions to global environmental degradation, States have common but differentiated responsibilities. The developed countries acknowledge the responsibility that they bear in the international pursuit of sustainable

development in view of the pressures their societies place on the global environment and of the technologies and financial resources they command.

• • •

Principle 11 ... commits all states to enact "effective environmental legislation," although the standards, objectives and priorities "should reflect the environmental and developmental context to which they apply." Principle 11 also recognises that standards applied by some countries "may be inappropriate and of unwarranted economic and social cost to other countries, in particular developing countries."

The Rio Declaration developed general principles of the international law of sustainable development. The "precautionary approach" is endorsed by Principle 15, and the "polluter pays" principle is implicitly recognised in Principle 16. The Rio Declaration took several steps beyond the Stockholm Declaration by supporting the development of "procedural" techniques for implementing international standards (including access to information and public participation), the use of environmental impact assessments, and enhanced notification, information exchange and consultation.

CARL BRUCH ET AL, ENVIRONMENTAL RULE OF LAW: FIRST GLOBAL REPORT
(Nairobi: United Nations Environment Programme, 2019), online (pdf): <https://wedocs.unep.org/bitstream/handle/20.500.11822/27279/ Environmental_rule_of_law.pdf> [footnotes omitted]

1.4 EVOLUTION OF ENVIRONMENTAL RULE OF LAW

• • •

While some countries adopted environmental laws in the 1970s and 1980s, most adopted their framework environmental laws starting in the 1990s, following the Rio Earth Summit. The 1990s also saw a rapid growth of environmental ministries and agencies. From 1972 to 1992, nations entered into more than 1,100 environmental agreements and other legal instruments. International and bilateral donors and partners focused money and energy in building human and institutional capacity.

By the time the 2002 World Summit on Sustainable Development was held, many countries' wherewithal for making new international commitments at global summits was exhausted. There was a sense among many that the Summit should focus on implementation of existing commitments, rather than on generating yet more commitments that countries may have difficulty implementing. This led to a focus at the Summit on voluntary public–private partnerships, which were viewed as not providing a substitute for effective environmental rule of law.

• • •

By the 2012 UN Conference on Sustainable Development (also known as "Rio+20"), there was substantial focus on environmental governance. *The Future We Want*, the outcome document from Rio+20, emphasized the importance of strong institutions, access to justice and information, and the political will to implement and enforce environmental law. It also expanded and refined a number of the public–private partnerships and other initiatives initiated at the World Summit on Sustainable Development. ...

• • •

The first United Nations Environment Assembly in 2014 adopted resolution 1/13, which calls upon countries "to work for the strengthening of environmental rule of law at the international, regional and national levels." And in 2016, the First World Environmental Law Congress, cosponsored by the International Union for Conservation of Nature and UN Environment, adopted the "IUCN World Declaration on the Environmental Rule of Law," which outlines 13 principles to serve as the foundation for developing and implementing solutions for ecologically sustainable development. It declares that "environmental rule of law should thus serve as the legal foundation for promoting environmental ethics and achieving environmental justice, global ecological integrity, and a sustainable future for all, including for future generations, at local, national, sub-national, regional, and international levels."

In 2015, the global community of nations recognized the importance of environmental rule of law to sustainable development. Sustainable Development Goal 16 emphasizes that environmental rule of law creates peaceful and inclusive societies premised upon access to justice and accountable and inclusive institutions. As such, Goal 16 cuts across all the other Sustainable Development Goals.

QUESTIONS

1. Identify and list environmental problems affecting Canada that can be addressed only by international cooperation and environmental challenges that Canada can regulate unilaterally using domestic law.

2. In your opinion, why it did take so long for the international community to create an international body of norms to protect the environment?

3. Should international environmental law treat all countries as equally responsible for global environmental problems such as climate change?

4. Do we need more environmental treaties to improve environmental protection?

III. IEL AND CANADA

The evolution of Canada's legal framework to protect the environment, addressed in the other chapters of this book, has been closely intertwined with the evolution of IEL. Canada's territory includes one quarter of the Earth's wetlands and boreal forests, the longest coastline on the planet, and 20 percent of the world's freshwater. As in other developed countries, social pressure from environmental organizations and social movements have consistently pushed concerns with environmental protection to the forefront of Canada's political agenda since the 1970s, with mixed results depending on the circumstances.

As a middle power, Canada relies heavily on international cooperation and the international rule of law to preserve its peace and security and to protect its values and interests, including those related to the national and international environment. Canada has been deeply engaged with IEL since its inception, being a party to a substantial number of important environmental agreements. Moreover, Canada has played an influential role in the development of key aspects of IEL. It was a Canadian diplomat, Maurice Strong, who served as secretary-general of both the 1972 Stockholm Conference on the Human Environment and the 1992 UN Conference on Environment and Development. Strong also served as the first head of UNEP, from 1972 to 1976. Canada has also played a leadership role in the negotiation of some of the key environmental law agreements, like the *Stockholm Convention on Persistent Organic Pollutants*, 22 May 2001, 2256 UNTS 119 (entered into force 17 May 2014).

As of April 2019, Canada is party to 115 international environmental agreements or legal instruments. (See "Canada Treaty Series" (last modified 3 March 2014), online: *Global Affair*

Canada <https://www.treaty-accord.gc.ca/cts-rtc.aspx?lang=eng>.) This includes 54 multilateral agreements (for example, the 1992 *United Nations Framework Convention on Climate Change*, 9 May 1992, 1771 UNTS 107 (entered into force 21 March 1994); the 2015 *Paris Agreement*; the 1992 *Convention on Biological Diversity*, 5 June 1992, 1760 UNTS 79 (entered into force 29 December 1993); and the 1989 *Basel Convention on the Control of Transboundary Movements of Hazardous Wastes and Their Disposal*, 22 March 1989, 1673 UNTS 57); 23 Canada–US environmental agreements (for example, the 1909 *Boundary Waters Treaty* and the 1991 *Agreement between the Government of Canada and the Government of the United States on Air Quality*, 13 March 1991, Can TS 1991, No 3 (entered into force 13 March 1991)); 28 cooperative bilateral agreements with various other countries (for example, the 2011 *Canada–Australia Cooperative Arrangement on Industrial Chemicals* and the 2017 *Canada–China Memorandum of Understanding Concerning Environmental Cooperation*); and various multilateral voluntary instruments (for example, the 1996 *Arctic Council* and the 2004 *Global Methane Initiative*) (see Environment and Climate Change Canada, "Participation in International Environmental Agreements and Instruments" for *Compendium of Canada's Engagement in International Environmental Agreements and Instruments*, 8th ed (2018), online: *Government of Canada* <https://www.canada.ca/en/environment-climate-change/corporate/international-affairs/partnerships-organizations/participation-international -environmental-agreements.html>).

This close engagement with IEL has affected Canada's environmental law in important ways. Canada's international commitments have often prompted the direct creation—or reform—of environmental laws and policies at the domestic level. Canadian legislators have incorporated some of the prominent legal principles of IEL—for example, sustainable development, precautionary principle, and polluter pays—into Canadian environmental law and policy regimes. Canadian courts have either applied customary IEL in concrete cases or indirectly applied IEL norms and principles that have been expressly incorporated into Canadian legislation. Finally, Canadian courts have used IEL to interpret national and sub-national environmental law provisions.

The following excerpt, from a paper by Charles-Emmanuel Côté, discusses the various ways in which IEL is applied to Canadian environmental law. The excerpt is followed by two concrete examples of the application of IEL in the areas of marine pollution and persistent organic pollutants to illustrate how IEL objectives and norms have been incorporated into Canadian statutory law (see Section III.A of this chapter).

CHARLES-EMMANUEL CÔTÉ, "APPLYING INTERNATIONAL LAW TO CANADIAN ENVIRONMENTAL LAW"
(Paper delivered at a Symposium on Environment in the Courtroom: Key Environmental Concepts and the Unique Nature of Environmental Damage, University of Calgary, 23-24 March 2012) [footnotes omitted]

INTRODUCTION

• • •

Canada's international obligations basically originate from two main sources. On the one hand, they arise from customary international practices (or customary international law), which consists of general domestic practices accepted as law. ...

On the other hand, Canada's international obligations flow from treaties entered into with other sovereign states or IO's [intergovernmental organizations]. ... For Canada to be bound by a treaty, it must have specifically consented to it. According to well established governmental practice and based on the principles of the *Constitution of the United Kingdom*, which are referred to in the preamble of the *Constitution Act of 1867* [(UK), 30 & 31 Vict, c 3], it is the federal government that has a monopoly over the correct procedures for entering into treaties, without any intervention on the part of the Federal Parliament or the provinces.

Canada is bound by numerous customary or conventional international obligations concerning environmental protection. These international obligations can be applied as sources of positive law or as interpretive sources for Canadian environmental law.

INTERNATIONAL LAW AS A SOURCE OF POSITIVE LAW
FOR CANADIAN ENVIRONMENTAL LAW

• • •

CUSTOMARY INTERNATIONAL LAW AS A SOURCE OF POSITIVE LAW

In the judicial ruling *R. v. Hape* [2007 SCC 26, [2007] 2 SCR 292] rendered in 2007, the Supreme Court of Canada ended the uncertainty surrounding the status of customary international practice in Canadian law. It is now clear that this is automatically accepted into *common law*, without the requirement for any special procedure or action on the part of the federal or provincial government, provided that it is not incompatible with the Constitution, federal legislation or provincial legislation. Only "prohibitive rules" in customary international law are automatically accepted: if a rule does not prohibit a course of conduct in Canada but rather the jurisdiction to act in a given manner, it is not automatically accepted and then requires the adoption of an act on the part of the legislator having jurisdiction.

• • •

A Canadian judge thus becomes a compliance officer for customary international law in Canadian environmental law, watching over Canada's compliance to its international obligations. He can also contribute by verifying the existence of a customary rule concerning environmental protection, not only for the purposes of the case he must decide, but also to advance international law for the benefit of environmental protection around the world. ...

THE TREATY AS A SOURCE OF POSITIVE LAW

Contrary to international custom, treaties entered into by Canada cannot apply to Canadian law without the legislator's intervention. Only an act can transform Canada's international obligations into a source of positive law under Canadian law. In its famous *Decision on the Conventions of the International Labour Organization* [*Canada (Attorney General) v Ontario (Attorney General)*, [1937] AC 326, 1937 CanLII 362], in 1937, the Judicial Committee of the Privy Council decided that the legislative authority required to implement a treaty under Canadian law is an ancillary power to the normal division of legislative jurisdictions. There is no general authority for the implementation of treaties in Canada: the federal or provincial legislator has the authority according to the matter targeted by the treaty. In spite of an old controversy concerning the denial of a general federal jurisdiction for the implementation of treaties, the 1937 ruling still constitutes the leading decision on this issue.

• • •

INCORPORATION ACT WITH ANNEXATION OF THE TREATY TEXT

The competent legislator may want to incorporate a treaty and attach its text to the Incorporation Act. ... The incorporated provisions thus form an integral part of the law in effect in Canada and are directly applicable under Canadian law.

INCORPORATION ACT WITHOUT ANNEXATION OF THE TREATY TEXT

On the other hand, even if the treaty text is not annexed to the Act, this does not necessarily mean that the legislator did not express a clear and unequivocal intention to incorporate the treaty into Canadian law. The legislator might well express his intention to render the text directly applicable under Canadian law without annexing it to the Incorporation Act. ...

• • •

IMPLEMENTATION ACT WITHOUT ANNEXATION OF THE TEXT OF A TREATY

The most common hypothesis is that of a treaty which is the subject of an implementation act on the part of the competent legislator, who has no intention to incorporate the treaty under Canadian law. The purpose of the implementing act is to change Canadian law in such a way as to ensure the performance by Canada of its conventional international obligations. This could be either a new act adopted specially for the implementation of a treaty, or else changes made to an already existing act. The provisions of the treaty itself remain inapplicable in Canadian law: only the legislative provisions for implementation are part of the law in effect in Canada. The text of the treaty itself cannot under any circumstances be invoked before the judge as the basis for a claim.

[Later case law on domestic application of international law in Canada includes *B010 v Canada (Citizenship and Immigration)*, 2015 SCC 58; *Kazemi Estate v Islamic Republic of Iran*, 2014 SCC 62; and *Araya v Nevsun Resources Ltd*, 2016 BCSC 1856.]

A. EXAMPLES OF THE INCORPORATION OF IEL INTO CANADIAN STATUTORY LAW

1. Marine Pollution

The 1973 *International Convention for the Prevention of Pollution from Ships*, 2 November 1973, *as Modified by the Protocol of 1978 Relating Thereto*, 17 February 1978, 1340 UNTS 62 (entered into force 2 October 1983) (MARPOL 73/78) is the main legal instrument for the prevention of marine pollution from ships—both accidental pollution and that from routine operations. MARPOL 73/78 combines the original 1973 Convention and the 1978 Protocol. Six MARPOL annexes serve to incorporate protocols covering a wide range of potential marine pollution sources, ranging from ship-generated fuel oil residues, sewage, and air pollution (including greenhouse gases) to cargo residues such as ballast water oil, wash-water chemicals, and dry cargo residue.

Most aspects of the MARPOL Convention have been incorporated into Canadian law through the *Canada Shipping Act, 2001*, SC 2001, c 26. The following excerpts illustrate how the objectives of the Act expressly include meeting international obligations and how the texts of the various protocols are included in Schedules that are part of the domestic statute. Finally, the excerpts of the *Canada Shipping Act, 2001* show how a national statute can set explicit conditions of application for certain international agreements.

CANADA SHIPPING ACT, 2001
SC 2001, c 26

Objectives of Act
6. The objectives of this Act are to

• • •

(c) protect the marine environment from damage due to navigation and ship-ping activities;

• • •

(g) ensure that Canada can meet its international obligations under bilateral and multilateral agreements with respect to navigation and shipping ... .

• • •

Schedule 1
29(1) Schedule 1 lists the international conventions, protocols and resolutions that Canada has signed that relate to matters that are within the scope of this Act and that the Minister of Transport has determined should be brought into force, in whole or in part, in Canada by regulation.
Schedule 2
(2) Schedule 2 lists the international conventions, protocols and resolutions that Canada has signed that relate to matters that are within the scope of this Act and that the Minister of Fisheries and Oceans has determined should be brought into force, in whole or in part, in Canada by regulation.

• • •

Salvage Convention
142(1) Subject to the reservations that Canada made ... , the International Conven-tion on Salvage, 1989, signed at London on April 28, 1989 ... , is approved and declared to have the force of law in Canada.
Inconsistent laws
(2) In the event of an inconsistency between the Convention and this Act or the regulations, the Convention prevails to the extent of the inconsistency.

2. Persistent Organic Pollutants

The *Stockholm Convention on Persistent Organic Pollutants* (POPs) is a legally binding mul-tilateral treaty with the objective to control the global production and use of chemicals that remain intact in the environment for long periods, become widely distributed geographically, accumulate in the fatty tissue of humans and wildlife, and have harmful impacts on human health or on the environment. The Stockholm Convention was adopted in May 2001 and entered into force in May 2004. Because POPs migrate long distances and tend to accumulate in northern climates, the uncontrolled global production and use of these chemicals places Canada—particularly the inhabitants of Canada's North—at greater risk of exposure to POPs. Canada signed and ratified the Stockholm Convention in May 2001.

There is no single legislative act implementing the Stockholm Convention in Canada. The production, the use, and the release of POPs in the country are managed through an overlap-ping legal and policy framework that involves both federal and provincial/territorial regulations and agencies. At the federal level, key policies and legislation used to comply with the Con-vention's obligations include the *Canadian Environmental Protection Act, 1999*, SC 1999, c 33 [CEPA] (which is the cornerstone of the federal regime of chemicals regulation); the *Pest Control Products Act*, SC 2002, c 28; and the Toxic Substances Management Policy (which controls the production and use of POPs and other chemical substances in food, drugs, pesticides, and other products). The federal government has included POPs in the list of chemicals under the Chemicals Management Plan, which assesses and takes action on chemicals that are found to be harmful.

QUESTIONS

1. Explain when Canadian courts can, and when they cannot, directly apply international environmental law.

2. Identify and list any Canadian environmental regulation, besides the ones cited in this chapter, that has been adopted to give effect to international commitments.

IV. PRINCIPLES OF IEL IN CANADA

Many of the general principles of IEL that developed since the 1992 *Rio Declaration on Environment and Development*—for example, sustainable development, public participation, and access to information—have been either expressly or implicitly incorporated into Canadian statutory law. Chapter 4 of this book addresses the implementation of the IEL principle of sustainable development in Canada in detail. This section includes examples of how the precautionary principle has been incorporated into the *Impact Assessment Act*, SC 2019, c 28, s 1 [IAA] and CEPA, and how the "polluter pays" principle has been incorporated into the *Canadian Energy Regulator Act*, SC 2019, c 28, s 10. This section also illustrates the way Canadian courts have navigated the intersection between IEL and domestic environmental law in the context of disputes related to the scope and application of principles of IEL. In *Morton v Canada (Fisheries and Oceans)*, 2019 FC 143, the court has clearly referenced the precautionary principle as an emerging principle of IEL and as part of a related treaty of which Canada was a part. The court has, however, used the precautionary principle as a tool to help interpret domestic statutory law, not to grant direct rights and obligations. In *Imperial Oil Ltd v Quebec (Minister of the Environment)*, 2003 SCC 58, [2003] 2 SCR 624 and *Midwest Properties Ltd v Thordarson*, 2015 ONCA 819, 128 OR (3d) 81, Canadian courts held that the "polluter pays" principle has become deeply entrenched in Canadian environmental law, making no references to specific treaties.

A. EXAMPLES OF THE INCORPORATION OF IEL PRINCIPLES INTO CANADIAN STATUTORY LAW

1. Precautionary Principle   -

Principle 15 of the 1992 Rio Declaration arguably contains the most accepted expression of the precautionary principle, stating: "Where there are threats of serious or irreversible damage, lack of full scientific certainty shall not be used as a reason for postponing cost-effective measures to prevent environmental degradation." In Canada, legislators have expressly incorporated this principle into various environmental statutes, including the *Federal Sustainable Development Act*, SC 2008, c 33; and the *Fisheries Act*, RSC 1985, c F-14 (last amended August 28, 2019). IAA and CEPA, for example, have incorporated this principle as follows.

IMPACT ASSESSMENT ACT
SC 2012, c 28, s 1 [emphasis added]

Purposes

6(1) The purposes of this Act are

• • •

(d) to ensure that designated projects that require the exercise of a power or performance of a duty or function by a federal authority under any Act of Parliament other than this Act to be carried out, *are considered in a careful and precautionary manner to avoid adverse effects within federal jurisdiction and adverse direct or incidental effects;*

• • •

(l) to ensure that projects, as defined in section 81, that are to be carried out on federal lands, or those that are outside Canada and that are to be carried out or financially supported by a federal authority, *are considered in a careful and precautionary manner to avoid significant adverse environmental effects;*

• • •

Mandate

(2) The Government of Canada, the Minister, the Agency and federal authorities, in the administration of this Act, must exercise their powers in a manner that fosters sustainability, respects the Government's commitments with respect to the rights of the Indigenous peoples of Canada *and applies the precautionary principle.*

CANADIAN ENVIRONMENTAL PROTECTION ACT, 1999
SC 1999, c 33, preamble, ss 2, 6, 76.1 [emphasis added]

Whereas the Government of Canada is *committed to implementing the precautionary principle* that, where there are threats of serious or irreversible damage, lack of full scientific certainty shall not be used as a reason for postponing cost-effective measures to prevent environmental degradation ... .

• • •

Duties of the Government of Canada

2(1) In the administration of this Act, the Government of Canada shall, having regard to the Constitution and laws of Canada and subject to subsection (1.1),

(a) exercise its powers in a manner that protects the environment and human health, *applies the precautionary principle* that, where there are threats of serious or irreversible damage, lack of full scientific certainty shall not be used as a reason for postponing cost-effective measures to prevent environmental degradation, and promotes and reinforces enforceable pollution prevention approaches ... .

• • •

National Advisory Committee

6(1) For the purpose of enabling national action to be carried out and taking cooperative action in matters affecting the environment and for the purpose of avoiding duplication in regulatory activity among governments, the Minister shall establish a National Advisory Committee ... .

Precautionary principle

(1.1) In giving its advice and recommendations, the Committee *shall use the precautionary principle.*

• • •

Weight of evidence and precautionary principle

76.1 When the Ministers are conducting and interpreting the results of

(a) a screening assessment under section 74,

(b) a review of a decision of another jurisdiction under subsection 75(3) that, in their opinion, is based on scientific considerations and is relevant to Canada, or

(c) an assessment whether a substance specified on the Priority Substances List is toxic or capable of becoming toxic,

the Ministers shall apply a weight of evidence approach and the precautionary principle.

2. Polluter Pays

Principle 16 of the 1992 Rio Declaration reads: "National authorities should endeavour to promote the internalization of environmental costs and the use of economic instruments, taking into account the approach that the polluter should, in principle, bear the cost of pollution, with due regard to the public interest and without distorting international trade and investment." Many Canadian environmental laws have expressly or implicitly incorporated the "polluter pays" principle, as illustrated by these excerpts from CEPA and the *Canadian Energy Regulator Act.*

CANADIAN ENVIRONMENTAL PROTECTION ACT, 1999
SC 1999, c 33, preamble, s 287 [emphasis added]

Whereas the Government of Canada *recognizes the responsibility of users and producers in relation to toxic substances and pollutants and wastes, and has adopted the "polluter pays" principle ... .*

• • •

Fundamental purpose of sentencing

287. The fundamental purpose of sentencing for offences under this Act is to contribute, in light of the significant and many threats to the environment and to human health and to the importance of a healthy environment to the well-being of Canadians, to respect for the law protecting the environment and human health through the imposition of just sanctions that have as their objectives

(a) to deter the offender and any other person from committing offences under this Act;

(b) to denounce unlawful conduct that damages or creates a risk of damage to the environment or harms or creates a risk of harm to human health; and

(c) *to reinforce the "polluter pays" principle by ensuring that offenders are held responsible for effective clean-up and environmental restoration.*

CANADIAN ENERGY REGULATOR ACT
SC 2019, c 28, s 10

POLLUTER PAYS PRINCIPLE

Purpose

136 The purpose of sections 137 to 142 [liability regime] is to reinforce the "polluter pays" principle by, among other things, imposing financial requirements on any company that is authorized under this Act to construct or operate a pipeline.

LIABILITY

Recovery of loss, damage, costs, expenses

137(1) If an unintended or uncontrolled release from a pipeline of oil, gas or any other commodity occurs, all persons to whose fault or negligence the release is attributable or who are by law responsible for others to whose fault or negligence the release is attributable are jointly and severally, or solidarily, liable for

(a) all actual loss or damage incurred by any person as a result of the release or as a result of any action or measure taken in relation to the release;

(b) the costs and expenses reasonably incurred by Her Majesty in right of Canada or a province, any Indigenous governing body or any other person in taking any action or measure in relation to the release; and

(c) all loss of non-use value relating to a public resource that is affected by the release or by any action or measure taken in relation to the release.

Contribution based on degree of fault

(2) The persons who are at fault or negligent or who are by law responsible for persons who are at fault or negligent are liable to make contributions to each other or to indemnify each other in the degree to which they are respectively at fault or negligent.

Vicarious liability

(3) The company that is authorized under this Act to construct or operate the pipeline from which the release occurred is jointly and severally, or solidarily, liable with any contractor — to whose fault or negligence the release is attributable — that performs work for the company for the actual loss or damage, the costs and expenses and the loss of non-use value, described in paragraphs (1)(a) to (c).

Absolute liability

(4) If an unintended or uncontrolled release of oil, gas or any other commodity from a pipeline occurs, the company that is authorized under this Act to construct or operate that pipeline is liable, without proof of fault or negligence, up to the applicable limit of liability that is set out in subsection (5) for the actual loss or damage, the costs and expenses and the loss of non-use value, described in paragraphs (1)(a) to (c).

B. IEL PRINCIPLES IN CANADIAN COURTS

1. Morton v Canada (Fisheries and Oceans) and the Precautionary Principle

Piscine Orthoreovirus (PRV) is a highly infectious virus that affects salmon known to be present in Norway, the United Kingdom, Ireland, Chile, the United States, and Canada. Heart and Skeletal Muscle Inflammation (HSMI) is an infectious disease that is currently among the top four diseases affecting salmon in Norway. A 2017 Norwegian study identified PRV as the cause of HSMI in Atlantic salmon. However, a 2016 study in Canada has concluded that while infectious, the PRV strain found in British Columbia has not been shown to cause disease or mortality.

The established policy of the Department of Fisheries and Oceans (DFO) was not to test for the presence of PRV or HSMI prior to issuing licences authorizing operators to transfer smolts (juvenile salmon) from inland hatcheries to ocean-based fish farms. (See DFO policies at Fisheries and Oceans Canada, "Fisheries Policies and Frameworks" (last modified 27 May 2019), online: *Government of Canada* <https://www.dfo-mpo.gc.ca/reports-rapports/regs/policies-politiques-eng.htm>.) Section 56 of the *Fishery (General) Regulations*, SOR/93-53 (FGRs) provides the minister of fisheries and oceans with the discretion to authorize such transfers. However, s 56(b) requires the minister to deny a transfer licence if fish have a disease or disease agent that "may be harmful to the protection and conservation of fish." DFO policy allowed operators themselves to determine that if the stock showed no signs of clinical disease requiring treatment, they could grant the licence without governmental testing.

Alexandra Morton challenged this policy in *Morton v Canada (Fisheries and Oceans)*, 2015 FC 575 (*Morton 2015*), arguing that it puts wild Pacific salmon at risk. The Federal Court held that s 56(b) of the FGRs requires the minister to take an approach consistent with the precautionary principle when considering transfer licences, and that the DFO policy constituted an impermissible delegation of the minister's regulatory authority to fish farm operators. Following the Federal Court's decision, DFO eliminated the licence condition held to be illegal, and adopted a new PRV policy that included a novel legal interpretation of the phrase "the protection and conservation of fish" in s 56(b). This interpretation allowed the transfer of any smolts that have a disease or disease agent unless they harm genetic diversity, species, or conservation units of fish "such that [they] cannot sustain biodiversity and the continuance of evolutionary and natural production processes."

'Namgis First Nation, alongside biologist Alexandra Morton, challenged this new iteration of the PRV policy, because it continued to put wild Pacific salmon at risk, as it continued to circumvent testing. 'Namgis additionally challenged a decision by DFO to issue a specific licence pursuant to the policy, authorizing a particular transfer of smolts to restock a fish farm situated in its territorial waters. While considering whether decisions under the PRV policy were reasonable, the court examined the following question: Did the minister derogate from the precautionary principle (when interpreting s 56 of the FGRs to design the PRV policy)? In finding that the minister's interpretation of s 56 is unreasonable because it derogates from the precautionary principle, the Federal Court referenced *114957 Canada Ltée (Spraytech, Société d'arrosage) v Hudson (Town)*, 2001 SCC 40, [2001] 2 SCR 241 and *Castonguay Blasting Ltd v Ontario (Environment)*, 2013 SCC 52 (in which the Supreme Court of Canada declared the precautionary principle as an emerging principle of IEL) as well as the Canadian commitment to a precautionary approach to fisheries under the United Nations *Agreement for the Implementation of the Provisions of the United Nations Convention on the Law of the Sea of 10 December 1982 Relating to the Conservation and Management of Straddling Fish Stocks and Highly Migratory Fish Stocks*, 4 August 1995, 2167 UNTS 88 (entered into force 11 December 2001). The court decision, however, was explicit in that the precautionary principle did not directly create or provide substantive rights.

MORTON V CANADA (FISHERIES AND OCEANS)
2019 FC 143

[1] The *Fishery (General) Regulations*, SOR/93-53 ("FGRs"), made pursuant to the *Fisheries Act*, RSC 1985, [c F-14] ("*Fisheries Act*" or "Act"), form part of Canada's fisheries management regime. The FGRs require the Minister of Fisheries ("Minister") to issue a licence before live fish can be transferred into any fish habitat or fish rearing

facility. The Minister may only issue such a licence if the conditions set out in s 56 of the FGRs are met. ...

• • •

[17] Pursuant to s 56, the Minister may issue a licence if three specified conditions are met:

> 56 The Minister may issue a licence if
> (a) the release or transfer of the fish would be in keeping with the proper management and control of fisheries;
> (b) the fish do not have any disease or disease agent that may be harmful to the protection and conservation of fish; and
> (c) the release or transfer of the fish will not have an adverse effect on the stock size of fish or the genetic characteristics of fish or fish stocks.

• • •

[39] ... Justice Rennie [in *Morton 2015*] found that s 56(b), properly construed, embodied the precautionary principle:

> [97] In my view, subsection 56(b) of the *FGRs*, properly construed, embodies the precautionary principle. First, subsection 56(b) prohibits the Minister from issuing a transfer licence if disease or disease agents are present that "may be harmful to the protection and conservation of fish." The phrase "may be harmful" does not require scientific certainty, and indeed does not require that harm even be the likely consequence of the transfer. Similarly, the scope of "any disease or disease agent" in subsection 56(b) should not be interpreted as requiring a unanimous scientific consensus that a disease agent (e.g., PRV) is the cause of the disease (e.g., HSMI).
>
> [98] The consequence of interpreting subsection 56(b) consistently with the precautionary principle is that the licence conditions must also reflect the precautionary principle. As the licence conditions cannot derogate from or be inconsistent with subsection 56(b), they therefore cannot derogate from the precautionary principle. As noted earlier, the Minister did not attempt to justify that licence condition 3.1(b)(iv) was consistent with the precautionary principle, but confined his argument in this respect to licence conditions 3.1(b)(i), (ii) and (iii).
>
> [99] In my view, the Minister's argument cannot stand. For the reasons given, conditions 3.1(b)(ii) and (iv) are inconsistent with section 56(b) and thus with the precautionary principle. The conditions dilute the requirements of subsection 56(b), a regulation designed to anticipate and prevent harm even in the absence of scientific certainty that such harm will in fact occur.

• • •

iv) Did the Minister derogate from the precautionary principle?

• • •

[155] [Cermaq Canada Inc] takes the position that the Minister's interpretation of harm with respect to s 56 is consistent with the precautionary principle as the focus of the principle is on serious or irreversible damage and that Justice Rennie's discussion of the principle is *obiter*. Further, DFO's approach to the PRV Policy in its regular review and assessment of developing science regarding PRV and HSMI takes an "adaptive management" approach which has developed in conjunction with the precautionary principle (*Pembina Institute for Appropriate Development v Canada (Attorney General)*, 2008 FC 302 at para 32), and the Delegate states in her decision that DFO will continue to actively monitor this area, and as new information becomes available, consider whether changes will be required. Further, s 56 itself is

reflective of the precautionary principle as it prohibits a transfer where a threat exists to the protection and conservation of fish, the principle does not provide additional substantive rights to limit the Minister's discretion. In any event, the Minister considered the risk of PRV and determined that it was not a risk to the protection and conservation of fish, therefore, the precautionary principle is not engaged and whether scientific certainty on that issue exists is irrelevant.

A) ANALYSIS

[156] In my view, Cermaq's position, that Justice Rennie's findings concerning s 56 and the precautionary principle are *obiter*, is of no merit. Justice Rennie devoted an entire section of his decision to considering the meaning of the precautionary principle. In that regard he referenced *114957 Canada Ltée (Spraytech, Société d'arrosage) v Hudson (Town)*, 2001 SCC 40 ("*Spraytech*") and *Castonguay Blasting Ltd. v Ontario (Environment)*, 2013 SCC 52 at para 20, in which the Supreme Court referred to the principle as an emerging principle of international law, which informed the scope and application of the legislative provision in question. Justice Rennie stated as follows:

[43] The precautionary [principle] recognizes, that as a matter of sound public policy the lack of complete scientific certainty should not be used as a basis for avoiding or postponing measures to protect the environment, as there are inherent limits in being able to predict environmental harm. Moving from the realm public policy [*sic*] to the law, the precautionary principle is at a minimum, an established aspect of statutory interpretation, and arguably, has crystallized into a norm of customary international law and substantive domestic law: *Spraytech* at paras 30-31. However, except as discussed in Part VII, the legal contours of the principle need not be determined here, as this decision does not rest or depend on the application of the principle.

• • •

[158] It is clear that Justice Rennie's findings are not *obiter*, but represent another basis upon which he found the impugned licence conditions to be invalid.

[159] I am also of the view that Justice Rennie's reasons serve to inform my analysis of the reasonableness of the PRV Policy in the sense that, as s 56 embodies the precautionary principle, the Minister's Interpretation of s 56 must also be informed by that principle. This, in turn, informs the PRV Policy, which applies the Interpretation, and any decisions made pursuant to s 56 and the Policy.

[160] In any event, the Minister acknowledges that it is intended that the precautionary principle will inform all aspects of fish management including the PRV Policy. For example, the Wild Salmon Policy references Article 6.2 of the 1995 *United Nations Agreement Relating to the Conservation and Management of Straddling Fish Stocks and Migratory Fish Stocks* whereby participating states will be more cautious when information is uncertain, unreliable or inadequate, and that the absence of adequate scientific information shall not be used as a reason for postponing or failing to take conservation and management measures. The Wild Salmon Policy states that the precautionary approach identifies important considerations for management: acknowledgment of uncertainty in information and future impacts and the need for decision-making in the absence of full information. It implies a reversal of the burden of proof and the need for longer term outlooks in the conservative of resources. And,

The application of precaution in the WSP will follow the guidance provided to Federal Departments by the Privy Council Office publication entitled "*A Framework for the Application of Precaution in Science-based Decision Making About Risk"* (Canada, Privy Council Office 2003). That Framework includes five principles of precaution:

- The application of the precautionary approach is a legitimate and distinctive decision-making approach within a risk management framework.
- Decisions should be guided by society's chosen level of risk.
- Application of the precautionary approach should be based on sound scientific information.
- Mechanisms for re-evaluation and transparency should exist.
- A high degree of transparency, clear accountability, and meaningful public involvement are appropriate.

• • •

[163] That said, the precautionary principle does not serve to create or to provide Ms. Morton or 'Namgis with substantive rights, such as requiring the Minister to test or gather information on the presence of PRV or HSMI in salmon before a transfer.

[164] And while paragraphs 97 to 99 of *Morton 2015* establish that the phrase "may be harmful" does not require scientific certainty or that harm will even be the likely consequence of the transfer, in my view, not requiring scientific certainty does not equate to total absence of uncertainty as 'Namgis submits. Within the confines laid out by s 56(b), the Minister or his delegate maintain the flexibility to assess the risk of harm including by weighing DFO's scientific advice, other and contrary scientific reports, and factual considerations in order to determine the allowable level of scientific uncertainty in a given situation. The Court must defer to that conclusion as long as "the decision was made in accordance with the governing legislation and that it is a reasonable decision in light of the evidence and information which was before the decision-maker" (*Mountain Parks Watershed Assn v Chateau Lake Louise Corp.*, 2004 FC 1222 at para 17).

[165] The difficulty that the Minister faces in this matter is that his interpretation of the phrase "the protection and conservation of fish" contained in s 56(b) of the FGRs, [sic] ascribes a level of harm that fails to embody and is inconsistent with the precautionary principle. In the result, decisions made under s 56 that apply the [sic] PRV Policy, which adopts that Interpretation, are also made in derogation of the precautionary principle.

• • •

[168] ... I do not understand the precautionary principle to mean that the risk of any level of potential harm is acceptable until it reaches the level of serious or irreversible harm, such as extirpation. Rather, its focus is to exercise more caution when information is uncertain and, where appropriate, to ensure that steps are taken to prevent irreversible harm, even when the potential risk of causing that harm is uncertain.

[169] As stated in "Science and the Precautionary Principle in International Courts and Tribunals":

While preventive action involves intervention prior to the occurrence in relation to known risks, precaution involves a preparedness by public authorities to intervene in advance in relation to potential, uncertain or hypothetical threats. If the risk is sufficiently serious in character, precaution may posit intervention even where a risk is simply suspected, conjectured or feared.

• • •

[214] Further, given the high degree of scientific uncertainty surrounding PRV and HSMI, the rapidly evolving science, the outstanding DFO comprehensive risk

assessment, and the known decline in wild salmon numbers, the Delegate's failure to address wild Pacific salmon health and status in making the PRV Policy Decision also fails to embody the precautionary principle.

• • •

[317] In any event, I have found above that the Minister's Interpretation of s 56 of the FGRs is unreasonable. This is because it permits transfers of fish carrying a disease agent or of fish that are diseased to a level or threshold of harm to wild Pacific salmon at the conservation unit or species level, it fails to embody and is inconsistent with the precautionary principle, and it fails to take into consideration the health of wild Pacific salmon. As a result of that finding, the PRV Policy Decision will be quashed.

2. "Polluter Pays" Principle: Imperial Oil and Midwest

Persistent problems with ground oil contamination in a residential complex built on land near the city of Levis led homeowners to file suit against the Quebec government for inadequate supervision of land remediation. The Quebec government had granted a licence for the residential building project on land that had previously served as storage for oil tanks belonging to Imperial Oil Limited and on which oil had leaked onto the ground. In 1998, the Quebec ministry of the environment issued Imperial Oil a cleanup order to decontaminate the soil. Imperial Oil asked a provincial administrative tribunal to quash the order, arguing that it had been motivated by the provincial government's desire to reduce its civil liability. After the administrative tribunal had rejected the appeal, a Quebec Superior Court judge ruled in favour of Imperial Oil, but the decision was later overturned by the Quebec Court of Appeal. The Supreme Court relied on the "polluter pays" principle to reject Imperial Oil's appeal against the Court of Appeal decision. The majority relied on the principle in its decision that those who had given cause to the contamination should be the ones responsible for remedying it, emphasizing, however, that this IEL principle is now "firmly entrenched in environmental law in Canada."

IMPERIAL OIL LTD V QUEBEC (MINISTER OF THE ENVIRONMENT)
2003 SCC 58, [2003] 2 SCR 624

LEBEL J:

I. INTRODUCTION

1 This environmental law case arises out of the application of the polluter-pay statutory principle that has now been incorporated into the environmental legislation of Quebec. When contamination caused problems at a site that had been operated by the appellant, Imperial Oil Limited ("Imperial"), Quebec's Minister of the Environment (the "Minister") ordered Imperial to prepare at its own expense a site characterization study which would also include appropriate decontamination measures and submit it to the Ministère. Imperial challenged that order before the Administrative Tribunal of Québec ("ATQ"), without success. The Superior Court allowed Imperial's application for judicial review because the Tribunal had committed what were, in the Court's opinion, unreasonable errors in interpreting the relevant legislation. In addition, the Court held that a situation of conflict of interest in which the Minister found himself at the time the order was issued would have

invalidated the order in any event. Because the Minister had been involved in supervising earlier decontamination work at the site and a number of purchasers of parts of the site had brought action against the Minister in civil liability, he did not have the appearance of impartiality required by the rules of procedural fairness applicable to his decision. The Quebec Court of Appeal set that judgment aside. In the opinion of that Court, the nature of the duties imposed on the Minister created a state of necessity which justified a situation that would otherwise have breached the principle of impartial administrative decision-making. The appeal decision also held that the ATQ had not unreasonably interpreted the *Environment Quality Act*, R.S.Q., c. Q-2 ("*EQA*").

2 ... For reasons differing in part from those of the Court of Appeal, I would dismiss this appeal. The Minister had the authority to issue the kind of order at stake in the present case under the *EQA*. Accordingly, by reason of the nature of the duties assigned to the Minister by the *EQA*, he did not violate any of the rules of procedural fairness that applied to the execution of his power to issue orders. The concept of impartiality was raised, interpreted and applied incorrectly in this case.

• • •

V. ANALYSIS

• • •

23 Section 31.42 *EQA*, which was enacted in 1990 (S.Q. 1990, c. 26, s. 4), applies what is called the polluter-pay principle, which has now been incorporated into Quebec's environmental legislation. In fact, that principle has become firmly entrenched in environmental law in Canada. It is found in almost all federal and provincial environmental legislation, as may be seen: *Canadian Environmental Protection Act, 1999*, S.C. 1999, c. 33; *Arctic Waters Pollution Prevention Act*, R.S.C. 1985, c. A-12, ss. 6, 7; *Fisheries Act*, R.S.C. 1985, c. F-14, s. 42; *Waste Management Act*, R.S.B.C. 1996, c. 482, ss. 26.5(1), 27(1), 27.1, 28.2, 28.5; *Environment Management Act*, R.S.B.C. 1996, c. 118, s. 6(3); *Environmental Protection and Enhancement Act*, R.S.A. 2000, c. E-12, ss. 2(i), 112, 113(1), 114(1), 116; *Environmental Management and Protection Act, 2002*, S.S. 2002, c. E-10.21, ss. 7, 9, 12, 14, 15, 46; *Contaminated Sites Remediation Act*, S.M. 1996, c. 40, ss. 1(1)(c)(i), 9(1), 15(1), 17(1), 21(a); *Environmental Protection Act*, R.S.O. 1990, c. E.19, ss. 7, 8, 43, 93, 97, 99, 150, 190(1); *Pesticides Act*, R.S.O. 1990, c. P.11, ss. 29, 30; *Ontario Water Resources Act*, R.S.O. 1990, c. O.40, ss. 16.1, 32, 84, 91; *Crown Forest Sustainability Act, 1994*, S.O. 1994, c. 25, s. 56(1); *Environment Act*, S.N.S. 1994-95, c. 1, ss. 2(c), 69, 71, 78(2), 88, 89, 90; *Environmental Protection Act*, S.N.L. 2002, c. E-14.2, ss. 8(1), 9, 28, 29, Part XIII; *Environmental Protection Act*, R.S.P.E.I. 1988, c. E-9, ss. 7, 7.1, 21; *Environmental Protection Act*, R.S.N.W.T. 1988, c. E-7, ss. 4(2), 5.1, 6, 7, 16. (See R. Daigneault, "La portée de la nouvelle loi dite 'du pollueur-payeur'" (1991), 36 *McGill L.J.* 1027.) That principle is also recognized at the international level. One of the best examples of that recognition is found in the sixteenth principle of *Rio Declaration on Environment and Development*, UN Doc. A/Conf. 151/5/Rev. 1 (1992).

24 To encourage sustainable development, that principle assigns polluters the responsibility for remedying contamination for which they are responsible and imposes on them the direct and immediate costs of pollution. At the same time, polluters are asked to pay more attention to the need to protect ecosystems in the course of their economic activities.

25 ... The Act authorizes the Minister to issue an order when he believes on reasonable grounds that a contaminant harmful to the environment is present in a place

and may cause harm to human beings or the ecosystem. The order may be made against whoever is responsible for the contamination, including anyone whose activity occurred before the coming into force of the Act in 1990. As discretionary and broad as the power to make orders appears to be, nonetheless important procedural requirements circumscribe it. We must now examine them.

John Thordarson and his company, Thorco Contracting, stored waste petroleum hydrocarbons (PHC) on their property inappropriately, in breach of the approvals and compliance orders issued by the Ministry of the Environment and Climate Change (MOE). Contaminated groundwater with significant concentrations of PHC resulting from this illegal storage migrated from the defendants' land onto adjoining property belonging to the plaintiff, Midwest Properties. Midwest launched a claim against Thorco Contracting and Thordarson based on three causes of action: (1) s 99 of the *Environmental Protection Act*, RSO 1990, c E.19 [*EPA*]; (2) nuisance; and (3) negligence. The plaintiff was successful on all three actions at the Ontario Court of Appeal and was awarded full remediation costs based on the "polluter pays" principle, in addition to punitive damages. The Supreme Court denied leave to appeal the decision.

MIDWEST PROPERTIES LTD V THORDARSON
2015 ONCA 819, 128 OR (3d) 81

[6] In my view, the trial judge erred in her interpretation and application of the private right of action contained in s. 99(2) of the *EPA*. This private right of action was enacted over 35 years ago and is designed to overcome the inherent limitations in the common law in order to provide an effective process for restitution to parties whose property has been contaminated. The trial judge's interpretation of the section is inconsistent with the plain language and context of this provision; it undermines the legislative objective of establishing a distinct ground of liability for polluters. This is remedial legislation that should be construed purposively. It is important that courts not thwart the will of the Legislature by imposing additional requirements for compensation that are not contained in the statute.

• • •

[49] In my view, the trial judge's interpretation undermines the legislative objective of establishing a separate, distinct ground of liability for polluters. It permits a polluter to avoid its no-fault obligation to pay damages solely on the basis that a remediation order is extant. The purposes of the *EPA* would be frustrated if a defendant could use an MOE order as a shield. Such an interpretation would also discourage civil proceedings, and may even discourage MOE officials from issuing remediation orders for fear of blocking a civil suit.

• • •

[68] This approach to damages reflects the "polluter pays" principle, which provides that whenever possible, the party that causes pollution should pay for remediation, compensation, and prevention: see Pardy [Bruce Pardy, *Environmental Law: A Guide to Concepts* (Markham, Ont: Butterworths, 1996)], at p. 187. As the Supreme Court has noted, the polluter pays principle "has become firmly entrenched in environmental law in Canada": *Imperial Oil Ltd. v. Quebec (Minister of the Environment)*, 2003 SCC 58, [2003] 2 S.C.R. 624, at para. 23. In imposing strict liability on polluters by focusing on only the issues of who owns and controls the pollutant, Part X of the *EPA*, which includes s. 99(2), is effectively a statutory codification of this principle.

QUESTIONS

1. Identify other principles of international environmental law in Canadian court decisions.
2. How have these courts engaged with these principles?

V. CASE STUDY: INTERNATIONAL CLIMATE REGIME AND CANADIAN CLIMATE LAW AND POLICY

Climate change, caused by greenhouse gas (GHG) emissions from everyday human activities (heating, transportation, industrial production, energy generation, food production, etc.) is a global problem *par excellence*. Because all states are responsible for climate change, and all states are affected by it, unilateral action by one state or action by a group of states is insufficient. An international response is inescapable. The international community has reached broad political consensus that climate change needs to be addressed, although there have been disputes over how urgent the problem is, what the remedies should be, and which countries should bear what burdens and what costs of climate action. Since 1992, states have been negotiating international responses to climate change under the *United Nations Framework Convention on Climate Change* (UNFCCC). In 2015, they signed the *Paris Agreement* to strengthen the global response to the threat of climate change by keeping the global temperature rise well below 2°C above pre-industrial levels and pursuing efforts to limit the temperature increase even further to 1.5°C, increase efforts to adapt to the impacts of climate change, and steer global financial flows toward a climate-friendly economy. Canada is a party to both the UNFCCC and the *Paris Agreement*.

The Canadian domestic legal framework to address climate change, discussed in Chapter 6 of this book, has been heavily influenced by international climate change law, especially at the federal level. Jurisdiction to regulate climate change in Canada, like other environmental issues, is shared between the different levels of government, although it is fair to say that many of the human activities that produce GHG emissions are under provincial jurisdiction. One significant challenge for Canada has been to coordinate provincial and federal regulation on climate. The *Pan-Canadian Framework on Clean Growth and Climate Change: Canada's Plan to Address Climate Change and Grow the Economy* (Gatineau, Qc: Environment and Climate Change Canada, 2016), online: *Government of Canada* <https://www.canada.ca/en/services/environment/weather/climatechange/pan-canadian-framework/climate-change-plan.html> is presented as a collective plan uniting the federal government, the provinces, and the territories (and engaging Indigenous peoples) to support Canada's efforts to implement its *Paris Agreement* commitment to reduce GHG emissions by 30 percent below 2005 emission levels by 2030. One of the cornerstones of the *Pan-Canadian Framework* is pricing GHG emissions across the country to steer behaviour toward a cleaner economy.

The *Greenhouse Gas Pollution Pricing Act*, SC 2018, c 12, s 186 [GGPPA], entered into force on June 21, 2018, establishing a federal GHG emissions pricing scheme that ensures the existence of carbon pricing throughout Canada. GGPPA allows provinces to establish their own carbon pricing schemes, provided they meet specified minimum federal benchmarks. If these minimum benchmarks are not met, a federal pricing regime (the federal backstop) will apply. Despite having broad support from most provinces and territories when it was agreed to in 2016 (Saskatchewan and Manitoba being the exceptions), by 2019, the GGPPA was facing resistance from several provinces, including from new conservative provincial governments in the two provinces with the largest shares of GHG emissions in Canada: Ontario and Alberta.

Four provinces have presented legal challenges against the GGPPA. In 2018, the government of Saskatchewan presented a reference case to the province's Court of Appeal to determine whether the GGPPA is "unconstitutional, in whole or in part." In August 2018, the government of Ontario filed a reference case questioning the constitutionality of the GGPPA to the Court of Appeal for Ontario. In April 2019, the Manitoba government applied for judicial review of GGPPA before the Federal Court of Canada, arguing that the federal carbon tax does not fall under Parliament's jurisdiction. In June 2019, the government of Alberta filed a reference question before the Alberta Court of Appeal on the constitutionality of the GGPPA. The Alberta case was heard in December 2019.

Thus far, provincial courts in two jurisdictions have confirmed the constitutionality of the GGPPA. In 2019, in a 3-2 decision (*Reference re Greenhouse Gas Pollution Pricing Act*, 2019 SKCA 40), the Saskatchewan Court of Appeal upheld the constitutionality of the GGPPA on the basis that the legislation falls within the scope of the federal government's "Peace, Order and Good Government" (POGG) jurisdictional authority. On May 31, the Saskatchewan government filed its appeal to the Supreme Court of Canada. In a 4-1 decision, the Court of Appeal for Ontario (in *Reference re Greenhouse Gas Pollution Pricing Act*, 2019 ONCA 544) ruled that federal Parliament has the power to enact a minimum national price on GHG emissions under the *Constitution Act, 1867*, based on the national concern branch of POGG. The Ontario government filed its appeal to the Supreme Court of Canada in August 2019.

The excerpt of the Ontario Court of Appeal decision below shows how, in deciding whether or not the federal Parliament has the power to enact GGPPA, the court referred to the international nature of the climate challenge (1) to discuss the context of the federal legislation, (2) to interpret the pith and substance of GGPPA, and (3) to analyze whether GGPPA met the three elements of POGG.

REFERENCE RE GREENHOUSE GAS POLLUTION PRICING ACT
2019 ONCA 544

II. BACKGROUND

GREENHOUSE GAS EMISSIONS AND CLIMATE CHANGE

[6] Climate change was described in the *Paris Agreement* of 2015 as "an urgent and potentially irreversible threat to human societies and the planet." It added that this "requires the widest possible cooperation by all countries, and their participation in an effective and appropriate international response."

[7] There is no dispute that global climate change is taking place and that human activities are the primary cause. ...

• • •

INTERNATIONAL COMMITMENTS TO MITIGATING CLIMATE CHANGE

[22] In 1992, growing international concern regarding the potential impacts of climate change led to the "Rio Earth Summit" and adoption of the *United Nations Framework Convention on Climate Change* (the "*UNFCCC*"). The objective of the *UNFCCC* is the "stabilization of greenhouse gas concentrations in the atmosphere at a level that would prevent dangerous anthropogenic interference with the climate system." Canada ratified the *UNFCCC* in December 1992, and it came into force on March 21, 1994. The *UNFCCC* has been ratified by 196 other countries.

[23] In December 1997, the parties to the *UNFCCC* adopted the *Kyoto Protocol* [*Kyoto Protocol to the United Nations Framework Convention on Climate Change*, 11 December 1997, 2303 UNTS 162 (entered into force 16 February 2005)], which established GHG emissions reduction commitments for developed country parties. Canada ratified the *Kyoto Protocol* on December 17, 2002 and committed to reducing its GHG emissions for the years 2008-2012 to an average of six percent below 1990 levels. Canada did not fulfill its commitment, and ultimately withdrew from the *Kyoto Protocol* in December 2012.

[24] In December 2009, most of the parties to the *UNFCCC* adopted the *Copenhagen Accord* [Decision 2/CP.15 in UNFCCC, *Report of the Conference of the Parties on its fifteenth session, held in Copenhagen from 7 to 19 December 2009, Addendum, Part Two: Action taken by the Conference of the Parties at its fifteenth session*, UN Doc FCCC/CP/2009/11/Add.1 (30 March 2010)]. The accord recognized that "climate change is one of the greatest challenges of our time." Parties to the accord recognized the need to hold global warming below 2 degrees Celsius above pre-industrial levels and to consider the need to limit it to 1.5 degrees. Under the accord, Canada committed to reducing its GHG emissions by 17 percent below 2005 levels by 2020. Canada is currently not on track to fulfill this commitment.

[25] In December 2015, the parties to the *UNFCCC* adopted the *Paris Agreement*. The Preamble to that agreement recognizes that climate change represents "an urgent and potentially irreversible threat to human societies and the planet." Parties to the agreement committed to holding global warming to "well below" 2 degrees Celsius above pre-industrial levels and to make efforts to limit it to 1.5 degrees above pre-industrial levels. Canada ratified the *Paris Agreement* on October 5, 2016 and committed to reducing its GHG emissions by 30 percent below 2005 levels by 2030. Canada's commitments under the *Paris Agreement* were part of the impetus for the *Act*.

• • •

CANADIAN EFFORTS TO ADDRESS CLIMATE CHANGE

• • •

[28] Shortly after announcing the *Pan-Canadian Approach* [*Pan-Canadian Approach to Pricing Carbon Pollution*], and after extensive discussions with the provinces, Canada ratified the *Paris Agreement*. Canada is required to report and account for progress towards achieving a "nationally determined contribution," which Canada stated at 30 percent below 2005 levels by 2030.

[29] On December 9, 2016, eight provinces, including Ontario, and the three territories adopted the *Pan-Canadian Framework on Clean Growth and Climate Change* (the *"Pan-Canadian Framework"*), which explicitly incorporated the Benchmark. ...

• • •

III. THE GREENHOUSE GAS POLLUTION PRICING ACT

[33] The *Act*'s long title is: "An Act to mitigate climate change through the pan-Canadian application of pricing mechanisms to a broad set of greenhouse gas emission sources and to make consequential amendments to other Acts." The Preamble of the *Act* includes, among other observations:

[R]ecent anthropogenic emissions of greenhouse gases are at the highest level in history and present an unprecedented risk to the environment, including its biological diversity, to human health and safety and to economic prosperity.

• • •

[T]he United Nations, Parliament and the scientific community have identified climate change as an international concern which cannot be contained within geographic boundaries.

• • •

[A]s recognized in the Pan-Canadian Framework ... climate change is a national problem that requires immediate action by all governments in Canada as well as by industry, non-governmental organizations and individual Canadians.

[34] The *Act* puts a price on carbon pollution in order to reduce GHG emissions and to encourage innovation and the use of clean technologies. ...

[35] The *Act* does not apply in all provinces. Rather, the *Act* and its regulations serve as the "backstop" contemplated by the *Pan-Canadian Framework* in those provinces that have not adopted sufficiently "stringent" carbon pricing mechanisms. ...

• • •

V. ANALYSIS

• • •

CHARACTERIZATION—THE "PITH AND SUBSTANCE" OF THE ACT

• • •

[70] This step of the analysis requires an examination of the purpose and effects of the law to identify its "main thrust": *Reference re Securities Act*, 2011 SCC 66, [2011] 3 S.C.R. 837, at para. 63. The purpose of a law is determined by examining both intrinsic evidence, such as the preamble of the law, and extrinsic evidence, such as the circumstances in which the law was enacted: *Rogers Communications Inc. v. Châteauguay (City)*, 2016 SCC 23, [2016] 1 S.C.R. 467, at para. 36. The effects of the law include both its legal effects and the practical consequences of the law's application: *Reference re Firearms Act (Can.)*, 2000 SCC 31, [2000] 1 S.C.R. 783, at paras. 18, 24.

• • •

[73] Not surprisingly, the parties characterize the pith and substance of the *Act* in different ways. Ontario puts it broadly: "a comprehensive regulatory scheme for the reduction of greenhouse gas emissions from all sources in Canada." Canada describes it more narrowly, as the "cumulative dimensions of GHG emissions." During oral argument, Canada indicated that it would, if necessary, accept some of the characterizations proposed by the interveners, such as Canada's Ecofiscal Commission, which defined the matter as "the control of extra-provincial and international pollution caused by GHG emissions."

[74] Neither Ontario's nor Canada's proposed characterization is persuasive. Ontario's description is too broad and is designed to support its submission that the law effectively gives Canada sweeping authority to legislate in relation to "local" provincial matters, thereby excluding any provincial jurisdiction in relation to GHGs. Canada's definition is too vague and confusing, since GHGs are inherently cumulative and the "cumulative dimensions" are undefined.

[75] The Preamble to the *Act* provides insight into its purpose:

Whereas there is broad scientific consensus that *anthropogenic greenhouse gas emissions contribute to global climate change*;

• • •

Whereas impacts of climate change, such as coastal erosion, thawing permafrost, increases in heat waves, droughts and flooding, and related risks to critical infrastructures and food security are already being felt throughout Canada and are impacting Canadians, in particular the Indigenous peoples of Canada, low-income citizens and northern, coastal and remote communities;

Whereas Parliament recognizes that it is *the responsibility of the present generation to minimize impacts of climate change on future generations*;

• • •

Whereas the Government of Canada is committed to achieving Canada's Nationally Determined Contribution – and increasing it over time – under the Paris Agreement by *taking comprehensive action to reduce emissions across all sectors of the economy, accelerate clean economic growth and build resilience to the impacts of climate change;*

Whereas it is recognized in the Pan-Canadian Framework on Clean Growth and Climate Change that *climate change is a national problem that requires immediate action by all governments in Canada as well as by industry, non-governmental organizations and individual Canadians;*

• • •

Whereas some provinces are developing or have implemented greenhouse gas emissions pricing systems;

Whereas *the absence of greenhouse gas emissions pricing in some provinces and a lack of stringency in some provincial greenhouse gas emissions pricing systems could contribute to significant deleterious effects on the environment,* including its biological diversity, on human health and safety and on economic prosperity;

And whereas *it is necessary to create a federal greenhouse gas emissions pricing scheme to ensure that, taking provincial greenhouse gas emissions pricing systems into account, greenhouse gas emissions pricing applies broadly in Canada ... .* [Emphasis added.]

[76] The purpose of the *Act*, as reflected in its Preamble and in Canada's international commitments and domestic initiatives, discussed earlier, is to reduce GHG emissions on a nation-wide basis. It does so by establishing national minimum prices for GHG emissions, through both the fuel charge and the OBPS [Output-Based Pricing System] excess emissions charge. Its effect is to put a price on carbon pollution, thereby limiting access to a scarce resource: the atmosphere's capacity to absorb GHGs. The pricing mechanisms also incentivize behavioural changes.

[77] The *Act*'s purpose and effects demonstrate that the pith and substance of the *Act* can be distilled as: "establishing minimum national standards to reduce greenhouse gas emissions." The means chosen by the *Act* is a minimum national standard of stringency for the pricing of GHG emissions.

CLASSIFICATION

• • •

(ii) Singleness, Distinctiveness and Indivisibility

[110] The requirement of *Crown Zellerbach* [*R v Crown Zellerbach Canada Ltd*, [1988] 1 SCR 401, 1988 CanLII 63] that a matter be single, distinct and indivisible is designed to limit the national concern branch to discrete matters with contained boundaries. It is aimed at preventing provincial jurisdiction from being overwhelmed with broad characterization of areas of national concern, such as "environmental protection," "inflation" or "preservation of national identity": see *Crown Zellerbach*, at pp. 452-453, per La Forest J., citing Gerald Le Dain, "Sir Lyman Duff and the Constitution" (1974) 12 Osgoode Hall L.J. 261, at p. 293; and Hogg, *Constitutional Law of Canada*, at para. 17.3(c).

• • •

[116] The international and interprovincial impacts of GHG emissions inform not only the "national" nature of the concern, but the singleness, distinctiveness and indivisibility of the matter of establishing minimum national standards to reduce GHG emissions. Like the production, use and application of atomic energy, which was considered in *Ontario Hydro v. Ontario (Labour Relations Board)*, 1993 CanLII 72 (SCC), [1993] 3 S.C.R. 327, the matter of establishing minimum national standards to reduce GHG emissions is "predominantly extra-provincial and international in character and implications, and possesses sufficiently distinct and separate characteristics to make it subject to Parliament's residual power": *Ontario Hydro*, at p. 379. Moreover, like the strategic and security aspects of atomic energy, the connection between minimum national standards to reduce GHG emissions and global climate change "bespeak[s] its national character and uniqueness": *Ontario Hydro*, at p. 379.

QUESTIONS

1. How would the Ontario Court of Appeal have decided the jurisdictional reference questions if Canada had no international climate change obligations?

2. Can the federal government meet international climate commitments without the cooperation of provinces? How?

FURTHER READINGS

Alam, Shawkat et al, eds, *International Environmental Law and the Global South* (New York: Cambridge University Press, 2015).

Bodansky, Daniel, Jutta Brunnée & Ellen Hey, "International Environmental Law: Mapping the Field" in Daniel Bodansky, Jutta Brunnée & Ellen Hey, eds, *The Oxford Handbook of International Environmental Law* (Oxford: Oxford University Press, 2008).

Bodansky, Daniel, Jutta Brunnée & Lavanya Rajamani, *International Climate Change Law* (Oxford: Oxford University Press, 2017).

Carlarne, Cinnamon Piñon, Kevin R Gray & Richard Tarasofsky, eds, *The Oxford Handbook of International Climate Change Law* (Oxford: Oxford University Press, 2016).

Côté, Charles-Emmanuel, "Applying International Law to Canadian Environmental Law" (Paper delivered at a Symposium on Environment in the Courtroom: Key Environmental Concepts and the Unique Nature of Environmental Damage, University of Calgary, 23-24 March 2012).

Daniel, Anne, "Canadian Contributions to International Environmental Law on Chemicals and Wastes: The Stockholm Convention as a Model" (2018) Canada in International Law at 150 and Beyond: Paper No 10, online (pdf): *Centre for International Governance Innovation* <https://www.cigionline.org/sites/default/files/documents/Reflections%20Series%20 Paper%20no.%2010%20DanielWEB.pdf>.

Freestone, David, ed, *Sustainable Development and International Environmental Law*, The International Library of Law and the Environment Series (Cheltenham: Edward Elgar, 2018).

French, Duncan & Louis J Kotzé, "'Towards a Global Pact for the Environment': International Environmental Law's Factual, Technical and (Unmentionable) Normative Gaps" (2019) 28:1 Rev of European, Comparative & Int'l Envtl L 25.

Klein, Daniel et al, eds, *The Paris Agreement on Climate Change: Analysis and Commentary* (Oxford: Oxford University Press, 2017).

Knox, John H & Ramin Pejan, eds, *The Human Right to a Healthy Environment* (Cambridge: Cambridge University Press, 2018).

Saunders, Phillip M et al, *Kindred's International Law, Chiefly as Interpreted and Applied in Canada*, 9th ed (Toronto: Emond, 2019).

van Ert, Gib, "The Domestic Application of International Law in Canada" in Curtis A Bradley, ed, *The Oxford Handbook of Comparative Foreign Relations Law* (New York: Oxford University Press, 2019).

van Ert, Gib, "The Reception of International Law in Canada: Three Ways We Might Go Wrong" (2018) Canada in International Law at 150 and Beyond: Paper No 2, online (pdf): *Centre for International Governance Innovation* <https://www.cigionline.org/sites/default/files/documents/Reflections%20Series%20Paper%20no.2web.pdf>.

CHAPTER SIX

DOMESTIC CLIMATE CHANGE

Sharon Mascher

I. INTRODUCTION

As United Nations Secretary General Ban Ki-Moon said in 2007, climate change is the "defining challenge of our age." The scientific consensus, as articulated in the Fifth Assessment Report of the Intergovernmental Panel on Climate Change (IPCC), emphasizes that global action is urgently needed to reduce the greenhouse gas (GHG) emissions into the atmosphere ("Summary for Policymakers" in *Climate Change 2014: Synthesis Report, Contribution of Working Groups I, II and III to the Fifth Assessment Report of the Intergovernmental Panel on Climate Change* (Geneva: IPCC, 2014), online (pdf): *IPCC* <https://www.ipcc.ch/site/assets/uploads/2018/05/SYR_AR5_FINAL_full_wcover.pdf>). Absent significant increases in emission reduction efforts, the IPCC predicts an increase in global average temperature of between 3.7°C and 4.8°C above the pre-industrial average by the end of the 21st century. This, it emphasizes, "will lead to high to very high risk of severe, widespread and irreversible impacts globally." Even if global average temperatures are held at a lower threshold, the IPCC makes clear that long-lasting changes will be felt in all components of the climate system. Already, sea levels are rising, oceans are acidifying, disease vectors are changing, and weather extremes are becoming more severe and frequent.

In Canada, temperatures are increasing at roughly double the average global rate, with the Arctic temperatures increasing at nearly three times the global average. A growing body of scientific evidence indicates that existing and anticipated impacts of climate change in Canada include changes in extreme weather events such as droughts, floods, longer fire seasons, and increased frequency and severity of heat waves; degradation of soil and water resources; and expansion of the ranges of life-threatening vector-borne diseases, such as Lyme disease and West Nile virus. Melting permafrost in the North is also a concern for infrastructure and winter roads. The economic costs associated with increasingly frequent and severe extreme weather events will also be significant. According to the Insurance Bureau of Canada, insurance companies were paying out approximately $400,000 per year due to severe weather events up until a decade ago. Since then, that number rose to an average of $1 billion per year, with insurers paying a record $1.9 billion in 2018, thirty times the yearly average of ten years ago.

While there is widespread consensus on the scientific evidence of climate change, the solutions are much more complicated. The global nature of the problem demands an international response. However, the fact that implementation must take place at the domestic level raises both economic and equity concerns. Economically, countries adopting ambitious policies and measures to mitigate their domestic GHG emissions are exposed to higher carbon costs, and their energy-intensive and trade-exposed industry suffers competitive disadvantage. From an equity perspective, those countries and communities who have contributed the least to the problem, together with future generations, will feel the impacts of climate change most severely.

The international climate law framework, as discussed earlier in Chapter 5, is striving to direct global action on climate change. This chapter focuses on the Canadian domestic climate change mitigation framework, constitutional jurisdiction, and climate change litigation.

II. DOMESTIC CLIMATE CHANGE MITIGATION FRAMEWORK

This section gives an overview of climate change law and policy in Canada by reproducing extracts of articles by Nathalie J Chalifour and Jessica Earle (on Canada's federal response to climate change) and Sharon Mascher (on comparative carbon pricing law in four Canadian provinces) and introducing key aspects of the *Pan-Canadian Framework on Clean Growth and Climate Change: Canada's Plan to Address Climate Change and Grow the Economy* (Gatineau, Qc: Environment and Climate Change Canada, 2016), online: *Government of Canada* <https://www.canada.ca/en/services/environment/weather/climatechange/pan-canadian-framework/climate-change-plan.html> and the *Greenhouse Gas Pollution Pricing Act*, SC 2018, c 12, s 186 [GGPPA].

A. OVERVIEW OF CANADA'S DOMESTIC POLICY RESPONSE

NATHALIE J CHALIFOUR & JESSICA EARLE, "FEELING THE HEAT: CLIMATE LITIGATION UNDER THE CANADIAN CHARTER'S RIGHT TO LIFE, LIBERTY, AND SECURITY OF THE PERSON"
(2018) 42 Vt L Rev 689 at 704-10 [in-text references and footnotes omitted]

2. Canadian Policy Response

It would be an understatement to say that Canada's history in dealing with climate change has been disappointing. Although Canada endorsed the UNFCCC [*United Nations Framework Convention on Climate Change*, 9 May 1992, 1771 UNTS 107 (entered into force 21 March 1994)] from the beginning, the country's response to climate change has been characterized by much rhetoric and little action, with the federal government historically alternating between failing to meet its own targets and ratcheting them back to less ambitious levels. For example, between 1990 and

II. DOMESTIC CLIMATE CHANGE MITIGATION FRAMEWORK

2008, the beginning of the first Kyoto Protocol [*Kyoto Protocol to the United Nations Framework Convention on Climate Change*, 11 December 1997, 2303 UNTS 162 (entered into force 16 February 2005)] commitment period, GHG emissions in Canada grew by 24% relative to the 1990 baseline. This means that, rather than reducing emissions by 6% as promised in Kyoto, Canada allowed them to climb 31% higher than its Kyoto target. With no plan in place to meaningfully change this trajectory, Canada became the first signatory country to withdraw from the Protocol in 2011.

While the federal government continued to participate in UNFCCC proceedings after this withdrawal, its underwhelming climate change commitments continued. Under the Copenhagen Accord [Decision 2/CP.15 in UNFCCC, *Report of the Conference of the Parties on its fifteenth session, held in Copenhagen from 7 to 19 December 2009, Addendum, Part Two: Action taken by the Conference of the Parties at its fifteenth session*, UN Doc FCCC/CP/2009/11/Add.1 (30 March 2010)] in 2010, Canada opted to lower the ambition of its target, committing to reduce emissions by 17% from 2005 levels by 2020 (the Copenhagen target). This is not only less ambitious than the Kyoto target, but even further removed from the IPCC 2020 benchmark [that is, the reduction targets established by the IPCC scenarios to align with established temperature goals]. Canada's INDC [intended nationally determined commitment], submitted prior to COP21 [the 21st Conference of the Parties in Paris], promised to cut GHG emissions 30% below 2005 levels by 2030 (the Paris target). The Paris target translates to emissions of 523 Mt CO2e [megatonnes of carbon dioxide equivalent] by 2030, a far cry from the 367-458 Mt by 2020 that the IPCC 2020 benchmark requires, as illustrated in Figure 1.

FIGURE 1   GHG-Reduction Targets

Commitment Year	International Agreement	Level of Emissions in Commitment Year (in Mt)	Target	Target Translated into Emissions (in Mt)
1992	Rio Earth Summit	621	Reduce emissions to 1990 levels by 2000	613
2005	Kyoto Protocol	738	Reduce emissions to 6 percent below 1990 levels by 2012	576
2010	Copenhagen Accord	701	Reduce emissions by 17 percent below 2005 levels by 2020	620
2010	IPCC Emissions Benchmark	701	Reduce emissions to 25-40 percent below 1990 levels by 2020	367-458
2015	Paris Agreement	722	Reduce emissions by 30 percent below 2005 levels by 2030	523

Between 1990 and today, the Canadian federal government has established seven national plans aimed at reducing the country's GHG emissions based on the target of the day. Although the federal government enacted during that time some policies aimed at reducing GHG emissions, such as requiring greater fuel efficiency from vehicles, requiring a minimum content of renewable fuel in gasoline and diesel, and a commitment to accelerate the phase-out of traditional coal-fired electricity by 2030, all seven national plans failed to achieve their goals. The country's emissions have risen by approximately 18% compared to 1990 levels, instead of falling to meet various commitments. A comprehensive audit by the federal, provincial and territorial Auditors General in Canada recently concluded that Canada is not expected to meet its 2020 GHG reduction target, and that "[m]eeting Canada's 2030 target will require substantial effort and actions beyond those currently planned or in place."

Governments may point to a variety of factors to explain their repeated failure to implement their own climate change plans and meet their GHG reduction commitments, including the complex nature of the division of powers over GHG emissions and the abundance of fossil fuel development in the country—including oil sands—and the changing ideologies in political leaders. We will neither excuse nor discuss these here, though we will note that the level of response to climate change has varied across the country, with some provinces showing considerable leadership at a time when the federal government was winning "fossil of the year" awards in international negotiations.

Following the election of Prime Minister Justin Trudeau and the renewed Canadian participation in international climate negotiations in Paris in 2015, the winds of federal climate policy changed. Shortly after the Paris Agreement [12 December 2015, UN Doc FCCC/CP/2015/10/Add.1 (entered into force 4 November 2016)], the Prime Minister met with his counterparts in the provinces and territories and consulted with indigenous leaders to determine actions that would be taken to meet the Paris target. The result was the Pan-Canadian Framework on Clean Growth and Climate Change (the Pan-Canadian Framework). The Framework includes a range of investments, as well as commitments to phase out fossil fuel subsidies by 2025 and reduce methane emissions from the oil and gas sector by 40-45% below 2012 levels by 2025 (though note that the implementation of the methane regulations has been delayed by three years). Perhaps most significantly, the Framework establishes a national benchmark carbon price equivalent to $10 per ton in 2018, rising by $10 per year to $50 per ton in 2022. If provinces and territories do not implement a carbon tax or cap-and-trade program equivalent to the benchmark, the federal government will impose one in that jurisdiction. Even with two provincial signatures missing, getting agreement on the Pan-Canadian Framework was in many ways a major achievement in Canada, given the intergovernmental dynamics at play. However, there remain reasons for concern. Clearly, the Framework comes too late to reduce emissions in accordance with the IPCC 2020 benchmark. Even more alarming is that the policies in the Framework are insufficient to meet Canada's Paris target. Taking into consideration actions in place as of September 2017, GHG emissions are projected to be 722 Mt of CO_2e in 2030. With additional measures under development but not yet implemented, those emissions will decrease to 641 or 583 Mt in 2030, with the latter including purchases of international allowances. The bottom line is that under none of these scenarios will Canada meet its Paris target.

These projections also assume full implementation, something that may be justifiably called into question given the government's consistently poor track record on implementing its past GHG-reduction plans. Several elements of the framework have yet to be implemented at the time of writing, including the federal clean fuel standard and the national carbon price. Early indications suggest that adoption of the national carbon price will not be easy. For instance, the province of Saskatchewan has promised to file a lawsuit challenging the constitutionality of the national carbon price. Also, the province of Manitoba has released a plan that does not meet the carbon price benchmark. In addition, the federal government acknowledged that it will be delaying implementation of new methane gas regulations from 2018-20 to 2020-23. Although the government maintains the delay will not jeopardize chances of reaching the target of reducing methane emissions by 40-45% by 2025, many are skeptical.

B. PAN-CANADIAN FRAMEWORK ON CLEAN GROWTH: CARBON PRICING SYSTEMS, BENCHMARK, AND BACKSTOP

PAN-CANADIAN FRAMEWORK ON CLEAN GROWTH AND CLIMATE CHANGE: CANADA'S PLAN TO ADDRESS CLIMATE CHANGE AND GROW THE ECONOMY
(Gatineau, Qc: Environment and Climate Change Canada, 2016), online: *Government of Canada* <https://www.canada.ca/en/services/environment/ weather/climatechange/pan-canadian-framework/climate-change-plan.html>

INTRODUCTION

• • •

PILLARS OF THE FRAMEWORK

The Pan-Canadian Framework has four main pillars: pricing carbon pollution; complementary measures to further reduce emissions across the economy; measures to adapt to the impacts of climate change and build resilience; and actions to accelerate innovation, support clean technology, and create jobs. ...

• • •

PRICING CARBON POLLUTION

OVERVIEW

Carbon pricing is broadly recognized as one of the most effective, transparent, and efficient policy approaches to reduce GHG emissions. Many Canadian provinces are already leading the way on pricing carbon pollution. British Columbia has a carbon tax, Alberta has a hybrid system that combines a carbon levy with a performance-based system for large industrial emitters, and Quebec and Ontario have cap-and-trade systems. [The Ontario cap-and-trade program was cancelled in July 2018. See note 1, below.] With existing and planned provincial action, broad-based carbon pricing will apply in provinces with nearly 85 per cent of Canada's economy and population by 2017, covering a large part of our emissions.

The federal government outlined a benchmark for pricing carbon pollution by 2018 ... . The goal of this benchmark is to ensure that carbon pricing applies to a broad set of emission sources throughout Canada and with increasing stringency over time either through a rising price or declining caps. The benchmark outlines that jurisdictions can implement (i) an explicit price-based system (a carbon tax or a carbon levy and performance-based emissions system) or (ii) a cap-and-trade system. Some existing provincial systems already exceed the benchmark. As affirmed in the Vancouver Declaration [*Vancouver Declaration on Clean Growth and Climate Change* (3 March 2016)], provinces and territories continue to have the flexibility to design their own policies to meet emissions-reduction targets, including carbon pricing, adapted to each province and territory's specific circumstances.

SHARON MASCHER, "STRIVING FOR EQUIVALENCY ACROSS THE ALBERTA, BRITISH COLUMBIA, ONTARIO AND QUÉBEC CARBON PRICING SYSTEMS: THE PAN-CANADIAN CARBON PRICING BENCHMARK"
(2018) 18:8 Climate Policy 1012 at 1015-24 [charts and references omitted]

3. INTRODUCTION TO ALBERTA, BC, ONTARIO AND QUÉBEC'S CARBON PRICING SYSTEMS

This section briefly introduces the four carbon pricing systems.

3.1. THE BC CARBON TAX

The BC carbon tax took effect on 1 July 2008. As North America's first comprehensive, revenue-neutral carbon tax, its implementation earned BC international recognition as a global climate leader. Simple in design and application, [Brian C] Murray and [Nicholas] Rivers [in "British Columbia's Revenue-Neutral Carbon Tax: A Review of the Latest 'Grand Experiment'" (2015) 86 Energy Policy 674] described it as "perhaps the closest example of an economist's textbook prescription for the use of a carbon tax to reduce GHG emissions." A Pigouvian tax, the BC carbon tax imposes a direct price on each tonne of CO2 equivalent (tCO2e) resulting from the combustion of fossil fuel. ...

• • •

3.2. ALBERTA'S HYBRID CARBON PRICING SYSTEM

Alberta's hybrid carbon pricing system is comprised of a carbon levy and an OBA [output-based allocation] system. The carbon levy, which took effect on 1 January 2017, operates much like the BC carbon tax. [The Alberta carbon levy was repealed and as of May 1, 2019 no longer applies in the province. See note 2, below.]

The OBA component, the Carbon Competitiveness Incentive Regulation [Alta Reg 255/2017] (CCIR), applies to facilities with annual emissions of 100,000 tCO2e or more and commenced 1 January 2018. The CCIR replaces an earlier OBA system, the Specified Gas Emitters Regulation (SGER) of 2007. The SGER required covered facilities to reduce emissions-intensity (emissions per unit of production) by a specified percentage ... relative to their historic performance. In addition to on-site reductions, covered facilities met compliance obligations by purchasing Alberta-based offsets and/or emission performance credits (EPCs) (banked or acquired in the secondary market) or paying into a Climate Change and Emissions Management Fund (CCEMF) at a fixed rate per tCO2e ... .

The CCIR continues the SGER's emissions-intensity focus and retains the same compliance options. However, the CCIR requires reductions relative to a benchmark rather than historic performance. ...

3.3. QUÉBEC AND ONTARIO'S CAP-AND-TRADE SYSTEMS

Québec and Ontario's cap-and-trade systems comply with the WCI [Western Climate Initiative] program design recommendations. Each system establishes caps on the number of tradable allowances (equivalent to 1 tCO2e) available each year. The allowances are distributed to covered emitters through a combination of free allocations and auctions. At the end of each compliance period, covered emitters must submit allowances equal to their actual emissions. Subject to price containment mechanisms, the market determines the price for allowances and thus the price/ tCO2e emitted. ...

4. COMPARATIVE ANALYSIS OF KEY DESIGN FEATURES

4.1. COVERAGE

The BC carbon tax applies to GHGs associated with the combustion of fossil fuels purchased or used within the province, subject to specified exemptions, and the use of combustibles (peat and tyres) to produce energy or heat. Initially covering 77% of provincial emissions, this number has dropped to 70% as the result of increases in non-combustion emissions, particularly vented and fugitive emissions associated with the production of gas. ... If it was updated to include those vented and fugitive emissions that can now be accurately measured, the BC carbon tax would cover approximately 80% of provincial emissions.

Alberta's carbon levy applies to GHGs associated with the combustion of fossil fuel purchased or used in the province, subject to specified exemptions. In order to avoid double-counting, heating fuels used on sites subject to Alberta's CCIR are exempt. The CCIR, in turn, covers the combustion and non-combustion emissions of covered facilities. The CCIR alone covers 50% of Alberta's emissions, with overall coverage rising to 70-90% when combined with the carbon levy.

Similar in scope, the Québec and Ontario cap-and-trade systems cover the combustion and non-combustion emissions of industrial facilities with annual GHG emissions of 25,000 MtCO2e or more; electricity generators and distributors; natural gas distributors; and electricity importers. Both systems also cover fuel distributors. This captures the combustion emissions associated with transportation, both juris-dictions' largest source of emissions. Each system covers approximately 85% of provincial emissions.

4.2. PRICE AND PRICE CONTAINMENT MECHANISMS

The BC carbon tax commenced in July 2008 at a rate of $10/tCO2e and rose by $5/ year until reaching its current rate of $30/tCO2e in 2012. The carbon tax was frozen at that rate until a newly elected BC government increased the carbon tax to $35/ tCO2e on 1 April 2018, with that rate increasing $5/year until it reaches $50/tCO2e in 2021.

Alberta's carbon levy commenced at $20/tCO2e in 2017 and rose to $30/tCO2e on 1 January 2018. Alberta's CCIR does not set an explicit carbon price. As there is no limit on paying into the CCEMF for compliance, the cost of doing so—currently set at $30/tCO2e—establishes a ceiling price. There is no floor price. The price of purchasing EPCs and offset credits is set by the market. ...

In the Ontario and Québec cap-and-trade systems, the sale of allowances at auc-tions and/or in the secondary market sets the carbon price. In the first joint auction held by the linked Ontario, Québec and California systems in February 2018, the carbon price was $18.44/tCO2e. However, both systems use price containment measures, floor prices and soft ceiling prices, to provide market stability. The floor price for auctioned allowances is established by reserve prices, with the highest reserve price (including California's) establishing the reserve price in linked auctions. Rising annually by 5% plus inflation, the 2018 reserve prices for Ontario and Québec are $14.68 (CAD) and $14.35 (CAD) respectively while California's reserve price is set at $14.53 (USD). A "soft ceiling price" is created by holding back a specified percentage of allowances to create a reserve. ...

Linking Québec and Ontario's cap-and-trade systems with California to create a larger market also affects the carbon price. ... [R]ecent legislation amending California's cap-and-trade system to control allowance prices with a hard ceiling price and impose stricter conditions and limits on offsets to satisfy Californian compliance obligations post-2020 may increase the price of Californian offset credits, with consequential effects on the carbon price in Québec and Ontario.

4.3. EMISSIONS CAPS AND BENCHMARKS

The Québec and Ontario cap-and-trade systems set an absolute cap on the allowances available for distribution each year. The caps therefore indirectly set the carbon price. ...

The Alberta CCIR does not cap absolute emissions [although Alberta's *Oil Sands Emissions Limit Act*, SA 2016, c O-7.5 caps oil sands emissions at 100 Mt/year]. ... Rather, it incentivizes reductions in emissions-intensity through benchmarks that, where possible, set a single product-based benchmark that applies across each industrial sector. The aim is to create competition within each sector to reduce emissions intensity ... .

4.4. TREATMENT OF EITE EMITTERS TO PROTECT AGAINST CARBON LEAKAGE

The BC carbon tax initially exposed all energy intensive, trade-exposed (EITE) sectors equally to the carbon price. However, despite a lack of evidence of competitiveness impacts, the agricultural sector now receives rebates and exemptions and the cement sector receives transitional support. ...

The Alberta CCIR and Québec and Ontario cap-and-trade systems afford more special protection to EITE sectors. Protecting competitiveness in the EITE sector is a particular concern for Alberta. Eighteen percent of Alberta's gross domestic product (GDP) is generated from EITE sectors, with those sectors responsible for 22% of provincial GHG emissions. The fact that these large emitters "tend to be trade-exposed facilities" is the principle reason for their separate treatment under the OBA system, which is itself a means of minimizing competitiveness impacts for EITE. Under the CCIR, only emissions that exceed the benchmark are fully exposed to the carbon price. While creating an incentive to reduce emissions, as signaled by the carbon price, the cost-weighted (total per-tonne) carbon price is therefore much lower. The benchmark can be further reduced ... when a particular risk of carbon leakage is demonstrated across a whole sector. ... This OBA system therefore operates to create a subsidy on production. With a 1% tightening rate, sectors covered by the CCIR, whether EITE or not, will receive this subsidy for many decades to come.

The Québec cap-and-trade system uses free allowances to offer targeted assistance to covered EITE sectors. ... Free allocations in both systems are based on emissions intensity benchmarks and decline on an annual basis.

• • •

5. PAN-CANADIAN CARBON PRICING BENCHMARK: STRIVING FOR EQUIVALENCY?

The Benchmark sets the goal of "ensuring that carbon pricing applies to a broad set of emission sources throughout Canada with increasing stringency over time to reduce GHG emissions at [the] lowest cost to business and consumers and to support innovation and clean growth." To achieve this, the Benchmark includes criteria related to "common scope" and "increases in stringency." ...

5.1. "COMMON SCOPE"

For all carbon pricing systems, minimum "common scope" is defined by reference to the BC carbon tax. Carbon pricing systems are to apply "at a minimum to substantively the same sources" or to "essentially the same sources and fuels" as the BC carbon tax. ...

5.2. "INCREASES IN STRINGENCY"

• • •

The increases in stringency criteria in the Benchmark focus primarily on achieving equivalency of carbon price. The Benchmark establishes a minimum carbon price of $10/tCO2e in 2018, which rises by $10/year to $50/tCO2e in 2022 (the Benchmark carbon price). The Benchmark carbon price applies directly to explicit price systems (the BC carbon tax and the Alberta carbon levy) and to the fixed price compliance option in the output-based component of the hybrid system (payment into the CCEMF under Alberta's CCIR). ... Beyond this, the Benchmark also requires emissions-intensity standards in the output-based component of a hybrid system to "be at levels that drive improved performance in carbon intensity over the 2018 to 2022 period" and account for "best-in-class" performance. ...

Translating the Benchmark carbon price into Québec and Ontario's cap-and-trade systems is more complex. To achieve this, the Benchmark requires cap-and-trade systems to set declining (more stringent) annual caps between 2018–2022 [sic] that are less than or equal to "the projected emissions reductions resulting from the carbon price that year in price-based systems." ... Leaving aside the disparity in coverage, the accuracy of these projections will largely determine whether equivalency of carbon price is achieved between the BC, Alberta, Québec and Ontario carbon pricing systems.

In addition, cap-and-trade provinces—and only cap-and-trade provinces—must have an emissions-reduction target equal to or greater than Canada's 2030 target (30% below 2005 levels). ... [There is] no corresponding expectation placed on the overall ambition of Alberta and BC's climate policies, [which] raises clear equivalency issues. Notably, Alberta and BC both have large fossil fuel resources, emissions profiles that are not consistent with Canada's 2030 target, and carbon pricing systems that do not cap emissions. ...

1. The Federal Carbon Pricing Backstop: Greenhouse Gas Pollution Pricing Act

On June 21, 2018, the federal GGPPA received royal assent. The Act establishes the federal carbon pricing "backstop" system that applies to any province or territory that requests it or that has not implemented a carbon pricing system that complies with the carbon pricing benchmark.

The GGPPA adopts a hybrid carbon pricing system that operates in much the same way as the Alberta system described in the extract from "Striving for Equivalency Across the Alberta, British Columbia, Ontario and Québec Carbon Pricing Systems," above. It consists of two main parts: (1) a fuel charge; and (2) an output-based pricing system (OBPS).

Under part 1 of the GGPPA, the fuel charge is applied to 22 kinds of fuels that emit GHGs when combusted. The specific fuels and their charge rates are set out in Schedule 2 of the Act, with the charge rates set at $10 per tonne of CO2e (tCO2e) in 2018 and rising by $10/tCO2e annually to $50/tCO2e in 2022. The fuel charge applies to fuels that are produced, delivered, or used in the backstop jurisdiction or brought into the backstop jurisdiction. Generally, fuel distributors and importers will be responsible to pay the fuel charge. It is expected that this cost will be passed on to consumers when they purchase fuel. Under the GGPPA, all direct revenues from the carbon levy are returned to the jurisdiction of origin.

Part 2 of the GGPPA establishes an output-based pricing system (OBPS) for prescribed industrial facilities with annual prescribed GHG emissions of 50,000 tonnes or more of CO2e. As with the Alberta OBA, the GGPPA is intended to minimize negative competitiveness impacts and avoid carbon leakage while still exposing large industrial emitters to a price signal to encourage GHG reductions. Under the OBPS, industrial facilities are subject to an output-based emissions limit (that is, emissions intensity) for the sector. Industrial facilities whose emissions fall below the applicable emissions limit will receive credits, while those whose emissions exceed the applicable emissions limit must remit compensation. Compensation may be provided in the form of surplus credits earned in the past or acquired from other facilities, offset credits, or the payment of an excess emissions charge. The excess emissions charge is equivalent to the fuel charges in part 1. Revenues from excess emissions charge payments may be distributed to the province or persons specified in the regulations.

NOTES

1. Commencing January 1, 2019, Nova Scotia implemented a cap-and-trade system. Meanwhile, on October 31, 2018, a newly elected Ontario provincial government passed legislation to repeal the Ontario cap-and-trade system (*Cap and Trade Cancellation Act, 2018*, SO 2018, c 13). Meanwhile, through Bill 1, *An Act to Repeal the Carbon Tax*, a newly elected Alberta government repealed the carbon levy effective May 30, 2019.

2. Following an assessment of the stringency of the provincial and territorial carbon pricing plans against the federal benchmark, the Government of Canada announced that (1) the federal OBPS for large industry would apply in Ontario, Manitoba, New Brunswick, and Prince Edward Island, and partially in Saskatchewan, starting in January 2019; (2) the federal fuel charge would apply in Saskatchewan, Ontario, Manitoba, and New Brunswick starting in April 2019; and (3) the federal fuel charge and OBPS would apply in Yukon and Nunavut starting on July 1, 2019. As a result of the repeal of its carbon levy, Alberta now also only partially meets the federal benchmark stringency requirements. As a result, the federal government has announced its intent to implement the federal fuel charge in Alberta as of January 1, 2020.

DISCUSSION

1. Explain the key differences between a carbon tax, a cap-and-trade system, and a hybrid system that includes a carbon levy and an output-based allocation system.

2. All carbon pricing systems, including the federal GGPPA, exempt gasoline and diesel used for farming purposes. What is the rationale for the exemption of this sector?

III. CONSTITUTIONAL JURISDICTION

The extent of the federal government's constitutional power to regulate GHG emissions has been the source of ongoing discussion. In *Syncrude Canada Ltd v Canada (Attorney General)*, 2016 FCA 160, the Federal Court of Appeal held that the criminal law power can be used to support market-based emissions trading schemes or other pricing mechanisms. However, there remain questions as to the ability of the national concern and emergency branches of the federal "peace, order and good government" (POGG) power to support climate policy such as GGPPA (as discussed above), which directs provinces to take particular action to mitigate provincial GHG emissions.

SYNCRUDE CANADA LTD V CANADA (ATTORNEY GENERAL)
2016 FCA 160

RENNIE JA:

I. INTRODUCTION

[1] Federal regulations require that all diesel fuel produced, imported or sold in Canada contain at least 2% renewable fuel. Syncrude Canada Ltd. produces diesel fuel at its oil sands operations in Alberta, which it uses in its vehicles and equipment.

[2] Syncrude commenced an application in the Federal Court seeking declarations of invalidity of the regulations on constitutional and administrative law grounds. The Federal Court dismissed the application (2014 FC 776) and Syncrude appeals to this Court. For the reasons that follow, I would dismiss the appeal.

II. LEGISLATIVE AND REGULATORY SCHEME

[3] Section 139 of the *Canadian Environmental Protection Act, 1999*, S.C. 1999, c. 33 (CEPA) prohibits the production, importation and sale in Canada of fuel that does not meet prescribed requirements.

[4] Subsection 140(1) of the CEPA provides that the Governor in Council may, on the recommendation of the Minister, make regulations for carrying out the purposes of section 139. Regulations may be made prescribing the concentrations or quantities of an element, component or additive in a fuel, the physical and chemical properties of fuel, the characteristics of fuel related to conditions of use and the blending of fuels. Subsection 140(2) requires that the Governor in Council be of the opinion that the regulation could make a significant contribution to the prevention of, or reduction in, air pollution resulting from, directly or indirectly, the combustion of fuel. It was under this provision that the *Renewable Fuels Regulations*, SOR/2010-189 (RFRs) were promulgated.

[5] Subsection 5(2) of the RFRs requires 2% of diesel fuel to be renewable fuel. ...

[6] Subsection 272(1) of CEPA makes it an offence to breach section 139. If prosecuted by indictment, an offender is liable for a fine of between $500,000 and $6,000,000. On conviction for a second offence these penalties double.

• • •

III. THE DEVELOPMENT OF THE RENEWABLE FUELS REGULATIONS

[8] Toxic substances are defined in section 64 of CEPA as those which "... may have an immediate or long-term harmful effect on the environment or its biological diversity; constitutes or may constitute a danger to the environment on which life depends; or constitutes or may constitute a danger in Canada to human life or health." Greenhouse gases (GHGs) are gases which, when released, lead to the retention of heat in the atmosphere. Since 2005, six of the most significant GHGs have been listed as toxic substances in Schedule 1 of the CEPA. These include carbon dioxide, methane, and nitrous oxide.

[9] The Regulatory Impact Analysis Statement (RIAS) accompanying the addition of GHGs to Schedule 1 in 2005 stated that they were added as toxic substances

because, as concluded in the Kyoto Protocol, they "have significant global warming potentials (GWPs), are long lived and therefore of global concern [and] have the potential to contribute significantly to climate change." The RIAS also noted that there has been a substantial rise in GHGs "as a result of human activity, predominately the combustion of fossil fuels" which could lead to an increase in frequency and intensity of heat waves, that in turn could "lead to an increase in illness and death": *Canada Gazette, Part II*, Vol. 139, No. 24, (November 21, 2005), pp. 2627, 2634 [2005 RIAS]. The 2005 RIAS cited both the *Montreal Protocol on Substances that Deplete the Ozone Layer* 16 September 1987, 1522 U.N.T.S. 3 and the Intergovernmental Panel on Climate Change, *Third Assessment Report*, 2000 (Cambridge, England: Cambridge University Press, 2002) as the scientific and policy basis for the addition of the six GHGs. The Panel concluded that "there is sufficient evidence to conclude that greenhouse gases constitute or may constitute a danger to the environment on which life depends, therefore satisfying the criteria set out in section 64 of the CEPA 1999" (2005 RIAS, p. 2634).

[10] A Notice of Intent to develop the RFRs was subsequently published in the *Canada Gazette Part I*, Vol. 140, No. 52, (December 30, 2006). ...

[11] The "Rationale for Action" in the Notice of Intent stated that "use of renewable fuels can significantly reduce emissions" and that the projected environmental benefit of replacing 5% of Canadian transportation fuel would represent a reduction in GHG emissions equivalent to the emissions of almost 675,000 vehicles.

[12] The RIAS accompanying the publication of the RFRs in 2010 (*Canada Gazette, Part II*, Vol. 144, No. 18, September 1, 2010) stated that GHGs are a significant air pollutant and contributor to climate change. The stated objective of the RFRs was to reduce GHGs, "thereby contributing towards the protection of Canadians and the environment from the impact of climate change and air pollution."

• • •

V. ISSUES ON APPEAL

[20] It is important to define at the outset what is, and what is not, in issue in this appeal. Syncrude does not challenge the constitutionality of the enabling provisions—sections 139 and 140 of CEPA. Syncrude does not contend that the definition of "air pollution" in subsection 140(2) of CEPA is overbroad, nor does it contest that GHGs contribute to air pollution, and that their reduction is a proper objective of the criminal law power. Syncrude concedes that, if the dominant purpose of the RFRs were in fact to combat climate change, there would be no constitutional infirmity. Rather, the core of Syncrude's challenge is that subsection 5(2) is not aimed at the reduction of air pollution, but is an economic measure aimed at the creation of a local market, a matter within subsection 92(13), or is directed to non-renewable natural resources, a matter of provincial legislative competence under section 92A of the *Constitution Act, 1867* [(UK), 30 & 31 Vict, c 3].

[21] Syncrude advances two main errors in the decision below.

[22] First, Syncrude submits that the judge erred by considering subsection 5(2) in the context of the CEPA regime as a whole before examining the subsection in isolation. It also submits that the judge failed to consider relevant evidence beyond the RIAS which, in its view, points to the true and colourable purpose of the RFRs. Before this Court, Syncrude maintains its position that, properly characterized, the RFRs are an economic measure, and intrude on provincial responsibility for natural resources, or are colourable attempts to achieve those purposes. It further argues that the RFRs are not a valid exercise of the criminal law power because, as a

requirement of 2%, and allowing certain exemptions, they do not completely prohibit or ban the use of fossil fuels.

[23] Syncrude contends that the consumption of fossil fuels is not inherently dangerous and that this undermines the notion that the RFRs have a valid criminal law purpose. Syncrude contrasts the pollutants it cites as legitimate evils, such as lead and sulphur, with GHGs. As the judge noted, "[i]n Syncrude's view, there is no evil to be suppressed": Reasons, para. 79.

[24] However, as the respondent points out, Syncrude's submission at paragraph 66 of its factum that "the production and consumption of petroleum fuels is not inherently dangerous" is inconsistent with its concession that GHG emissions contribute to the evil of climate change. Syncrude's position is problematic and at times concedes the correlation between GHGs, global warming and the consumption of fossil fuels.

[25] Syncrude's second ground of appeal is that the judge erred in failing to conclude that the Governor in Council did not, and could not, hold the requisite opinion under subsection 140(2) that the RFRs would reduce air pollution. ...

VI. ANALYSIS

A. STANDARD OF REVIEW

• • •

[30] In sum, the question of whether subsection 5(2) of the RFRs is constitutional is reviewed on a standard of correctness. The question of whether the Governor in Council validly enacted subsection 5(2) pursuant to CEPA is assessed against the *Katz* [*Katz Group Canada Inc v Ontario (Health and Long-Term Care)*, 2013 SCC 64, [2013] 3 SCR 810] standard of inconsistency with the enabling statute. Any factual findings made by the judge in the course of his analysis are reviewed on a standard of palpable and overriding error.

• • •

C. CHARACTERIZATION OF SUBSECTION 5(2) OF THE RFRS

[38] There are two stages to the division of powers analysis. The first is an inquiry into the essential character of the law, or, as is often said, its pith and substance. The second is "to classify that essential character" by reference to the heads of power under the *Constitution Act, 1867*: *Reference re Firearms Act (Can.)*, 2000 SCC 31 at para. 15, [2000] 1 S.C.R. 783 [*Firearms Reference*].

[39] The characterization exercise is informed by both the law's purpose and its effect. Purpose is gleaned first, from the law itself, as stated by Parliament, but also from extrinsic sources such as Hansard and government policy papers ... . The purpose can also be informed by reference to the mischief to which the law is directed.

[40] Following identification of purpose, the inquiry turns to the legal effect of the law—how does the law operate and what effect does it have? At this stage, the court may consider both the legal and practical effect of the law. Having regard to Syncrude's argument, which is predicated on the ineffectiveness of a renewable fuel requirement, the language of the Supreme Court in *Firearms Reference*, at paragraph 18, is highly instructive:

> Determining the legal effects of a law involves considering how the law will operate and how it will affect Canadians. The Attorney General of Alberta states that the law

will not actually achieve its purpose. Where the legislative scheme is relevant to a criminal law purpose, he says, it will be ineffective (e.g., criminals will not register their guns); where it is effective it will not advance the fight against crime (e.g., burdening rural farmers with pointless red tape). These are concerns that were properly directed to and considered by Parliament. Within its constitutional sphere, Parliament is the judge of whether a measure is likely to achieve its intended purposes; efficaciousness is not relevant to the Court's division of powers analysis: *Morgentaler*, ... [*R v Morgentaler*, [1993] 3 SCR 463, 1993 CanLII 74], at pp. 487-88, and *Reference re Anti-Inflation Act*, 1976 CanLII 16 (SCC), [1976] 2 S.C.R. 373. Rather, the inquiry is directed to how the law sets out to achieve its purpose in order to better understand its "total meaning": W.R. Lederman, *Continuing Canadian Constitutional Dilemmas* (1981), at pp. 239-40. In some cases, the effects of the law may suggest a purpose other than that which is stated in the law: see *Morgentaler, supra*, at pp. 482-83; *Attorney-General for Alberta v. Attorney-General for Canada*, 1938 CanLII 251 (UK JCPC), [1939] A.C. 117 (P.C.) *(Alberta Bank Taxation Reference)*; and *Texada Mines Ltd. v. Attorney-General of British Columbia*, 1960 CanLII 43 (SCC), [1960] S.C.R. 713; see generally P.W. Hogg, *Constitutional Law of Canada* (loose-leaf ed.), at pp. 15-14 to 15-16. In other words, a law may say that it intends to do one thing and actually do something else. Where the effects of the law diverge substantially from the stated aim, it is sometimes said to be "colourable."

[41] The application of these principles to the regulation in issue leads to the conclusion that subsection 5(2) is directed to maintaining the health and safety of Canadians, as well as the natural environment upon which life depends. At the risk of repetition, the following points can be derived from the enabling statutory framework in support of this conclusion:

- The RFRs were enacted under subsection 140(2) of CEPA, which requires the Governor in Council be of the opinion that the regulation could make a significant contribution to the reduction of air pollution.
- Subsection 3(1) of CEPA defines "air pollution" as a condition of the air arising from any substance that directly or indirectly endangers health and safety.
- Six substances which comprise GHGs were added to Schedule 1 of CEPA in 2005. Section 64 of CEPA defines a toxic substance as one which may have an immediate or long-term harmful effect on the environment, or its diversity, or may constitute a danger to human life or health.
- Subsection 140(1) contemplates a wide range of regulations in respect of fuel, including "the concentrations or quantities of an element, component or additive in a fuel; the physical or chemical properties of a fuel; the characteristics of a fuel [...] related to [...] conditions of use; [and] the blending of fuels [...]" [ellipses in original].
- In imposing a 2% renewable fuel requirement subsection 5(2) is directed to the reduction of toxic substances in the atmosphere. The Order in Council promulgating subsection 5(2) stated that the regulation "would make a significant contribution to the prevention of, or reduction in, air pollution, resulting from, directly or indirectly, the presence of renewable fuel gasoline, diesel fuel or heating distillate oil."

[42] The RFRs impose requirements respecting the concentration of renewable fuels and thus limit the extent to which GHGs that would otherwise arise from the combustion of fossil fuel are emitted. GHGs are listed as toxic substances under Schedule 1 of CEPA. By displacing the combustion of fossil fuels, the renewable fuel

requirement reduces the amount of "air pollution" arising from the GHGs (toxic substance) which would otherwise enter the atmosphere. In sum, the purpose and effect of subsection 5(2) is unambiguous on the face of the legislative and regulatory scheme in which it is situated. It is directed to the protection of the health of Canadians and the protection of the natural environment.

[43] Resort to the RIAS confirms this conclusion. ...

[44] The September 1, 2010 RIAS expressly stated that the RFRs were aimed at a reduction of GHG emissions. ...

[45] The July 20, 2011 RIAS, (*Canada Gazette, Part II*, Vol. 145, No 15) notes at page 1429 that the Governor in Council was of the opinion that the proposed regulations "could, through the presence of renewable fuel, make a significant contribution to the prevention of, or reduction in, air pollution." It observed that "[t]he most significant source of GHGs [...] is the combustion of fossil fuels" and that GHGs are "the primary contribution to climate change": pp 1435-36 [ellipses in original]. The RIAS reiterates, at considerable length and in considerable detail the environmental and health benefits of a renewable fuel requirement.

• • •

D. SCOPE OF THE CRIMINAL LAW POWER

[47] In broad terms, the jurisprudence of the Supreme Court of Canada establishes a three-part test for a valid exercise of the criminal law power. A valid exercise of the criminal law power requires a) a prohibition, b) backed by a penalty, c) for a criminal purpose: *AHR* [*Reference re Assisted Human Reproduction Act*, 2010 SCC 61, [2010] 3 SCR 457]. Only the last of these is contested in the case at bar.

[48] Supreme Court jurisprudence as far back as the *Reference re Validity of Section 5(a) Dairy Industry Act*, 1948 CanLII 2 (SCC), [1949] S.C.R. 1, [1949] 1 D.L.R. 433 [*Margarine Reference*] has described the nature of the criminal purpose requirement as a requirement that the law be aimed at suppressing or reducing an "evil." Put in more contemporary language, to have a valid criminal law purpose the law must address a public concern relating to peace, order, security, morality, health or some other purpose (*AHR* at para. 43), but it must stop short of pure economic regulation.

[49] Protection of the environment is, unequivocally, a legitimate use of the criminal law purpose. The Supreme Court of Canada has held that "the protection of a clean environment is a public purpose [...] sufficient to support a criminal prohibition [...] to put it another way, pollution is an 'evil' that Parliament can legitimately seek to suppress": *Hydro-Québec* [*R v Hydro-Québec*, [1997] 3 SCR 213, 1997 CanLII 318] at para. 123 [ellipses in original]. In dissent although not on this point, at paragraph 43, Chief Justice Lamer and Iacobucci J. echoed La Forest J.'s view:

> To the extent that La Forest J. suggests that this legislation is supportable as relating to health, therefore, we must respectfully disagree. We agree with him, however, that the protection of the environment is itself a legitimate criminal public purpose, analogous to those cited in the *Margarine Reference, supra*. We would not add to his lucid reasoning on this point, save to state explicitly that this purpose does not rely on any of the other traditional purposes of criminal law (health, security, public order, etc.). To the extent that Parliament wishes to deter environmental pollution specifically by punishing it with appropriate penal sanctions, it is free to do so, without having to show that these sanctions are ultimately aimed at achieving one of the "traditional" aims of criminal law. The protection of the environment is itself a legitimate basis for criminal legislation.

[50] It is useful to recall that, in *Hydro-Québec* at paragraph 150, the disputed regulation was directed to "providing or imposing requirements respecting the quantity or concentration of a substance listed in Schedule 1 that may be released into the environment either alone or in combination with others from any source" and therefore was a valid use of the criminal law power. Subsection 5(2) of the RFRs operates in the same manner.

[51] More recently, in *AHR* the Supreme Court observed that pollution was one of the "new realities" facing Canada, and that Parliament needed flexibility in making decisions as to the types of conduct or activity that required the sanction of criminal law: para. 235.

E. THE INEFFECTIVENESS OF THE RFRS

[52] I turn to Syncrude's principal argument—that the RFRs are ineffective in achieving their purpose. Syncrude urges that "the evidence of practical effects of the RFRs overwhelmingly contradict the suggestion that the dominant purpose of the RFRs is to reduce GHG emissions."

[53] This argument does not succeed on either an evidentiary or legal basis.

[54] Syncrude points to evidence which suggests, on certain assumptions, that the actual reduction in GHGs arising from the transition to renewable fuels is illusory, and in fact, [*sic*] the RFRs contribute to GHGs. ...

[55] Suffice to say, the Governor in Council considered this issue and concluded otherwise. ...

• • •

[59] Syncrude contends that the evidence (which, as noted, is not compelling) that the RFRs would not in fact reduce GHG emissions is relevant to the characterization of the dominant purpose because it addresses *the legal and practical* effect of the provision. It contends that the evidence that the RFRs will not be effective in reducing GHGs is not addressed to the question of whether the provision is *in fact* efficacious. It concedes, correctly, that whether the measure is worthwhile or useful is not germane to the characterization exercise.

[60] This distinction simply seeks to circumvent the proposition ... that the effectiveness of the legislation is irrelevant for the purposes of characterization. There is no doubt as to what the regulations seek to achieve, how they operate, and their practical effect. The argument that there may be a better, more efficacious way to reduce GHGs does not alter the conclusion. ... Syncrude's argument that, because the RFRs are ineffective, an assertion which fails on the evidence, the dominant purpose must have been to establish a local market, fails.

F. THE REGULATION IS NOT AN ECONOMIC MEASURE

[61] As noted, Syncrude contends that the dominant purpose of the RFRs was to create a market in renewable fuels. The RIAS reveals careful consideration of the refining industry, transportation to the consumer, and the effect of subsection 5(2) on agriculture. There is also evidence that the creation of long-term demand for renewable fuels was an integral part of the strategy to reduce GHGs.

[62] It must be recalled that it is uncontroverted that GHGs are harmful to both health and the environment and as such, [*sic*] constitute an evil that justifies the exercise of the criminal law power. Syncrude concedes that GHGs are air pollution within the definition of CEPA. Nevertheless, Syncrude urges that subsection 5(2) is *ultra vires* because the government foresaw and hoped for the development of a market whereby more renewable fuels would be available for consumption, replacing

the consumption of fossil fuels which produce the GHGs. It also contends that the RFRs do not in fact, [sic] achieve the goal of reducing air pollution, indeed, it says that the renewable fuel requirement would lead to a net increase in GHGs, arising from the GHG emissions associated with the planting, harvesting, transportation and refining of bio-fuel crops.

• • •

[66] The environment and economy are intimately connected. Indeed, it is practically impossible to disassociate the two. This point was well-made in *Friends of Oldman River Society v Canada (Ministry of Transport)*, 1992 CanLII 110 (SCC), [1992] 1 S.C.R. 3, 88 D.L.R. (4th) 1 where the Court said "it defies reason to assert that Parliament is constitutionally barred from weighing the broad environmental repercussions, including socio-economic concerns, when legislating with respect to decisions of this nature."

[67] The existence of the economic incentives and government investments, while relevant to the characterization exercise, do not detract from the dominant purpose of what the RFRs do and why they do it. The inquiry does not end with proof of an incentive or market subsidy. Consistent with *Ward*, one must inquire as to the purpose and effect. ... Here, the RIAS (*Canada Gazette, Part I*, Vol. 145, No. 15, (July 20, 2011), p. 699) states the purpose of collateral investments in infrastructure costs related to the production of renewable fuels was "to generate greater environmental benefits in terms of GHG emission reductions."

[68] The evidence demonstrates that part of the objective of the RFRs was to encourage next-generation renewable fuels production and to create opportunities for farmers in renewable fuels. However, the evidence also demonstrates that a market demand and a market supply for renewable fuels and advanced renewable fuels technologies had to be created to achieve the overall goal of greater GHG emissions reduction.

[69] The criminal law power is not negated simply because Parliament hoped that the underlying sanction would encourage the consumption of renewable fuel and spur a demand for fuels that did not produce GHGs. All criminal law seeks to deter or modify behaviour, and it remains a valid use of the power if Parliament foresees behavioural responses, either in persons or in the economy.

[70] To close on this point, the consequential shifts in agriculture and the market for fuel arising from the renewable fuel requirement is not inconsistent with the dominant purpose of subsection 5(2) being the reduction of GHGs, with their uncontroverted costs to the health of the human and natural environment; rather, it reinforces the dominant purpose.

G. THE ABSENCE OF AN ABSOLUTE PROHIBITION

[71] Syncrude also argues that the RFRs cannot be a valid exercise of the criminal law power given certain exemptions in the RFR regime, and that in imposing a 2% renewable fuel requirement, they do not ban outright the presence of GHGs in fuel.

• • •

[73] A prohibition need not be total, and it can admit exceptions: *Firearms Reference* at para. 39 and *RJR-MacDonald Inc. v. Canada (Attorney General)*, 1995 CanLII 64 (SCC), [1995] 3 S.C.R. 199 at paras. 52-57, 127 D.L.R. (4th) 1 [*RJR-MacDonald*]. Indeed, environmental regulations often set limits, or concentrations of listed substances; so too do regulations of the food industry. Recall that in *Hydro-Québec* the majority observed, at paragraph 150, that regulations imposing requirements prescribing *the manner and condition of release or the source of release* of substances listed in

Schedule 1 to CEPA into the environment were a valid use of the criminal law power. Recall as well that paragraph 140(1)(a) of CEPA authorizes regulations respecting "the concentration or quantities of an element, component or additive in fuel."

[74] Syncrude points to the fact that the regulation is, in some circumstances, suspended during the winter due to technical challenges in blending traditional and renewable fuels. There are two answers to this, one legal, the other pragmatic. It may be that a criminal law requires exceptions in circumstances where a total prohibition would either be unjust or contrary to other interests which Parliament is charged with safeguarding. Many uncontroversial exercises of the criminal law establish a regime whereby, if certain measures or steps are taken otherwise-prohibited conduct becomes permissible. ... Indeed, other regulations made pursuant to CEPA, such as the *Gasoline Regulations*, SOR/90-247, sections 4 and 6, prescribe a maximum amount of a harmful substance that is allowed in fuel without prohibiting that substance completely.

[75] There is no constitutional threshold of harm that must be surpassed before the criminal law power is met, provided there is a reasonable apprehension of harm. Syncrude has no answer to the question of whether the RFRs become constitutional at a 10%, 25%, 50% or 100% renewable fuel requirement. There is no magic number. ...

[76] Turning to the pragmatic answer; if the winter exemption is engaged, the RFRs require a greater than 2% utilization during the summer months. The regulatory obligation is met by purchasing compliance units from another user. On a national basis, the net effect is the same.

[77] To conclude, Syncrude's argument that the regulation is invalid because it is not a blanket prohibition has no doctrinal support. Further, Syncrude concedes that other regulations, such as those limiting concentration of lead and sulphur in fuel are valid: *Sulphur in Diesel Fuel Regulations*, SOR/2002-254. Nothing distinguishes the prohibition of a certain amount of sulphur or lead in fuel from a positive requirement of a certain amount of renewable fuel in fuels. Both seek to prevent the emission of toxic substances, whether sulphur dioxide or GHGs, and both are addressed to the reduction of air pollution.

H. INTRUSION INTO PROVINCIAL JURISDICTION OVER NON-RENEWABLE NATURAL RESOURCES

• • •

[80] [S]ubsection 5(2) applies to Syncrude as a consumer of diesel fuel in its operations, not its production of synthetic crude oil. Syncrude meets the requirements of the RFRs by purchasing compliance units from another producer. The RFRs do nothing to affect the rate or timing of resource extraction, which Syncrude describes as its core business. Simply put, Syncrude stands no different than any other consumer of diesel fuel in Canada, whether a trucking company, a municipal transit authority or a contractor with a diesel fuel requirement. The RFRs are laws of general application, and not directed to the management of natural resources.

I. THE INDIRECT MEANS ARGUMENT

[81] Syncrude argues that the use of the RFRs to create a demand for renewable fuels which would in turn reduce GHG emissions is an indirect, and not direct, means of addressing GHGs. ... I have already found above that such creation of demand for renewables was not the dominant purpose of the RFRs. This suffices to dispose of this argument.

• • •

J. THE COLOURABILITY ARGUMENT

• • •

[89] The Supreme Court of Canada in *Hydro-Québec* made it clear that colourability requires Parliament's declared valid purpose to be a mere pretence for incursion into provincial jurisdiction. This is a high standard. Again, as in the case of characterization of the dominant purpose, Syncrude points to the evidence which it submits demonstrates that the government knew that renewable fuels do not in fact have lower life cycle GHG emissions. Syncrude also submits that the government understood that the RFRs would spur the development of a domestic market for renewable fuels, create collateral economic incentives to agriculture and industry to assist in the transition to planting and refining of biofuels, and have other positive effects on some sectors of agriculture. This, Syncrude submits, establishes that the primary purpose must have been to intrude into provincial responsibilities to create a market for Canadian renewable fuels.

[90] Here, however, the evidence supports the opposite conclusion. When the references in the evidence to the creation of a domestic market for renewable fuels is considered in its context, including the evidence that the purpose of subsection 5(2) in particular, [sic] was to make a significant contribution to the prevention and reduction in air pollution through a reduction of GHGs as well as the evidence that anticipated the market related consequences and goals were part of the strategy to reduce GHG emissions of fossil fuels, the colourability argument fails.

[91] Indeed, this observation highlights the degree to which the valid use of the criminal law power to protect the environment may have consequential economic effects. It would be extremely easy for Parliament to use the criminal law to protect the environment if Parliament had no concern for the economy; it could simply ban the consumption of fossil fuels. The challenge lies in protecting the environment while avoiding or compensating for negative economic side effects. In some cases, crafting the regime so as to mitigate the economic side effects may be the majority of the work. The fact that managing economic effects plays a role, even a large role, in a given law does not mean that the law is a colourable attempt to pursue an unconstitutional objective.

[92] Syncrude points to the concomitant capital incentives and subsidies to agriculture and industry to promote the renewable fuels industry as evidence that the RFRs were a colourable attempt to intrude into areas of provincial legislative competence. However, the analysis must go further, and inquiry must be made as to the reason and purpose which underlies these measures. When this is done, it is clear that their objective was to facilitate access to renewable fuels and spur the development of new technologies which would "generate greater environmental benefits in terms of GHG emissions reduction": *Canada Gazette*, Part I, Vol. 145, No. 15, (July 20, 2011), p. 699. As the judge observed, the creation of a demand for renewable fuels was a necessary part of the overall strategy to reduce GHG emissions, but it was not the dominant purpose.

[93] These consequential market responses do not detract from the dominant purpose. The RFRs were designed to combat the deleterious effect of GHGs on the atmosphere by mandating that a type of fuel that was foreseeably less GHG-emitting be used in at least 2% of the fuel supply. The evidence points overwhelmingly to the fact that the RFRs were in pith and substance directed to the reduction of air pollution by reducing GHG emissions from the use of fossil fuels.

• • •

VII. CONCLUSION

[101] I find that subsection 5(2) of the RFRs is *intra vires* both the *Constitution Act 1867* and CEPA and I would dismiss the appeal with costs.

NOTES AND QUESTION

In a reference before the Ontario Court of Appeal on the constitutionality of the GGPPA (court file no C65807), the Attorney General of Canada, in a factum dated February 8, 2019, argued (at para 2):

Parliament's enactment of the *Greenhouse Gas Pollution Pricing Act* ("*Act*") falls within its jurisdiction to legislate for the peace, order, and good government of Canada on matters of national concern. The cumulative dimensions of GHG emissions is a matter of national concern that only Parliament can address. The means chosen to address this matter, carbon pricing, is widely recognized as an effective and essential measure to encourage the behavioural changes needed to reduce GHG emissions. The *Act* sets national standards to ensure that every province and territory encourages this essential behavioural modification.

The Attorney General of Ontario, on the other hand, argued that regulating GHG emissions is not a novel federal power under the national concern doctrine.

In *Reference re Greenhouse Gas Pollution Pricing Act*, 2019 ONCA 544, the majority of the Ontario Court of Appeal held that the GGPPA was a valid exercise of the Parliament's POGG power and did not involve an unconstitutional intrusion into provincial jurisdiction. However, rather than accepting the argument of the Attorney General of Canada that the GGPPA's purpose was to regulate the "cumulative dimensions of GHG emissions," the majority identified the purpose of the law as "establishing minimum national standards to reduce GHG emissions." Given the nature of GHG emissions, the Ontario Court of Appeal was also satisfied that there is a need for these minimum standards to be satisfied by one national law rather than provincial cooperation—the most important element of the "national concern" test—because failure of one province to cooperate would carry with it adverse consequences for the residents of other provinces. The court was also satisfied that the impact on provincial jurisdiction is not so serious that it would "disrupt the fundamental distribution of power that characterizes Canadian federalism," since provinces retain the ability to design their own regulatory regimes, provided they meet the minimum national standards established by the GGPPA.

In a similar reference brought before the Saskatchewan Court of Appeal (*Reference re Greenhouse Gas Pollution Pricing Act*, 2019 SKCA 40), the majority also held that the GGPPA is a valid exercise of Parliament's POGG power, but it again disagreed with Canada that "the cumulative dimensions of GHG emissions" are a matter of national concern within the exclusive legislative jurisdiction of Parliament. The Saskatchewan Court of Appeal instead held, much more narrowly, that "the establishment of minimum national standards of price stringency for GHG emissions" is a valid exercise of Parliament's POGG power.

The province of Alberta has also brought a reference in the Alberta Court of Appeal, and the province of Manitoba has applied for judicial review before the Federal Court. The constitutionality of the GGPPA will ultimately be decided by the Supreme Court of Canada, which is scheduled to hear appeals from the decisions of the Ontario of Appeal and the Saskatchewan Court of Appeal together in January, 2020.

1. Based on the cases considered in Chapter 10, particularly *Friends of the Oldman River Society v Canada (Minister of Transport)*, [1992] 1 SCR 3, 1992 CanLII 110, 132 NR 321; *Ontario v Canadian Pacific Ltd*, [1995] 2 SCR 1031; and *R v Hydro-Québec*, 1997 CanLII 318, 217 NR 241; as well as the cases *British Columbia v Canadian Forest Products Ltd*, 2004 SCC 38, [2004] 2 SCR 74; and *114957 Canada Ltée (Spraytech, Société d'arrosage) v Hudson (Town)*, 2001 SCC 40, [2001] 2 SCR 241, which are discussed in other chapters, consider how you would articulate the arguments in both sides of the dispute.

IV. CLIMATE CHANGE LITIGATION

Citizens around the world are turning to litigation to force their governments to adopt more ambitious climate change mitigation goals or to implement national policies and measures to achieve mitigation commitments.

In the ground breaking ruling in *Urgenda Foundation v The State of the Netherlands*, HAZA C/09/456689 13-1396 (9 October 2018) (Hague CA), the Court of Appeal upheld a decision of the District Court, finding (at para 76) that the Netherlands is breaching its duty of care by "failing to pursue a more ambitious reduction" of GHG emissions, and agreed with the lower court's finding that the state should reduce its emissions by at least 25 percent by the end of 2020. After highlighting important scientific facts related to climate change, the court (at para 45) spoke of "a real threat of dangerous climate change, resulting in the serious risk that the current generation of citizens will be confronted with loss of life and/or a disruption of family life" and concluded that "the State has a duty to protect against this real threat."

Drawing on the success of this case, citizen-led litigation is also progressing against governments in the United States, New Zealand, Ireland, Norway, the United Kingdom, France, the European Union, Switzerland, Belgium, Colombia, India, and Canada.

In November 2018, ENvironnement JEUnesse launched a class action lawsuit against the Canadian government on behalf of all Quebec youth under the age of 35. The statement of claim, filed in the Quebec Superior Court, argues that by not imposing emission reduction targets that it knows to be necessary, the Canadian government has "undermine[d] the rights of all Canadians, but especially those of young people, who will have to live and survive with the consequences of the previous generations' neglect." Some of the questions that ENvironnement JEUnesse seeks to have decided in the class action are: "Does the Canadian government have an obligation to implement measures to prevent dangerous global warming and thereby safeguard the constitutional rights of class members under ss. 7 and 15 of the *Canadian Charter* (*Canadian Charter of Rights and Freedoms*, Part I of the *Constitution Act, 1982*, being Schedule B to the *Canada Act 1982* (UK), 1982, c 11) and 1, 10 and 46.1 of the *Quebec Charter* (*Charter of Human Rights and Freedoms*, CQLR c C-12)?" and "Has the Canadian government failed to meet this obligation, notably by adopting GHG reduction targets that it knows to be dangerous?" (unofficial translation of the Motion for Authorization to Institute a Class Action and Obtain the Status of Representative).

While this case will take several years to progress through the courts, it raises several novel questions to be considered by the courts. In the extract below, Nathalie J Chalifour and Jessica Earle consider some of the essential issues in applying s 7 of the Canadian Charter to the climate change challenge.

NATHALIE J CHALIFOUR & JESSICA EARLE, "FEELING THE HEAT: CLIMATE LITIGATION UNDER THE CANADIAN CHARTER'S RIGHT TO LIFE, LIBERTY, AND SECURITY OF THE PERSON"

(2018) 42 Vt L Rev 689 at 714-53 [footnotes omitted]

II. APPLYING SECTION 7 TO CLIMATE

According to section 7 of the Charter, "[e]veryone has the right to life, liberty and security of the person and the right not to be deprived thereof except in accordance with the principles of fundamental justice." As already noted, applying this guarantee to the facts of climate change raises more novel questions than a typical Charter challenge. For instance, there is the threshold issue of whether the Charter applies, given that most GHG emissions are emitted from the private sector. There is also the issue of finding the most appropriate claimants who would have standing to bring the case, since there are multiple ways to do so and the analyses would vary in each instance. ...

A. DOES THE CHARTER APPLY?

• • •

Section 32 of the Charter states that the Charter applies to "all matters within the authority of Parliament" and the legislature of each province. The Supreme Court takes a broad approach to this provision, finding that the Charter applies not only to laws and regulations, but also to government policies, programs, practices, and decisions. ...

[A]ctions of private actors can be subject to Charter scrutiny if there is a sufficient nexus between the action and government policy. What matters is that there is a "direct and ... precisely-defined connection" between a government's policy and the third party's impugned conduct. ...

While the majority of GHG emissions in Canada are created by private parties, most of these emissions are directly or indirectly authorized by government through permits, licenses, or regulatory standards for fossil-fuel extraction, development, transportation, or sale. In some cases, the projects responsible for the emissions are directly or indirectly subsidized by the government. The reality is that federal, provincial, and territorial governments authorize, enable, and facilitate the majority of GHG emissions in Canada: private actors would not be able to emit GHGs to the extent they do but for the active permission of the government. The fact that the government itself does not emit the majority of GHGs is not a barrier to a Charter challenge. What matters is that the government's policies allow, enable, and often encourage those emissions.

• • •

C. POTENTIAL CLAIMANTS

In light of the impacts of climate change and the above requirements for standing, it is possible to imagine a broad range of potential claimants for a section 7 climate challenge. Consider the following examples:

- An Inuit woman living in a northern community experiencing severe stress due to the inability to access (or leave) her community because of melting ice and permafrost roads;
- A First Nations man whose ability to hunt and provide food for his family and community is significantly compromised by changing weather and wildlife migratory patterns;
- A senior woman living in a large urban area experiencing respiratory disease and other health problems as a result of extreme heat waves;
- A woman experiencing PTSD after going into labor while stranded in her car alone during a catastrophic flood;
- The wife of a farmer who committed suicide after a period of depression brought on by repeated crop failure associated with extreme drought conditions;
- A coastal community, such as Lennox Island First Nation, where a receding coastline is threatening the community's homes, cultural rights, and future livelihoods; or
- A group of youth and a representative of future generations, similar to the plaintiffs in *Juliana* [*Juliana v United States*, 217 F Supp (3d) 1224 (D Or 2016)].

This list of potential claimants is extensive and diverse. A claim could be brought on behalf of one or a combination of such plaintiffs, or even by a public interest organization representing everyday citizens, as was the case in the *Urgenda* litigation [*Urgenda Foundation v The State of the Netherlands*, HAZA C/09/00456689 (24 June 2015) (Hague Dist Ct)] (where the plaintiffs were 900 citizens and a public interest organization). As illustrated by cases such as *Bedford* [*Canada (Attorney General) v Bedford*, 2013 SCC 72, [2013] 3 SCR 1101] and *Carter* [*Carter v Canada (Attorney General)*, 2015 SCC 5, [2015] 1 SCR 331], the ideal claimant is often a combination of a public interest group and a mixed group of individuals experiencing harms.

• • •

D. THE SECTION 7 ANALYSIS

A section 7 analysis typically proceeds in two steps. First, has the claimant's right to life, liberty, or security of the person been violated? If so, is the deprivation in accordance with the principles of fundamental justice? According to the courts, a deprivation can relate to one or more of the three interests at once. However, for ease, we will examine each in turn.

[The authors turn to examine deprivation of life, liberty, or security of the person in the light of the scientific record of the impacts of climate change on human health associated with extreme weather events, the expanding range of vector-borne disease and contaminated water supplies, air pollution, restricted ability to leave or access communities (particularly in the North), and interference with physical and psychological integrity.]

III. CENTRAL ISSUES TO A SECTION 7 CLIMATE CHALLENGE

As the preceding discussion demonstrated, climate change does and will continue to cause serious harm to Canadians. Yet those harms do not fit neatly into the grooves of typical section 7 analyses. In this Part, we discuss three central questions that will require the courts to be flexible and purposeful in their adjudication of a section 7 climate Charter challenge.

A. WHAT STATE CONDUCT TO CHALLENGE

A critical strategic issue in a section 7 climate claim is determining what government conduct created the infringement. In many section 7 cases, this is a simple issue because there is a single provision (e.g., a provision from the *Criminal Code*) or a single government decision or action that allegedly violates someone's right to life, liberty, or security of the person. A climate claim is more complicated because plaintiffs have many ways to frame the infringement, and the choice of framing may determine the outcome of the case.

For example, plaintiffs could take a conventional approach and challenge a single, specific decision (e.g., the authorization of a major fossil-fuel extraction project or the building of a fossil-fuel pipeline), which they would argue leads to harmful levels of GHG emissions. However, governments might escape responsibility if plaintiffs only challenge a single decision by pointing to the limited impact of that one decision.

It would be more compelling to focus attention on the network of policies, plans, and decisions that cumulatively cause harm. For instance, the Canadian government routinely grants permits and licenses authorizing activities that emit GHGs, such as oil and gas extraction projects, refineries, and pipelines. The government has a long history of financing a wide range of fossil-fuel activity, including exploration, development, extraction, production, consumption, and exportation. Plaintiffs could frame the lawsuit around a series of government decisions to authorize, allow, enable, encourage, and subsidize fossil-fuel exploration, development, and exploitation at a level that collectively and over time has the effect of contributing to harmful levels of emissions. This is similar to the plaintiffs' approach in *Juliana*. Professor Lynda Collins's ["Safeguarding the Longue Durée: Environmental Rights in the Canadian Constitution" (2015) 71 SCLR (2d) 519] description of the potential for these types of decisions to constitute "state-sponsored environmental harm" offers a tidy way to characterize a variety of overt government decisions that could be the basis of a section 7 violation.

Plaintiffs could also frame the claim as a failure on the part of the federal government to meet its international and national commitments to reduce GHG emissions and avoid dangerous levels of warming. Relatedly, plaintiffs could orient the claim around the federal government's repeated failure to meet its own GHG-reduction targets—especially when those targets are already less than what the IPCC has said was necessary for developed countries to avoid dangerous levels of warming. A claim might also focus on the government's ineffective implementation of GHG-reduction plans. This would be similar to the claims made in *Urgenda* or *Leghari* [*Leghari v Federation of Pakistan*, WP No 25501/2015 (Lahore H Ct)], which focused on the inadequacy of the government's response to climate change. Framing a Charter challenge in terms of government inaction, however, adds a level of difficulty to the claim.

Finally, plaintiffs could argue that governments have a positive duty to take actions necessary to provide a stable climate or avoid dangerous levels of GHG emissions. However, this opens up the Pandora's box of debate around positive obligations and the inclusion of socio-economic rights in the Charter.

[The authors proceed to a detailed examination of each option in turn.]

B. THE EVIDENTIARY BURDEN AND CAUSATION CHALLENGE

Causation has been a challenge in many environmental cases. However, the same problems that arise in establishing causation in those cases may not arise in the context of a climate challenge. ...

1. The Challenge of Establishing Causation in Environmental Cases

In evaluating the issue of causation, courts must remember that the burden of proof is a balance of probabilities, meaning claimants are only required to prove that it is more likely than not that the government's actions or lack of action is causing climate change harm. The causation threshold in Charter cases is lower than the but-for causation test used in torts cases. Chief Justice McLachlin [in *Bedford*] underlined the importance of being flexible in applying the evidentiary thresholds for section 7, noting that all that is required is a sufficient causal connection, as this is "a fair and workable threshold for ... the port of entry for [section] 7 claims." The Court recognized that holding otherwise would risk barring meritorious lawsuits.

While it is true that environmental rights cases under section 7 have, to date, failed on causation, a closer look suggests causation is not the barrier it might appear to be. ...

• • •

3. Causation in a Climate Case

Given the Supreme Court's emphasis on flexibility and drawing inferences, we are of the view that causation should not be a major hurdle in climate cases. Even if the more stringent standard from *Operation Dismantle* [*Operation Dismantle v The Queen*, [1985] 1 SCR 441, 1985 CanLII 74] is used, claimants would likely succeed. In contrast to fear of missile testing leading to nuclear war, there is clear evidence that GHG emissions cause harm. As noted earlier, there is a thorough and robust evidentiary record, signed off on by governments, which clearly outlines the science of climate change and its impacts. For instance, the IPCC's latest assessment report shows that: (1) climate change is caused by anthropogenic GHG emissions; (2) those emissions are leading to warming of average surface temperatures; (3) this warming has many impacts, including rising sea levels, ocean acidification, and increased severity and frequency of extreme weather events, from wildfires to droughts to floods; and (4) these impacts will have many negative implications, including increased mortality and negative human health effects. The causal connection between GHG emissions and harm is thus clearly established in the IPCC's reports.

Claimants have an even stronger chance of succeeding if the more flexible standard articulated in *Bedford* is used, which allows judges to consider strong statistical data and expert evidence to make the link between global warming and harm. As per *Kelly* [*Kelly v Alberta (Energy Resources Conservation Board)*, 2011 ABCA 325] and *Domke* [*Domke v Alberta (Energy Resources Conservation Board)*, 2008 ABCA 232], claimants would have a particularly strong case because the government's own documents outline the level of unacceptable climate-change risk, while the government itself engages in action and inaction that exacerbates this risk.

The federal government has essentially laid the evidentiary foundation for climate claimants since it explicitly recognizes its responsibility to reduce GHG emissions and has articulated its obligations in the form of specific mitigation targets, yet repeatedly failed to meet this target while still underscoring the grave risks and harms that climate change causes. Additionally, the federal government has selected a mitigation target that is below the threshold required for Canada to do its part in avoiding crossing the global 2°C threshold. The Dutch court in the *Urgenda* decision relied upon a similar set of evidence to hold the government accountable, and we believe Canadian courts should use this threshold as well since it quantifies what Canada must do to avoid dangerous levels of climate change.

In addition, the Supreme Court has made clear that claimants establish a section 7 breach when they present prima facie evidence that government action exposes them to substantial risk of harm. As such, there is no requirement that the claimant provide proof that the harm will actually occur. Translated into a climate change context, claimants will meet their burden of proof when they show that the government's conduct, both over the last 25 years and in the present, exposes them to a substantial risk of harm; they do not need to meet the more difficult burden of showing a direct cause-and-effect relationship between government action and specific harm that has already taken place. Notably, government conduct does not have to be the only or dominant cause of the harm, which is important for a climate case because all nations contribute to the problem. ...

• • •

Even with the strong evidentiary foundation for climate change, there are two arguments that the government would likely raise to avoid a finding that it has violated the Charter. First, in cases concerning extreme weather events, it could argue that, while climate change contributes to increased severity and frequency of storms, it is impossible to conclusively say that any one particular flood or storm was attributable to climate change (the attribution problem). Second, it could argue that Canada contributes only a small proportion of global GHG emissions, and thus it is not responsible for resulting harm (the *de minimis* argument).

While it is clear that climate change is causing more frequent and severe weather, and that the science is rapidly evolving, it may still be challenging to definitively tie one particular event to climate change since some extreme weather events would have happened even in the absence of warming temperatures. However, there is very clear science showing that the probability of extreme weather events and their severity have both increased as a result of GHG emissions. As such, a plaintiff whose claim is based on the harm caused by one particular extreme weather event might have a greater challenge establishing causation than a plaintiff whose claim is based on the harms caused by more systemic, widespread damage such as rising sea levels, overall patterns of change in weather, or serious risks to physical and psychological health (e.g., children who are not yet harmed but for whom the risk of harm is serious). However, as the weather attribution science matures, this evidentiary threshold will become easier to meet.

The argument that the Canadian government should be able to avoid responsibility because it is only one of many contributors to the global problem of climate change should also fail. The Dutch government raised this *de minimis* argument in the *Urgenda* case, suggesting that it should not be forced to reduce its emissions because doing so would have a trivial impact on a global scale. The Court rejected this argument, finding "that a sufficient causal link can be assumed to exist between the Dutch greenhouse gas emissions, global climate change and the effects (now and in the future) on the Dutch living climate." The Court emphasized that there is political consensus with regards to the 2°C threshold for preventing "hazardous climate change" and held that the Netherlands must make mitigation efforts that contribute to avoiding this threshold. As such, because the Dutch GHG emissions were contributing to climate change, the State's actions were part of the problem, which was sufficient to establish fault. This approach in some ways mirrors the way tort law addresses the problem of multiple causal agents, holding that, in cases involving scientific uncertainty, a wrongdoer may be held liable on proof of a material contribution to the risk of harm that ultimately befell the plaintiff. This risk-based approach meshes well with jurisprudence that has already recognized that section 7 of the Charter may be violated by serious state-sponsored risk to life or health.

We argue Canadian courts should adopt a similar tack in deciding a climate-change Charter challenge. Although at 1.6%, Canada's emissions as a proportion of global emissions might be argued to be relatively small and thus insignificant, Canada is still among the top ten global emitters of GHGs on an absolute basis, and in the top three on a per capita basis. Cast in this light, any argument that Canada's contribution is so minor that it should absolve the country of its responsibility to do its share to mitigate emissions and solve a global problem is irresponsible and unjust. It would be unconscionable for a wealthy, privileged nation that bears responsibility for creating the problem of climate change—a problem that is wreaking havoc in small island states and less developed countries—to argue that it is not accountable to do its part in addressing climate change. This argument would also fly in the face of public statements made by the Canadian government about the importance of taking action.

NOTES

1. In *Turp v Canada (Justice)*, 2012 FC 893, the claimants challenged the federal government's decision to pull out of the Kyoto Protocol, alleging that this decision was contrary to the *Kyoto Protocol Implementation Act*, SC 2007, c 30, and violated the rule of law, the principle of separation of powers, and the democratic principle. The Federal Court upheld the government's decision, reasoning (at para 18) that the Act had not limited the royal prerogative (as it might have by way of clear language) and that the government had acted pursuant to the royal prerogative, under which "the conduct of foreign affairs and international relations, including the decision to conclude or withdraw from a treaty, falls exclusively under the executive branch of government." Consequently, the separation of powers was not violated as the executive retained authority to withdraw (see para 28). Significantly in *Turp,* the Federal Court (at para 18) held "[i]n the absence of a Charter challenge" it appears a decision made in the exercise of prerogative powers would not be justiciable.

2. Governments are not the only focus of climate change litigation. Individual citizens, municipalities, and states have also commenced actions against corporations responsible for significant GHG emissions, seeking damages for climate change-related harms.

QUESTIONS

1. Does a private action based on negligence and/or nuisance against corporations raise different questions relating to causation than an action based on the Charter does? See, for example, *Native Village of Kivalina v ExxonMobil Corp*, 663 F Supp (2d) 863 at 870 (ND Cal 2009).

2. If climate change mitigation is the desired goal, is climate change litigation more appropriately directed at governments or corporations? Or is there a role for both?

3. In *Environnement Jeunesse (ENJEU) v Attorney General of Canada*, 2019 QCCS 2885, the Quebec Superior Court held that an application to bring a class action against the Canadian government alleging a violation of rights under the Canadian Charter and the Quebec Charter for failing to take adequate action to prevent climate action should not be authorized. The decision, which is subject to appeal, was based on a finding that ENJEU had not established a factual or rational justification for the class—which is made up of Quebec residents aged 35 and under. In coming to this conclusion, Justice Morrison reasoned that all residents of Quebec who have reached the age of majority will share an increased burden from climate change and the choice of class was therefore arbitrary, subjective and inappropriate. In light of the Chalifour and Earle reasoning, how would you frame the class?

4. On October 25, 2019, 15 youths ranging in age from 11 to 18 and coming from eight provinces and the Northwest Territories commenced an action against the Canadian government, alleging that the government is violating their rights to life, liberty, and security of the person under s 7 of the Charter and, given the disproportionate effect of climate change on youths and future generations, also violating their rights to equality under s 15 of the Charter. The youths are also alleging the Canadian government is failing to protect essential public trust resources. What are choices in the statement of claim filed in *La Rose v Her Majesty the Queen* (25 October 2019), Vancouver T-1750-19 (BCFC) regarding the choice of claimants and the state conduct challenged? How is causation addressed?

FURTHER READINGS

Secondary Sources

Chalifour, Nathalie J, "Jurisdictional Wrangling over Climate Policy in the Canadian Federation: Key Issues in the Provincial Constitutional Challenges to Parliament's Greenhouse Gas Pollution Pricing Act" (2019) 50:2 Ottawa L Rev 157.

Gage, Andrew & Michael Byers, *Payback Time? What the Internationalization of Climate Litiga-tion Could Mean for Canadian Oil and Gas Companies* (Ottawa: Canadian Centre for Policy Alternatives, 2014), online (pdf): *West Coast Environmental Law* <https://www.wcel.org/sites/default/files/publications/Payback%20Time.pdf>.

Gorrie, Melissa, "Addressing the Elephant in the Climate Change Room: Using the Law to Reduce Individual and Household Consumption" (2018) 31:2 J Envtl L & Prac 137.

Klaudt, Dustin, "Can Canada's 'Living Tree' Constitution and Lessons from Foreign Climate Liti-gation Seed Climate Justice and Remedy Climate Change?" (2018) 31:3 J Envtl L & Prac 185.

Olszynski, Martin, Sharon Mascher & Meinhard Doelle, "From Smokes to Smokestacks: Lessons from Tobacco for the Future of Climate Change Liability" (2017) 30:1 Geo Envtl L Rev 1.

Pan-Canadian Framework on Clean Growth and Climate Change: Canada's Plan to Address Climate Change and Grow the Economy (Gatineau, Qc: Environment and Climate Change Canada, 2016), online: *Government of Canada* <https://www.canada.ca/en/services/environment/weather/climatechange/pan-canadian-framework/climate-change-plan.html>.

Stein, Eleanor & Alex Geert Castermans, "Case Comment—Urgenda v. The State of the Neth-erlands: The 'Reflex Effect'—Climate Change, Human Rights, and the Expanding Definitions of the Duty of Care" (2017) 13:2 McGill J Sustainable Development L 303.

Legislation

Bill 37, *Liability for Climate-Related Harms Act, 2018*, 1st Sess, 42nd Parl, Ontario, 2018 (sec-ond reading, lost on division 25 October 2018).

Carbon Competitiveness Incentive Regulation, Alta Reg 255/2017.

Carbon Tax Act, SBC 2008, c 40.

Determination of annual caps on greenhouse gas emission units relating to the cap-and-trade system for greenhouse gas emission allowances for the 2013-2020 period, OC 1185-2012, (2012) Q Gaz II, 3612.

Greenhouse Gas Pollution Pricing Act, SC 2018, c 12, s 186.

Cases

Leghari v Federation of Pakistan, WP No 25501/2015 (Lahore H Ct).

Native Village of Kivalina v ExxonMobil Corp, 663 F Supp (2d) 863 (ND Cal 2009).

Reference re Greenhouse Gas Pollution Pricing Act, 2019 SKCA 40.

Urgenda Foundation v The State of the Netherlands, HAZA C/09/00456689 (24 June 2015) (Hague Dist Ct), aff'd HAZA C/09/456689 13-1396 (9 October 2018) (Hague CA).

CHAPTER SEVEN

THE WATER – ENERGY – FOOD NEXUS

Damilola S Olawuyi and Walters Nsoh

I. OVERVIEW

This chapter examines the inextricable linkages between water, energy, and food (WEF) systems and how the sustainable functioning of one depends on the other. It reviews frameworks and models that have been proposed in international, regional, and domestic law to help policy-makers understand the complexity of the nexus and to increase synergies between those regulating these resources. It then discusses the need for greater integration and coordination of governance efforts aimed at addressing WEF scarcities. Accordingly, this chapter examines hybrid approaches for addressing some of the sectoral environmental issues identified in other chapters in this book.

An underlying theme of the chapter, therefore, is that enhanced levels of legislation and rule linkage, elaboration of common and shared principles by institutional actors in WEF domains, as well as integration of WEF-related decision-making and administration both internally (for example, through the creation of one single regulatory authority) and externally (for example, by promoting knowledge, expertise, and information sharing by WEF-related institutions) are significant steps toward advancing systemic and integrated governance of WEF resources.

At the end of this chapter, you should be able to do the following:

- identify the linkages between water, energy, and food systems and how the sustainable functioning of one depends on the other;
- describe the specific WEF nexus challenges in global systems and the normative features of a nexus approach to WEF governance;

- understand legal frameworks and institutional structures that have been proposed to help policy-makers understand the complexity of the nexus and to increase synergies with regulating these resources;
- appreciate the idea of systemic integration as an important concept in international environmental law; and
- identify the practical gaps and barriers in WEF nexus integration in decision-making and planning.

II. INTRODUCTION

Water, energy, and food are inextricably linked to all aspects of human life, that is, our ability to work, live, survive, and execute tasks.[1] Without water, we cannot produce food and energy, and without energy, we cannot process or distribute food and water. For example, a collapse of energy systems could result in the disruption of food preservation and supply. Similarly, a water shortage could hinder food production and energy production, especially the effective functioning of hydropower stations.[2] Also, without food, human and animal contributors to the energy and water supply value chain may not be able to function well.[3] Global water, energy, and food systems are evidently so interlinked that disruption of one resource could result in disruptions of the other two.[4] Energy production can result in the contamination of water and food systems, while food and agricultural processes could result in water pollution and energy inefficiency.[5]

Given these interdependencies, addressing the interplay and trade-offs between water, energy, and food systems, often described as the WEF nexus, is of increasing interest to a wide community of natural and social scientists, policy-makers, governments, international development agencies, and academic scholars.[6] The WEF nexus topic investigates technological, legal, and institutional innovations for addressing common threats to water, energy, and food security. Recent studies, including the World Economic Forum reports of 2011 and 2014, have underlined the need to develop integrated policy responses that address common threats to the availability, accessibility, and affordability of WEF.[7] Similarly, the National Intelligence Council

---

1   See Jamie Pittock, Karen Hussey & Stephen Dovers, eds, *Climate, Energy and Water: Managing Trade-offs, Seizing Opportunities* (Cambridge: Cambridge University Press, 2015) at 1-27; see also Mairi Dupar & Naomi Oates, "Getting to Grips with the Water–Energy–Food 'Nexus'" (13 April 2012), online: *Climate and Development Knowledge Network* <https://cdkn.org/2012/04/getting-to-grips-with-the-water-energy-food-nexus/?loclang=en_gb>.

2   Beatriz Mayor et al, "The Role of Large and Small Scale Hydropower for Energy and Water Security in the Spanish Duero Basin" (2017) 9:10 Sustainability 1807.

3   Dupar & Oates, *supra* note 1.

4   Morgan Bazilian et al, "Considering the Energy, Water and Food Nexus: Towards an Integrated Modelling Approach" (2011) 39:12 Energy Policy 7896, DOI: <https://doi.org/10.1016/j.enpol.2011.09.039>

5   H Jeswani, R Burkinshaw & A Azapagic, "Environmental Sustainability Issues in the Food–Energy–Water Nexus: Breakfast Cereals and Snacks" (2015) 2 Sustainable Production and Consumption 17.

6   Dupar & Oates, *supra* note 1; see also Food and Agricultural Organization of the United Nations (FAO), *The Water–Energy–Food Nexus: A New Approach in Support of Food Security and Sustainable Agriculture* (Rome: FAO, 2014) at 1-5, online (pdf): <http://www.fao.org/3/a-bl496e.pdf> [FAO, "Food Security and Sustainable Agriculture"]; Karen Hussey & Jamie Pittock, "The Energy–Water Nexus: Managing the Links between Energy and Water for a Sustainable Future" (2012) 17:1 Ecol & Soc 31 at 32.

7   World Economic Forum, *Water Security: The Water–Food–Energy–Climate Nexus* (Washington, DC: Island Press, 2011), online (pdf): <http://www3.weforum.org/docs/WEF_WI_WaterSecurity_WaterFoodEnergyClimateNexus_2011.pdf>; World Economic Forum, *Insight Report: Global Risks 2014*, 9th ed (Geneva: World Economic Forum, 2014), online (pdf): <http://www3.weforum.org/docs/WEF_GlobalRisks_Report_2014.pdf>.

of the United States identified the holistic management of the WEF nexus as one out of four megatrends that could result in major and transformational global shifts by 2030.[8] The European Union (EU) has also canvassed the need for integrated management of water, energy, and land resources in order to address common threats to WEF security.[9] In international water law, the nexus approach has been considered within the regime of the United Nations Economic Commission for Europe (UNECE) Water Convention[10] as providing a way "to enhance water, energy and food security by increasing efficiency, reducing trade-offs, building synergies and improving governance, while protecting ecosystems."[11] These studies emphasize the need to strengthen synergies and policy coherence between water, food, and agriculture and land management sectors in the national and transboundary context.[12]

However, despite the increased prominence of the WEF nexus discourse in science, engineering, policy, and development literature, a detailed case on the legal and institutional considerations for building cross-sectoral cooperation amongst WEF actors in private and public spheres has yet to be developed.[13] This chapter explores WEF nexus debates from a legal perspective in order to reveal legal preconditions for, and practical complexities of, a nexus approach to WEF governance. It investigates frameworks and models that have been proposed to help policy-makers understand the complexity of the nexus and to increase synergies in regulating these resources. It then discusses the need for enhanced levels of legislation and rule linkage; elaboration of common and shared principles by institutional actors in WEF domains; epistemic pluralism; and multi-perspective knowledge, expertise, and information sharing in WEF-related decision-making. These are significant steps toward advancing systemic and integrative governance of WEF resources.

The chapter is organized into five sections, this introduction being the second. Section III explores the inextricable linkages between water, energy, and food systems and how the sustainable functioning of one depends on the other. It provides specific examples of WEF nexus challenges in global systems, especially in Canada and the United Kingdom, two countries where the WEF nexus discourse has received significant interest and attention. Section IV discusses the scope and elements of the WEF nexus, while Section V discusses frameworks and models that have been proposed to address the complexity of the nexus and to increase

---

8   United States, National Intelligence Council, *Global Trends 2030: Alternative Worlds* (Washington, DC: NIC, 2012) at iv, online (pdf): <https://www.dni.gov/files/documents/GlobalTrends_2030.pdf>, noting, "Tackling problems pertaining to one commodity won't be possible without affecting supply and demand for the others." It called for proactive and holistic responses by policy-makers and private-sector partners to avoid water, energy, and food scarcities.

9   European Union, *Confronting Scarcity: Managing Water, Energy and Land for Inclusive and Sustainable Growth*, The 2011/2012 European Report on Development (Belgium: European Union, 2012) at iii, 2, online (pdf): <https://ecdpm.org/wp-content/uploads/2013/10/ERD-2011-2012-Confronting-Scarcity-Managing-water-energy-land.pdf>.

10   *Convention on the Protection and Use of Transboundary Watercourses and International Lakes*, 17 March 1992, 1936 UNTS 269 (entered into force 6 October 1996).

11   *Reconciling Resource Uses in Transboundary Basins: Assessment of the Water-Food-Energy-Ecosystems Nexus*, UN Doc ECE/MP.WAT/46, November 2015 at iii, online (pdf): *UNECE* <https://www.unece.org/fileadmin/DAM/env/water/publications/WAT_Nexus/ece_mp.wat_46_eng.pdf> [UNECE, *Reconciling Resource Uses in Transboundary Basins*].

12   See National Intelligence Council, *supra* note 8. See also Nina Weitz et al, "Closing the Governance Gaps in the Water-Energy-Food Nexus: Insights from Integrative Governance" (2017) 45 Global Environ Change 165.

13   Many of the existing studies have not provided exhaustive legal analysis, while law texts on this theme have focused on specific sectors. See Jorge E Viñuales, "The Protocol on Water and Health as a Strategy for Global Water Governance Integration" (2018) 68:1 ICLQ 175; Antti Belinskij, "Water–Energy–Food Nexus Within the Framework of International Water Law" (2015) 7 Water 5396.

synergies with regulating these resources. Section VI provides some lessons and recommendations on the required steps and processes for advancing systemic and integrative governance of WEF resources.

III. THE WEF NEXUS DISCOURSE: SCOPE AND SIGNIFICANCE

The WEF nexus discourse recognizes the interlocking pressures and trade-offs facing WEF systems.[14] It identifies the need for legal and institutional coordination of governance efforts aimed at addressing water, energy, and food scarcities in order to address overlap, interdependencies, constraints, synergies, and trade-offs.[15] It also investigates how technological advancements, policies, rules, and/or legislation in one domain affect and reinforce other domains. The nexus approach advocates a fundamental shift from sectoral and "one pipe at a time" governance approaches to a cross-sectoral, coherent, and integrated approach to WEF management in order to overcome unintended consequences of uncoordinated policy between different sectors.[16]

The WEF nexus discourse is not new.[17] As far back as the 1980s, researchers and policy-makers began to highlight the need for cross-sector, cross-scale, and hybrid reasoning and planning in WEF sectors.[18] However, the impetus and calls for a nexus approach to WEF governance in decision-making and planning have grown significantly over the last decade due to four main reasons.[19] The first is an unprecedented rise in demand for WEF.[20] Demand for food, water,

---

14 Rose Cairns & Anna Krzywoszynska, "Anatomy of a Buzzword: The Emergence of 'The Water—Energy—Food Nexus' in UK Natural Resource Debates" (2016) 64 Environ Sci & Pol'y 164; see also Holger Hoff, "Understanding the Nexus" (Background paper for the Bonn2011 Nexus Conference: The Water, Energy and Food Security Nexus Bonn, Germany, 16—18 November 2011), online (pdf): <https://www.water-energy -food.org/uploads/media/understanding_the_nexus.pdf>.

15 UK Economic and Social Research Council (ESRC) defines the nexus as "a way of thinking about the interdependencies, tensions and trade-offs between food, water and energy security, in the wider context of environmental change with a focus on the impact on social systems." See UK, Parliamentary Office of Science & Technology, *The Water-Energy-Food Nexus* (POSTnote 543) by Jonathan Wentworth (London: POST, 2016) at 2, online (pdf): <http://researchbriefings.files.parliament.uk/documents/POST-PN-0543/POST-PN-0543.pdf>.

16 Weitz et al, *supra* note 12 at 165-66; see also P Hellegers et al, "Interactions between Water, Energy, Food and Environment: Evolving Perspectives and Policy Issues" (2008) 10:1 Water Pol'y 1.

17 See J Bird, "The Water, Energy and Food Security Nexus—Is It Really New?" (The Gerald Lacey Memorial Lecture, delivered at the Institution of Civil Engineers, Westminster, 12 May 2014), online: *The Irrigation and Water Forum* <https://iwaterforum.org.uk/gerald-lacey-memorial-lectures/>; see also Felix Dodds & Jamie Bartram, "The History of the Nexus at the Intergovernmental Level" in Felix Dodds & Jamie Bartram, eds, *The Water, Food, Energy and Climate Nexus: Challenges and an Agenda for Action* (Abingdon, Oxon: Routledge, 2016) 7-46; Hayley Leck et al, "Tracing the Water—Energy—Food Nexus: Description, Theory and Practice" (2015) 9:8 Geography Compass 445.

18 For example, calls for integrated water resources management (IWRM) and integrated coastal zone management (ICZM) have featured prominently in the literature since the 1980s. However, they were seen as too narrow and inadequate to respond to emerging challenges in food and energy sectors. For a detailed overview, see Leck et al, *supra* note 17.

19 Cairns and Krzywoszynska trace the recent focus on the WEF nexus to the year 2008, where business leaders of the World Economic Forum issued a call to engage with nexus issues between economic growth and water, energy, and food resource systems. See Cairns & Krzywoszynska, *supra* note 14.

20 Viviana Wiegleb & Antje Bruns, "What Is Driving the Water—Energy—Food Nexus? Discourses, Knowledge, and Politics of an Emerging Resource Governance Concept" (2018) 6:128 Front Environ Sci, DOI:

and energy has grown over the last decade and is projected to grow further by approximately 35, 40, and 50 percent, respectively, by 2030, owing to an increase in the global population and rise in consumption patterns across the world, especially in developing countries.[21] As countries develop, their populations will require more energy, food, and water.[22] For example, demand for food and energy is increasing in developed countries, such as Canada and the United Kingdom, with a high concentration of industries, especially thermal power generation, manufacturing, oil and gas, and agricultural sectors.[23] Canada has the second highest water use per capita in the world, only surpassed by the United States.[24] An average annual growth rate of 4 percent per year in water use, coupled with significant disturbances to freshwater ecosystems from human activities such as pollution, agricultural run-off, transportation incidents, habitat loss, invasive species, climate change, oil and gas development, and hydropower dams are all threats that can affect the long-term availability, affordability, and accessibility of water resources in Canada.[25]

Also, as population increases, so does the demand for energy. For example, intertwined with economic diversification and expansion in Canada, especially in oil- and gas-producing provinces such as Alberta, is a significant rise in population and electricity consumption at a median rate of 4-10 percent per year.[26] Similarly, in the United Kingdom, estimates show that overall domestic energy consumption was 8.8 percent higher in 2017 than in 1970.[27] Given these energy demand patterns, there has been an urgency to increase installed capacity of

---

<https://doi.org/10.3389/fenvs.2018.00128>. See also National Intelligence Council, *supra* note 8; Hoff, *supra* note 14 at 4.

21 According to UN estimates, the world population of 7.4 billion (in 2016) will increase by 1 billion over the next ten years and reach 9.6 billion by 2050. See United Nations Department for Economic and Social Affairs, "World Population Projected to Reach 9.7 Billion by 2050" (29 July 2015), online: *United Nations* <http://www.un.org/en/development/desa/news/population/2015-report.html>; see also *BP Energy Outlook*, 2018 ed (2018) at 4, 20, online (pdf): *bp.com* <https://www.bp.com/content/dam/bp -country/de_ch/PDF/Energy-Outlook-2018-edition-Booklet.pdf>, stating that global energy consumption is to increase by one-third or so (30 percent) by 2040.

22 For example, the United Nations Water 2013 factsheet on water scarcity estimates that by 2025, two-thirds of the world's population will live in regions where demand for water exceeds supply by more than 50 percent (see online: <http://www.un.org/waterforlifedecade/scarcity.shtml>).

23 In 2009, the then-UK Chief Scientific Adviser, John Beddington, noted that the world will face a "perfect storm" of food, water, and energy shortages by 2030, and this could be further complicated by climate change. Stephen Mulvey, "Averting a Perfect Storm of Shortages," *BBC News* (24 August 2009), online: <http://news.bbc.co.uk/2/hi/8213884.stm>. See also "Water Withdrawal and Consumption by Sector" (last modified 10 March 2017), online: *Government of Canada* <https://www. canada.ca/en/environment-climate-change/services/environmental-indicators/water-withdrawal-consumption-sector.html>.

24 Statistics Canada noted a high threat to water availability in southern Ontario, southern Alberta, southern Saskatchewan, southwestern Manitoba, and the Okanagan Valley in British Columbia, where more than 40 percent of the water in rivers was withdrawn for human use in 2009. See "Water Availability in Canada" (last modified 10 April 2017), online: *Government of Canada* <https://www.canada.ca/en/ environment-climate-change/services/environmental-indicators/water-availability.html>.

25 World Wildlife Fund (WWF), *Watershed Reports: A National Assessment of Canada's Freshwater* (2017), online (pdf): <http://assets.wwf.ca/downloads/WWF_Watershed_Reports_Summit_FINAL_web.pdf>.

26 For example, since 2003, primary electricity consumption in Alberta has risen on average by 2.2 percent a year, with peak demand expected to grow by an average 3.3 percent per year for the period from 2009 to 2029. See Alberta Electric System Operator (AESO), *Future Demand and Energy Outlook (2009-2029)* (2009) at 1-3.

27 UK, Department for Business, Energy & Industrial Strategy, *Energy Consumption in the United Kingdom* by Liz Waters (July 2018) at 22, online (pdf): <https://assets.publishing.service.gov.uk/government/ uploads/system/uploads/attachment_data/file/729317/Energy_Consumption_in_the_UK__ ECUK__2018.pdf>.

electric power plants in order to meet the increasing peak demand load.[28] Similarly, a number of countries have intensified efforts to reduce the current electricity demand rate by promoting energy efficiency in water, food, and industrial sectors and eliminating waste.[29] Addressing energy demand, without understanding the implications of energy efficiency measures and activities on food and agricultural productivity, may result in counterproductive policies. Also, advancing agricultural expansion projects without addressing the impacts of such projects on electricity usage and demand could provide counterproductive effects on energy efficiency and security. For example, the food and agricultural sector is currently the largest consumer of water (70 percent) and one of the largest users of energy (30 percent).[30] Food prices are, therefore, projected to increase as energy, fertilizer, and water transportation costs rise.[31] Also, addressing energy demand through expansion of alternative and renewable energy projects, for example, could affect both land access for agricultural purposes and food security.[32] The WEF nexus model allows policy-makers to understand the implications of increasing energy demand on food and water supply and the implications of rising food production and agriculture sector demand for water and energy.[33]

A second driver of the WEF nexus discourse is the unique threats posed by climate change to water, energy, and food systems.[34] Apart from climate-induced fatal heat waves and debilitating sea level rise, climate change could have wide-ranging effects on food production, water availability, and energy generation.[35] For example, a rise in the frequency of droughts as a result of drier summers, changes in forest fire patterns, a decrease in water availability, an increase in the number pests and insects, and a rise in insect-borne diseases, as well as changes in climate variables such as temperature, precipitation, and humidity, could significantly affect the entire value chain of food production, distribution, storage, and transportation.[36] To effectively limit and address the catastrophic impacts of climate change, the international climate change regime has emphasized the importance of cooperating across relevant sectors in both the

---

28 Damilola Olawuyi, "Advancing Innovations in Renewable Energy Technologies as Alternatives to Fossil Fuel Use in the Middle East: Trends, Limitations, and Ways Forward" in Donald Zillman et al, eds, *Innovation in Energy Law and Technology: Dynamic Solutions for Energy Transitions* (Oxford: Oxford University Press, 2018) 354.

29 *Ibid.* See also Claudia Ringler, Anik Bhaduri & Richard Lawford, "The Nexus Across Water, Energy, Land and Food (WELF): Potential for Improved Resource Use Efficiency?" (2013) 5:6 Curr Opin Environ Sustain 617.

30 Rabia Ferroukhi et al, *Renewable Energy in the Water Energy & Food Nexus* (Abu Dhabi: International Renewable Energy Agency, 2015) at 12, online: <https://www.irena.org/publications/2015/Jan/Renewable-Energy-in-the-Water-Energy--Food-Nexus> [IRENA].

31 FAO, *'Energy-Smart' Food for People and Climate* (Issue Paper) (Rome: FAO, 2011) at iv-v, online (pdf): <http://www.fao.org/3/i2454e/i2454e00.pdf>.

32 See Chidi Oguamanam, "Sustainable Development in the Era of Bioenergy and Agricultural Land Grab" in Shawkat Alam et al, eds, *International Environmental Law and the Global South* (Cambridge: Cambridge University Press, 2015) 237 at 238-40.

33 IRENA, *supra* note 30 at 12-15.

34 See Intergovernmental Panel on Climate Change (IPCC), "Summary for Policymakers" in *Climate Change 2013: The Physical Science Basis—Working Group I Contribution to the IPCC Fifth Assessment Report* (New York: Cambridge University Press, 2013) 3 at 3-10, online: <https://www.ipcc.ch/report/ar5/wg1/>.

35 See J Carter et al, "Climate Change and the City: Building Capacity for Urban Adaptation" (2015) 95 Progress in Planning 1; Leck et al, *supra* note 17.

36 See Ellen Wall, Barry Smit & Johanna Wandel, eds, *Farming in a Changing Climate: Agriculture Adaptation in Canada* (Vancouver: UBC Press, 2007) at 273; Budong Qian et al, "Changing Growing Season Observed in Canada" (2012) 112:2 Climatic Change 339.

preparation and implementation of National Adaptation Plans (NAPs).[37] Addressing climate change impacts in one domain, without addressing trade-offs and impacts in other domains, may result in maladaptation and ineffectiveness.[38] Also, given the cross-cutting implications of climate change for water, energy, and food infrastructure, promoting the design of smart and climate-resilient infrastructure can enhance efficiency and reduce emissions across entire WEF domains.[39] Infrastructure upgrades for climate adaptation, for example, can be coordinated to promote smart water systems and energy efficiency, as well as smart food storage and preservation. Furthermore, infrastructure integration can help promote multiple and flexible use of infrastructure (for example, dams and irrigation and drainage systems) for WEF purposes.[40]

A third and related driver of the WEF discourse is the need to address the interactions and implications of climate and energy expansion projects on human rights, most especially human rights to property, water, and food.[41] Several energy access projects—such as the Muskrat Falls hydroelectric project in Labrador, Canada; construction of the Site C hydroelectric dam on British Columbia's Peace River; Mambilla hydropower project in Nigeria; renewable energy projects in Senegal and Tanzania; rural electrification projects in the Philippines; the Three Gorges Dam project in China; hydroelectric projects in Honduras and Panama; and large energy pipeline projects such as the West African Gas Pipeline project in Ghana—have been linked with complex human rights violations.[42] Furthermore, the production of bioenergy crops, such as sugarcane, could reduce land and water availability, resulting in a sharp rise in food prices.[43] Similarly, low-carbon energy projects implemented under the Clean Development Mechanism (CDM) and the reducing emissions from deforestation and forest degradation, sustainable management of forests and conservation, and enhancement of forest carbon stocks (REDD+) schemes have been linked with severe human rights violations in developing countries.[44] These human rights concerns include compulsory acquisition of lands as project sites, forced displacement, marginalization, exclusion, concentration of energy access projects

---

37 United Nations Framework Convention on Climate Change (UNFCCC), *National Adaptation Plans: Technical Guidelines for National Adaptation Plan Process* (Germany: United Nations Climate Change Secretariat, 2012) at 11-13, online (pdf): <https://unfccc.int/files/adaptation/cancun_adaptation_framework/application/pdf/naptechguidelines_eng_high__res.pdf>, stating that all relevant sectors and ministries should develop a common understanding of adaptation plans, including efforts to cooperate across sectors, regions, and cities.

38 *Ibid.*

39 IRENA, *supra* note 30 at 13-15. See also Pittock et al, *supra* note 1.

40 Ringler, Bhaduri & Lawford, *supra* note 29 at 618-20.

41 Despite ongoing controversies about the nature, scope, and content of the right to water, as well as the right to food, in international law, they are both recognized rights in international human rights law with substantive and procedural dimensions. For a recent analysis, see Virginie Barral, "Towards Judicial Coordination for Good Water Governance?" (2018) 67:4 ICLQ 931; see also M Arden, "Water for All? Developing a Human Right to Water in National and International Law" (2016) 65:4 ICLQ 771.

42 For a recent and detailed discussion of these debates, see Damilola Olawuyi, "Energy (and Human Rights) for All: Addressing Human Rights Risks in Energy Access Projects" in Raya Salter, Carmen Gonzalez & Elizabeth Kronk Warner, eds, *Energy Justice: US and International Perspectives* (Cheltenham: Edward Elgar, 2018) 73 [Olawuyi, "Energy (and Human Rights) for All"]; M Hall & D Weiss, "Avoiding Adaptation Apartheid: Climate Change Adaptation and Human Rights Law" (2012) 37:2 Yale J Int'l L 309.

43 Oguamanam, *supra* note 32 at 237-40. See also CF Runge & B Senauer, "How Biofuels Could Starve the Poor," *Foreign Affairs* 86:3 (May/June 2007) 41 at 41.

44 Damilola Olawuyi, "Climate Justice and Corporate Responsibility: Taking Human Rights Seriously in Climate Actions and Projects" (2016) 34:1 J Energy & Nat'l Res L 27; Naomi Roht-Arriaza, "Human Rights in the Climate Change Regime" (2010) 1:2 J Hum Rts & Env't 211.

in poor and vulnerable communities, and governmental repression in developing countries.[45] The gaps and the high incidence of human rights violations resulting from energy access projects have increased calls for a more transparent, accountable, and human rights-based approach to energy access.[46] Emerging debates on energy justice, therefore, recognize the growing indirect impacts that WEF projects have on human rights and examine how international law could provide legal frameworks to address these impacts.[47] The WEF model allows countries to develop a systemic view of the implications of energy expansion projects on human rights as well as on long-term economic planning.

The need for coherent and holistic implementation of the Sustainable Development Goals (SDGs) is a fourth and related driver of the WEF nexus discourse.[48] The nexus approach has become increasingly recognized as an important vehicle through which countries can holistically implement and achieve the SDGs to avoid overlap.[49] SDG 6 (water), SDG 7 (energy), and SDG 2 (food) encourage countries to develop projects and initiatives aimed at eliminating water, energy, and food scarcities by 2030.[50] The 2030 UN Agenda for sustainable development also highlights the need for a common approach to implement all the SDGs in order to reduce access inequalities.[51] The nexus approach allows policy-makers to have a systemic understanding and view of the trade-offs and synergies between the SDGs and to avoid overlapping and duplicative sector-specific actions and programs. It also provides a coordinated platform to pursue and implement related international obligations on WEF security as contained in other instruments. Through information sharing and cooperation between the different institutions responsible for the various SDGs, a country can formulate and implement a multiscale, holistic, and integrated plan for achieving the SDGs.[52]

Given these main drivers, the appetite to integrate WEF considerations into planning and decision-making is very high in developed and developing countries, and could remain sustained for the next decade. Despite the policy awareness, however, many countries continue to develop, manage, and regulate WEF systems and technological innovations independently. To advance integrated WEF governance, there is a need to further the conceptual understanding of the features of the integration of WEF governance as well as the theoretical possibilities and practical problems associated with such integration.

---

45 See Damilola Olawuyi, *The Human Rights-Based Approach to Carbon Finance* (Cambridge: Cambridge University Press, 2016) at 1-25; see also Roht-Arriaza, *supra* note 44.

46 See United Nations Environment Programme (UNEP), *Climate Change and Human Rights* (Nairobi: UNON Publishing Services Section, 2015) at 9-10, online (pdf): *UN Environment Document Repository* <https://wedocs.unep.org/bitstream/handle/20.500.11822/9530/-Climate_Change_and_Human_Rightshuman-rights-climate-change.pdf.pdf>.

47 Olawuyi, "Energy (and Human Rights) for All," *supra* note 42.

48 Raya Marina Stephan et al, "Water–Energy–Food Nexus: A Platform for Implementing the Sustainable Development Goals" (2018) 43:3 Water Int'l 1 at 3, noting that "[a]n overall guiding principle of the WEF nexus approach is the concept of achieving *sustainable development*" (emphasis in original). See also "Nexus and the SDG's: Water–Energy–Food Nexus Serves the SDG's" (last accessed 7 May 2019), online: *Nexus Dialogue Programme* <https://www.nexus-dialogue-programme.eu/about/nexus-and-the-sdgs/>.

49 J Terrapon-Pfaff et al, "Energising the WEF Nexus to Enhance Sustainable Development at Local Level" (2018) 223 J Environ Mgmt 409. See also United Nations, *Policy Brief 9: Water–Energy–Food Nexus for the Review of SDG 7* (2018), online (pdf): *Sustainable Development Goals* <https://sustainabledevelopment.un.org/content/documents/17483PB9.pdf> [Policy Brief 9].

50 Policy Brief 9, *supra* note 49. See also FAO, "Walking the Nexus Talk: Assessing the Water–Energy–Food Nexus in the Context of the Sustainable Energy for All Initiative" (2014) FAO Environment and Natural Resources Management Working Paper No 58 [FAO, "Walking the Nexus Talk"].

51 FAO, "Walking the Nexus Talk," *supra* note 50.

52 Terrapon-Pfaff, *supra* note 49 at 410.

IV. CONTOURS AND FEATURES OF THE WEF NEXUS

A central tenet of the nexus governance model is the idea of integration, that is, integrating or harmonizing WEF obligations, rules, and norms into policy-making through a coordinated or holistic approach. The nexus approach is characterized by the UNECE to include five core features. These are the integration of (1) institutions; (2) information sharing; (3) instruments, laws, and policies to address trade-offs and exploit synergies; (4) infrastructure and techno-logical solutions; and (5) international coordination and cooperation at regional levels (the "5-I Principles").[53]

In practical terms, WEF nexus governance entails assessing the benefits and impacts of pro-jects, programs, and infrastructure in one sector and mainstreaming them in the other two sectors. It draws attention to the potential impacts of actions, measures, and projects in one sector on the most vulnerable groups, such as poor and racial minority communities, women, children, disabled persons, and Indigenous peoples.[54] For example, rather than focus on energy benefits alone, the WEF nexus allows project planners in the energy sector to understand the shared benefits and impacts of energy projects for water access, land use, and food security on vulnerable communities. By implementing the 5-I Principles in the design, approval, finance, and implementation of WEF projects, policy-makers are better positioned to anticipate and consider the impacts of a project in one domain on the other domains, and on the public, and then take steps to mitigate those impacts. The WEF nexus model aims to reduce fragmentation and strengthen policy coherence between water, food, and agriculture and land management sec-tors at local and regional levels.[55]

The WEF nexus governance approach builds on dominant discussions in international law on the need to address fragmentation and lack of coherence in the interpretation and applica-tion of the various international law instruments on water, energy, environment, food, trade, climate change, and human rights.[56] There have been concerns and evidence that projects at national levels that are designed to implement obligations under one treaty produce conflicting or overlapping implications under other treaty provisions and rules of customary international law.[57] Such overlap has resulted in increased discussion of the principle of systemic integration and coherent interpretation of international law obligations, laid down in

---

53 On the meaning and scope of each of the elements, see UNECE, *Reconciling Resource Uses in Trans-boundary Basins, supra* note 11 at 8. See also UNECE, *Methodology for Assessing the Water–Food–Energy–Ecosystems Nexus in Transboundary Basins*, UN Doc ECE/MP.WAT/WG.1/2015/8 (15 June 2015), online (pdf): <http://www.unece.org/fileadmin/DAM/env/water/publications/WAT_55_NexusSynthesis/ECE-MP-WAT-55_NexusSynthesis_Final-for-Web.pdf> [UNECE, *Methodology for Assessing the Nexus*].

54 Eloise Biggs et al, "Sustainable Development and the Water–Energy–Food Nexus: A Perspective on Livelihoods" (2015) 54 Envtl Sci & Pol'y 389.

55 See UNECE, *Reconciling Resource Uses in Transboundary Basins, supra* note 11 at iii, stating that a nexus assessment can "assist countries in optimizing their use of resources, to increase efficiency and to ensure greater policy coherence and co-management."

56 For detailed discussions of the need for greater integration and coherence in international law, see Viñuales, *supra* note 13; see also Frank Biermann et al, "The Fragmentation of Global Governance Architectures: A Framework for Analysis" (2009) 9:4 Global Envtl Pol 14; M Young, ed, *Regime Inter-action in International Law: Facing Fragmentation* (Cambridge: Cambridge University Press, 2012). See also Harro Van Asselt, Francesco Sindico & Michael Mehling, "Global Climate Change and the Fragmen-tation of International Law" (2008) 30:4 Law & Pol'y 423.

57 Olawuyi, "Energy (and Human Rights) for All," *supra* note 42; see also Sean Stephenson, "Jobs, Justice, Climate: Conflicting State Obligations in the International Human Rights and Climate Change Regimes" (2010) 42:1 Ottawa L Rev 155; Joost Pauwelyn, "Bridging Fragmentation and Unity: International Law as a Universe of Inter-Connected Islands" (2004) 5 Mich J Int'l L 903.

art 31(3)(c) of the *Vienna Convention on the Law of Treaties*,[58] as a potential solution to the problem of fragmentation in international law.[59]

Despite debates on the scope and ambit of the principle of systemic integration and coherent interpretation of international law obligations, it is generally agreed that it provides a legal basis for harmonizing and coordinating international law obligations on water, energy, food, and climate change, as well as human rights obligations, such that an attempt to perform one obligation does not lead to conflict with or the violation of another.[60] Article 31(3)(c) reinforces the significance of interpreting and applying international law instruments in mutually supportive ways.[61] Several of the international obligations on access to water, energy, and food—as reflected in treaties such as the *United Nations Framework Convention on Climate Change*[62] and the *Paris Agreement*;[63] core international human rights instruments such as the *International Covenant on Civil and Political Rights*[64] and the *International Covenant on Economic, Social and Cultural Rights*;[65] and non-binding declarations and action plans such as the UN SDGs and the *Universal Declaration of Human Rights*,[66] amongst others—all establish important principles on WEF security that cannot be implemented in isolation.[67] The nexus governance approach is a logical step that could bring about hybrid reasoning in the harmonization and integration of international law obligations on the right to water, the right to food, energy security, and climate change mitigation and adaptation, as well as procedural rights on access to information and stakeholder participation, to make them operate as part of a coherent and meaningful whole.

Similarly, considering that many of the parties to global climate change treaties are also parties to core international human rights treaties that address access to water and food, an integrative and coherent approach provides an avenue for countries to respect, protect, and fulfill human rights on water and food while combatting climate change.[68] The *Paris Agreement*

---

58 23 May 1969, 1155 UNTS 331 (entered into force 27 January 1980) [VCLT].

59 See C Mclachlan, "The Principle of Systemic Integration and Article 31(3)(c) of the Vienna Convention" (2005) 54:2 ICLQ 279; V Tzevelekos, "The Use of Article 31(3)(c) of the VCLT in the Case Law of the ECtHR: An Effective Anti-Fragmentation Tool or a Selective Loophole for the Reinforcement of Human Rights Teleology? Between Evolution and Systemic Integration" (2010) 31 Mich J Int'l L 621 at 631.

60 Van Asselt, Sindico & Mehling, *supra* note 56 at 423; Meinhard Doelle, "Linking the Kyoto Protocol and Other Multilateral Environmental Agreements: From Fragmentation to Integration?" (2004) 14 J Envtl L & Prac 75; P-M Dupuy, "Unification Rather than Fragmentation of International Law? The Case of International Investment Law and Human Rights Law" in P-M Dupuy, F Francioni & E-U Petersmann, eds, *Human Rights in International Investment Arbitration* (Oxford: Oxford University Press, 2009) 45. See also United Nations General Assembly, International Law Commission, *Fragmentation of International Law: Difficulties Arising from the Diversification and Expansion of International Law—Report of the Study Group of the International Law Commission*, UNGAOR, 58th Sess, UN Doc A/CN.4/L.682 (13 April 2006). [ILC]

61 ILC, *supra* note 60.

62 9 May 1992, 1771 UNTS 107 (entered into force 21 March 1994).

63 12 December 2015, UN Doc FCCC/CP/2015/10/Add.1 (entered into force 4 November 2016).

64 16 December 1966, 999 UNTS 171 (entered into force 23 March 1976) [ICCPR].

65 16 December 1966, 993 UNTS 3 (entered into force 3 January 1976) [ICESCR].

66 Adopted 10 December 1948, GA Res 217A9 (III), 3 UN GAOR, UN Doc A/810 at 71 (1948) [UDHR].

67 See art 11 of the ICESCR; *Optional Protocol to the International Covenant on Economic, Social and Cultural Rights*, 10 December 2008 (entered into force 5 May 2013); and art 25(1) of the UDHR.

68 There are 160 parties to the ICESCR and 166 parties to the ICCPR. The majority of these parties have also signed and ratified the *United Nations Framework Convention on Climate Change* and the *Paris Agreement*, which contain obligations to address the implications of climate change on water, energy, and food systems. See the preamble to the *Paris Agreement*.

recognizes that "[p]arties should, when taking action to address climate change, respect, promote and consider their respective obligations on human rights."[69]

This speaks to the need for a mutually reinforcing approach that enables a country to ensure that projects, actions, and measures designed to meet obligations under the climate change regime do not violate international human rights obligations on water, energy, and food. A nexus approach to WEF governance is a methodological approach through which human rights obligations on water and food can be incorporated into energy and climate actions and projects to avoid trade-offs, overlaps, and inconsistencies.

Furthermore, through knowledge mobilization and information sharing, a WEF nexus governance model can provide opportunities for policy-makers to better understand how energy access initiatives under SDG 7 can affect food security and supply that is within the ambit of SDG 2. It can also provide a basis for addressing the implications of increased agricultural production on water and energy use. Synergies, trade-offs, and challenges to the interface between WEF policies (such as access to water, energy, and land for the poorest; the reduction of resource-intensive consumption and production patterns; and the effective deployment of technologies relevant to all domains) cannot be addressed in isolation. Examining the interplay and nexus between food, energy, and water policies enables a holistic management and systemic view of the complex and critical stress points.[70] Furthermore, rather than considering trade-offs and risks on a piecemeal, sectoral, and technology-by-technology basis, a WEF nexus governance model supports the development of integrated, systemic, and multisectoral governance and monitoring systems.

The nexus approach to WEF governance provides a normative framework for reducing the fragmentation of international law obligations relating to water, energy, and food, as well as climate change and human rights.[71] Through a nexus assessment, actions and measures that negatively affect one sector could be spotted and reconsidered before approval.[72] Furthermore, a WEF nexus governance model can allow countries to integrate their obligations to respect human rights on water, energy, and food into climate and environmental programs through a holistic framework.

However, while the potential and promise of the WEF nexus governance model is clear, what is required in practice, especially in terms of legal and governance frameworks to integrate the fundamental goals of regulating water, energy, and food, remains very much a work-in-progress. This has led to the charge that the WEF nexus is fuzzy and ambiguous.[73] Identifying the WEF nexus and interdependencies without addressing legal and institutional challenges to practical application in local contexts may not be enough to drive action. Some of the frameworks and models that have been proposed to advance integrated WEF governance are discussed in the next section.

V. THE WEF NEXUS WITHIN THE FRAMEWORK OF INTERNATIONAL AND DOMESTIC LAW

While drivers that give impetus to adopting a WEF nexus approach are global in nature, translating WEF nexus governance to practical impacts will vary according to different legal

---

69 *Paris Agreement*, preamble.

70 Ringler, Bhaduri & Lawford, *supra* note 29 at 618-20.

71 Van Asselt, Sindico & Mehling, *supra* note 56; see also Stephenson, *supra* note 57 at 180.

72 UNECE, *Reconciling Resource Uses in Transboundary Basins*, *supra* note 11 at iii.

73 See Wiegleb & Bruns, *supra* note 20; see also Cairns & Krzywoszynska, *supra* note 14 at 164-65; UK Houses of Parliament, *supra* note 15 at 2.

contexts, regimes, and actors, including domestic-level institutions; regional organizations; international development agencies; UN human rights bodies; and international food, water, and energy regimes. This section discusses some of the key instruments at international, regional, and national levels that help contextualize and explain the WEF nexus.

A. INTERNATIONAL LAW INSTRUMENTS ON WEF GOVERNANCE

As discussed earlier, international law supports the idea of the nexus approach to secure human rights to water, energy, and food. However, there is currently no international treaty that specifically codifies the nexus approach to WEF governance. A large part of the nexus literature is underpinned by UN resolutions, declarations, general comments, and normative recommendations of treaty bodies, as well as policy reports, position papers, working papers, or strategy documents compiled by international agencies (such as the World Bank) that have no legally binding force under international law.[74] For example, the UN and EU Commission have advocated a need for a nexus perspective to implement the UN SDGs.[75] Similarly, the nexus approach has been well elaborated by the UNECE as a strategic framework for increasing good water governance and cooperation between riparian countries and across different sectors.[76] In its reports on the WEF nexus, the UNECE emphasizes the need to strengthen synergies and policy coherence between water, food, and agriculture and land management sectors in national and transboundary context.[77] For example, in the context of international water law, the UNECE has elaborated the need to strengthen synergies and policy coherence between water, energy, and food sectors through a step-by-step approach that will involve (1) identification of the socioeconomic context and conditions of the basin; (2) identification of key sectors and stakeholders to be included; (3) analysis of the key sectors to be included; (4) identification of interlinkages and intersectoral and transboundary issues, (5) nexus dialogue, sharing of sectoral perspectives, and the emergence of potential solutions; and (6) in-depth analysis of issues to reveal possible solutions for synergies.[78]

Similarly, the value of institutional coordination and cooperation in implementing WEF programs has been emphasized by UN agencies.[79] For example, United Nations Water (UN-Water) was established in 2003 to coordinate efforts of UN entities and international organizations working on water and sanitation issues.[80] Similarly, in 2009, the United Nations Development Group launched the Human Rights Mainstreaming Mechanism (UNDG-HRM), which aims to strengthen coherence in human rights mainstreaming policies and practices across UN systems and enhance UN system-wide knowledge codification and sharing, capacity development, collaboration, and policy dialogue on human rights mainstreaming across the UN.[81] Despite

---

74 On the status and normative importance of these instruments, see David Forsythe, *Human Rights in International Relations* (Cambridge: Cambridge University Press, 2006) at 12. See also Antonio Cassese, *International Law* (Oxford: Oxford University Press, 2001).

75 The Nexus Dialogue Programme, *supra* note 48.

76 UNECE, *Reconciling Resource Uses in Transboundary Basins, supra* note 11 at iii.

77 *Ibid.*

78 UNECE, *Methodology for Assessing the Nexus, supra* note 53. See also Belinskij, *supra* note 13 at 5399.

79 Policy Brief 9, *supra* note 49; see also FAO, "Walking the Nexus Talk," *supra* note 50.

80 "About United Nations Water" (last visited 6 May 2019), online: *UN-Water* <http://www.unwater.org/about-unwater/>; see also UN-Water, *The United Nations World Water Development Report 2015: Water for a Sustainable World* (Paris: UNESCO, 2015) at 1-5.

81 See "Priority Focus 1: Promoting a coordinated & coherent UN system wide approach to human rights integration" in UNDG, *UNDG Human Rights Mainstreaming Mechanism: Operational Plan 2011-2013* (November 2011).

ongoing debates on the efficiency of the UN coordination efforts, it is generally accepted that institutional coherence and coordination in the design and implementation of development projects, especially with respect to food, water, energy, the environment, and human rights, can help leverage strengths and reduce inconsistencies.[82]

Even though these soft law instruments are not international treaties and, therefore, do not have legally binding force, they provide practical interpretations and guidelines on how a country can coordinate its water, energy, and food regulatory approaches in order to fulfill its international obligations.[83] Not only do soft law instruments provide flexible guidelines on how to tackle emerging concerns, they provide a template on how international policies can be implemented. They also serve as forbearers to binding hard law instruments in the future.[84] The UN efforts can also provide normative guidelines and lessons on how to achieve institutional coordination for WEF-related activities and programs at the national level.

B. NATIONAL INSTRUMENTS ON THE WEF NEXUS

Traditionally, WEF sectors are governed in several countries, including in Canada and the United Kingdom, by separate sets of laws, rules, and institutions. For example, in Alberta, energy activities are governed by laws that do not comprehensively address water and food security issues.[85] The different laws on water and food also do not comprehensively address energy security challenges. Similarly, within the legislative domain in the United Kingdom, WEF nexus issues are yet to be fully addressed. The energy legislation does not include direct and comprehensive reference to food, land use, and water.[86] Likewise, the water legislation does not make direct mention of energy, land use, and food production.[87] Also, the food legislation does not comprehensively address the link with water and energy security issues.[88] While there is some link to food production, this is only as far as the obligation imposed on water suppliers to licensees is concerned.[89] This creates interpretation gaps in the legal basis and source of responsibility when it comes to detecting the nexus. The different legislation also prescribes approval processes that are not interlinked and coordinated.

However, this is not to suggest that different instruments on WEF do not make mention of the other sectors. Alberta's *Responsible Energy Development Act* (REDA) in fact provides an example of the nature of hybrid reasoning and rule linkage that is required for WEF nexus implementation.[90] Section 2 of the Act empowers the Alberta Energy Regulator (AER) to regulate water conservation and management, environmental protection, and public lands management with respect to energy resource activities in Alberta. Section 67(1) also creates an obligation on the AER to ensure that its activities are consistent with programs, policies, and

---

82 See Viñuales, *supra* note 13; Belinskij, *supra* note 13; see also Olawuyi, "Energy (and Human Rights) for All," *supra* note 42.

83 Rosalyn Higgins, *Problems and Process: International Law and How We Use It* (Oxford: Oxford University Press, 1994).

84 Alan Boyle, "Some Reflections on the Relationship of Treaties and Soft Law" (1999) 48:4 ICLQ 901; H Hillgenberg, "A Fresh Look at Soft Law" (1999) 10:3 EJIL 499 at 502.

85 See *Coal Conservation Act*, RSA 2000, c C-17; *Gas Resources Preservation Act*, RSA 2000, c G-4; *Oil and Gas Conservation Act*, RSA 2000, c O-6; *Oil Sands Conservation Act*, RSA 2000, c O-7; *Pipeline Act*, RSA 2000, c P-15; *Turner Valley Unit Operations Act*, RSA 2000, c T-9.

86 See e.g. *Petroleum Act 1998* (UK), c 17 and *Energy Act 2016* (UK), c 20 and related regulations.

87 See e.g. *Water Act 2014* (UK), c 21.

88 See e.g. *Food Safety Act 1990* (UK), c 16 and the *Food Standards Act 1999* (UK), c 28.

89 *Water Act 2014*, Schedule 2, s 66B(4)(b)(ii).

90 *Responsible Energy Development Act*, SA 2012, c R-17.3.

work of the government in respect of energy resource development, public lands management, environmental management, and water management. This provision aims to ensure systemic coherence of activities and programs related to water, energy, and public lands management in Alberta. By empowering the AER to consider water, energy, and land protection in energy resource development, the AER is responsible for streamlining the licensing, permitting, and project approval processes for energy activities to avoid negative impacts across the diverse domains. However, this is as far as the Act goes, and it does not address issues of promoting energy efficiency in water and food projects, nor does it address questions of climate change impacts on food and water security. Furthermore, the AER's mandate and activities relate mainly to the approval of energy resource projects and do not extend to broader issues relating to low carbon and renewable energy projects.

Similarly, in the United Kingdom, the *Environmental Permitting (England and Wales) Regulations 2016*[91] offers an example of innovative legislation that integrates the administration of a range of environmental regimes.[92] The system requires regulators to control certain activities that could harm the environment or human health, and covers facilities such as the energy industry,[93] waste operations,[94] food industry,[95] and water discharge and groundwater activities.[96] The system also allows a single permit to cover more than one regulated facility if they are on the same site. Although, in practice, this has raised questions about the extent to which physically unrelated facilities could be part of the same site, such an approach could allow the permit-issuing authority to draw on its combined expertise to address intersectoral issues on the site covered by the permit.[97] Furthermore, the *Infrastructure Act 2015*,[98] which simplifies the procedure for obtaining the right to use underground land for the purpose of exploiting oil and gas and deep geothermal energy, introduces safeguards that aim to ensure that fracking does not take place within protected groundwater source areas. The safeguards also include an obligation to monitor the level of methane in groundwater for a period of 12 months before fracking begins, and in so doing, the Act recognizes the interlink between the energy exploitation and the need to protect groundwater sources.[99] However, this is as far as the Act goes, and it does not address issues of food security, nor does it address issues of water and energy security.[100] Although the *Infrastructure Act 2015* imposes a duty on the Secretary of State to regularly request advice on the impact of emissions from the onshore petroleum sector on the ability of the United Kingdom to meet the carbon limits imposed by the *Climate Change Act 2008*,[101] such

---

91   (UK) (SI 2016/1154) [EPEWR].

92   These regulations provide for a consolidated system of environmental permitting in England and Wales under multiple legislation, including the *Environment Act 1995* (UK), c 25; *Pollution Prevention and Control Act 1999* (UK), c 24; *Environmental Protection Act 1990* (UK), c 43; *Water Resources Act 1991* (UK), c 57; *Radioactive Substances Act 1993* (UK), c 12; *Water Industry Act 1991* (UK), c 56; and *Infrastructure Act 2015* (UK), c 7. See UKELA and King's College London, *The State of UK Environmental Legislation in 2011: Is There a Case for Reform? Interim Report* (2011) at 9-10.

93   EPEWR, reg 8; see also Schedule 1, part 2, c 1.

94   EPEWR, reg 12.

95   EPEWR, Schedule 1, part 2, c 6, s 6.8.

96   EPEWR, regs 12 and 38.

97   See *United Utilities Water plc v Environment Agency for England & Wales* [2006] EWCA 633.

98   (UK), s 50.

99   *Ibid.*

100 See e.g. *Petroleum Act 1998* (UK), c 17 and *Energy Act 2016* (UK), c 20 and related regulations.

101 (UK), c 27.

TABLE 7.1 Potential for WEF Nexus Integration: Examples from Canada and United Kingdom

Jurisdiction	Key Legislation/ Institution	Strengths and Gaps
Canada (Alberta)	*Responsible Energy Development Act*, SA 2012, c R-17.3	Section 3 of this Act establishes the Alberta Energy Regulator (AER) as the single regulator for oil, gas, oil sands, and coal. One of the mandates of the AER is to '[ensure] the safe, efficient, orderly, and environmentally responsible development of oil, oil sands, natural gas, and coal resources" in Alberta.[a]
		The AER has powers to regulate water management, environmental protection, and land management in proposed energy resource activities in Alberta. The AER's mandate as the regulatory body responsible for reviewing applications and related environmental impact assessments (EIAs) relating to water, land, and environment in the energy context could enhance regulatory efficiency and internal integration of environmental protection goals contained in multiple enactments.
		While the AER exemplifies the possibility of a nexus approach to environmental protection, pollution control, and regulation of WEF resources, the AER's mandate is currently limited to energy resource activities and does not cover important industries and activities relating to the WEF nexus such as renewable energy; the utilities sector; natural gas; electricity markets; animal health and welfare; farming; the fisheries policy; horticulture; energy efficiency; food and drink; and plants and seeds, including genetically modified amongst others. The permitting functions in these other industries and sectors remain within the purview of different government departments and agencies. Furthermore, the AER's mandate is currently limited to permitting, licensing, and pollution control. It does not address issues relating to energy security, food security, and water security.

a "Who We Are" (last visited 22 May 2019). online: *Alberta Energy Regulator* <https://www.aer.ca/providing-information/about-the-aer/who-we-are>.

(Continued on next page.)

TABLE 7.1   Potential for WEF Nexus Integration: Examples from Canada and United Kingdom *(Continued)*

Jurisdiction	Key Legislation/ Institution	Strengths and Gaps
Canada (Federal)	Office of the Commissioner of the Environment and Sustainable Development	The commissioner represents another example of internal integration of multiple environmental objectives under the supervision of a central "watchdog." The commissioner is an independent unit, which is housed within the Office of the Auditor General of Canada and which oversees, reviews, and appraises sustainable development programs across all government departments. It "provides parliamentarians with objective, independent analysis and recommendations on the federal government's efforts to protect the environment and foster sustainable development."[b] The commissioner produces regular reports covering different aspects of sustainable development, ranging from environmental protection to water management, climate change, localized air quality, coastal and marine environment, waste management, agriculture, and fisheries to children and future generations.
		The commissioner audits the federal government's management of environmental and sustainable development issues, and "is responsible for assessing whether federal government departments are meeting their sustainable development objectives, and overseeing the environmental petitions process."[c]
		Appointing a commissioner for sustainable development has presented some great positive changes for integrated governance of WEF resources. The commissioner contributes to coherence, accountability, and transparency in the implementation of sustainable development programs in government as a whole. However, the commissioner performs largely advisory functions and does not play a part in the licensing, permitting, and approval of water, energy, and food projects. Furthermore, the commissioner's audit mandate does not provide enormous potential for integrated and cross-departmental solutions on how decisions in relation to how WEF considerations are made. For example, the obligation to give weight to sustainable development considerations in programs and activities may not necessarily lead ministries and departments to consider the implications of their activities and programs for other domains and sectors.

b "Who We Are" (last visited 8 May 2019), online: *Office of the Auditor General of Canada* <http://www.oag-bvg.gc.ca/internet/English/au_fs_e_370.html>

c "Members" ("Commissioner of the Environment and Sustainable Development—Canada") (last visited 22 May 2019). online: *Network of Institutions for Future Generations* <http://futureroundtable.org/en/web/network-of-institutions-for-future-generations/roundtable>.

United Kingdom	*Environmental Permitting (England and Wales) Regulations 2016* (UK) (SI 2016/1154)	These regulations "provide a consolidated system of *environmental permitting in England and Wales*."[d] The regulations grant the regulator (i.e., Environment Agency [EA] in England and Natural Resources Wales [NRW] in Wales) powers to regulate and enforce water management, environmental protection, and land management policies in proposed development activities and projects across multiple industries, including water, energy, and food sectors. The EA is the main body responsible for issuing environmental permits to cover projects across different sectors in England. The system also allows a single permit to cover more than one regulated facility if they are on the same site. While the EA exemplifies the possibility of a nexus approach to environmental protection, pollution control, and regulation of WEF resources, the EA's mandate is currently limited to permitting, licensing, and pollution control. It does not address issues of energy security, food security, and water security.
United Kingdom	Environmental Audit Select Committee Sustainable Development in Government Policy (SDiG)	The Environmental Audit Select Committee is a select committee of the House of Commons in the Parliament of the United Kingdom. The "remit of the Environmental Audit Committee is to consider the extent to which the policies and programmes of government departments and non-departmental public bodies contribute to environmental protection and sustainable development, and to audit their performance against sustainable development and environmental protection targets."[e] The committee conducts performance audits to assess how government departments are meeting their sustainable development objectives in line with the SDiG. The committee contributes to coherence, accountability, and transparency in the implementation of sustainable development programs in government as a whole. However, the committee performs largely advisory and auditing functions and does not play a part in the licensing, permitting, and approval of water, energy, and food projects. Furthermore, the committee's audit mandate does not provide enormous potential for integrated and cross-departmental solutions on how decisions in relation to WEF considerations are made. For example, the obligation to give weight to sustainable development considerations in programs and activities may not necessarily lead ministries and departments to consider the implications of their activities and programs for other domains and sectors.

d   Explanatory Note, *Environmental Permitting (England and Wales) Regulations 2016* (UK) (SI 2016/1154), online: <https://www.legislation.gov.uk/ukdsi/2016/9780111150184/note>.

e   "Role—Environmental Audit Committee" (last accessed 8 May 2019), online: *Parliament (UK)* <https://www.parliament.uk/business/committees/committees-a-z/commons-select/environmental-audit-committee/role/>

an obligation does not go as far as setting limits on energy production and efficiency or regulating water usage.[102]

Table 7.1, above, sets out examples of ongoing efforts in Canada and the United Kingdom to integrate and coordinate the orderly supervision and development of water, energy, and food sectors across different legislation, regulations, and policy documents, as well as the challenges that remain. The integration of WEF considerations across different sector-based legal frameworks remains a complex challenge due to the absence of direct recognition of the WEF nexus interplay and linkages.

As seen in Table 7.1, above, the WEF nexus concept is still evolving in both jurisdictions and will require further elaboration. While some of the legal obligations to achieve energy efficiency in water and food projects can be inferred or drawn from existing legislation and other cross-sectoral policy documents, such an approach is indeterminate and may not provide an opportunity for a clear and robust understanding of the critical interplay, trade-offs, and synergies that exist in decision-making and planning across the domains.[103] Speaking of a nexus in such a context will, therefore, appear to lack legal foundation and basis.[104] The absence of linked rules, procedures, and obligations across the WEF domains makes it difficult to reflect WEF nexus considerations in the design, approval, financing, and implementation of multiscale and multisectoral projects.[105] Furthermore, a lack of linked rules and processes could also complicate the process of obtaining approvals and permits, and demonstrate compliance for multisectoral projects across WEF domains.

To develop linked legal frameworks and rules for WEF action and projects, one should start by creating a common understanding of the WEF nexus among the various public and private actors on water, energy, food, land, and climate change. Such a common understanding can help develop an expansive understanding of the WEF nexus to ensure wide coverage of the impacts of WEF policies and projects for localized air quality, water quality, land quality, climate change, nature conservation, agricultural productivity, food preservation, public health, and resource management amongst others. Such a common understanding can also enable regulators to detect and address conflicting or overlapping provisions and rules across the WEF domains. It can also allow for the development of consistent and coherent processes, procedures, and legal knowledge on the WEF nexus. For example, a single permit can be issued to cover more than one regulated facility in the different sectors.

C. INSTITUTIONS ON WEF

The overarching mandate to implement, supervise, and enforce WEF programs remains under the purview of separate institutions such as transboundary water commissions and planning ministries/departments. The fragmentation of WEF responsibilities across different agencies and institutions, with distinct financial and resource allocations and most times competing and conflicting priorities, raises complex questions in terms of potential for developing and implementing integrated solutions across the sectors.[106] For example, in the United Kingdom, the Department for Business, Energy and Industrial Strategy (BEIS) oversees energy governance and policy, whereas food and water are the remit of the Department of Food and Rural Affairs.

---

102 *Supra* note 99, s 49.

103 Joseph N Lekunze & Angwe R Lekunze, "Linking Energy Efficiency Legislation and the Agricultural Sector in South Africa" (2017) 13:1 Journal for Transdisciplinary Research in Southern Africa 359, stating that legislation is vital in order to achieve energy efficiency in the agricultural sector.

104 Weitz et al, *supra* note 12 at 166; Dennis Wichelns, "The Water–Energy–Food Nexus: Is the Increasing Attention Warranted, from Either a Research or Policy Perspective?" (2017) 69 Envtl Sci & Pol'y 113; Cairns & Krzywoszynska, *supra* note 14.

105 Weitz et al, *supra* note 12 at 166.

106 UNECE, *Reconciling Resource Uses in Transboundary Basins*, *supra* note 11 at 8–11.

Similar patterns can be observed in Canada, where responsibilities for WEF policies are fragmented across a number of ministries. In Alberta, for example, Alberta Energy oversees energy and mineral resource policy, while food and water are under the supervision of Alberta Agriculture and Food, and Alberta Environment and Parks, respectively. All of these ministries have key responsibilities for activities and issues that have implications for water, energy, and food security, ranging from building new power stations to the building of major infrastructure projects such as airports, roads, river dams, and food processing plants. Such diffusion and fragmentation of responsibilities in a wide range of ministries and agencies can lead to a lack of coherent implementation and coordination of WEF policies.

Administrative integration and coordination of diverse policy actors and sectors can be achieved internally or externally.[107] The idea of internal integration refers to drawing regulatory oversight and responsibility for WEF sectors in one single authority and/or within one single permit to promote the consideration of WEF issues across all policy areas in the three domains. The AER provides an example of internal integration of water, environmental, and land management goals in energy development activities within one single authority. A single regulatory approach can provide an opportunity to draw together regulatory responsibility for diverse sectors into one entity. External integration, on the other hand, refers to the unified integration of WEF protection requirements by the different departments, institutions, and ministries through bilateral and interministerial cooperation initiatives. An example of external integration is the joint responsibility of departments or ministries for coordinating approvals, planning, and supervising projects.

In the United Kingdom, over the last 15 years, attempts to deal with the issue of coordination has led to greater external integration across different government departments (such as those for transport, energy, agriculture, and trade and industry) by promoting the consideration of environmental issues across all policy areas.[108] For example, the Sustainable Development in Government (SDiG) initiative requires diverse ministries to consider the sustainable development impacts of their policies and programs. However, this loose policy approach to promoting external integration of numerous institutions, with different budgets and inconsistent objectives, processes, and priorities, has not been without great difficulties.[109]

Domestic-level implementation of intersectoral coordination is often stifled by capacity questions.[110] For example, assessing the interplay of water laws and policies in an energy institution or ministry would require expanding staff capacity or recruiting experts in water management. Similarly, implementing energy efficiency policies in the food sector would require recruiting staff that can understand, analyze, and implement energy legislation and rules. Furthermore, assessing the human rights implications of an energy access project on the right to water, food, land, and property would require significant human rights knowledge and expertise. These are complex transformations that could expand the scope of activities of entities into uncharted areas such as interpreting energy efficiency and making decisions on the human rights implications of an energy project for water and food security.

More importantly, given that these respective institutions are currently not constituted or designed to analyze and implement WEF knowledge, their ability to carry out such functions is limited. For example, some human rights advocates consider it dangerous to place the function of interpreting human rights in the hands of professional administrators.[111] As Tallant J

---

107 See Stuart Bell & Donald McGillivray, *Environmental Law*, 7th ed (Oxford: Oxford University Press, 2008) at 99-100.

108 See Andrea Ross, "The United Kingdom Approach to Delivering Sustainable Development in Government: A Case Study in Joined-Up Working" (2005) 17 J Envtl L 27.

109 *Ibid.*

110 Stephan et al, *supra* note 48 at 7; Weitz et al, *supra* note 12.

111 See Martti Koskenniemi, "Human Rights Mainstreaming as a Strategy for Institutional Power" (2010) 1:1 Humanity: An International Journal of Human Rights, Humanitarianism, and Development 47; Philip

rightly notes, epistemic distinctions can be fueled by the tendency of actors to remain within the formal confines of their areas of mandate.[112] Such distinction is also fueled by the divergent training, styles, and perspectives of actors in the respective fields.[113] Similarly, institutional requirements such as fiduciary and non-disclosure obligations in some water, energy, and food utilities, and the risk of being in breach of their legal and institutional responsibilities, can serve as a disincentive for actors to be willing to cooperate across sectors.[114]

This problem of practical operationalization can be addressed through pragmatic and standardization approaches that foster cooperation and minimize duplication. This will require building shared and common understanding by institutional actors in WEF domains, sharing information and knowledge in open and linked systems, and constituting cross-sectoral panels and committees that can provide an informed picture of WEF interdependencies and interplay. Operationalization could also be achieved through the internalization of diverse functions, which should address the problem of fragmentation among diverse institutions by drawing together the regulatory responsibilities for different sectoral environmental problems within one single authority/institution. Internalizing diverse regulatory responsibilities within one single authority might address the issues of coordination and trade-offs across sectors by bringing together actors with different interests, perceptions, and practices.[115] Whatever the approach adopted, a necessary starting point will be to elaborate and develop cross-sector analysis of the key institutions at the municipal, local, national, basin, transboundary, and regional levels governing the use of water, energy, and land resources.[116] Such analysis will examine to what extent the mandates of existing institutions are coherent, conflicting, and/or duplicative and also whether there are linked platforms in place to support knowledge and information sharing and intersectoral cooperation. For example, institutions can leverage on their respective expertise, facilities, and best practices by engaging with staffs and experts across sectors to assist with reviewing and assessing multisector projects. Interagency linkages and partnerships, through joint initiatives and knowledge sharing, could increase trust and enhance synergic solutions that enhance WEF governance.[117]

Linked to the question of capacity and institutional coordination is the question of resources. Integrating WEF knowledge and practices across the domains will come at considerable costs. These costs may include, for example, those of upgrading existing infrastructure, expanding current institutions, staffing, training, field inspections, project review panels, and program design to

Alston, "Resisting the Merger and Acquisition of Human Rights By Trade Law: A Reply to Petersmann" (2002) 13 EJIL 815.

112   J Tallant, "Forging Stronger Cooperation Between Human Rights and Climate Change Communities" (Presentation at United Nations Seminar to Address the Adverse Impacts of Climate Change on the Full Enjoyment of Human Rights, Palais des Nations, Salle XII, Geneva, Switzerland, 23-24 February 2012), online (pdf): <https://www.ohchr.org/Documents/Issues/ClimateChange/Seminar2012/DanielTaillant_24Feb2012.pdf>. Young also argues that actors sometimes resist integrative measures and try to avoid pressures to compromise on priority issues. See OR Young, "Institutional Linkages in International Society: Polar Perspectives" (1996) 2:1 Glob Gov 1.

113   Stephan et al, *supra* note 48 at 7.

114   Andy Stirling, "Developing 'Nexus Capabilities': Towards Transdisciplinary Methodologies" (ESRC Nexus Network, 2015) at 22-23, identifying institutional pressures as a key reason for the closure of WEF nexus integration.

115   Jeremy Allouche, Carl Middleton & Dipak Gyawali, "Nexus Nirvana or Nexus Nullity? A Dynamic Approach to Security and Sustainability in the Water–Energy–Food Nexus" (2014) STEPS Working Paper 63; Christian Stein, Jennie Barron & Timothy Moss, "Governance of the Nexus: From Buzz Words to a Strategic Action Perspective" (November 2014) Nexus Network Think Piece Series, Paper 003.

116   On the methodology for conducting governance analysis on the WEF nexus, see UNECE, *Reconciling Resource Uses in Transboundary Basins*, *supra* note 11 at 108-9.

117   *Ibid.*

integrate WEF perspectives.[118] Due to limited resources and competing budget priorities, WEF nexus integration may run into implementation problems, especially in developing countries with limited financial capabilities.[119] For example, water, energy, and food security programs have been stifled in many African and Latin American countries due to inadequate funding, understaffing, budget mismanagement, and lack of sustained commitment by governments.[120]

However, WEF nexus governance could be met at lower costs and deliver greater cost saving in the long run if planners in each sector develop opportunities for sharing resources and infrastructure. For example, designing energy-efficient water infrastructure and programs can reduce spending on electricity.[121] Also, when food is wasted, energy, water, and land are also wasted.[122] Therefore, promoting sustainable food consumption and sustainable agriculture could reduce public spending on energy and water infrastructure in the long run.

Furthermore, to reduce the cost of WEF nexus governance, it is essential for actors across the domains to build on existing capacities and resources. As suggested above, this will require building on internal programs and capacities and streamlining them to avoid duplication and waste. Linking new programs to already existing ones would save some cost and provide ready infrastructures with which to work. As noted earlier, instead of focusing on expert recruitment, ministries can build joint committees and panels that allow them to explore co-benefits in WEF nexus implementation. This may require appointing an ombudsperson, a coordination agency, or an audit committee to spearhead synergic use of resources across the domains. A good example is the Office of the Commissioner of the Environment and Sustainable Development, an independent unit housed within the Office of the Auditor General of Canada that oversees, reviews, and appraises sustainable development programs across all government departments.[123] The commissioner conducts performance audits, oversees the work of government ministries, and assists them in harmonizing their working methods and reporting requirements on sustainable development.[124] Such a coordinating entity or unit would bring together key actors to address intersectoral impacts and opportunities and to avoid duplication of roles. It could also be well placed to identify areas of priority and distribute resources in accordance with the priorities identified.

The aforementioned gaps and barriers to the application of a nexus approach to WEF governance can be addressed through an integrative and comprehensive legal framework, such as the REDA in Alberta and the Environmental Permitting regime in England and Wales, that foster synergies and rule linkage across WEF domains.

VI. CONCLUSION

Despite the emergence of international, regional, and domestic-level instruments and institutions designed to reduce the fragmentation of responsibilities in the management and

---

118 Stephan et al, *supra* note 48 at 7; Stirling, *supra* note 114.

119 As a recent UN study notes, "there may be lack of motivation to coordinate by relevant sectoral bodies because the transaction costs of coordination are perceived to be higher than the benefits." See Policy Brief 9, *supra* note 49 at 4.

120 Olawuyi, "Energy (and Human Rights) for All," *supra* note 42 at 101-2.

121 FAO, "Food Security and Sustainable Agriculture," *supra* note 6 at 1-5.

122 *Ibid.*

123 "Who We Are" ("The Commissioner of the Environment and Sustainable Development") (last visited 22 May 2019), online: *Office of the Auditor General of Canada* <http://www.oag-bvg.gc.ca/internet/English/au_fs_e_370.html#Commissioner>.

124 *Ibid.*

regulation of WEF resources, the full-scale implementation of a nexus approach to WEF governance remains a work-in-progress. Given the interdependencies between water, energy, and food sectors, common threats to the availability, affordability, and accessibility of these resources cannot be effectively addressed in isolation. Integrated governance of WEF resources can help address trade-offs; inconsistencies; and fragmentations in the design, approval, finance, and implementation of WEF projects. When considered as a whole, through a nexus approach, common challenges facing WEF security can be coherently addressed across the diverse domains.

As learned from the United Kingdom, a loose policy approach to WEF nexus may not foster the required level of institutional coordination and integrated solutions across the diverse sectors. To effectively implement a nexus approach to WEF governance, a comprehensive linkage of legislation, rules, and procedures across the WEF domains is essential. Integration of rules can be achieved by linking applicable procedures and rules on the design, approval, financing, and implementation of projects across the sectors. For example, the approval of a water project could require project proponents to demonstrate the impact of such a project on energy efficiency as well as food production. This goes beyond environmental impact analysis and assessment alone to include comprehensive evaluation and consideration of the implications of a water development project on food and energy policies and vice versa. Such rule linkage can also detect and address conflicting or overlapping provisions and rules across the WEF domains that may hinder cross-sector cooperation and coordination.

Designating a focal institution or administrative unit that will coordinate knowledge, expertise, and information sharing across the sectors is essential to adequately promote WEF consideration across the sectors. Apart from serving as a one-stop shop or single window that will facilitate and integrate permit and approval processes for projects, such an institution can also provide capacity development opportunities for administrators to acquire technical knowledge about the methods, requirements, and data in other sectors. This could help ensure standardized and systematized understanding and documentation of plans and programs across WEF domains. A focal institution can also facilitate and simplify data collection and information sharing across the WEF sectors. By creating a platform for data sharing, such a focal unit can help detect conflicting projects, rules, and procedures. Similarly, by empowering and establishing a focal institution on projects, stakeholders across private and public sectors can obtain relevant information and develop an institutional understanding of the process and methodology for implementing projects that are of common interest to the sectors.

QUESTIONS

1. What is the water–energy–food (WEF) nexus? What are the linkages between WEF systems, and how specifically is the sustainable functioning of one dependent on the other?

2. What are the cross-cutting challenges facing WEF systems? What common patterns and drivers are there across Canada and in the United Kingdom?

3. How important is a nexus approach to WEF governance? What are the core elements of a nexus approach to WEF governance?

4. Traditionally, WEF sectors are governed by separate sets of laws, rules, and institutions. What are the disadvantages of fragmentation of rules and responsibilities across WEF sectors?

5. The concept of systemic integration can provide a strong basis for a coherent application and implementation of water, energy, and food instruments. What are the barriers and constraints to effective rule linkage across the sectors in practice?

6. Do existing international institutions, such as the UN, provide adequate framework for domestic level implementation of the nexus approach to WEF governance?

7. What do the examples from Canada and the United Kingdom tell us about the requirements for integrating WEF systems? What kinds of similarities and differences do we find in both countries?

8. Considering the country examples, in what ways has the administration of WEF sectors become more integrated over the last years? Evaluate the effectiveness and limits of internal and external integration of institutions and rules across the WEF domains.

9. What criteria should be applied in determining the success or otherwise of rule linkage across WEF domains?

FURTHER READINGS

Abdul Salam, P et al, eds, *Water–Energy–Food Nexus: Principles and Practices* (Hoboken, NJ: Wiley; Washington, DC: American Geophysical Union, 2017).

Bielicki, JM et al, "Stakeholder Perspectives on Sustainability in the Food–Energy–Water Nexus" (2019) 7:7 Front Environ Sci 1.

Boas, I, F Biermann & N Kanie, "Cross-Sectoral Strategies in Global Sustainability Governance: Towards a Nexus Approach" (2016) 16 Int Environ Agreements: Politics, Law Econ 449.

Machell, J et al, "The Water Energy Food Nexus—Challenges and Emerging Solutions" (2015) 1:1 Environ Sci: Water Res & Technol 15.

Pahl-Wostl, C, "Governance of the Water–Energy–Food Security Nexus: A Multi-Level Coordination Challenge" (2019) 92 Environ Sci Policy 356.

Siddiqi, A, A Kajenthira & LD Anadón, "Bridging Decision Networks for Integrated Water and Energy Planning" (2013) 2:1 Energy Strat Rev 46.

Simpson, Gareth & Graham PW Jewitt, "The Development of the Water–Energy–Food Nexus as a Framework for Achieving Resource Security: A Review" (2019) 8:7 Front Environ Sci 1.

Wicaksono, A, G Jeong & D Kang, "Water, Energy, and Food Nexus: Review of Global Implementation and Simulation Model Development" (2017) 19:3 Water Policy 440.

CHAPTER EIGHT

ENERGY, TECHNOLOGY, AND ENVIRONMENT

Allan Ingelson and Kristen van de Biezenbos

I. INTRODUCTION

Environmental law is primarily concerned with addressing the negative impacts that human activities have on ecosystems. Those activities include natural resource extraction. Often, new extractive methods can pose new dangers to the surrounding environment, and new technologies must be developed to address them. For example, technological innovation has resulted in a shale oil and gas revolution in the United States,[1] and it has spilled over to Canada. Shale gas development in western Canada is supplying the increased demand for natural gas reserves to generate electricity and replace coal-fired power plants in Canada and supporting the transition to a lower carbon economy. The policy of the Canadian federal government and the policies of British Columbia, Alberta, and Saskatchewan are to promote continued natural gas development. However, the US shale gas development experience has demonstrated that there are potential negative environmental impacts to water, soil, wildlife, and the atmosphere from shale gas development. These impacts are being mitigated through new regulations and innovative technologies. At the same time, rigorous provincial and federal scrutiny of the potential environmental impacts resulting from new technology are crucial to building public trust for the development of natural gas as an electricity resource with much lower greenhouse gas (GHG) emissions than coal.

An understanding of government policies, legislation, and the evolving specific regulations that govern the deployment and operation of new technology that limits emissions from the oil and gas industry will assist environmental law students in becoming more effective counsel.

Three decades of technological innovation that incorporates horizontal drilling with hydraulic fracturing (HF), making previously uneconomic oil and natural gas production from shales profitable, has produced a shale gas "revolution" in the US. A similar "revolution" is now proceeding in Canada. This technological innovation is permitting the US and Canada to increase their gas production for electricity generation, replacing coal with natural gas that emits significantly less GHGs responsible for global warming. In addition to increased shale gas production for electricity generation domestically, the Canadian federal government has endorsed the export of shale gas to generate increased export revenues for the Canadian economy. On October 2, 2018, Prime Minister Justin Trudeau and BC Premier John Horgan announced the approval of a $40 billion liquefied natural gas (LNG) export project facility in Kitimat, BC.[2] Most shale oil and gas development in BC occurs near the borders with Yukon and Alberta. Current active plays include the Montney Basin, which spans the Alberta–BC border near Dawson Creek, and the Horn River Basin play, which extends into the Yukon.[3] The Liard Basin and Cordova Embayment, proximate to the Horn River Basin, are smaller and still in early development.[4] Horn River potentially contains 448 trillion cubic feet (Tcf) of shale gas, of which 78 Tcf is marketable.[5] The Montney is larger, with an estimated 1,965 Tcf of combined tight gas and shale gas, of which 271 Tcf is marketable.[6] Since these plays became areas of interest in 2005, BC's shale natural gas production has risen from negligible levels to parity

---

1   Daniel Yergin, *The Quest: Energy, Security and the Remaking of the Modern World* (New York: Penguin Press, 2011).

2   Dan Healing, "Massive LNG Project in B.C. Gets Shareholders' Final Approval," *Toronto Star* (2 October 2018), online: <https://www.thestar.com/business/2018/10/02/massive-lng-project-in-bc-gets-shareholders-final-approval.html>.

3   Natural Resources Canada, "British Columbia's Shale and Tight Resources" (last modified 25 July 2017), online: *Government of Canada* <http://www.nrcan.gc.ca/energy/sources/shale-tight-resources/17692>.

4   *Ibid.*

5   *Ibid.*

6   *Ibid.* Tight gas is natural gas commonly found in sandstones and limestones, while shale gas is found in shale formations. Both forms tend to require hydraulic fracturing to make gas production economic.

with production from conventional formations in 2011.[7] By 2015, shale oil and gas production formed 80 percent of BC's gas production.[8]

HF has prompted concerns from residents and non-governmental organizations about its potential environmental, health, and safety impacts on surface and underground water, the land, and the atmosphere, the latter in regard to GHG emissions and climate change. As more shale gas wells are drilled in western Canada to provide baseload generation, there will be increased GHG emissions from operations at new wells if natural gas emissions and the associated volatile organic hydrocarbons (VOCs) are not captured and prevented from being released directly into the atmosphere. Natural gas is mostly made up of methane, a potent GHG, and so the extraction of natural gas always creates the potential for the release of methane and other VOCs into the atmosphere. Thus, although generating electricity from shale gas emits fewer GHG emissions than coal, it does emit more than wind and solar energy, especially if there are also emission leaks in the extraction and transportation processes. In response to these concerns, provincial and federal regulators have revised existing regulations and are creating new ones to prevent and/or mitigate the potential environmental and health and safety impacts of HF.

The regulation of shale gas provides a case study of the new regulatory requirements for unconventional shale gas development and the deployment of innovative energy technologies to mitigate the negative environmental impacts. In this chapter, we will examine the current policies and laws that govern shale oil and gas development in Canada, and we will outline the associated regulatory challenges. First, however, we will discuss the constitutional framework for provincial and federal regulation of energy and the environment before examining three significant issues: water impacts, induced earthquakes, and GHG emissions.

II. CONSTITUTIONAL FRAMEWORK FOR ENERGY AND ENVIRONMENTAL REGULATION

Canada's Constitution provides for the division of legislative powers between the federal and provincial governments to regulate oil and gas exploration, development, and production on lands under their respective jurisdiction.[9] Pursuant to ss 92(5), (13), and 109 of the *Constitution Act, 1867*, provincial governments have the authority to regulate oil and gas development on provincial lands. This includes HF of oil and gas wells on those lands. Since most of the HF of shale oil and gas wells has occurred on provincial lands in BC, Alberta, and Saskatchewan, provincial regulators have led the process of updating existing regulations and developing new ones to address novel environmental issues that arise in unconventional shale oil and gas development.

A. PROVINCIAL AND FEDERAL AUTHORITY TO LIMIT EMISSIONS TO PROTECT THE ENVIRONMENT

Sections 91(7), (10), (12), and (24) of the *Constitution Act, 1867* provide the federal government with the authority to regulate HF on lands under the jurisdiction of the federal government. Canada's national regulator, the Canadian Energy Regulator (CER) (previously the National Energy

---

7   *Ibid.*

8   *Ibid.*

9   *Constitution Act, 1867* (UK), 30 & 31 Vict, c 3, part VI (Distribution of Legislative Powers); *Constitution Act, 1930* (UK), 20-21 Geo V, c 26 (as amended by item 16 of the Schedule to the *Constitution Act, 1982*, being Schedule B to the *Canada Act 1982* (UK), 1982, c 11); see e.g. *Alberta Natural Resources Act*, SC 1930, c 3, s 2.

Board (NEB)), regulates HF operations on military lands and offshore in Atlantic Canada (jointly with the governments of Newfoundland and Labrador and Nova Scotia) pursuant to the *Canada Oil and Gas Operations Act.*[10] In addition, pursuant to s 91(24) of the *Constitution Act, 1867,* Parliament enacted the *Indian Oil and Gas Act*[11] and created another federal oil and gas regulator called Indian Oil and Gas Canada, which regulates HF operations on Indigenous lands addressed by this legislation.

Provincial governments are granted power to protect the environment and the property, health, and safety of provincial residents under ss 92(5) and (13) of the *Constitution Act, 1867.* Statutes such as the *Environmental Management Act*[12] and *Climate Change Accountability Act*[13] in British Columbia and the *Environmental Protection and Enhancement Act*[14] and *Climate Change and Emissions Management Act*[15] in Alberta have been adopted to protect the environment. One recent example of action taken by the BC government to protect the health of residents in the northeastern part of the province is commissioning a health risk assessment of the impacts from shale gas development and reporting the results.[16]

With respect to the authority of the federal government to regulate and protect the environment, the constitutionality of the *Clean Air Act,*[17] a predecessor statute to the *Canadian Environmental Protection Act,*[18] was affirmed in *R v Canada Metal Co.*[19] More recently, Peter Hogg analyzed the constitutional authority of the federal government to regulate GHG emissions and argued that the criminal law and the broad-based "peace, order, and good government" power are the main sources of federal authority under the *Constitution Act, 1867* that can be relied on by the federal government to regulate GHG emissions.[20] As he states in his article, "[t]here is no doubt that mandatory reduction in greenhouse gas emissions would be upheld as an exercise of the Criminal Law power of Parliament,"[21] and he cites *R v Hydro-Québec*[22] as a leading authority to support this conclusion.

The federal government, in some cases, can also rely on its jurisdiction over interprovincial and international matters to limit methane emissions.[23] In light of the potential national and international environmental impacts from the release of substances that include methane emissions, the ruling of the Supreme Court of Canada in *R v Crown Zellerbach Canada Ltd*[24] supports the authority of the federal government to reduce methane emissions to protect the environment, as a matter of national concern.[25]

With respect to shale gas, methane, which is a substantial component of natural gas, has been emitted by the oil and gas industry for more than a century. Provincial governments have the constitutional authority to restrict the volume of methane emissions from oil and gas operations on provincial lands for the purpose of natural gas conservation to prevent the waste of

---

10 RSC 1985, c O-7.

11 RSC 1985, c I-7.

12 SBC 2003, c 53 [EMA].

13 SBC 2007, c 42.

14 RSA 2000, c E-12 [EPEA].

15 SA 2003, c C-16.7.

16 Government of British Columbia, "Oil and Gas Activities in Northeastern B.C.: Human Health Risk Assessment" (last visited 24 September 2019), online: *Government of British Columbia* <https://www2.gov.bc .ca/gov/content/health/keeping-bc-healthy-safe/oil-and-gas-activities>.

17 RSC 1985, c C-32.

18 SC 1988, c 22.

19 1982 CanLII 2994, [1983] 2 WWR 307 (Man QB).

20 Peter W Hogg, "Constitutional Authority over Greenhouse Gas Emissions" (2009) 46:2 Alta L Rev 507 at 514.

21 *Ibid.*

22 [1997] 3 SCR 213, 1997 CanLII 318.

23 *Constitution Act, 1867,* s 92A(1)(c).

24 [1988] 1 SCR 401, 1988 CanLII 63.

25 See *Reference re Greenhouse Gas Pollution Pricing Act,* 2019 SKCA 40.

methane, which is a valuable energy resource, and they have done so for decades through provincial agency regulations. Likewise, the federal government limits methane emissions from oil and gas operations on lands under federal management. The Constitution also provides the federal and provincial governments with the authority to limit emissions for the different objective of environmental protection, which includes responding to global climate change and minimizing the negative local health effects from increased methane emissions. The more precise manner in which provincial and federal governments regulate these local health effects, which include potential water and land impacts from induced earthquakes and atmospheric impacts from GHG emissions, will be discussed below.

III. POTENTIAL IMPACTS ON WATER RESOURCES—WATER CONTAMINATION AND AQUIFER DEPLETION

The technological innovation that has led to increased HF in Canada has promoted increased concerns about the potential negative impacts on groundwater and surface water. The prior shale oil and gas development experience in the US has made it clear that there is the potential for negative environmental impacts in Canada on water quality and the volume of water that may be used for other purposes.[26] In 2014, the Council of Canadian Academies (CCA) released a report prepared by leading Canadian scientists called *Environmental Impacts of Shale Gas Extraction in Canada*.[27] The media backgrounder to the report concluded that "[h]uman health and well-being may be affected by various environmental effects (e.g. water and air quality) … . However, health impacts are not well understood and additional research is required."[28] According to the CCA experts, it is difficult to evaluate the environmental impacts from HF of oil and gas wells because of the lack of information surrounding many key issues, especially the problem of fracking fluids escaping from incorrectly or incompletely sealed wells.[29] The expert report noted that as of 2014, there was limited existing information, and it concluded that "industry has researched and assessed upstream impacts on groundwater only minimally" and that government and academia have paid little attention to this type of impact.[30] In regard to groundwater, the CCA scientific expert reported:

> The greatest threat to groundwater is gas leakage from wells for which the impacts are not being systematically monitored and predictions remain unreliable. Potable groundwater can also be at risk from underground pathways for gases, fracturing chemicals, and saline fluids that migrate upwards.[31]

The report also concluded that leaky oil and gas wells, due to either improperly placed cement seals or damage from repeated HF treatments and cement deterioration over time, could have the potential to cause risks to groundwater from the upward migration of natural gas and saline waters from leaky well casings.[32] According to the CCA experts, if wells are

---

26 Allan Ingelson, "Shale Gas Law and Regulation in North America" in Tina Hunter, ed, *Handbook of Shale Gas Law and Policy: Economics, Access, Law and Regulation in Key Jurisdictions*, Energy & Law, vol 18 (Cambridge: Intersentia, 2016) 305.

27 (Ottawa: Council of Canadian Academies, 2014), online (pdf): *CCA* <https://cca-reports.ca/wp-content/uploads/2018/10/shalegas_fullreporten.pdf> [CCA, *Environmental Impacts of Shale Gas Extraction*].

28 CCA, Media Backgrounder, "Environmental Impacts of Shale Gas Extraction in Canada" (1 May 2014) at 2, online (pdf): *CCA* <https://cca-reports.ca/wp-content/uploads/2018/10/shalegas_newsen.pdf> [CCA, Media Backgrounder].

29 CCA, *Environmental Impacts of Shale Gas Extraction*, *supra* note 27 at xiii.

30 *Ibid* at 63.

31 CCA, Media Backgrounder, *supra* note 28 at 1.

32 CCA, *Environmental Impacts of Shale Gas Extraction*, *supra* note 27 at xiii.

properly sealed, the risk to groundwater sources appears to be minimal, although little is known about the movement of fracking chemicals and wastewater in the subsurface.[33] Surface water can be contaminated by chemicals or additives in HF fluids that may be spilled on the land surface during or after HF operations. As shale gas development requires a high density of wells to sustain a stable production rate, the need for well integrity is paramount, especially in areas that depend on groundwater for potable water supply. Improved technologies as well as long-term monitoring are required to manage the impacts. Leaks could also lead to increased GHG emissions.

The HF process uses a significant volume of water to inject fracturing fluids into shale formations. Fracturing ingredients added to the water include surfactants, friction reducers, and biocides, along with structural proppants like sand and ceramic particles. These ingredients are amalgamated into the injection water in order to assist with the fracturing process. The compositional characteristics of this fluid have been a topic of concern, given its movement between the surface and subsurface and the resulting risk of surface water and groundwater contamination.[34] Produced water, which is water that comes up with oil and gas during production and is generally contaminated by fossil fuels and, in the case of HF, fracturing fluid, is also an issue. Given the potential for adverse effects, the proper treatment of produced water is critical to develop public confidence in HF, and both BC and Alberta are addressing this issue by amending existing oil and gas regulations and developing new legislation, regulations, directives, and orders.

In Alberta, the largest oil-and-gas-producing province in Canada, the *Oil and Gas Conservation Act*[35] is the main statute used to regulate HF in the province. The OGCA provides the Alberta Energy Regulator (AER) with the authority to regulate oil and gas operations in order to prevent and mitigate significant adverse environmental impacts on any air, water, soil, or biological resource resulting from oil and gas operations to the extent necessary to protect public health. The AER has adopted new standards that emphasize more diligent planning to avoid water contamination from HF operations. Directive 083 requires that HF have no adverse effect on aquifers and no adverse effect on water quality in water wells located near oil and gas wells.[36] To minimize the risk of aquifer contamination, a detailed aquifer risk assessment must be completed prior to approval of the proposed operations.[37] Well operators must apply for a well licence that specifies the proposed location where the well will be drilled and HF operations will proceed, and the location of nearby water wells and other sources of water

---

33 *Ibid*.

34 E Michael Thurman et al, "Analysis of Hydraulic Fracturing Flowback Fluids and Produced Waters Using Accurate Mass: Identification of Ethoxylated Surfactants" (2014) 86:19 Anal Chem 9653.

35 SA 2000, c O-6 [OGCA].

36 AER, Directive 083, "Hydraulic Fracturing—Subsurface Integrity" (21 May 2013), s 5.3, online (pdf): *AER* <https://www.aer.ca/documents/directives/Directive083.pdf>.

37 AER, Directive 083, s 4.3.2:

19) A risk assessment must be prepared if conducting hydraulic fracturing operations above, or within 100 m below, the BGWP [base of groundwater protection].

20) Licensees' risk assessment must include the following:

a) an evaluation of the potential for direct fracture communication from the subject well to a nonsaline aquifer,

b) the true vertical depth (TVD) of the top and base of any nonsaline aquifers above the BGWP,

c) the TVD of the fracture interval(s) within the wellbore,

d) the modelled vertical fracture distance (i.e., vertical half length),

e) the minimum distance between vertical fracture propagation and the adjacent nonsaline aquifers along the entire fracture interval.

within a certain distance from the proposed well.[38] Where the injection of HF fluids is proposed, the well must be cased with steel pipe designed to prevent the release of fluids that contain chemicals into the surrounding subsurface shale formations and that might also flow up the borehole and spill onto the land surface. Operators must also provide details on the types of HF fluids and their chemical contents to be injected.[39]

Another element of HF that is regulated by the Alberta government is the construction of pits used to store waste products. Pits used to manage the waste from oil and gas production must be constructed so that they are not a public or wildlife hazard or do not adversely affect air, soil, or surface water or groundwater.[40] Chemical spills and the release of waste products must be reported to the provincial regulator immediately upon discovery of a spill or release. The oil and gas operator must describe the impacts resulting from that spill or release[41] and must take action to mitigate the environmental damage.[42]

Both the AER and the BC Oil and Gas Commission (BCOGC) have revised their regulatory requirements with respect to well integrity.[43] Well integrity refers to the prevention of the escape of fluids (for example, liquids or gases) to subsurface formations or the surface.[44] A loss of well integrity can cause negative subsurface impacts and/or the release of fluids to the surface, either of which creates a public safety and environmental risk. Oil and gas wells[45] can be subject to significant stresses during HF, leading to a loss of well integrity. The AER Directive 083 provides a comprehensive set of regulatory requirements that must be satisfied by shale gas well licensees to prevent a loss of well integrity during HF.[46]

---

38 Directive 065, "Resources Applications for Oil and Gas Reservoirs" (5 April 2016), online (pdf): *AER* <https://www.aer.ca/documents/directives/Directive065.pdf>; Directive 051, "Injection and Disposal Wells—Well Classifications, Completions, Logging, and Testing Requirements" (March 1994), online (pdf): *AER* <https://www.aer.ca/documents/directives/Directive051.pdf>.

39 AER, Directive 051, s 4.

40 Directive 050, "Drilling Waste Management" (1 August 2019), ss 6.2(3), (4), online (pdf): *AER* <https://www.aer.ca/documents/directives/Directive050.pdf>; Alberta Energy and Utilities Board, Information Letter IL 96-13, "Revision of Guide 50 Drilling Waste Management" (1996).

41 *Oil and Gas Conservation Rules*, Alta Reg 151/1971, ss 8.050(2)-(3); EPEA, ss 110, 111.

42 *Oil and Gas Conservation Rules*, s 8.050(1); EPEA, s 112.

43 "Managing Well Integrity" (last visited 24 September 2019), online: *BCOGC* <https://www.bcogc.ca/public-zone/managing-well-integrity>.

44 NORSOK Standard D-010, "Well Integrity in Drilling and Well Operations," Rev 4 (June 2013), online: *Standards Norway* <https://www.standard.no/en/sectors/energi-og-klima/petroleum/norsok-standard-categories/d-drilling/d-0104/>.

45 Defined in appendix 1 to AER Directive 083 as "a well at which a licensee proposes to conduct hydraulic fracturing."

46 According to s 2.3.3 of the directive, if the well licensee proposes using a single-barrier system, the licensee must submit the following technical information to the AER for consideration as to whether this type of barrier system will be adequate:

1. the load capacity and safety factors used in the design of the casing relative to the loads and the well environment that the casing will be exposed to;
2. adjusted maximum pressure;
3. the proposed operating practice to be used (for example, the *Primary and Remedial Cementing Guidelines* [Drilling and Completions Committee] or a technically equivalent standard) when planning and executing the cementing program;
4. the demonstrated integrity of both casing and cement prior to initial fracture operations;
5. the demonstrated integrity of casing during fracture operations;
6. the demonstrated integrity of casing with final completion operations or within 90 days of the fracture operation; and
7. the results of a surface casing vent flow/gas migration test before the initial fracturing operations occur and between 60 and 90 days after completing the fracturing operations.

A. VOLUME OF WATER USED

In BC, as in Alberta and Saskatchewan, HF requires large amounts of water. In 2015, seven companies had water licences in BC and withdrew roughly 2.2 million cubic metres of water.[47] An additional 54 companies held short-term use approvals and used approximately 2 million cubic metres of water.[48] In total, over 7.7 million cubic metres were used in HF operations on 534 wells by 26 different operators in 2015.[49] This is the largest use of water for oil and gas activities in the province.[50] Private acquisition and produced water (38.5 percent), flowback fluids (15 percent), and small amounts of water from municipal waste treatment account for the discrepancy between the total amount of water used and the amount withdrawn under water authorizations.[51] Despite the significant fraction of produced water recycled by these operations, the majority was disposed of by injection into disposal wells.

As of 2014, there have been roughly 110 wells used for wastewater disposal in BC, and most of them were completed before 1991.[52] Of total wastewater, 60 percent has been injected into wells more than 43 years old.[53] Well #2240, the biggest disposal well by volume by a large margin, was completed in 1968; since then, it has been injected with 41 billion litres of various oil and gas waste liquids, mostly produced water.[54] The amount of fluid injected into disposal wells and wellbore integrity testing under the terms of the operator's permit must be monitored and reported to the BCOGC.[55] Monthly reports detailing total injection hours and volume must also be filed.[56] In some cases, shallow groundwater monitoring near disposal wells is required by permit.[57] The BCOGC requires operators to pressure test disposal wells annually,[58] although it should be noted that questionable industry compliance rates invalidate this requirement to a degree.[59]

Perhaps most concerning is the fact that little is known about produced water quality once it has been injected into disposal wells. There is information available regarding produced water before injection, but the fate of the wastewater in these wells is unknown. There is no post-disposal testing requirement, and, in some cases, the water is not reused.[60] Compounding this issue is the fact that there is no requirement for baseline testing of surrounding water systems before produced water is injected, creating a lack of information about any changes injection might have on nearby water systems.[61]

---

47 *2015 Annual Report on Water Management for Oil and Gas Activity* (6 June 2016) at 8, online: *BCOGC* <http://www.bcogc.ca/node/13261/download> [BCOGC, *2015 Annual Report*].

48 *Ibid.*

49 *Ibid.*

50 *Quarterly Oil and Gas Water Management Summary—Second Quarter 2017 (Apr-Jun)* (6 December 2017) at 5, online: *BCOGC* <https://www.bcogc.ca/node/14651/download>.

51 BCOGC, *2015 Annual Report, supra* note 47 at 19.

52 Savannah Carr-Wilson, "Improving the Regulation of Fracking Wastewater Disposal in BC" (Environmental Law Centre, University of Victoria, May 2014) at 10, 29, online (pdf): *Environmental Law Centre* <http://www.elc.uvic.ca/press/documents/2014-01-04-ELC-Report_ImprovingFrackingWastewater DisposalRegulation.pdf>. Figure 2 in appendix A to the report illustrates the number of wells used for disposal in BC as well as the decade of their drilling.

53 *Ibid* at 11.

54 *Ibid* at 11, 29. This figure represents approximately 39 percent of all oil and gas liquid waste disposed of in BC until 2014.

55 *Water Service Wells: Summary Information*, version 3.1 (October 2019) at 19, 24-25, online: *BCOGC* <http://www.bcogc.ca/node/5997/download> [BCOGC, *Water Service Wells*].

56 *Ibid*; see Form BC-S18, Monthly Acid Gas Disposal Template.

57 BCOGC, *Water Service Wells, supra* note 55. It should be noted that produced water is injected much deeper than the level of groundwater monitoring wells.

58 *Ibid* at 14; see also s 16(3) of the *Drilling and Production Regulation*, BC Reg 282/2010.

59 Carr-Wilson, *supra* note 52 at 12.

60 *Ibid* at 10.

61 *Ibid.*

B. WATER DISPOSAL IN A WATER-INTENSIVE INDUSTRY

Shale oil and gas extraction, particularly HF, is a water-intensive process. Depending on a number of factors, water requirements can be in the millions of litres per well.[62] For example, in 2010, Apache conducted 274 hydraulic fractures on a 16-well pad in the Horn River Basin, using an average of 61 million litres per well.[63] Oil and gas water use is increasing at the same time that northeast BC is experiencing pressure on water resources, both from increased demand and from climate change. Climate projections published by the Pacific Climate Impacts Consortium anticipated future reductions in streamflow in the Peace River watershed during the summer and fall months.[64] This has been borne out by subsequent events. In the summer of 2010, the BCOGC was forced to suspend surface water withdrawals on public land for four river basins in the Peace River watershed due to drought conditions, which resulted in low river levels.[65] Similar suspensions followed in the summers of 2012 and 2014.[66] Since shale oil and gas operations require most of their water in short timespans,[67] banning the use of surface water during summer months essentially halted operations until the ban was lifted, forcing operators to source water elsewhere in the meantime.[68] Gas production and concurrent water consumption in northeastern BC have only increased since 2014, putting more pressure on water resources in the area.

Despite water scarcity in the northeast, BC's regulatory regime still requires operators to dispose of their produced water by injection into disposal wells. Also known as injection wells, these are deep boreholes in porous formations able to accommodate large amounts of fluid,[69] often depleted oil or gas reservoirs or deep saline aquifers.[70] Once produced water is injected into these wells, it cannot be reused.[71] The BCOGC sets a number of requirements that operators must meet before applying or submitting an application to use a disposal well, including

- information on location, age, pressure, and other data of the disposal well and any other wellbores within a 3 km radius;
- evidence of hydraulic isolation of the disposal zone, often demonstrated by drilling logs showing signs of impermeable rock above the disposal zone or temperature logs;

---

62 Karen Campbell & Matt Horne, *Shale Gas in British Columbia: Risks to B.C.'s Water Resources* (September 2011) at 10, online (pdf): *Pembina Institute* <https://www.pembina.org/reports/shale-and-water.pdf>.

63 *Ibid.*

64 Francis Zwiers, Markus Schnorbus & Greg Maruszeczka, *Hydrologic Impacts of Climate Change on BC Water Resources: Summary Report for the Campbell, Columbia and Peace River Watersheds* (July 2011) at 8, online (pdf): *Pacific Climate Impacts Consortium* <https://pacificclimate.org/sites/default/files/publications/Zwiers.HydroImpactsSummary-CampbellPeaceColumbia.Jul2011-SCREEN.pdf>.

65 Water Use Suspension Directive 2010-05, "Suspension of Surface Water Withdrawals (Peace River)" (11 August 2010), online: *BCOGC* <https://www.bcogc.ca/node/5839/download>.

66 See Directive 2012-01, "Suspension of Short-Term Water Use in Northeast BC" (2 August 2012), online: *BCOGC* <https://www.bcogc.ca/node/8026/download> and Directive 2014-01, "Suspension of Short-Term Water Withdrawals (Peace River)" (28 July 2014), online: *BCOGC* <https://www.bcogc.ca/node/11274/download>.

67 Campbell & Horne, *supra* note 62 at 11.

68 It should be noted that in the oil and gas industry, summer months are often used for major infrastructure work instead of drilling and completions, which generally require more water. See James Waterman, "Going Through a Dry Spell," *Pipeline News North* (31 August 2012), online: <http://www.pipelinenewsnorth.ca/news/industry-news/going-through-a-dry-spell-1.1122675>.

69 Greg Goss et al, *Unconventional Wastewater Management: A Comparative Review and Analysis of Hydraulic Fracturing Wastewater Management Practices Across Four North American Basins* (October 2015) at 20, online (pdf): *Canadian Water Network* <http://cwn-rce.ca/wp-content/uploads/2015/10/Goss-et-al.-2015-CWN-Report-Unconventional-Wastewater-Management.pdf>.

70 *Ibid.*

71 Ernst & Young, *Review of British Columbia's Hydraulic Fracturing Regulatory Framework* (3 March 2015) at 96, online: *BCOGC* <http://www.bcogc.ca/node/12471/download>.

- a pressure integrity test of the disposal well;
- maps showing any known faults or seismicity within a 20 km radius; and
- groundwater data, including groundwater depth and any freshwater wells within a 3 km radius.[72]

Due in part to these requirements, there are a limited number of disposal wells in BC. Of 261 available wells, only 82 are currently active.[73] In addition, most active disposal wells are located relatively far from the highest concentrations of hydraulically fractured wells,[74] leading to increased transport time, distance, and costs, as well as a higher likelihood of accidental discharge.

Decades of water injection practice in Alberta, BC, and Saskatchewan indicate that it is uneconomic to retrieve and treat that water from disposal wells; therefore, it is essentially unusable for other applications, and it is removed from the hydrological cycle.[75] Because injected water is not monitored after injection, there is no water quality information available for the contents of disposal wells.[76] However, it is reasonable to assume water quality only worsens after injection, given that HF fluids often return to the surface more toxic than injected due to exposure to heat, pressure, contaminants, bacterial growth, and industry waste.[77] Consequently, injected produced water is unfit for other purposes. The disposal well is meant to be its final resting place. The unusable nature of produced water, once the water is in disposal wells, puts pressure on fresh surface water and groundwater sources, as operators are forced to obtain water for gas production from fresh sources. The issue of water scarcity in northeastern BC compounds this problem.

C. BC REGULATORY REGIME

In 2010, the government of British Columbia adopted the *Oil and Gas Activities Act*[78] to streamline the oil and gas regulatory process by providing for the BCOGC to handle all oil and gas regulatory matters within the province under the OGAA. The BCOGC manages all permitting of oil and gas activities (as defined in s 1 of the OGAA) and compliance with other Acts, including the *Land Act*,[79] the EMA, and the *Water Sustainability Act*[80] (formerly the *Water Act*),[81] for licensing and monitoring activities. The BC Ministry of Environment and Climate Change Strategy is responsible for ongoing enforcement of general EMA environmental protection regulations as they relate to the oil and gas industry.

---

72 *Application Guideline for: Deep Well Disposal of Produced Water/Deep Well Disposal of Nonhazardous Waste* (8 September 2017), online: *BCOGC* <https://www.bcogc.ca/node/8206/download>.
73 Fact Sheet, "Disposal Wells" (July 2019), online: *BCOGC* <https://www.bcogc.ca/node/11468/download>.
74 Goss et al, *supra* note 69 at 44–45.
75 Ben Parfitt, *Fracking, First Nations, and Water: Respecting Indigenous Rights and Better Protecting Our Shared Resources* (Vancouver: Canadian Centre for Policy Alternatives, June 2017) at 8, online (pdf): *Canadian Centre for Policy Alternatives* <https://www.policyalternatives.ca/sites/default/files/uploads/publications/BC%20Office/2017/06/ccpa-bc_Fracking-FirstNations-Water_Jun2017.pdf>; see also Ernst & Young, *supra* note 71 at 96.
76 Carr-Wilson, *supra* note 52 at 11.
77 Daniel Alessi et al, "Comparative Analysis of Hydraulic Fracturing Wastewater Practices in Unconventional Shale Development: Water Sourcing, Treatment, and Disposal Practices" (2017) 42:2 Can Water Resources J 105 at 107.
78 SBC 2008, c 36 [OGAA].
79 RSBC 1996, c 245.
80 SBC 2014, c 15 [WSA].
81 RSBC 1996, c 483. For a brief discussion of the WSA and the *Water Act*, see Section III.D of this chapter.

Section 7(1) of the BC *Oil and Gas Waste Regulation*,[82] created under authority of the EMA, authorizes well operators to reinject produced or flowback water from operations into a subsurface formation following well completion. No treatment of the wastewater is required prior to reinjection. Division 6 of part 8 of the *Drilling and Production Regulation*, created under the OGAA, also deals with the injection and disposal of produced and flowback water from operations in subsurface formations. Section 74 provides that any volume of fluid (inclusive of any air, water, or gas) injected into a subsurface formation must be measured via a metering system. Section 75 of the Regulation requires the quantity of all injected fluids to be reported to the BCOGC no later than 20 days after the end of the month in which the injection or disposal occurred.

Section 51 of the BC *Drilling and Production Regulation* provides that operators may store produced or flowback water from well operations in open pits on site during operations. These pits must be constructed of clay or other impermeable materials, and the bottom-most depth must be above the groundwater table (s 51(3)(c)). The pit must be located so as not to collect runoff from rain or melting snow (s 51(3)(d)) and never to be filled to more than 1 metre at any point from the brim of the pit (s 51(3)(e)). In addition, the pits must be located at least 100 metres from a natural boundary (as defined in s 1 of the *Land Act*) of a water body (as defined in s 1 of the OGAA) (s 51(3)(a)) and at least 200 metres from any water supply well (s 51(3)(b)). More generally, s 51(1) of the Regulation states:

> 51(1) A well permit holder must ensure that formation water, oil, drilling fluid, completion fluid, waste, chemical substances or refuse from a well, tank or other facility do not do any of the following:
> (a) create a hazard to public health or safety;
> (b) run into or contaminate any water supply well, usable aquifer or water body or remain in a place from which it might contaminate any water supply well, usable aquifer or water body;
> (c) run over, pollute or damage any land or public road;
> (d) pass into or, on ice, over any water body that is frequented by fish or wildlife or that flows into any such water body.

In BC, all schemes for the gathering, storage, and disposal of produced water require an approval from the provincial regulator. Disposal of produced water must be in accordance with an approved scheme or by a method determined acceptable to the BCOGC. Reuse of produced water is not prohibited, but the regulatory system does not explicitly provide for such reuse. In BC, s 6 of the EMA requires a permit or approval for the discharge of waste from prescribed industries or activities. Since produced water from the oil and gas industry—a prescribed industry subject to Schedule 1 to the *Waste Discharge Regulation*[83]—can be classified as a "waste," oil and gas operators are required to obtain a permit from the Ministry of Environment and Climate Change Strategy before discharging produced water.

Produced water in BC can be recycled in HF operations pursuant to the BC *Management of Saline Fluids for Hydraulic Fracturing Guideline*.[84] According to the guideline, "[p]roduced water and completion fluid returns may be re-used for subsequent hydraulic fracturing operations"; however, once there is "no longer any operational use for saline fluid," it requires disposal in a well permitted by the BCOGC.[85]

---

82 BC Reg 254/2005.
83 BC Reg 320/2004.
84 Version 1.1 (April 2019), online: *BCOGC* <https://www.bcogc.ca/node/12440/download>.
85 *Ibid* at 11.

D. BC WATER SUSTAINABILITY ACT

In early 2016, the *Water Act* was essentially replaced by the WSA. The WSA renamed the *Water Act* the *Water Users' Communities Act* and repealed many of its provisions. The WSA vested surface water and groundwater in the Crown.[86] It requires authorization for water use and contains provisions that affect the issue of recycling produced water, both in terms of how fresh water and groundwater are treated and in terms of new water protections.[87]

E. NEW ALBERTA HYDRAULIC FRACTURING WATER USE REQUIREMENTS

Increased concerns about the deployment of the innovative combination of HF and horizontal drilling in shales have prompted closer scrutiny by provincial oil and gas regulators in Alberta to prevent the negative environmental impacts on water resources. On February 22, 2018, Alberta Environment and Parks (AEP) issued a new directive: "Directive for Water Licensing of Hydraulic Fracturing Projects—Area of Use Approach."[88] The directive became effective on the date of its release and does not replace or override requirements specified in other Acts, regulations, policy directives, or guidelines that were in effect at the time of an application for a licence under the *Water Act*.[89] The directive applies to HF projects that have longer development horizons, that are planned to take place in a specific geographic area, and that have ongoing water demands throughout the projects' life. These types of HF projects can be distinguished by operating areas constrained by mineral tenure rights, multiple hydrocarbon wells to be developed within the operating areas, hydrocarbon wells completed by using multi-stage HF techniques, well pad and hydrocarbon well development staged over many years, and ongoing water demands during the projects' lifetime.[90] The directive outlines the duration of water use licences and the water release requirements.[91]

AEP indicates that it will apply the directive to provide a consistent approach to the assessment of water licence applications for HF projects with multi-year operations that occur in an area constrained by mineral tenure rights. In addition, the directive will serve as a guide for operators of HF programs if they apply for a water use licence under the *Water Act*.[92] AEP has transitioned from a "well by well" licensing approach to an "area of use" approach that will grant long-term licences for the entire project area. The directive stipulates the criteria and requirements that must be satisfied before a water use licence can be issued. The requirements include the following: an alternative water source assessment, the demonstrable need for water throughout the life of the project, identification of a Point of Diversion,[93] an appurtenance statement, and the identification of a Point of Use Area (PUA) boundary.

With regard to alternative water source assessments, AEP expects applicants to investigate the use of alternative water sources before considering the use of non-saline water for their projects. Examples of such water sources are, but are not limited to, recycled flowback water, recycled municipal or industrial wastewater, saline groundwater, groundwater that contains

---

86 WSA, s 5(1).

87 WSA, ss 9, 10.

88 Bulletin 2018-04, "New Alberta Environment and Parks Water Directive" (22 February 2018), online (pdf): *AER* <https://www.aer.ca/documents/bulletins/Bulletin-2018-04.pdf>; AEP, Water Quantity, 2018, No 1, "Directive for Water Licensing of Hydraulic Fracturing Projects—Area of Use Approach" (22 February 2018), online (pdf): *Alberta Government* <https://open.alberta.ca/dataset/ef2df211-1091-4470-9b42 -defe6529a862/resource/abce01b3-2011-494c-bc50-a42774d49995/download/directivehydraulic fracturing-feb16-2018.pdf>. [AEP, Water Quantity, 2018, No 1]

89 RSA 2000, c W-3.

90 AEP, Water Quantity, 2018, No 1 at 1.

91 AEP, Water Quantity, 2018, No 1 at 2.

92 *Ibid*.

93 The Point of Diversion is the precise physical location where water is withdrawn from a specified source.

hydrocarbon compounds (excluding methane), and/or non-water technologies.[94] Applicants must include an alternative assessment that shows that no other economically and environmentally feasible water sources are available during the term of the proposed licence. AEP notes that guidance on conducting alternative assessments can be found in s 3.2.3 of its 2006 *Water Conservation and Allocation Guideline for Oilfield Injection.*[95]

The applicant must demonstrate the need for the allocation of water by submitting the following information: the project area; the mineral lease boundaries to be developed as well as any boundaries of major river basins as defined in the *Water Act*; a project development plan at the concept/scoping level that identifies the well density required to develop oil and gas in the area (that is, the number of wells in each section); the project development schedule at the concept/scoping level that identifies the estimated volume of water required annually from the first year of the project until the end of the project; the total volume of water required for each well (that is, m³/well); the data, models, and assumptions used to justify the water allocation request; and the number of years expected before project completion.[96]

In addition, applicants are required to provide reports that demonstrate an ongoing need for water throughout the life of the project during the period specified by the executive director of the water policy branch of AEP. The reports must include the following information: the volume of water diverted from a source; the volume of water used and the water use per oil and/or gas well—all compared to estimates submitted with the application and any previous reports; an estimate of the monthly volume of water that is expected to satisfy the project operations for the upcoming reporting period; and any changes to the mineral lease boundaries within the project area and to the well density plan that may result in a change from the original schedule of development and that might affect the timelines to complete the project.[97]

Future licences may include a condition that allows the director to reduce the allocation of water and/or reduce the term of the licence. Prior to any consideration of a reduction in water volume and/or the term for which the volume will be reduced, a 30-day written notice (or other time-period specified by the director) will be provided to a water licensee to request additional information to justify the ongoing and future water needs under an existing licence. In cases when there is a significant deviation from the operator's development plan, and the need for water in HF operations cannot be demonstrated, the director has the discretion to reduce the annual allocation and/or the licence term.

In regard to the Point of Diversion, only one point will be granted per licence from either a surface or groundwater source. The directive indicates that one Point of Diversion is a well or multiple wells contained within the equivalent area of one quarter section and completed within the same aquifer.[98] The Point of Diversion must be known at the time of application and can be amended only in accordance with s 54(1)(b)(vi) of the *Water Act.*[99]

With regard to the appurtenance,[100] conditions must be included in all licences, and a licence must specify the appurtenance to either the land or an undertaking, not both. Licences are

---

94 AEP, Water Quantity, 2018, No 1 at 3.

95 (1 January 2006), online (pdf): *Alberta Government* <https://open.alberta.ca/dataset/f4f40c00-5e52
    -4ea0-a1cf-3ecdafd61b95/resource/db3ccf86-5b54-4cc5-bfce-a5b42f9282bf/download/water
    -oilfieldinjectionguideline-2006.pdf>.

96 AEP, Water Quantity, 2018, No 1 at 3.

97 *Ibid.*

98 AEP, Water Quantity, 2018, No 1 at 4.

99 *Ibid.*

100 Appurtenance "means belonging to; accessory or incident to; adjunct to; appended or annexed to." Refer
    to ESRD, Water Quantity, 2014, No 1, "Guidelines Regarding Appurtenance" (20 March 2014), online (pdf):
    Alberta Government <https://open.alberta.ca/dataset/c1bcfc26-f1bd-4c66-92f4-8bc6572be37d/
    resource/59a52ba2-e41e-40b2-b76f-e81bb7491b0e/download/guidelinesregardingappurtenance
    -apr23-2014.pdf> for additional explanation.

typically appurtenant to the Point of Diversion but can also be appurtenant to a Point of Use. This is not the case for multi-stage large scale HF projects that can be appurtenant only to the Point of Diversion. In addition, the appurtenance statement with regard to a Point of Diversion should refer to land, not the undertaking.

As far as the PUA is concerned, applicants are required to identify a subsurface mineral lease area(s) (SSMLA) and specify where the water will be used in the drilling, HF, and completion operations. If the applicant intends to include multiple SSMLAs under one licence, the SSMLAs should be contiguous or within close proximity to one another. The PUA is an extension of the SSMLA to the surface, with a small buffer allowing for related surface activities such as road access, dust suppression, construction, and related infrastructures that require water. The PUA should align with the applicant's mineral leases and must encompass the entire SSMLA, usually indicated on a detailed map. In addition, all licences that are granted will specify the purpose(s) and use(s) of water within both the PUA and SSMLA.

If granted a licence, the licensee will be required to report intermittently on the surface locations where the water allocated under the licence is being used within the PUA. The surface locations must align with the PUA defined in the licence. The size of an SSMLA cannot be larger than the PUA, which, itself, will be no larger than 16 townships. However, the director may consider a larger PUA if there are clear net environmental benefits. Examples of such environmental benefits may be, but are not limited to, a reduced or a less significant spatial footprint, the need for fewer independent water sources, and the use of a source that has fewer potential adverse environmental impacts.[101]

Once a licence is granted, the PUA cannot be expanded but only reduced, through a licence amendment, and in accordance with s 54 of the *Water Act*. With respect to the SSMLA, all proposed changes are to be submitted to the director, who will determine if the changes are significant enough to require an amendment to the licence. If licensees acquire new mineral leases within the existing PUA, they may apply under the *Water Act* to amend and increase the SSMLA in the licence. However, if an increase in the SSMLA requires additional water, the applicant must apply for a new licence. In circumstances where there is a decrease in the SSMLA, the director may consider a reduction in the volume of the allocated water, a change in the diversion rate, or timing to reflect the disposition of the lands. Furthermore, operators that acquire new mineral leases through the disposition of another must apply for a separate water licence for the newly acquired lease(s).

The term of a water use licence is a maximum of ten years, unless otherwise established in the water guidelines or subject to an amendment to the *Water (Ministerial) Regulation*.[102] Renewals for subsequent terms of up to ten years are available unless the director has previously specified otherwise. Any other terms or conditions within the licence may be revised in accordance with s 59 of the *Water Act*.

The increased attention that the 2018 AEP directive gives to reducing the volume of non-saline water consumed in HF activities should prompt operators to deploy technologies that will facilitate increasing the volume of water recycled and reused for HF in additional wells, or for other reuse purposes.

In regard to the release of wastewater, the directive indicates that the management of the produced water is governed under the standard licence conditions. Before any release of fresh or non-saline water into the environment, the licensee must ensure the following actions are taken: all recommended practices to prevent the spread of aquatic invasive species are implemented; the water meets acceptable surface water quality and groundwater quality guidelines; the water is to flow into the watershed where the original diversion occurred; erosion prevention and other precautionary environmental protection measures are taken; and the consent of the immediate and downstream landowner(s) have been obtained. The increased emphasis

101 AEP, Water Quantity, 2018, No 1 at 6.
102 Alta Reg 205/1998.

on protecting the quality of surface water and groundwater should encourage the increased deployment of water remediation technologies.

It should be noted that the injection of saline water into disposal wells has been linked to induced seismic events in the US states of Oklahoma, Colorado, and Arkansas.[103] There have also been seismic events near HF sites in Alberta and BC, but they have been more closely linked to the HF process itself, as opposed to wastewater injection wells.[104] See the following section for a further discussion of induced seismicity.

IV. LAND AND PROPERTY IMPACTS FROM INDUCED SEISMICITY

Induced seismicity (IS) is an emerging issue in Alberta and BC that refers to earthquakes caused by human industrial activities that include the injection of HF fluids and may also include the injection of wastewater such as saline water produced by some oil and gas operations into subsurface disposal wells. New federal guidelines adopted by the NEB in 2013 and more recently enacted provincial regulatory requirements in Alberta and BC to deploy seismometers to monitor for IS (and also in Alberta, requirements to create a traffic-light system to prevent IS caused by HF) are responding to the novel issue that has resulted from the deployment of new technology to produce oil and gas from shales. Canadian regulatory responses to IS are drawing on the earlier US regulatory experience.

A. INTRODUCTION TO INDUCED SEISMICITY

In light of the much larger geographic area of shale oil and gas development in the US, American seismologists have been monitoring for IS for a longer time and across a broader geographic area than in Canada; therefore, due to the increased number of human-generated seismic events in the US, the American experience is a valuable consideration in evaluating and responding to seismic risks in Canadian shale oil and gas development. The United States Geological Survey (USGS) defines an earthquake as a "sudden slip on a fault, and the resulting ground shaking and radiated seismic energy caused by the slip ... or other sudden stress changes in the earth."[105] In essence, earthquakes are created by natural (tectonic) forces "when one block of rock moves suddenly (over a few seconds) relative to another" and causes vibrations that, if strong enough, can be felt at the surface of the Earth.[106] In 2012, the US National Research Council reported that some seismic events can be induced by fluid injection activities.[107] Under certain geologic and reservoir conditions, a limited number of injection wells

---

103 Justin L Rubinstein & Alireza Babaie Mahani, "Myths and Facts on Wastewater Injection, Hydraulic Fracturing, Enhanced Oil Recovery, and Induced Seismicity" (2015) 86:4 Seismological Research Letters 1060, DOI: <https://doi.org/10.1785/0220150067>.

104 Gail M Atkinson et al, "Hydraulic Fracturing and Seismicity in the Western Canada Sedimentary Basin" (2016) 87:3 Seismological Research Letters 631 at 643, DOI: <https://doi.org/10.1785/0220150263>.

105 "Earthquake Glossary" (last visited 29 September 2019), online: *USGS* <https://earthquake.usgs.gov/learn/glossary/?term=earthquake>.

106 *Assessing the Impact of Shale Gas on the Local Environment and Health: Second Interim Report* (2015), online (pdf): *Task Force on Shale Gas* <https://darkroom.taskforceonshalegas.uk/original/e4d05cb29b0269c2a394685dad7516e6:c48ffe7884e9b668b8d4b7799a027874/task-force-on-shale-gas-assessing-the-impact-of-shale-gas-on-the-local-environment-and-health.pdf>.

107 National Research Council, *Induced Seismicity Potential in Energy Technologies: Report in Brief* (2012), online (pdf): *The National Academies of Sciences, Engineering, and Medicine* <http://dels.nas.edu/resources/static-assets/materials-based-on-reports/reports-in-brief/Induced-Seismicity-Report-Brief-Final.pdf>.

have been found to be associated with inducing earthquakes that have resulted in felt levels of ground shaking.[108] The geological explanation for the assumed causation in this regard, at least in part, has to do with faults:

> In general, existing faults and fractures are stable, but a change in subsurface pore pressure—the pressure of fluid in the pores and fractures of rock—for example due to the injection or extraction of fluid from Earth's subsurface, may change the crustal stresses acting on a nearby fault, creating a seismic event.[109]

In the 1960s and 1970s, the injection of fluids that contained chemical waste into subsurface disposal wells in Colorado was linked to a number of earthquakes.[110] The Association of American State Geologists (AASG) has now reported a link between the injection of oilfield wastewater into disposal wells and induced seismic events:

> Earthquake activity has increased recently in parts of the U.S. midcontinent. ... Disposal of fluids from oil and gas production ... can cause induced seismicity.[111]

In response to an increased number of earthquakes in the state, the Colorado Oil and Gas Conservation Commission (COGCC) has adopted a "traffic light" protocol to reduce the risk of IS from injection of oilfield wastewater into disposal wells.[112] The COGCC created a permit review process that includes consideration of the potential for IS from wastewater injection, the implementation of a stoplight system to shut down injection wells if certain seismic event levels are recorded, and a compensation fund into which operators pay for persons affected by IS.[113] Also, the COGCC limits the maximum volume and pressure of fluid injection in order to reduce the possibility of IS.[114]

Oklahoma is another state that has experienced an increase in IS from oil industry wastewater injection. With shale oil and gas development, the cumulative volume of monthly wastewater injection increased from 80 million barrels per month in 1997 to 160 million barrels per month in 2013, with most of the increased volume of saltwater injected into disposal wells from HF wells.[115]

On April 21, 2015, the Oklahoma Geological Survey released a "Summary Statement on Oklahoma Seismicity." In this document, Interim Director and State Geologist Richard Andrews stated: "The primary source for suspected triggered seismicity is not from hydraulic fracturing, but from the injection/disposal of water associated with oil and gas production."[116]

---

108 *Ibid.*

109 *Ibid* at 2.

110 StatesFirst, *Potential Injection-Induced Seismicity Associated with Oil & Gas Development: A Primer on Technical and Regulatory Considerations Informing Risk Management and Mitigation* (2015) at ii, online (pdf): *Ground Water Protection Council* <http://www.gwpc.org/sites/default/files/finalprimerweb.pdf>; see also JH Healy et al, "The Denver Earthquakes" (1968) 161:3848 Science 1301.

111 Fact Sheet, "Induced Seismicity" (25 February 2015) at 1, online (pdf): *AASG* <http://stategeologists.americangeosciences.org/sites/default/files/aasg/AASG%20Induced%20Seismicity%20statement.pdf>.

112 "Engineering Unit Seismicity Review for Class II Underground Injection Control Wells" (last visited 29 September 2019) at 2–3, online (pdf): *COGCC* <https://cogcc.state.co.us/documents/about/TF_Summaries/GovTaskForceSummary_Sesimicity_Review_for_Class_II_Underground_Injection_Control_Wells.pdf> [COGCC, "Engineering Unit Seismicity Review"]; *2017 Annual Report to the Water Quality Control Commission and Water Quality Control Division of the Colorado Department of Public Health and Environment* (30 December 2017) at 6, online (pdf): *COGCC* <https://www.colorado.gov/pacific/sites/default/files/SB181arCOGCC2017_1.pdf> [COGCC, *2017 Annual Report*].

113 COGCC, *2017 Annual Report, supra* note 112 at 12.

114 COGCC, "Engineering Unit Seismicity Review," *supra* note 112 at 1–2.

115 Meredith A Wegener, "Shake, Rattle, and Palsgraf: Whether an Actionable Negligence Claim Can Be Established in Earthquake Damage Litigation" (2016) 11 Tex J Oil, Gas & Energy L 123.

116 See Richard D Andrews & Austin Holland, "Summary Statement on Oklahoma Seismicity" (Oklahoma Geological Survey, 21 April 2015), online (pdf): *Earthquakes in Oklahoma* <https://earthquakes.ok.gov/wp-content/uploads/2015/04/OGS_Summary_Statement_2015_04_20.pdf>.

In June of 2015, the USGS co-published an article pertaining to increased seismic activity in the US Midwest, stating:

> Earthquake activity has undergone a manifold increase in the U.S. midcontinent since 2009, principally in Oklahoma but also in Arkansas, Colorado, Kansas, New Mexico, and Texas. The nature of the space-time distribution of the increased seismicity, as well as numerous published case studies, strongly indicates that the increase is of anthropogenic origin, principally driven by injection of wastewater coproduced with oil and gas from tight formations.[117]

The Oklahoma Corporation Commission (OCC) regulates oil and gas activities in the state and also has authority over Class II injection wells (wells that are used only to inject fluids associated with oil and natural gas production).[118] On July 17, 2015, the OCC issued a press release about a new directive on earthquake response.[119] The effect of the directive includes adding 200 additional disposal wells to those that are to undergo monitoring as mandated by an initial directive issued by the Commission in March of 2015. The amended directive "expands the total size" of the "areas of interest" that are covered under the directive and now monitors 511 disposal wells in the Arbuckle formation to ensure that operators are not injecting into this formation. The release also states: "There is broad agreement among seismologists that disposal below the Arbuckle poses a potential risk of causing earthquakes, as it puts the well in communication with the 'basement' rock."[120] On March 7, 2016, the OCC expanded the area of interest governing disposal wells in the Arbuckle area to cover over 10,000 square miles of disposal well locations, with an objective to reduce the total volume of produced water disposed by more than 300,000 barrels a day.[121]

In 2018, a study indicated that the increase in seismic events in Oklahoma is due to the deep wastewater injection.[122] In response to IS, the OCC released new regulations to identify and monitor areas where most of the IS has been experienced, and it requires operators to have access to a seismic array in order to receive real-time seismicity readings. It has also introduced a stoplight system.[123]

The most significant changes to Oklahoma's oil and gas regulations include the revision of OAC s 165:10-5-4(b)(7), which changed reporting requirements for injection well amounts from a monthly to a daily record, and amended s 165:10-5-6(d)(1)(A), which requires operators

---

117 William L Ellsworth et al, "Increasing Seismicity in the U.S. Midcontinent: Implications for Earthquake Hazard" (2015) 34:6 The Leading Edge 618 at 625, DOI: <https://doi.org/10.1190/tle34060618.1>.

118 *Oklahoma Administrative Code*, s 165:10-1-6 ("Duties and authority of the Conservation Division") [OAC]; OAC, s 165:10-5-2 ("Approval of enhanced recovery injection wells or disposal wells"), respectively.

119 Press Release, "OCC Announces Next Step in Continuing Response to Earthquake Concerns" (17 July 2015), online (pdf): *OCC* <http://www.occeweb.com/News/DIRECTIVE-2.pdf> [OCC, Press Release]. See also Andrews & Holland, *supra* note 116, and US Environmental Protection Agency, "Underground Injection Control (UIC): Class II Oil and Gas Related Injection Wells" (last modified 26 August 2019), online: *EPA* <https://www.epa.gov/uic/class-ii-oil-and-gas-related-injection-wells>.

120 OCC, Press Release, *supra* note 119 at 1.

121 OCC, "Media Advisory Regarding Expanded Regional Earthquake Response" (7 March 2016), online (pdf): *Earthquakes in Oklahoma* <http://earthquakes.ok.gov/wp-content/uploads/2015/01/03-07-16ADVISORY-AOI-VOLUME-REDUCTION.pdf>.

122 Thea Hincks et al, "Oklahoma's Induced Seismicity Strongly Linked to Wastewater Injection Depth" (2018) 359:6381 Science 1251.

123 Corey Jones, "Regulators Bolster Protocols to Reduce Chances of Fracking-Induced Earthquakes Felt in Oklahoma," *Tulsa World* (27 February 2018), online: <http://www.tulsaworld.com/earthquakes/regulators-bolster-protocols-to-reduce-chances-of-fracking-induced-earthquakes/article_21d1fea5-acae-5721-ba22-78fd145c0162.html>; Liz Hampton, "Oklahoma Regulator Issues New Regional Protocol to Curb Earthquakes," *Reuters* (27 February 2018), online: <https://www.reuters.com/article/us-oklahoma-drilling-regulation/oklahoma-regulator-issues-new-regional-protocol-to-curb-earthquakes-idUSKCN1GB2MC>.

to conduct the mechanical integrity testing for disposal wells that are injecting 20,000 barrels of respective fluid per day and to perform reservoir pressure testing every 60 days.[124]

In April 2016, the USGS released a report that updated previous findings and reiterated that "earthquake rates have recently increased markedly in multiple areas of the Central and Eastern United States ... especially since 2010, and scientific studies have linked the majority of this increased activity to wastewater injection in deep disposal wells."[125]

Note that the US experience forms the basis for action taken by provincial and federal regulators in Canada, and we will examine the Canadian regulatory regime below.

B. CANADIAN FEDERAL REGULATION

In 2013, the NEB (now the Canadian Energy Regulator) implemented HF guidelines that require well operators to collect and submit baseline subsurface geological data in order for the oil and gas regulator to evaluate the potential for IS from HF operations on federal frontier lands as part of the well-permitting review and approval process.[126]

To date, most of the oilfield shale IS in Canada has been reported to occur on provincial lands under the jurisdiction of the BC and Alberta governments. As a result, the BCOGC and the AER have taken the provincial lead in evaluating and responding to resident concerns about IS from shale oil and gas development in western Canada.[127] Both the BC and Alberta regulators and their associated agencies are actively monitoring for IS.[128]

C. BRITISH COLUMBIA

A report on IS in the Horn River Basin released by the BCOGC in 2012 concluded that 272 seismic events were "caused by fluid injection during HF in proximity to pre-existing faults" and that "[n]one of the ... events caused any injury, property damage or posed any risk to public safety or the environment" in the sparsely populated area of northeastern BC under consideration.[129] In a December 2014 report that followed increasing seismic activity in the Montney formation, the BCOGC stated that the "effectiveness of mitigation methods for induced seismicity related to hydraulic fracturing is difficult to assess"; however, the BCOGC did state that there were possible ways to effect this mitigation, including "limiting injection rates and pressures, and locating disposal wells distal from faults."[130]

---

124 Press Release, *supra* note 119 at 2-3. For new rules for wells and seismicity, effective August 1, 2019, refer to OAC, s 165:10-5-7-(c)(5)(A) (see *Title 165: Corporation Commission, Chapter 10: Oil and Gas Conservation* (1 August 2019) at 95, online (pdf): *OCC* <https://www.occeweb.com/rules/CH10eff-080119searchable.pdf>).

125 Mark D Petersen et al, *2016 One-Year Seismic Hazard Forecast for the Central and Eastern United States from Induced and Natural Earthquakes*, revised version 1.1 (Reston, Va: United States Geological Survey, 2016) at 2, online (pdf): <http://pubs.usgs.gov/of/2016/1035/ofr20161035.pdf>.

126 Canadian Energy Regulator, "Filing Requirements for Onshore Drilling Operations Involving Hydraulic Fracturing" (September 2013), s 4.3, online: *Canada Energy Regulator* <https://www.cer-rec.gc.ca/bts/ctrg/gnthr/flrqnshrdrllprtn/index-eng.html#s4_3>.

127 The BCOGC regulates development of the Horn River and Montney shales; the AER regulates exploration and production of shale gas in the Montney, Duvernay, Colorado, and Fernie/Nordegg shales within the province.

128 KM Haug, JM Dongas & JE Warren, *A Review of the Potential Correlation Between Low-Magnitude Earthquakes and Oil and Gas Industry Activity in Alberta*, Open File Report 2013-16 (Alberta Energy Regulator; Alberta Geological Survey, February 2014), online (pdf): *Alberta Geological Survey* <https://ags.aer.ca/document/OFR/OFR_2013_16.pdf>.

129 *Investigation of Observed Seismicity in the Horn River Basin* (August 2012) at 3, online: *BCOGC* <https://www.bcogc.ca/node/8046/download>.

130 *Investigation of Observed Seismicity in the Montney Trend* (December 2014) at 13, online: *BCOGC* <https://www.bcogc.ca/node/12291/download>.

The BCOGC has also employed a traffic-light system wherein seismic events with a magnitude of 4.0 or greater on the Richter scale will result in the cessation of production operations until the BCOGC implements a mitigation plan to address seismicity.[131] In 2015, the regulator updated its *Drilling and Production Regulation* to address seismicity. Pursuant to s 21.1(1) of the Regulation, a well permit holder "must immediately report to the Commission any seismic event within a 3 km radius of the drilling pad that is recorded by the well permit holder or reported to the well permit holder"[132] for any seismic event that "has a magnitude of 4.0 or greater"[133] or if "ground motion is felt on the surface by any individual within the 3 km radius."[134] If a 4.0 event occurs, the well permit holder must suspend HF operations and/or fluid disposal operations on the well immediately.[135] This Regulation applies to both producing oil and gas wells and wastewater disposal wells.

D. ALBERTA

After more than four decades of monitoring for IS from fluid injection activities in and near provincial oilfields, the Alberta Geological Survey and the AER have concluded that in Alberta, there is a clear connection between HF operations and IS at a limited number of sites in the province.[136] Earthquakes have occurred in the Fox Creek area, north of Edmonton, where HF programs have been carried out, and they have prompted the AER to adopt traffic-light protocols (TLPs), as has been done in Oklahoma, to reduce the potential for triggering earthquakes from HF. However, unlike in the US, in Alberta, no property damage has been reported to date, and no lawsuits claiming damage from seismicity induced by oilfield activities have been initiated.

The University of Calgary has undertaken the multidisciplinary Hydraulic Fracturing Innovation Initiative (HFII), which includes the first comprehensive Canadian law and policy investigation of IS. Building on the research results of the geologists and engineers in the multidisciplinary initiative, the university is evaluating the adequacy of existing provincial and federal laws and regulations to address the novel legal issues associated with HF and IS. The research program is developing approaches that are suitable for establishing scientifically sound data, and it is developing and deploying new methods for hazard assessment of IS. The research comprises baseline and post-HF assessments surrounding IS.

Notwithstanding the lack of property damage from IS associated with HF reported to date,[137] the AER, as part of its approach to unconventional shale oil and gas development, has adopted a "risk-based" approach that considers different types of geological environments in which IS may arise in order to better manage the impacts and liability from HF.[138] To evaluate potential environmental and human impacts from IS, the AER has defined the term "risk assessment" and is applying a "systematic analysis of the risks from activities and a rational evaluation of their significance by comparison against predetermined standards, target risk

---

131 *Ibid* at 16.

132 *Drilling and Production Regulation*, s 21.1(1).

133 *Drilling and Production Regulation*, s 21.1(1)(a).

134 *Drilling and Production Regulation*, s 21.1(1)(b).

135 *Drilling and Production Regulation*, s 21.1(2).

136 K Parks, "Shale-Gas Development, Hydraulic Fracturing, and Water in Alberta: AER's Regulatory Program" (Presentation made at Synergy Alberta Conference, Red Deer, Alberta, 29 October 2013) at 20, online: *Synergy Alberta* <http://www.synergyalbertaregistration.ca/conference/2013/downloads/presentations/WaterPanelKParks.pdf>.

137 *Ibid.*

138 J Stewart, A Lucas & G Bruno, "A Comparative Analysis of Public Participation in the Regulation of Hydraulic Fracturing in the Bakken" (2017) Occasional Paper No 59, online: *Canadian Institute of Resources Law* <https://cirl.ca/publications/occasional-papers/50-59>.

levels, or other risk criteria."[139] The "play-focused approach" considers different geographic areas in which shale oil and gas are being developed in a variety of geologic settings, exploring and testing the different physical and chemical properties of each. As Alastair Lucas, Theresa Watson, and Eric Kimmel noted in 2014:

> The AER selected a management-based regulatory approach as the preferred intervention strategy to influence oil and gas sector firms to manage or reduce the subsurface risks associated with hydraulic fracturing. ...
>
> The AER's regulatory response specifies the planning elements that operators must consider, and that they be able to demonstrate that the subsurface risks associated with hydraulic fracturing operations are properly managed. These requirements direct industry to provide assurances and demonstrate that the risks to social and environmental values (predominantly water resources) are safely managed.[140]

In light of the significantly higher pressures at which HF fluids are injected into the surface relative to wastewater injected into disposal wells, subsurface geologic mapping to identify where faults are located and careful site selection to avoid HF at sites near faults are actions that should be taken to minimize the potential for triggering an earthquake. In addition, monitoring for increased seismic activity in the area where a HF program is proceeding, changing the HF parameters, or suspending operations are additional steps that can be taken to reduce the potential for triggering earthquakes that may cause property damage and/or physical injury.

In the event that well licensees do not comply with the regulatory requirements, their operations can be suspended or terminated by the energy regulator, and in the event that shale gas operators cause environmental damages, fines can be imposed under the Alberta *Environmental Protection and Enhancement Act* (EPEA).

In addition to concerns over seismicity, HF has also raised climate change concerns over the accidental or deliberate release of methane from onshore HF wells.

V. CLIMATE CHANGE AND ATMOSPHERIC IMPACTS— FEDERAL REGULATION TO REDUCE METHANE EMISSIONS FROM THE OIL AND GAS INDUSTRY THROUGH TECHNOLOGICAL INNOVATION

For decades, the volume of natural gas emitted by the oil and gas industry has been limited by provincial and federal regulators under oil and gas conservation legislation and regulations to avoid wasting the valuable energy resource. However, equipment leaks and the industry practice of venting at major natural gas facilities continue to be significant sources of national GHG emissions. As mentioned previously, natural gas contains methane, a potent GHG that has a global warming potential of more than 25 times carbon dioxide (CO_2) over a 100-year period (though it does not stay in the atmosphere for as long as CO_2).[141] Environment and Climate Change Canada (ECCC) has reported that the Canadian oil and gas sector was responsible for 25 percent of the national GHG emissions during the period of 1990 to 2012. In 2017, 27 percent

---

139 AER, Directive 083, appendix 1.

140 "Regulating Multistage Hydraulic Fracturing: Challenges in a Mature Oil and Gas Jurisdiction" in DN Zillman et al, eds, *The Law of Energy Underground: Understanding New Developments in Subsurface Production, Transmission, and Storage* (Oxford: Oxford University Press, 2014) 127 at 137.

141 Environment and Climate Change Canada, "Proposed Methane Regulations: A Significant Step in Addressing Climate Change in Canada" (Ottawa: Environment and Climate Change Canada, June 2017), online (pdf): *Global Methane Initiative* <https://www.globalmethane.org/documents/1_Canada_James%20Diamond_post_508.pdf>.

of Canada's GHG emissions were from the same industry.[142] The development of new technology to detect the level of methane emissions from Canadian oil and gas operations has allowed federal and provincial regulators in Alberta to create new regulations to monitor and reduce the level of emissions as part of the *Pan-Canadian Framework on Clean Growth and Climate Change*, which is a national plan directed toward reducing the effects of climate change, as discussed in more detail in Chapter 6.[143]

On June 29, 2016, as part of the North American initiative on Climate, Energy, and the Arctic, Prime Minister Justin Trudeau announced that Canada would reduce its national methane emissions from the oil and gas industry by 40 to 45 percent below the level of emissions in 2012 by 2025.[144] In the two years since the federal government facilitated the emergence of the *Pan-Canadian Framework on Clean Growth and Climate Change*, first ministers created provincial–national–territorial groups to consult with Indigenous peoples, the business sector, civil society, and the general public to discuss options and propose recommendations as to how to best respond to climate change. Following the consultation process, four pillars were created under the plan: pricing carbon pollution; complementary climate actions such as implementing more stringent emission standards; adapting and building resilience to the effects of climate change; and investing in clean technology, innovation, and jobs.[145]

In April 2018, under s 332(1) of the *Canadian Environmental Protection Act, 1999*,[146] the minister of environment and climate change published *Regulations Respecting Reduction in the Release of Methane and Certain Volatile Organic Compounds (Upstream Oil and Gas Sector)*, in part II of the *Canada Gazette*.[147] Consistent with responding to climate change and protecting the health of Canadians by improving air quality, s 1 of the Methane Regulations provides that the regulations are designed to "reduc[e] the immediate or long-term harmful effects of the emission of methane and certain volatile organic compounds." The Methane Regulations fall under the second pillar of the Pan-Canadian Framework, which provides for more stringent emission standards. The Methane Regulations focus on reducing methane emissions and VOCs from the upstream oil and gas industry.[148] Some of the provisions in the Methane Regulations will be phased in to allow facility operators to plan and budget for equipment upgrades and/or the purchase of new equipment. Some provisions will come into force

---

142 ECCC, "Greenhouse Gas Emissions" (last modified 17 April 2019), online: *Government of Canada* <https://www.canada.ca/en/environment-climate-change/services/environmental-indicators/greenhouse-gas-emissions.html>.

143 *Pan-Canadian Framework on Clean Growth and Climate Change: Canada's Plan to Address Climate Change and Grow the Economy*, (Gatineau, Qc: Environment and Climate Change Canada, 2016), online: *Government of Canada* <https://www.canada.ca/en/services/environment/weather/climatechange/pan-canadian-framework/climate-change-plan.html>.

144 Drew Nelson, "The Power of Three: Mexico Aligns with U.S. and Canada on Oil and Gas Methane Pollution" (29 June 2016), online (blog): *Environmental Defense Fund* <http://blogs.edf.org/energyexchange/2016/06/29/the-power-of-three-mexico-aligns-with-u-s-and-canada-on-oil-and-gas-methane-pollution/>; see also "U.S.–Canada Joint Statement on Climate, Energy, and Arctic Leadership" (10 March 2016), online: *Prime Minister of Canada* <https://pm.gc.ca/en/news/statements/2016/03/10/us-canada-joint-statement-climate-energy-and-arctic-leadership>.

145 ECCC, "Pan Canadian Framework for Clean Growth and Climate Change" (last modified 14 March 2019), online: *Government of Canada* <https://www.canada.ca/en/services/environment/weather/climatechange/pan-canadian-framework.html>.

146 SC 1999, c 33.

147 SOR/2018-66 (in force 1 January 2020) [Methane Regulations]; ECCC, News Release, "Canada Finalizes Major Commitment to Reduce Carbon Pollution" (26 April 2018), online: *Government of Canada* <https://www.canada.ca/en/environment-climate-change/news/2018/04/canada-finalizes-major-commitment-to-reduce-carbon-pollution.html>.

148 The term "upstream" refers to drilling, exploration, and production operations and the associated facilities.

on January 1, 2020, and others, in 2023.[149] The federal government estimates that by 2025, the regulations will result in a decrease of the equivalent of 232 million tonnes of CO_2 in national methane emissions from the oil and gas industry.[150]

The Methane Regulations were not created in a vacuum. For decades, both the provincial and federal governments have restricted the volume of methane emitted from oil and gas operations to prevent wasting a valuable economic resource and to optimize Crown and oil and gas industry revenues. Since there is significantly more onshore oil and gas development on provincial lands in BC, Alberta, and Saskatchewan than on federal lands, historically, the provincial regulators developed more comprehensive systems to limit methane emissions than the federal government. As a result, the new federal regulations incorporate by reference some of the provincial standards used in BC, Alberta, and Saskatchewan to limit methane emissions.[151] To assist in appreciating the interplay between the existing provincial systems and the more stringent federal regulations, we will analyze the provincial laws of BC and Alberta that limit upstream oil and gas industry emissions in the following sections of this chapter.

A. THE NEW, STRICTER FEDERAL REGULATIONS BUILD ON EXISTING PROVINCIAL FRAMEWORKS TO SIGNIFICANTLY REDUCE EMISSIONS

The methane emissions from the two provinces with expanding shale development that could increase Canada's national emissions if more stringent regulatory steps are not taken by the federal government has prompted the adoption of the new federal regulations. For decades, the provincial oil and gas regulator in Alberta has recommended that operators detect and repair facility equipment leaks.[152] An understanding of the weaknesses of the Alberta and BC regimes will assist in appreciating the regulatory reform recently undertaken by the federal government to significantly reduce the current level of methane emissions from the largest industry sources.

In 2013, the Alberta government adopted a new act called the *Responsible Energy Development Act*[153] to better regulate its oil and gas industry by creating the AER[154] to, among other things, enforce the EPEA to minimize oil and gas industry emissions. Under REDA, the AER administers "energy resource enactments" that include acts, regulations, and directives that are sometimes incorporated into regulations by reference.[155] A regulation called the *Oil and Gas Conservation Rules* is employed along with the AER directives 060,[156] 017,[157] and

149 ECCC, "Canada's Methane Regulations for the Upstream Oil and Gas Sector: Methane Regulations" (last modified 26 April 2018), online: *Government of Canada* <https://www.canada.ca/en/environment-climate-change/services/canadian-environmental-protection-act-registry/proposed-methane-regulations-additional-information.html>.

150 ECCC, "Federal Regulations to Reduce Methane Emissions in the Oil and Gas Sector: Greenhouse Gas Emission Reductions" (last modified 26 April 2018), online: *Government of Canada* <https://www.canada.ca/en/environment-climate-change/news/2018/04/federal-regulations-to-reduce-methane-emissions-in-the-oil-and-gas-sector.html>.

151 Methane Regulations, s 9.

152 Directive 060, "Upstream Petroleum Industry Flaring, Incinerating, and Venting" (13 December 2018), online (pdf): *AER* <https://www.aer.ca/documents/directives/Directive060_2020.pdf>.

153 SA 2012, c R-17.3 [REDA].

154 REDA, s 3.

155 REDA, s 1(1)(j); see also AER, "Acts, Regulations, and Rules" (last visited 2 October 2019), online: *AER* <https://www.aer.ca/regulating-development/rules-and-directives/acts-regulations-and-rules.htm>.

156 "Methane Reduction" (last visited 19 October 2019), online: *AER* <https://www.aer.ca/providing-information/by-topic/methane-reduction>.

157 Directive 017, "Measurement Requirements for Oil and Gas Operations" (13 December 2018), online (pdf): *AER* <https://www.aer.ca/documents/directives/Directive017.pdf>.

084[158] to limit methane emissions. The directives managed by the AER contain detailed information on the expectations of the regulator to limit emissions from oilfield operations.

The current oil and gas conservation (OGC) rules and directives that cover all of Alberta are similar to the BC guideline in that they lack specific requirements to compel operators to detect and prevent equipment leaks.[159] They also lack a specific deadline by which equipment repairs must be completed. As in BC, the OGC regulations in Alberta do not prescribe as many inspections to be carried out within a specified time period as is required under the Methane Regulations. Recommendations, rather than requirements, characterize the provincial OGC systems, and this leads to a higher level of methane and VOC emissions from facilities than is necessary. The significant weakness of the BC and Alberta regulatory systems—failing to require timely detection and repair of equipment leaks—is evident in the Saskatchewan system as well.

The BCOGC employs the OGAA to limit emissions from upstream oil and gas operations for OGC purposes.[160] The BCOGC manages permitting of oil and gas activities as defined in s 1 of the OGAA,[161] and the BC Ministry of the Environment is responsible for ongoing enforcement of the environmental protection regulations under the EMA. In regard to methane leaks from equipment in BC upstream facilities, the provincial guideline does not specify a precise deadline by which operators must complete preventative maintenance actions.[162] In BC, there is a lack of concrete requirements to ensure that facility equipment leaks are repaired in a timely manner to minimize the volume of methane emissions released into the atmosphere. The BC Guideline does not specify the number of annual facility inspections that must be completed at facilities.[163] The Alberta and BC regulatory systems draw heavily on industry guidelines prepared by the Canadian Association of Petroleum Producers (CAPP), a national oil industry association that represents most of the oil companies in Canada.[164] The voluntary industry guidelines provide suggestions to operators about where the most common sources of equipment leaks are and how to most efficiently manage the volume of emissions by focusing on larger leaks of process fluid. They also recommend early leak detection and repairs.[165] The industry guidelines recommend that industry operators prioritize the most common types of equipment leaks for regular and more frequent screenings as part of directed leak inspection and maintenance programs.[166]

B. FACILITY AND EQUIPMENT LEAKS

The provisions in part 1 of the Methane Regulations address leaks at onshore oil and gas facilities, and those in part 2 cover leaks at offshore facilities. The new regulations create uniform,

---

158 Directive 084, "Requirements for Hydrocarbon Emission Controls and Gas Conservation in the Peace River Area" (11 September 2018), online (pdf): *AER* <https://www.aer.ca/documents/directives/Direc tive084.pdf>.

159 One exception to the province-wide requirements in Directive 084 are the more stringent requirements that apply to the Peace River Area, as indicated in ss 6.1-6.2.6, which became effective on September 27, 2018.

160 "Reducing Methane Emissions" (last visited 19 October 2019), online: *BCOGC* <https://www.bcogc.ca/ public-zone/reducing-methane-emissions>.

161 OGAA, s 6.

162 *Flaring and Venting Reduction Guideline*, version 5.1 (May 2018) at 55, online: *BCOGC* <https://www .bcogc.ca/node/5916/download> [BC Guideline].

163 *Drilling and Production Regulation*, s 41.1. See also *ibid*, ch 7, for venting requirements generally.

164 "Best Management Practice: Management of Fugitive Emissions at Upstream Oil and Gas Facilities" (January 2007), online (download): *CAPP* <https://www.capp.ca/publications-and-statistics/publica tions/116116>.

165 *Ibid* at 1.

166 *Ibid* at 8.

national standards to significantly reduce methane emissions in all provinces and territories. The term "fugitive emissions" in s 2 of the Methane Regulations refers to gas leaks from equipment and venting natural gas from facilities, and it is defined as "the emission of hydrocarbon gas from an upstream oil and gas facility in an unintentional manner." The regulations focus on reducing emissions from larger facilities, which are classified in the regulations as facilities that receive more than 60,000 standard m^3 of hydrocarbon gas during a 12-month period.[167] Initially, addressing a smaller number of larger sources of emissions that account for most of the methane that is released into the atmosphere reflects a high leverage approach. One of the weaknesses of the provincial OGC systems is the absence of concrete provisions that compel leak prevention, detection, and timely repair of equipment leaks that will further reduce emissions. The Methane Regulations address this first deficiency by clearly mandating the completion of leak detection and repair programs in s 29 as follows:

> 29(1) An operator for a facility must—in order to limit fugitive emissions containing hydrocarbon gas from equipment components at the facility—establish and carry out at the facility
>> (a) a regulatory leak detection and repair program that satisfies the requirements of sections 30 to 33; or
>> (b) an alternative leak detection and repair program referred to in subsection 35(1) that results in at most the same quantity of those fugitive emissions as would result from a regulatory program referred to in paragraph (a), as demonstrated in a record, with supporting documents, made by the operator before the program is established and, at least once per year and at least 90 days after a previous demonstration, while the program is being carried out.
>
> (2) An operator for a facility that establishes a leak detection and repair program referred to in paragraph (1)(b) must, without delay, notify the Minister to that effect.

A second weakness of the BC, Alberta, and Saskatchewan OGC systems that is addressed in the Methane Regulations is the failure to require timely leak repairs to reduce emissions. To remedy this deficiency, s 32 of the Regulations stipulates that in most cases, a leak must be repaired within 30 days of the leak being detected:

> 32. A leak from an equipment component that is detected, whether as a result of an inspection or otherwise, must be repaired
>> (a) if the repair can be carried out while the equipment component is operating, within 30 days after the day on which it was detected; and
>> (b) in any other case, within the period before the end of the next planned shutdown unless that period is extended under section 33.

Clearly, this provision mandates timely leak repair.

A third weakness of the existing provincial regulatory systems is the failure to specify the time by which facility equipment must be inspected. The Methane Regulations address this third deficiency by requiring that equipment components at an upstream oil and gas facility be inspected on or before the later of May 1, 2020, and the day that occurs 60 days after the day on which production of the facility first began as well as at least three times per year and at least 60 days after a previous inspection.[168] The Regulations mandate three annual inspections, which is more frequent than the number prescribed in the provincial OGC systems. The types of technology that will be used during inspections (for example, infrared cameras, sniffers, drones, and satellite systems) are specified in the Regulations to prevent potential arguments and disputes as to whether there have been emissions that exceed the level permitted under the Regulations.

The requirements in the Methane Regulations clearly convey to facility operators the emphasis that the minister of environment and climate change is placing on preventing, detecting, and repairing equipment leaks in a timely manner to significantly further reduce

---

167 Methane Regulations, ss 20, 26-45.
168 Methane Regulations, ss 30(1)-(3).

emissions from large oil and gas facilities. The fact that the Regulations specify time periods in which operators must complete equipment repairs will prompt facility operators to pay closer attention to the current volume of emissions from equipment leaks. When these provisions are enforced, they may result in a decrease in the volume of methane that is released from a foreseeable and preventable source of emissions.

In addition to the general equipment leak provisions in the Methane Regulations, there are more specific provisions that apply to different types of equipment, including pneumatic devices and compressors, discussed below.[169]

C. LEAKS FROM PNEUMATIC DEVICES AND COMPRESSORS

A variety of automated instruments called pneumatic devices that use natural gas to pump liquids and for other purposes are employed throughout the industry. Some of these devices leak methane. As with other types of oil industry equipment, the Methane Regulations prescribe operating efficiency standards for pneumatic controllers and pumps.[170] The regulations prompt the installation of more recent technology by requiring operators to replace certain types of pneumatic controllers that produce a larger volume of emissions (high-bleed controllers) with low-bleed or no-bleed controllers, which release a much smaller volume of emissions. As with the other types of equipment, the repairs and/or equipment replacements must be completed within the time period specified in the regulations. In order to provide facility operators with reasonable notice to allow them to budget for new equipment purchases to replace the existing equipment, the provisions in the regulations that apply to pneumatic devices are scheduled to come into force in 2023.[171]

D. VENTING

Another source of methane emissions is venting. Venting is the practice by which natural gas is released directly into the atmosphere.[172] As natural gas is used to control pressurized equipment, including pumps in multiple industry operations, methane is released from equipment in processing facilities through vents. The Methane Regulations are designed to reduce the volume of methane that is vented from larger oil and gas facilities by 95 percent. To achieve this objective, s 26 of the Methane Regulations creates an annual venting limit of not more than 15 000 m³ of hydrocarbon gas for an upstream oil and gas facility during a year. This annual venting limit should prompt facility operators to innovate to further reduce emissions. At the same time, the Methane Regulations incorporate existing technology used in the western Canadian oil-and-gas-producing provinces to manage the level of emissions. For example, s 9 of the Methane Regulations refers to the current provincial methane destruction (gas combustion) standards and requirements used by regulators in BC, Saskatchewan, and Alberta to limit methane emissions as follows:

> 9. Hydrocarbon gas destruction equipment that is used at an upstream oil and gas facility[173] must satisfy the requirements related to the destruction of hydrocarbon gas set out in
> (a) sections 3.6 and 7 of Version 4.5 of the guideline entitled *Flaring and Venting Reduction Guideline*, published by the Oil and Gas Commission of British Columbia in June 2016, if the facility is located in British Columbia;

---

169 Methane Regulations, ss 37, 39, 49, 50.
170 Methane Regulations, ss 37(1), (2), 39(1).
171 ECCC, "Canada's Methane Regulations for the Upstream Oil and Gas Sector," *supra* note 149.
172 "Methane Emissions" (last visited 20 October 2019), online: *CAPP* <https://www.capp.ca/responsible-development/air-and-climate/methane-emissions>.
173 Robert Bott, David M Carson & David Coglon, *Our Petroleum Challenge: Canadian Resources, Global Markets*, 8th ed (Calgary: Canadian Centre for Energy Information, 2013). Upstream facilities are those connected to oil and gas drilling, exploration, and production operations.

(b) section 3 of the directive entitled *Directive S-20: Saskatchewan Upstream Flaring and Incineration Requirements*,[174] published by the Government of Saskatchewan on November 1, 2015, if the facility is located in Manitoba or Saskatchewan; and

(c) sections 3.6 and 7 of the directive entitled *Directive 060: Upstream Petroleum Industry Flaring, Incinerating, and Venting*, published by the Alberta Energy Regulator on March 22, 2016, in any other case.

In non-emergency situations, as an alternative to venting gas, the Methane Regulations require operators to capture and use at least 95 percent of the methane in facilities for a beneficial purpose rather than wasting the gas. They stipulate that at a minimum, 95 percent of the gas must be captured and used for one of three beneficial purposes prescribed in the regulations. Section 5 of the Methane Regulations requires a minimum equipment operating efficiency as follows:

5(1) Hydrocarbon gas conservation equipment that is used at an upstream oil and gas facility must

(a) be operated in such a manner that at least 95% of the hydrocarbon gas ... is captured and conserved.

Section 7 of the Methane Regulations stipulates that the gas must be captured and conserved by using one of the three following methods:

(a) used at the facility as fuel in a combustion device that releases at most 5% of the combusted hydrocarbon gas to the atmosphere as hydrocarbon gas;

(b) delivered; or

(c) injected into an underground geological deposit for a purpose other than to dispose of the gas as waste.

In regard to the first method, the Methane Regulations specify that no more than 5 percent of the gas can be released. This emissions limit should prompt technological innovation to reduce the level of methane that is currently released into the atmosphere. The second method, "delivered," refers to piping the gas to be sold and used, again another option recommended and sometimes used in the OGC regimes. The third method, subsurface injection, is also referred to as "enhanced recovery," which requires the gas to be reinjected into an oil and gas reservoir to avoid the release of methane into the atmosphere. These three emissions reduction practices recommended in the BC, Alberta, and Saskatchewan OGC systems are required under the Regulations.

E. VENTING FROM COMPRESSORS

Beyond the general provisions in the Methane Regulations to decrease emissions from venting at facilities, since there are different types of compressors that emit at different levels, the new regulations contain special provisions tailored to the type of compressor. There are special provisions in the Regulations that limit the volume of emissions that can be vented from compressors.[175] To reduce the volume of emissions from each type of compressor, industry operators are required to complete annual measurements to ensure that the emissions limits stipulated in the Regulations are satisfied. Section 15 requires the measurement of gas flow volumes as the first step toward further reducing the volume of emissions. Section 16(3) requires operators to take initial and subsequent gas flow measurements during specific time periods. The flow rate must be initially measured on "January 1, 2021, if the compressor is

---

174 (November 2015), online (download): *Saskatchewan* <https://publications.saskatchewan.ca/#/products/75523>.

175 Methane Regulations, ss 14(b), 16(3).

installed at the facility before January 1, 2020," and "the 365th day after the day on which the compressor was installed at the facility in any other case," and it must be subsequently measured in "the period that ends on the 365th day after the day on which a previous measurement was taken."

Section 14 of the Methane Regulations provides for optimal equipment performance that takes into account the different types of compressors used at different sites, and the new regulations focus on optimal equipment maintenance and efficiency to minimize the level of emissions from the different types of compressors.[176] This section will require the deployment of technology to further reduce emissions. As with other types of equipment that we have considered, operators of compressors will be required to take action to conserve or destroy methane or else to meet the applicable venting limits for the compressor. Corrective action is required if emissions exceed the limit applicable to the compressor, which depends on the installation date, the type of compressor, and its rated brake power.[177] A specific timeline of 90 days is stipulated in the Regulations to complete the required work on compressors to reduce methane emissions.[178]

F. HYDRAULIC FRACTURING AND SHALE WELL COMPLETIONS

A third potential source of methane emissions that is addressed in the Methane Regulations is HF operations and well completions at newly drilled oil and gas wells. Historically, venting of methane at oil and gas well sites has been allowed, and this has contributed to an increased volume of emissions. What sets this source apart from the larger facilities that we have discussed is the much greater number of oil and gas wells in Canada and the potential for an increase in the volume of emissions in the future as additional shale oil and gas wells are drilled and completed in BC to supply natural gas to the major LNG export project recently endorsed by the prime minister and the BC premier.

Recently, technology has been refined to detect and monitor methane releases from oil and gas wells. Employing satellite data, scientists and engineers have analyzed and compared atmospheric methane emission trends in North America before and after unconventional shale gas development.[179] It has been reported that fugitive methane concentrations have increased dramatically in areas with shale oil and gas development.[180]

To prevent methane emissions from new oil and gas wells throughout Canada, s 11(2) of the Methane Regulations (which includes the section heading "No venting") prohibits venting at new well sites and requires the capture and use of natural gas for a beneficial purpose or combustion/destruction of the gas. The section requires that "[h]ydrocarbon gas associated with flowback at a well ... not be vented during flowback but ... instead be captured and routed to hydrocarbon gas conservation equipment or hydrocarbon gas destruction equipment." This is consistent with the Pennsylvania state "no venting" requirement.[181] As a condition of well permitting in Pennsylvania, venting is prohibited, and, therefore, natural gas must be captured and directed into a combustion device to prevent emissions at new oil and gas wells.[182]

---

176 ECCC, "Canada's Methane Regulations for the Upstream Oil and Gas Sector," *supra* note 149.

177 Methane Regulations, s 18(2).

178 Methane Regulations, s 18(4).

179 See e.g. Jian-Xiong Sheng et al, "2010–2016 Methane Trends over Canada, the United States, and Mexico Observed by the GOSAT Satellite: Contributions from Different Source Sectors" (2018) 18 Atmos Chem Phys 12257.

180 Oliver Scheising et al, "Remote Sensing of Fugitive Methane Emissions from Oil and Gas Production in North American Tight Geologic Formations" (2014) 2:10 Earth's Future 548.

181 Allan Ingelson, "Plugging the Holes—New Canadian and US Regulations to Reduce Upstream Methane Emissions" (2019) 12:4 J of World Energy L & Bus 294.

182 Ibid.

Arguably, if shale oil and gas producers in Pennsylvania can develop shale oil and gas econom-ically without venting, operators in BC should be able to do so as well.

In summary, the Methane Regulations create new emissions reduction requirements that should further significantly decrease the volume of methane that enters the atmosphere from equipment leaks and venting at facilities as well as from HF and completions at new oil and gas wells. Starting January 1, 2020, facility operators must start implementing equipment leak detection and repair (LDAR) programs. The Methane Regulations incorporate by reference the US Environmental Protection Agency national leak testing method and require timely imple-mentation of LDAR programs within a specified time period.[183] In regard to facility inspections, the regulations require three inspections be completed per year, every year, which is more frequent than in existing provincial systems. Like the regulations in the US, the Methane Regu-lations specify the types of technology (such as infrared cameras, sniffers, drones, and satellite systems) to be used during large facility inspections. Some provisions in the Regulations will be phased in during the next five years to allow facility operators to budget for equipment upgrades that will further reduce emissions.

VI. CONCLUSION

The combination of HF and horizontal drilling has transformed the oil and gas industry in the US and Canada. New energy technologies often create new environmental challenges and prompt new regulations and technological innovation to mitigate the environmental impacts; HF is no exception. Examples of innovation are new HF fluid and produced water remediation and recycling technologies to mitigate soil, surface, and groundwater contamination and to reduce the volume of water used. New regulations require monitoring and responding to the emerging issue of IS from HF as well as the deployment of technologies and the new "stop-light" operating regulatory requirements in Alberta to reduce the risk of earthquakes. In response to climate change, in order to respond to new environmental, health, and safety challenges, federal and provincial regulators have developed and implemented new regulatory requirements that promote technological innovation. New technology allows regulators to detect and measure the volume of methane emissions to enable the enforcement of the new regulations. The 2018 federal and Alberta methane emissions reduction regulations provide recent examples of guidelines that compel technological innovation to capture and benefi-cially use a much larger volume of methane, a potent GHG that contributes to global warming, one of the major environmental challenges facing Canada and the global community.

QUESTIONS

1. As mentioned in the text, both the Alberta and BCOGC regulatory systems draw heavily on industry guidelines prepared by a national oil industry association that represents most of the oil companies in Canada. This is not uncommon. Why do you think regulators chose to do this? What are the potential problems with this approach?

2. The use of natural gas as a replacement for coal can be characterized as a GHG emis-sions reduction strategy, but even if its use helps combat climate change, is continuing to rely on natural gas to generate electricity good for the environment? Why should we continue to develop natural gas in some provinces instead of relying only on wind or solar throughout Canada?

3. Because natural gas is more diffuse than oxygen, it is extremely difficult to transport. Facil-ities to either compress the gas or convert it to liquid natural gas are required on or near the extraction site. In some jurisdictions, such as Nigeria and North Dakota, natural gas producers are

---

183 Methane Regulations, ss 29(1)(a), 30(3)(b), 32.

permitted to "flare" or burn the natural gas instead of processing it. Why do you think these jurisdictions permit flaring? What could be done to discourage it?

4. HF is associated with IS in some jurisdictions. In Oklahoma, parties are permitted to sue the company responsible for the HF operation that caused the earthquake, but it can be difficult to identify which HF operation caused the seismicity. Aside from geological reasons, why do you think this might be?

5. HF uses enormous quantities of water, and disposing of the water plus any associated liquid that was locked into the shale with the oil and gas is very expensive. Instead, many producers have injected the used water back into the ground, where it is not monitored. Why might this be a problem? What is the likelihood that injected water could be recovered and treated?

6. The provincial and the federal governments have separate schemes for the regulation of methane. What problems do you see arising from inconsistent methane regulations applying to interprovincial versus intraprovincial projects?

7. Throughout this chapter, we have discussed complex technical regulations aimed at preventing environmental damage from fossil fuel extraction. What role do you think lawyers play in developing and enforcing these regulations? To what extent must they work with scientists and engineers in either endeavour?

FURTHER READING

Ingelson, Allan, "Plugging the Holes—New Canadian and US Regulations to Reduce Upstream Methane Emissions" (2019) 12:4 J World Energy L & Bus 294.

CHAPTER NINE

ENVIRONMENTAL AND TOXIC TORTS: LEGAL REALITIES AND CONTEMPORARY CHALLENGES*

Cameron SG Jefferies

I. INTRODUCTION

Though environmental torts are extremely common, private litigation is not an ideal route to secure environmental protection and cannot replace the need for long-term planning and comprehensive environmental regulation. Unlike sound planning processes and pollution mitigation efforts, private litigation is often time-consuming and prohibitively costly. Private lawsuits tend to be reactive and adversarial. A final challenge that is common to environmental law more generally is the need to consider scientific and technical uncertainties that may

---

* This chapter updates the work done by William Charles and David VanderZwaag on chapter 3 in the previous edition of *Environmental Law and Policy* (Toronto: Emond Montgomery, 2003).

constitute a significant hurdle in establishing factual causation and harm deserving of compensation. The most common awards in tort cases are monetary damages and injunctive relief (either temporary or permanent), which are discretionary. Class action litigation in instances of widespread environmental harm presents its own set of challenges. As is the case with remedies in environmental law more generally, it is appropriate to question the efficacy of these awards in remedying environmental harm that has already occurred.

Despite these limitations, private litigation plays an important role in environmental protection, serving as a backstop when sufficient regulation does not exist or when it is not being enforced. While there are various theories and justifications for tort law, it operates, at its core, to provide a measure of compensation for individuals who suffer an injury to themselves or their property and also to deter future wrongdoers (*British Columbia v Canadian Forest Products Ltd*, 2004 SCC 38 at para 68, [2004] 2 SCR 74 [*Canadian Forest*]). Litigation may be the only way to air legitimate grievances where government officials have refused to act or polluters have behaved inappropriately. The profile of an environmental issue can be elevated through a lawsuit, and a court offers a decision-making forum less prone to political pressures. Successful private litigation, especially if pursued as a class action, has the ability to alter "business as usual" scenarios for major polluters.

Just how active judges should be in policy-making and how prepared they are to tackle perplexing scientific and technical dilemmas remain controversial issues. On one hand, a conservative approach to these issues may be justified on the basis that elected officials are the more proper vehicle for complex social policy decisions and detailed consideration of scientific knowledge. On the other hand, many common law doctrines are inherently imbued with value-based considerations that are open to creative and incremental jurisprudential evolutions based on changing societal perspectives. Furthermore, while judges are expert in common law reasoning, the realities of 21st-century life make scientific and technical considerations a mainstay of contemporary litigation.

Long-standing common law actions of negligence, nuisance, strict liability, riparian rights, trespass to land, and trespass to the person have been developed and used to protect individual rights to physical integrity and property. In Canada, we have nonetheless failed to enact laws to guarantee our safety from the harmful effects of toxic substances in spite of our growing awareness of the danger. We may remain tethered to the tradition that "English law reduces environmental problems to questions of property" (LA Scarman, *English Law—The New Dimension* (London: Stevens & Sons, 1974) at 51), but there is also reason to believe that tort law can rise to the challenge to help "realize the possibility of justice in the chemical era" (L Collins & H McLeod-Kilmurray, *The Canadian Law of Toxic Torts* (Toronto: Canada Law Book, 2014) at 305).

The following section of this chapter surveys the basic legal requirements of negligence, including public authority liability, private nuisance, public nuisance, strict liability, riparian rights, trespass to land, and trespass to the person. The section thereafter focuses on contemporary issues and judicial challenges in toxic torts where plaintiffs are exposed to toxic agents (chemical, biological, or radiological), and introduces tort law's role in litigating climate change.

II. OVERVIEW OF APPLICABLE COMMON LAW DOCTRINES

A. NEGLIGENCE

The most important tort action today is negligence. In a broad sense, negligence law deals with the compensation of losses caused by unintentional but unreasonable conduct that harmfully affects legally protected interests. Unreasonable conduct has been defined as "the omission to do something which a reasonable [person] guided by those considerations which ordinarily regulate the conduct of human affairs, would do, or doing something which a prudent, reasonable [person] would not do" (per Alderson B in *Blyth v Birmingham Water Works Co* (1856), 156 ER 1047 at 1049 (Ex Ct)).

A negligence action, in which a defendant is held to the standard of care of a reasonable person, may be effectively used in the area of environmental litigation. To be successful, a plaintiff must establish, on the balance of probabilities, five key elements of the tort. These elements are legal duty, breach of the standard of care, cause in fact, proximate cause, and damage to the plaintiff. The court will also consider whether the plaintiff's conduct warrants a reduction—or even elimination—of the award that would otherwise follow.

SMITH BROTHERS EXCAVATING WINDSOR LTD V CAMION EQUIPMENT & LEASING INC (TRUSTEE OF)
[1994] OJ No 1380 (QL) (Gen Div)

[The case deals with vandalized storage tanks on the Camion property, where the valves on each tank were intentionally opened to permit the escape of in excess of 1,300,000 litres of methanol. The methanol crossed the Camion property line, causing surface damage on the plaintiff's property and seeping into the underground water system. In its judgment, the court found that the escape of the fluid and the tampering of the tanks had resulted from intentional acts by unknown parties who had some specialized knowledge of their operation (and were not children).

At trial, the plaintiff argued that Camion had fallen short of the standard of care required to secure the methanol from interference or escape. In its defence, Camion gave evidence that there was at least one staff member located at the property at all times and that this accorded with the minimum standard of care.]

189 ... In the evenings and after midnight, a dispatcher was present for Camion's trucking business and while not in attendance specifically to guard the tank, there was a people presence. To add to this presence, Camion after 5:00 PM each day or when the business was closed from pedestrian traffic, located 3 German Shepherd dogs in the vicinity of the tanks. These dogs were located in different areas of the yard and were controlled by a 25 foot leash and a 200 foot slide cable. A security company was also retained for weekends and holidays to carry out periodic inspections when the business was closed.

[Camion argued that it did not employ a full-time security officer because of the expense of doing so but that this was not required within the industry (no evidence of licensing requirements or minimum security compliance standards with government or regulatory bodies was tendered).

The court examined the duty of the defendants to its neighbours and the standard of care required.]

196 Although, [sic] hindsight is a useful tool as to what could have been done at least in the area of its obligations, the real question is whether what was done fell below the accepted standard of care imposed within the industry, and constitutes negligence.

197 If liability were to be determined alone based on the principles of negligence, I do not find from the evidence that the plaintiff has established a breach of the duty of care or that this defendant Camion has fallen below the standard of care acceptable within the industry. In the evidence of Fire Chief Tessier, he confirms

that he is not aware of any special security that is required or provided for tank farms.

198 I accept from the evidence that additional security measures could have been implemented and put in place not only for accidental causes but intentional.

199 That is, not [sic] however, the test for liability in negligence since we first commence with a duty and a breach of this duty to establish liability.

· · ·

205 Upon the evidence, the defendants met the standard of care within the industry which as it relates to security for tank farms is minimal. Although greater security could have been provided, if the obligation does not exist and the standard of care as required is met, the failure to provide additional security does not alone constitute negligence.

[In addition to the security question, the plaintiffs also alleged delay in Camion's cleanup efforts and remediation. The court concluded that the defendants had acted without delay. Specifically, they had hired a firm to assess environmental problems, and this had resulted in immediate action in consultation with the Ministry of the Environment. The court found that remediation had been conducted appropriately and within reasonable time limits. For these reasons, the plaintiff failed on this ground of negligence.]

B. PUBLIC AUTHORITY LIABILITY

A field of negligence law that is increasingly important in the area of environmental protection is the liability of public authorities in preventing or controlling polluting activities. The doctrine of Crown immunity, historically protecting public authorities from civil liability, has been significantly limited in recent years through statute and judicial decisions. *Just v British Columbia*, [1989] 2 SCR 1228, 1989 CanLII 16 [*Just* cited to SCR] remains a leading authority in Canada for determining governmental civil liability. It has been applied by the Alberta Court of Appeal in the environmental case that follows.

TOTTRUP V LUND
2000 ABCA 121, [2000] 9 WWR 21

[The plaintiff brought a negligence action against the minister of Alberta environmental protection and two former ministers of the environment, seeking damages for flooding and contamination of his lands. The plaintiff alleged that, as a result of the negligence of the ministers, his property had flooded, had been contaminated, and had ultimately been rendered unfit for agricultural or recreational use. The ministers were successful in having the plaintiff's claim struck for having no prospect of success; the plaintiff appealed.]

[19] [The Court of Appeal articulated the test of whether public authorities owe a duty of care from *Anns v Merton London Borough Council*, [1977] UKHL 4 and *Kamloops v Nielsen*, [1984] 2 SCR 2 at 10, 1984 CanLII 21 as follows:]

(1) is there a sufficiently close relationship between the parties ... so that, in the reasonable contemplation of the authority, carelessness on its part might cause damage to that person? If so, (2) are there any considerations which ought to negative or limit (a) the scope of the duty and (b) the class of persons to whom it is owed or (c) the damages to which a breach of it may give rise?

[The court opined that in applying the test to public authorities, determination of whether the matter is within the "policy" or "operational" sphere of decision-making constitutes an overriding consideration and that policy decisions and actions are excluded from the duty of care. The court highlighted the distinction by reciting the reasoning of the Supreme Court of Canada in *Just v British Columbia*, where the court (at 1242) indicated that the division between policy and operation is part of the exclusionary considerations referred to in the *Anns* test.]

[20] ... The duty of care should apply to a public authority unless there is a valid basis for its exclusion. A true policy decision undertaken by a government agency constitutes such a valid basis for exclusion. What constitutes a policy decision may vary infinitely and may be made at different levels although usually at a high level.

The decisions in *Anns v. Merton London Borough Council* and *Kamloops v. Nielsen* indicate that a government agency in reaching a decision pertaining to inspection must act in a reasonable manner which constitutes a *bona fide* exercise of discretion. To do so they must specifically consider whether to inspect and if so, the system of inspection must be a reasonable one in all the circumstances.

For example, at a high level there may be a policy decision made concerning the inspection of lighthouses. If the policy decision is made that there is such a pressing need to maintain air safety by the construction of additional airport facilities with the result that no funds can be made available for lighthouse inspection, then this would constitute a *bona fide* exercise of discretion that would be unassailable. Should then a lighthouse beacon be extinguished as a result of the lack of inspection and a shipwreck ensue, no liability can be placed upon the government agency. The result would be the same if a policy decision were made to increase the funds for job retraining and reduce the funds for lighthouse inspection so that a beacon could only be inspected every second year and as a result the light was extinguished. Once again this would constitute the *bona fide* exercise of discretion. Thus, a decision either not to inspect at all or to reduce the number of inspections may be an unassailable policy decision. This is so provided it constitutes a reasonable exercise of *bona fide* discretion based, for example, upon the availability of funds.

On the other hand, if a decision is made to inspect lighthouse facilities the system of inspections must be reasonable and they must be made properly: see *Indian Towing Co.*, 350 U.S. 61 (1955). Thus, once the policy decision to inspect has been made, the court may review the scheme of inspection to ensure it is reasonable and has been reasonably carried out in light of all the circumstances, including the availability of funds, to determine whether the government agency has met the requisite standard of care.

• • •

Thus, a true policy decision may be made at a lower level provided that the government agency establishes that it was a reasonable decision in light of the surrounding circumstances.

[The Alberta Court of Appeal noted that all factors of the case are to be considered when one is assessing whether a matter is policy or operational. These factors include the degree to which the public relied on the authority (and the extent to which reliance was encouraged by the authority) and the extent to which the authority brought the duty upon itself through its interactions with the individual in question. Whether or not a duty of care exists is a question of law, assessed in view of the allegations found in the statement of claim. The court's application of this approach proceeded as follows:]

[22] In this case, the issue is whether there is a duty of care owing by these Ministers, or any one of them, to Tottrup.

[23] In both the pleadings and in argument counsel for the plaintiff relied on particular statutes as the basis of the duty of care. There is no independent tort of breach of statutory duty: *Saskatchewan Wheat Pool v. Canada*, [1983] 1 S.C.R. 205 (S.C.C.). The provisions of the statute form part of the circumstances which may give rise to a duty of care. The reference in the pleadings to a duty owed under various statutes "... or at law" is consistent with the law that a duty of care on a public authority arises only at common law, though it may derive from powers and duties conferred on a public authority by statute. In this case, reliance was placed on the statutory duties.

[24] An examination of the pleadings leads me to conclude that the plaintiff seeks liability against the Ministers on two bases. First, the essence of [the] plaintiff's claim is that the Ministers knew of contamination and flooding and did nothing, and thereby failed to enforce regulations and perform their duties under the statute. Secondly, the Ministers are being sued as vicariously responsible for the acts of their subordinates.

· · ·

[32] In the present case, the plaintiff alleges that the various Ministers were aware of the discharge of contaminants, sewage, waste water and storm water as well as the effects on Atim Creek and Big Lake and took no action. The allegation that the Ministers took no action to stop the flooding and enforce compliance of all regulations takes these pleadings to their highest level.

[33] There is no allegation that the Ministers acted irresponsibly or carelessly in the exercise of any discretionary decision, or failed to give due consideration to the exercise of their discretion. There is no assertion that these Ministers, or any of them, acted in any way with respect to Tottrup so as to create a duty to him. There is not even an allegation that the Ministers were directly involved in any decision made relating to enforcement of any statutory provisions as it affected Tottrup. Nor is it alleged that they were careless in any supervisory powers with respect to any subordinates and decisions made by them. There are no facts pled that could support a finding that a policy decision had been made, which resulted in any of these Ministers making an operational decision affecting the plaintiff. As noted by Berger J.A., the pleadings do not allege facts supporting any conclusion that the Ministers acted negligently in the execution of any policy or discretionary decision already taken. Finally, there is no allegation that any of these Ministers were guilty of the tort of misfeasance in office.

[In conclusion, the court did not find any mandatory statutory duty or common law duty imposing upon the ministers a duty to prevent flooding of the plaintiff's land. Additionally, the court agreed with the chambers judge that the facts, as pleaded, did not support a duty owed by the ministers to Tottrup.]

QUESTION

In your opinion, is it appropriate to apply private law doctrine to instances of potential public authority liability? This is currently a live issue. In the case of *Paradis Honey Ltd v Canada*, 2015 FCA 89, leave to appeal to SCC refused, 2015 CanLII 69423 [*Paradis Honey* cited to FCA], a group of commercial beekeepers brought a negligence action against the Canadian government, alleging that a series of regulations prohibited the importation of honeybees from the

United States into Canada. These regulations had a significant economic impact on Canadian commercial beekeeping, which could not rely on bee imports to replace bee colonies that died over winter. In *obiter* the court opined (at para 127) that "[i]n cases involving public authorities, we have been using an analytical framework built for private parties, not public authorities. We have been using private law tools to solve public law problems. So to speak, we have been using a screwdriver to turn a bolt." The court proposed that such issues ought to be dealt with in accordance with public law principles, specifically referencing the applicability of administrative law.

C. PRIVATE NUISANCE

A private nuisance is classically defined as an activity that unreasonably and substantially interferes with the use and enjoyment of land that is owned or occupied by another person (*Antrim Truck Centre Ltd v Ontario (Transportation)*, 2013 SCC 13). Liability may be imposed, even if the defendant did not intend and was not negligent in causing the interference. If the interference involves a form of actual, substantial, physical damage to land itself or personal injury to occupants, courts will be, as they have been, quick to find nuisance, given the substantial gravity of interference. Where the interference involves the hindrance to the plaintiff's enjoyment of the property (that is, the property's "amenity")—for example, by loud noises or noxious odours—courts will weigh various factors to determine whether a nuisance exists. Key factors include duration and gravity of the interference, the neighbourhood (for example industrial/urban versus rural), utility of the defendant's activity, and whether the plaintiff has abnormal sensitivities.

One of Canada's first environmental tort cases, *Groat v Edmonton (City)*, [1928] SCR 522, 1928 CanLII 49 [*Groat* cited to SCR], brought the issue of private nuisance resulting from environmental contamination before the Supreme Court. Here, the plaintiff landowners alleged that the expanding waste water management infrastructure and municipal garbage facility of the city of Edmonton had fouled a creek running across their land. In finding for the plaintiffs, Rinfret J opined (at 532) that environmental pollution, "in itself, constitutes a nuisance." While this broad endorsement of the application of private nuisance to environmental harm has proved overly optimistic, private nuisance has been successfully argued in a number of environmental cases involving pollutants such as pesticides (*Bridges Brothers Ltd v Forest Protection Ltd*, 1976 CanLII 1251, 14 NBR (2d) 91 (QB)) and sewage (*Roberts v City of Portage la Prairie*, [1971] SCR 481, 1971 CanLII 128).

The defence most commonly asserted in private nuisance cases is that of statutory authority. This defence is available where the impugned activity has been carried out, by a public authority, pursuant to statute (L Klar & C Jefferies, *Tort Law*, 6th ed (Toronto: Thomson Reuters, 2017) at 888). The scope of the statutory authority defence has been considered by the Supreme Court in two key decisions: *Tock v St John's Metropolitan Area Board*, 1989 CanLII 15, 64 DLR (4th) 620 and *Ryan v Victoria (City)*, 1999 CanLII 706, 168 DLR (4th) 513. In *Tock*, the court considered three different applications of the defence. In *Ryan*, the court declared that the appropriate test to use to determine whether the defence of statutory authority was available was the traditional rule as restated by Sopinka J in *Tock*, which can be summarized as follows: a public body is immunized from liability if it shows there is no practical possibility of carrying out its mandate without causing a nuisance to others. The burden of proof is on the party advancing the defence. This is not easy because the courts strain against a conclusion that private rights are intended to be sacrificed to the common good. The defendant must negate that there are alternate methods of carrying out the work. The mere fact that one is considerably less expensive will not avail. If only one method is practically feasible, it must be established that it was practically impossible to avoid the nuisance. It is insufficient for the defendant to negate negligence.

Plaintiffs pursuing nuisance actions often ask the court for the discretionary remedy of injunctive relief. This is a logical course of action, given that damages alone will most likely fail to correct the interference. This is especially true in situations of continuing nuisance.

The following case demonstrates some of the difficulties in pursuing a private nuisance claim in the context of environmental damage.

SMITH V INCO LTD
2011 ONCA 628, 62 CELR (NS) (3d) 92

[This class action case concerns the historical emissions from Inco's nickel refinery, which operated in Port Colborne, Ontario for 66 years before closing in 1985. The class member claimants lived proximate to the refinery, and their properties had been contaminated by nickel particles that had been deposited on their lands from Inco's emissions. Their claim for damages was based on an argument that, owing to public concern over nickel contamination, the value of their properties had failed to appreciate at the same rate as that of other analogous properties. They alleged various causes of action, including private nuisance, and received a $36 million damage award at trial.

In reviewing the applicability of private nuisance on these facts, the Ontario Court of Appeal offered the following reasoning.]

[39] People do not live in splendid isolation from one another. One person's lawful and reasonable use of his or her property may indirectly harm the property of another or interfere with that person's ability to fully use and enjoy his or her property. The common law of nuisance developed as a means by which those competing interests could be addressed, and one given legal priority over the other. Under the common law of nuisance, sometimes the person whose property suffered the adverse effects is expected to tolerate those effects as the price of membership in the larger community. Sometimes, however, the party causing the adverse effect can be compelled, even if his or her conduct is lawful and reasonable, to desist from engaging in that conduct and to compensate the other party for any harm caused to that person's property. In essence, the common law of nuisance decided which party's interest must give way. That determination is made by asking whether in all the circumstances the harm caused or the interference done to one person's property by the other person's use of his or her property is unreasonable: *Royal Anne Hotel Co. v. Ashcroft (Village)* (1979), 95 D.L.R. (3d) 756 (B.C. C.A.), at pp. 760-61.

[40] The reasonableness inquiry focuses on the effect of the defendant's conduct on the property rights of the plaintiff. Nuisance, unlike negligence, does not focus on or characterize the defendant's conduct. The defendant's conduct may be reasonable and yet result in an unreasonable interference with the plaintiff's property rights.

[The court was clear that private nuisance, while always predicated on indirect interference with property rights, can be characterized either as an actual physical injury to land or as a substantial interference with the use and enjoyment of property, which is also called an amenity nuisance. The plaintiffs' position in this case was that their property was physically injured by the nickel particles becoming part of the soil, and this significantly affected the property value owing to public concerns about potential health consequences of nickel-contaminated soil. The court was clear that the form of private nuisance that is pleaded affects the reasonableness analysis.]

[45] ... Where amenity nuisance is alleged, the reasonableness of the interference with the plaintiff's property is measured by balancing certain competing factors, including the nature of the interference and the character of the locale in which that interference occurred. Where the nuisance is said to have produced physical damage to land, that damage is taken as an unreasonable interference without the balancing of competing factors.

[The court did point to some *dicta* suggesting that there might still be a limited role for balancing competing factors when the alleged nuisance is in the form of physical damage to land but did not take the opportunity to decide this issue; instead, the court proceeded on the basis of the claimant's contention that balancing cannot occur when nuisance involving actual physical damage to land is considered. The court then turned its attention to the type of harm or injury to property that would constitute nuisance.]

[49] In *St. Helen's Smelting Co.* [*St Helen's Smelting Co v Tipping* (1865), 11 HLC 642, [1861-1873] All ER Rep Ext 1389], the Lord Chancellor used different phrases to describe the kind of harm to land that would suffice to establish nuisance. He referred to "material injury to the property" and to "circumstances the immediate result of which is sensible injury to the value of the property." Subsequent cases have used somewhat different terminology, some of which now seems outdated and inappropriate: *e.g.* see *Salvin v. North Brancepeth Coal Co.* (1874), L.R. 9 Ch. App. 705 (Eng. Ch. Div.), at p. 709. In our view, the requirement of "material injury to property" referred to in *St. Helen's Smelting Co.* is satisfied where the actions of the defendant indirectly cause damage to the plaintiff's land that can be properly characterized as material, actual and readily ascertainable.

[50] Material damage refers to damage that is substantial in the sense that it is more than trivial: *Barrette c. Ciment du St-Laurent inc.*, [2008] 3 S.C.R. 392 (S.C.C.), at para. 77. Actual damage refers to damage that has occurred and is not merely potential damage that may or may not occur at some future point: *Walker v. McKinnon Industries Ltd.* [[1949] OR 549 (H Ct J)] at pp. 558-59. Damage that is readily ascertainable refers to damage that can be observed or measured and is not so minimal or incremental as to be unnoticeable as it occurs. We do agree, however, with counsel for the claimants that the damage may be readily ascertainable even if it is not visible to the naked eye and does not produce some visibly noticeable change in the property. In our view, a change in the chemical composition of the soil measurable through established scientific techniques would constitute a readily ascertainable change in the soil: see *Gaunt v. Fynney* (1872), L.R. 8 Ch. App. 8 (U.K. H.L.). For the reasons we will develop below, the claimants' problem is not with the ascertainability of the change caused by the nickel particles, but with the characterization of that change as damage or harm to the property.

• • •

[67] In our view, actual, substantial, physical damage to the land in the context of this case refers to nickel levels that at least posed some risk to the health or wellbeing of the residents of those properties. Evidence that the existence of the nickel particles in the soil generated concerns about potential health risks does not, in our view, amount to evidence that the presence of the particles in the soil caused actual, substantial harm or damage to the property. The claimants failed to establish actual, substantial, physical damage to their properties as a result of the nickel particles becoming part of the soil. Without actual, substantial, physical harm, the nuisance claim as framed by the claimants could not succeed.

[The court allowed the appeal and set aside the trial judgment.]

QUESTIONS

1. The Ontario Court of Appeal in *Smith* is clear that, to find private nuisance, there must be "actual, substantial, physical damage to the land" (para 67). Should occupiers lacking proprietary interests have the right to sue in private nuisance, relying on principled legal arguments such as the "polluter pays" principle or the precautionary principle? For additional discussion on this point, see *Saik'uz First Nation and Stellat'en First Nation v Rio Tinto Alcan Inc*, 2015 BCCA 154 at paras 38-40.

2. In view of concerns about exposure to chemical substances, should the courts expand the existing nuisance categories? Collins and McLeod-Kilmurray, in *The Canadian Law of Toxic Torts* at 67-68, propose that "courts may wish to create a new category of 'material chemical damage'" to complement existing nuisance categories. This new category would account for contemporary technical capacity to quantify the sort of "micro-level adverse changes" and any associated harmful impacts to property that, historically, could not be observed with the naked eye. They note that "environmental harms are a major category of concern for Canadians and it would make sense for tort law to address this through the recognition of material chemical damage as a third stream of nuisance."

D. PUBLIC NUISANCE

A public nuisance is an "action brought to protect the public interest in freedom from damages to health, safety, morality, comfort or convenience" (OM Reynolds, "Public Nuisance: A Crime in Tort Law" (1978) 31 Okla L Rev 318). This civil action is rooted in the criminal law and in the 18th and 19th century common law offence of common nuisance that developed to supplement the criminal offence. Originally designed to deal with obstructions of public highways, rights of way, or navigable waters, this tort has expanded to cover the pollution of beaches and shoreline properties, as well as noise-generating activities and street prostitution. In order to determine whether a particular activity interferes unreasonably with the public interest, a court must balance the defendant's right to engage in an activity, without undue restriction, against the public right to have its interests protected. Several factors may be considered by the court. These include the trouble or inconvenience caused by the activity, the ease or difficulty involved in taking steps to avoid the risk, the general practice of others, the utility of the activity, and the character of the neighbourhood. Essentially, "[t]he more harmful and less useful the activity, the more likely it is that it will be termed a (public) nuisance." Contrarily, if the impugned activity simply affects public convenience and does not cause material damage to public property, the outcome is less certain (Klar & Jefferies at 856, citing *Chessie v JD Irving Ltd*, 1982 CanLII 2918, 140 DLR (3d) 501 (NBCA)).

On the theory that public rights are vested in the Crown, public nuisance actions must be commenced by the attorney general. The only exception to this rule occurs when the public right interference is such that some private right is interfered with at the same time. For example, if an obstruction is placed on a highway such that the owner of an adjacent premises has his or her private access to and from the property interfered with, that person will have suffered "special damage." It is clear that in cases where a public nuisance results in personal injury or damage to or interference with the plaintiff's property, the special damages requirement is met. However, where the plaintiff suffers a purely economic loss or is merely inconvenienced, the issue is more difficult and the answer as to whether this sort of loss qualifies as special damage less clear. Courts have differed in their views as to whether the plaintiff's loss must be particular or special in kind (as compared to public loss) or whether a greater degree of damage of the same kind is sufficient. In several cases, Canadian courts have taken a narrow view of special damages (see *Hickey v Electric Reduction Co of Canada, Ltd*, which is discussed below).

HICKEY V ELECTRIC REDUCTION CO OF CANADA, LTD
1970 CanLII 907, 21 DLR (3d) 368 (Nfld SC)

[The case concerns the defendant's discharge of poisonous material from its phosphorous plant on Placentia Bay. The plant polluted the bay, contaminating fish and making them unfit for commercial fishing. At the outset, the court (at 369) distinguished between private nuisance and public nuisance, with particular reference to the following definition:]

Salmond, *The Law of Torts*, 15th ed. (1969), expresses it [being the distinction between private and public nuisance] more succinctly at p. 64:

> A public or a common nuisance is a criminal offence. It is an act or omission which materially affects the reasonable comfort or convenience of life of a class of Her Majesty's subjects ...

and he adds:

> A public nuisance falls within the law of torts only in so far as it may in the particular case constitute some form of tort also. Thus the obstruction of a highway is a public nuisance; but if it causes any special and peculiar damage to an individual, it is also a tort actionable at his suit.

[The court (at 371-72) observed that not only the plaintiff but all fishermen using the polluted bay suffered economically. In the court's view, this was fatal to the plaintiff's action.]

[W]hen a public nuisance has been created anyone who suffers special damage, that is direct damage has a right of action. I am unable to agree to this rather wide application of Salmond's view that a public nuisance may become a tortious act. I think the right view is that any person who suffers peculiar damage has a right of action, but where the damage is common to all persons of the same class, then a personal right of action is not maintainable. Mr. Wells suggests that the plaintiffs' right to outfit for the fishery and their right to fish is a particular right and this right having been interfered with they have a cause of action. This right which they enjoy is a right in common with all Her Majesty's subjects, an interference with which is the whole test of a public nuisance; a right which can only be vindicated by the appropriate means, which is an action by the Attorney-General, either with or without a relator, in the common interest of the public.

Other cases since *Hickey* have recognized some economic losses as a special injury, allowing private actions for recovery under public nuisance to proceed. In *Gagnier v Canadian Forest Products Ltd*, 1990 CanLII 538, 51 BCLR (2d) 218, the British Columbia Supreme Court allowed the claim of a crab fisher to proceed against the defendant operators of pulp mills for economic loss resulting from the closure of his business caused by pollution of a crab fishery. The court in *Gagnier* referred to the *Hickey* decision as being too narrow. The court indicated that economic losses could be recovered under public nuisance if a plaintiff shows a significant difference in degree of damage between him or her and the public generally. The action was later dismissed because of inadequate records of income earned and circumstantial evidence that Mr Gagnier did not intend to continue fishing for crab. See MD Faieta et al, *Environmental Harm: Civil Actions and Compensation* (Toronto: Butterworths, 1996) at 178; see also Collins & McLeod-Kilmurray, *The Canadian Law of Toxic Torts* at 54. Other cases, however, have confirmed what appears to be a preference by Canadian courts for the strict approach. See *Stein v Gonzalez*, 1984 CanLII 344, 31 CCLT 19 (BCSC).

QUESTIONS

1. If the standing requirement is too narrow, is the legislative branch justified in its efforts to liberalize standing for private actions? For example, the Northwest Territories *Environmental Rights Act*, RSNWT 1988, c 83 (Supp), s 6 grants every resident the right to protect the environment from the release of contaminants by commencing an action in the Supreme Court. A person commencing an action would not have to establish a pecuniary or property right or interest, nor would that person have to establish any greater or different harm than any other person. See also the Yukon *Environment Act*, SY 2002, c 76, s 8 and the Ontario *Environmental Bill of Rights, 1993*, SO 1993, c 28, s 84.

2. If public nuisance is failing to protect public resources, should Canadian courts engage with other common law doctrines like the public trust doctrine? This issue came before the Supreme Court in *Canadian Forest* (cited in Section I of this chapter), where the court considered various justifications for the Crown to recover damages for injuries to public natural resources and other environmental losses. The facts of this case involved a forest fire that had burned nearly 1,500 hectares of interior British Columbia. The cause of the fire had been attributed to the appellant company, Canadian Forests Products Ltd, which had failed to extinguish a flare-up that had resulted from a controlled burn; the Crown was also partially responsible for failing to provide adequate firefighting efforts. The area that had burned included forested areas licensed for logging, forested areas deemed too immature to log, and other areas off limits to logging because of their environmental value. The attorney general sought damages for three categories of loss: (1) firefighting expenditures and land restoration; (2) lost profits ("stumpage revenue") from the loss of harvestable trees; and (3) losses associated with the destruction of non-harvestable trees that had been set aside for environmental reasons. Pursuant to the third category of damages, the Crown sought compensation at one-third the commercial value of the non-harvestable trees, with an additional premium attributed to their environmental purpose. The Crown failed to secure these damages; however, the court's consideration of doctrinal sources for potential compensation for environmental damage, including the public trust doctrine (which protects the public's interest in certain natural resources) and *parens patriae* jurisdiction (which allows the Crown to protect public interests), is a notable development.

Binnie J, writing for the majority, articulated (at para 76) that "public rights and jurisdiction over these cannot be separated from the Crown. This notion of the Crown as holder of inalienable 'public rights' in the environment and certain common resources was accompanied by the procedural right of the Attorney General to sue for their protection representing the Crown as *parens patriae*." He then proceeded to canvass the application of *parens patriae* and the public trust doctrine in the US, before concluding (at para 81) that, in Canada,

> [i]t seems to me there is no legal barrier to the Crown suing for compensation as well as injunctive relief in a proper case on account of public nuisance, or negligence causing environmental damage to public lands, and perhaps other torts such as trespass, but there are clearly important and novel policy questions raised by such actions. These include the Crown's potential liability for *inactivity* in the face of threats to the environment, the existence or non-existence of enforceable fiduciary duties owed to the public by the Crown in that regard, the limits to the role and function and remedies available to governments taking action on account of activity harmful to public enjoyment of public resources, and the spectre of imposing on private interests an indeterminate liability for an indeterminate amount of money for ecological or environmental damage.

Binnie J held (at para 82) that "[t]his is not a proper appeal for the Court to embark on a consideration of these difficult issues." Subsequent judicial consideration of *Canadian Forest* has not significantly advanced application of these doctrinal justifications. For example, in

Burns Bog Conservation Society v Canada, 2014 FCA 170 at para 44, the Federal Court of Appeal agreed with the Federal Court's observation that Binnie J's reasoning, at best, "opens the door to the application of the public trust doctrine developed in the United States in respect of land owned by the Crown" (para 44). It remains possible that, given the correct fact pattern, the public trust doctrine may yet emerge as a viable justification for compensation. See Jerry V DeMarco, Marcia Valiante & Marie-Ann Bowden, "Opening the Door for Common Law Environmental Protection in Canada" (2005) 15 J Envtl L & Prac 233; and Anna Lund, "Canadian Approaches to America's Public Trust Doctrine: Classic Trusts, Fiduciary Duties & Substantive Review" (2012) 23 J Envtl L & Prac 135.

E. STRICT LIABILITY

Strict liability is liability regardless of fault on the part of the defendant. In the environmental context, this is found in cases where the defendant collects things on his or her land that are likely to cause mischief if they escape. If they do escape, the defendant will be held strictly liable—that is, liable for the damages resulting from such an escape, even if the defendant may not have been careless or at fault in allowing the escape. This so-called rule originates in the case of *Rylands v Fletcher* (1868), LR 3 HL 330. The essential elements of the tort created by the decision can be listed as follows: (1) the defendant is in lawful occupation of property, (2) on which is stored a dangerous agent or thing constituting a non-natural use of land, and (3) an agent or thing escapes from the defendant's property, (4) causing damage to the plaintiff. The non-natural use requirement has, traditionally and historically, been the factor most frequently considered by courts, but they have given it both a broad and a narrow meaning. Considered broadly, a non-natural use has been held to be any use that exposes the neighbourhood to special dangers. More narrowly, it requires that the use be not only hazardous but also unusual or special in the sense that it is not one originally conducted on land. See Klar & Jefferies at 745-50.

In *Cambridge Water Co v Eastern Counties Leather plc*, [1994] 1 All ER 53 (HL), a case involving the pollution of a plaintiff's water supply by chemicals previously considered "safe" but later coming under government regulation, the House of Lords embraced the traditional technical distinctions of non-natural use and escape from land but added the requirement of foreseeability of damage. There, the trial judge had found the storage of organochlorines in the vicinity of an industrial village to be a natural use of land. The House of Lords (at 75) expressed the opinion that the storage of substantial quantities of chemicals on industrial premises was to be regarded as an "almost classic case" of non-natural use. Lord Goff (at 75) also rejected the US interpretation and application of *Rylands* that imposes strict liability in cases where damage is caused by "ultra-hazardous operations." The court concluded (at 76) that because *Rylands* was, in essence, "an extension of the law of nuisance to cases of isolated escapes from land" and because foreseeability was already an element of nuisance, the defendant could not be held liable for the unforeseeable damage from escaped chemicals.

Following *Cambridge Water*, the status of *Rylands* was addressed by the Ontario Court of Appeal in *Smith* (at para 68), where the court noted that "[i]n Canada, *Rylands v. Fletcher* has gone largely unnoticed in appellate courts in recent years. However, in 1989 in *Tock*, the Supreme Court of Canada unanimously recognized *Rylands v. Fletcher* as continuing to provide a basis for liability distinct from liability for private nuisance or negligence." The Court of Appeal in *Smith* dismissed the strict liability claim on the basis of the non-natural use requirement. However, in *obiter*, the court addressed the trial judge's observation that foreseeability was not a requirement for *Rylands* in Ontario by suggesting (at para 110) that there are "compelling reasons to require foreseeability of the kind of damages alleged to have been suffered by the plaintiffs."

F. RIPARIAN RIGHTS

Riparian rights are rights held by the owner of land bordering a river, lake, or stream. Riparian rights are often asserted in environmental cases because of the potential for courts to impose a strict environmental standard for water protection. The most important riparian rights for environmental purposes are those that pertain to both the natural quantity and the natural quality of water flow. See *KVP Co v McKie*, [1949] SCR 698, 1949 CanLII 8.

The extent to which courts may weaken the application of strict riparian rights is subject to some uncertainty. A "domestic use" or "ordinary use" exception where a riparian owner may use water for domestic purposes such as drinking, stock watering, and washing without incurring liability to a lower riparian is quite clear. See GV LaForest, QC & Associates, *Water Law in Canada—The Atlantic Provinces* (Ottawa: Department of Regional Economic Expansion, 1972) at 224 (note also that it is common for provincial legislation to alter common law definitions; see, for example, Alberta's *Water Act*, RSA 2000, c W-3, s 1(1)(x), which defines and scopes permissible "household purposes"). Other secondary uses, such as waste disposal, may also be argued, and actions may lie only if the use is "unreasonable," a standard that is subject to a case-by-case interpretation.

Some courts have endorsed a strict approach to environmental protection. For example, in *Gauthier v Naneff*, 1970 CanLII 517, 14 DLR (3d) 513 (Ont H Ct J), the court interpreted "unreasonable" in the light of present-day knowledge of pollution problems, indicating that every riparian proprietor has an entitlement to water quality without "sensible alteration"— meaning the water retains the natural quality that the rights holder has come to expect. Other courts have been less strict and more willing to consider social and economic interests, particularly at the stage of deciding whether to grant injunctive relief for riparian interferences. See, for example, *Lockwood v Brentwood Park Investments Ltd*, 1970 CanLII 929, 10 DLR (3d) 143 (NSSC (AD)). Riparian rights have also been stated to extend to lands abutting the sea or other tidal waters. See GV LaForest, QC & Associates at 200.

G. TRESPASS TO THE PERSON IN THE FORM OF BATTERY

The general tort of trespass to the person covers three specific subtorts: battery, assault, and false or wrongful imprisonment. The most relevant action in the environmental context is battery, defined as the deliberate application of force to another person resulting in harm or offensive contact to that person. To make out a claim in battery, the plaintiff must demonstrate, amongst other requirements, that the defendant acted intentionally (that is, desired the consequence or should have been substantially certain that the consequence would result) and also that the physical contact resulted directly from the defendant's action. See Klar & Jefferies at 53-54. Intention and directness have proven to be two significant obstacles in pleading battery in the context of environmental harm or chemical contamination. See, generally, L Collins & H McLeod-Kilmurray, "Toxic Battery: A Tort for our Time?" (2008) 16 Tort L Rev 131.

Macdonald v Sebastian, 1987 CanLII 5371, 81 NSR (2d) 189 (SC (TD)) is a case of battery in the environmental context, where a mother and her children were exposed to unacceptable levels of arsenic in the water supply of their leased premises. Since the defendant, a medical doctor, had knowledge of the high arsenic levels and obvious damages to the health and safety of tenants, the court was willing to find a deliberate act of battery.

In *MacQueen v Sydney Steel Corp*, 2011 NSSC 484, rev'd 2013 NSCA 143, 369 DLR (4th) 1, leave to appeal to SCC refused, [2015] 1 SCR ix [*MacQueen* cited to NSCA], individuals living proximate to the Sydney Tar Ponds in Nova Scotia initiated a class action alleging battery and nuisance and seeking remediation of the pond, the implementation of a medical monitoring program, and damages. The tar ponds formed in the tidal estuary of the Muggah Creek where, over time, contaminated effluent from an upstream steelworks settled out and became concentrated. In alleging battery, the plaintiffs claimed that people living proximate to the industrial site and the ponds would inhale and ingest or otherwise be exposed to contaminants through dermal contact. The class action initially received certification to proceed, but certification was set aside upon appeal. In considering each alleged cause of action, the appellate court emphasized the directness requirement, which could not be proven on the facts. With respect to battery in particular, the court (at para 98) stated that "exposure to the contaminants alleged was not direct, but an indirect consequence of the industrial activities carried on by the appellants."

H. TRESPASS TO PROPERTY

Trespass to property is any direct and intentional invasion of land by another person, substance, or object absent legal authorization. No physical damage to the property need occur to maintain an action; interference with the legal right of possession is sufficient.

The tort consists of an act of direct physical entrance upon land in the possession of another, remaining upon such land after being told to leave, or placing or projecting any object upon the land. In each case, the act must be done without lawful justification. The two key elements of the tort are intention and directness. The latter requirement has been particularly problematic for plaintiffs in cases involving the spraying of insecticides and other toxic chemicals where wind drift carries the chemicals from their intended target and deposits them on the plaintiff's property (see Klar & Jefferies at 134). Another example of the problems posed by the directness requirement is the case involving oil being jettisoned into the water by the defendant and carried into the plaintiff's foreshore yet found not to constitute a trespass because the interference with the plaintiff's land was not the direct result of the defendant's act in *Southport Corp v Esso Petroleum Co*, [1954] 2 QB 182 (CA), rev'd on other grounds, [1955] 3 All ER 864 (HL). Similarly, in *Hoffman v Monsanto Canada Inc*, 2007 SKCA 47, [2007] 6 WWR 387, leave to appeal to SCC refused, 2007 CanLII 55334, the drift of genetically modified seeds from one farm onto neighbouring organic farms did not qualify as a trespass by the companies that had developed and marketed these seeds because significant interventions had occurred between developing and marketing of the seeds and their eventual deposition on the plaintiffs' property. There is weight to the argument that in circumstances where the interference was "set in motion by the defendants assisted only by natural and inevitable forces," they ought to be treated as sufficiently direct to constitute a trespass (Klar & Jefferies at 133–34).

A further legal issue is the question of what constitutes a physical entry upon land. It is likely that non-physical interferences, such as vibrations, fumes, and odours, do not constitute physical entry (*Phillips v California Standard Co*, 1960 CanLII 525, 31 WWR (NS) 331 (Alta SC (TD))). Some US courts grappling with the problem have insisted upon the entry of something tangible, having appreciable mass and visible to the naked eye, with intangible intrusions more suitably addressed through nuisance or negligence actions (*Babb v Lee County Landfill SC, LLC*, No 2012-212741 (SC US Sup Ct 2013)). This approach would not allow for the recognition of industrial dust or noxious fumes (see WP Keeton et al, eds, *Prosser and Keeton on Law of Torts*, 5th ed (St Paul, Minn: West, 1984) at 71). However, other US court decisions have found a trespass to land in the entry of invisible gases and microscopic particles where they do harm or cause a substantial interference. See, for example, *Martin v Reynolds Metals Co*, 342 P (2d) 790 (Or 1959); *Bradley v American Smelting and Refining Co*, 709 P (2d) 782 (Wash 1985)).

III. CHALLENGES AND JUDICIAL STRUGGLES IN TOXIC TORTS

Toxic torts tend to fall into major categories, each with jurisprudential challenges. First, plaintiffs may try to prevent a threatened exposure to toxic agents. For example, they may try to stop the spraying of herbicides on a nearby property by arguing that the defendant's planned activity is tortious and should be prohibited or restricted by way of injunctive relief. Scientific uncertainties regarding toxic substances abound, with limited and sometimes conflicting studies making conclusions on effects difficult.

For the judiciary, various challenges are raised. Should traditional burden and standards of proof be followed, with plaintiffs having to establish all the elements of causes of action, including causation, on a balance of probabilities? In light of the precautionary principle under international environmental law, where decision-makers are urged to err on the side of caution in situations of scientific uncertainty, should the burden of proof shift to defendants? What type and level of risk should form the basis for judicial and injunctive action?

A second category of cases involves plaintiffs suffering a present injury, such as cancer, where establishing a causal link to a defendant's tortious activity is a central obstacle. Two types of situations are prevalent. In the indeterminate-plaintiff scenario, the plaintiff struggles to prove causation because of limitations in scientific evidence and the reality that non-tortious causes such as lifestyle and genetic predisposition may also explain an illness. A related inquiry involves situations where plaintiffs are exposed to a toxic agent but have no present injury in the traditional sense of a manifest physical or personal injury. In this indeterminate-harm scenario, "all that a given plaintiff can demonstrate is that the defendant has exposed him or her to a material risk of harm," which is insufficient to sustain a tort action (Collins & McLeod-Kilmurray, *The Canadian Law of Toxic Torts* at 126). Nevertheless, various types of damage may be claimed, including recovery for an enhanced risk of future disease, money for health monitoring, compensation for fear of getting a serious illness, and compensation for a reduction in property value linked to public perceptions of risk or the stigma attached to the property.

In the "indeterminate defendant" situation, the plaintiff is able to establish an illness linked to a tortious activity but is unable to identify a specific defendant. Long latency periods for disease may make it difficult to point the legal finger at a particular defendant, especially where numerous defendants may have been involved in the manufacture and distribution of a particular toxic agent. Generic marketing further complicates the indeterminate-defendant situation. Again, challenges arise. Should the traditional common law "but for" test for causation (that is, the plaintiff must establish on the balance of probabilities that but for the defendant's tortious activity, injury would not have occurred) be rejected? If so, what is the appropriate replacement?

A. PREVENTION OF THREATENED EXPOSURE TO TOXIC AGENTS

PALMER V NOVA SCOTIA FOREST INDUSTRIES
1983 CanLII 2898, 2 DLR (4th) 397 (NSSC (TD))

[This case involves an application by the plaintiffs to enjoin the defendant forestry company from spraying certain areas with phenoxy herbicides. The chemicals in question (dioxins and chlorophenols) were the subject of considerable political and regulatory scrutiny at the time this action for injunctive relief was brought. The plaintiffs claimed that if these chemicals entered their lands, they would create a serious health risk and constitute a nuisance (assuming the plaintiffs could prove that the defendant company caused the risk).

Importantly, the plaintiffs' action had been commenced *before* any spraying occurred and the relief was sought—a *quia timet* injunction. This remedy serves to prevent the occurrence of harm and, to be warranted, requires a "strong case of probability" of the alleged potential harm. The plaintiffs must prove the essential elements of a regular injunction (that is, irreparable harm and the inadequacy of damages) and otherwise convince the court that this is an appropriate circumstance to deliver a discretionary remedy.

The court, convinced that damages would not suffice if a serious health risk would result from spraying, focused its attention on whether the plaintiffs had offered sufficient proof of a serious risk to health.]

[552] Because of the nature of the issues in dispute, the witnesses produced and the testimony given, the enormous publicity attached to the trial and the public interest involved, the evidence went far beyond the particular substances involved and related to all the phenoxy herbicides and their derivatives. The whole trial took on the aura of a scientific inquiry as to whether the world should be exposed to dioxins. Scientists from all over North America, as well as from Sweden were called and testified. Scientific reports and studies from scientists the world over were filed as part of the evidence. In order to give both sides full opportunity to present their cases fully, it was necessary to grant this latitude although both parties were aware that the final decision would have to relate to the particular facts between the parties before the court.

[553] As to the wider issues relating to the dioxin issue, it hardly seems necessary to state that a court of law is no forum for the determination of matters of science. Those are for science to determine, as facts, following the traditionally accepted methods of scientific inquiry. A substance neither does nor does not create a risk to health by court decree and it would be foolhardy for a court to enter such an inquiry. If science itself is not certain, a court cannot resolve the conflict and make the thing certain.

[554] Essentially a court is engaged in the resolution of private disputes between parties and in the process follows certain time-honoured and well-established procedures and applies equally well-established principles of law, varying and altering them to adjust to an ever-changing society. Part of the process is the determination of facts and another part the application of the law to those facts, once determined, and designing the remedy. As to the occurrence of events, the court is concerned with "probability" and not with "possibility."

[The plaintiffs also raised the concern that certain diseases, like cancer, have long incubation periods and that the full effect of chemicals may not be known for many decades. The court expressed similar reservations in its approach to long-term risk.]

[590] If all substances which are carcinogenic or otherwise toxic were removed from use, we would have no air to breathe or potable water and many common everyday products, necessary to our life, would be removed. The key to the use of all these is dosage. Where it can be determined that there is a safe dosage, according to acceptable scientific standards, then a substance can be used. Our regulatory agencies and scientists around the world are daily involved in this very area.

[591] As well, virtually all chemicals are toxic, but those in use generally are safe if used below the toxic levels, i.e., if the dose received is below the safety levels. Scientists also determine a "no observable effect level." That is a level of intake of any particular substance where no effect is observed. It is, in most cases, far below the safe level, at least several orders of magnitude (each order being a multiple of 10) lower.

[592] In these determinations effect on humans is assessed by extrapolation from animal studies. This is a well-known and widely-accepted approach and some of the evidence here was based on this method.

[593] I am satisfied that the overwhelming currently accepted view of responsible scientists is that there is little evidence that, for humans either 2,4-D or 2,4,5-T is mutagenic or carcinogenic and that TCDD is not an effective carcinogen, and

further, that there are no-effect levels and safe levels for humans and wildlife for each of these substances.

• • •

[595] Having reached this point it is appropriate to add that the evidence of risk assessments clearly indicates that any risk here in Nova Scotia, if, indeed, there is a risk at all, is infinitesimally small and many, many times less than one in a million which level, apparently, is regarded as a safe and acceptable risk by most of the world's regulatory agencies.

[In conclusion, the court declined to grant a *quia timet* injunction on the basis that the plaintiffs had failed to prove a strong probability or sufficient degree of any risk to health.

An additional issue raised in the *Palmer* case was whether a group of plaintiffs could maintain a representative action (on behalf of other persons living near the spray sites) under Nova Scotia's *Civil Procedure Rules*. Nunn J found that the key legal requirements of numerous persons and common interest (in this case, risk to health) had been met. All provinces save the smallest—Prince Edward Island—have enacted class action legislation. In *Hollick v Toronto (City)*, 2001 SCC 68, the Supreme Court noted three advantages of class actions: judicial economy; distributed litigation costs, improving access to justice; and behaviour of wrongdoers modified to fully account for public harm. For further discussion, see Meinhard Doelle, "The Sydney Tar Ponds Case: Shutting the Door on Environmental Class Action Suits in Nova Scotia?" (2015) 27 J Envtl L & Prac 279.]

QUESTIONS

1. According to Nunn J, a serious health risk was required to find a substantial interference with the use and enjoyment of land and, thus, a nuisance. Is this an appropriate threshold, or should courts also consider something lesser, such as reasonable medical concern or reasonable ecological concern?

2. The precautionary principle, which is an important principle of international environmental law and a common feature of Canada's environmental laws, functions to err on the side of environmental and human health protection in the face of uncertainty. Should the precautionary principle affect our approach to assessing causation? Prominent Canadian scholars argue that the precautionary approach could shift the burden of proof from the plaintiff to the defendant, who would have to satisfy the court of the absence of reasonable concern regarding the potential environmental impact of his or her proposed activity. Furthermore, a reversed burden of proof could prompt companies to produce more complete data sets on chemical safety. See D VanderZwaag, *Canada and Marine Environmental Protection: Charting a Course Towards Sustainable Development* (London: Kluwer Law International, 1995) at 407-8 and Collins & McLeod-Kilmurray, *The Canadian Law of Toxic Torts* at 153.

B. PROVING CAUSATION OF PRESENT INJURY

1. Addressing the Indeterminate Plaintiff Challenge

JONES V MOBIL OIL CANADA LTD
1999 ABQB 520, 248 AR 1

[In this case, the plaintiff rancher alleged that his cattle had been exposed to or ingested harmful chemicals and that the defendant, Mobil, was at fault for failing to erect adequate fencing around its operations and for spilling chemicals that polluted the ground and water on his land. Mobil denied that it was the cause of the failure of the plaintiff's herd of cattle. The court held that Mobil had breached its duty to erect effective fencing and also found nuisance.

The court assessed the plaintiff's ability to prove on a balance of probabilities that Mobil had caused or materially contributed to the herd's failure.]

[161] The onus of proving that Mobil's negligence or nuisance materially contributed to the failure of his herd is on Mr. Jones. However, as established by the Supreme Court of Canada in *Farrell v Snell* (1990), 72 DLR (4th) 289, causation need not be determined with scientific precision, and it is essentially a question of fact that can be answered by the application of ordinary common sense.

[162] As pointed out by Sopinka, J. in [that case], although the burden of proof remains on the plaintiff throughout the trial, in the absence of evidence to the contrary put forward by the defendant, an inference of causation may be drawn, even in the absence of positive or scientific proof of causation. If some evidence has been adduced by the defendant, that evidence must be weighed against the evidence put forward by the plaintiff. In weighing such evidence, it is necessary to have regard to what evidence it was in the power of one side to have produced and in the power of the other to have contradicted. ...

• • •

[164] The Supreme Court continued its analysis of the principles of causation in *Athey v. Leonati et al.* (1996), 140 DLR (4th) 235, and confirmed that causation is not to be applied too rigidly. It is now clear that it is not necessary for a plaintiff to establish that the negligence of the defendant is the sole cause of the injury. As stated by Major, J. at page 239 of *Athey* (*supra*), as long as a defendant is part of a cause of the damage, such defendant is liable, even if there exist other preconditions to the injury, as long as the actions or inactions of the defendant caused or materially contributed to the damage. A defendant is not excused from liability merely because other causal factors for which the defendant is not responsible exist.

[The plaintiff had tendered evidence indicating that between 1982 and 1992, his cattle had had access to harmful oilfield chemicals and that his animals had suffered various symptoms. The plaintiff had had his animals tested periodically, but veterinary experts had been unable to provide a positive diagnosis of poisoning. The evidence did, however, support the conclusion that the herd had been exposed to noxious substances and that cattle have a tendency to consume these contaminate types when the opportunity presents itself. In reply, Mobil's experts had opined on the difficulty of diagnosing oilfield poisoning of this type and had offered reports that did not support, but also did not rule out, contamination.

In evaluating this evidence in view of the causation analysis, the court returned to the plaintiff's burden of proof.]

[168] Mr. Jones does not have to prove conclusively that exposure to contaminants or ingestion of them led to the symptoms suffered by the herd: the test is the balance of probabilities. There must be more than conjecture for an inference to be drawn in the absence of exact proof. Such inference must be reasonable. However, the inability of the experts to give a firm diagnosis, or to agree on a diagnosis, is not fatal to such an inference. All the evidence must be considered in considering whether such an inference is reasonable.

[The court concluded that it could reasonably infer that the herd's failure had been caused or materially contributed to by contamination from oilfield chemicals and that Mobil had been unable to present a sufficiently strong alternate theory. Thus, it was more than likely that the damage had resulted from Mobil's negligence and the nuisance it had created.]

The material contribution approach as an alternative to the traditional "but for" test for causation continues to be rather elusive. In *Athey v Leonati*, [1996] 3 SCR 458 at 466, 1996 CanLII 183, Major J provided only minimal guidance suggesting a "contributing factor is material if it falls outside the *de minimis* range."

Lord Wilberforce in *McGhee v National Coal Board*, [1973] 3 All ER 1008 (HL) suggested that where a defendant's negligence has materially increased the risk of injury and the injury occurs within the scope of the risk, the defendant should bear the burden of disproving causation. Canadian courts have had a number of opportunities to consider application of material contribution to risk. In *Snell v Farrell*, 1990 CanLII 70, 72 DLR (4th) 289, the Supreme Court rejected the "material increase of risk" and/or "reverse onus" approach. Then, in *Resurfice Corp v Hanke*, 2007 SCC 7 at paras 21-25, 278 DLR (4th) 643, McLachlin CJ, in *obiter*, clarified that the "material contribution" test remains an alternative to the "but for" test available in exceptional cases where it is impossible for the defendant to prove causation, owing to reasons beyond the plaintiff's control, and where the defendant's negligence exposed the plaintiff to an unreasonable risk of injury, and that injury materialized. Most recently, the Supreme Court revisited *Hanke* in *Clements v Clements*, 2012 SCC 32, [2012] 2 SCR 181 and confirmed (at para 14, citing *MacDonald (Litigation Guardian of) v Goertz* 2009 BCCA 358, 275 BCAC 68 (*sub nom Chambers v Goertz*) favourably) that the material contribution exception to the "but for" test substitutes factual causation with "proof of material contribution to risk" but also that it has yet to be applied by the Supreme Court. With respect to "impossibility," McLachlin CJ is clear that this requirement is not met simply because of evidentiary difficulties; rather, it will "typically" operate in scenarios where "there are a number of tortfeasors. All are at fault, and one or more has in fact caused the plaintiff's injury," and the plaintiff "would not have been injured 'but for' their negligence, viewed globally. However, because each can point the finger at the other, it is impossible for the plaintiff to show on a balance of probabilities that any one of them in fact caused her injury" (para 39).

A related line of inquiry is indeterminate harm, which entails questions of what constitutes a present injury and what is properly compensable. For example, a prospective plaintiff might seek to initiate a claim against a polluter, seeking recovery for the fear/anxiety of contracting a serious illness, such as cancer. In the American context, courts have developed various tests to address this problem. Consider, for example, *Potter v Firestone Tire & Rubber Co*, 863 P (2d) 795 (Cal 1993). In this toxic exposure case, the plaintiff landowners lived adjacent to a landfill where the defendant had disposed of waste in a manner that exposed the community to carcinogenic substances over an extended period of time. The Supreme Court of California reasoned as follows:

> To summarize, we hold with respect to negligent infliction of emotional distress claims arising out of exposure to carcinogens and/or other toxic substances: Unless an express exception to this general rule is recognized: in the absence of a present physical injury or illness, damages for fear of cancer may be recovered only if the plaintiff pleads and proves that (1) as a result of the defendant's negligent breach of a duty owed to the plaintiff, the plaintiff is exposed to a toxic substance which threatens cancer; *and* (2) the plaintiff's fear stems from a knowledge, corroborated by reliable medical or scientific opinion, that it is more likely than not that the plaintiff will develop the cancer in the future due to the toxic exposure. ... ["2.c. Likelihood of Cancer in the Future," 1993, para 27]

• • •

When a defendant acts with oppression, fraud or malice, no reason, policy or otherwise, [*sic*] justifies application of the more likely than not threshold. Any burden or consequence to society from imposing liability is offset by the deterrent impact of holding morally blame-worthy defendants fully responsible for the damages they cause, including damage in the form of emotional distress suffered by victims of the misconduct who reasonably fear future cancer. [Emphasis added.] ["3. Likelihood of Cancer in the Future," 1993, para 5.]

In Canada, such cases are considered by the courts as negligence actions alleging mental injury. To qualify, the alleged mental injury must be "serious and prolonged and rise above the ordinary annoyances, anxieties and fears that people living in society routinely, if sometimes reluctantly, accept" (*Mustapha v Culligan of Canada Ltd*, 2008 SCC 27 at para 9, [2008] SCR 114). The Supreme Court's consideration of mental injury in *Saadati v Moorhead*, 2017 SCC 28 at para 2, [2017] 1 SCR 543 makes clear, however, that recovery is not premised on the plain-tiff's ability to prove a recognizable psychiatric illness because "[t]his and other mechanisms by which some courts have historically sought to control recovery for mental injury are, in my respectful view, premised upon dubious perceptions of psychiatry and of mental illness in general, which Canadian tort law should repudiate." The court was confident that the general elements of any negligence action and the threshold elucidated in *Mustapha* are sufficient to guard against "unworthy claims."

Another important issue is the sort of remedial awards that can be sought by those exposed to hazardous substances. In the American context, "medical surveillance expenses" are regu-larly sought in toxic tort cases. As explained by the court in *Ayers v Jackson TP*, 525 A (2d) 287 (NJ 1987), "[t]he claim for medical surveillance expenses ... seeks to recover the cost of peri-odic medical examinations intended to monitor plaintiffs' health and facilitate early diagnosis and treatment of disease caused by plaintiffs' exposure to toxic chemicals."

In the Canadian context, which includes public health care, medical testing has been certi-fied in a number of class actions. See *Wilson v Servier Canada Inc*, 2000 CanLII 22407, 50 OR (3d) 219 (Sup Ct J), which is the main decision on point. In the environmental context, see *Ring v Canada (Attorney General)*, 2007 NLTD 146, rev'd 2010 NLCA 20 and *MacQueen*. In both these cases, the class action was certified at trial and then overturned on appeal. For detailed treatment of medical monitoring, see Brandon Stewart, "Just What the Doctor Ordered: A Canadian Approach to Medical Monitoring and Toxic Risk" (2013) 8:2 Can Class Action Rev 271.

A final noteworthy issue is the plaintiff's ability to recover for public perception of risk/fear and reduced property value associated with contaminated property. In *Smith*, the claimants alleged (at para 22) that "their property values had not increased at the same rate as compar-able property values in other small cities located nearby" and that this discrepancy was explained by "the reasonable, widespread public health concerns over the nickel deposits in the soil on their properties" that had accumulated during the 60 years that the defendant's refinery had operated. To prove damages, the claimants proposed a "market comparison approach" to compare rates of property appreciation in comparable communities. At trial, Henderson J concluded that the evidence supported a $36 million award to the aggregated class. The Court of Appeal, however, disagreed and concluded (at para 128) that "the record conclusively demonstrates that the claimants have suffered no loss."

In *Tridan Developments Ltd v Shell Canada Products Ltd*, 2002 CanLII 20789, 57 OR (3d) 503 (CA), the courts considered damages associated with "stigmatized" property. Here, the Ontario Court of Appeal reversed a lower court's award of $350,000 for the loss of property value due to stigma associated with the contamination of Tridan's land following a gas leak from Shell's service station. The case is a limited precedent, however, because the court con-cluded that since the contaminated site was required to be remediated to pristine condition, there was no stigma loss. The court, however, did not foreclose such a head of damage, at least where a site was not cleaned to a pristine state. For further discussion, see *Steadman v Corporation of the County of Lambton*, 2015 ONSC 101 at paras 62-71; J Hierlmeier, "The Enigma of Stigma: A New Environmental Contamination Challenge Facing Canada's Judiciary" (2002) 11 Dal J Legal Stud 179.

2. Addressing the Indeterminate Defendant Challenge

SINDELL V ABBOTT LABORATORIES
607 P (2d) 924 (Cal 1980)

[In this case, the plaintiff, representing herself and a class of similarly situated women, brought an action against 11 drug companies that had manufactured, promoted, and distributed diethylstilbesterol (DES) between 1941 and 1971. DES is a synthetic compound of the female hormone estrogen that had been administered to the plaintiff's mother to prevent miscarriage; in 1947, the Food and Drug Administration (FDA) had authorized DES marketing for miscarriage prevention on an experimental basis so long as it was labelled accordingly.

The plaintiff asserted that the defendants had known, or ought to have known, that DES was ineffective as a miscarriage preventative measure and was also a carcinogenic substance that posed a significant cancer risk to the daughters of the mothers who had taken the drug. Additionally, the defendants had failed to properly test DES, had not adhered to the FDA's experimental authorization, and had advertised DES as both safe and effective. The plaintiff had suffered a malignant bladder tumour that had been surgically removed but left her requiring constant monitoring.

The plaintiff advanced two causes of action. First, the defendants were jointly and individually negligent for manufacturing, marketing, and promoting DES as safe and effective without adequately testing, warning, or monitoring its effects. Second, the defendants were jointly liable regardless of which DES brand had caused the specific harm because they had collaborated in marketing, testing, and promoting the drug, utilized the same chemical formula, and relied on an industry-wide safety standard.

The court characterized the issue as follows:]

This case involves a complex problem both timely and significant: may a plaintiff, injured as the result of a drug administered to her mother during pregnancy, who knows the type of drug involved but cannot identify the manufacturer of the precise product, hold liable for her injuries a maker of a drug produced from an identical formula?

[With respect to causation, the court endorsed the application of a "market share" approach to liability.]

[T]he imposition of liability depends upon a showing by the plaintiff that his or her injuries were caused by the act of the defendant or by an instrumentality under the defendant's control. ...

• • •

But we approach the issue of causation from a different perspective: we hold it to be reasonable in the present context to measure the likelihood that any of the defendants supplied the product which allegedly injured plaintiff by the percentage which the DES sold by each of them for the purpose of preventing miscarriage bears to the entire production of the drug sold by all for that purpose. ...

If plaintiff joins in the action the manufacturers of a substantial share of the DES which her mother might have taken, the injustice of shifting the burden of proof to defendants to demonstrate that they could not have made the substance which injured plaintiff is significantly diminished. While 75 to 80 percent of the market is suggested as the requirement by the Fordham Comment (at p. 996), we hold only that a substantial percentage is required.

The presence in the action of a substantial share of the appropriate market also provides a ready means to apportion damages among the defendants. Each defendant will be held liable for the proportion of the judgment represented by its share of that market unless it demonstrates that it could not have made the product which caused plaintiff's injuries. ...

Under this approach, each manufacturer's liability would approximate its responsibility for the injuries caused by its own products. Some minor discrepancy in the correlation between market share and liability is inevitable; therefore, a defendant may be held liable for a somewhat different percentage of the damage than its share of the appropriate market would justify. It is probably impossible, with the passage of time, to determine market share with mathematical exactitude. But just as a jury cannot be expected to determine the precise relationship between fault and liability in applying the doctrine of comparative fault ... or partial indemnity ... , the difficulty of apportioning damages among the defendant producers in exact relation to their market share does not seriously militate against the rule we adopt.

Sindell left numerous issues unresolved, including what constitutes a substantial share of the market; what is the appropriate scope of market analysis (local, county, state/provincial, national); whether a plaintiff's overall recovery should be limited to the percentage of market share represented by defendants sued; and how far market share liability should be extended outside the generic drug context. In *Brown v Superior Court*, 44 Cal (3d) 1049, 751 P (2d) 470 (1988), the California Supreme Court clarified that a plaintiff's recovery should be limited by the proportion of the market share represented by defendants impleaded.

Canadian courts have not endorsed a market share approach to liability; however, a version of this theory of liability appears in provincial legislation enabling governments to take direct action against tobacco manufacturers to recover for the costs of treating individuals exposed to tobacco products. Each defendant can be held liable for a proportion of the costs equivalent to its market share of the product, which can be calculated by the court based on a statutory formula. British Columbia's *Tobacco Damages and Health Care Costs Recovery Act*, SBC 2000, c 30 was challenged on the basis of its constitutionality in *British Columbia v Imperial Tobacco Canada Ltd*, 2005 SCC 49, [2005] 2 SCR 473, where the Supreme Court held that legislation was constitutionally valid. Similar legislation has been enacted in every province.

Market share liability is not the only approach available for addressing the indeterminate defendant challenge. Other approaches include legislative reform (addressing common causation hurdles), concert of action theory (acting pursuant to a common design to harm the plaintiff), and enterprise liability (adhering to an inadequate industry standard through industry-wide cooperation). See KJ Owen, "Industry-Wide Liability: Protecting Plaintiffs and Defendants" (1992) 44 Baylor L Rev 45; J Pizzirusso, "Increased Risk, Fear of Disease and Medical Monitoring: Are Novel Damage Claims Enough to Overcome Causation Difficulties in Toxic Torts?" (2000) 7 Envtl L 183; and Collins & McLeod-Kilmurray, *The Canadian Law of Toxic Torts* at 146-57.

IV. TORT LAW AND CLIMATE CHANGE

Anthropogenic climate change is the critical environmental issue of our time. The Earth's atmosphere is a global commons, and greenhouse gases are emitted by every country. Accordingly, the most appropriate legal response remains cooperative international action that mitigates against dangerous levels of climate change and simultaneously supports adaptation and resilience. Unfortunately, the international response, embodied in treaties such as the *United National Framework Convention on Climate Change*, 9 May 1992, 1771 UNTS 107 (entered into force 21 March 1994) and the *Paris Agreement*, 12 December 2015, UN Doc FCCC/CP/2015/10/Add.1 (entered into force 4 November 2016), has failed to address anthropogenic climate change effectively.

Climate change litigation has emerged as a parallel response from citizens and nongovernmental organizations, primarily as lawsuits against governments (based on public law administrative and constitutional grounds) and against corporations (based on private law tort grounds). The most famous (and successful) tort-based action is *Urgenda Foundation v The State of the Netherlands*, HAZA C/09/00456689 (24 June 2015) (Hague Dist Ct), aff'd HAZA C/09/456689 13-1396 (9 October 2018) (Hague CA), where a Dutch environmental group alleged that the State of the Netherlands acted negligently toward its citizens by failing to take sufficient action to reduce its contribution to global climate change. In this landmark decision, the District Court of the Hague held that the Netherlands owed its citizens a duty to take action to reduce the "high risk of hazardous climate change" (at para 4.65) as "quickly and as much as possible" (at para 4.73). Importantly, the court also held that this duty was not abrogated by the fact that the Dutch "contribution to the present global greenhouse gas emissions is currently small" (at para 4.83) nor was causation a barrier to the claim because "a sufficient causal link can be assumed to exist between the Dutch greenhouse gas emissions, global climate change and the effects (now and in the future) on the Dutch living climate" (at para 4.90). Ultimately, the court found the State of Netherlands to be negligent and ordered the government to limit its greenhouse gas emissions by 25 percent, compared to 1990 levels, by the end of 2020. The Hague Court of Appeal upheld the trial decision in October 2018. For further discussion, see Josephine van Zeben, "Establishing a Governmental Duty of Care for Climate Change Mitigation: Will Urgenda Turn the Tide?" (2015) 4:2 Transnat'l Envtl L 339; Roger Cox, "A Climate Litigation Precedent: Urgenda Foundation v The State of the Netherlands" (November 2015) CIGI Paper No 79, online (pdf): *Centre for International Governance Innovation* <https://www.cigionline.org/sites/default/files/cigi_paper_79.pdf>; and Michael Slattery, "Pathways from Paris: Does Urgenda Lead to Canada?" (2017) 30:3 J Envtl L & Prac 241.

Significant tort-based climate litigation has also occurred in the US, with large corporate emitters rather than the government being the target. In *Comer v Murphy Oil USA*, 585 F (3d) 855 (5th Cir 2009), vacated *en banc* review, 607 F (3d) 1049 (5th Cir 2010), the plaintiff property owners in Mississippi claimed that the corporate defendants' emissions had contributed to climate change, which had increased the severity of Hurricane Katrina, which had damaged their property. The claim alleged multiple torts, including trespass, negligence, private nuisance, and public nuisance. The District Court dismissed the claim on the basis that the plaintiffs lacked standing and also that the claims raised non-justiciable political questions. The Court of Appeal overturned the trial decision; however, the case was never heard on its merits because of procedural quirks.

In *Connecticut v American Electric Power Co Inc*, 406 F Supp (2d) 265 (SDNY 2005), rev'd 582 F (3d) 309 (2nd Cir 2009), rev'd 131 S Ct 2527 (2011), eight states and three conservation groups sued five power companies in a public nuisance action seeking injunctive relief. The power companies successfully argued that the federal *Clean Air Act*, 42 USC § 7401 (1970) and the regulatory scheme it created for greenhouse gases displaced federal nuisance law.

In *Native Village of Kivalina v ExxonMobil Corp*, 663 F Supp (2d) 863 (ND Cal 2009), aff'd 696 F (3d) 849 (9th Cir 2012), the village of Kivalina, which is inhabited by Alaskan Iñupiat and situated on a small spit of land stretching into the Bering Sea, brought a public nuisance action against large fossil fuel companies, alleging that the greenhouse gas emissions associated with the defendants' products had contributed to the erosion of the village site. The plaintiffs sought compensation for damages associated with sea ice erosion, land subsidence, and community relocation. The Court of Appeal confirmed that the federal *Clean Air Act* comprehensively dealt with the issues raised by the village of Kivalina, thus displacing and precluding a public nuisance action. For further discussion, see Jacqueline Peel, *Climate Change Litigation: Regulatory Pathways to Cleaner Energy* (Cambridge: Cambridge University Press, 2015); Douglas A Kysar, "What Climate Change Can Do About Tort Law" (2011) 41:1 Envtl L 1; DA Grossman, "Tort-Based Climate Litigation" in WCG Burns & HM Osofsky, eds, *Adjudicating Climate Change* (New York: Cambridge University Press, 2009).

Most recently, American tort-based climate litigation has featured cities in California and Washington State, as well as New York City and the state of Rhode Island, suing large fossil fuel companies and seeking compensation for the costs of climate change adaptation. The District Court of the Southern District of New York dismissed the New York City action, which asserted nuisance (both public and private) and trespass, against five multinational energy companies. In *City of New York v BP plc*, 325 F Supp (3d) 466 (SDNY 2018), the District Court dismissed the action on the basis that both federal and state tort law had been displaced by the federal *Clean Air Act*, which governs domestic greenhouse gas regulation. Additionally, to the extent that New York City had attempted to hold the defendants accountable for emissions outside the US, the court concluded that the City's claims were "barred by the presumption against extraterritoriality and the need for judicial caution" (at 475) in considering issues that have serious foreign policy implications. The City of New York has appealed to the Second Circuit Court of Appeals.

Canadian courts have yet to adjudicate a tort-based climate change action. Litigation, to date, has been limited to the administrative challenges to executive inaction. See, for example, *Friends of the Earth v Canada (Governor in Council)*, 2008 FC 1183, 299 DLR (4th) 583, aff'd 2009 FCA 297, leave to appeal to SCC refused, 2010 CanLII 14720; see also *Turp v Canada (Minister of Justice)*, 2012 FC 893. That said, it is apparent that Canadian courts assessing a tort-based climate action would have to grapple with the issues that have recurred in American jurisprudence, including causation, the indeterminate defendant problem, and justiciability.

In January 2019, the City of Victoria, British Columbia voted in favour of pursuing class action litigation against major fossil fuel companies to recover damages associated with climate change. Specifically, Victoria City Council resolved to initiate tracking expenditures made in response to climate change and endorsed the following resolution for consideration at the meetings of the Union of British Columbia Municipalities (UBCM) and the Association of Vancouver Island and Coastal Communities (City of Victoria, Minutes—Victoria City Council (17 January 2019) at 22):

Recovering Municipal Costs Arising from Climate Change

WHEREAS local governments are incurring substantial costs in relation to the impacts of climate change, including volatile weather patterns, drought, wildfires, erosion and other impacts;

AND WHEREAS it is fiscally prudent to recover these costs from corporations that have profited from the burning of fossil fuels, with knowledge that these economic activities contribute to climate change;

THEREFORE BE IT RESOLVED THAT UBCM explore the initiation of a class action lawsuit on behalf of member local governments to recover costs arising from climate change from major fossil fuels corporations;

AND BE IT FURTHER RESOLVED THAT the Province of British Columbia consider legislation to support local governments in recovering costs arising from climate change from major fossil fuel corporations.

FURTHER READINGS

Collins, L & H McLeod-Kilmurray, *The Canadian Law of Toxic Torts* (Toronto: Canada Law Book, 2014).

Faieta, MD, et al, *Environmental Harm: Civil Actions and Compensation* (Toronto: Butterworths, 1996).

Klar, L & C Jefferies, *Tort Law*, 6th ed (Toronto: Thomson Reuters, 2017).

Mansell, R, "Civil Liability for Environmental Damage" in AR Lucas, ed, *Canadian Environmental Law*, 3rd ed (Toronto: LexisNexis, 2017) (loose-leaf, vol 1) ch 18.

CHAPTER TEN

CONSTITUTIONAL JURISDICTION*

Alastair R Lucas

I. INTRODUCTION

P MULDOON & B RUTHERFORD, "ENVIRONMENT AND THE CONSTITUTION: SUBMISSION TO THE HOUSE OF COMMONS STANDING COMMITTEE ON ENVIRONMENT"

(Toronto: Canadian Environmental Law Association and Pollution Probe, 1991), appendix E (edited)

DIVISION OF POWERS

The *Constitution Act, 1867* [(UK), 30 & 31 Vict, c 3, reprinted in RSC 1985, Appendix II, No 5] sets out the division of powers between the federal and the provincial governments. The list of powers is meant to be exhaustive and the federal and provincial governments are to be supreme within their own sphere.

---

* Based in part on the third edition chapter by Marie-Ann Bowden.

PROVINCIAL JURISDICTION

The provinces have jurisdiction to regulate with respect to pollution matters by virtue of their primary jurisdiction over "Property and Civil Rights in the Province" (s. 92(13)) and "Generally all matters of a merely local or private nature in the Province" (s. 92(16)). It can be said that property and civil rights are the provincial equivalent of the federal peace, order and good government. Given that a good deal of pollution arises in the context of land use and land use planning, pollution regulation appears to be of a local and regional nature. Provinces do not, however, have the right to regulate out of province companies. Other sources of provincial jurisdiction are found in their control and ownership of their land, mines and minerals (s. 109) and non-renewable natural resources, forestry and electrical energy (s. 92A).

FEDERAL JURISDICTION

The federal power to legislate over environmental matters is clear where such matters have interprovincial and international effects; however, it is unclear that the power to legislate national environmental standards would survive a jurisdictional challenge. [The ongoing Ontario and Saskatchewan reference cases concerning the validity of the federal *Greenhouse Gas Pollution Pricing Act*, SC 2018, c 12, s 186, which establishes a charge on carbon emitters, may shed light on this issue (see "Problems" in Section II.B, below).]

Parliament's jurisdiction to regulate the environment comes from a number of different heads of power. It is questionable that any one head of power gives Parliament the jurisdiction that it needs to play a strong role in providing national standards and policy. Especially in areas where land pollution, land use and resource conservation are involved, the federal government would undoubtedly be challenged for stepping into provincial jurisdiction.

The significant federal powers involved can be characterized into two groups: functional and conceptual. The functional powers are as follows:

- "Navigation and Shipping" (s. 91(10))
- "Sea Coast and Inland Fisheries" (s. 91(12))
- "Canals, Harbours, Rivers and Lake Improvements" (s. 108)
- "Federal Works and Undertakings" (s. 91(29) and 92(10))

While "Agriculture" (s. 95) might be added to this list, and although it is framed as a concurrent power that is shared with the provinces, it has essentially been emptied of meaning by judicial pronouncement. It is difficult to see it as a true concurrent power.

It is clear that the above exclusive powers allow Parliament to legislate over specific activities which necessarily involve matters of environmental quality.

The conceptual powers, however, arguably provide Parliament with general authority to legislate over broadly defined activities which by analogy or implication include matters of environmental quality. They are as follows:

- "Criminal Law" (s. 91(27))
- "Peace, Order and Good Government" (s. 91)
- "Taxation" (s. 91(3))
- "Trade and Commerce" (s. 91(2))
- "Public Debt and Property" (the Spending Power, s. 91(1A)).

II. FEDERAL–PROVINCIAL CONFLICTS

A. FUNCTIONAL POWERS

FOWLER V THE QUEEN
[1980] 2 SCR 213, 1980 CanLII 201

[The appellant operated a logging business in coastal British Columbia. As part of the operation, logs were removed from the forest and dragged across a small stream, resulting in the deposit of debris in the stream bed. The stream, which flowed into the coastal salt waters of the province, at times contained fish and was used for spawning and rearing of salmon. No evidence established that the deposit of the debris in any way affected the fish or the fry. The appellant was charged pursuant to s 33(3) of the *Fisheries Act*, RSC 1970, c F-14.]

MARTLAND J: The sole issue to be determined in this appeal is that which is raised in the constitutional question propounded in the order of the Chief Justice of this Court: "Is Section 33(3) of the *Fisheries Act*, R.S.C. 1970, c. F-14, within the legislative competence of the Parliament of Canada?"

Section 33 of the *Fisheries Act* appears under the heading "Injury to Fishing Grounds and Pollution of Waters" and contains, *inter alia*, the following subsections:

33(1) No one shall throw overboard ballast, coal ashes, stones, or other prejudicial or deleterious substances in any river, harbour or roadstead, or in any water where fishing is carried on, or leave or deposit or cause to be thrown, left or deposited, upon the shore, beach or bank of any water or upon the beach between high and low water mark, remains or offal of fish, or of marine animals, or leave decayed or decaying fish in any net or other fishing apparatus; such remains or offal may be buried ashore, above high water mark.

• • •

(3) No person engaging in logging, lumbering, land clearing or other operations, shall put or knowingly permit to be put, any slash, stumps or other debris into any water frequented by fish or that flows into such water, or on the ice over either such water, or at a place from which it is likely to be carried into either such water.

• • •

(11) For the purposes of this section and sections 33.1 and 33.2, "deleterious substance" means
    (a) any substance that, if added to any water, would degrade or alter or form part of a process of degradation or alteration of the quality of that water so that it is rendered or is likely to be rendered deleterious to fish or fish habitat or to the use by man of fish that frequent that water, or
    (b) any water that contains a substance in such quantity or concentration, or that has been so treated, processed or changed, by heat or other means, from a natural state that it would, if added to any other water, degrade or alter or form part of a process of degradation or alteration of the quality of that water so that it is rendered or is likely to be rendered deleterious to fish or fish habitat or to the use by man of fish that frequent that water ... .

The respondent contends that subs. (3) of s. 33 is valid legislation because of the legislative authority of Parliament in respect of "Sea Coast and Inland Fisheries" under s. 91(12) of the *British North America Act* [now *Constitution Act, 1867*, 30 & 31 Victoria, c 3 (UK)]. The appellant submits that subs. (3) falls within provincial legislative powers, relying upon ss. 92(5), 92(10), 92(13) and 92(16) of the Act.

• • •

The legislation in question here does not deal directly with fisheries, as such, within the meaning of those definitions. Rather, it seeks to control certain kinds of operations not strictly on the basis that they have deleterious effects on fish but, rather, on the basis that they might have such effects. *Prima facie*, subs. 33(3) regulates property and civil rights within a province. Dealing, as it does, with such rights and not dealing specifically with "fisheries," in order to support the legislation it must be established that it provides for matters necessarily incidental to effective legislation on the subject-matter of sea coast and inland fisheries.

• • •

The criteria for establishing liability under subs. 33(3) are indeed wide. Logging, lumbering, land clearing and other operations are covered. The substances which are proscribed are slash, stumps and other debris. The amount of the substance which is deposited is not relevant. The legislation extends to cover not only water frequented by fish but also water that flows into such water, ice over any such water and any place from which slash, stumps and other debris are likely to be carried into such water.

Subsection 33(3) makes no attempt to link the proscribed conduct to actual or potential harm to fisheries. It is a blanket prohibition of certain types of activity, subject to provincial jurisdiction, which does not delimit the elements of the offence so as to link the prohibition to any likely harm to fisheries. Furthermore, there was no evidence before the Court to indicate that the full range of activities caught by the subsection do, in fact, cause harm to fisheries. In my opinion, the prohibition in its broad terms is not necessarily incidental to the federal power to legislate in respect of sea coast and inland fisheries and is *ultra vires* of the federal Parliament.

Appeal allowed with costs.

NORTHWEST FALLING CONTRACTORS LTD V THE QUEEN
[1980] 2 SCR 292, 1980 CanLII 210

[Three thousand gallons of diesel fuel stored on the appellant's property were spilled into the tidal waters of British Columbia. The appellant was charged with violating s 33(2) of the *Fisheries Act*, RSC 1970, c F-14.]

MARTLAND J: The main issue which is to be determined in this appeal is as to whether it was within the legislative competence of the Parliament of Canada to enact subs. 33(2) of the *Fisheries Act*, RSC 1970, c. F-14, as amended [now RSC 1985, c F-14, s 36(3)].

Subsection (2) is one of a number of provisions appearing in the section which comes under the heading "Injury to Fishing Grounds and Pollution of Waters." The following are the relevant subsections of s. 33:

• • •

33(2) Subject to subsection (4), no person shall deposit or permit the deposit of a deleterious substance of any type in water frequented by fish or in any place under any conditions where such deleterious substance or any other deleterious substance that results from the deposit of such deleterious substance may enter any such water.

[Other subsections of s 33 are reproduced in *Fowler v The Queen*, above.]

• • •

The appellant's main argument was that the legislation under attack is really an attempt by Parliament to legislate generally on the subject matter of pollution and thus to invade the area of provincial legislative power over property and civil rights. He points to the very broad definition of "water frequented by fish" in subs. 33(11) which refers to "Canadian fisheries waters" which, under s. 2, includes "all waters in the territorial sea of Canada and all internal waters of Canada." He also refers to the broad scope of the definition of "deleterious substance." When these definitions are applied to subs. 33(2) it is said that the subsection is really concerned with the pollution of Canadian waters.

The charges laid in this case do not, however, effectively bring into question the validity of the extension of the reach of the subsection to waters that would not, in fact, be fisheries waters "or to substances other than those defined in paragraph (a) of subsection 33(11)." The charges relate to diesel fuel spilled into tidal waters. The task of the Court in determining the constitutional validity of subs. 33(2) is to ascertain the true nature and character of the legislation. It is necessary to decide whether the subsection is aimed at the protection and preservation of fisheries. In my opinion it is.

Basically, it is concerned with the deposit of deleterious substances in water frequented by fish, or in a place where the deleterious substance may enter such water. The definition of a deleterious substance is related to the substance being deleterious to fish. In essence, the subsection seeks to protect fisheries by preventing substances deleterious to fish entering into waters frequented by fish. This is a proper concern of legislation under the heading of "Sea Coast and Inland Fisheries."

The situation in this case is different from that which was considered in *Dan Fowler v. Her Majesty the Queen*, a judgment of this Court recently delivered. That case involved the constitutional validity of subs. 33(3) of the *Fisheries Act* and it was held to be *ultra vires* of Parliament to enact. Unlike subs. (2), subs. (3) contains no reference to deleterious substances. It is not restricted by its own terms to activities that are harmful to fish or fish habitat. The basis of the judgment in the *Fowler* case is set out in the following passage:

Subsection 33(3) makes no attempt to link the proscribed conduct to actual or potential harm to fisheries. It is a blanket prohibition of certain types of activity, subject to provincial jurisdiction, which does not delimit the elements of the offence so as to link the prohibition to any likely harm to fisheries.

In my opinion, subs. 33(2) was *intra vires* of the Parliament of Canada to enact. The definition of "deleterious substance" ensures that the scope of subs. 33(2) is restricted to a prohibition of deposits that threaten fish, fish habitat or the use of fish by man.

Appeal dismissed.

NOTES AND QUESTIONS

1. Although the cases included in this section address alleged federal intrusions into provincial jurisdiction, provincial environmental legislation has not been immune from constitutional challenge. For example, in *Ontario v Canadian Pacific Ltd*, [1995] 2 SCR 1031, 17 CELR (NS) 129 (*sub nom R v Canadian Pacific Ltd*), Canadian Pacific (CP) was charged with unlawfully discharging a contaminant (smoke) into the natural environment and causing adverse effects pursuant to s 13(1)(a) of the *Environmental Protection Act*, RSO 1980, c 141 [EPA]. CP's controlled burns to clear weeds and brush from its right-of-way had adversely affected adjoining residential properties.

At trial, CP was able to establish due diligence and was acquitted. This was overturned upon appeal. CP then appealed to the Ontario Court of Appeal and ultimately to the Supreme Court of Canada, challenging the legislation on two constitutional grounds: first, that the section of the EPA was vague and uncertain and, thus, in violation of s 7 of the *Canadian Charter of Rights and Freedoms*, Part I of the *Constitution Act, 1982*, being Schedule B to the *Canada Act 1982* (UK), 1982, c 11; and second, that interjurisdictional immunity applied in relation to the section because CP is a federally regulated undertaking.

The court determined that the legislation applied to the appellant's maintenance along the right-of-way. With regard to the s 7 arguments, the court, although divided in its reasons, unanimously upheld s 13(1)(a), finding that it was not "unconstitutionally vague or overbroad." The court strengthened the cause for statutory protection of the environment by stating (at para 87):

> Section 13(1)(a) is sufficiently precise to provide for a meaningful legal debate, when the provision is considered in light of the purpose and subject matter of the EPA, the nature of the provision as a regulatory offence, the societal value of environmental protection, related provisions of the EPA, and general interpretive principles. Section 13(1)(a) is also proportionate and not overbroad. The objective of environmental protection is itself broad, and the legislature is justified in choosing broad, flexible language to give effect to this objective.

2. Does a provincial energy regulator lack power to require reclamation of abandoned oil and gas wells because its actions conflict with federal bankruptcy laws? This was the issue before the Supreme Court in *Orphan Well Association v Grant Thornton Ltd*, 2019 SCC 5. The problem was that the Alberta Energy Regulator (AER), under the *Oil and Gas Conservation Act*, RSA 2000, c O-6, ordered Redwater Energy Corporation's bankruptcy trustee (Grant Thornton) to clean up Redwater's inactive wells. This meant applying funds from the sale of producing wells instead of "disclaiming" inactive wells under the federal *Bankruptcy and Insolvency Act*, RSC 1985, c B-3 [BIA], leaving no funds to pay Redwater's secured creditors. The trustee argued that the BIA authorized it to disclaim the inactive wells and required it to respect the BIA's priority for secured creditors.

The Supreme Court had to determine whether the federal BIA and the Alberta *Oil and Gas Conservation Act* came into conflict. If so, under the paramountcy doctrine, the federal law would prevail.

A court majority reasoned that there is no operational conflict or frustration of purpose because the BIA deals with trustees' personal liability; it does not permit bankruptcy trustees to ignore the bankrupt company's environmental liabilities. Furthermore, the abandonment order requirements were not claims provable in bankruptcy under the BIA creditor priority scheme. Thus, funds from the sale of the producing wells would be used to pay abandonment costs and not creditors' claims. The AER's powers to make abandonment and remediation orders does not give the regulator a monetary claim provable in the bankruptcy. It is not a creditor. Rather, it acts in the public interest and for the public good. Thus, the federal statutes and provincial statutes can coexist.

"Bankruptcy," said Wagner CJ (at para 160), writing for the majority, "is not a licence to ignore rules, and insolvency professionals are bound by and must comply with valid provincial laws during bankruptcy."

The majority (at para 66), in considering whether the BIA came into conflict with the Alberta statute, stated:

[T]he application of the doctrine of paramountcy should also give due weight to the principle of co-operative federalism. This principle allows for interplay and overlap between federal and provincial legislation. While co-operative federalism does not impose limits on the otherwise valid exercise of legislative power, it does mean that courts should avoid an expansive interpretation of the purpose of federal legislation which will bring it into conflict with provincial legislation.

The minority (at para 186), per Côté J, took issue with this approach:

In my view, my colleague places undue reliance on the principle of cooperative federalism to narrow the scope of federal law and find a harmonious interpretation where no plausible one exists. Courts must be especially careful about using cooperative federalism to interpret legislative provisions narrowly in a case like this where Parliament expressly envisioned that the disclaimer right could come into conflict with provincial law. This is evident from the very first line of s. 14.06(4) [of the BIA], which states that the disclaimer power applies "[n]otwithstanding anything in any federal or provincial law." The notion that judicial restraint should compel a different interpretation is therefore belied by the fact that Parliament considered, acknowledged and *accepted* the potential for conflict. [Emphasis in original.]

Question: What role (if any) should the idea of "cooperative federalism" play in the application of the paramountcy doctrine?

3. In 2018, British Columbia proposed amendments to its *Environmental Management Act*, SBC 2003, c 53 that would require permits for increasing the volume of "hazardous substances" (with "heavy oil" the only substance mentioned) transported or possessed in the province (BC OIC No 211/2018 (25 April 2018)).

The definition of "heavy oil" in the schedule of the proposed legislation is consistent with the chemical composition of bitumen produced in the Alberta oil sands region. In issuing permits, the provincial director of waste management requires the applicant to consider environmental and health risks of a potential spill, demonstrate "to the satisfaction of the director" appropriate measures to respond to and compensate in respect of spills, and establish funds and agree to compensate persons as well as local and First Nation governments (s 22.4). The director can attach conditions to permits and has a discretion to suspend or cancel permits in the event of noncompliance. This would in principle authorize the province to refuse to issue heavy oil transportation permits and, thus, prohibit bitumen pipelines such as the Trans Mountain Expansion.

On numerous occasions before enacting the amendments to the *Environmental Management Act*, members of the BC government made statements to the effect that they oppose the Trans Mountain Expansion oil pipeline project (the pipeline is now owned by the federal government) and that they are prepared to use every available tool to stop this pipeline.

In 2018, the BC government filed a reference case concerning the constitutional validity of these amendments in the BC Court of Appeal. The federal government argued that the proposed BC legislation is in pith and substance in relation to the regulation of interjurisdictional pipelines an exclusive federal matter under s 92(10)(a) of the *Constitution Act, 1867*. Under the paramountcy doctrine, it either is in operational conflict with, or frustrates the legislative purpose of, the federal *National Energy Board Act*, RSC 1985, c N-7 (under which the Trans Mountain Expansion Project was approved). Alternatively, under the interjurisdictional immunity doctrine, it is inapplicable to interjurisdictional pipelines because it impairs the essential core of these undertakings.

The first constitutional question was whether the province has constitutional authority to enact the amendments. A unanimous court in *Reference re Environmental Management Act (British Columbia)*, 2019 BCCA 181 at para 105 concluded:

Both the law relating to the division of powers and the practicalities surrounding the TMX project lead to the conclusion, then, that the pith and substance of the proposed Part 2.1 is to place conditions on, and if necessary, prohibit, the carriage of heavy oil [through] an interprovincial undertaking. Such legislation does not in its pith and substance relate to "Property ... in the Province" or to "Matters of a merely local or private Nature," but to Parliament's jurisdiction in respect of federal undertakings under s. 92(10) of the *Constitution Act*.

Addressing the provincial argument that the amendment is a valid law of general application that does not purport to address federally regulated interprovincial pipelines, the court (at para 101) stated:

Even if it were not intended to '"single out" the TMX pipeline, it has the potential to affect (and indeed "stop in its tracks") the entire operation of Trans Mountain as an interprovincial carrier and exporter of oil. It is legislation that in pith and substance relates to, and relates *only* to, what makes the pipeline "specifically of federal jurisdiction." By definition, an interprovincial pipeline is a continuous carrier of liquid across provincial borders. ... Unless the pipeline is contained entirely within a province, federal jurisdiction is the only way in which it may be regulated. [I]t is simply not practical—or appropriate in terms of constitutional law—for different laws and regulations to apply to an interprovincial pipeline (or railway or communications infrastructure) every time it crosses a border.

This led to the conclusion that it was unnecessary for the court to consider the paramountcy or interjurisdictional immunity doctrines. Nor was it necessary to assess whether, on the assumption that the amendment would be valid, it would be applicable to bitumen entering the province through interprovincial pipelines.

Question: What are the strongest arguments to support provincial jurisdiction to enact legislation authorizing provincial officials to attach enforceable conditions (including potential permit denial or shutdown) to environmental approvals for interprovincial oil or gas pipelines?

B. CONCEPTUAL POWERS

R V CROWN ZELLERBACH CANADA LTD
[1988] 1 SCR 401, 1988 CanLII 63

[Crown Zellerbach, a logging operator, was charged with contravening s 4(1) of the *Ocean Dumping Control Act*, SC 1974-75-76, c 55 (now part 7, division 3 of the *Canadian Environmental Protection Act, 1999*, SC 1999, c 33), which prohibited anyone from dumping any substance into the sea without obtaining and complying with a permit. The "sea" as defined by the Act included the internal waters of Canada other than fresh waters. Although the respondent had a permit to dump under the legislation, it did not cover Beaver Cove, the area in question. The navigable waters of the cove were within the province of British Columbia and, through Johnstone Strait, were connected to the Pacific Ocean. There was no evidence that the dumping of the woodwaste by the respondent in any way interfered with either navigation or marine life.

Both at trial and at the Court of Appeal, it was held that s 4(1) was *ultra vires* the federal government.]

LE DAIN J: ... As the constitutional question indicates, the issue raised by the appeal is the constitutionality of the application of s. 4(1) of the Act to the dumping of waste in waters, other than fresh waters, within a province. The respondent concedes, as it must, that Parliament has jurisdiction to regulate dumping in waters lying outside the territorial limits of any province. It also concedes that Parliament has jurisdiction to regulate the dumping of substances in provincial waters to prevent pollution of those waters that is harmful to fisheries, if the federal legislation meets the tests laid down in the *Fowler* and *Northwest Falling* cases. It further concedes, in view of the opinion expressed in this Court in *Interprovincial Co-operatives Ltd. v. The Queen*, [1976] 1 SCR 477, that Parliament has jurisdiction to regulate the dumping in provincial waters of substances that can be shown to cause pollution in extra-provincial waters. What the respondent challenges is federal jurisdiction to control the dumping in provincial waters of substances that are not shown to have a pollutant effect in extra-provincial waters. The respondent contends that on the admitted facts that is precisely the present case. The respondent submits that in so far as s. 4(1) of the Act can only be read as purporting to apply to such dumping it is *ultra vires* and, alternatively, that it should be read, if possible, so as not to apply to such dumping. In either case the appeal must fail. ...

In this Court the Attorney General of Canada [principally submitted] that the control of dumping in provincial marine waters, for the reasons indicated in the Act, was part of a single matter of national concern or dimension which fell within the federal peace, order and good government power. He characterized this matter as the prevention of ocean or marine pollution. His reliance on the specific heads of federal jurisdiction with respect to navigation and shipping and seacoast and inland fisheries, as well as others of a maritime nature, was rather as indicating, in his submission, the scope that should be assigned to federal jurisdiction under the peace, order and good government power to regulate the dumping of substances for the prevention of marine pollution. The Attorney General of Canada made it plain that he was not relying in this Court on ancillary or necessarily incidental power. His contention was that the control of dumping in provincial marine waters was an integral part of a single matter of national concern. Nor did he rely in this Court on the peace, order and good government power as a basis of federal jurisdiction to enact the *Ocean Dumping Control Act* in implementation of the *Convention on the Prevention of Marine Pollution by Dumping of Wastes and other Matter* [26 UST 2403, 1046 UNTS 120, 11 ILM 1294 (1972)]. He referred to the Convention and its Annexes as indicating the mischief to which the act is directed and supporting his characterization of the matter in relation to which the Act was enacted. ...

Before considering the relationship of the subject-matter of the Act to the possible bases of federal legislative jurisdiction something more should be said about the characterization of that subject-matter, according to the respective contentions of the parties. As I have indicated, the appellant contends that the Act is directed to the control or regulation of marine pollution, the subject-matter of the *Convention on the Prevention of Marine Pollution by Dumping of Wastes and other Matter*. The respondent, on the other hand, contends that by its terms the Act is directed at dumping which need not necessarily have a pollutant effect. It prohibits the dumping of *any* substance, including a substance not specified in Schedule I or Schedule II, except in accordance with the terms and conditions of a permit. In my opinion, despite this apparent scope, the Act, viewed as a whole, may be properly characterized as directed to the control or regulation of marine pollution, in so far as that may be relevant to the question of legislative jurisdiction. The chosen, and perhaps only effective, regulatory model makes it necessary, in order to prevent marine pollution, to prohibit the dumping of any substance without a permit. Its purpose is to require a permit so that the regulatory authority may determine before the proposed dumping has occurred whether it may be permitted upon certain terms and conditions, having regard to the factors or concerns specified in ss. 9 and 10 of the Act and Schedule III.

• • •

I agree with Schmidt Prov Ct J and the British Columbia Court of Appeal that federal legislative jurisdiction with respect to seacoast and inland fisheries is not sufficient by itself to support the constitutional validity of s. 4(1) of the Act because that section, viewed in the context of the Act as a whole, fails to meet the test laid down in *Fowler* and *Northwest Falling*. While the effect on fisheries of marine pollution caused by the dumping of waste is clearly one of the concerns of the Act it is not the only effect of such pollution with which the Act is concerned. A basis for federal legislative jurisdiction to control marine pollution generally in provincial waters cannot be found in any of the specified heads of federal jurisdiction in s. 91 of the *Constitution Act, 1867*, whether taken individually or collectively.

IV

It is necessary then to consider the national dimensions or national concern doctrine (as it is now generally referred to) of the federal peace, order and good government power as a possible basis for the constitutional validity of s. 4(1) of the Act, as applied to the control of dumping in provincial marine waters.

· · ·

From this survey of the opinion expressed in this Court concerning the national concern doctrine of the federal peace, order and good government power I draw the following conclusions as to what now appears to be firmly established:

1. The national concern doctrine is separate and distinct from the national emergency doctrine of the peace, order and good government power, which is chiefly distinguishable by the fact that it provides a constitutional basis for what is necessarily legislation of a temporary nature;
2. The national concern doctrine applies to both new matters which did not exist at Confederation and to matters which, although originally matters of a local or private nature in a province, have since, in the absence of national emergency, become matters of national concern;
3. For a matter to qualify as a matter of national concern in either sense it must have a singleness, distinctiveness and indivisibility that clearly distinguishes it from matters of provincial concern and a scale of impact on provincial jurisdiction that is reconcilable with the fundamental distribution of legislative power under the Constitution;
4. In determining whether a matter has attained the required degree of singleness, distinctiveness and indivisibility that clearly distinguishes it from matters of provincial concern it is relevant to consider what would be the effect on extra-provincial interests of a provincial failure to deal effectively with the control or regulation of the intra-provincial aspects of the matter.

This last factor, generally referred to as the "provincial inability" test and noted with apparent approval in this Court in *Labatt* [*Labatt Breweries of Canada Ltd v Attorney General of Canada*, [1980] 1 SCR 914, 1979 CanLII 190], *Schneider* [*Schneider v The Queen*, [1982] 2 SCR 112, 1982 CanLII 26] and *Wetmore* [*R v Wetmore*, [1983] 2 SCR 284, 1983 CanLII 29], was suggested, as Professor Hogg acknowledges, by Professor Gibson in his article, "Measuring 'National Dimensions'" (1976), 7 *Man. LJ* 15, as the most satisfactory rationale of the cases in which the national concern doctrine of the peace, order and good government power has been applied as a basis of federal jurisdiction. As expounded by Professor Gibson, the test would appear to involve a limited or qualified application of federal jurisdiction. ...

As expressed by Professor Hogg in the first and second editions of his *Constitutional Law of Canada*, the "provincial inability" test would appear to be adopted simply as a reason for finding that a particular matter is one of national concern falling within the peace, order and good government power: that provincial failure to deal effectively with the intra-provincial aspects of the matter could have an adverse effect on extra-provincial interests. In this sense, the "provincial inability" test is one of the indicia for determining whether a matter has that character of singleness or indivisibility required to bring it within the national concern doctrine. It is because of the interrelatedness of the intra-provincial and extra-provincial aspects of the matter that it requires a single or uniform legislative treatment. The "provincial inability" test must not, however, go so far as to provide a rationale for the general notion, hitherto rejected in the cases, that there must be a plenary jurisdiction in one order of government or the other to deal with any legislative problem. In the context of the national concern doctrine of the peace, order and good government power, its utility lies, in my opinion, in assisting in the determination whether a matter has the requisite singleness or indivisibility from a functional as well as a conceptual point of view.

• • •

V

Marine pollution, because of its predominantly extra-provincial as well as international character and implications, is clearly a matter of concern to Canada as a whole. The question is whether the control of pollution by the dumping of substances in marine waters, including provincial marine waters, is a single, indivisible matter, distinct from the control of pollution by the dumping of substances in other provincial waters. The *Ocean Dumping Control Act* reflects a distinction between the pollution of salt water and the pollution of fresh water. The question, as I conceive it, is whether that distinction is sufficient to make the control of marine pollution by the dumping of substances a single, indivisible matter falling within the national concern doctrine of the peace, order and good government power.

Marine pollution by the dumping of substances is clearly treated by the *Convention on the Prevention of Marine Pollution by Dumping of Wastes and other Matter* as a distinct and separate form of water pollution having its own characteristics and scientific considerations. ... The limitation of the undertaking in the Convention, presumably for reasons of state policy, to the control of dumping in the territorial sea and the open sea cannot, in my opinion, obscure the obviously close relationship, which is emphasized in the UN Report, between pollution in coastal waters, including the internal marine waters of a state, and pollution in the territorial sea. Moreover, there is much force, in my opinion, in the appellant's contention that the difficulty of ascertaining by visual observation the boundary between the territorial sea and the internal marine waters of a state creates an unacceptable degree of uncertainty for the application of regulatory and penal provisions. This, and not simply the possibility or likelihood of the movement of pollutants across that line, is what constitutes the essential indivisibility of the matter of marine pollution by the dumping of substances.

There remains the question whether the pollution of marine waters by the dumping of substances is sufficiently distinguishable from the pollution of fresh waters by such dumping to meet the requirement of singleness or indivisibility. In many cases the pollution of fresh waters will have a pollutant effect in the marine waters into which they flow, and this is noted by the UN Report, but that report, as I have suggested, emphasizes that marine pollution, because of the differences in the composition and action of marine waters and fresh waters, has its own characteristics and scientific considerations that distinguish it from fresh water pollution. Moreover, the distinction between salt water and fresh water as limiting the application of the *Ocean Dumping Control Act* meets the consideration emphasized by a majority of this Court in the *Anti-Inflation Act* reference [*Re: Anti-Inflation Act*, [1976] 2 SCR 373, 1976 CanLII 16]—that in order for a matter to qualify as one of national concern falling within the federal peace, order and good government power it must have ascertainable and reasonable limits, in so far as its impact on provincial jurisdiction is concerned.

For these reasons I am of the opinion that s. 4(1) of the *Ocean Dumping Control Act* is constitutionally valid as enacted.

NOTE

In *Reference re Greenhouse Gas Pollution Pricing Act*, 2019 SKCA 40, a majority of the Saskatchewan Court of Appeal upheld the constitutionality of the federal *Greenhouse Gas Pollution Pricing Act*, SC 2018, c 12, s 186 under the national concern branch of the federal peace, order, and good government (POGG) power. The Act imposes a charge on greenhouse gas (GHG) producing fuels and combustible waste. It is intended to operate as a backstop, applying only in provinces that have not priced those emissions in the same manner. The court (at para 11) identified "the establishment of minimum national standards of price stringency for GHG emissions" as the relevant POGG subject matter.

The federal Act was also upheld by a majority of the Ontario Court of Appeal: *Reference re Greenhouse Gas Pollution Pricing Act*, 2019 ONCA 544. Supreme Court of Canada appeals by both provinces were pending in January 2020. In 2019, Alberta filed a similar reference with the Alberta Court of Appeal. The case was heard in December 2019. Also in 2019, Manitoba initiated a judicial review in Federal Court challenging on constitutional grounds the federal implementation of a carbon levy in Manitoba in the face of that province's arguably equally effective carbon tax.

FRIENDS OF THE OLDMAN RIVER SOCIETY V CANADA (MINISTER OF TRANSPORT)
[1992] 1 SCR 3, 1992 CanLII 110

[In response to an application by the province of Alberta to construct a dam on the Oldman River, the federal minister of transport issued an approval pursuant to s 5 of the *Navigable Waters Protection Act*, RSC 1985, c N-22. In reviewing the application, the minister considered the effect of the project on marine navigation and attached appropriate conditions relating thereto, but he did not subject the application to an environmental assessment as provided in the *Environmental Assessment and Review Process Guidelines Order*, SOR/84-467. The Friends of the Oldman River Society applied for an order in the nature of *certiorari* to quash the approval as well as *mandamus* to require the minister of transport and the minister of fisheries and oceans to comply with the guidelines order.]

LA FOREST J: The protection of the environment has become one of the major challenges of our time. To respond to this challenge, governments and international organizations have been engaged in the creation of a wide variety of legislative schemes and administrative structures. In Canada, both the federal and provincial governments have established Departments of the Environment, which have been in place for about twenty years. More recently, however, it was realized that a department of the environment was one among many other departments, many of which pursued policies that came into conflict with its goals. Accordingly at the federal level steps were taken to give a central role to that department, and to expand the role of other government departments and agencies so as to ensure that they took account of environmental concerns in taking decisions that could have an environmental impact.

To that end, s. 6 of the *Department of the Environment Act*, RSC 1985, c. E-10, empowered the Minister for the purposes of carrying out his duties relating to environmental quality, by order, with the approval of the Governor-in-Council, to establish guidelines for use by federal departments, agencies and regulatory bodies in carrying out their duties, functions and powers. Pursuant to this provision the *Environmental Assessment and Review Process Guidelines Order* ("*Guidelines Order*") was established and approved in June 1984; SOR/84-467. In general terms, these guidelines require all federal departments and agencies that have a decision-making authority for any proposal, i.e., any initiative, undertaking or activity that may have an environmental effect on an area of federal responsibility, to initially screen such proposal to determine whether it may give rise to any potentially adverse environmental effects. If a proposal could have a significant adverse effect on the environment, provision is made for public review by an environmental assessment panel whose members must be unbiased, free of political influence and possessed of special knowledge and experience relevant to the technical, environmental and social effects of the proposal.

The present case raises the constitutional and statutory validity of the *Guidelines Order* as well as its nature and applicability.

[See Chapter 17 of this text for a discussion of the issues directly related to environmental assessment.]

• • •

Is the *Guidelines Order* so broad as to offend ss. 92 and 92A of the *Constitution Act, 1867* and therefore constitutionally inapplicable to the Oldman River Dam owned by Alberta?

• • •

CONSTITUTIONAL QUESTION

The constitutional question asks whether the *Guidelines Order* is so broad as to offend ss. 92 and 92A of the *Constitution Act, 1867.* However, no argument was made with respect to s. 92A for the apparent reason that the Oldman River Dam project does not, in the appellant's view, fall within the ambit of that provision. The process of judicial review of legislation which is impugned as *ultra vires* Parliament was recently elaborated on in *Whitbread v. Walley* [[1990] 3 SCR 1273, 1990 CanLII 33] ... and does not bear repetition here, save to remark that if the *Guidelines Order* is found to be legislation that is in pith and substance in relation to matters within Parliament's exclusive jurisdiction, that is the end of the matter. It would be immaterial that it also affects matters of property and civil rights (at p. 1286). The analysis proceeds first by identifying whether in pith and substance the legislation falls within a matter assigned to one or more of the heads of legislative power.

While various expressions have been used to describe what is meant by the "pith and substance" of a legislative provision, in *Whitbread v. Walley* I expressed a preference for the description "the dominant or most important characteristic of the challenged law." Naturally, the parties have advanced quite different features of the *Guidelines Order* as representing its most important characteristic. For Alberta, it is the manner in which it is said to encroach on provincial rights, although no specific matter has been identified other than general references to the environment. Alberta argues that Parliament has no plenary jurisdiction over the environment, it being a matter of legislative jurisdiction shared by both levels of government, and that the

Guidelines Order has crossed the line which circumscribes Parliament's authority over the environment. The appellant Ministers argue that in pith and substance the *Guidelines Order* is merely a process to facilitate federal decision-making on matters that fall within Parliament's jurisdiction—a proposition with which the respondent substantially agrees.

The substance of Alberta's argument is that the *Guidelines Order* purports to give the Government of Canada general authority over the environment in such a way as to trench on the province's exclusive legislative domain. Alberta argues that the *Guidelines Order* attempts to regulate the environmental effects of matters largely within the control of the province and, consequently, cannot constitutionally be a concern of Parliament. In particular, it is said that Parliament is incompetent to deal with the environmental effects of provincial works such as the Oldman River Dam.

I agree that the *Constitution Act, 1867* has not assigned the matter of "environment" *sui generis* to either the provinces or Parliament. The environment, as understood in its generic sense, encompasses the physical, economic and social environment touching several of the heads of power assigned to the respective levels of government. Professor Gibson put it succinctly several years ago in his article "Constitutional Jurisdiction over Environmental Management in Canada" (1973), 23 *UTLJ* 54, at p. 85:

> "environmental management" does not, under the existing situation, constitute a homogeneous constitutional unit. Instead, it cuts across many different areas of constitutional responsibility, some federal and some provincial. And it is no less obvious that "environmental management" could never be treated as a constitutional unit under one order of government in any constitution that claimed to be federal, because no system in which one government was so powerful would be federal.

• • •

It must be recognized that the environment is not an independent matter of legislation under the *Constitution Act, 1867* and that it is a constitutionally abstruse matter which does not comfortably fit within the existing division of powers without considerable overlap and uncertainty. A variety of analytical constructs have been developed to grapple with the problem, although no single method will be suitable in every instance. ...

In my view the solution to this case can more readily be found by looking first at the catalogue of powers in the *Constitution Act, 1867* and considering how they may be employed to meet or avoid environmental concerns. When viewed in this manner it will be seen that in exercising their respective legislative powers, both levels of government may affect the environment, either by acting or not acting. This can best be understood by looking at specific powers.

• • •

[The judgment proceeds to examine the example of exclusive federal jurisdiction over interprovincial railways, as well as navigation and shipping.]

• • •

Environmental impact assessment is, in its simplest form, a planning tool that is now generally regarded as an integral component of sound decision-making. Its fundamental purpose is summarized by R. Cotton and D.P. Emond in "Environmental Impact Assessment," in J. Swaigen, ed., *Environmental Rights in Canada* (1981), 245, at p. 247:

> The basic concepts behind environmental assessment are simply stated: (1) early identification and evaluation of all potential environmental consequences of a proposed undertaking; (2) decision making that both guarantees the adequacy of

this process and reconciles, to the greatest extent possible, the proponent's development desires with environmental protection and preservation.

As a planning tool it has both an information-gathering and a decision-making component which provide the decision maker with an objective basis for granting or denying approval for a proposed development. ... In short, environmental impact assessment is simply descriptive of a process of decision-making.

• • •

Because of its auxiliary nature, environmental impact assessment can only affect matters that are "truly in relation to an institution or activity that is otherwise within [federal] legislative jurisdiction"; see *Devine v. Quebec (Attorney General)*, [1988] 2 S.C.R. 790 ... . Given the necessary element of proximity that must exist between the impact assessment process and the subject matter of federal jurisdiction involved, this legislation can, in my view, be supported by the particular head of federal power invoked in each instance. In particular, the *Guidelines Order* prescribes a close nexus between the social effects that may be examined and the environmental effects generally. Section 4 requires that the social effects examined at the initial assessment stage be "directly related" to the potential environmental effects of a proposal, as does s. 25 in respect of the terms of reference under which an environmental assessment panel may operate. Moreover, where the *Guidelines Order* has application to a proposal because it affects an area of federal jurisdiction, as opposed to the other three bases for application enumerated in s. 6, the environmental effects to be studied can only be those which may have an impact on the areas of federal responsibility affected.

I should make it clear, however, that the scope of assessment is not confined to the particular head of power under which the Government of Canada has a decision-making responsibility within the meaning of the term "proposal." Such a responsibility, as I stated earlier, is a necessary condition to engage the process, but once the initiating department has thus been given authority to embark on an assessment, that review must consider the environmental effect on all areas of federal jurisdiction. There is no constitutional obstacle preventing Parliament from enacting legislation under several heads of power at the same time ... . In the case of the *Guidelines Order*, Parliament has conferred upon one institution (the "initiating department") the responsibility, in the exercise of its decision-making authority, for assessing the environmental implications on all areas of federal jurisdiction potentially affected. Here, the Minister of Transport, in his capacity of decision maker under the *Navigable Waters Protection Act*, is directed to consider the environmental impact of the dam on such areas of federal responsibility as navigable waters, fisheries, Indians and Indian lands, to name those most obviously relevant in the circumstances here.

• • •

In the end, I am satisfied that the *Guidelines Order* is in pith and substance nothing more than an instrument that regulates the manner in which federal institutions must administer their multifarious duties and functions. Consequently, it is nothing more than an adjunct of the federal legislative powers affected. In any event, it falls within the purely residuary aspect of the "Peace, Order and Good Government" power under s. 91 of the *Constitution Act, 1867.* Any intrusion into provincial matters is merely incidental to the pith and substance of the legislation. It must also be remembered that what is involved is essentially an information gathering process in furtherance of a decision-making function within federal jurisdiction, and the recommendations made at the conclusion of the information gathering stage are not binding on the decision maker. ...

For the foregoing reasons I find that the *Guidelines Order* is *intra vires* Parliament and would thus answer the constitutional question in the negative.

NOTE

Ultimately, the federal environmental impact assessment of the Oldman River Dam was completed. Unfortunately, the project was virtually complete by the time the recommendations of the Environmental Assessment Panel were made public. Interestingly, the panel concluded that "[t]he environmental, social and economic costs of the project are not balanced by corresponding benefits and finds that, as presently configured, the project is unacceptable." The panel did recognize the realities of the situation, however, and therefore, their first recommendation suggested that the minister "decommission the dam by opening the low level diversion tunnels to allow unimpeded flow of the river." In the event that the recommendation was not accepted by the minister, further recommendations regarding conditions for approval were included in the report (*Oldman River Dam: Report of the Environmental Assessment Panel* (Hull, Qc: FEARO, 1992)).

R V HYDRO-QUÉBEC
[1997] 3 SCR 213, 1997 CanLII 318

[Hydro-Québec was charged with breaching a 1989 interim order restricting the emission of polychlorinated biphenyls (PCBs). The interim order was made by the minister of the environment under the authority of ss 34 and 35 of the *Canadian Environmental Protection Act*, RSC 1985, c 16 (4th Supp) (now the *Canadian Environmental Protection Act, 1999*, SC 1999, c 33), which provided for the regulation of toxic substances. Hydro-Québec sought to have these sections and the interim order declared *ultra vires* the federal government.]

LA FOREST J (L'Heureux-Dubé, Gonthier, Cory, and McLachlin JJ): This Court has in recent years been increasingly called upon to consider the interplay between federal and provincial legislative powers as they relate to environmental protection. Whether viewed positively as strategies for maintaining a clean environment, or negatively as measures to combat the evils of pollution, there can be no doubt that these measures relate to a public purpose of superordinate importance, and one in which all levels of government and numerous organs of the international community have been increasingly engaged. In the opening passage of this Court's reasons in what is perhaps the leading case, *Friends of the Oldman River Society v. Canada (Minister of Transport)*, [1992] 1 SCR 3, at pp. 16-17, the matter is succinctly put this way:

> The protection of the environment has become one of the major challenges of our time. To respond to this challenge, governments and international organizations have been engaged in the creation of a wide variety of legislative schemes and administrative structures.

> The all-important duty of Parliament and the provincial legislatures to make full use of the legislative powers respectively assigned to them in protecting the environment has inevitably placed upon the courts the burden of progressively defining the extent to which these powers may be used to that end. In performing this task, it is incumbent on the courts to secure the basic balance between the two levels of government envisioned by the Constitution. However, in doing so, they must be mindful that the Constitution must be interpreted in a manner that is fully responsive to emerging realities and to the nature of the subject matter sought to be regulated. Given the pervasive and diffuse nature of the environment, this reality poses particular difficulties in this context.

This latest case in which this Court is required to define the nature of legislative powers over the environment is of major significance. The narrow issue raised is the extent to and manner in which the federal Parliament may control the amount of and conditions under which Chlorobiphenyls (PCBs)—substances well known to pose great dangers to humans and the environment generally—may enter into the environment. However, the attack on the federal power to secure this end is not really aimed at the specific provisions respecting PCBs. Rather, it puts into question the constitutional validity of its enabling statutory provisions. What is really at stake is whether Part II ("Toxic Substances") of the *Canadian Environmental Protection Act*, RSC 1985, c. 16 (4th Supp.), which empowers the federal Ministers of Health and of the Environment to determine what substances are toxic and to prohibit the introduction of such substances into the environment except in accordance with specified terms and conditions, falls within the constitutional power of Parliament.

• • •

In considering how the question of the constitutional validity of a legislative enactment relating to the environment should be approached, this Court in *Oldman River, supra*, made it clear that the environment is not, as such, a subject matter of legislation under the *Constitution Act, 1867*. As it was put there, "the *Constitution Act, 1867* has not assigned the matter of 'environment' *sui generis* to either the provinces or Parliament" ... . Rather, it is a diffuse subject that cuts across many different areas of constitutional responsibility, some federal, some provincial ... . Thus Parliament or a provincial legislature can, in advancing the scheme or purpose of a statute, enact provisions minimizing or preventing the detrimental impact that statute may have on the environment, prohibit pollution, and the like. In assessing the constitutional validity of a provision relating to the environment, therefore, what must first be done is to look at the catalogue of legislative powers listed in the *Constitution Act, 1867* to see if the provision falls within one or more of the powers assigned to the body (whether Parliament or a provincial legislature) that enacted the legislation ... . If the provision in essence, in pith and substance, falls within the parameters of any such power, then it is constitutionally valid.

• • •

I have gone on at this length to demonstrate the simple proposition that the validity of a legislative provision (including one relating to environmental protection) must be tested against the specific characteristics of the head of power under which it is proposed to justify it. For each constitutional head of power has its own particular characteristics and raises concerns peculiar to itself in assessing it in the balance of Canadian federalism. This may seem obvious, perhaps even trite, but it is all too easy (see: *Fowler v. The Queen*, [1980] 2 SCR 213) to overlook the characteristics of a particular power and overshoot the mark or, again, in assessing the applicability of one head of power to give effect to concerns appropriate to another head of power when this is neither appropriate nor consistent with the law laid down by this Court respecting the ambit and contours of that other power. ...

• • •

What appears from the analysis in *RJR-MacDonald* [*RJR-MacDonald Inc v Canada (Attorney General)*, [1995] 3 SCR 199, 1995 CanLII 64] is that as early as 1903, the Privy Council ... had made it clear that the power conferred on Parliament by s. 91(27) is "the criminal law in its *widest sense*" (emphasis added). Consistently with this approach, the Privy Council in *Proprietary Articles Trade Association v. Attorney-General for Canada*, 1931 CanLII 385, [1931] AC 310 (hereafter PATA), at p. 324, defined the criminal law power as including any prohibited act with penal consequences.

As it put it, at p. 324: "The criminal quality of an act cannot be discerned ... by reference to any standard but one: Is the act prohibited with penal consequences?" This approach has been consistently followed ever since and, as *RJR-MacDonald* relates, it has been applied by the courts in a wide variety of settings. Accordingly, it is entirely within the discretion of Parliament to determine what evil it wishes by penal prohibition to suppress and what threatened interest it thereby wishes to safeguard, to adopt the terminology of Rand J in the *Margarine Reference* [*Reference re Validity of Section 5(a) of the Dairy Industry Act*, [1949] SCR 1, 1948 CanLII 2] ... .

Contrary to the respondent's submission, under s. 91(27) of the *Constitution Act, 1867*, it is also within the discretion of Parliament to determine the extent of blameworthiness that it wishes to attach to a criminal prohibition. So it may determine the nature of the mental element pertaining to different crimes, such as a defence of due diligence like that which appears in s. 125(1) of the Act in issue. This flows from the fact that Parliament has been accorded plenary power to make criminal law in the widest sense. This power is, of course, subject to the "fundamental justice" requirements of s. 7 of the *Canadian Charter of Rights and Freedoms*, which may dictate a higher level of *mens rea* for serious or "true" crimes; cf. *R v. Wholesale Travel Group Inc.*, [1991] 3 SCR 154, and *R v. Rube*, [1992] 3 SCR 159 ... but that is not an issue here.

The *Charter* apart, only one qualification has been attached to Parliament's plenary power over criminal law. The power cannot be employed colourably. ...

• • •

This approach is entirely consistent with the recent pronouncement of this Court in *Ontario v. Canadian Pacific Ltd.*, [1995] 2 SCR 1031, where Gonthier J, speaking for the majority, had this to say, at para. 55:

> It is clear that over the past two decades, citizens have become acutely aware of the importance of environmental protection, and of the fact that penal consequences may flow from conduct which harms the environment. ... Everyone is aware that individually and collectively, we are responsible for preserving the natural environment. I would agree with the Law Reform Commission of Canada, *Crimes Against the Environment*, ... [(Ottawa: The Commission, 1985) Working Paper 44], which concluded at p. 8 that:
>
>> ... a fundamental and widely shared value is indeed seriously contravened by some environmental pollution, a value which we will refer to as the *right to a safe environment*.
>
>> To some extent, this right and value appears to be new and emerging, but in part because it is an extension of existing and very traditional rights and values already protected by criminal law, its presence and shape even now are largely discernible. Among the new strands of this fundamental value are, it may be argued, those such as *quality of life*, and *stewardship* of the natural environment. At the same time, traditional values as well have simply expanded and evolved to include the environment now as an area and interest of direct and primary concern. Among these values fundamental to the purposes and protections of criminal law are the *sanctity of life*, the *inviolability and integrity of persons*, and the *protection of human life and health*. It is increasingly understood that certain forms and degrees of environmental pollution can directly or indirectly, sooner or later, seriously harm or endanger human life and human health. [Italics in original (*Canadian Pacific Ltd*); underlining added (in *Hydro-Québec*).]

• • •

What the foregoing underlines is what I referred to at the outset, that the protection of the environment is a major challenge of our time. It is an international problem, one that requires action by governments at all levels. And, as is stated in the preamble to the Act under review, "Canada must be able to fulfil its international obligations in respect of the environment." I am confident that Canada can fulfil its international obligations, in so far as the toxic substances sought to be prohibited from entering into the environment under the Act are concerned, by use of the criminal law power. The purpose of the criminal law is to underline and protect our fundamental values. While many environmental issues could be criminally sanctioned in terms of protection of human life or health, I cannot accept that the criminal law is limited to that because "certain forms and degrees of environmental pollution can directly or indirectly, sooner or later, seriously harm or endanger human life and human health," as the paper approvingly cited by Gonthier J in *Ontario v. Canadian Pacific, supra,* observes. But the stage at which this may be discovered is not easy to discern, and I agree with that paper that the stewardship of the environment is a fundamental value of our society and that Parliament may use its criminal law power to underline that value. The criminal law must be able to keep pace with and protect our emerging values.

• • •

It constitutes a definition of the crime, defining the reach of the offence, a constitutionally permissive exercise of the criminal law power, reducing the area subject to criminal law prohibition where certain conditions exist. I cannot characterize it as an invasion of provincial power any more than the appellants were themselves able to do.

• • •

In *Crown Zellerbach,* I expressed concern with the possibility of allocating legislative power respecting environmental pollution exclusively to Parliament. I would be equally concerned with an interpretation of the Constitution that effectively allocated to the provinces, under general powers such as property and civil rights, control over the environment in a manner that prevented Parliament from exercising the leadership role expected of it by the international community and its role in protecting the basic values of Canadians regarding the environment through the instrumentality of the criminal law power. Great sensitivity is required in this area since, as Professor Lederman has rightly observed, environmental pollution "is no limited subject or theme, [it] is a sweeping subject or theme virtually all-pervasive in its legislative implications" ... .

Turning then to s. 35, I mentioned that it is ancillary to s. 34. It deals with emergency situations. The provision, it seems to me, indicates even more clearly a criminal purpose, and throws further light on the intention of s. 34 and of the Act generally. It can only be brought into play when the Ministers believe a substance is not specified in the List in Schedule I or is listed but is not subjected to control under s. 34. In such a case, they may make an interim order in respect of the substance if they believe "immediate action is required to deal with a significant danger to the environment or to human life and health."

[The majority of the court held that the legislation fell "wholly within Parliament's power to enact laws under s. 91(27) of the *Constitution Act, 1867,*" and that it was "not necessary to consider" whether it could be upheld using peace, order, and good government.]

QUESTIONS

1. Examine the provisions of the federal *Species at Risk Act*, reproduced in Chapter 21 of this book. What federal powers did the draftspersons have in mind to justify the legislative scheme?

2. Ontario and Saskatchewan argued in constitutional references before their courts of appeal in 2019 that the federal *Greenhouse Gas Pollution Pricing Act* intrudes on the provinces' jurisdiction over provincial property (*Constitution Act, 1987*, s 92(13)), local works and undertakings (*Constitution Act, 1867*, s 92(10)), and non-renewable natural resources (*Constitution Act, 1867*, s 92A). The Act came into force in Manitoba, New Brunswick, Ontario, and Saskatchewan—provinces that, at the time of writing, did not have equivalent carbon pricing legislation—on April 1, 2019. Under the Act, "distributors" who deliver prescribed fuels must pay a specified "charge." Can the federal government rely on the POGG power? What other federal heads of power may be available? For a further discussion of the Saskatchewan case, see the Note section following the *Crown Zellerbach* extract, above.

C. HARMONIZATION

CANADIAN COUNCIL OF MINISTERS OF THE ENVIRONMENT, A CANADA-WIDE ACCORD ON ENVIRONMENTAL HARMONIZATION (1998)
online (pdf): <https://www.ccme.ca/files/Resources/harmonization/accord_harmonization_e.pdf>

VISION

Governments working in partnership to achieve the highest level of environmental quality for all Canadians.

PURPOSE OF THE ACCORD

To provide a framework and mechanisms to achieve the vision and to guide the development of sub-agreements pursuant to the Accord.

THE OBJECTIVES OF HARMONIZATION

The objectives of harmonization are to:

- enhance environmental protection;
- promote sustainable development; and
- achieve greater effectiveness, efficiency, accountability, predictability and clarity of environmental management for issues of Canada-wide interest, by:
  1. using a cooperative approach, to develop and implement consistent environmental measures in all jurisdictions, including policies, standards, objectives, legislation and regulations;
  2. delineating the respective roles and responsibilities of the Federal, Provincial and Territorial governments within an environmental management partnership by ensuring that specific roles and responsibilities will generally be undertaken by one order of government only;

3. reviewing and adjusting Canada's environmental management regimes to accommodate environmental needs, innovation, expertise and capacities, and addressing gaps and weaknesses in environmental management; and
4. preventing overlapping activities and inter-jurisdictional disputes.

PRINCIPLES

Governments agree that their environmental management activities will reflect the following:

1. those who generate pollution and waste should bear the cost of prevention, containment, cleanup or abatement (polluter pays principle);
2. where there are threats of serious or irreversible environmental damage, lack of full scientific certainty shall not be used as a reason for postponing cost-effective measures to prevent environmental degradation (precautionary principle);
3. pollution prevention is the preferred approach to environmental protection;
4. environmental measures should be performance-based, results-oriented and science-based;
5. openness, transparency, accountability and the effective participation of stakeholders and the public in environmental decision-making is necessary for an effective environmental management regime;
6. working cooperatively with Aboriginal people and their structures of governance is necessary for an effective environmental management regime;
7. Canada-wide approaches on how to meet the objectives of this Accord will allow for flexible implementation required to reflect variations in ecosystems and local, regional, provincial and territorial conditions;
8. decisions pursuant to the Accord will be consensus-based and driven by the commitment to achieve the highest level of environmental quality within the context of sustainable development;
9. nothing in this Accord alters the legislative or other authority of the governments or the rights of any of them with respect to the exercise of their legislative or other authorities under the Constitution of Canada;
10. legislation, regulations, policies and existing agreements should accommodate the implementation of this Accord;
11. the environmental measures established and implemented in accordance with this Accord will not prevent a government from introducing more stringent environmental measures to reflect specific circumstances or to protect environments or environmental values located within its jurisdiction;
12. this Accord and sub-agreements do not affect Aboriginal or treaty rights;
13. all Canadians should be confident that their environment is respected by neighbouring Canadian jurisdictions.

SUB-AGREEMENTS

1. The governments will enter into multi-lateral sub-agreements to implement the commitments set out in this Accord. These sub-agreements will be related to specific components of environmental management or environmental issues to be addressed on a Canada-wide partnership basis.

2. These sub-agreements or their implementation agreements will delineate specific roles and responsibilities to provide a one-window approach to the implementation of environmental measures; in the case of environmental assessment that means a single assessment and a single review process which may involve more than one jurisdiction.

3. Roles and responsibilities will be undertaken by the order of the government best situated to effectively discharge them. In assessing which government is best situated, governments will give consideration to applicable criteria, such as:
   - scale, scope and nature of environmental issue
   - equipment and infrastructure to support obligations
   - physical proximity
   - efficiency and effectiveness
   - human and financial resources to deliver obligations
   - scientific and technical expertise
   - ability to address client or local needs
   - interprovincial/interterritorial/international considerations.

4. Pursuant to this Accord, governments may also enter into regional or bilateral implementation agreements on regional or local issues, for specific ecosystems, for the purposes of providing for necessary variations in the implementation of environmental measures, or for facilitating cooperation in matters not specifically covered under this general multi-lateral Accord.

5. In undertaking a role under a sub-agreement, a government will assume results-oriented and measurable obligations for the discharge of that role, and commit to regular public reporting to demonstrate that its obligations have been met.

6. When a government has accepted obligations and is discharging a role, the other order of government shall not act in that role for the period of time as determined by the relevant sub-agreement.

7. In instances where a government is unable to fulfil its obligations under this Accord, the concerned governments shall develop an alternative plan to ensure that no gaps are created within the environmental management regime. As a general guideline, these plans will be completed within six months.

8. In areas where governments have been unable to reach consensus on a Canada-wide approach, each government is free to act within its existing authority and will advise the other governments accordingly.

9. When a sub-agreement or implementation agreement assigns specific roles or responsibilities to one order of government, the other order of government will review and seek to amend as necessary their legislation, regulations, policies and existing agreements to provide for the implementation of that sub-agreement.

10. Nothing in this Accord will prevent a government from taking action within its authority to respond to environmental emergencies consistent with existing emergency response agreements.

ADMINISTRATION

1. It is the intention of Ministers to conclude sub-agreements on all areas of environmental management that would benefit from Canada-wide coordinated action.

2. Through the Canadian Council of Ministers of the Environment (CCME), ministers will set priorities and establish workplans for addressing issues of Canada-wide significance pursuant to this Accord. Any government may bring forward issues for consideration by the Council of Ministers.
3. Ministers will review progress under the Accord and will provide regular public reports on meeting obligations under the Accord.
4. The resource implications of any adjustments to government programming resulting from this Accord and its sub-agreements will be examined and addressed.
5. This Accord and its sub-agreements may be amended from time to time with the consent of the governments.
6. This Accord comes into force as of January 29, 1998. A government may withdraw from this Accord six months after giving notice.
7. The Council of Ministers in consultation with the public will review this Accord 2 years after the date of its coming into force to evaluate its effectiveness and determine its future.
8. Each government will make the Accord and Canada-wide sub-agreements available to the public.

NOTES AND QUESTIONS

1. What is the Canadian Council of Ministers of the Environment (CCME)? What is its mandate and to whom is it accountable? See the CCME website: <www.ccme.ca>.

2. The *Canada-Wide Accord on Environmental Harmonization* did not receive universal support. In particular, the House of Commons Standing Committee on Environment and Sustainable Development, which held hearings prior to the signing of the accord to survey the diverse opinions of business, labour, industry, Indigenous, and environmental groups, was highly critical of the initiative. The consequent committee report disputed the underlying justification for the agreement of the duplication and overlap of responsibility, and questioned the environmental benefits associated with devolving responsibility for environmental management from the federal government to the provinces. The committee recommendations bluntly suggested a delay of the ratification of the accord until its specific concerns could be addressed and full public consultation completed. In spite of the committee's opinion, the accord was signed in January 1998. See House of Commons Standing Committee on Environment and Sustainable Development, *Report on the Harmonization Initiative of the Canadian Council of Ministers of the Environment* (Ottawa: The Committee, December 1997).

3. The challenges to the accord continued in court when the Canadian Environmental Law Association sought a declaration that the agreements were of no force and effect because the then minister of the environment had exceeded her authority in signing them or had fettered her discretion by agreeing not to act with respect to matters within her statutory authority. Although the Federal Court—Trial Division held that the matter was justiciable, it found that the minister had been within her authority to enter such agreements by virtue of s 7 of the *Department of the Environment Act*, RSC 1985, c E-10 and ss 6, 98, and 99 of the *Canadian Environmental Protection Act*, RSC 1985, c 16 (4th Supp). With regard to the issue of fettering her discretion, the court held that the argument was premature because there was insufficient factual basis on which to make a determination; whether fettering might occur was dependent upon the content of the future sub-agreements. See *Canadian Environmental Law Association v Canada (Minister of the Environment)*, [1999] 3 FC 564, 1999 CanLII 7906.

4. Is the accord a *de facto* amendment of the Constitution, albeit not a *de jure* change? Over time, could this practice become a constitutional convention?

5. On problems with the transparency and enforceability of interdepartmental and intergovernmental agreements generally, see F Gertler, "Lost in (Intergovernmental) Space:

Cooperative Federalism in Environmental Protection" in S Kennett, ed, *Law and Process in Environmental Management* (Calgary: CIRL, 1993) ch 4.

III. EMERGING JURISDICTIONS

A. MUNICIPALITIES

In addition to municipalities potentially exceeding their powers under provincial municipal acts, their by-laws may also be outside provincial legislative powers under the *Constitution Act, 1867*. Thus, in *Burnaby (City) v Trans Mountain Pipeline UCL*, 2015 BCSC 2140, the British Columbia Supreme Court first declined to address the constitutional questions because the National Energy Board (NEB), as it was then (it is now the Canada Energy Regulator), had decided that Burnaby by-laws that restricted Trans Mountain pipeline construction did not apply to the Trans Mountain Expansion Project, and the Federal Court of Appeal had denied leave to appeal. These NEB powers are based on federal jurisdiction in relation to extraprovincial undertakings under s 92(10)(a) of the *Constitution Act, 1867*. However, the court went on to consider and answer these constitutional questions. Macintosh J concluded (at para 75), "Burnaby's by-laws can have no application so as to impede or block the location of the Pipeline or the studies needed to determine its location," and further stated (at para 77),

> [w]here valid provincial laws conflict with valid federal laws in addressing interprovincial undertakings, paramountcy dictates that the federal legal regime will govern. The provincial law remains valid, but becomes inoperative where its application would frustrate the federal undertaking.

The by-laws were also inoperative under the interjurisdictional immunity doctrine because they impair the core competence of the pipeline, a matter within the exclusive jurisdiction of Parliament.

The British Columbia Court of Appeal (in *Burnaby (City) v Trans Mountain Pipeline ULC*, 2017 BCCA 132) dismissed an appeal, holding that the NEB did have the authority to determine the constitutional validity of the Burnaby by-laws.

B. ABORIGINAL JURISDICTIONS

ABORIGINAL SELF-GOVERNMENT: THE GOVERNMENT OF CANADA'S APPROACH TO IMPLEMENTATION OF THE INHERENT RIGHT AND THE NEGOTIATION OF SELF-GOVERNMENT
(Ottawa: Minister of Indian Affairs and Northern Development, 1995)

THE INHERENT RIGHT OF SELF-GOVERNMENT IS A SECTION 35 RIGHT

The Government of Canada recognizes the inherent right of self-government as an existing Aboriginal right under section 35 of the *Constitution Act, 1982* [being Schedule B to the *Canada Act 1982* (UK), 1982, c 11]. It recognizes, as well, that the inherent right may find expression in treaties, and in the context of the Crown's relationship with treaty First Nations. Recognition of the inherent right is based on the view that the Aboriginal peoples of Canada have the right to govern themselves in relation to matters that are internal to their communities, integral to their unique cultures, identities, traditions, languages and institutions, and with respect to their special relationship to their land and their resources.

• • •

[For greater detail on Indigenous peoples' jurisdiction over the environment, see Chapter 12.]

FURTHER READINGS

Chalifour, N, "Drawing Lines in the Sand: Parliament's Jurisdiction to Consider Upstream and Downstream Greenhouse Gas (GHG) Emissions in Interprovincial Pipeline Project Reviews" (2019) 23:1 Rev Const Stud 129.

Chalifour, N, "Jurisdictional Wrangling over Climate Policy in the Canadian Federation: Key Issues in the Provincial Constitutional Challenges to Parliament's Greenhouse Gas Pollution Pricing Act" (2019) Ottawa Law Review Working Paper Series No 2019-2.

Harrison, K, *Passing the Buck: Federalism and Canadian Environmental Policy* (Vancouver: UBC Press, 1996).

Olszynski, M, "Testing the Jurisdictional Waters: The Provincial Regulation of Interprovincial Pipelines" (2019) 23:1 Rev Const Stud 91.

Saunders, JO, ed, *Managing Natural Resources in a Federal State* (Scarborough, Ont: Carswell, 1986).

Valiante, M, "Legal Foundations of Canadian Environmental Policy: Underlining Our Values in a Shifting Landscape" in D Van Nijnatten & R Boardman, eds, *Canadian Environmental Policy: Context and Cases,* 2nd ed (Don Mills, Ont: Oxford University Press, 2002) ch 1.

CHAPTER ELEVEN

ENVIRONMENTAL LAW IN CANADA'S NORTH

Nigel Bankes and David Wright

I. INTRODUCTION: NORTHERN CONTEXT AND ENVIRONMENT

Canada's North, comprising the land mass covering the three northern territories (see the map in Figure 11.1, below), is distinctly different from the rest of the country in several ways. In terms of human populations, Northern Canada is very sparsely populated compared with jurisdictions in the South. While the land mass covers 3,921,739 km²,[1] an area comparable to all of

---

1 Statistics Canada, *Table 15.7: Land and Freshwater Area, by Province and Territory*, Catalogue No 11-402-X (Ottawa: Statistics Canada, 7 October 2016), online: <https://www150.statcan.gc.ca/n1/pub/11-402-x/2010000/chap/geo/tbl/tbl07-eng.htm>.

Western Europe, the combined population of all three territories is just 118,400.[2] A significant proportion of the population is made up of Indigenous peoples: 85.9 percent in Nunavut, 50.7 percent in Northwest Territories, and 23.3 percent in Yukon.[3] Much of the Indigenous population, which comprises Inuit, First Nations, and Métis, continues to engage in traditional hunting, gathering, trapping, and fishing activities.[4]

FIGURE 11.1 Map of Northern Canada

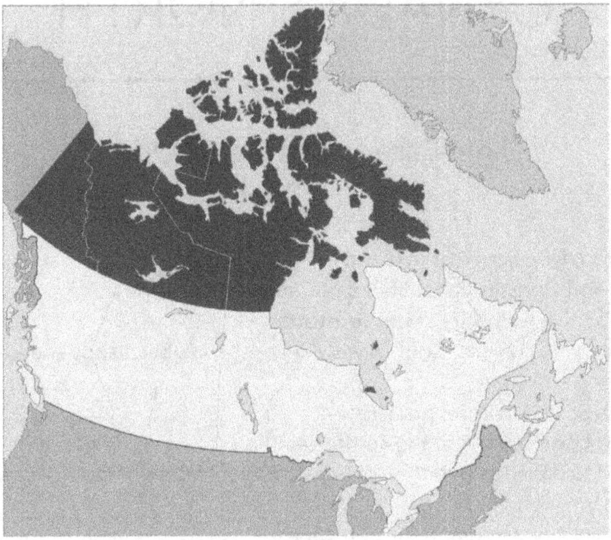

Source: "Northern Canada, defined politically to comprise (from west to east) Yukon, Northwest Territories, and Nunavut" (11 January 2009), online: *Wikipedia* <https://en.wikipedia.org/wiki/Northern_Canada#/media/File:Northern_Canada.svg>.

In terms of the natural environment, this region of Canada is made up of Arctic and Sub-Arctic zones. The Arctic zone, where the Indigenous population is primarily Inuit, is characterized by a treeless tundra landscape that sits atop permanently frozen ground ("permafrost," notwithstanding intensifying climate change impacts). It is home to many species, including cotton grass, sedge, dwarf heath, shrubs, mosses, lichens,[5] as well as iconic animals such as polar bears,

---

2   Intergovernmental Affairs, *Provinces and Territories: Information on Provinces and Territories* (last modified 25 July 2018), online: *Government of Canada* <https://www.canada.ca/en/intergovernmental-affairs/services/provinces-territories.html>.

3   Northwest Territories, NWT Bureau of Statistics, *Indigenous Peoples 2016 Census* (2 November 2017) at 1, online (pdf): newstats <https://www.statsnwt.ca/census/2016/Indigenous_Peoples_2016_Census.pdf>.

4   See *First Nation of Nacho Nyak Dun v Yukon*, 2017 SCC 58, [2017] 2 SCR 576 [*First Nation of Nacho Nyak Dun* 2017]. See also Thomas R Berger, *Northern Frontier, Northern Homeland: The Report on the Mackenzie Valley Pipeline Inquiry*, vol 1 (Ottawa: Minister of Supply and Services Canada, 1977), online (pdf): *Prince of Wales Northern Heritage Centre* <https://www.pwnhc.ca/extras/berger/report/BergerV1_complete_e.pdf> [Berger Inquiry].

5   Doreen Aun et al, "Flora of the Canadian Arctic" (Geography 351 Term Project, Simon Fraser University, Fall 2002), online: *Canada Arctic: Exploration of the Canadian Arctic* <http://www.sfu.ca/geog-351fall02/gp2/WEBSITE/2_content_v.html>.

snowy owls, muskoxen, Arctic wolves, and barren-ground caribou.[6] The Sub-Arctic zone has more extensive vegetative coverage and a higher diversity of species. This area is an extension of Canada's boreal zone, which contains a large range of mammals, including bears, wolves, wolverines, and caribou, as well as insects, fungi, and microorganisms.

For an accessible overview of Canada's North, see the excerpt below from Thomas Berger's 1977 report of the Mackenzie Valley Pipeline Inquiry.

THOMAS R BERGER, NORTHERN FRONTIER, NORTHERN HOMELAND: THE REPORT ON THE MACKENZIE VALLEY PIPELINE INQUIRY, VOL 1

(Ottawa: Minister of Supply and Services Canada, 1977) at 2, 4, online (pdf): *Prince of Wales Northern Heritage Centre* <https://www.pwnhc.ca/extras/berger/report/BergerV1_complete_e.pdf>

Biologists divide the North into two great regions called "biomes": the boreal forest and the tundra. The boreal forest is characterized in the minds of most people by spruce trees and muskeg. It is the broad band of coniferous forest that extends right across Canada from Newfoundland to Alaska. The tundra, extending from the boreal forest northward to the Arctic Ocean, comprises one-fifth of the land mass of Canada, but most of us who have never seen it, and know of it simply as a land without trees, sometimes call it "the barrens." Yet the tundra biome includes landscapes as varied and as beautiful as any in Canada—plains and mountains, hills and valleys, rivers, lakes and sea coasts. In winter, land and water merge into white and grey desert, but the summer brings running water, explosively rapid plant growth, and a remarkable influx of migratory birds.

The two northern biomes—the tundra and the boreal forest—meet along the tree line. The tree line is not really a line, but a transitional zone that is commonly many miles in width. This biologically important boundary, which separates forest and tundra, also separates the traditional lands of the Indians and the Inuit. The tree line may also be viewed as the southern limit of the Arctic, the boundary between the Arctic and the sub-Arctic ... .

• • •

To understand the impact of industrial development on the northern ecosystem and the appropriateness of mitigative measures, it is essential first to understand its general nature and the features that set it apart from more familiar ecosystems in the South. Merely to characterize the North as sensitive, vulnerable or even fragile will not help. Granted, certain species are sensitive: falcons, for example, cannot tolerate disturbances near their nesting sites. The massing of some species such as caribou, white whales and snow geese in certain areas at certain times will make whole populations of them vulnerable. And the response of permafrost to disturbance suggests that its very existence is fragile. But anyone who has visited the North during the long winters and the short mosquito-infested summers will know that northern species must be hardy to survive.

Every ecosystem is built on both living and non-living elements. The two are inextricably linked, and the characteristics of the one are reflected in those of the other. It is not surprising that the combinations of climate and topography in the

---

6   Conservation of Arctic Flora and Fauna, *Arctic Biodiversity Assessment: Report for Policy Makers*, (Akureyri, Iceland: Conservation of Arctic Flora and Fauna, 2013) at 4, online (pdf): *Canada Foundation for Innovation* <https://www.innovation.ca/sites/default/files/Rome2013/files/Arctic%20Council%20-%20Biodiversity%20Assessment.pdf>.

northern biomes have produced plant and animal populations unique to the North. The relations within the northern ecosystems are not well understood, but at least three characteristics appear to distinguish them: the simplicity of the food chains, the wide oscillations in populations, and the slow growth rates.

NOTES AND QUESTIONS

Berger J framed his famous report around two views of Canada's North: as a "last frontier" and as a "homeland." How do you think each of these viewpoints could influence environmental law and policy for the region?

As you read the remainder of this chapter, consider which framing you think has acted as the predominant driver and how the framings are (or are not) reflected in the case law and legislation.

From an environmental assessment perspective, the Berger Inquiry was a major turning point. It influenced the architecture of project-level assessment regimes in Canada for decades to come. Meinhard Doelle, in his text on Canada's federal environmental assessment regime, called the Berger Inquiry "a catalyst" for evolution of environmental assessment.[7]

II. THE LEGAL AND CONSTITUTIONAL STATUS OF CANADA'S TERRITORIES

Section 146 of the *Constitution Act, 1867*[8] deals with the expansion of Confederation from the original four provinces of Ontario, Quebec, New Brunswick, and Nova Scotia. It contemplated that in addition to the possibility of the separate colonies of Newfoundland, Prince Edward Island, and British Columbia being invited to join the Union as provinces, Rupert's Land (that is, the lands granted under the terms of the Hudson Bay Charter) and the Northwestern Territory might also be admitted into the Union "on Address from the Houses of the Parliament of Canada." These vast territories did join Canada by Imperial Order in Council in 1870,[9] and the Arctic Islands followed in 1880. While some of these lands south of 60 degrees latitude were subsequently carved out as the provinces of Alberta, Saskatchewan, and Manitoba or added to the existing provinces of Ontario and Quebec, the balance of these lands remain as the three territories of Yukon, Northwest Territories, and (since 1999) Nunavut. Section 4 of the *Constitution Act, 1871*[10] confirms that the federal Parliament has plenary legislative authority with respect to these three territories:

> The Parliament of Canada may from time to time make provision for the administration, peace, order, and good government of any territory not for the time being included in any Province.

In the last two decades, however, the federal Parliament and the executive have devolved considerable legislative authority to the legislative assemblies of the three territories and have

---

7   See *The Federal Environmental Assessment Process: A Guide and Critique* (Toronto, Ont: LexisNexis Canada, 2008).

8   (UK), 30 & 31 Vict, c 3.

9   *Rupert's Land and North-Western Territory Order* (23 June 1870) (UK), reprinted in RSC 1985, App II, No 9. This Order in Council and the terms of the transfer continue to be the subject of litigation especially in Yukon. See e.g. *Ross River Dena Council v Canada (Attorney General)*, 2017 YKSC 58.

10   (UK), 34-35 Vict, c 28.

also devolved the administration and control of publicly owned lands and resources to each of Yukon and Northwest Territories. The terms of the transfers have been effected in each case by means of a devolution agreement: see *Yukon Northern Affairs Program Devolution Transfer Agreement*[11] and *Northwest Territories Lands and Resources Devolution Agreement.*[12]

Publicly owned lands and resources within Nunavut, however, have yet to be transferred to that government, and remain, for the most part, under the administration and control of the federal government. As a result, federal resource laws such as the *Canada Petroleum Resources Act*,[13] the *Canada Oil and Gas Operations Act*,[14] and the federal *Nunavut Mining Regulations*[15] continue to apply in Nunavut.

A. LEGISLATIVE AUTHORITY IN THE TERRITORIES

The legislative authority for each of the territorial governments is established by the terms of a federal statute, respectively, *Yukon Act*,[16] *Northwest Territories Act*,[17] and *Nunavut Act*.[18]

Below are the sections of the *Yukon Act* dealing with legislative authority over matters relating to the environment and the management and conservation of natural resources.

YUKON ACT
SC 2002, c 7, ss 18-22, 26

18(1) The Legislature may make laws in relation to the following classes of subjects in respect of Yukon:

• • •

(e) municipal and local institutions;

(f) direct taxation and licensing in order to raise revenue for territorial, municipal or local purposes;

(g) the levying of a tax on furs or any portions of fur-bearing animals to be shipped or taken from Yukon to any place outside Yukon;

• • •

(j) property and civil rights;

• • •

(m) the conservation of wildlife and its habitat, other than in a federal conservation area;

---

11 29 October 2001, online (pdf): *Government of Canada* <https://www.aadnc-aandc.gc.ca/DAM/DAM-INTER-HQ/STAGING/texte-text/nth_pubs_yna_yna_1316538556192_eng.pdf>.

12 (25 June 2013), online (pdf): *Devolution of Lands and Resources in the Northwest Territories* <https://devolution.gov.nt.ca/wp-content/uploads/2013/09/Final-Devolution-Agreement.pdf>.

13 RSC 1985, c 36 (2nd Supp).

14 RSC 1985, c O-7.

15 SOR/2014-69.

16 SC 2002, c 7.

17 SC 2014, c 2, s 2.

18 SC 1993, c 28.

(n) waters, other than waters in a federal conservation area, including the deposit of waste in those waters, the definition of what constitutes waste and the disposition of any right in respect of those waters under subsection 48(2);

• • •

(q) public real property—including the timber and wood on that property—under the administration and control of the Commissioner ...;

• • •

(t) agriculture;

(u) the entering into of intergovernmental agreements by the Commissioner ...;

• • •

(x) generally, all matters of a merely local or private nature;

• • •

[Section 19 follows the text of s 92A (the "resources" amendment adopted in 1982) and the sixth schedule of the *Constitution Act, 1867.*]

20(1) Nothing in subsections 18(1) and (2) and section 19 shall be construed as giving the Legislature greater powers than are given to legislatures of the provinces under sections 92, 92A and 95 of the *Constitution Act, 1867.*

(2) Despite subsections 18(1) and (2) and section 19, the Legislature may not make laws in respect of the right to the use and flow of waters for the production or generation of water-power to which the *Dominion Water Power Act* applies.

21 Despite subsection 20(1), the Legislature may, in exercising its powers under sections 18 and 19 for the purpose of implementing aboriginal land claim agreements or aboriginal self-government agreements, make laws that are in relation to the matters coming within class 24 of section 91 of the *Constitution Act, 1867.*

22(1) Despite subsection 20(1), any law of the Legislature in relation to the conservation of wildlife, unless the contrary intention appears in it, applies to and in respect of Indians and Inuit.

(2) Nothing in paragraph 18(1)(m) or subsection (1) shall be construed as authorizing the Legislature to make laws restricting or prohibiting Indians and Inuit from hunting for food on unoccupied public real property, other than a species that is declared by order of the Governor in Council to be in danger of becoming extinct. This subsection does not apply to laws that implement the Agreement given effect by the *Western Arctic (Inuvialuit) Claims Settlement Act.*

• • •

26 In the event of a conflict between a law of the Legislature and a federal enactment, the federal enactment prevails to the extent of the conflict.

NOTES AND QUESTIONS

1. To what extent do the provisions of s 18 of the *Yukon Act* differ from those of s 92 of the *Constitution Act, 1867*? How important are these differences?

2. What do you think the role of s 26 of the *Yukon Act* is? What are the implications of s 26 when a territorial government assumes additional legislative responsibilities? What else must the federal government do to make the assumption of territorial jurisdiction effective?

3. The relevant provisions in the *Northwest Territories Act* are essentially identical to those in the Yukon. In the case of Nunavut, however, the *Nunavut Act* has no equivalent to s 19 of

the *Yukon Act*, which in turn is evidently modelled on s 92A of the *Constitution Act, 1867*. There is no equivalent provision for Nunavut, since, as noted above, Nunavut has yet to assume administration and control of the public lands located within Nunavut.

B. ADMINISTRATION AND CONTROL WITH RESPECT TO PUBLIC LANDS AND RESOURCES IN THE TERRITORIES

Below are the provisions of the *Yukon Act* dealing with the administration and control of public lands.

YUKON ACT
SC 2002, c 7, ss 45, 48-49

45(1) Subject to this Act ... the Commissioner has the administration and control of public real property and of oil and gas in the adjoining area and may, with the consent of the Executive Council, use, sell or otherwise dispose of that property, or any products of that property, that oil or gas, or any interest in that oil or gas, and retain the proceeds of the disposition.

• • •

48(1) The rights in respect of all waters in Yukon belong to Her Majesty in right of Canada.

(2) Subject to this Act, the Commissioner has the administration and control of all rights in respect of waters in Yukon—other than waters in a federal conservation area—and, with the consent of the Executive Council, may exercise those rights or sell or otherwise dispose of them and may retain the proceeds of the disposition.

• • •

(4) Subsection (2) does not apply to the right to the use and flow of waters for the production or generation of water-power to which the *Dominion Water Power Act* applies.

• • •

49(1) The Governor in Council, on the recommendation of the Minister, may take from the Commissioner the administration and control of public real property and transfer the administration of the property to a federal minister or a federal agent corporation if the Governor in Council considers it necessary to do so for

(a) the national interest, including
(i) national defence or security,
(ii) the establishment, or changes to the boundaries, of a national park, historic site or other area protected under an Act of Parliament, and
(iii) the creation of the infrastructure required for initiatives in respect of transportation or energy;
(b) the welfare of Indians and Inuit; or
(c) the settlement of an aboriginal land claim or the implementation of an aboriginal land claim agreement.

• • •

(3) [This subsection imposes an obligation on the minister of Indian affairs and Northern development to consult Yukon before making a recommendation.]

NOTES AND QUESTIONS

1. How do these provisions of the *Yukon Act* differ from the public property provisions of the *Constitution Act, 1867* (ss 108 and 109) and the similar provisions in the Natural Resources Transfer Agreements of 1930?[19]

2. The *Canadian Charter of Rights and Freedoms*[20] applies to the territories in much the same way as it applies to provincial governments by virtue of s 32(1)(a), which provides that the Charter applies "to the Parliament and government of Canada in respect of all matters within the authority of Parliament including all matters relating to the Yukon Territory and Northwest Territories."

What sorts of environmental issues do you think that the parties might have had to deal with in the course of devolution negotiations with respect to the transfer of the administration and control of public lands and resources from Canada to Yukon and the Northwest Territories, particularly with respect to old mining sites?[21]

While a territory has a distinct constitutional status within Canada, it is worth recalling that s 35 of the federal *Interpretation Act*[22] provides that "province," when used in an enactment, "means a province of Canada, *and includes Yukon, the Northwest Territories and Nunavut*" (emphasis added).

Another crucially important influence on the environmental laws of the three territories is the terms of land claims agreements. These agreements include the Yukon *Umbrella Final Agreement*,[23] as implemented by individual final agreements with most of Yukon's individual First Nations;[24] the Inuvialuit Final Agreement, covering the Western Arctic region, the northern part of the Mackenzie Delta, and Yukon's North Slope; the Nunavut Final Agreement with Inuit of the central and eastern Arctic; and the Gwich'in, Sahtu, and Tlicho agreements in the Mackenzie Valley.[25] Note that some First Nations and Métis communities in the southern part of Northwest Territories have not entered into land claims agreements.

The agreements above are all constitutionally protected by s 35 of the *Constitution Act, 1982*:[26]

> 35(1) The existing aboriginal and treaty rights of the aboriginal peoples of Canada are hereby recognized and affirmed.
>
> (2) In this Act, "aboriginal peoples of Canada" includes the Indian, Inuit and Métis peoples of Canada.
>
> (3) For greater certainty, in subsection (1) "treaty rights" includes rights that now exist by way of land claims agreements or may be so acquired.

---

19 As scheduled to the *Constitution Act, 1930* (UK), 20-21 Geo V, c 26.

20 Part I of the *Constitution Act, 1982*, being Schedule B to the *Canada Act 1982* (UK), 1982, c 11.

21 For a consideration of some of the issues associated with old mining sites, see *Yukon v BYG Resources Inc*, 2017 YKSC 2.

22 RSC 1985, c I-21.

23 (29 May 1993), online (pdf): *Council of Yukon First Nations* <https://cyfn.ca/wp-content/uploads/2013/08/umbrella-final-agreement.pdf> [UFA].

24 The following groups have not entered into final agreements: White River First Nation, Liard First Nation, and Ross River Dena Council. "Council of Yukon First Nations" (last visited 1 July 2019), online: *Land Claims Agreement Coalition* <http://landclaimscoalition.ca/coalition_members/council-of-yukon-first-nations/>.

25 All land claims agreements can be accessed online at Crown–Indigenous Relations and Northern Affairs Canada, "Final Agreements and Related Implementation Matters" (last modified 18 June 2018), online: *Government of Canada* <https://www.rcaanc-cirnac.gc.ca/eng/1100100030583/1529420498350>.

26 Being Schedule B to the *Canada Act 1982* (UK), 1982, c 11.

(4) Notwithstanding any other provision of this Act, the aboriginal and treaty rights referred to in subsection (1) are guaranteed equally to male and female persons.

All of these agreements contain provisions dealing with matters such as land use planning, environmental impact assessment, wildlife, and water management. In practice, therefore, these agreements establish principles and substantive standards and procedures that any legislation dealing with these matters (whether federal or territorial) must follow. This is well illustrated in the following sections of this chapter. As you read these sections, you might reflect on what you see as being the consequences of this constitutional foundation for much of northern environmental law.

III. LANDSCAPE-SCALE ENVIRONMENTAL LAW

A. LAND USE PLANNING IN THE TERRITORIES

Land use planning is a fundamental part of environmental law in Canada's northern territories. The Yukon Land Use Planning Council provides the following comprehensive description of land use planning:

> It is a value-based process that guides decision-making regarding the land, and attempts to consider the various land-based needs. Land Use Planning is the process of making educated judgments about how the land should be shared and used. These judgments are based on what we know about the land, and how we hope to relate to the land as humans. In other words, there are two important elements to Land Use Planning: understanding the land and its users and making decisions about how to manage that land.[27]

In short, land use planning is a tool for balancing economic, social, and environmental priorities across a specific region. Once a land use plan (LUP) is in place, it typically guides decision-making throughout the delineated region, specifying where certain activities may and may not take place. In this way, a LUP serves an important role in project-level decision-making across Canada's North. Generally, once a LUP is in place, it is integrated into project-level assessments and becomes an important step in the assessment process. This step is typically very early in the project-level assessment, requiring the land use planning body to make a determination as to whether the proposed project conforms with the LUP for that region.

The land use planning legal context in Canada's northern territories is based on commitments in the land claims agreements.[28] These planning regimes are then typically integrated with respective territorial legislation.[29] At the institutional level, implementation of LUPs is carried out by a land use planning body, such as a board or commission.

For example, art 11 of the *Nunavut Agreement*[30] sets out the land use planning regime for all of Nunavut, and the regime is then implemented through part 2 of the *Nunavut Planning and Project Assessment Act*.[31] The Nunavut Planning Commission administers and implements the

---

27 "Frequently Asked Questions (FAQs) About Regional Land Use Planning in the Yukon" (last visited 1 July 2019) at 1, online (pdf): *Yukon Land Use Planning Council* <http://www.planyukon.ca/index.php/documents-and-downloads/reference-documents/107-faqs-sheet/file>.

28 See e.g. *Gwich'in Comprehensive Land Claim Agreement*, vol 1 (22 April 1992) ch 24, online (pdf): *Gwich'in Tribal Council* <https://gwichintribal.ca/sites/default/files/gtc-comprehensive-land-claim.pdf> [GCLCA].

29 See e.g. *Mackenzie Valley Resource Management Act*, SC 1998, c 25 [MVRMA].

30 (25 May 1993), online: *Nunavut Tunngavik* <https://nlca.tunngavik.com> [NA].

31 SC 2013, c 14, s 2 [NUPPAA].

regime, as required by part 4 of art 11 of the NA. As of 2019, Nunavut has two approved land use plans: the *North Baffin Regional Land Use Plan* and the *Keewatin Regional Land Use Plan*.[32]

In the Mackenzie Valley context in Northwest Territories, land use planning requirements are set out in the three existing land claims agreements. Chapter 24 of the GCLCA, for example, sets out the regime for land use planning in the Gwich'in Settlement Area,[33] and the regime is then implemented through part 2 of the MVRMA. The Gwich'in Land Use Planning Board is responsible for preparing and implementing the Gwich'in LUP, which was finalized in 2003. There are three approved land use plans in Northwest Territories, one for each of the Gwich'in,[34] Sahtu,[35] and Tlicho regions.[36]

In Yukon, chapter 11 of the UFA specifies how regional land use planning should be carried out. These requirements have become part of the 11 final agreements negotiated by individual Yukon First Nations.[37] Unlike Northwest Territories and Nunavut, Yukon has no dedicated territorial land use planning legislation, though statutes such as the *Territorial Lands (Yukon) Act*[38] and the *Yukon Environmental and Socio-economic Assessment Act*[39] have roles to play.[40] Rather, the UFA required the establishment of the Yukon Land Use Planning Council[41] as well as the establishment of regional land use planning councils to develop specific regional land use plans.[42] There are eight planning regions in Yukon: North Yukon, Northern Tutchone, Dawson, Teslin, Whitehorse, Kluane, Kaska, and the Peel River Watershed. As of 2019, only one LUP has been finalized—the *Final Recommended North Yukon Use Plan*.[43] Two others are in development: that of Dawson and that of the Peel River Watershed. The latter was the subject of litigation that reached the Supreme Court of Canada in 2017 and is discussed in detail in the next section.

---

32 "Land Use Plans" (last visited 1 July 2019), online: *Nunavut Planning Commission* <https://www.nunavut.ca/land-use-plans>.

33 GCLCA, 24.2.

34 *Nành' Geenjit Gwitr'it T'igwaa'in: Working for the Land—Gwich'in Land Use Plan* (7 August 2003), online (pdf): *Gwich'in Planning Board* <http://www.gwichinplanning.nt.ca/publications/lupd/final%20 2003/Gwichin_Plan_2003.pdf>.

35 *Sahtu Land Use Plan* (8 August 2013), online (pdf): *Sahtu Land Use Planning Board* <https://sahtulanduseplan.org/sites/default/files/final_sahtu_land_use_plan_april_29_2013.pdf>.

36 *Tlicho Land Use Plan* (2012), online (pdf): *Tlicho Government* <https://www.tlicho.ca/sites/default/files/105-LandUsePlan_FINAL%20VERSION%5B2%5D.pdf>.

37 See e.g. *Tr'ondëk Hwëch'in Final Agreement* (16 July 1998; updated 10 January 2019), online (pdf): *Yukon* <https://yukon.ca/en/trondek-hwechin-final-agreement>. See also *The Kwanlin Dun First Nation Final Agreement* (19 February 2005), online (pdf): *Kwanlin Dun First Nation* <http://www.kwanlindun.com/images/uploads/Final_Agreement.pdf>.

38 SY 2003, c 17.

39 SC 2003, c 7 [YESAA].

40 See, generally, Yukon, Department of Energy, Mines and Resources, "Overview of Legislation and Policies Pertaining to Regional Land Use Plans in the Yukon" (January 2011), online (pdf): *Yukon Land Use Planning Council* <https://www.planyukon.ca/index.php/documents-and-downloads/reference-documents/common-land-use-planning-process-1/509-overview-of-legislation-and-policies-pertaining-to-regional-land-use-plans-in-the-yukon>.

41 UFA, 11.3.0.

42 UFA, 11.4.0.

43 (January 2009), online (pdf): *Yukon Land Use Planning Council* <https://www.planyukon.ca/index.php/documents-and-downloads/north-yukon-planning-commission-documents/regional-plans/final-recommended-plan/275-final-recommended-north-yukon-land-use-plan>.

B. LAND USE PLANNING IN THE YUKON—THE FIRST NATION OF NACHO NYAK DUN V YUKON

The Peel Watershed is an area in northwest Yukon approximately 68,000 square kilometers in size and covering roughly 14 percent of the territory.[44] The First Nations of Na-Cho Nyak Dun, Tr'ondëk Hwëch'in, Vuntut Gwitchin, and Tetlit Gwich'in all have traditional territory in the region.[45] While there was natural resource exploration and development in the area in the past,[46] and there continues to be considerable interest in mineral development and oil and gas potential today,[47] the Peel Watershed is considered to be largely pristine[48] and an internationally significant wilderness.[49] Consequently, all parties involved in the development of the Peel LUP recognized that some areas needed to be excluded from future development and "afforded high levels of protection."[50]

Precisely which areas and what level of protection, however, became contentious during the development of the Peel Watershed LUP. In 2009, the Peel Watershed Planning Commission (established in 2006) provided its recommended plan to the Government of Yukon, proposing that approximately 80 percent of the region be afforded a high degree of protection as "special management areas" and the remaining portions be "integrated management areas" open to mineral and oil and gas development under certain terms.[51]

Near the end of the approval process, and after the commission had released a final recommended plan, the Government of Yukon unilaterally proposed and adopted a final plan that made substantial changes to increase access to and development of the region.

First Nations and environmental groups litigated the matter, seeking orders quashing Yukon's plan and directing Yukon to redo consultations required under chapter 11 of the UFA.

At trial, Veale J declared that Yukon did not act in conformity with the process set out in the final agreements, and quashed Yukon's plan.[52] On appeal, the Yukon Court of Appeal ruled that Yukon had failed to properly exercise its rights to propose modifications to the recommended plan, and returned the parties to the earlier stage in the process where Yukon could articulate its priorities in a valid manner.[53] First Nations and environmental groups appealed to the Supreme Court of Canada, seeking a different remedy. The unanimous court upheld the trial judge's order quashing Yukon's approval of the plan and returned the parties to the latter consultation stage.[54] This was considered to be a victory for the First Nations and environmental groups, and the ruling provided further clarity with respect to implementation of land claims agreements and associated Crown consultation obligations.

At the trial level, Veale J offered an overview of the Yukon land use planning process, extracted below.

---

44 *The First Nation of Nacho Nyak Dun v Yukon (Government of)*, 2014 YKSC 69 at para 5 [*First Nation of Nacho Nyak Dun 2014*].

45 *Ibid* at para 6.

46 See, generally, Canadian Parks and Wilderness Society, Yukon Chapter, *Peel Watershed Atlas* (2004), online: US Geological Survey <https://www.sciencebase.gov/catalog/item/5771b8a4e4b07657d1a6cb9c>.

47 *First Nation of Nacho Nyak Dun 2017, supra* note 4 at para 13.

48 *First Nation of Nacho Nyak Dun 2014, supra* note 44 at para 70.

49 Michael J Green et al, *Peel Watershed Yukon: International Significance from the Perspective of Parks, Recreation and Conservation*, Report prepared for Yukon Parks (March 2008).

50 *First Nation of Nacho Nyak Dun 2014, supra* note 44 at para 70.

51 *Ibid* at paras 57-61.

52 *First Nation of Nacho Nyak Dun 2017, supra* note 4 at para 27.

53 *First Nation of Nacho Nyak Dun v Yukon*, 2015 YKCA 18.

54 *First Nation of Nacho Nyak Dun 2017, supra* note 4.

THE FIRST NATION OF NACHO NYAK DUN V YUKON
(GOVERNMENT OF)
2014 YKSC 69

C) THE LAND USE PLANNING PROCESS

[20] The Final Agreements established new constitutional arrangements for Yukon, Canada and Yukon First Nations, including provisions for land use planning under Chapter 11. The provisions incorporated from the UFA provide for land use planning commissions, that may be established jointly by the Government of Yukon and any affected Yukon First Nation, to develop land use plans for discrete regions of Yukon.

[21] Chapter 11 ("Land Use Planning") of the Final Agreements sets out the objectives of land use planning, which include the following:

> 11.1.1.1 to encourage the development of a common Yukon land use planning process outside community boundaries;
> 11.1.1.2 to minimize actual or potential land use conflicts both within Settlement Land and Non-Settlement Land and between Settlement Land and Non-Settlement Land;

> • • •

> 11.1.1.6 to ensure that social, cultural, economic and environmental policies are applied to the management, protection and use of land, water and resources in an integrated and coordinated manner so as to ensure Sustainable Development.

> • • •

[23] Section 11.3.0 establishes a Yukon Land Use Planning Council, with Government and First Nation representation. The Council:

> 11.3.3 ... shall make recommendations to Government and each affected Yukon First Nation on the following:
> 11.3.3.1 land use planning, including policies, goals and priorities, in the Yukon;
> 11.3.3.2 the identification of planning regions and priorities for the preparation of regional land use plans;
> 11.3.3.3 the general terms of reference, including timeframes, for each Regional Land Use Planning Commission;
> 11.3.3.4 the boundary of each planning region; and
> 11.3.3.5 such other matters as Government and each affected Yukon First Nation may agree.

[24] Regional Land Use Planning Commissions may be established to develop regional land use plans:

> 11.4.1 Government and any affected Yukon First Nation may agree to establish a Regional Land Use Planning Commission to develop a regional land use plan.

> • • •

> 11.4.4 Each Regional Land Use Planning Commission shall prepare and recommend to Government and the affected Yukon First Nation a regional land use plan within a timeframe established by Government and each affected Yukon First Nation.

D) REGIONAL LAND USE PLANS

[26] Chapter 11 of the Final Agreements also sets out the approval process for regional land use plans developed by planning commissions.

[27] Specifically, s. 11.6.0 sets out the procedure for First Nation and Government approval of land use plans for Settlement and Non-Settlement Land. First Nations and the Government of Yukon must engage in intergovernmental consultation during the approval process, but the requirements differ in that the Government of Yukon is obliged to consult not only with affected Yukon First Nations but also any affected Yukon community about plans for Non-Settlement Land. Yukon First Nations need only consult with the Government of Yukon when Settlement Land is at issue. The dispute in the case at bar concerns the approval process for Non-Settlement Land contained within the Peel Watershed.

The excerpt below from the decision of the Supreme Court of Canada provides a succinct summary of the operation of UFA provisions in relation to the Peel Watershed LUP, as well as an overview of interpretive principles for modern treaties and a discussion of the disagreement between First Nations and the Government of Yukon.

FIRST NATION OF NACHO NYAK DUN V YUKON
2017 SCC 58, [2017] 2 SCR 576

[16] Throughout the planning process, the Commission engaged in intensive stakeholder, expert, and public consultation and published various reports which informed its development of the Recommended Plan.

[17] In 2009, after more than four years of research and consultation, the Commission initiated the land use plan approval process by submitting its Recommended Peel Watershed Regional Land Use Plan to Yukon and the affected First Nations (s. 11.6.1). This process is found in ss. 11.6.1 to 11.6.5.2 of Chapter 11, set out in an Appendix to these reasons.

[18] After consultation, Yukon was required to approve, reject, or propose modifications to the part of the plan that applied to non-settlement land (s. 11.6.2). If Yukon chose to reject it or propose modifications, it was required to provide written reasons (s. 11.6.3). The First Nations have similar rights and responsibilities with respect to the part of the Recommended Plan that applies to settlement land (ss. 11.6.4 and 11.6.5).

• • •

[35] I agree with the parties and both courts below that Yukon's changes to the Final Recommended Plan did not respect the land use planning process in the Final Agreements. However, the reasoning and the focus of the parties and courts below lead to different conclusions and different remedies. In my view, Yukon's approval of the plan was not valid as Yukon's changes to this plan were not authorized. To explain why, I must interpret s. 11.6.3.2 of the Final Agreements, which sets out Yukon's right to modify a Final Recommended Plan.

[36] The provisions of Chapter 11 must be interpreted in light of the modern treaty interpretation principles set out in this Court's jurisprudence and the interpretation principles in the Final Agreements (ss. 2.6.1 to 2.6.8). Because modern treaties are "meticulously negotiated by well-resourced parties," courts must "pay close attention to [their] terms" (*Quebec (Attorney General) v. Moses*, 2010 SCC 17, [2010] 1 SCR S.C.R.

557, at para. 7). "[M]odern treaties are designed to place Aboriginal and non-Aboriginal relations in the mainstream legal system with its advantages of continuity, transparency, and predictability" (*Little Salmon* [*Beckman v Little Salmon/Carmacks First Nation*, 2010 SCC 53, [2010] 3 SCR 103], at para. 12). Compared to their historic counterparts, modern treaties are detailed documents and deference to their text is warranted (*Little Salmon*, at para. 12; see also Julie Jai, "The Interpretation of Modern Treaties and the Honour of the Crown: Why Modern Treaties Deserve Judicial Deference" (2010), 26 *N.J.C.L.* 25, at p. 41).

[37] Paying close attention to the terms of a modern treaty means interpreting the provision at issue in light of the treaty text *as a whole* and the treaty's objectives (*Little Salmon*, at para. 10; *Moses*, at para. 7; ss. 2.6.1, 2.6.6 and 2.6.7 of the Final Agreements; see also the *Interpretation Act*, R.S.C. 1985, c. I-21, s. 12). Indeed, a modern treaty will not accomplish its purpose of fostering positive, long-term relationships between Indigenous peoples and the Crown if it is interpreted "in an ungenerous manner or as if it were an everyday commercial contract" (*Little Salmon*, at para. 10; see also D. Newman, "Contractual and Covenantal Conceptions of Modern Treaty Interpretation" (2011), 54 *S.C.L.R.* (2d) 475). Furthermore, while courts must "strive to respect [the] handiwork" of the parties to a modern treaty, this is always "subject to such constitutional limitations as the honour of the Crown" (*Little Salmon*, at para. 54).

[38] By applying these interpretive principles, courts can help ensure that modern treaties will advance reconciliation. Modern treaties do so by addressing land claims disputes and "by creating the legal basis to foster a positive long-term relationship" (*Little Salmon*, at para. 10). Although not exhaustively so, reconciliation is found in the respectful fulfillment of a modern treaty's terms.

NOTES AND QUESTIONS

1. How will *First Nation of Nacho Nyak Dun* affect the development and adoption of land use plans in modern treaty contexts in the future? To what extent do you think the decision may slow or accelerate development of land use plans? Why?

2. The latest step in the broader Yukon land use planning process is in the Dawson region, which is an area of relatively heavy industrial activity due to rich gold deposits. The Land Use Planning Commission for that region was reformed in early 2019 after slow progress in earlier years.[55]

One oft-cited rationale behind regional environmental assessment and land use planning is that it may result in efficiencies in project-level assessments later on. To what extent do you think that rationale is tenable in the northern regimes? What differences in the northern context may affect this calculation?

3. A climate change report released by the federal government in spring 2019 documented changes across Canada in temperature, precipitation, snow, ice, and permafrost, reporting that Northern Canada has warmed and will continue to warm at even more than double the global rate.[56] Relatedly, the Vuntut Gwitchin, a self-governing First Nation in northern Yukon, declared a state of emergency with respect to climate change in June 2019, declaring that "climate

---

55 For the commission's terms of reference, see "Dawson Regional Planning Commission: Terms of Reference 2018" (18 September 2018), online (pdf): *Yukon Land Use Planning Council* <https://www.planyukon.ca/index.php/documents-and-downloads/dawson-regional-planning-commission/863-drpc2018tor/file>.

56 Environmental and Climate Change Canada, Fisheries and Oceans Canada, and Natural Resources Canada, *Canada's Changing Climate Report* (Gatineau, Qc: Environment and Climate Change Canada, 2019), online: *Government of Canada* <https://www.nrcan.gc.ca/environment/impacts-adaptation/21177>.

change constitutes a state of emergency for our lands, waters, animals and people."[57] What do you think the changing climate means for land use planning in Canada's North? From a legal perspective, what challenges might this present, and what legal tools could be used to respond?

IV. PROJECT-LEVEL ASSESSMENT IN THE TERRITORIES

A. OVERVIEW

In each of the three territories, the legal regime for project-level assessment is set out in legislation, which, as explained above, flows from commitments in land claims agreements and associated land use planning processes and institutions.[58] In Yukon, project-level assessment is addressed in chapter 12 of the UFA and implemented through YESAA (see note 39). The assessment process requires an evaluation of environmental, social, cultural, and economic effects of development projects undertaken in Yukon. Institutionally, the Yukon Environmental and Socio-economic Assessment Board is responsible for administering YESAA.

In Nunavut, the project-level assessment regime is set out in art 12 of the NA and is implemented through part 3 of the NUPPAA (see note 31). The institution primarily responsible for these reviews is the Nunavut Impact Review Board, though the Nunavut Land Use Planning Commission performs initial reviews for conformance with any applicable LUP.[59] All of these northern regimes are designed around a model of co-management whereby the Indigenous communities are directly involved in project-level assessment and decision-making. The remainder of this section provides a more detailed look at the Mackenzie Valley regime in the Northwest Territories.

B. PROJECT-LEVEL ASSESSMENT IN THE MACKENZIE VALLEY

In the Mackenzie Valley context, similar to that of Yukon and Nunavut, each of the land claims agreements (Gwich'in, Sahtu, and Tlicho) recognizes the Indigenous communities as co-managers and joint decision-makers with respect to land and water and developments in each settlement area. The MVRMA essentially implements the key parts relating to lands and resources in these modern treaties. The co-management regimes and linkages between the land claims agreements and the MVRMA are succinctly described by the Northwest Territories Supreme Court in relation to the Tlicho Agreement[60] in *Tlicho Government v Canada (Attorney General)*,[61] a case involving an application by the Tlicho government for interlocutory injunctive relief in the context of broader Indigenous-led litigation aimed at stopping amendments to the MVRMA.[62]

---

57 *Yeendoo Diinehdoo Ji'heezrit Nits'oo Ts'o' Nan He'aa Declaration* (June 2019), online (pdf): *Vuntut Gwitchin First Nation* <https://www.vgfn.ca/pdf/CC%202019%20Declaration.pdf>.

58 Although the focus here is on the project-level assessment provisions of the northern land claim agreements and associated legislation, the discrete water provisions of the Nunavut and Yukon agreements are also significant, especially in the context of the regulation of mining projects. See e.g. *Western Copper Corporation v Yukon Water Board*, 2011 YKSC 16.

59 NUPPAA, s 77(1).

60 *Land Claims and Self-Government Agreement Among the Tlicho and the Government of the Northwest Territories and the Government of Canada,* 25 August 2003, online (pdf): *Government of Canada* <https://www.aadnc-aandc.gc.ca/DAM/DAM-INTER-HQ/STAGING/texte-text/ccl_fagr_nwts_tliagr_tliagr_1302089608774_eng.pdf>.

61 2015 NWTSC 9.

62 David V Wright, "Bill C-88 Will Finally Eliminate the MVRMA 'Superboard' ... But Where's the Rest?" (8 January 2019), online (blog): *ABlawg.ca* <https://ablawg.ca/2019/01/08/bill-c-88-will-finally-eliminate-the-mvrma-superboard-but-wheres-the-rest>.

Design and operation of the MVRMA was discussed in *De Beers Canada Inc v Mackenzie Valley Environmental Impact Review Board*,[63] a case in which De Beers Canada Inc (De Beers) was attempting to quash the Board's decision to conduct a full environmental impact review of the proposed Kennady Lake Project (diamond mine). The following excerpt discusses the purposes of the regime and how it works.

DE BEERS CANADA INC V MACKENZIE VALLEY ENVIRONMENTAL IMPACT REVIEW BOARD
2007 NWTSC 24

[18] The *Act* was designed to implement the Gwich'in and Sahtu Land claims agreements by providing an integrated system of water and land management in the MacKenzie [sic] Valley region of the Northwest Territories. *North American Tungsten Corporation Ltd. v. MacKenzie* [sic] *Valley Land and Water Board*, ... [2003 NWTCA 5], at para.14.

[19] Section 9.1 specifically sets out the *Act's* purpose in establishing boards:

> 9.1 The purpose of the establishment of boards by this Act is to enable residents of the MacKenzie [sic] Valley to participate in the management of its resources for the benefit of the residents and of other Canadians.

[20] Section 112 of the *Act* deals with the constitution and quorum of the Review Board. That provision demonstrates a clear intent by Parliament to have the perspective of the Gwich'in First Nation, the Sahtu First Nation and the Tlicho Government represented on the Review Board.

[21] Section 112 is in Part 5 of the *Act*. Part 5 sets out the procedure for assessing the environmental impact of developments in the MacKenzie [sic] Valley and includes the provisions at issue in this case. The purpose of Part 5 is outlined at section 114:

> 114. The purpose of this Part is to establish a process comprising a preliminary screening, an environmental assessment and an environment [sic] impact review in relation to proposals for development [sic], and
>
>> (a) to establish the Review Board as the main instrument in the MacKenzie [sic] Valley for the environmental assessment and environmental impact review of developments;
>>
>> (b) to ensure that the impact on the environment of proposed developments receives careful consideration before actions are taken in connection with them; and
>>
>> (c) to ensure that the concerns of aboriginal people and the general public are taken into account in that process.

[22] This provision suggests that the impact on the environment and public concern are factors of comparable importance in the context of the *Act*. This is reflected in a number of other provisions that also refer to both possible impacts on the environment and public concern, such as section 128.

[23] Section 115 sets out guiding principles to be followed in the process established in Part 5:

---

63 2007 NWTSC 24.

115. The process established by this Part shall be carried out in a timely and expeditious manner and shall have regard to

(a) the protection of the environment from the significant adverse impacts of proposed developments;

(b) the protection of the social, cultural and economic well-being of residents and communities in the MacKenzie [sic] Valley;

(c) the importance of conservation to the well-being and way of life of the aboriginal peoples of Canada ... who use an area of the MacKenzie [sic] Valley.

[24] Section 115.1 directs the Review Board to consider traditional knowledge as well as scientific information in the exercise of its powers.

[25] In my view, certain conclusions flow from these provisions. Parliament intended the Review Board to be the main instrument in the assessment of projects for development in the region. Aboriginal people were intended to have meaningful input in this process. Parliament intended that potential environmental impacts and public concern be important factors for the Review Board in making decisions. Parliament also intended that the preservation of social, cultural and economic well-being of the residents of the region and the importance of conservation to well-being and way of life of aboriginal people be taken into account.

[26] In this context, the Review Board's mandate is to balance many complex and potentially conflicting factors. The specificity of requirements in the Review Board's composition and quorum reflect the unique context of the *Act*'s adoption. There is a clear link between the composition of the Review Board and some of the factors it is mandated to take into account.

• • •

[32] De Beers argues that what the Review Board did in this case was an inadequate and incomplete [environmental assessment] that did not meet the requirements of the *Act*. In support of this position, De Beers relies on Section 117 of the *Act* and on the opening words of section 128. The relevant portions of these provisions read as follows:

117(1) Every environmental assessment of a proposal for development shall include a determination by the Review Board of the scope of the development, subject to any guidelines made under section 120.

(2) Every environmental assessment and environmental impact review of a proposal for a development shall include a consideration of

(a) the impact of the development on the environment, including the impact of malfunctions or accidents that may occur in connection with the development and any cumulative impact that is likely to result from the development in combination with other developments;

(b) the significance of any such impact;

(c) any comments submitted by members of the public in accordance with the regulations or the rules of practice and procedure of the Review Board

(d) where the development is likely to have a significant adverse impact on the environment, the need for mitigative or remedial measures; and

(e) any other matter, such as the need for the development and any available alternatives to it, that the Review Board or any other responsible minister, after consulting with the Review Board, determines to be relevant.

(...)

128(1) On completing an environmental assessment of a proposal for development, the Review Board shall,

(a) where the development is not likely in its opinion to have any significant adverse impact on the environment or to be a cause of significant public concern, determine that an environment [*sic*] impact review of the proposal need not be conducted;

(b) where the development is likely in its opinion to have a significant adverse impact on the environment,

(i) order that an environment [*sic*] impact review of the proposal be conducted, subject to paragraph 130(1)(c), or

(ii) recommend that the approval of the proposal be made subject to the imposition of such measures as it considers necessary to prevent the significant adverse impact;

(c) where the development is likely in its opinion to be a cause of significant public concern, order that an environmental impact review of the proposal be conducted, subject to paragraph 130(1)(c); and

(d) where the development is likely in its opinion to cause an adverse impact on the environment so significant that it cannot be justified, recommend that the proposal be rejected without an environmental impact review.

(...)

(4) The Review Board shall identify in its report any area within or outside the MacKenzie [*sic*] Valley in which the development is likely, in its opinion, to have a significant adverse impact on the environment or to be a cause of significant public concern and specify the extent to which the area is affected.

Ultimately, the court found that the review board's conclusion was not unreasonable, citing Parliament's intent for public concern to be an important factor in decisions about proposed developments.[64]

NOTES AND QUESTIONS

1. How does the MVRMA's conception of environmental assessment differ from environmental assessment (that is, project-level assessment) regimes in the other territories? How does it differ from such regimes in southern Canada? To what extent do you think these differences are justifiable and why?

2. For some discussion of the potentially distinctive nature of northern assessment regimes in light of the participatory and co-management goals of northern land claims agreements, see Sari Graben's "Living in Perfect Harmony: Harmonizing Sub-Arctic Co-Management Through Judicial Review."[65]

3. In 2007, the federal government commissioned "The Review of the Regulatory Systems Across the North." The final report recommended two options for reform in the Mackenzie Valley, one of which was "fundamental restructuring".[66] What changes to this regime do you think would make sense? What challenges and barriers would you expect to arise?

4. In 2016, the Trudeau government pledged to "fully implement" the *United Nations Declaration on the Rights of Indigenous Peoples*.[67] To what extent to you think the existing

---

64 *De Beers, supra* note 63 at paras 66, 67.

65 (2011) 49 Osgoode Hall LJ 199.

66 Neil McCrank, *Road to Improvement* (Ottawa: Indian and Northern Affairs Canada, 2008) at ii, online (pdf): *Government of Canada* <http://publications.gc.ca/collections/collection_2010/ainc-inac/R3-74-2008-eng.pdf>.

67 GA Res 61/295, UNGAOR, 61st Sess, UN Doc A/RES/61/295 (2007), online (pdf): *United Nations* <https://www.un.org/esa/socdev/unpfii/documents/DRIPS_en.pdf>.

project-level assessment regime under the MVRMA is consistent with that commitment? What gaps, friction, or challenges do you think may arise in this context?

V. WILDLIFE AND FISHERIES MANAGEMENT IN NORTHERN CANADA

A. OVERVIEW

Wildlife and fisheries management in northern Canada is largely a function of the terms of modern land claims agreements. These agreements not only establish co-management institutions of public government for wildlife (for example, the Nunavut Wildlife Management Board [NWMB], the Gwich'in Renewable Resources Board, and the Yukon Fish and Wildlife Management Board) but also confirm the wildlife harvesting rights of beneficiaries under the respective land claims agreements.[68] The statement of principles, objectives, and conservation in art 5 (Wildlife) of the NA captures the balance between Inuit rights and the importance of sustainable management of wildlife:

Principles

5.1.2 This Article recognizes and reflects the following principles:

(a) Inuit are traditional and current users of wildlife;

(b) the legal rights of Inuit to harvest wildlife flow from their traditional and current use;

(c) the Inuit population is steadily increasing;

(d) a long-term, healthy, renewable resource economy is both viable and desirable;

(e) there is a need for an effective system of wildlife management that complements Inuit harvesting rights and priorities, and recognizes Inuit systems of wildlife management that contribute to the conservation of wildlife and protection of wildlife habitat;

(f) there is a need for systems of wildlife management and land management that provide optimum protection to the renewable resource economy;

(g) the wildlife management system and the exercise of Inuit harvesting rights are governed by and subject to the principles of conservation;

(h) there is a need for an effective role for Inuit in all aspects of wildlife management, including research; and

(i) Government retains the ultimate responsibility for wildlife management.

Objectives

5.1.3 This Article seeks to achieve the following objectives:

(a) the creation of a system of harvesting rights, priorities and privileges that

(i) reflects the traditional and current levels, patterns and character of Inuit harvesting,

(ii) subject to availability, as determined by the application of the principles of conservation, and taking into account the likely and actual increase in the population of Inuit, confers on Inuit rights to harvest wildlife sufficient to meet their basic needs, as adjusted as circumstances warrant,

(iii) gives DIOs [Designated Inuit Organizations] priority in establishing and operating economic ventures with respect to harvesting, including sports and other commercial ventures,

(iv) provides for harvesting privileges and allows for continued access by persons other than Inuit, particularly long-term residents, and

(v) avoids unnecessary interference in the exercise of the rights, priorities and privileges to harvest;

---

68 For a discussion of the role of the NWMB in academic literature, see Nigel Bankes, "Implementing the Fisheries Provisions of the Nunavut Claim: Re-Capturing the Resource?" (2003) 12 J Envtl L & Prac 141 and S Boudreau & L Fanning, "Nunavut Fisheries Co-management and the Role of the Nunavut Land Claim Agreement in Fisheries Management and Decision Making" (2016) 30 Ocean YB 207.

(b) the creation of a wildlife management system that

(i) is governed by, and implements, principles of conservation,

(ii) fully acknowledges and reflects the primary role of Inuit in wildlife harvesting,

(iii) serves and promotes the long-term economic, social and cultural interests of Inuit harvesters,

(iv) as far as practical, integrates the management of all species of wildlife,

(v) invites public participation and promotes public confidence, particularly amongst Inuit, and

(vi) enables and empowers the NWMB to make wildlife management decisions pertaining thereto.

Conservation

5.1.4 The principles of conservation will be interpreted and applied giving full regard to the principles and objectives outlined in Sections 5.1.2 and 5.1.3 and the rights and obligations set out in this Article.

5.1.5 The principles of conservation are:

(a) the maintenance of the natural balance of ecological systems within the Nunavut Settlement Area;

(b) the protection of wildlife habitat;

(c) the maintenance of vital, healthy, wildlife populations capable of sustaining harvesting needs as defined in this Article; and

(d) the restoration and revitalization of depleted populations of wildlife and wildlife habitat.

The agreement establishes the NWMB (s 5.2.33) as the "main instrument of wildlife management in the Nunavut Settlement Area." Amongst other things, the NWMB has the responsibility to establish total allowable harvest levels for species (s 5.6.16) and must approve the "designation of rare, threatened and endangered species" (s 5.2.34(f)). Board decisions, however, are subject to disallowance by the relevant minister (for example, the federal minister in the case of fisheries and the territorial minister in the case of other forms of wildlife) in recognition of the fact that the agreement recognizes that "Government retains ultimate responsibility for wildlife management" (s 5.2.33). However, according to s 5.3.3, both the board's and the minister's decisions may serve to restrict or limit Inuit harvesting only

to the extent necessary:

(a) to effect a valid conservation purpose;

(b) to give effect to the allocation system outlined in this Article ... ; or

(c) to provide for public health or public safety.

The interrelationship between these provisions was considered by the Nunavut Court of Justice in the following decision.

B. THE INTERACTION BETWEEN LAND CLAIMS AGREEMENT AND TERRITORIAL LAW

KADLAK V NUNAVUT (MINISTER OF SUSTAINABLE DEVELOPMENT)
2001 NUCJ 1

[1] Noah Kadlak lives on Southampton Island in the vastness of Canada's eastern arctic. He is an experienced Inuk hunter, and a beneficiary under the Nunavut Land

Claims Agreement [now known, at the request of Nunavut Tunngavik Inc (NTI, the organization representing Nunavut Inuit) as the *Nunavut Agreement*: see NTI Annual General Meeting, Resolution RSA-16-10-11-Terminology: Use of Terms in Nunavut Agreement (Rankin Inlet, Nunavut: 18-20 October 2016), online (pdf): *Nunavut Tunngavik Inc* <https://www.tunngavik.com/files/2016/11/RSA-16-10-11-Terminology-eng.pdf>]. ...

[2] Mr. Kadlak wishes to hunt a polar bear using the traditional methods and technology of his ancestors. ...

• • •

PROCEDURAL HISTORY:

• • •

[5] In response to Noah Kadlak's application, the NWMB granted Mr. Kadlak permission to carry out the traditional hunt, but made this subject to a number of conditions [including]

• • •

> c) That the person be accompanied by at least one other experienced hunter with a firearm ... ;
> d) That the person first obtain the written endorsement of their HTO [Hunters and Trappers Organization] and the NWMB.

[6] [T]he NWMB forwarded its decision ... to the Minister of Resources, Wildlife and Economic Development of the NWT ... .

[7] ... The NWT Minister advised the NWMB that he was exercising his jurisdiction under Article 5.3.11 of the Nunavut Land Claims Agreement to disallow the Board's decision ... on the basis that the proposed hunt presented an unwarranted risk to public safety [see NA art 5.3.3].

[8] The NWMB then reconsidered its original decision as required by Article 5.3.12. The Board reaffirmed the original decision granting the applicant permission to conduct a traditional hunt. ...

[9] The Minister of Sustainable Development for the new Nunavut Territory responded on October 25th, 1999. He confirmed that he was disallowing the Board's decision to grant permission for a traditional bear hunt on the grounds of public safety. It is this decision by the Minister of Sustainable Development that is now under review in this Court.

THE SOCIAL AND LEGAL CONTEXT OF THE NUNAVUT LAND CLAIMS AGREEMENT:

[10] Before the coming of organized government, the Inuit lived in scattered camps in the remote regions of what is now the new Territory of Nunavut. They survived in this harsh environment through nomadic hunting activities. The Inuit have developed a close symbiotic relationship to the land, and all the creatures of the air, sea and land upon which they have traditionally depended as a people for their survival. The traditions of the hunt are an important focus of Inuit culture. Even today, Inuit language, art, diet and clothing celebrate the hunt and the animals of the hunt. The preservation of Inuit culture remains closely linked to this traditional way of life. The Inuit right to hunt is understandably the central focus of the Nunavut Land Claims Agreement. This is key to their social and cultural identity as a people.

[11] The Inuit right to harvest wildlife is set out in Article 5.6.1 of the Nunavut Land Claims Agreement. This Article provides that:

"... an Inuk shall have the right to harvest up to the full level of his or her economic, social and cultural needs, subject to this Article."

Article 5.1.42 further provides that:

"An Inuk may employ any type, method, or technology to harvest pursuant to the terms of this Article that does not ... conflict with the laws of general application regarding humane killing of wildlife, public safety and firearms control."

• • •

THE APPROPRIATE STANDARD OF JUDICIAL REVIEW:

• • •

[16] ... The decision made by the Minister in this case restricts or limits a constitutionally protected right of harvest that I have found to be the central focus of the Nunavut Land Claims Agreement. The decision under review does not involve a delicate balancing of polycentric rights as in the Turbot case recently before the Federal Court (see *NTI vs. Minister of Fisheries and Oceans* (1997) [*sic*] 1997 CanLII 16940 (FC), 149 DLR (4th) 519). It involves an individual's right of harvest. I find that the individual's right to determine the method of harvest has been directly impacted by the impugned decision. There is a "prima facie infringement of an aboriginal right" within the meaning of the *Sparrow* judgment of the Supreme Court of Canada (1990) 1990 CanLII 104 (SCC), 70 DLR (4th) 385.

[17] I find that the highest level of judicial review, the standard of correctness, is demanded by the facts of this case. Any lesser standard of review would not be adequate to effectively protect the right proclaimed under the Nunavut Land Claims Agreement; a right that is both recognized and affirmed by section 35 of the *Constitution Act*. Any lesser standard of review would potentially undermine and erode the very objective that the Nunavut Land Claims Agreement seeks to protect.

[18] In this case, there is no privative clause to limit Court reviews of Ministerial decisions made under Part 6 that limit or restrict the Inuit right of harvesting. The decision under review does not involve difficult technical issues, or issues involving special expertise or competence. It does involve the application of broad public policy considerations to the proposed exercise by the applicant of his right of harvest. It does involve consideration of the legal meaning to attach to the phrase "public safety" as this is found in Article 5.3.3 of the Nunavut Land Claims Agreement. I find that there is nothing about the issues behind this decision that cannot be closely examined by a reviewing Court on a standard of correctness.

• • •

[20] I infer that a primary objective of the Nunavut Land Claims Agreement is to protect Inuit harvesting rights from unwarranted state interference ... . It is entirely appropriate to ask the Court to intervene when government decisions adversely impact, or infringe upon those rights protected by the Constitution of this country. By conferring constitutional status and priority upon the Inuit right to harvest wildlife, Parliament and this Territory have sanctioned challenges to social and economic policy objectives embodied in legislation to the extent that this right is, has been, or will be affected. This Court finds that it is well equipped to monitor and maintain the delicate balance between the public interest represented by

government and the private interests defined and protected by the Constitution, on the other. Curial deference has very little place in a review involving constitutional issues of this kind.

• • •

THE STANDARD OF CORRECTNESS:

[22] Section 35(1) of the *Constitution Act* does not promise that the rights under the Nunavut Land Claims Agreement will be immune from all forms of government regulation. It does require the Territorial and Federal Crown to justify any decision that impacts adversely upon the promises made and rights conferred in the Nunavut Land Claims Agreement. A decision by government that affects the exercise of a substantive aboriginal right will only be upheld if it meets the test for justifying an interference with a right recognized and affirmed under section 35(1). This test, and the analysis that precedes it, has been outlined by the Supreme Court of Canada in ... *Regina vs. Sparrow* 1990 CanLII 104 (SCC), [1990] 3 CNLR 160; (1990) 70 DLR (4th) 385. The Territorial Crown thus has the burden in this case of justifying a decision that clearly restricts the right of harvest, and the right to determine the means of harvest, conferred upon Inuit by the Nunavut Land Claims Agreement.

• • •

[27] The second stage of the "Sparrow" analysis outlined by the Supreme Court of Canada requires that this Court examine the legislative objective behind the impugned decision. I am satisfied that the decision to restrict the Inuit harvesting right in this case was made pursuant to a "valid" legislative objective within the meaning of the *Sparrow* case. I further find that the decision to prohibit Noah Kadlak from pursuing the bear with a spear falls lawfully within this valid legislative objective of "public safety."

[28] In making this finding, the Court accepts that the broader definition of public safety advanced by the government is correct in law. If this Court adopted the narrow definition advanced by the applicant, then many of the restrictions initially imposed by the NWMB upon Noah Kadlak would also be rendered "invalid." These restrictions appear to have been imposed in an effort to address the risk to the individual hunter pursuing the traditional bear hunt. The provisions of Article 5.3.3 of the Nunavut Land Claims Agreement equally bind the Minister and the NWMB. If the Minister cannot validly restrict hunting activities on the basis of risks assumed by individual hunters, then the NWMB had no basis in law to do so.

[29] While the Court is thus prepared to accord the phrase "public safety" with a broad and expansive definition that would include the assumption of risks by individual hunters, the 2nd stage of the Sparrow type analysis requires that the Minister strictly comply with a "principle" of minimal interference when making his or her decision. Was the Minister's decision to effectively prohibit the traditional hunt the minimum infringement or restriction of the harvesting right possible in order to achieve the desired objective of public safety as I have defined it? Are there reasonable conditions, short of outright prohibition, that could substantially address the Minister's concerns? The principle of minimal interference is to be applied liberally, in accordance with constitutional principles of interpretation, to ensure that the rights recognized and affirmed by section 35 of the *Constitution Act* are not unduly restricted or denied through overzealous government regulation. ...

[30] The "principle" of minimal interference is well entrenched in constitutional litigation ... I find that it is also a "principle" that has been expressly built into the

criteria circumscribing the Minister's decision under Article 5.3.3 of the Nunavut Land Claims Agreement. [This article is quoted above.]

[31] Before any decision is made to prohibit a particular form of harvesting activity, traditional or otherwise, the NWMB or the Minister must first consider whether other reasonable conditions could effectively address the legitimate public safety or public health concerns arising from the activity. It is clear that the NWMB did this when first authorizing the traditional hunt subject to conditions. There is no evidence before me that the Minister has done so.

[32] The outright prohibition of a traditional Inuit harvesting activity is a drastic step. It is a step of last resort. This is so particularly given the principles and objectives of the Nunavut Land Claims Agreement that appear to recognize and accept the validity of traditional harvesting activities, and their continued importance to contemporary Inuit society. For the reasons given earlier, Government must be prepared to have the justification for such a decision closely scrutinized by the Courts. I am not satisfied on the evidence before me that the Minister's decision to disallow the NWMB decision in this case satisfied this principle of minimal interference. I am not satisfied in the circumstances of this case, and on the evidence now before me, that reasonable conditions could not have been crafted to address the Minister's concerns. In the result, the decision of the Minister disallowing the NWMB authorization for a traditional hunt is quashed. It has not met the necessary standard of correctness. The Crown has failed to discharge the burden of justifying the decision under review. This matter is accordingly remitted back to the Minister for his further consideration.

NOTES AND QUESTIONS

1. Kilpatrick J (at para 13) purported to apply "a large, liberal and purposive interpretation so as to best attain the objectives" of the agreement. However, the Supreme Court of Canada has tended to emphasize the importance of text, as already noted in the extract from *Nacho Nyak Dun* (the "Peel Watershed" case), above. How might these seemingly different approaches be reconciled?

2. The Nunavut *Wildlife Act*[69] was adopted in 2003 with the aim of implementing the provisions of the NA. A key element of the legislation is its recognition of the importance of Inuit traditional knowledge (or "Inuit Qaujimajatuqangit"):

Inuit Qaujimajatuqangit
Guiding principles and concepts
8. The following guiding principles and concepts of Inuit Qaujimajatuqangit apply under this Act:

(a) *Pijitsirniq/Ihumaliukti*, which means that a person with the power to make decisions must exercise that power to serve the people to whom he or she is responsible;

(b) *Papattiniq/Munakhinik*, which means the obligation of guardianship or stewardship that a person may owe in relation to something that does not belong to the person;

(c) *Aajiiqatigiingniq/Pitiakatigiiklotik*, which means that people who wish to resolve important matters or any differences of interest must treat each other with respect and

---

69 SNu 2003 c 26.

discuss them in a meaningful way, keeping in mind that just because a person is silent does not necessarily mean he or she agrees;

(d) *Pilimmaksarniq/Ayoikyumikatakhimanik*, which means that skills must be improved and maintained through experience and practice;

(e) *Piliriqatigiingniq/Havakatigiiklutik*, which means that people must work together in harmony to achieve a common purpose;

(f) *Avatimik Kamattiarniq/Amiginik Avatimik*, which means that people are stewards of the environment and must treat all of nature holistically and with respect, because humans, wildlife and habitat are inter-connected and each person's actions and intentions towards everything else have consequences, for good or ill;

(g) *Qanuqtuurunnarniq/Kaujimatukanut*, which means the ability to be creative and flexible and to improvise with whatever is at hand to achieve a purpose or solve a problem;

(h) *Qaujimanilik/Ihumatuyuk*, which means a person who is recognized by the community as having in-depth knowledge of a subject;

(i) *Surattittailimaniq/Hugattittailimanik*, also called *Iksinnaittailimaniq/Ikhinnaittailimanik*, which means that hunters should hunt only what is necessary for their needs and not waste the wildlife they hunt;

(j) *Iliijaqsuittailiniq/Kimaitailinik*, which means that, even though wild animals are harvested for food and other purposes, malice towards them is prohibited;

(k) *Sirliqsaaqtittittailiniq/Naklihaaktitihuiluhi*, which means that hunters should avoid causing wild animals unnecessary suffering when harvesting them;

(l) *Akiraqtuutijariaqanginniq Nirjutiit Pijjutigillugit/Hangiaguikluhi Nekyutit InuupPiutigingitait*, which means that wildlife and habitat are not possessions and so hunters should avoid disputes over the wildlife they harvest or the areas in which they harvest them; and

(m) *Ikpigusuttiarniq Nirjutilimaanik/Pitiaklugit nekyutit*, which means that all wildlife should be treated respectfully.

What are the implications of this provision for the way in which the NWMB goes about its work?

C. THE INTERACTION BETWEEN LAND CLAIMS AGREEMENTS AND FEDERAL LAW

Kadlak deals with the minister's power of disallowance with respect to matters that fall under the jurisdiction of the territorial government, but it is also important to consider the interaction between the provisions of land claims agreements and federal law. This is well illustrated by one of the so-called "turbot cases": *Nunavut Tunngavik Inc v Canada (Minister of Fisheries and Oceans)*.[70] The case involved the allocation of fisheries quotas for turbot in Davis Strait. The substantive question for the court was the extent to which the minister of fisheries and oceans had to take the terms of the NA into account in making the quota allocation. The litigation deals with an area in Davis Strait that lies beyond the Nunavut Land Claims Settlement Area, and, thus, the role of the NWMB is somewhat different from that described in *Kadlak*.

---

70 [1998] 4 FC 405, 1998 CanLII 9080, [1998] FCJ No 1026 (QL) (CA).

NUNAVUT TUNNGAVIK INC V CANADA (MINISTER OF FISHERIES AND OCEANS)
[1998] 4 FC 405, 1998 CanLII 9080, [1998] FCJ No 1026 (QL) (CA)

[The court emphasized the power that the minister ordinarily has under the *Fisheries Act.*]

[13] The Minister possesses absolute discretion under subsection 7(1) of the *Fisheries Act*, R.S.C. 1985, c. F-14, to issue or authorize to be issued leases and licences for fisheries or fishing. The rationale for such discretion is that Canada's fisheries are a common property resource belonging to all the people of Canada and licensing is a tool to manage fisheries which is given to the Minister whose duty it is to manage, conserve and develop that resource in the public interest (see *Comeau's Sea Foods Ltd. v. Canada (Minister of Fisheries and Oceans)*, 1997 CanLII 399 (SCC), [1997] 1 S.C.R. 12, at pages 25-26).

[However, the court went on to note the following:]

[14] The actual exercise of such discretionary power is influenced by numerous fluctuating policy concerns which go beyond the necessary issue of conservation and protection of fish to include cultural, political, scientific, technical and socio-economic considerations or policies (see *Comeau's Sea Foods Ltd.*, *supra*, at 30 ...). Also of relevance to the exercise of such discretion are any international policies that Canada promotes or adheres to as well as any legislative obligation that the Government may have assumed which bears directly on the issue of fishery and fetters either the Minister's discretion itself or the manner in which his discretion is to be exercised.

[15] In our view, the Agreement between the Government and the Nunavut Inuit is one such obligation. The Agreement was implemented legislatively by the *Nunavut Land Claims Agreement Act*, S.C. 1993, c. 29 and subsection 6(1) of the Act, in case of inconsistency or conflict between the Agreement and any federal law, gives paramountcy to the Agreement to the extent of the inconsistency or conflict (see also, to the same effect, Section 2.2.3 of the Agreement).

[The particular provision at issue was s 15.3.7 of the agreement, which provides:

15.3.7 Government recognizes the importance of the principles of adjacency and economic dependence of communities in the Nunavut Settlement Area on marine resources, and shall give special consideration to these factors when allocating commercial fishing licences within Zones I and II. Adjacency means adjacent to or within a reasonable geographic distance of the zone in question. The principles will be applied in such a way as to promote a fair distribution of licences between the residents of the Nunavut Settlement Area and the other residents of Canada and in a manner consistent with Canada's interjurisdictional obligations.

The court then turned to examine the record to assess whether the minister had discharged his responsibilities under the agreement, and concluded that the evidence did not support that conclusion.]

[57] First, the Nunavut Inuit who, in their December 4, 1996 letter to the Minister already requested additional quotas from the usual 5 500t [5,500 metric tonnes] Canadian share of the TAC [total allowable catch] on the basis of these principles in Section 15.3.7 of the Agreement, were given only 100t out of the 1 100t increase of the share of the TAC. This means that the Nunavut Inuit obtained only 9% of Canada's unilateral increase of its share of the TAC. At the same time, Labrador Inuit who are

not adjacent to Zone I and Nunavik Inuit received 36% of the increase (400t). Finally, Newfoundland fishermen who also are not adjacent to Zone I were allocated 55% (600t) of the quotas (see the memorandum of the Deputy Minister to the Minister pointing out that Sub-area 0 in which Zone I is located is not adjacent to Newfoundland and Labrador ... . In terms of individual increases, the percentages were as follows: Nunavut: 7%; Nunavik and Labrador Inuit: 108%; Newfoundland: 40% (see the Atlantic Groundfish Management Plan 1996, Vol. I, Appeal Book, at page 86).

[58] Second, as a result of the Minister's decision, the Nunavut Inuit share of the TAC was reduced from 27% to 24%.

[59] Third, while the Nunavut Inuit share of the TAC was reduced, the share of the competitive fishery increased from 27% to 32%. The fishermen in that category of licensees do not satisfy the definition of adjacency since they are primarily from Newfoundland and, therefore, not within a reasonable geographic distance from Zone I.

[60] Fourth, the Minister knew both of the demands of the Nunavut Inuit for additional quotas based on the adjacency and economic dependence principles, and the fact that the Nunavut Inuit considered their actual share of the TAC to be an absolute minimum ... . Yet, notwithstanding a 20% increase by Canada of its share of the TAC which is 10% of the overall TAC, he allocated to them only a slight portion of the increase which had the effect of reducing their share of that overall TAC.

[61] Fifth, the Minister was informed by his Deputy Minister that the increase of 100t out of the 1 100t increase to the Nunavut Inuit, who are the most adjacent to the resource, was open to criticism especially when compared to the increased access (400t) by Labrador and Northern Quebec Inuit ... .

[62] Finally, in a memorandum to the Minister dated March 4, 1997, the Deputy Minister recommended an allocation to the Nunavut Inuit of 300t from the 1 100t increase in Canada's quota ...

[63] There is no doubt that the allocation of fishing quotas is a daunting task for the Minister and requires a balancing of competing interests. As our colleague Décary J.A. said in the *Carpenter Fishing Corp.* case [*Carpenter Fishing Corp v Canada*, [1998] 2 FC 548 (CA)] ... at page 565:

> Quotas invariably and inescapably carry with them some element of arbitrariness and unfairness. Some fishermen may win, others may lose, some may win or lose more than others, most if not all will find themselves with less catches than before.

[64] However, in the present case, what was involved was not a reduction but rather an increase of the fishing quotas whose allocation was subject to some specific provisions of the Agreement which constrained the exercise of the Minister's discretion. The Minister may have had good and valid reasons to come to the conclusion that he did. We do not know and we cannot guess. But in the absence of explanations or reasons for coming to that conclusion which would indicate not whether the decision was right or wrong, but whether the decision was lawful ... we are left with the curious result and the surrounding circumstances of the exercise of his discretion which, in our view, lead to a reasonable inference that the Minister either did not give special consideration to the adjacency and economic dependence principles as required by the Agreement or misconstrued these principles when allocating commercial fishing licences within Zone I.

• • •

[71] ... Therefore, the order of the motions judge should be varied to read:

> I set aside the Minister's decision of April 7, 1997 as being contrary to law, and refer the matter to the present Minister for reconsideration.

QUESTION

1. Can you think of other examples in which a broad discretionary power in a statute will now have to be interpreted in light of disciplines imposed in a land claims agreement?

VI. INTERNATIONAL DIMENSIONS OF WILDLIFE MANAGEMENT AND HARVESTING RIGHTS

There is frequently an international dimension to the conservation and management of wildlife resources if populations of wildlife such as polar bears or caribou are shared between different jurisdictions.

A. POLAR BEARS

The *Agreement on the Conservation of Polar Bears* was signed by all five of the polar bear range states (Canada, Russia, United States, Norway, and Denmark (in respect of Greenland)) and provides in part as follows:

> ### AGREEMENT ON THE CONSERVATION OF POLAR BEARS
> (15 November 1973), online: *Polar Bear Range States* <https://polarbearagreement.org/resources?task=document.viewdoc&id=1>
>
> Recognizing the special responsibilities and special interests of the States of the Arctic Region in relation to the protection of the fauna and flora of the Arctic Region;
> Recognizing that the polar bear is a significant resource of the Arctic Region which requires additional protection;
> Having decided that such protection should be achieved through co-ordinated national measures taken by the States of the Arctic Region;
> Desiring to take immediate action to bring further conservation and management measures into effect;
> Having agreed as follows:
>
> Article I
>
> 1. The taking of polar bears shall be prohibited except as provided in Article III.
> 2. For the purposes of this Agreement, the term "taking" includes hunting, killing and capturing.
>
> Article II
>
> Each Contracting Party shall take appropriate action to protect the ecosystems of which polar bears are a part, with special attention to habitat components such as denning and feeding sites and migration patterns, and shall manage polar bear populations in accordance with sound conservation practices based on the best available scientific data.
>
> Article III
>
> 1. Subject to the provisions of Articles II and IV any Contracting Party may allow the taking of polar bears when such taking is carried out:
>   a) for bona fide scientific purposes; or

b) by that Party for conservation purposes; or

c) to prevent serious disturbance of the management of other living resources, subject to forfeiture to that Party of the skins and other items of value resulting from such taking; or

d) by local people using traditional methods in the exercise of their traditional rights and in accordance with the laws of that Party; or

e) wherever polar bears have or might have been subject to taking by traditional means by its nationals.

2. The skins and other items of value resulting from taking under sub-paragraph (b) and (c) of paragraph 1 of this Article shall not be available for commercial purposes.

• • •

Article V

A Contracting Party shall prohibit the exportation from, the importation and delivery into, and traffic within, its territory of polar bears or any part or product thereof taken in violation of this Agreement.

Article VI

1. Each Contracting Party shall enact and enforce such legislation and other measures as may be necessary for the purpose of giving effect to this Agreement.

2. Nothing in this Agreement shall prevent a Contracting Party from maintaining or amending existing legislation or other measures or establishing new measures on the taking of polar bears so as to provide more stringent controls than those required under the provisions of this Agreement.

Note that there are considered to be 19 subpopulations of polar bears, depicted in Figure 11.2, below.

NOTES AND QUESTION

1. What is the scope of the Indigenous harvesting exception in art III? When Canada ratified the agreement, it included an interpretive declaration in which it declared its understanding that a traditional hunt could continue onshore and offshore and that the traditional hunt also allowed a community to sell a quota entitlement to a non-resident hunter using a native guide and a dog team. The declaration is included in the official Canada Treaty Series version of the agreement: Can TS 1976 No 24 (ratification by Canada 14 December 1974). By this declaration, Canada purported to allow a "trophy harvest" of polar bears where a community wished to allocate a portion of its quota to a foreign hunter in order to reap the economic and cultural benefits associated with continuing to practise a traditional hunt. Trophy hunting is controversial with respect to both polar bears and other charismatic megafauna.[71]

The agreement does not say anything about how the parties should apportion the harvest of polar bears where the same population is harvested by Indigenous communities in different jurisdictions. For three different models for dealing with how to deal with the issue of apportioning a harvest, see the following agreements: (1) the agreement between the Inuvialuit

---

71 For an exploration of some of the issues, see Milton MR Freeman & Lee Foote, eds, *Inuit, Polar Bears, and Sustainable Use: Local, National and International Perspectives* (Edmonton: CCI Press, 2009). And for an exploration of the legal issues, see Nigel Bankes & David S Lee, "The Legal Framework for the Conservation Hunting of Polar Bears in Nunavut" in that volume at 199.

(Canada) and Inupiat (Alaska) for the management of the Southern Beaufort Sea population;[72] (2) the *Memorandum of Understanding between the Government of Canada, the Government of Nunavut, and the Government of Greenland for the Conservation and Management of Polar Bear Populations;*[73] and (3) the *Agreement between the Government of the United States of America and the Government of the Russian Federation on the conservation and management of the Alaska–Chukotka polar bear population.*[74]

FIGURE 11.2   Subpopulations of Polar Bears and Protected Areas

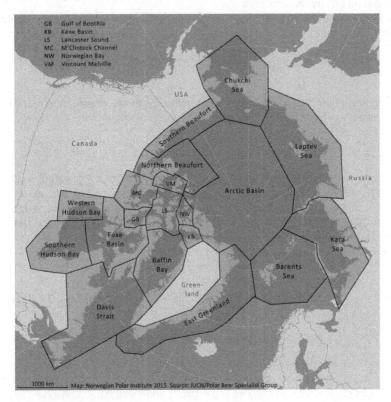

Source: "Maps of Subpopulations of Polar Bears and Protected Areas: Circumpolar Polar Bear Subpopulation and Status Map 2018." © IUCN/Polar Bear Specialist Group (last modified 6 June 2018), online: *Government of Canada* <https://www.canada.ca/en/environment-climate-change/services/biodiversity/maps-sub-populations-polar-bears-protected.html>.

72 *Inuvialuit–Inupiat Polar Bear Management Agreement in the Southern Beaufort Sea* (4 March 2000), online: *IUCN/SCC Polar Bear Specialist Group* <http://pbsg.npolar.no/en/agreements/USA-Canada.html>.

73 A signed text of the 2009 MOU is available online (pdf): *IUCN/SCC Polar Bear Specialist Group* <http://pbsg.npolar.no/export/sites/pbsg/en/docs/GN-MOU-PB.pdf>. The text is undated, but press reports suggest that the text was signed on October 30, 2009: "Canada, Nunavut and Greenland Sign Polar Bear Pact," *Environment News Service*, online: <http://www.ens-newswire.com/ens/oct2009/2009-10-30-01.html>. Note that according to the 2018 "Compendium of Canada's Engagement in International Environmental Agreements and Instruments," the Memorandum of Understanding expired in 2014; another one was expected in early 2019, but did not arrive.

74 (16 October 2000), online: *IUCN/SCC Polar Bear Specialist Group* <http://pbsg.npolar.no/en/agreements/US-Russia.html>. For a recent decision dealing with a shared population of polar bears within Canada see *Makivik Corporation v Canada (Environment and Climate Change)*, 2019 FC 1297. This decision is a judicial review of decisions of two land claim agreement wildlife management boards establishing a total allowable take and non-quota limitations for the harvesting of Southern Hudson Bay (SHB) polar bears.

B. PORCUPINE CARIBOU HERD

Another example of an Arctic species that is of international interest is the Porcupine caribou herd. The herd, which migrates annually between Yukon and Alaska, is the subject of a 1987 agreement between the United States and Canada.

AGREEMENT BETWEEN THE GOVERNMENT OF CANADA AND THE GOVERNMENT OF THE UNITED STATES OF AMERICA ON THE CONSERVATION OF THE PORCUPINE CARIBOU HERD
Can TS 1987 No 31 (entered into force 17 July 1987)

The Government of Canada and the Government of the United States of America, hereinafter called the "Parties":

RECOGNIZING that the Porcupine Caribou Herd regularly migrates across the international boundary between Canada and the United States of America and that caribou in their large free-roaming herds comprise a unique and irreplaceable natural resource of great value which each generation should maintain and make use of so as to conserve them for future generations;

ACKNOWLEDGING that there are various human uses of caribou and that for generations certain people of Yukon Territory and the Northwest Territories in Canada have customarily and traditionally harvested Porcupine Caribou to meet their nutritional, cultural and other essential needs and will continue to do so in the future, and that certain rural residents of the State of Alaska in the United States of America have harvested Porcupine Caribou for customary and traditional uses and will continue to do so in the future; and that these people should participate in the conservation of the Porcupine Caribou Herd and its habitat;

RECOGNIZING the importance of conserving the habitat of the Porcupine Caribou Herd, including such areas as calving, post-calving, migration, wintering and insect relief habitat;

UNDERSTANDING that the conservation of the Porcupine Caribou Herd and its habitat requires goodwill among landowners, wildlife managers, users of the caribou and other users of the area;

RECOGNIZING that the Porcupine Caribou Herd should be conserved according to ecological principles and that actions for the conservation of the Porcupine Caribou Herd that result in the long-term detriment of other indigenous species of wild fauna and flora should be avoided;

RECOGNIZING that the Parties wish to establish co-operative bilateral mechanisms to co-ordinate their activities for the long-term conservation of the Porcupine Caribou Herd and its habitat;

RECOGNIZING that co-operation and co-ordination under this Agreement should not alter domestic authorities regarding management of the Porcupine Caribou Herd and its habitat and should be implemented by existing rather than new management structures;

HAVE AGREED as follows:

1. Definitions

For the purpose of this Agreement only:

a. "Porcupine Caribou Herd" means those migratory barren ground caribou found north of 64°, 30' north latitude and north of the Yukon River which usually share common and traditional calving and post-calving aggregation grounds between the Canning River in the State of Alaska and the Babbage River in Yukon Territory and which historically migrate within the State of Alaska, Yukon Territory, and the Northwest Territories.

b. "Conservation" means the management and use of the Porcupine Caribou Herd and its habitat utilizing methods and procedures which ensure the long-term productivity and usefulness of the Porcupine Caribou Herd. Such methods and procedures include, but are not limited to, activities associated with scientific resources management such as research, law enforcement, census taking, habitat maintenance, monitoring and public information and education.

c. "Habitat" means the whole or any part of the ecosystem, including summer, winter and migration range, used by the Porcupine Caribou Herd during the course of its long-term movement patterns, as generally outlined on the map attached as an Annex.

2. Objectives

The objectives of the Parties are:

a. To conserve the Porcupine Caribou Herd and its habitat through international co-operation and co-ordination so that the risk of irreversible damage or long-term adverse effects as a result of use of caribou or their habitat is minimized;

b. To ensure opportunities for customary and traditional uses of the Porcupine Caribou Herd by:

1. in Alaska, rural Alaska residents in accordance with 16 U.S.C. 3113 and 3114, AS 16.05.940(23), (28) and (32), and AS 16.05.258(c); and

2. in Yukon and the Northwest Territories, Native users as defined by sections A8 and A9 of the Porcupine Caribou Management Agreement (signed on October 26, 1985) and those other users identified pursuant to the process described in section E2(e) of the said Agreement;

c. To enable users of Porcupine Caribou to participate in the international co-ordination of the conservation of the Porcupine Caribou Herd and its habitat;

d. To encourage co-operation and communication among governments, users of Porcupine Caribou and others to achieve these objectives.

3. Conservation

a. The Parties will take appropriate action to conserve the Porcupine Caribou Herd and its habitat.

b. The Parties will ensure that the Porcupine Caribou Herd, its habitat and the interests of users of Porcupine Caribou are given effective consideration in evaluating proposed activities within the range of the Herd.

c. Activities requiring a Party's approval having a potential impact on the conservation of the Porcupine Caribou Herd or its habitat will be subject to impact assessment and review consistent with domestic laws, regulations and processes.

d. Where an activity in one country is determined to be likely to cause significant long-term adverse impact on the Porcupine Caribou Herd or its habitat, the other Party will be notified and given an opportunity to consult prior to final decision.

e. Activities requiring a Party's approval having a potential significant impact on the conservation or use of the Porcupine Caribou Herd or its habitat may require mitigation.

f. The Parties should avoid or minimize activities that would significantly disrupt migration or other important behavior patterns of the Porcupine Caribou Herd or that would otherwise lessen the ability of users of Porcupine Caribou to use the Herd.

g. When evaluating the environmental consequences of a proposed activity, the Parties will consider and analyze potential impacts, including cumulative impacts, to the Porcupine Caribou Herd, its habitat and affected users of Porcupine Caribou.

h. The Parties will prohibit the commercial sale of meat from the Porcupine Caribou Herd.

4. International Porcupine Caribou Board

a. The Parties will establish an advisory board to be known as the International Porcupine Caribou Board, hereinafter called the Board.

b. The Parties will each appoint four members of the Board within a reasonable period following the entry into force of the present Agreement.

c. The Board will:

1. adopt rules and procedures for its operation, including those related to the chairmanship of the Board; and

2. give advice or make recommendations to the Parties, subject to concurrence by a majority of each Party's appointees.

d. The Board, seeking, where appropriate, information available from management agencies, local communities, users of Porcupine Caribou, scientific and other interests, will make recommendations and provide advice on those aspects of the conservation of the Porcupine Caribou Herd and its habitat that require international co-ordination, including but not limited to the following:

1. the sharing of information and consideration of actions to further the objectives of this Agreement at the international level;

2. the actions that are necessary or advisable to conserve the Porcupine Caribou Herd and its habitat;

3. co-operative conservation planning for the Porcupine Caribou Herd throughout its range;

4. when advisable to conserve the Porcupine Caribou Herd, recommendations on overall harvest and appropriate harvest limits for each of Canada and the United States of America taking into account the Board's review of available data, patterns of customary and traditional uses and other factors the Board deems appropriate;

5. the identification of sensitive habitat deserving special consideration; and

6. recommendations, where necessary, through the Parties as required, to other boards and agencies in Canada and the United States of America on matters affecting the Porcupine Caribou Herd or its habitat.

e. It is understood that the advice and recommendations of the Board are not binding on the Parties; however, by virtue of this Agreement, it has been accepted that the Parties will support and participate in the operation of the Board. In particular they will:

1. provide the Board with information regarding the conservation and use of the Porcupine Caribou Herd and its habitat;

2. promptly notify the Board of proposed activities that could significantly affect the conservation of the Porcupine Caribou Herd or its habitat and provide an opportunity to the Board to make recommendations;

3. consider the advice and respond to the recommendations of the Board; and

4. provide written reasons for the rejection in whole or in part of conservation recommendations made by the Board.

5. International Responsibility

The Parties will consult promptly to consider appropriate action in the event of:

a. significant damage to the Porcupine Caribou Herd or its habitat for which there is responsibility, if any, under international law; or

b. significant disruption of migration or other important behavior patterns of the Porcupine Caribou Herd that would significantly lessen the ability of users of Porcupine Caribou to use the Herd.

6. Implementation

Co-operation and co-ordination under and other implementation of this Agreement shall be consistent with the laws, regulations and other national policies of the Parties and is subject to the availability of funding.

7. Interpretation and Application

All questions related to the interpretation or application of the Agreement will be settled by consultation between the Parties.

8. Entry into force—Amendments

a. This Agreement which is authentic in English and French shall enter into force on signature and shall remain in force until terminated by either Party upon twelve months written notice to the other.

b. At the request of either Party, consultations will be held with a view to convening a meeting of the representatives of the Parties to amend this Agreement.

The map in Figure 11.3, below, illustrates the annual range of the herd as well as protected areas on both sides of the border, including the Arctic National Wildlife Refuge (ANWR) in the US and Vuntut and Ivvavik National Parks in Canada.

FIGURE 11.3   Porcupine Caribou Range and Protected Areas

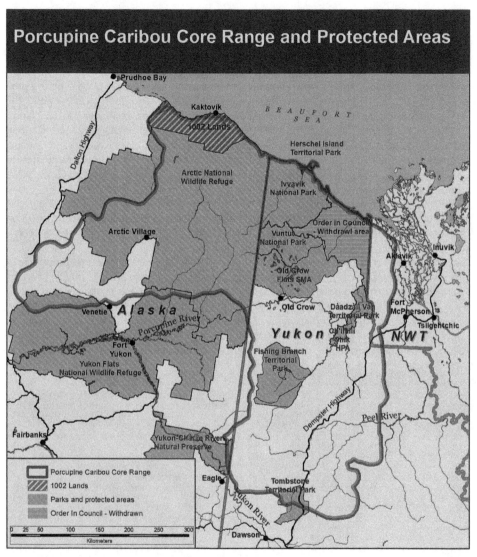

Source: Published by permission of the Porcupine Caribou Management Board, online: *Porcupine Caribou Management Board* <https://www.pcmb.ca>.

NOTES AND QUESTIONS

There is one area within ANWR that has an uncertain legal status. This is the area known as the "1002 lands," which is shown on the map and named after s 1002 of the federal *Alaska National Interest Lands Conservation Act* of 1980.[75] This section contemplated that the coastal plain area should be assessed for both its oil and gas potential as well as its wildlife values. The subsequent environmental assessment report ultimately concluded (in 1987) that the entire area of the 1002 lands should be made available for oil and gas activities. However, the proposed Act to authorize leasing was subsequently dropped by Congress. More recently, the Trump Administration is once again actively considering oil and gas leasing for the 1002 lands.

The coastal plain in Alaska constitutes the key calving ground of the Porcupine Caribou Herd, and the herd is a key resource for Indigenous communities in both Alaska and Canada, but more particularly in Canada. About 85 percent of the herd is taken by communities in Canada, including Aklavik, Inuvik, Tuktoyaktuk, Fort McPherson, Tsiigehtchic, Old Crow, Dawson City, and Mayo.

1. Consider how you might use the terms of the agreement to argue against oil and gas leasing of these lands. Your argument might be made on behalf of Canada, on behalf of Yukon or the Northwest Territories, or on behalf of any of the user communities listed above. Would your argument differ depending on your client, and, if so, how?[76]

2. Can you also use the *Agreement on the Conservation of Polar Bears* to support your argument? As noted above, there is one subpopulation of polar bears (the Southern Beaufort Population) that is shared between Inupiat (Alaska) and Inuvialuit (Canada) harvesters.

In addition to the international agreement, there is also a domestic agreement between Canada, Yukon, Northwest Territories, and Indigenous user groups.[77] The PCMA is explicitly contemplated in the relevant land claims agreements, and each provides that the PCMA prevails over the land claims agreement in the event of a conflict.[78]

---

75   94 Stat 2371.

76   If you would like to compare your response with that of the submissions filed with the Bureau of Land Management, see "Submission of The Inuvialuit Game Council (IGC), Wildlife Management Advisory Council (North Slope) (WMAC(NS)), Wildlife Management Advisory Council (Northwest Territories) (WMAC(NWT)), and Fisheries Joint Management Committee (FJMC)" (March 2019), online (pdf): *Porcupine Caribou Management Board* <https://www.pcmb.ca/PDF/EIS/IGC-WMAC(NS)-WMAC(NWT)-FJMC%20submission%20to%20BLM%20March%2012%202019.pdf>.

77   *Porcupine Caribou Management Agreement* (26 October 1985), online (pdf): *Porcupine Caribou Management Board* <http://www.pcmb.ca/PDF/general/Board-Operations/Canada%20Porcupine%20Caribou%20Management%20Agreement.pdf> [PCMA].

78   UFA, 16.3.11, GCLCA, 12.6.4.

CHAPTER TWELVE

INDIGENOUS PEOPLES' JURISDICTION OVER THE ENVIRONMENT

Heather Fast and Brenda L Gunn

I. INTRODUCTION

In Canada, discussions of legal jurisdiction over the environment usually focus on the division of legal authority between the federal government, the provincial and territorial governments, and the courts as set out in the *Constitution Act, 1867*.[1] However, with respect to management and protection of the environment, jurisdiction is shared not only between the federal and provincial government but also with Indigenous peoples. Indigenous peoples' jurisdiction is inherent, stemming from their own legal systems. As increasingly recognized by the Canadian

---

1   (UK), 30 & 31 Vict, c 3.

courts, Indigenous peoples have specific rights and jurisdiction due to the fact that they lived in organized societies that pre-date European arrival.[2]

This chapter focuses on the jurisdiction of Indigenous peoples over the environment, including jurisdiction over natural resources and environmental protection as recognized under s 35(1) of the *Constitution Act, 1982*.[3] The goal is to provide background on Indigenous peoples' jurisdiction and current issues so they can be better incorporated into environmental decision-making in Canada. According to s 35(2), "Aboriginal peoples" includes First Nations, Métis, and Inuit peoples, with a diverse range of cultural practices and languages. (A note about terminology in this chapter: we have used "Indigenous" generally and "Aboriginal" when the specific context requires it [e.g., in the context of the Constitution or in quoted material].)

The constitutional recognition of Aboriginal rights in s 35 and the adjudication of these rights have provided some clarification and confirmation of Indigenous peoples' jurisdiction and role in environmental regulation. This chapter focuses on court decisions and the implications such decisions have had for Indigenous peoples' access to and control of natural resources and the environment in Canada today. There will also be a discussion of other legal developments and their impact on Indigenous peoples' jurisdiction, such as self-government agreements and the *United Nations Declaration on the Rights of Indigenous Peoples*.[4]

A. INDIGENOUS PEOPLES' CONNECTION TO TRADITIONAL LANDS

The following excerpt from the 2010 report of the Inter-American Commission of Human Rights, *Indigenous and Tribal Peoples' Rights over Their Ancestral Lands and Natural Resources: Norms and Jurisprudence of the Inter-American Human Rights System*,[5] provides an example of the recognition that has long been given to the rights of Indigenous peoples within international law. This excerpt is provided to help explain why Indigenous peoples continue to push for greater recognition of the role of Indigenous governments in the management of natural resources:

> 1. Indigenous and tribal peoples have unique ways of life, and their worldview is based on their close relationship with land. The lands they traditionally use and occupy are critical to their physical, cultural and spiritual vitality. This unique relationship to traditional territory may be expressed in different ways, depending on the particular indigenous people involved and its specific circumstances; it may include traditional use or presence, maintenance of sacred or ceremonial sites, settlements or sporadic cultivation, seasonal or nomadic gathering, hunting and fishing, the customary use of natural resources or other elements characterizing indigenous or tribal culture. As the Inter-American Court of Human Rights has pointed out, "for indigenous communities, relations to the land are not merely a matter of possession and production but a material and spiritual element which they must fully enjoy, even to preserve their cultural legacy and transmit it to future generations." "[T]o guarantee the right of indigenous peoples to communal property, it is necessary to take into account that the land is closely linked to their oral expressions and traditions, their customs and languages, their arts and rituals, their knowledge and practices in connection with nature, culinary art, customary law, dress, philosophy, and values." ...

---

2   *R v Van der Peet*, [1996] 2 SCR 507, 1996 CanLII 216.

3   Being Schedule B to the *Canada Act 1982* (UK), 1982, c 11.

4   GA Res 61/295, UNGAOR, 61st Sess, UN Doc A/RES/61/295 (2007), online (pdf): *United Nations* <https://undocs.org/A/RES/61/295> [UN Declaration or UNDRIP].

5   OEA/Ser.L/V/II, Doc 56/09 (Washington, DC: Organization of American States, 2010), online (pdf): *Organization of American States* <https://www.oas.org/en/iachr/indigenous/docs/pdf/Ancestral-Lands.pdf>.

2. The ... guarantee of the right to territorial property is a fundamental basis for the development of indigenous communities' culture, spiritual life, integrity and economic survival. It is a right to territory that encompasses the use and enjoyment of its natural resources. It is directly related, even a pre-requisite, to enjoyment of the rights to an existence under conditions of dignity, to food, water, health, life, honor, dignity, freedom of conscience and religion, freedom of association, the rights of the family, and freedom of movement and residence. Throughout the Americas, indigenous and tribal peoples insist that the State "effectively guarantee their right to live in their ancestral territory and thus to not only carry out their traditional subsistence activities, but also preserve their cultural identity."

3. The organs of the Inter-American system have long paid particular attention to indigenous and tribal peoples' right to communal property over their lands and natural resources, as a right in itself, and as a guarantee of the effective enjoyment of other basic rights. For the IACHR, "protection of the right of indigenous peoples to their ancestral territory is an especially important matter, as its enjoyment involves not only protection of an economic [unit] but also protection of the human rights of a collectivity whose economic, social and cultural development is based on its relationship with the land." The Inter-American Court, for its part, has underscored that indigenous peoples' territorial rights concern "the collective right to survival as an organized people, with control over their habitat as a necessary condition for reproduction of their culture, for their own development and to carry out their life aspirations." [Footnotes omitted.]

B. ASSERTION OF COLONIAL JURISDICTION

Long before European settlers first came to the region that is now known as Canada, Indigenous peoples had their own cultural practices, legal systems, and natural resource management practices over these lands and resources. Although discussions of legal jurisdiction in Canada often focus on interpreting the rights and powers recognized in the Canadian Constitution, it is important to recognize that Indigenous governments and the jurisdiction they exercised over lands and resources pre-date colonial and Canadian governments' jurisdiction. The inherent jurisdiction of Indigenous governments is slowly being recognized by Canadian courts. The Supreme Court of Canada recognized that the purpose of s 35 of the *Constitution Act, 1982* is "to extend constitutional protection to the practices, customs and traditions central to the distinctive culture of aboriginal societies prior to contact with Europeans."[6] Indigenous peoples' jurisdiction originates from their occupation of and relationship with their traditional territories prior to contact with Europeans and includes the exercise of jurisdiction and laws over these lands. To understand why there is a need for Indigenous peoples and governments to be better included in environmental decision-making in Canada, it is helpful to understand how Canada has asserted sovereignty and how this affected Indigenous peoples' inherent jurisdiction.

When European settlers and explorers eventually came to the region that is now Canada, they encountered Indigenous peoples and their established legal systems. The colonial government began to assert sovereignty over these lands through the "doctrine of discovery," a legal principle through which colonial powers asserted jurisdiction over the lands they "discovered," regardless of the Indigenous peoples already occupying such lands.

In *Guerin v R*, the Supreme Court explained the doctrine:

The exclusion of all other Europeans, [sic] necessarily gave to the nation making the discovery the sole right of acquiring the soil from the natives, and establishing settlements upon it. ... It was a right which all asserted for themselves, and to the assertion of which, by others, all assented.

---

6   *R v Adams*, [1996] 3 SCR 101, 1996 CanLII 169 at para 33.

Those relations which were to exist between the discoverer and the natives, [sic] were to be regulated by themselves. The rights thus acquired being exclusive, no other power could interpose between them.

In the establishment of these relations, the rights of the original inhabitants were, in no instance, entirely disregarded; but were necessarily, to a considerable extent, impaired. *They were admitted to be the rightful occupants of the soil, with a legal as well as just claim to retain possession of it,* and to use it according to their own discretion; but their rights to complete sovereignty, as independent nations, were necessarily diminished, and their power to dispose of the soil at their own will, to whomsoever they pleased, was denied by the original fundamental principle, that discovery gave exclusive title to those who made it. [Emphasis added by the court.][7]

Colonial governments asserted what they perceived as their sovereign rights over Indigenous peoples' land, in some cases through the negotiation of treaties, in others, through occupation or seizure of such land.[8] Indigenous peoples who had exercised jurisdiction over and relied upon the natural environment for their identity and survival for thousands of years were removed from their traditional lands to make room for increasing numbers of European settlers.[9] These settlers had a different environmental perspective and viewed nature as something to be conquered and developed, leading them to cut down forests, overfish rivers, and plough and fence in land for agricultural purposes.[10] Thus, in most cases, legal and physical control of the traditional territories historically (and presently) occupied by Indigenous peoples was taken away from them. These exploitative natural resource practices of colonial governments and settlers alike fundamentally altered the territories. However, despite the culturally and ecologically destructive practices of the colonial powers, there continued to be some legal recognition of Indigenous peoples' rights to ownership and use of their traditional territories and the natural resources contained within. This legal recognition includes the *Royal Proclamation of 1763*,[11] the *Constitution Act, 1867*, and the *Indian Act, 1876*.[12]

---

7   *Guerin v R*, [1984] 2 SCR 335 at 378, 1984 CanLII 25, quoting *Johnson v M'Intosh*, 21 US (8 Wheat) 543 at 573-74 (1823); *Van der Peet, supra* note 2 at para 36. For a further exploration of this doctrine from an Indigenous perspective, see Tracey Lindberg, "The Doctrine of Discovery in Canada" and "Contemporary Canadian Resonance of an Imperial Doctrine" in Robert J Miller et al, *Discovering Indigenous Lands: The Doctrine of Discovery in the English Colonies* (Oxford: Oxford University Press, 2010) ch 4 and ch 5, respectively; Felix Hoehn, "Back to the Future—Reconciliation and Indigenous Sovereignty After Tsilhqot'in" (2016) 67 UNBLJ 109. As noted by LaForme JA in *Tyendinaga Mohawk Council v Brant*, 2014 ONCA 565 at para 62, "the legal principle that 'discovery' by European nations in colonial times gave rise to the astounding consequences to indigenous peoples ... has come under criticism for its use as a valid legal principle." See also United Nations Permanent Forum on Indigenous Issues, 11th Sess, "The North American Indigenous Peoples' Caucus Statement" (8 May 2012).

8   Truth and Reconciliation Commission of Canada, *Canada's Residential Schools: The History, Part 1: Origins to 1939—The Final Report of the Truth and Reconciliation Commission of Canada*, vol 1 (Montreal & Kingston; London; Chicago: McGill-Queen's University Press, 2015) at 4, 15, online (pdf): *Government of Canada* <http://www.trc.ca/assets/pdf/Volume_1_History_Part_1_English_Web .pdf> [TRC, *Canada's Residential Schools*]; Patrick Wolfe, "Settler Colonialism and the Elimination of the Native" (2006) 8:4 J Genocide Research 387 at 388, 391, 399.

9   CA Bayly, *The Birth of the Modern World, 1780-1914: Global Connections and Comparisons* (Malden, Mass: Blackwell Publishers, 2004) at 439-440.

10 TRC, *Canada's Residential Schools, supra* note 8 at 14; Bayly, *ibid* at 434, 439; Patricia Seed, "Houses, Gardens, and Fences: Signs of English Possession in the New World" in *Ceremonies of Possession in Europe's Conquest of the New World: 1492-1640* (New York: Cambridge University Press, 1995) 16.

11 RSC 1970, Appendix II, No 1.

12 SC 1876, c 18.

While the *Royal Proclamation of 1763* created systems of British governance in areas formerly controlled by France, it also included legal protections for "Indian" (or First Nations) territories and jurisdiction.[13] This was accomplished by prohibiting "European settlement, occupation, or infringement" on First Nations' territories without consent of the First Nations.[14] It further prohibited individual settlers from acquiring First Nations land; only the Crown would be able to acquire First Nations' territories where First Nations consented. The Proclamation also protected First Nations' occupation and use of territories.[15] Although often discussed as a "unilateral declaration of the Crown's will,"[16] the Proclamation was presented to First Nations, and this resulted in the negotiation of the *Treaty of Niagara* in 1764.[17] Together, these developments represent a nation-to-nation agreement that captured promises to respect the sovereignty of First Nations, including jurisdiction over their territories that they had not voluntarily ceded to the Crown.[18]

A second development that recognizes First Nations jurisdiction over lands is s 91(24) of the *Constitution Act, 1867*, which grants the federal government authority over "Indians, and Lands reserved for the Indians."[19] Section 91(24) transferred responsibility for Indigenous peoples from the British to the Canadian government. The federal government was granted sole authority to negotiate treaties with the Indigenous peoples and purchase their land.[20] Implicitly, this recognizes that Indigenous peoples do have jurisdiction over their lands and that the Crown must take some positive step to acquire jurisdiction.

Finally, the *Indian Act, 1876* was enacted to provide a legal framework for the exercise of federal jurisdiction over "Indians" and governance of most aspects of their lives. However, even under the *Indian Act*,[21] there is some limited recognition of jurisdiction, including regulation of band government and membership, taxation, lands and resources, and money management.[22] This Act gave very limited recognition of First Nations' jurisdiction over land and resources, and it imposed new governance requirements on the First Nations occupying reserve lands. The resulting band councils, however, have limited jurisdiction to make decisions about reserve lands. Today, the regime imposed on First Nations by the *Indian Act* has been recognized as "fundamentally ill-suited to their needs and aspirations."[23]

These developments sought to assert British sovereignty over the lands in Canada. They served to legally entrench colonial rule over Indigenous peoples and their lands, often significantly affecting Indigenous peoples' ability to assert jurisdiction over the lands, thus having an impact on their traditional ways of life. The assertion of power over Indigenous peoples has led

---

13 "Pre-Confederation Treaties" (last visited 11 September 2019), online: *Treaty Relations Commission of Manitoba* <http://www.trcm.ca/treaties/pre-confederation-treaties/>.

14 *Ibid.*

15 *Ibid.*

16 John Borrows, "Wampum at Niagara: The Royal Proclamation, Canadian Legal History, and Self-Government" in *Aboriginal and Treaty Rights in Canada: Essays on Law, Equality, and Respect for Difference* (Vancouver: University of British Columbia Press, 1997) 155.

17 *Ibid.*

18 *Ibid* at 169.

19 In *Reference as to Whether the Term "Indians" in Head 24 of Section 91 of the British North America Act 1867 Includes Eskimo Inhabitants of the Province of Quebec*, [1939] SCR 104, 1939 CanLII 22, "Indians" was interpreted to include Inuit peoples, and in *Daniels v Canada (Indian Affairs and Northern Development)*, 2016 SCC 12, "Indians" was interpreted to include Métis peoples.

20 Mary C Hurley, *The Indian Act* (Ottawa: Library of Parliament, 2009) 1 at 1.

21 RSC 1985, c I-5.

22 Hurley, *supra* note 20 at 1.

23 *Ibid.*

to the destruction of traditional lands and the development of environmental governance processes that often do not allow for the meaningful participation of the Indigenous peoples who are often most affected by natural resource development projects. It should be noted, though, that the failure of the Canadian legal system to provide robust recognition and protection of Indigenous peoples' jurisdiction over their traditional territories does not negate Indigenous peoples' inherent jurisdiction. The constitutional recognition of Aboriginal and treaty rights in s 35(1) of the *Constitution Act, 1982* provided better protection of Indigenous peoples' traditional territories and ways of life, and it expanded the recognized scope of Indigenous jurisdiction over natural resources and the environment.

QUESTIONS

1. What are some of the similarities and differences between Indigenous peoples' relationship with their traditional territories and broader Canadian perspectives on the use and management of lands? Can these two relationships be reconciled or better aligned?

2. The report *Truth and Reconciliation Commission of Canada: Calls to Action*[24] urges all levels of government to repudiate the doctrine of discovery. What changes need to be made to environmental law in Canada to repudiate the doctrine of discovery? How would repudiating the doctrine of discovery contribute to better recognition of Indigenous peoples' jurisdiction over the environment?

3. As you read through the next section, think about how the different relationships Indigenous peoples have with land and resources influence the scope of their s 35 rights.

II. CURRENT STATE OF CANADIAN LAW: INDIGENOUS CONTROL AND PROTECTION OF THE ENVIRONMENT

Today, under Canadian law, Indigenous jurisdiction over the environment is largely determined through the interpretation of s 35 of the *Constitution Act, 1982*, which recognizes and affirms Aboriginal and treaty rights. Section 35 did not create new rights but, instead, recognized the inherent legal rights of Indigenous peoples already existing in 1982.[25] The Supreme Court has interpreted the Aboriginal rights protected by s 35 as limited to activities that are an element of a practice, custom, or tradition integral to the distinctive culture of the Indigenous peoples asserting such rights[26] and that have not otherwise been extinguished prior to the enactment of the *Constitution Act, 1982* or by treaty.[27] Protected treaty rights are those established through the historic treaties made prior to 1982 as well as through modern treaties made after this time, such as the land claim settlement agreements.[28] This means that Aboriginal rights vary based on the Indigenous peoples claiming such rights and the historical activities undertaken by those specific people. This section will discuss the current state of the law in relation to Aboriginal rights, with a focus on the decisions of the Supreme Court, and the implications of such rights in relation to use and control of Indigenous traditional territories and the natural resources they contain. This will involve consideration of a range of recognized rights,

---

24 (Winnipeg: Truth and Reconciliation Commission of Canada, 2015), online (pdf): *Truth and Reconciliation Commission of Canada* <http://nctr.ca/assets/reports/Calls_to_Action_English2.pdf>.

25 *Delgamuukw v British Columbia*, [1997] 3 SCR 1010, 1997 CanLII 302 at para 133.

26 *Van der Peet, supra* note 2 at para 46.

27 *Ibid* at paras 125, 126, 133.

28 *Constitution Act, 1982*, s 35(3).

including Aboriginal title and the right to self-government, as well as the justified infringement of such rights, including the duty of consultation and accommodation.

Aboriginal rights "fall along a spectrum with respect to their degree of connection with the land."[29] At one end of the spectrum are the Aboriginal rights deriving from cultural practices, customs, and traditions, and, at the other end of the spectrum, is Aboriginal title, which recognizes a right to the land itself.[30] Depending on the right(s) asserted, there will be different levels of access to and control over the traditional lands and resources recognized in the exercise of that right.[31]

A. ABORIGINAL TITLE

Aboriginal title is a subcategory of Aboriginal rights that recognizes communal Indigenous land rights.[32] Aboriginal title "encompasses the right to exclusive use and occupation of the land held pursuant to that title for a variety of purposes."[33] Thus, Indigenous peoples with recognized Aboriginal title have a higher level of recognized legal control (and broader jurisdiction over the environment) than communities that do not have recognized title. Aboriginal title shares some similarities with Western property rights—for example,

> the right to decide how the land will be used; the right of enjoyment and occupancy of the land; the right to possess the land; the right to the economic benefits of the land; and the right to pro-actively use and manage the land.[34]

Aboriginal title also encompasses mineral rights and may also confer exclusive rights to other natural resources on the land.[35] A titleholding Indigenous community has jurisdiction to engage in a range of activities on the associated land, regardless of whether such activities are recognized as Aboriginal rights on their own.[36]

To establish Aboriginal title, an Indigenous community must be able to show that its ancestral community occupied the land over which title is being claimed prior to the assertion of sovereignty by the Crown sufficiently and exclusively.[37] To meet the sufficient occupation requirement, "the Aboriginal group in question must show that it has historically acted in a way that would communicate to third parties that it held the land for its own purposes."[38] If the Indigenous community relies on its present-day occupation of the land to support its claim of sufficient and exclusive occupation, the community must also establish continuity of occupation since pre-sovereignty times.[39]

Although Aboriginal title recognizes exclusive use and occupation of the land to the titleholding Indigenous community, there are still inherent limits on the way the community can use the respective land.[40] These limits distinguish Aboriginal title from Western property rights.

---

29 *Delgamuukw, supra* note 25 at para 138.

30 *Ibid.*

31 *Adams, supra* note 6 at paras 25-30.

32 *Van der Peet, supra* note 2 at para 33.

33 *Delgamuukw, supra* note 25 at para 117.

34 *Tsilhqot'in Nation v British Columbia,* 2014 SCC 44 at para 73.

35 *Delgamuukw, supra* note 25 at para 122; *Tsilhqot'in, ibid* at para 88.

36 *Delgamuukw, supra* note 25 at para 117.

37 *Ibid* at para 143; *Tsilhqot'in, supra* note 34 at paras 26, 38.

38 *Tsilhqot'in, supra* note 34 at para 38.

39 *Delgamuukw, supra* note 25 at para 143; *Tsilhqot'in, ibid* at paras 26, 45-46.

40 *Delgamuukw, supra* note 25 at paras 124-25, 128.

Aboriginal title lands cannot be used in a way that is "irreconcilable with the nature of the occupation of that land and the relationship that the particular group has had with the land."[41] For example, if an Indigenous community has claimed title on the basis of that land being used by the community for a specific purpose, such as hunting, the land may not be used in a manner that would prevent it from being used for that purpose, for example, strip mining.[42] Aboriginal title is also considered to be a collective title "held not only for the present generation but for all succeeding generations."[43] This means the land cannot be used in a way that would prevent future generations from using and enjoying it.[44] Titleholding communities are also limited in how they can dispose of their lands and the legal interests they hold:[45] Aboriginal title can be alienated only to the federal Crown.[46]

Governments and others seeking to use the land must obtain consent of the Aboriginal titleholders.[47] However, if the Indigenous community does not consent, one may still justify the proposed incursion on the land using the *Sparrow* test,[48] discussed further below. However, justifying an infringement of Aboriginal title is generally more difficult to establish than an infringement of other Aboriginal rights. This is especially true in situations where a third-party interest (for example, timber licences) in Aboriginal title has been granted without the consent of the titleholding community.[49]

B. ABORIGINAL RIGHTS

Although s 35 ensures Aboriginal rights have constitutional protection, it provides little clarity in terms of what constitutes an Aboriginal "right." Thus, it has largely been left to the courts to determine the scope of s 35. As discussed, Aboriginal title is a subcategory of Aboriginal rights. Beyond title, courts have recognized a range of other Aboriginal rights, including fishing, hunting and trapping wildlife, and harvesting natural resources.[50] These other Aboriginal rights recognize specific use of or access to certain geographic areas and natural resources, but they do not recognize jurisdiction over these resources.

In *Van der Peet*, the Supreme Court adopted a two-stage test for establishing an Aboriginal right under s 35(1). The first stage requires identifying the precise nature of the Aboriginal right being claimed;[51] this involves considering "the nature of the action which the applicant is claiming was done pursuant to an aboriginal right, the nature of the governmental regulation, statute or action being impugned, and the practice, custom or tradition being relied upon to establish the right."[52] The second stage of the test requires proving that the activity is an "element of a practice, custom or tradition integral to the distinctive culture of the Aboriginal

---

41 *Ibid* at para 128.

42 *Ibid*.

43 *Tsilhqot'in, supra* note 34 at para 74.

44 *Ibid*.

45 *Delgamuukw, supra* note 25 at para 113; *Tsilhqot'in, ibid*.

46 *Ibid*.

47 *Tsilhqot'in, supra* note 34 at para 76.

48 *R v Sparrow*, [1990] 1 SCR 1075, 1990 CanLII 104, [1990] CarswellBC 105 [*Sparrow* cited to CarswellBC].

49 *Tsilhqot'in, supra* note 34 at para 127.

50 For example, see *Adams, supra* note 6; *R v Côté*, [1996] 3 SCR 139, 1996 CanLII 170; *R v Sappier; R v Gray*, 2006 SCC 54; *R v Powley*, 2003 SCC 43.

51 *Van der Peet, supra* note 2 at para 51.

52 *Ibid* at para 53.

group claiming the right,"[53] proving that the activity was an integral part of the Indigenous society prior to the arrival of Europeans in North America, and proving that there is reasonable continuity between the ancestral practice, custom, or tradition and its modern form.[54] For Métis peoples, the activity must be one exercised "after a particular Métis community arose and before it came under the effective control of European laws and customs."[55]

Aboriginal rights are communal rights and cannot "be exercised by any member of the aboriginal community independently of the aboriginal society [they are] meant to preserve."[56] The recognition of such rights creates a legal connection between an Indigenous community and the wildlife, natural resources, and traditional territory involved. However, there are limitations on the exercise of such rights and the Indigenous community's ability to control or protect the associated resources and land. Aboriginal rights have been identified by the courts as *sui generis*, meaning they are unique and distinct from other legally recognized rights.[57] They have been distinguished from Western property rights and cannot be characterized as a right to a particular resource.[58] Instead, the jurisdiction over natural resources afforded to Indigenous communities on the basis of Aboriginal rights is generally limited to the undertaking of certain activities and does not include legal control of the resource involved. The exercise of Aboriginal rights is also generally site specific and restricted to a particular geographic area. Such geographic limitation is typical for Aboriginal rights that involve harvesting a specific resource such as fish, game, or trees.[59] However, Aboriginal rights to undertake an activity in a particular area do not require the recognition of Aboriginal title.[60] Thus, even when an Indigenous community is not found to have a legal interest in the land that encompasses a geographic region, they may still have legal rights to access specific resources in that area.

Aboriginal rights can also be limited by valid federal and provincial laws if such limitation can be justified. To determine when a justified infringement has occurred, the Supreme Court established a test in *R v Sparrow*.[61] The court emphasized that the test must be applied on a case-by-case basis, with consideration of the specific factual context.[62] First, it must be shown whether the government has infringed the rights (this could include demonstrating that the limitation of the Aboriginal right by the law is unreasonable), whether the law imposes undue hardship, or whether the law denies the rights holders their preferred means of exercising that right.[63] If there is a *prima facie* infringement, the court must then consider whether the infringement was justified.[64] To justifiably infringe an Aboriginal right, the law must serve an objective that is "compelling and substantial,"[65] such as conservation and resource management;[66] public safety;[67] "development of agriculture, forestry, mining, and hydroelec-

---

53 *Ibid* at para 46.

54 *Ibid* at paras 60-65.

55 *Powley, supra* note 50 at para 37.

56 *Sappier, supra* note 50 at para 26.

57 *Sparrow, supra* note 48 at para 68.

58 *Sappier, supra* note 50 at para 21; *Sparrow, ibid.*

59 *Adams, supra* note 6 at para 30; *Côté, supra* note 50 at para 39.

60 *Côté, supra* note 50 at para 38.

61 *Supra* note 48.

62 *Ibid* at para 66; *Delgamuukw, supra* note 25 at paras 165, 201.

63 *Sparrow, supra* note 48 at para 70.

64 *Ibid* at para 71.

65 *Ibid.*

66 *Ibid* at paras 72, 73; *Adams, supra* note 6 at para 57; *Delgamuukw, supra* note 25 at para 165.

67 *Sparrow, supra* note 48 at para 71; *R v Badger,* [1996] 1 SCR 771, 1996 CanLII 236 at para 89.

tric power";[68] general economic development;[69] and building infrastructure.[70] If a valid legislative objective is found, the court must then consider whether the infringement is consistent with the honour of the Crown and the special relationship that exists between Indigenous peoples and the Crown.[71] This part of the justification test involves considering how the Aboriginal right was prioritized, the extent of the infringement (minimal impairment), whether there was adequate consultation with the affected Indigenous community, and if fair compensation was awarded.[72]

The tests to prove Aboriginal rights and the government's ability to justify infringements have long been subject to criticism. For further discussion, see the following articles:

- Gordon Christie, "Aboriginal Rights, Aboriginal Culture, and Protection" (1998) 36:3 Osgoode Hall LJ 447.
- John Borrows, "Frozen Rights in Canada: Constitutional Interpretation and the Trickster" (1997) 22:1 Am Indian L Rev 37.
- John Borrows, "Sovereignty's Alchemy: An Analysis of Delgamuukw v British Columbia" (1999) 37:3 Osgoode Hall LJ 537.
- Senwung Luk, "Justified Infringement—A Minimal Impairment Approach" (2013) 25 J Envtl L & Prac 169.

NOTES

In setting out the test for Aboriginal rights, the Supreme Court has indicated that rights must be allowed to evolve to avoid a "frozen rights" approach. In *Sappier*, the Supreme Court discussed the idea of ensuring that rights can continue to evolve, explaining, "The right to harvest wood for the construction of temporary shelters must be allowed to evolve into a right to harvest wood by modern means to be used in the construction of a modern dwelling."[73] However, in *Lax Kw'alaams Indian Band v Canada (Attorney General)*,[74] the court took a very limited approach to understanding the evolution of rights:

[49] If established, an Aboriginal right is not frozen at contact, but is subject to evolution both in terms of the subject matter and the method of its exercise, depending on the facts.

• • •

[51] However, when it comes to "evolving" the subject matter of the Aboriginal right, the situation is more complex. A "gathering right" to berries based on pre-contact times would not, for example, "evolve" into a right to "gather" natural gas within the traditional territory. The surface gathering of copper from the Coppermine River in the Northwest Territories in pre-contact times would not, I think, support an "Aboriginal right" to exploit deep shaft diamond mining in the same territory. While courts have recognized that Aboriginal rights must be allowed to evolve within limits, such limits are both quantitative and qualitative. A "pre-sovereignty aboriginal practice cannot be transformed into a different modern right" (*Marshall (2005)* [*R v Marshall; R v Bernard*, 2005 SCC 43, [2005] 2 SCR 220], at para 50).

• • •

---

68 *Delgamuukw, supra* note 25 at para 165.

69 *Ibid.*

70 *Ibid.*

71 *Sparrow, supra* note 48 at para 75; *Delgamuukw, ibid* at para 162.

72 *Sparrow, supra* note 48 at paras 76, 82.

73 *Sappier, supra* note 50 at para 48.

74 2011 SCC 56, [2011] 3 SCR 535.

[55] Counsel for the Lax Kw'alaams argues that, even if pre-contact trade had been limited to eulachon grease (which they deny), the modern right should not be "frozen" but should be generalized and "evolved" to include all other fish species and fish products.

[56] However, such an "evolution" would run counter to the trial judge's clear finding that the ancestors of the Lax Kw'alaams fished all species but did not trade in any significant way in species of fish or fish products other than eulachon. Extension of a modern right to all species would directly contradict her view that only the "species-specific" trade in eulachon grease was integral to the distinctive culture of the pre-contact society. A general commercial fishery would represent an outcome qualitatively different from the pre-contact activity on which it would ostensibly be based, and out of all proportion to its original importance to the pre-contact Tsimshian economy.

In *Côté*, the Supreme Court explained the idea of site specificity of right: "an aboriginal right will frequently be limited to a specific territory or location, depending on the actual pattern of exercise of such an activity prior to contact. As such, an aboriginal right will often be defined in site-specific terms, with the result that it can only be exercised upon a specific tract of land."[75] The court continued to explain that Aboriginal rights include incidental activities: "to ensure the continuity of aboriginal practices, customs and traditions, a substantive aboriginal right will normally include the incidental right to teach such a practice, custom and tradition to a younger generation."[76]

Ensuring priority in allocating the resource is one factor to consider in justifying infringements. The idea of priority was explained in *R v Gladstone*:

the doctrine of priority requires that the government demonstrate that, in allocating the resource, it has taken account of the existence of aboriginal rights and allocated the resource in a manner respectful of the fact that those rights have priority over the exploitation of the fishery by other users.[77]

C. MÉTIS RIGHTS

Métis peoples also have constitutionally protected rights under s 35(1) of the *Constitution Act, 1982*. The Supreme Court recognized that Métis people have a unique and distinct heritage and culture, as indicated by the following excerpt from *Powley*:

10 The term "Métis" in s. 35 does not encompass all individuals with mixed Indian and European heritage; rather, it refers to distinctive peoples who, in addition to their mixed ancestry, developed their own customs, way of life, and recognizable group identity separate from their Indian or Inuit and European forebears. Métis communities evolved and flourished prior to the entrenchment of European control, when the influence of European settlers and political institutions became pre-eminent. The Royal Commission on Aboriginal Peoples describes this evolution as follows:

Intermarriage between First Nations and Inuit women and European fur traders and fishermen produced children, but the birth of new Aboriginal cultures took longer. At first, the children of mixed unions were brought up in the traditions of their mothers or (less often) their fathers. Gradually, however, distinct Métis cultures emerged, combining European and First Nations or Inuit heritages in unique ways. Economics played a major role in this process. The special qualities and skills of the Métis population made them indispensable members of Aboriginal/non-Aboriginal economic partnerships, and that association

---

75 *Côté, supra* note 50 at para 39.

76 *Ibid* at para 56.

77 *R v Gladstone*, [1996] 2 SCR 723, 1996 CanLII 160 at para 62.

contributed to the shaping of their cultures.... As interpreters, diplomats, guides, couriers, freighters, traders and suppliers, the early Métis people contributed massively to European penetration of North America. [Ellipses in original.]

• • •

The Métis developed separate and distinct identities, not reducible to the mere fact of their mixed ancestry: "What distinguishes Métis people from everyone else is that they associate themselves with a culture that is distinctly Métis" ([*Report of the Royal Commission on Aboriginal Peoples: Perspectives and Realities*], vol. 4, at 202).

• • •

12 ... A Métis community can be defined as a group of Métis with a distinctive collective identity, living together in the same geographic area and sharing a common way of life. ... [78]

Three broad factors were identified by the court in *Powley* to assist with determinations of Métis identity for the purposes of claiming Métis rights under s 35. These include self-identification as a member of the Métis community, evidence of an ancestral connection to an historic Métis community, and a demonstrated acceptance by a modern Métis community.[79] The court in the *Powley* decision also modified the *Van der Peet* test, as discussed above, to apply to the establishment of Métis rights and "account for the unique post-contact emergence of Métis communities, and the post-contact foundation of their aboriginal rights."[80]

D. TREATY RIGHTS

In 1701, the British Crown began entering into treaties with Indigenous peoples. Treaties are often divided into different categories: pre-confederation, post-confederation, and modern treaties. Pre-confederation treaties are often considered peace and friendship treaties whereby European settlers and First Nations allied themselves militarily or for trade purposes. These treaties, signed mostly in Eastern Canada with the Mi'kmaq, made no reference to land cession or British assertion of sovereignty. Post-confederation treaties include the Numbered Treaties, that is, Treaties 1-11, which were signed throughout central Canada. Indigenous peoples and Canada continue to disagree on whether these treaties were land cession treaties, since the written text of the treaties generally indicates that the Indigenous peoples agree to "cede, surrender and release" all claims to the lands other than small lands reserved for the exclusive use of Indigenous peoples. However, the Indigenous signatories to the treaties express that the spirit and intent of the treaties were to share the land and the resources, and that they never gave up "ownership and jurisdiction" over the lands. Modern treaties encompass those signed after 1923 and are known as comprehensive land claim settlements and exist in British Columbia and the North.

The terms of such treaties and land claim settlements vary considerably; therefore, the impact of treaty rights on Indigenous jurisdiction over land and resources also varies and is often dependent on court interpretation. The Supreme Court recognized that a "treaty represents an exchange of solemn promises between the Crown and the various Indian nations. It is an agreement whose nature is sacred."[81] Although characterized as such historically, the Supreme Court recognized that treaties are far more than written contracts.[82] As noted in

---

78 *Powley, supra* note 50.

79 *Ibid* at paras 31-33.

80 *Ibid* at para 18.

81 *Badger, supra* note 67 at para 41; *R v Sioui*, [1990] 1 SCR 1025, 1990 CanLII 103, 1990 CarswellQue 103 at para 96 [*Sioui* cited to CarswellQue].

82 *Simon v R*, [1985] 2 SCR 387, 1985 CanLII 11, (*sub nom R v Simon*) 1985 CarswellNS 226 at para 24.

Badger, "treaties, as written documents, recorded an agreement that had already been reached orally and they did not always record the full extent of the oral agreement."[83] Thus, when Canadian courts consider a treaty, the court "must take into account the context in which the treaties were negotiated, concluded and committed to writing."[84] This means that a treaty is not limited to the written text of the treaty but must be interpreted to include the oral promises made during the negotiations.

In terms of legal rights to lands and natural resources, treaty rights vary depending on the agreement from which they originate. For example, many treaties explicitly recognize rights providing for the preservation and protection of traditional hunting, fishing, or trapping activities for subsistence or ceremonial use.[85] In some cases, the Supreme Court interpreted such treaty rights to also include harvesting activities undertaken for commercial purposes.[86] Treaties between the Crown and Indigenous peoples have in many cases resulted in the creation of reserve lands.[87]

Although subject to federal legislation governing reserves (for example, the *Indian Act*), Indigenous interests in reserve lands have been found by the Supreme Court to be fundamentally similar to Aboriginal title.[88] The Supreme Court has also found that Indigenous interest in reserve lands may include subsurface rights to those lands, including the rights to oil and gas deposits underlying those lands.[89] Thus, if an Indigenous community has not ceded the subsurface rights associated with its reserve lands through the signing of a treaty or land claim agreement with the Crown, it ought to play a direct role in the management of oil, gas, and mineral resources on that land. Treaty rights may also entitle Indigenous communities to a share in Crown revenues associated with their traditional territories.[90]

E. DUTY TO CONSULT AND ACCOMMODATE

The Crown's duty to consult was first articulated by the Supreme Court in *Sparrow* and later affirmed in *Delgamuukw* as a factor to consider in justifying infringements of Aboriginal and treaty rights. In 2004 and 2005, the Supreme Court extended the duty to consult and accommodate to Crown decisions that may adversely affect Aboriginal rights where the rights are

---

83 *Badger, supra* note 67 at para 52.

84 *Ibid.*

85 *R v Marshall*, [1999] 3 SCR 456, 1999 CanLII 665; *R v Morris*, 2006 SCC 59, [2006] 2 SCR 915. See also Peace and Friendship Treaties (1725 to 1779); Robinson Treaties (1850); Douglas Treaties (1850-1854); Post-Confederation Numbered Treaties 1-11 (1871-1921).

86 *Marshall, supra* note 85; *R v Horseman*, [1990] 1 SCR 901, 1990 CanLII 96.

87 A "reserve," as defined in s 2 of the *Indian Act*, RSC 1985, c I-5, is "a tract of land, the legal title to which is vested in Her Majesty, that has been set apart by Her Majesty for the use and benefit of a band."

88 *Osoyoos Indian Band v Oliver (Town)*, 2001 SCC 85 at para 41, [2001] 3 SCR 746; *Guerin, supra* note 7 at 379; *Delgamuukw, supra* note 25 at paras 116-21.

89 *Blueberry River Indian Band v Canada (Department of Indian Affairs and Northern Development)*, [1995] 4 SCR 344, 1995 CanLII 50; *Delgamuukw, supra* note 25 at para 122. See also "Aboriginal & Treaty Rights: Subsurface Resources" in *Report of the Aboriginal Justice Inquiry of Manitoba: The Justice System and Aboriginal People*, vol 1 (1999) ch 5, online: *The Aboriginal Justice Implementation Commission* <http://www.ajic.mb.ca/volumel/chapter5.html#36>.

90 See, for example, *Restoule v Canada (Attorney General)*, 2018 ONSC 7701. In this case, the Supreme Court found that the Robinson Treaties provide the Anishinaabe with a constitutionally protected right to share in the Crown revenues from the territory. The court also found that the Crown has a mandatory and reviewable obligation to increase the annuities when the economic circumstances warrant.

asserted but not yet proven.[91] In *Haida Nation*, the Supreme Court confirmed that the duty to consult arises "when the Crown has knowledge, real or constructive, of the potential existence of the aboriginal right or title and contemplates conduct that might adversely affect it."[92] Depending on the Aboriginal rights that have triggered the duty to consult, the Crown may also be required to accommodate the affected Indigenous community.

The Supreme Court identified the duty to consult as a means of protecting Aboriginal and treaty rights and furthering the goals of reconciliation.[93] Although the recognition of the duty to consult and accommodate emerged from the recognition and affirmation of Aboriginal and treaty rights in s 35(1), it is not considered to be an Aboriginal right itself but, instead, is an obligation owed to Indigenous peoples by the Crown and is "a corollary of the Crown's obligation to achieve the just settlement of Aboriginal claims through the treaty process."[94] The duty to consult and accommodate can be seen as recognizing Indigenous peoples' jurisdiction, including Indigenous peoples' legal interests in the land and legal rights to undertake certain resource-related activities, when Indigenous peoples are fully engaged in the decision-making processes.

In *Haida Nation*, the Supreme Court described the scope and content of the duty to consult and accommodate as follows:

> 39 The content of the duty to consult and accommodate varies with the circumstances. Precisely what duties arise in different situations will be defined as the case law in this emerging area develops. In general terms, however, it may be asserted that the scope of the duty is proportionate to a preliminary assessment of the strength of the case supporting the existence of the right or title, and to the seriousness of the potentially adverse effect upon the right or title claimed.
>
> • • •
>
> 43 ... In this respect, the concept of a spectrum may be helpful, not to suggest watertight legal compartments but rather to indicate what the honour of the Crown may require in particular circumstances. At one end of the spectrum lie cases where the claim to title is weak, the Aboriginal right limited, or the potential for infringement minor. In such cases, the only duty on the Crown may be to give notice, disclose information, and discuss any issues raised in response to the notice. ...
>
> 44 At the other end of the spectrum lie cases where a strong *prima facie* case for the claim is established, the right and potential infringement is of high significance to the Aboriginal peoples, and the risk of non-compensable damage is high. In such cases deep consultation, aimed at finding a satisfactory interim solution, may be required. While precise requirements will vary with the circumstances, the consultation required at this stage may entail the opportunity to make submissions for consideration, formal participation in the decision-making process, and provision of written reasons to show that Aboriginal concerns were considered and to reveal the impact they had on the decision. This list is neither exhaustive, nor mandatory for every case. The government may wish to adopt dispute resolution procedures like mediation or administrative regimes with impartial decision-makers in complex or difficult cases.
>
> 45 Between these two extremes of the spectrum just described, [sic] will lie other situations. Every case must be approached individually. Each must also be approached flexibly,

---

91 *Haida Nation v British Columbia (Minister of Forests)*, 2004 SCC 73, [2004] 3 SCR 511; *Taku River Tlingit First Nation v British Columbia (Project Assessment Director)*, 2004 SCC 74, [2004] 3 SCR 550; *Mikisew Cree First Nation v Canada (Minister of Canadian Heritage)*, 2005 SCC 69, [2005] 3 SCR 388.

92 *Haida Nation*, *supra* note 91 at para 35.

93 *Rio Tinto Alcan Inc v Carrier Sekani Tribal Council*, 2010 SCC 43 at para 34, [2010] 2 SCR 650.

94 *Ibid* at para 32.

since the level of consultation required may change as the process goes on and new information comes to light. The controlling question in all situations is what is required to maintain the honour of the Crown and to effect reconciliation between the Crown and the Aboriginal peoples with respect to the interests at stake. Pending settlement, the Crown is bound by its honour to balance societal and Aboriginal interests in making decisions that may affect Aboriginal claims. The Crown may be required to make decisions in the face of disagreement as to the adequacy of its response to Aboriginal concerns. Balance and compromise will then be necessary.[95]

The duty to accommodate arises when the consultation process suggests that an amendment of Crown policy may be required: "Where a strong *prima facie* case exists for the claim, and the consequences of the government's proposed decision may adversely affect it in a significant way, addressing the Aboriginal concerns may require taking steps to avoid irreparable harm or to minimize the effects of infringement, pending final resolution of the underlying claim."[96]

However, as recognized by the Supreme Court, the process of accommodation "does not give Aboriginal groups a veto over what can be done with land."[97] Instead, "[w]here consultation is meaningful, there is no ultimate duty to reach agreement. Rather, accommodation requires that Aboriginal concerns be balanced reasonably with the potential impact of the particular decision on those concerns and with competing societal concerns."[98]

In *Mikisew Cree First Nation v Canada (Governor General in Council)*,[99] the Supreme Court held that the duty to consult and accommodate does not apply directly to the development and reform of legislation, even if such legislation has the potential to negatively affect Aboriginal rights: "[e]xtending the duty to consult doctrine to the legislative process would oblige the judiciary to step beyond the core of its institutional role and threaten the respectful balance between the three pillars of our democracy. It would also transpose a consultation framework and judicial remedies developed in the context of executive action into the distinct realm of the legislature."[100] However, the court recognized that once passed, the legislation could be declared invalid if it unjustifiably infringes Aboriginal or treaty rights.[101] Also, as noted above, in *Sparrow*, consultation is one of the factors to consider when justifying infringements of Aboriginal and treaty rights.

Although the duty to consult and accommodate does not explicitly recognize the jurisdiction of Indigenous peoples over lands and resources, it plays an important role in protecting Indigenous peoples' jurisdiction by ensuring Indigenous peoples play a role in environmental decision-making processes. For example, at the federal level, the failure of the Crown to fulfill its legal duty to consult the Indigenous peoples who were affected by pipeline projects that had been granted approval by the National Energy Board has had a significant impact on the progress of such developments. In several recent decisions, the Federal Court of Appeal quashed government pipeline approvals and required additional consultation with Indigenous peoples and further consideration of potential environmental impacts before the projects could progress.[102] In *Gitxaala*, this resulted in the eventual cancellation of the Northern

---

95 *Haida Nation, supra* note 91.

96 *Ibid* at para 47.

97 *Ibid* at para 48.

98 *Taku River, supra* note 91 at para 2.

99 2018 SCC 40.

100 *Ibid* at para 2.

101 *Ibid* at para 3.

102 *Tsleil-Waututh Nation v Canada (Attorney General)*, 2018 FCA 153; *Gitxaala Nation v Canada*, 2016 FCA 187.

Gateway project as the federal government determined that the project was likely to cause significant adverse environmental effects that were not justified in the circumstances.[103] The following excerpt from *Tsleil-Waututh* discusses the strengths and weaknesses of the consultation and accommodation processes examined by the Federal Court of Appeal in both cases.

TSLEIL-WAUTUTH NATION V CANADA (ATTORNEY GENERAL)
2018 FCA 153

[553] Without doubt, the consultation process for this project was generally well-organized, less rushed (except in the final stage of Phase III) and there is no reasonable complaint that information within Canada's possession was withheld or that requests for information went unanswered.

[554] Ministers of the Crown were available and engaged in respectful conversations and correspondence with representatives of a number of the Indigenous applicants.

[555] Additional participant funding was offered to each of the applicants to support participation in discussions with the Crown consultation team following the release of the Board's report and recommendations. The British Columbia Environmental Assessment Office also offered consultation funding.

[556] The Crown Consultation Report provided detailed information about Canada's approach to consultation, Indigenous applicants' concerns and Canada's conclusions. An individualized appendix was prepared for each Indigenous group ... .

[557] However, for the reasons developed below, Canada's execution of Phase III of the consultation process was unacceptably flawed and fell short of the standard prescribed by the jurisprudence of the Supreme Court. As such, the consultation process fell short of the required mark for reasonable consultation.

[558] To summarize my reasons for this conclusion, Canada was required to do more than receive and understand the concerns of the Indigenous applicants. Canada was required to engage in a considered, meaningful two-way dialogue. Canada's ability to do so was constrained by the manner in which its representatives on the Crown consultation team implemented their mandate. For the most part, Canada's representatives limited their mandate to listening to and recording the concerns of the Indigenous applicants and then transmitting those concerns to the decision-makers.

[559] On the whole, the record does not disclose responsive, considered and meaningful dialogue coming back from Canada in response to the concerns expressed by the Indigenous applicants. While there are some examples of responsiveness to concerns, these limited examples are not sufficient to overcome the overall lack of response. The Supreme Court's jurisprudence repeatedly emphasizes that dialogue must take place and must be a two-way exchange. The Crown is required to do more than to receive and document concerns and complaints. As this Court wrote in *Gitxaala*, at paragraph 265, speaking of the limited mandate of Canada's representatives:

> When the role of Canada's representatives is seen in this light, it is of no surprise that a number of concerns raised by Aboriginal groups—in our view, concerns very

---

103 See "Northern Gateway Pipelines Project" (last modified 24 July 2017), online: *Natural Resources Canada* <https://www.nrcan.gc.ca/energy/resources/19184>.

central to their legitimate interests—were left unconsidered and undiscussed. This fell well short of the conduct necessary to meet the duty to consult.

[560] Further, Phase III was to focus on two questions: outstanding concerns about Project-related impacts and any required incremental accommodation measures. Canada's ability to consult and dialogue on these issues was constrained by two further limitations: first, Canada's unwillingness to depart from the Board's findings and recommended conditions so as to genuinely understand the concerns of the Indigenous applicants and then consider and respond to those concerns in a genuine and adequate way; second, Canada's erroneous view that it was unable to impose additional conditions on Trans Mountain.

[561] Together these three factors led to a consultation process that fell short of the mark and was, as a result, unreasonable. Canada then exacerbated the situation by its late disclosure of its view that the Project did not have a high level of impact on the established and asserted rights of the Indigenous applicants—a disclosure made two weeks before they were required to submit their final response to the consultation process and less than a month before the Governor in Council approved the Project.

In *Clyde River (Hamlet) v Petroleum Geo-Services Inc*,[104] the Supreme Court also described what is necessary to fulfill deep consultation and accommodation.

CLYDE RIVER (HAMLET) V PETROLEUM GEO-SERVICES INC
2017 SCC 40

[45] Bearing this in mind, the consultation that occurred here fell short in several respects. First, the inquiry was misdirected. While the NEB [National Energy Board] found that the proposed testing was not likely to cause significant adverse environmental effects, and that any effects on traditional resource use could be addressed by mitigation measures, the consultative inquiry is not properly into environmental effects *per se*. Rather, it inquires into the impact on the *right*. No consideration was given in the NEB's environmental assessment to the source—in a treaty—of the appellants' rights to harvest marine mammals, nor to the impact of the proposed testing on those rights.

[46] Furthermore, although the Crown relies on the processes of the NEB as fulfilling its duty to consult, that was not made clear to the Inuit. The significance of the process was not adequately explained to them.

[47] Finally, and most importantly, the process provided by the NEB did not fulfill the Crown's duty to conduct deep consultation. Deep consultation "may entail the opportunity to make submissions for consideration, formal participation in the decision-making process, and provision of written reasons to show that Aboriginal concerns were considered and to reveal the impact they had on the decision" (*Haida*, at para. 44). Despite the NEB's broad powers under *COGOA* [*Canada Oil and Gas Operations Act*, RSC 1985, c O-7] to afford those advantages, limited opportunities for participation and consultation were made available to the appellants. [T]here

104 2017 SCC 40.

were no oral hearings. Although the appellants submitted scientific evidence to the NEB, this was done without participant funding. ...

• • •

[49] While these procedural safeguards are not always necessary, their absence in this case significantly impaired the quality of consultation. Although the appellants had the opportunity to question the proponents about the project during the NEB meetings in the spring of 2013, the proponents were unable to answer many questions, including basic questions about the effect of the proposed testing on marine mammals. The proponents did eventually respond to these questions; however, they did so in a 3,926 page [sic] document which they submitted to the NEB. This document was posted on the NEB website and delivered to the hamlet offices in Pond Inlet, Clyde River, Qikiqtajuak and Iqaluit. Internet speed is slow in Nunavut, however, and bandwidth is expensive. The former mayor of Clyde River deposed that he was unable to download this document because it was too large. Furthermore, only a fraction of this enormous document was translated into Inuktitut. To put it mildly, furnishing answers to questions that went to the heart of the treaty rights at stake in the form of a practically inaccessible document dump months after the questions were initially asked in person is not true consultation. ... No mutual understanding on the core issues—the potential impact on treaty rights, and possible accommodations—could possibly have emerged from what occurred here.

NOTES

In *Clyde River*, the court also affirmed that regulatory bodies can play a role in fulfilling the duty to consult.[105]

In *Rio Tinto*, the Supreme Court discussed the "adverse impacts" necessary to trigger the duty to consult and accommodate: "Adverse impacts extend to any effect that may prejudice a pending Aboriginal claim or right. Often the adverse effects are physical in nature. However, ... high-level management decisions or structural changes to the resource's management may also adversely affect Aboriginal claims or rights even if these decisions have no 'immediate impact on the lands and resources.'"[106] However, the court clarified that in the context of consultation and accommodation, adverse impacts must be on the future exercise of the right and does not include prior and continuing breaches or impacts on the negotiating position of an Indigenous group.[107]

In *Mikisew Cree First Nation v Canada (Minister of Canadian Heritage)*, the Supreme Court considered the duty of consultation and accommodation in relation to post-confederation treaties and recognized that "the honour of the Crown infuses every treaty and the performance of every treaty obligation."[108] Thus, Treaty 8 of the Numbered Treaties was found to give rise to both *Mikisew* procedural rights (for example, consultation) and substantive rights (for example, hunting, fishing, and trapping rights). The court found that in situations where procedural rights have been violated, for example, through conduct that is not compatible with the honour of the Crown, it is not necessary to move directly into the *Sparrow* justification analysis; instead, a First Nation may be able to succeed in setting aside a government decision regardless of whether the decision and facts of the case would support an infringement of substantive rights.

---

105 *Ibid* at paras 21-23.

106 *Rio Tinto, supra* note 93 at para 47.

107 *Ibid* at paras 47-50.

108 *Mikisew Cree First Nation v Canada (Minister of Canadian Heritage), supra* note 91 at para 57.

F. SELF-GOVERNANCE

Another recognized means of protecting and potentially extending the jurisdiction of Indigenous peoples over lands and natural resources is Indigenous self-government. The Supreme Court recognized that Indigenous peoples were historically self-governing; however, this has not translated into the explicit recognition of a general Aboriginal right of self-government under s 35.[109] Instead, the Supreme Court held that claims to self-government under s 35(1) of the Constitution must be measured against the same standard as other Aboriginal rights set out in *Van der Peet*.[110] Thus, an Aboriginal right to self-government may be justifiably infringed, and the jurisdiction of Canadian governments continues to be recognized as paramount. Despite the restrictions on Indigenous self-governance recognized by the Supreme Court, there are a growing number of examples of self-government in Canada as a result of various agreements, treaties, and legislation.

For example, in Yukon, the *Umbrella Final Agreement*, signed in 1993, provided a framework for the negotiation of self-government agreements by Yukon First Nations.[111] The *Umbrella Final Agreement* has contributed to the completion of 11 land claim agreements with Yukon First Nations.[112] Under the terms of their respective agreements, self-governing First Nations have had a range of control over their recognized "settlement lands," from "rights, obligations and liabilities equivalent to fee simple" to fee simple title to subsurface mineral rights.[113] Self-governing First Nations may also have the power to enact laws related to the "[u]se, management, administration, control and protection of settlement land"; "[a]llocation or disposition of rights and interests in and to settlement land"; "[u]se, management, administration and protection of natural resources under the ownership, control or jurisdiction of the first nation"; "[g]athering, hunting, trapping and fishing and the protection of fish, wildlife and their habitat"; "[c]ontrol of the sanitary condition of buildings and property"; "[p]lanning, zoning and land development"; "[c]ontrol or prohibition of the operation and use of vehicles"; "[c]ontrol or prevention of pollution and protection of the environment"; and "[c]ontrol or prohibition of the transport of dangerous substances."[114] They also have the ability to play a more significant role in environmental governance processes, including the ability to grant project authorizations as the "decision body" in the environmental assessment process under the *Yukon Environmental and Socio-economic Assessment Act*.[115]

In British Columbia, the *Nisga'a Final Agreement*, enacted in 1999, includes recognition of self-governance rights for the Nisga'a Lisims Government.[116] Through this agreement, Canada and British Columbia formally recognized Nisga'a ownership of just under 2,000 km² of Nisga'a

109 *Sioui, supra* note 81 at paras 69-70, 74, 76; *Sparrow, supra* note 48 at para 49; *Delgamuukw, supra* note 25 at para 170.

110 *R v Pamajewon*, [1996] 2 SCR 821, 1996 CanLII 161.

111 *Umbrella Final Agreement* (1993), online: *Council of Yukon First Nation* <https://cyfn.ca/ufa>; *Yukon First Nations Self-Government Act*, SC 1994, c 35.

112 This includes Champagne and Aishihik First Nations, First Nation of Nacho Nyak Dun, Little Salmon/ Carmacks First Nation, Selkirk First Nation, Ta'an Kwach'an Council, Teslin Tlingit Council, Tr'ondëk Hwëch'in, Vuntut Gwitchin First Nation, Kluane First Nation, Kwanlin Dun First Nation, and Carcross/ Tagish First Nation (*Yukon First Nations Self-Government Act*, Schedule II).

113 *Umbrella Final Agreement*, 5.4.1.

114 *Yukon First Nations Self-Government Act*, Schedule III, part III.

115 SC 2003, c 7, s 2(1).

116 *Nisga'a Final Agreement* (1999), online (pdf): *Nisga'a Lisims Government* <https://www.nisgaanation.ca/sites/default/files/Nisga%27a%20Final%20Agreement%20-%20Effective%20Date.PDF>; *Nisga'a Final Agreement Act*, SC 2000, c 7; British Columbia *Nisga'a Final Agreement Act*, SBC 1999, c 2.

lands as well as mineral resources on or under those lands.[117] As a result, the Nisga'a Nation has been able to establish Nisga'a laws related to the access and use of Nisga'a lands and resources including procedures for land use planning and environmental assessment.[118] However, in the event of a conflict between a Nisga'a law and a federal or provincial law of general application, the federal or provincial law will prevail to the extent of the conflict.[119]

NOTES

For other examples of agreements that resulted in Indigenous self-government, see below:

- *James Bay and Northern Quebec Agreement* (1975) and *Northeastern Quebec Agreement* (1978): These agreements established a framework for the land and local government regimes for the James Bay Crees and the Naskapi of Kawawachikamach.[120]
- *Nunavut Land Claims Agreement* (1993): This agreement resulted in the transfer of lands to the Inuit, the creation of the Nunavut territory in 1999, and the establishment of its own legislative assembly and public government. Under the terms of the agreement, jurisdiction over some territorial matters, including wildlife management, land use planning, and development and natural resource management, was transferred to the new government.[121]
- *Labrador Inuit Land Claims Agreement* (2003): This agreement resulted in the creation of the Nunatsiavut Government and five regional community governments with powers of administration, control, and management over the lands and waters contained within the Settlement Area.[122]
- Although not necessarily an expansion of Indigenous peoples' jurisdiction over lands and resources, the movement toward self-government has been paralleled by the development of co-management arrangements between Indigenous peoples and Canadian governments where decision-making authority and responsibility over lands, wildlife, and natural resources is shared. For example, in British Columbia, the Nisga'a Lisims Government shares management of the Nass River salmon fishery with the Governments of

---

117 British Columbia *Nisga'a Final Agreement Act*, Schedule, c 3, paras 1-8, 19-20.

118 British Columbia *Nisga'a Final Agreement Act*, Schedule, c 5, paras 6-12; c 8, paras 69-70; c 9, paras 37-38; c 10, para 3-4; c 11, para 44-52. See, for example, the *Nisga'a Land Act*, NLGSR 2000/10 and the *Nisga'a Land Regulation*, NLGSR 2015/10 (for Nisga'a legislation, see the Nisga'a Lisims Government website: <www.nisgaanation.ca/legislation>).

119 British Columbia *Nisga'a Final Agreement Act*, Schedule, c 10, para 3.

120 *The James Bay and Northern Quebec Agreement* (1975), online (pdf): *Naskapi* <http://www.naskapi.ca/documents/documents/JBNQA.pdf>; *The Northeastern Quebec Agreement* (1978), online (pdf): *Christian Aboriginal Infrastructure Developments* <http://caid.ca/AgrNorEasQueA1974.pdf>; *James Bay and Northern Quebec Native Claims Settlement Act*, SC 1976-77, c 32; *An Act approving the Agreement concerning James Bay and Northern Quebec*, CQLR c C-67; *Naskapi and the Cree-Naskapi Commission Act*, SC 1984, c 18. See also Thomas Isaac, "Aboriginal Self-Government in Canada: Cree-Naskapi (of Quebec) Act" (1991) 7 Native Studies Rev 15.

121 *The Nunavut Land Claims Agreement* (1993), online (pdf): *Government of Nunavut* <https://www.gov.nu.ca/sites/default/files/Nunavut_Land_Claims_Agreement.pdf>; *Nunavut Land Claims Settlement Act*, SC 1993, c 29; *Nunavut Act*, SC 1993, c 28; *Nunavut Waters and Nunavut Surface Rights Tribunal Act*, SC 2002, c 10; *Nunavut Planning and Project Assessment Act*, SC 2013, c 14, s 2.

122 *The Labrador Inuit Land Claims Agreement* (2003), online (pdf): *Nunatsiavut* <https://www.nunatsiavut.com/wp-content/uploads/2014/07/Labrador-Inuit-Land-Claims-Agreement.pdf>; *Labrador Inuit Land Claims Agreement Act*, SNL 2004, c L-3.1; *Labrador Inuit Land Claims Agreement Act*, SC 2005, c 27.

Canada and British Columbia, an arrangement facilitated through the Joint Fisheries Management Committee.[123] A collaborative approach has also been used in the management of the transboundary waters of the Mackenzie River basin and the development of the Mackenzie River Basin Bilateral Water Management Agreements.[124]

G. CONCLUSION

The broad scope of Indigenous jurisdiction that arises from applicable s 35 Aboriginal and treaty rights means that Indigenous communities must be dealt with on a case-by-case basis when natural resource development approvals and other government actions may have an impact on their legal rights.[125] Different communities, even when existing in similar geographic areas, may have different legal rights in terms of access to and protection of their territorial lands and associated natural resources and may require different standards of consultation and accommodation. However, even when a community has broad jurisdiction due to the Aboriginal or treaty rights they possess, there is still the possibility that the community may not be able to prevent a restriction on the exercise of their rights if it can be justified under the *Sparrow* test. Thus, the duty to consult plays an important role in ensuring that even when a justified infringement of an Indigenous community's rights occurs, the community has direct input into the situation and potential influence on the final approval and/or project design, if, for example, the infringement occurs as a result of a natural resource development project. As briefly discussed in Section II.F, Indigenous jurisdiction over lands and resources may be extended through negotiated self-government agreements and statutory developments. Although it may not result in an expansion of jurisdiction, there is also potential for an expanded role of Indigenous peoples and representation of their s 35 rights in environmental governance processes through the development of collaborative approaches to environmental protection and natural resource development.

QUESTIONS

1. Does the current scope of s 35(1) assist in promoting greater environmental protection in Canada?

2. How does the limited definition of Aboriginal rights undermine greater recognition of Indigenous peoples' jurisdiction over the environment?

3. Can the justified infringement test be compatible with recognition of Indigenous peoples' jurisdiction over the environment? If so, what additional safeguards might be necessary?

---

123 *Nisga'a Fisheries and Wildlife Act*, NLGSR 2000/16, ss 20-22.

124 *Mackenzie River Basin Transboundary Waters Master Agreement* (1997), online (pdf): *Government of Alberta* <https://open.alberta.ca/dataset/a9d6c809-b7f1-4c3a-ac50-5a2194a1b7a0/resource/e0681073-168b-4204-b433-aa41322bedab/download/mackenzie-river-basin-transboundary-waters-master-agreement.pdf>; *Alberta–Northwest Territories Mackenzie River Basin Bilateral Water Management Agreement* (2015), online (pdf): *Government of Northwest Territories* <https://www.enr.gov.nt.ca/sites/enr/files/ab-nwt_water_management_agreement_final_signed_2.pdf>; *British Columbia–Northwest Territories Mackenzie River Basin Bilateral Water Management Agreement* (2015), online (pdf): *Government of Northwest Territories* <https://www.enr.gov.nt.ca/sites/enr/files/nwt-bc_transboundary_water_management_agreement_oct_15_2015.pdf>. See also Andrea Beck, "Aboriginal Consultation in Canadian Water Negotiations: The Mackenzie Bilateral Water Management Agreements" (2016) 39:2 Dal LJ 487; Alex Latta, "Indigenous Rights and Multilevel Governance: Learning from the Northwest Territories Water Stewardship Strategy" (2018) 9:2 The International Indigenous Policy Journal, art 4, online: *Western Libraries* <https://ojs.lib.uwo.ca/index.php/iipj/article/view/7546/6190>.

125 *Sparrow, supra* note 48 at para 66; *Delgamuukw, supra* note 25 at para 165.

III. FUTURE DIRECTIONS FOR GREATER RECOGNITION OF INDIGENOUS PEOPLES' JURISDICTION OVER THE ENVIRONMENT

Thus far, this chapter has focused on the existing protections and recognition of Indigenous peoples' jurisdiction over the environment. This section considers areas where Canadian law, including environmental law, needs to be further developed to ensure a better and robust protection of Indigenous peoples' jurisdiction, including expanding the protection of s 35(1) and the implementation of the UN Declaration.

A. EXPANDING EXISTING SECTION 35 RIGHTS

The exercise of Aboriginal and treaty rights is often dependent on access to healthy environmental resources, yet Canadian law has not recognized Indigenous peoples' environmental rights to better enable the protection of traditional lands and the natural elements they contain. However, there are a number of legal scholars who have suggested that a right to conservation is inherent in a number of constitutionally recognized Aboriginal and treaty rights and should, therefore, receive explicit legal recognition.[126] For example, Lynda Collins and Meghan Murtha have focused their analysis on the treaty and Aboriginal rights to hunt, fish, and trap and suggest that such rights are a possible source of Indigenous environmental rights in Canada.[127] The following excerpt discusses their proposed expansion of Aboriginal rights.

> ### LYNDA M COLLINS & MEGHAN MURTHA, "INDIGENOUS ENVIRONMENTAL RIGHTS IN CANADA: THE RIGHT TO CONSERVATION IMPLICIT IN TREATY AND ABORIGINAL RIGHTS TO HUNT, FISH, AND TRAP"
> (2010) 47:4 Alta L Rev 959 at 983-86 [footnotes omitted]
>
> Claims to environmental protection can also be grounded in Aboriginal rights where there is no governing treaty, or where it is arguable that a treaty or land surrender failed to extinguish the Aboriginal right in issue. ...
>
> • • •
>
> Unlike treaty rights, which derive from an agreement between a given First Nation and the Crown, Aboriginal rights arise by virtue of Aboriginal peoples' prior use and occupation of an area of land. Thus, arguments put forward in the treaty rights context regarding Aboriginal expectations of the Crown do not readily apply to found

---

126   Lynda M Collins & Meghan Murtha, "Indigenous Environmental Rights in Canada: The Right to Conservation Implicit in Treaty and Aboriginal Rights to Hunt, Fish, and Trap" (2010) 47:4 Alta L Rev 959; Randy Kapashesit & Murray Klippenstein, "Aboriginal Group Rights and Environmental Protection" (1991) 36 McGill LJ 925; Theresa McClenaghan, *Molested and Disturbed: Environmental Protection by Aboriginal Peoples Through Section 35 of The Constitution Act, 1982* (Toronto: Canadian Environmental Law Association, 1999); Bradford Monse, "Indigenous Rights as a Mechanism to Promote Environmental Sustainability" in Laura Westra, Klaus Bosselmann & Richard Westra, eds, *Reconciling Human Existence with Ecological Integrity* (London: Earthscan, 2008) 159.

127   Collins & Murtha, *supra* note 126 at 967.

an Aboriginal right to environmental preservation. Rather, in the context of Aboriginal rights, the right to conservation derives from two bases.

First, Aboriginal peoples may argue, as in the treaty context, that an Aboriginal right to hunt, fish, or trap must be interpreted as including a right to conservation if the Aboriginal right is to be given any substance. The argument that rights to harvest resources are meaningless in the absence of a corresponding right to the conservation thereof applies to Aboriginal rights as well as it does to treaty rights. Where an Aboriginal group can demonstrate that sustainable resource use is a part of its traditional culture, there will be a strong argument for interpreting the content of an Aboriginal resource right as including a right to conservation. This flows from the principle that courts must be "sensitive to the aboriginal perspective ... on the meaning of the rights at stake." Further, since it has been recognized that conservation and sustainable management is consistent with the enhancement of aboriginal rights, it follows that environmental degradation may be inconsistent with those rights.

Second, Aboriginal peoples may also enjoy a free-standing Aboriginal right to govern the environmental preservation of their lands. Aboriginal systems of sustainable environmental management will meet the *Van der Peet* test in many cases. In virtually every case, these systems will meet the requirement of being a central and significant part of the distinctive Aboriginal culture, or of being "one of the things that truly *made the society what it was.*" Indeed, self-regulation of environmental resources has been treated as a defining characteristic of Indigenous societies globally, and this is no less true with respect to Indigenous peoples in Canada.

Although Aboriginal peoples generally may not have great difficulty demonstrating that engaging in environmental preservation was integral to their culture prior to contact, there may be some difficulty in meeting the continuity requirement in many cases. As noted above, to qualify as an Aboriginal right an activity must have continuity with pre-contact practice, though there need not be "an unbroken chain of continuity." Kapashesit and Klippenstein assert that Aboriginal ecological management systems, "while often severely stressed, have the ability to survive." Nevertheless, it is likely that this part of the *Van der Peet/Sappier* test will constitute the biggest hurdle for Aboriginal peoples claiming a right to engage in environmental regulation. Despite the potential difficulty of demonstrating continuity, there is a strong argument that Aboriginal environmental governance systems persist. John Borrows explains:

> Indigenous legal principles form a system of "empirical observations and pragmatic knowledge," which have both value in themselves, and also in demonstrating how people structure information; they embrace ecological protection and could be woven into the very fabric of North American legal ideas. Indigenous laws sometimes find their expression in traditional stories, which are a primary source to discover precedents guiding environmental and land-use planning. These narratives often pre-date the common law, have enjoyed their persuasiveness for centuries, and have yet to be overturned or extinguished from the tribal memory. Placing Indigenous traditions in an inter-societal context, through a culturally appropriate methodology that allows access to oral tradition and community knowledge, illustrates how traditional legal knowledge could enhance democracy and facilitate sustainability.

Similarly, Kapashesit and Klippenstein argue that, "where a viable Aboriginal [ecological] management system exists," government has a constitutional duty to accommodate that system. They contend that there is an Aboriginal right to environmental preservation and that where an Aboriginal resource management system exists, it is the preferred means of exercising that right. Further, they assert that where such a system is in place, the Crown would be unable to justify externally imposed conservation legislation, since such legislation would fail the minimal impairment subtest of the *Sparrow* justificatory test. With respect to the nature and scope of the right to environmental self-governance, Theresa McClenaghan explains that

> [a] particular right of self-government may arise from establishment of an environmental aboriginal right which in turn might imply a right of governance as to the scope of that right. Another approach would see aboriginal peoples exercising environmental governance by rule making about activities on the aboriginal peoples' "own" lands (aboriginal title or reserve lands) and about members' activities. Another possibility is to insist that neighbouring or other orders of government require persons under their jurisdiction to comply with rules to avoid specified impacts on aboriginal peoples. Canadian common law courts could enforce decisions that aboriginal peoples have made about allowable impacts on the environment of their "own" lands.

Thus, the independent right to environmental self-government may complement conservation rights inherent in Aboriginal and treaty rights to hunt, fish, and trap."

QUESTIONS

1. What are the benefits for environmental law in Canada if s 35 were to include a right to conservation as argued above?

2. What might be some of the challenges to gaining recognition of a right to conservation as described above? How could these challenges be overcome?

3. In reading the discussion below, would implementing the UN Declaration require recognizing a right to conservation?

B. IMPLEMENTATION OF THE UNITED NATIONS DECLARATION ON THE RIGHTS OF INDIGENOUS PEOPLES

Another key development for increasing recognition of Indigenous peoples' jurisdiction over the environment and natural resources is the UN Declaration. The UN Declaration recognizes several rights relevant to Indigenous peoples' jurisdiction, including the right to self-determination; the right to self-government; the right to participation in decision-making (including free, prior, and informed consent); and the right to their lands, territories, and natural resources. The UN Declaration includes recognition that "respect for indigenous knowledge, cultures and traditional practices contributes to sustainable and equitable development and proper management of the environment."[128]

The following excerpts explore the meaning and legal impact of the ratification of the UN Declaration and the future development of Indigenous jurisdiction in Canada.

---

128 UNDRIP, *supra* note 4, preamble at 2.

BRENDA L GUNN, "BEYOND VAN DER PEET: BRINGING TOGETHER INTERNATIONAL, INDIGENOUS AND CONSTITUTIONAL LAW"

in *UNDRIP Implementation: Braiding International, Domestic and Indigenous Laws: Special Report* (Waterloo, Ont: Centre for International Governance Innovation, 2017) 29

Recently, Canada has expressed its full commitment to UNDRIP: "We intend nothing less than to adopt and implement the Declaration in accordance with the Canadian Constitution. ... By adopting and implementing the Declaration, we are breathing life into section 35 and recognizing it as a full box of rights for Indigenous peoples. Canada believes that our constitutional obligations serve to fulfill all the principles of the Declaration, including 'free, prior and informed consent.'" [Footnote 23: Minister of Indigenous and Northern Affairs Carolyn Bennett, "Announcement of Canada's Support for the United Nations Declaration on the Rights of Indigenous Peoples" [sic] (Statement delivered at the 15th Session of the United Nations Permanent Forum on Indigenous Issues, 10 May 2016), online: *Northern Public Affairs* <http://www.northernpublicaffairs.ca/index/fully-adopting-undrip-minister-bennetts-speech/>.]

• • •

Some may attempt to limit the impact of UNDRIP by emphasizing the non-binding nature of declarations. While a declaration does not create directly enforceable, binding legal obligations on a state in and of itself, "soft law cannot be simply dismissed as non-law." [Footnote 24: Mauro Barelli, "The Role of Soft Law in the International Legal System: The Case of the United Nations Declaration on the Rights of Indigenous Peoples" (2009) 58 ICLQ 957 at 959.] ... Much of the debate around the technical status of the international instrument has been a political manoeuvre to undermine its domestic application; hopefully, we can move beyond these debates, now that Canada has expressed its unconditional support, and begin the process of implementing UNDRIP in Canada. ...

UNDRIP recognizes the essential humanity of Indigenous peoples ... [and] proclaims that Indigenous peoples can no longer be denied fundamental human rights based on imperialist/racist ideas that Indigenous peoples are "fierce savages whose occupation was war" [Footnote 29: Johnson v M'Intosh, 21 US (8 Wheat) 543 (1823).] and resultant doctrines such as discovery and *terra nullius*. [Footnote 30: UNDRIP, preamble.] The United Nations also recognized that Indigenous peoples have a right to be recognized as Indigenous and that special protections may be necessary to ensure their inherent rights are realized. [Footnote 31: UNDRIP, arts 1, 2.] UNDRIP recognizes that colonization occurred and had a negative impact on Indigenous peoples, in particular the dispossession from their lands, territories and resources. [Footnote 32: UNDRIP, preamble.] ...

The United Nations is "*convinced* that the recognition of the rights of indigenous peoples in this declaration will enhance harmonious and cooperative relations between the state and indigenous peoples, based on principles of justice, democracy, respect for human rights, non-discrimination and good faith." [Footnote 33: UNDRIP, preamble (emphasis in original).] ... This is an important point because many people in Canada believe that recognizing special rights for Indigenous peoples will tear Canada apart. ...

[A]chieving the ends of UNDRIP requires Indigenous peoples and Canada to work together. The Canadian federal and provincial governments cannot unilaterally implement UNDRIP. ...

• • •

> To implement UNDRIP, Canadian constitutional law must shift in its approach to defining Indigenous peoples' rights toward ensuring that the rights are defined according to Indigenous peoples' legal traditions.

One of the key rights in the UN Declaration that is relevant to environmental law and increasing recognition of Indigenous peoples' jurisdiction is the right to participate in decision-making. The United Nations Expert Mechanism on the Rights of Indigenous Peoples (EMRIP) conducted a study on the right to participate in decision-making.[129] In the final report, the expert mechanism addressed key aspects of the right and highlighted factors to determine good practices in fulfilling Indigenous peoples' right to participate in decision-making.

UNHRC, FINAL REPORT OF THE STUDY ON INDIGENOUS PEOPLES AND THE RIGHT TO PARTICIPATE IN DECISION-MAKING: REPORT OF THE EXPERT MECHANISM ON THE RIGHTS OF INDIGENOUS PEOPLES
UNHRC, 18th Sess, UN Doc A/HRC/18/42 (2011)

II. DEFINING GOOD PRACTICES

• • •

13. ... The most significant indicator of good practice is likely to be the extent to which indigenous peoples were involved in the design of the practice and their agreement to it. Other indicators include the extent to which the practice:

(a) Allows and enhances indigenous peoples' participation in decision-making;

(b) Allows indigenous peoples to influence the outcome of decisions that affect them;

(c) Realizes indigenous peoples' right to self-determination;

(d) Includes, as appropriate, robust consultation procedures and/or processes to seek indigenous peoples' free, prior and informed consent.

• • •

ANNEX

EXPERT MECHANISM ADVICE NO. 2 (2011): INDIGENOUS PEOPLES AND THE RIGHT TO PARTICIPATE IN DECISION-MAKING

1. Indigenous peoples are among the most excluded, marginalized and disadvantaged sectors of society. ... Decision-making rights and participation by indigenous peoples in decisions that affect them is necessary to enable them to protect, inter alia, their cultures, including their languages and their lands, territories and resources. ...

2. The right of indigenous peoples to participation is well established in international law. More recently, the indigenous-rights discourse has seen increased focus on rights not only allowing indigenous peoples to participate in decision-making processes affecting them, but to actually control the outcome of such processes.

• • •

---

129 UNHRC, *Final Report of the Study on Indigenous Peoples and the Right to Participate in Decision-Making: Report of the Expert Mechanism on the Rights of Indigenous Peoples*, UNHRC, 18th Sess, UN Doc A/HRC/18/42 (2011).

14. The participation of indigenous peoples in external decision-making is of crucial importance to good governance. One of the objectives of international standards on indigenous peoples' rights is to fill the gap between their rights on the one hand and their implementation on the other hand.

• • •

MEASURES

• • •

29. States have a duty to respect indigenous peoples' right to participate in all levels of decision-making, including in external decision-making, if the indigenous peoples concerned so choose and in the forms of their choosing, including, where appropriate, in co-governance arrangements.

30. States should respect and assist both traditional and contemporary forms of indigenous peoples' governance structures, including their collective decision-making practices.

• • •

32. Indigenous women often face exceptional impediments to participation in decision-making. States, international organizations, indigenous peoples and other decision-making entities should therefore conduct more intensive studies and design appropriate mechanisms to facilitate the participation of indigenous women in their activities and increase their access to address difficulties facing indigenous women seeking to fully participate in decision-making. ...

One often discussed aspect of the right to participate in decision-making is free, prior, and informed consent. The EMRIP study also addressed this aspect and provided insight into what is required to obtain Indigenous peoples' free, prior, and informed consent.[130]

UNHRC, FREE, PRIOR AND INFORMED CONSENT: A HUMAN RIGHTS-BASED APPROACH: STUDY OF THE EXPERT MECHANISM ON THE RIGHTS OF INDIGENOUS PEOPLES
UNHRC, 39th Sess, UN Doc A/HRC/39/62 (2018)

III. FREE, PRIOR AND INFORMED CONSENT AS A HUMAN RIGHTS NORM

• • •

13. Free, prior and informed consent operates fundamentally as a safeguard for the collective rights of indigenous peoples. ...

• • •

15. States' obligations to consult with indigenous peoples should consist of a qualitative process of dialogue and negotiation, with consent as the objective (see A/HRC/18/42, annex, para. 9). The Declaration does not envision a single moment or action but a process of dialogue and negotiation over the course of a project, from planning to implementation and follow-up. Use in the Declaration of the combined

---

130 UNHRC, *Free, Prior and Informed Consent: A Human Rights-Based Approach: Study of the Expert Mechanism on the Rights of Indigenous Peoples*, UNHRC, 39th Sess, UN Doc A/HRC/39/62 (2018), online (pdf): <https://documents-dds-ny.un.org/doc/UNDOC/GEN/G18/245/94/PDF/G1824594.pdf? OpenElement>.

terms "consult and cooperate" denotes a right of indigenous peoples to influence the outcome of decision-making processes affecting them, not a mere right to be involved in such processes or merely to have their views heard (see A/HRC/18/42). It also suggests the possibility for indigenous peoples to make a different proposal or suggest a different model, as an alternative to the one proposed by the Government or other actor.

• • •

19. The rights of indigenous peoples over their lands, resources and territories are also integral parts of free, prior and informed consent, as construed in the Declaration. The right to "own, use, develop and control" the lands, territories and resources (art. 26) gives rise to a right to free, prior and informed consent consistent with indigenous peoples' right of self-determination. In this regard, the role of free, prior and informed consent is to safeguard indigenous peoples' cultural identity, which is inextricably linked to their lands, resources and territories.

• • •

25. Consent is a key principle that enables indigenous peoples to exercise their right to self-determination, including development that involves control over or otherwise affects their lands, resources and territories. With such an understanding, indigenous peoples are considered to engage with and are entitled to give or withhold consent to proposals that affect them.

26. Indigenous peoples' decision to give or withhold consent is a result of their assessment of their best interests and that of future generations with regard to a proposal. When they give their consent it provides an important social licence and a favourable environment to any actor operating on and around their lands, territories and resources, as many studies and research have shown, including by the private sector. [Footnote 23: Cathal M Doyle, *Indigenous Peoples, Title to Territory, Rights and Resources: The Transformative Role of Free Prior and Informed Consent*, Routledge Research in Human Rights Law (London; New York: Routledge, 2014) ch 5.] Indigenous peoples may withhold their consent in a number of situations and for various purposes or reasons ... .

• • •

30. If indigenous peoples choose to give their consent to a project, consent should be consistent with indigenous peoples' own laws, customs, protocols and best practices, including representation by legal counsel whenever possible and as required by law. In many, if not all, instances, consent must be recorded in a written instrument, negotiated by the parties, and signed affirmatively by a legitimate authority or leader of the relevant indigenous peoples, which may include more than one group (see paras. 42-45 below). Full understanding by indigenous peoples must be ensured and additional measures should be taken by the State in cases involving indigenous peoples of recent contact.

• • •

35. As to impact, if a measure or project is likely to have a significant, direct impact on indigenous peoples' lives or land, territories or resources then consent is required (see A/HRC/12/34, para. 47). It has been referred to as a "sliding scale approach" to the question of indigenous participatory rights, which means that the level of effective participation that must be guaranteed to indigenous peoples is essentially a function of the nature and content of the rights and activities in question. [Footnote 29: Gaetano Pentassuglia, *Minority Groups and Judicial Discourse in International Law: A Comparative Perspective*, International Studies in Human Rights, vol 102 (Leiden; Boston: Brill/Nijhoff, 2009) at 113.] ... Assessment of the

impact requires consideration of the nature, scale, duration and long-term impact of the action, such as damage to community lands or harm to the community's cultural integrity.

• • •

[In the annex to the study, the EMRIP includes the following advice:]

ANNEX

• • •

6. States should ensure that consent is always the objective of consultations, bearing in mind that in certain cases consent will be required. Consultations should start at the planning phase (i.e., prior to the State or enterprise committing to under-take a particular project or adopting a particular measure, such as the licensing of a project) so indigenous peoples can influence final decisions. The measures to be consulted on should be clear. Consultations should occur throughout the evolution of the project, entailing "constant communication between the parties" [Footnote 1: *Saramaka People v Suriname* (2007) at para 133 (Inter-American Court of Human Rights).] and should not be confused with public hearings for environment and regulatory statutes.

A final aspect of the UN Declaration that is critical to increasing recognition of Indigenous peoples' jurisdiction is realizing Indigenous peoples' right to self-determination and self-government. The excerpt below begins to highlight some key aspects of self-determination in Canada.

BRENDA GUNN, "MOVING BEYOND RHETORIC: WORKING TOWARD RECONCILIATION THROUGH SELF-DETERMINATION"
(2015) 38:1 Dal LJ 237 at 251–54 [footnotes omitted]

Self-determination is more than a question of Indigenous peoples having their own governing institutions—it is about choice and the freedom to make decisions on their way of life. ...

• • •

The first aspect of the right to self-determination is the right to freely determine one's own political status. ...

... Erica-Irene Daes describes this aspect of self-determination as "a kind of belated state-building, through which indigenous peoples are able to join with all the other peoples that comprise the state on mutually agreed-upon and just terms after many years of isolation and exclusion."

... While this nation-building process can be daunting, there are resources to draw upon. A noteworthy starting point for understanding the intended Indige-nous–Crown relationship is the Royal Proclamation of 1763, which confirmed the nation-to-nation relationship whereby each nation retained its sovereignty. ...

Likewise, in much of Canada treaties are the foundational legal instruments setting out the terms of the relationship between Indigenous peoples and the Crown. ...

Treaties are an exercise of Indigenous peoples' right to self-determination. Treaties must be implemented in light of modern day realities without diminishing their original spirit and intent, given their constitutional status to fulfill self-determination and promote reconciliation. ...

• • •

As part of the internal aspect to self-determination, the Declaration recognizes Indigenous peoples' right to their own political institutions. Article 4 confirms Indigenous peoples' right to autonomy or self-government over internal and local affairs, and the means for financing these activities. The Declaration identifies some areas where Indigenous institutions have continuing jurisdiction: articles 20, 33, 34 and 35 include the right to have their own institutions, including legal systems; the right to pursue economic activities; the right to determine their own identity or membership according to their own membership laws; and the right to determine the responsibilities of members. Indigenous peoples' also have the right to maintain their political systems.

QUESTIONS

1. When discussing increased recognition for Indigenous peoples' jurisdiction, some people raise concerns regarding accessibility and intelligibility of Indigenous laws, as well as having different environmental laws throughout Canada, or even within a single province. Consider how general principles of federalism and division of powers may assist in addressing concerns over multiple governments involved in regulating the environment and having different laws exist within a single province.

2. How does the duty of consultation and accommodation compare with the right to participate in decision-making and free, prior, and informed consent?

3. There is increasing recognition of Indigenous peoples' involvement in international environmental decision-making to ensure broad participation of Indigenous peoples and consideration of Indigenous peoples' rights. For example, see the platform for local communities and Indigenous peoples at the United Nations Framework Convention on Climate Change: <unfccc.int/LCIPP>.

4. Given Indigenous peoples' relationship with their traditional territories as discussed above, how might greater recognition of Indigenous peoples' jurisdiction over the environment improve environmental decision-making in Canada?

IV. CONCLUSION

Indigenous governments and the jurisdiction they exercise over lands and resources pre-date colonial and Canadian governments. This inherent jurisdiction has slowly been recognized in Canada through s 35 of the *Constitution Act, 1982* and the interpretation of Aboriginal rights by the Canadian courts. Although the constitutional recognition and adjudication of Aboriginal rights in s 35 has provided some guidance in terms of Indigenous peoples' jurisdiction and role in environmental regulation, there is considerable potential for the expansion of such jurisdiction in the future. Under Canada's current legal regime, Indigenous jurisdiction over lands and resources varies depending on the Aboriginal and treaty rights of a specific community, resulting in range of legal rights in terms of access to and protection of traditional lands. The required standards of consultation and accommodation also vary depending on the Aboriginal and treaty rights that trigger the duty. However, even when an Indigenous community has rights that result in a high level of legal control over lands and resources, there is still potential for those rights to be infringed under the *Sparrow* test.

Indigenous jurisdiction over the environment has been expanded in Canada as Indigenous communities have negotiated self-government agreements and developed collaborative approaches to environmental decision-making and land management. Despite these developments, further expansion of Indigenous jurisdiction is still needed in order to ensure traditional territories and cultural practices are adequately protected. One means of increasing Indigenous jurisdiction over the environment may be through an expanded interpretation of s 35 rights, such as the recognition of an inherent right to conservation as proposed by Collins and Murtha. Another promising means of expansion is through the implementation of the UN Declaration, including recognition of Indigenous peoples' rights to participation in decision-making, self-determination, and self-government.

CHAPTER THIRTEEN

ENVIRONMENTAL LAW IN QUEBEC*

Paule Halley

I. INTRODUCTION

The development of a large body of environmental legislation and regulation raises the question of whether private litigation can still prove to be an efficient legal tool for the protection of the environment. The question derives mainly from the fact that the state is playing a more active and prominent role in the prevention and reduction of environmental degradation.

---

* The author gratefully acknowledges the contribution of the Honourable Justice Lorne Giroux, Court of Appeal of Quebec, as co-author of the previous version of this chapter.

In Quebec, this same question can be asked about the civil law. The development of a regulatory regime centred on the *Environment Quality Act*, CQLR c Q-2 (EQA) highlights the limits of using private civil law remedies in this sphere. As will be discovered in this chapter, the theoretical basis for private litigation is different in Quebec, and yet there are great similarities between the common law and the civil law with respect to the issues, the problems, and the outcome. This chapter begins with an explanation of the legal context and the theoretical foundations of the civil law as applied in the area of private environmental litigation. The chapter explores the recurring problem of causation and looks at a more promising procedural development: the class action. The final section provides an overview of three interrelated areas of law that have been developed to address public participation: environmental rights, public right to participate in the enforcement of the EQA, and public participation and environmental assessment.

II. LEGAL CONTEXT

The province of Quebec is a bijural legal system. Since the *Quebec Act, 1774* (UK), 14 Geo III, c 83, the rights of the citizens of Quebec to "hold and enjoy their Property and Possessions, together with all Customs and Usages relative thereto, and all other their Civil Rights" (s 8) has been held to apply to private law: the law as between subject and subject, that is, involving the rights of one subject against another. See WF O'Connor, "Property and Civil Rights in the Province" (1940) 18:5 Can Bar Rev 331 at 337.

At the time of the *Quebec Act*, Quebec private law was governed by the *coutume de Paris* (Custom of Paris) but was later codified in the *Civil Code of Lower Canada*, 29 Vict, c 41, which was assented to September 18, 1865 and came into force on August 1, 1866. On January 1, 1994, the *Civil Code of Lower Canada* was replaced by the *Civil Code of Québec*, CQLR c CCQ-1991 (CCQ), enacted by SQ 1991, c 64.

On the other hand, in Quebec, starting with the British conquest, public law, that is, the law as between the subject and the institutions of government, has been the domain of British law. Even today, in such areas as constitutional and administrative law, should Quebec statutory law be silent on any given question, resort has to be had to common law principles (R Dussault & L Borgeat, *Administrative Law Treatise*, vol 1 (Toronto: Carswell, 1985) at 18-21).

FEDERAL LAW—CIVIL LAW HARMONIZATION ACT, NO 1
SC 2001, c 4, preamble

WHEREAS all Canadians are entitled to access to federal legislation in keeping with the common law and civil law traditions;

WHEREAS the civil law tradition of the Province of Quebec, which finds its principal expression in the *Civil Code of Québec*, reflects the unique character of Quebec society;

WHEREAS the harmonious interaction of federal legislation and provincial legislation is essential and lies in an interpretation of federal legislation that is compatible with the common law or civil law traditions, as the case may be;

• • •

WHEREAS the objective of the Government of Canada is to facilitate access to federal legislation that takes into account the common law and civil law traditions, in its English and French versions;

III. THE CIVIL LIABILITY AND THE ENVIRONMENT

This duality covers the field of environmental law as well. In Quebec, as with most other provinces, there is a regulatory regime in place whereby the state has assumed a large part of the responsibilities of protecting the environment. On the other hand, the civil law is also fertile ground for private environmental litigation based on the maxim "*[s]ic utere tuo ut alienum non laedas*" (or, "use your own property in such a manner as not to injure that of another").

While the issues dealt with in litigation and the practical results reached by the civil law in private environmental disputes present many similarities with those of the common law, the theoretical underpinnings are somewhat different. For example, the civil law makes no distinction between private and public nuisance. As will be seen in the following discussion, the civil law concepts of "abuse of rights" and "neighbourhood annoyances" can be said to be analogous to the concept of private nuisance in the common law.

A. FAULT-BASED LIABILITY

CIVIL CODE OF QUÉBEC
CQLR c CCQ-1991, art 1457

1457. Every person has a duty to abide by the rules of conduct incumbent on him, according to the circumstances, usage or law, so as not to cause injury to another.

Where he is endowed with reason and fails in this duty, he is liable for any injury he causes to another by such fault and is bound to make reparation for the injury, whether it be bodily, moral or material in nature.

He is also bound, in certain cases, to make reparation for injury caused to another by the act, omission or fault of another person or by the act of things in his custody.

ST LAWRENCE CEMENT INC V BARRETTE
2008 SCC 64, [2008] 3 SCR 392

LEBEL and DESCHAMPS JJ:

• • •

II. ANALYSIS

• • •

C. FAULT-BASED LIABILITY

[21] ... The first rule imposes a general duty to abide by the rules of conduct that lie upon a person having regard to the law, usage or circumstances (Ministère de la Justice, *Commentaires du ministre de la Justice: Le Code civil du Québec—Un mouvement de société* (1993), vol. I, at p. 886). Civil fault [TRANSLATION] "is the difference between the agent's conduct and the abstract, objective conduct of a person who is reasonable, prudent and diligent" (J.-L. Baudouin and P. Deslauriers,

La responsabilité civile (7th ed. 2007), vol. I, at p. 171; see also J. Pineau and M. Ouellette, *Théorie de la responsabilité civile* (2nd ed. 1980), at p. 7). The standard of civil fault thus corresponds to an obligation to act reasonably, prudently and diligently and can be characterized as an obligation of means ... . The basis for civil liability remains the same whether the impugned conduct is intentional or unintentional (Baudouin and Deslauriers, at p. 165). The purpose of civil liability is [TRANSLATION] "not to blame or punish but only to compensate for loss" (Baudouin and Deslauriers, at p. 9; see also Pineau and Ouellette, at p. 60). Intent to injure is therefore not necessary to trigger liability ... .

[22] In the context of neighbourhood disturbances, civil fault may relate either to the abusive exercise of a right of ownership or to a violation of standards of conduct that are often set out in statutory or regulatory provisions relating to the use of property. ...

• • •

(3) Fault and Violation of a Law

• • •

[34] In Quebec civil law, the violation of a legislative standard does not in itself constitute civil fault ... . For that, an offence provided for in legislation must also constitute a violation of the standard of conduct of a reasonable person under the general rules of civil liability set out in art. 1457 *C.C.Q.* ... . The standard of civil fault corresponds to an obligation of means. Consequently, what must be determined is whether there was negligence or carelessness having regard to the specific circumstances of each disputed act or each instance of disputed conduct. This rule applies to the assessment of the nature and consequences of a violation of a legislative standard.

• • •

[36] In Quebec, art. 1457 *C.C.Q.* imposes a general duty to abide by the rules of conduct that lie upon a person having regard to the law, usage or circumstances. As a result, the content of a legislative standard may influence the assessment of the duty of prudence and diligence that applies in a given context. In a civil liability action, it will be up to the judge to determine the applicable standard of conduct—the content of which may be reflected in the relevant legislative standards—having regard to the law, usage and circumstances.

QUEBEC (ATTORNEY GENERAL) V GIRARD
2004 CanLII 47874, [2005] RRA 13 (Qc CA) (SOQUIJ Translation)

I. MAIN APPEAL OF THE MINISTÈRE DE L'ENVIRONNEMENT ET DE LA FAUNE AND OF THE MUNICIPALITY

(A) THE FAULT OF THE MINISTÈRE DE L'ENVIRONNEMENT ET DE LA FAUNE

[3] The trial judge rightly concluded that environmental standards were contravened in the operation of a dry material disposal site at Shipshaw and that the Ministère de l'Environnement et de la Faune (hereinafter MEF)—well aware of the

contraventions since the operation of the site began—had not implemented the recommendations in its own inspection reports in a timely manner. On the contrary, through its own laxity and inaction, the MEF had permitted the situation to deteriorate to the critical point that led to the class action. The trial judge was therefore justified in concluding that the MEF had committed a fault.

(B) THE FAULT OF THE MUNICIPALITY

[4] Having authorized the creation of a dry material disposal site in a residential neighbourhood in the heart of the town, the municipality was required to exercise constant vigilance in ensuring the respect of environmental standards. The evidence shows that by 1996 the director general of the municipality had lost all confidence in the operator of the dry material disposal site due to the operator's repeatedly unacceptable behaviour. Moreover, the contractual agreement of May 8, 1995 expressly authorized the municipality to take recourse by interlocutory injunction in addition to enforcing municipal bylaws. Nevertheless, the municipality chose not to intervene or crack down on the operator, despite the inaction of the MEF and the operator's wrongdoing and bad faith. By remaining apathetic and indifferent to the actions of the operator and the laxity of the MEF, despite the means at its disposal, the municipality also committed a fault giving rise to liability.

NOTE

Since the enactment of art 1376 CCQ, the civil law principles of civil liability apply, as a rule, to wrongful acts by the state and its bodies and other legal persons established in the public interest. If the state intends to avoid the general rules of civil liability by invoking immunity from public law in order to discharge its obligations, it then has the burden of showing that this ground of defence applies to its situation. Although in the 2008 case discussed above the court did not discuss governmental civil liability in any detail, in many cases, it is an issue that has prompted much judicial analysis and comment: *Prud'Homme v Prud'Homme*, 2002 SCC 85, [2002] 4 SCR 663; *Carrier c Québec (Procureur général)*, 2011 QCCA 1231.

B. NO-FAULT LIABILITY IN RESPECT OF NEIGHBOURHOOD ANNOYANCES

In the area of environmental litigation, the most important civil cause of liability is neighbourhood annoyances under art 976 CCQ. The no-fault obligations to all neighbours (owners, lessees, or occupants) make it much easier for those affected by a neighbourhood source of environmental harm to seek remedies. Unlike the general tort regime laid down in art 1457 CCQ that is fault-based, successful claims under art 976 CCQ are based on the actual environmental effects rather than on the care taken by the defendant in light of applicable standards.

CIVIL CODE OF QUÉBEC
CQLR c CCQ-1991, art 976

976. Neighbours shall suffer the normal neighbourhood annoyances that are not beyond the limit of tolerance they owe each other, according to the nature or location of their land or local usage.

ST LAWRENCE CEMENT V BARRETTE
2008 SCC 64, [2008] 3 SCR 392

LEBEL and DESCHAMPS JJ:

• • •

II. ANALYSIS

• • •

D. NO-FAULT LIABILITY

(1) Preliminary Comments

[37] In addition to the general rules applicable to fault-based civil liability, it is necessary to consider the possibility of liability in situations where neighbours suffer abnormal annoyances but the owner who causes the damage has not committed a fault.

• • •

(3) Coming into Force of the Civil Code of Québec: Art. 976 C.C.Q. and No-Fault Liability

• • •

(D) SUMMARY OF THE LEGISLATIVE HISTORY, OF THE CASE LAW, AND OF COMMENTARIES ON ART. 976 C.C.Q.

• • •

[73] Next, it must be remembered that the actual words of art. 976 *C.C.Q.* do not require evidence of wrongful conduct to establish the liability of an owner who has caused excessive neighbourhood annoyances ... .

• • •

(5) General Policy Considerations

[80] Finally, it must be mentioned that the acceptance of no-fault liability furthers environmental protection objectives. ... No-fault liability also reinforces the application of the polluter-pay principle ... .

• • •

(7) Conclusion

[86] Even though it appears to be absolute, the right of ownership has limits. Article 976 *C.C.Q.* establishes one such limit in prohibiting owners of land from forcing their neighbours to suffer abnormal or excessive annoyances. This limit relates to the *result* of the owner's act rather than to the owner's *conduct*. It can therefore be said that in Quebec civil law, there is, in respect of neighbourhood disturbances, a no-fault liability regime based on art. 976 *C.C.Q.* which does not require recourse to the concept of abuse of rights or to the general rules of civil liability. With this form of liability, a fair balance is struck between the rights of owners or occupants of neighbouring lands.

• • •

E. APPLICATION OF THE PRINCIPLES OF CIVIL LIABILITY TO THE FACTS OF THIS CASE

• • •

(3) Finding of No-Fault Liability Under Art. 976 C.C.Q.

[95] After hearing the evidence, Dutil J. said she was convinced that, even though SLC had operated its plant in compliance with the applicable standards, the representatives and members of the group had suffered abnormal annoyances that were beyond the limit of tolerance neighbours owe each other according to the nature or location of their land (para. 304). First, clinker dust or cement dust had caused the most serious annoyances in all the zones she had identified, namely the red, blue, yellow and purple zones. Because of the dust deposits, many residents had to wash their cars, windows and garden furniture frequently and could not enjoy their property. This led to considerable annoyances associated with maintenance and painting and with the use of outdoor spaces (paras. 305 *et seq.*). As well, sulphur, smoke and cement odours caused abnormal annoyances in all zones except the purple zone (paras. 323 *et seq.*). Finally, the noise from the cement plant's operation caused annoyances that were beyond the limit of tolerance in the red zone and, to a lesser extent, in the blue zone (paras. 328 *et seq.*). In view of Dutil J.'s findings of fact, it seems clear to us that the group members suffered abnormal annoyances that varied in their intensity but were beyond the limit of tolerance neighbours owe each other. The trial judge was therefore justified in finding SLC liable under art. 976 *C.C.Q.*

[96] We note in closing that Dutil J. did not misinterpret the word "neighbour" as used in art. 976 *C.C.Q.* when she concluded that all members living in the neighbourhoods adjacent to the plant were neighbours of the plant for the purposes of that provision on the basis that they lived close enough to it (paras. 354-59). Article 976 *C.C.Q.* does not define the scope of the concept of "neighbour." Obviously, the plaintiff must prove a certain geographic proximity between the annoyance and its source. However, the word must be construed liberally. The leading case on this point, which dates back to 1975, is *Carey Canadian Mines Ltd. v. Plante*, [1975] C.A. 893. In that case, the plaintiff claimed damages from Carey Canadian Mines after a river crossing his land became polluted; the evidence showed that the pollution came from an asbestos deposit two miles away. The Quebec Court of Appeal confirmed that the obligation extended to the entire neighbourhood and that the properties concerned did not have to be adjacent.

QUEBEC (ATTORNEY GENERAL) V GIRARD
2004 CanLII 47874, [2005] RRA 13 (Qc CA) (SOQUIJ Translation)

II. INCIDENTAL APPEAL

• • •

(A) EXCLUSION OF CHILDREN

[9] The trial judge erred in fact and in law in concluding that the children residing on the properties located within the perimeter of the dry material disposal site and in the recognized damage zones suffered neither damage nor injury as such.

[10] First, we should note that the class action was authorized for a group comprising [TRANSLATION] "... any person, in any capacity whatsoever ... who has suffered and continues to suffer damages from contaminants, pollutants, odours, leaching waters, vermin or any other cause whatsoever ... ." It is therefore beyond doubt that children were included in this group and covered by the class action. Second, there is no evidence showing that the children had developed a threshold of tolerance that protected them from the serious problems that affected the adults. Finally, nothing in the evidence supported the trial judge's conclusion that the injury suffered by the adults was not experienced by the children as well. The record also shows that the children spent more time outside, engaged in recreational activities. Consequently, the children who resided with the adults during the periods covered by the class action should be included within the group of persons subject to compensation.

DAVID E ROBERGE, "NUISANCE LAW IN QUEBEC (ARTICLE 976 C.C.Q.): 10 YEARS AFTER CIMENT DU SAINT-LAURENT, WHERE DO WE STAND?"
(2017) 76 R du B 321 at 336-37, 340 [footnotes omitted]

(B) THE TRENDS SINCE CIMENT DU SAINT-LAURENT

• • •

As recognized by courts and doctrine, the normality of neighbourhood disturbances must be appreciated from the point of view of a reasonable person placed in similar circumstances.

Article 976 C.C.Q. has been described as requiring the demonstration of two main criteria, i.e. that the neighbourhood annoyances are recurring and severe. Since 2015, when the Court of Appeal suggested in *Plantons* [*Plantons A et P inc c Delage*, 2015 QCCA 7] a test in two steps along the concepts of recurrence and severity of the inconveniences, this analytical framework has been regularly followed by the courts when dealing with claims pursuant to article 976 C.C.Q. Some cases have also drawn a parallel between the requirement of the common law of nuisance to prove a "substantial and unreasonable" interference as described in *Antrim* [*Antrim Truck Centre Ltd v Ontario (Transportation)*, 2013 SCC 13, [2013] 1 SCR 594], and the need to show recurrent and severe annoyances pursuant to article 976 C.C.Q.

The concept of recurrence requires proof of an element of repetition and continuity over time. However, recurrence pertains to the inconveniences suffered, and not necessarily to the activity which caused them: hence, it has been decided that a unique act which occurred at a specific point in time may not prevent article 976 C.C.Q. to apply, insofar as the consequences of that act persist.

As for severity, article 976 C.C.Q. calls more specifically for analysing the normality of the inconveniences according to the location of the lands, their nature and local usage, to which should be added the timing of the inconveniences. These factors must be pondered according to overall circumstances, and their respective value can therefore vary from one case to another. In assessing severity, the courts have often reiterated that the evidence must reveal something beyond the mere deprivation of an advantage.

• • •

– Type of Neighbourhood

Article 976 C.C.Q. recognizes that the location of the lands and their nature are relevant factors. This contextual approach has led the courts to review the type of neighbourhood in which the inconveniences take place, including zoning regulations, in order to determine the fair expectations of neighbours.

It is obvious that what neighbours must tolerate will be different for those living in the country or in a city, in a residential or in a commercial zone.

C. ABUSE OF RIGHTS

CIVIL CODE OF QUÉBEC
CQLR c CCQ-1991, art 7

7. No right may be exercised with the intent of injuring another or in an excessive and unreasonable manner, and therefore contrary to the requirements of good faith.

ST LAWRENCE CEMENT V BARRETTE
2008 SCC 64, [2008] 3 SCR 392

[24] Article 7 *C.C.Q.* thus gives effect to the principle of the relativity of rights, which applies to rights as absolute in theory as the right of ownership. According to this principle, one person's right necessarily limits that of another person, and to uphold all such rights concurrently will reduce the absoluteness of each ... .

• • •

[25] Article 7 *C.C.Q.* places two limits on rights: a right may be exercised neither with the intent of causing injury nor in an excessive and unreasonable manner. ... An abuse of rights relates to the exercise of a right whose legitimacy is not at issue ... .

[26] This leads to the following question: Does the concept of abuse of rights under art. 7 *C.C.Q.* correspond to a scheme of civil liability separate from that of arts. 1457 and 1458 *C.C.Q.*? Civil law commentators in Quebec generally answer that abuse of rights constitutes civil fault in the exercise of a right ... .

• • •

[29] Where a right exists, therefore, the usual application of the concept of fault is qualified. The holder of a right has a sphere of autonomy in exercising that right. In such a context, it thus becomes crucial, when analysing civil liability, to consider the nature of the right in issue and the circumstances in which it is exercised, since, as Ghestin and Goubeaux note [in *Traité de droit civil—Introduction générale*, 3rd ed (Paris: LGDJ, 1990)], an *abuse* of rights must be found in order to show fault. Once an abuse is found, the holder of the right loses the protection of the sphere of autonomy that flows from the right. Violation of a standard of conduct is therefore inextricably linked to the concept of abuse of rights.

(2) Abuse of Rights, Abnormal Annoyances and Art. 976 C.C.Q.

[30] However, conduct is not the deciding criterion when it comes to abnormal annoyances under art. 976 *C.C.Q.* ... An owner who causes abnormal annoyances

without either intent to injure or excessive and unreasonable conduct [TRANSLA-TION] "does not abuse his or her rights, because he or she cannot be accused of wrongful conduct" (Lafond, at p. 404). The word "abuse" implies blame and [TRANS-LATION] "is ill-suited to an attitude that may in itself be beyond reproach" (Ghestin and Goubeaux, at p. 686).

[31] A finding that abnormal annoyances were caused will therefore not be enough to establish fault in the exercise of a right. On the other hand, an owner who commits a fault may be held liable for damage even if the damage does not reach the level of abnormal annoyances. Article 976 *C.C.Q.* does not guarantee immunity from the consequences of civil fault. ... Even though art. 976 *C.C.Q.* incorporates a duty to tolerate normal neighbourhood annoyances, this does not mean that it authorizes wrongful conduct.

D. PRESUMED FAULTS AND SERVITUDES

The CCQ contains many servitudes and presumptions. In the context of civil liability and the environment, actions are primarily taken under arts 1465 CCQ and 982 CCQ.

CIVIL CODE OF QUÉBEC
CQLR c CCQ-1991, art 1465

§ 3. ACT OF A THING

1465. The custodian of a thing is bound to make reparation for injury resulting from the autonomous act of the thing, unless he proves that he is not at fault.

OUIMETTE C (CANADA) ATTORNEY GENERAL
2002 CanLII 30452, [2002] RJQ 1228 (Qc CA) (SOQUIJ Translation)

[72] That liability regime is independent of the regime in article 1457 of the *Civil Code of Québec* (*Quebec Railway, Light, Heat and Power Co. v. Vandry*, [1920] A.C. 662). The *Civil Code of Québec* confirms that duality, although the concept of fault underlies that liability. However, a fault is presumed only inasmuch as the damage stems from the autonomous act of a thing. Jean-Louis Baudouin wrote the following on the subject:

[TRANSLATION]

The Québec courts have established in various ways that, in order to benefit from the presumption in article 1054 of the *Civil Code of Lower Canada*, which is now article 1465 of the *Civil Code of Québec*, the victim must prove that *the accident was due to the thing itself, not to the conduct of the one controlling, manipulating or directing it at the time the harm was caused*. Hence, the presumption does not apply in favour of an employee who is injured because he or she slipped his or her hand into a meat grinder when using it. It therefore distinguishes between a personal act engaged in through or by means of an inanimate object and the act of a thing that, through its own activity, harms another. However, the exact, precise line of demarcation between the two regimes is often difficult to identify. [References omitted.] [Emphasis added.]

– *La responsabilité civile*, 4th ed. (Cowansville, Qc.: Yvon Blais, 1994) at 400 and 401, No 713.

[73] In this case, the appellant specifically reproached the respondent for improperly managing the Témiscamingue reservoir by tolerating water levels that are higher than necessary during free water periods. His expert advocated a different management method that would stop the erosion.

[74] It must be concluded that, in the opinion of the appellant himself, it is the conduct of the respondent, the respondent's way of doing things, that is at the root of the increased erosion, not the dam or the water it accumulates. The dam merely responds to the commands of its manager and the water level varies accordingly. The autonomous act is not at the root of the claim from the respondent.

CIVIL CODE OF QUÉBEC
CQLR c CCQ-1991, art 982

DIVISION III

WATER

• • •

982. Unless it is contrary to the general interest, a person having a right to use a spring, lake, sheet of water, underground stream or any running water may, to prevent the water from being polluted or depleted, require the destruction or modification of any works by which the water is being polluted or depleted.

MARK L SHEPHEARD, "FARMING, GOOD NEIGHBOURS, AND PROTECTING THE GENERAL INTEREST IN WATER RESOURCES: HOW EFFECTIVE IS THE PROMISE OF SUSTAINABLE WATERSHED MANAGEMENT IN QUEBEC?"
(2017) 13:2 McGill J of Sustainable Development L 271 at 280-82, 297-98
[footnotes omitted]

Jurisprudence interpreting article 976 of the *Civil Code of Québec* (the good neighbour principle) is important for the implementation of sustainable watershed management in Quebec as it delineates the general interest in water. Interpretation of article 976 by the Supreme Court of Canada (SCC) provides guidance about community tolerance of environmental harms. The Court has set the overall tone for natural resource use obligations and the consequences of subjecting neighbours to intolerable annoyance by establishing that the good neighbour principle limits absolute rights of private ownership. ...

The *good neighbour* principle in article 976 functions as the preamble, or general provision, for the entire section of the *Civil Code of Québec* that deals with special rules about the ownership of immovables. This contextual role cannot be underestimated. When the National Assembly introduced this principle into the *Civil Code of Québec*, it explicitly did so to take greater account of environmental concerns, the value of water, and quality of life. Of particular note for this discussion is the level of tolerance described by article 982, giving a person with water access rights the ability to prevent water sources from being polluted or depleted by seeking the modification or destruction of water access and use works. The practical implication of this article is to make water quality and quantity relevant considerations of good neighbourly conduct. The general interest in water is pivotal to the assessment because it provides the standard—defined in particular circumstances—beyond which a neighbour has grounds to act. The *Water Protection Act* [*Act to affirm the collective nature of water resources and to promote better governance of water and associated environments*, CQLR c C-6.2] specifies the general interest as protection, restoration, improvement, and management of water in pursuit of sustainable development. This has the potential to link farm water management practice and accountability with sustainable management outcomes at a watershed scale, making community interests and environmental concerns relevant to defining what it means for a farmer to be a good neighbour in the use and management of resources.

• • •

The administrative arrangements for sustainable watershed management provide formal expectations about anticipated behaviour and good neighbourly relations. The *Civil Code of Québec* promotes good neighbourly conduct, protects the legitimate use of watercourses by riparian landowners, and emphasizes water as a chose commune (something common to all) and in the general interest. The expectations of good neighbourly conduct, legitimate use, and water as a common thing are reinforced by the *Water Protection Act*. Together these sources of legal expectation establish a public interest in private natural resource use and its impacts on the sustainability of resource management in a watershed. ...

• • •

With this in mind, bringing the general interest to the fore in farmer decision making about land and water management involves making the duty for water protection enforceable in the general interest. Article 982 of the *Civil Code of Québec* enables this by allowing private claimants to seek an injunction or damages for environmental harm. Such private enforcement is likely to enhance the definition of responsibility under the statutory duty to protect water resources and improve its behavioural effectiveness as a standard for the sustainable use of resources.

QUESTION

Compare the civil law and the common law on matters such as nuisance and proof of fault. Which model is better suited to environmental protection?

IV. CAUSAL LINK

The problem of causation with respect to environmental litigation is as acute in the civil law as it is in the common law. It shows that, even if we know that industrial, agricultural, domestic, and other activities produce pollutants, the consequences that these pollutants may have on humans are very difficult to prove.

Current judicial thinking on causation in Quebec civil law is summarized in the following observations by Gonthier J of the Supreme Court of Canada in *Laferrière v Lawson*, [1991] 1 SCR 541 at 608-9, 1991 CanLII 87:

By way of summary, I would make the following brief, general observations:

- The rules of civil responsibility require proof of fault, causation and damage.
- Both acts and omissions may amount to fault and both may be analyzed similarly with regard to causation.
- Causation in law is not identical to scientific causation.
- Causation in law must be established on the balance of probabilities, taking into account all the evidence: factual, statistical and that which the judge is entitled to presume.
- In some cases, where a fault presents a clear danger and where such a danger materializes, it may be reasonable to presume a causal link, unless there is a demonstration or indication to the contrary.
- Statistical evidence may be helpful as indicative but is not determinative. In particular, where statistical evidence does not indicate causation on the balance of probabilities, causation in law may nonetheless exist where evidence in the case supports such a finding.
- Even where statistical and factual evidence do not support a finding of causation on the balance of probabilities with respect to particular damage (e.g. death or sickness), such evidence may still justify a finding of causation with respect to lesser damage (e.g. slightly shorter life, greater pain).
- The evidence must be carefully analyzed to determine the exact nature of the fault or breach of duty and its consequences as well as the particular character of the damage which has been suffered, as experienced by the victim.
- If after consideration of these factors a judge is not satisfied that the fault has, on his or her assessment of the balance of probabilities, caused any real damage, then recovery should be denied.

NOTES AND QUESTION

1. Perhaps the most spectacular example of the difficulties in proving causation in private environmental litigation lies with the case of *Berthiaume c Val Royal Lasalle Ltée*, [1992] RJQ 76 (Qc Sup Ct).

Berthiaume was a consolidation of six civil suits in damages arising from the installation of urea formaldehyde foam insulation (UFFI) in private residences. Plaintiffs sued in damages both UFFI installation contractors and manufacturers for alleged impairment of their health resulting from toxic vapours and microscopic dust given off by the foam insulation. They claimed pecuniary compensation for property damage caused by noxious odours and other material damage caused by the product itself and by its faulty installation in the walls of their houses. They also claimed damages for the resulting loss in property value. Some of the defendant installation contractors have also filed a warranty action against both manufacturers of UFFI and their own insurers. The foam had been installed in the plaintiffs' homes from March 1977 to September 1990. UFFI was finally banned in Canada in 1981.

The trial lasted a record six years and five months, with 460 days of trial. The transcript of the evidence (114,000 pages) and of the arguments ran to 809 volumes. There were 1,820 exhibits, and 122 witnesses gave testimony. Hurtubise J took the case under advisement on February 20, 1990 and rendered a 1,099-page judgment on December 13, 1991.

The plaintiffs ultimately failed because the trial judge held that they had not established a causal relationship between the alleged injury and damage and the use of the products in question. The trial judge expressly stated that, with the rejection of risk theory in *Lapierre v AG*

(Que), [1985] 1 SCR 241, 1985 CanLII 66, liability rested on the need to establish fault or harm and causation on the balance of probabilities. The judge found that some of the plaintiffs did suffer symptoms as alleged, but those symptoms were relatively minor and non-specific in nature. They could thus have resulted from a variety of causes.

While the average levels of formaldehyde (given off by UFFI) were slightly higher in UFFI-insulated homes, there were other potentially relevant factors, such as the age of the house, the type of walls, and the existence of other sources of formaldehyde within the house. Furthermore, existing instruments capable of measuring such levels were "fragile," thus making it impossible to trace a "dosage response" curve between formaldehyde levels and the seriousness of the symptoms. As for the risk of cancer, the trial judge held that, on the preponderance of evidence, the plaintiff had not established the existence of such a risk but that the weight of the evidence pointed in fact to the opposite. The claims for material damages and loss of property value were also dismissed.

On appeal, the Court of Appeal rejected all claims. Since the appellants had failed to prove the materiality of any health risk, they could not bypass the requirement to prove causation by simply claiming that the respondent installers had deprived them of a chance to avoid future health problems likely to cause a depreciation of their homes. The rules of civil liability did not allow them to rely on the concept of loss of opportunity in such a way. Furthermore, by putting forward such an argument based on future health problems, the appellants were, in fact, asking for a re-evaluation of the whole of the findings of fact upon which rested the fundamental conclusion of the judgment at trial. Since the appellants could not demonstrate manifest or overriding error on the part of the trial judge, the Court of Appeal refused to make such a re-evaluation. (*Berthiaume c Réno-Dépôt inc*, [1995] RJQ 2796, 21 CELR (NS) 188, *(sub nom Denicourt c Construction Marc-André Noël inc)* 1995 CanLII 4831 (Qc CA).

2. The decision in *Spieser c Canada (Procureur général)*, 2012 QCCS 2801, another important precedent, illustrates the very complex nature of a claim for health-related injuries alleged to be attributed to environmental contamination and the challenges that the parties face in the context of such litigation, in particular in demonstrating the link between pollutants and health-related injuries. The plaintiff, Marie-Paule Spieser, sued the Government of Canada, a research centre, and a munitions manufacturer on the grounds that they had allegedly spilled trichloroethylene (TCE) on the ground, leading to a contamination of the water table and drinking water wells of the residents of the municipality of Shannon. The plaintiff alleged that this TCE contamination was the cause of an abnormally high number of cases of cancer, illnesses, and other ill effects among the residents of Shannon. Spieser sought compensation, damages, and injunctive relief, requiring the defendants to take measures to decontaminate the water table. She also claimed punitive damages related to injuries to the physical integrity of class members and to the enjoyment of their property.

The trial judge dismissed the claim in civil liability, being of the view that the evidence did not show on a balance of probabilities that the spilling of TCE that contaminated ground water was the cause of the elevated number of cancers and diseases among the residents of Shannon. However, the Superior Court did award compensatory damages, on the grounds that the defendants were subject to the no-fault liability regime of art 976 CCQ and that the contamination of the water table and water wells amounted to an abnormal nuisance exceeding tolerance limits. It will be interesting to see whether the Court of Appeal will uphold the judgment at first instance.

Such cases are perfects examples of the complexity of litigation, notably the interaction between the environment and health, and the challenges for the judicial system.

3. Compare the civil law and the common law on the approach for establishing causation. Is there any difference? Which model is better suited to environmental protection?

V. CIVIL LIABILITY AND ADMINISTRATIVE APPROVALS

In practice, a review of the cases shows that, in litigation based on the theory of "neighbourhood disturbances," judges are less concerned with finding a fault, whether proven or presumed, than they are with establishing whether the environmental prejudice or inconvenience suffered exceeds that which should be normal in the circumstances.

In this context, the defendant cannot escape liability by establishing that his or her activity has been authorized by governmental authority as evidenced by the issuance of the necessary permits *if* the activity is conducted in a manner that exceeds the normal measure of inconvenience that should be acceptable in the circumstances. Most of the existing cases deal with authorizations, such as municipal permits, allowing only the establishment of the activity. It is likely that a defence based on specific environmental approvals, especially those setting allowable effluent levels, will be more problematic for the courts.

The defence based on environmental approvals came before the Quebec Court of Appeal in *Gestion Serge Lafrenière inc c Calvé*, 1999 CanLII 13814, [1999] RJQ 1313 (Qc CA). The case involved a request for an interlocutory injunction by a riparian owner of Lake Heney in the Outaouais Region seeking the closure of a fish farming operation whose phosphorus-rich final effluent was discharged into a stream flowing into the lake. Scientific evidence showed rapid eutrophication of the lake on a scale likely to cause irreparable harm.

Among the issues tackled by the Court of Appeal in *Gestion Serge Lafrenière* was whether or not arts 976, 981, and 982 CCQ have precedence over the EQA.

The petitioner, the president of the *Association pour la protection du lac Heney*, submitted the argument that, even if the respondent was operating its fish farm in accordance with a valid ministerial authorization issued under the authority of the EQA, those provisions of the CCQ, especially art 982 and the private right of a neighbour to a clean environment, should have precedence. Therefore, such private right could be enforced by the court not withstanding a valid authorization granted under the statute.

In a carefully reasoned opinion, Gendreau JA, writing for a unanimous bench, rejected as too absolute a petitioner's reasoning that that would deprive the holder of a ministerial authorization of any legal protection with respect to the effluents covered by such authorization. Thus, in principle, the administration of the statute should have precedence over private law rules as expressed in the CCQ.

However, according to the court, there could arise situations whereby an activity likely to have an impact on environmental quality is authorized without the establishment of any specific limits by law, by regulation, or in the ministerial authorization itself as to the permissible level of contaminants discharged in the environment during the course of such activity. In such an instance, private law rules could then be invoked as backup to impose limits on an environmental authorization granted by public authority. As stated by Gendreau JA (at 1326-27):

> I am of the view that the administration of the *Environment Quality Act* should ordinarily have precedence over private law rules. However, there may be circumstances where, as in the present case, an activity is authorized without any emission levels being set down under statute, by regulation or in the certificate authorization. In such a case might not a neighbour be able to avail of civil law rules of good neighbourliness to compel the operators to take reasonable measures to minimize the disruption caused by their operation? Private law provisions in such a context would be suppletive rules that would serve as a check on an authorization granted by a public authority for the use of land. There may be other similar scenarios. [Translated by author.]

As will be seen later, in situations such as that arising in *Gestion Serge Lafrenière*, the plaintiffs could also try to seek redress by attacking the validity of the ministerial authorization relied upon by the defendant whose activity the plaintiff complains is causing environmental harm.

QUESTION

Compare the civil law and the common law about the specific defence of environmental approvals. When an activity is operated under an environmental authorization granted by public authority, to what extent can the common law rules be applied as suppletive law in this context?

VI. THE SPECIAL CASE OF AGRICULTURAL ACTIVITIES

Agricultural activities carried out in agricultural zones established under the *Act respecting the preservation of agricultural land and agricultural activities*, CQLR c P-41.1 enjoy specific statutory protection from civil proceedings seeking damages or injunctive relief regarding dust, odors, or noise arising from the conduct of such activities. Quebec's "right to farm" legislation not only reinstates the defence of prior occupation (s 100) but grants what amounts to total immunity from civil recourse as long as there is compliance with regulatory standards. The Quebec statute goes so far as to exclude dust, odors, and noise produced by agricultural activities from the standard of neighbourhood annoyances laid down in art 976 CCQ.

ACT RESPECTING THE PRESERVATION OF AGRICULTURAL LAND AND AGRICULTURAL ACTIVITIES
CQLR c P-41.1, ss 79.17–17.19.2

79.17. In an agricultural zone, no person shall incur liability toward a third person by reason of dust, noise or odours resulting from agricultural activities, or shall be prevented by a third person from exercising such agricultural activities, if they are exercised, subject to section 100,

(1) in accordance with the regulatory standards adopted under the *Environment Quality Act* (chapter Q-2) that relate to dust and noise or, as regards odours, in accordance with the standards aimed at reducing the inconvenience caused by odours resulting from agricultural activities, originating from the exercise of the powers provided for in subparagraph 4 of the second paragraph of section 113 of the *Act respecting land use planning and development* (chapter A-19.1);

(2) in accordance with the provisions of the *Environment Quality Act* as regards any matter not covered by regulatory standards.

79.18. Where a plaintiff or an applicant in an action or proceedings brought against a person exercising agricultural activities in an agricultural zone

(1) claims damages to compensate for the dust, noise or odours resulting from the activities, or

(2) applies for an injunction to prevent or modify the exercise of the activities,

it is incumbent upon the plaintiff or applicant, to establish liability, to prove that the person exercising the agricultural activities has contravened the applicable regulatory standards or the *Environment Quality Act* (chapter Q-2), as the case may be.

79.19. In an agricultural zone, the inconvenience caused by dust, noise or odours resulting from agricultural activities does not exceed the limit of tolerance neighbours owe each other, insofar as the activities are exercised, subject to section 100,

(1) in accordance with the regulatory standards adopted under the *Environment Quality Act* (Chapter Q-2) that relate to dust and noise or, as regards odours, in accordance with the standards aimed at reducing the inconvenience caused

by odours resulting from agricultural activities, originating from the exercise of the powers provided for in subparagraph 4 of the second paragraph of section 113 of the *Act respecting land use planning and development* (chapter A-19.1);

(2) in accordance with the provisions of the *Environment Quality Act* as regards any matter not covered by regulatory standards.

79.19.1. Nothing in this division shall be interpreted as enabling a person who carries on an agricultural activity to avoid liability for a gross or intentional fault committed in carrying on that activity.

79.19.2. The agricultural activities of a breeding unit that are carried on in accordance with subdivisions 1.1 and 1.2 of Division I of this chapter are, for the purposes of sections 79.17 to 79.19, deemed to be carried on in compliance with the standards aimed at reducing the inconvenience caused by odours resulting from agricultural activities, originating from the exercise of the powers provided for in subparagraph 4 of the second paragraph of section 113 of the *Act respecting land use planning and development* (chapter A-19.1).

NOTE

Under the Quebec statute, regulatory compliance is the only condition for granting immunity. Those provisions do not even require that agricultural activities be conducted according to "normal farming practice" as is the case with similar "right to farm" legislation elsewhere in Canada. Thus, the underlying purpose of those provisions would appear to be to prevent the courts from granting relief to victims of dust, odour, and noise generated by agricultural activities when those activities are conducted in accordance with regulatory standards, even where there is a finding that those activities cause nuisances of an abnormal and exorbitant character.

Given the scope of the definition of "agricultural activities" in the Quebec statute (s 1(0.1)), which extends to "activities relating to the storage, packaging, processing and sale of farm products" "carried out by a producer on his farm with respect to farm products from his operation or, secondarily, from the operations of other producers," Quebec's "right to farm" provisions are undoubtedly the most indulgent of farming interests. (For a critical review, see L Giroux, "Où s'en va le droit québécois l'environnement?" in *Développements récents en droit de l'environnement (1997)*, Barreau du Québec, Formation permanente, vol 90 (Cowansville, Qc: Éditions Yvon Blais, 1997) 381 at 440-49.)

VII. CLASS ACTIONS

Since 1979, the *Code of Civil Procedure*, CQLR c C-25 has authorized class actions in Quebec (arts 999-1051). Class actions remain authorized under the revised *Code of Civil Procedure*, CQLR c C-25.01 (CCP) (arts 571-604). Unlike other Canadian legislation authorizing class actions, the conditions set out in the CCP do not include the requirement that the class action be the best means of settling the matter in dispute. The conditions required for class actions are provided for in art 575 CCP:

575. The court authorizes the class action and appoints the class member it designates as representative plaintiff if it is of the opinion that

(1) the claims of the members of the class raise identical, similar or related issues of law or fact;

(2) the facts alleged appear to justify the conclusions sought;

(3) the composition of the class makes it difficult or impracticable to apply the rules for mandates to take part in judicial proceedings on behalf of others or for consolidation of proceedings; and

(4) the class member appointed as representative plaintiff is in a position to properly represent the class members.

The usefulness of class actions in environmental litigation was greatly strengthened with the 1990 decision of the Court of Appeal in *Comité d'environnement de la Baie inc c Société d'électrolyse et de chimie Alcan ltée*, 1990 CanLII 3338, [1990] RJQ 655, 6 CELR (NS) 150 (Qc CA) [cited to RJQ], leave to appeal refused, [1990] 2 SCR xi.

In that case, the court was sitting on appeal from a Superior Court judgment refusing to grant authorization to institute a class action (then art 1002, now art 574 CCP) on the ground that the requirements of the CCP had not been met (then art 1003, now art 575 CCP).

The case arose out of the defendant's operations at its docking facilities for the unloading of mineral ore required in its aluminum smelting process. It was argued that dust from the fallout of these mineral substances caused damages to the houses of the 2,400 members of the group of residents, making maintenance and cleaning more costly and depriving the owners of the enjoyment of their property.

In the Superior Court, Alcan had argued successfully that, in particular, the causes of action of the members of the group did not raise "identical, similar or related questions of law or fact" as required by then art 1003(a) (now art 575(1) CCP).

The Court of Appeal reversed this decision and granted the authorization. The court held that art 1003(a) did not require that all or even most of the questions raised be identical, similar, or closely related. It was enough for members of the group to raise a number of issues of law or fact that were sufficiently related to justify a class action. In rendering the unanimous judgment of the court, Rothman JA (at 661) extolled the advantages and virtues of this remedy in environmental matters:

> The class action recourse seems to me a particularly useful remedy in appropriate cases of environmental damage. Air or water pollution rarely affect just one individual or one piece of property. They often cause harm to many individuals over a large geographic area.
>
> The issues involved may be similar in each claim but they may be complex and expensive to litigate, while the amount involved in each case may be relatively modest.
>
> The class action, in these cases, seems an obvious means for dealing with claims for compensation for the harm done when compared to numerous individual law suits, each raising many of the same issues of fact and law.

Since the decision of the Supreme Court in *St Lawrence Cement*, class action is increasingly used in environmental law matters. The liberal approach to the authorization to bring a class action in Quebec favours the exercise of claims pursuant to art 976 CCQ. However, the authorization requirement still plays an important part in avoiding vexatious claims.

A. IDENTICAL, SIMILAR, OR RELATED QUESTIONS OF LAW OR FACT

VIVENDI CANADA INC V DELL'ANIELLO
2014 SCC 1, [2014] 1 SCR 3

LEBEL and WAGNER JJ:

• • •

[48] Caution must be exercised when applying the principles from *Dutton* [*Western Canadian Shopping Centres Inc v Dutton*, 2001 SCC 46, [2001] 2 SCR 534] and *Rumley* [*Rumley v British Columbia*, 2001 SCC 69, [2001] 3 SCR 184] to the rules of

Quebec civil procedure relating to class actions. Although those decisions have now been recognized in Quebec law and have been cited and applied many times by Quebec courts, the issue that is central to this appeal nonetheless shows that it is necessary to clarify the relevance and scope of the principles in question in the context of Quebec procedural law. ...

• • •

[50] The source of the commonality requirement in Quebec civil procedure is art. 1003 *C.C.P.* [now art 575], which requires that "the recourses of the members raise identical, similar or related questions of law or fact."

[51] Two observations are in order with respect to the wording of art. 1003(a) *C.C.P.* First, this paragraph provides that a class action can be authorized only if the questions are common. Nowhere has the legislature stated that there must be common answers.

[52] Second, if art. 1003(a) is compared with the legislation of the common law provinces, it can be seen that the wording used to establish the commonality requirement is different in the latter. For example, the requirement is expressed in broader and more flexible terms in Quebec's *C.C.P.* than in Ontario's legislation, which requires the existence not merely of similar or related questions, but of "common issues": *Class Proceedings Act*, 1992, S.O. 1992, c. 6, s. 5(1)(c). Moreover, the wording of the Ontario statute is used in the legislation of all the other common law provinces of Canada that have legislated with respect to class actions ... .

[53] Although the expression "common issues" is frequently used by Quebec judges and authors, its content is not exactly the same as that of the expression "identical, similar or related questions of law or fact." It would be difficult to argue that a question that is merely "related" or "similar" could always meet the "common issue" requirement of the common law provinces. The test that applies in Quebec law therefore seems to be less stringent. ...

[54] In addition, it can be seen from the Quebec courts' interpretation of art. 1003(a) *C.C.P.* that their approach to the commonality requirement has often been broader and more flexible than the one taken in the common law provinces. The Quebec courts propose a flexible approach to the common interest that must exist among the group's members ... .

• • •

[57] Thus, the Quebec approach to authorization is more flexible than the one taken in the common law provinces, although the latter provinces do generally subscribe to an interpretation that is favourable to the class action. The Quebec approach is also more flexible than the current approach in the United States ... .

[58] There is one common theme in the Quebec decisions, namely that the *C.C.P.*'s requirements for class actions are flexible. As a result, even where circumstances vary from one group member to another, a class action can be authorized if some of the questions are common: ... . To meet the commonality requirement of art. 1003(a) *C.C.P.*, the applicant must show that an aspect of the case lends itself to a collective decision and that once a decision has been reached on that aspect, the parties will have resolved a not insignificant portion of the dispute ... . All that is needed in order to meet the requirement of art. 1003(a) *C.C.P.* is therefore that there be an identical, related or similar question of law or fact, unless that question would play only an insignificant role in the outcome of the class action. It is not necessary that the question make a complete resolution of the case possible.

B. FACTS ALLEGED APPEAR TO JUSTIFY THE CONCLUSIONS SOUGHT

CARRIER C QUÉBEC (PROCUREUR GÉNÉRAL)
2011 QCCA 1231 (SOQUIJ Translation)

[37] At the authorization stage, when the sufficiency of the evidence is assessed only in a *prima facie* manner, as a rule, it is premature to find that an immunity defence applies in favour of the State. What amounts to one of several grounds of defence, the immunity argued in this case by the respondent cannot, in considering the authorization, be raised to the ranks of grounds for dismissal. Failing a finding that the motion is *prima facie* frivolous or bound to fail or else that the facts alleged are insufficient or that it is [TRANSLATION] "undisputable" that the right claimed is without merit, it seems to me that, apart from these circumstances, it is not advisable at the start of the analysis to decide the absolute value of such a defence.

• • •

[45] Except in the case of clear and express statutory immunity, and considering that in general, an analysis of the value of a line of defence based on State immunity is more a question of mixed law and fact than it is a question of law alone, it was appropriate under the circumstances of the present case, and in light of the allegations in the motion, to leave it up to the trial judge to decide this issue.

C. COMPOSITION OF THE GROUP

As for the possibility that collective recovery (art 595 CCP) would not be feasible or convenient, the provisions of the CCP give the judge to whom a motion for authorization is presented some discretion in deciding what questions are to be dealt with collectively and what questions are to be decided individually. She does not have to dismiss the motion simply because the applicant has proposed collective recovery when individual recovery would be more expedient (art 599 CCP). In the circumstances, the basis of responsibility has to be the same for all members of the group. The principal differences between the claims would relate to the damages suffered by individual members, and, even then, there might be some similar categories of damage. The trial judge might then decide to limit the common questions in an appropriate manner and order individual recovery of the damages.

DAVID E ROBERGE, "NUISANCE LAW IN QUEBEC (ARTICLE 976 C.C.Q.): 10 YEARS AFTER CIMENT DU SAINT-LAURENT, WHERE DO WE STAND?"
(2017) 76 R du B 321 at 355-56, 357 [footnotes omitted]

When assessing damages in class actions, it is recognized that each class member does not need to testify to establish the injury actually sustained. In [*St Lawrence Cement*], the Supreme Court stated that "the court can draw from the evidence a presumption of fact that the members of the group have suffered a similar injury" to that of the plaintiff. In Quebec, these presumptions must be serious, precise and concordant, pursuant to article 2849 C.C.Q.

What must be proven is an element of damage common to everyone, and while the injury of the class members may vary in intensity, courts can infer that each member has sustained injury based on similarities between the claimants' characteristics.

Accordingly, courts can divide the class into subgroups, each of them made up of members who have suffered a similar injury. ...

• • •

Given the judicial discretion and the difficulty in assessing environmental annoyances, the Supreme Court recognized that the use of average amounts to indemnify class members may be reasonable and appropriate in certain circumstances.

NOTES

1. In *Nadon c Anjou (Ville)*, 1994 CanLII 5900, [1994] RJQ 1823, 28 MPLR (2d) 139 (Qc CA) [cited to RJQ], the Court of Appeal again emphasized the particularly well-adapted nature of class actions for litigation raising environmental protection issues. The application was for authorization to institute a class action for damages and an injunction, on behalf of approximately 200,000 people who were allergic to ragweed pollen, against 23 municipalities for contravening the by-law obliging them to eradicate ragweed from their land by August 1.

The Court of Appeal reversed the Superior Court decision and authorized the class action. In this connection, the court stressed (at 1827-28) that the conditions set out in art 1003 (now art 575 CCP) are to be interpreted in a non-restrictive manner and that once they have been met there is little discretion left to the court, which does not need to rule on the validity in law of the arguments relied on by petitioners or in the respondent defence. The action was ultimately dismissed, since the plaintiff could not show that the hay fever resulted from plants on land owned or controlled by the municipalities. The court also held that the EQA protected human beings in general, not individuals that had specific medical problems (see *Nadon c Montréal (Ville de)*, 2008 QCCA 2221, leave to appeal to SCC refused, [2009] SCCA No 11 (QL)).

2. Let us now examine some case law where class actions were authorized. In "*Snowmobiles on the Parc linéaire « Petit train du Nord »*," the members of the group were granted injunctive relief to prohibit the circulation of snowmobiles on the Parc linéaire « Petit train du Nord ». From 1997 to 2004, a monetary relief in the amount of $1,200 per year (plus interests and additional indemnity) was also granted to all persons who lived at a distance of 100 metres or less from the snowmobile track during the winter season. See *Coalition pour la protection de l'environnement du parc Linéaire « Petit train du nord » c Comté des Laurentides (Municipalité régionale)*, 2004 CanLII 45407, [2005] RJO 116 (Qc Sup Ct).

Class actions have also been authorized for victims of the severe floods in the Saguenay and Lac St-Jean regions in the summer of 1996. In these actions, the victims claimed damages against the owners and operators of dams and dikes, whom they held partially or totally responsible for loss of property and personal injury. They alleged that, due to negligence and carelessness on the part of the owners and operators, some of which were agents of the Crown, the floods had not been properly controlled. For an overview of some of the complex issues involved in these actions, see *Arseneault c Québec (Société immobilière)*, 1997 CanLII 8910 (Qc Sup Ct) (settlement agreement).

In *Regroupement des citoyens du quartier St-Georges inc c Alcoa Canada ltée*, 2007 QCCS 2691, the members of the group sought the environmental rehabilitation of their land and houses in the St-Georges neighbourhood, financial compensation for the members who had developed an illness caused by emissions from the plant, and injunctive relief for the reduction of the plant's harmful emissions.

QUESTION

Review your provincial class actions statute. Do any elements or provisions differ fundamentally from those of the Quebec model?

VIII. ECOLOGICAL PREJUDICE

With the *Act to affirm the collective nature of water resources and to promote better governance of water and associated environments*, CQLR c C-6.2 adopted in 2009, the province of Quebec formally recognized ecological harm as a category of indemnifiable damage. This development is symbolically significant and builds on the recognition of this category of damages by the Supreme Court in the 2004 decision *British Columbia v Canadian Forest Products Ltd*, 2004 SCC 38, [2004] 2 SCR 74.

> ## ACT TO AFFIRM THE COLLECTIVE NATURE OF WATER RESOURCES AND TO PROMOTE BETTER GOVERNANCE OF WATER AND ASSOCIATED ENVIRONMENTS
> ### CQLR c C-6.2, s 8
>
> 8. If damage to water resources, including impairment of their physical, chemical or biological properties, ecological functions or quantitative status, is caused by a person or through a person's fault or illegal act, the Attorney General may institute an action against that person, in the name of the State as custodian of the interests of the nation in water resources, with a view to obtaining one or more of the following:
>
> (1) restoration of the water resources to their original state or a state similar to their original state;
>
> (2) reparation through compensatory measures;
>
> (3) reparation by payment of compensation in a lump sum or otherwise.
>
> For the purposes of this section, "original state" means the state of the water resources and of their ecological functions as it would have existed had the damage not occurred, determined on the basis of the best available information.
>
> The obligation to make reparation for damage to water resources or their ecological functions caused through the fault or illegal act of two or more persons is solidary.

NOTE

The compensation obtained as a result of an action for damage to water resources filed under s 8 above is credited to the Green Fund established by s 15.1 of the *Act respecting the Ministère du Développement durable, de l'Environnement et des Parcs*, CQLR c M-30.001 to finance water governance measures, including water protection and development measures, and measures to ensure there is an adequate quality and quantity of water in a sustainable development perspective. There is a limitation period of ten years after the date on which the minister becomes aware of the damage (s 11 of the *Act to affirm the collective nature of water resources and to promote better governance of water and associated environments*).

IX. STATUTORY RIGHTS

As mentioned at the outset, Quebec follows the rest of Canada in relying on regulatory legislation as the main component of its environmental protection policy. Quebec's EQA contains the main elements of the basic provincial regulatory model as outlined in Chapter 15 of this text. However, there are a few differences in that province worth mentioning.

A. ENVIRONMENTAL RIGHTS

CHARTER OF HUMAN RIGHTS AND FREEDOMS
CQLR c C-12, ss 46.1, 49

46.1. Every person has a right to live in a healthful environment in which biodiversity is preserved, to the extent and according to the standards provided by law.

• • •

49. Any unlawful interference with any right or freedom recognized by this Charter entitles the victim to obtain the cessation of such interference and compensation for the moral or material prejudice resulting therefrom.

In case of unlawful and intentional interference, the tribunal may, in addition, condemn the person guilty of it to punitive damages.

BERDAH C PROCUREURE GÉNÉRALE DU QUÉBEC/ATTORNEY GENERAL OF QUEBEC
2018 QCCS 4379

[119] In its decision *Aubry v Éditions Vice-Versa* [[1998] 1 SCR 591, 1998 CanLII 817], the Supreme Court of Canada has confirmed that the infringement of a right guaranteed by the *Charter of Human Rights and Freedoms* [footnote omitted] will give rise to an action in damages only if a fault, damage and causal connection are established. The relevant passage reads as follows:

> 49. The case at bar raises a problem of civil law and it is in light of that law that it must be resolved. The infringement of a right guaranteed by the (*Charter of Human Rights and Freedoms*) (hereinafter the "Quebec Charter") gives rise, under s. 49 para.1, to an action for moral and material prejudice. Such an action is subject to the civil law principles of recovery. As a result, the traditional elements of liability, namely fault, damage and causal connection, must be established.

DE MONTIGNY V BROSSARD (SUCCESSION)
2010 SCC 51, [2010] 3 SCR 64

(2) OBJECTIVES OF EXEMPLARY DAMAGES

[47] While compensatory damages are awarded to compensate for the prejudice resulting from fault, exemplary damages serve a different purpose. An award of such damages aims at expressing special disapproval of a person's conduct and is tied to the judicial assessment of that conduct, not to the extent of the compensation required for reparation of actual prejudice, whether monetary or not. ...

[48] In Quebec law, the system of exemplary damages remains exceptional in nature. Article 1621 *C.C.Q.* states that such damages may be awarded only where this is provided for by law. As we have seen, the *Charter* so provides by allowing

exemplary damages to be awarded in cases involving unlawful and intentional interference with the rights and freedoms it guarantees. ...

[49] Because of the exceptional nature of this right, the Quebec courts have so far been quite strict in giving effect to the preventive purpose of exemplary damages under art. 1621 *C.C.Q.* by using them only for punishment and deterrence (both specific and general) of conduct that is considered socially unacceptable (*Béliveau St-Jacques* [*Béliveau St-Jacques v Fédération des employées et employés de services publics inc*, [1996] 2 SCR 345, 1996 CanLII 208], at paras. 21 and 126; *St-Ferdinand* [*Quebec (Public Curator) v Syndicat national des employés de l'hôpital St-Ferdinand*, [1996] 3 SCR 211, 1996 CanLII 172], at para. 119). An award of exemplary damages seeks to punish a person who commits an unlawful act for doing so intentionally and to deter that person, and members of society generally, from repeating the act by condemning it as an example.

ENVIRONMENT QUALITY ACT
CQLR c Q-2, s 19.1

CHAPTER III

THE RIGHT TO A HEALTHY ENVIRONMENT AND TO THE PROTECTION OF LIVING SPECIES

19.1. Every person has a right to a healthy environment and to its protection, and to the protection of the living species inhabiting it, to the extent provided for by this Act and the regulations, orders, approvals and authorizations issued under any section of this Act and, as regards odours resulting from agricultural activities, to the extent prescribed by any standard originating from the exercise of the powers provided for in subparagraph 4 of the second paragraph of section 113 of the *Act respecting land use planning and development* (chapter A-19.1).

ACT TO AFFIRM THE COLLECTIVE NATURE OF WATER RESOURCES AND TO PROMOTE BETTER GOVERNANCE OF WATER AND ASSOCIATED ENVIRONMENTS
CQLR c C-6.2, s 2

2. Under the conditions and within the limits defined by the law, it is the right of every natural person to have access to water that is safe for drinking, cooking and personal hygiene.

B. PUBLIC RIGHT TO PARTICIPATE IN THE ENFORCEMENT OF THE EQA

Since 1978, one of the special features of the Quebec statute is the important right, given to the public, to participate in the enforcement of the environmental regulatory regime. Participation is accomplished by a liberalization of the rules governing standing. Today, the Quebec

Superior Court has a unique and progressive statutory power to grant injunctive relief. See Paule Halley, « Recours en protection de l'environnement : le recours de la loi sur la qualité de l'environnement » in S Lavallée & P Issalys, dir, *Vastes mondes, Études en l'honneur du professeur Denis Lemieux*, ed (Montreal: Éditions Yvon Blais, 2018) at 363-95.

ENVIRONMENT QUALITY ACT
CQLR c Q-2, ss 19.2-19.7

19.2. A judge of the Superior Court may grant an injunction to prohibit any act or operation which interferes or might interfere with the exercise of a right conferred by section 19.1.

19.3. The application for an injunction contemplated in section 19.2 may be made by any natural person domiciled in Québec frequenting a place or the immediate vicinity of a place in respect of which a contravention is alleged.

It may also be made by the Attorney General and by any municipality in whose territory the contravention is being or about to be committed.

19.4. In the case where an interlocutory injunction is applied for, the security contemplated in article 511 of the *Code of Civil Procedure* (chapter C-25.01) shall not exceed $500.

19.5. Every application made pursuant to this division must be served on the Attorney General.

19.6. Every application for an injunction made under this division shall be heard and decided by preference.

19.7. Sections 19.2 to 19.6 do not apply in the case where a depollution project, land rehabilitation plan or program has been duly authorized or approved under this Act, or in the case where a depollution attestation has been issued under this Act, except with regard to any act contrary to the provisions of an authorization, a rehabilitation plan, a depollution program, a depollution attestation or any applicable regulation.

The Superior Court is empowered to grant an injunction, "to prohibit any act or operation which interferes ... with the exercise" of the right to a healthy environment and to its protection, and to the protection of the living species inhabiting it (s 19.2 EQA). It should be pointed out that those rights, granted by s 19.1 of the EQA, are illustrative of a certain category of certain environmental rights sought by those wishing to strengthen environmental laws in Canada.

In practice, because of the provisions of ss 19.1 and 19.7, the scope of this right is limited to cases where there has been a contravention of the Act; of a regulation; or of an order, approval, or authorization issued under the Act. This would include, for example, the right to enjoin a promoter from carrying on an activity or development project undertaken without first subjecting it to the environmental assessment process and obtaining the governmental approval required by ss 31.1 to 31.9 of the EQA (*Québec (Procureur général) c Béchard*, 1989 CanLII 403, [1989] RJQ 261, 3 CELR (NS) 307 at 322 (Qc CA)).

Under s 19.7 of the EQA, the holding of a ministerial authorization is a valid defence barring a plaintiff from obtaining an injunction under ss 19.1 and 19.2 unless the plaintiff can establish that the holder of such a certificate is acting contrary to its terms and conditions.

In such an instance, the Court of Appeal in *Gestion Serge Lafrenière* (discussed in Section V, above) recognized that the plaintiff in an injunction is entitled to seek a declaration that the ministerial authorization delivered to the defendant under the statutory scheme is null and void. Such a declaration by the court would lift the obstacle represented by s 19.7 of the EQA to the granting of injunctive relief to enforce the plaintiff's right to environmental quality as provided by ss 19.1 and 19.3 of the EQA:

> In such a context [where a plaintiff seeks a declaration of nullity], a citizen, who has suffered damage to his environment through the actions of a third party, has a sufficient interest to seek the vitiation of the authorization to carry on that activity. Such an interest is derived from the need to provide for a legal remedy to guarantee the right to a healthy environment, a right to the value of which has been recognized by both the legislator and the courts. [Translated by author.]

In that case, the Court of Appeal decided that the plaintiff had made a strong case that the ministerial authorization delivered by the minister of the environment should be declared null and void. The court said that, in delivering a ministerial authorization allowing the plaintiff to increase its phosphorous discharges from its fish farming operation, the minister had acted in an unreasonable manner because he was well aware that the lake into which the effluents flowed was already at risk. In addition, the minister had created an estoppel situation by not respecting his prior commitment to residents that there would be more studies and research on the effects of an increase in discharges on the lake prior to the issuance of the approval. The court thus came to the conclusion that the plaintiff was entitled to interlocutory injunctive relief in spite of s 19.7 of the EQA.

While the statutory injunction of the EQA does not prevent access to the common law remedy of injunction (arts 509-515 CCP), the advantages of using the statutory remedy lie with the fact that not only is standing much easier to achieve (because it is granted to "any natural person domiciled in Québec frequenting a place or the immediate vicinity of a place in respect of which a contravention is alleged" (s 19.3 EQA) but, also, in the case of an interlocutory injunction, security for costs that could be required from the applicant cannot exceed $500.

In a significant and early decision rendered in 1984, the Quebec Court of Appeal defined the boundaries of the regulatory regime and the civil law theory of neighbourhood disturbances as grounds for injunctive relief (*Enterprises BCP ltée c Bourassa* (1984), JE 84-279 (Qc CA), digested in *Canadian Environmental Law*, 2nd, vol 1, ref Q-4.8.). On an appeal from a Superior Court judgment issuing an injunction under s 19.2 of the EQA, the Court of Appeal held as follows:

1. Under s. 19.1 of the EQA, the court can, upon request, order the cessation of any activity conducted or operated without the authorization required under the EQA.
2. Under the statutory regime, this judicial stop order can only remain in force until the authorization has been obtained. The court thus held that the injunction should expire upon (appellant industry's) reception of it.
3. A court can grant injunctive relief based upon both (a) sections 19.1 of the EQA (for a contravention to the regulatory regime) and (b) the civil law theory of abuse of rights and abnormal annoyances. In such a case, that part of the order based on s. 19.1 is subject to the limitations set out in s. 19.7, but not the order based on the civil law principles.
4. Thus, an order requiring the cessation of all operations of an industrial plant—because environmental approval has not yet been granted—is limited by the proviso in s. 19.7, to the period until the environmental authorization is granted. However, those orders with respect to the manner of conducting the industrial operations (shutting off idling truck engines, prohibiting dumping of waste in the open) are not subject to the limitations of s. 19.7.

Hence, *Enterprises BCP ltée* shows the willingness of the courts to try to integrate traditional civil law concepts and contemporary regulatory legislation in order to fashion a more efficient environmental protection remedy available to private citizens.

NOTES

1. The Quebec Court of Appeal has refused to restrict the scope of the statutory recourse granted by ss 19.1 to 19.7 of the EQA. In *Nadon c Anjou* (as discussed in Section VII.C, above), the appellant had been refused authorization by the Superior Court to institute a class action against the city of Montreal and 22 other municipalities of the Montreal Urban Community (MUC). In her action, the appellant sought an injunction under s 19.1 to compel the respondent municipalities to eradicate ragweed from the lands they owned as mandated by a clean air by-law enacted by the MUC and approved by the minister of the environment under ss 124 and 124.2 of the EQA.

The Court of Appeal reversed and granted the authorization to institute the class action. The court pointed out that ss 19.1 to 19.7 had been inserted into the EQA in 1978 to liberalize access to the courts for citizens seeking to enforce the Act and the regulations. It rejected the argument, based on a strict reading of s 19.2, that it could not allow for the granting of a mandatory injunction.

2. An interlocutory injunction can also be granted under these sections, but the Court of Appeal has stated that they do not excuse the petitioner from establishing that the granting of the interlocutory injunction is "necessary in order to avoid serious or irreparable injury ... or a factual or legal situation of such a nature as to render the final judgment ineffectual" as required by art 511 of the CCP.

According to consistent case law, the Court of Appeal has ruled that, in the case of a violation of an objective norm contained in a public interest statute, there is an almost irrefutable presumption that there is serious or irreparable injury (see *Val-Bélair c Entreprises Raymond Denis inc*, 1993 CanLII 3664, [1993] RJQ 637 (Qc CA), leave to appeal to SCC refused [1993] 3 SCR vi; *Constantineau c Saint-Adolphe d'Howard (Municipalité)*, 1996 CanLII 6103 (Qc CA); *Filion c Vallée-du-Richelieu (Municipalité régionale de comté de la)*, 2006 QCCA 385; *Groupe CRH Canada inc c Beauregard*, 2018 QCCA 1063). The undertaking of an activity or the conduct of an operation without prior authorization having been obtained when it is required under the EQA is a typical example of the violation of an objective norm. Furthermore, in the total absence of prior authorization, the court does not have to inquire about the balance of convenience and inconvenience, and the interlocutory injunction will then issue. Because of s 126 of the EQA, this is the case, even against the government or one of its agencies (see *Maltais c Procureure générale du Québec*, 2018 QCCS 527).

3. As stated earlier, there is a great similarity between Quebec and the other provinces regarding fundamental problems of environmental law such as matters of causation. In the area of judicial enforcement of environmental rights, however, Quebec has taken the lead by codifying environmental rights and granting broad standing to residents and special injunction powers to the courts.

QUESTION

Compare the standing rules in the EQA with common law standing rules and those set out in other Canadian legislation. Which model is better suited to environmental protection?

C. PUBLIC PARTICIPATION AND ENVIRONMENTAL ASSESSMENT

Quebec has had an accessible public participation process for environmental issues since 1978 (SQ 1978, c 64), when the Bureau d'audiences publiques sur l'environnement (BAPE) was established. BAPE is a permanent, quasi-judicial agency that is separate from Quebec's Ministry of Environment and operates under its mandate (ss 6.3 and 31.3.5 EQA). The role of the BAPE is to provide government a perspective on sustainable development in its decision-making by presenting analysis and notices that take into account the 16 principles in s 6 of the *Sustainable Development Act*, CQLR c D-8.1.1. The purpose of this law is to set up a new management framework within the administration to ensure, in particular through the establishment of a set of principles, that powers and responsibilities are exercised in the pursuit of sustainable development.

To carry out its mission, the BAPE informs and consults the public on environmental issues or projects subject to public consultation. At the request of the minister, BAPE can proceed with inquiries, mediation, and public hearings in the environmental assessment process. It can also undertake special consultations, such as public review of government policies and programs (hazardous waste, forest protection, waste, and water management).

In 1978, Quebec became the first province in Canada to enshrine an environmental impact assessment process in its legislation (ss 31.1 to 31.9 EQA). The purpose of the environmental assessment and review process is to ensure that environmental concerns are integrated into project development and implementation planning. At two points during this process, the public has an opportunity to participate. First, BAPE provides the public with information, and any citizens who consider that the project should be publicly discussed and assessed can submit a request for public hearings to the minister (ss 31.3.1 and 31.3.5 EQA). In the case of hearings, the procedure followed by BAPE is based on public exchanges between the board, citizens, agencies and ministries, and the promoter (*Rules of procedure of the Bureau d'audiences publiques sur l'environnement*, CQLR c Q-2, r 45.1). At the end of the process, BAPE submits its report to the ministry, to be released to the public within 15 days (ss 6.7 and 31.3.7 EQA). The ministry then submits its own recommendations to the government, and the government may then issue or refuse to issue an authorization for the project (s 31.5 EQA).

QUESTION

Compare the public participation process for environmental assessment of the EQA with rules set out in other Canadian legislation. How is it similar? How is it different?

FURTHER READINGS

Desjardins, Marie-Claude & Hélène Mayrand, « Les recours des citoyens en vertu du droit commun » dans *JurisClasseur Québec*, collection « Droit public », Droit de l'environnement, fascicule 16 (Montréal: LexisNexis Canada, 2012) (feuilles mobiles).

Halley, P, « Recours en protection de l'environnement : le recours de la loi sur la qualité de l'environnement » dans S Lavallée & P Issalys, dir, *Vastes mondes, Études en l'honneur du professeur Denis Lemieux* (Montreal: Éditions Yvon Blais, 2018) à 363-95.

Thériault, Sophie & Charles Tremblay-Potvin, « Droit à l'environnement » dans *JurisClasseur Québec*, collection « Droit public », Droit de l'environnement, fascicule 4 (Montréal: LexisNexis Canada, 2012) (feuilles mobiles).

CHAPTER FOURTEEN

JUDICIAL REVIEW AND PUBLIC PARTICIPATION*

Alastair Lucas and Brett Carlson

I. INTRODUCTION

This chapter covers the territory of administrative law, which is concerned with the rights of citizens in relation to the exercise of power by the state. Administrative law is a common law–statute law amalgam that limits the exercise of state power on citizens by means of procedural fairness and substantive legal rights. It is closely connected with the rule of law in both its legal supremacy and its anti-arbitrariness manifestations. The increasing complexity of environmental regulation since the 1970s has produced a labyrinth of administrative bodies, tribunals, and appeal boards that exercise decision-making powers in relation to the environment. Administrative law in this context has assumed greater importance as citizens, businesses, and civil society resort increasingly to judicial review of regulatory decisions and seek greater participation in public environmental decision-making. Public participation has become particularly important in the last decade as attitudes toward major infrastructure projects have become increasingly polarized among civil society, Indigenous communities, and municipal and provincial governments, which desire greater participation in decision-making and judicial review. In addition, we have seen the emergence of "social licence," an extra-legal concept that, nevertheless, implies legally sanctioned consent.

---

* Based in part on the third edition chapter by Chris Tollefson.

II. ADMINISTRATIVE LAW AND JUDICIAL REVIEW: THE BASICS FOR ENVIRONMENTAL LAW

A. WHAT IS ADMINISTRATIVE LAW?

Administrative law is the body of law that governs government officials and administrative tribunals that are empowered to make decisions or pass regulations that affect people's rights or interests. In the environmental law context, this means that a broad range of decisions are subject to administrative law requirements. This extends to decisions made by cabinet, officials, and tribunals that have statutorily delegated powers. This is known as "tribunal law"—the administrative law of tribunals and decision-makers. Examples of this are approvals for contaminant release and for infrastructure granted by ministers, their designated officials, and the federal and provincial Cabinets. Tribunal law encapsulates legislative decision-making powers and decision-makers' rules of practice and procedure, as well as relevant common law principles.

This tribunal administrative law is the first stage encountered by aspiring public participants. Legislation, along with potentially applicable common law, prescribes the criteria for a citizen's "standing" to participate in environmental decisions. These rules offer persons the right to participate if they can demonstrate to a decision-maker that they meet the relevant statutory criteria—for example, that they are "directly affected" by a decision. This is not the same as general public opportunities to participate, which may or may not be available depending on what legislators say about public participation in their statutes or how decision-makers exercise discretionary statutory powers.

Where persons are granted the right to participate in a decision, the procedural elements of participation such as notice, disclosure, right to present information, and argument are determined, even if this is restrictive, by the relevant legislation. However, unless reasonably clearly excluded, the common law of "procedural" fairness will provide a person at least basic rights to an impartial decision-maker, reasonable notice, and appropriate means to be heard. In some circumstances, constitutional rights such as Aboriginal rights to consultation and accommodation may be available even where statutory participatory rights are restricted. It is common to find judicial appeal rights in environmental statutes to challenge procedural or substantive environmental decisions. However, these may be subject to obtaining leave to appeal from the court.

If there is no appeal, the common law (buttressed by rules of court) provides rights to superior court "judicial review." In this way, the procedural fairness and the substance of environmental decisions by tribunals and officials can be challenged.

III. THE ADMINISTRATIVE PROCESS

In the first instance, decisions affecting the environment are made within the bureaucracy by ministerial officials charged with responsibility for exercising statutory powers relating to environmental protection, public health, and resource development. Whether the decision relates to permitting waste, locating landfill sites, or developing resources, usually a statutory appeal lies to an administrative appeal board.

Since appointments to such tribunals are made at the discretion of Cabinet, a perennial concern is tribunal independence. Because these tribunals exercise quasi-judicial powers and rely on public confidence to discharge these powers effectively, there has been considerable debate over how to minimize the inevitably political dimension of the appointments process: see W Tilleman, "Environmental Appeal Boards: A Comparative Look at the United States, Canada and England" (1996) 21 Colum J Envtl L 1 at 18-29.

Another recurring issue in this area concerns tribunal rules and procedures. Although they may be appellate bodies, tribunals will often "retry" the matter before them as a trial *de novo*. This means that the parties are entitled to call evidence instead of merely relying on the written record relating to the decision on appeal. Most tribunals also possess a broad discretion to confirm, alter, or overturn the decision under appeal. Tribunals are not expected to follow the legal formalities and rules of evidence that govern court proceedings. To expedite the hearing process (which will often involve unrepresented laypersons), many tribunals issue policy directives with respect to hearing procedures. In some provinces, notably Ontario and Alberta, such hearings are also subject to statutory codes of procedure. Perhaps most important, all tribunals are bound by a common law duty of procedural fairness to the parties appearing before them, the discharge of that duty being overseen by the superior courts.

A. JUDICIAL SUPERVISION OF ADMINISTRATIVE ACTION

When reviewing tribunal decisions, courts will determine the appropriate standard of review. Often the court will defer to the tribunal's decision, particularly where the decision-maker is interpreting its governing statute. Other factors in determining relative deference include the decision-maker's expertise in the subject area, whether the issue is one of law or fact, whether the decision involves assessing a range of societal factors, and whether the legislature has attempted to exclude judicial review by inserting a privative clause into the statute. This is called the "reasonableness standard." A reasonable decision has been described by the Supreme Court of Canada as one that is transparent, intelligible, and justified and "falls within a range of possible, acceptable outcomes which are defensible in respect of the facts and law" (*Dunsmuir v New Brunswick*, 2008 SCC 9 at para 47).

However, where the issue is constitutional or there is a clear question whether the decision-maker is acting within its statutory power (particularly where the question involves potential overlap with another decision-maker's power or is considered centrally important for the legal system), the court will not defer. In these scenarios, the standard will be "correctness," and the court may substitute its own decision for that of the tribunal.

Standard of review is a notoriously confusing area of administrative law that is rapidly developing. In 2018, the Supreme Court of Canada agreed to hear appeals in three cases (none of them environmental) specifically to review these standard of review principles.

In the environmental law context, the threshold question of standard of review was considered in *Canada (Fisheries and Oceans) v David Suzuki Foundation*.

CANADA (FISHERIES AND OCEANS) V DAVID SUZUKI FOUNDATION
2012 FCA 40

MAINVILLE JA:

• • •

THE STANDARD OF REVIEW

THE MINISTER'S POSITION

[65] At its core, the principal question before this Court concerns the meaning of the words "legally protected by provisions in, or measures under, this or any other Act of Parliament" found in subsection 58(5) of the SARA [*Species at Risk Act*, SC

2002, c 29]. That is a question of statutory interpretation, and that is not disputed by the Minister.

[66] However, the Minister submits that Parliament has entrusted him with the responsibility to manage the regulatory schemes under the SARA and the *Fisheries Act* [RSC 1985, c F-14], and that consequently, his interpretation of section 58 of the SARA—and of the provisions of the *Fisheries Act* and of its regulations as they relate to that section—should be given deference.

[67] The Minister relies for this proposition on *Dunsmuir* and recent decisions of the Supreme Court of Canada which have all clearly emphasized the deference which courts must show to an administrative tribunal when it interprets a provision of its enabling (or "home") statute or statutes closely connected to its functions. ...

• • •

DUNSMUIR AND THE SUBSEQUENT CASE LAW

[83] The Minister submits in this appeal that in view of the responsibilities conferred on him by the SARA and the *Fisheries Act*, his interpretation of those statutes is not susceptible to judicial review on a standard of correctness. The Minister's position implies that the standard of review analysis ends as soon as Parliament confers on a minister the responsibility to administer a federal statute. This, the Minister submits, is the conclusion which must be drawn from the recent jurisprudence of the Supreme Court of Canada. I disagree.

• • •

[85] As Justices Bastarache and LeBel jointly noted in *Dunsmuir* at paragraphs 27 to 31, judicial review is intimately connected with the preservation of the rule of law and with maintaining legislative supremacy. While developing a more coherent and workable framework for judicial review—notably by merging the "patently unreasonable" and "reasonableness *simpliciter*" standards of review into a single "reasonableness" standard—*Dunsmuir* still requires that a proper standard of review analysis be carried out in appropriate circumstances.

[86] For this purpose, *Dunsmuir* has set out a two step process: first, courts ascertain whether the jurisprudence has already determined in a satisfactory manner the degree of deference to be accorded with regard to a particular question; second, where the first inquiry proves unfruitful, courts must proceed to a standard of review analysis involving the factors making it possible to identify the proper standard of review: *Dunsmuir* at para. 62.

[87] In the case of an administrative tribunal exercising adjudicative functions in the context of an adversarial process, and explicitly or implicitly empowered by its enabling statute to decide questions of law, judicial deference will normally extend to its interpretation of its enabling statute or of a statute closely connected to its functions. ...

[88] However, deference on a question of law will not always apply, notably where the administrative body whose decision or action is subject to review is not acting as an adjudicative tribunal, is not protected by a privative clause, and is not empowered by its enabling legislation to authoritatively decide questions of law. A standard of review analysis is still required in appropriate cases. ...

[89] What *Dunsmuir* has made clear is that "[a]n exhaustive review is not required in every case to determine the proper standard of review": *Dunsmuir* at para. 57. Further, *Dunsmuir* has also made clear that "at an institutional level, *adjudicators* ... can be underlined{presumed} to hold relative expertise in the interpretation of the legislation that gives them their mandate, as well as related legislation that they might often

encounter in the course of their functions": *Dunsmuir* at para. 68 (emphasis added); *Nor-Man Regional Health Authority Inc. v. Manitoba Association of Health Care Professionals*, 2011 SCC 59 (S.C.C.) at para. 53.

[90] Consequently, since *Dunsmuir*, unless the situation is exceptional, the interpretation by an adjudicative tribunal of its enabling statute or of statutes closely related to its functions should be presumed to be a question of statutory interpretation subject to deference on judicial review: *Alberta (Information and Privacy Commissioner) v Alberta Teachers' Association*, 2011 SCC 61 (S.C.C.) at paras. 34 and 41, per Justice Rothstein ("*Alberta Teachers' Association*").

• • •

[95] The analytical framework and the presumption set out in *Dunsmuir* have been recently described as follows by Justice Fish in *Nor-Man Regional Health Authority Inc. v. Manitoba Association of Health Care Professionals*, above at paras. 35 and 36:

> [35] An administrative tribunal's decision will be reviewable for correctness if it raises a constitutional issue, a question of "general law 'that is both of central importance to the legal system as a whole and outside the adjudicator's specialized area of expertise,'" or a "true question of jurisdiction or *vires*." It will be reviewable for correctness as well if it involves the drawing of jurisdictional lines between two or more competing specialized tribunals (*Dunsmuir*, at paras 58-61; *Smith* [*Smith v Alliance Pipeline Ltd*, 2011 SCC 7, [2011] 1 SCR 160], at para. 26; *Toronto (City) v. C.U.P.E., Local 79*, 2003 SCC 63, [2003] 3 S.C.R. 77, at para. 62, *per* LeBel J.).
>
> [36] The standard of reasonableness, on the other hand, normally prevails where the tribunal's decision raises issues of fact, discretion or policy; involves inextricably intertwined legal and factual issues; or relates to the interpretation of the tribunal's enabling (or "home") statute or "statutes closely connected to its function, with which it will have particular familiarity" (*Dunsmuir*, at paras. 51 and 53-54; *Smith*, at para. 26).

[96] This analytical framework and this presumption must be understood in the context in which they were developed: they concern adjudicative tribunals. The presumption is derived from the past jurisprudence which had extensively considered the standard of review applicable to the decisions of such tribunals. By empowering an administrative tribunal to adjudicate a matter between parties, Parliament is presumed to have restricted judicial review of that tribunal's interpretation of its enabling statute and of statutes closely connected to its adjudicative functions. That presumption may however be rebutted if it can be found that Parliament's intent is inconsistent with the presumption.

[97] The Minister is inviting this Court to expand the above-described *Dunsmuir* analytical framework and presumption to all administrative decision makers who are responsible for the administration of a federal statute. I do not believe that *Dunsmuir* and the decisions of the Supreme Court of Canada which followed *Dunsmuir* stand for this proposition.

[98] What the Minister is basically arguing is that the interpretation of the SARA and of the *Fisheries Act* favoured by his Department and by the government's central agencies, such as the Department of Justice, should prevail. The Minister thus seeks to establish a new constitutional paradigm under which the Executive's interpretation of Parliament's laws would prevail insofar as such interpretation is not unreasonable. This harks back to the time before the *Bill of Rights* of 1689 where the Crown reserved the right to interpret and apply Parliament's laws to suit its own policy objectives. It would take a very explicit grant of authority from Parliament in order for this Court to reach such a far-reaching conclusion.

[99] The issues in this appeal concern the interpretation of a statute by a minister who is not acting as an adjudicator and who thus has no implicit power to decide questions of law. Of course, the Minister must take a view on what the statute means in order to act. But this is not the same as having a power delegated by Parliament to decide questions of law. The presumption of deference resulting from *Dunsmuir*, which was reiterated in *Alberta Teachers' Association* at paras. 34 and 41, does not extend to these circumstances. The standard of review analysis set out at paragraphs 63 and 64 of *Dunsmuir* must thus be carried out in the circumstances of this case in order to ascertain Parliament's intent.

[100] In other words, does Parliament intend to shield the Minister's interpretation of the pertinent provisions of the SARA and of the *Fisheries Act* from judicial review on a standard of correctness? On the basis of the standard of review analysis further set out below, I answer in the negative.

STANDARD OF REVIEW ANALYSIS

[101] First, neither the SARA nor the *Fisheries Act* contains a privative clause. This is a strong indication of Parliament's intent *not* to shield the Minister's legal interpretation of these statutes from judicial review.

[102] Second, as provided in section 57 of the SARA, the purpose of section 58 is "to ensure that [...] all the critical habitat is protected." Hence, under subsection 58(5), the Minister "must" make a protection order to protect identified critical habitat unless that habitat is "legally protected by provisions in, or measures under, this or any other Act of Parliament." These are all indications that Parliament has greatly restricted the Minister's discretion. It would be strange indeed if the Minister's interpretation of such restrictive legislative language could somehow prevail in order to curtail Parliament's intent in adopting these provisions. Here again, Parliament's intent not to shield the Minister's legal interpretation from judicial review appears clear.

[103] Third, the Minister acts in an administrative capacity, and not as an adjudicator, when preparing and issuing a protection statement under subsection 58(5) of the SARA. The fact that Parliament has not had to set up an independent administrative tribunal to adjudicate legal issues under the SARA—including legal issues resulting from section 58—is a further indication of the legislative intent to empower the courts with authority to adjudicate these issues on a standard of correctness. The question in issue is one of statutory interpretation which the courts are best equipped to answer in the circumstances of this case.

[104] Finally, though the Minister—acting on the advice of the officials of the Department of Fisheries and Oceans—can certainly claim expertise in the management of the fisheries and of fish habitat, this does not confer on the Minister expertise in the interpretation of statutes. Expertise in fisheries does not necessarily confer special legal expertise to interpret the statutory provisions of the SARA or of the *Fisheries Act*.

[105] For these reasons, the issues of statutory interpretation raised by this appeal will be reviewed and determined on a standard of correctness.

NOTE

In *Minister of Citizenship and Immigration v Vavilov*, 2019 SCC 65, released December 19, 2019, the Supreme Court of Canada explicitly invited submissions from the parties and interveners on the legal framework for determining the appropriate standard of review and application of the reasonableness standard. The result of the court's analysis is that the *Dunsmuir* approach should be modified in several ways. Please see *Vavilov* at paras 16-17 for the revised framework.

B. GROUNDS FOR REVIEW

There are a limited number of recognized grounds upon which courts are prepared to review administrative action. In the federal realm, these grounds for review have been codified in s 18(1) of the *Federal Courts Act*, RSC 1985, c F-7; in most other jurisdictions, however, grounds are defined through precedent. Common legal grounds upon which judicial review is sought include:

- substantive *ultra vires* (decisions or actions that are outside a body's statutory powers);
- unlawful fettering of discretion;
- improper delegation of discretionary power;
- reliance on irrelevant considerations or lack of reliance on relevant considerations;
- administrative discrimination;
- breach of procedural fairness;
- exercising discretion for an improper purpose or in bad faith;
- justification of reasons; and
- in restricted circumstances, errors of law and/or fact.

Given the broad and far-reaching objectives of environmental policy, decision-makers are often granted broad discretionary powers to pursue the objects set out in legislation. As a result, decisions are frequently challenged on the basis that the decision-maker failed to take into consideration relevant factors or was bound by considerations that unlawfully fettered discretion. For example, in *W-4 Industrial Park (Sturgeon Industrial Estates) v Alberta (Environment)*, 1983 ABCA 256, (*sub nom Wimpey Western Ltd v Alberta (Department of the Environment)*) 28 Alta LR (2d) 193, the appellants sought an order to compel a director in the Department of the Environment to issue a permit for the construction of a wastewater treatment plant on the grounds that the director had taken into account irrelevant considerations related to policy objectives of favoring larger regional facilities. Notwithstanding that these policy objectives were not explicitly mentioned in the legislation, the court noted (at para 29) that they were consistent with the broad purposes of the act regarding environmental protection and remediation. The legislation granted far-reaching powers to pursue these objects, and, therefore, "it is relevant for the Director to consider the policies of the Minister keeping in mind that he must neither act under dictation nor fetter his discretion." The decision was upheld and the appeal dismissed.

In *Imperial Oil Ltd v British Columbia (Ministry of Water, Land and Air Protection)*, 2002 BCSC 219, the court reached the opposite conclusion and compelled the Ministry of Water, Land and Air Protection to issue an approval in principle for the remediation of contaminated lands. Imperial argued that the sole consideration of the ministry was whether the civil claims of the owners of the contaminated lands had been settled. The court found that this was an irrelevant consideration that was not set out in the act, and further noted that it effectively placed the decision-making authority at the mercy of the civil claims settlements. According to the court, this constituted an improper delegation of discretionary authority.

Environmental regulation also tends to encroach on various commercial interests. Decision-makers, for example, in Canada's national parks, often distinguish between different classes of businesses or persons in the application of law. In administrative law, this raises questions concerning discrimination. *Sunshine Village Corp v Canada (Parks)*, 2004 FCA 166 involved Sunshine Village's application for judicial review of a Parks Canada decision to charge higher building permit fees in Banff and Jasper national parks than elsewhere in the country. The legislation granted broad authority to the superintendent and did not expressly limit the ability to set fees. Sunshine Village pointed to the historic rules that prevent municipalities from discriminating unless expressly provided in the legislation. The court found that the fact that Parliament confers general regulation-making authority with respect to crown fees deserves deference. In this scenario, the courts permitted a level of administrative discrimination. See also *Moresby Explorers Ltd v Canada (Attorney General)*, 2007 FCA 273.

Decision-makers have a duty of procedural fairness. Broadly, this duty, according to *Baker v Canada (Minister of Citizenship and Immigration)*, [1999] 2 SCR 817 at para 22, 1999 CanLII 699, requires that "administrative decisions are made using a fair and open procedure, appropriate to the decision being made and its statutory, institutional, and social context, with an opportunity for those affected by the decision to put forward their views and evidence fully and have them considered by the decision-maker." In *Le Chameau Exploration Ltd v Nova Scotia (Attorney General)*, 2007 NSSC 386, the applicant sought judicial review of an order to determine ownership under the *Special Places Protection Act*, RSNS 1989, c 438 on the basis of not observing the rules of natural justice. The court held that the applicant was denied an opportunity to make submissions on the legal ownership claim of a historic shipwreck, and the appeal was upheld.

However some courts have emphasized that the idea of nominate grounds such as irrelevant considerations and fettering of discretion are no longer good law (see *Forest Ethics Advocacy Association v Canada (National Energy Board)*, 2014 FCA 245 at paras 66-67). This leaves broader qualitative reasonableness criteria (see *Dunsmuir*, above), including justification, transparency (reasons for decision), and intelligibility. However, this approach has not been applied consistently.

Thus, in *Tsleil-Waututh Nation v Canada (Attorney General)*, 2018 FCA 153, applicants brought an application for judicial review of Cabinet's decision to approve the Trans Mountain Expansion Project. Among several grounds of review, the applicants made submissions with respect to the various deficiencies in the National Energy Board's report on which Cabinet ultimately relied to justify its decision on the project. The court found (at paras 468 and 469) that the board had unjustifiably excluded project-related marine shipping from the project's definition, which led the board to conclude erroneously that the project would not cause significant adverse environmental effects under the *Species at Risk Act*, SC 2002, c 29. These errors led to a deficient report on which Cabinet unreasonably relied in rendering its decision.

QUESTION

Canadian courts have traditionally given Cabinet a wide berth in the exercise of discretionary powers while keeping bureaucratic discretion under much closer check. What rationale(s) support(s) this approach? Do you agree with such an approach?

C. REMEDIES

A critical question is that of remedy. The principal remedies available on judicial review are orders to (1) quash the administrative action (*certiorari*); (2) prohibit the action (*prohibition*); (3) require the decision-maker to act (*mandamus*); and (4) declare existing rights, duties, or powers (*declaratory relief*).

To preserve their rights pending the hearing of an application for review, litigants may also seek interim injunctive relief (although public interest litigants often find it difficult to obtain such relief for reasons to be discussed below). Even where an applicant successfully establishes that grounds for judicial review exist, courts have discretion to deny relief for various reasons, including that the jurisdictional breach is minor, that the application for review is premature, or that alternative remedies (that is, other avenues of appeal) have not been exhausted: see, for example, *Berg v British Columbia (Attorney General)* (1991), 48 Admin LR 82 (BCSC).

The principles governing appeals and judicial review are not necessarily the same. Appeal rights and procedures are determined completely by the governing statute. However, some courts have essentially ignored the distinction. In *Gitxaala Nation v Canada*, 2016 FCA 187, the Federal Court of Appeal, which was faced with a group of consolidated actions, including statutory appeals and judicial review applications concerning the National Energy Board approval of the Northern Gateway pipeline application, said simply that it would review the challenges in the same way that it proceeds when considering applications for judicial review.

IV. PUBLIC PARTICIPATION AND THE PUBLIC INTEREST

The public has come to play a much larger role in environmental decision-making. This expansion has occurred on various fronts, including land-use planning processes, environmental assessment, pollution and resource permitting procedures, and public interest environmental litigation. In recent years, a debate has emerged with respect to who ought to have standing in the decision-making process and the judicial review stage, as well as the role of extralegal concepts such as "social licence."

R ANAND & IG SCOTT, QC, "FINANCING PUBLIC PARTICIPATION IN ENVIRONMENTAL DECISION MAKING"
(1982) 60:1 Can Bar Rev 81 at 87-94 [footnotes omitted]

A. ACCESS TO JUSTICE

The objection that encouraging public participation would have the effect of stirring up unmeritorious litigation is only one aspect of a wider attack on "public interest" advocacy that is commonly mounted by critics who argue that conflict resolution is the sole legitimate purpose of civil actions. Another aspect of this approach is the assumption that when claims are not enforced through litigation, it is because they are unimportant to the affected individuals. ...

It is clear that the failure to advance a particular cause in a given piece of litigation often results from barriers to legal redress that have nothing to do with the merit of the cause or the relative importance of the harm that is perceived by the "victim." Economic barriers to participation in decision-making are well documented in all forms of litigation, and apply most severely to those who suffer in addition from social, psychological and cultural impediments to the redressing of their grievances.

Additional barriers present themselves in the case of public interest groups. Professor Michael Trebilcock ... has identified three such barriers that have analogous effects on environmental groups. Firstly, the environmental concerns of the average citizen are spread across a great range of projects, issues and locations. On the other hand, a business interest that is concerned with the particular project, issue or location has "a sufficiently concentrated stake in any prospective regulation of it to make [its] views known very forcefully to government." ...

Secondly, unlike highly concentrated producer interests, environmental interests are not generally homogeneous. Most environmentalists are also both consumers and producers of goods and services, and in these roles will often see things differently. ...

The third barrier is commonly known as the "free rider" phenomenon. Olson, for example, argues that unless the membership in a public interest group is small, or unless some special incentive is provided to encourage individuals to act in the common interests of the group, rational and self-interested individuals will not act to achieve their common or group interests. ...

In the result, public interest groups never achieve the strength that their number of potential beneficiaries would indicate, since many of the possible contributors of money, time and expertise either require or are permitted to take a "free ride" at the expense of existing members.

It is by overcoming these "barriers to litigation" that the encouragement of public participation achieves the significant benefit of obtaining confidence in our system of civil justice. A significant "process" value is attached by the community to enhanced public involvement in collective decision-making. ...

B. PRIVATE ENFORCEMENT OF PUBLIC RIGHTS

A common response to the argument for increased citizen involvement in environmental decision-making is the assertion that intervenors have no useful purpose to serve, given that the public agencies such as administrative tribunals and courts have been entrusted with the dual roles of regulators of industry and representatives of the public interest. Yet enforcement of public policies can be achieved by private individuals by supplementing the work of the various tribunals or by "energizing the agencies." ...

[T]hree principal factors ... combine to produce what has become known as agency "capture" by regulated interests. Firstly, the limited resources that are allocated to administrative agencies, considered in relation to the sheer mass of activity that is required to monitor and test proposals and applications, necessitates close co-operation between the regulator and the regulated industry. Administrative boards thus become dependent upon industry as providers of information. A second cause of industry orientation is the dependence of regulatory agencies on the regulated interests for political support. Independent tribunals cannot rely upon the government to protect them from legislative attack and must therefore develop their own constituencies that are capable of generating support in the legislatures. In this regard, a natural ally can often be found in the regulated interests.

Most importantly, two other characteristics of the administrative process have combined to form a third source of agency deference to industry positions. ...

"[G]overnmental agencies rarely respond to interests that are not represented in their proceedings." The mere setting up by governments of regulatory agencies is insufficient to protect the public interest. ...

At the very least, even if the interests of the regulated industry and the adjudicator do not fully coincide, it is clear that the "public interest" which is the theoretical mandate of the decision-maker is not unitary. It has diverse and indeed countervailing components, and so the environmental tribunal or court cannot be expected to become its guardian with unqualified success. Public intervention "softens the artificial two-sidedness which is often a by-product of the adversarial adjudicative process."

C. IMPROVEMENT OF ADMINISTRATIVE AND JUDICIAL PROCESSES

Four distinct benefits accrue to the investigative and adjudicative processes as a result of increased public participation.

Firstly, public participation provides decision-makers with a greater range of ideas and information on which to base their decisions. ...

This substantive contribution to environmental decision-making has two aspects. Firstly, public participants bring important factual information and legal submissions to the attention of the adjudicator. ... The second element of substantive contribution is the presentation of a viewpoint or perspective that is not otherwise available to the decision-maker. Intervenors are often able to put forward a legal or factual argument which places a unique emphasis or interpretation upon existing issues or causes the tribunal to examine a new issue. ...

The second major benefit is that public participation can enhance public acceptance of judicial and administrative decisions ... . Public acceptability, in turn, can be expected to ease the implementation and enforcement of judicial and administrative decisions that rely upon public co-operation.

Third, problems of agency dependence on industry for political support may be alleviated by the broad participation of other parties. Such participation may promote the actual autonomy of the agency, both by giving it a broader perspective from which to view its own role, and by providing alternative potential bases of political support.

Fourth, the presentation of alternative view points at the board or lower court level is said to induce these decision-makers to be more thorough in their analyses and to articulate more clearly and precisely the reasons for their decisions. These improvements may in turn contribute to the building of a record on which a reviewing or appellate court might reverse the initial decision.

While the goal of making bureaucracies more open and accountable to the public is generally uncontroversial, there is less support for the idea that we should aspire to a similar openness and accountability in our court system.

Kristen Van De Biezenbos charts the rise, and she argues the decline, of social licence in her article "The Rebirth of Social Licence."

KRISTEN VAN DE BIEZENBOS, "THE REBIRTH OF SOCIAL LICENCE"
(2019) 14:2 MJSDL 153 at 162-65 [footnotes omitted]

2.2 SOCIAL LICENCE TAKES FLIGHT: FROM METAPHOR TO MANDATE

Social licence was originally intended to describe an approach to establishing positive community relations in countries with an underdeveloped rule of law, but it began to take on a broader, more normative cloak when it moved into the context of Western democracies with highly developed natural resource sectors. At first blush, this development seems unexpected. Why would countries with a strong rule of law need something like social licence to gain local and community approval? And yet, social licence has become so prevalent an idea in Canada that even the Prime Minister emphasizes the need for social licence in support of the government's carbon pricing plans. One explanation for this might be the greater power of community groups, neighbourhood associations, and non-governmental organizations (NGOs), especially environmental advocacy groups, in these countries. Generally speaking, a strong civil society is able to exert significant pressure on unpopular energy projects, and the concept of social licence worked for both communities and project proponents because of its signalling power: when a project proponent was able to claim social licence, it served to indicate the project's acceptance or approval by those community groups.

Yet another possible explanation for the rise of social licence in Canada is the formation of alliances between Indigenous groups and environmental groups, both national and international. By combining the concerns of local groups with larger organizations, the reasons for protesting energy projects became more divorced from community-based concerns. In response, energy companies began to seek a social licence that would meet, in some way, the demands of both the local and the national. Thus, social licence grew to encompass the steps taken by large natural resources companies—including oil & gas firms—to respond to the demands of these powerful new alliances, to "meet the expectations of society and avoid activities that societies (or influential elements within them) deem unacceptable." And, because of the power these alliances wield in Western countries like Canada, addressing their concerns to prevent retaliation (whether economic or political) has become necessary as opposed to discretionary. There is also a sense that the law is often too slow to reflect shifting attitudes about certain projects and industries, while social licence reflects those shifts more accurately.

In some cases, what the community wants is unrelated to economic impacts or local health or safety needs, but it is key to local acceptance. For example, paper mill owners in the United States have voluntarily undertaken measures at their facilities such as odour control, water tinting, and steam suppression to appease the nearby communities. As one mill owner said, "we wanted to be a good neighbour; it's the local stakeholders that give us the right to operate." Or, as Prime Minister Justin Trudeau has said, "[g]overnments may be able to issue permits, but only communities can grant permission." Many of the industry concerns that social licence is able to address are thus reputational; it offers benefits beyond what strict legal compliance can confer. This may explain why social licence became so important to Canada's oil and gas industry (and its opponents) so quickly. Avoiding boycotts and other forms of negative publicity are major concerns of the energy industry, as a poor public image can discourage investment and drive up costs.

Energy companies face significant challenges from environmental groups, "not in my backyard" (or NIMBY) concerned landowners, and Indigenous communities and groups, as well [as] the Canadian public's growing concerns over the industry's contribution to climate change. At the same time, these same companies continue to emphasize the oil and gas industry's importance to the national and provincial economies. This makes social licence a powerful and attractive tool for these companies, since the considerable efforts needed to obtain the requisite provincial and local permits may assure the relevant government that a particular project is in the best interests of the nation or province and meets the applicable standards, but obtaining those permits may do little or nothing to move the needle of public opinion. Social licence offers a tantalizing way to win the ever-elusive war for the people's approval.

However, this is when the vagueness of the term bites back. Companies may take measures to respond to what they perceive national, provincial, and local concerns to be, and in doing so they (or their supporters) may claim that they have acquired the social licence to operate. After all, social licence has no definition or objective criteria, so the company is not clearly wrong when it says that it has acquired the social licence. However, opponents of these companies or particular projects are equally able to argue, no matter what a company may say or do, that they have not earned social licence for their projects. Their proof of this may simply be the fact that some opposition remains, in spite of the steps a company has taken to win popular support. Further complicating matters is the fact that some groups are fundamentally opposed to certain energy projects, which means that if one accepts their definition of social licence, certain projects may never gain the social licence to operate, and thus may never legitimately operate at all.

As a result, we end up with oil and gas companies claiming to have acquired social licence, opposing groups arguing that the companies do not have social licence, while directly impacted local groups and communities are being left out of the conversation altogether.

A. PUBLIC INTEREST STANDING IN JUDICIAL REVIEW

Opportunities for public participation exist at both the decision-making stage and the judicial review stage. At the judicial review stage, the courts have developed a three-part test for granting public interest standing:

1. there is a justiciable issue;
2. the party has a genuine interest in the matter; and
3. there is no other reasonable and effective manner to bring the issue before the court.

(See *Finlay v Canada (Minister of Finance)*, [1986] 2 SCR 607, 1986 CanLII 6.)

The Supreme Court has relaxed the application of the three-part *Finlay* test, stating that it must be applied flexibly and purposively (see *Canada (Attorney General) v Downtown Eastside Sex Workers United Against Violence Society*, 2012 SCC 45; *Delta Air Lines Inc v Lukács*, 2018 SCC 2). Given the widespread public interest in environmental law and litigation, courts often have to grapple with the issue of whether a party has a sufficiently "genuine interest" in the matter or is "directly affected." Further complicating matters are the subtle differences in granting standing between tribunals (often involving statutory rights of appeal) and courts (which typically use the common law approach set out in *Finlay*). These issues are discussed in the following cases.

FOREST PRACTICES BOARD V MINISTRY OF FORESTS AND RIVERSIDE FOREST PRODUCTS LTD
(11 June 1996), Decision No 95/01(a) (BC Forest Appeals Commission), online: <http://www.fac.gov.bc.ca/forestPracCode/95-01a.pdf>

[Riverside Forest Products was issued a stop work order and remediation order regarding damaging road construction and hauling. A review panel overturned the decision; on appeal, the Cariboo-Chilcotin Conservation Council (CCCC) applied for intervener status, a matter within the discretion of the commission, pursuant to s 131 of the *Forest Practices Code of British Columbia Act*, SBC 1994, c 41.]

In deciding whether intervenor status should be granted under sub-section 131(9) of the *Act* the CCCC and Riverside submit, and the Commission agrees, that the test is whether the applicant has a valid interest in participating and can be of assistance in the proceedings ... .

In this case CCCC has provided some indication that they have a valid interest in participating. They represent a coalition of groups in the Cariboo-Chilcotin area that have a particular interest in the protection of the environment and sustainable development. The Commission is satisfied that the CCCC being a local group with a particular environmental interest does have a valid interest in participating in this procedure.

The second prong of the test is whether the CCCC can be of assistance in the proceedings. Riverside submits that the CCCC will not be of assistance to the proceeding because their interest is already represented by the Board. Riverside suggests that the legislature provided the Board with its broad authority to bring appeals before the Commission for the very reason that they represent the public interest and therefore represent the CCCC's interest. The Board itself has submitted that it does not agree with this characterisation of the Board's role. Indeed the Board's own Values and Guiding Principles which are found at page 14 of the Board's 1995 Annual Report state that, "The Board will represent the public's interests, not those of any single group." The Commission cannot agree that the Board will represent the CCCC's interests. Had the legislature anticipated that the Board would have such a broad mandate it surely would not have provided for intervenors within the same legislative scheme.

· · ·

The question still remains can the CCCC be of assistance to these proceedings. The CCCC submits that they bring a unique environmental perspective to the proceedings. This is particularly so in that they are active users of the provincial forest that is the subject of this appeal. The Commission notes that the Preamble to the *Act* provides:

> WHEREAS British Columbians desire sustainable use of the forests they hold in trust for future generations;
>   AND WHEREAS sustainable use includes ...
>   (c) balancing productive, spiritual, ecological and recreational values of forests to meet the economic and cultural needs of peoples and communities, including first nations ... .

Considering the above, it is the decision of the Commission that a local environmental coalition can be of assistance to the proceedings and in particular may be of assistance in determining the meaning and scope of "damage to the environment" as it is used in section 45 of the *Act*.

The final question to consider is to what extent should the CCCC be permitted to participate. Riverside submits that the participation should be in writing and that it should be limited to the interpretation of section 45 of the *Act*. The CCCC submits that full submissions including an environmental perspective be put before the Commission. The Board submits that they do not object to the CCCC application because the CCCC may choose to raise issues that the Board will not.

Riverside suggests that the Commission should come to the same conclusion that the Forest Appeal Board reached in *MacMillan Bloedel Ltd. v. Chief Forester*, June 19, 1992. In that case the Appeal Board was considering an application for intervenor status by the Sierra Club of Western Canada into an appeal under the *Forest Act*. The appeal was over the annual allowable cut that had been arrived at between the licensee and the Ministry. The Appeal Board granted the Sierra Club limited standing to provide written argument only. Their reason for doing so was that the Board did not want to prejudice the parties by forcing them to respond to grounds of attack other than those which they chose to raise.

There are, however, differences between that case and this one. In this case the *Act* specifically provides for intervenors while the *Forest Act* does not. Similarly, in this case there is an issue under appeal that can benefit from the balancing of ecological interests against economic interests as is contemplated in the Preamble. The *Forest Act* has no such provision. Finally, the issue under appeal in the *MacMillan Bloedel* case was contractual in nature. In this case it is not.

Given the above it is the decision of the Commission that the Commission will benefit from the full participation of the CCCC as it applies to the appeal that has been commenced by the Board.

[Intervener status was granted.]

QUESTION

In *Forest Ethics Advocacy Association*, an NGO and an individual challenged a National Energy Board approval of a major oil pipeline project, particularly the board's decisions on the relevance of certain issues, and the parties' standing to participate in the board hearing. The court stated (at paras 29-34):

[29] Under subsection 18.1(1) of the *Federal Courts Act*, R.S.C. 1985, c. F-7, only those who are "directly affected" can ask this Court to review a decision.

[30] Forest Ethics is not "directly affected" by the Board's decisions. The Board's decisions do not affect its legal rights, impose legal obligations upon it, or prejudicially affect it in any way ... . Therefore, Forest Ethics does not have direct standing to bring an application for judicial review and invoke the Charter against the Board's decisions.

[31] In oral argument, Forest Ethics submitted that it had status in this Court as a litigant with public interest standing.

[32] However, Forest Ethics falls well short of establishing that it satisfies the criteria for public interest standing ... .

[33] Indeed, in this application and on this record, Forest Ethics is a classic "busybody," as that term is understood in the jurisprudence. Forest Ethics asks this Court to review an administrative decision it had nothing to do with. It did not ask for any relief from the Board. It did not seek any status from the Board. It did not make any representations on any issue before the Board. In particular, it did not make any representations to the Board concerning the three interlocutory decisions.

[34] The record filed by Forest Ethics does not show that it has a real stake or a genuine interest in freedom of expression issues similar to the one in this case. Further, a judicial review brought by Forest Ethics is not a reasonable and effective way to bring the issue before this Court. Forest Ethics' presence is not necessary—Ms. Sinclair, represented by Forest Ethics' counsel, is present and is directly affected by the Board's decision to deny her an opportunity to participate in its proceedings.

After reading the *Forest Practices Board* decision and the discussion of *Forest Ethics Advocacy Association*, above, do you agree, in general, that administrative tribunals should adopt a more liberal approach to standing than the courts? Why or why not?

SIERRA CLUB OF CANADA V CANADA (MINISTER OF FINANCE)
[1999] 2 FC 211, 1998 CanLII 9124, 1998 CarswellNat 2384

[The Minister of Finance appealed dismissal of a motion to strike the Sierra Club's application for judicial review of the minister's refusal to require an environmental assessment of a proposed sale of two CANDU nuclear reactors by Canada to China.]

(2) THE STANDING OF THE APPLICANT

22 [T]he applicant has not contended that the administrative action that it impugns in the application for judicial review affects the private legal rights of the Sierra Club or its members, or inflicts on either it or them "special damage" that is over and above that sustained by the public at large. Thus, the applicant's claim to standing is based solely on the appropriateness of the Sierra Club as a representative of the public interest to bring before the Court the allegations that the respondents are in breach of their statutory duty under the *CEAA*. The grant of standing in such circumstances is, of course, a matter within the discretion of the Court: *Finlay v. Canada (Minister of Finance)*, [1986] 2 S.C.R. 607 (S.C.C.).

• • •

(i) Standing and the Federal Court Act, Subsection 18.1(1)

27 The first argument made by the intervenor [Atomic Energy of Canada Limited] was that standing to make an application for judicial review in the Federal Court is governed by subsection 18.1(1) of the *Federal Court Act* which provides that:

18.1(1) An application for judicial review may be made by the Attorney General of Canada or by anyone *directly affected by the matter in respect of which relief is sought*. [Emphasis added.]

28 Counsel for the intervenor contended that, by definition, a person who relies on public interest standing, rather than on the infringement of a private right or the infliction of special damage, is not "directly affected," and therefore lacks standing under subsection 18.1(1). He also referred to case law involving the words "directly affected" in other statutes, where they had been interpreted as requiring the applicant to have an interest similar to that required at common law for a person to be eligible for injunctive or declaratory relief on the basis of "private right" standing.

• • •

30 Counsel frankly conceded that *Sunshine Village Corp. v. Superintendent of Banff National Park* (1996), 20 C.E.L.R. (N.S.) 171 (Fed. C.A.) was against him. In that case, which also concerned a challenge by a public interest group concerned with environmental protection, Desjardins J.A. said (at 191):

It is evident from the facts that the appellant is not "directly affected by the matter in respect of which relief is sought," namely with regard to the construction agreement of September 17, 1995, and the Charest approval of August 31, 1992. CPAWS does not, therefore, have standing as of right.

I agree, however, with Reed J. in *Friends of the Island Inc. v. Canada (Minister of Public Works)* [[1993] 2 F.C. 229 (F.C.T.D.)] that it was not the intention of Parliament, by including the words "directly affected" in subsection 18.1(1) of the *Federal Court Act*, to restrict the public interest standing to the pre *Thorson* [cited below], *Borowski* [cited below], *Finlay* test. She suggested that:

... the wording in subsection 18.1(1) allows the Court discretion to grant standing when it is convinced that the particular circumstances of the case and the type of interest which the applicant holds justify status being granted.

Thus Reed J. reasoned that if an applicant is able to meet the above criteria and, assuming that there is a justiciable issue and no other effective and practical means of getting the issue before the courts, standing will be granted.

• • •

32 ... *Sunshine Village, supra*, clearly holds that a person who satisfies the requirements for discretionary public interest standing may seek relief under subsection 18.1(1), even though not "directly affected." In my opinion, this is the preferable view, even though the language of subsection 18.1(1) suggests that only those who meet the pre-*Finlay* test may seek judicial review. In the absence of an explicit statutory provision excluding public interest applicants from the Federal Court, it would be so incongruous to subject the Court's ability to entertain applications for judicial review to a limitation not imposed on other courts, that I am unwilling to adopt the narrower interpretation of subsection 18.1(1) for which the intervenor in this case has contended.

• • •

(II) PUBLIC INTEREST STANDING AT COMMON LAW

35 Whether a public interest applicant should be granted standing is determined by reference to the three well known factors established by the Supreme Court of Canada in *Finlay, supra*, and the preceding trilogy of cases dealing with public interest standing and constitutional challenges, namely, *Thorson v. Canada (Attorney General) (No. 2)* (1974), [1975] 1 S.C.R. 138 (S.C.C.), *Borowski v. Canada (Minister of Justice)*, [1981] 2 S.C.R. 575 (S.C.C.) and *McNeil v. Nova Scotia (Board of Censors)*, [1978] 2 S.C.R. 662 (S.C.C.).

36 Thus, a reviewing court must consider whether the litigation raises a serious or justiciable issue; whether the applicant has a genuine interest in the outcome or subject-matter of the litigation; and whether there are persons other than the applicant who are more directly affected and who can reasonably be expected to litigate the issues raised by the applicant. ...

• • •

(b) A Genuine Interest

49 Whether the applicant has a genuine interest in the outcome of the application for judicial review ... is a more difficult question. The intervenor advanced a novel theory [about the genuine interest test]. ... "Has the applicant demonstrated a reasonably apprehended harm to a vulnerable constituency, and is it the appropriate body to represent that constituency? ..."

• • •

52 I agree that one function performed by the "genuine interest" requirement is to help to ensure that those granted public interest standing have an experience and expertise with respect to the underlying subject-matter of the litigation that will inform their written and oral submissions made in support of the application for judicial review, and will assist the Court to reach an appropriate result. I consider below whether the Sierra Club has a genuine interest in this sense.

53 However, I do not agree that the case law supports, even implicitly, the notion that public interest standing is *only* ever granted to protect members of vulnerable groups from reasonably apprehended harm. No doubt there will continue to be instances in which standing is granted in such situations: members of vulnerable groups are, after all, often not in a position to defend their interests through litigation, and it is therefore quite appropriate that organizations that have an involvement with the issues should be allowed to litigate on their behalf.

54 But in my view, the intervenor's theory of public interest standing is too narrow because it overlooks the fact that an important reason for the extension of public interest standing beyond the Attorney General has been to protect the constitutional precepts of the rule of law and democratic accountability. If public interest standing were confined in the manner suggested by the intervenor, then a wide range of administrative action would potentially be exempted from the restraints of legality, and the need to comply with the duly express[ed] will of Parliament. ...

55 The next aspect of the "genuine interest" element of the public interest standing test is whether the Sierra Club has demonstrated a degree of involvement with the subject-matter of the application for judicial review ... .

56 The subject-matter of the application ... is whether there is a statutory duty to subject the export of the CANDU nuclear reactors to China, and their construction and operation there, to a full environmental assessment, and whether the approval

of the partial financing of the transaction from public funds is unlawful in the event that an assessment has not been conducted as required by the *CEAA*.

57 The Sierra Club's interest in these issues of legality stems from its concern with the protection of the environment, and its belief that the project under review may endanger the environment, especially in the event of an accident. The Sierra Club takes the position that the *CEAA* and the environmental assessment process that it mandates are important legal and administrative tools for ensuring a degree of transparency and public accountability that will help to avoid the making of decisions that may prove to be environmentally costly.

58 In other words, the Sierra Club's interest in the legal issues that they raise is intimately linked to its corporate objectives. Accordingly, I do not accept the intervenor's submission that the Sierra Club's interest is confined to "legal process" as an abstract principle. Similarly, I do not accept their submission that the Sierra Club's opposition to the use of nuclear power establishes that it is litigating for political reasons, and is inconsistent with its having a genuine interest in the outcome of the application for judicial review. Litigants go to court to advance their own interests or those that they support; challenges to the legality of governmental action are normally fuelled by more than an abstract concern for ensuring the supremacy of the law.

· · ·

62 The intervenor and the respondents relied heavily on *Shiell v. Canada (Atomic Energy Control Board)* (1995), 98 F.T.R. 75 (Fed. T.D.) to demonstrate that the Sierra Club lacks a genuine interest. In that case, the applicant sought to set aside an amendment by the Atomic Energy Control Board of an operating licence held by Cameco Corp. enabling it to construct an expanded tailing management system in connection with the operation of its uranium mine and mill at Key Lake in Saskatchewan. The applicant, Ms. Shiell, had a long record of appearances at hearings held with respect to the development of uranium mining in Saskatchewan. Heald D.J. dismissed the application on the ground that the applicant lacked standing. He said (at p. 79):

> As in *Amok* [cited below], the applicant does not have a direct personal interest in these proceedings and, accordingly, the decision in *Finlay v. Canada*, ([1986] 2 S.C.R. 607, 71 N.R. 338, [1987] 1 W.W.R. 603, 33 D.L.R. (4th) 321) has no relevance. She lives at Nipawin, Saskatchewan, several hundred miles from the respondent's Key Lake operation. Her interest is neither direct nor personal. The decision *a quo* will not affect her in any way different from that felt by any other member of the general public.

63 Let me make three points about this decision. First, with all respect, a requirement of a "direct personal interest" is not now the test required by the common law for public interest standing: "genuine interest" is significantly broader. "Direct personal interest" is much closer to the test used to determine whether a person has standing as of right, on the ground that the person's legal rights or interests are affected, or that the person has sustained harm that is different from that suffered by other members of the public.

64 Second, the case of *Shiell v. Amok Ltd.* (1987), 27 Admin. L.R. 1 (Sask. Q.B.) on which Heald D.J. relied is distinguishable from the case at bar on the ground that, in that case, Barclay, J. regarded the dispute as one that was essentially between two private individuals, and not as one involving an allegation of unlawful conduct by agencies of government. Barclay, J. stated: "public interest standing should not be conferred to enable a party to sue a private individual or a corporation." Accordingly,

he applied the standing test applicable to the tort of public nuisance by asking whether the plaintiff had suffered special damage over and above that of the public at large.

65 Third, *Shiell* is probably best understood as a case in which there were persons more directly affected than the plaintiff, because they lived much closer to the uranium mine. This case is therefore more relevant to the third element of the public interest standing test than to whether the plaintiff has a genuine interest.

66 In support of its contention that the Sierra Club's level of involvement is sufficient to demonstrate that it has a genuine interest in the subject matter of this litigation, its counsel relied upon *Sunshine Village Corp.*, *supra*, where the Canadian Parks and Wilderness Society (CPAWS) was granted standing to challenge the legality of a proposed development in Banff National Park, largely on the basis of the applicant's track record of general interest in preserving "the integrity of eco-systems in Canada's parks and wilderness areas." This seems to me quite similar to the facts of the present case.

• • •

68 In my view, the intervenor and respondents have not demonstrated that the Sierra Club lacks a genuine interest in the subject matter of this litigation by virtue of its limited involvement with the export of nuclear reactors.

B. AVAILABILITY OF INTERIM INJUNCTIVE RELIEF

While courts have displayed an increasing willingness to grant standing to public interest litigants, they have been much less sympathetic to arguments that existing legal doctrine should be adapted to accommodate public interest litigation in other ways. One area where this has been particularly true concerns the availability of interim injunctive relief.

ALGONQUIN WILDLANDS LEAGUE V ONTARIO (MINISTER OF NATURAL RESOURCES)
(1996), 21 CELR (NS) 102 (Ont Gen Div)

SAUNDERS J: The stay order sought is analogous to an injunction. There is no dispute as to the general nature of the test to be applied. It is the test set out in *RJR-MacDonald Inc. v. Canada (Attorney General)* (1994), 111 DLR (4th) 385 (SCC). It is a threefold test:

  (i)   Is there a serious issue to be tried?;
  (ii) Would the applicants suffer irreparable harm if the stay were refused?; [and]
  (iii) What is the balance of convenience? That is, which of the parties would suffer the greater harm from the granting or refusing the interim relief ... .

Initially this is the test with the lowest threshold. As stated in *RJR-MacDonald* at p. 411 unless the case on the merits is frivolous or vexatious or is a pure question of law, the judge as a general rule should go on to the next stage. The nature of the issues may be revisited at the end of the day when reaching a conclusion on the balance of convenience test. In dealing with this issue, the court should do no more at this stage than make a preliminary investigation of the merits. Indeed it is undesirable to go into the merits in any detail, having regard for the fact that they will be fully canvassed by the panel.

The applicant's attack on the municipal action is based on a noncompliance with the *Crown Forest Sustainability Act, 1994* [SO 1994, c. 25], and the conditions imposed by the Environmental Assessment Board. In my opinion the applicants have raised issues of statutory interpretation and ministerial conduct which are not frivolous and which require consideration before they can be determined. It is accordingly appropriate to pass to the second stage ... .

The applicants allege irreparable harm, in effect, on the simple straightforward position, that once you cut down a tree you cannot put it back. The extent or even the existence of the harm is disputed by the respondents. Furthermore the Minister submits that even if there were to be harm demonstrated, there has been no harm to these applicants, which the Minister submits is a necessary element of the test ... .

The cases suggest that the three tests should be considered in order and that if the applicant fails at any stage, that should be the end of the matter. It is important to note that neither the applicants in *Metropolitan Stores* [*Manitoba (Attorney General) v Metropolitan Stores Ltd*, [1987] 1 SCR 110, 1987 CanLII 79, (*sub nom Metropolitan Stores Ltd v Manitoba Food & Commercial Workers, Local 832*) 38 DLR (4th) 321] nor the applicants in *RJR-MacDonald* were public interest applicants. The cases cited by the Minister in support of the submission that the irreparable harm must be suffered by the applicants either involved the issue of standing or were not binding on this court. It would be a rare case where a public interest applicant such as the organizations which are making this application would directly suffer irreparable harm. It would be illogical to grant these applicants standing and then turn around and deny them relief because they had not suffered harm. It would seem to me that a better approach would be to consider the public interest harm alleged by the applicants along with the harm to the respondents at the third stage of the inquiry. In my opinion there is nothing in the passage of Mr. Justice Beetz that would be inconsistent with that approach, bearing in mind that in *Metropolitan Stores* there was no public interest applicant. In short, in this situation, we should skip stage two and move to stage three. ...

The third stage is the balance of convenience or as it is sometimes called the balance of inconvenience. The factors to be considered vary from case to case. In this case the public interest is very much involved. The applicants say there would be irreparable harm to the public interest if this stay is not granted. Conversely the respondents say there would be irreparable harm to the public interest if the stay were to be granted.

As I have said the applicants take the simple and straightforward position that if you cut down the trees you cannot put them back. The respondents dispute there will be any significant harm or indeed any harm at all. There is considerable conflicting evidence on this point and it is not possible to make any meaningful determination. For the purpose of this motion, I am prepared to assume there will be some irreparable harm to the natural growth and wildlife in the area in spite of the efforts to keep it to a minimum.

The harm to the respondents is of a different nature. The Crown will be hampered in pursuing its policy for the use of Crown lands. Crown revenue will be at least deferred and perhaps lost. It is uncontradicted that needed wood supply will be unavailable and the Goulard mill will not be able to operate at full capacity. It is also uncontradicted that if this occurs there will be loss of employment which will have a ripple effect in the community. Again it is hard to quantify the extent of the harm, but it must be assumed that there will be some harm.

What is going on here is part of a worldwide controversy or debate carried on in an effort to achieve a sustainable environment. In assessing the balance of convenience it is suggested in *RJR-MacDonald* that the court in determining whether to grant or withhold interlocutory relief should have regard not only to the harm which the parties contend they will suffer, but also to the nature of the relief sought, the nature of the legislation which is under attack, and where the public interest lies. To this I would add the nature of the authority of the Ministry which is under attack. This was not an issue in the *RJR-MacDonald* case, but in my opinion is an appropriate member of the group.

For a number of years the Ministry and interested segments of the public have been struggling with the issue of forest management. It is the obvious goal of all to achieve and maintain a sustainable environment while balancing the interests of the various segments. It is a complicated, ongoing and developing process. The details are set out in the material filed. In the course of argument it was not suggested that there had been anything other than good faith on the part of all parties to this application. The cutting of the forest at Owain Lake is clearly part of a comprehensive government policy with respect to the use of its land carried out in accordance with the principles I have tried to describe. While the applicants raised serious issues with respect to the compliance with the legislation and with the Environmental Assessment Board conditions, they have not, as submitted by the respondents for the industry, demonstrated anything that is substantially inconsistent with the draft manual or any connection between the alleged deficiencies and the alleged harm. The government action has been consistent with its declared policy.

In all of the circumstances I considered the balance favours the respondents. In my opinion it would be inappropriate to interfere with the action of the government, even for a short time. The motion therefore will be dismissed.

In May 1991, MacMillan Bloedel, a major forest company, began cutting a roadway into the lower Tsitika Valley, a remote area in western British Columbia, in preparation for future logging of old-growth forest. The Western Canada Wilderness Committee launched an action claiming the road building was unlawful. It contended that the Ministry of Forests had no authority to issue a road-building permit to the company until the ministry had approved the logging activities that the road would support. When their application for judicial review was dismissed in the BC Supreme Court, the Wilderness Committee filed an appeal and sought an injunction against further road building (completing the last 400 M of the road) until the appeal was heard.

This injunction application was dismissed by Toy JA (in chambers). He held that the balance of convenience weighed against granting the injunction sought: *Western Canada Wilderness Committee v British Columbia (Attorney General)*, 1991 CanLII 525, 4 BCAC 296. Among the factors that he said supported this conclusion were that:

1. the applicants had no direct or indirect interest that would be adversely affected if the road building continued;
2. the applicants had not proffered an undertaking to indemnify the company as to damages; and
3. completion of the road in this remote location would not amount to irreparable harm.

QUESTIONS

1. What arguments can be made that the Western Canada Wilderness Committee was directly and adversely affected? How does this question relate to the interlocutory injunction test?
2. What are the arguments against the undertaking to indemnify damages?
3. What is the basis for the court's irreparable harm conclusion?

NOTES

1. In *SPEC v Vancouver Parks Board*, 2000 BCSC 372, (*sub nom Friends of Stanley Park v Vancouver (City) Board of Parks and Recreation*) 10 MPLR (3d) 25, the applicant sought an interim injunction to halt a road-widening project in Vancouver's Stanley Park. Although he dismissed the application, Davies J offered these views with respect to the undertaking requirement:

> [45] As I said during argument, it seems to me that if an applicant who applies for injunctive relief in a matter concerning serious public interests is able to establish a serious question to be tried, and that the balance of convenience, including the public interest, favours the granting of injunctive relief, such relief should not generally, at the interlocutory stage, be rendered ineffectual by reason of the fact that the applicant may not have the financial wherewithal to provide a viable undertaking as to damages.
>
> [46] Had the applicants been successful in obtaining an interim injunction in this case, I would have exercised my discretion to allow that injunction without an undertaking as to damages.

2. Courts have also been increasingly willing to regard logging activity in parks as irreparable for the purposes of applications for injunctive relief. See C Tollefson, "Advancing an Agenda? Recent Developments in Public Interest Environmental Law in Canada" (2002) 51 UNBLJ 175. In *Caddy Lake Cottagers Assn v Florence-Nora Access Road Inc*, 1998 CanLII 6302, 126 Man R (2d) 230 (CA), the court opined that if the injunction was not granted, irreparable harm would ensue in that "damages will not compensate for a destroyed forest" and that a failure to grant such relief would trigger a "non-reversible process, even in the event that the applicant [were ultimately] successful." Similarly, in *Friends of Point Pleasant Park v Canada (Attorney General)*, 2000 CanLII 15928, 188 FTR 280 (TD), the petitioners sought an interim injunction pending an application to block a plan to log trees suspected of being infested with spruce beetle. In granting the injunction, O'Keefe J stated (at para 42):

> The applicants maintain that irreparable harm will be caused because if the interlocutory injunction is not granted and the judicial review application succeeds, then 10,000 trees would have been cut down under an invalid order. These trees could not be replaced in a person's lifetime, as many are older trees and the harm caused to the applicants' interests could not be repaired. As well, the applicants argued that an award of damages would not replace the trees. The applicants also allege irreparable harm to themselves as individuals and as representing the public interest. Based on the above facts, I find that the applicants will suffer irreparable harm.

C. COSTS AND PUBLIC INTEREST LITIGANTS

Liability of public interest litigants for adverse costs awards has been an issue, as the following excerpt shows.

CHRIS TOLLEFSON, "WHEN THE 'PUBLIC INTEREST' LOSES: THE LIABILITY OF PUBLIC INTEREST LITIGANTS FOR ADVERSE COSTS AWARDS"
(1995) 29 UBC L Rev 303 at 304-5, 314-19 [footnotes omitted]

Traditionally, Canadian courts have followed the English approach in awarding costs. In so doing, they have applied a "two-way" costs rule under which a litigant's liability for or entitlement to costs depends on whether the litigant is judicially deemed to have succeeded in the litigation. Increasingly, however, courts are being asked to recognize an exception to this rule where the unsuccessful party is "a responsible public interest litigant." Proponents of a "one-way" public interest costs rule, often referred to as the "public interest costs exception," invoke American jurisprudence where this approach to allocating costs has become well established and has displaced, for this and other designated types of litigation, the so-called "American rule" under which each side bears its own legal fees.

• • •

[The article then discusses *Sierra Club of Western Canada v British Columbia (Chief Forester)* (1993), 22 Admin LR (2d) 129 (BCSC), a challenge to the ecological sustainability of the manner in which the chief forester had calculated the company's allowable timber cut. The BC Supreme Court dismissed the action and awarded costs against the Sierra Club: 1994 CanLII 6510, 117 DLR (4th) 395.]

US public law has seen a series of lawsuits by corporate interests aimed at individuals and public interest organizations that participate in lawful activities such as demonstrations, offence reporting, and attending meetings. These SLAPP suits ("strategic lawsuits against public participation"), intended to intimidate public opponents, have also emerged in Canada.

CHRIS TOLLEFSON, "STRATEGIC LAWSUITS AND ENVIRONMENTAL POLITICS: DAISHOWA INC. V. FRIENDS OF THE LUBICON"
(1996) 31:1 J Can Studies 119 [footnotes omitted]

Even if the courts ultimately decide to extend the protection of the *Charter* to SLAPP targets, there is still a compelling need for direct legislative response to the SLAPP problem. SLAPP suits characteristically represent an attempt to convert economic power into legal advantage at the expense of democratic participation. In recognition of this, the goal of anti-SLAPP legislation must be to protect democratic participation by countering the corrosive effects of money in the legal process. In recent years, legislation of this kind has been enacted in nine American states.

NOTE

Some governments have acted to prevent SLAPP suits. BC's *Protection of Public Participation Act*, SBC 2001, c 19 (PPPA) is an example. The Act created a statutory public participation right protecting communications with government on issues of public interest. It prohibited actions that harmed persons or property, violated a court order, or were otherwise "unwarranted interference by the defendant with the rights or property of a person." It also changed the common law of defamation to accommodate communications within the statutory definition of "public participation." A court could summarily dismiss an action where the court was satisfied, on a balance of probabilities, that it targeted conduct that fell within this definition and was for an "improper purpose"—to chill public participation. If satisfied that there was a "reasonable possibility" that the defendant could meet these conditions should the case go to trial, the court could order the plaintiff to post security for the full amount of costs and damages to which a defendant might ultimately be entitled. However, a new government repealed the Act only a few months after it had come into force. In 2019, another new government enacted the *Protection of Public Participation Act*, SBC 2019, c 3.

To date, the only anti-SLAPP laws enacted in Canada are in Quebec, Ontario, and BC, although there are more than 20 such laws in the United States.

FURTHER READINGS

Ingelson, A, ed, *Environment in the Courtroom* (Calgary: University of Calgary Press, 2019).

McKenzie, J, *Environmental Politics in Canada* (Oxford: Oxford University Press, 2002).

Tilleman, W & A Lucas, eds, *Litigating Canada's Environment: Leading Canadian Environmental Cases by the Lawyers Involved* (Toronto: Thomson Reuters, 2017).

Tollefson, C, "SLAPPs: Developing a Canadian Response" (1994) 73 Can Bar Rev 200.

CHAPTER FIFTEEN

ENVIRONMENTAL REGULATORY LEGISLATION*

Alastair Lucas and Brett Carlson

I. INTRODUCTION

Environmental regulatory legislation at the federal and provincial levels has developed over the last 50 years. Legislative approaches have changed in several stages so that today, while environmental legislation retains classic approval and regulatory offence provisions at its core, it has evolved to include sophisticated alternatives such as economic instruments, consultation processes, and an array of enforcement and compliance tools. This chapter charts this evolution by examining various regulatory approaches, presenting a legislative model that captures the essential elements of the provincial statutes, and providing an overview of the federal *Canadian Environmental Protection Act, 1999*, SC 1999, c 33 [CEPA 1999]. Attention is given to the role and the development of environmental standards. The last part of the chapter focuses on judicial interpretation of environmental legislation in a range of contexts.

---

* The authors gratefully acknowledge the research assistance of Cheryl Sharvit, Joseph Chan, and Diego Almedia.

401

ALASTAIR LUCAS, "THE NEW ENVIRONMENTAL LAW"
in Ronald Watts & Douglas Brown, eds, *Canada: The State of Federation: 1989* (Kingston, Ont: Queen's University, Institute for Intergovernmental Relations, 1989) 167 at 168-71 [endnotes omitted]

WASTE CONTROL LAWS

This first generation of environmental statutes includes the basic air, water and land pollution statutes enacted by Canada, and by the provinces in the early 1970s. One category of these statutes is those that established separate environment departments for the first time. The essential object of these Acts was control of waste that was being deposited on land or discharged into water or air. Regulatory systems were established to identify waste sources, to bring these sources under permit, then by means of permit terms or conditions, to control the quality and quantity of waste discharged. Failure to comply with these requirements was made an offence punishable upon summary conviction by modest fines. Waste discharge likely to cause harm to human life or health or to the environment upon which human life depends, [*sic*] was often established as a general offence.

These statutes were clean-up laws, designed to minimize discharge of human and industrial waste into the environment. The underlying assumption was that the natural environment, with its air, water and land components, could, through careful management, be used to dispose of, dilute and cleanse the waste produced by human activity. It was a matter of measuring, then carefully and fairly allocating this environmental assimilative capacity.

It was recognized by governments and their advisors that civil legal actions, designed to resolve disputes between private parties and compensate persons damaged, were an ineffective legal tool for general systematic control of environmentally harmful waste discharge. It was also recognized that existing statute law, such as the common nuisance provision of the *Criminal Code* [RSC 1985, c C-46], public health statutes and miscellaneous provisions scattered through natural resource development statutes were not equal to the task of comprehensive environmental control.

Waste control statutes include comprehensive environmental statutes such as the *Ontario Environmental Protection Act* [RSO 1980, c 141], and the *Quebec Environment Quality Act* [RSQ 1977, c Q-2], which deal with air, water and land pollution from the base of comprehensive definitions of "pollution," "contaminant" and "environment," and single resource statutes such as the Alberta *Clean Air, Clean Water*, and *Land Surface Conservation and Reclamation* Acts [*Clean Air Act*, RSA 1980, c C-12; *Clean Water Act*, RSA 1980, c C-13; and *Land Surface Conservation and Reclamation Act*, RSA 1980, c L-3], which covered much of the same ground but established a separate regulatory system for each environmental medium [these are now consolidated in the *Environmental Protection and Enhancement Act*, RSA 2000, c E-12]. Federal first generation environmental statutes include the *Clean Air Act* [RSC 1985, c C-32], the *Canada Water Act* [RSC 1985, c C-11], and the *Fisheries Act* [RSC 1985, c F-14] Pollution Amendments and Industry Regulations [industry-related regulations, such as the *Metal Mining Liquid Effluent Regulations*, CRC, c 819, and *Petroleum Refinery Liquid Effluent Regulations*, CRC, c 828.]. Gaps were filled and Acts were fine-tuned through development of regulations, policies and procedures during the late 1970s and early 1980s.

These environmental laws were administered by environment departments, [*sic*] that were largely technical agencies, staffed by the scientific and engineering experts necessary to implement the permit schemes and develop "safe" standards for waste discharge. Initially a great deal of effort was expended simply to bring all waste sources under permit.

SECOND GENERATION ENVIRONMENTAL LAWS

A second generation of environmental statutes is now emerging. These laws are a response to overwhelming evidence that the waste control approach, while significant, is only one aspect of an effective environmental protection regime. A central objective of these new laws is control of persistent toxic substances. These materials either accumulate in the environment to produce conditions dangerous to the natural environment, or are simply so toxic and so persistent that even small amounts create serious danger over large periods of time. Such small dose toxicity and slow decomposition characteristics make the established assimilative waste regulation approach unsuitable for dealing effectively with toxic substances.

The new laws thus recognize that environmental protection is a long-term process that must address potential intergenerational effects of environmental damage. Because new scientific knowledge about the toxicity of particular substances is continually developing, the laws must be flexible and include the means for identification and effective regulation of new contaminants. The approach is preventive, but also anticipatory.

Also reflected in these second generation statutes is that fact that toxic substances respect no boundaries—provincial or international. The second generation environmental laws are consequently outward looking, and international in their development, implementation and administration. Provincial laws must reflect interprovincial and federal–provincial understandings and commitments, and must also, if they are to contribute to the solution of the global problem, reflect current international conditions and Canada's international obligations. Federal laws such as CEPA [*Canadian Environmental Protection Act*, SC 1988, c 22] must clearly implement specific international environmental commitments and must also be consistent with current international thinking about global environmental protection.

Another characteristic of the new environmental statutes is that enforcement provisions are far more sophisticated than the simple offence sections of the clean-up legislation. There is greater flexibility to permit the regulators a choice of appropriate enforcement tools, ranging from expeditious tickets for minor offenses, to serious indictable criminal offenses for actions that endanger life or health, mandatory administrative orders and civil legal actions. Negotiation techniques may be used in appropriate circumstances and provision is made for citizen involvement in regulatory processes, particularly in enforcement.

The serious criminal offenses which carry large fines and even potential imprisonment, [sic] have caught the attention of the corporate sector. Interest is particularly keen, [sic] when these offenses are combined with officer and director liability provisions that may render corporate officials personally liable for environmental offenses and subject to fine or imprisonment even if they merely acquiesced or failed to make appropriate inquiries into activity that resulted in serious environmental harm. The clear message is that environmental offenses are serious crimes, and that nothing short of demonstrating that all reasonable care was taken in the circumstances will excuse corporate employees and even officers and directors. This has provided strong incentives for corporations to review or audit their compliance with environmental requirements, take any necessary corrective action, and prepare and implement environmental protection polices and plans so that environmentally damaging actions can be avoided.

STEFAN AMBEC ET AL, "THE PORTER HYPOTHESIS AT 20: CAN ENVIRONMENTAL REGULATION ENHANCE INNOVATION AND COMPETITIVENESS?"

(2013) 7:1 Rev Envtl Econ & Policy 2, DOI: <https://doi.org/10.1093/reep/res016> [footnotes omitted]

Historically, the conventional wisdom among economists, policymakers, and business managers concerning environmental protection was that it comes at an additional cost to firms that may erode their global competitiveness. According to this traditional view, environmental regulations such as technological standards, environmental taxes, or tradable emissions forces [*sic*] firms to allocate some inputs (labor, capital) to pollution reduction, which is unproductive from a business perspective even if it offers environmental or health benefits to society. Technological standards restrict the choice of technologies or inputs in the production process. Taxes and tradable permits charge firms for emitting pollutants, a by-product of the production process that was previously free. These fees necessarily divert capital away from productive investments.

About twenty years ago, this traditional paradigm was contested by a number of economists, notably Professors Michael Porter (Porter 1991) and Claas van der Linde (Porter and van der Linde 1995a). Relying primarily on case studies, these researchers argue that pollution is often a waste of resources and that a reduction in pollution may lead to an improvement in the productivity with which resources are used. They argue that more stringent but properly designed environmental regulations (in particular, market-based instruments such as taxes or cap-and-trade emissions allowances) can "trigger innovation [broadly defined] that may partially or [in some instances] more than fully offset the costs of complying with them" (Porter and van der Linde 1995a, 98).

Porter was not the first to question mainstream economic views about the cost of environmental regulation. Arguments that pollution controls can spur the reduction of waste by businesses date back to the 1800s (Desrochers and Haight 2012). By the 1980s, some researchers had begun to examine whether environmental regulations could boost technology innovation without necessarily harming competitiveness (Ashford 1993). But it is Porter who, building on this foundation, can be credited with bringing these ideas into the mainstream business and policy debate—and inspiring two decades of research into the "Porter Hypothesis."

• • •

Porter and van der Linde (1995a, 99–100) go on to explain that there are at least five reasons why properly crafted regulations may lead to these outcomes:

- "First, regulation signals companies about likely resource inefficiencies and potential technological improvements."
- "Second, regulation focused on information gathering can achieve major benefits by raising corporate awareness."
- "Third, regulation reduces the uncertainty that investments to address the environment will be valuable."
- "Fourth, regulation creates pressure that motivates innovation and progress."
- "Fifth, regulation levels the transitional playing field. During the transition period to innovation-based solutions, regulation ensures that one company cannot opportunistically gain position by avoiding environmental investments."

Finally, they note, "We readily admit that innovation cannot always completely offset the cost of compliance, especially in the short term before learning can reduce the cost of innovation-based solutions" (Porter and van der Linde 1995a, 100).

• • •

More than twenty years ago, Michael Porter generated enormous interest among scholars, policymakers, businesses, and interest groups in the idea that well-designed regulation could actually enhance competitiveness. Indeed, much has been written since then about what has become known as the Porter Hypothesis. This article has provided an overview of the theoretical and empirical literature on the Porter Hypothesis. First, we find that the theoretical arguments for the Porter Hypothesis appear to be more solid now than when they were first discussed as part of the heated debate in the *Journal of Economic Perspectives* in 1995 (see Palmer et al. 1995). On the empirical side, the evidence for the "weak" version of the Porter Hypothesis (that stricter environmental regulation leads to more innovation) is fairly clear and well established. However, the empirical evidence on the strong version of the Porter Hypothesis (that stricter regulation enhances business performance) is mixed, but with more recent studies providing clearer support.

Porter's suggestion that more stringent environmental protection may lead to "win–win" outcomes for society overall has stimulated extensive academic research and policy debates over the last twenty years and has no doubt contributed to significant environmental and economic improvements through better designed regulation.

NOTES

Voluntary agreements for environmental protection based on discretionary statutory powers and the exercise of enforcement discretion became a preferred approach to the implementation of environmental legislation in most jurisdictions during the 1990s. This was a consequence, as Neil Gunningham and Darren Sinclair pointed out in *Leaders & Laggards: Next-Generation Environmental Regulation* (Sheffield: Greenleaf, 2002) ch 9, of market-based ideology and government cost-cutting. They saw the way forward as regulatory reconfiguration involving a variety of instruments and approaches, including reflexive regulation (which uses indirect means to achieve social objectives) and regulatory pluralism ("smart regulation"—multiple instruments used strategically). However, there is also evidence of a focus in provinces such as Ontario on statutory requirements and stricter enforcement as well as legislative changes to reflect this new focus.

D Paul Emond presents another analysis of the development of environmental legislation in "The Greening of Environmental Law" (1991) 36 McGill LJ 742. His focus is on process and emphasizes preventive assessment and consensual decision-making. (Environmental impact assessment concepts, legislation, and processes are treated specifically in Chapter 17 of this book.) This emphasis on public participation and consultation may also be seen as an element of an emerging third generation of environmental legislation—namely, laws to promote sustainability or "sustainable development." Sustainability draws much of its inspiration from the definition of sustainable development offered by the World Commission on Environment and Development in *Our Common Future* (Oxford: Oxford University Press, 1987) (the Brundtland commission report) at 43—it is "development that meets the needs of the present without compromising the ability of future generations to meet their own needs."

This definition was expanded in subsequent international instruments, and legal "principles" have emerged, particularly from the work done by the International Law Association's Committee on the Legal Aspects of Sustainable Development. In its fifth report in 2002 (*New Delhi*

Declaration of Principles of International Law Relating to Sustainable Development, Resolution 3/2002 (2002); see Int'l L Ass'n Rept Conf 70, 2002), it presented seven principles and their definitions: (1) the duty of states to ensure sustainable natural resource development; (2) equity and eradication of poverty; (3) common but differentiated responsibilities of developed and developing countries; (4) a precautionary approach to human health, natural resources, and ecosystems; (5) public participation and access to information and justice; (6) democratic and transparent governance; and (7) integration of economic development, human rights, and social and environmental objectives.

The preamble to CEPA 1999 declares that "the primary purpose of this Act is to contribute to sustainable development through pollution prevention." As discussed below, it also incorporates the precautionary principle (the idea that where there are threats of serious or irreversible damage, the lack of full scientific certainty is not a reason for postponing cost-effective measures to prevent environmental degradation), both generally and specifically, in relation to assessment of toxic substances. According to Supreme Court of Canada dicta in *114957 Canada Ltée (Spraytech, Société d'arrosage) v Hudson (Town)*, 2001 SCC 40, [2001] 2 SCR 241, there may be sufficient state practice to allow a good argument that the precautionary principle is a principle of customary international law that must be taken into account in establishing the context for interpretation of Canadian legislation. Other provisions of CEPA 1999 that address these sustainability principles include the parts on pollution prevention (part 4), life-cycle management or virtual elimination of toxics (part 5), the establishment of advisory and consultative processes (part 2), an environmental protection cause of action (s 22), citizen investigation submissions (s 17), and an environmental registry (s 12).

> ## ENVIRONMENTAL COMMISSIONER OF ONTARIO, HAVING REGARD: ANNUAL REPORT, 2000-2001
> (Toronto: ECO, 2001) at 78, online (pdf): *Office of the Auditor General of Ontario* <http://www.auditor.on.ca/en/content/reporttopics/envreports/env01/2000-01-AR.pdf>
>
> [As Ontario's Environmental Commissioner reported in 2001, in the 1990s, the province had increased its use of voluntary abatement agreements. However, the report noted a change.]
>
> ### THE SHIFT BACK TO MANDATORY ABATEMENT
>
> • • •
>
> [D]uring the Walkerton Inquiry, an internal MOE [Ministry of the Environment] memorandum, disclosed as part of the Inquiry evidence, announced a major shift in MOE's internal policy—from voluntary to mandatory abatement. The MOE memo, distributed to all district managers and supervisors in March 2000, called for strict compliance with MOE's Compliance Guideline and announced a movement away from voluntary abatement and towards mandatory abatement. The memorandum put forward a new interpretation of the section of the Compliance Guideline that previously permitted MOE to use voluntary abatement measures in specific situations. The memorandum sets out an expectation that, where even one of the mandatory criteria exists, a control document will be issued and mandatory abatement pursued.

II. PROVINCIAL REGULATORY LEGISLATION

Provincial legislation that regulates discharge of environmental contaminants is by no means uniform. There are, however, enough common elements to suggest a basic legislative model. Typically, the province establishes a regime for licensing and controlling contaminant discharges. Breaches of licensing requirements or terms and conditions of licences are quasi-criminal offences. Another central element is an array of powers to issue mandatory administrative orders in the event of unapproved release of contaminants.

The following is a more complete outline of the basic model:

1. Interpretation (definitions of key application and limitation terms)
2. Statement of purposes
3. Scope of application, including whether the Crown is bound as well as general exclusions
4. Prohibition against discharge of contaminants without an approval
5. Application procedure provisions and power in a designated official or authority to grant approvals
6. Enforcement order powers
7. Exemption or variance powers
8. Appeals
9. Enabling powers for economic instruments and market-based approaches
10. Offences and penalties
11. Regulation-making powers

QUESTION

1. Review your provincial environmental regulatory statute. How many elements of the basic model can you identify? Do any parts or provisions differ fundamentally from the model? If so, what are the particulars?

NOTES

In each statute, certain key terms delineate the application of the regime and establish standards for environmental harm. For example, "environment" or some version of the term is defined as follows:

- Alberta *Environmental Protection and Enhancement Act*, RSA 2000, c E-12, s 1(t):

  "environment" means the components of the earth and includes
  (i) air, land and water,
  (ii) all layers of the atmosphere,
  (iii) all organic and inorganic matter and living organisms, and
  (iv) the interacting natural systems that include components referred to in subclauses (i) to (iii).

- Ontario *Environmental Protection Act*, RSO 1990, c E.10, s 1(1):

  "natural environment" means the air, land and water, or any combination or part thereof, of the Province of Ontario.

  This includes private land and is not limited to public land within the province: *Rockcliffe Park Realty Ltd v Ontario (Director of the Ministry of the Environment)*, 1975 CanLII 518, 62 DLR (3d) 17 (Ont CA).

Things subject to regulation are defined, as in the following examples:

- Alberta *Environmental Protection and Enhancement Act*, s 1(mmm):

"substance" means
   (i) any matter that
     (A) is capable of becoming dispersed in the environment, or
     (B) is capable of becoming transformed in the environment into matter referred
to in paragraph (A),
   (ii) any sound, vibration, heat, radiation or other form of energy, and
   (iii) any combination of things referred to in subclauses (i) and (ii).

- Ontario *Environmental Protection Act*, s 1(1):

"contaminant" means any solid, liquid, gas, odour, heat, sound, vibration, radiation or combination of any of them resulting directly or indirectly from human activities that causes or may cause an adverse effect.

- Nova Scotia *Environment Act*, SNS 1994-95, c 1, ss 3(k) and (ba), respectively:

"contaminant" means, unless otherwise defined in the regulations, a substance that causes or may cause an adverse effect;

• • •

"waste" means a substance that would cause or tend to cause an adverse effect if added to the environment, and includes rubbish, slimes, tailings, fumes, smoke from mines or factories, other air emissions, or other industrial wastes, effluent, sludge, sewage, garbage, refuse, scrap, litter or other waste products of any kind.

- British Columbia *Environmental Management Act*, SBC 2003 c 53, s 1(1):

"waste" includes
   (a) air contaminants,
   (b) litter,
   (c) effluent,
   (d) refuse,
   (e) biomedical waste,
   (f) hazardous waste, and
   (g) any other substance prescribed by the Lieutenant Governor in Council, or the
minister under section 22 [minister's regulations—codes of practice], or, if either of them prescribes circumstances in which a substance is a waste, a substance that is present in those circumstances,

whether or not the type of waste referred to in paragraphs (a) to (f) or prescribed under paragraph (g) has any commercial value or is capable of being used for a useful purpose.

Application of statutes may be defined in terms of pollution sources rather than or in addition to contaminants or substances. See the following examples:

- Alberta *Environmental Protection and Enhancement Act*, s 1(a):

"activity" means an activity or part of an activity listed in the Schedule of Activities.

- Ontario *Environmental Protection Act*, s 1(1):

"source of contaminant" means anything that discharges into the natural environment any contaminant.

"Source of contaminant" must be a source outside the natural environment and not part of the natural environment itself: *Canadian National Railway Co v Ontario (Director under the Environmental Protection Act)*, 1991 CanLII 7169, 6 CELR (NS) 211 at 223 (Ont Div Ct), aff'd 1992 CanLII 7705, 8 CELR (NS) 1 at 5 (Ont CA).

While standards for environmental harm are established by definitions of activities or conditions such as "pollution" or things such as "contaminant" or "waste," they may also be defined in terms of effects, as in the following examples:

- Alberta *Environmental Protection and Enhancement Act*, s 1(b):

  "adverse effect" means impairment of or damage to the environment, human health or safety or property.

- Ontario *Environmental Protection Act*, s 1(1):

  "adverse effect" means one or more of,

    (a) impairment of the quality of the natural environment for any use that can be made of it,
    (b) injury or damage to property or to plant or animal life,
    (c) harm or material discomfort to any person,
    (d) an adverse effect on the health of any person,
    (e) impairment of the safety of any person,
    (f) rendering any property or plant or animal life unfit for human use,
    (g) loss of enjoyment of normal use of property, and
    (h) interference with the normal conduct of business.

- Nova Scotia *Environment Act*, s 3(c):

  "adverse effect" means an effect that impairs or damages the environment or changes the environment in a manner that negatively affects aspects of human health.

QUESTIONS

1. Do purpose sections have any practical use, or are they merely elaborate political statements?

2. Is it necessary to include exemption or variance provisions in environmental regulatory statutes?

3. Is it necessary to include appeal provisions in environmental regulatory statutes, or will general law rights to judicial review suffice? Judicial review is discussed in Chapter 14.

III. FEDERAL REGULATORY LEGISLATION: THE TOXICS CONTROL MODEL

A. OVERVIEW OF CEPA 1999

CEPA 1999, the successor to the original *Canadian Environmental Protection Act*, SC 1988, c 22, is the cornerstone federal environmental regulatory statute. For constitutional as well as historical and federal administrative policy reasons, the Act's structure and elements differ somewhat from the provincial regulatory model. It incorporates several matters that were once the subject of separate legislation, including disposal at sea, control of nutrients, standards for fuels, and emissions from engines.

The Act is also the formal articulation of federal environmental policy on a number of matters. It includes the ideas of the "polluter pays" principle and pollution prevention, and it sets out requirements for pollution prevention plans. The precautionary principle is included in the Act's preamble and is used as a specific criterion in determining whether substances are toxic for the purposes of the Act. It also provides context for the interpretation of other sections. The principle, as stated in the preamble, is that a "lack of full scientific certainty shall not be used as a reason for postponing cost-effective measures to prevent environmental degradation" where there are threats of serious or irreversible damage. Other principles include "virtual elimination of persistent and bioaccumulative toxic substances" (preamble), which is embedded in the toxics control part of the Act, and the need to protect and "remove threats to biological diversity" (preamble), which is implemented in the part on the regulation of biotechnology (part 6) as well as in the toxics control (part 5) and pollution prevention (part 4) provisions.

Equivalency agreements are the main technique for harmonizing CEPA 1999 requirements with those of provincial regulatory legislation. Provisions of CEPA 1999 do not apply in any jurisdiction for which there is an order declaring that the provisions do not apply. Such orders may be made by Cabinet on the recommendation of the minister of the environment if the minister and a provincial or territorial government agree in writing that the jurisdiction has in force laws that are equivalent to the standards and requirements established by CEPA 1999 regulations and has provisions for citizen requests for investigation of alleged offences similar to those in CEPA 1999.

The major difference between CEPA 1999 and the provincial regulatory statutes is the apparent lack of broad contaminant discharge prohibitions supported by a permit or approval system in CEPA 1999 (there is a limited permit system for ocean discharges). CEPA 1999 also contains a part on toxics control (part 5), which establishes a basis, although not a complete statutory scheme, for a prohibition and approval system for the regulation and management of toxic substances. This is potentially the regulatory heart of CEPA 1999. According to s 64 of the Act, a substance is "toxic" (except where the expression "inherently toxic" appears) if

> it is entering or may enter the environment in a quantity or concentration or under conditions that
>> (a) have or may have an immediate or long-term harmful effect on the environment or its biological diversity;
>> (b) constitute or may constitute a danger to the environment on which life depends; or
>> (c) constitute or may constitute a danger in Canada to human life or health.

"Inherently toxic" is not defined. However, according to s 3(1) of the Act,

> "substance" means any distinguishable kind of organic or inorganic matter, whether animate or inanimate, and includes
>> (a) any matter that is capable of being dispersed in the environment or of being transformed in the environment into matter that is capable of being so dispersed or that is capable of causing such transformations in the environment,
>> (b) any element or free radical,
>> (c) any combination of elements of a particular molecular identity that occurs in nature or as a result of a chemical reaction, and
>> (d) complex combinations of different molecules that originate in nature or are the result of chemical reactions but that could not practically be formed by simply combining individual constituents,
> and, except for the purposes of sections 66, 80 to 89 and 104 to 115, includes
>> (e) any mixture that is a combination of substances and does not itself produce a substance that is different from the substances that were combined,

(f) any manufactured item that is formed into a specific physical shape or design during manufacture and has, for its final use, a function or functions dependent in whole or in part on its shape or design, and

(g) any animate matter that is, or any complex mixtures of different molecules that are, contained in effluents, emissions or wastes that result from any work, undertaking or activity.

The toxics provisions then establish a series of process stages. First, information on whether a substance is toxic or capable of becoming toxic may be gathered. Next, substances are assessed to determine if they are toxic. This stage involves a priority substances list of substances for which, once listed, the health and environment ministers must carry out an assessment and determine toxicity. Persons using, manufacturing, supplying, or importing substances on two other lists, the domestic substances list and the non-domestic substances list, are required to supply specified information to the minister of the environment, who then assesses it to determine whether the substance is toxic before allowing its import, manufacture, or use.

If a substance is found to be toxic, the final stage is regulation. The governor in council may, on the recommendation of the ministers, decide that the substance should be added to the toxic substances list. The ministers are expressly required to apply a "weight of evidence approach and the precautionary principle" when interpreting the results of a screening assessment (s 76.1). Where they are satisfied that a substance meets the criteria for virtual elimination, they must propose the implementation of such elimination of the substance. Otherwise, a listed substance may then be made the subject of regulations by the governor in council; this must be done within two years of listing. The regulation of toxics under CEPA 1999 has been characterized as "life-cycle" management, in which the full range of actions in relation to a substance, from production or importation to disposal, is regulated.

Regulations with respect to substances on the list of toxic substances may, pursuant to s 93(1) of the Act, "provid[e] for, or impos[e] requirements respecting," a series of matters, including

(a) the quantity or concentration of the substance that may be released into the environment either alone or in combination with any other substance from any source or type of source;

(b) the places or areas where the substance may be released;

(c) the commercial, manufacturing or processing activity in the course of which the substance may be released;

(d) the manner in which and conditions under which the substance may be released into the environment, either alone or in combination with any other substance;

• • •

(l) the total, partial or conditional prohibition of the manufacture, use, processing, sale, offering for sale, import or export of the substance or a product containing it;

• • •

(r) the manner, conditions, places and method of disposal of the substance or a product containing it, including standards for the construction, maintenance and inspection of disposal sites.

B. VIRTUAL ELIMINATION

Where a substance is screened and the ministers propose to recommend that it be added to the list of toxic substances, and they are satisfied that the substance is persistent and bioaccumulative, that it results primarily from human activity, and that it is not a naturally occurring radionuclide or inorganic substance, the ministers must propose implementation of virtual elimination under the Act (s 77(4)). This means "the ultimate reduction of the quantity or concentration of the substance in the release below the level of quantification specified by the ministers" (s 65(1)) in a virtual elimination list. "Level of quantification" means "the lowest concentration that can be accurately measured using sensitive but routine sampling and analytical methods" (s 65.1), and in specifying this concentration, the ministers must take into account a variety of factors, including environmental or health risks as well as other relevant social, economic, or technical matters (s 65(3)). Implementation of virtual elimination requires preparation and submission to the minister of a plan to accomplish the purpose (s 79). However, it seems to be contemplated that although elimination plan measures may be incorporated into regulations, there does not appear to be a mechanism for direct enforcement of obligations under virtual elimination plans themselves.

The toxics control part of CEPA 1999 provides the legislative power to create a regulatory system for any substance that fits the broad definition of "toxic" on the basis of standards for quantity, concentration, and place of release of substances, including prohibitions and regulation of substance disposal. Control is then achieved though the wide array of classic and innovative compliance mechanisms that range from prosecutions to economic instruments and market-based approaches. It is unlikely that these powers would support a permit or approval system. Rather, regulation is through the toxicity assessment process itself—toxics are identified and then managed according to generic standards, and requirements are prescribed by regulation.

C. POLLUTION PREVENTION PLANS

The minister of the environment has broad powers to publish notices requiring specified persons to prepare and implement pollution prevention plans for substances or groups of substances that are on the Act's Schedule I list of toxic substances or that are likely to cause international air or water pollution. Though there is provision for guidelines and model plans, there is no requirement that plans be submitted to or reviewed by Environment and Climate Change Canada. Preparers are required merely to file a declaration within the specified time that a plan has been prepared and is being implemented and to keep a copy of the plan in their files.

Marcia Valiante has lamented the wide ministerial discretion and approach, and characterizes these as

> a middle ground between a completely voluntary system and a comprehensive mandatory system, ... [one that] accepts that industry is the central designer of pollution prevention, but [that fits the] design into a minimal administrative framework.

("The Legal Foundations of Canadian Environmental Policy" in D Van Nijnatten & R Broadman, eds, *Canadian Environmental Policy*, 2nd ed (Toronto: Oxford University Press, 2002) at 1, 14.)

D. INTERNATIONAL AIR AND WATER POLLUTION

The ministers of environment and health are authorized to act to prevent, control, or correct international air or water pollution. This includes substances from a Canadian source likely to create or contribute to pollution in a country other than Canada or to violate an international agreement binding on Canada (CEPA 1999, part 7, divisions 6, 7). There are provisions for consultation with other governments, but, subject to reciprocity with the other country, the minister is ultimately required to take action either by requiring pollution prevention plans or by recommending necessary regulations to Cabinet. Release of substances in contravention of the regulations is prohibited. There are specific ministerial powers in place to require proponents of activities likely to produce international pollution to submit plans and specifications and, if necessary, to issue interim remedial and preventive orders.

E. ECONOMIC INSTRUMENTS

The minister of the environment is authorized to establish "guidelines, programs and other measures for the development and use of economic instruments and market-based approaches" (s 322). There are specific powers to enable the federal Cabinet to make regulations concerning deposits and refunds (s 325) and tradeable units systems (s 326). The latter may provide the authority for the establishment of emission-trading systems for greenhouse gas emission reduction in order to meet international climate change agreement obligations. There is also a provision for regulations concerning fees and charges that may encompass emission fees (s 328).

F. ENFORCEMENT AND COMPLIANCE TECHNIQUES

Apart from market-based techniques such as emissions trading and the citizen "application for investigation" process, which is continued from its predecessor statute, CEPA 1999 includes a range of new and innovative enforcement and compliance techniques. "Environmental protection alternative measures" may be adopted under agreement where an offence of a specified category is alleged to have been committed and the attorney general, after consulting the minister of the environment, is satisfied that this would be appropriate with regard to a series of factors. These factors include the nature of the offence; compliance history; protection of the environment, human life and health, and other interests of society; whether the person charged accepts responsibility; and whether there is sufficient evidence to proceed with a prosecution. Agreements may contain appropriate terms and conditions, including reasonable costs of verifying compliance. Upon filing of an agreement, charges will be stayed or adjourned.

Enforcement officers may issue administrative orders, called "environmental protection compliance orders," for periods up to 180 days, where officers have reasonable grounds to believe that any provision of the Act or the regulations has been contravened (ss 234-241). Orders may prescribe a range of requirements, including the shutdown of any activity, work, or undertaking for a specified period. Persons to whom orders may be issued are those who own or have charge, management, or control of the contaminant substance in question or the property on which it is located or those who cause or contribute to the alleged contravention.

The standard of proof for the offence and the resulting significant harm is specified to be judged on a balance of probabilities. Defences include due diligence, authorized conduct, and officially induced mistake of law. There is a fuller discussion of issues related to enforcement and compliance in Chapter 19.

QUESTIONS

1. What is the purpose of the complex CEPA 1999 scheme for assessment and rescheduling of a toxic substance before regulations can be adopted? Why not list toxic substances in Schedule I directly?

2. Are the equivalency provisions of CEPA 1999 likely to prevent duplication and potential inconsistency of CEPA 1999 regulations with provincial legislation? What problems do you foresee?

3. To what extent can CEPA 1999 be used to address global environmental issues such as ocean pollution and global warming? What specific questions should be asked?

IV. ENVIRONMENTAL STANDARDS

In approving contaminant discharges under provincial or federal statutes, decisions must be based on standards established by regulation or by non-binding guidelines. How are these standards or guidelines established? What is their scientific or technical basis? Do they relate to substances discharged, or do they relate to the ambient environment into which the substances are discharged? What is the procedure for standard setting?

In the following extract, these questions are discussed in the context of a generalized model for setting environmental standards. To make legal sense of the model it is necessary to consider how or to what extent it applies to the specific structure, scheme, and requirements of each provincial and federal environmental regulatory statute.

MAH FRANSON, RT FRANSON & AR LUCAS, ENVIRONMENTAL STANDARDS

(Edmonton: Environment Council of Alberta, 1982) at 23-25

A MODEL PROCEDURE FOR SETTING ENVIRONMENTAL STANDARDS

WHAT ARE STANDARDS?

One of the first barriers that must be overcome is terminological. Writers in different fields clearly mean different things when they write about standards, guidelines, and objectives. Some legal writers distinguish between guidelines and standards, for example, on the basis of their legal impact. For them, a standard is a legally enforceable specification of the amount of pollutant that may be discharged or present in the ambient medium. There is a tendency for the popular press to follow this distinction. In contrast, technical writers would not necessarily follow this distinction. For them, an objective might refer to the particular uses that are desired for the water or air. A standard would specify the amount of contaminant that could be discharged, but it might or might not be legally enforceable. The model we will outline in this report is intended to establish a consistent terminology for the purposes of this report. When we come to evaluate the particular practices and standards of each jurisdiction we shall relate our findings to the terminology we have used in this model.

DEFINITION OF TERMS

"Objective" denotes a goal or purpose toward which an environmental control effort is directed. Examples of objectives are as follows: to preserve and enhance the salmon fishery in these waters; to prevent crop damage caused by air pollution; to protect the public health.

"Criteria" are compilations or digests of scientific data that are used to decide whether or not a certain quality of air or water is suitable for the chosen objectives. A simple example of a criterion that might be used to judge the suitability of water quality for a certain species of fish might be:

Concentration of Pollutant	Effect
A mg/L	No adverse effects noted
B mg/L	Lowest level at which sublethal effects noted
C mg/L	Lowest level at which mortalities noted
D mg/L	No survival

"Standard" denotes a prescribed numerical value or set of values to which concentrations or amounts actually occurring in the ambient medium or the discharge to that medium may be compared, whether legally enforceable or not. Examples of standards are:

- Average concentration of Pollutant X in the air shall not exceed Y micrograms per cubic metre during any 24-hour period. (Ambient)
- Maximum daily discharge of Pollutant A from Point Source B shall not exceed Z kg. (Effluent)

HOW SHOULD STANDARDS BE SET?

The traditional, technically based approach to setting standards is as follows:

1. Identification of uses of the ambient resource to be protected or *objectives* to be met.
2. Formulation of *criteria* through collection and/or generation of scientific information.
3. Formulation of *ambient quality standards* from the criteria.
4. Development of *effluent standards* for discharges into the environment that will produce a quality meeting the ambient standard.
5. Development of *monitoring and other information-gathering programs* that will refine the data inputs to the previous steps and provide feedback on whether the objectives are being met.

The following extract illustrates (in the case of Ontario) how the standard-setting process fits into the legislative framework.

KATHLEEN COOPER ET AL, ENVIRONMENTAL STANDARD SETTING AND CHILDREN'S HEALTH: A REPORT BY THE CHILDREN'S HEALTH PROJECT

(Toronto: CELA and OCFP Environmental Health Committee, 2000)
at 107-8, 175-76 [footnotes omitted]

3.5.1.3 CANADA-WIDE ACCORD ON ENVIRONMENTAL HARMONIZATION

In 1993, the CCME [Canadian Council of Ministers of the Environment, which remains active: <www.ccme.ca/index.html>] identified harmonization of environmental management in Canada as a top priority and developed the Canada-Wide Accord on Environmental Harmonization ... . On January 29, 1998, all jurisdictions except for Quebec signed the Accord. While not a statute, the Accord holds the potential to have a dramatic impact on the way that standards are developed at both the federal and provincial levels.

The Accord is a multilateral umbrella agreement, whose intent is to provide a framework for achieving harmonization. It provides a framework for the development of ancillary Sub-agreements on specific areas of environmental management. [One of these sub-agreements is the Canada-Wide Environmental Standards Sub-Agreement.]

• • •

CANADA-WIDE ENVIRONMENTAL STANDARDS SUB-AGREEMENT: CANADA-WIDE STANDARDS

The Canada-Wide Environmental Standards Sub-agreement "sets out the principles underpinning the development of Canada-wide Standards (CWS) for environmental quality and human health, and commits the governments to participate in their development. Such standards could include guidelines and objectives, as well as legally enforceable standards." The focus of the Sub-agreement is on "ambient standards, so that all Canadians can expect a common high degree of environmental quality." Ambient standards are described as levels of environmental quality for specific media (for example, air, water, soil, or sediment).

One of the stated underpinnings of the development and attainment of Canada-wide Environmental Standards is the Precautionary Principle. The agreement states that, "where there are threats of serious or irreversible environmental damage, lack of full scientific certainty shall not be used as a reason for postponing the development and implementation of standards."

The Sub-[a]greement "calls for governments to establish priorities for the development of CWSs and to allow for public involvement." The priority setting phase consists of three stages; nomination, screening, and selection.

In November of 1999, the ministers agreed on draft Canada-Wide Standards for four priority pollutants: particulate matter; ground-level ozone; benzene; and mercury. Ministers agreed to take the standards back to their Cabinet colleagues, who have six months to consult on these before they are finalized and formally adopted at the CCME meeting in the spring of 2000.

[CCME standards were used in the development of provincial contaminant substance standards. Ontario, for example, by Guideline A-8 (Ontario Environment and Energy, *Guideline for the Implementation of Canada-wide Standards for Emissions of Mercury* (19 August 2004; last modified 1 May 2019), online: *Government of Ontario* <https://www.ontario.ca/page/guideline-8-guideline-implementation-canada-wide-standards-emissions-mercury>), adopted CCME Canada-wide standards for emissions of mercury, dioxins and furans from municipal waste, biomedical waste, sewage sludge, hazardous waste incineration systems, and dioxin and furan emissions from steel manufacturing electric arc furnaces and iron sintering plants. These standards, which continue to be reviewed and updated, are used to establish discharge conditions in certificates of approval for specific facilities.]

• • •

5.2.1 AMBIENT AIR QUALITY CRITERIA

Ambient Air Quality Criteria (AAQC) are established under the *EPA* [Ontario *Environmental Protection Act*] and limit total atmospheric contaminant levels. The Criteria are established for different time periods and set the maximum average contaminant concentration that is permissible during a particular time period. Hence, a one hour AAQ Criterion for a contaminant would limit the average atmospheric quantity of the contaminant that is present during a one-hour period at a particular point or receptor. AAQC are based on either human health or environmental effects, whichever is the most sensitive, and are normally set at a level that is not expected to cause adverse effects to a sensitive receptor, based on continuous exposure. Consequently, socio-economic factors including costs and technological feasibility are not considered in the setting of an AAQC. If odour or irritant effects are experienced at levels below health effects, then the AAQC are established based on that more sensitive impact. The Criteria are not themselves standards, but they may become indirectly enforceable by way of being included in a particular Certificate of Approval issued to a particular applicant for a specific facility or mobile source. Where relevant, they are used to guide the setting of individual Certificate of Approval limits. Where National Ambient Air Quality Objectives ... exist, they inform the setting of AAQC. The Canada Wide Standards process under CCME has largely usurped development of additional National Ambient Air Quality Objectives (NAAQO), in the sense that the federal government is devoting its resources to the CWS process although the authority to enact NAAQO is still in place. The Ontario Ministry of the Environment expects that in the future as new standards are developed, " ... all of the criteria will be adopted as standards and there will no longer be air 'guidelines' in use. This approach will be more consistent with current practice and more consistent with enforceability requirements."

5.2.2 POINT OF IMPINGEMENT STANDARDS

Regulation 346 [*General Air Pollution Regulation*, RRO 1990, Reg 346] under the *EPA* sets out Point of Impingement (POI) standards for non-vehicular contaminant sources. These legally-binding standards limit the contaminant content of the emissions that are produced by individual facilities. A point of impingement is the location at which a contaminant first makes contact with a sensitive receptor following emission. The receptor may be human, animal or plant. For any given emission source, there exist multiple points of impingement, as the contaminant reaches different receptors (people, plants, wildlife) that are situated at different distances and in different directions from the emission source. Schedule 1 to Regulation 346 establishes Point of Impingement limits for a number of contaminants. These standards are maximum average contaminant concentrations that are permitted over a half hour period at the Point of Impingement. They may not be exceeded unless an emission source is explicitly exempted by regulation.

QUESTIONS

1. What are the advantages and disadvantages of specifying contaminant standards in regulations and making the breach of any standard an offence? If standards are directly enforceable in this way, should they be in the form of ambient standards or effluent standards? Would it be more efficient and effective not to specify standards in regulations but, instead, to publish standards in guideline form so that they may be adopted, if appropriate, as terms and conditions in operating licences or approvals?

2. What form should public participation in standard setting take? Should public hearings be held? If so, at what stage or stages of the process? Would it suffice to invite interested individuals or groups to submit written comments on proposed standards? If standard setting does involve some form of government–industry bargaining, is there a place for public involvement?

3. How can federal Canada-wide standards be implemented and enforced under provincial regulatory statutes?

V. INTERPRETATION OF ENVIRONMENTAL STATUTES

The ordinary principles of statutory interpretation, which involve reading the relevant words in their entire context and in their grammatical and ordinary sense harmoniously with the scheme and object of the Act and the intention of Parliament, apply to the interpretation of environmental legislation.

Since the scope of discretionary powers under environmental statutes is often at issue, purpose clauses and statute processes assume particular importance.

In *Quebec (Attorney General) v Canada (National Energy Board)*, [1994] 1 SCR 159, 14 CELR (NS) 1 at 30, Iacobucci J said:

> I am of the view that the Court of Appeal erred in limiting the scope of the [National Energy] Board's environmental inquiry to the effects on the environment of the transmission of power by a line of wire across the border. To limit the effects considered to those resulting from the physical act of transmission is an unduly narrow interpretation of the activity contemplated by the arrangements in question. The narrowness of this view of the Board's inquiry is emphasized by the detailed regulatory process that has been created. I would find it surprising that such an elaborate review process would be created for such a limited inquiry. As the Court of Appeal in this case recognized, electricity must be produced, either through existing facilities or the construction of new ones, in order for an export contract to be fulfilled. Ultimately, it is proper for the Board to consider in its decision-making process the overall environmental costs of granting the licence sought.

"Environmental quality" was interpreted as including social as well as biophysical elements in *Friends of the Oldman River Society v Canada (Minister of Transport),* [1992] 1 SCR 3, 7 CELR (NS) 1 at 25, where La Forest J stated:

> I cannot accept that the concept of environmental quality is confined to the biophysical environment alone; such an interpretation is unduly myopic and contrary to the generally held view that the "environment" is a diffuse subject matter: See: *R v. Crown Zellerbach Canada Ltd.,* [1988] 1 SCR 401, 3 CELR (NS) 1, 25 BCLR (2d) 145, 40 CCC (3d) 289, 48 DLR (4th) 151, 84 NR 1. The point was made by the Canadian Council of Resource and Environment Ministers, following the "Brundtland Report" of the World Commission on Environment and Development, in the *Report of the National Task Force on Environment and Economy,* September 24, 1987, at 2:
>
>> Our recommendations reflect the principles that we hold in common with the World Commission on Environment and Development (WCED). These include the fundamental belief that environmental and economic planning cannot proceed in separate spheres. Long-term economic growth depends on a healthy environment. It also affects the environment in many ways. Ensuring environmentally sound and sustainable economic development requires the technology and wealth that is generated by continued economic growth. Economic and environmental planning and management must therefore be integrated. Surely the potential consequences for a community's livelihood, health and other social matters from environmental change are integral to decision-making on matters affecting environmental quality, subject, of course, to the constitutional imperatives, an issue I will address later.

In the *Friends of the Oldman River* case, the Supreme Court held that the effect of the federal *Environmental Assessment and Review Process Guidelines Order,* SOR/84-467 (subsequently replaced by the *Canadian Environmental Assessment Act,* SC 1992, c 37, which was in turn replaced by the *Impact Assessment Act,* SC 2019, c 28, s 1.) was to add environmental factors to the decision criteria mentioned in s 5 of the *Navigable Waters Protection Act,* RSC 1985, c N-22 (as it then was), notwithstanding that the Guidelines Order was merely delegated legislation and that it did not explicitly add environmental decision criteria to any powers under federal statutes. The issue was treated by the court as one of consistency between the Guidelines Order and the *Navigable Waters Protection Act* approval power. The test was whether the two statutes were contradictory. The doctrinal similarity to the principle of paramountcy in cases involving constitutional division of powers was noted. According to La Forest J, broad interpretation of the Guidelines Order was consistent with its objectives and those of the provisions in its parent *Department of the Environment Act*, RSC 1985, c E-10—to make environmental assessment an essential component of federal decision-making (see Chapter 17).

The contextual approach to statutory interpretation includes, as L'Heureux-Dubé J observed in *Spraytech*, above, respecting the relevant values and principles enshrined in both customary and conventional international law. She concluded that there may be sufficient state practice to support arguments that the precautionary principle is a principle of customary international law. Thus, the principle must be respected in determining whether s 410 of the Quebec *Cities and Towns Act*, RSQ, c C-19, which empowered municipalities to pass by-laws for the "peace, order, good government, health and general welfare ... of the municipality" authorized a pesticides by-law that included a prohibition on pesticide use.

"Every now and then, a case comes along that causes some people to question the reach of our environmental laws," said Joseph Castrilli and Ramani Nadarajah ("Protecting and Expanding the Scope of Environmental Legislation: Castonguay Blasting v Ontario" in W Tilleman & A Lucas, eds, *Litigating Canada's Environment: Leading Canadian Environmental Cases by the Lawyers Involved* (Toronto: Thomson Reuters, 2017) at 173.)

In *Castonguay Blasting Ltd v Ontario (Environment)*, 2013 SCC 52, Castonguay Blasting Ltd was charged under the Ontario *Environmental Protection Act* (EPA) with failing to report an incident in which its highway construction blasting threw "fly-rock" into the air, causing property damage. The issue was whether the EPA applied only where a discharge (the rock) may cause non-trivial harm to the "natural environment," as opposed to where it may cause harm to people, animals, plants, or property but not to the "natural environment." Abella J for the Supreme Court majority said in the following extract:

CASTONGUAY BLASTING LTD V ONTARIO (ENVIRONMENT)
2013 SCC 52

[13] The issue in this appeal is the proper interpretation of the reporting requirement in s. 15(1). This provision states:

15.—(1) Every person who discharges a *contaminant* or causes or permits the *discharge* of a contaminant into the *natural environment* shall forthwith notify the Ministry if the discharge is out of the normal course of events, the discharge causes or is likely to cause an *adverse effect* and the person is not otherwise required to notify the Ministry under section 92. [Emphasis added by authors.]

[14] The terms "discharge," "contaminant," "natural environment" and "adverse effect" are defined in s. 1(1) of the *EPA*, as follows:

"natural environment" means the air, land and water, or any combination or part thereof, of the Province of Ontario;
"discharge," when used as a verb, includes add, deposit, leak or emit and, when used as a noun, includes addition, deposit, emission or leak;
"contaminant" means any solid, liquid, gas, odour, heat, sound, vibration, radiation or combination of any of them resulting directly or indirectly from human activities that causes or may cause an adverse effect;
"adverse effect" means one or more of,
    (a) impairment of the quality of the natural environment for any use that can be made of it,
    (b) injury or damage to property or to plant or animal life,
    (c) harm or material discomfort to any person,

(d) an adverse effect on the health of any person,

(e) impairment of the safety of any person,

(f) rendering any property or plant or animal life unfit for human use,

(g) loss of enjoyment of normal use of property, and

(h) interference with the normal conduct of business;

[15] Castonguay conceded that the discharge of fly-rock caused property damage, but argued that injury or damage to private property alone is insufficient to engage the reporting requirement. Since the discharge did not impair the natural environment—the air, land or water—Castonguay was not required to report the incident to the Ministry.

[16] Castonguay's argument is, in essence, an argument that while the definition of "adverse effect" has eight components—paras. (a) to (h)—para. (a) is an umbrella clause. In other words, there *must* be, in the language of para. (a), "impairment of the quality of the natural environment for any use that can be made of it" before any of the other seven elements come into play. They are not stand-alone elements and only constitute an "adverse effect" if they are accompanied by the impairment to the quality of the natural environment set out in para. (a). An adverse effect as defined in paras. (b) through (h) *without* any accompanying impairment to the quality of the natural environment under para. (a) will not be sufficient to trigger s. 15(1).

· · ·

[21] Parsing the language of s. 15(1) illuminates its clear preventative and protective purposes. First, a person must discharge a *contaminant*. Second, the contaminant must be discharged *into the natural environment*. Third, the discharge must be *out of the normal course of events*. Fourth, the discharge must be one that *causes or is likely to cause an adverse effect*. Finally, the person must not be otherwise required to notify the Ministry under s. 92, which refers to the spill of pollutants from a structure, vehicle or container and is therefore not applicable to the circumstances of this case.

[22] Taking each phrase in turn, the full scope of the reporting requirement is revealed. Section 15(1) applies to the discharge of "contaminant[s]" as defined by the *EPA*. The definition of contaminant in s. 1(1) of the *EPA* includes "any solid liquid, gas, odour, heat, sound, vibration, radiation or combination of any of them resulting directly or indirectly from human activities that causes or may cause an adverse effect." The reference to human activities in the definition of contaminant, when read in the context of s. 15 and the *EPA* as a whole, recognizes that the *EPA* applies only to those activities which engage the natural environment—the air, land or water in the province. This ensures that the definition of contaminant and s. 15 of the *EPA* maintain a nexus to the statutory objective of environmental protection.

[23] The discharge must be *into the natural environment*, defined as the air, land and water of Ontario. Section 15(1) does not impose any restrictions on the length of time the contaminant remains in the natural environment, nor does it require that the contaminant become part of the natural environment.

[24] Only discharges that are *out of the normal course of events* are required to be reported to the Ministry. This restricts the application of s. 15(1) by excluding many everyday, routine activities. Although driving a car, for example, discharges fumes into the natural environment, the discharge is not out of the normal course of events and no report to the Ministry is required.

[25] The key, in my view, to understanding s. 15(1) is that the discharge of the contaminant caused or was likely to cause an "adverse effect." As previously noted, adverse effect is defined as:

"adverse effect" *means one or more of,*

    (a) impairment of the quality of the natural environment for any use that can be made of it,

    (b) injury or damage to property or to plant or animal life,

    (c) harm or material discomfort to any person,

    (d) an adverse effect on the health of any person,

    (e) impairment of the safety of any person,

    (f) rendering any property or plant or animal life unfit for human use,

    (g) loss of enjoyment of normal use of property, and

    (h) interference with the normal conduct of business;

• • •

[31] To interpret "adverse effect" restrictively not only reads out the plain and obvious meaning of the definition, it narrows the scope of the reporting requirement, thereby restricting its remedial capacity and the Ministry's ability to fulfill its statutory mandate.

• • •

[34] The effects set out in paras. (a) to (h) are designed to capture a broad range of impacts. Some are limited to impacts on animals, people or property and do not require any impairment of the air, land or water in Ontario. Since the *EPA* protects the natural environment *and those who use it*, this is consistent with the broader protections the *EPA* was intended to provide. Paragraphs (a) through (h) also reflect a statutory recognition that protecting the natural environment requires, among other strategies, maximizing the circumstances in which the Ministry of the Environment may investigate and remedy environmental harms, including those identified in paras. (a) to (h).

[35] Moreover, it is important to note that the words "adverse effect" appear in many provisions of the *EPA*. Sections 6, 14, 18, 91.1, 93, 94, 97, 132, 156, 157.1, and 188.1 deal with a range of environmental concerns such as when an order to take preventative measures may be issued or the development of spill prevention and contingency plans. Restricting the definitional scope of "adverse effect" would therefore also limit the scope of the *EPA*'s protective and preventative capacities and, consequently, the Ministry's ability to respond to the broad purposes of the statute.

[36] In summary, the requirement to report "forthwith" in s. 15(1) of the *EPA* is engaged where the following elements are established:

    i. a "contaminant" is discharged;

    ii. the contaminant is discharged into the natural environment (the air, land and water or any combination or part thereof, of the Province of Ontario);

    iii. the discharge is out of the normal course of events;

    iv. the discharge causes, *or is likely to cause*, an adverse effect, namely one or more of the effects listed in paras. (a) to (h) of the definition;

    v. the adverse effect or effects are not trivial or minimal; and

    vi. the person is not otherwise required to notify the Ministry under s. 92, which addresses the spill of pollutants.

[37] Applying these elements to this case, s. 15(1) was clearly engaged. Castonguay "discharged" fly-rock, large pieces of rock created by the force of a blast, into the "natural environment." There is also no doubt that fly-rock meets the definition of "contaminant." The discharge in this case was "out of the normal course of events"—it was an accidental consequence of Castonguay's blasting operation. Had the blast been conducted routinely, the fly-rock would not have been thrust into the air.

[38] Finally, the discharge of fly-rock caused an "adverse effect" under paras. (b) and (g) of the definition, namely, it caused injury or damage to property and loss of enjoyment of the normal use of the property. Because the reporting requirement is also engaged when the discharge is "likely to cause an adverse effect," para. (e) is also applicable since the potential existed for "impairment of the safety of any person."

VI. THE QUASI-CRIMINAL OFFENCE MODEL

A. STRICT ENFORCEMENT

Quasi-criminal offences, or "strict enforcement," are traditional and fundamental elements of the provincial regulatory model outlined above. They are, therefore, considered in this chapter, while more detailed material is presented in Chapter 19. Though the main vehicle used here is the central offence provision under the federal *Fisheries Act*, RSC 1985, c F-14, analogous legal issues arise in the case of offences under the provincial regulatory statutes. The *Fisheries Act* includes several classic regulatory offence sections, and there is a long history of prosecution of these offences. In fact, there was even a dedicated report series, the *Fisheries Pollution Reports* (FPR) (available online at Environmental Law Centre: <www.elc.ab.ca>), that was published by the Enforcement Section of Environment Canada in the 1970s.

Section VI.C, below, discusses interpretive issues that have arisen in prosecutions under these *Fisheries Act* offence provisions. Emphasis is on s 36(3) (which is reproduced below).

In addition to CEPA 1999, the *Fisheries Act* is a major federal environmental regulatory regime (see K Webb, *Pollution Control in Canada: The Regulatory Approach in the 1980s* (Ottawa: Law Reform Commission of Canada, 1988)). Under this regulatory system, which establishes industry-specific regulatory limits for contaminant discharges, emphasis continues to be given to enforcement through prosecution of quasi-criminal offences.

B. REGULATORY PROVISIONS

The core regulatory provisions are based on the s 35(1) offence that, before 2012, prohibited projects and activities likely to result in "harmful alteration, disruption or destruction of fish habitat" (HADD). The minister could authorize a project or activity, subject to prescribed conditions.

Amendments in 2012 transformed the *Fisheries Act* regulatory scheme into what Martin Olszynski (in "In Search of #BetterRules: An Overview of Federal Environmental Bills C-68 and C-69" (15 February 2018), online: *ABlawg.ca* <https://ablawg.ca/2018/02/15/in-search-of-betterrules-an-overview-of-federal-environmental-bills-c-68-and-c-69/>) describes as a "'serious harm to fish' regime." The scope of s 35 was limited to serious harm to fish that are "part of a commercial, recreational or Aboriginal fishery."

Bill C-68, *An Act to amend the Fisheries Act and other Acts in consequence*, 1st Sess, 42nd Parl, 2018 (assented to 21 June 2019) SC 2019, c 14, which was introduced in 2018 and partially came into force on August 28, 2019, repeals the "commercial, recreational or Aboriginal fishery" restriction, largely returning to the HADD regime. Olszynski notes:

> As was the case before 2012, there will once again be two standalone prohibitions, the first against the death of fish by means other than fishing; and the second against impacts to fish habitat:
>
> **Death of fish**
>   34.4(1) No person shall carry on any work, undertaking or activity, other than fishing, that results in the death of fish.

Harmful alteration, disruption or destruction of fish habitat
35(1) No person shall carry on any work, undertaking or activity that results in the harmful alteration, disruption or destruction of fish habitat.

Both prohibitions continue to be subject to Ministerial and regulatory authorization. These provisions will require further scrutiny but the following scheme seems to emerge. Under Bill C-68, there will be three kinds of projects that may be subject to some kind of oversight: (i) projects with the *potential* to impact fish and fish habitat but which impacts may be avoided or minimized to a level of insignificance; (ii) projects with moderate impacts, and (iii) projects with potentially significant impacts.

C. THE MAJOR OFFENCES

The following is the key *Fisheries Act* offence provision designed to protect fish and, thus, the quality of fish-bearing waters, by prohibiting the deposit of any "deleterious substance" in "water frequented by fish."

Deposit of deleterious substance prohibited
36(3) Subject to subsection (4), no person shall deposit or permit the deposit of a deleterious substance of any type in water frequented by fish or in any place under any conditions where the deleterious substance or any other deleterious substance that results from the deposit of the deleterious substance may enter any such water.

Deposits authorized by regulation
(4) No person contravenes subsection (3) by depositing or permitting the deposit in any water or place of
(a) waste or pollutant of a type, in a quantity and under conditions authorized by regulations applicable to that water or place made by the Governor in Council under any Act other than this Act;
(b) a deleterious substance of a class and under conditions—which may include conditions with respect to quantity or concentration—authorized under regulations made under subsection (5) applicable to that water or place or to any work or undertaking or class of works or undertakings; or
(c) a deleterious substance the deposit of which is authorized by regulations made under subsection (5.2) and that is deposited in accordance with those regulations.

Regulations for authorizing certain deposits
(5) The Governor in Council may make regulations for the purpose of paragraph (4)(b) prescribing
(a) the deleterious substances or classes thereof authorized to be deposited notwithstanding subsection (3);
(b) the waters or places or classes thereof where any deleterious substances or classes thereof referred to in paragraph (a) are authorized to be deposited;
(c) the works or undertakings or classes thereof in the course or conduct of which any deleterious substances or classes thereof referred to in paragraph (a) are authorized to be deposited;
(d) the quantities or concentrations of any deleterious substances or classes thereof referred to in paragraph (a) that are authorized to be deposited;
(e) the conditions or circumstances under which and the requirements subject to which any deleterious substances or classes thereof referred to in paragraph (a) or any quantities or concentrations of those deleterious substances or classes thereof are authorized to be deposited in any waters or places or classes thereof referred to in

paragraph (b) or in the course or conduct of any works or undertakings or classes thereof referred to in paragraph (c); and

(f) the persons who may authorize the deposit of any deleterious substances or classes thereof in the absence of any other authority, and the conditions or circumstances under which and requirements subject to which those persons may grant the authorization.

NOTE

The elements of the s 36(3) offence must be proven by the Crown beyond a reasonable doubt. They are as follows:

1. a person (natural or artificial)
2. deposited (act) or permitted the deposit of (omission)
3. a deleterious substance
4. in water frequented by fish or in a place or under conditions where such deleterious substance or another deleterious substance that results from the deposit may enter water frequented by fish.

"Deposit" is defined as "any discharging, spraying, releasing, spilling, leaking, seeping, pouring, emitting, emptying, throwing, dumping or placing" (s 34(1)).

"Deleterious substance" is defined in s 34(1), in para (a) of "deleterious substance," as "any substance that, if added to any water, would degrade or alter or form part of a process of degradation or alteration of the quality of that water so that it is rendered or is likely to be rendered deleterious to fish or fish habitat or to the use by man of fish that frequent that water."

Note that the due diligence defence is discussed in Chapter 19.

QUESTIONS

1. Does s 36(3) include only intentional deposits?
2. Is dredging contaminated material from a water body and depositing it in another part of the water body a "deposit"? (See *Société pour Vaincre La Pollution v Canada (Minister of the Environment)*, 1996 CanLII 12448, 114 FTR 213, 22 CELR (NS) 64 (TD).)
3. What about when silt that is stirred up from a streambed by the operation of heavy equipment in the water settles on fish eggs located on another part of the streambed? (See *R v Stearns-Roger Engineering Co*, 1973 CanLII 1691, [1974] 3 WWR 285 (BCCA).)

FURTHER READINGS

Benedickson, J, *Environmental Law*, 4th ed (Toronto: Irwin Law, 2013), chs 8, 9.

Berger, S, *The Prosecution and Defence of Environmental Offences* (Aurora, Ont: Canada Law Book) (loose-leaf).

Gunningham, N & D Sinclair, *Leaders and Laggards: Next Generation Environmental Regulation* (Sheffield: Greenleaf, 2002).

Halsbury's Laws of Canada, *Environment* at HEN-70-350 "Regulation of the Environment in Canada" (2018 Reissue).

Wood, S, G Tanner & B Richardson, "Whatever Happened to Canadian Environmental Law?" (2010) 37 Ecology LQ 51.

CHAPTER SIXTEEN

THE ECONOMIC APPROACH AND BEYOND*

Georgios Dimitropoulos

I. INTRODUCTION

If there is one social science that can claim dominance in terms of its influence on public policy over the last two centuries, it is certainly economics. Much of this dominance is explained by the success of the economic model, a model that attempts to replicate the approach found in the natural sciences. The model provided by the natural sciences is particularly attractive to policy-makers, given its predictive value. At the same time, it is a model that reduces social life down to certain (independent and dependent) variables, failing, thus, to account for the complexity of social life.

The science of economics has had a great impact on the law as well. Under the influence of American legal realism, both the impact of economics on the law and the economic analysis of law became part of the mainstream, mainly in the United States, and more recently in Canada, Europe, and the rest of the world. The strong position of the "law and economics" movement started being challenged only more recently—namely since the beginning of the 21st century—by one rather unanticipated discipline of the social sciences: psychology, specifically its cognitive strand. It was through economics that psychology started exercising its influence on public policy-making. The influence of cognitive psychology on economics led to the development of the field of behavioural economics, which made its way into the law and gave rise to behavioural law and economics. These two disciplines helped develop the field of behavioural public policy.

---

* The chapter for this edition of the book is based on Chapter 10 of the previous edition, by J Owen Saunders.

Economic approaches to public policy have played a particularly important role with respect to environmental policy. This has led to some controversy: can and should environmental goods be measured and given a price? The behavioural approach moves beyond the use of the price system by dealing with environmental problems through the use of "nudges" and tries to address potential "cognitive biases" to which consumers may be subject. This has led to some further controversy: are nudges a sufficient means to address the pressing environmental problems of our times?

Many environmental issues can be considered examples of market failure, that is, exceptions to the "normal" model that economists use to describe the world. At least two prominent examples of market failure are of special interest in environmental law and policy: public goods and (negative) externalities, or spillover effects. The failure of the market is rooted in an inability to assert ownership over a particular resource. As a result, the market fails to provide the "correct" price signals, and the good is not produced in the optimal quantities.

The issue of market failure in environmental law and policy is discussed in Section II of this chapter. Section III moves on to discuss a policy tool that has been used to assess regulatory interventions in environmental law and policy: cost–benefit analysis. The chapter concludes with Section IV, which discusses the three main pillars of contemporary environmental law and policy and shows the transition from command-and-control to market-based to behavioural regulation. The three pillars should be understood as complementing rather than competing with each other.

II. MARKET FAILURE

BC FIELD & ND OLEWILER, ENVIRONMENTAL ECONOMICS, 1ST ED (CDN)
(Toronto: McGraw-Hill Ryerson, 1995) at 69-78

EXTERNAL COSTS

When entrepreneurs in a market economy make decisions about what and how much to produce, they will normally take into account the price of what they will produce and also the cost of items for which they will have to pay: labour, raw materials, machinery, energy, and so on. We call these the *private* costs of the firm, [sic] they are the costs that show up in the profit-and-loss statement at the end of the year. Any firm, assuming it has the objective of maximizing its profits, will try to keep its production costs as low as possible. This is a worthwhile outcome for both the firm and society because inputs always have opportunity costs; they could have been used to produce something else. Furthermore, firms will be alert to ways of reducing costs when the relative prices of inputs change.

But in many production operations there is another type of cost that, while representing a true cost to society, does not show up in the firm's profit-and-loss statement. These are called *external costs*. They are called "external" because, although they are real costs to some members of society, they will not normally be taken into account by firms when they go about making their decisions about output rates. Another way of saying this is that there are costs that are external to firms but internal to society as a whole.

One of the major types of external cost is the cost inflicted on people through environmental degradation. An example is the easiest way to see this. Suppose a paper mill is located somewhere on the upstream reaches of a river and that, in the course of its operation, it discharges a large amount of wastewater into the river. The wastewater is full of organic matter that arises from the process of converting wood to paper. This waste material gradually is converted to more benign materials by the natural assimilative capacity of the river water but, before that happens, a number of people downstream are affected by the lower quality of water in the river. Perhaps the waterborne residuals reduce the number of fish in the river, affecting down-stream fishers. The river may be also less attractive to look at, affecting people who would like to swim or sail on it. Worse, the river water perhaps is used downstream as a source of water for a public water supply system, and the degraded water quality means that the town has to engage in more costly treatment processes before the water can be sent through the water mains. All of these downstream costs are real costs associated with producing paper, just as much as the raw materials, labour, energy, etc., used internally by the plant. But from the mill's standpoint these down-stream costs are *external costs*. They are costs that are borne by someone other than the people who make decisions about operating the paper mill. At the end of the year the profit-and-loss statement of the paper mill will contain no reference whatever to these real downstream external costs.

If we are to have rates of output that are socially efficient, decisions about resource use must take into account both types of costs—the private costs of producing paper plus whatever external costs arise from adverse environmental impacts. In terms of full social cost accounting:

Social Costs = Private Costs + External (Environmental) Costs.

• • •

Most of the cases of environmental destruction involve external costs of one type or another. Electricity generating plants emit airborne residuals that affect the health of people living downwind. Users of chemicals emit toxic fumes that affect people living in the vicinity. Developers build on land without taking into account the deg-radation of the visual environment of local inhabitants, and so on. Nor is it only businesses who are responsible for external environmental costs. When individuals drive their automobiles, exhaust gases add to air pollution, and when they dispose of solid waste materials (like old batteries), they may affect the quality of the local environment.

• • •

EXTERNAL BENEFITS

An external benefit is a benefit that accrues to somebody who is outside, or external, to the decision about consuming or using the good or resource that causes the externality. When the use of an item leads to an external benefit, the market willing-ness to pay for that item will understate the social willingness to pay.

• • •

As another example of an external benefit, consider a farmer whose land is on the outskirts of an urban area. The farmer cultivates the land and sells his produce to people in the city. Of course, the farmer's main concern is the income he can derive from the operation, and he makes decisions about inputs and outputs accord-ing to their effect on that income. But the land kept in agriculture produces several other benefits, including habitat for birds and other small animals, and scenic values for passers-by. These benefits, while internal from the standpoint of society, are external from the standpoint of the farmer. They don't appear anywhere in his profit-and-loss position: they are external benefits of his farming decisions. In this case the agricultural value of the land to the farmer understates the social willingness to pay to have the land in agriculture.

When economists discuss the rudiments of supply and demand, we usually use as examples very simple goods that do not have external benefits. Farmers produce and supply so many million apples per year. Individual and market demand curves for apples are easy to comprehend. If we want to know the total number of apples bought, we can simply add up the number bought by each person in the market. Each person's consumption affects no one else. In this case the market demand curve will represent accurately the aggregate marginal willingness to pay of consumers [sic] for apples. But in cases involving external benefits, this no longer holds. We can see this by considering a type of good that inherently involves large-scale external benefits, what economists have come to call "public goods."

PUBLIC GOODS

Consider the provision of national defence services. Once the defence system with all its hardware and people are in place, everyone in the country receives the service. Once the services are made available to one person, others cannot be excluded from making use of the same services. This is the distinguishing characteristic of a *public good*. It is a good which, if made available to one person, automatically becomes available to others.

Another example of a public good is clean air. If the air around a city is free of serious contaminants, anyone in the city can breathe the air without diminishing its availability to all other people within the city. Note carefully that it is not the ownership of the supplying organization that makes a public good public. Although our two examples require government involvement, a public good is distinguished by the technical nature of the good, not by the type of organization making it available. For example, radio signals are free to anyone with a receiver. But most radio stations are privately owned.

We are interested in public goods because environmental quality is essentially a public good. If the quantity of stratospheric ozone is increased, everyone worldwide benefits. Private markets are likely to undersupply public goods, relative to efficient levels. To see why, let's take another very simple example: a small freshwater lake on the shores of which there are three occupied homes. The people living in the houses use the lake for recreational purposes but, unfortunately, the water quality of the lake has been contaminated by an old industrial plant that has since closed. The contaminant is measured in parts per million (ppm). At present the lake contains 5 ppm of this contaminant. It is possible to clean the water by using a fairly expensive treatment process. Each of the surrounding homeowners is willing to pay a certain amount to have the water quality improved. Table 4-2 shows these individual marginal willingnesses to pay for integer values of water quality. It also shows the total marginal willingness to pay, which is the sum of the individual values.

The table also shows the marginal cost of cleaning up the lake, again just for integer values of water quality. Note that we have increasing marginal cost; as the lake becomes cleaner, the marginal cost of continued improvement increases. Marginal cost and aggregate marginal willingness to pay are equal at a water quality of 2 ppm. At levels less than this (higher ppm), aggregate marginal willingness to pay for a cleaner lake exceeds the marginal cost of achieving it, hence from the standpoint of these three homeowners together, improved water quality is desirable. But at quality levels better than 2 ppm, total willingness to pay falls below marginal costs. Thus 2 ppm is the socially efficient level of water quality in the lake.

TABLE 4-2 Individual and Aggregate Demand for Lowering Lake Pollution

Level of contaminant (ppm)	Marginal willingness to pay ($ per year)			Total	Marginal cost of cleanup
	Homeowner A	Homeowner B	Homeowner C		
4	110	60	30	200	50
3	85	30	20	140	65
2	70	10	15	95	95
1	55	0	10	65	150
0	45	0	5	50	240

• • •

Having identified the efficient level of water quality, could we rely on a competitive market system, where entrepreneurs are on the alert for new profit opportunities, to get the contaminant in the lake reduced to that level? Suppose a private firm attempts to sell its services to the three homeowners. The firm goes to person A and tries to collect an amount equal to that person's true willingness to pay. But that person will presumably realize that once the lake is cleaned up, it's cleaned up for everybody no matter how much they actually contributed. And so A may have the incentive to underpay, relative to their true willingness to pay, in the hopes that the other homeowners will contribute enough to cover the costs of the cleanup. But, of course, the others may react in the same way. When a public good is involved, each person may have an incentive to "free ride" on the efforts of others. A free rider is a person who pays less for a good than her/his true marginal willingness to pay, a person who underpays, that is, relative to the benefits they receive.

Free riding is a ubiquitous phenomenon in the world of public goods, or in fact any good the consumption of which produces external benefits. Because of the free-riding impulse, private, profit-motivated firms will have difficulty covering their costs if they go into the business of supplying public goods. Private firms will be unable to determine a person's true willingness to pay for the public good. Thus, private firms will normally *under supply* goods and services of this type, if they can supply the good or service at all. Environmental quality improvements are essentially public goods. Since we cannot rely on the market system to provide efficient quantities of "goods" of this type, we must fall back on some type of nonmarket institution involving collective action of one type or another. In the lake example, the homeowners may be able to act collectively, perhaps through a homeowner association, to secure contributions for cleaning up the lake. Of course, the free-rider problem will still exist even for the homeowner's association, but if there are not too many of them, personal acquaintance and the operation of moral pressure may be strong enough to overcome the problem. When there are many thousands or millions of people, however, as there usually are in most environmental issues, the free-rider problem may be handled effectively only with more direct collective action through a governmental body that has taxing power. It is not that we wish completely to replace market processes in these cases. What we want to do is add sufficient public oversight to the market system that we do finally end up with efficient levels of environmental quality that are equitably distributed.

NOTE

It has been established so far that the market generates externalities. There are multiple ways to control negative externalities. According to mainstream economics, external costs can be addressed through regulation, taxes, or subsidies. Regulation is sometimes a very efficient means to control negative externalities, while at the same time being straightforward and relatively easy to impose. Often, it will be the most effective means of controlling externalities; for example, prohibition may be the only solution in the face of acute environmental disasters.

Despite the benefits of direct regulation, commands and prohibitions may sometimes be very costly or very difficult to enforce. Discontinuing a certain factory or a certain industry may lead to great social costs. It is also difficult for the government to control and may lead to illicit activities in the shadow of the law. Taxation presents itself as an alternative to direct regulation in some instances. Taxation allows polluters to continue polluting; however, it makes them pay for each unit of pollution. Taxes for pollution and environmental taxes present an effort to impose a cost where there was none previously. This cost is to be borne by the firm or individual that creates the negative externality; taxation is an attempt to internalize externalities. Ideally, the tax should raise the marginal costs of continuing the activity for the polluting firm or individual to equal the costs that the continued activity imposes on society. According to mainstream economics, the tax mechanism allows the market itself to take all costs into account and allocate the resources in the public interest under the conditions of the pricing mechanism. Still, taxes are difficult to administer for both the private firms and the government. For example, accurate devices for monitoring the amount of pollutants may be difficult to acquire.

When taxation may not be the most effective means to control externalities, yet another solution would be to offer polluters outright payments or subsidies to stop polluting; for example, to install antipollution equipment. This may sometimes be more efficient, but it could create resentment among the public about using taxpayers' money to subsidize polluting activities by the private sector.

The management of the common resources or the common physical infrastructure raises further issues of negative externalities. Garrett Hardin raised this issue in dramatic terms with his illustration of the progressive "tragedy of the commons." Can the obvious path to collective disaster—spearheaded by the rational self-interest of welfare-maximizing individuals—be prevented?

G HARDIN, "THE TRAGEDY OF THE COMMONS"
(1968) 162 Science 1243 at 1244

The tragedy of the commons develops in this way. Picture a pasture open to all. It is to be expected that each herdsman will try to keep as many cattle as possible on the commons. Such an arrangement may work reasonably satisfactorily for centuries because tribal wars, poaching and disease keep the numbers of both man and beast well below the carrying capacity of the land. Finally, however, comes the day of reckoning, that is, the day when the long-desired goal of social stability becomes a reality. At this point, the inherent logic of the commons remorselessly generates tragedy.

As a rational being, each herdsman seeks to maximize his gain. Explicitly or implicitly, more or less consciously, he asks, "What is the utility *to me* of adding one more animal to my herd?" This utility has one negative and one positive component.

1) The positive component is a function of the increment of one animal. Since the herdsman receives all the proceeds from the sale of the additional animal, the positive utility is nearly +1.

2) The negative component is a function of the additional overgrazing created by one more animal. Since, however, the effects of overgrazing are shared by all the herdsmen, the negative utility for any particular decision-making herdsman is only a fraction of −1.

Adding together the component partial utilities, the rational herdsman concludes that the only sensible course for him to pursue is to add another animal to his herd. And another; and another … . But this is the conclusion reached by each and every rational herdsman sharing a commons. Therein is the tragedy. Each man is locked into a system that compels him to increase his herd without limit—in a world that is limited. Ruin is the destination toward which all men rush, each pursuing his own best interest in a society that believes in the freedom of the commons. Freedom in a commons brings ruin to all.

NOTES AND QUESTIONS

Both mainstream economics and law focus on the need to create strong institutions of contract and property, with equally strong and enforceable individual rights for resolving the problem of the failure of the market to deal with cases where the prices of certain factors are not adequately accounted for in the production decision, for example, the difficulty in asserting ownership rights over the right to enjoy a mountain sunset. The solution to externalities according to this view is the clear and enforceable allocation of property rights. Also in the case of the commons, a solution derived from the tragedy of the commons may thus be to privatize the commons and vest property rights in one or more owners to manage them.

What about the allocation of property rights? Does economics tell us anything about who should be the recipient of such rights if an economically efficient result is to be pursued? Let us imagine a large steel mill polluting agricultural land and damaging the surrounding crops. How can the negative externalities created by pollution from the mill be internalized by allocating enforceable rights to air quality? Is it important who is given such property rights? Is the initial allocation of the entitlements important? Accordingly, does it make any difference whether the legal system imposes no penalty on the factory owner for polluting the air or whether it shows its disapproval of such pollution by allowing farmers to sue for the damage to the crop yield? According to the Coase Theorem, the initial allocation of rights and entitlements is not important to the economically efficient outcome for society. The same result, in the sense of economic efficiency, will be achieved independent of whether the rights are allocated to the farmer or the factory owner. Society as a whole will not be affected by the initial allocation of entitlements. It is only important for social welfare that rights be allocated. The Coase Theorem is, of course, subject to certain assumptions that do not hold true in real life. What is probably even more important is that it raises serious questions of fairness. Efficiency in such cases does not mean a "fair" allocation of the relevant rights.

AM POLINSKY, AN INTRODUCTION TO LAW AND ECONOMICS, 2ND ED
(Toronto: Little, Brown & Co, 1989) at 11-14

THE COASE THEOREM

One of the central ideas in the economic analysis of law was developed in an article by Ronald Coase in 1960 ["The Problem of Social Cost" (1960) 3 JL & Econ 1]. This idea, which has since been named the *Coase Theorem*, is most easily described by an example. Consider a factory whose smoke causes damage to the laundry hung outdoors by five nearby residents. In the absence of any corrective action each resident would suffer $75 in damages, a total of $375. The smoke damage can be eliminated in either of two ways: A smokescreen can be installed on the factory's chimney, at a cost of $150, or each resident can be provided an electric dryer, at a cost of $50 per resident. The efficient solution is clearly to install the smokescreen since it eliminates total damage of $375 for an outlay of only $150, and it is cheaper than purchasing five dryers for $250.

ZERO TRANSACTION COSTS

The question asked by Coase was whether the efficient outcome would result if the right to clean air is assigned to the residents or if the right to pollute is given to the factory. If there is a right to clean air, then the factory has three choices: pollute and pay $375 in damages, install a smokescreen for $150, or purchase five dryers for the residents at a total cost of $250. Clearly, the factory would install the smokescreen, the efficient solution. If there is a right to pollute, then the residents face three choices: suffer their collective damages of $375, purchase five dryers for $250, or buy a smokescreen for the factory for $150. The residents would also purchase the smokescreen. In other words, the efficient outcome would be achieved regardless of the assignment of the legal rights.

It was implicitly assumed in this example that the residents could costlessly get together and negotiate with the factory. In Coase's language, this is referred to as the assumption of *zero transaction costs*. In general, transaction costs include the costs of identifying the parties with whom one has to bargain, the costs of getting together with them, the costs of the bargaining process itself, and the costs of enforcing any bargain reached. With this general definition in mind, we can now state the simple version of the Coase Theorem: If there are zero transaction costs, the efficient outcome will occur regardless of the choice of legal rule.

Note that, although the choice of the legal rule does not affect the attainment of the efficient solution when there are zero transaction costs, it does affect the distribution of income. If the residents have the right to clean air, the factory pays $150 for the smokescreen, whereas if the factory has the right to pollute, the residents pay for the smokescreen. Thus, the choice of the legal rule redistributes income by the amount of the least-cost solution to the conflict. Since it is assumed for now that income can be costlessly redistributed, this distributional effect is of no consequence—if it is not desired, it can be easily corrected.

POSITIVE TRANSACTION COSTS

The assumption of zero transaction costs obviously is unrealistic in many conflict situations. At the very least, the disputing parties usually would have to spend time and/or money to get together to discuss the dispute. To see the consequences of positive transaction costs, suppose in the example that it costs each resident $60 to get together with the others (due, say, to transportation costs and the value attached to time). If the residents have a right to clean air, the factory again faces the choice of paying damages, buying a smokescreen, or buying five dryers. The factory would again purchase the smokescreen, the efficient solution. If the factory has a right to pollute, each resident now has to decide whether to bear the losses of $75, buy a dryer for $50, or get together with the other residents for $60 to collectively buy a smokescreen for $150. Clearly, each resident will choose to purchase a dryer, an inefficient outcome. Thus, given the transaction costs described, a right to clean air is efficient, but a right to pollute is not.

• • •

We can now state the more complicated version of the Coase Theorem: If there are positive transaction costs, the efficient outcome may not occur under every legal rule. In these circumstances, the preferred legal rule is the rule that minimizes the effects of transaction costs. These effects include the actual incurring of transaction costs and the inefficient choices induced by a desire to avoid transaction costs.

The distributional consequences of legal rules are somewhat more complicated when there are transaction costs. It is no longer true, as it was when there were zero transaction costs, that the choice of rule redistributes income by the amount of the least-cost solution. In the example, if the residents have the right to clean air, the factory pays $150 for the smokescreen, whereas if the factory has the right to pollute, the residents pay $250 for five dryers.

Although the simple version of the Coase Theorem makes an unrealistic assumption about transaction costs, it provides a useful way to begin thinking about legal problems because it suggests the kinds of transactions that would have to occur under each legal rule in order for that rule to be efficient. Once these required transactions are identified, it may be apparent that, given more realistic assumptions about transaction costs, one rule is clearly preferable to another on efficiency grounds. The more complicated version of the Coase Theorem provides a guide to choosing legal rules in this situation.

NOTE

One of the limitations of the Coase Theorem, and modern welfare economics, is that it does not engage in any effective way the issue of interpersonal utility comparisons. Twentieth-century economics has not addressed the issue of the initial allocation, nor has it addressed the distribution of costs and benefits or whether there are more or less fair distributions. Economics provides no answer, for example, as to whether a certain individual would get greater utility from an additional $100 of income than would another. To avoid this obstacle, economists sometimes assume that so long as the outcome of a particular action means that losers *could* be compensated and there remain net social benefits, then the welfare of society is increased. This is a dubious result not only when viewed from the point of view of other disciplines, but also when viewed through the lens of the rationality of the law as such. It needs to be noted that Adam Smith, the founder of modern economics, first became a professor of Logic and then held the Chair of Moral Philosophy at the University of Glasgow.

FURTHER READINGS

Coase, RH, "The Problem of Social Cost" (1960) 3 JL & Econ 1.

Elliott, H, "A General Statement of the Tragedy of the Commons" (1997) 18:6 Population and Environment: A Journal of Interdisciplinary Studies 515.

Frischmann, BM, *Infrastructure: The Social Value of Shared Resources* (Oxford: Oxford University Press, 2012).

Hahn, RW, "The Impact of Economics on Environmental Policy" (2000) 39:3 J Envtl Econ & Mgmt 375.

Mathis, K & BR Huber, eds, *Environmental Law and Economics, Economic Analysis of Law* in European Legal Scholarship, vol 4 (Berlin: Springer, 2017).

Revesz, RL, P Sands & RB Stewart, eds, *Environmental Law, the Economy, and Sustainable Development: The United States, the European Union, and the International Community* (New York: Cambridge University Press, 2000).

Samuels, WJ, "The Coase Theorem and the Study of Law and Economics" (1974) 14 Nat Resources J 1.

Wilen, JE, "Renewable Resource Economics and Policy: What Differences Have We Made?" (2000) 39:6 J Envtl Econ & Mgmt 306.

III. COST–BENEFIT ANALYSIS

The discussion in the previous section concentrated on the inefficiencies that were introduced by the failure of the market to adequately reflect all the relevant costs and benefits inherent in the use of some environmental resources. The identification of all such costs and benefits, especially in the context of environmental decision-making, is the subject of the large and often controversial practice in policy-making and literature on cost–benefit analysis. The controversy is the result of the effort to monetize and quantify values and solutions to environmental problems for which values and solutions are not necessarily quantifiable or on which society is not always ready to put a value. Contemporary policy-makers need to consider whether there are, and should be, any values that are non-pecuniary and whether there are, and there should be, any assets that are to be perceived as priceless.

The following two excerpts discuss the application of the cost–benefit analysis in policy-making, as well as the issues its widespread use is raising.

TS VEEMAN, "THE APPLICATION OF ECONOMIC ANALYSIS TO PUBLIC LAND AND RESOURCE MANAGEMENT: AN OVERVIEW"
in TJ Cottrell, ed, *Role of Economics in Integrated
Resource Management, Proceedings held October 16-18, 1985*
(Edmonton: Alberta Energy/Forestry, Lands and Wildlife, 1985) 17 at 17-24.
[internal references omitted]

ECONOMICS AND VALUE

THE CONCEPT OF VALUE

• • •

Since money is the current medium of exchange (and not gold, salt, or cigarettes as in previous times and places), the exchange value of a commodity is measured in terms of its price, that is, the quantity of money for which the commodity can be exchanged. The price or exchange value of goods, in turn, is determined simultaneously by considerations of supply (cost) and demand (utility or preference). Underlying the pattern of demand is the doctrine of consumers' sovereignty—the notion that each individual is the best judge of what he or she wants. Moreover, the marginal utility associated with goods is tied to a person's marginal willingness to pay. Implicit, too, is the assumption that the consumer's wants are insatiable—more is preferred to less. Such assumptions clearly can be criticized, but are unlikely to be abandoned completely.

The fact that goods have value can be ascribed ultimately to the scarcity of resources and the aspect that the resources have competing uses. If goods were available in unlimited supply, they would be free. Typically that is not the case, and price must serve as a rationing device for goods or resources, particularly those with exclusive property rights. In so far as the valuation of natural resources is concerned, it is also important to remember that natural resources are multi-attribute and thus have quantity, quality, time and space dimensions.

Economic values are regarded to be relative values and not "intrinsic" values. Economic values are typically couched in terms of opportunity cost. The value of an extra gun is the amount of butter you would be willing to give up to obtain the gun. Economists do not try to determine what something, like education or clean air, is worth in and of itself. Economic values are typically marginal or incremental values, rather than total values.

• • •

GENERAL APPROACHES AND CRITERIA FOR RESOURCE MANAGEMENT

• • •

EFFICIENCY AND EQUITY

The criterion or goal of efficiency deals essentially with the relationship of social benefits and social costs exclusive of their distribution. Any project having net social benefits greater than zero or, alternatively, having a benefit–cost ratio exceeding unity, passes the limited test of economic feasibility. A more stringent efficiency test requires that the project be compared with alternative projects or uses of scarce investment funds.

The goal of equity, on the other hand, refers to the incidence of social benefits and costs—in a nutshell, who reaps the benefits and who bears the costs? Any project or policy typically has impacts on the personal or size distribution of income (among income recipients such as individuals or households), the functional distribution of income (in terms of labor [sic] income, projects, and rent), and the spatial or regional distribution of income (say as between northern and southern Alberta).

THE MARKET SYSTEM AND PARETO-OPTIMALITY

Economists extol the virtues of price systems as useful, de-centralized, administrative devices. It is also a tenet of economics that a perfectly competitive market system will tend to be efficient. Given the initial endowment of resources, which may be unequal, and given the state of technology, a Pareto-optimal state is achieved wherein total social product—"the size of the economic pie"—is maximized from our scarce resources. Pareto-optimality occurs when there is no way to make one economic agent better off without making someone else worse off, and is associated with a host of marginality conditions in production and consumption.

The concept of Pareto-optimality is of rather limited use as a criterion for public policy. Most projects or policies generate gains to some individuals and losses to others. This led, in the 1940s, to a further refinement of modern applied welfare economics—the "compensation principles" of Hicks [John R Hicks, "The Foundations of Welfare Economics" (1939) 49:196 Econ J 696] and Kaldor [Nicholas Kaldor, "Welfare Propositions in Economics and Interpersonal Comparisons of Utility" (1939) 49:195 Economic J 549]. Any project or policy change improved social welfare, it was argued, if the gainers could (hypothetically) compensate the losers and there was some positive net gain remaining. Indeed, benefit–cost analysis rests on these very theoretical underpinnings—the "Pareto criterion with compensation." These refinements are not without criticism. Indeed, [Kenneth] Arrow, the Nobel laureate, has argued that it is impossible to aggregate individual preferences into a social preference over various states of the world. Even "majority rule" can be shown not to be an ideal social welfare function. Despite these theoretical difficulties, econo-mists continue to use benefit–cost analysis as a practical tool, and legislatures continue to use the principle of "majority rule."

SUSAN ROSE-ACKERMAN, "PUTTING COST–BENEFIT ANALYSIS IN ITS PLACE: RETHINKING REGULATORY REVIEW"
(2011) 65 U Miami L Rev 335 at 335-36, 337-39, 348-51 [footnotes omitted]

Policymakers need to reassess the role of cost–benefit analysis (CBA) in regulatory review. Although it remains a valuable tool, a number of pressing current problems do not fit well into the CBA paradigm. In particular, climate change, nuclear accident risks, and the preservation of biodiversity can have very long-run impacts that may produce catastrophic and irreversible effects. ...

CBA is suitable for many conventional policy issues that have limited but signifi-cant effects on society in the short to medium run. The best analogy is to the deci-sions made by large corporations when they decide how to invest to maximize profits. In such cases, both public agencies and firms seek to maximize net gains, holding conditions in the rest of the world constant. However, that is not an appro-priate analogy for policies with a significant global impact.

Since 1981, the Office of Information and Regulatory Affairs (OIRA) in the White House has reviewed significant proposed and final regulations for conformity with cost–benefit tests. Under a series of executive orders, OIRA has performed this role through Republican and Democratic presidencies. These policy reviews are contro-versial: Some claim that OIRA promotes the use of sound social–scientific reasoning; others see it as a front for business interests and a triumph of cold and heartless economic reasoning.

• • •

The failure to rethink the executive order is unfortunate—especially given the global trend to institutionalize something called impact assessment (IA). IA is not quite the same thing as CBA, but it is grounded in an identical commitment to promulgating policies that have positive net benefits while at the same time improv-ing public accountability and incorporating other values. A bandwagon may be starting that needs to be subject to critical scrutiny before it acquires the status of conventional wisdom.

With no change in the executive order, CBA will continue to be enshrined as the ideal standard for regulation in the United States. Even if the actual cost–benefit studies performed by U.S. government agencies are highly variable in quality and often lack key components, the technique remains a benchmark for analysis.

I seek to challenge the hegemony of CBA on two grounds. First, cost–benefit analysis should be used to evaluate only a limited class of regulatory policies, and even then it should be supplemented with value choices not dictated by welfare economics. Second, CBA presents an impoverished normative framework for policy choices that do not fall into this first category. Policy ought to be made on other grounds even though consideration of the costs and the benefits of a program is obviously a requirement for sound policymaking.

I do not wish to be misunderstood. I favor technocratic analysis that measures both costs and benefits in the most accurate way possible and that uses these data to make intelligent policy choices. Problems arise, however, when the search for a single "best" policy forces analysts to make controversial assumptions simply to produce an answer that "maximizes" social welfare. The debate often conflates two related problems. First, analysts must resolve a set of difficult conceptual issues even where CBA is an appropriate technique on normative grounds. More fundamentally, the second set of problems strikes at the heart of the technique and make[s] it an inappropriate metric for the analysis of some policy issues.

First, difficult issues arise even if net-benefit maximization is a plausible public goal. In the best case for cost–benefit analysis, the program seeks to correct a failure in private markets, and the law's distributive consequences are not a major concern. Overall distributive effects may be small or, if large, tilt in an egalitarian direction, as when a regulation limits the monopoly power of large businesses. Here, the main problems are measurement difficulties that are sometimes so fundamental that better analysis or consultation with experts cannot solve them. I am thinking mainly of debates over the proper discount rate for future benefits and costs; efforts to incorporate attitudes toward risk; and the vexing problems of measuring the value of human life, of aesthetic and cultural benefits, and of harm to the natural world. Disputes over these issues turn on deep philosophical questions—for example, valuing future generations versus balancing capital and labor in the production of goods and services; acknowledging the value of extra years of life versus "life" itself; taking risk preferences into account; and giving culture, ecosystems, and natural objects a place in the calculus. These issues do not have "right" answers within economics. They should not be obscured by efforts to put them under the rubric of a CBA. Politically responsible officials in the agencies and the White House should resolve them in a transparent way.

Sometimes one policy is much better than many others under a wide range of assumptions. Sensitivity tests can explore this possibility. There is no need to resolve difficult conceptual and philosophical issues if the preferred outcome does not depend on the choice of a discount rate or the value given to human life. Such tests should be a routine part of the analytic toolkit and of the options presented to the ultimate policymakers.

Second, many policies raise important issues of distributive justice, individual rights, and fairness, especially between generations. Talk of "net-benefit maximization" does not help illuminate these value choices. These issues raise measurement problems, but the difficulties with CBA run deeper. Even if everything could be measured precisely, CBA would be an inappropriate metric. Attempts to add distributive weights to CBA are fundamentally misguided. They suppose that technocrats, especially economists, can resolve distributive justice questions. The distributive consequences of policies should be part of the public debate over policies, aided by technocrats who can help to outline the distributive consequences of various policies. The main analytic problem is familiar to students of tax incidence. The nominal cost bearer may pass on some of the costs to others. Distributive impacts are often difficult to measure and trace.

This second category includes policy issues that have a large impact on society, at present and over multiple generations. Choices taken today may be irreversible or very costly to change, and they may risk large negative consequences for future generations. In these cases, the marginal, microanalytic framework characteristic of cost–benefit analysis is not appropriate even if one stays within a utilitarian framework. The problems—climate change, risks from the storage of nuclear waste, loss of biodiversity, to give a few examples—may have large pervasive impacts that stretch far into the future. Catastrophes are possible, even if not likely. These issues raise broad economic and social issues that require a different normative framework.

• • •

CASE 3: LARGE-SCALE MULTI-GENERATION PROBLEMS: IRREVERSIBILITIES AND CATASTROPHES

Welfare economists often study long-run macroeconomic policies where nothing is held constant. The normative framework has traditionally aimed to maximize the sustainable rate of economic growth, a policy position that obviously calls for the present generation to give up consumption in the interest of long-run economic growth. Others have pointed out that there is no sound philosophical reason to favor the future over the present so that the goal should be to maximize the steady-state level of per capita income over time. These models assumed an infinitely lived civilization that could save and invest at different rates over time. If we add in the possibility that the present can impose large, irreversible, and possibly catastrophic costs on the distant future, this raises the question of intergenerational obligation with particular salience.

To see the problem, consider the issue of climate change. Society will experience many of the benefits of climate change policy far in the future. Using even a low-end discount rate, say five percent, implies that a one dollar benefit obtained fifty years in the future has a present value of nine cents. At three percent, the present value is twenty-three cents and at six percent it is five cents. Suppose to keep things simple that all the benefits will accrue in year fifty and that they will be five billion dollars. At five percent, the discounted present value of these benefits is $450,000, but it could be much higher or lower depending upon the discount rate chosen. Should that choice determine the global policy on climate change?

Even those who advocate the equal worth of all generations accept a long-run positive growth rate as a fact of human history, in spite of the doubt cast on this claim as a result of climate change or other systemic risks. In other words, they assume that the market will generate a positive interest rate. That assumption produces much of the agonizing over the social rate of discount. Some claim that the lives of those in future generations should count equally to present lives and that that implies a zero discount rate for saved lives or sacrifices under some policy. With a positive rate of return on capital, however, such a philosophical commitment to equity would imply that, under a cost–benefit test, it will always be optimal to accept present risks to life that will reduce comparable future risks by a small amount.

If instead one considers the welfare of future generations, and not just the number of people alive, then one can avoid this extreme result. As Samida and Weisbach [Dexter Samida & David A Weisbach, "Paretian Intergenerational Discounting" (2007) 74 U Chicago L Rev 145] point out, treating all generations as equally worthy is not the same thing as putting aside the same amount of money in the present for all generations. The present generation must only put aside enough so that compound interest will produce an amount equal to what it has kept for itself. It is one thing to value all generations equally in the social-welfare calculation and quite another to use a discount rate of zero when evaluating the value of saved lives and morbidity. The former assumes a policy goal and asks the state to achieve it by means of choices that take account of the opportunity cost of capital to investors. The latter takes the choice of a discount rate to reflect the social values of benefits and costs occurring at different points in time. If we assume a civilization of infinite (or at least several centuries) duration, with no irreversible links between catastrophe risks and today's policies, then the interests of the future are reflected in the discount rates that exist at present. However, two problems remain: converting wellbeing to a metric that can be measured and compared and dealing with the possibility of catastrophic, irreversible downside risks.

As to the former, Louis Kaplow ["Discounting Dollars, Discounting Lives: Inter-generational Distributive Justice and Efficiency" (2007) 74 U Chicago L Rev 79] has tried to get around this problem by assuming that utility at any point in time can be converted to dollars, discounted back to the present at the opportunity cost of capital, and then compared with a similarly monetized value for present lives. That technique is consistent with the Samida and Weisbach approach, but it downplays the problem of making the required conversion. There would be no difficulty if we could assume that different generations are essentially similar on average, that we only care about the average, and that the distortions introduced to the welfare measure by using a monetary proxy are not so severe as to seriously skew the ranking of options. Further-more, there must not be important irreversibilities that threaten overall wellbeing in a way that cannot be balanced by other compensating measures. Unfortunately, even if the other assumptions hold, the issue of climate change and other large-scale risks do not satisfy the irreversibility condition. For such issues, one should not waste time worrying about problems that arise in ordinary policy analytic exercises.

If catastrophic and irreversible harms are possible, then conventional cost–benefit analysis is not an appropriate tool. If our present actions increase the chances of a global disaster, this behavior will show up in the long-run rate of interest. The rate on long-run investments ought to rise to reflect that risk so that the certainty equivalents of different investments are kept in line. The supply of funds for projects that will only pay off in the distant future ought to shrink. Those shifts might be sufficient to per-suade the government to initiate policies to limit those risks, but note that, because of the logic of discounting, very long-run harms will have little impact on current markets. The debate ought not to be framed as a debate over the discount rate. Rather, it concerns the obligations of the present towards the future. Some economic analysts have dismissed this concern with the claim that future generations will be richer than we are and so we need not worry about them, beyond the incentives for saving and investment given by market interest rates and inter-familiar affection. Today, the ground has shifted as climate change and other risks appear to threaten future generations' hold on prosperity. We can still use economics to discuss the cost-effective ways to deal with climate change, but it is not going to resolve the basic issue.

FURTHER READINGS

Cropper, ML, "Has Economic Research Answered the Needs of Environmental Policy?" (2000) 39:3 J Envtl Econ & Mgmt 328.

Daly, HE & JB Cobb Jr, *For the Common Good* (Boston: Beacon Press, 1989).

Revesz, RL & MA Livermore, *Retaking Rationality: How Cost–Benefit Analysis Can Better Protect the Environment and Our Health* (Oxford: Oxford University Press, 2008).

Sagoff, M, "Some Problems with Environmental Economics" (1988) 10 Envtl Ethics 55.

IV. THREE PILLARS OF ENVIRONMENTAL REGULATION

The section above dealt with the evaluation of economic costs and benefits in environmental decision-making. It introduced the notion that there might be different ways of regulatory intervention to assure that the costs are properly reflected in the market. Much of environ-mental legislation has historically relied on command-and-control approaches to this end (see Chapter 15). For example, once it is decided that a certain level of pollution is unacceptable to society, amounts above this level may be prohibited.

The 20th century saw the rise of incentives, and other regulatory instruments that use the market forces more generally to achieve certain results, in environmental regulation. Is the creation of a market an appropriate and socially and morally acceptable response on behalf of policy-makers and regulators? Environmentalists often disagree, suggesting that putting a price on environmental goods in a way legitimizes pollution.

Beyond command-and-control and market-based instruments, a third pillar has been added to the repertoire of contemporary policy-makers: behavioural interventions and nudges. Behavioural interventions and nudges were, of course, developed before their identification as such at the turn of the century. They were usually identified as "consumer approaches" to environmental regulation. Command-and-control interventions are interventions by the government in the production process—whether that intervention is characterized by direct command and control or by the rearrangement of property rights—that concentrate on the supply side. Consumer approaches suggest demand-side interventions—namely interventions addressing the consumer directly, for example, through the use of eco-labelling. The consumer approaches to environmental regulation were developed later in time and were systematized even more recently under the category of behavioural interventions and nudges.

While the excerpt following immediately below introduces readers to a wide array of market-based instruments, the last excerpts of this chapter discuss the transition of environmental regulation toward consumer approaches as well as their development and consolidation under the new category of nudges.

DG MCFETRIDGE, "THE ECONOMIC APPROACH TO ENVIRONMENTAL ISSUES"
in GB Doern, ed, *The Environmental Imperative: Market Approaches to the Greening of Canada* (Toronto: CD Howe Institute, 1990) 84 at 95-102

MARKETABLE PERMITS

DEFINITION

Under a marketable-permit scheme, the appropriate level of environmental quality is defined in terms of allowable emissions. Permits are allocated to firms, generally on the basis of historic emissions or output. These permits enable the owner to emit a specified amount of pollution. Permits can be traded and sometimes banked. As a result, abatement is undertaken by the firms with the lowest abatement costs. Firms with higher costs buy the permits. This system minimizes the cost of achieving the desired level of abatement, provided that the market is competitive.

EXAMPLES

Marketable Effluent Permits: ...

Emissions Trading: The EPA [US Environmental Protection Agency] allows limited trading in the right to emit carbon monoxide, sulphur dioxide, and nitrous oxides. Trading may take any of four forms: netting, offsets, bubbles and banking.

- *Netting* allows new emissions from a plant provided they are offset by emission reductions elsewhere in the same plant. This is also called "internal trading."
- *Offsets* is the practice of allowing new emissions in areas in which air-quality standards have not been met provided they are offset by greater reductions in the same plant or other plants in the same area. Offsets can thus be obtained either by "internal or external trading."

- *Bubbles* are an aggregation of all sources of a given pollutant in a particular plant. Required emissions reductions can take place where it is least costly.
- *Banking* is the process by which emissions below a required level can be "saved" and used or sold in the future.

• • •

Lead Trading: During the 1982-87 period, the United States reduced the lead content of motor gasoline. Each refinery received lead rights equal to its current production times the current lead-control standard. If the lead content of a refiner's gasoline production was below the total allowed amount, remaining lead rights could be sold or banked.

• • •

EMISSIONS CHARGES

DEFINITION

In principle, an emissions charge is levied on a per-unit-of-pollutant basis. The unit charge can vary with the nature of the pollutant and with the concentration and time period of emission. Again, in principle, the fee should be equal to the damages imposed on competing users. In other words, the fees should be equal at the margin to the decline in the value of the resource to other users.

If emissions charges are set in this fashion, several results will follow:

- the value derived from emissions must be at least as great as the sum of the costs imposed on competing users;
- emissions abatement will be introduced to the point at which the cost of abatement equals the emissions fee; and
- investments in abatement will be distributed efficiently among polluters.

EXAMPLES

Emissions or effluent charges tend to differ significantly from the ideal. They are often not related directly to emissions and, as far as can be discerned, are not based on the damages inflicted on competing users. In France, for example, effluent charges do not vary with the volume or content of effluent, although the sewage tax is volume-related and discharge permits are priced according to discharge content. In West Germany, effluent charges cover a wide range of pollutants and are related to volume and concentration.

• • •

A number of Canadian cities levy effluent charges based on BOD [biological oxygen demand], suspended solids, and grease. Some have found their system of charges to be effective and easy to administer [J Chant, DG McFetridge & D Smith, "The Economics of the Conserver Society" in W Block, ed, *Economics and the Environment: A Reconciliation* (Vancouver: Fraser Institute, 1990)]. Response elasticities of BOD and suspended solids discharge to changes in effluent fees on the order of 0.5 have also been found in Canada.

FURTHER READINGS

Ackerman, BA & RB Stewart, "Reforming Environmental Law" (1985) 37 Stan L Rev 1333.

Biggs, HM, RF Kosobud & DL Schreder, eds, *Emissions Trading: Environmental Policy's New Approach* (New York: Wiley, 2000).

Canada, Task Force on Economic Instruments and Disincentives to Sound Environmental Practices, *Economic Instruments and Disincentives to Sound Environmental Practices: Final Report of the Task Force* (Ottawa: Environment Canada, 1994).

Dales, JH, *Pollution, Property and Prices* (Toronto: University of Toronto Press, 1968).

Hahn, RW & RN Stavins, "Incentive-Based Environmental Regulation: A New Era from an Old Idea" (1991) 18 Ecology LQ 1.

Organisation for Economic Co-operation and Development, *Managing the Environment: The Role of Economic Instruments* (Paris: OECD, 1994).

Sandler, T, *Global Challenges: An Approach to Environmental, Political and Economic Problems* (Cambridge: Cambridge University Press, 1997).

Schubert R, "Purchasing Energy-Efficient Appliances—To Incentivise or to Regulate?" in K Mathis & BR Huber, eds, *Environmental Law and Economics*, Economic Analysis of Law in European Legal Scholarship, vol 4 (Berlin: Springer, 2017) 215.

Tietenberg, T, ed, *The Economics of Global Warming* (Aldershot, UK: Edward Elgar, 1997).

JP KIMMEL JR, "DISCLOSING THE ENVIRONMENTAL IMPACT OF HUMAN ACTIVITIES: HOW A FEDERAL POLLUTION CONTROL PROGRAM BASED ON INDIVIDUAL DECISION MAKING AND CONSUMER DEMAND MIGHT ACCOMPLISH THE ENVIRONMENTAL GOALS OF THE 1970S IN THE 1990S"

(1989) 138 U Pa L Rev 505 at 526, 527-29 [footnotes omitted]

Until now, most proposed economic charge approaches have sought to achieve environmental quality by targeting only the business sector of the economy. Proponents of such charge approaches assume that most externalities occur during production. The charge approach alters the cost variable of the producer's output equation in an effort to influence production decisions and create a more efficient market. The regulatory approach, while addressing economic factors, also targets only producers by implementing production constraints.

• • •

The consumer is an appropriate target of environmental enhancement legislation because consumer behavior greatly influences production decisions. Additionally, consumers themselves cause pollution while consuming and disposing of products.

Reducing the demand for highly polluting products could produce a number of environmental benefits. First, it would decrease aggregate pollutant emissions as either inefficient production decreased or more environmentally efficient methods of production, use, and disposal were adopted. The direct regulatory approach cannot achieve these results because it fails to address pollution occurring through the use and disposal of products and packages. Additionally, targeting the demand component in producer decisions removes producers from the difficult position in which they are placed by both the regulatory and charge systems. Under those systems, producers face the same consumer demands, needs, and desires regardless of the additional costs of productions that are imposed. The result is that only one component of consumer demand—price—may be affected. The other factors of demand are left weighing in favor of continued consumption of the same products, regardless of their environmental impact.

Second, making the demand for products sensitive to the pollution generated throughout the product's life cycle would provide an incentive to producers and disposal firms to satisfy that demand by developing products and disposal methods that meet consumers' overall desires. Pollutants would be reduced because of the consumer demand for more environmentally efficient products and processes.

Third, a system operating within the free market by influencing consumer demand would be more efficient because a central planning agency would no longer be making pollution control decisions based on information that is nearly impossible to gather or assimilate. Each producer and consumer would make her own decisions based on market information that would guide those decisions toward environmental goals. Moreover, this approach recognizes that some pollution is an unavoidable by-product of economic and social progress; individual economic decision making will sometimes demand that certain products be produced regardless of their environmental impact. In those situations, however, costs could be imposed on the consumer to compensate society for the use and cleanup of the environment.

Finally, developing demand-driven economic incentives to encourage compliance with environmental goals greatly reduces the difficulties of attempting to force thousands of ambivalent producers to comply with regulatory standards. If the market in which producers sell their goods and services demands that those items be pollution-lean, the need to monitor producers disappears; voluntary compliance would be more certain.

MF TEISL, B ROE & RL HICKS, "CAN ECO-LABELS TUNE A MARKET? EVIDENCE FROM DOLPHIN-SAFE LABELING"
(2002) 43:3 J Envtl Econ & Mgmt 339 at 339-40 [footnotes omitted]

The environmental characteristics of products have become increasingly important to consumers. Firms have responded by placing eco-labels on products that highlight the item's environmental attributes and by introducing new, or redesigned, "green" products. Governments and nongovernmental organizations have also responded by organizing, implementing, and verifying eco-labeling programs that cover thousands of products in more than 20 countries, while international efforts to standardize environmental labeling schemes have also emerged. From a policy perspective, one aim of eco-labels is to educate consumers about the environmental impacts of the product's manufacture, use, and disposal, thereby leading to a change in purchasing behavior and ultimately, to a reduction in negative impacts. Further, eco-labeling policies may promote environmental objectives without production site command and control methods and are seen as a way of meeting global environmental objectives while complying with international trade agreements.

In order for eco-labels to achieve policy objectives, consumers must hold preferences for certain environmental amenities and respond to the information presented on eco-labels by altering purchases toward eco-labeled goods. Their widespread use suggests that eco-labeling is perceived as an effective method of altering consumer behavior. However, few studies have attempted to identify the behavioral effectiveness of eco-labeling programs. Evaluating the policy effectiveness of eco-labeling programs requires understanding how information affects market behavior. Evaluating the economic efficiency of labeling programs requires measuring the benefits and costs of such information.

NOTE

Since the 19th century, the rational choice paradigm of human agency has led to the develop-ment of two major categories of regulatory instruments for the steering of human behaviour: command-and-control and market-based regulation. Both are founded on the paradigm of the rational individual as developed by the rational choice theory. According to rational choice theory, people respond to opportunities and incentives available to them, as well as to screens and sanctions. Screens are procedures guaranteeing that only individuals who have some specific qualities will be the beneficiaries of a system; they can be positive by favouring a specific category of people, or they can be negative by disfavouring another category. The procedures and mecha-nisms include appointment, search procedures, constraints, and desiderata on eligibility for office. Sanctions are also important for the rational design of public policies, since it is believed that rational individuals will avoid financial and other sanctions. Finally, positive and negative incen-tives, which have a financial impact, are believed to direct the conduct of individuals.

The two more traditional pillars of environmental regulation have started giving way more recently to a third pillar of environmental regulation: "environmental" or "green" nudges. Nudges, as well as other forms of behavioural regulation, have been made possible with the move from supply to demand-side/consumer-side interventions. Nudges aim to guide consumer behaviour toward more environmentally friendly choices. This breaking away from command-and-control and incentives corresponds to a shift away from rational choice models of human agency to an understanding of human action as "boundedly rational." Nudges are based on a different under-standing of the individual as well as of the drivers of behaviour. It is an understanding based on the individual as boundedly rational—namely an individual who is subject to "cognitive biases."

This continuous development of environmental regulation and policy-making does not sig-nify a radical break with the past but proceeds as an evolutionary process of adopting new instru-ments without abandoning older ones. Behavioural regulation and nudging are theoretically supported by a political philosophy of "libertarian paternalism," as developed by the Nobel laure-ate Richard Thaler and Harvard Law School professor and former US Office of Information and Regulatory Affairs administrator Cass R Sunstein, that tries to bring together libertarian and paternalistic understandings of society and the role of the government in it.

RICHARD THALER & CASS R SUNSTEIN, NUDGE: IMPROVING DECISIONS ABOUT HEALTH, WEALTH, AND HAPPINESS
(New Haven: Yale University Press, 2008) at 5-6 [endnotes omitted]

The libertarian aspect of our strategies lies in the straightforward insistence that, in general, people should be free to do what they like—and to opt out of undesirable arrangements if they want to do so. To borrow a phrase from the late Milton Fried-man, libertarian paternalists urge that people should be "free to choose." We strive to design policies that maintain or increase freedom of choice. When we use the term libertarian to modify the word paternalism, we simply mean liberty-preserving. And when we say liberty-preserving, we really mean it. Libertarian paternalists want to make it easy for people to go their own way; they do not want to burden those who want to exercise their freedom.

The paternalistic aspect lies in the claim that it is legitimate for choice architects to try to influence people's behavior in order to make their lives longer, healthier, and better. In other words, we argue for self-conscious efforts, by institutions in the private sector and also by government, to steer people's choices in directions that will improve their lives. In our understanding, a policy is "paternalistic" if it tries to influence choices in a way that will make choosers better off, as judged by them-selves. Drawing on some well-established findings in social science, we show that in many cases, individuals make pretty bad decisions—decisions they would not have made if they had paid full attention and possessed complete information, unlimited cognitive abilities, and complete self-control.

Libertarian paternalism is a relatively weak, soft, and nonintrusive type of pater-nalism because choices are not blocked, fenced off, or significantly burdened. If people want to smoke cigarettes, to eat a lot of candy, to choose an unsuitable health care plan, or to fail to save for retirement, libertarian paternalists will not force them to do otherwise—or even make things hard for them. Still, the approach we recom-mend does count as paternalistic, because private and public choice architects are not merely trying to track or to implement people's anticipated choices. Rather, they are self-consciously attempting to move people in directions that will make their lives better. They nudge.

A nudge, as we will use the term, is any aspect of the choice architecture that alters people's behavior in a predictable way without forbidding any options or significantly changing their economic incentives. To count as a mere nudge, the intervention must be easy and cheap to avoid. Nudges are not mandates. Putting the fruit at eye level counts as a nudge. Banning junk food does not.

P HACKER & G DIMITROPOULOS, "BEHAVIOURAL LAW & ECONOMICS AND SUSTAINABLE REGULATION: FROM MARKETS TO LEARNING NUDGES"

in K Mathis & BR Huber, eds, *Environmental Law and Economics*, Economic Analysis of Law in European Legal Scholarship, vol 4 (Berlin: Springer, 2017) 155 at 159-170 [footnotes omitted]

2.1 FIRST PILLAR: COMMAND-AND-CONTROL—THE EXAMPLE OF CHEMICALS REGULATION

Historically, command-and-control regulation came first and was perceived as a natural way to address environmental problems. For example, water quality legislation attempts to keep a high standard of water quality by limiting the release of pollutants into water resources. The relevant legislation may include restrictions on the changing of the physical, biological and chemical characteristics of water resources. Command-and-control regulation represents the traditional and still-prevalent way of regulating life by government, and all the more so in environmental law.

A very characteristic example in the European Union is the regulation of chemi-cals. Chemicals are regulated in the European Union by Regulation 1907/2006 on Registration, Evaluation, Authorisation and Restriction of Chemicals (REACH) that was adopted to serve various purposes, including the protection of human health, animal welfare and the environment from risks posed by chemicals. It entered into force in 2007 as one of the most important legal instruments in the history of the European Union: it represents the most complete regulation of chemicals in the world. The EU is a global leader in this field: Several other countries, including China, India, Russia, South Korea, Switzerland, and the US have either adopted similar regulatory frameworks, or have drawn inspiration from REACH.

• • •

The REACH framework represents an excellent example of command-and-control regulation in environmental law that combines more strict—e.g., authorisation and restriction—, [sic] and less strict—e.g., registration—interventions by the relevant regulatory authorities. While some authors have presented it as a means of experimental governance, this does not change the fact that it includes more traditional elements of regulation.

2.2 SECOND PILLAR: INCENTIVISING ENVIRONMENTALLY-FRIENDLY BEHAVIOUR—THE EXAMPLE OF EU EMISSIONS TRADING SCHEME

The European Union was also one of the first polities to establish a mandatory Emissions Trading Scheme (EU ETS) to combat climate change under the obligations undertaken by the EU and its Member States under the Kyoto Protocol to the United Nations Framework Convention on Climate Change (UNFCCC). The purpose of the EU ETS is to reduce industrial greenhouse gas (GHG) emissions in a cost-effective way. It is based on the idea—that is also to be found in the Kyoto Protocol—of creating a market for trading with greenhouse gas emission allowances. Introducing a market for a non-market good is the main idea of the EU ETS.

The differentiation from the first pillar of environmental regulation should be clear. In the first case, companies and citizens are obliged by legislation to behave in a particular way. In the second case, their behaviour is not directly dictated by the law, but rather is the result of decentralized coordination by market forces. It is true that the basic rules of the trading game of the GHG emissions allowances market are provided for in a command-and-control way by the EU legislator. For example, the EU legislator sets a limit—the so called "cap"—on the total amount of certain greenhouse gases that can be emitted by the factories, power plants and other installations taking part in the market. The cap is reduced over time so that total emissions also fall over time. But setting a solid legal framework is a prerequisite for every market, where for example contract and property are regulated and sanctions are put in place to guarantee the smooth functioning of the relevant market. The mandatory framework of the GHG emission allowances does not change anything about how the behaviour of the participants in the system is steered, namely by economic incentives provided to players in the market.

2.3 GREEN NUDGES: A THIRD PILLAR?

In more recent years, a further paradigm has started to appear in environmental law. Following the findings of behavioural economics and cognitive psychology, this new paradigm is based on an understanding of the individual as boundedly rational. The new regulatory approach informed by this understanding is commonly referred to as "nudging." Environmental nudges are spreading across various fields and countries. ...

The following section gives examples of green nudges and categorizes them as pollution reducing nudges, energy efficiency nudges and climate change nudges. In a second step, it explains how nudges influence human behaviour.

2.3.1 Examples of Green Nudges

Examples of green nudges can be sorted into three categories: pollution reducing nudges, energy efficiency nudges, and climate change nudges (with some overlap between the last two, see below, Sect. 2.3.1.3).

2.3.1.1 POLLUTION REDUCING NUDGES

2.3.1.1.1 *The Green Footprint*

Nudges can be used for pollution reduction, both in natural habitats and city environments. One successful example is the so-called "green footprint" that has been used in Copenhagen for litter reduction. The city of Copenhagen implemented the Green Footprint nudge in 2012 to steer people towards keeping the city cleaner by painting green footprints on the ground leading to the city's bins. This very low-cost nudge is reported to have reduced total waste in the city by 46%.

2.3.1.2 ENERGY EFFICIENCY NUDGES

Another important category of environmental nudges are energy efficiency nudges. Their aim is to induce consumers and firms to consume less energy. Three specific subcategories are surveyed here: default settings of a green energy provider, social norms to reduce energy and water consumption, and finally energy efficiency labels.

2.3.1.2.1 *Preference of the "Green" Energy Provider*

The choice of energy provider presents a puzzle to apologists of rational choice: many people state that they prefer "green," i.e., environment friendly for sustainable sources of energy. However, even in markets in which providers of such energy sources are easily available, they are not often chosen.

Daniel Pichert and Konstantinos Katsikopoulos ["Green Defaults: Information Presentation and Proenvironmental Behaviour" (2008) 28 J Envtl Psychology 63] ran a large study including two natural studies and two laboratory experiments to investigate whether default effects are responsible for this gap between stated and revealed preferences. In the natural studies, they found that when the green provider was [the] default option, it was used by the majority of people. The laboratory experiments further supported the status quo bias in the choice of the energy provider: participants exhibited significant default effects, choosing the green provider more often when it was the default option, and significant "green endowment effects" (WTA [willingness to accept] > WTP [willingness to pay] for green energy). This shows the potential of spurring sustainable energy use through adequate green defaults. This would serve a dual cause: Communities, regions or nation states could choose to adopt green defaults in order to align choice with stated preference and to simultaneously support sustainable energy production.

2.3.1.2.2 *Electricity and Water Bills—Mention of the Average Consumption of Neighbours and Use of Smiley Face*

Other experiments have used the power not of defaults but of social norms to influence behaviour in a pro-environmental away. Most prominently, such strategies are employed to reduce electricity and water consumption. Hunt Allcott ["Social Norms and Energy Conservation" (2011) 95 J Public Econ 1082] analysed a natural field experiment in which households were provided not only with information about their own but also their neighbours' electricity use (social comparison module); furthermore, the electricity provider included emoticons based on whether the household paired "great," "good" or "below average" (efficiency standing emoticons). The treatment reduced total electricity use by 2%. Allcott concluded that the social comparison module drove most of the reduction in electricity use; the efficiency

FIGURE 16.1   US EnergyGuide

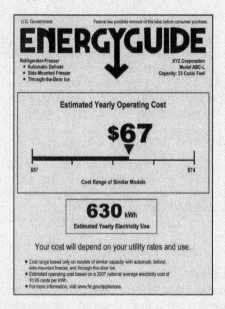

standing emoticons played a negligible role according to his regression discontinuity analysis. The greatest effect could be measured in the highest decile of pre-treatment consumption as users apparently adapted their consumption to what they perceived as a social norm: the mean electricity used in the neighbourhood. Similar results were obtained by Ian Ayres and colleagues [Ian Ayres, Sophie Raseman & Alice Shih, "Evidence from Two Large Field Experiments That Peer Comparison Feedback Can Reduce Residential Energy Usage" (2013) 29 JL Econ & Org 992] in two large-scale field experiments (N=35,000 and 40,000) using social comparison messages and efficiency standing emoticons to lower energy consumption.

Yet another similar result was reported for a natural field experiment on water use. In this setting, the social comparison treatment, combined with a prosocial message and technical advice on how to conserve water, resulted in a decrease in water consumption of 4.8%. Technical advice only (a list of tips on how to conserve water) had close to no effect at all. Again, the effect was strongest among users with high pre-treatment water consumption.

2.3.1.2.3 Energy Efficiency Labels

In recent years, over 40 countries have introduced energy efficiency labels that come in different formats and aim to steer household appliance purchase choices (e.g. of refrigerators) in energy-efficient directions. The most widely-used labels are the mandatory EnergyGuide developed by the US Federal Trade Commission (FTC) (see Fig. 1), the Energy Star, a voluntary but more selective program run by the US Environmental Protection Agency (EPA) (see Fig. 2), and the Energy Efficiency Grade which is mandatory in the European Union (see Fig. 3) and used similarly in parts of Asia (e.g. China, Russia) and South America. In fact, energy efficiency labelling was introduced in the EU by Directive 92/75/EEC as early as 1992; an amended directive in 2010 introduced further high-quality energy efficiency grades (A+, A++, A+++), adapting the scale to more energy-efficient appliances.

FIGURE 16.2 US Energy Star

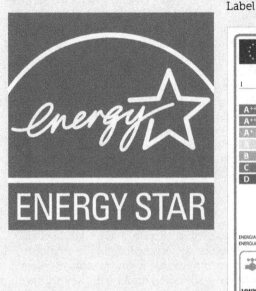

FIGURE 16.3 EU Energy Efficiency Label

A large-scale laboratory experiment by Newell and Siikamäki [Richard G Newell & Juha Siikamäki, "Nudging Energy Efficiency Behavior: The Role of Information Labels" (2014) 1:4 JAERE 555] tested the effectiveness of these labels and several variations in guiding household decisions. The key result was that all three labels (EnergyGuide, Energy Star and Energy Efficiency Grade) are generally effective. An enhanced version of the EU efficiency grade proved to be the most effective of all three individual labels, nearly doubling the probability of a household choosing an energy efficient appliance that is more expensive up front but reduces operating costs by 10%. The greatest driver of energy efficient choice in the experiment was the provision of information on the economic value of saving energy. In another online randomized experiment, Davis and Metcalfe [sic] [Lucas W Davis & Gilbert E Metcalf, "Does Better Information Lead to Better Choices? Evidence from Energy-Efficiency Labels" (2014) National Bureau of Economic Research Working Paper No 20720, online: *The National Bureau of Economic Research* <https://www.nber.org/papers/w20720>] found that providing state specific information (e.g. about energy prices and expected energy consumption which vary from region to region) can have an even greater effect on energy efficiency, with consumers in high-use and high-price states willing to invest more in energy efficiency than their counterparts in low-use or low-price states. Furthermore, some experiments attest to the necessity of providing disclosure of lifetime energy costs instead of annual information.

However, many of the studies mentioned were undertaken in laboratory environments. These results should be tested with field experiments to generate more valid results, particularly in view of the possibility of rational inattention with respect to energy efficiency in the real world. In fact, in a field experiment in Norway, the amended Energy Efficiency Grade (coupled with estimated annual total operational costs, as in the Newell and Siikamäki study) was deployed in a number of stores.

However, significant effects could only be achieved for an energy-intensive appliance (tumble dryers, not for refrigerators), and only when the label was matched with specifically instructed sales personnel who were trained to highlight the importance of energy efficiency in individual sales conversations. A similar result was reported in a UK field experiment in which enhanced energy labels were effective (without trained sales personnel) for washer dryers, but not for tumble dryers or for washing machines; again, buyers were only reactive to the label for the most energy-intensive appliance. Finally, and perhaps most interestingly, Schubert and Stadelmann [Renate Schubert & Marcel Stadelmann, "Energy-Using Durables—Why Consumers Refrain from Economically Optimal Choices" (2015) 3 Frontiers in Energy Research 1] in a field experiment found a "volume effect" of energy labels, which induced consumers to buy more energy-efficient, but also larger appliances, resulting in greater net energy consumption than if people had chosen a smaller, less efficient appliance.

• • •

2.3.1.3 CLIMATE CHANGE NUDGES

A final category of green nudges sets out to combat climate change. While energy consumption reduction also contributes indirectly to slowing climate change (by reducing fossil energy resources use), interventions that we term "climate change nudges" directly tackle the problem of global warming by limiting the key drivers of global warming, namely atmospheric greenhouse gas emissions. A particularly noteworthy candidate for the combat against climate change is the shift toward more fuel-efficient vehicles, an area where there is currently much room for regulatory improvement: the fossil fuel dependence of global transport in general and cars in particular makes vehicle emissions a crucial contributor to global warming.

2.3.1.3.1 Fuel Economy Label

Many countries around the globe have now introduced initiatives to convey information about the fuel efficiency of cars to retail clients and firms via fuel economy labels. In this domain, there is a preference-action gap similar to the one mentioned with respect to green energy providers: while many car owners acknowledge that car pollution is a main driver of the greenhouse effect, and state that they intend to buy an electric or hybrid car (33% in a recent survey), the use of hybrid or electric cars in Europe (according to the same survey) is stuck at 1.9% of total cars used. This is all the more surprising since the purchase of fuel-efficient cars could save drivers substantial amounts of money. Often referred to as the energy-efficiency gap, i.e., the difference between actual and optimal energy use, the US government has named this the "energy paradox" and claimed: "the problem is that consumers appear not to purchase products that are in their economic self-interest." The US government suspects that myopia, loss aversion, and lack of salience of the benign monetary effects of fuel efficiency may explain the unwillingness to invest in products like cars that are more expensive up front but cheaper over their lifetime; a recent study by Renate Schubert and Marcel Stadelmann [cited earlier] points in the same direction.

• • •

2.3.2 The Effect of Green Nudging

As has been described above, green or environmental nudging affects human behaviour in different ways than either command-and-control or market-based interventions. The distinguishing characteristic and effectiveness of nudges lies in the fact that they intervene in market transactions (or non-market decisions) with environmental implications at the very moment the relevant actors decide. Therefore, they are often vastly more effective—both in absolute terms and relative to their costs—than more traditional forms of regulation. For example, reductions in electricity use and water supply generated by messages incorporating social norms are equivalent to the price effect of a rise in electricity or water prices by approximately 11 to 20% (electricity) or 12 to 15% (water). While such extreme economic incentives often cannot be provided in the marketplace, green nudges are generally relatively cheap to generate and easy to administer.

Green nudges use three main instruments to achieve the desired result: salience, default rules, and social norms. All three instruments are very different from the incentives, screens and sanctions used by a rational choice approach to regulation because they are based on a different understanding of the individual. According to this understanding, individuals are "boundedly rational," they have "bounded willpower," and are "boundedly self-interested." Bounded rationality means that individuals make mistakes in judgment and perception because information cannot be processed rationally. This can be seen in the case of the use of salience. The driving force of human behaviour for example in the case of Copenhagen's green footprints is salience. The citizen throwing the garbage into the trash bin does not decide to act this way based on a cost–benefit analysis, but rather is prompted to act by the footprint on the street. The hassle factor of her action (cognitive costs) is diminished rather than financial costs increased. A similar force also lies behind labels, including energy efficiency labels and the fuel economy label.

Bounded willpower means that individuals are subject to weaknesses of will. For example, they decide to consume food they know is bad for their health and even when they had planned to go on a diet. The regulator can take advantage of bounded willpower in order to nudge in the direction that most people would have wanted to behave, reinforcing second order rather than first-order preferences. This can be done with the use of defaults, for example by giving preference to the green energy provider over the grey one.

Finally, people are boundedly self-interested, which means that they sometimes act through motives beyond self-interest, like fairness. This can be shown in the case of the use of social norms by the regulator. Mentioning the average consumption of neighbours and the use of a smiley face in electricity bills can have a significant impact on individual behaviour in reducing electricity consumption towards the average. Furthermore, peer comparison reminders have been shown to encourage towel reuse in hotels. These studies add to a growing literature about the effectiveness of social norms in shaping behaviour.

NOTES AND QUESTIONS

Any additional policy instrument in the regulatory toolbox of the government leading to the further protection of the environment should be received positively. One may suggest though that green nudges and other behavioural interventions are not sufficient to address the problems of contemporary rapid environmental degradation. Additionally, the behavioural approach does not challenge the foundations of the rational choice paradigm; rather, it seeks ways to improve it.

1. Is the concept of bounded rationality sufficient to address contemporary environmental concerns?

2. Can the social sciences present environmental policy-makers with a more radical understanding of the individual and society that would potentially place them in a better position to address environmental problems in the Anthropocene?

3. Is the dominance of one (or more) discipline for environmental policy-making acceptable? Or should policy-makers be informed—and create organizations that are in the position to be informed—by all social sciences?

FURTHER READINGS

Akerlof, K & C Kennedy, *Nudging Toward a Healthy Natural Environment: How Behavioral Change Research Can Inform Conservation* (Fairfax, Va: George Mason University, 2013), online: *Issuelab* <http://www.issuelab.org/resource/nudging_toward_a_healthy_natural_environment_how_behavioral_change_research_can_inform_conservation>.

Goldstein, NJ, RB Cialdini & V Griskevicius, "A Room with a Viewpoint: Using Social Norms to Motivate Environmental Conservation in Hotels" (2008) 35 J Consumer Research 472.

Künzler, A & D Kysar, "Environmental Law" in Eyal Zamir & Doron Teichman, eds, *The Oxford Handbook of Behavioral Economics and the Law* (Oxford: Oxford University Press, 2014) 748.

Pichert, D & KV Katsikopoulos, "Green Defaults: Information Presentation and Proenvironmental Behaviour" (2008) 28 J Envtl Psychology 63.

Simon, HA, "A Behavioral Model of Rational Choice" (1955) 69 QJ Econ 99.

Stavins, R & B Whitehead, "Market-Based Environmental Policies" in MR Chertow & DC Esty, eds, *Thinking Ecologically: The Next Generation of Environmental Policy* (New Haven: Yale University Press, 1997) 105.

Sunstein, CR & LA Reisch, "Automatically Green: Behavioral Economics and Environmental Protection" (2014) 38 Harv Envtl L Rev 127.

Sunstein, CR & LA Reisch, "Green by Default" (2013) 66 Kyklos 398.

Thaler, R, "Doing Economics Without Homo Economicus" in SG Medema & WJ Samuels, eds, *Foundations of Research in Economics: How Do Economists Do Economics?* (Cheltenham, UK: Edward Elgar, 1996) 227.

CHAPTER SEVENTEEN

IMPACT ASSESSMENT*

Martin Z Olszynski

---

*   I acknowledge the previous contributions of Paul Emond (first edition), Rod Northey (second edition), and William A Tilleman (first, second, and third editions). I am grateful also to David V Wright for comments and suggestions on an earlier version of this chapter.

Human welfare itself depends on the health of ecosystems—for the very good reason that our bodies, like our industries, are maintained by constantly taking in and digesting parts of the external world. When the quality of the environment deteriorates, so do we, along with our economies. This simple linkage has often been overlooked, but now its truth is coming home.

> Environment Canada, *The State of Canada's Environment* (Ottawa: Minister of Supply and Services Canada, 1991) at p 1-3.

While more food, energy and materials than ever before are now being supplied to people in most places, this is increasingly at the expense of nature's ability to provide such contributions in the future, and frequently undermines nature's many other contributions, which range from water quality regulation to sense of place. ... Biodiversity—the diversity within species, between species and of ecosystems—is declining faster than at any time in human history.

> Intergovernmental Science–Policy Platform on Biodiversity and Ecosystem Services, "Summary for Policymakers of the Global Assessment Report on Biodiversity and Ecosystem Services of the Intergovernmental Science–Policy Platform on Biodiversity and Ecosystem Services," addendum to *Report of the Plenary of the Intergovernmental Science–Policy Platform on Biodiversity and Ecosystem Services on the Work of Its Seventh Session*, ISPPBES, 7th Sess, UN Doc IPBES/7/10/Add.1 (2019) at 3.

I. INTRODUCTION

Almost three decades separate the two passages excerpted above (the first of which was used to introduce this chapter in previous editions of this book). In that same period, Canada has seen four different environmental assessment regimes at the federal level, the most recent one having just been brought into force on August 28, 2019, when Bill C-69, *An Act to enact the Impact Assessment Act and the Canadian Energy Regulator Act, to amend the Navigation Protection Act and to make consequential amendments to other Acts*, 1st Sess, 42nd Parl, 2018 (assented to 21 June 2019) SC 2019, c 28, was proclaimed.

These facts, as well as others considered throughout this chapter, suggest that all is not well in Canadian environmental assessment law and policy. Conventionally regarded as an integral tool in the global push toward "sustainable development," that is, "development that meets the needs of the present without compromising the ability of future generations to meet their own needs" (World Commission on Environment and Development, *Our Common Future* (Oxford: Oxford University Press, 1987) at 43), many observers suggest that as currently practised in Canada, environmental assessment has resulted in mostly incremental improvements in environmental and natural resources decision-making:

Canada's first generation environmental assessment regimes have made important contributions. They have won greater attention to environmental considerations. They have opened
some significant decision making to public scrutiny. In their brightest moments, they have
been instrumental in forcing re-examination of prevailing priorities and practices. But environmental assessment laws and practices in Canada have not achieved the initially desired transformation in proponent and associated decision-maker culture to integrate habitual attention
to environmental concerns. And they have not yet moved effectively to take on new understandings and imperatives—especially growing recognition of complex interactions in socio-
ecological systems and increasingly pressing needs to ensure progress towards sustainability.

(Robert B Gibson, Meinhard Doelle & A John Sinclair, "Fulfilling the Promise: Basic Components of Next Generation Environmental Assessment" (2016) 29 J Envtl L & Prac 257 at 258.)

Although a definitive explanation for these shortcomings is beyond the scope of this chapter, several features of most modern environmental assessment regimes undoubtedly play
some role. These include the procedural focus of environmental assessment laws, their primary
preoccupation with significant impacts, and their project-by-project approach. Before these
are considered, however, it is useful to first set out the approach and contents of this chapter.

Like previous editions of this book, this chapter focuses on *federal* environmental assessment law and policy; although reference is made to various provincial regimes throughout,
these are not discussed in any detail. Not only does each province have a distinct regime (see
Table 17.1), but some provinces also have more than one regime, varying according to territories and sectors.

TABLE 17.1   Provincial and Territorial Environmental Assessment Regimes

British Columbia	*Environmental Assessment Act*, SBC 2018, c 51
Alberta	*Environmental Protection and Enhancement Act*, RSA 2000, c E-12
Saskatchewan	*The Environmental Assessment Act*, SS 1979-80, c E-10.1
Manitoba	*The Environment Act*, CCSM c E125
Ontario	*Environmental Assessment Act*, RSO 1990, c E.18
Quebec	*Environment Quality Act*, CQLR c Q-2
Nova Scotia	*Environment Act*, SNS 1994-95, c 1
New Brunswick	*Clean Environment Act*, RSNB 1973, c C-6
Prince Edward Island	*Environmental Protection Act*, RSPEI 1988, c E-9
Newfoundland and Labrador	*Environmental Protection Act*, SNL 2002, c E-14.2
Yukon	*Yukon Environmental and Socio-economic Assessment Act*, SC 2003, c 7
Northwest Territories	*Mackenzie Valley Resource Management Act*, SC 1998, c 25
Nunavut	*Nunavut Planning and Project Assessment Act*, SC 2013, c 14, s 2

Following this introduction, Section II of the chapter sets out a brief overview of Canada's previous environmental assessment regimes. The objective is to convey their main features, strengths, weaknesses, and the underlying policy debates that have driven reforms over the past three decades. To a large extent, these debates have been enmeshed in broader debates regarding the nature of Canadian federalism (that is, the balance of power between the federal and provincial governments) and the merits—or not—of (de)regulation. Section III focuses on the main provisions and mechanics of the two most recent regimes, the recently repealed *Canadian Environmental Assessment Act, 2012*, SC 2012, c 19, s 52 [CEAA 2012] and the most recently proclaimed *Impact Assessment Act*, SC 2019, c 28, s 1 [IAA]. Because these regimes are structured nearly identically, and because CEAA 2012 will continue to apply to projects currently being assessed under that Act (including any future litigation with respect to those projects), this section includes a discussion of both regimes, highlighting the key differences in particular. Section IV considers the primary legal issues that arise in the environmental assessment context, especially the relevant constitutional law, administrative law, and Aboriginal rights issues.

A. ENVIRONMENTAL ASSESSMENT AS (MERE) DECISION-MAKING PROCESS

As defined by the International Association for Impact Assessment (IAIA) on its homepage at <www.iaia.org>, environmental or impact assessment is simply "the *process of identifying* the future consequences of a current or proposed action" (emphasis added). The emphasis on process and identification is key because most environmental assessment laws, including all of Canada's impact assessment laws (past and present), do not impose any limits or constraints on the kinds of actions or projects that governments may approve. Some limits may be found in related legislation (for example, effluent limits under the *Metal and Diamond Mining Effluent Regulations*, SOR/2002-222, pursuant to the federal *Fisheries Act*, RSC 1985, c F-14), and these inform the assessment process, but environmental assessment laws do not contain any such requirements in and of themselves. Rather, and as is the case with the world's first modern environmental assessment law, the United States' *National Environmental Policy Act*, 42 USC §§ 4321 et seq [NEPA], the primary objective has been "to force agencies to *consider* the environmental effects of their actions and to provide a means to *involve and inform the public* in federal agency decision-making" (emphasis added) (Courtney A Schultz, "History of the Cumulative Effects Analysis Requirement Under NEPA and Its Interpretation in US Forest Service Case Law" (2012) 27 J Envtl L & Litig 125 at 126). As the Supreme Court of the United States put it in *Robertson v Methow Valley Citizens Council*, 490 US 332 (1989), "NEPA merely prohibits uninformed—rather than unwise—agency action" (at 351).

This perspective is reflected in the landmark decision of the Supreme Court of Canada in *Friends of the Oldman River Society v Canada (Minister of Transport)*, [1992] 1 SCR 3, 1992 CanLII 110, 132 NR 321 [*Friends of the Oldman River Society* cited to SCR], which involved Canada's first formal environmental assessment regime, the *Environmental Assessment and Review Process Guidelines Order*, SOR/84-467 [EARPGO], passed under the authority of the *Department of the Environment Act*, RSC 1985, c E-10. The Supreme Court (at 71) described environmental assessment as follows:

> Environmental impact assessment is, in its simplest form, a planning tool that is now generally regarded as an integral component of sound decision-making. ... As a planning tool it has both an information-gathering and a decision-making component which provide the decision maker with an objective basis for granting or denying approval for a proposed development ... . *In short, environmental impact assessment is simply descriptive of a process of decision making* [sic]. [Emphasis added.]

The critical assumption underlying such regimes is that identifying potential environmental (and other) impacts in a transparent and rigorous manner should lead to decision-making that better accounts for those impacts, because decision-makers (which in the Canadian context generally means the minister of the environment or entire Cabinet) can be held politically accountable for their decisions (for example, through letter-writing campaigns, editorials, and social media, as well as at the ballot box). As noted by American law professor Bradley Karkkainen, NEPA's "logic and legislative history ... suggest that [its] authors expected the resulting public scrutiny to act as an independent constraint on agency discretion ... that public disclosure would lead to political accountability that would compel agency managers to curb their most environmentally destructive practices" ("Toward a Smarter NEPA: Monitoring and Managing Government's Environmental Performance" (2002) 102:4 Colum L Rev 903 at 912).

The same assumption is reflected in the *Hansard* related to Canada's first *legislated* environmental assessment regime, the *Canadian Environmental Assessment Act*, SC 1992, c 37 [CEAA]. As further set out in Section II of this chapter, the basic test under that regime was to determine whether a project was or was not likely to result in "significant adverse environmental effects." If not, or if such effects were deemed by Cabinet to be "justified in the circumstances" (which was widely—and, as it turns out, accurately—regarded as a loophole by opposition members of Parliament at the time), then the relevant federal department(s) could issue the permit or provide the funding that triggered that Act's application in the first place. Shortly before CEAA's passage, Parliament debated an opposition amendment that would have restricted the availability of the "justified in the circumstances" provision to projects that contributed "to the goal of achieving sustainable development" (*House of Commons Debates*, 34-3, vol 7 (16 March 1992) at 8291 [Chas L Caccia]). While acknowledging that promoting sustainable development was one of several enumerated purposes of CEAA, the then parliamentary secretary to the minister of the environment expressed concern that such an explicit limitation (essentially a substantive limit) would give the courts too much of a role in project approval (for example, deciding whether a project met this requirement in litigation challenging such determinations). The unconstrained version that ultimately prevailed reflected the government's policy "that politicians, elected representatives, are in the best position to accept this responsibility today" (*House of Commons Debates*, 34-3, vol 7 (16 March 1992) at 8302 [Lee Clark]). The essence of this policy was subsequently captured by the Federal Court in *Greenpeace Canada v Canada (Attorney General)*, 2014 FC 463 at para 237: "In short, Parliament has designed a decision-making process under the CEAA that is, when it functions properly, both evidence-based and democratically accountable."

The fundamental question facing environmental law practitioners, scholars, and students in the 21st century is whether this mechanism of political accountability is suited to the challenge of sustainability and, if not, how it might be supplemented or even replaced. When considering this question, it is useful to recall that the practice of environmental assessment came to prominence in the 1970s—an era of heightened environmental awareness and concern. While such concerns are still prevalent today, especially with respect to anthropogenic climate change, they generally have to compete with other pressing societal concerns, including equality, national security, and economic growth and disparity. The advent of the Internet has also resulted in a surge of publicly available information, including that with respect to environmental assessments (all current federal environmental assessments, along with some of their supporting documents, can be accessed online through the recently renamed Canadian Impact Assessment Registry [CIA Registry]: <iaac-aeic.gc.ca/050/evaluations/050?culture=en-CA>). And while this increased access to information enables broader and more informed public debate, the amount of potentially relevant information can also be overwhelming. Either or both of these considerations may explain why the number of projects deemed likely to result in "significant adverse environmental effects" (SAEE) has actually *increased* in recent years (see Figure 17.1, below[†]), the vast majority of them being deemed "justified in the circumstances"

---

† I am grateful to Christopher Philip, UCalgary Law JD 2017, for permission to use this graph.

(see Marla Orenstein, "What Now? The Fate of Projects: A Review of Outcomes from the Federal
EA Approvals Process," Canada West Foundation Policy Brief (7 November 2018), online: *Canada West Foundation* <https://cwf.ca/research/publications/what-now-the-fate-of-projects-a
-review-of-outcomes-from-the-federal-ea-approvals-process>).

FIGURE 17.1   CEAA Assessments Concluding Significant Adverse Environmental
Effects Likely (1993-2016)

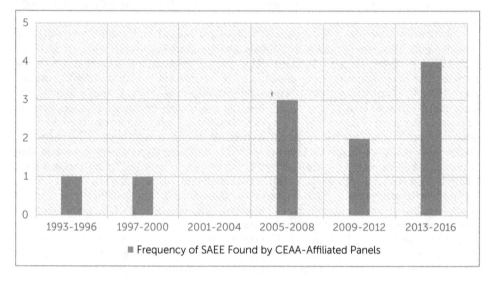

■ Frequency of SAEE Found by CEAA-Affiliated Panels

QUESTIONS

1. Is it reasonable, in your opinion, to expect political accountability to drive more environmentally sound decision-making? What other factors and considerations do politicians take
into account when making decisions about resource projects? Consider this passage from
Labrador Inuit Association v Newfoundland (Minister of Environment and Labour), 1997 Can-
LII 14612 at para 11, 155 Nfld & PEIR 93 (NLSC (AD)):

> Both the Parliament of Canada and the Newfoundland Legislature have enacted environ-
> mental assessment legislation ... . The regimes created by these statutes represent a public
> attempt to develop an appropriate response that takes account of the forces which threaten
> the existence of the environment. ... Environmental laws must be construed against their
> commitment to future generations and against a recognition that, in addressing environ-
> mental issues, we often have imperfect knowledge as to the potential impact of activities
> on the environment. *One must also be alert to the fact that governments themselves, even
> strongly pro-environment ones, are subject to many countervailing social and economic
> forces*, sometimes legitimate and sometimes not. Their agendas are often influenced by non-
> environmental considerations. [Emphasis added.]

2. Does the potential for political accountability to drive better environmental decision-
making vary depending on the type of project being assessed? Consider that there are currently over 100 projects listed in the CIA Registry; how many have you heard of? Consider also
the controversy surrounding interprovincial pipelines in Canada (for example, the since abandoned Northern Gateway pipeline project and the recently approved Trans Mountain pipeline
expansion project). Why might this be the case?

3. Notwithstanding some important improvements (further discussed in Section III of this chapter), the IAA retains the basic "assessment-as-decision-making-process" paradigm: the final determination made by the relevant minister or Cabinet will be whether a project is "in the public interest." What legal, scientific, and policy conditions appear necessary to you in order for political accountability to play its intended role in such a scheme?

4. If political accountability is not up to the task, what are some potential alternatives? Could independent and specialized tribunals, instead of a minister or Cabinet, be given broad authority to make final decisions on major projects? Why or why not?

B. AVOIDING SIGNIFICANT IMPACTS, ONE PROJECT AT A TIME

Two additional and interrelated features have invariably diminished the effectiveness of environmental assessment as a tool for achieving sustainable development. The first is the tendency to focus on *significant* adverse environmental effects to the neglect of lesser but not insignificant effects. The second is the persistence of a *project-by-project* approach without sufficient regard for the cumulative effect of multiple projects and activities on a given landscape or ecosystem.

With respect to significant adverse effects and seeking first and foremost to merely avoid these as the primary objective, Robert Gibson correctly observes that such schemes "move us further away from sustainability, though usually only in small steps" ("Favouring the Higher Test: Contribution to Sustainability as the Central Criterion for Reviews and Decisions Under the Canadian Environmental Assessment Act" (2000) 10:1 J Envtl L & Prac 39 at 43). This is because such regimes presume that projects without significant adverse environmental effects are consistent with sustainable development, when in fact these are nevertheless likely to result in dozens of adverse effects ranging from minor to moderate (setting aside the ambiguity in such qualifiers for the time being).

Furthermore, while individually such projects may not result in readily demonstrable environmental harm, when combined with other projects and activities on the landscape, they can lead to the so-called "death by a thousand cuts," or what ecologist William E Odum describes as the "tyranny of small decisions" ("Environmental Degradation and the Tyranny of Small Decisions" (1982) 32:9 BioScience 728). With respect to the eutrophication (i.e., oxygen depletion) of lakes, for example, Odum has noted (at 728) that

> [f]ew cases ... are the result of intentional and rational choice. Instead, lakes gradually become more and more eutrophic through the cumulative effects of small decisions: the addition of increasing numbers of domestic sewage and industrial outfalls along with increasing run-off from more and more housing developments, highways, and agricultural fields.

Although some of the projects and activities referred to in Odum's example would have been caught by the original Act (CEAA), most of them would not trigger the recently repealed CEAA 2012 or the new IAA. And while cumulative effects analysis has long been a standard feature of project-based impact assessment, it has also long been recognized that its implementation in this context has generally yielded unsatisfactory results (see Peter N Duinker & LA Greig, "The Impotence of Cumulative Effects Assessment in Canada: Ailments and Ideas for Redeployment" (2006) 37:2 Envtl Mgmt 153). Rather, most observers support a move toward higher-order decision-making, including regional assessments and land use planning, to effectively manage cumulative effects (see The Expert Panel on the State of Knowledge and Practice of Integrated Approaches to Natural Resource Management in Canada, *Greater than the Sum of Its Parts: Toward Integrated Natural Resource Management in Canada* (Ottawa: Council of Canadian Academies, 2019), online (pdf): *Council of Canadian Academies* <https://cca-reports.ca/wp-content/uploads/2019/04/Report-Greater-than-the-sum-of-its-parts-toward-integrated-natural-resource-management-in-Canada.pdf>). The province of Alberta is the most recent Canadian jurisdiction to move in this direction, with the passage of the *Alberta Land Stewardship Act*, SA 2009, c A-26.8 and the establishment of seven planning regions, although this regime has been plagued with delays and incomplete implementation (for example, only two regional plans have been completed, and even those are missing some critical elements). In the meantime, the limited data that exists (The Expert Panel on the State of Knowledge and Practice, above, at 15) suggests that the cumulative pace and scale of human activity in Canada is significant and ill-suited to project-by-project approaches (see Figure 17.2).

FIGURE 17.2   Relative Densities (Low to High) of Human Access in Canada

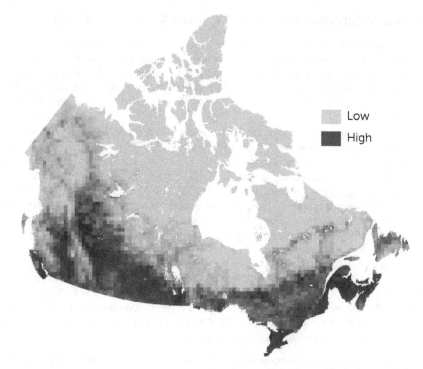

Low
High

Data Source: Global Forest Watch Canada, 2014

Map Source: Expert Panel, *Greater Than the Sum of Its Parts*, Figure 2.1 at 16.

As further discussed in Section III.B.3, compared to CEAA 2012, the IAA does contain more detailed provisions with respect to regional assessments, but whether such assessments will actually be carried out remains at the discretion of the minister.

QUESTIONS

1. The CEAA 2012 regime was significantly narrower than the original CEAA regime; roughly 3,000 assessments (98 percent of the total) were terminated when the former regime came into force, and approximately 70 major projects have been assessed in any given year (see Figure 17.3 for total projects undergoing federal assessment in Canada in 2019). Bearing in mind what is known about cumulative effects, what are some of the reasons that the federal government may have chosen to move in this direction?

2. Although improved in several important ways, the IAA maintains CEAA 2012's major project focus. Compare Figures 17.2 (above) and 17.3 (below). What are the implications of such a narrowly focused regime for Canada's environment and its management?

FIGURE 17.3   Federal Assessments in Progress (July 2019)

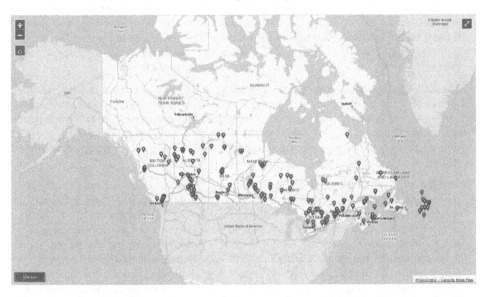

Reproduced with the permission of the Impact Assessment Agency of Canada. Please note there is a potential variation in projects from day to day. The locations are approximate, and some projects have more than one marker. Note that since the IAA came into force in August 2019, the Canadian Environmental Assessment Registry has been renamed the Canadian Impact Assessment Registry, and the relevant web page has moved to <https://iaac-aeic.gc.ca/050/evaluations/exploration?active=true&showMap=true&selection[document_type]=project>.

II. A BRIEF HISTORY OF CANADIAN IMPACT ASSESSMENT LAW

In Canada, the starting point for federal environmental assessment was a 1972 task force report. Soon thereafter, the government initiated the environmental assessment and review process (EARP) through Cabinet policy. To implement the EARP, the government established the Federal Environmental Assessment Review Office (FEARO) in April 1974 (now the Impact Assessment Agency of Canada). EARP's focus was the public review of significant projects, programs, and activities.

A. ENVIRONMENTAL ASSESSMENT AND REVIEW PROCESS GUIDELINES ORDER (EARPGO) (1984-1995)

Following internal and external review of the EARP, the government promulgated the EARPGO. At the time, the EARPGO was conceived of as simply a planning tool for government actions and not a legally binding directive. However, in 1989, and to the surprise of many (including the federal minister of the environment), the Federal Court of Appeal affirmed a lower court decision that the EARPGO was legally binding: *Canadian Wildlife Federation Inc v Canada (Minister of the Environment)*, [1989] 3 FC 309, 1989 CanLII 7273 (TD), aff'd 1989 CanLII 7280, 99 NR 72 (FCA).

In *Friends of the Oldman River Society*, the Supreme Court (at 17-18) described the EARPGO scheme as follows:

> In general terms, these guidelines require all federal departments and agencies that have a decision-making authority for any proposal, i.e., any initiative, undertaking or activity that

may have an environmental effect on an area of federal responsibility, to initially screen such proposal to determine whether it may give rise to any potentially adverse environmental effects. If a proposal could have a significant adverse effect on the environment, provision is made for public review by an environmental assessment panel whose members must be unbiased, free of political influence and possessed of special knowledge and experience relevant to the technical, environmental and social effects of the proposal.

The EARPGO was actually quite similar to both the CEAA 2012 and IAA regimes; all three could be described as "major project" regimes. However, whereas the latter are both triggered on the basis of a relatively clear project list contained within a regulation, in *Friends of the Oldman River Society*, the EARPGO was interpreted by the Supreme Court (at 47) as applying only to those projects with respect to which a federal department or agency had what it described as an "affirmative regulatory duty":

> That is not to say that the [EARPGO] is engaged every time a project may have an environmental effect on an area of federal jurisdiction. There must first be a "proposal" which requires an "initiative, undertaking or activity for which the Government of Canada has a *decision making responsibility*." (Emphasis added.) In my view the proper construction to be placed on the term "responsibility" is that the federal government, having entered the field in a subject matter assigned to it under s. 91 of the *Constitution Act, 1867* [(UK), 30 & 31 Vict, c 3], must have an affirmative regulatory duty pursuant to an Act of Parliament which relates to the proposed initiative, undertaking or activity. It cannot have been intended that the [EARPGO] would be invoked every time there is some potential environmental effect on a matter of federal jurisdiction. Therefore, "responsibility" within the definition of "proposal" should not be read as connoting matters falling generally within federal jurisdiction. Rather, it is meant to signify a legal duty or obligation. Once such duty exists, it is a matter of identifying the "initiating department" assigned responsibility for its performance, for it then becomes the decision-making authority for the proposal and thus responsible for initiating the process under the [EARPGO].

Applying this test, the Supreme Court in *Friends of the Oldman River Society* held that the federal minister of transport was obligated to comply with the EARPGO on the basis of her regulatory responsibility with respect to interferences with navigation under s 5 of the *Navigable Waters Protection Act*, RSC 1985, c N-22 [NWPA] (as it then was) but that the minister of fisheries and oceans, who was requested to issue a s 35(2) *Fisheries Act* authorization for impacts to fish habitat caused by the Oldman River dam, was not. This latter power was described (at 49) as "*ad hoc*." That being said, the Supreme Court (at 72-73) held that once the EARPGO was triggered, the "initiating department" had an obligation to consider all impacts on areas of federal jurisdiction:

> I should make it clear, however, that the scope of assessment is not confined to the particular head of power under which the Government of Canada has a decision-making responsibility within the meaning of the term "proposal." Such a responsibility, as I stated earlier, is a necessary condition to engage the process, but once the initiating department has thus been given authority to embark on an assessment, that review must consider the environmental effect on all areas of federal jurisdiction. There is no constitutional obstacle preventing Parliament from enacting legislation under several heads of power at the same time ... Here, the Minister of Transport, in his capacity of decision maker under the *Navigable Waters Protection Act*, is directed to consider the environmental impact of the dam on such areas of federal responsibility as navigable waters, fisheries, Indians and Indian lands, to name those most obviously relevant in the circumstances here.

As it turned out, the "affirmative regulatory duty" concept proved notoriously difficult to apply. Subsequent jurisprudence has confirmed that the "affirmative regulatory duty" concept applied only to the EARPGO and did not establish any kind of constitutional limit on the triggering of federal environmental assessment (see *Moses c Canada (Procureur général)*, 2008 QCCA 741 at paras 93-115, aff'd *Quebec (Attorney General) v Moses*, 2010 SCC 17).

QUESTIONS

Using previous versions of the legislation (for example, on CanLII), compare the 1992 versions of s 5 of the NWPA and s 35 of the *Fisheries Act*. Can you spot the "affirmative regulatory duty"? Now read the relevant passages of the *Friends of the Oldman River Society* decision. Do you agree with La Forest J that these regimes are fundamentally different in kind? What might have motivated him to read such a duty into the EARPGO regime?

B. CANADIAN ENVIRONMENTAL ASSESSMENT ACT (CEAA) (1995-2012)

An initial draft of CEAA was released in 1990 and, much like the legislative process involving Bill C-69 (see Section III of the chapter), involved both House and Senate Committee hearings that resulted in many modifications to the draft bill. It was given royal assent in June 1992, the same year as the United Nation's Earth Summit and Canada's signing of the United Nations' landmark *Rio Declaration on Environment and Development*, UNGA, UN Doc No A/CONF.151/26/ Rev.1 (Vol 1), annex I (1992), but the then–Progressive Conservative government of Prime Minister Brian Mulroney postponed its proclamation (that is, coming into force). Following the election of a Liberal government in 1994, CEAA was proclaimed on January 19, 1995. At that time, four regulations required to implement CEAA were also promulgated: the *Inclusion List Regulations*, SOR/94-637; the *Law List Regulations*, SOR/94-636; the *Exclusion List Regulations*, SOR/94-639; and the *Comprehensive Study List Regulations*, SOR/94-638. Their role is further discussed in the following section, most of which is adapted from Martin Z Olszynski & Marie-Ann Bowden, "Old Puzzle, New Pieces: Red Chris and Vanadium and the Future of Federal Environmental Assessment" (2011) 89 Can Bar Rev 445.

1. Triggering an Assessment

In contrast to the EARPGO, CEAA was intended to provide certainty in the triggering process. Pursuant to s 5 of the Act, a federal environmental assessment of a "project" (essentially a physical work) was required whenever a "federal authority" did one or more of the following "for the purpose of enabling the project to be carried out in whole or in part":

1. was the proponent;
2. provided any form of financial assistance to the proponent;
3. sold, leased, or otherwise disposed of federal lands, or
4. under a provision listed in the above-noted *Law List Regulations*, issued a permit or licence, granted an approval, or took any other action listed there.

Unless the project was listed in the *Exclusion List Regulations* (which set out mostly minor or routine projects), it required a federal environmental assessment, a scheme that came to be known as "all in unless out." The result was several thousands of federal environmental assessments annually, with the most common (roughly 30 percent of all assessments) initiated by what became known as the "Law List trigger" (a reference to the *Law List Regulations*). As in the case of the EARPGO, the issuance of a permit for works that interfered with navigation pursuant to s 5 of the then NWPA was a "Law List trigger" (that is, this permitting power was listed in the Regulations), but in contrast to the EARPGO (as interpreted by the Supreme Court), so were numerous provisions under the federal *Fisheries Act*, including the issuance of a s 35(2) authorization for works and undertakings that were likely to result in the harmful alteration, disruption, or destruction of fish habitat. Where an environmental assessment was required, s 11(1) of CEAA stated that the federal authority became a "responsible authority" in relation to that project and had to ensure that an assessment was carried out. Where a project had several triggers, several responsible authorities would be involved (for example, Fisheries and Oceans Canada [DFO], Transport Canada, the National Energy Board [NEB] (now the Canadian Energy Regulator), and the Canadian Nuclear Safety Commission [CNSC]). In such instances, one responsible authority would play a lead role or the assessment would be coordinated by the agency. Under CEAA, the agency played no substantive role in the actual assessment of projects.

CEAA contemplated three different levels of assessment (or tracks) of increasing rigour: screenings, comprehensive studies, and panel reviews (mediations were also contemplated but never used). Pursuant to s 18, screenings were the presumptive track unless a project was one as described in the *Comprehensive Study List Regulations*, which included a list of projects determined most likely to result in significant adverse effects. The vast majority of federal assessments were done at the screening level.

While each of the different assessment tracks had specific requirements, the general requirements were outlined in ss 14 to 17. Section 14 set out the elements of the assessment process: an environmental assessment (that is, the preparation and submission of an environmental impact statement [EIS] by the proponent and its analysis by the responsible authority or authorities and other stakeholders); a report; and, where applicable, the implementation of "follow-up programs." Section 15 gave responsible authorities or, in the case of a panel review, the minister of the environment the power to determine the "scope of the project" for the purposes of assessment. Section 16 gave those same persons the power to determine the "scope of factors" to be considered in the assessment (usually referred to as the "scope of the assessment"). Scoping became one of the most contentious and litigated steps under CEAA, as further set out below.

2. Scoping

Prior to a Supreme Court ruling in 2010 (*MiningWatch Canada v Canada (Fisheries and Oceans)*, 2010 SCC 2, further discussed below), the approach of many responsible authorities—with Canadian courts' blessing—was that the "project" referred to in s 18 (which determined the assessment track) was not necessarily the actual project proposed by a proponent (for example, a metal mine) but, rather, the "project as scoped" by the responsible authority. Under this approach, many development proposals that would have otherwise required comprehensive studies did not require them, especially as federal departments increasingly—although not uniformly—embraced an approach known as "scoping to trigger." This practice involved separating a development proposal into a list of components and then "scoping-in" only those that required federal regulatory approval or funding (for example, a minor dam and stream crossing for a mine access road requiring *Fisheries Act* authorization, as opposed to the entire mine requiring such authorization because it includes a dam and stream crossing).

To the uninitiated, it might appear that Canadian courts allowed what seems like a clear circumvention of the Act, and the *Comprehensive Study List Regulations* in particular, for most of the legislation's life. Behind this willingness, however, appears to lie a concern for some kind of proportionality, or nexus, between the triggering federal power and the federal government's consequent involvement in project assessment and management, a preoccupation that finds some support in the Supreme Court's *Friends of the Oldman River Society* decision, including the "affirmative regulatory duty" concept discussed above.

In the CEAA context, this preoccupation may have been first expressed in *Manitoba's Future Forest Alliance v Canada (Minister of the Environment)*, 1999 CanLII 8362 (FC), where the question was whether an assessment triggered by an application for a s 5 NWPA permit for a bridge should also include within its scope the forestry operation that the bridge was intended to serve. Nadon J (as he then was) adopted the respondent forestry company's concerns (at para 86):

What happens if a city within Canada, or a province for that matter, decides to build a bridge? When they seek approval under section 5 of the *NWPA*, does everything that city or province does become one big "project" which must be environmentally assessed under the *CEAA*? Surely not, but this might well be the result if the Applicants' arguments are accepted. Unless the environmental assessment is connected with the regulatory authority which triggers the *CEAA*, there is simply no reasonable limit placed on what the responsible authority in any given case would have to consider.

It was in *Prairie Acid Rain Coalition v Canada (Minister of Fisheries and Oceans)*, 2006 FCA 31 that such concerns took on a distinctively constitutional flavour. The project at issue was the Fort Hills oil sands mine, the construction of which required the dewatering—that is, the destruction—of Fort Creek, a fish-bearing tributary of the Athabasca River in northeastern Alberta. This latter aspect required a s 35(2) *Fisheries Act* authorization, thus triggering CEAA. The *Prairie Acid Rain Coalition* sought judicial review of the DFO decision to "scope" the project as the destruction of Fort Creek, leaving out the oil sands operation and, in so doing, avoiding a comprehensive study (the mine's production levels exceeded the relevant threshold in the *Comprehensive Study List Regulations*). The coalition argued that the general tenor of the Supreme Court's *Friends of the Oldman River* decision envisioned a more expansive approach to federal environmental assessment, one that would be thwarted by narrow scoping. Rothstein JA (as he then was) disagreed and suggested that limiting the scope of the project was necessary in order to respect constitutional limits:

> [24] The purpose of the [*Comprehensive Study List Regulations*] appears to be that when a listed project is scoped under subsection 15(1), a comprehensive study, rather than a screening, will be required in respect of that project. ... In this case, the oil sands undertaking is subject to provincial jurisdiction. The *Comprehensive Study List Regulations* do not purport to sweep under a federal environmental assessment undertakings that are not subject to federal jurisdiction. Nor are the Regulations engaged because of some narrow ground of federal jurisdiction, in this case, subsection 35(2) of the *Fisheries Act*. See *Friends of the Oldman River Society v. Canada (Minister of Transport)*, [1992] 1 S.C.R. 3, at pages 71-72.

> • • •

> [26] ... the subject of the environment is not one within the exclusive legislative authority of the Parliament of Canada. Constitutional limitations must be respected and that is what has occurred in this case.

Four years later, however, in *MiningWatch*, Rothstein J (then sitting as a judge of the Supreme Court) held that CEAA did *not* permit federal authorities to first "scope" projects down to certain components for the purposes of determining what environmental assessment track applies. Rather, it was the entire "project as proposed by the proponent" that determined whether a screening or the more rigorous comprehensive study track applied. While acknowledging that the proponent and government respondents relied heavily on *Prairie Acid Rain Coalition* (also referred to as *"True North"* after the then proponent of the project), Rothstein J did not engage in any analysis of the reasons underpinning those earlier decisions but, rather, merely held that to the extent that they were inconsistent with the analysis in *MiningWatch*, the latter now governs (see para 26). Just over a year and a half later, CEAA would be repealed and replaced with CEAA 2012.

Determining the scope of factors was generally a less contentious step. Pursuant to s 16 of CEAA, all assessments had to take into account certain factors, the scope of which was determined by the responsible authority or, in the case of a panel review, the minister of the environment. First and foremost, the assessment had to consider "the environmental effects of the project, including the environmental effects of malfunctions or accidents that may occur in connection with the project," the significance of those effects, as well as "measures that are technically and economically feasible and that would mitigate any significant adverse environmental effects of the project." This list of factors was somewhat contracted under CEAA 2012 but then considerably expanded under the IAA (see Section III.C.2 of the chapter). Much of the litigation in the assessment context challenges the adequacy or completeness of the consideration given to these factors in a particular assessment or whether the analysis reflects the legislation's commitments to sustainable development and the precautionary principle (as set out in the legislation's "purpose" section). Both types of challenges are rendered relatively difficult by Canadian courts' deferential approach to such issues (see Section IV of the chapter).

3. Decision-Making

Once an environmental assessment was completed, a report—informed by but subsequent to and distinct from the proponent's EIS—had to be completed and a two-step "course of action" taken. The first step was for responsible parties to determine the project's likelihood of causing "significant adverse environmental effects" after they took into account any appropriate mitigation measures. If such effects were deemed not likely or likely but "justified in the circumstances," the federal permit, decision, or other action that triggered CEAA could proceed (the second step). If such effects were deemed likely and not justified, then no authorization or approval could be issued. As noted above, in the vast majority of cases (99 percent under CEAA), projects were deemed not likely to result in significant adverse effects.

In addition, when responsible authorities relied on mitigation measures in making the effects determination, CEAA imposed an obligation to ensure, or at least to be satisfied, of their implementation. Generally, the former was supposed to be accomplished through conditions contained in the permit or authorization that triggered CEAA in the first place (for example, a s 35(2) authorization), but in practice, this was seldom the case. The latter option (to be satisfied) was added to CEAA after the Federal Court's decision in *Environmental Resource Centre v Canada (Minister of Environment)*, 2001 FCT 1423, 40 Admin LR (3d) 217, which held that the term "ensure" precluded responsible authorities from relying on mitigation measures contained in provincial permits and approvals over which they had no control. The term "to be satisfied" is presumed to allow such reliance.

QUESTIONS

1. Although the "scoping to trigger" approach was widely criticized by environmental groups and scholars, there is another side to the argument. For example, DFO analysts could legitimately argue that their expertise lies in matters of fish and fish habitat—not the myriad other—often complex—issues and challenges associated with mining (whether metal or oil sands). CEAA contained provisions requiring other federal departments to provide their expertise when requested (as did CEAA 2012 and as does the IAA), but this apparently was not sufficient. Can you think of reasons why?

2. CEAA also contained provisions for joint reviews with provincial authorities (for CEAA 2012, see s 40; for the IAA, see s 39), and federal and provincial ministers of the environment signed many agreements toward harmonizing assessment processes, but this was also not sufficient to prevent the "scoping to trigger" phenomenon. Again, can you think of reasons why?

III. CANADIAN ENVIRONMENTAL ASSESSMENT ACT, 2012 (CEAA 2012) AND THE IMPACT ASSESSMENT ACT (IAA)

A. LEGISLATIVE HISTORY

CEAA 2012 was formally introduced in the House of Commons as but one part of the unprecedented (in substance) omnibus budget bills of 2012 (Bill C-38, *Jobs, Growth and Long-term*

Prosperity Act, 1st Sess, 41st Parl, 2012 (assented to 29 June 2012), SC 2012, c 19, and Bill C-45, *Jobs and Growth Act, 2012*, 1st Sess, 41st Parl, 2012 (assented to 14 December 2012), SC 2012, c 31). As the centerpiece of what was referred to by the government of the day as its "responsible resource development" initiative, CEAA 2012 fundamentally altered the federal environmental assessment regime from one that assessed the effects of federal decision-making broadly to one that focused almost exclusively on major resource projects. As noted above, nearly 3,000 screening-level environmental assessments were terminated with the coming into force of CEAA 2012, pursuant to which only about 70 projects underwent assessment in any given year (see Figure 17.4, below). There are consequently only two assessment tracks: reviews by responsible authorities (for the general rules, see ss 22-27) and panel reviews (see ss 38-46).

The number of federal authorities responsible for assessment was also reduced: the NEB and CNSC became responsible for projects falling within their mandates (ss 29-31 set out a distinct regime for NEB-regulated projects), and—for the first time—the agency was responsible for all other projects (s 15).

CEAA 2012 also restricted public participation to those deemed "directly affected" (see Section III.E of this chapter).

Other aspects of these omnibus budget bills drastically reduced the scope of Canada's *Fisheries Act*, and the protections for fish habitat in particular (see Chapter 15 of this book as well as Martin Z Olszynski, "From 'Badly Wrong' to Worse: An Empirical Analysis of Canada's New Approach to Fish Habitat Protection Laws" (2015) 28:1 J Envtl L & Prac 1). What was then still called the *Navigable Waters Protection Act* was also fundamentally altered. Renamed the *Navigation Protection Act*, RSC 1985, c N-22, it applied to only a fraction of the water bodies that were subject to the pre-2012 regime (the Act has once again been renamed, as the *Canadian Navigable Waters Act*, with the coming into force of Bill C-69). Finally, the *National Energy Board Act*, RSC 1985, c N-7 [NEBA], was amended to give Cabinet, rather than the NEB, the final authority to either approve or reject interprovincial pipeline projects. (NEBA has also now been repealed and replaced by the *Canadian Energy Regulator Act*, SC 2019, c 28, s 10, although Parliament has retained its final authority over interprovincial pipeline projects.)

FIGURE 17.4   Number of Federal Assessments in Progress per year (2009-2018)

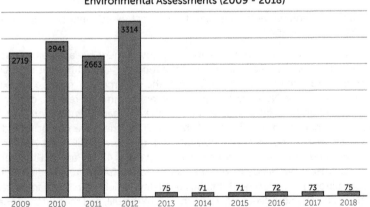

Number of ongoing federal environmental assessments based on data compiled by Martin Olszynski from the Canadian Environmental Assessment Agency, "Accountability, Performance and Financial Reporting" (last modified 11 April 2019), online: *Government of Canada* <https://www.canada.ca/en/impact-assessment-agency/corporate/transparency/accountability-performance-financial-reporting.html>.

Because all of these changes were contained within budget bills, they barely received any parliamentary scrutiny. That is not to suggest, however, that they went unnoticed or unchallenged. They were met with considerable opposition from Indigenous peoples (giving rise to the "Idle No More" movement: <www.idlenomore.ca/story>), environmental law scholars (see, for example, Meinhard Doelle, "CEAA 2012: The End of Federal EA as We Know It?" (2012) 24:1 J Envtl L & Prac 1), environmental non-governmental organizations (eNGOs), scientists, as well as former politicians from across the political spectrum (for a comprehensive listing of science-based critiques, see Alana Westwood et al, "The Role of Science in Contemporary Canadian Environmental Decision-Making: The Example of Environmental Assessment" (2019) 52:1 UBC L Rev 243).

Ultimately, "restoring lost protections" became a key plank of the federal Liberal campaign in 2015. Upon winning that election, the Liberal government undertook a four-year process of study by parliamentary committees, expert panels, and senate committees. With respect to environmental assessment, the government appointed a four-person panel, the Expert Panel for the Review of Environmental Assessment Processes, to undertake nationwide consultations with experts, Indigenous groups, and the public, including invitations for written submissions and in-person presentations. Its report, *Building Common Ground: A New Vision for Impact Assessment in Canada—The Final Report of the Expert Panel for the Review of Environmental Assessment Processes* (Ottawa: Canadian Environmental Assessment Agency, 2017), online: *Government of Canada* <https://www.canada.ca/en/services/environment/conservation/assessments/environmental-reviews/environmental-assessment-processes/building-common-ground.html>, was released in April 2017 and recommended a *major* overhaul of CEAA 2012, calling for the following:

- a broadening of the scope of assessment beyond biophysical impacts to include social, health, economic, and cultural effects, both positive and negative, and a move toward sustainability rather than merely the avoidance of significant adverse effects;
- the creation of a new, independent, and quasi-judicial commission to conduct impact assessment in Canada (similar to the Canadian Radio-Television and Telecommunications Commission);
- the incorporation of the *United Nations Declaration on the Rights of Indigenous Peoples*, GA Res 61/295 UNGAOR, 61st Sess, UN Doc A/RES/61/295 (2007), online (pdf): <https://www.un.org/esa/socdev/unpfii/documents/DRIPS_en.pdf> [UNDRIP], and mandatory consideration of Indigenous knowledge as part of the objective of reconciliation with Indigenous peoples;
- the introduction of a new, legislated planning phase to precede the assessment phase; and
- new legislative requirements to ensure that impact assessment is evidence-based and contains the best science.

Following a period of public consultation, the government released a discussion paper outlining how it proposed to respond to all of the reports that had by that time been completed (in addition to *Building Common Ground*, the government received an expert panel report on modernizing the NEB and two parliamentary committee reports, one with respect to the *Fisheries Act* and the other with respect to the *Navigation Protection Act*). Following another period of public consultation, in February 2018, the government tabled Bill C-69 (amendments to the *Fisheries Act* were also tabled in the form of Bill C-68, *An Act to amend the Fisheries Act and other Acts in consequence*, 1st Sess, 42nd Parl, 2018 (assented to 21 June 2019), SC 2019, c 14). Bill C-69 was then subjected to further review, first by the House Standing Committee on Environment and Sustainability, which, with a few important exceptions, introduced mostly housekeeping amendments to the Bill, and then by the Senate Standing Committee on Energy, Environment and Resources, which travelled across Canada and introduced nearly 200 amendments. Approximately 60 of these amendments were accepted by the government, while another 30 were accepted with modification. Bill C-69 received royal assent on June 21, 2019, and was proclaimed into force on August 28, 2019.

The IAA reflects relatively few of the expert panel's recommendations and, for the most part, can be described as a modest improvement on CEAA 2012. Like CEAA 2012, the IAA is built around a designated project list rather than being triggered by federal decision-making generally (as CEAA was). The main differences include a new "planning phase" (as recommended by the expert panel), whereas under CEAA 2102, there was only a screening decision; the elimination of the "directly affected" standing test introduced in CEAA 2012; and an expansion of the scope of assessments to include social, economic, and health effects that fall within Parliament's jurisdiction (hence the change from environmental assessment to impact assessment). The federal government will also have to consider, among other things, a project's contribution to sustainability and whether it contributes to or hinders Canada's ability to meet its climate change commitments.

The discussion below sets out the main elements of CEAA 2012 and the IAA, following the same order as in the discussion of CEAA, in Section II.B, above (triggering, scoping, and decision-making), with a few additional headings and accompanied by relevant legislative excerpts. Some provisions have been omitted or shortened in light of space constraints. Because the IAA is virtually identical in terms of its structure, the corresponding provisions of that legislation are included, often side by side for comparison.

B. TRIGGERING: DESIGNATED PROJECTS, PROJECTS ON FEDERAL LANDS, REGIONAL AND STRATEGIC ASSESSMENTS

1. Designated Projects

Under CEAA 2012, the primary starting point was the *Regulations Designating Physical Activities*, SOR/2012-147, which largely reproduced CEAA's *Comprehensive Study List Regulations*. Projects in the *Regulations Designating Physical Activities* were referred to as "designated projects" in the Act. If a proponent planned to carry out a designated project, for example, "the construction, operation, decommissioning and abandonment of a new ... metal mine ...with an ore production capacity of 3 000 t/day or more" (see the Schedule to the Regulations), s 8(1) of the Act required the proponent to provide the agency with a description of the designated project in accordance with applicable regulations. Upon receipt and review for completeness, the agency would then post certain information to the Canadian Environmental Assessment Registry (CEA Registry) and conduct a "screening" to determine whether or not a federal assessment would be required. This was a true screening decision (that is, a limited analysis), not the screening track assessment set out in CEAA. Thus, with the exception of designated projects regulated by the NEB and the CNSC for which assessment was always required (see s 13), the mere presence of a project in the Regulations did not guarantee that a federal assessment would follow. Rather, the agency had discretion to determine whether an assessment would be required.

The table below sets out the relevant provisions of the CEAA 2012 screening process (left column) as well as the new planning phase provisions of the IAA that were essentially superimposed onto the CEAA 2012 screening process (right column).

CEAA 2012	IAA
Screening	**Planning Phase**

<table>
<tr><td>

Proponent's obligation—description of designated project
8(1) The proponent of a designated project—other than one that is subject to an environmental assessment under section 13 or subsection 14(1)—must provide the Agency with a description of the designated project that includes the information prescribed by regulations made under paragraph 84(b).

• • •

Posting of description of designated project and public notice on Internet site
9 When the Agency is satisfied that the description of the designated project includes all of the required information, it must post the following on the Internet site:

(a) a summary of the description;
(b) an indication of how a copy of the description may be obtained; and
(c) a notice that indicates that the designated project is the subject of a screening, invites the public to provide comments respecting the designated project within 20 days after the posting of the notice and indicates the address for filing those comments.

Screening decision
10 Within 45 days after the posting of the notice on the Internet site, the Agency must

(a) conduct the screening, which must include a consideration of the following factors:
  (i) the description of the designated project provided by the proponent,
  (ii) the possibility that the carrying out of the designated project may cause adverse environmental effects,

</td><td>

Obligations
Proponent's obligation—description of designated project
10(1) The proponent of a designated project must provide the Agency with an initial description of the project that includes the information prescribed by regulations made under paragraph 112(1)(a).

Copy posted on Internet site
(2) The Agency must post a copy of the description on the Internet site.

Public participation
11 The Agency must ensure that the public is provided with an opportunity to participate meaningfully, in a manner that the Agency considers appropriate, in its preparations for a possible impact assessment of a designated project, including by inviting the public to provide comments within the period that it specifies.

Agency's obligation—offer to consult
12 For the purpose of preparing for a possible impact assessment of a designated project, the Agency must offer to consult with any jurisdiction that has powers, duties or functions in relation to an assessment of the environmental effects of the designated project and any Indigenous group that may be affected by the carrying out of the designated project.

Federal authority's obligation
13(1) Every federal authority that is in possession of specialist or expert information or knowledge with respect to a designated project that is the subject of the Agency's preparations must, on the Agency's request and within the period that it specifies, make that information or knowledge available to the Agency.

</td></tr>
</table>

(iii) any comments received from the public within 20 days after the posting of the notice, and

(iv) the results of any relevant [regional] study ... ; and

(b) on completion of the screening, decide if an environmental assessment of the designated project is required.

Federal authority's obligation

11 Every federal authority that is in possession of specialist or expert information or knowledge with respect to a designated project that is subject to a screening must, on request, make that information or knowledge available to the Agency within the specified period.

Posting notice of decision on Internet site

12 The Agency must post a notice of its decision made under paragraph 10(b) on the Internet site.

Engaging proponent

(2) Every federal authority that has powers, duties or functions conferred on it under any Act of Parliament other than this Act with respect to a designated project that is the subject of the Agency's preparations—including the Canadian Energy Regulator, the Canadian Nuclear Safety Commission, the Canada–Nova Scotia Offshore Petroleum Board and the Canada–Newfoundland and Labrador Offshore Petroleum Board—must, on the Agency's request, engage the proponent of the designated project in order that the federal authority may specify to the proponent the information, if any, that it may require in order to exercise those powers or perform those duties or functions.

Agency's obligation—summary of issues

14(1) The Agency must provide the proponent of a designated project with a summary of issues with respect to that project that it considers relevant, including issues that are raised by the public or by any jurisdiction or Indigenous group that is consulted under section 12, and with any information or knowledge made available to it by a federal authority that the Agency considers appropriate.

Copy posted on Internet site

(2) The Agency must post on the Internet site a copy of the summary of issues that it provided to the proponent.

Proponent's obligation—notice

15(1) The proponent must provide the Agency with a notice that sets out, in accordance with the regulations, how it intends to address the issues referred to in section 14 and a detailed description of the designated project that includes the information prescribed by regulations made under paragraph 112(1)(a).

• • •

Copy posted on Internet site

(3) When the Agency is satisfied that the notice includes all of the information or details that it specified, it must post a copy of the notice on the Internet site.

(Continued on next page.)

CEAA 2012	IAA
Screening	**Planning Phase**

<table>
<tr><td></td><td>

Decisions Regarding Impact Assessments
Agency's Decision
Decision
16(1) After posting a copy of the notice on the Internet site under subsection 15(3), the Agency must decide whether an impact assessment of the designated project is required.

Factors
(2) In making its decision, the Agency must take into account the following factors:
- (a) the description referred to in section 10 and any notice referred to in section 15;
- (b) the possibility that the carrying out of the designated project may cause adverse effects within federal jurisdiction or adverse direct or incidental effects;
- (c) any adverse impact that the designated project may have on the rights of the Indigenous peoples of Canada recognized and affirmed by section 35 of the *Constitution Act, 1982*;
- (d) any comments received within the time period specified by the Agency from the public and from any jurisdiction or Indigenous group that is consulted under section 12;
- (e) any relevant assessment referred to in section 92, 93 or 95 [regional and strategic];
- (f) any study that is conducted or plan that is prepared by a jurisdiction—in respect of a region that is related to the designated project—and that has been provided to the Agency; and
- (g) any other factor that the Agency considers relevant.

Posting notice on Internet site
(3) The Agency must post a notice of its decision and the reasons for it on the Internet site.

</td></tr>
</table>

Under the IAA, CEAA 2012's screening step has been transformed into the new expert panel-recommended planning phase. Where a project is described in the amended *Physical Activities Regulations*, SOR/2019-285 (having been modified from the CEAA 2012 version, including the raising of thresholds for certain types of mines), the planning phase begins with an *initial* project description and not only public participation but also an offer to consult with other relevant jurisdictions and Indigenous groups (s 12). The agency will then provide the proponent with a list of issues that it considers relevant and that it must also post in the CIA

Registry (s 14(2)), and the proponent will be required to respond with a *detailed* description of its project. At this juncture, after considering specified factors (s 16(2), in which the list of factors is marginally longer than that in s 10 of CEAA 2012), the agency will make its decision as to whether an impact assessment will be required. If one is required, the entire planning phase is to take 180 days from the time that the proponent posted its initial project description (s 18). This stands in contrast to the screening decision under CEAA 2012, which must be made 45 days after a project description is deemed complete (s 10). A direct comparison of these two phases is not entirely appropriate, however, because the new planning phase is intended to facilitate planning that proponents were already doing but that was not formally part of the process. As explained by the expert panel in *Building Common Ground*,

> [a] Planning Phase should lead to a more effective and efficient process. In the development of projects today, some proponents may already undertake a conceptual Planning Phase, prior to the initiation of the current assessment process. Bringing this conceptual Planning Phase into the formal IA process would aid both proponents and communities by helping facilitate relationship-building and trust. It would also provide clarity to the proponent early in the process with regard to the main issues of concern. For communities and Indigenous Groups, the Planning Phase would allow them to identify important information that can be inputted into the IA. [Footnote omitted.]

Connecting this planning phase to the assessment phase is the information-gathering provision set out in s 18 of the IAA, which requires the agency to post a notice of commencement that sets out the information or studies that it will require from the proponent, taking into account the factors set out in s 22(1) (see Section III.C.2) in determining what information or which studies it considers necessary.

2. Projects on Federal Lands or Outside Canada

CEAA 2012 also contained a secondary, informal regime for projects carried out on federal lands or outside Canada (ss 67-72). There was no formal assessment process set out in these provisions; relevant federal authorities simply had to be satisfied that no significant adverse environmental effects were likely or, if they were, that these were deemed justified in the circumstances by Cabinet. The IAA retains this secondary scheme in ss 81-90, but as with the designated project regime, this secondary regime is improved in some respects. Whereas under CEAA 2012 there was almost no way of knowing when such determinations were made (except by filing an access to information request), under the IAA, relevant federal authorities are required to post notices when they intend to make such determinations and, in some instances and at their discretion, to accept comments from the public prior to finalizing their determinations. There is also a new power to designate classes of projects that will be exempt from this regime:

Designation of class of projects
    88. The Minister may, by order, designate a class of projects if, in the Minister's opinion, the carrying out of a project that is a part of the class will cause only insignificant adverse environmental effects.
Projects excluded
    (2) Sections 82 and 83 do not apply to an authority in respect of a project that is part of a class of projects that is designated under subsection (1).

Such a power is probably necessary, as there are many routine projects that are carried out on federal lands and do not require additional scrutiny. Moreover, and consistent with the general thrust of the IAA, this power is constrained by the fact that any federal authority that proposes such a class must post a notice of its intent, consider public comments, and provide reasons when making a final determination (see s 89).

3. Regional and Strategic Assessments

Finally, both pieces of legislation contain provisions for carrying out what CEAA 2012 referred to as "regional studies": "a study of the effects of existing or future physical activities carried out in a region that is entirely on federal lands" (s 73) or the same kind of study but "in a region that is composed in part of federal lands or in a region that is entirely outside federal lands" (s 74), in which case the minister could enter into agreements with other relevant jurisdictions for the joint establishment of a committee to conduct such an assessment. Under CEAA 2012, there was only one regional study conducted: the "Regional Assessment of Offshore Oil and Gas Exploratory Drilling East of Newfoundland and Labrador," which is currently ongoing.

Once again, under the IAA, these provisions are expanded and somewhat improved. The IAA refers to not only "regional assessments" (in ss 92 and 93) but also "strategic assessments" (in s 95), which are described as assessments of "(a) any Government of Canada policy, plan or program—proposed or existing—that is relevant to conducting impact assessments; or (b) any issue that is relevant to conducting impact assessments of designated projects or of a class of designated projects." The federal government is currently undertaking a strategic assessment with respect to climate change (a draft of the assessment is currently available at <www.strategic assessmentclimatechange.ca>). Whether more will follow and at what pace is uncertain, since both regional and strategic assessments are still subject to the minister's discretion. Perhaps the most significant change in the IAA is a new ability to request such assessments. Pursuant to s 97, the minister must respond, with reasons and in a prescribed time period, to any request that such assessments be conducted.

C. SCOPING: PROJECTS, FACTORS, AND ENVIRONMENTAL EFFECTS

1. Projects

Because CEAA 2012 was a major project regime built first and foremost on a project list, the controversy over project scoping has largely dissipated. Both proponents and the government appear to have accepted that a project's scope will largely mirror that which is described in the regulations. This may also be attributable to having consolidated and assigned assessment responsibilities to federal agencies that have authority over entire projects rather than merely aspects of them. The one recent exception is with respect to activities that are "incidental to" a "designated project," the definition of which (in both CEAA 2012 and the IAA) is as follows:

CEAA 2012	IAA
Definitions	**Definitions**
2(1) ...	2 ...
• • •	• • •
"designated project" means one or more physical activities that (a) are carried out in Canada or on federal lands; (b) are designated by regulations made under paragraph 84(a) or designated in an order made by the Minister under subsection 14(2); and (c) are linked to the same federal authority as specified in those regulations or that order. It includes any physical activity that is incidental to those physical activities.	"designated project" means one or more physical activities that (a) are carried out in Canada or on federal lands; and (b) are designated by regulations made under paragraph 109(b) or designated in an order made by the Minister under subsection 9(1). It includes any physical activity that is incidental to those physical activities, but it does not include a physical activity designated by regulations made under paragraph 112(1)(a.2).

It was the last part of this definition that in part compelled the Federal Court of Appeal to overturn the governor in council approval for the Trans Mountain pipeline expansion project in *Tsleil-Waututh Nation v Canada (Attorney General)*, 2018 FCA 153, relevant passages of which are excerpted below.

TSLEIL-WAUTUTH NATION V CANADA (ATTORNEY GENERAL)
2018 FCA 153 at paras 1-2, 5, 391-404

I. INTRODUCTION

[1] On May 19, 2016, the National Energy Board issued its report concerning the proposed expansion of the Trans Mountain pipeline system. The Board's report recommended that the Governor in Council approve the expansion. The Board's recommendation was based on the Board's findings that the expansion is in Canada's public interest, and that if certain environmental protection procedures and mitigation measures are implemented, and if the conditions the Board recommended are implemented, the expansion is not likely to cause significant adverse environmental effects.

[2] On November 29, 2016, the Governor in Council accepted the Board's recommendation and issued Order in Council P.C. 2016-1069. ...

• • •

[5] Applying largely uncontested legal principles established by the Supreme Court of Canada to the factual record, a factual record that is also largely not contested, I conclude that most of the flaws asserted against the Board's process and findings are without merit. However, the Board made one critical error. The Board unjustifiably defined the scope of the Project under review not to include Project-related tanker traffic. The unjustified exclusion of marine shipping from the scope of the Project led to successive, unacceptable deficiencies in the Board's report and recommendations. ...

• • •

X. CONSIDERATION OF THE ISSUES

• • •

[391] The definition of "designated project" is found in section 2 of the *Canadian Environmental Assessment Act, 2012* ... . The parties agree that the issue of whether Project-related marine shipping ought to have been included as part of the defined designated project turns on whether Project-related marine shipping is a "physical activity that is incidental" to the pipeline component of the Project. This is not a pure issue of statutory interpretation. Rather, it is a mixed question of fact and law heavily suffused by evidence [see Section IV of the chapter for a discussion of the standard of review applicable to project assessments].

[392] In response to the submissions of Tsleil-Waututh, Raincoast and Living Oceans, Canada and Trans Mountain make two submissions. First, they submit that the Board reasonably concluded that the increase in marine shipping was not part of the designated project. ...

[393] Before commencing my analysis, it is important to situate the Board's scoping decision and the exclusion of Project-related shipping from the definition of the Project. The definition of the designated project truly frames the scope of the Board's analysis. Activities included as part of the designated project are assessed under the

Canadian Environmental Assessment Act, 2012 with its prescribed list of factors to be considered. Further, as the Board acknowledged in Chapter 10 of its report, the *Species at Risk Act* [SC 2002, c 29] imposes additional obligations on the Board when a designated project is likely to affect a listed wildlife species. ...

• • •

[395] I begin my analysis with Trans Mountain's application to the Board for a certificate of public convenience and necessity for the Project. In Volume 1 of the application, at pages 1-4, Trans Mountain describes the primary purpose of the Project to be "to provide additional transportation capacity for crude oil from Alberta to markets in the Pacific Rim including BC, Washington State, California and Asia." ... To place this in perspective, currently in a typical month five tankers are loaded with diluted bitumen at the Westridge Marine Terminal, some of which are the smaller, Panamax tankers. The expanded system would be capable of serving up to 34 of the larger, Aframax tankers per month (with actual demand influenced by market conditions).

[396] This evidence demonstrates that marine shipping is, at the least, an element that accompanies the Project. Canada argues that an element that accompanies a physical activity while not being a major part of the activity is not "incidental" to the physical activity. Canada says that this was what the Board implicitly found.

[397] The difficulty with this submission is that it is difficult to infer that this was indeed the Board's finding, albeit an implicit finding. I say this because in its scoping decision the Board gave no reasons for its conclusion ...

[398] Having defined the designated project not to include the increase in marine shipping, the Board dealt with the Project-related increase in marine shipping activities in Chapter 14 of its report. Consistent with the scoping decision, at the beginning of Chapter 14 the Board stated, at page 323:

> As described in Section 14.2, marine vessel traffic is regulated by government agencies, such as Transport Canada, Port Metro Vancouver, Pacific Pilotage Authority and the Canadian Coast Guard, under a broad and detailed regulatory framework. *The Board does not have regulatory oversight of marine vessel traffic, whether or not the vessel traffic relates to the Project*. There is an existing regime that oversees marine vessel traffic. *The Board's regulatory oversight of the Project, as well as the scope of its assessment of the Project under the Canadian Environmental Assessment Act (CEAA 2012), reaches from Edmonton to Burnaby, up to and including the Westridge Marine Terminal (WMT)*. ... [Emphasis added by the court; footnote omitted.]

[399] Two points emerge from this passage. The first point is the closest the Board came to explaining its scoping decision was that the Board did not have regulatory oversight over marine vessel traffic. There is no indication that the Board grappled with this important issue.

[400] The issue is important because the Project is intended to bring product to tidewater; 71% of this product could be delivered to the Westridge Marine Terminal for shipment by tanker. Further, as explained below, if Project-related shipping forms part of the designated project additional requirements apply under the *Species at Risk Act*. Finally, Project-related tankers carry the risk of significant, if not catastrophic, adverse environmental and socio-economic effects should a spill occur.

[401] Neither Canada nor Trans Mountain point [*sic*] to any authority to the effect that a responsible authority conducting an environmental assessment under the *Canadian Environmental Assessment Act, 2012* must itself have regulatory oversight over a particular subject matter in order for the responsible authority to be able to define a designated project to include physical activities that are properly incidental to the Project. The effect of the respondents' submission is to impermissibly write the following italicized words into the definition of "designated project": "It includes

any physical activity that is incidental to those physical activities *and that is regulated by the responsible authority."*

[402] In addition to being impermissibly restrictive, the Board's view that it was required to have regulatory authority over shipping in order to include shipping as part of the Project is inconsistent with the purposes of the *Canadian Environmental Assessment Act, 2012* enumerated in subsection 4(1). These purposes include protecting the components of the environment that are *within the legislative authority of Parliament* and ensuring that designated projects are considered in a careful and precautionary manner to avoid significant adverse environmental effects.

[403] The second point that arises is that the phrase "incidental to" is not defined in the *Canadian Environmental Assessment Act, 2012*. It is not clear that the Board expressly directed its mind to whether Project-related marine shipping was in fact an activity "incidental" to the Project. Had it done so, the Canadian Environmental Assessment Agency's "Guide to Preparing a Description of a Designated Project under the Canadian Environmental Assessment Act, 2012" provides a set of criteria relevant to the question of whether certain activities should be considered "incidental" to a project. These criteria are:

i.   the nature of the proposed activities and whether they are subordinate or complementary to the designated project;
ii. whether the activity is within the care and control of the proponent;
iii. if the activity is to be undertaken by a third party, the nature of the relationship between the proponent and the third party and whether the proponent has the ability to "direct or influence" the carrying out of the activity;
iv. whether the activity is solely for the benefit of the proponent or is available for other proponents as well; and,
v.   the federal and/or provincial regulatory requirements for the activity.

[404] The Board does not advert to, or grapple with, these criteria in its report. Had the Board grappled with these criteria it would have particularly considered whether marine shipping is subordinate or complementary to the Project and whether Trans Mountain is able to "direct or influence" aspects of tanker operations.

[The court remitted the matter to the board for reconsideration. The board ultimately included marine shipping within the scope of the project under CEAA 2012.]

QUESTIONS

The Court of Appeal noted that neither Canada nor Trans Mountain could point to any authority to the effect that a responsible authority conducting an environmental assessment must itself have regulatory oversight over a particular subject matter in order to define a designated project to include physical activities that are properly incidental to the project. Can you think of one such authority considered in this chapter? What about *Manitoba's Future Forest Alliance v Canada (Minister of the Environment)* (discussed in Section II.B.2)? Between that approach and the agency's criteria, which do you prefer? Which is better suited to the CEAA 2012 and IAA regimes?

2. Factors to Assess

With respect to the scope of assessment, the relevant factors are laid out in ss 19 and 22 of CEAA 2012 and the IAA, respectively, excerpted below (underlining indicates new wording). Under CEAA 2012, the scope of these factors was determined by the responsible authority or, in the case of a panel review, the minister. Under the IAA, the scope of these factors in all cases is determined by the agency.

CEAA 2012	IAA
Factors	**Factors—impact assessment**

CEAA 2012	IAA

19(1) The environmental assessment of a designated project must take into account the following factors:
  (a) the environmental effects of the designated project, including the environmental effects of malfunctions or accidents that may occur in connection with the designated project and any cumulative environmental effects that are likely to result from the designated project in combination with other physical activities that have been or will be carried out;
  (b) the significance of the effects referred to in paragraph (a);
  (c) comments from the public—or, with respect to a designated project that requires that a certificate be issued in accordance with an order made under section 54 of the *National Energy Board Act*, any interested party—that are received in accordance with this Act;
  (d) mitigation measures that are technically and economically feasible and that would mitigate any significant adverse environmental effects of the designated project;
  (e) the requirements of the follow-up program in respect of the designated project;
  (f) the purpose of the designated project;
  (g) alternative means of carrying out the designated project that are technically and economically feasible and the environmental effects of any such alternative means;
  (h) any change to the designated project that may be caused by the environment;
	22(1) The impact assessment of a designated project, whether it is conducted by the Agency or a review panel, must take into account the following factors:
	  (a) the changes to the environment or to health, social or economic conditions and the positive and negative consequences of these changes that are likely to be caused by the carrying out of the designated project, including
	    (i) the effects of malfunctions or accidents that may occur in connection with the designated project,
	    (ii) any cumulative effects that are likely to result from the designated project in combination with other physical activities that have been or will be carried out, and
	    (iii) the result of any interaction between those effects;
	  (b) mitigation measures that are technically and economically feasible and that would mitigate any adverse effects of the designated project;
	  (c) the impact that the designated project may have on any Indigenous group and any adverse impact that the designated project may have on the rights of the Indigenous peoples of Canada recognized and affirmed by section 35 of the Constitution Act, 1982;
	  (d) the purpose of and need for the designated project;
	  (e) alternative means of carrying out the designated project that are technically and economically feasible, including through the use of best available technologies, and the effects of those means;
	  (f) any alternatives to the designated project that are technically and economically feasible and are directly related to the designated project;

(i) the results of any relevant study conducted by a committee established under section 73 or 74; and

(j) any other matter relevant to the environmental assessment that the responsible authority, or—if the environmental assessment is referred to a review panel—the Minister, requires to be taken into account.

• • •

Community knowledge and Aboriginal traditional knowledge

(3) The environmental assessment of a designated project may take into account community knowledge and Aboriginal traditional knowledge.

(g) Indigenous knowledge provided with respect to the designated project;

(h) the extent to which the designated project contributes to sustainability;

(i) the extent to which the effects of the designated project hinder or contribute to the Government of Canada's ability to meet its environmental obligations and its commitments in respect of climate change;

(j) any change to the designated project that may be caused by the environment;

(k) the requirements of the follow-up program in respect of the designated project;

(l) considerations related to Indigenous cultures raised with respect to the designated project;

(m) community knowledge provided with respect to the designated project;

(n) comments received from the public;

(o) comments from a jurisdiction that are received in the course of consultations conducted under section 21;

(p) any relevant assessment referred to in section 92, 93 or 95;

(q) any assessment of the effects of the designated project that is conducted by or on behalf of an Indigenous governing body and that is provided with respect to the designated project;

(r) any study or plan that is conducted or prepared by a jurisdiction—or an Indigenous governing body not referred to in paragraph (f) or (g) of the definition jurisdiction in section 2—that is in respect of a region related to the designated project and that has been provided with respect to the project;

(s) the intersection of sex and gender with other identity factors; and

(t) any other matter relevant to the impact assessment that the Agency requires to be taken into account.

Some of the IAA's new factors, such as impacts on the rights of Indigenous peoples, are essentially a codification of current law (as further discussed in Section IV), while others do expand that which the agency or a review panel considers when reviewing a project, including alternatives to the project (rather than merely alternative means, as under CEAA 2012), traditional knowledge of Canada's Indigenous peoples (discretionary under CEAA 2012), a project's contribution to sustainability, and whether it hinders or contributes to Canada's attainment of its climate change commitments. Section 22(1)(s)—"the intersection of sex and gender with other identity factors"—was the subject of particular controversy in the lead up to Bill C-69's passage. At its core, this factor merely recognizes that resource development can have different impacts depending on identity factors such as gender, race, and sexuality. For further reading, see Jennifer Koshan, "Bills C-68 and C-69 and the Consideration of Sex, Gender and Other Identity Factors" (2 May 2018), online (blog pdf): *ABlawg.ca* <http://ablawg.ca/wp-content/uploads/2018/05/Blog_JK_Bills_C68_69.pdf>; and Impact Assessment Agency of Canada, "Interim Guidance: Gender-Based Analysis Plus in Impact Assessment" (last modified 21 August 2019), online: *Government of Canada* <https://www.canada.ca/en/impact-assessment-agency/services/policy-guidance/practitioners-guide-impact-assessment-act/gender-based-analysis.html>.

3. Environmental Effects

Finally, both CEAA 2012 and the IAA limit the kinds of effects that federal impact assessment can consider. This is fundamentally a scoping issue. This is done by defining "effects" in a restrictive—and arguably convoluted—manner, an aspect of these regimes not found in CEAA. Under CEAA 2012, this definition consisted of two basic parts: environmental effects that fall within Parliament's legislative authority (s 5(1)) and effects that are "directly linked or necessarily incidental to" the exercise of a federal power (s 5(2)):

Environmental effects

5(1) For the purposes of this Act, the environmental effects that are to be taken into account in relation to an act or thing, a physical activity, a designated project or a project are

(a) a change that may be caused to the following components of the environment that are within the legislative authority of Parliament:

(i) fish and fish habitat as defined in subsection 2(1) of the *Fisheries Act*,

(ii) aquatic species as defined in subsection 2(1) of the *Species at Risk Act*,

(iii) migratory birds as defined in subsection 2(1) of the *Migratory Birds Convention Act, 1994* [SC 1994, c 22], and

(iv) any other component of the environment that is set out in Schedule 2;

(b) a change that may be caused to the environment that would occur

(i) on federal lands,

(ii) in a province other than the one in which the act or thing is done or where the physical activity, the designated project or the project is being carried out, or

(iii) outside Canada; and

(c) with respect to aboriginal peoples, an effect occurring in Canada of any change that may be caused to the environment on

(i) health and socio-economic conditions,

(ii) physical and cultural heritage,

(iii) the current use of lands and resources for traditional purposes, or

(iv) any structure, site or thing that is of historical, archaeological, paleontological or architectural significance.

Exercise of power or performance of duty or function by federal authority

(2) However, if the carrying out of the physical activity, the designated project or the project requires a federal authority to exercise a power or perform a duty or function

conferred on it under any Act of Parliament other than this Act, the following environmental effects are also to be taken into account:

(a) a change, other than those referred to in paragraphs (1)(a) and (b), that may be caused to the environment and that is directly linked or necessarily incidental to a federal authority's exercise of a power or performance of a duty or function that would permit the carrying out, in whole or in part, of the physical activity, the designated project or the project; and

(b) an effect, other than those referred to in paragraph (1)(c), of any change referred to in paragraph (a) on

(i) health and socio-economic conditions,

(ii) physical and cultural heritage, or

(iii) any structure, site or thing that is of historical, archaeological, paleontological or architectural significance.

Schedule 2

(3) The Governor in Council may, by order, amend Schedule 2 to add or remove a component of the environment.

Considering some of the commentary that followed the introduction and passage of CEAA 2012, one might reasonably conclude that ss 5(1) and (2) were relatively straightforward—even an improvement on the previous approach under CEAA, which did not distinguish between effects. In ecological reality, however, there are actually "many linkages between and among environmental changes" that are "complex" and require "careful" consideration, as the federal panel for the New Prosperity mining project observed in a passage worthy of quoting at length.

REPORT OF THE FEDERAL REVIEW PANEL—NEW PROSPERITY GOLD–COPPER MINE PROJECT

(31 October 2013) at 21, online (pdf): *Canadian Environmental Assessment Agency* <https://www.ceaa-acee.gc.ca/050/documents/p63928/95631E.pdf>

The Panel interprets the two branches of [the s 5(2)] definition of effects as follows:

- "directly linked" environmental effects to be [sic] effects that are the direct and proximate result of a federal decision; and
- "necessarily incidental" environmental effects are other effects that are substantially linked to a federal decision although they may be secondary or indirect effects.

All direct environmental effects resulting from the loss of Little Fish Lake (Y'anah Biny) and the upper reaches of Fish Creek (Teztan Yeqox) that are not captured under subsection 5(1) would be considered under subsection 5(2). Also, if the loss of the above-mentioned areas results in the loss of habitats used by the moose or grizzly bear [generally regarded as falling within provincial jurisdiction], for example, those indirect and substantial effects on the grizzly bear and moose would be considered environmental effects that are necessarily incidental to a federal decision, and would therefore be captured under subsection 5(2) of CEAA 2012.

· · ·

There are many linkages between and among environmental changes, including changes that are environmental effects defined under CEAA 2012 and those that are not. For example, the Panel determined that the Project would generate seepage of pore waters from the tailings storage facility. This would be considered a change in the environment—i.e. a change in the quantity and quality of groundwater influenced by seepage originating from the tailings storage facility. This seepage would also result in a change in surface water quality when it would seep into Fish Lake (Teztan Biny) which is located down slope from the tailings storage facility. That change in water quality in Fish Lake would be considered an environmental effect under the former Act but it would not, by itself, fall within one of the listed categories defining an environmental effect under subsection 5(1) of CEAA 2012. Fish Lake, however, consists of fish habitat which sustains a viable population of fish, namely rainbow trout. The change in the water quality in Fish Lake would have an adverse effect on both the fish habitat and the fish which are both within the listed environmental effect categories.

Moreover, Fish Lake (Teztan Biny) is used by the Tsilhqot'in for traditional purposes and as part of their cultural heritage. The changes caused to the Lake would affect the Aboriginal cultural heritage as well as the current use of land and resources by Aboriginal peoples for traditional purposes. These too would be environmental effects under subsection 5(1) of CEAA 2012.

Since the effects and linkages are a complex and interactive web, the Panel was careful to consider those interactions when deciding how to categorize the environmental effects).

While there is no formal case law interpreting these provisions, the foregoing passage suggests considerable breadth to the scope of the effects to be considered where, as in the case of the New Prosperity mine project, federal decision-making is engaged (essentially a return to the outcome in *MiningWatch*). Under the IAA, these provisions have been moved to the interpretation section of the Act (see s 2, "direct or incidental effects," "effects," and "effects within federal jurisdiction").

QUESTION

In *Tsleil-Waututh Nation* (excerpted above), the Federal Court of Appeal held that the NEB had unlawfully excluded project-related marine shipping from the scope of the project under CEAA 2012. The court noted, however, that marine shipping was discussed in chapter 14 of the NEB's report pursuant to its "public interest" mandate under s 52(2)(e) of the NEBA. Review that section of the NEBA, as well as its current wording pursuant to s 183(2)(l) of the *Canadian Energy Regulator Act*. What, if any, are the implications for the interpretation of the relevant definitions under the IAA, bearing in mind the New Prosperity Panel's analysis?

D. DECISION-MAKING

As in the case of CEAA, the basic test under CEAA 2012 was whether a designated project "is likely to cause significant adverse environmental effects" (ss 52-54). If not, or if Cabinet determined that such effects were likely but "justified in the circumstances," the project was approved. In contrast to CEAA, however, both CEAA 2012 and the IAA conclude with the issuance of a "decision statement," which sets out the effects determination and binding conditions, including mitigation measures and monitoring. Importantly, the effects determination under CEAA 2012 was simply that: a recitation, including whether such effects were justified in the circumstances; no effort was made to actually justify such determinations (for a critique of this approach, see Martin Olszynski, "Shell Jackpine Mine Expansion Project: The Mysterious

Case of the Missing Justification" (12 December 2013), online: *ABlawg.ca* <https://ablawg
.ca/2013/12/12/shell-jackpine-mine-expansion-project-the-mysterious-case-of-the-missing
-justification>).

The IAA more or less retains CEAA 2012's political decision-making structure but has abandoned the dual concepts of "significance" and "justified in the circumstances" as the bright line
test here. Rather, the test is whether a project is "in the public interest," which takes into
account significant adverse effects but also considers a project's impacts on Indigenous
peoples, its contribution to sustainability, and the implications for Canada's climate change
commitments, all of which must be based on the impact assessment report and set out in
reasons that demonstrate their consideration:

Decision-Making
Minister's decision
60(1) After taking into account the report with respect to the impact assessment of a
designated project that is submitted to the Minister ... the Minister must

(a) determine whether the adverse effects within federal jurisdiction—and the adverse
direct or incidental effects—that are indicated in the report are, in light of the factors
referred to in section 63 and the extent to which those effects are significant, in the public
interest; or

(b) refer to the Governor in Council the matter of whether the effects referred to in
paragraph (a) are, in light of the factors referred to in section 63 and the extent to which
those effects are significant, in the public interest.

Notice posted on Internet site
(2) If the Minister refers the matter to the Governor in Council, he or she must ensure
that a notice of the referral and the reasons for it are posted on the Internet site.

• • •

Governor in Council's determination
62 If the matter is referred to the Governor in Council under paragraph 60(1)(b) or section 61, the Governor in Council must, after taking into account the report with respect to
the impact assessment of the designated project that is the subject of the referral, determine
whether the adverse effects within federal jurisdiction—and the adverse direct or incidental
effects—that are indicated in the report are, in light of the factors referred to in section 63
and the extent to which those effects are significant, in the public interest.

Factors—public interest
63 The Minister's determination under paragraph 60(1)(a) in respect of a designated
project referred to in that subsection, and the Governor in Council's determination under
section 62 in respect of a designated project referred to in that subsection, must be based
on the report with respect to the impact assessment and a consideration of the following
factors:

(a) the extent to which the designated project contributes to sustainability;

(b) the extent to which the adverse effects within federal jurisdiction and the adverse
direct or incidental effects that are indicated in the impact assessment report in respect
of the designated project are significant;

(c) the implementation of the mitigation measures that the Minister or the Governor
in Council, as the case may be, considers appropriate;

(d) the impact that the designated project may have on any Indigenous group and
any adverse impact that the designated project may have on the rights of the Indigenous
peoples of Canada recognized and affirmed by section 35 of the *Constitution Act, 1982*
[being Schedule B to the *Canada Act 1982* (UK), 1982, c 11]; and

(e) the extent to which the effects of the designated project hinder or contribute to
the Government of Canada's ability to meet its environmental obligations and its commitments in respect of climate change.

Conditions—effects within federal jurisdiction

64(1) If the Minister determines under paragraph 60(1)(a), or the Governor in Council determines under section 62, that the effects that are indicated in the report … are in the public interest, the Minister must establish any condition that he or she considers appropriate in relation to the adverse effects within federal jurisdiction with which the proponent of the designated project must comply.

Conditions—direct or incidental effects

(2) If the Minister determines under paragraph 60(1)(a), or the Governor in Council determines under section 62, that the effects that are indicated in the report … are in the public interest, the Minister must establish any condition that he or she considers appropriate—that is directly linked or necessarily incidental to the exercise of a power or performance of a duty or function by a federal authority that would permit a designated project to be carried out, in whole or in part, or to the provision of financial assistance by a federal authority to a person for the purpose of enabling the carrying out, in whole or in part, of that designated project—in relation to the adverse direct or incidental effects with which the proponent of the designated project must comply.

Conditions subject to exercise of power or performance of duty or function

(3) The conditions referred to in subsection (2) take effect only if the federal authority exercises the power or performs the duty or function or provides the financial assistance.

Mitigation measures and follow-up program

(4) The conditions referred to in subsections (1) and (2) must include

(a) the implementation of the mitigation measures that the Minister takes into account in making a determination under paragraph 60(1)(a), or that the Governor in Council takes into account in making a determination under section 62, other than those the implementation of which the Minister is satisfied will be ensured by another person or by a jurisdiction; and

(b) the implementation of a follow-up program and, if the Minister considers it appropriate, an adaptive management plan.

Decision Statement

Decision statement issued to proponent

65(1) The Minister must issue a decision statement to the proponent of a designated project … .

Detailed reasons

(2) The reasons for the determination must demonstrate that the Minister or the Governor in Council, as the case may be, based the determination on the report with respect to the impact assessment of the designated project and considered each of the factors referred to in section 63.

Whether this new requirement to consider the above-noted factors in a transparent way that demonstrates their consideration will have an effect on the types of projects that the federal government approves (that is, nudges the government toward sustainability), or whether such reasons will be first and foremost a communications exercise that seeks to justify any given project decision, is something that all stakeholders and participants will be following in the years ahead.

E. PUBLIC PARTICIPATION

As noted in Section III.A, CEAA 2012 restricted public participation in environmental assessments carried out by the NEB and review panels to "interested parties," which the Act defined as persons who, in the opinion of the NEB or a review panel, were "directly affected by the carrying out of the designated project or [had] relevant information or expertise" (s 2(2)). The term "directly affected" is not defined but commonly found throughout Alberta's environmental legislation and is generally understood as connoting a private legal interest of some kind.

Shaun Fluker and Nitin Kumar Srivastava examined the application of the CEAA 2012 standing test across four projects (the New Prosperity Mine, Shell's Jackpine Mine Expansion, Site C, and Kinder Morgan's Trans Mountain Expansion) and found "inconsistent rulings on public participation" ("Public Participation in Federal Environmental Assessment under the Canadian Environmental Assessment Act 2012: Assessing the Impact of 'Directly Affected'" (2016) 29 J Envtl L & Prac 65).

The IAA does not contain any explicit restrictions on public participation. On the contrary, references to "participate meaningfully" abound in nearly every phase of assessment (see, for example, ss 11, 27, and 33). At the same time, this reference is usually qualified—see, for example, s 27: "The Agency must ensure that the public is provided with an opportunity to participate meaningfully, *in a manner that the Agency considers appropriate, within the time period specified by the Agency,* in the impact assessment of a designated project" (emphasis added).

F. DEALING WITH UNCERTAINTY: FOLLOW-UP PROGRAMS, THE PRECAUTIONARY PRINCIPLE, AND ADAPTIVE MANAGEMENT

Once an assessment is complete and a decision statement is issued, the proponent is required to comply with all relevant conditions, including with respect to monitoring and what CEAA, CEAA 2012, and the IAA all describe as "follow-up programs": "a program for verifying the accuracy of the environmental assessment of a designated project; and determining the effectiveness of any mitigation measures." These were and are required for all designated projects under CEAA 2012 (s 19) and the IAA (s 22), respectively, and their results are supposed to be included in the public CIA Registry (IAA, s 105(2)(e)).

Follow-up programs are necessary because there is often some uncertainty in an impact assessment, whether in predicting adverse effects, their significance, or the effectiveness of mitigation measures. It is in this context of uncertainty that the "precautionary principle" (that is, "[w]here there are threats of serious or irreversible damage, lack of full scientific certainty shall not be used as a reason for postponing cost-effective measures to prevent environmental degradation" [Principle 15 of the *Rio Declaration*]) also becomes relevant. Both CEAA 2012 and the IAA commit the federal government to adhering to the precautionary principle (sections 4 and 6, respectively), as shown below.

CEAA 2012	IAA
Mandate	**Mandate**
4(2) The Government of Canada, the Minister, the Agency, federal authorities and responsible authorities, in the administration of this Act, must exercise their powers in a manner that protects the environment and human health and applies the precautionary principle.	6(2) The Government of Canada, the Minister, the Agency and federal authorities, in the administration of this Act, must exercise their powers in a manner that fosters sustainability, respects the Government's commitments with respect to the rights of the Indigenous peoples of Canada and applies the precautionary principle.

It is also in this context that the concept of "adaptive management" has come to play a prominent role. CEAA explicitly referred to adaptive management in its provisions regarding follow-up programs (s 38(5)) but reference to it was removed in CEAA 2012. Nevertheless, proponents and government agencies continue to invoke it; a 2017 survey of the CEA Registry revealed that 91 percent of the projects listed there contained at least one reference—and usually several—to adaptive management. Most recently, the joint review panel report for Teck's Frontier Oil Sands Project contains 340 references to adaptive management. (See *Report of the*

Joint Review Panel—Teck Resources Limited Frontier Oil Sands Mine Project (25 July 2019), online (pdf): *Canadian Environmental Assessment Agency* <https://www.ceaa-acee.gc.ca/050/documents/p65505/131106E.pdf>.) Unfortunately, while the concept is sound, in the Canadian assessment context, there is often considerable divergence between the theory and actual practice, as the following excerpt demonstrates.

MARTIN OLSZYNSKI, "FAILED EXPERIMENTS: AN EMPIRICAL ASSESSMENT OF ADAPTIVE MANAGEMENT IN ALBERTA'S ENERGY RESOURCES SECTOR"
(2017) 50:3 UBC L Rev 697 [footnotes omitted]

II. BACKGROUND AND CONTEXT

A. ADAPTIVE MANAGEMENT

Most historical accounts of the origins of adaptive management begin with the publication of *Adaptive Environmental Assessment and Management* by Canadian ecologists C.S. Holling and Carl J. Walters in the late 1970s. Since that time, adaptive management has undergone considerable evolution, and it is now commonly applied to a wide variety of resource issues. The unfortunate, and perhaps inevitable, result of this evolution and variety of application is that adaptive management has also become "a highly malleable term. It has been defined and applied in a variety of ways, ranging from highly detailed and rigorous to nearly vacuous."

Nevertheless, most scholars agree on certain core principles: adaptive management is supposed to be a structured or systemic process through "which decisions are made and modified as a result of what is known and learned about the effect of previous decisions." Most scholars also agree that adaptive management should not to be confused or conflated with "trial and error" approaches ... . Current policy guidance from both the U.S. Department of the Interior and the Canadian Environmental Assessment Agency appear to capture the essence of adaptive management adequately. The former defines adaptive management as "a systematic approach for improving resource management by learning from management outcomes." The latter defines the term as "a planned and systematic process for continuously improving Envtl Mgmt practices by learning about their outcomes."

Adaptive management is also generally associated with a six-step cycle (see Figure 1), although the number of steps varies as some steps are combined while others are separated. In their recent article ["Designing Administrative Law for Adaptive Management" (2014) 67:1 Vand L Rev 1] examining the administrative law barriers to the implementation of adaptive management in the U.S., Professors Robin Craig and J.B. Ruhl set out the following basic elements of what they refer to as a "structured, multistep protocol: (1) definition of the problem, (2) determination of goals and objectives for management, (3) determination of the baseline, (4) development of conceptual models, (5) selection of future actions [(1)–(5) constituting Steps 1 and 2 in Figure 1], (6) implementation of management actions, (7) monitoring, and (8) evaluation and return to step (1)" ... .

The Adaptive Management Cycle

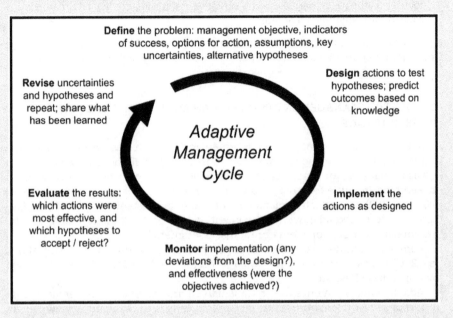

Define the problem: management objective, indicators of success, options for action, assumptions, key uncertainties, alternative hypotheses

Design actions to test hypotheses; predict outcomes based on knowledge

Revise uncertainties and hypotheses and repeat; share what has been learned

Adaptive Management Cycle

Implement the actions as designed

Evaluate the results: which actions were most effective, and which hypotheses to accept / reject?

Monitor implementation (any deviations from the design?), and effectiveness (were the objectives achieved?)

Adaptive management practitioners and scholars distinguish between two kinds of adaptive management: active and passive. As explained by Professor Brad Karkkainen [in "Adaptive Ecosystem Management and Regulatory Penalty Defaults: Toward a Bounded Pragmatism" (2003) 87:4 Minn L Rev 943],

> "Active" adaptive management ... consists of conscious generation and testing of specific scientific hypotheses through narrowly tailored, scientifically designed management experiments. "Passive" adaptive management ... involves heightened monitoring of key indicators and adjustment of policies in response ... while foregoing the conscious experimental hypothesis-testing of the "active" model.

While a detailed discussion about the theory of adaptive management is beyond the scope of this paper, a few additional comments are warranted. First, and perhaps most importantly, adaptive management is not "fail-safe": "no form of adaptive management, no matter how rigorous, can guarantee successful resource protection. ... Adaptive management can help us recognize management mistakes and limit the damage they cause ... . But it does not prevent mistakes, nor does it guarantee that the mistakes we make will be reversible." Second, adaptive management is not a panacea: there are environmental problems for which adaptive management is not suitable. In fact, most U.S. scholars now suggest that it is probably not appropriate for most environmental problems. Ideal conditions for adaptive management have been described as those where the "management-problem context presents a dynamic system for which uncertainty and controllability are high and risk is low." Finally, in order to be effective, adaptive management must be fully and rigorously implemented:

> If the management actions are implemented in a way that strays from the design, if the experimental design does not isolate the signal of interest from background

noise (through spatial/temporal contrasts, replicates and controls), or if monitoring focuses on the wrong variables, scale or frequency, it will be difficult if not impossible to learn anything meaningful.

As will be seen, almost all of the actual and proposed applications of adaptive management considered in this paper do not reflect any of these limitations.

• • •

C. ADAPTIVE MANAGEMENT IN CANADIAN ENVIRONMENTAL LAW JURISPRUDENCE

Although references to adaptive management in Canadian environmental law jurisprudence and scholarship predate 2008, most Canadian scholars would agree that it was in that year, and specifically with the release of the Federal Court's decision in *Pembina Institute for Appropriate Development v Canada (Attorney General)* [2008 FC 302], that adaptive management made its substantive debut. Tremblay-Lamer J. described adaptive management as one of the "guiding tenets" in the interpretation of Canadian environmental assessment law.

Pembina Institute involved a challenge by several environmental organizations to a 2007 report by the Joint Review Panel on the Kearl Oil Sands Project proposed by Imperial Oil Resources. ...

Adaptive management's role in Canadian environmental assessment law arose in response to the environmental groups' challenges to the Joint Review Panel's treatment of end-pit lakes and peatland restoration. The Court in *Pembina Institute* described adaptive management as countering "the potentially paralyzing effects of the precautionary principle" by "permit[ting] projects with uncertain, yet potentially adverse environmental impacts to proceed based on flexible management strategies capable of adjusting to new information regarding adverse environmental impacts where sufficient information regarding those impacts and potential mitigation measures already exists." Applying this approach to the Joint Review Panel's treatment of end-pit lakes ... the Court accepted that there was "some uncertainty with respect to end-pit lake technology," but it was not such that it should "paralyze the entire project." With respect to peatlands, the restoration of which the applicants argued was "not even known in general terms," the Court held that "while uncertainties ... remained, they could be addressed through adaptive management given the existence of generally known replacement measures contained in Imperial Oil's mine closure plan."

The *Pembina Institute* decision was quickly and widely criticized. Professor Arlene Kwasniak [in "Use and Abuse of Adaptive Management in Environmental Assessment Law and Practice: A Canadian Example and General Lessons" (2010) 12:4 J Environmental Assessment Policy & Management 425] argued that the Court's approach "[ran] contrary to the CEAA [1992] for numerous reasons," including the explicit and relatively minor role for adaptive management envisioned by the legislation at that time. Professor Nathalie Chalifour [in "Case Comment: A (Pre)Cautionary Tale About the Kearl Decision: The Significance of Pembina Institute for Appropriate Development et al. v. Canada (Attorney-General) for the Future of Environmental Assessment" (2009) 5:2 JSDLP 251] pointed out that the Court's approach rendered "virtually meaningless" the statutory requirement that, to be considered, mitigation measures must be "technically and economically feasible." She also expressed doubts about its consistency with the statutory requirement to apply the precautionary principle: "A precautionary approach would place the onus on Imperial Oil to demonstrate that the reclamation technology relating to end pit lakes and peatlands was sufficient to ensure that they would not cause serious environmental impacts." Reflecting on the absence of any detailed discussion surrounding the proposed application of adaptive management by the panel (e.g., objectives, indicators, alternative actions, monitoring plans), this author suggested that in such instances there would be "little to no basis for concluding that the uncertainty associated with proposed mitigation measures will actually be reduced, let alone that these measures will prove effective."

Anecdotally, at least, these concerns appear to have been well-founded. The reclamation of peatlands in the oil sands context is a good example. Five years after the *Pembina Institute* decision, this issue was revisited by the Joint Review Panel for Shell Canada's ("Shell") proposed expansion of the Jackpine Oil Sands Project ... . This time around, adaptive management was discussed in the context of air quality, climate change considerations, end-pit lake remediation, surface water quality, and the loss of fish habitat. However, Shell "acknowledged that peatlands cannot be reclaimed." Consequently, the Joint Review Panel concluded that their loss (approximately 8,500 football fields worth) was a significant adverse environmental effect. Not surprisingly, environmental groups at the Jackpine Mine Expansion Project hearings argued against adaptive management generally, suggesting that it "has proven to be a failure." The Athabasca Chipewyan First Nation also expressed its frustration that adaptive management "is often no more than a general commitment to do something if it becomes necessary." ...

Since (and arguably because of) *Pembina Institute*, reliance on adaptive management has only increased. ... In *Greenpeace Canada v Canada (Attorney General)*, government respondents argued that Canadian courts "have endorsed 'adaptive management' as a necessary counterbalance [to the precautionary principle] to ensure that socially and economically desirable projects can come to fruition." Thus, there appears to have emerged a *quasi*-common law that fails to reflect any of the principles and limitations of genuine adaptive management, i.e., that it is not fail-safe, that it is not a panacea, and that it must be rigorously implemented.

• • •

VI. CONCLUSION

The results in this paper confirm that adaptive management, as applied in Alberta's energy resources sector, is suffering from most, if not all, of the shortcomings currently identified in the literature. At the environmental assessment stage, adaptive management has erroneously been cast as a routine and fail-safe strategy that will ensure the effective mitigation of any and all adverse environmental effects. Virtually no attention is being paid to experimental design (i.e., the selection of objectives, indicators, uncertainties and hypotheses), nor is consideration given as to whether adaptive management is even an appropriate response to the problem for which it is being proposed. At the approval stage, there appears to be a significant gap in terms of the number and kinds of issues for which adaptive management is being required compared to those for which it has been proposed. Where it is required, as approval terms are generally vague and ambiguous; none require the preparation of a detailed adaptive management plan. Finally, at the reporting stage, implementation is generally poor: It was non-existent for the oil sands mines considered here. Coalmines and *in situ* developments demonstrated some compliance and implementation but were beset by deficiencies, including vague and unenforceable triggers ... .

QUESTIONS

1. What, in your view, is the proper relationship between the precautionary principle and adaptive management? What about the impact assessment process more generally? Consider the following recent passage by Phelan J in *Taseko Mines Limited v Canada (Environment)*, 2017 FC 1099:

> [123] It was reasonable for the Panel not to accept Taseko's "vague assurances" that it would engage in adaptive management in order to deal with adverse environmental effects. The Panel sought information on environmental effects and mitigation measures, and Taseko refused to provide this information. It was entirely reasonable, and in line with the Panel's (reasonable) interpretation of the precautionary principle, for the Panel to conclude that the concentration of water quality variables in Fish Lake (Teztan Biny) and Wasp Lake would likely be a significant adverse environmental effect.
>
> [124] Indeed, acceptance of vague adaptive management schemes in circumstances such as these would, in my view, tend to call into question the value of the entire review panel process—if all such decisions could be left to a later stage, then the review panel process would simply be for the sake of appearances.

2. Adaptive management has been reintroduced in s 64(4)(b) of the IAA (contents of a decision statement), with the addition of the word "plan": "The conditions referred to in subsections (1) and (2) must include ... (b) the implementation of a follow-up program and, if the Minister considers it appropriate, *an adaptive management plan*" (emphasis added). What effect, if any, would you expect this reintroduction—in this modified form—to have on the practice of adaptive management in the Canadian impact assessment context?

3. In addition to the reintroduction of the term "adaptive management," the IAA also contains provisions authorizing the minister to modify the conditions of a decision statement (ss 68 and 69), subject to the limitation that such modification cannot increase the adverseness of any impacts. Why do you think such provisions were added?

IV. LEGAL ISSUES IN FEDERAL IMPACT ASSESSMENT

There are numerous issues that lawyers involved in impact assessment are bound to encounter. This section considers three such issues: constitutional issues, administrative law issues, and Indigenous law issues.

A. CONSTITUTIONAL ISSUES

As reflected in various parts of this chapter (for example, project scoping under CEAA, in Section II.B.2, and the definition of "environmental effects" under CEAA 2012 and the IAA, in Section III.C.3), constitutional concerns have always been a fixture of Canadian environmental assessment law. While the provinces have traditionally been viewed as having primary jurisdiction over resource development, nearly three decades have passed since the Supreme Court first confirmed Parliament's ability to enact an assessment law. Nevertheless, with the passage of Bill C-69, several provinces are once again asserting their primacy in the natural resources context. The following excerpt begins by setting out one such assertion of provincial primacy. It then summarizes the relevant jurisprudence and constitutional principles that have evolved over the past 30 years and concludes by applying them to the IAA.

MARTIN OLSZYNSKI & NIGEL BANKES, "SETTING THE RECORD STRAIGHT ON FEDERAL AND PROVINCIAL JURISDICTION OVER THE ENVIRONMENTAL ASSESSMENT OF RESOURCE PROJECTS IN THE PROVINCES"

(24 May 2019), online (pdf): *ABlawg.ca* <http://ablawg.ca/wp-content/uploads/2019/05/Blog_MO_NB_BillC69.pdf>

Alberta's new premier has recently threatened to sue the federal government over Bill C-69, the Liberal government's attempt to restore some credibility to Canada's environmental assessment regime. More specifically, Premier Kenney has recently been asserting that section 92A of the *Constitution Act, [1867]*, which gives the provinces jurisdiction over the development of non-renewable natural resources, precludes the federal government from assessing what the Premier describes as "provincial projects": "[Bill C-69] gives a new federal agency the power to regulate provincial projects, such as *in situ* oil sands developments and petrochemical refineries, which are entirely within a province's borders and already subject to provincial regulation. It disregards a landmark Supreme Court ruling on jurisdiction and the balance between federal and provincial powers spelled out in the Constitution—including section 92A[,] in which provinces have exclusive authority over non-renewable resource projects." In making these comments, the Premier contradicts almost three decades of settled jurisprudence with respect to the federal and provincial division of powers over the environment generally, and federal jurisdiction to conduct environmental assessments specifically.

• • •

Indeed, the Supreme Court of Canada has already decided this issue in favor of the federal government—not once but twice. The first time was in *Friends of the Oldman River Society v Canada* ... , alluded to by the Premier in the excerpt introducing this post. That decision, from 1992, involved the then–controversial Oldman River dam and Canada's first federal environmental assessment regime, [*EARPGO*] ... :

> What is not particularly helpful in sorting out the respective levels of constitutional authority over a work such as the Oldman River dam, however, is the characterization of it as a "provincial project" or an undertaking "primarily subject to provincial regulation" as the appellant Alberta sought to do. That begs the question and posits an erroneous principle that seems to hold that there exists a general doctrine of interjurisdictional immunity to shield provincial works or undertakings from otherwise valid federal legislation. ...
>
> What is important is to determine whether either level of government may legislate. One may legislate in regard to provincial aspects, the other federal aspects. Although local projects will generally fall within provincial responsibility, federal participation will be required if the project impinges on an area of federal jurisdiction as is the case here. ...
>
> In essence, then, the [*EARPGO*] has two fundamental aspects. First, there is the substance of the [*EARPGO*] dealing with environmental impact assessment to facilitate decision-making under the federal head of power through which a proposal is regulated. As I mentioned earlier, this aspect of the [*EARPGO*] can be

sustained on the basis that it is legislation in relation to the relevant subject matters enumerated in s. 91 of the *Constitution Act, 1867.* The second aspect of the legislation is its procedural or organizational element that coordinates the process of assessment, which can in any given case touch upon several areas of federal responsibility, under the auspices of a designated decision maker, or in the vernacular of the [*EARPGO*], the "initiating department." This facet of the legislation has as its object the regulation of the institutions and agencies of the Government of Canada as to the manner in which they perform their administrative functions and duties. This, in my view, is unquestionably *intra vires* Parliament. It may be viewed either as an adjunct of the particular legislative powers involved, or, in any event, be justifiable under the residuary power in s. 91. (at 68-69, 73-74, emphasis [omitted]) [Ellipses in original article.]

Thus, environmental assessment is to be understood first and foremost as a process for decision-making—one that both federal and provincial governments may deploy when exercising their respective authorities over resource projects. Two years later, in *Quebec (Attorney General) v Canada (National Energy Board)* 1994 CanLII 113 (SCC), the Supreme Court recognized that while the existence of regimes at both levels of government may result in overlapping assessments, this was "neither unusual [n]or unworkable":

If in applying [the *National Energy Board Act,* whose application triggered an environmental assessment pursuant to the [*EARPGO*] in this case], the [National Energy] Board finds environmental effects within a province relevant to its decision to grant an export licence, a matter of federal jurisdiction, it is entitled to consider those effects. So too may the province have, within its proper contemplation, the environmental effects of the provincially regulated aspects of such a project. This co-existence of responsibility is neither unusual nor unworkable ... [the Court went on to cite the provisions in the [*EARPGO*] for harmonizing assessments between both levels of government]. (at 193) [Interpolation in original.]

Shortly thereafter, in 1995, [*CEAA*] was brought into force. For our purposes here, it is sufficient to note that *CEAA* was broader in both scope and application than [*EARPGO*] at issue in Oldman River insofar as it was triggered by federal decision-making generally. ...

Like [*EARPGO*], *CEAA* ... was also eventually challenged, this time by Quebec. In *Quebec (Attorney General) v Moses,* 2010 SCC 17 (CanLII), the Supreme Court was first and foremost concerned with the potential conflict between *CEAA* and the *James Bay and Northern Quebec Agreement.* Quebec intervened early in the proceedings, however, resulting in the certification of a constitutional question regarding the applicability of *CEAA* ... and its regulations to a proposed vanadium mine, construction and operation of which was expected to impact fish and fish habitat .... While recognizing that such projects fall within provincial jurisdiction under section 92A, the Court [reiterated the applicability of the "double aspects" doctrine in this context]:

There is no doubt that a vanadium mining project, considered in isolation, falls within provincial jurisdiction under s. 92A of the *Constitution Act, 1867* over natural resources. There is also no doubt that ordinarily a mining project anywhere in Canada that puts at risk fish habitat could not proceed without a permit from the federal Fisheries Minister, which he or she could not issue except after compliance with the *CEAA.* The mining of non-renewable mineral resources aspect falls within provincial jurisdiction, but the fisheries aspect is federal. (at para 36)

Critical to understanding the constitutional significance of *Moses* is that the Supreme Court had just rendered its only other *CEAA*-related decision a few months earlier. The main issue in *Miningwatch* [sic] *Canada* ... was whether the federal government could restrict the scope of the projects that required assessment to those aspects that required federal approval (e.g. the destruction of a creek requiring *Fisheries Act* approval rather than the construction of an oil sands mine)—an approach that was often justified on constitutional grounds (see e.g. *Prairie Acid Rain Coalition* ...). The Supreme Court held that the project subject to assessment was the project *as proposed by a proponent*, not as scoped by federal departments. Combining these two decisions, there appears to be no constitutional barrier preventing the federal government from assessing resource projects—in their entirety— on the basis that they may have impacts on areas of federal jurisdiction, such as fisheries, navigation, migratory birds, and transboundary effects ... .

To summarize, jurisdiction over the environment is shared between the federal and provincial governments. This sharing results in some "overlap" (*Friends of the Oldman River, supra*), which is neither "unusual nor unworkable" (*Quebec (Attorney General) v Canada (National Energy Board, supra*). Although structured somewhat differently, in both instances where the federal environmental assessment regime has been challenged ([*EARPGO*] and *CEAA* ...), the federal government has prevailed. As further set out below, it is also likely to prevail in any challenge to Bill C-69.

• • •

The *Impact Assessment Act* (*IAA*) is found in Part 1 of Bill C-69. If passed, it will be the fourth environmental assessment regime to be implemented at the federal level in as many decades. This is because ... the *IAA* is a response to the previous Conservative government's 2012 omnibus budget bills, which among other things repealed the original *CEAA* (Canada's second regime) and replaced it with the current [*CEAA, 2012*] (the third regime). We focus our analysis on *CEAA, 2012* because, from a constitutional perspective and despite so much rhetoric, the *IAA* is structured identically.

The most important difference between *CEAA* ... and *CEAA, 2012* is that while the former was triggered by federal decision-making ... *CEAA, 2012* is first triggered on the basis of a "major project" list contained in a regulation ... . A second difference is that *CEAA, 2012* process ends with its own "decision-statement" (i.e. certificate) setting out whether a project is approved and, if so, any applicable terms and conditions, whereas the original *CEAA*, being an adjunct to other federal regimes (e.g. the *Fisheries Act*, the *National Energy Board Act*), relied on those regimes for implementation.

Were this to be it, we acknowledge that there might be some uncertainty as to the constitutionality of the *CEAA, 2012* regime [and with it, the *IAA*]. At the very least, considerable care would have to be taken in drafting the project list to ensure that the projects contained there had a reasonable likelihood of impacting areas of federal jurisdiction. Critically, with the exception of projects regulated by the National Energy Board and the Canadian Nuclear Safety Commission (where federal jurisdiction is obvious), the presence of a project on the list *does not automatically* mean that an assessment will be required. Pursuant to section 10, the Canadian Environmental Assessment Agency must then make a decision (referred to as a screening decision) as to whether to require an assessment, taking into account several factors, including "the possibility that the carrying out of the designated project may cause adverse environmental effects" (para 10(1)(b)). Pursuant to subsection 5(1)," ... environmental effects" are defined as [see the definition of environmental effects in Section III.C.3]. ... Simply put, a key consideration in the screening decision is whether the project is *in fact* likely to have adverse effects on matters falling within federal jurisdiction.

In our view, this screening decision secures both *CEAA, 2012*'s and the *IAA*'s constitutionality (for the *IAA*, see section 16 and related definitions). Such a step is necessary because while in practice most projects on the project list will also require some kind of federal approval or authorization, and this would be sufficient to render the regime's application to such projects constitutional (as in *Moses ...* , *supra*), strictly speaking that is not necessary to trigger the Act's application. In such instances, the screening decision secures Parliament's jurisdiction. Viewed this way, *CEAA, 2012* is not merely an adjunct like its predecessors; it is more of a hybrid, having both procedural elements but also a substantive one for "protect[ing] the components of the environment that are within the legislative authority of Parliament from signifi-cant adverse environmental effects caused by a designated project" (*CEAA, 2012* at para 4(1)(a)). Like [*EARPGO*], then, it can be upheld by reference to those various subject matters enumerated in s. 91 of the *Constitution Act, 1867.* Where federal approvals are necessary, the Act recognizes the government's jurisdiction to consider the effects of its own decisions, although this is limited to those that are "directly linked or necessarily incidental" to the issuance of such approvals.

Although the scope of assessment under the *IAA* will be broader than the *CEAA, 2012*, in that it explicitly contemplates not just environmental effects but also social, economic, and health effects, like environmental effects these are all tethered back to those that fall within Parliament's legislative authority or which can be considered directly linked or necessarily incidental to the exercise of a federal power or function (*IAA* at section 2). In our view, the *CEAA, 2012* and *IAA* regimes are actually more timid, constitutionally, than the original *CEAA* as interpreted by the Supreme Court of Canada in *Miningwatch* [*sic*] *Canada, supra*.

QUESTIONS

In *Friends of the Oldman River Society*, La Forest J expressed incredulity at the idea that the EARPGO "would be invoked every time there is some potential environmental effect on a mat-ter of federal jurisdiction." Is this a problem for CEAA 2012 and the IAA? Why or why not?

B. ADMINISTRATIVE LAW ISSUES

For the vast majority of cases, legal challenges to assessments are by way of judicial review (see Chapter 14 for an overview of the relevant judicial review principles generally). In the environmental assessment context, recent administrative law issues have revolved around the reviewability (or not) of assessment reports and Canadian courts' approach to the substantive analysis contained therein (including determinations with respect to significance, mitigation, and the adequacy of assessments). As will be seen, Canadian courts have been reluctant to scrutinize the science of assessment, applying a relatively lax form of reasonableness review out of an apparent and arguably exaggerated fear of becoming "an academy of science" (*Van-couver Island Peace Society v Canada*, [1992] 3 FC 42 at 51 (TD)).

1. Legal Status of Assessments and Their Reviewability

The issue of the legal status of assessments and their reviewability was widely considered settled until the Federal Court of Appeal's recent decisions in *Gitxaala Nation v Canada*, 2016 FCA 187 (the litigation surrounding the since-abandoned Northern Gateway project) and

Tsleil-Waututh Nation. The first case excerpted below, *Alberta Wilderness Assn v Canada (Minister of Fisheries and Oceans)*, 1998 CanLII 9122, [1999] 1 FC 483 (CA), reflects what was previously the consensus view that environmental assessment reports were directly reviewable (that is, could be challenged in court) as prerequisites to subsequent decision-making. The second case is the relevant excerpt from *Tsleil-Waututh Nation* wherein the court held that the NEB's environmental assessment was *not* directly reviewable but, rather, that it was the governor in council's decision to accept that report as conforming with the relevant legislation that was reviewable on a standard of reasonableness. It is not currently clear, however, whether this decision is restricted to the specialized regime for NEB assessments under CEAA 2012 or whether it may be applied more broadly in subsequent litigation. While such an approach seems unnecessarily convoluted, the difference between the two approaches may be more academic than practical. The real difficulty lies in the uncertain and uneven application of the reasonableness standard in this context. In *Tsleil-Waututh Nation*, reasonableness review required over 200 paragraphs. In *Gitxaala*, on the other hand, it took just one stunningly brief one. The application of the reasonableness standard in the assessment context is considered in Section IV.B.3.

ALBERTA WILDERNESS ASSN V CANADA (MINISTER OF FISHERIES AND OCEANS)
[1999] 1 FC 483, 1998 CanLII 9122 (CA)

The view that the panel report is an essential statutory prerequisite to the issuance of approvals is supported by previous case law. I agree with the decisions of *Bowen v. Canada (Attorney General)*, 1997 CanLII 6383 (FC), [1998] 2 F.C. 395 (T.D.); *Friends of the West Country, ...* [*Friends of the West Country Assn v Canada (Minister of Fisheries & Oceans)*, [1998] 4 FC 340, 1998 CanLII 7113 (TD)]; and *Union of Nova Scotia Indians v. Canada (Attorney General)*, 1996 CanLII 3847 (FC), [1997] 1 F.C. 325 (T.D.) which hold that an environmental assessment carried out in accordance with the Act is required before a decision such as the Minister's authorization in the present case can be issued. This view is reinforced by the decision in *Friends of the Oldman River Society v. Canada (Minister of Transport)*, 1992 CanLII 110 (SCC), [1992] 1 S.C.R. 3 which confirmed that the guidelines that were a pre-cursor to CEAA (the *Environmental Assessment and Review Process Guidelines Order*, SOR/84-467) were mandatory rather than directory in nature and, thus, failure to comply with them would deny the responsible authority the jurisdiction to proceed.

The requirements of CEAA are legislated directions that are explicit in mandating the necessity of an environmental assessment as a prerequisite to ministerial action. It is clear that the Minister has no jurisdiction to issue authorizations in the absence of an environmental assessment. It is equally clear that any assessment must be conducted in accordance with the Act, including for example, the requirement imposed under section 16 of CEAA. The fact that a federal response has been issued and remains unchallenged does not change these requirements. Thus, the appellants are entitled to argue the merits of their case.

The appellants are entitled to seek prohibition against the Minister on the basis that the panel report is materially deficient. The fact that the federal response was not challenged is irrelevant to the appellants' claim. In my view, the federal response does not supersede the panel report, nor can it, as the respondents suggest, potentially cure any deficiencies in the panel report. The two are separate statutory steps with distinct purposes and functions.

Section 37 of CEAA dictates that the Minister must consider the panel report before embarking on a course of action. Subparagraph 34(c)(i) establishes that this report must set out the "rationale, conclusions and recommendations of the panel relating to the environmental assessment of the project." Paragraph 34(d) makes it clear that it is this report that contains the results of the environmental assessment that must be submitted to the Minister. Finally, subsection 2(1) defines "environmental assessment" as "an assessment of the environmental effects of the project that is conducted in accordance with this Act." Thus the report that must be submitted to the Minister pursuant to paragraph 34(d) must contain, pursuant to subparagraph 34(c)(i) and subsection 2(1), the results of an environmental assessment conducted in compliance with the requirements of CEAA.

In sum, the combined effect of paragraphs 34(c), (d), subsection 2(1) and section 37 is that before taking a course of action, the Minister must consider an environmental assessment, that was conducted in accordance with the Act. Therefore, the appellants are entitled to bring into question the report and are not barred from doing so because they did not challenge the federal response.

TSLEIL-WAUTUTH NATION V CANADA (ATTORNEY GENERAL)
2018 FCA 153 at paras 185-201

(C) THE JURISPRUDENCE WHICH REVIEWED ENVIRONMENTAL ASSESSMENT REPORTS

[185] The City of Vancouver also points to jurisprudence in which environmental assessment reports prepared by joint review panels were judicially reviewed, and argues that this Court erred by failing to deal with this jurisprudence. The authorities relied upon by Vancouver are: *Alberta Wilderness Assn. v. Cardinal River Coals Ltd.*, [1999] 3 F.C. 425, 15 Admin. L.R. (3d) 25 (F.C.); *Friends of the West Country Assn. v. Canada (Minister of Fisheries and Oceans)*, [2000] 2 F.C.R. 263, (1999), 169 F.T.R. 298 (C.A.); *Pembina Institute for Appropriate Development v. Canada (Attorney General)*, 2008 FC 302, 80 Admin. L.R. (4th) 74; *Grand Riverkeeper, Labrador Inc. v. Canada (Attorney General)*, 2012 FC 1520, 422 F.T.R. 299; and, *Greenpeace Canada v. Canada (Attorney General)*, 2014 FC 463, 455 F.T.R. 1, rev'd on appeal, 2015 FCA 186, 475 N.R. 247.

[186] All of these authorities predate *Gitxaala*. They do not deal with the "complete code" of legislation that was before the Court in *Gitxaala*. But, more importantly, in none of these decisions was the availability of judicial review put in issue—this availability was assumed. In *Gitxaala* the Court reviewed the legislative scheme and explained why the report of the Joint Review Panel was not justiciable. The Court did not err by failing to refer to case law that had not considered this issue.

(D) THE REFERENCE TO INAPPLICABLE PROVISIONS OF THE CANADIAN ENVIRONMENTAL ASSESSMENT ACT, 2012

[187] The City of Vancouver also argues that *Gitxaala* is distinguishable because it dealt with section 38 of the *Canadian Environmental Assessment Act, 2012*, a provision that has no application to the process at issue here. The City also notes that *Gitxaala*, at paragraph 124, referred to sections 30 and 31 of the *Canadian*

Environmental Assessment Act, 2012. These sections are said not to apply to the Joint Review Panel at issue in *Gitxaala*.

• • •

[189] It followed that sections 29 through 31 of the *Canadian Environmental Assessment Act, 2012* did not apply to the Northern Gateway project, and ought not to have been referenced by the Court in *Gitxaala* in its analysis of the legislative scheme.

[190] This said, the question that arises is whether these references were material to the Court's analysis. To assess the materiality, if any, of this error I begin by reviewing the content of the provisions said to be erroneously referred to in *Gitxaala*.

[191] Section 29 of the *Canadian Environmental Assessment Act, 2012*, discussed above at paragraph 62, requires a responsible authority to ensure that its environmental assessment report sets out its recommendation to the Governor in Council concerning the decision the Governor in Council must make under paragraph 31(1)(a) of the *Canadian Environmental Assessment Act, 2012*. Section 30 allows the Governor in Council to refer any recommendation made by a responsible authority back to the responsible authority for reconsideration. Section 31 sets out the options available to the Governor in Council after it receives a report from a responsible authority. Paragraph 31(1)(a), discussed at paragraph 67 above, sets out the three choices available to the Governor in Council with respect to its assessment of the likelihood that a project will cause significant adverse environmental effects and, if so, whether such effects can be justified.

[192] These provisions, without doubt, do apply to the Project at issue in these proceedings. Therefore, the Project is to be assessed under the legislative scheme analyzed in *Gitxaala*. It follows that *Gitxaala* cannot be meaningfully distinguished.

• • •

[196] It follows that the analysis in *Gitxaala* was based upon a proper understanding of the legislative scheme, notwithstanding the Court's reference to sections 29 and 31 of the *Canadian Environmental Assessment Act, 2012* instead of the applicable provisions.

[197] Put another way, the error was in no way material to the Court's analysis of the respective roles of the Joint Review Panel, which prepared the report to [*sic*] the Governor in Council, and the Governor in Council, which received the panel's recommendations and made the decisions required under the legislative scheme.

• • •

(E) GITXAALA THWARTS REVIEW OF THE DECISION OF THE NATIONAL ENERGY BOARD

[200] Finally, Vancouver argues that subsection 54(1) of the *National Energy Board Act* and 31(1) of the *Canadian Environmental Assessment Act, 2012* both make the Board's report a prerequisite to the decision of the Governor in Council. As the Governor in Council is not an adjudicative body, meaningful review must come in the form of judicial review of the report of the Board. The decision in *Gitxaala* thwarts such review.

[201] I respectfully disagree. As this Court noted in *Gitxaala* at paragraph 125, the Governor in Council is required to consider any deficiency in the report submitted to it. The decision of the Governor in Council is then subject to review by this Court under section 55 of the *National Energy Board Act*. The Court must be satisfied that the decision of the Governor in Council is lawful, reasonable and constitutionally

valid. If the decision of the Governor in Council is based upon a materially flawed report the decision may be set aside on that basis. Put another way, under the legislation the Governor in Council can act only if it has a "report" before it; a materially deficient report, such as one that falls short of legislative standards, is not such a report. In this context the Board's report may be reviewed to ensure that it was a "report" that the Governor in Council could rely upon. The report is not immune from review by this Court and the Supreme Court.

Although the IAA regime is different from that of CEAA and CEAA 2012 in some respects, an "impact assessment" is similarly defined in s 2 of the IAA as "an assessment ... that is conducted *in accordance with this Act*" (emphasis added) and is similarly a prerequisite to subsequent government decision-making, including not only by the minister (s 60) and the governor in council (s 62) but also by other federal authorities who are *prohibited* from exercising any power or duty under any other Act that could permit a project to be carried out in whole or in part unless an impact assessment has been determined not to be required or a decision statement has been issued (see s 8). Viewed this way—as a constraint on government decision-making—it seems untenable to suggest that Parliament intended those very decision-makers, rather than the courts, to be the arbiters of whether a given assessment conforms to the requirements of the legislation. It should also be noted that the Senate Committee on Energy, Environment, and Resources proposed several privative clauses during its review of Bill C-69 (see "Report of the Committee" (28 May 2019) (Chair: Rosa Galvez), online: *Senate of Canada* <https://sencanada .ca/en/committees/report/74834/42-1>), but they all were ultimately rejected by Parliament.

2. Significance and Mitigation

The primary test under CEAA and CEAA 2012 was whether a project was likely to result in significant adverse environmental effects. Although this test's prominence has been reduced under the IAA to one of five factors that inform the government's "public interest" determination (alongside sustainability and climate change commitments, per s 63), it is still likely to carry considerable weight in framing the desirability, or not, of a project and, therefore, to generate litigation. The following excerpt sets out Canadian courts' general approach to the issue of significance and the related concept of mitigation under CEAA and CEAA 2012. Whether or not this approach, which can be described as somewhat subjective, will be carried over to the IAA or replaced with a more objective test remains to be seen. The addition of "principles of scientific integrity" (s 6(3), further discussed below) and the foundational jurisprudence (for example, *Friends of the Oldman River Society*) point toward a more objective test.

PEMBINA INSTITUTE FOR APPROPRIATE DEVELOPMENT V CANADA (ATTORNEY GENERAL)
2008 FC 302

[22] With respect to assessing the significance of environmental effects, the jurisprudence reveals that this assessment is not a wholly objective exercise but rather contains "a large measure of opinion and judgement." The Federal Court of Appeal has asserted that "[r]easonable people can and do disagree about the adequacy and completeness of evidence which forecasts future results and about the significance of such results [...]" (*Alberta Wilderness Assn. v. Express Pipelines Ltd.*, 1996 CanLII 12470 (FCA), [1996] F.C.J. No. 1016 (QL), at para. 10). [Ellipses in original.]

• • •

[24] Similarly, it is evident that the assessment of environmental effects, including mitigation measures, is not to be conceptualized as a single, discrete event. Instructively, in *Union of Nova Scotia Indians v. Canada (Attorney General)*, 1996 CanLII 3847 (FC), [1997] 1 F.C. 325, [1996] F.C.J. No. 1373 (QL), Mackay J. indicated, at para. 32 that he was not persuaded that the CEAA requires that all the details of mitigating measures be resolved before the acceptance of a screening report. He further asserted that the nature of the process of assessment was "ongoing and dynamic" with continuing dialogue between the proponent, the responsible authorities and interested community groups.

[25] Moreover, jurisprudence relating to the EARPGO is also instructive as to the content of the legal duty to consider mitigation measures. In *Tetzlaff v. Canada (Minister of the Environment (F.C.A.)*, [1991] 1 F.C. 641, at p. 657, Iacobucci C.J.A. described the assessment of mitigation measures in s. 12(c) of the EARPGO in the following terms: "If the initial assessment procedure reveals that the potentially adverse environmental effects that may be caused by the proposal "are insignificant or mitigable with known technologies" the proposal [...] may proceed or proceed with mitigation, as the case may be." [Ellipses in original.] In the case of *Canadian Wildlife Federation Inc. v. Canada (Minister of the Environment)* (1990), 31 F.T.R. 1, at p. 12, the decision which was upheld by the Court in *Tetzlaff*, Muldoon J. analysed s. 12(c) of the EARPGO and asserted that "since the Minister did not identify any known technologies but only vague hopes for future technology, it is not possible to consider that the recited adverse water quality effects are mitigable." Thus, in the context of a panel assessment, the possibilities of future research and development do not constitute mitigation measures.

[26] I note also that s. 16(1)(d) of the CEAA ..., the provision mandating consideration of mitigation measures, adds the proviso that mitigation measures must be technically *and economically* feasible as opposed to solely technically feasible ("known technologies" in the wording of the EARPGO). This second condition, in effect, imposes an additional requirement for measures to be classified as mitigating under the CEAA: under the current Act mitigation measures must also be economically feasible in order to qualify as such.

QUESTIONS

The passage from *Alberta Wilderness Assn v Express Pipelines Ltd* cited with approval in *Pembina Institute* is somewhat at odds with *Friends of the Oldman River Society*, which held that the assessment phase is intended to provide "an objective basis" for decision-making. Consider also these subsequent passages from *Pembina Institute*, written with a view toward panel reviews but applicable to all assessments:

[73] ... [G]iven that the Report is to serve as an objective basis for a final decision, the Panel must, in my opinion, explain in a general way why the potential environmental effects, either with or without the implementation of mitigation measures, will be insignificant.

[74] ... The assessment of the environmental effects of a project and of the proposed mitigation measures occur outside the realm of government policy debate, which by its very nature must take into account a wide array of viewpoints and additional factors that are necessarily excluded by the Panel's focus on project related environmental impacts. ...

What is the most appropriate approach to significance, in your view?

3. Adequacy and Completeness of Assessments

In addition to determinations with respect to significance and mitigation, parties have also challenged the adequacy and completeness of assessments. In part, this can be understood as a desire for those authoring assessment reports to "show their math," without which it can be difficult to evaluate whether determinations with respect to significance and mitigation are accurate or even simply reasonable. This issue will undoubtedly arise in relation to some of the new factors that an impact assessment must consider, including a project's contribution to sustainability and whether or not it furthers or hinders Canada's climate change commitments. The agency has already prepared some interim guidance on these two matters (see "Further Readings" at the end of this chapter). The following excerpt exemplifies the Canadian judiciary's current formalistic and highly deferential approach to adequacy and completeness.

ONTARIO POWER GENERATION INC V GREENPEACE CANADA
2015 FCA 186

[In the fall of 2006, Ontario Power Generation applied to the CNSC for a site preparation licence for several new reactors at its existing Darlington nuclear plant in Bowmanville, Ontario. Application for this licence, as well as for authorizations under the federal *Fisheries Act* and the then *Navigable Waters Protection Act*, triggered the application of the then applicable CEAA. The project was referred to a joint review panel in 2008. Following 284 information requests (IRs) and 17 days of hearings in the spring of 2011, the panel submitted its final report to the minister in August of that same year, concluding that the project was not likely to result in significant adverse environmental effects. The applicants challenged the adequacy of the environmental assessment (EA) shortly thereafter. At trial (in *Greenpeace Canada v Canada (Attorney General)*, 2014 FC 463), Russell J found gaps in the panel's assessment (specifically with respect to hazardous substance emissions [HSEs], spent nuclear fuel, and a failure to consider the effects of a severe "common cause" accident) that in his view were unreasonable in light of the purpose and scheme of the Act. The majority of the Federal Court of Appeal, on the other hand, endorsed a formal approach to judicial review in this context, as set our below.]

V. STANDARD OF REVIEW

[120] Since the decision of the Supreme Court of Canada in *Dunsmuir v. New Brunswick*, 2008 SCC 9, [2008] 1 S.C.R. 190 [*Dunsmuir*], there are only two standards of review: correctness and reasonableness. When a question is reviewed on the correctness standard, the reviewing court is free to substitute its judgment on the question for that of the tribunal whose decision with respect to that question is under review. When the question is reviewed on the reasonableness standard, the reviewing court may not intervene by simply substituting its opinion for that of the tribunal. Rather, the reviewing court can only intervene if the decision is not reasonable.

• • •

VI. DISCUSSION

A. DID THE JUDGE SELECT THE CORRECT STANDARD OF REVIEW?

[122] The Judge selected reasonableness as the standard of review with respect to the question of whether the Panel considered or failed to consider the environmental effects of HSEs from the Project and their significance, as required by

paragraphs 16(1)(a) and (b) of the Act. We are of the view that this is a question of mixed fact and law in respect of which we can discern no readily extricable legal issue. Accordingly, we agree with the Judge that this question must be reviewed on the standard of review of reasonableness.

B. DID THE JUDGE CORRECTLY APPLY THE REASONABLENESS STANDARD?

[123] In the circumstances, the Panel made no specific finding that it had complied with the consideration requirements ... . However, it is our view that in conducting the EA and preparing the EA Report, the Panel must be taken to have implicitly satisfied itself that it was in compliance with those statutory requirements. In applying the reasonableness standard to this question, we must consider the Panel's decision as a whole, in the context of the underlying record, to determine whether the Panel's implicit conclusion that it had complied with the consideration requirements is reasonable (see *Agraira [Agraira v Canada (Public Safety and Emergency Preparedness*, 2013 SCC 36, [2013] 2 SCR 559] at paragraph 53).

The Consideration Requirements

[124] The consideration requirements in paragraphs 16(1)(a) and (b) of the Act have been interpreted by the Courts.

[125] In *Friends of the West Country Assn. v. Canada (Minister of Fisheries and Oceans)*, [2000] 2 F.C. 263, 248 N.R. 25 (CA) [*Friends of the West Country Assn*], Justice Rothstein stated at paragraph 26:

> The use of the word "shall" in subsection 16(1) indicates that *some consideration* of each factor is mandatory. [Emphasis added by the court.]

[The relevant portions of s 16 of CEAA stated that an assessment "shall include a consideration of the following factors." This wording has been changed in both CEAA 2012 (s 19) and the IAA (s 22): assessments "must *take into account* the following factors" (emphasis added).]

[126] We also endorse the finding of Justice Pelletier at paragraph 71 of *Inverhuron & District Ratepayers' Assn. v. Canada (Minister of the Environment)*, 2000 CanLII 15291 (FC), 191 F.T.R. 20, [2000] F.C.J. No. 682 (QL) [*Inverhuron*], as follows:

> [71] It is worth noting again that the function of the Court in judicial review is not to act as an "academy of science" or a "legislative upper chamber." In dealing with any of the statutory criteria, the range of factual possibilities is practically unlimited. No matter how many scenarios are considered, it is possible to conceive of one which has not been. The nature of science is such that reasonable people can disagree about relevance and significance. *In disposing of these issues, the Court's function is not to assure comprehensiveness but to assess, in a formal rather than substantive sense, whether there has been some consideration of those factors in which the Act requires the comprehensive study to address. If there has been some consideration, it is irrelevant that there could have been further and better consideration.* [Emphasis added by the court.]

• • •

[128] The [Trial] Judge appears to have reached the same conclusion with respect to the level or type of the consideration requirements in ... the Act. He acknowledged that the "form and extent" of any such consideration was not stipulated in the Act and that the Panel is "required to use its expertise to gauge the extent and form of 'consideration' required in each particular case" (Reasons at paragraph 195).

[129] In addition, at paragraph 198 of the Reasons, the Judge confirmed that it is not the role of the Court to assess and reweigh the methodology and conclusions of an expert panel, stating:

[198] In attacking the EA Report as inadequate, the Applicants are to a considerable extent asking the Court to assess and reweigh the methodology and conclusions of an expert panel. This is not the role of the Court. It is true that s. 16(1) and (2) of the CEAA mandate the *"consideration"* of certain factors, *but the way this is done and the weight to be ascribed to each factor is left to the expert Panel to be assessed in accordance with the purposes of the Act.* [Emphasis added by the court.]

[130] It has not been asserted by any party to the appeals that the Panel Agreement, Terms of Reference or EIS Guidelines required, or the Panel itself stipulated, any particular type or level of consideration that it would give to the HSE environmental effects. Thus, in our view, the type or level of consideration that the Panel was required to give to those effects was simply that which is mandated in *Friends of the West Country Assn and Inverhuron*, namely, "some consideration." It follows, in our view, that a failure of the Panel to consider the HSE environmental effects can only be established if it is demonstrated that the Panel gave no consideration at all to those environmental effects.

QUESTIONS

1. Review the introductory part of this chapter about the role that political accountability is supposed to play in impact assessment. Does the Federal Court of Appeal's approach to reviewing assessments enable or frustrate the mechanism of political accountability?

2. One of the more prominent themes to emerge in the lead up to Bill C-69 is that the science of impact assessment has lacked rigour. This led Green Party Leader Elizabeth May to introduce the following amendment to s 6 of the IAA (purpose and mandate provisions), which was unanimously approved by the House Standing Committee on the Environment and Sustainability:

Application of principles to powers
6(3) The Government of Canada, the Minister, the Agency and federal authorities must, in the administration of this Act, exercise their powers in a manner that adheres to the principles of scientific integrity, honesty, objectivity, thoroughness and accuracy.

What effect, if any, do you expect this provision will have on the science of assessment? Should it be expected to change the way that Canadian courts approach disputes over the adequacy of assessments (that is, their approach to reasonableness review in this context)? For American jurisprudence interpreting requirements with respect to scientific integrity, see *Idaho Sporting Congress v Thomas*, 137 F (3d) 1146 at para 10 (9th Cir 1998).

C. ABORIGINAL RIGHTS AND THE DUTY TO CONSULT

As noted in Chapter 12, in Canada there is a strong connection between environmental law and Aboriginal rights. This connection is particularly important in the resource development context, where project permitting—whether federal or provincial—will often trigger the duty to consult. Most such permitting regimes are linked to an environmental or impact assessment regime. In this context and with varying levels of success, both federal and provincial governments have tried to discharge their consultation obligations through various assessment regimes, including CEAA 2012. The following passage sets out some of the legal principles that have emerged as a result of such efforts.

DAVID V WRIGHT, "FEDERAL LINEAR ENERGY
INFRASTRUCTURE PROJECTS AND THE RIGHTS OF
INDIGENOUS PEOPLES: CURRENT LEGAL LANDSCAPE
AND EMERGING DEVELOPMENTS"
(2018) 23:1 Rev Const Stud 175 [footnotes omitted]

Since the very earliest of the duty to consult cases, the courts have had to confront the relationship between the duty to consult and administrative law processes and associated bodies and tribunals. In [*Haida Nation v British Columbia (Minister of Forests)*, 2004 SCC 73, [2004] 3 SCR 511], the court stated, "[i]t is open to governments to set up regulatory schemes to address the procedural requirements appropriate to different problems at different stages, thereby strengthening the reconciliation process and reducing recourse to the courts" (at para 51). Consistent with that finding, in [*Taku River Tlingit First Nation v British Columbia (Project Assessment Director)*, 2004 SCC 74, [2004] 3 SCR 550], the Court held that the unique environmental assessment process that was applicable in that case was sufficient to meet the procedural requirements of the duty to consult and that the province did not have to develop special consultation measures outside of the EA process.

In the years following *Haida* and *Taku*, there was considerable confusion regarding the role of the NEB [and other administrative bodies] in fulfilling the duty to consult. While not all questions have been answered by the courts, significant clarity has emerged. In short, questions hinged on whether and to what extent the NEB's process could be relied on by the Crown to fulfill the duty to consult, and to what extent the NEB itself could assess whether the duty had been fulfilled.

The answers to these two questions are now relatively clear. The Crown need not set up a separate process for fulfilling the duty to consult (though the Crown may do so, as discussed further below). Rather, participation by affected Indigenous communities in a forum created for other purposes, such as an environmental assessment, can fulfill the Crown's duty to consult. Further, the Crown may rely on an administrative body to fulfill the duty to consult "*so long as the agency possesses the statutory powers to do what the duty to consult requires in the particular circumstances*" [citing *Chippewas of the Thames First Nation v Enbridge Pipelines Inc*, 2017 SCC 41 at para 32, [2017] 1 SCR 1099].

... It is now relatively clear that "Tribunals that consider resource issues that impinge on Aboriginal interests may be given: the duty to consult; the duty to determine whether adequate consultation has taken place; both duties; or, no duty at all" [citing *Gitxaala Nation v Canada*, 2016 FCA 187 at para 175]. Building on this principle, if the Crown intends to rely on the regulatory body to fulfill the duty to consult, it must make that clear to the affected Indigenous groups(s) (*Chippewas of the Thames, supra* at para 44). In recent years, this is a practice that has indeed been followed by the Crown [citing *Tsleil-Waututh Nation v Canada (Attorney General)*, 2018 FCA 153 at para 548].

Applying this to the NEB specifically, the Supreme Court has now clearly stated that the Crown may, subject to circumstances discussed below, rely on the NEB review process to *completely* fulfill the duty. However ... the Crown has an obligation to undertake further consultation (and, if appropriate, accommodation) in a situation where there was inadequate consultation in the regulatory forum [for example, the EA process]. In all situations, the court has been clear in stating that the duty to consult must be fulfilled before the Governor in Council gives its approval for the issuance of a certificate by the NEB.

The foregoing excerpt touches on only one of the many issues that arise at the intersection of impact assessment, Indigenous law, and the rights of Indigenous peoples, an area that undoubtedly merits its own chapter. For the purposes of this chapter, however, a final note about Bill C-69 and the IAA in particular is required. As already noted, the IAA contains several new provisions that give heightened prominence to the rights of Indigenous peoples. These include the recognition of Indigenous rights (s 3), mandatory consultation with affected Indigenous groups during the planning phase (s 12), mandatory consideration of Indigenous knowledge (ss 22(1)(g) and 119), and recognition of Indigenous peoples' own laws and associated assessment regimes (s 22(1)(q)). These provisions, as well as others, are expected to play a major role in furthering the goal of reconciliation. For an early overview and assessment, see David Laidlaw, "Bill C-69, the Impact Assessment Act, and Indigenous Process Considerations" (15 March 2018), online (pdf): *ABlawg.ca* <http://ablawg.ca/wp-content/uploads/2018/03/Blog _DL_BillC69.pdf>; and David V Wright, "Indigenous Engagement and Consideration in the Newly Proposed Impact Assessment Act: The Fog Persists" (27 February 2018), online (pdf): *ABlawg.ca* <http://ablawg.ca/wp-content/uploads/2018/02/Blog_DVW_Indigenous_IAA.pdf>.

FURTHER READINGS

Doelle, Meinhard, "CEAA 2012: The End of Federal EA as We Know It?" (2012) 24:1 J Envtl L & Prac 1.

Expert Panel for the Review of Environmental Assessment Processes, *Building Common Ground: A New Vision for Impact Assessment in Canada—The Final Report of the Expert Panel for the Review of Environmental Assessment Processes* (Ottawa: Canadian Environmental Assessment Agency, 2017), online: *Government of Canada* <https://www.canada.ca/en/services /environment/conservation/assessments/environmental-reviews/environmental-assessment -processes/building-common-ground.html>.

Gibson, Robert B, Meinhard Doelle & A John Sinclair, "Fulfilling the Promise: Basic Components of Next Generation Environmental Assessment" (2016) 29 J Envtl L & Prac 257.

Impact Assessment Agency of Canada, *Practitioner's Guide to Federal Impact Assessments Under the Impact Assessment Act* (last modified 27 August 2019), online: *Government of Canada* <https://www.canada.ca/en/impact-assessment-agency/services/policy-guidance /practitioners-guide-impact-assessment-act.html>.

Olszynski, Martin, "Failed Experiments: An Empirical Assessment of Adaptive Management in Alberta's Energy Resources Sector" (2017) 50:3 UBC L Rev 697.

Westwood, Alana et al, "The Role of Science in Contemporary Canadian Environmental Decision-Making: The Example of Environmental Assessment" (2019) 52:1 UBC L Rev 243.

CHAPTER EIGHTEEN

POLLUTION PREVENTION AND ENVIRONMENTAL LIABILITY: THE EVOLUTION OF THE LAW OF TOXIC REAL ESTATE, CONTAMINATED LANDS, AND INSURANCE

Joseph F Castrilli

I. INTRODUCTION

Healthy land and soil are vital for sustaining life and human habitat. Industrialization, mining, urban and transportation infrastructure, waste generation and disposal, and intensification of agricultural activities have left a legacy of soil and land contaminated by heavy metals, organic chemicals, radionuclides, and other pollutants around the world. Soil pollution refers to the presence of a chemical or substance that is out of place or present at higher than normal concentration and that has adverse effects on any non-target organism. Unless properly managed, contaminated lands can (1) lead to significant contamination of water, soil, and air and threaten human health and the environment; (2) result in land being taken out of productive agricultural use; and (3) jeopardize the use of land for recreational, residential, and commercial purposes.

United Nations agencies have described soil or land pollution as an alarming issue globally. In China, 16 percent of all Chinese soils and 19 percent of its agricultural soils are categorized as polluted. There are approximately 3 million potentially polluted sites in the European Economic Area. In the United States, there are more than 1,300 designated contaminated sites on that country's Superfund National Priorities List, and in Australia, the total number of contaminated sites is estimated at approximately 80,000. See "What's the Big Deal About Dirt?" (5 December 2018), online: *United Nations Environment Programme* <https://www.unenvironment .org/news-and-stories/story/whats-big-deal-about-dirt>; and Natalia Rodriguez Eugenio, Michael McLaughlin & Daniel Pennock, *Soil Pollution: A Hidden Reality* (Rome: Food and Agriculture Organization of the United Nations (FAO), 2018) at 1, online (pdf): *FAO* <http:// www.fao.org/3/i9183en/i9183en.pdf>.

Contaminated land also poses numerous risks to human health and the environment in Canada. The increase in the number of such sites has also grown substantially. As early as 1989, the federal government and the provinces recognized the importance of their remediation. When the Auditor General of Canada first audited contaminated sites on federal lands or arising from federal activities in the mid-1990s, there were a few thousand sites. By 2017, the federal government had identified approximately 23,000 sites that were suspected of being or were actually contaminated. These sites ranged from small areas of soil contaminated by spilled fuel to very large abandoned mine sites contaminated by heavy metals and other toxic substances for which the federal government had assumed responsibility. The contaminated site problem exists in each province on both public and private lands. The environmental impact and the financial costs associated with these sites can be felt decades after an activity has ended. See Commissioner of the Environment and Sustainable Development, "Federal Contaminated Sites and Their Impacts" in *2012 Spring Report of the Commissioner of the Environment and Sustainable Development* (Ottawa: CESD, 2012) ch 3, online: *Office of the Auditor General of Canada* <http://www.oag-bvg.gc.ca/internet/English/parl_cesd_201205_ 03_e_36775.html>; and "About Federal Contaminated Sites" (last modified 24 August 2017), online: *Government of Canada* <https://www.canada.ca/en/environment-climate-change/ services/federal-contaminated-sites.html>.

For decades, a variety of advisory and regulatory bodies have raised concerns about the environmental contamination of land in Canada. The former National Round Table on the Environment and the Economy (NRTEE) stated in 1998 that

> [a]cross Canada, thousands of contaminated sites lie abandoned or underutilized, the result of a century of industrialization. Their current condition poses health and economic threats. Many of these sites have not been identified because of insufficient information on the environmental condition of land. Although many of these sites are capable of being cleaned up economically and brought into productive use, the rate of clean-up is slow.

See *State of the Debate on the Environment and the Economy: Greening Canada's Brownfield Sites* (Ottawa: NRTEE, 1998) at 3, online (pdf): <http://publications.gc.ca/collections/collection_ 2013/ec/En133-36-1998-eng.pdf>.

In a similar vein and around the same time, the Canadian Council of Ministers of the Environment (CCME) noted:

Decades of human activity have left a legacy of contaminated land throughout Canada. Virtually every sector of the Canadian economy has contributed to the problem, ranging from resource industries (mining and forestry), heavy industries (steel-making) and petro-chemical production to small manufacturing plants and retail gasoline stations. Historical practices, most of them environmentally unacceptable today, have created current conditions that could potentially harm human health and the environment.

See *Guidance Document on the Management of Contaminated Sites in Canada* (April 1997) at 1, online (pdf): <https://www.ccme.ca/files/Resources/csm/pn_1279_e.pdf>.

An early recommendation to governments of a consistent nationwide approach on how to address the problem was the implementation of CCME's principles on contaminated site liability. See *Contaminated Site Liability Report: Recommended Principles for a Consistent Approach Across Canada*, prepared by the Core Group on Contaminated Site Liability (Winnipeg: CCME, 1993), online (pdf): <https://www.ccme.ca/files/Resources/csm/pn_1122_e.pdf>. The CCME principles addressed matters such as (1) adopting the "polluter pays" principle in framing contaminated site remediation policy and legislation, (2) defining and exempting persons potentially responsible for cleanup, (3) developing factors to address the allocation of responsibility, (4) issuing certificates of compliance when cleanup is satisfactorily completed, and (5) applying fairness principles to any regime adopted.

The 1990s saw governments across the country begin to address questions of land contamination, particularly issues relating to remediation and liability. A number of provinces enacted legislation regulating the problem and incorporated many of the CCME principles into their regimes. Laws adopted in several provinces in the 1990s addressed matters such as (1) investigation and identification of contaminated sites; (2) persons responsible for remediation; (3) development of remediation plans; (4) joint, several, absolute, and retroactive liability; (5) apportionment or allocation of remediation responsibility; and (6) cost recovery from responsible persons by those who incur remediation costs. A prime example of the adoption of these principles is the contaminated site remediation provisions of the British Columbia *Environmental Management Act*, SBC 2003, c 53, part 4.

As a result of these legislative initiatives, the sale, ownership, and management of lands contaminated with toxic substances, wastes, and other hazardous materials increasingly occupied the interest of the real estate, business, industrial, and financial communities due to the potential for liability for cleanup and compensation costs. Potentially responsible persons within these sectors began seeking means of limiting their liability through a variety of measures designed to mitigate and, if possible, prevent pollution from activities within their ownership, management, or control.

Among the measures developed by the private sector on a voluntary basis have been environmental audits and environmental management systems. Both these measures are internal evaluations of company activity designed to verify compliance with legal requirements, company policies, and standards, as well as to identify compliance problems, weaknesses in management systems, or areas of environmental risk. The reasons for the development of these voluntary private sector efforts include the need to (1) avoid future corporate or personal civil or administrative liability for environmental cleanup and compensation by determining whether current operations are in compliance with environmental laws, (2) establish a defence of due diligence to possible quasi-criminal liability by putting in place a proper system of environmental management, and (3) obtain financing from lending institutions that may require as a condition of such funding an environmental audit or development of an environmental management system. See R Cotton et al, "Environmental Considerations in Business Transactions" in *Canadian Environmental Law*, 2nd ed (Markham, Ont: Butterworths, 1991); and JD Wolfe, "Environmental Management Systems: Due Diligence and State of the Art—ISO 14000" in Law

Society of Upper Canada, *Advanced Environmental Law* (Toronto: Continuing Legal Education, LSUC, 1996).

More recently, a second generation of land remediation legislation to address "brownfields," or abandoned or underutilized properties where past actions have caused real or suspected environmental contamination, has begun to evolve in Canada. Regarded as a subset of contaminated sites, brownfields are viewed as sites that exhibit good potential for other uses and economically viable business opportunities. See NRTEE, *Greening Canada's Brownfield Sites*, above, at 4. They also have been defined as "vacant or underused sites with potential for redevelopment. They may be contaminated, often due to former industrial or commercial use." See Ontario Ministry of Municipal Affairs and Housing, *Brownfields Ontario* (Toronto: MMAH, 2018). The impetus for brownfield laws is twofold. First, it arises from increased concern in government and the private sector over the impact of stringent contaminated site legislation on the ability and willingness of the real estate, business, industrial, and financial communities to engage in the environmental cleanup of abandoned or orphaned lands. Second, it arises from a desire to avoid residential, commercial, and industrial development in new "greenfield" areas when rehabilitated lands could be used.

This chapter provides an overview of three interrelated areas of the law that have developed to address these matters: (1) private rights of action between purchasers, vendors, and other persons involved in the sale of toxic real estate; (2) regulatory control of, and civil and administrative liability for, contamination of land involving potentially responsible parties such as owners, operators, parent corporations, lenders, receivers, receiver-managers, trustees in bankruptcy, and governments; and (3) insurance coverage for damage arising from environmentally contaminated property.

II. TOXIC REAL ESTATE

A. THE LIABILITY OF VENDORS—CONTRACT PRINCIPLES

The liability of vendors to purchasers for the sale of contaminated real estate may arise under contract principles. The following case illustrates the application of the doctrine of *caveat emptor* and the circumstances under which a vendor has a duty to disclose information regarding the contaminated state of a property.

TONY'S BROADLOOM & FLOOR COVERING LTD V NCM CANADA INC
1995 CanLII 7153, 17 CELR (NS) 22 (Ont Gen Div)

WHITE J:

BACKGROUND

The plaintiff purchaser, Tony's Broadloom and Floor Covering Ltd. ("Tony's Broadloom"), in Trust, moved for summary judgment to rescind an agreement of purchase and sale, primarily on the ground that the vendor failed to advise the plaintiff that the land had been contaminated by varsol, which, in the plaintiffs' submission, was a latent defect.

The defendant vendor, SKD Company ("SKD"), brought a cross-motion for summary judgment to dismiss the plaintiff's action, primarily on the ground that the defect was patent, and, in any event, the contamination did not prevent the purchaser from continuing to use the land for its current use as a factory.

• • •

ISSUES

1. Is hazardous waste contamination of industrially zoned land a patent or a latent defect?
2. Is the vendor of land contaminated by hazardous waste obliged to disclose such defect to the purchaser when no inquiry is made by the purchaser, and the vendor is unaware of the purchaser's intention to use the land for anything other than its current use?

LAW

PATENT OR LATENT DEFECT

The distinction between a patent and latent defect is described by Ron Milner Stonham in his text, *The Law of Vendor and Purchaser* (Sydney: The Law Book Co. of Australia Pty. Ltd., 1964), at p. 229:

> A patent defect is a defect which a purchaser is likely to discover if he inspects the property with ordinary care. A latent defect is one which a purchaser, inspecting the property with ordinary care, would not be likely to discover. Whether a defect is patent or latent is a question of degree ... . It is not enough that there exists on the land an object of sense, that might put a careful purchaser on inquiry; but, in order to be a patent defect, the defect must either be visible to the eye, or arise by necessary implication from something visible to the eye. [Citations omitted.]

Similarly, in 42 *Halsbury's Laws of England*, 4th ed. (London: Butterworths, 1983), s. 51, under the subheading *Disclosure by the Vendor—Defects of Quality* it is stated at p. 47:

> Defects of quality may be either patent or latent. Patent defects are such as are discoverable by inspection and ordinary vigilance on the part of a purchaser, *and latent defects are such as would not be revealed by any inquiry which a purchaser is in a position to make before entering into the contract for purchase.*
>
> The vendor is not bound to call attention to patent defects; the rule is "caveat emptor." Therefore a purchaser should make inspection and inquiry as to what he is proposing to buy. *If he omits to ascertain whether the land is such as he desires to acquire, he cannot complain afterwards on discovering defects of which he would have been aware if he had taken ordinary steps to ascertain its physical condition.* ... [Emphasis added.]

• • •

I am of the view that a reasonable purchaser, purchasing industrially zoned land which it knew, or ought to have known, was used as a factory, and upon which it intended to construct a residential development, would have exercised its right to inspect the Property to discover whether there was any contamination before submitting an offer to purchase. Further, a prudent purchaser would have seen the pipes on the Property, and would have inspected the contents of the shed on the Property, and would have been drawn to inquire of the vendor for what purpose these structures existed.

Thus, I find that since the varsol contamination was readily discoverable by the purchaser in these circumstances, it constitutes a patent defect. The rule of caveat emptor applies to contracts of sale of land. The purchaser takes that which he sees, or which, as a prudent and diligent purchaser, he ought to have seen, and is not entitled to have anything better ... . In the case of a patent defect, as distinguished from a latent defect as to quality or condition, and where the means of knowledge are equally open to both parties, and no concealment is made or attempted, a prudent purchaser will inspect, and exercise ordinary care—caveat emptor: V Di Castri, *The Law of Vendor and Purchaser*, at p. 173.

Caveat emptor applies where an inspection by a reasonably competent person would have revealed the defect. The purchaser made no inquiry of the vendor as to whether the Property was fit for development as a residential complex. ... The vendor had no indication from the purchaser that the purchaser did not intend to continue the extant use of the Property as a factory.

I am asked to determine whether the vendor's silence regarding the varsol contamination, and, in particular, in not [proffering] to the purchaser the contents of the May Letter and the August Report, amounted to fraudulent or negligent misrepresentation. In other words, was there a positive duty on the vendor to come forward with the information that the land was contaminated by varsol, notwithstanding that the contamination would not affect the purchaser's ability to carry on employing the land for its current use?

The plaintiff charges that the vendor has perpetrated fraud. I disagree. There may indeed be a moral obligation to have disclosed the contamination; there is no legal obligation to have done so, where the contamination does not render the land unusable for any purpose, and where the vendor took no steps to conceal the contamination.

• • •

There is no fiduciary relationship between the vendor and purchaser in the negotiation of a contract for the sale and purchase of land. Prima facie the vendor is not obliged to disclose matters, not being defects in title, merely affecting the value or price or the use to which the property may be put, whether such defects be patent or latent: Stonham, *The Law of Vendor and Purchaser, supra*, at p. 221.

I note the result in *John Levy Holdings Inc. v. Cameron & Johnstone Ltd.* (1992), 26 RPR (2d) 130, appeal dismissed March 24, 1993 (Ont. CA), where Philp J found that while contaminants on the property in that case exceeded [Ministry of the Environment] guidelines for agricultural/residential/parkland use, the contaminants did not affect the current use of the property, which was commercial/industrial. As the vendor had no way of knowing the purchaser's intention to some day rezone the property to develop a residential condominium complex, the vendor was not bound to disclose the fact that the property was contaminated for the purpose of this higher use.

• • •

If the purchaser intended to use the property for residential purposes after seeking planning approval, the onus was on the purchaser to ensure that the Property could be so used. The plaintiff should have: (i) conducted a proper inspection of the Property before entering the agreement of purchase and sale; (ii) asked the vendor pertinent questions particularly related to the pipes and equipment in the shed, and, (iii) insisted that a provision be inserted in the agreement, making it conditional on the Property being appropriate for residential use. See *McGeek Enterprises Ltd. v. Shell Canada Ltd.* (1991), 6 OR (3d) 216. ...

In the circumstances, I am unable to find that there was a legal duty on the vendor to advise the purchaser about the May Letter and the August Report, both of which disclose that varsol contamination of the Property is an ongoing problem.

[The plaintiff's motion was dismissed. The defendant's cross-motion was granted because the court found the defect to be patent, because it was readily discoverable by reasonable inspection.]

NOTES

1. The Ontario Court of Appeal affirmed the decision of White J in *Tony's Broadloom & Floor Covering Ltd v NMC Canada Inc*, 1996 CanLII 680, 31 OR (3d) 481 at 487-88 (CA). The Court of Appeal would have treated the presence of the contaminant as neither a latent nor a patent defect in the property because the vendors had had no reason to believe that the purchasers would use the property for any purpose other than an industrial one. The purchasers "got exactly what they bargained for—industrial land. Their undisclosed intention to use the property for residential purposes does not alter the bargain" they had made or "create a latent defect in the industrial property" that the purchasers had agreed to acquire. The Court of Appeal went on to suggest that if it was wrong, and the presence of the contaminant was a defect, then it agreed with the conclusion at trial that the defect was a patent one because it would have been readily discoverable by the purchasers had they exercised reasonable vigilance in the circumstances. In the context of this case, reasonable vigilance would have included inspection of the property and inquiries of the vendors and local and provincial authorities, as well as the taking of soil samples early enough in time to learn of the existence of the contaminant before closing. Instead, according to the appeal court, the purchasers had chosen "not to disclose their intended use of the property and to take no steps to satisfy themselves that the property could be used for that purpose."

2. Another toxic real estate case exemplifying the application of the doctrine of *caveat emptor* is *801438 Ontario Inc v Badurina* (2000), 34 RPR (3d) 306 (Ont Sup Ct J). In *Badurina*, the court dismissed the purchaser's action against the defendant vendor because the court found that the latter had made no representations as to the environmental condition of the vacant land or its development potential. The court held that the purchaser could, in any event, have readily ascertained for itself the condition and development potential of the property and that of adjacent derelict and contaminated property. The *Badurina* court also affirmed the proposition that what constitutes a defect in the quality of land must be determined in the context of the intended use of the land.

3. Some provinces have responded to the problems posed by the doctrine of *caveat emptor* by imposing disclosure requirements on vendors of real property. In British Columbia, s 40(6) of the province's *Environmental Management Act* requires that if a vendor of real property knows or reasonably should know that the property has been used for an industrial or commercial purpose, the vendor must provide a site profile to a prospective purchaser of the property and, subject to the regulations, to a director of the Ministry of Environment and Climate Change Strategy. Pursuant to s 3(7) of the *Contaminated Sites Regulation*, BC Reg 375/96, a vendor of real property must provide a site profile to a prospective purchaser at least 30 days before the actual transfer of real property. Under s 4(13) of the Regulation, vendors are exempt from the requirement to provide a site profile if (1) the purchaser waives the requirement in writing, (2) at the time of contract for purchase and sale, the subject property of the sale is used primarily for residential purposes, or (3) the property has never been zoned for any use other than residential. Schedule 1 to the Regulation sets out the information that must be included in a site profile, including identification of areas of the site that are of potential environmental concern as a result of pollution from (1) more than 100 litres of petroleum, solvent, or other substance spilled to the environment; (2) residue of chemicals or other substances after removal of piled materials; (3) discarded barrels, drums, or tanks; or (4) "contamination resulting from migration of substances from other properties" (part IV of the Schedule).

B. THE LIABILITY OF VENDORS—TORT PRINCIPLES

Vendors may also be liable under tort principles. The doctrine of *caveat emptor* does not apply to fraudulent representations or conduct. Where a defect is latent and may pose a risk of danger to life, health, or the environment, the failure of a vendor to disclose this information to a purchaser may constitute fraud and allow the purchaser to sue for deceit.

SEVIDAL V CHOPRA
1987 CanLII 4262, 2 CELR (NS) (2d) 173 at 190-92, 197 (Ont H Ct J)

[Prior to entering into an agreement of purchase and sale, the vendors failed to disclose to the purchasers the existence of radioactive material in the neighbourhood. Before closing, the vendors learned that the subject property itself also was contaminated with radioactive material but did not disclose this information to the purchasers.]

LIABILITY OF THE CHOPRAS

The issues with respect to the Chopras relate to disclosure. Did the Chopras owe a duty to the Sevidals to disclose the presence of radioactive material in the McClure Crescent area before the agreement to purchase was signed, or to disclose the discovery of radioactive material in the backyard of 63 McClure Crescent before the closing?

Here we are dealing with a latent defect. Latent defects with respect to the sale of land, [sic] have been described succinctly in 42 *Hals.* (4th ed.), p. 47, para. 51:

> latent defects are such as would not be revealed by any inquiry which a purchaser is in a position to make before entering into the contract for purchase.

Redican v. Nesbitt, [1924] SCR 135, ... stands for the proposition that the doctrine of caveat emptor does not apply to fraud, error in substantialibus or where there is a warranty, contractual condition or collateral contract.

In reviewing whether a cause of action existed in the case of *McGrath v. Maclean* (1979), 22 OR (2d) 784 ... (Ont. CA), Dubin JA, at p. 791-92 [OR], quoted favourably from a lecture by Professor Bora Laskin, as he then was, ... :

> Does the vendor have any duty of disclosure in matters of quality and fitness which do not constitute defects of title? Here we deal with the classical notion of caveat emptor as applied to the physical amenities and condition of the property unrelated to any outstanding claims of third parties or public authorities such as would impinge on the title. *Absent fraud, mistake or misrepresentation, a purchaser takes existing property as he finds it*, whether it be dilapidated, bug-infested or otherwise uninhabitable or deficient in expected amenities, unless he protects himself by contract terms. ...
>
> *I do not propose to dwell on fraud, mistake or misrepresentation save to make a few observations about the way in which, if established, they relieve a purchaser from the binding effect of caveat emptor. Fraud can be a rather elastic conception, and there are cases which show a tendency to find fraud when there has been concealment by the vendor of latent defects. Rowley v. Isley,* [1951] 3 DLR 766, a British Columbia decision entitling a purchaser to rescind (even after paying the price and taking possession) where there was a failure to disclose infestation by roaches, illustrates the proposition, and goes quite far in allowing rescission after the transaction had been closed. *On the other hand, a latent defect of quality going to fitness for habitation and which is either unknown to the vendor or such as not to make him chargeable with concealment or reckless disregard of its truth or falsity*

will not support any claim of redress by the purchaser. He must find his protection in warranty. [Dubin JA's emphasis.]

• • •

An exception to the general rule of caveat emptor will be found where there is fraud or fraudulent misrepresentation and, where there is such a finding, failure on the part of the vendor to disclose will give rise to a cause of action.

Fraud arises when a statement is made "knowingly, or without belief in its truth, or recklessly, careless whether it be true or false": Per Lord Herschell in *Derry v. Peek* (1889), 14 App. Cas. 337 (HL) at p. 374. Fraud can also arise where there is active concealment, *Abel v. McDonald*, ... [1964 CanLII 190, [1964] 2 OR 256 (CA)]. Finally, fraud arises where there is failure to disclose a potential danger, *Rivtow Marine*, ... [*Rivtow Marine Ltd v Washington Iron Works*, [1974] SCR 1189, 1973 CanLII 6]; *McGrath v. Maclean*, ... [1979 CanLII 1691, 22 OR (2d) 784 (CA)]; *CRF Holdings*, ... [*CRF Holdings Ltd v Fundy Chemical Int'l Ltd*, 1981 CanLII 488, [1982] 2 WWR 385 (BCCA)]; *Ford v. Schmitt*, ... [(1984), 29 ACWS (2d) 64 (Ont Co Ct)].

Counsel for the Sevidals argued that failure to disclose the presence of radioactive contamination both in the area and later on the property itself amounted to a fraudulent misrepresentation, and that the Chopras intended to deceive the Sevidals.

[The court reviewed cases.]

• • •

In all the circumstances of this case, I find that the Chopras had a duty to disclose the change of circumstances to the Sevidals prior to closing. Accordingly, with regard to the second issue, I find that the Chopras should have disclosed the discovery of radioactive material on their property, and I find the Chopras were guilty of concealment of facts so detrimental to the Sevidals that it amounted to a fraud upon them. Therefore, the Chopras are liable in deceit.

NOTES

1. Fraud is a serious allegation requiring a high standard of proof. In *Ban v Keleher*, 2017 BCSC 1132, a British Columbia Supreme Court judge noted, in summarizing the authorities, that to succeed in a claim for fraudulent misrepresentation, a plaintiff must establish that (1) a defendant made a representation of fact to the plaintiff; (2) the representation was false in fact; (3) the defendant knew that the representation was false when making it, or made the false representation recklessly, not knowing if it was true or false; (4) the defendant intended for the plaintiff to act on the representation; and (5) the plaintiff was induced to enter into the contract while relying on the false representation and thereby suffered a detriment. The court held that the defendant in *Ban* was not liable in fraudulent misrepresentation despite failing to advise the plaintiff purchaser in the property disclosure statement, which formed part of the contract of purchase and sale, that the defendant had received two notices of likely or actual offsite migration of contaminants from environmental consultants acting for a neighbouring property owner. Nor had the defendant advised the plaintiff that the consultants had attended on the defendant's property to conduct drilling, install monitoring wells, and conduct sampling to determine if chemical contaminants from the neighbouring property, a former dry cleaning business, had migrated to the defendant's property. The court noted that for a misrepresentation to be fraudulent, it requires proof of intention, and in the circumstances of the case in *Ban*, the "clear and convincing proof" of the mental element of fraud, that is, the deliberate intention to induce the purchaser to enter into the contract to purchase the property by relying on the false representation, had not been made out by the plaintiffs.

2. In *Godin v Jenovac* (1993), 35 RPR (2d) 288 (Ont Gen Div), a vendor failed to disclose the existence of a closed municipal landfill in the vicinity of the subject property. The court held that there was no duty to disclose this information to the purchaser in the absence of any evidence that the site posed a health hazard or danger. Similarly, in *Ceolaro v York Humber Ltd*, 1994 CanLII 7524, 37 RPR (2d) 1 (Ont Gen Div), a vendor developer failed to advise condominium purchasers that the property had formerly been a site for sewage treatment and that it had been subject to extensive remedial engineering to remove a methane gas hazard. The *Ceolaro* court followed *Godin* and distinguished *Sevidal* on the basis that there was no duty on the vendor to disclose the information unless there was a health or safety risk.

3. Vendors may be liable under other tort principles such as negligent misrepresentation and negligence in circumstances where the same facts that are insufficient to found liability on the basis of fraudulent misrepresentation can give rise to liability under these principles. In *Ban*, cited above, the court (at para 31) noted that a misrepresentation in a property disclosure statement is capable of giving rise to a claim for damages for negligent misrepresentation. The test is fivefold:

 a) there must be a duty of care based on a "special relationship" between the representor and the representee;
 b) the representation in question must be untrue, inaccurate, or misleading;
 c) the representor must have acted negligently in making said misrepresentation;
 d) the representee must have relied, in a reasonable manner, on said negligent misrepresentation; and
 e) the reliance must have been detrimental to the representee in the sense that damages resulted.

The court in *Ban* held that while the defendant was not liable in fraudulent misrepresentation, the facts, as noted above, gave rise to liability in negligent misrepresentation.

4. In *Sassy Investments Ltd v Minovitch*, 1996 CanLII 8635, 21 CELR (NS) 126 (BCSC), vendors of a gasoline station were liable for negligently misrepresenting to the purchasers that they had monitored and recorded the gasoline inventory at the station, and they were liable in negligence for failing to complete inventory records and not exercising the requisite degree of care in controlling the gasoline inventory when uninventoried gasoline leaked from the station's underground pipes and contaminated the wells of nearby residents.

C. THE LIABILITY OF REAL ESTATE AGENTS AND SOLICITORS

It is possible for real estate agents or lawyers to attract environmental liability in any type of land transaction. Real estate agents may be liable in contract or tort if they fail to exercise a reasonable degree of care and skill that persons of ordinary prudence and ability might be expected to show in the capacity of agent. Solicitors in real estate transactions also may be liable in contract or tort if they fail to exercise the due care and attention expected of the reasonably competent solicitor. The *Sevidal* case illustrates the application of these principles in an environmental context.

SEVIDAL V CHOPRA
1987 CanLII 4262, 2 CELR (NS) (2d) 173 at 203-7 (Ont H Ct J)

LIABILITY OF ANTONIO AND NORTHGATE

The issue with respect to Antonio is: did she meet the appropriate level of competence expected from a real estate agent for the work which she undertook for the Sevidals?

[The court found that the real estate agent had exercised the appropriate level of competence with respect to finding a suitable house and property for the Sevidals, except for the radioactivity problem, about which, the court found, the agent had not known until after the agreement had been signed. The court further held that it could not find that the agent ought to have known of the problem. The court also found that neither the agent's employer, Northgate, the Sevidals' lawyer, Clapp, nor the loan mortgage officer had known of a radioactivity problem at McClure Crescent, although all of them had had experience in dealing with real estate in the Scarborough area. Moreover, the court found that nothing would have alerted Antonio to the fact that the McClure Crescent development was any different from numerous others in the Scarborough area.]

Having the waiver of the condition [regarding financing] signed before the mortgage was applied for is a different situation. In *Charter-York Ltd. v. Hurst; Hurst v. Charter-York Ltd.* (1978), 2 RPR 272 (Ont. HC) [leave to appeal to SCC refused (1979), 28 NR 616n], Labrosse J considered the claim of a vendor against his real estate agent based on a breach of the obligations under the listing agreement. At p. 279 with respect to the standard of care required by a real estate agent under the contract, he cited with approval an extract from 22 *Hals.* (3d ed.), at pp. 47-48:

All agents, whether paid or unpaid, skilled or unskilled, are under a legal obligation to exercise due care and skill in performance of the duties which they have undertaken, a greater degree of care being required from a paid than from an unpaid, and from a skilled than from an unskilled, agent. The question in all such cases is whether the act or omission complained of is inconsistent with that reasonable degree of care and skill which persons of ordinary prudence and ability might be expected to show in the situation and profession of the agent.

Labrosse J also found at p. 280 that the standard of care by the agent and the quantum of damages in the *Charter-York* case would be the same whether the breach was based in contract or in tort. His reasoning would be applicable to this case and I adopt it.

The Sevidals were immigrants to Canada. They were purchasing their first home and they were unfamiliar with the laws affecting the purchase. Antonio had emigrated from their homeland and spoke the same dialect. The Sevidals relied on her to a large extent as their real estate agent. Antonio was the Sevidals' agent. The Chopras were represented by another agent. In view of my earlier findings that Antonio failed to explain the waiver and that the Sevidals did not understand it, I find that, in having the Sevidals sign the waiver before the mortgage was applied for, Antonio did not meet the level of competence expected of her.

[The court found that the Sevidals' loss was foreseeable because the agent had taken the chance of removing the condition, expecting that, in her experience, the mortgage would not be refused, and, even if it were, she could arrange other financing.]

Nevertheless she knew she was exposing the Sevidals to some risk which, I have found, she failed to explain to them. The uncontroverted testimony of Clapp was that, if the condition had remained, he would have had no difficulty in getting the Sevidals out of the transaction once the radioactivity problem in the area was discovered. By her action, Antonio prevented the Sevidals from using the condition in a manner in which their lawyer testified it could have been used to prevent loss to them. Antonio, therefore, is responsible for the resulting loss.

[Since Antonio was an employee of Northgate, acting within the scope of her duties, the court also found Northgate responsible for the acts of its employee.]

LIABILITY OF CLAPP

The issues with respect to Clapp are: first, what was his retainer and, second, did Clapp meet an appropriate level of competence expected from a solicitor for the work which he undertook?

• • •

I find that Clapp did consider, to the extent necessary in the 2 days after he was retained, the avenues open to the Sevidals for backing out of the transaction. I have no doubt that, had the Sevidals not changed their instructions to him, he would have continued to pursue his original retainer in an appropriate fashion and would have continued to advise them when the next appropriate step was contemplated.

Since Clapp himself had substantial experience in the residential real estate field, I do not find it was necessary for Clapp, before his retainer changed, to consult a person more experienced than himself.

I find as well that it was reasonable for Clapp not to make independent inquiries of AECB [Atomic Energy Control Board] since Mrs. Sevidal had told him she had been advised by a responsible government agency that there was no contamination on the property at 63 McClure Crescent.

[The court found that Clapp had carried out his duties in acting for the Sevidals as a reasonably competent solicitor. He had not been careless in his advice to, or representation of, them.]

NOTE

In *Dobara Properties Limited v Arnone*, 2016 ONSC 3599, the plaintiffs sued (1) their former solicitors for damages concerning the purchase of contaminated land and (2) their former litigation counsel whom they had retained to sue the solicitors for missing the limitation period in the action. The plaintiffs sought recovery of damages against the counsel for what they otherwise could have recovered against the solicitors. The court held that the plaintiffs were entitled to compensation from the litigation counsel for all reasonably foreseeable damages resulting from the loss of opportunity to avoid the consequences of the negligence of the solicitors. This amounted to over $50,000 for environmental remediation costs expended by the plaintiffs on cleanup of the property.

D. THE LIABILITY OF GOVERNMENT AGENCIES

A government agency may attract environmental liability in the context of real estate matters as a vendor or purchaser of land or as a regulator.

The situation of regulatory negligence was considered in *Heighington v Ontario*, 1989 CanLII 4314, 4 CELR (NS) 65 at 67 (Ont CA). In this case, the provincial department of health became aware in the 1940s that soil on the subject property had high levels of radioactive contamination. The province expropriated the lands in the 1950s, and a provincial crown housing agency, unaware of the contamination, leased the land to builders in the 1970s, and they subdivided the land into lots to construct houses. In 1980, radiation levels exceeding acceptable limits were found in some of the yards of the subdivision. The owners and former owners of residences in the subdivision brought action against the province in negligence and were successful at trial (1987 CanLII 5417, 2 CELR (NS) 93 (Ont H Ct J)). The province appealed the trial judgment, but the Court of Appeal held that the *Public Health Act*, RSO 1937, c 299 "imposed a duty on the Department of Health to take such measures as necessary to abate conditions injurious or dangerous to health," and that "[i]n all the circumstances, the provincial officials were negligent in that, in breach of the *Public Health Act*, they failed to take reasonable steps to cause to be removed such radioactive material, including contaminated soil, as might endanger the health of future occupants of the land."

NOTES AND QUESTIONS

1. In the *Sevidal* case, the Atomic Energy Control Board (AECB) was found liable in negligent misrepresentation. The agency, pursuant to statutory powers under the former *Atomic Energy Control Act*, RSC 1970, c A-19 (now the *Nuclear Safety and Control Act*, SC 1997, c 9), assumed responsibility for disseminating information about radioactivity in the area. However, the agency gave the Sevidals inaccurate information about whether there was radioactive soil on the property. In addition, the agency failed to give the family other pertinent information about the status of ongoing investigations, in part because of an agency policy of non-disclosure about soil contamination except to landowners, a policy not communicated to the Sevidals. Because the Sevidals had sought advice in order to help them make a judgment whether to back out of the transaction, the agency's representations failed to meet the standard of care required in the circumstances and contributed to the damages suffered by the Sevidals (at 197-200). The agency also was found liable in negligence because there was a sufficient relationship of proximity between the agency and the public due to the agency's assumption of responsibility to provide the public information regarding radioactivity in the area. A duty of care arose because it was also within the contemplation of agency employees that carelessness on their part would be likely to cause damage to the Sevidals. The agency in this instance was not protected from a negligence claim by arguing that its action was based on a policy decision. The court noted that the agency had a right, as a matter of policy, to decide to whom information would be disseminated. In this case, however, the agency had provided some incomplete and inaccurate information to the Sevidals without advising them of the agency's policy of non-disclosure, which would have alerted the family to the need to make other inquiries. In *Sevidal*, "[t]he actions of the A.E.C.B almost set a trap for the unwary purchasers. Parliament certainly never intended a public authority to exercise its policy-making powers in such a way that non-disclosure of the policy would mislead a member of the public who made an appropriate inquiry" (at 203).

2. Because of concerns over the federal government attracting liability upon the purchase or sale of land, the Treasury Board of Canada adopted a management policy on federal contaminated sites in 2002. The policy required that (1) before federal departments or agencies acquired or disposed of real property, they ascertain its environmental condition; and (2) when disposing of federal real property, departments and agencies, upon request, disclose available environmental information on the property to potential purchasers. See "Treasury Board Federal Contaminated Sites Management Policy" (1 July 2002), online: *Government of Canada* <https://www.tbs-sct.gc.ca/pol/doc-eng.aspx?id=12033>. In 2006, the treasury board rescinded this policy and replaced it with a new one requiring "custodians" of federal property (defined as federal departments whose ministers have responsibility for real property), prior to disposing of it, to ensure they can provide interested parties with sufficient information on the property's environmental condition to allow them to make an informed decision on its acquisition. See "Policy on Management of Real Property" (1 November 2016; last modified 11 April 2019), online: *Government of Canada* <https://www.tbs-sct.gc.ca/pol/doc-eng.aspx?id=12042>; "Directive on the Sale or Transfer of Surplus Real Property" (1 November 2006; last modified 22 December 2015), online: *Government of Canada* <https://www.tbs-sct.gc.ca/pol/doc-eng.aspx?id=12043>.

3. What difference, if any, would the 2002 treasury board policy have had on the outcome of the *Sevidal* case had the policy been in effect at the time and been applied by the AECB? Would the 2006 policy be applicable to a fact situation like *Sevidal*?

III. CONTAMINATED LAND

In addition to private rights of action by purchasers against vendors and others in connection with the sale of toxic real estate, a variety of other parties with interests in contaminated lands increasingly are subject to a myriad of controls and liabilities imposed by legislatures, regulators, and courts. Liability may attach to the interests of owners, operators, parent corporations, lenders, receivers, receiver-managers, trustees in bankruptcy, or governments. A preliminary issue that all such potentially responsible parties must face is the level of cleanup that must be achieved.

A. THE CLEANUP STANDARD

Determining "how clean is clean" has been an ongoing debate in the context of the cleanup of contaminated lands. Federal–provincial bodies, such as the CCME, have developed a variety of guidelines and standards to address contaminants in soil and groundwater. In some provincial jurisdictions, these standards have been adopted as regulations. In others, they have been retained as guidelines. The following case illustrates the extent to which remediation may be required to satisfy civil liability claims.

**TRIDAN DEVELOPMENTS LTD V SHELL CANADA
PRODUCTS LTD**
2002 CanLII 20789, 57 OR (3d) 503 (CA)

[The appellant, Shell Canada Products Limited, operated a service station in Ottawa adjacent to a car dealership owned by the respondent, Tridan Developments Limited. In 1990, 9,000 litres of gasoline leaked from an underground fuel line on Shell's property. Shell undertook remediation of its property in accordance with government standards applicable at the time but did not remove all of the contaminated soil. In 1991, Tridan discovered that some of the gasoline had migrated to its property. Shell accepted responsibility for the cleanup of Tridan's property, but a dispute concerning the appropriate level of cleanup arose. The trial judge held that Tridan was entitled to have its property remediated to a pristine condition and assessed that cost at $550,000. The trial judge further awarded Tridan $350,000 for loss of property value due to the stigma associated with the contamination. Shell appealed the assessment of damages.]

[1] CARTHY J.A.: ... .

• • •

THE FACTS

• • •

[7] Several sets of [Ministry of Environment] MOE guidelines were in place during the period between the spill and trial ... [T]he "Guideline for Use at Contaminated Sites in Ontario," revised February 1997 ("1997 MOE guideline") ...

[8] ... currently applies. Its stated purpose is to provide, [sic]

... advice and information to property owners and consultants to use when assessing the environmental condition of a property, when determining whether or not restoration is required, and in determining the kind of restoration needed to allow continued use or reuse of the site. The ministry has provided the guideline, along with the supporting documentation, to assist landowners in making decisions on soil and/or groundwater quality for proposed or existing property uses.

[9] Under the 1997 MOE guideline, the level of permissible pollutants varies depending on whether the property is used for agricultural, residential or commercial purposes. The relevant criteria for land used for commercial purposes is set out in Table B. Within Table B, permissible concentration levels vary depending on whether the groundwater is used for drinking purposes and on whether the soil at the contaminated site is fine, medium or [coarse]. Lower concentration levels of pollutants are permitted for [coarse] grain soil, since pollutants can travel more easily through [coarse] soil than fine soil.

[10] No one suggests that the guidelines supplant the common law standard of compensation for injury to land. However, Shell asserts that the MOE guideline represents a reasonable standard to apply to commercial lands that are contaminated but unaffected for the purpose being served. The difference in cost between meeting the 1997 MOE guideline and achieving a site which is clean of all contaminants, referred to in the evidence as a pristine site, is approximately $250,000, mostly referable to the amount of soil that must be removed and replaced.

DAMAGES FOR REPARATION OF THE TRIDAN PROPERTY

[11] The trial judge found that the plaintiffs were entitled to have their property remediated to pristine condition and assessed the cost of doing so at $550,000. ...

[12] The trial judge might have relied upon those expert witnesses supporting the MOE guidelines as a reasonable measure of reparation and thus the damages suffered. This is a commercial property on a busy thoroughfare and unlikely to ever be a site for residential use. It might be concluded that, in a practical sense, Tridan is not likely to need or want to clean its soil at depth of every particle of pollutant. However, in the circumstances of this case, I cannot say the trial judge erred in deciding that Tridan was entitled to reparation to a pristine state. Where a product that may cause mischief escapes to a neighbour's property, there is responsibility "for all the damage which is the natural consequence of its escape." See *Rylands v. Fletcher* (1866), [1861-73] All ER Rep. 1 at 7 ... . Of course, they must be reasonable. On all the evidence, it is fair to conclude that the damages would not be eliminated by reparations to the point of the MOE guidelines. There would be residual loss of value, referred to as stigma, which would be reduced, as the trial judge found, or eliminated, as I am about to find, by remediation to the pristine level.

STIGMA

[13] An analysis of all the evidence brings me to the conclusion that there is no support for the trial judge's conclusion that there is a residual reduction of value in a pristine site caused by the knowledge that it was once polluted. It would appear that the trial judge simply misapprehended the evidence of the two principal witnesses for Tridan [who testified that there would be no impact on market value if the site were cleaned to a pristine condition].

• • •

[17] In sum, the evidence compels me to conclude that there is no stigma loss at the pristine cleanup level. This conclusion also makes sense of the trial judge's holding that cleanup to the pristine standard was justified in this case. If the trial judge's assessment of stigma damage at $350,000 is taken as the diminution in value at cleanup to the guideline standard, then the more economical route is to proceed to the pristine level at an additional cleanup cost of $250,000 with no stigma damage.

[18] In my view, the only reasonable conclusion from the totality of the evidence is that a pristine site has no residual loss of value and that ... the judgment should be amended to reduce the amount awarded by $350,000.

[The court allowed the appeal in part.]

NOTES

1. *Tridan* establishes two important propositions. First, in appropriate circumstances, a defendant who permits a contaminant to migrate offsite may be required to remediate the neighbour's property back to its original pristine condition, even if that remediation level is more stringent or protective than standards established by government cleanup guidelines. Second, while a court can order the cleanup of neighbouring land to a pristine condition, landowners that benefit from such a 100 percent remediation cannot claim thereafter that there is a contamination stigma attached to their land and that it warrants additional damages.

2. The *Tridan* case also is important because an appellate court recognized that there may be a reduction in a property's value based on the concept of stigma attaching to it, notwithstanding that the court disallowed stigma damages in that case. See *Steadman v Corporation of the County of Lambton*, 2015 ONSC 101 at para 63. *Steadman* (at paras 64-65) also referred to a paper prepared by Katherine M van Rensburg, now of the Ontario Court of Appeal ("Deconstructing Tridan: A Litigator's Perspective" (2006) 24:4 Advocates' Soc J 16), discussing the ramifications of the *Tridan* decision:

[C]laims for stigma damages will have to be based on *compelling and persuasive expert evidence* and ... the courts may greet such claims with skepticism, especially in the absence of evidence of residual contamination at the property. ... [T]he recognition of stigma as a head of damages must recognize that contaminated lands carry risk and liability, as well as post-remediation value. (p. 15) [*sic*] [Emphasis added.]

3. The principles arising from *Tridan* have been applied by the courts of other provinces. See *618369 Alberta Ltd v Canadian Turbo (1993) Inc*, 2004 ABQB 283 (court awarding damages for diminution of the plaintiff's land value for contamination of the property by leakage from a service station despite payment of remediation costs by the defendants).

4. In 2001, Ontario enacted Bill 56, the *Brownfields Statute Law Amendment Act, 2001*, SO 2001, c 17, which amended several environmental, planning, and municipal laws in the province. As part of the amendments, Bill 56 established rules for contaminated site assessment and cleanup. In particular, Bill 56 amended the *Environmental Protection Act*, RSO 1990, c E.19, to do three things. First, it made environmental site assessment and cleanup to prescribed standards mandatory where there is a change in land use from industrial/commercial to residential/parkland. Second, it authorized regulations to provide clear rules for site assessment, cleanup, and standards for contaminants based on a proposed land use. This change largely codified MOE's 1997 guidelines into standards having the force of law. Third, it required the acceptance of a site-specific risk assessment by MOE as prepared by a certified professional, and it allowed for conditions to be placed on the use of a property. See R Fishlock,

"Brownfields Reform in Ontario" in *Key Developments in Environmental Law: 2010 Edition* (Toronto: Canada Law Book, 2010).

B. LIABILITY PRINCIPLES

Principles of contaminated site liability have embraced two competing approaches under legislation in Canada. One approach is exemplified by the adoption of the "polluter pays" principle. The Supreme Court of Canada described this principle in *Imperial Oil Ltd v Quebec (Minister of the Environment)*, 2003 SCC 58 at paras 1, 23-24, [2003] 2 SCR 624, a case involving contamination at a site owned by Imperial Oil Ltd, which challenged an order from the Minister of the Environment that required the company to prepare at its own expense, and submit to the ministry, a site characterization study that would also include decontamination measures. In upholding the order on appeal, the Supreme Court noted that the "polluter pays" principle "has now been incorporated into the environmental legislation of Quebec. ... In fact, that principle has become firmly entrenched in environmental law in Canada. It is found in almost all federal and provincial environmental legislation ... [and] is also recognized at the international level. ... To encourage sustainable development, that principle assigns polluters the responsibility for remedying contamination for which they are responsible and imposes on them the direct and immediate costs of pollution." However, a second approach of environmental legislation is the imposition of liability irrespective of fault. The competing statutory principles have been reflected in the case law.

1. Polluter Pays Versus No-Fault Liability

KAWARTHA LAKES (CITY) V ONTARIO (ENVIRONMENT)
2013 ONCA 310

GOUDGE JA:

[1] This proceeding arises from a fuel oil spill that occurred on December 18, 2008 on residential property owned by Mr. and Mrs. Gendron. The Gendron property is adjacent to a road allowance owned by the appellant City of Kawartha Lakes, which is in turn adjacent to the shore of Sturgeon Lake. The fuel oil was delivered to the Gendrons that day by Thompson Fuels Ltd.

[2] Following the spill, fuel oil migrated on to the appellant's property and into Sturgeon Lake. As a consequence, the Ministry of the Environment (the MOE) ordered the appellant to remediate the adverse effects of the spill on its property. The appellant appealed unsuccessfully, first to the Environment Review Tribunal, and then to the Divisional Court. With leave, it now appeals to this court.

[3] All parties agree that the appellant bore no responsibility for the spill. The issue is whether the Tribunal erred in preventing the appellant from calling evidence to show who was at fault for the spill. The Divisional Court found that the Tribunal was correct in doing so.

[4] I would dismiss the appeal. ...

• • •

[10] ... The appellant's position was that while the MOE had jurisdiction to issue a s. 157.1 [no fault] order [under the Ontario *Environmental Protection Act*] against it as a property owner, to do so was unfair and contrary to the "polluter pays" principle, which assigns polluters the responsibility for, and the cost of, remedying the

contamination for which they are responsible. To make this case, the appellant sought to call evidence that each of the home owners, the fuel provider and/or the maker of the fuel tank was at fault for the spill.

• • •

[19] ... I agree with the Tribunal and the Divisional Court that evidence that others were at fault for the spill is irrelevant to whether the order against the appellant should be revoked. That order is a no fault order. It is not premised on a finding of fault on the part of the appellant but on the need to serve the environmental protection objective of the legislation.

[20] The tribunal had to determine whether revoking the Director's order would serve that objective. Deciding whether others are at fault for the spill is of no assistance in answering that question. Evidence of the fault of others says nothing about how the environment would be protected and the legislative objective served if the Director's order were revoked. Indeed, by inviting the Tribunal into a fault finding exercise, permitting the evidence might even impede answering the question in the timely way required by that legislative objective.

[The court dismissed the appeal].

NOTES

1. In *Hamilton Beach Brands Canada Inc v Ministry of the Environment and Climate Change*, 2018 ONSC 5010 at paras 63-67 (Div Ct), the Divisional Court of Ontario dismissed an appeal from a decision of the province's Environmental Review Tribunal that upheld an MOE order under s 18 of the *Environmental Protection Act* that required current owners of property to delineate offsite migration of contaminants even though they alleged that they were innocent owners of the property contaminated by the previous owners. The court noted that the tribunal's interpretation of s 18 as being applicable to existing and not just future offsite migration of contaminants was consistent with the Act's 2001 brownfield amendment requirements that extinguish any protections under the Act for owners of property where contamination migrates offsite. Compare this result with that of the following case.

2. In *JI Properties Inc v PPG Architectural Coatings Canada Ltd*, 2015 BCCA 472 at paras 29, 53, 59-60, a former owner of contaminated land who had obtained a "comfort letter" from the regulator stating that it had cleaned up the site to the standards applicable at the time was held liable for $4.75 million in additional remediation costs incurred by the current owner of the site. The former owner could not rely on the comfort letter as a defence to paying for the costs of remediation because the letter was not the equivalent of a certificate of compliance and, thus, was not what s 46(1)(m) of the *Environmental Management Act* required. The British Columbia Court of Appeal noted that the policy that was reflected in the section was that historic polluters who have left land contaminated in the sense that it does not meet the standards prescribed by regulation and required to qualify for a certificate of compliance are liable for the cost of remediating land to current standards. The court described a foundation of the scheme that became law in the province in the late 1990s: the "polluter pays" principle, whose statutory objective was to require polluters to pay the cost of cleanup of contamination from which they have benefited in the past, even where their polluting activities had not been prohibited or had been authorized at the time they occurred.

2. Retroactive, Retrospective, and Prospective Liability

A variation of the debate whether polluter pays or no-fault liability principles should apply in the context of contaminated land is the question of whether legislation should impose liability retroactively, retrospectively, or merely prospectively. That is, should legislation (1) reach back in time to impose liability for events that occurred before the law's enactment, (2) be restricted to operating with respect to events subsequent to its enactment, or (3) apply to something in between? Statute and case law in various provinces have provided a number of answers.

Under British Columbia's *Environmental Management Act*, s 47(1) states that a "person who is responsible for remediation of a contaminated site is absolutely, retroactively and jointly and separately liable to any person or government body for reasonably incurred costs of remediation of the contaminated site, whether incurred on or off the contaminated site." The term "retroactive" is not defined in the statute, and it attracted judicial comment in the following case, interpreting the *Waste Management Act*, RSBC 1996, c 482 (the predecessor legislation to the *Environmental Management Act*).

BRITISH COLUMBIA HYDRO AND POWER AUTHORITY V BRITISH COLUMBIA (ENVIRONMENTAL APPEAL BOARD)
2003 BCCA 436

NEWBURY JA:

• • •

[67] ... Professor Driedger states that a retroactive statute is "easy to recognize" since it must contain a provision that ["]changes the law as of a time prior to its enactment." (See also Côté, ... [J-P Côté, *The Interpretation of Legislation in Canada*], 3rd ed. [(2000)], at 127.) The *Waste Management Act as a whole* does not contain any statement that it is meant to apply as of a date earlier than April 1, 1997, nor that it shall be deemed always to have been law, or that it has always been the law. The only express reference in Part 4 to retroactivity is the word "retroactively" in s. 27(1), which applies to the liability of persons "who are responsible for remediation" of a contaminated site—a phrase which all counsel assumed, correctly in my view, is meant to refer to "responsible persons" as defined by s. 26.5(1). The definition does not suggest that such persons "are and have always been" responsible persons or that they "are and have since British Columbia entered Confederation, been" responsible for remediation. Nor is any reference made to the predecessor corporations of previous or present owners or operators, or to the estates of deceased owners or operators.

• • •

[75] ... if all of Part 4 or the definition of "responsible person," [sic] did operate retroactively, the implications would be breathtaking in terms of legal theory. Any individual or body corporate who had contributed to the contamination of real property in British Columbia since the time it entered Confederation would be caught in the net as of the time of the contamination. Individuals have died, estates and corporations have been wound up, businesses and properties have been bought and sold, financial statements have been relied upon—the finality of a host of transactions and representations would be cast into doubt by a statute that imposes liability retroactively to 1871—subject, I suppose, to any bar arising under the *Limitation Act* [RSBC 1996, c 266, replaced by *Limitation Act*, SBC 2012, c 13] (concerning which we received no submissions). Quite apart from any presumption of construction, this fact should cause any court to require that clear language be used to effect such a result.

[76] In short, I agree with Deputy Director Driedger, who stated in his reasons:

... for the purpose of the power to issue a remediation order in s. 27.1(1) [sic] of the Act, the definitions of responsible person in the 1993 amendments to the *Waste*

Management Act are not retroactive. *Nothing in the language of s. 26.5 suggests that definitions operate backward in time and change the law from what it was in 1965. The provisions are instead a clear example of retrospective legislation which—in relation to the definition of responsible person—operates for the future but in so doing imposes new legal consequences in respect of past actions, events or status.* Thus, on April 1, 1997, a person who was a past or present owner or operator of a contaminated site, or a person who in the past was a producer or transporter, became a responsible person subject to a remediation order. While the effect of the amendments was to dramatically expand in the present the responsibility of persons for their past actions or status, the amendments do not change the law *as it existed before the legislation came into force.* [Emphasis added.]

(I note that in an article entitled *"Retrospectivity in Law"* (1995) 29 *U.B.C. Law Rev.* 5, Professor E. Edinger takes a similar view concerning Part 4 (see paras 10-12), as does Professor M. McDonald ... ["An Enquiry into the Ethics of Retrospective Liability: The Case of British Columbia's Bill 26" (1995) 29 UBC L Rev 63] at 63-71.)

LEGAL OIL AND GAS LTD V ALBERTA (MINISTER OF ENVIRONMENT)
2000 ABQB 388, 34 CELR (NS) 303

[An environmental protection order, under s 113 of Alberta's *Environmental Protection and Enhancement Act*, RSA 2000, c E-12, was issued to an oil well owner to clean up a spill. The spill had migrated offsite and contaminated neighbouring land decades before the law was enacted. Section 113 authorizes a director of the provincial environment ministry to issue an order to the person responsible for the substance where the director is of the opinion that a release of a substance into the environment has occurred, and the release has caused an adverse effect. The owner contended that any contamination of these lands would have occurred before it took possession and acquired ownership of the well. Following a hearing by the provincial Environmental Appeal Board, the minister of environment adopted the recommendation of the board to affirm the order. The owner applied for judicial review of the minister's approval of the order. The court stated the following about the issue of retrospectivity:]

[47] The Applicants submit that ministerial approval of the Director's order has the effect of determining that s. 102 [now s 113] of the Act is retrospective in its application. They argue that as the Act does not expressly state that it operates with respect to transactions which occurred prior to its enactment, the Board should have applied the presumption against retrospective application.

• • •

[49] However, the Board ... concluded that to the extent the [order] has a retrospective element, s. 102 of the Act is intended to operate in that fashion.

[50] I do not consider the conclusions of the Board in relation to this issue to be patently unreasonable, particularly given that the Supreme Court of Canada has recognized an exception to the presumption against retrospective application when the purpose of the provision is to protect the public rather than to punish (*Brosseau v. Alberta Securities Commission*, [1989] 1 S.C.R. 301). Section 102 of the Act certainly falls in the "protection of the public" category.

HUANG V FRASER HILLARY'S LIMITED
2018 ONCA 527

[In the 1960s and 1970s, solvents used in the defendant's dry cleaning operations spilled onto the ground. In the mid-1980s, the defendant purchased an additional property that was determined in 2002 to be the source of solvent contamination of a property purchased by the plaintiff.]

HOURIGAN JA:

• • •

(3) SECTION 99 OF THE EPA

[29] Fraser's submission is that the trial judge erred because he retrospectively applied Part X of the [*Environmental Protection Act*]. That part of the legislation deals with liability and other obligations as a consequence of spills. Fraser notes that Part X was not proclaimed into force until 1985. Because the spills on its property ceased in 1974, Fraser submits that the *EPA* can have no application. I would not give effect to this ground of appeal.

[30] The relevant sections of the *EPA* to consider in analyzing this submission are as follows:

93(1) The owner of a pollutant and the person having control of a pollutant that is spilled and that causes or is likely to cause an adverse effect shall forthwith do everything practicable to prevent, eliminate and ameliorate the adverse effect and to restore the natural environment.

• • •

99(2) Her Majesty in right of Ontario or in right of Canada or any other person has the right to compensation,
(a) for loss or damage incurred as a direct result of,
(i) the spill of a pollutant that causes or is likely to cause an adverse effect,
(ii) the exercise of any authority under subsection 100(1) or the carrying out of or attempting to carry out a duty imposed or an order or direction made under this Part, or
(iii) neglect or default in carrying out a duty imposed or an order or direction made under this Part;
(b) for all reasonable cost and expense incurred in respect of carrying out or attempting to carry out an order or direction under this Part,
from the owner of the pollutant and the person having control of the pollutant.

[31] In my view, the trial judge did not retrospectively apply the *EPA*. Time does not freeze in 1974 for the purposes of liability under s. 99(2). Accepting for the purposes of this argument that the spills ceased in that year, there was an ongoing obligation under s. 93 of the *EPA* to remediate the damage. That remediation has not been done. Therefore, there is liability under s. 99(2)(a)(i) and (ii) because Fraser has not fulfilled a duty imposed on it under Part X of the *EPA*. In short, while the spills may have occurred before Part X of the *EPA* was enacted, Fraser's obligations under that part of the legislation are ongoing.

NOTES AND QUESTIONS

1. In *Épiciers Unis Métro-Richelieu Inc, division "Éconogros" v Collin*, 2004 SCC 59 at para 46, [2004] 3 SCR 257, in a non-contaminated land case, the Supreme Court adopted the following statement from an article by EA Driedger ("Statutes: Retroactive Retrospective Reflections" (1978) 56 Can Bar Rev 264 at 268-69; copyright © 1978 Can Bar Rev by EA Driedger) on the retroactivity/retrospectivity question:

> A retroactive statute is one that operates as of a time prior to its enactment. A retrospective statute is one that operates for the future only. It is prospective, but it imposes new results in respect of a past event. A retroactive statute *operates backwards*. A retrospective statute *operates forwards*, but it looks backwards in that it attaches new consequences *for the future* to an event that took place before the statute was enacted. A retroactive statute changes the law from what it was; a retrospective statute changes the law from what it otherwise would be with respect to a prior event. [Emphasis in original.]

2. The British Columbia Court of Appeal in *British Columbia Hydro*, excerpted above, cast doubt on the legislatively expressed intention to apply liability for contaminated sites retroactively, viewing the provision in what is now the *Environmental Management Act* as, instead, retrospective in nature, given the statutory language employed. The Alberta Court of Queen's Bench decision in *Legal Oil* stated that a statutory provision can operate *against* the presumption against retrospective application of the law, particularly where the purpose of the provision is to protect the public. The Ontario Court of Appeal in *Huang* stated that an ongoing statutory obligation to remediate environmental contamination did not constitute retrospective application of the law. Are all of these characterizations of the issue from the British Columbia, Alberta, and Ontario courts in accord with the Supreme Court excerpt from *Épiciers*?

3. Allocation of Liability

In order to introduce fairness principles into the process of assigning liability for contaminated lands, provinces have adopted principles of apportionment or allocation into their legislation. Under British Columbia's *Environmental Management Act*, s 49(2) allows potentially responsible persons to seek an opinion from an allocation panel, established under the statute, regarding whether the person is a responsible person or a minor contributor and, if liable, the person's share of liability for contamination.

Other provinces have developed similar regimes. The process in Manitoba, for example, is established under *The Contaminated Sites Remediation Act*, CCSM c C205. Following the identification of remediation measures that are necessary at a contaminated property, the Act authorizes the province to issue remediation orders to potentially responsible persons (PRPs). The Act sets out a process for apportionment of liability among PRPs based on a set of factors derived from the 1993 CCME principles for contaminated site liability (discussed in Section I of this chapter). The factors include (1) the "polluter pays" principle, (2) subjective or objective knowledge of the person regarding the contaminated state of the property, (3) effect on fair market value or permitted uses of the site, (4) reasonable steps, if any, taken to prevent contamination, (5) whether the PRP disposed of the site while knowing it was contaminated, (6) compliance with industry standards in handling contaminants, and (7) steps that the PRP took to limit contamination and notify regulatory authorities after becoming aware of the contamination (ss 1(1)(c), 21). PRPs are responsible only for their proportionate share of remediation costs as determined by agreement or following a provincial apportionment hearing. They are not jointly and severally liable for cleanup unless they are in default (s 30).

NOTES AND QUESTIONS

Is it sound environmental policy for Manitoba law to contemplate that less than 100 percent of remediation liability could be allocated among PRPs, leaving the provincial taxpayer potentially responsible for the costs of remaining "orphaned" shares? See J Stefaniuk, "The Green Greenfields of Home: Contaminated Sites Legislation in the Prairie Provinces—An Overview" (Paper delivered at the Canadian Bar Association National Environmental Law Section Annual Legal Education Program, "Contaminated Properties and the Redevelopment of Brownfield Sites," Toronto, April 2002) at 3.

C. DAMAGES PRINCIPLES

Another way of looking at the issue of the appropriate cleanup standard for land that has been contaminated is as a question of the measure of damages. Cases across the country have taken a number of approaches to the issue.

MIDWEST PROPERTIES LTD V THORDARSON
2015 ONCA 819, 128 OR (3d) 81

[The plaintiff and defendant owned adjoining properties in an industrial area of Toronto. The defendant stored large volumes of waste petroleum hydrocarbons (PHC) on its property for several decades, and the PHC contaminated the soil and groundwater on its property and eventually the plaintiff's property. The plaintiff discovered the contamination after it had acquired its property in 2007 and sued the defendant under several common law causes of action and also pursuant to s 99(2) of the *Environmental Protection Act*. The trial judge held that the defendants were not liable under any of the causes of action, finding that the plaintiff had failed to prove that it had suffered damages, in particular because it had not proven that the PHC contamination lowered the value of its property. The plaintiff appealed the trial judgment.

The following excerpts from the Ontario Court of Appeal judgment address the treatment of damages under s 99(2) of the Act.]

HOURIGAN JA:

• • •

(II) FAILURE TO PROVE DAMAGES

[56] The trial judge also dismissed ... Midwest's s. 99(2) claim on the ground that it "did not introduce evidence of damage or loss pursuant to section 99 of the *EPA*, such as actual loss in property value or its inability to use its property or operate its business on its property, or business losses." The respondents assert three arguments in support of the trial judge's conclusion on damages.

[57] First, the respondents argue that any damages awarded to Midwest should be measured by the diminution in the value of Midwest's property rather than by the cost of remediation.

[58] The respondents note that, while Mr. Vanin and Mr. Tossell suggested that there would be negative financial impacts from the contamination, neither was qualified as an expert in mortgages or property valuation. Midwest also did not tender any appraisal reports or property valuations. Therefore, the respondents submit that there is no basis to conclude that the value of Midwest's property has been adversely affected, and accordingly, no basis on which to award damages.

[59] I would not give effect to these arguments.

[60] There is a significant debate in the case law about whether diminution in value or restoration costs is the appropriate measure of damages in cases of

environmental harm: see Faieta et al. [Mario D Faieta et al, *Environmental Harm: Civil Actions and Compensation* (Markham, Ont: Butterworths, 1996)], at p. 293.

[61] At common law, the traditional view was that damages for any type of injury to property should be measured by the diminution in value caused by the injury: see *Hosking v. Phillips* (1848), 154 E.R. 801, 3 Exch. Rep. 168 (Eng. Ex. Ct.). More recently, courts have awarded damages based on restoration costs, even if those costs exceed the amount of the decrease in property value: see Katherine M. van Rensburg, "Deconstructing *Tridan*: A Litigator's Perspective" (2004) 15 J. Envtl. L. & Prac. 85, at p. 89; see e.g. *Jens v. Mannix Co.* (1978) [sic], 1978 CanLII 1962 (BC SC), 89 D.L.R. (3d) 351 (B.C.S.C.); *Horne v. New Glasgow*, 1953 CanLII 335 (NS SC), [1954] 1 D.L.R. 832 (N.S.S.C.).

[62] The restoration approach is superior, from an environmental perspective, to the diminution in value approach. Since the cost of restoration may exceed the value of the property, an award based on diminution of value may not adequately fund clean-up: Bruce Pardy, *Environmental Law: A Guide to Concepts* (Markham, ON: Butterworths, 1996), at p. 223.

• • •

[80] ... As noted above, there is really no dispute on the evidence regarding the costs of the remediation. Midwest led expert evidence that the reasonable costs of remediating its property would be $1,328,000 and the respondents, while challenging that expert evidence, did not lead positive evidence on the costs of remediating Midwest's property. In my view, the future remediation costs for Midwest's property are recoverable and Midwest is entitled to judgment for the full amount of its estimated costs, being $1,328,000.

NOTES AND QUESTIONS

1. In *Cousins v McColl-Frontenac Inc*, 2006 NBQB 406, aff'd 2007 NBCA 83, the New Brunswick Court of Appeal upheld a trial judgment based on common law nuisance and strict liability principles that found the plaintiff entitled to recover damages from the defendant (owner of a closed service station that leaked gasoline) for contamination of land the plaintiff had acquired from a third party. However, the Court of Appeal also agreed with the trial judge that it would be unreasonable to assess damages on the basis of the cost of remediation. The basis for the trial judgment conclusion was that it rejected the assumption that the plaintiff would spend enormous sums (approximately $1-2 million) for the remediation of the property acquired from the third party, which the court regarded as speculative remediation expenses of undeveloped land or theoretical assumptions about lost profits from development that had not occurred. Instead, the trial court awarded $125,000 to the plaintiff on the basis of the net investment made.

2. Should injured parties be entitled to compensation on the basis of restoring land to the condition it was in before it was contaminated, or on the basis of the diminution in its value arising from the contamination? Or on some other basis? See Ramani Nadarajah, "Appropriate Measure of Damages Part 1: No Award"; Janet Bobechko, "Appropriate Measure of Damages Part 2: Clean to Pristine"; Jennifer Fairfax, "Appropriate Measure of Damages Part 3: Clean to 'Restoration'"; Matthew Gardner, "Appropriate Measure of Damages Part 4: Clean to Risk Assessment Acceptance"; and Natalie Mullins, "Appropriate Measure of Damages Part 5: Diminution in Value" (Presentations made at the Law Society of Ontario's "The Six-Minute Environmental Lawyer 2018" program, Toronto, 3 October 2018).

D. LIMITATION PERIOD IMPACTS ON CONTAMINATED LAND LIABILITY

Contamination of land can consist of soil and groundwater pollution that is often difficult to discover without the assistance of technical and scientific experts, and sometimes even with their assistance. The resulting uncertainty can have an impact on recovery in an action by barring a claim due to an expiring limitation period in the absence of judicial recognition of the special problems posed in "discovering" knowledge of actual contamination.

CROMBIE PROPERTY HOLDINGS LIMITED V MCCOLL-FRONTENAC INC (TEXACO CANADA LIMITED)
2017 ONCA 16

[The plaintiff (appellant) brought an action for damages resulting from the contamination of its property by hydrocarbons, which were alleged to have migrated from an adjacent property that had been used as a gas station until 2004. In its action, commenced on April 28, 2014, the plaintiff asserted that it had not been aware of soil and groundwater contamination on its property caused by the migration of hydrocarbons from the gas station property until September 17, 2012, though it had purchased the property on April 10, 2012. The plaintiff had hired a consultant to assist with its environmental due diligence. The defendant (respondent) owner of the gas station property claimed that the plaintiff had discovered the contamination more than two years before commencing the action, and, therefore, the action was barred by the *Limitations Act, 2002*, SO 2002, c 24, Schedule B. A motion for summary judgment brought by the defendant was granted and the action dismissed, the motions judge holding that (1) the plaintiff had become aware of sufficient material facts to form the basis for the action by March 9, 2012, when the plaintiff had waived all conditions for the purchase, including environmental conditions, for 22 properties; or (2) although in possession of a draft Phase II report prepared and submitted by its consultant on May 9, 2012, the plaintiff had had more than sufficient basis for an action by March 30, 2012, when laboratory results had been made available to it. The plaintiff appealed the decision.]

VAN RENSBURG JA:

• • •

(2) FRAMING THE LIMITATIONS ISSUE

[33] In order to obtain a summary dismissal of the action, the moving parties were required to establish that there was no issue requiring a trial about their limitation defence. The specific issue was whether Crombie's claim in respect of the environmental contamination of its property was "discovered" within the meaning of s. 5 of the *Limitations Act, 2002* before April 28, 2012.

[34] Section 5(1) of the *Limitations Act, 2002* provides that a claim is discovered on the earlier of:

    (a) the day on which the person with the claim first knew,

        (i) that the injury, loss or damage had occurred,

        (ii) that the injury, loss or damage was caused by or contributed to by an act or omission,

        (iii) that the act or omission was that of the person against whom the claim is made, and

(iv) that, having regard to the nature of the injury, loss or damage, a proceeding would be an appropriate means to seek to remedy it; and

(b) the day on which a reasonable person with the abilities and in the circumstances of the person with the claim first ought to have known of the matters referred to in clause (a).

[35] The limitation period runs from when the plaintiff is actually aware of the matters referred to in s. 5(1)(a)(i) to (iv) or when a reasonable person with the abilities and in the circumstances of the plaintiff first ought to have known of all of those matters: *Longo* [*Longo v MacLaren Art Centre Inc*, 2014 ONCA 526, 323 OAC 246], at para. 41. The knowledge sufficient to commence the limitations clock has been described as "subjective" knowledge or "objective" knowledge. The prospective plaintiff must have known or ought reasonably to have known of the material facts necessary for a claim. It is "reasonable discoverability" and not "the mere possibility of discovery" that triggers a limitation period: *Van Allen v. Vos*, 2014 ONCA 552, 121 O.R. (3d) 72, at paras. 33 and 34.

[36] The central issue in this case, as framed by the parties, is when the appellant knew or ought reasonably to have known that the Crombie Property was contaminated by hydrocarbons, and in particular whether that occurred before April 28, 2012. ...

• • •

[38] [T]he motion judge ... made two palpable and overriding errors.

(3) EQUATING SUSPICION OF CONTAMINATION WITH ACTUAL KNOWLEDGE OF CONTAMINATION

• • •

[40] The motion judge did not point to any evidence that Crombie had actual knowledge of the hydrocarbon contamination at the Crombie Property [in March 2012]. ...

• • •

[42] [T]he motion judge equated Crombie's knowledge of possible contamination with knowledge of actual contamination ... . It was not sufficient that Crombie had suspicions or that there was possible contamination. The issue under s. 5(1)(a) of the *Limitations Act, 2002* for when a claim is discovered, [sic] is the plaintiff's "actual" knowledge. The suspicion of certain facts or knowledge of a potential claim may be enough to put a plaintiff on inquiry and trigger a due diligence obligation, in which case the issue is whether a reasonable person with the abilities and in the circumstances of the plaintiff ought reasonably to have discovered the claim, under s. 5(1)(b). Here, while the suspicion of contamination was sufficient to give rise to a duty of inquiry, it was not sufficient to meet the requirement for actual knowledge. The subsurface testing, while confirmatory of the appellant's suspicions, was the mechanism by which the appellant acquired actual knowledge of the contamination.

[43] Finally, I note that the motion judge stated that the appellant's claims were "available and discoverable" well before April 28, 2012. While not determinative, this suggests that the motion judge adopted too low a threshold for discoverability and did not focus on what was necessary to her analysis: she was required to determine when the appellant had actual knowledge of the elements of its claim, and in particular that the property was contaminated by hydrocarbons, and when a reasonable

person with the appellant's abilities and in its circumstances, [sic] ought to have known of the contamination. The fact that contamination was there to be discovered was of course not sufficient to start the limitations clock.

[44] For these reasons, I conclude that it was a palpable and overriding error for the motion judge to equate knowledge of potential contamination with knowledge of actual contamination.

NOTE

In allowing the appeal in *Crombie*, the Ontario Court of Appeal also held that the motions judge had failed to consider the surrounding circumstances of the transaction, in particular the multi-property nature of the transaction, which involved the purchase and sale of 22 separate properties, the plaintiff's waiver of conditions, and the resulting impact on the ability of the plaintiff to obtain knowledge of actual contamination at an earlier point in time.

E. PARTIES LIABLE

As noted at the beginning of this section, liability may attach to the interests of owners, operators, parent corporations, lenders, receivers, receiver-managers, trustees in bankruptcy, or governments, each of which is discussed below.

1. Owners and Operators—Past and Present

Many provinces have vested ministries of the environment with broad authority to order the cleanup of contaminated property, including soil and groundwater. These orders are often directed at owners and operators of sources of contamination. Some of these jurisdictions also have attempted to apply their legislative powers to past owners and operators.

Canadian National Railway Co v Ontario (Director under the Environmental Protection Act), 1991 CanLII 7169, 6 CELR (NS) (2d) 211 at 214, 218 (Ont Div Ct) exemplifies judicial treatment of current and past owners and operators under early versions of these statutory authorities. On land owned by Canadian National Railway (CNR), Abitibi-Price Inc (AP Inc) operated a wood treatment business in Thunder Bay harbour from 1974 to 1982. At that point, AP Inc assigned the lease and sold the business to Northern Wood Preservers Inc (NWP Inc) and took back a mortgage by way of sublease to secure the sale. Over the years, soil, groundwater, and sediments in and around the site became contaminated by creosote and other chemicals arising from current and past operations at the site. In 1987, a director of the Ministry of the Environment issued a control order under the *Environmental Protection Act*, RSO 1980, c 141, as amended, to CNR (the landowner), AP Inc (the past plant owner and operator), and NWP Inc (the current plant owner and operator) to study and clean up the problem. All three appealed the order to the province's Environmental Appeal Board. The board confirmed the order against CNR and NWP Inc, both of which appealed to the Divisional Court, while the director appealed the dismissal of the order against AP Inc. The Divisional Court confirmed the order against NWP Inc, dismissed it against CNR, and upheld the dismissal of the order against AP Inc. The Ontario Court of Appeal affirmed the decision of the Divisional Court (1992 CanLII 7705, 8 CELR (NS) (2d) 1 at 5-6 (Ont CA)). With respect to CNR, the Court of Appeal agreed with the Divisional Court that in the factual circumstances of the case, the soil that constitutes the natural medium through which the contaminant percolates is not a "source of contaminant" within the meaning of s 6 of the Act, and that CNR was not, as a result of its interest as a reversionary owner of the contaminated soil, a "person responsible for a source of contaminant" under that section. With regard to AP Inc, the Court of Appeal agreed with the Divisional Court that ss 6 and 17, as drafted at the time, were restricted to present, not former, owners and operators, and that the director's order could not be addressed to AP Inc as a result of activities conducted by it during the period of its ownership or operation prior to 1982. The Court of Appeal further noted that although not determinative of the issue, amendments to ss 6 and 17 (now ss 7 and 18) of the *Environmental Protection Act* in 1990 extend the scope of these provisions to previous owners and occupiers as well as to persons who "had" the charge, management, or control of a source of contaminant, undertaking, or property. The Court of Appeal agreed that the order was properly directed to NWP Inc, which was the owner and person in control and management of the plant that the board had found was a continuing source of the contamination.

NOTES AND QUESTIONS

1. If the 1990 amendments had been in force at the time of the 1987 order in *Canadian National Railway*, what would be the result for AP Inc? What about CNR? Do the 1990 amendments change CNR's legal position?

2. In 2001, Bill 56, Ontario's brownfield law, amended several pieces of environmental, planning, and municipal legislation to provide liability protection from future environmental orders for current and past owners and operators (those in charge, management, or control) of contaminated property if they follow the prescribed site assessment and cleanup process. This includes filing a record of site condition with the province under the site registry regime established by the amendments, using a certified consultant, and following other requirements prescribed by regulation (see part XV.1, Records of Site Condition, of the Ontario *Environmental Protection Act*, particularly s 168.7, Consequences of filing record of site condition). See Fishlock, "Brownfields Reform in Ontario," cited in Section III.A of this chapter.

3. Other provinces have developed extensive contaminated site liability provisions for owners and operators. British Columbia's *Environmental Management Act* (Part 4—Contaminated Site Remediation) treats current and past owners and operators as persons responsible for remediating contaminated sites, subject to certain exemptions. Excerpts from the statute follow.

ENVIRONMENTAL MANAGEMENT ACT
SBC 2003, c 53, ss 39(1), 45(1), 46(1)

DIVISION 1—INTERPRETATION

Definitions and interpretation

39(1) In this Part ... :

• • •

"operator" means ... a person who is or was in control of or responsible for any operation located at a contaminated site, but does not include a secured creditor unless the secured creditor is described in section 45(3) ... ;

• • •

"owner" means a person who
   (a) is in possession,
   (b) has the right of control, or
   (c) occupies or controls the use

of real property, and includes, without limitation, a person who has an estate or interest, legal or equitable, in the real property, but does not include a secured creditor unless the secured creditor is described in section 45(3) ... ;

• • •

DIVISION 3—LIABILITY FOR REMEDIATION

Persons responsible for remediation of contaminated sites

45(1) Subject to section 46 ... , the following persons are responsible for remediation of a contaminated site:

(a) a current owner or operator of the site;

(b) a previous owner or operator of the site;

• • •

Persons not responsible for remediation

46(1) The following persons are not responsible for remediation of a contaminated site:

• • •

(d) an owner or operator who establishes that

(i) at the time the person became an owner or operator of the site,

(A) the site was a contaminated site,

(B) the person had no knowledge or reason to know or suspect that the site was a contaminated site, and

(C) the person undertook all appropriate inquiries into the previous ownership and uses of the site and undertook other investigations, consistent with good commercial or customary practice at that time, in an effort to minimize potential liability,

(ii) if the person was an owner of the site, the person did not transfer any interest in the site without first disclosing any known contamination to the transferee, and

(iii) the owner or operator did not, by any act or omission, cause or contribute to the contamination of the site;

(e) an owner or operator who

(i) owned or occupied a site that at the time of acquisition was not a contaminated site, and

(ii) during the ownership or operation, did not dispose of, handle or treat a substance in a manner that, in whole or in part, caused the site to become a contaminated site ... .

NOTES AND QUESTIONS

1. British Columbia's contaminated site liability provisions for current and past owners and operators are modeled on the 1980 US *Comprehensive Environmental Response, Compensation, and Liability Act* (CERCLA), 42 USC, § 9607(a). CERCLA makes the following person a potentially responsible party: "(1) the owner and operator of a vessel or a facility" or "(2) any person who at the time of disposal of any hazardous substance owned or operated any facility at which such hazardous substances were disposed of." CERCLA contains exemptions from liability that are similar to those in BC's legislation. Amendments to CERCLA in 2002 added exemptions for *bona fide* prospective purchasers and contiguous property owners. They also clarified the innocent purchaser defence added to the law by

amendments in 1986. See EE Smary, "The New Federal Superfund Amendments—New Transactional and Brownfield Standards in the United States" (Paper delivered at the Canadian Bar Association National Environmental Law Section Annual Legal Education Program, "Contaminated Properties and the Redevelopment of Brownfield Sites," Toronto, April 2002) at 3-8.

2. In the early 2000s, the British Columbia Advisory Panel on Contaminated Sites (BCAPCS) recommended that the *Waste Management Act* (predecessor to the current law) narrow the range of persons currently caught within what is now s 45(1) of the *Environmental Management Act* and the definitions of "owner" and "operator" in what is now s 39(1) of the Act. According to the advisory panel, "responsibility should be connected primarily to a person's control over and causal link to the activity or substance causing the contamination, rather than to considerations of who has the 'deepest pockets.'" See BCAPCS, *Advisory Panel on Contaminated Sites Interim Report* (3 September 2002) (Panel Chair: Margaret Eriksson) at 15-16, online (pdf): *Legislative Assembly of British Columbia—Legislative Library* <http://www.llbc .leg.bc.ca/public/PubDocs/bcdocs/356959/interim_report_final.pdf>. While the recommendations were not incorporated into what is now the *Environmental Management Act*, the proposal raises a number of questions. What are the advantages and disadvantages of this approach to identifying potentially responsible persons? Is not the deepest pocket that of the taxpayer who will be forced to pay for cleanups if those persons with some connection to, or who benefited from activity on, a contaminated site are exempt from liability? Moreover, if the net of potentially responsible persons is narrowed, will this encourage or undermine the trend to act preventively in business practices by performing due diligence inspections and environmental audits on property?

2. Parent Corporations

There are a number of liability theories that may be applicable to parent corporations under contaminated site legislation. One theory is based on simply owning shares in a subsidiary. A second theory is based on the control exercised by the parent over the subsidiary. The following case explores these theories.

BEAZER EAST INC V BRITISH COLUMBIA (ENVIRONMENTAL APPEAL BOARD)
2000 BCSC 1698, 36 CELR (NS) 195

[For a number of years, Beazer East Inc was the parent corporation (through share ownership) of the operator of a wood treatment facility that had contaminated the site as a result of its operations. The Environmental Appeal Board upheld a site remediation order of the provincial environment ministry against Beazer. The company sought judicial review of the board decision.]

[76] The Board did not find s 35(5) of the Contaminated Sites Regulation [BC Reg 375/96] to be the test for determining whether a parent corporation is an operator. The Board found that the Legislature did not intend to "pierce the corporate veil" in the sense that liability for remediation as an operator does not occur simply because of the legal relationship between a company and its shareholders. Thus, a parent which owns 100% of its subsidiary's shares does not, on that fact alone, become an operator under the [*Waste Management Act*]. By implication, the Board also made these same findings with respect to the ownership issue.

[77] The Board relied on the broad language used by the Legislature in the definition of "owner" to reject the narrow approach advocated by Beazer to the effect that corporate principles dictate that parent corporations should not be treated as owners of real property belonging to their subsidiaries. The Board concluded that Beazer had the right to "control the use of" the real property as a result of the fact that all leases of the Site had to be approved by Beazer before they could be entered into by the Principal Operator.

• • •

[90] ... In my view, this case is not about lifting the corporate veil in the sense of making the shareholders of a corporation liable for the actions of the corporation. Rather, this case is about the interpretation of the *Act*. ...

• • •

[95] The Board concluded that Beazer had "the right of control of ... the use of real property." It did not expressly consider dictionary definitions of the word "right." The relevant definition of the word "right" in the *Concise Oxford Dictionary of Current English*, 9th ed. (Clarendon Press: Oxford, 1998) is: "a thing one may legally or morally claim." The word "right" in the definition of "owner" is not referring to a moral claim. Rather, it is referring to a legal claim.

[96] To be a right within the meaning of the *Act*, it is my view that it must be a right recognized by law. Put another way, it must be a legally enforceable right. A parent corporation does not have the legal right to control a subsidiary's use of its assets. The rights of a parent corporation vis-à-vis its subsidiary flow from its shares. The rights attached to shares typically include the rights to vote for, among other things, the directors and auditors of the subsidiary, to attend shareholder meetings, to receive dividends and to receive a return of capital. It has been well established since *Salomon v. Soloman & Company*, [1897] A.C. 22 (H.L.) that a corporation has a separate existence from its shareholders. A shareholder does not have a legally enforceable right to control or direct the use of the corporation's assets.

[97] Of course, a parent corporation may have *de facto* control over the use of a subsidiary's assets. With the knowledge that a parent corporation can change the directors of a subsidiary and that the directors can change the officers, the management of the subsidiary may follow the directions of the parent corporation with respect to the use of its assets because the officers realize that they may be removed if they ignore those directions. However, there is a difference between a right to control and an ability to control.

• • •

[99] ... It was open to the Legislature to define "owner" to include persons who had the capacity or ability to control the use of real property but it chose to confine the definition to persons who had the right of control of the use of the property (and persons who occupied the property or who actually controlled the use of the property).

[The court held that Beazer was properly named in the order as a responsible person by virtue of being a previous operator of the site, but the portion of the board's decision finding Beazer to be a previous owner of the site was set aside.]

NOTES

1. Tysoe J in *Beazer* found that the right to control means a legally enforceable right and that Beazer, the parent corporation and sole shareholder of the subsidiary that held title to the site, did not have a right of control over the subsidiary's property because the subsidiary was a separate legal entity.

2. Under British Columbia's *Contaminated Sites Regulation*, BC Reg 375/96, s 35(5), as amended, a parent corporation will not be liable in a cost recovery civil claim brought under s 47(5) of the *Environmental Management Act* for the costs of remediation arising from the acts of a subsidiary corporation unless the plaintiff can prove that the parent authorized, permitted, or acquiesced in the activity of the subsidiary corporation that gave rise to the costs of remediation.

3. Courts in other jurisdictions have imposed liability on parent corporations by piercing the corporate veil or assigning tort liability directly to the parent company. In the international investment context, what are the implications for parent corporations with foreign subsidiaries under various statutory, corporate, or tort theories of responsibility? See W Braul, "Parent Corporation Liability for Foreign Subsidiaries" (2001) 4:4 Envtl L 258.

3. Lenders

Lenders can potentially be held liable for the costs of remediating the contaminated property of those who borrow from them if they assume the ownership of the property or exercise control or management of the property. Realizing on security taken on assets that happen to be environmentally contaminated lands may constitute "control" sufficient for lenders to incur liability for cleanup costs.

Uncertainty in the law in the 1990s resulted in a cycle of lenders either being held liable or refusing to finance new or expanded development of sites where contamination existed because of fear of attracting liability. This left the impression that existing law rewarded lenders who did nothing and penalized those who got involved. Accordingly, legislatures began to address the problem. To resolve the unsettled state of affairs, in 2001, Ontario enacted Bill 56, which includes two categories of amendments to the *Environmental Protection Act* designed to protect secured creditors and others (see part XV.2, Special Provisions Applicable to Municipalities, Secured Creditors, Receivers, Trustees in Bankruptcy, Fiduciaries and Property Investigators). The first category provides secured creditors with protection from environmental liability while they protect their security interests. In particular, secured creditors not in possession are now permitted to undertake a variety of prescribed actions without attracting liability for specific ministry orders. These actions include investigating and providing services to property, paying taxes, collecting rent, and responding to the presence or discharge of a contaminant on the property (s 168.17). The second category protects secured creditors when they foreclose on a property. Secured creditors that foreclose on a property are protected from the issuance of a ministry order for five years from the date of foreclosure unless they engage in gross negligence, wilful misconduct, or other circumstances that may be prescribed by the regulations (s 168.18).

Despite the amendments, Bill 56 has not eliminated the potential for imposing environmental liability on secured creditors in Ontario. The amendments allow the ministry to issue orders to a secured creditor who has foreclosed on a property where the province believes that a contaminant on the property poses a danger to human health or safety, serious risk of impairment to the natural environment, or serious risk of injury to property (s 168.20). Although these instances are characterized as "exceptional circumstances" under Bill 56, this characterization has not entirely eliminated liability concerns in the financial community. See R Curpen, S Elliot & D Kirby, "Ontario Brownfields Bill Passed with Mixed Opinions" (2002) 5:2 Envtl L 290 at 293-94.

Other jurisdictions also have dealt with the issue of lender liability through legislation. British Columbia's *Environmental Management Act* (part 4—Contaminated Site Remediation) treats lenders as persons responsible for remediating contaminated sites, subject to certain exemptions. Statutory excerpts follow.

ENVIRONMENTAL MANAGEMENT ACT
SBC 2003, c 53, ss 39(1), 45(3), (4)

DIVISION 1—INTERPRETATION

Definitions and interpretation

39(1) In this Part ... :

• • •

"secured creditor" means a person who holds a mortgage, charge, debenture, hypothecation or other security interest in property at a contaminated site, and includes an agent for that person;

• • •

DIVISION 3—LIABILITY FOR REMEDIATION

Persons responsible for remediation of contaminated sites

• • •

45(3) A secured creditor is responsible for remediation of a contaminated site if

(a) the secured creditor at any time exercised control over or imposed requirements on any person regarding the manner of treatment, disposal or handling of a substance and the control or requirements, in whole or in part, caused the site to become a contaminated site, or

(b) the secured creditor becomes the registered owner in fee simple of the real property at the contaminated site.

(4) A secured creditor is not responsible for remediation if it acts primarily to protect its security interest, including, without limitation, if the secured creditor

(a) participates only in purely financial matters related to the site,

(b) has the capacity or ability to influence any operation at the contaminated site in a manner that would have the effect of causing or increasing contamination, but does not exercise that capacity or ability in such a manner as to cause or increase contamination,

(c) imposes requirements on any person, if the requirements do not have a reasonable probability of causing or increasing contamination at the site, or

(d) appoints a person to inspect or investigate a contaminated site to determine future steps or actions that the secured creditor might take.

NOTES AND QUESTIONS

1. The attempt to limit the liability of lenders under British Columbia law is based on CERCLA (§ 9607(a)(2)), as amended in 1996. See W Braul, "Liability Features of Bill 26" (1994) 4 J Envtl L 139 at 151-55. As long as the lender has not participated in management, it is not liable under CERCLA, even if it later forecloses. However, the lender must seek to sell at the "earliest practicable, commercially reasonable time, on commercially reasonable terms, taking into account market conditions and legal and regulatory requirements" (CERCLA, § 9601(20)(F)).

2. Pursuant to s 25 of the *Contaminated Sites Regulation*, secured creditors in British Columbia also will not become responsible for contaminated site remediation if they impose requirements on persons to comply with environmental laws; participate in loan workout actions; take steps to preserve, protect, and enhance the value of secured assets or reduce environmental contamination; or undertake realization proceedings, as long as they do not become the "fee simple" owner of the contaminated site.

3. Compare the Ontario, British Columbia, and US approaches to issues of lender liability. Which approach is preferable? To what extent can cautious lenders prevent potentially "dirty" developments by refusing financing?

4. Receivers and Receiver-Managers

Receivers are appointed by creditors or pursuant to court order to take possession and control of the property of bankrupt or insolvent persons. Receiver-managers have the further responsibility of carrying on the business of the debtor. Receivers and receiver-managers can attract environmental liability where such properties are contaminated and can be made the subject of cleanup orders under environmental legislation. The following case was the first in Canada to find that the costs of environmental cleanup take priority over a secured party's claim in the distribution of the assets of an insolvent party.

PANAMERICANA DE BIENES Y SERVICIOS, SA V NORTHERN BADGER OIL & GAS LIMITED
1991 ABCA 181, 7 CELR (NS) 66

LAYCRAFT CJA:

[1] The issue on this appeal is whether the *Bankruptcy Act* [now *Bankruptcy and Insolvency Act*], RSC 1985, c. B-3, prevents the court-appointed receiver-manager of an insolvent and bankrupt oil company from complying with an order of the Energy Resources Conservation Board of the province of Alberta. The order required the receiver-manager, in the interests of environmental safety, to carry out proper abandonment procedures on seven suspended oil wells. In Court of Queen's Bench, Mr. Justice MacPherson held [in *Panamericana de Bienes y Servicios SA v Northern Badger Oil & Gas Ltd*, 1989 CanLII 3232 at paras 30, 23 (Alta QB)] that the order requiring "the abandonment and the securing of potentially dangerous well sites is at the expense of the secured creditors' entitlement" under the *Bankruptcy Act* and is "beyond the province's constitutional powers." He directed the receiver-manager not to comply with the order. For the reasons which follow, I respectfully disagree with that conclusion and would allow the appeal by the board.

• • •

V THE DUTIES OF THE RECEIVER

• • •

[42] In the present case it is clear that almost from the commencement of the receivership, the receiver was aware of the obligation, in law, of Northern Badger to see the oil and gas wells properly abandoned. The correspondence from the board detailed the obligation for the proper operation of the wells and the ultimate abandonment of them.

• • •

VI CONCLUSION

[45] In my opinion the board had the power, when authorized by the Lieutenant Governor in Council, to order the abandonment of the wells by some person. The order was clearly within the general regulatory scheme, and within the expressed purposes, of both of the statutes regulating the oil and gas industry. ...

. . .

[55] The receiver has had complete control of the wells and has operated them since May 1987, when it was appointed receiver and manager of them. It has carried out for more than three years activities with respect to the wells which only a licensee is authorized to do under the provisions of the *Oil and Gas Conservation Act* [RSA 1980, c O-5]. In that position, it cannot pick and choose as to whether an operation is profitable or not in deciding whether to carry it out. If one of the wells of which a receiver has chosen to take control should blow out of control or catch fire, for example, it would be a remarkable rule of law which would permit him to walk away from the disaster saying simply that remedial action would diminish distribution to secured creditors.

[56] While the receiver was in control of the wells, there was no other entity with whom the board could deal. An order addressed to Northern Badger would have been fruitless. That is so because, by order of the court, upon the application of the debenture holder, neither Northern Badger nor its trustee in bankruptcy had any right even to enter the well sites or to undertake any operation with respect to them. Moreover, under the regulatory scheme for Alberta oil wells, only a licensee is entitled to produce oil and gas. The receiver cannot be heard to say that, while functioning as a licensee to produce the wells and to profit from them, it assumed none of a licensee's obligations.

. . .

[63] ... The Alberta legislation regulating oil and gas wells ... is a statute of general application within a valid provincial power. It is general law regulating the operation of oil and gas wells, and safe practices relating to them, for the protection of the public. It is not aimed at subversion of the scheme of distribution under the *Bankruptcy Act* though it may incidentally affect that distribution in some cases. It does so, not by a direct conflict in operation, but because compliance by the receiver with the general law means that less money will be available for distribution.

NOTES AND QUESTIONS

1. The Alberta Court of Appeal's affirmation of the board's order in *Northern Badger* resulted in the receiver-manager having to allocate approximately $200,000 from the funds realized on the sale of the bankrupt company's assets for proper environmental cleanup and sealing of the abandoned wells. This left virtually nothing to be distributed to the secured creditor. What if the cleanup had cost more than the funds available to the receiver-manager from the sale of the bankrupt's assets? Would the receiver-manager have been liable for the difference?

2. In 1997, Parliament answered this question by enacting a series of amendments (SC 1997, c 12, s 15) to the *Bankruptcy and Insolvency Act*, RSC 1985, c B-3, ss 14.06(2)-(8). These amendments expanded and extended to receivers (and interim receivers) the protection from personal liability already available under the statute to trustees in bankruptcy. In particular, the amendments remove personal liability from receivers under federal or provincial law for any environmental condition or damage that arose before the receiver's appointment. For environmental conditions or damage arising after the appointment, liability attaches to the receiver only if there has been gross negligence or wilful misconduct. In addition, if an order requiring the receiver to remedy an environmental condition is made under federal or provincial law, the receiver may comply with the order, abandon the property, contest the order, or apply for a stay of the order. The purpose of the application for a stay of the order is to allow the receiver the opportunity to assess the economic viability of complying with the order (s 14.06(5)). If the receiver abandons any interest in the real property (for example, if the costs of remedying environmental damage exceed the value of the property), the costs to remedy the damage do

not rank as a cost of administration but are only an unsecured claim (s 14.06(6)). However, any federal or provincial government claim for the costs of remedying environmental damage affecting real property of the debtor is a secured claim and ranks in priority to all other claims (s. 14.06(7)).

3. Have the 1997 amendments struck the right balance between protecting the public from environmental harm and protecting receivers (and trustees in bankruptcy) and the social function that they perform in a bankruptcy? See D Saxe, "Trustees' and Receivers' Environmental Liability Update" (1998) 49 CBR (3d) 138. The issue has been addressed by the courts from time to time since the decision in *Northern Badger*, most recently by the Supreme Court in the following case.

ORPHAN WELL ASSOCIATION V GRANT THORNTON LTD
2019 SCC 5

[Redwater Energy Corporation (Redwater), an oil and gas company, was granted licences by Alberta's energy regulator. While a few of Redwater's licensed wells still produced and were profitable, the majority were spent and had abandonment and reclamation liabilities that exceeded their value. A lending institution provided funds to Redwater and was granted a security interest in its property. When Redwater began experiencing financial difficulties, Grant Thornton Limited (GTL) was appointed as its receiver. At that point in time, Redwater owed the lender over $5 million and had over 70 inactive or spent wells, pipelines, and related facilities. In response to the regulator's notice to GTL that it was legally obligated to fulfill abandonment obligations for all of its licensed assets before distributing any funds to creditors, GTL, having determined that it could not meet those requirements because the cost of doing so would exceed sale proceeds for the remaining productive wells, informed the regulator that it was taking possession of only Redwater's most productive wells and not the remainder, and that it had no obligation to fulfill any regulatory requirements with respect to the latter. The regulator issued orders because it regarded the inactive or spent infrastructure as an environmental and safety hazard and, with the Orphan Well Association (OWA), sought a declaration requiring GTL to comply with the orders up to the financial limit of the assets remaining in Redwater's estate. GTL brought a cross-application for an order that would allow it to pursue the sale of the productive wells and prevent the regulator from requiring it to comply with its orders. GTL was appointed trustee of Redwater's estate pursuant to a bankruptcy order and relied on s 14.06(4)(a)(ii) of the *Bankruptcy and Insolvency Act* [(*BIA*)] with respect to the abandoned assets. The lower courts held that the regulator's orders under Alberta law conflicted with the federal Act because (1) they imposed obligations on GTL with respect to the abandoned assets contrary to s 14.06(4), and (2) they gave priority to the claims of the regulator, an unsecured creditor, instead of to those of Redwater's secured creditors. The Supreme Court allowed the appeal of the regulator and OWA. The following excerpts discuss the court's treatment of *Northern Badger*.]

THE CHIEF JUSTICE:

• • •

[130] *Northern Badger* established that a regulator enforcing a public duty by way of non-monetary order is not a creditor. I reject the claim in the dissenting reasons that *Northern Badger* should be interpreted differently. First, I note that whether the Regulator has a contingent claim is relevant to the sufficient certainty test, which presupposes that the Regulator is a creditor. I cannot accept the proposition in the

dissenting reasons that *Northern Badger* was concerned with what would become the third prong of the *Abitibi* [*Newfoundland and Labrador v AbitibiBowater Inc*, 2012 SCC 67, [2012] 3 SCR 443] test. In *Northern Badger*, Laycraft C.J.A. accepted that abandonment was a liability and identified the issue as "whether that liability is to the Board so that it is the Board which is the creditor" (para. 32). Second, the underlying scenario here with regards to Redwater's end-of-life obligations is exactly the same as in *Northern Badger*—a regulator is ordering an entity to comply with its legal obligations in furtherance of the public good. This reasoning from *Northern Badger* was subsequently adopted in cases such as *Strathcona (County) v. Fantasy Construction Ltd. (Trustee of)*, 2005 ABQB 794, 261 D.L.R. (4th) 221, at paras. 23-25, and *Lamford Forest Products Ltd. (Re)* (1991), 1991 CanLII 8243 (BC SC), 86 D.L.R (4th) 534.

[131] I cannot agree with the suggestion by the majority of the Court of Appeal in this case that *Northern Badger* "is of limited assistance" in the application of the *Abitibi* test (para. 63). Rather, I agree with Martin J.A. that *Abitibi* did not overturn the reasoning in *Northern Badger*, but instead "emphasized the need to consider the substance of provincial regulation in assessing whether it creates a claim provable in bankruptcy" (para. 164). As Martin J.A. noted, even following *Abitibi*, the law continues to be that "public obligations are not provable claims that can be counted or compromised in the bankruptcy" (para. 174). *Abitibi* clarified the scope of *Northern Badger* by confirming that a regulator's environmental claims will be provable claims under certain circumstances. It does not stand for the proposition that a regulator exercising its enforcement powers is always a creditor. The reasoning in *Northern Badger* was simply not applicable on the facts of *Abitibi*, given the actions of the Province as outlined above.

[132] In *Abitibi*, Deschamps J. noted that insolvency legislation had evolved in the years since *Northern Badger*. That legislative evolution did not, however, change the meaning to be ascribed to the term "creditor." In this regard, I agree with the conclusion in *Strathcona County v. Fantasy Construction Ltd. (Trustee of)*, 2005 ABQB 559, 256 D.L.R. (4th) 536, that the amendments to the *BIA* dealing with environmental matters in the years following *Northern Badger* cannot be interpreted as having overturned the reasoning in that case. As should be clear from the earlier discussion of s. 14.06, the amendments to the *BIA* do not speak to when a regulator enforcing an environmental claim is a creditor.

[133] The conclusion that the reasoning in *Northern Badger* continues to be relevant since *Abitibi* and the amendments to insolvency legislation also finds support in the writings of academic commentators. Stewart's position is that, while *Abitibi* discussed *Northern Badger*, it did not overturn it [FL Stewart, "How to Deal with a Fickle Friend? Alberta's Troubles with the Doctrine of Federal Paramountcy" in JP Sarra & B Romaine, eds, *Annual Review Insolvency Law 2017* (Toronto: Thomson Reuters, 2018)]. He urges this Court to clarify that there remains "a distinction between a regulatory body that is a creditor because it is enforcing a debt, and a regulatory body that is not a creditor because it is enforcing the law" (p. 221). Similarly, Lund argues that a court should "consider the importance of the public interests protected by the regulatory obligation when deciding whether the debtor owes a debt, liability or obligation to a creditor" (p. 178).

[134] For the foregoing reasons, *Abitibi* cannot be understood as having changed the law as summarized by Laycraft C.J.A. I adopt his comments at para. 33 of *Northern Badger*:

> The statutory provisions requiring the abandonment of oil and gas wells are part of the general law of Alberta, binding every citizen of the province. All who become

licensees of oil and gas wells are bound by them. Similar statutory obligations bind citizens in many other areas of modern life ... But the obligation of the citizen is not to the peace officer, or public authority which enforces the law. The duty is owed as a public duty by all the citizens of the community to their fellow citizens. When the citizen subject to the order complies, the result is not the recovery of money by the peace officer or public authority, or of a judgment for money, nor is that the object of the whole process. Rather, it is simply the enforcement of the general law. The enforcing authority does not become a "creditor" of the citizen on whom the duty is imposed.

[135] Based on the analysis in *Northern Badger*, it is clear that the Regulator is not a creditor of the Redwater estate. The end-of-life obligations the Regulator seeks to enforce against Redwater are public duties. Neither the Regulator nor the Government of Alberta stands to benefit financially from the enforcement of these obligations. These public duties are owed, not to a creditor, but, rather, to fellow citizens, and are therefore outside the scope of "provable claims." I do not intend to suggest, however, that a regulator will be a creditor only where it acts exactly as the province did in *Abitibi*. There may very well be situations in which a regulator's actions fall somewhere between those in *Abitibi* and those in the instant case. Notably, unlike some previous cases, the Regulator has performed no environmental work itself. I leave such situations to be addressed in future cases in which there are full factual records. Here, it is clear that the Regulator is seeking to enforce Redwater's public duties, whether by issuing the Abandonment Orders or by maintaining the LMR [Liability Management Rating] requirements. The Regulator is not a creditor within the meaning of the *Abitibi* test.

NOTES AND QUESTIONS

1. In *Newfoundland and Labrador v AbitibiBowater Inc*, 2012 SCC 67 at paras 26-30, [2012] 3 SCR 443, the Supreme Court stated that there are three requirements that orders must meet in order to be subject to the federal insolvency process: (1) "there must be a debt, a liability or an obligation to a creditor"; (2) "the debt, liability or obligation must be incurred" at a specific time; and (3) "it must be possible to attach a monetary value to the debt, liability or obligation." In *Orphan Well Association*, the court made it clear that the Alberta energy regulator was not acting as a creditor of Redwater's estate but was acting in the public interest. Therefore, its order was allowed to stand notwithstanding federal bankruptcy law.

2. The environmental liability of receivers has also been expressly limited in provincial legislation. Under s 107 of Alberta's *Environmental Protection and Enhancement Act*, a receiver or receiver-manager is a "person responsible for the contaminated site" who can be issued environmental protection orders in connection with contaminated sites. However, s 240(3) limits the liability of receivers or receiver-managers to the value of the assets that they are administering unless the situation identified in the order resulted from or was aggravated by their gross negligence or wilful misconduct.

3. British Columbia does not obligate receivers to personally remediate sites that were contaminated on the date that the receiver became the owner or operator of the site unless the receiver exercised control or imposed requirements over persons regarding the management of substances, was grossly negligent or guilty of wilful misconduct in the exercise of such control, and the control requirements caused the site to become contaminated. Sections 26(3) and (3.1) of the *Contaminated Sites Regulation* requires a receiver to carry out remediation at a contaminated site only to the extent of available funds and only during the term of the appointment. Under s 26(1) of the Regulation, "available funds" refers to those funds left after

the receiver and secured and trade creditors have been paid and borrowed funds by the receiver have been taken into account.

4. Bill 56, Ontario's "brownfield law," which in 2001 amended the *Environmental Protection Act*, limits the province's authority to issue a cleanup order to a receiver unless the order arises from the gross negligence or wilful misconduct of the receiver or from other circumstances prescribed by the regulations. This is the case even in situations of environmental emergency if the receiver also notifies the province within a prescribed time period after being served with the order of its abandonment or disposal of interest in the property to which the order relates, or if the order has been stayed under the federal bankruptcy legislation. See ss 168.19(1), 168.20(1), (2), and (7) of the Act.

5. Compare the laws of Alberta, British Columbia, and Ontario, above, with federal requirements under the *Bankruptcy and Insolvency Act*. Has consistency in approach across the country on the issue of the liability of receivers for environmental damage been achieved? To what extent, if any, are any of the provincial laws above pre-empted by the 1997 federal amendments? Note that the provincial rules also apply to trustees in bankruptcy.

6. Injured third parties also have applied to the courts for leave to commence actions against receivers and receiver-managers for environmental damage arising from the management of the bankrupt's business. See *Mortgage Insurance Co of Canada v Innisfil Landfill Corp* (1995), 20 CELR (NS) 19 (Ont Gen Div—Comm List); *Mortgage Insurance Co of Canada v Innisfil Landfill Corp* (1996), 20 CELR (NS) 37 (Ont Gen Div—Comm List); and; *Mortgage Insurance Co of Canada v Innisfil Landfill Corp* (1997), 23 CELR (NS) 288 (Ont Gen Div—Comm List). The Bill 56 amendments, above, do not protect receivers from civil liability. Should they?

7. Alberta's energy regulator has used judicial proceedings to enforce its well abandonment and reclamation directions to oil and gas companies: see *Alberta Energy Regulator v Lexin Resources Ltd*, 2017 ABQB 219.

5. Trustees in Bankruptcy

Federal bankruptcy and insolvency law permits trustees in bankruptcy to be appointed by courts to administer the estates of bankrupt persons. Property owned by the bankrupt becomes the responsibility of the trustee for the purposes of selling assets and distributing the sale proceeds to creditors. If the bankrupt's property is contaminated, a trustee confronts the same potential liability problems faced by other potentially responsible persons. However, even before amendments by Parliament to federal bankruptcy law, the courts had been prepared to treat trustees somewhat better than other potentially responsible parties, as illustrated by *Re Lamford Forest Products Ltd*, 1991 CanLII 8243, 8 CELR (NS) (2d) 186 at 188 (BCSC). In that case, a bankrupt sawmill made a voluntary assignment in bankruptcy in 1990. The site was contaminated with heavy metals and other toxic substances as a result of lumber treatment activities connected with the sawmill business. The regional waste manager issued the company a provincial pollution abatement order that, if complied with, would absorb, if not exceed, all the proceeds without payment to secured or other creditors. If the order was not complied with, substantial penalties would follow. The official receiver brought a motion for directions, and the court (at 194) held:

> The balancing of values in this case falls in favour of protecting the health and safety of society over the rights of creditors, as it did in the *Bulora* [*Canada Trust Co v Bulora Corp* (1980), 34 CBR (NS) 145 (Ont SC), aff'd (1981), 39 CBR (NS) 152 (Ont CA)] and the *Panamericana* case, but there is also a need in modern society for trustees to take on the duty of winding up insolvent estates. ... [N]o trustee can be found who will take on the bankruptcy of Lamford without a guarantee that he or she will be entitled to trustee's fees to be deducted from the amount paid out under the order, and will have no personal liability for the costs of

clean-up of the contaminated site ... I direct that in the event that there are insufficient funds to meet the requirements of the order, the payment of funds pursuant to the order must be subject to a reduction equal to the amount of the trustee's fees.

Amendments in 1992 (SC 1992, c 27, s 9(1)) to s 14.06(2) of the *Bankruptcy and Insolvency Act* exempted a trustee in bankruptcy from personal liability under environmental legislation if the harm occurred before the trustee's appointment, or after the appointment, unless the damage occurred as a result of the trustee's failure to exercise due diligence.

NOTES AND QUESTIONS

1. Did the 1992 amendments to the *Bankruptcy and Insolvency Act* codify the result in *Lamford* respecting exemption of the trustee from liability for environmental contamination occurring prior to the appointment of the trustee? In 1997, further amendments to the Act extended this exemption from liability to receivers and receiver-managers. In addition, the 1997 amendments also changed the standard of care during the administration of the bankrupt's estate for trustees (and receivers or receiver-managers) from due diligence to gross negligence or wilful misconduct. Do you agree with the standard of care chosen? See V Dumoulin & AM Sheahan, "Environmental Liability: Proposed Amendments to the Bankruptcy and Insolvency Act" (1996) 5 Digest Env L & Assess 85 at 86, 105-6.

2. *Lamford* has been commented upon favourably in cases such as *Strathcona County v PriceWaterhouseCoopers Inc*, 2005 ABQB 559 at para 34 as an example of how the reluctance of trustees and receivers to accept assignments in cases involving environmental issues was overcome judicially, particularly in the period before Parliament and provincial legislatures reformed the law.

6. Government

In theory, any level of government may be liable for environmental cleanup of contaminated land. In practice, municipal governments may be more exposed than any other government level for several reasons. First, municipalities may have abandoned or derelict land within their territory. Second, under provincial planning and related legislation, municipalities are responsible for both controlling and fostering real property development and redevelopment. Third, municipalities may acquire property as a result of unpaid municipal taxes.

Accordingly, to facilitate the redevelopment of brownfields, some provinces have enacted legislation that limits municipal environmental liability in a manner that parallels the protections provided to secured creditors and their representatives. Bill 56, Ontario's brownfield law, which amended the province's *Environmental Protection Act* (by adding s 168.12(2)) in 2001, exempts municipalities from a variety of environmental orders in connection with, for example, any action taken on non-municipal property for the purpose of collecting rents, preserving services, or responding to environmental risks from the presence of contaminants on, in, or under the property.

NOTES AND QUESTIONS

1. The law reforms also allow municipalities who become owners of contaminated properties because of failed tax sales from becoming subject to environmental orders with respect to the properties for five years. However, municipalities can lose this protection if there is gross negligence or wilful misconduct by the municipality or if there are exceptional circumstances such as harm or risk to persons, the natural environment, or other property (see ss 168.13 and 168.14 of the Ontario *Environmental Protection Act*). Also, there are other exceptions to the liability protections offered, and there is no protection from civil (or quasi-criminal) liability. Some

commentators have described the protections offered to municipalities and other potentially responsible persons as "qualified immunities" that may or may not result in the redevelopment of brownfields. Do you agree? See, for example, Curpen, Elliot & Kirby, "Ontario Brownfields Bill Passed with Mixed Opinions," cited in Section III.E.3 of this chapter, at 294.

2. What are the environmental risks and benefits associated with rapid facilitation of brownfield redevelopment? See JF Castrilli, "Hazardous Wastes and Brownfields" in *Sixth Annual Report on Ontario's Environment* (Toronto: Canadian Institute for Environmental Law and Policy, 2002) 55 at 69-70.

IV. INSURANCE

As private actions and government regulatory initiatives increase the scope and magnitude of environmental liability for contaminated lands, potentially responsible persons seek insurance protection to cover the costs of environmental claims and government orders. The extent to which comprehensive general liability insurance, special purpose environmental impairment liability insurance, or other type of insurance provides coverage for such persons is governed by exclusion clauses contained in these insurance policies. As this chapter already has noted, governments themselves may face environmental liability. The following case illustrates the effect of a pollution exclusion clause in a policy of insurance in the context of a claim of negligence against the government.

R V KANSA GENERAL INSURANCE CO
1994 CanLII 626, 13 CELR (NS) 59 (Ont CA)

[In 1988, a landowner commenced an action against an adjacent landowner, RK, and her tenants, alleging that environmental pollutants had escaped from their lands onto those of the plaintiff. RK issued a third-party claim against the Crown, alleging the negligence of its officers in responding to the pollution problem. The Crown advised its insurer, Kansa General Insurance Co (KGI), of the third-party claim. KGI undertook to defend the claim without prejudice to its right to dispute coverage or indemnity in light of the pollution exclusion clause in the insurance policy. KGI subsequently asked the Crown to assume the defence of the proceedings. The Crown applied for an order requiring KGI to defend the action. A motions judge held that the pollution exclusion clause applied only to exclude coverage to an insured who actively engaged in polluting activities. He ordered KGI to defend the action without prejudice to its right to deny coverage at a later time if the Crown was shown to be a polluter within the meaning of the exclusion clause. KGI appealed the order to defend.

KGI had issued the Crown a comprehensive general liability insurance policy (Policy) that provided that the insurer would pay all sums that the insured became obliged to pay for damages arising from property damage caused by accident or occurrence as covered by the Policy. The Policy contained the following exclusion:

This Policy shall not apply to claims arising out of:

• • •

(i) the discharge, dispersal, release or escape of smoke, vapours, soot, fumes, acids, alkalis, toxic chemicals, liquids or gases, waste materials or other irritants, contaminants or pollutants into or upon land, the atmosphere or any water of any description no matter where located or how contained, or into any water-course, drainage or sewage system, but this exclusion does not apply if such discharge, dispersal, release or escape is caused by accident insofar as the Insured is concerned.

The Ontario Court of Appeal held that American cases are not persuasive in the Canadian context and would not form a sound basis for the interpretation of the pollution exclusion clause in the Policy because the pollution exclusion clauses in those cases were all less absolute than the clause in question, which excluded coverage even for sudden and accidental pollution.]

LABROSSE JA: ...

• • •

Even if I assume, for the sake of argument, that the pollution exclusion clause in the Policy operates only against an "active" or "actual" polluter, the Crown is faced with a serious difficulty in light of s. 14(1) of the *Environmental Protection Act*, RSO 1990, c. E.19 ... .

• • •

Section 14(1) creates three kinds of polluters: those who discharge a contaminant, those who cause the discharge of a contaminant and those who permit the discharge of a contaminant. The Crown concedes that, if the allegations of the [RK] claim are made out, it would be included in the third class of polluter. Under Ontario law, the passive polluter who permits pollution to take place is just as much a polluter as the active polluter who discharges or causes the discharge of pollution. The Crown's argument that it could not be considered an active polluter, within the meaning of the American cases, therefore does not assist it under Ontario law.

There is no dispute between the parties regarding the principles which are relevant to the insurer's duty to defend. They were stated by McLachlin J in *Nichols v. American Home Assurance Co.*, [1990] 1 SCR 801. The duty to defend arises when the allegations in the pleadings raise claims which might be payable under the agreement to indemnify in the insurance contract: the mere possibility that a claim may succeed is sufficient. If there is any ambiguity in the contract, it must be resolved in favour of the insured. The duty to defend is broader than the duty to indemnify since it is not necessary for the insured to establish that the obligation to indemnify will, in fact, arise in order to trigger the duty to defend.

The Policy issued to the Crown provided very broad coverage. The insurer agreed to pay all sums which the insured became obligated to pay, by law or by agreement, for damages arising from property damage caused by an accident or occurrence. The claim to which the Policy refers, in relation to the insurer's duty to defend, is any action brought against the Crown for an occurrence under the Policy. ... [I]t has been conceded that the Crown's alleged negligence in fulfilling its regulatory duty falls within the definition of "occurrence" under the Policy and, therefore, obliges [KGI] to defend the [RK] claim. The exclusion clause, however, denies coverage where the claim arises out of the discharge of pollutants upon land. The issue then becomes whether the Crown's alleged regulatory negligence falls within the pollution exclusion clause. The negligence relates to a failure to recognize, advise and respond to environmental contamination. The third party seeks contribution and indemnity for damages caused by the unstemmed pollution as a result of the Crown's failure to act.

• • •

To succeed the appellant must ... show that the [RK] claim is based on circumstances in which it is possible to trace a continuous chain of causation, unbroken by the interposition of a new act of negligence, between the pollution at #39 Fenmar Drive and the damages sustained by [RK]. In my opinion, the Crown's alleged negligence cannot be divorced from the discharge of pollutants which caused the damages and, therefore, the claim falls within the exclusion. The damages claimed by [RK] arise from the contamination of the lands at #39 Fenmar Drive and the alleged regulatory negligence does not constitute an intervening act, ... which breaks the chain of causation. The fact that it is the negligence of the Crown's officers in carrying out their regulatory duty to enforce the environmental legislation rather than the negligence of the Crown's officers in, for example, transporting toxic material which gave rise to the discharge of pollutants, does not change the nature of the occurrence and, hence, of the claim. The regulatory negligence can do no more than exacerbate the damages: there would be no loss without the pollution.

[The court allowed the appeal, set aside the order, and dismissed the Crown's application for a declaration that KGI must defend the third-party claim brought against the Crown.]

NOTES AND QUESTIONS

1. *Kansa* is one of the first cases in Canada to consider absolute pollution exclusion clauses in a comprehensive general liability insurance policy. What are the implications of this decision for insurance coverage of environmental damage? See AR Hudson & JK Friesen, "Environmental Coverage Under Comprehensive General Liability Insurance Policies in Canada" (1995) 5 J Envtl L & Prac 141 at 156-60.

2. Despite the result in *Kansa*, insurance law experts note that comprehensive general liability insurance policies are probably the most common insurance policies issued to Canadian businesses. They note that while many people in the insurance industry will say that such policies are not intended to cover pollution losses, that view is not entirely accurate. They suggest that it is important to examine the actual policy wording to determine whether (1) a loss falls within the insuring agreement, (2) an exclusion takes away coverage, and (3) an exception to the exclusion restores the coverage that would have otherwise been excluded. See T Donnelly, "Finding Pollution Coverage Under the CGL Insurance Policy" (Presentation made at the Law Society of Ontario's "The Six-Minute Environmental Lawyer 2018" program, Toronto, 3 October 2018).

3. Special purpose environmental liability insurance policies that attempt to cover, not exclude, pollution are increasingly considered by persons engaging in activities with a high risk of environmental harm. However, these policies present their own problems for insured persons and insurers. See DR Cameron, *Environmental Concerns in Business Transactions: Avoiding the Risks* (Toronto: Butterworths, 1993) at 79; and LA Reynolds, "New Directions for Environmental Liability Insurance in Canada" (1996) 6 J Envtl L & Prac 89.

4. The use of *environmental* insurance policies is seen as another method of facilitating redevelopment of brownfields because it can facilitate transactions by reducing risk and uncertainty for developers and lenders. See D Kirby, S Elliot & K Dobson, "Insurance Is a Risk Management Tool for Brownfields" (2001) 4:4 Envtl L 263 at 265.

5. What role do insurers play in ensuring that the polluter pays? To the extent that an insurer provides environmental impairment liability insurance coverage to high-risk industrial and commercial interests under strict standards, does the insurer effectively become a *de facto* environmental regulator? Is that good or bad? See Reynolds, cited above, at 207-8.

FURTHER READINGS

Benedickson, J, "Remediation and Restoration of Contaminated Land" in *Environmental Law*, 4th ed (Toronto: Irwin Law, 2013) ch 11.

Commissioner of the Environment and Sustainable Development (CESD), *Federal Contaminated Sites and Their Impacts* (Ottawa: CESD, 2012).

CHAPTER NINETEEN

ENVIRONMENTAL ENFORCEMENT

Shaun Fluker

I. INTRODUCTION

This chapter looks at environmental enforcement. The sections that follow examine the characteristics of an environmental offence, explain the due diligence defence, and describe the principles applicable to the sentencing of an environmental offender. This chapter does not cover other mechanisms such as licensing, administrative penalties, enforcement orders, market-based incentives, or negotiated arrangements.

The prosecution of a statutory offence is one of several available environmental enforcement tools. Prosecution is often noted as being reserved for the more serious instances of non-compliance. However, some commentators assert that prosecutions should be used more often because the high profile of a successful conviction has the greatest deterrent effect. Similarly, an increasing use of creative sentencing orders and less emphasis on fines as the sanction for an environmental offence means that prosecutions can also lead to environmental research or restoration projects that support the underlying public welfare objectives of environmental legislation.

II. ENVIRONMENTAL OFFENCES

Most environmental offences result from activity that contravenes a regulatory standard or are otherwise conducted without legislative authorization (see Chapter 15, which examines the establishment of regulatory standards and related functions of environmental legislation). Canadian courts have characterized an environmental offence as a regulatory offence, which constitutes a breach of societal interests and is distinguishable from a "true crime." In *R v Wholesale Travel Group Inc*, [1991] 3 SCR 154 at 218-19, 1991 CanLII 39, the Supreme Court of Canada described the basis for this distinction as follows:

> It has always been thought that there is a rational basis for distinguishing between crimes and regulatory offences. Acts or actions are criminal when they constitute conduct that is, in itself, so abhorrent to the basic values of human society that it ought to be prohibited completely. Murder, sexual assault, fraud, robbery and theft are all so repugnant to society

that they are universally recognized as crimes. At the same time, some conduct is prohibited, not because it is inherently wrongful, but because unregulated activity would result in dangerous conditions being imposed upon members of society, especially those who are particularly vulnerable.

The objective of regulatory legislation is to protect the public or broad segments of the public (such as employees, consumers and motorists, to name but a few) from the potentially adverse effects of otherwise lawful activity. Regulatory legislation involves a shift of emphasis from the protection of individual interests and the deterrence and punishment of acts involving moral fault to the protection of public and societal interests. While criminal offences are usually designed to condemn and punish past, inherently wrongful conduct, regulatory measures are generally directed to the prevention of future harm through the enforcement of minimum standards of conduct and care.

Canadian courts have characterized a regulatory offence as either *mens rea*, strict liability, or absolute liability. In *R v Sault Ste Marie*, [1978] 2 SCR 1299 at 1325-26, 1978 CanLII 11, the Supreme Court set out these three categories as follows:

1. Offences in which *mens rea*, consisting of some positive state of mind such as intent, knowledge, or recklessness, must be proved by the prosecution either as an inference from the nature of the act committed, or by additional evidence.
2. Offences in which there is no necessity for the prosecution to prove the existence of *mens rea*; the doing of the prohibited act *prima facie* imports the offence, leaving it open to the accused to avoid liability by proving that he took all reasonable care. This involves consideration of what a reasonable man would have done in the circumstances. The defence will be available if the accused reasonably believed in a mistaken set of facts which, if true, would render the act or omission innocent, or if he took all reasonable steps to avoid the particular event. These offences may properly be called offences of strict liability. ...
3. Offences of absolute liability where it is not open to the accused to exculpate himself by showing that he was free of fault.

In *Sault Ste Marie*, the Supreme Court also held that a regulatory offence is presumptively a strict liability offence.

In *Lévis (City) v Tétreault; Lévis (City) v 2629-4470 Québec inc*, 2006 SCC 12 at paras 13-19, the Supreme Court reaffirmed this categorization of regulatory offences as well as the presumption of strict liability in the absence of statutory language that suggests otherwise. The essential point for people charged with committing environmental offences is that they will usually escape liability if they can establish that they took reasonable care to avoid the impugned act.

While the overwhelming majority of environmental offences are strict liability, it is still important to have some understanding of how courts distinguish between the three categories of a regulatory offence. In this regard, note that the use of words such as "knowingly" and "wilfully" in legislation is not always determinative that an offence is *mens rea* rather than strict liability. Likewise, while *Sault Ste Marie* left open the possibility that a legislator may create an absolute liability offence with clear language, courts will generally be reluctant to impose liability in the absence of any fault by the offender. Thus, in order to properly categorize an environmental offence, it is necessary to fully decipher the intention of the legislator by looking at the purpose of the legislation, the context of the provision in question, the nature of the offence, and other factors such as the severity of the penalty in relation to the offence.

NOTES AND QUESTIONS

1. Consider the language used in the following sections of Alberta's *Environmental Protection and Enhancement Act*, RSA 2000, c E-12 and distinguish between the *mens rea*, strict liability, and absolute liability offences:

108(1) No person shall knowingly release or permit the release of a substance into the environment in an amount, concentration or level or at a rate of release that is in excess of that expressly prescribed by an approval, a code of practice or the regulations.

(2) No person shall release or permit the release of a substance into the environment in an amount, concentration or level or at a rate of release that is in excess of that expressly prescribed by an approval or the regulations.

• • •

179(1) No person shall dispose of waste on a highway except in a container placed for the purpose of collecting it.

(2) No person shall transport waste in or on a vehicle on a highway unless the waste is adequately contained, secured or covered to prevent it from falling off or being blown off the vehicle while being transported.

• • •

227 A person who

(a) knowingly provides false or misleading information pursuant to a requirement under this Act to provide information,

(b) provides false or misleading information pursuant to a requirement under this Act to provide information,

(c) fails to provide information as required under this Act ...

• • •

is guilty of an offence.

228(1) A person who commits an offence referred to in section ... 108(1), ... or 227(a), ... is liable

(a) in the case of an individual, to a fine of not more than $100 000 or to imprison-ment for a period of not more than 2 years or to both fine and imprisonment, or

(b) in the case of a corporation, to a fine of not more than $1 000 000.

(2) A person who commits an offence referred to in section ... 108(2), ..., 227(b), (c), ... is liable

(a) in the case of an individual, to a fine of not more than $50 000, or

(b) in the case of a corporation, to a fine of not more than $500 000.

(3) A person who commits an offence referred to in section ... 179, ... is liable

(a) in the case of an individual, to a fine of not more than $250, or

(b) in the case of a corporation, to a fine of not more than $1000.

229 No person shall be convicted of an offence under section ... 108(2), ... 227(b), (c), ... if that person establishes on a balance of probabilities that the person took all reasonable steps to prevent its commission.

PAUL MCCULLOCH & DANIELLE MEULEMAN, "STRATEGIC DECISIONS IN ENVIRONMENTAL PROSECUTIONS"

in Allan Ingelson, ed, *Environment in the Courtroom* (Calgary: University of Calgary Press, 2019) ch 15 [endnotes omitted]

WHAT CHARGE?

If a decision is made to launch an investigation, the investigator will assess the range of possible offences and proceed to gather evidence. There are many different types of environmental offences. Common offences include:

- failure to comply with administrative orders;
- failure to obtain licence/approval/permit;

- failure to comply with conditions in licence/approval/permit;
- failure to keep records;
- depositing waste without an approval or in [an] area not approved for disposal;
- discharges that exceed approved limits.

Typically, some of the more serious offences include:

- discharging contaminants that cause adverse effect or impair the environment;
- failure to report discharges/spills/upsets/accidents;
- obstruction;
- submitting false and misleading information;
- offences involving toxic/hazardous substances;
- habitat destruction.

A single complaint, incident or inspection can lead to a mix of different types of offences, and can involve a single offence over a period of time or discreet offences on the same day. Therefore, once an investigator determines that he or she has reasonable and probable grounds, the next important step is to decide what charge(s) to proceed with. Some of the considerations that go into this determination are the seriousness of the offences, the number of offences, the complexity of the evidence needed to prove each charge, and what statutory regime to proceed under. As well, some statutes have prescribed minimum penalties for certain offences and the investigator may consider (and the defendant may want to try to influence) whether to charge with a more serious or with a lesser offence.

• • •

WILL THE EVIDENCE BE ADMISSIBLE?

Environmental prosecutions are no different than any other trial, and inevitably involve a myriad of tactical decisions regarding the presentation of evidence by both the prosecutor and the defence. Two topics that are perhaps more common to environmental prosecutions are the admissibility of statements made by agents of the defendant and the introduction of lab results.

Environmental regulation is full of self-reporting requirements which have generally been upheld as constitutional in a regulatory context. One question that often arises is: What do you do when the sole evidence that forms the basis of an offence was supplied to the enforcement agency by the defendant, either directly or through an agent? Many licences require companies to test emissions or effluent on a regular basis, and the reports must be submitted to the regulator periodically. The results are generally reported by submitting a letter or, more recently, uploading the data into a database through a Web-enabled portal. These reports may contain lab results demonstrating that the company exceeded an emission limit which constitutes an offence.

So how should the prosecutor go about proving this offence? One avenue would be to call all the witnesses involved in obtaining the sample, delivering it to the lab, and conducting the testing. In this scenario, the prosecutor would have to call a large number of witnesses: the employee who took the sample, any employee who handled it and transported it to the lab, or perhaps an employee of the courier company, the person who received it at the lab, all the technicians who processed the samples for testing, and the analyst who signs the final test result. This evidence would likely take days of trial time. Alternatively, the prosecutor could call one witness: the inspector who received the letter and attached lab results from the company and maybe followed up with the environmental manager at the facility and discussed the results afterward. The second avenue is permitted under the evidentiary rule allowing admissions made by an agent of the defendant to be entered into evidence through a third party (the inspector). This is potentially a much more efficient use of court time and avoids the prosecutor needing to call employees from the defendant company. Defence counsel should of course consider whether to challenge through a *voir dire* the use of the hearsay exception in this manner, considering, for example: Was the report made to the enforcement agency by an agent or employee authorized to make the admissions? Can it be demonstrated that the sampling and testing procedures are unreliable?

As described above, proving the reliability of test results can involve a significant amount of evidence detailing the entire chain of events from the time the sample was taken, in what type of container, how it was handled and transported, what control methods were employed (multiple samples, travel blanks, background samples), the test method used, the quality control and assurance processes employed by the lab, and the qualifications and background of the lab technicians. Some statutes create an evidentiary rule dispensing with the need for any of this evidence where the lab or personnel meet certain qualifications, permitting the prosecutor to simply enter the test result as evidence. However, it is left open to the defendant to provide evidence to the contrary. Furthermore, most test results have standard margins of error. A prosecution should rarely proceed where the exceedance of a limit is within the margin of error.

As Chapter 15 notes, the *Fisheries Act*, RSC 1985, c F-14 establishes a significant federal environmental regulatory regime that sets out prohibitions against harm to fish and fish habitat. Sections 34 to 42.1 of the *Fisheries Act* include several offence provisions concerning fisheries protection and pollution for which there is a long history of prosecutions. (Note: s 30 of Bill C-68, *An Act to amend the Fisheries Act and other Acts in consequence* added ss 42.2 to 42.5 to the *Fisheries Act*. These sections also deal with enforcement; however, at the time of writing, these amendments were not in force.) Environment Canada published a dedicated reporting series on these prosecution cases entitled the Fisheries Pollution Reports, which is still available as archival material on the Environmental Law Centre website (<www.elc.ab.ca>).

Section 42.1 requires the minister responsible for the legislation to report annually to Parliament on the administration and enforcement of these provisions. These *Fisheries Act* offence provisions offer a good illustration of the range of interpretive and evidentiary issues that can arise in an environmental prosecution.

R V KINGSTON (CITY)
(2004), 70 OR (3d) 577, 240 DLR (4th) 734 (CA)

[The city of Kingston operated a municipal landfill from the 1950s to the early 1970s. After closing the landfill, the city created a recreational area on the site. Subsequently, it was discovered that leachate from the site was entering the Cataraqui River. In the 1990s, citizens pressed the city and the Ontario Ministry of the Environment to develop an abatement plan. Eventually a citizen volunteer group carried out sampling at the site, had the samples analyzed, and laid charges against the city under s 36(3) of the *Fisheries Act*. A parallel investigation by the ministry led to the laying of additional charges under the *Fisheries Act*. The city was convicted at trial, but the Ontario Superior Court of Justice subsequently ordered a new trial. The convictions were restored by the Ontario Court of Appeal.]

[60] Subsection 36(3) of the *Fisheries Act*, reproduced again below for ease of reference, prohibits persons from (1) depositing or permitting the deposit of (2) a

deleterious substance of any type (3) in water frequented by fish or in any place where the deleterious substance may enter such water.

36(3) Subject to subsection (4) [deposits authorized by regulation], no person shall deposit or permit the deposit of a deleterious substance of any type in water frequented by fish or in any place under any conditions where the deleterious substance or any other deleterious substance that results from the deposit of the deleterious substance may enter any such water.

• • •

[62] In s. 34(1)(a), "deleterious substance" is defined as:

(a) any substance that, if added to any water, would degrade or alter or form part of a process of degradation or alteration of the quality of that water so that it is rendered or is likely to be rendered deleterious to fish or fish habitat or to the use by man of fish that frequent that water[.]

[63] On an ordinary and plain reading of para. (a), a substance is deleterious if, when added to any water, it would alter the quality of the water such that it is likely to render the water deleterious to fish, fish habitat or to the use by man of fish that frequent the water. There is no stipulation in para. (a) that the substance must be proven to be deleterious to the receiving water. There is no reference to the receiving water in para. (a). On the contrary, the language makes it clear that the substance is deleterious if, when added to any water, it degrades or alters the quality of the water to which it has been added. The "any water" referred to in para. (a) is not the receiving water. Rather, it is any water to which the impugned substance is added, after which it can be determined whether the quality of that water is rendered deleterious to fish, fish habitat or the use by man of fish that frequent that water.

• • •

[78] Accordingly, in my view, ss. 36(3) and 34(1) cannot be taken as requiring the Crown to prove the nature of the allegedly deleterious substance. The prohibition in s. 36(3) is against the deposit of a deleterious substance "of any type." What must be proven is that the substance, whatever it might be, is a deleterious substance within the meaning of para. (a) of the definition of that term in s. 34(1). In this case, it meant that the prosecution had to prove that the leachate, when added to any water, was likely to render the water deleterious to fish or fish habitat or to the use by man of fish that frequent the water. It did not have to prove which component of the leachate was responsible for the degradation or alteration of the quality of the water such that the water was likely to be rendered deleterious to fish. Nor was it obliged to show that fish living in the vicinity of the seep were harmed. It was required only to prove the elements of the offence as set out above.

• • •

[81] On the record, there can be no doubt that the trial judge was entirely justified in finding that the respondents had deposited waste in the dump site; that when it rained, some part of the waste or its residue combined with rain water to become leachate; that the leachate seeped into the Cataraqui River; and, that the Cataraqui River is frequented by fish. In the language of s. 36(3), the trial judge was entitled to find that the respondents permitted the deposit of leachate into water frequented by fish.

[82] Did the trial judge err in concluding that the leachate was a deleterious substance within the meaning of the definition of that term in s. 34(1)(a)? That is, did the trial judge err in concluding that the leachate, if added to any water, would alter the quality of that water so that the water was likely rendered deleterious to fish?

[83] The Ministry's acute lethality tests were performed on the Ministry samples at a variety of concentrations. The diluted concentrations were made by adding the leachate to a proportionate amount of water. Given the trial judge's acceptance of the protocols employed and the test results on the diluted Ministry samples, I see no error in his conclusion that the leachate contained in those samples was a deleterious substance within the meaning of para. (a) of the definition of that term in s. 34(1).

NOTES AND QUESTIONS

1. Statutory interpretation plays a key role in making out the elements of an environmental offence. Recall the discussion in Chapter 15 on the interpretation of environmental legislation, and, in particular, the excerpts provided from *Castonguay Blasting Ltd v Ontario (Environment)*, 2013 SCC 52 in that chapter. A key issue in *Castonguay Blasting* was whether the reporting requirement in s 15(1) of Ontario's *Environmental Protection Act*, RSO 1990, c E.19 applied only to a discharge that may result in an adverse effect to the "natural environment." The Supreme Court gave the reporting requirement in s 15 a broader interpretation than this. What was the Supreme Court's ruling on the scope of s 15, and what does this decision suggest about the proper approach toward the interpretation of an offence provision in environmental legislation?

2. In *R v Kingston (City)*, the court noted the elements of the offence in s 36(3) of the *Fisheries Act* as (1) depositing or permitting the deposit of (2) a deleterious substance (3) in water frequented by fish or where the substance may enter such water. The Crown bears the onus of proving each of these elements beyond a reasonable doubt, and various interpretive and evidentiary issues can arise in the midst of the trial. The court agreed with the interpretation of "deleterious substance" provided by the British Columbia Court of Appeal in *R v MacMillan Bloedel (Alberni) Ltd* (1979), 47 CCC (2d) 118, [1979] 4 WWR 654 (BCCA). In *MacMillan Bloedel*, the defendant was charged under s 36(3) in relation to a spill of oil that had occurred during unloading at a marine dock. On the interpretation of a "deleterious substance," the British Columbia Court of Appeal in *MacMillan Bloedel* rejected the argument that the Crown had to prove the oil spill rendered the received waters deleterious:

[10] What is being defined is the substance that is added to the water, rather than the water after the addition of the substance. To re-phrase the definition section in terms of this case: oil is a deleterious substance if, when added to any water, it would degrade or alter or form part of a process of degradation or alteration of the quality of that water so that that water is rendered deleterious to fish or to the use by man of fish that frequent that water. Applying that test to the findings of fact here, bunker C oil is a deleterious substance. Once it is determined that bunker C oil is a deleterious substance and that it has been deposited, the offence is complete without ascertaining whether the water itself was thereby rendered deleterious. I do not think that the words "that water" in the definition section mean the water into which it is alleged the accused deposited the substance. Those words refer back to "any water," at the beginning of the definition: the hypothetical water which would degrade if the oil was added to it.

[11] The appellant says that the purpose of this legislation is to prevent waters being rendered deleterious to fish and that, if given the plain meaning of the words, an absurdity will result. It is said that if a teaspoon of oil was put in the Pacific Ocean and oil was a deleterious substance, that would constitute an offence. In its submission that absurdity can be avoided by reading the Act to require that the water be made deleterious. There are some attractions to that reasoning, but I think that the result would be at least as unsatisfactory. Nothing could be done to prevent damage to the water that fell short of rendering the water deleterious. To prove that the damage had gone that far would be difficult indeed.

[12] Had it been the intention of Parliament to prohibit the deposit of a substance in water so as to render that water deleterious to fish, that would have been easy to express. A different prohibition was decided upon. It is more strict. It seeks to exclude each part of the process of degradation. The thrust of the section is to prohibit certain things, called "dele-terious substances," being put in the water. That is the plain meaning of the words used and is the meaning that I feel bound to apply.

The primary issue in *R v Kingston (City)* arose from the fact that ammonia was the substance that had rendered the leachate harmful to fish, even though it is a naturally occurring substance that is not inherently toxic. This fact had led the Ontario Superior Court of Justice in *Fletcher v Kingston (City)*, [2002] OJ No 2324 (QL) to settle on an interpretation of "deleterious substance" under the *Fisheries Act* that included a consideration of the effect of the substance on the receiving waters, making reference to how the Ontario Court of Appeal in *R v Inco Ltd* (2001), 54 OR (3d) 495, 155 CCC (3d) 383 interpreted s 30(1) of the *Ontario Water Resources Act*, RSO 1990, c O.40 as follows:

30(1) Every person that discharges or causes or permits the discharge of any material of any kind into or in any waters or on any shore or bank thereof or into or in any place that may impair the quality of the water of any waters is guilty of an offence.

The different language used in s 30(1) compared with that in s 36(3) of the *Fisheries Act* was noted by the Ontario Court of Appeal in concluding that the Superior Court of Justice had erred in finding that it was necessary for the prosecution under s 36(3) to establish that the substance renders the receiving water deleterious to fish. Does the plain language in the two sections support these different interpretations of the phrase "deleterious substance"?

3. The excerpt of *R v Kingston (City)* omits the court's lengthy discussion of the methods employed to collect and test the leachate samples and the arguments made by the City of Kingston to challenge the validity of the test results. The trial judge who had heard the evidence in *Fletcher v Kingston (City)*, [1998] OJ No 6453 (QL) (Prov Div) at paras 35, 37-39 had rejected these challenges by the City:

[T]he Defence attempts to discredit the methods used in the testing procedures by alleging that a pH shift results from the standard procedures utilized in warming the samples of effluent to fifteen degrees centigrade before the bioassays are performed. PH shift, I should explain to those who were not here for all of the trial, is the measurement of acidity or alkalin-ity of the samples and a pH of seven is a neutral, halfway in between. They claim that the resultant pH shift results in the increase in temperature of the effluent samples produces [*sic*] greater portions of unionized ammonia as opposed to the ionized portion which their experts claim is the toxic element of ammonia, that is, the unionized portion is the toxic element of ammonia. Through their expert's testimony, they further claim that the protocol which lays down precise methods for dealing with the testing, including doing the tests at fifteen degrees centigrade temperature and warming or cooling the samples to achieve this tem-perature and using rainbow trout as the fish in the bioassay tests is not what is required in this element of the charge.

• • •

However, having assessed the arguments and considered the reasoned counter argu-ments by the Prosecution and the Crown which negated these claims, again by charts, calculations and reference to other studies, this Trier of Fact must conclude that any change in the protocols, that is, laying down a method of testing which has been well established should take place in the scientific realm.

The so called protocols are the 1990 publications of Environment Canada: (1) the Bio-logical Test Method. Acute Lethality Test Using Rainbow Trout and that is Exhibit 18 filed in this trial, and (2) The Biological Test Method—Determining Acute Lethality of Effluents to Daph-nia Magna, Exhibit 19. They were developed with input and guidance from many scientific authorities throughout Canada and North America, were reviewed before publication and comments and suggestions were actively sought from the academic, scientific, industrial and laboratory community before final review. They were updated with amendments in 1996. This was a 1990 publication first of all. In the scientific realm, a serious challenge to an accepted protocol would involve experimentation, publication in an acknowledged periodical, attempted replication of the challenger's experimental results by other experts and an eventual forum of the experts in the field. Undoubtedly, a successful challenge by scientific experts would result in an immediate amendment to the protocol. The protocol, Exhibit 18 ... , specifically notes the conditions under which testing must be done, among them a temperature of fifteen degrees centigrade plus or minus one centigrade degree. So, what is acceptable is a range of temperature between fourteen degrees centigrade and sixteen degrees centigrade. ... [T]he same document also gives the rationale for using rainbow trout, which focuses on their availability, the knowledge of how toxicants affect them, and the extensive data bank for comparisons, etcetera. Since they have been used extensively throughout North America for more than two decades, a lot is known about them. Similar procedures are set out in section four of the Daphnia Magna protocol, Exhibit 19.

This Court, based on that evidence, declines to make a ruling which impinges on the well researched, referenced and reasoned methodology of such documents as "The Protocol," which has such widespread scientific support. By happenstance, in looking at all of the data, the Court does not agree with the Defence's arguments in support of the pH shift as causing the deaths in the bioassays. The argument of the Defence is entirely theoretical and scientific experts who wish to overturn accepted science, in this court's opinion, have to do more than testify in Court.

This excerpt from the decision of the trial judge in *Fletcher v Kingston (City)*, as well as the discussion by McCulloch and Meuleman set out above in "Strategic Decisions in Environmental Prosecutions," demonstrates how the collection, admissibility, and probative weight of evidence is a crucial aspect in the prosecution of an environmental offence. This can often prove to be a difficult burden for the prosecution. For an illustration, see *R v Vale Newfoundland & Labrador Limited*, 2016 CanLII 5779 (NL Prov Ct), where the court held that the prosecution had failed to establish that discharged effluent was a "deleterious substance" under s 34 of the *Fisheries Act*, citing evidentiary difficulties in how the effluent samples were tested.

4. *R v Kingston (City)* began as a private prosecution. Similarly, the *R v Syncrude Canada Ltd* and *Podolsky v Cadillac Fairview Corp* decisions set out in Section III of this chapter were also initiated by way of a private prosecution. While the common law recognizes the right of a citizen to prosecute for a statutory offence, this right is subject to the power of the attorney general to intervene in the prosecution. This intervention typically leads to either a stay in the proceedings or the Crown taking over the prosecution.

One of the more troubling aspects of private environmental prosecutions in Canada is that some provinces implement a blanket policy of intervention by the attorney general to stay or withdraw private prosecutions, while others are more tolerant of the proceedings. For a detailed discussion on private prosecutions of environmental offences, see John Swaigen, Albert Koehl & Charles Hatt, "Private Prosecutions Revisited: The Continuing Importance of Private Prosecutions in Protecting the Environment" (2013) 26 J Envtl L & Prac 31.

5. One of the more noteworthy unsuccessful private prosecutions in Canada that highlights some of its structural difficulties is Martha Kostuch's unsuccessful attempts to prosecute the Government of Alberta in relation to its construction of the Oldman River Dam in the late 1980s. Martha Kostuch alleged that Alberta had committed an offence by violating s 35(1) of the *Fisheries Act*, which prohibited any work or undertaking that resulted in the harmful alteration, disruption, or destruction of fish habitat. The attorney general intervened and stayed the Kostuch prosecution several times over approximately half a decade. For an overview of these proceedings, see Shaun Fluker, "Remembering Martha Kostuch: The Private Prosecution and

the Oldman River Dam" (29 September 2008), online: *ABlawg* <https://ablawg.ca/2008/09/29/remembering-martha-kostuch-the-private-prosecution-and-the-oldman-river-dam/>.

6. Environmental legislation may also impose liability on corporate directors and officers for offences committed by the corporation. Section 280(1) of the *Canadian Environmental Protection Act, 1999*, SC 1999, c 33 provides as follows:

> 280(1) If a corporation commits an offence under this Act, any director, officer, agent or mandatary of the corporation who directed, authorized, assented to, acquiesced in or participated in the commission of the offence is a party to and guilty of the offence, and is liable on conviction to the penalty provided for by this Act for an individual in respect of the offence committed by the corporation, whether or not the corporation has been prosecuted or convicted.

A similar provision is set out in s 232 of the *Environment Protection and Enhancement Act*, RSA 2000, c E-12. In Ontario, s 194 of the *Environmental Protection Act* explicitly states that a director or officer has a duty to take all reasonable care to prevent the corporation from committing the offence, and that the onus is on the director or officer to prove that he or she has satisfied the obligation.

III. DUE DILIGENCE DEFENCE

The most common defence to the prosecution of an environmental offence is that the accused took all reasonable care to avoid committing the act. In *R v Sault Ste Marie*, above, the Supreme Court described this due diligence defence as an inherent characteristic of a strict liability offence: once the prosecution proves the *actus reus* beyond a reasonable doubt, the onus in a proceeding shifts to the accused to establish that it took reasonable measures specific to the offence for which it has been charged. In the context of an environmental offence, this often requires the accused to establish on the balance of probabilities that it implemented proper systems or that it followed best industry practices in conducting the activity. In *Fletcher v Kingston (City)*, above, the trial judge rejected the due diligence argument on the basis that the City had known of the leachate discharge from the landfill site and had failed to establish that it had had a plan to monitor or otherwise deal with the problem. Environmental legislation often explicitly provides for a due diligence defence to an offence.

The following list set out in *R v Commander Business Furniture Inc* (1992), 9 CELR (NS) 185 (Ont Prov Div) at 212 is often cited by Canadian courts as factors to consider in assessing a due diligence defence:

1) the nature and gravity of the adverse effect;
2) the foreseeability of the effect including abnormal sensitivities;
3) the alternative solutions available;
4) legislative or regulatory compliance;
5) industry standards;
6) the character of the neighbourhood;
7) what efforts have been made to address the problem;
8) over what period of time and promptness of response;
9) matters beyond the control of the accused including technological limitations;
10) skill level expected of the accused;
11) the complexities involved;
12) preventative systems;
13) economic considerations; and
14) actions of officials.

Consider these factors as you read through the following two decisions.

R V SYNCRUDE CANADA LTD
2010 ABPC 229

[On April 28, 2008, approximately 1,600 migratory birds died when they landed on a tailings pond located on Syncrude's Aurora North oil sands mine along the Athabasca River, north of Fort McMurray, Alberta. The Aurora mine, along with other oil sands operations in this region, falls under the pathway for migratory birds flying to and from breeding grounds in Wood Buffalo National Park. Weather or fatigue will force birds to rest along their route, and a tailings pond located under the flyway can be an attractive resting spot, particularly in early spring as the warm bitumen floating on the water surface keeps it free of ice and snow. A member of the Sierra Club of Canada commenced a private prosecution against Syncrude in January 2009, and the Crown subsequently took control of the proceedings and prosecuted Syncrude under s 5.1(1) of the *Migratory Birds Convention Act, 1994*, SC 1994, c 22 and s 155 of the *Environmental Protection and Enhancement Act*, RSA 2000, c E-12. The relevant federal and provincial statutory provisions read as follows:

Migratory Birds Convention Act, 1994

5.1(1) No person or vessel shall deposit a substance that is harmful to migratory birds, or permit such a substance to be deposited, in waters or an area frequented by migratory birds or in a place from which the substance may enter such waters or such an area.

Environmental Protection and Enhancement Act

155 A person who keeps, stores or transports a hazardous substance or pesticide shall do so in a manner that ensures that the hazardous substance or pesticide does not directly or indirectly come into contact with or contaminate any animals, plants, food or drink.

The trial judge found that the Crown had proved the elements of both offences beyond a reasonable doubt, and the onus shifted to Syncrude to establish a due diligence defence. Syncrude also raised several additional defences to the charges, including impossibility, act of God, abuse of process, and *de minimus*.]

7. DUE DILIGENCE

[95] The defence of due diligence will be available in a prosecution for a strict liability offence if the accused reasonably believed in a mistaken set of facts which, if true, would render the act or omission innocent; or if it took all reasonable steps to avoid the particular event. *R v. Sault Ste. Marie (City)* at p. 1326.

[96] The defence would apply if Syncrude established on a balance of probabilities that it could not have reasonably foreseen the contravention of the statutes. Syncrude's actions must be judged on the basis of the information available to it at the time of the alleged offence. *R. v. MacMillan Bloedel Ltd.*, 2002 BCCA 510 (CanLII) at paras. 44-49; *R. v. Starosielski*, 2001 ABPC 208 (CanLII) at para. 134; *R. v. Edmonton (City)* at para. 701.

[97] There is no evidence of any mistake of fact here. Syncrude should have known that the proscribed conduct would occur. Bitumen would be deposited into the Aurora Settling Basin and Syncrude would not be able to ensure, i.e., make certain, that birds would not be contaminated by the bitumen in the Basin. It was reasonably foreseeable that those events could occur on April 28, 2008 at the Aurora Settling Basin.

[98] The defence would also apply if Syncrude established that it took all reasonable care to avoid the contraventions.

... The due diligence which must be established is that of the accused alone. Where an employer is charged in respect of an act committed by an employee acting in the course of employment, the question will be whether the act took place without the accused's direction or approval, thus negating wilful involvement of the accused, and whether the accused exercised all reasonable care by *establishing a proper system* to prevent commission of the offence and by taking *reasonable steps to ensure the effective operation of the system*. The availability of the defence to a corporation will depend on whether such due diligence was taken by those who are the directing mind and will of the corporation, whose acts are therefore in law the acts of the corporation itself. [emphasis added] *R. v. Sault Ste. Marie (City)* at p. 1331.

[99] To meet the onus, Syncrude is not required to show that it took all possible or imaginable steps to avoid liability. It was not required to achieve a standard of perfection or show superhuman efforts. It is the existence of a "proper system" and "reasonable steps to ensure the effective operation of the system" that must be proved. The conduct of the accused is assessed against that of a reasonable person in similar circumstances. *Lévis (City) v. Tétreault, supra*, at para. 15; *R. v. Edmonton (City)*, 2006 ABPC 56 (CanLII) at para. 703; *R. v. J.D. Irving Ltd.*, [2008] N.B.J. No. 371 at paras. 42-43; Libman [*Libman on Regulatory Offences in Canada*] at pp. 7-2 to 7-3, 7-21 to 7-24.

[100] Various factors should be taken into account to determine whether the defence has established reasonable care. The defence applies in many different situations and so there can be no single comprehensive list of appropriate considerations for all cases. The decision must be based on the particular circumstances of the case. [The court cites the list of considerations set out in *R v Commander Business Furniture Inc*, above.] ...

[101] The question then is whether Syncrude has established that it took all reasonable steps to ensure that waterfowl would not be contaminated in its tailings pond. Whether or not Syncrude could ensure against the contamination, it must still be determined whether it took all reasonable steps toward that end.

[102] Although reasonable care to prevent the contamination of wildlife would not ordinarily be a defence to the federal charge, the federal Crown has conceded that, in the particular circumstances of this case, Syncrude should be acquitted of the federal charge if that reasonable care is proved.

A. GRAVITY OF THE EFFECT

[103] The gravity of the potential harm caused by Syncrude's conduct will influence the efforts it would reasonably be expected [to] undertake to prevent the harm. Libman at pp. 7-50 to 7-51.

[104] Until better technology is available, tailings ponds will be a part of tar sands operations, and a risk to wildlife. Operators cannot remove all of the bitumen from the tailings with current technology so this substance is found in smaller bits throughout the pond, as well as being more concentrated in a sticky mat in some parts of the pond. As the events of April 28, 2008 demonstrate, severe contamination with bitumen has dreadful and deadly consequences for waterfowl and the evidence indicates that there can be serious longer term adverse consequences from relatively mild contamination.

[105] In assessing the gravity of the loss of waterfowl, it is important to consider the broader context. There is some evidence, particularly the testimony of Dr. Robertson, suggesting that the loss of migrating waterfowl in this case, and consequent loss of their offspring, would likely affect particularly mallard populations available for hunting. However, large numbers of ducks are killed by licenced hunters. In addition many migratory birds will be contaminated or killed in other industrial circumstances.

[106] I doubt that the number of ducks lost on or about April 28, 2008 at the Aurora Settling Basin would have any significant impact on total duck populations and it may be a small number compared with the loss from hunting or total losses in industrial settings. In addition the evidence indicates that the loss on April 28, 2008 would probably have occurred even with deterrents in place. However, it is important to remember the purpose of the provincial and federal legislation. The legislation is designed to protect the environment and maintain migratory bird populations, respectively. As with most regulatory offences, the legislation is not just directed at the immediate and direct effect of the proscribed conduct but also at the potential harm if that conduct was widespread. See, for example: *R. v. Carriere*, 2005 SKPC 84 (CanLII) at paras. 45-47.

B. COMPLEXITY

[107] The volume of tailings produced by tars sands operations results in very large ponds, the Aurora pond being the size of about 640 football fields. There are usually more appealing water bodies for waterfowl and shorebirds to use for rest or food but they will be attracted to these ponds nonetheless. Because the Aurora facility is located under major migratory flyways there are large numbers of birds in the vicinity during migration. It is evident from the expert testimony that the challenge of deterring birds from the pond is complex. The proper design and operation of bird deterrent programs demands a high level of expertise and, when a company creates a risk such as a tar sands tailings pond, it is reasonable that the company should have in place or access the expertise to effectively manage the risk to wildlife. Libman at pp. 7-99 to 7-101. See, respecting expertise expected of property owners: *R. v. Heinrichs*, [1995] B.C.J. No. 2546 (B.C.S.C.).

[108] In the past Syncrude had commissioned expert studies and its employees had participated in the Oil Sands Bird and Wildlife Protection Committee. The employees directly involved in the bird deterrence program, the Bird and Environmental Team, were experienced in the operation and maintenance of the bird deterrent devices. While they may have learned of bird behaviour and deterrence from their job experience, they had no real training in those areas. Dave Matthews, BET Leader and Senior Construction Specialist, stated that he had no training in managing wildlife. He relied on his experience and on the experience of the Team members to determine where cannons would be placed.

[109] The BET experience is valuable but it is not a sufficient basis for an effective bird deterrent program for tar sands operations. One example of the problem with relying exclusively on experience is found in the statement of BET member Gordon Grandjambe. He said that sound cannons cannot be placed too close together because the birds get used to the sound. He said shore-based cannons were kept roughly 1000 yards apart. The expert evidence indicates that waterfowl will become habituated to frequent firing of the cannons but does not suggest that cannons should be placed further apart to address this problem and certainly not 1000 yards

apart. A more important example is the decision to commence deploying deterrents on April 14, 2008, a decision which was clearly not informed by proper training or expertise.

C. PREVENTIVE SYSTEM

[110] Syncrude was obliged to have in place a system to prevent waterfowl from landing on the tailings pond and to ensure the effective operation of that deterrent system. See: Libman at pp. 7-105 to 7-106.

[111] Syncrude's bird deterrent system in 2008 was based on the use of sound cannons and human effigies. The evidence indicates that these devices can be effective. While Syncrude had documents that set out procedures for bird deterrence, the documents are not in any way comprehensive and do not reflect the complexity of effective bird deterrence. One document, apparently a job description for a Bird Deterrent Tech, indicated that deterrents were to be activated in all contaminated waters beginning on April 1, depending on the weather and arrival of birds. Dave Matthews said there was no formal schedule however. Another document concerning cannon set-up called for the cannons to be placed no further than 240 metres apart on land or water. The evidence indicates that Syncrude did not have enough cannons to achieve this density. It does not appear that these documents played any significant part in Syncrude's bird deterrent program.

[112] Syncrude had, in previous years, cut back substantially on the number of deterrents. Staff had also been reduced, primarily by retirements. Dave Matthews said that he and his supervisor, Gary Bourque, felt they could do the work with the reduced staff. Mr. Matthews and the BET members decided to stop using booms to confine the mat. Mr. Matthews said that the decision was based on the problem of keeping up with the pouring of the tailings and their conclusion that the mat was sinking before it became a problem.

[113] Most significantly, Mr. Matthews and his supervisor Gary Bourque made the decision to bring the BET team to work on April 14, 2008. Their statements indicate that this decision was based on the weather. The hire letters specifying the April 14 start date are dated March 19, 2008. For various reasons some members of the crew were unable to start work on April 14. When the BET did get to work, there was only one truck available even though they usually used four trucks. Apparently there was a problem renting vehicles and one truck had been lent to an operations team.

[114] As a result of the late start, Syncrude did not have sound cannons deployed on the perimeter of Aurora Settling Basin before the bird landings discovered on April 28, 2008. Certain employee statements indicate that cannons were deployed at the Basin on April 16 or 17 but I am convinced that their statements are mistaken on this point. Gordon Grandjambe thought he placed eight cannons at the north end of the Basin on April 17. Fred Cardinal said he and Lawrence Powder placed six cannons at Aurora Recycling Pond and four on the tailings pond on April 16. However, Lawrence Powder indicated that he was not at Aurora until April 17 and he placed only six cannons on the recycling pond. Lloyd Benio's statement suggests that there were a few cannons near the Basin prior to April 28. These contradictory statements do not establish that the cannons had been placed on the Basin on April 28. I do not doubt that these are the employees' best recollections at the time of their statements but I am satisfied that they are mistaken. For them it was simply a matter of trying to remember what they were doing on an ordinary work day.

[115] I accept the sworn testimony of Todd Powell that the cannons had not been placed at the Basin by the time he arrived on April 28. This is confirmed by Dave Matthews' statement. The presence or absence of the cannons on April 28 would

have been a matter of some importance to both Mr. Powell and Mr. Matthews. In Mr. Powell's case it would bear directly on the investigation and in Mr. Matthews' case he would be accountable for the decision as to when cannons were deployed. This conclusion is also consistent with the cannon update maps for April 24 described in Steve Gaudet's statement. For the purpose of the due diligence defence that finding would be sufficient, but for other defences advanced by Syncrude it may not be. I will make it clear here that I am convinced beyond reasonable doubt that the cannons were not placed at the Aurora Settling Basin prior to April 28.

D. ALTERNATIVE SOLUTIONS

[116] Stewart, C.J. held in *R. v. Gonder* [1981 CanLII 3207, 62 CCC (2d) 326 (Y Terr Ct)] at para. 25:

> Reasonableness of care is often best measured by comparing what was done against what could have been done. The reasonableness of alternatives the accused knew or ought to have known were available is a primary measure of due diligence. To successfully plead the defence of reasonable care the accused must establish on a balance of probabilities there were no reasonable feasible alternatives that might have avoided or minimized injury to others. See also: Libman at pp. 7-135 to 7- 141.

[117] The evidence here, while disclosing no real industry standard for bird deterrence, offered a number of reasonable alternatives. The most obvious alternative was to have sufficient equipment and staff ready for deployment of adequate deterrents no later than early April. Shell Albian Sands Muskeg River Mine and Suncor were both able to commence deployment in early April in 2008. These operators also had more comprehensive written procedures, oversight by individuals with appropriate training and advance planning and preparation of equipment. I am not suggesting that Syncrude was required to adopt either of these systems, simply that there were reasonable alternatives available.

[118] I was impressed with the evidence of Dr. St. Clair who offered an opinion respecting a minimum reasonable deterrent system. Oil sands operators would be well advised to accept Dr. St. Clair's advice but I do not find that oil sands operators must meet these requirements to establish reasonable care. Dr. St. Clair's opinion does, however, provide evidence of reasonable alternatives available to Syncrude. Of particular note is the advice that the system should be operational in early spring, i.e.: March, not late April. Dr. St. Clair also suggested appropriate training for those involved in the deterrent program, including training in bird behaviour and identification, experimental design and monitoring protocols.

[119] In my view, there existed several reasonable and feasible alternatives of which Syncrude did or should have known. I have heard no evidence to suggest that these alternatives would not be economically feasible.

E. FORESEEABILITY

[120] Foreseeability is properly considered to determine if the accused has taken reasonable steps. It is only required to take steps to avoid that which it can reasonably foresee. *R. v. MacMillan Bloedel Ltd.*, [2002] B.C.J. No. 2083 (B.C.C.A.) at para. 52.

[121] Due diligence does not require clairvoyance or that the accused should have foreseen every possible failure. *R. v. Lonkar Well Testing Limited*, 2009 ABQB 345 (CanLII) at para. 40; *R. v. Daishowa Canada Co.* (1991), 118 A.R. 112 at 116, aff'd. (1993) A.R. 179 (C.A.).

[122] In *R. v. Rio Algom Ltd.* (1988), 1988 CanLII 4702 (ON CA), 66 O.R. (2d) 674 the Ontario Court of Appeal discussed the test for foreseeability in connection with

occupational health and safety legislation. Libman, at p. 7-70, described the test quoting *Rio Algom*:

> The test is not whether the particular accident was foreseeable, but whether a reasonable person would have foreseen that "the circumstances that [led] to the accident created a hazard requiring remedial intervention." See also: *R. v. Lonkar Well Testing Limited* at para. 41.

[123] Syncrude argues that it had in place a system which worked for many years to prevent the loss of all but a small numbers of birds. It says that it could not reasonably have anticipated the confluence of circumstances that resulted in the deaths of more than 1600 water fowl. There was a record snowfall on April 20 to 22 which interfered with plans to deploy deterrents. The weather and the fact that adjacent water bodies were frozen over also made it more likely that waterfowl would land.

[124] However, Syncrude's management should have known of the circumstances that make it more likely that migratory birds will land on the tailings pond in the spring. When nearby water bodies remain frozen while the tailings pond is open, waterfowl are more likely to be attracted to the tailings pond. Adverse weather, which is not uncommon in early April, will also make it more likely that birds will land. It would be impossible to predict with certainty when break-up will occur, what the weather conditions will be prior to break-up and that migratory birds will start to appear on a specific date. It is not, however, difficult to predict that there will be years when these circumstances converge. On the evidence I have heard, this convergence is not a remote possibility. The expert evidence respecting the conspecific behaviour of birds also leads to the conclusion that, once a few birds landed, many more might follow.

[125] The magnitude of the storm was rare but not completely unprecedented. There was more snowfall on April 20 and 21 of 1985. The prospect that weather would interfere with deployment of deterrents at some times in April was foreseeable.

[126] It was apparent that deterrents should be in place as early in the spring as reasonably and safely possible and that they should be deployed as quickly as reasonably possible. Syncrude did not deploy the deterrents early enough and quickly enough. This failure can be attributed to the absence of an effective documented procedure, inadequate training and expertise, the reduction in staff, the late hiring dates, delay in getting staff to work and not having equipment ready soon enough. Syncrude's reduction in the number of deterrents and the decision to stop using booms bring into question the effectiveness of the deterrents even if they were in place. There is no evidence to suggest that these acts or omissions were in any way the product of scientific or expert analysis.

[127] The argument that there had been low numbers of detected fatalities in previous years is a factor to be considered but it is not a persuasive basis for concluding that it was not reasonably foreseeable that more birds would be contaminated without the prompt deployment of deterrents. Firstly, there was no adequate monitoring to determine how many birds actually landed, were contaminated or died in the tailings pond. In addition there was no scientific or expert basis for predicting that the relatively low numbers would continue despite cutbacks in staff and deterrents or the later deployment of the deterrents.

[128] It may be reasonable that Syncrude did not anticipate the severity of the weather conditions or the total number of birds that would be killed but a reasonable person in Syncrude's place would have foreseen that Syncrude's acts and omissions leading up to the events of April 28, 2008 would cause an unacceptable hazard for waterfowl. Syncrude did not establish a proper system to ensure that wildlife would not be contaminated in the Aurora Settling Basin or take reasonable steps to ensure the effective operation of the system.

PODOLSKY V CADILLAC FAIRVIEW CORP
2013 ONCJ 65

[Ecojustice launched a private prosecution against the owners and managers of the Yonge Corporate Centre (YCC) office buildings in northern Toronto. The defendants were charged under provincial and federal environmental legislation in relation to harm or death suffered by migratory birds resulting from collisions with the highly reflective glass windows of the buildings. The court found that the prosecution established beyond a reasonable doubt the elements of the offences set out by s 14(1) of the *Environmental Protection Act*, RSO 1990, c E.19 (EPA), which provided that "[A] person shall not discharge a contaminant or cause or permit the discharge of a contaminant into the natural environment, if the discharge causes or may cause an adverse effect," and s 32(1) of the *Species at Risk Act*, SC 2002, c 29 (SARA), which provided that "No person shall kill, harm, harass, capture or take an individual of a wildlife species that is listed as an extirpated species, an endangered species or a threatened species." The onus shifted to the defendants to establish on the balance of probabilities that reasonable steps were implemented to avoid the bird collisions.]

(F) THE DEFENCE OF DUE DILIGENCE

[86] Having found the *actus reus* for the *EPA* and *SARA* offences, the burden shifts to the defendants to establish their lack of fault. As put simply in *Sault Ste. Marie*, at para. 67: "Proof of the prohibited act *prima facie* imports the offence, but the accused may avoid liability by proving that he took reasonable care." Proof, in this context, is satisfied on the civil standard, a balance of probabilities. Failing same, the defendants will necessarily be found guilty of the two offences.

[87] A determination of whether a defendant has exercised due diligence involves, as said in *Lévis (Ville) c. Tétreault, supra*, at para. 15, the application of an "objective standard ... under which the conduct of the accused is assessed against that of a reasonable person in similar circumstances." The exercise is largely fact-driven and depends, as many cases have repeated, on "an assessment of all the circumstances of the case." On conducting this analysis I am persuaded, for the reasons that follow, that the defendants have met their onus.

[88] I appreciate, in reaching this conclusion, that the YCC did not retain external consultants to address the problem of bird strikes. I appreciate, as well, that a corporate defendant, as here, cannot relieve itself of liability by effectively delegating or outsourcing its responsibility. (See, for example, *R. v. Canadian Tire Corp.*, [2004] O.J. No. 312 (Ont. S.C.), at para. 89.) The defendants, through Patricia Poyntz, relied on Michael Mesure and Bob Alsip, both of whom, she rightly assumed, were in contact with Dr. Klem. She reached no further in her search for expert assistance but, in the circumstances, I do not think her efforts unreasonable. Mesure was and remains the executive director of FLAP, Toronto's leading source of information and contacts respecting avian collisions and their remedy. Alsip headed the Convenience Group—the "only game in town," as was widely accepted, in the field of technological solutions to the problem. And Dr. Klem is generally acknowledged as the leading North American expert in the discipline pertaining to the causes of avian collisions and strategies for averting them. If there were other reputable sources of consulting expertise prior to the conclusion of the timeframe set out in the charges, their names or affiliations were not advanced by the prosecution during the course of this trial.

[89] It is also the case that Cadillac Fairview's investment in bird deterrent applications at the YCC appears to have accelerated in the period immediately following the company's first becoming aware that it faced prosecution for environmental and

animal welfare offences. Some may read this as a reaction to the litigation and infer that the defendants could therefore have acted with greater dispatch. I do not see it that way. As I construe the evidentiary record, the defendants had committed themselves to moving forward on the bird strike problem before, as one might say, the writ was dropped. The prior delays, on my assessment, were attributable to technological or logistic challenges presented by the YCC's physical setting and the development of a suitable product. The more salient question is whether the YCC ought earlier to have contracted to install an alternative application that, although inferior in efficacy, cost and tenant satisfaction, would at least have gone some way to mitigating the terrible harm caused to migrating birds. The difficult balancing of the factors germane to this question is the critical analysis that led me to my verdict and the one to which I now turn.

[90] One helpful and oft-cited catalogue of factors relevant to this determination is that devised by Hackett J. in *R. v. Commander Business Furniture Inc.* [The court cites the list of considerations set out in *Commander Business Furniture*, above.] ... .

[91] Cost considerations, while in no way dispositive, factor into many if not most assessments of due diligence. The following passage from *Commander Business*, at paras. 110-11, is of assistance to the task at hand:

> In my view, the degree of control that an accused can exercise over a problem must have an air of reality and therefore must include some consideration of cost. ...
>
> Having said that, economic concerns must be properly balanced against other factors. For example, *phasing in an operational change which will both protect the environment and the economic viability of a company may be duly diligent in all the circumstances.* It is difficult to imagine that any industrial standards or reasonable person would support a non-phased-in approach which would destroy a company when a realistic phased-in timely approach would have reasonable success over a reasonable period of time and thereby accommodate both interests. *On the other hand, if a phased-in approach that complied with the industry standard would destroy the environment or cause or risk of [sic] serious harm, no cost would be too great.* The degree or level of harm or adverse effect must therefore be reasonably balanced with economic considerations and the other factors set out earlier for a due diligence defence. [Emphasis added.]

[92] I do not intend to here retrace the factual review that occupies much of this judgement or conduct a detailed factor-by-factor analysis. I do note that the YCC apparently complied with municipal building and industry standards, that only a handful, at most, of buildings in the GTA had adopted a more aggressive strategy in deterring bird strikes by 2010, that the YCC implemented and maintained a policy to respond to nocturnal light pollution, that it had co-operated with FLAP's bird retrieval, rescue and documentation efforts for more than a decade, and that it had endeavoured, if intermittently and without tangible success, to find solutions to the problem of daytime collisions since the late 1990s. The YCC, through Patricia Poyntz, had consulted with FLAP about the problem of avian collisions and, on at least a few occasions, conducted test installations of window treatments that proved ineffective, unappealing to its tenants, or both.

[93] The presenting problems were complex and the necessarily site-specific solutions were constantly evolving. What worked elsewhere did not work at the YCC. As said Hill J. in *Canadian Tire, supra,* at para. 85,

> In assessing the efficacy of a due diligence defence, the court must guard against the correcting, but at times distorting, influences of hindsight. In considering the

defendant's efforts, the court "does not look for perfection" (*R. v. Safety-Kleen Canada Ltd.* (1997), 1997 CanLII 1285 (ON CA), 114 C.C.C. (3d) 214 (Ont. C.A.) at 224) nor some "superhuman effort" on the defendant's part (*R. v. Courtaulds Fibres Canada* (1992), 1992 CanLII 12826 (ON CJ), 76 C.C.C. (3d) 68 (Ont. Prov. Ct.) at 77). If the facts suggest a discoverable causative flaw "could readily" have been remedied, due diligence will fail: *R. v. Rio Algom Ltd.* [1988 CanLII 4702, 46 CCC (2d) 242 (Ont CA)], *supra* at 249, 252.

There were no quick-fix solutions to the problem of daytime bird strikes at the YCC and the measures that were proposed were expensive and, prior to 2011, of dubious efficacy. It must not be forgotten that the standard to be applied in assessing due diligence is that of the reasonable person in like circumstances, not one of immediate perfection upon recognition of an environmental problem.

[94] All that said, many hundreds of birds met their untimely deaths and many others were undoubtedly injured in the eight months bracketed by March and November of 2010. This single factor, particularly given its foreseeability, weighs heavily in the calculus of reasonable care. Balancing this against the other considerations (including, as I find, Poyntz's good faith effort to advance the bird file at the YCC), I conclude that the defendants did exercise due diligence in addressing the problem of avian collisions. Accordingly, acquittals must follow.

NOTES AND QUESTIONS

1. Identify all of the considerations noted in *Syncrude* and *Cadillac Fairview* in determining whether the accused exercised reasonable care. Note the type of evidence on which the court relied for its assessment of due diligence. What do the court's reasons in *Syncrude* suggest needed to be established in order for Syncrude to successfully defend itself? How does this compare with the court's reasoning in *Cadillac Fairview*, another case involving the death of migratory birds? What is distinct about the measures taken, or the circumstances of the offences, to explain the different results in these two cases?

2. In *Cadillac Fairview*, the court heard evidence that some of the birds killed were members of a species listed as threatened under the federal *Species at Risk Act*. Does the court give sufficient weight to this evidence in its due diligence assessment?

3. In *R v Syncrude*, Syncrude raised a number of defences other than due diligence. Syncrude argued that any sanction for the death of the migratory birds should be based on evidence that it had failed to comply with the conditions in its regulatory licence to operate the Aurora mine. In the absence of such a finding, Syncrude argued it would be an abuse of process for the Crown to prosecute. The court dismissed this argument, but the trial judge noted that he would have been inclined to accept the abuse of process argument in relation to the federal charge if the federal Crown had not conceded that it would not seek a conviction under s 5.1(1) of the *Migratory Birds Convention Act* if Syncrude was successful in defending against the provincial charges based on due diligence. What do you think was the basis of this concession by the federal Crown? For some discussion on the abuse of process argument in this case, see Shaun Fluker, "R. v Syncrude Canada: A Clash of Bitumen and Birds" (2011) 49 Alta L Rev 237. Syncrude also sought to defend itself on the basis of *de minimus*, arguing its actions were of trivial consequence because birds die in the tailings ponds regardless of deterrence efforts. The court did not accept this argument either. Other courts have questioned the applicability of a *de minimus* defence to a regulatory offence (for some discussion, see *Peel (Region, Department of Public Health) v Le Royal Resto and Lounge Inc*, 2017 ONCJ 767).

4. For a discussion of principles in relation to assessing the due diligence of directors and officers charged with an offence under environmental legislation in relation to a corporate act, see *R v Bata Industries Ltd* (1992), 9 OR (3d) 329, 7 CELR (NS) 245 (Prov Div).

IV. SENTENCING FOR AN ENVIRONMENTAL OFFENCE

Canadian courts hold that sentencing principles for an environmental offence are unique from those for other regulatory infractions. In *R v United Keno Hill Mines Ltd* (1980), 10 CELR 43 (Y Terr Ct), the accused corporation pleaded guilty to discharging effluent into a nearby watercourse contrary to its water licence. As part of his consideration of an appropriate sentence, the trial judge set out a list of considerations relevant to the sentencing of an environmental offender (see also *R v Van Waters & Rogers Ltd*, 1998 ABPC 55). As the next case demonstrates, a sentencing court will refer to these considerations in deciding on an appropriate sanction for an environmental offence.

R V TERROCO INDUSTRIES LIMITED
2005 ABCA 141

[A driver with Terroco Industries, a company in the business of transporting dangerous materials, incorrectly mixed two products into the tank of a transport truck, and this then resulted in an escape of chlorine gas. Another person at the site was exposed to the gas, and this resulted in serious injury to his respiratory system. After this incident, the driver went to his destination and pumped the mixture of products into a disposal well. The mixture sprayed onto the ground near the well. Terroco was convicted of a breach of s 98(2) of the *Environmental Protection and Enhancement Act*, SA 1992, c E-13.3 (EPEA). This section stated that "no person shall release or permit the release into the environment of a substance in an amount, or concentration or level or at a rate of release that causes or may cause a significant adverse effect." Terroco was also convicted of a breach of s 19(a) of the *Dangerous Goods Transportation and Handling Act*, SA 1998, c D-3.5 (DGTHA). This section stated that "a person shall not handle, offer for transportation or transport any dangerous goods unless the person complies with all applicable safety requirements." Terroco was sentenced to a fine of $50,000 for the EPEA offence and $5,000 for the DGHTA offence. Terroco appealed the sentence and obtained leave under the *Provincial Offences Procedure Act*, RSA 2000, c P-34 for a determination of the appropriate principles to be applied in sentencing for an offence under environmental legislation.]

ANALYSIS

[34] Although leave was granted on the question of which general sentencing principles are to be applied, these reasons will be restricted to the discussion of general principles that have a role to play in this appeal. I therefore propose to deal with (1) culpability, (2) prior records and past involvement with the authorities, (3) acceptance of responsibility, (4) damage/harm and (5) deterrence. To adopt the wording of Morrow, J. in *R. v. Kenaston Drilling (Arctic) Ltd.* (1973), 1973 CanLII 1297 (NWT SC), 41 D.L.R. (3d) 252, 12 C.C.C. (2d) 383 (N.W.T. S.C.), sentencing principles for environmental offences require "a special approach."

1. CULPABILITY

[35] Culpability should be a dominant factor in sentencing for environmental offences. The EPEA provides that the maximum sentence for intentional acts is twice that for unintentional acts. On some occasions the Crown will come close to establishing that the release was intentional. Conversely, there are acts which cause harm

despite the exercise of due diligence which provides an absolute defence. In between these two extremes are a myriad of circumstances ranging from cases of recklessness to those where the defence of due diligence failed but the evidence showed a near miss. It is evident that offences which involve recklessness will call for more severe penalties than those which are near due diligence misses. The degree of carelessness is a factor in sentencing for environmental offences. Due diligence in sentencing for environmental offences is to be assessed on a sliding scale: the more diligent the offender, the lower the range of fit sentences; alternatively, the less diligent the offender, the higher the range of fit sentence.

[36] In determining the degree of culpability, the failure to take simple and inexpensive steps to avoid the unwanted consequence prior to the contamination is an aggravating factor ... . Reasonable foreseeability impacts the sentence. If the danger is obvious rather than obscure, the failure to take reasonable care demonstrates a higher level of culpability and is an aggravating factor ... .

• • •

2. PRIOR RECORD AND PAST INVOLVEMENT WITH THE AUTHORITIES

[38] A prior record indicates that an offender is more concerned about profit than compliance. It can be an aggravating factor. Similarly if the offender has been warned by the authorities about its conduct but persists, that is an aggravating factor ... .

3. ACCEPTANCE OF RESPONSIBILITY/REMORSE

[39] An early guilty plea to an environmental offence is a mitigating factor. ... An offender who sees no error is more prone to re-offend than is one who recognizes guilt and takes responsibility. ...

• • •

[42] ... If there is a failure to take remedial steps, such an omission is an aggravating factor, while early reporting, cooperation and the exercise of remedial actions is a mitigating factor ... .

• • •

4. DAMAGE/HARM

[45] The existence, potential, duration and degree of harm are factors to be fully considered in sentencing for environmental offences. If actual harm is established that is an aggravating factor, especially when the harm is a readily foreseeable consequence of the underlying action ... . Sentencing judges should therefore be alive to whether harm occurred to persons, property, the environment or all of them. The degree of actual harm is also a relevant factor. Damage that is trifling is not nearly as aggravating as damage to persons and the environment that is long lasting and of significant degree. If the harm consists of death that is a serious aggravating factor.

• • •

[47] In many environmental offences, harm is not easily identified. However, the absence of ascertainable harm is not a mitigating but merely a neutral factor ...

[48] Furthermore, the potential for harm is also a relevant consideration ... . The greater the potential for harm, the greater the warranted penalty. The potential for harm is informed by the probability of the risk, the nature of the product, the likely magnitude of damage if the risk materializes and the sensitivity of the site including its proximity to population and fragile environments ...

[49] The unexceptional nature of an environmental offence site is also not a mitigating factor, however, a delicate site that is not easily rejuvenated may be cited as an aggravating factor ... . It logically follows that a site such as a waterway that causes the harm to be rapidly spread over a large area creates aggravating circumstances.

[50] A site that is person-sensitive also calls for special protection. If the spill or release of [a] substance occurs next to a school or playground, the potential for harm is greater thus an exacerbating factor exists. Such potential for harm calls for a more severe sentence than if the release or spill occurs in an isolated, unpopulated rural area. ...

[51] The cost of repairing or addressing the damages caused by the offence may also be a significant factor in determining harm ...

• • •

5. DETERRENCE

[53] A key component of sentences imposed for breaches of environmental protection statutes should be specific and general deterrence. ...

• • •

[56] When considering specific deterrence sentencing judges should consider many of the factors I have already outlined. For example, the degree of remorse informs the need for specific deterrence. An offender that takes responsibility for its actions and cooperates with the authorities is on a different footing than an offender that increases its culpability by, for example, attempting a surreptitious cleanup of a spill to avoid civil and penal consequences.

• • •.

[58] ... Whenever a corporate offender is being sentenced the sentencing court should be made aware of the offender's general ability to pay. Individual deterrence is achieved at a much lesser cost when a small corporation of limited means is to be sentenced than when the corporation is large enough that maximum sentences have limited significance.

• • •

[60] The penalty imposed should also have a deterrent effect on others in that industry who may risk offending. ... What will be a severe fine for one offender may be a pittance to another. The starting point for sentencing a corporate offender must be such that the fine imposed appears to be more than a licensing fee for illegal activity or the cost of doing business ... . The other side of this coin must be that, in the majority of cases, the sentence should not result in economic inviability ...

PETER J CRAIG, "NEGOTIATING SENTENCES"
in Allan Ingelson, ed, *Environment in the Courtroom* (Calgary: University of Calgary Press, 2019) ch 30

To say the sentencing process is more art than science is not exactly relaying an insightful observation. I personally find the identification and application of notionally precedent sentencing decisions in environmental cases very challenging. ...

I am always mindful of the purpose of the sentencing exercise in a regulatory prosecution. Environmental offences, like many others, are violations of public welfare legislation. I fully acknowledge the significance of deterrence, both general and specific in this context. But to my way of thinking, the focus of an environmental sentencing should be squarely placed on how deterrence is achieved, while at the same time addressing remediation causally connected to an offence, if applicable, and also promoting public or industry education and awareness which could change behaviour. I do not see these as mutually exclusive objectives.

So, how does all this theory manifest itself when dealing with environmental offence sentence negotiation? ... I believe that a fine should always be a component of a global sentence package. However, my point is, how big should the fine piece of this global sentence pie be, and as a result, should counsel be fixating on fine quantum exclusively when discussing sentence? [A]re funds and human resources better directed elsewhere, particularly if there is an unresolved remediation problem or significant educational/awareness need tied to the root cause of an offence?

My general approach when considering sentence discussion with counsel is to first educate myself about the offence and the defendant, and my principal conduit in these respects is always the investigator. I lean heavily on investigators to school me about enforcement issues connected to a geographic area or industry sectors. I know few prosecutors positioned to gauge these things themselves, and I certainly include myself with the majority. I will provide an example to illustrate the exercise, and I will fudge a little bit of detail to protect identifying any individuals or entities.

Suppose you are a woe-begotten prosecutor who shows up for work one day and there is a multi-banker box file on your desk. It is a case involving the owner of a commercial premises which has its own on-site sewage disposal system. The corporate owner has been charged with an offence under the *Environment Act* for violating terms and conditions of its system approval. The particulars of the charge involve effluent exceedences outflowing into the lake adjacent to the property. The investigation reveals that, quite commonly, the owner hired a certified consultant to design, install, and secure approval for the system, and has further retained the consultant to monitor the system and forward to the department the quarterly produced effluent level data which is a further condition of the approval.

The owner, once charged, takes responsive action and corrects the problem. The principal of the company tells the investigator that everyone working in his industry essentially operates this end of their business the same way he does and virtually defers all compliance decisions and compliance filing responsibilities to consultants, for a commensurate fee, of course. The investigator tells you, the beleaguered prosecutor, when she calls you prior to the defendant's initial court date that this is very typical, and, indeed, is something of a macro-enforcement/education issue. You, the noble warrior of justice, recognize that contracting out responsibility under the Act in this fashion certainly doesn't constitute due diligence, but you do also acknowledge the lesser degree of moral culpability on the part of this owner that the situation entails.

The defendant's counsel speaks to you on the arraignment date (i.e. the initial court appearance in answer to the charge). He is kicking the tires a little bit, and seeks your position on sentence if an early guilty plea is forthcoming. The parties agree to adjourn the defendant's plea for a month or so to allow discussions to occur in the interim.

You arrange a meeting with the investigator the following week. She elaborates on her case a little more. She has found the defendant, in the person of its principal, to have been very cooperative with the investigation and to have taken practical responsibility for the offence. What is more, this person is an active member of a *bona fide* provincial industry association which works periodically with the department and which encompasses most of the businesses carrying on similar operations in the province. The investigator elaborates further about the very tangible enforcement need to educate members of this industry about the practice of delegating statutory responsibility under the Act to consultants, which in her opinion is widespread and prevalent throughout the entire province.

You, the savvy prosecutor, quickly deduce that perhaps this is a case tailor-made for creative sentencing options. ...

• • •

You then write the defendant's counsel and communicate your position on plea resolution and *joint* sentence recommendation. You use the fine range as a guide for the defendant's global financial penalty, so to speak, as you will be proposing several creative sentence initiatives for which there will be a hard cost to the defendant attached. You propose that the defendant:

- Fund a presentation at the industry association AGM in the amount of $5000 which will reflect the circumstances of this offence. ...;
- Make a donation to a local Watercourse Preservation Society in the amount of $5,000;
- Publish the circumstances of the offence in a media outlet(s) mutually agreed as between the defendant and the department, with the content also to be mutually agreed, the total approximate cost of which shall be $5000; and
- Pay a fine in the amount of $500.

• • •

My experience with this negotiating process, and particularly utilizing creative sentencing, has been overwhelmingly positive. ... My respectful observation is that judges view these types of sentences as more directly responsive to the offence, and more congruent with the sentencing principles for public welfare offences than sentences based on fines only.

NOTES AND QUESTIONS

1. Some environmental legislation sets out specific factors for consideration in sentencing for offences committed under that legislation. For example, s 102(e) of the *Species at Risk Act*, SC 2002, c 29 requires a sentencing judge to consider any evidence of non-compliance with legislation designed to protect wildlife species, and s 27.7(2) of the *Canada National Parks Act*, SC 2000, c 32 provides that a history of non-compliance with federal or provincial legislation that relates to environmental protection is an aggravating factor in determining an appropriate sentence for an offence committed in a national park. In *R v The Lake Louise Ski Area Ltd*, 2018 ABPC 280, the court referenced these factors in sentencing the ski resort to a $2.1 million fine for cutting down endangered whitebark pine trees.

Sections 718 to 718.21 of the *Criminal Code*, RSC 1985, c C-46 also set out principles that should be considered, including the need to ensure that an overall sentence is proportionate to the gravity of the offence and the culpability of the offender.

2. In *R v Syncrude Canada Ltd*, above, the sentence imposed on Syncrude included the maximum statutory fines, as well as three creative orders. The total quantum of the sentence was $3 million, which remains one of the largest sentences ever imposed in Canada for an environmental offence. Explain how the sentencing principles set out in *Terroco* would support the imposition of such a large penalty in *Syncrude*. To what extent do these principles overlap with the considerations relevant to an assessment of a due diligence defence?

3. While the maximum statutory fines for an environmental offence have increased significantly over the years, a monetary penalty alone may be an inadequate sanction for an

environmental offence. Canadian legislators turned to "creative" measures in the late 1980s in an attempt to enhance the effectiveness of environmental enforcement. Section 291 of the *Canadian Environmental Protection Act, 1999*, SC 1999, c 33 is illustrative of the typical creative penal options now found in many Canadian environmental statutes, and this section provides for sentencing orders that require the forfeiture of benefits accruing from the offence; direct the payment of restitution for cleanup or remediation; revoke licences or prohibit activity; direct funding for environmental research, education, or remedial projects; require the performance of community service; require an offender to publish the details of its offence; or require a performance bond to secure compliance with a sentence. For a detailed discussion of these creative sentencing options, see Elaine L Hughes & Larry A Reynolds, "Creative Sentencing and Environmental Protection" (2009) 19 J Envtl L & Prac 105. Consider the extent to which a creative sentencing order, as opposed to just a monetary fine, aligns more closely with the nature of a regulatory offence and the purpose of environmental enforcement.

4. The excerpt from "Negotiating Sentences" by Peter J Craig, above, offers a glimpse into the role of a prosecutor in an environmental sentencing. Craig provides a sense of why creative environmental sentences have grown in popularity over the past couple of decades in Canada. In *Syncrude*, the parties presented the court with a joint submission on sentencing that included a direction to provide $1.3 million to the University of Alberta to fund research on improving the effectiveness of bird monitoring and deterrence in the oil sands. The trial judge in *Syncrude* accepted this submission and ordered Syncrude to fund the research as a part of its sentence.

A creative sentence may require the court to retain supervisory jurisdiction over the duration of a project funded by a creative order. What problems or issues might arise in the administration of a creative sentence, such as the one in *Syncrude*, that would require ongoing judicial supervision? What factors or criteria should guide the Crown on whether to recommend a creative sentence for an environmental offence, and how do you think recipients or beneficiaries of funded projects should be selected? In answering this question, consider the rationale for the joint submission in *Syncrude* directing that funding be provided for research on bird monitoring and deterrence in the oil sands.

5. One of the amendments to federal environmental legislation implemented in 2009 by the *Environmental Enforcement Act*, SC 2009, c 14 was to add a provision that directs fines levied under the legislation into the Environmental Damages Fund. For example, s 294.1 of the *Canadian Environmental Protection Act, 1999* directs all fines imposed under the legislation into the fund. The overall purpose of the fund is described as supporting projects related to environmental restoration and conservation. See "Environmental Damages Fund" (last modified 15 November 2018), online: *Government of Canada* <https://www.canada.ca/en/environment-climate-change/services/environmental-funding/programs/environmental-damages-fund.html>. Environment and Climate Change Canada solicits applications for projects that meet prescribed criteria and also maintains a database of information on funded projects since 2015 on its website: see "Environmental Damages Fund: Project Map" (last modified 15 November 2018), online: *Government of Canada* <https://www.canada.ca/en/environment-climate-change/services/environmental-funding/programs/environmental-damages-fund/map-projects.html>. Consider the similarities and differences between the federal Environmental Damages Fund, which directs all fines into a single fund administered by Environment and Climate Change Canada, and the case-specific creative sentences that, as Peter Craig describes, are usually the product of negotiation and a joint submission by the prosecutor and defence counsel to the sentencing court. What strengths and weaknesses can you identify in comparing these two models for creative sentencing?

6. Another mechanism related to creative environmental sentencing is the use of environmental protection alternative measures. These are essentially negotiated compliance agreements where a person who has committed an environmental offence avoids a conviction by agreeing to binding measures that will be implemented to help prevent subsequent

contraventions or to remediate damages that occurred as a result of the infraction. For an illustration of a statutory provision that allows for the use of these measures, see s 296 of the *Canadian Environmental Protection Act, 1999.*

FURTHER READINGS

Berger, Stanley D, *The Prosecution and Defence of Environmental Offences* (Toronto: Thomson Reuters, 2009) (loose-leaf).

Ingelson, Allan E, ed, *Environment in the Courtroom* (Calgary: University of Calgary Press, 2019).

Libman, Rick, *Libman on Regulatory Offences in Canada* (Salt Spring Island, BC: Earlscourt Legal Press, 2002) (loose-leaf).

Swaigen, John, *Regulatory Offences in Canada: Liability & Defences* (Scarborough, Ont: Carswell, 1992).

CHAPTER TWENTY

HUMAN RIGHTS AND ANIMAL RIGHTS

Sara Bagg and Katie Sykes

I. THE HUMAN RIGHT TO A HEALTHY ENVIRONMENT[1]

A. THE MORAL VIEW OF HUMAN RIGHTS

Whether or not a global right to a healthy environment has been formally legally recognized, arguably such a right already exists on the moral plain.

> [A]ctivists, courts, and even governments oftentimes make rights-based demands long before the respective entitlement has been acknowledged in a formal legal document. Women's movements and courts around the world invoked women's right to be free from domestic violence long before national constitutions recognized it and the United Nations adopted the 1993 Declaration on the Elimination of Violence Against Women [GA Res 48/104, UNHR (1993)]. Socioeconomic rights advocacy and litigation preceded the adoption of the 1966 International Covenant on Economic, Social and Cultural Rights [16 December 1966, 993 UNTS 3 (entered into force 3 January 1976)] by several decades. The fact that the 2007 UN Declaration on the Rights of Indigenous Peoples [GA Res 61/295, UNDESA (2007)] required over twenty years of international negotiations for its adoption did not prevent indigenous peoples' movements from effectively using the language of human rights in the meantime, as a means to demand the protection of their territories, cultures, and livelihoods.
>
> Similarly, at least since the 1972 Stockholm Declaration of the UN Conference on the Human Environment [UN Doc A/Conf.48/14/Rev.1, UNEP (1972)], civil society and state actors have invoked the right to a healthy environment regardless of the fact that it has not been formally incorporated into an international legal instrument.[2]

This idea that environmental rights exist on a moral plain and may be leveraged to influence policy and state action regardless of explicit legal recognition was affirmed by the Supreme Court of the Philippines, which found that

> the right to a balanced and healthful ecology need not even be written in the Constitution for it is assumed, like other civil and political rights guaranteed in the Bill of Rights, to exist from the inception of mankind and it is an issue of transcendental importance with intergenerational implications. Even assuming the absence of a categorical legal provision specifically prodding petitioners to clean up the bay, they and the men and women representing them cannot escape their obligation to future generations of Filipinos to keep the waters of the Manila Bay clean and clear as humanly as possible. Anything less would be a betrayal of the trust reposed in them.[3]

1. The Status of Environmental Rights in Canada

While a moral right to a healthy environment may exist, and there are examples of such a right being leveraged by rights advocates or referred to in legal arguments, the concept has not yet influenced Canada's approach to managing or protecting the environment or our way of making sense of our relationship to the environment. In 1995, the Supreme Court of Canada decided *Ontario v Canadian Pacific Ltd*, discussing for the first time "[the] fundamental and widely shared

---

1   While there are specific references in this chapter to David R Boyd, *The Right to a Healthy Environment: Revitalizing Canada's Constitution* (Vancouver: UBC Press, 2012) [Boyd, *The Right to a Healthy Environment*] and other works by Boyd, pinpoint references do not capture the degree to which this chapter was inspired by him. With permission, his words and ideas were a heavy influence.

2   César Rodríguez-Garavito, "A Human Right to a Healthy Environment? Moral, Legal and Empirical Considerations" in John H Knox & Ramin Pejan, eds, *The Human Right to a Healthy Environment* (Cambridge: Cambridge University Press, 2018) 155 at 157-58 (internal citations omitted).

3   *Metropolitan Manila Development Authority v Concerned Residents of Manila Bay*, GR Nos 171947-48, December 18, 2008, 574 SCRA 661.

value ... [of our] *right to a safe environment*."[4] Citing a working paper of the Law Reform Commission of Canada, "Crimes Against the Environment," the court found:

> To some extent, this right and value appears to be new and emerging, but in part because it is an extension of existing and very traditional rights and values already protected by criminal law, its presence and shape even now are largely discernible. Among the new strands of this fundamental value are, it may be argued, those such as *quality of life*, and *stewardship* of the natural environment. At the same time, traditional values as well have simply expanded and evolved to include the environment now as an area and interest of direct and primary concern. Among these values fundamental to the purposes and protections of criminal law are the *sanctity of life*, the *inviolability and integrity of persons*, and the *protection of human life and health*.[5]

While the court made reference in this decision to weighty concepts such as "traditional rights and values," neither this language nor the court's reasoning has caught on. Since *Canadian Pacific* was decided, the "right to a safe environment" has rarely been referenced in Canadian case law, even more rarely in the context of the environment. In 2001, the Supreme Court decided *114957 Canada Ltée (Spraytech, Société d'arrosage) v Hudson (Town)*, referring to the notion of a "healthy environment" and considering "what type of an environment we wish to live in, and what quality of life we wish to expose our children [to]."[6] Again, since this case, these considerations have occasionally been referred to, but the reasoning has not been embraced as a means of driving more rights-based or environmentally focused interpretations of the law.

Significantly, in *R v Hydro-Québec*,[7] the Supreme Court found that Parliament's regulation of toxic substances under the *Canadian Environmental Protection Act, 1999*[8] was a valid exercise of its criminal law power under s 91(27) of the *Constitution Act, 1867*.[9] While four out of nine members of the Supreme Court did not agree that CEPA fit within a criminal law framework, a five-member majority held that because CEPA's administrative processes culminated in a prohibition enforced by a penalty, the scheme was sufficiently prohibitory to count as criminal law. Here, the court discussed Parliament's clear intent to rely on the criminal law to underline the value of respect for the environment. While the court in *Hydro-Québec* again referred to "the right to a healthy environment," it did not unpack this idea in its decision. Following these cases, references to the right to either a "safe environment" or a "healthy environment" are rarely mentioned in further Supreme Court jurisprudence. At its most basic level, *Hydro-Québec* marked Canada's environmental law as punitive at its core.[10]

QUESTIONS

1. Based on a review of Chapter 2 of this book, why has the moral right to a healthy environment not been more seriously considered in Canadian jurisprudence? Consider explanations that may be historical, theoretical, economic, political, or legal.

---

4 [1995] 2 SCR 1031 at para 55, 1995 CanLII 112 (emphasis in original).

5 (1985) Working Paper 44 at 8 (emphasis in original).

6 2001 SCC 40 at para 1, [2001] 2 SCR 241 [*Spraytech*].

7 [1997] 3 SCR 213, 1997 CanLII 318.

8 SC 1999, c 33 [CEPA].

9 (UK), 30 & 31 Vict, c 3. Once a substance is classified as toxic, CEPA and its regulations set out the rules for the manufacture, importation, processing, transport, sale, use, discard, or release of the substance into the environment.

10 For a more fulsome discussion of the impact of this decision on Canada's environmental law, see Chapter 2.

2. Consider the excerpt from the Law Reform Commission's Working Paper 44, referred to in *Canadian Pacific* and referenced above. In your view, have Canadians' values or their sense of their rights (with regard to environmental protection) changed since this time? Generally speaking, would you say that the Law Commission's recommendations have been heeded or ignored?

3. In *Hydro-Québec*, the Supreme Court considered whether Parliament held the constitutional jurisdiction to create laws regulating toxic substances under CEPA. Can you identify any implications that have followed from the fact that our national environmental laws were grounded in Parliament's criminal law power? The Supreme Court arguably could have explored Parliament's ability to protect the environment as a matter of national concern in reference to Parliament's "peace, order, and good government" jurisdiction under s 91 of the *Constitution Act, 1867*. Would this have been a better fit? What difference might it have made?

B. THE LEGAL RIGHT TO A HEALTHY ENVIRONMENT

1. Procedural Rights[11]

Legal rights can be either substantive or procedural. Substantive rights are in place to protect the most fundamental aspects of our humanity, for example, those rights entrenched in the *Canadian Charter of Rights and Freedoms*.[12] Substantive rights guarantee that our interactions with the state are in line with our basic humanity and the dignity we are owed as humans. Procedural rights, in contrast, apply to the processes according to which such substantive rights can be enforced. Procedural rights guarantee things like our right to information, our right to be consulted by decision-makers, our right to a fair hearing, and our right to be provided with reasons for a decision that may affect us. Procedural rights are "normatively defensible only by reference to a complete elaboration of the substantive rights at stake when [they] are invoked."[13] In other words, procedural rights lack force and meaning when there is no substantive right to protect.

While it may be true that the effect of a procedural right depends upon its having something of value to safeguard, in the context of procedural environmental rights, they are at least a first step for holding industry, decision-makers, and legislators accountable to the public. Beginning in the 1970s in Canada, there were numerous unsuccessful attempts to obtain environmental bills of rights. A series of bills that attempted to address existing deficiencies in the law at the time was introduced in the following jurisdictions: in British Columbia (1971, 1973, and 1994); Alberta (1979); Saskatchewan (1982 and 1992); and Ontario (1979, 1980, 1987, and 1989). However, each time such bills were introduced, they either died on the order paper or were blocked by the majority government of the day. The only rights legislation successfully enacted between 1970 and 1980 was s 19.1 of Quebec's *Environment Quality Act*, which gave every natural person "a right to a healthy environment and to its protection ... to the extent provided for by this Act and the regulations, orders, approvals and authorizations issued under any section of this Act."[14] Because of the restrictive wording, the section has had only a mild

---

11 Parts of this procedural rights section were taken from Elaine Hughes' Chapter 11 in the previous edition of this text: *Environmental Law and Policy*, 3rd ed (Toronto: Emond Montgomery, 2003). I thank her for this contribution.

12 Part I of the *Constitution Act, 1982*, being Schedule B to the *Canada Act 1982* (UK), 1982, c 11 [*Charter*].

13 Larry Alexander, "Are Procedural Rights Derivative Substantive Rights?" (1998) 17:1 Law & Phil 19 at 19.

14 CQLR c Q-2.

effect, but it has granted the public increased access to the judicial system by eliminating the requirement to prove standing before bringing an action under the law.[15]

In 1991, both the Yukon Territory and the Northwest Territories passed legislation conferring environmental rights. Yukon's *Environment Act*[16] states the following in its preamble:

> Recognizing that a healthful environment is indispensable to human life and health;
>
> Recognizing that every individual in the Yukon has the right to a healthful environment;
>
> • • •
>
> Recognizing that the Government of the Yukon is the trustee of the public trust and is therefore responsible for the protection of the collective interest of the people of the Yukon in the quality of the natural environment.

Additionally, s 6 of the Act states:

> 6. The people of the Yukon have the right to a healthful natural environment.

The Northwest Territories *Environmental Rights Act*[17] (which was also adopted by the territory of Nunavut)[18] provides in its preamble:

> Whereas the people of the Northwest Territories have the right to a healthy environment and a right to protect the integrity, biological diversity and productivity of the ecosystems in the Northwest Territories.

Section 6 of the Act is titled "Right to Protect the Environment," and s 6(1) provides:

> 6(1) Every person resident in the Territories has the right to protect the environment and the public trust from the release of contaminants by commencing an action in the Supreme Court against any person releasing any contaminant into the environment.

Section 6(2) eliminates the need to prove standing under the Act:

> (2) No person is prohibited from commencing an action under subsection (1) by reason only that he or she is unable to show
>
> (a) any greater or different right, harm or interest than any other person; or
>
> (b) any pecuniary or proprietary right or interest in the subject matter of the proceeding.[19]

In 1993, Ontario passed the *Environmental Bill of Rights, 1993*,[20] protecting Ontarians' procedural rights to participate in environmental decision-making, including the right to be notified and to comment on environmentally significant government proposals, to ask a ministry to review a law or to investigate harm to the environment, to appeal a ministry decision, to sue for harm to a public resource, to sue for public nuisance causing environmental harm, and to be protected from employer reprisals for asserting these rights. The Ontario Bill of Rights also makes the ministry responsible for developing and publishing a statement of environmental

---

15 See *Nadon c Anjou (Ville)*, 1994 CanLII 5900, [1994] RJQ 1823, 28 MPLR (2d) 139 (CA); *Gestion Serge Lafrenière inc c Calvé*, 1999 CanLII 13814, [1999] RJQ 1313 (CA); *Imperial Oil Ltd v Quebec (Minister of the Environment)*, 2003 SCC 58.

16 RSY 2002, c 76.

17 RSNWT 1988, c 83 (Supp).

18 *Environmental Rights Act*, RSNWT (Nu) 1988, c 83 (Supp).

19 In spite of the broadly worded protections extended in this legislation, there are few cases to reference. Among the examples are *Western Copper Corporation v Yukon Water Board*, 2010 YKSC 61 and *Talbot v Northwest Territories (Commissioner)*, 1997 CanLII 4520, 5 Admin LR (3d) 102 (NWTSC).

20 SO 1993, c 28.

values to guide the ministry in making environmentally significant decisions or in deciding to conduct a review or investigation under the legislation. The legislation includes s 27(3), which specifies certain "rights of participation," including the right to submit written comments, in some cases opportunities for oral representations, public meetings, mediation among persons with different views on issues, "[a]ny other process that would facilitate more informed public participation in decision-making on the proposal," and "[a]ny additional rights of public partici-pation that the minister giving the notice considers appropriate."[21]

While at the federal level there has never been legislation specifically designed to promote or protect procedural environmental rights,[22] the *Canadian Environmental Assessment Act*[23] actively promoted the value of public participation through its preamble, which provided:

> [T]he Government of Canada is committed to facilitating public participation in the environ-mental assessment of projects to be carried out by or with the approval or assistance of the Government of Canada and providing access to the information on which those environ-mental assessments are based.

The stated purpose of CEAA 1992 was "ensur[ing] that there be opportunities for timely and meaningful public participation throughout the environmental assessment process" (s 4(1)). CEAA 1992 entitled any interested person to participate in the environmental decision-making process, and federal authorities were obligated to allow all interested persons to participate in comprehensive studies and panel reviews conducted under the legislation. However, CEAA 1992 was repealed and replaced by the *Canadian Environmental Assessment Act, 2012*.[24] In CEAA 2012, the preamble was omitted, and the purpose section was slightly but significantly altered to ensure that opportunities for meaningful public participation be provided "during" as opposed to "throughout" an environmental assessment. CEAA 2012 restricted participation in federal environmental assessments to "interested parties" only, meaning where "the person is *directly affected* by the carrying out of the designated project or if, in its opinion, the person has relevant information or expertise" (s 2(2) [emphasis added]). In August 2019, CEAA 2012 was repealed and replaced by the *Impact Assessment Act*.[25]

QUESTION

What is your view of the suggestion that procedural rights are derivative and lacking in effect-iveness unless backed by substantive rights? Consider the idea that in an environmental con-text, procedural rights minimally ensure standing and the right to be informed and to participate.

---

21 There is little significant case law to reference. *Lafarge Canada Inc v Ontario (Environmental Review Tribunal)*, 2008 CanLII 30290, 36 CELR (3d) 191 (Ont Div Ct), leave to appeal refused (26 November 2008) Doc M36552, confirming citizen rights to appeal approvals of the Ministry of the Environment to the Environmental Review Tribunal, is a rare example; see Joseph Castrilli & Richard Lindgren, "Leave to Appeal Under Ontario's Environmental Bill of Rights: Lafarge Canada Inc. v Ontario (Environmental Appeal Tribunal)" in W Tilleman & A Lucas, eds, *Litigating Canada's Environment: Leading Canadian Environ-mental Cases by the Lawyers Involved* (Toronto: Thomson Reuters, 2016) 151. For a discussion of the effectiveness of this legislation, see Boyd, *The Right to a Healthy Environment, supra* note 1 at 63-65.

22 Noting that on April 5, 2019, Edmonton MP Linda Duncan introduced private member's Bill C-438, *An Act to enact the Canadian Bill of Rights*, 1st Sess, 42nd Parl, 2019 (second reading 6 June 2019), which included the right to a healthy environment. The Bill did not pass second reading. Previously, Duncan had introduced Bill C-469, *An Act to establish a Canadian Environmental Bill of Rights*, 2nd Sess, 40th Parl, 2009 (first reading 29 October 2009) and Bill C-634, *An Act to establish a Canadian Environmental Bill of Rights*, 2nd Sess, 41st Parl, 2014 (first reading 29 October 2014) with the same desired outcome. Those bills did not pass first reading.

23 SC 1992, c 37 [CEAA 1992]

24 SC 2012, c 19, s 52 [CEAA 2012].

25 SC 2019, c 28, s 1.

2. The Substantive Right to a Healthy Environment

Almost 30 years ago, John Swaigen and Richard Woods made the following observations in "A Substantive Right to Environmental Quality":

> The right to enter the forum is only the beginning. If participants in the forum find that one party—the party seeking to develop land or discharge pollutants—consistently comes to the forum armed with rights which compel a decision in its favour and against the environment, those with counter-balancing rights will become disillusioned and abandon the forum, seek other forums, retreat into apathy, strike out against the system, or demand similar rights.
>
> There is evidence that the failure of institutional arrangements to result in decisions in favour of environmental protection has led to such disillusionment. The adjustments to the legal process that have taken place over the past decade have not led to a balancing of environmental concerns against private property rights, or against the discretion of government agencies to make decisions favouring immediate economic benefits over environmental protection. Perhaps this is the time to renew the search for a substantive right to environmental quality—one which ensures advocates of environmental quality more than a mere right to participate and entrenches environmental quality in the legal system as a value equivalent to private property rights and a fetter on government discretion to permit environmentally-harmful activities; a right that draws lines and sets limits on how much environmental degradation is permissible.[26]

Taking up this call, David Boyd (currently the United Nations' special rapporteur on human rights and the environment) has argued in numerous books and essays in favour of the right to a healthy environment in Canada. According to Boyd, the constitutional right to a healthy environment imposes three distinct duties upon governments: (1) to respect the right by not infringing on it through state action; (2) to protect the right from infringement by third parties (which may require regulations, implementation, and enforcement); and (3) to take actions to fulfill the right (such as by providing environmental services, including clean water, sanitation, and waste management).[27] Courts in some countries have consistently held that laws, regulations, and administrative actions that violate the right will be struck down. Furthermore, where the right to a healthy environment is constitutionalized, both the public and the judiciary are newly empowered to hold governments accountable for their protection.

In Argentina, for example, political leaders promised to clean up the Matanza-Riachuelo River but took few concrete steps until citizens exercised their constitutional right to a healthy environment. This led to strict and detailed court-imposed obligations with independent monitoring bodies, special reporting requirements, and penalties, which proved difficult for political leaders to avoid.[28]

Boyd has argued that a constitutionally protected right to a healthy environment comes with the following advantages:[29]

- *Stronger environmental laws.* In at least 78 of the nations where the right to a healthy environment is explicitly recognized, the recognition resulted in strengthened environmental laws (incorporating both substantive and procedural environmental rights). Where legislation is the main tool to protect environmental rights, then legislators are empowered to act, and properly enforced legislation applies to all instances of a problem. In contrast, where litigation is the alternative, courts can respond only to the issues

---

26 J Swaigen, ed, *Environmental Rights in Canada* (Toronto: Butterworths and CELRF, 1981) 195 at 199–200.

27 Boyd, *The Right to a Healthy Environment, supra* note 1 at 98.

28 *Mendoza v Estado Nacional,* [2008] File M 1569 XL (SC) (Argentina), online: *Global Health and Human Rights Database* <https://www.globalhealthrights.org/health-topics/chronic-diseases/mendoza-beatriz-silva-et-al-v-the-national-state-et-al/>.

29 Boyd, *The Right to a Healthy Environment, supra* note 1 at 18–23.

brought before them, and their decisions are case by case—addressed only to the litigating parties.

- *Advanced screening of new laws and regulations.* Where a constitutionally protected environmental right is in place, all prospective laws and regulations must be drafted in a manner consistent with the government's duty to respect, protect, and fulfill the right.

- *Safety net.* In addition to providing an impetus for strengthening the law, the right to a healthy environment closes gaps in the law. In the Nepalese case *Dhungel v Godavari Marble Industries*,[30] Godawari Marble was found to have seriously degraded the surrounding forest during its marble mining processes. While the company had not technically violated any act or rule, the court found that the constitutional right to life included the right to a healthy environment. The court ordered that previously proposed amendments to the *Minerals Act, 2043* be fully enforced or that the ministry enact new legislation to better protect the environment (including air, water, and, in particular, the Godawari forest).

- *Preventing rollbacks.* When the right to a healthy environment is constitutionally protected, then the laws and policies that are in place to enforce its protection cannot be weakened. Courts have articulated the principle that, based on the right to a healthy environment, current environmental laws and policies represent a baseline that can be improved but not weakened.[31]

- *Improved implementation and enforcement.* Recognition of the constitutional right to a healthy environment can facilitate increased implementation and enforcement of environmental laws. Enforcement efforts may be taken up by the public, drawing attention to violations and providing an impetus for the allocation of additional resources to environmental monitoring and protection. For example, the Ministerio Publico in Brazil hears public reports of alleged violations of constitutional rights and environmental law, thereby resulting in a dramatic increase in environmental enforcement.[32] Between 1984 and 2004 in the state of São Paulo, the Ministerio Publico filed over 4,000 public civil actions addressing issues ranging from deforestation to air pollution.[33]

- *Increased public involvement.* The right to a healthy environment has been consistently interpreted by legislators, executives, and the judiciary to include procedural environmental rights. In many nations that recognize the right to a healthy environment, administrative processes and courthouses are now open to citizens who had previously lacked economic or personal interest but who are now seeking to protect society's collective interest in a healthy environment.

In addition to these benefits, Boyd further suggests that the arguable drawbacks of an entrenched right to a healthy environment, such as the law being too vague to be useful, being redundant because of already existing human rights and environmental laws, being a threat to democracy, or being likely to cause a flood of litigation, have not transpired in countries where the right has been entrenched.[34]

30 WP 35/1992 (1995.10.31) (SC) (Nepal).

31 See, for example, Belgian Constitutional Court, no 135/2006; Constitutional Court, no 137/2006; Constitutional Court, no 145/2006; and L Lavrysen, "Presentation of Aarhus-Related Cases of the Belgian Constitutional Court" (2007) 2 Environ L Network Intl L Rev 5 at 8.

32 LK McAllister, "Public Prosecutors and Environmental Protection in Brazil" in A Romero & S West, eds, *Environmental Issues in Latin America and the Caribbean* (New York: Springer, 2005) 207 at 207.

33 LK McAllister, *Making Law Matter: Environmental Protection and Legal Institutions in Brazil* (Stanford, Cal: Stanford University Press, 2008) at 99.

34 David R Boyd, "Catalyst for Change, Evaluating Forty Years of Experience: Implementing the Right to a Healthy Environment" in John H Knox & Ramin Pejan, eds, *The Human Right to a Healthy Environment* (Cambridge: Cambridge University Press, 2018) 17 at 17 [Boyd, "Catalyst for Change"].

QUESTIONS

1. Go to the "Notes and Questions" section at the end of Chapter 2. Review question 3, referring to the sweeping changes made, without public consultation, to Canada's environmental law under Bill C-38, *Jobs, Growth and Long-Term Prosperity Act*[35] (including to CEAA 1992). In light of this example, what are your thoughts about Boyd's assertion that Canadian environmental laws are too easily changed or "rolled back"? What is your view of the fact that the Canadian government can make these changes to environmental legislation without public consultation or approval?

2. The case of *Talbot v Northwest Territories (Commissioner)*, cited earlier, concerned the presence of arsenic in the air and water in Yellowknife produced by the Royal Oak (Giant) Yellowknife Mine. Talbot brought a claim against the Government of the Northwest Territories under s 6(1) of the Northwest Territories *Environmental Rights Act*, which permits residents to commence an action in the Supreme Court against any person releasing contaminants into the environment. Since Talbot sued the government as opposed to the polluter, the court rejected the claim, referring to it as a "political issue." What are your thoughts on the court framing the plaintiff's claim as "political" rather than legal? Can this be reconciled with the broad language provided in the preamble to the Act, which addresses the right to a healthy environment? Could the court have been more open to the claim based on the language of the legislation or in light of other possible interpretive aids? Compare this with *Dhungel v Godavari Marble Industries*, discussed above.

C. THE PREVALENCE OF ENVIRONMENTAL RIGHTS

Despite the fact that the conversation about a constitutional right to a healthy environment was started before the 1982 enactment of the Charter, Canada stands out for its continued failure to protect the right to a healthy environment.[36] Internationally, of 193 UN member states, only 38 fail to recognize the right to a healthy environment in either (1) a regional treaty, (2) national legislation, or (3) a constitution.[37] Canada is among those that are failing.

Numerous countries have signed non-binding soft-law declarations that include the right to a healthy environment. An example of such a declaration is the *Malé Declaration on the Human Dimension of Global Climate Change*, "[r]eaffirming the *United Nations Charter* and the *Universal Declaration of Human Rights*" and

> noting that the fundamental right to an environment capable of supporting human society and the full enjoyment of human rights is recognized, in varying formulations, in the constitutions of over one hundred states and directly or indirectly in several international instruments.[38]

---

35 1st Sess, 41st Parl, 2012 (assented to 29 June 2012), SC 2012, c 19.

36 An exception is the addition of s 46.1 in 2006 to Quebec's *Charter of Human Rights and Freedoms*, CQLR c C-12, which states, "Every person has a right to live in a healthful environment in which biodiversity is preserved, to the extent and according to the standards provided by law." In addition, as a result of David Suzuki's grassroots campaign, The Blue Dot Movement, 173 communities in Canada have passed a *Declaration to the Right to a Healthy Environment*. See online: *Blue Dot* <http://www.bluedot.ca>.

37 Boyd, "Catalyst for Change," *supra* note 34 at 18. Much of the information in this section was taken from this referenced Boyd article.

38 *Malé Declaration on the Human Dimension of Global Climate Change* (2007) at 1, online (pdf): *Center for International Environmental Law* <http://www.ciel.org/Publications/Male_Declaration_Nov07.pdf>. See also the 18-member Association of Southeast Asian Nations' *ASEAN Human Rights Declaration* (2012), online: <https://asean.org/asean-human-rights-declaration>.

Over 100 countries have recognized the right to a healthy environment in national legislation, for example, Cuba, Gambia, and Lithuania.[39]

Further, the substantive right to a healthy environment is constitutionally protected in 100 countries. No other social or economic right has spread as quickly through the world's constitutions.[40] In the United States, more than 30 of 50 states have added constitutional provisions referring to environmental rights or to state duties to protect the environment.[41]

A final means by which the right to a healthy environment may come to be nationally recognized is by the judiciary.[42] Internationally, courts have found the right to a healthy environment to be an implicit but essential element of the constitutionally protected right to life.[43] In *Farooque v Bangladesh*, the right to a healthy environment was implicitly recognized in Bangladesh, where the court found various authorities had failed to sufficiently mitigate air and noise pollution caused by motor vehicles in the capital city of Dhaka. The court found that the constitutional protection of the right to life encompasses "the protection and preservation of environment, ecological balance free from pollution of air and water, and sanitation without which life can hardly be enjoyed. Any act or omission contrary thereto will be violative of the said right to life."[44]

QUESTIONS

1. According to Boyd, the majority of Canadians falsely believe they have a right to a healthy environment.[45] Did you believe this? What is your reaction to the fact that Canada stands out internationally for its failure to protect the right to a healthy environment?

2. Article 28H(1) of the Indonesian Constitution sets out the right to a healthy environment in Indonesia and provides: "Every person shall have the right to live in physical and spiritual prosperity, to have a home and to enjoy a good and healthy environment, and shall have the right to obtain medical care."[46] The language of the right is aspirational in the sense that it is difficult to imagine a government securing physical and spiritual prosperity for every person within its borders. Compare this language to that used in the Canadian Charter. Compare the protection of human rights in Canada (considering in particular the limiting language of ss 1, 7, and 33 of the Charter). What is the effect of the difference?

---

39 Note that the vast majority of the countries that protect the right to a healthy environment in national legislation also have constitutional protection. Those above are among rare exceptions.

40 Davis S Law & Mila Versteeg, "The Evolution and Ideology of Global Constitutionalism" (2011) 99:5 Cal L Rev 1163.

41 Dana Drugmand, "Hawaii Joins Trend: Recognizes Constitutional Right to Safe Climate and Environment," *Climate Liability News* (5 January 2018), online: <https://www.climateliabilitynews.org/2018/01/05/hawaii-climate-environment-constitutional-right/>.

42 Dinah Shelton, "Complexities and Uncertainties in Matters of Human Rights and the Environment: Identifying the Judicial Role" in John H Knox & Ramin Pejan, eds, *The Human Right to a Healthy Environment* (Cambridge: Cambridge University Press, 2018) 97 at 98.

43 For example, Bangladesh, Estonia, Guatemala, India, Israel, Italy, Malaysia, Nigeria, Pakistan, Sri Lanka, Tanzania, and Uruguay. For details, see David R Boyd, "The Implicit Constitutional Right to a Healthy Environment" (2011) 20:2 RECIEL 171.

44 *Farooque v Bangladesh* (1997), 49 DLR 1 (Bangladesh).

45 Boyd, *The Right to a Healthy Environment, supra* note 1 at 3.

46 *Constitution of the Republic of Indonesia* (last amended 2002), online: *UNHRC* <https://www.refworld.org/docid/46af43f12.html>.

3. The Inter-American Commission on Human Rights

has emphasized that each state has a duty to enforce its internal law and international commitments in the field of environmental protection; although the right to development implies that the state is free to exploit its natural resources and grant concessions, the authorities must apply and enforce the legal provisions that protect the rights to life, health, and to live in a healthy environment.[47]

Could Canada's hesitation to entrench a constitutional right to a healthy environment relate to our commitment to the rule of law and the inevitable challenges the government would face in protecting this right? Is this a valid justification for not entrenching the right?

4. Can Canada's hesitation to entrench the right to a healthy environment be reconciled with Boyd's warning that "Canada lags behind other wealthy industrialized nations in terms of the big picture related to reducing or eliminating environmental impacts on health,"[48] where in saying this Boyd is comprehensively referring to our failures in the following areas: outdoor air quality, indoor air quality, drinking water quality, pesticide regulations, toxic substances, and climate change?

5. In consideration of the position of the Inter-American Commission on Human Rights, is it reasonable that a country may simply avoid the obligation to respect international human rights by failing to adopt them? See Chapter 2 for a deeper understanding of this moral obligation and its relationship to law.

D. SECURING THE RIGHT TO A HEALTHY ENVIRONMENT IN CANADA

In Canada, the right to a healthy environment could, theoretically, come to be recognized through a constitutional amendment, federal legislation, or a judicial decision in which the right to a healthy environment is read in to a previously existing Charter right. On October 25, 2019, after this chapter was finalized, fifteen young Canadians filed a statement of claim in Canada's Federal Court asking the Canadian government to develop a climate recovery plan using the best available science. This claim relies upon Charter ss 7 and 15(1). The likelihood of the claim's success is indirectly considered below.

1. Constitutional Amendment

Though not impossible, given the process established under part V of the *Constitution Act, 1982*,[49] immense procedural challenges stand in the way of a constitutional amendment entrenching environmental rights. Amending Canada's Constitution requires a proclamation, issued by the governor general and authorized by resolutions from the House of Commons, the Senate, and the legislative assemblies of two-thirds (or seven) of the provinces, representing at least 50 percent of all Canadians—with a three-year deadline for securing resolutions. Furthermore, the *Constitutional Amendments Act* requires that resolutions introduced federally be supported by Quebec, Ontario, British Columbia, two or more Atlantic provinces (with at least 50 percent of the region's population), and two or more Prairie provinces (with at least 50 percent of the region's population).[50] Based on a lack of enthusiasm, both federally and provincially (as previously outlined), the possibility of a constitutional amendment seems extremely low.

47 Shelton, *supra* note 42 at 97, note 1.

48 David R Boyd, *Cleaner, Greener, Healthier* (Vancouver: UBC Press, 2015). In particular, see "A Comparative Analysis of Environmental Health Laws and Policies" ch 7 at 129.

49 Being Schedule B to the *Canada Act 1982* (UK), 1982, c 11.

50 *An Act respecting constitutional amendments*, SC 1996, c 1.

2. Federal Legislation

In 2017, the House of Commons Standing Committee on Environment and Sustainable Development conducted a statutory five-year review of CEPA and recommended that the federal government reference the right to a healthy environment in CEPA. The committee recommended

- that "the preamble of CEPA be amended to recognize a right to a healthy environment";
- that "the government consider amending CEPA to include the right to a healthy environment in the administrative duties of the Government of Canada (section 2), in the development of objectives, guidelines, and codes of practice (sections 54 and 55), in the assessment of the risks of toxic substances (section 76.1), and the development of risk management tools (section 91)"; and
- "that a series of substantive and procedural improvements be incorporated into the various sections of CEPA to give greater force and effect to environmental rights, including as set out in recommendations."[51]

While the Government of Canada responded to the recommendation by commending the members of the committee "for their insight and their commitment to enhance the protection of the environment and human health for present and future generations of Canadians,"[52] it was not prepared to act on these recommendations.[53] This was despite the opportunity it had to make such amendments when making other changes to CEPA in the *Miscellaneous Statute Law Amendment Act, 2017* (Bill C-60).[54] Based on this recent rejection of the recommendation to include the right to a healthy environment in federal legislation, if the substantive right to a healthy environment is to be recognized in Canada anytime soon, it will most likely occur as a result of litigation (with the courts finding that some form of environmental harm has breached a protected right under the Charter).

3. Judicial Decision

a. *The Right to Life, Liberty, and Security of the Person*

Outside Canada, a number of courts have interpreted the right to life as including the right not to suffer from environmental harms. In *Kumar v State of Bihar*, the Supreme Court of India found that the

[r]ight to live is a fundamental right under Art 21 of the Constitution and it includes the right of enjoyment of pollution free water and air for full enjoyment of life. If anything endangers or impairs that quality of life in derogation of laws, a citizen has the right to have recourse to Art 32 of the Constitution, for removing the pollution of water or air, which may be detrimental to the quality of life.[55]

---

51 House of Commons, Standing Committee on Environment and Sustainable Development, *Report 8—Healthy Environment, Healthy Canadians, Healthy Economy: Strengthening the Canadian Environmental Protection Act, 1999—Report of the Standing Committee on Environment and Sustainable Development* (June 2017) (Chair: Deborah Schulte) at 7–8, online (pdf): <https://www.ourcommons.ca/Content/Committee/421/ENVI/Reports/RP9037962/envirp08/envirp08-e.pdf>.

52 Environment and Climate Change Canada, *Follow-Up Report to the House of Commons Standing Committee on Environment and Sustainable Development on the Canadian Environmental Protection Act, 1999* (29 June 2018) at 3, online (pdf): <https://www.canada.ca/content/dam/eccc/documents/pdf/cepa/FollowUpCepaReport-eng.pdf>.

53 Mia Rabson, "Feds Still Mulling over Making a Healthy Environment a Right in Canada," *CBC News* (29 June 2018), online: <https://www.cbc.ca/news/politics/mckenna-environment-right-1.4727851>.

54 SC 2017, c 26.

55 *Kumar v State of Bihar*, AIR 1991 SC 420 (India). A businessman filed a public interest litigation claim against iron and steel companies for dumping sludge from factory washeries into the Bokaro River. The

In *Leghari v Federation of Pakistan*,[56] a farmer suffering from a prolonged drought sued the national government for failing to carry out the *National Climate Policy, 2012* and the *Framework for Implementation of Climate Change Policy (2014-2030)*. In its decision, the Lahore High Court Green Bench considered whether the government's inaction in addressing vulnerabilities associated with climate change violated the fundamental constitutional rights to life and dignity. The court found the right to life includes the right to an environment that is healthy and clean, which is to be read with the constitutional principles of democracy, equality, social, economic, and political justice, as well as the international environmental principles of sustainable development, the precautionary principle, environmental impact assessment, inter- and intra-generational equity, and the public trust doctrine.[57]

The right to life and security are entrenched in Canada under s 7 of Canada's Charter, which provides: "Everyone has the right to life, liberty and security of the person and the right not to be deprived thereof except in accordance with the principles of fundamental justice." A successful claimant under s 7 must first meet the test for standing to bring the case, meaning that the claimant has either directly affected interests or public interest standing (meaning the applicant has a genuine interest in the case, which presents a serious legal issue, and there is no other way to bring the issue before the court).

The case of *Re BC Motor Vehicle Act*[58] established that under s 7, the "principles of fundamental justice" (clearly identifiable legal principles, which are fundamental to our sense of how the legal system ought fairly to operate) include not only procedural justice but also substantive justice, and, therefore, s 7 protects both substantive and procedural rights. Claims under s 7 must first prove that some government action (which in an environmental context could include the creation of a law, an investment, a project on Crown land, or the issuance of a permit or licence authorizing some activity) has resulted in a deprivation of the right to life, liberty, or security of the person, and, furthermore, that this deprivation is not in accordance with the principles of fundamental justice.[59] Section 7 is often referenced in a criminal justice context but has also been used to challenge Canada's abortion laws, laws preventing medically assisted suicide, and the criminalization of prostitution.[60]

Arguably in Canada, as in other countries, the right to life and/or security includes the right to a healthy environment. According to the Supreme Court, "the right to life is engaged where the law or state action imposes death or an increased risk of death on a person, either directly or indirectly."[61] The court has found that security of the person includes the right to control one's own bodily integrity; where state action has a likely effect of seriously impairing a person's physical or mental health, this violates that right.[62] Notably, in *Canadian Pacific*, the

---

petitioner argued that the State Pollution Control Board had failed to take appropriate steps to prevent the pollution. While the court dismissed the petition, it made the comments above *in obiter*.

56 (2016) WP No 25501/2015 (Lahore H Ct).

57 Brian J Preston, "The Evolving Role of Environmental Rights in Climate Change Litigation" (2018) 2:2 Chinese J Envtl Law 131 at 149.

58 [1985] 2 SCR 486, 1985 CanLII 81. A further hurdle not discussed in detail here is that to succeed with any Charter claim, a claimant must first establish that (1) a government action breached his or her protected right, and (2) the breach is not saved by s 1 of the Charter—which allows violations that are "reasonable limits prescribed by law as can be demonstrably justified in a free and democratic society."

59 In terms of additional hurdles, *Gosselin v Quebec (Attorney General)*, 2002 SCC 84, [2002] 4 SCR 429 found that s 7 protects rights *infringements* but cannot compel rights *protections* (though this hurdle may be overcome in ideal circumstances).

60 *R v Morgentaler*, [1993] 3 SCR 463, 1993 CanLII 74; *Carter v Canada (Attorney General)*, 2015 SCC 5, [2015] 1 SCR 331; *Canada (Attorney General) v Bedford*, 2013 SCC 72, [2013] 3 SCR 1101.

61 *Carter, supra* note 60 at para 62.

62 *R v Morney*, [1999] 1 SCR 652 at para 55, 1999 CanLII 678.

Supreme Court referred to the concepts of "quality of life" and "sanctity of life" in the context of preserving the natural environment,[63] and in *Spraytech*, the court referred to "quality of life" in the context of safeguarding the health of future generations.[64] In *Operation Dismantle v The Queen*[65] (in which anti-nuclear groups argued that US cruise missile testing in Canada infringed s 7), the relationship between government action and potential harm was found too remote, since the case sought to prevent a future and theoretical disaster. However, in *Chaoulli v Quebec (Attorney General)*,[66] the court found that future risk of infringement could constitute the basis for a breach, depending on the seriousness of the impact of the potential breach. Without question, the current effects of Canada's weak legislation, pollution, and climate change are becoming less remote and more concerning. Consequently, the relationship between these effects and individuals' life and security is becoming less remote.

While courts have considered the application of s 7 in environmental cases, there has not yet been a successful claim. *Domke v Alberta (Energy Resources Conservation Board)* is an appeal of a decision by Alberta's Energy Resources Conservation Board granting two sour gas well licences (such wells having the potential to release toxic hydrogen sulfide [H_2S] and sulfur dioxide [SO_2]) in Drayton Valley, Alberta. The Court of Appeal in this case denied leave to appeal because the court found that a s 7 Charter claim was not made out.[67] In assessing whether there had been a s 7 infringement of life, liberty, or security of the person, the board had found that since the company had offered to relocate residents with health concerns during the drilling of the wells, neither the life nor security of these individuals had been infringed. Furthermore, because the relocation of such individuals was to have been elective, there was no loss of liberty. The Alberta Court of Appeal found this circular reasoning, which requires focusing exclusively on either the forest or the trees but not both together, unassailable.

In *Locke v Calgary (City)*, Locke challenged the City of Calgary by-law providing for fluoridation of the City's water supply, arguing that the by-law breached his security of the person pursuant to s 7.[68] Locke's argument was based on the reasoning articulated in *Rodriguez v British Columbia (Attorney General)* (and other cases) that the "right to choose how one's body will be dealt with, even in the context of beneficial medical treatment, has long been recognized."[69] The court accepted that water fluoridation at approximately one part per million is safe and endorsed by the World Health Organization. Locke's claim was, therefore, rejected because it failed to establish that security of the person was implicated by communal water fluoridation.

b. The Equal Right to a Healthy Environment

One may make a further argument that the right to a healthy environment is a matter of environmental justice, demanding

---

63 *Canadian Pacific, supra* note 4 at para 55.

64 *Spraytech, supra* note 6 at para 1.

65 [1985] 1 SCR 441, 1985 CanLII 74; in reference to environmental effects, review Chapter 2 of this text or Boyd's *Cleaner, Greener, Healthier, supra* note 48.

66 2005 SCC 35, [2005] 1 SCR 791.

67 *Domke v Alberta (Energy Resources Conservation Board)*, 2008 ABCA 232.

68 1993 CanLIII 7225 (Alta QB).

69 [1993] 3 SCR 519 at 588, 1993 CanLII 75.

the fair treatment and meaningful involvement of all people regardless of race, color, national origin, or income, with respect to the development, implementation, and enforcement of environmental laws, regulations, and policies. This goal will be achieved when everyone enjoys:

- the same degree of protection from environmental and health hazards, and
- equal access to the decision-making process to have a healthy environment in which to live, learn, and work.[70]

Pursuant to s 15(1) of the Charter,

every individual is equal before and under the law and has the right to the equal protection and equal benefit of the law without discrimination and, in particular, without discrimination based on race, national or ethnic origin, colour, religion, sex, age or mental or physical disability.

Section 15(1) protects individuals' right to *substantive* equality—which entails "the promotion of a society in which all are secure in the knowledge that they are recognized at law as human beings equally deserving of concern, respect and consideration."[71]

Section 15(1) aims to correct and inhibit discrimination against certain groups "suffering social, political and legal disadvantage in our society."[72] To make a *prima facie* discrimination claim, there must be evidence of a legal distinction made on an enumerated or analogous ground, with evidence that the distinction's impact on the claimant perpetuated an arbitrary disadvantage.[73]

Nathalie Chalifour has observed that there are increasing levels of environmental injustice in Canada, and that while either s 7 or s 15(1) of the Charter may be leveraged in arguments that attempt to safeguard against such injustices, there are specific advantages to each. First, the scope of protections offered by s 7 apply to all Canadians, and, second, the courts have recently interpreted s 7 extremely progressively. In the case of s 15(1), while the section focuses on "discriminatory treatment" without the need to prove a causal connection between a claimant's harm and the government's actions, the claimant must fall under one of the enumerated or analogous grounds in the section. The effect is that people experiencing environmental injustice for a reason not enumerated, for example, based on income level, would not be captured by s 15(1) protections.[74] According to Chalifour, the lack of access to safe drinking water on many Indigenous reserves, the disproportionate pollution levels on the Amjiwnaang First Nation, and Inuit food security issues are among the examples of environmental justice issues that fall under s 15(1).[75]

70 "Environmental Justice" (last modified 2 April 2018), online: *United States Environmental Protection Agency* <http://www.epa.gov/environmentaljustice>.

71 *Andrews v Law Society of British Columbia*, [1989] 1 SCR 143 at 171, 1989 CanLII 2.

72 *Eldridge v British Columbia (Attorney General)*, [1997] 3 SCR 624 at para 54, 1997 CanLII 327.

73 *Quebec (Attorney General) v A*, 2013 SCC 5 at para 325.

74 Nathalie Chalifour, "Environmental Justice and the Charter: Do Environmental Injustices Infringe Sections 7 and 15 of the Charter?" (2015) 28:1 J Envtl L & Prac 89, Ottawa Faculty of Law Working Paper No 2017-12, online: *SSRN* <https://ssrn.com/abstract=2922653> [Chalifour cited to Working Paper No 2017-12]; see also Madiha Vallani, "Sections 7 and 15 of the Canadian Charter of Rights and Freedoms in the Context of the Clean Water Crisis on Reserves: Opportunities and Challenges for First Nations Women" (2018) Master of Laws Research Papers Repository, 2, online: *Western Libraries* <https://ir.lib.uwo.ca/llmp/2/>.

75 Chalifour, *supra* note 74 at 18.

QUESTIONS FOR DISCUSSION

The members of the Aamjiwnaang First Nation (including Ada Lockridge and Ron Plain) live next to industrial facilities within Chemical Valley, which is in Sarnia, Ontario and which accounts for roughly 40 percent of Canada's petrochemical industry. In 2011, Lockridge and Plain sought a judicial review of a decision made under Ontario's *Environmental Protection Act*[76] respecting the sulphur output of Suncor Energy Products in Sarnia. Lockridge and Plain argued that Ontario's failure to conduct a cumulative effects assessment infringed on the applicants' Charter rights under both ss 7 and 15, as well as their rights to procedural fairness. The recorded environmental effects of the petrochemical industry on the Aamjiwnaang First Nation include (1) physical health impacts—cancers, asthma, birth defects, miscarriages, still-births, a skewed female-to-male birth ratio, skin rashes, chronic headaches, and high blood pressure; and (2) mental health impacts—including fear and anger from the proximity of indus-trial facilities and the related smells and sirens from pollution accidents and practice drills, stress from living in a constant state of emergency preparedness and awaiting the next acci-dent that releases pollutants at a dangerous level, and the inability to undertake cultural activ-ities (hunting) because of the fear of pollution (contaminated animals).[77] Suncor argued that the application should be dismissed on the basis that the issues raised were a collateral attack on its operations and the past approvals that Suncor had previously obtained in full compliance with the regulatory requirements. The Ontario Divisional Court denied the motion to strike the application.[78] While Lockridge and Plain's claim was withdrawn after the Ontario government committed to conduct a review of Sarnia's Chemical Valley and associated regulations,[79] the most current information suggests that in fact little has been done to address the issue.[80]

1.a. Based on the information about the applicability of ss 7 and 15 of the Charter provided in the chapter, make the strongest argument you can on behalf of Lockridge and Plain.

b. What do you take from the fact that the Ontario Divisional Court refused to dismiss Lockridge and Plain's claim?

c. What do you take from the fact that little has changed since the time it was dismissed?

2.a. In *Clean Air Foundation Ltd v Government of the HKSAR*,[81] the applicants brought a judicial review application in relation to the authorities' failure to ensure that adequate laws or effective policies were in place to take action against air pollution. In their arguments, the applicants relied on Hong Kong's *Bill of Rights*[82] and also on art 12 of the *International Coven-ant on Economic, Social and Cultural Rights*,[83] which recognizes the "the right of everyone to

---

76 RSO 1990, c E.19.

77 Environmental Law Centre, University of Victoria, "Environmental Rights: Human Rights and Pollution in Sarnia's Chemical Valley" (Backgrounder for the ELC Associates teleconference on Environmental Rights: Human Rights and Pollution in Sarnia's Chemical Valley) (13 June 2011) at 3, online (pdf): <http://www.elc.uvic.ca/associates/documents/ChemicalValleyAssociatesBackgrounder_June13.11.pdf>.

78 *Lockridge v Director, Ministry of the Environment*, 2012 ONSC 2316 (Div Ct).

79 "Defending the Rights of Chemical Valley Residents—Charter Challenge" (last visited 20 May 2019), online: *Ecojustice* <https://www.ecojustice.ca/case/defending-the-rights-of-chemical-valley-residents-charter-challenge/>.

80 Carolyn Jarvis, "'It's a Disgrace': One Year After Ontario Promised Change, Toxic Emissions Are Still Spilling into Sarnia," *Canada's National Observer* (14 November 2018), online: <https://www.nationalobserver.com/2018/11/14/news/its-disgrace-one-year-after-ontario-promised-change-toxic-emissions-are-still>.

81 [2007] HKCFI 757 (Hong Kong).

82 CAP 383 *Hong Kong Bill of Rights Ordinance* (online): *Hong Kong Legal Information Institute* <http://www.hklii.hk/eng/hk/legis/ord/383/>.

83 16 December 1966, 993 UNTS 3 (entered into force 3 January 1976), online: *UNHR* <https://www.ohchr.org/en/professionalinterest/pages/cescr.aspx>.

the enjoyment of the highest attainable standard of physical and mental health." In its decision, the Hong Kong High Court found that the issue was not justiciable because it found that the central issues in the case were not matters of law but related to why government had chosen not to pursue certain policies.[84] What is your view of the court's refusal to consider the issue of air pollution in this case?

3. Look back at the earlier discussion concerning the Canadian government's failure to accept the recommendation to include references to the right to health in CEPA. Is this a simple policy decision?

II. ANIMAL RIGHTS[85]

A. THE PROPERTY PARADIGM: ANIMALS AS OBJECTS, NOT SUBJECTS, OF RIGHTS

Animals are defined as property in Canadian law. This basic principle was reaffirmed by the Newfoundland Court of Appeal in 2018, in a case involving a dispute over the ownership of Miya, a Bernese mountain dog–poodle cross, between a couple who had been romantically involved but had split up. The court observed that "[i]n the eyes of the law a dog is an item of personal property,"[86] and the only question to be resolved was who owned Miya. Wild animals, like domestic animals, are also property. Provincial wildlife statutes typically deem wild animals to be the property of the provincial government until they are killed by a hunter in accordance with applicable legal requirements, at which point ownership passes to the hunter.[87]

Non-human animals are "objects" rather than "subjects" of rights.[88] Humans have legal rights with respect to the animals they own, but animals themselves are not rights-bearers. Relatedly (although it is not exactly the same point), animals have no legal standing. They cannot sue on their own behalf, nor can lawyers or legal organizations seeking to assert their interests.

But that summary, while accurate as far as it goes, oversimplifies the legal status of animals. There are various laws that protect animals from certain kinds of treatment and from being harmed in certain ways. In this sense, they do have a legal status that differs from that of other kinds of property.

It is a criminal offence to wilfully cause unnecessary pain, suffering, or injury to an animal or a bird.[89] Under provincial and territorial animal protection laws, it is illegal for a person who

---

84 Shelton, *supra* note 42 at 101-2.

85 This section of the chapter is written by Katie Sykes.

86 *Baker v Harmina*, 2018 NLCA 15 at para 12. Hoegg JA (at para 48), in dissent in the same case, agreed that dogs are property, but would have taken a more flexible approach, noting that "[o]wnership of a dog is more complicated to decide than, say, a car, or a piece of furniture" because people form strong relationships with their dogs, and because dogs have "personality, affection, loyalty, intelligence, the ability to communicate and follow orders, and so on."

87 For example, under British Columbia's *Wildlife Act*, RSBC 1996, c 488, "[o]wnership in all wildlife in British Columbia is vested in the government" (s 2(1)), and "[a] person who lawfully kills wildlife and complies with all applicable provisions of this Act and the regulations acquires the right of property in that wildlife" (s 2(3)).

88 Richard A Epstein, "Animals as Objects, or Subjects, of Rights" in Cass R Sunstein & Martha C Nussbaum, eds, *Animal Rights: Current Debates and New Directions* (Oxford: Oxford University Press, 2004) 143 at 144: "[u]nder traditional conceptions of law, animals were typically regarded as objects of rights vested in their owners but not as subjects of rights against human beings."

89 *Criminal Code*, RSC 1985, c C-46, s 445.1(1)(a).

is responsible for an animal to abuse or neglect it; to deprive it of adequate food, water, or shelter; or to cause it or allow it to continue to be injured, in pain, sick, or suffering.[90]

Animals are, therefore, not exactly like other "items of personal property," such as cars or furniture. There are no laws prohibiting us from neglecting or abusing our cars or our chairs. In a limited sense, animals can be said to have legal rights if a right can be defined as a legal rule requiring someone to refrain from doing something to the rights-bearer. Although there are pervasive shortcomings in the effectiveness and adequate enforcement of animal protection laws,[91] at least formally the protections do exist, and (depending on one's view of what "rights" are) they could be described as animal rights.

B. PROCEDURAL RIGHTS AND LEGAL STANDING FOR ANIMALS

1. Expanding Rights Versus Enforcing Existing Rights

Cass Sunstein draws an analogy between efforts to expand legal rights for animals and other struggles to vindicate rights and increase social justice (such as the civil rights movement in the US).[92] Sunstein observes that

> [f]or those interested in expanding rights of any kind, there are two historically honored strategies. The first is to enlarge the category of legal rights beyond what the legal system now recognizes ... [and a] second, more modest legal strategy is simply to try to ensure that the rights that are now on the books actually exist in the world.[93]

Sunstein argues that (as noted above) animals do have a fairly wide array of rights "on the books." For example, endangered and threatened species have legal protections, and animals are entitled not to be subjected to cruelty. But "[a] major problem is that the relevant laws are rarely enforced. They exist, but for too many animals, they are worth little more than the paper they are written on."[94] To remedy this problem, Sunstein argues that the existing laws to protect animals from cruelty and abuse "should be amended or interpreted to give a private right of action against those who violate them."[95]

a. Private Prosecution

In a limited sense, there is a mechanism in Canadian law for private individuals and organizations to enforce animal cruelty law: private prosecution. The *Criminal Code* preserves the ancient right to initiate a private prosecution against someone who has violated criminal law.[96] The ability to start a private prosecution applies to most summary offences in the *Criminal Code*, including animal cruelty offences, as well as to offences under other federal legislation,

---

90 See e.g. *Prevention of Cruelty to Animals Act*, RSBC 1996, c 372, s 24 (prohibiting causing an animal to be in distress or permitting it to remain in distress) and s 1(2) (definition of "distress"). See also the discussion of similar provisions under Alberta's *Animal Protection Act*, below.

91 For further discussion of the deficiencies of Canadian animal protection laws and some proposals for reform, see, generally, Peter Sankoff, Vaughan Black & Katie Sykes, eds, *Canadian Perspectives on Animals and the Law* (Toronto: Irwin, 2015).

92 Cass R Sunstein, "Can Animals Sue?" in Cass R Sunstein & Martha C Nussbaum, eds, *Animal Rights: Current Debates and New Directions* (Oxford: Oxford University Press, 2004) 251 at 251.

93 *Ibid* at 251-52.

94 *Ibid* at 252.

95 *Ibid*.

96 Peter Sankoff & Sophie Gaillard, "Bringing Animal Abusers to Justice Independently: Private Prosecutions and the Enforcement of Canadian Animal Protection Legislation" in Peter Sankoff, Vaughan Black & Katie Sykes, eds, *Canadian Perspectives on Animals and the Law* (Toronto: Irwin, 2015) 307.

including provisions related to animal protection (for example, those that apply to the transportation and slaughter of food animals).[97] Provincial and territorial law may also permit private prosecution, depending on the jurisdiction.[98]

This means that individuals and animal protection organizations can initiate the enforcement of criminal animal cruelty laws themselves, bypassing public prosecutors and law enforcement agencies that may be reluctant to do so or may not prioritize animal protection.[99] Private prosecutions can be a way to bring public attention to underenforcement or inaction by the public authorities, a strategy that has been used successfully by environmental activists with respect to the enforcement of environmental law.[100]

However, private prosecution (discussed in Chapter 19 of this text) is a much less powerful enforcement mechanism than the full-fledged private right of action that Sunstein argues for. The main limitation of private prosecution is that it remains subject to the Crown's ultimate control of the criminal process. The attorney general can step in and take over or end the proceedings at any point after they are initiated.[101] Private prosecutions are also expensive and challenging for private citizens or non-profits to investigate and litigate, especially because they do not have access to the resources and legal powers of the public law enforcement authorities.[102]

b. Reece v Edmonton (City): The Need for Legal Standing for Animals

Private citizens and groups seeking to ensure meaningful legal protections for animals have tried to find other ways to represent animal interests in court. In *Reece v Edmonton (City)*,[103] the applicants sought a declaration from a civil court that the City of Edmonton was violating Alberta's animal welfare laws by keeping Lucy, an elephant, in unsuitable conditions at the Edmonton Valley Zoo.

The applicants alleged that Lucy suffered from a long list of debilitating health conditions related to her captivity, and that since 2007 she had been kept at the zoo alone—a sad and lonely living situation given that female elephants are exceptionally social animals.[104] They argued that the City was committing an offence under Alberta's *Animal Protection Act*,[105] which prohibits keeping an animal in a condition of being injured, sick, in pain, or suffering.[106]

The City of Edmonton moved to dismiss the proceedings as an abuse of process, and that motion was granted by a chambers judge.[107] The Alberta Court of Appeal upheld the dismissal of the application. It held that a private individual cannot use civil proceedings as a way to

97   *Ibid* at 313-14.

98   *Ibid* at 314.

99   *Ibid* at 315.

100 *Ibid* at 316-17; see also Kernaghan Webb, "Taking Matters into Their Own Hands: The Role of the Citizen in Canadian Pollution Control Enforcement" (1991) 36 McGill LJ 770.

101 Sankoff & Gaillard, *supra* note 96 at 320-21.

102 *Ibid* at 323-27.

103 2011 ABCA 238, leave to appeal to SCC refused, 2012 CanLII 22074 [*Reece* cited to ABCA].

104 See the discussion of the appellants' evidence in *Reece, supra* note 103 at paras 103-27, Fraser CJ dissenting.

105 RSA 2000, c A-41 [APA].

106 APA, ss 2(1) and 1(2). The applicants also argued that Lucy's living conditions were contrary to zoo industry guidelines for the care of elephants, so that s 2.2 of the APA, which creates an exemption for activities carried on in accordance with "reasonable and generally accepted practices of animal care," therefore, did not apply.

107 *Reece v Edmonton (City)*, 2010 ABQB 538.

enforce criminal law.[108] This meant that the application was dismissed on procedural grounds without a trial or other hearing of the evidence concerning Lucy's situation.

But one member of the three-judge panel at the Court of Appeal, Fraser CJ, dissented. Fraser CJ's dissenting opinion is probably the most extensive and thoughtful discussion of the concept of animal rights and the nature of animal protection law in Canadian jurisprudence. Ultimately, her argument was that, if laws to protect animals exist, there must be some way to make those laws effective—so *someone* should have the legal standing to go before a court and show that the law is not being enforced.

Fraser CJ argued that the case raised a fundamental issue: "who, if anyone, is entitled to access the courts, and under what circumstances, to protect animals to the extent the Alberta Legislature has defined?"[109] In her view,

> courts should not diminish the full import of animal protection laws by creating unnecessary barriers to those seeking to ensure compliance with them. Animals, including Lucy, cannot commence lawsuits on their own to protect themselves. They must rely on humans to give voice to the truly voiceless. Thus, courts should take a generous, not impoverished, approach to the grant of public interest standing for those attempting to enforce the restrictive animal rights that do exist.[110]

c. *Intervener Status*

Another mechanism that can provide space for legal submissions to be made from the point of view of animals' interests—although it is not the same as legal standing—is intervener status. Intervener status allows an individual or entity, with leave of the court, to participate in legal proceedings in which he or she is not a principal litigant, in order to present arguments and advocate for interests that are engaged by the litigation and that otherwise would not be represented.

The national animal advocacy organization Animal Justice Canada (Animal Justice) has been granted leave to make submissions as an intervener in a number of important cases involving animal protection laws and animals' interests.[111] The most prominent of these so far is *R v DLW*,[112] a rare Supreme Court decision on animal protection.

---

108 *Reece, supra* note 103 at paras 29-31. Although the relevant statute was the APA, rather than the *Criminal Code*, the Alberta Court of Appeal reasoned that s 2(1) of the APA created an offence and imposed penalties—that is, that cruelty to animals under provincial animal protection law was in the nature of a criminal offence.

109 *Ibid* at para 53.

110 *Ibid* at para 90.

111 These cases include *Vancouver Aquarium Marine Science Centre v Charbonneau*, 2017 BCCA 395 (a copyright case that involved an independent filmmaker's critical documentary about the cetacean program at the Vancouver Aquarium and in which Animal Justice argued that copyright law should not be applied in a way that risks chilling or silencing critical discussion of the treatment of animals); *Ocean Wise Conservation Association v Vancouver Board of Parks and Recreation*, 2018 BCSC 196 (overruled in *Ocean Wise Conservation Association v Vancouver Board of Parks and Recreation*, 2019 BCCA 58) (a case concerning the legality of the by-law amendment of the Vancouver Parks Board to prohibit keeping whales in Stanley Park, where the Vancouver Aquarium is located; Animal Justice and Zoocheck both intervened to make submissions countering the argument that the by-law amendment infringed on Vancouver Aquarium's freedom of expression contrary to s 2(b) of the Charter); and *Bogaerts v Attorney General of Ontario*, 2019 ONSC 41 (a case that challenged the constitutionality of certain provisions of Ontario's animal protection statute and in which the court substantially adopted Animal Justice's argument that the principles of fundamental justice under s 7 of the Charter include governmental obligations of transparency and accountability).

112 2016 SCC 22.

The case concerned the interpretation and scope of the offence of bestiality under s 160(1) of the *Criminal Code*. Animal Justice was granted leave to intervene and presented arguments that at least part of the purpose of the criminal offence of bestiality in modern law is to protect vulnerable animals and to punish sexual abuse of animals, which do not have the capacity to consent.[113] Abella J, in dissent, expressly referred to Animal Justice's factum in her reasons.[114]

DLW and other cases where animal advocates have been granted intervener status show that it is possible to add an animal-focused perspective to litigation, and, potentially, to influence the development of the law in a way that is better informed about what is at stake for animals. But an intervener is, by definition, limited to participating in litigation between other parties, and cannot initiate a case independently.

d. Developments in the United States on Standing for Animals

In the US, lawyers advocating for animals and animal advocacy groups like the Animal Legal Defense Fund and People for the Ethical Treatment of Animals (PETA) have tried novel legal arguments to attempt to establish standing on behalf of animals. One reason there are more cases like this in the US than in Canada is the standard costs rule in Canada that the loser must pay the costs of the winning side, which can deter litigants from attempting novel strategies that have a high chance of losing even though their arguments may also contribute to the development of the law.

In *Cetacean Community v Bush*,[115] the Ninth Circuit Court of Appeals ruled that animals can potentially have standing under art III of the US Constitution (constitutional standing), provided that standing is granted under the specific statute under which the plaintiff brings suit (statutory standing).

In *Naruto v Slater*,[116] PETA asserted the right to act as a litigation guardian of or "next friend" to Naruto, a crested macaque on whose behalf PETA asserted a claim of copyright ownership. (The case involved copyright claims over a photograph apparently taken by the macaque with a camera belonging to wildlife photographer David Slater when it pressed the shutter button while pointing the camera at itself; it is colloquially known as the "monkey selfie" case.) The Ninth Circuit Court of Appeals found that, absent express authorization from Congress, there was no right for next friends to bring suit on behalf of animals.[117] Smith J, in concurring reasons, raised concerns about the potential for abuse and the special problems that could arise from allowing lawyers and organizations to assert rights on behalf of animals:

> Animal-next-friend standing is particularly susceptible to abuse. Allowing next-friend standing on behalf of animals allows lawyers ... and various interest groups ... to bring suit on behalf of those animals or objects *with no means or manner to ensure the animals' interests are truly being expressed or advanced.* Such a change would fundamentally alter the litigation landscape. Institutional actors could simply claim some form of relationship to the animal or object to obtain standing and use it to advance their own institutional goals with no means to curtail those actions. We have no idea whether animals or objects wish to own copyrights or open bank accounts to hold their royalties from sales of pictures. To some extent, as humans, we have a general understanding of the similar interests of other humans. In the habeas corpus context, we presume other humans desire liberty. Similarly, in actions on behalf of infants, for example, we presume the infant would want to retain ownership of the property she inherited. But the interests of animals? We are really asking what *another*

113 *Ibid* at para 69.

114 *Ibid* at para 140.

115 386 F (3d) 1169 (9th Cir 2004).

116 888 F (3d) 418 (9th Cir 2018).

117 *Ibid* at 421-22 (internal citations omitted).

species desires. Do animals want to own property, such as copyrights? Are animals willing to assume the duties associated with the rights PETA seems to be advancing on their behalf? Animal-next-friend standing is materially different from a competent person representing an incompetent person. We have millennia of experience understanding the interests and desire of humankind. This is not necessarily true for animals. Because the "real party in interest" can actually *never credibly articulate its interests or goals*, next-friend standing for animals is left at the mercy of the institutional actor to advance its own interests, which it *imputes* to the animal or object with *no accountability*. This literally creates an avenue for what Chief Justice Rehnquist feared: making the actual party in interest a "pawn to be manipulated on a chessboard larger than his own case."[118]

QUESTIONS

1. Is the lack of effective enforcement of animal protection laws a rule-of-law problem? Does it undermine the rule of law if there are protections for animals "on the books" but those provisions are systematically underenforced or "worth little more than the paper they are written on"?

2. Do you agree with Fraser CJ that animals must have some form of legal standing if they are to be legally protected in a meaningful way? If so, what would be an appropriate mechanism for giving them standing? Should private individuals or organizations have a private right of action to sue those who violate laws intended to protect animals? Should there be a right for lawyers to represent an animal as its "next friend" or litigation guardian? How would you address the potential problems identified by Smith J in the *Naruto* case, such as the difficulty of identifying an animal's interest in the case, or the risk of making the animal litigant "a pawn to be manipulated on a chessboard larger than his [or her] own case"?

3. Would a different approach, such as a public guardian or advocate responsible for representing animals (perhaps along the lines of the children's lawyer offices that exist in some jurisdictions),[119] be preferable—and feasible?

4. Whatever model is best for giving animals a voice in the courts, could it also extend to advocacy on behalf of other non-human entities that are legally protected, such as natural phenomena or ecosystems? Consider, for example, Christopher Stone's arguments concerning standing and rights for trees and other natural objects.[120]

C. SUBSTANTIVE ANIMAL RIGHTS

Recall Sunstein's argument that there are two possible strategies for expanding animal rights: enlarging the category of rights beyond what the legal system now recognizes and ensuring that the rights that are now on the books actually exist in the world. With respect to the first strategy, expanding substantive rights, there are efforts on numerous fronts to improve legal protections for animals. For example, in 2019, Canada passed three new federal laws that improve protection for animals:

---

118   *Ibid* at 432 (internal citations omitted) (emphasis in original).

119   For example, the Office of the Children's Lawyer of Ontario's Ministry of the Attorney General, which represents children under the age of 18 in court cases involving custody and access and child protection, as well as in civil, and estates and trusts cases. See "The Office of the Children's Lawyer" (last visited 20 May 2019), online: Ontario Ministry of the Attorney General <https://www.attorneygeneral.jus.gov.on.ca/english/family/ocl>.

120   "Should Trees Have Standing? Towards Legal Rights for Natural Objects" (1972) 45 S Cal L Rev 450.

- a law that prohibits keeping, breeding, and displaying cetaceans (whales, dolphins, and porpoises) in captivity;[121]
- a law that strengthens criminal prohibitions on bestiality and animal fighting, closing some loopholes; and[122]
- a law banning imports and exports of shark fins.[123]

Bill S-214, which aimed to outlaw testing cosmetic products on animals and selling animal-tested cosmetics in Canada, did not make it past the third reading.[124]

Some scholars argue that legal protections for animals will always be inadequate unless the legal system recognizes animals themselves as having rights—not just procedural rights to be heard or represented in court, but the legal right not to be treated as an object used for human purposes.

1. Welfarism, Humane Treatment, and the Rights–Welfare Debate

It is often said that our animal protection laws are based on a philosophy of "welfarism." Welfarism involves determining whether a given activity imposed on animals is justified by balancing its costs against its benefits, which usually means weighing the suffering involved for the animal against the benefit to humans.

In *R v Menard*,[125] the leading case interpreting what it means to cause "unnecessary" suffering to animals within the meaning of what is now s 445.1(a) of the *Criminal Code*, Lamer JA (as he then was) construed the statute to require this kind of balancing test:

> [I]n setting standards for the behaviour of men towards animals, we have taken into account our privileged position in nature and have been obliged to take into account at the outset the purpose sought. We have, moreover, wished to subject all behaviour, which would already be legalized by its purpose, to the test of the "means employed." ...
>
> [T]he legality of a painful operation must be governed by the necessity for it, and even where a desirable and legitimate object is sought to be attained, the magnitude of the operation and the pain caused thereby must not so far outbalance the importance of the end as to make it clear to any reasonable person that it is preferable that the object should be abandoned rather than that disproportionate suffering should be inflicted.[126]

Canadian animal law scholar Jessica Eisen argues that the law truly reflects not the proportionality analysis described in *Menard* but rather a principle of "humane treatment."[127] Humane treatment, Eisen argues, accepts human purposes as legitimate and important in all cases short of outright sadistic abuse and merely seeks to achieve incremental improvement in the treatment of animals being used for those purposes.[128]

---

121 Bill S-203, *An Act to amend the Criminal Code and other Acts (ending the captivity of whales and dolphins)*, 1st Sess, 42nd Parl, 2015 (assented to 21 June 2019).

122 Bill C-84, *An Act to amend the Criminal Code (bestiality and animal fighting)*, 1st Sess, 42nd Parl, 2018 (assented to 21 June 2019).

123 Bill S-238, *An Act to amend the Fisheries Act and the Wild Animal and Plant Protection and Regulation of International and Interprovincial Trade Act (importation and exportation of shark fins)*, 1st Sess, 42nd Parl, 2017 (assented to 21 June 2019).

124 Bill S-214, *An Act to amend the Food and Drugs Act (cruelty-free cosmetics)*, 1st Sess, 42nd Parl, 2015 (third reading in the House 19 June 2019).

125 1978 CanLII 2355, 43 CCC (2d) 458 (Qu CA) [*Menard* cited to CCC].

126 *Ibid* at 464-65.

127 Jessica Eisen, "Beyond Rights and Welfare: Democracy, Dialogue, and the Animal Welfare Act" (2018) 51:3 U Mich JL Ref 469.

128 *Ibid* at 491.

Laws based on the "welfarist" or "humane treatment" model have not done much in practice to improve the treatment of animals, and this failure is often cited as evidence that welfarism is inherently incapable of bringing about meaningful legal protection for animals. Some argue that meaningful reform can be achieved only by rejecting the welfarist model and recognizing animals as having legal rights themselves. Others prefer to focus on achieving practical improvements in the situation of animals within the welfarist framework, either because they believe that it is justifiable within limits to use animals for human ends, or because they support incremental reform with the recognition of animal rights as a more distant goal, or both. The debate between these points of view is known as the rights–welfare debate.[129]

2. Peter Singer and Speciesism

The most famous philosopher of animal welfare is Peter Singer, who is a utilitarian. Utilitarianism generally assesses the moral legitimacy of actions by balancing the aggregate costs against the benefits of that action. Singer accepts that we can justifiably subject animals to treatment that causes them suffering as long as the total welfare or benefit that results from the action outweighs that suffering.

Singer is sharply critical, however, of the way the balancing of suffering and benefits is actually applied to animals. Applying utilitarian balancing fairly requires that "the interests of every being affected by an action ... be taken into account and given the same weight as the like interests of any other being."[130] Singer argues that, in fact, we systematically devalue animal interests and overvalue human interests because we have an ethically unjustifiable bias in favour of the interests of members of our own species and against those of members of other species.[131] Singer calls this bias "speciesism," which is analogous to other unfair prejudices like sexism and racism.[132] Because our decisions are distorted by speciesism, Singer argues, we support "practices that require the sacrifice of the most important interests of members of other species in order to promote the most trivial interests of our own species."[133]

3. Gary Francione and Abolitionism

Gary Francione is a proponent of animal rights and rejects welfarism. He argues that welfarism, which permits the use of animals as a means to human ends, is really just a cover for institutionalized exploitation.[134] Francione argues that the legal classification of non-human animals as property is the root of legalized animal exploitation and abuse, and should be abolished:

> The property aspect of animals is almost always a major component in the resolution of human/animal conflicts, because even if the property status is not explicit, in almost all circumstances in which human and animal interests conflict a human is seeking to act upon her property. As far as the law is concerned, it is as if we were resolving a conflict between

129 See Gary L Francione & Robert Garner, *The Animal Rights Debate* (New York: Columbia University Press, 2010).

130 Peter Singer, *Animal Liberation* (New York: Harper Perennial, 2009; first published 1975) at 5.

131 *Ibid* at 6.

132 *Ibid*. The term "speciesism" was originally coined by Richard Ryder, a psychologist and animal rights advocate who, in 1977, was involved in organizing the first animal rights symposium at Cambridge University (where a "Declaration Against Speciesism" was signed by 150 people).

133 *Ibid* at 9.

134 Gary L Francione, *Animals, Property and the Law* (Philadelphia: Temple University Press, 2012; first published 1995).

a person and a lamp, or some other piece of personal property. The winner of the dispute is predetermined by the way in which the conflict is conceptualized in the first place.[135]

Francione argues that the law should recognize animal rights; that is, as he argues, it should recognize their right to not be treated as property.[136] Consciously echoing the language (and arguments) of the movement to abolish human chattel slavery, Francione describes his position as "abolitionism."[137] He argues that the use of sentient animals for human ends should be abolished, not just regulated or modified.[138]

4. Tom Regan: Kantian Rights and Animals as "Subjects-of-a-Life"

Tom Regan was an animal rights philosopher who developed an account of animal rights based on Immanuel Kant's conception of individual rights. Kant (as explained by Regan) considered "rights" to be the entitlement of rational beings to be treated as "ends in themselves" with "independent value, in their own right, quite apart from how useful they happen to be to others."[139] Regan argues that at least some non-human animals, like humans, have rights in the Kantian sense that they are entitled to be treated as ends in themselves, not as a means to the ends of others.

Regan departs from Kant in rejecting the proposition that the precondition of being a rights-bearer is rationality. For Regan, the basis of an animal's status as a being with rights is the experience of being the "subject-of-a-life," that is, having a life that matters to the animal itself:

> [I]ndividuals are subjects-of-a-life if they have beliefs and desires; perception, memory, and a sense of the future, including their own future; an emotional life together with feelings of pleasure and pain; preference- and welfare-interests; the ability to initiate action in pursuit of their desires and goals; a psychophysical identity over time; and an individual welfare in the sense that their experiential life fares well or ill for them, logically independently of their utility for others and logically independently of their being the object of anyone else's interests. Those who satisfy the subject-of-a-life criterion themselves have a distinctive kind of value—inherent value—and are not to be viewed or treated as mere receptacles.[140]

Regan argues that all animals who meet the subject-of-a-life criterion have the "equal basic right to be treated with respect." For Regan, it is never justifiable to harm such individuals "on the grounds that all those affected by the outcome will thereby secure 'the best' aggregate balance of intrinsic values (e.g. pleasures) over intrinsic disvalues (e.g. pains)"—because that would be treating them as a means for the ends of others and denying their inherent value.[141] This position rejects the interest-balancing underlying welfarism.

5. Science-Based Arguments for Animal Rights

Recent advances in scientific understanding of animal minds, intelligence, consciousness, communications, and social organization have undermined the idea that there is a strict dividing line between human beings and all other species. Some people believe that evidence of

---

135 *Ibid* at 24.

136 Francione & Garner, *supra* note 129 at 1 (emphasis in the original).

137 *Ibid*.

138 *Ibid*.

139 Tom Regan, *The Case for Animal Rights* (Berkeley: University of California Press, 1983) at 175.

140 *Ibid* at 243.

141 *Ibid* at 286-87.

connections and continuity between humans and other animal species supports the case for recognizing certain animals as being entitled to basic rights.

For example, the Great Ape Project was a collaboration between scientists, philosophers, and ethicists in the 1990s.[142] The Great Ape Project built on increasing scientific evidence of the cognitive and social sophistication of non-human great apes—that is, chimpanzees, orangutans, gorillas, and bonobos—as well as their evolutionary kinship with humans (zoologists classify humans, along with the non-human great ape species, our closest relatives, as members of the family Hominidae). The evolving scientific consensus on both of these points was cited as supporting evidence for a "Declaration on Great Apes" that defined the non-human great apes as members of a community that are the equal of humans, sharing the basic rights to life, liberty, and freedom from torture.[143]

Similarly, science has been invoked to support proposals of rights for cetaceans (whales and dolphins). Marine biologists, including Canadian scientists Hal Whitehead and Luke Rendell, have found abundant evidence from studying the behaviour of cetaceans that they have sophisticated minds, social organization, communicative abilities, and (as Whitehead and Rendell argue) their own cultures.[144] In 2010, a conference at the University of Helsinki put forward the *Declaration of Rights for Cetaceans: Whales and Dolphins*, asserting that individual cetaceans have various rights (including the right to life, freedom, residence in their natural environment, and protection of their culture) and that they are not property.[145] The preamble to this declaration notes that "scientific research gives us deeper insights into the complexities of cetacean minds, societies and cultures."

6. Steven Wise and the Nonhuman Rights Project

American lawyer Steven Wise and his colleagues at the Nonhuman Rights Project seek to secure recognition of legal personhood and fundamental rights for non-human animals through strategic litigation. The Nonhuman Rights Project brings *habeas corpus* claims on behalf of individual great apes, elephants, dolphins, and whales that are living in captivity in various US states.[146]

One such case, in New York State, involved a *habeas corpus* claim advanced on behalf of two chimpanzees, Tommy and Kiko.[147] The Appellate Division, First Department, reasoned that the chimpanzees could not have legal rights because they did not have the "capacity or ability, like humans, to bear legal duties, or to be held legally accountable for their actions."[148]

The Nonhuman Rights Project's motion for leave to appeal this decision to the New York Court of Appeals was denied, but one of the judges wrote a concurring opinion calling into question whether the Appellate Division's reasoning really supported the categorical denial of legal rights to non-human animals:

---

142 Paola Cavalieri & Peter Singer, eds, *The Great Ape Project* (London: Fourth Estate, 1993).

143 "A Declaration on Great Apes" in *The Great Ape Project, ibid* at 5.

144 Hal Whitehead & Luke Rendell, *The Cultural Lives of Whales and Dolphins* (Chicago: University of Chicago Press, 2015).

145 *Declaration of Rights for Cetaceans: Whales and Dolphins* (last visted 20 May 2019), online: *Cetacean Rights* <https://www.cetaceanrights.org>. For a discussion of the genesis and significance of this Declaration, see "Declaration of Rights for Cetaceans: Whales and Dolphins" (2011) 14:1 J Intl Wildlife L & Pol'y 75.

146 "Litigation" (last visited 20 May 2019), online: *Nonhuman Rights Project* <https://www.nonhuman-rights.org/litigation/>.

147 *Matter of Nonhuman Rights Project Inc v Lavery*, 152 AD (3d) 73 (NY 1st Dept 2017).

148 *Ibid* at 78.

Can a nonhuman animal be entitled to release from confinement through the writ of habeas corpus? Should such a being be treated as a person or as property, in essence a thing?

• • •

Even if it is correct ... that nonhuman animals cannot bear duties, the same is true of human infants or comatose human adults, yet no one would suppose that it is improper to seek a writ of habeas corpus on behalf of one's infant child ... or a parent suffering from dementia ... . In short, being a "moral agent" who can freely choose to act as morality requires is not a necessary condition of being a "moral patient" who can be wronged and may have the right to redress wrongs ... .

• • •

The record before us in the motion for leave to appeal contains unrebutted evidence, in the form of affidavits from eminent primatologists, that chimpanzees have advanced cognitive abilities, including being able to remember the past and plan for the future, the capacities of self-awareness and self-control, and the ability to communicate through sign language. Chimpanzees make tools to catch insects; they recognize themselves in mirrors, photographs, and television images; they imitate others; they exhibit compassion and depression when a community member dies; they even display a sense of humor. ...

Does an intelligent nonhuman animal who thinks and plans and appreciates life as human beings do have the right to the protection of the law against arbitrary cruelties and enforced detentions visited on him or her? This is not merely a definitional question, but a deep dilemma of ethics and policy that demands our attention. To treat a chimpanzee as if he or she had no right to liberty protected by habeas corpus is to regard the chimpanzee as entirely lacking independent worth, as a mere resource for human use, a thing the value of which consists exclusively in its usefulness to others. Instead, we should consider whether a chimpanzee is an individual with inherent value who has the right to be treated with respect.[149]

QUESTIONS

1. Is it (sometimes) justifiable for humans to use animals for human purposes? If you think it is, how would you evaluate whether an animal-use practice is justified? Do you think existing laws fit with your sense of what is justified and what is not?

2. Do animals need to be granted some form of legal rights in order to have real legal protection from abuse? Do they need to be classified as legal "persons," instead of "property"?

3. If animals do have rights, what rights do they have, and which animals have them? How would you draw a principled line between those that have rights and those that do not?

4. What do you think about the argument that animals cannot have legal rights because they do not have legal obligations or responsibilities?

D. BEYOND RIGHTS AND WELFARE

The debate between proponents of animal rights and advocates of welfarist approaches to animal protection has continued for a long time—although the problems that both camps see with existing animal protection law can be very similar. Some argue that the rights–welfare debate may not be very fruitful in terms of increasing the likelihood of practical improvements

---

149 *Matter of Nonhuman Rights Project Inc v Lavery*, 2018 NY Slip Op 03309 (Fahey J concurring) at 3-5. Fahey J concurred with the decision not to grant leave to appeal because, had leave been granted and the appeal proceeded, he would probably have voted to affirm—presumably for reasons different from those given by the Appellate Division.

in legal protection for animals, and that it may be more productive to analyze human–animal relationships through a different lens. We will briefly look at ideas proposed by Canadian scholars that supplement rights and welfare theories by engaging with questions that are beyond the scope of those theories.

1. Moving the Needle: Law and Social Change

Jessica Eisen argues that one dimension missing from both the rights and welfare approaches is attention to the relationship between law and social change. Even if we had (or could have) an answer to which framework is superior philosophically, the best philosophical argument does not lead to real-world change unless social attitudes and public values are in favour of that change. Especially in a democratic society, a prerequisite for legal reform is broad public support. As Eisen says,

> both rights and welfarism, in their most essential forms, purport to offer theoretical frame-works that can be productively employed here and now, and in any place or time, to produce just outcomes. While this may be appropriate to the philosophical projects in which Singer and Regan are most directly engaged, such an approach is inadequate to considering animal justice as a legal and political project. Reasoned philosophical argument of the kind that Singer and Regan engage can play a crucial role in moving the needle on these problems. But a workable legal theory of animal justice must incorporate the necessity of that moving needle. This is especially so where advocates call for drastic changes to current practices, as both Regan and Singer do. A theory of animal legal protection that aspires to broad social change requires a framework that acknowledges the need for a range of argumentation, from the traditional to the critical. Rather than seeking determinate moral frameworks, animal legal theory must embrace the role that shifting public opinions and mainstream "common sense" play in defining human–animal relationships, including through democratic legislative change.[150]

Therefore, Eisen advocates building the foundation for an "evolving ethic" of human–animal relationships, by analogy with Laurence Tribe's model of an evolving framework of conceptions of the human relationship with nature.[151]

2. Relational Rights: Human and Animal Communities

Sue Donaldson and Will Kymlicka are animal rights theorists, but their theory of human–animal relationships goes beyond animal rights accounts (such as Regan's theory of animal rights, summarized earlier in this chapter) that focus on intrinsic qualities of individual animals and the associated negative individual rights, such as the rights not to be killed, held in captivity, or tortured. Donaldson and Kymlicka agree with rights theorists that all sentient animals have basic rights and that respecting those rights would require the end of many of the ways in which humans exploit animals.[152] But they see traditional, individualistic animal rights theory as failing to provide an account of the principles that should govern relationships between human societies and different communities of animals. Donaldson and Kymlicka's theory focuses on how human and animal communities can coexist in a way that reflects justice. Their work is based on political philosophy and citizenship theory.

---

150 Eisen, *supra* note 127 at 494.

151 *Ibid* at 496-97; see also Laurence Tribe, "Ways Not to Think About Plastic Trees: New Foundations for Environmental Law" (1974) 83:7 Yale LJ 1315 at 1338-39.

152 Sue Donaldson & Will Kymlicka, *Zoopolis: A Political Theory of Animal Rights* (Oxford: Oxford University Press, 2011).

Donaldson and Kymlicka classify animals into three groups, reflecting three different types of relationships between animal and human communities. They argue that different principles are required to regulate human relationships with each group. Domesticated animals are, by reason of domestication, members of our communities, and they are entitled to have their interests taken into account in our social and political arrangements; the appropriate framework for their relationship to human communities is citizenship. Wilderness animals live independently of humans, but they are vulnerable to harm from human activities. They constitute self-determined sovereign communities, and human relationships with them should be governed by norms analogous to those that govern state-to-state relationships in international law. The third category is "liminal" animals: wild animals that live in human settlements, for example, squirrels, raccoons, crows, and starlings. Donaldson and Kymlicka classify their status with respect to human communities as that of "denizens," similar to human denizens who are co-residents of communities but are not co-citizens, for example, refugees, migrant workers, and isolationist communities that choose not to integrate into the mainstream society (for example, the Amish). Donaldson and Kymlicka argue that in each of these models, justice requires the recognition of different kinds of rights and obligations between the animal and human communities—not only negative rights of animals not to be subjected to certain kinds of treatment but also positive rights, such as the right of "citizen" animals to have their interests taken into account in our definition of the public good, and the right of "sovereign" animals to positive assistance and intervention.[153]

QUESTIONS FOR DISCUSSION

1. Are public opinion and mainstream consensus about human–animal relationships changing? Consider, for example, the various bills to change federal animal protection law described above. Are they examples of real change that further justice for animals? What might bring about changes in social attitudes and public values concerning human–animal relationships?

2. What do you think about rights and obligations that apply between human and animal *communities*, as distinct from rights of individual animals? Are you persuaded by Donaldson and Kymlicka's framework of domestic animal "citizens," wild animal sovereignty, and liminal animal "denizens"? How do those concepts need to be modified when applied to animal, rather than human, communities?

FURTHER READINGS

Human Rights

Atapattu, Sumudu & Andrea Schapper, *Human Rights and the Environment: Key Issues*, (New York: Routledge, 2019).

Boyd, David R, *The Environmental Rights Revolution: A Global Study of Constitutions, Human Rights, and the Environment* (Vancouver: UBC Press, 2012).

Boyd, David R, *The Right to a Healthy Environment: Revitalizing Canada's Constitution* (Vancouver: UBC Press, 2012).

Bulto, Takele Soboka, *The Extraterritorial Application of the Human Right to Water in Africa* (Cambridge: Cambridge University Press, 2014).

---

153 *Ibid.*

Chalifour, Nathalie, "Environmental Justice and the Charter: Do Environmental Injustices Infringe Sections 7 and 15 of the Charter?" (2015) 28:1 J Envtl L & Prac 89, Ottawa Faculty of Law Working Paper No 2017-12, online: *SSRN* <https://ssrn.com/abstract=2922653>.

Chalifour, Nathalie & Jessica Earle, "Feeling the Heat: Climate Litigation Under the Charter's Right to Life, Liberty and Security of the Person" (20 November 2017), Ottawa Faculty of Law Working Paper No 2017-48, online: *SSRN* <https://ssrn.com/abstract=3080379>.

Fluker, Shaun, "The Right to Public Participation in Resources and Environmental Decision-Making in Alberta" (2015) 52:3 Alta L Rev 567.

Hajjar Leib, Linda, *Human Rights and the Environment: Philosophical, Theoretical and Legal Perspectives* (Leiden, NL: Martinus Nijhoff Publishers, 2011).

Knox, John H, *Framework Principles and Human Rights and the Environment,* UNHRSP (2018), online (pdf): *UN Special Rapporteur on Human Rights and the Environment* <https://www.ohchr.org/Documents/Issues/Environment/SREnvironment/FrameworkPrinciplesUserFriendlyVersion.pdf>.

Knox, John H & Ramin Pejan, eds, *The Human Right to a Healthy Environment* (Cambridge: Cambridge University Press, 2018).

Vallani, Madiha, "Sections 7 and 15 of the Canadian Charter of Rights and Freedoms in the Context of the Clean Water Crisis on Reserves: Opportunities and Challenges for First Nations Women" (2018) Master of Laws Research Papers Repository, 2, online: *Western Libraries* <https://ir.lib.uwo.ca/llmp/2/>.

Animal Rights

Bisgould, Lesli, *Animals and the Law* (Toronto: Irwin, 2011).

Cavalieri, Paola & Peter Singer, eds, *The Great Ape Project* (London: Fourth Estate, 1993).

Donaldson, Sue & Will Kymlicka, *Zoopolis: A Political Theory of Animal Rights* (Oxford: Oxford University Press, 2011).

Eisen, Jessica, "Beyond Rights and Welfare: Democracy, Dialogue, and the Animal Welfare Act" (2018) 51:3 U Mich JL Ref 469.

Francione, Gary L, *Animals, Property and the Law* (Philadelphia: Temple University Press, 2012).

Francione, Gary L & Robert Garner, *The Animal Rights Debate* (New York: Columbia University Press, 2010).

Reece v Edmonton (City), 2011 ABCA 238.

Regan, Tom, *The Case for Animal Rights* (Berkeley: University of California Press, 1983).

Sankoff, Peter, Vaughan Black & Katie Sykes, eds, *Canadian Perspectives on Animals and the Law* (Toronto: Irwin, 2015).

Singer, Peter, *Animal Liberation* (New York: Harper Perennial, 2009).

Sunstein, Cass R & Martha C Nussbaum, eds, *Animal Rights: Current Debates and New Directions* (Oxford: Oxford University Press, 2004).

Wise, Steven M, *Rattling the Cage: Towards Legal Rights for Animals* (Boston: Da Capo Press, 2000).

CHAPTER TWENTY-ONE

PROTECTED SPACES AND ENDANGERED SPECIES*

Stewart Elgie

* The author thanks Annie Arko for her invaluable research assistance on this chapter.

In wildness is the preservation of the world ... . Life consists of wildness. The most alive is the wildest. Not yet subdued to man, its presence refreshes him ... . When I would re-create myself, I seek the darkest wood, the thickest and most interminable and to the citizen, most dismal, swamp. I enter it as a sacred place, a Sanctum Sanctorum. There is the strength, the marrow, of Nature. In short, all good things are wild and free.

Henry David Thoreau, "Walking," *The Atlantic Monthly* 9:56 (June 1862)

I. PARKS AND PROTECTED AREAS

A. THE HISTORY OF PARKS

Most Canadians take for granted the fact that we have wilderness parks. However, parks, in the modern sense, are a relatively recent North American creation:

Today we look upon parks as special places that provide a sanctuary for both man and nature, places where some relief from everyday stress can be found. Special places serving contemplative or spiritual needs have existed in eastern cultures since 500 B.C. The eastern religions of Shintoism, Taoism, and Buddhism held a reverence for nature not reflected in Christianity. Thus shrines such as the Bo Tree in Sri Lanka have protected nature and provided places for contemplation for more than 2000 years. In contrast, Christian [and Judaic] theology often casts wilderness as the antithesis of paradise. As exemplified in the writings of Joel (Joel 2:3): "The land is like the garden of Eden before them, but after them a desolate wilderness."

Skipping a few centuries, we find new benchmarks in the royal forests and game preserves of England and France. ... In the new world, Boston Common (1603) is often acknowledged as the first formal public open space in North America. The next major landmark was the establishment of Yosemite as a twenty-square-kilometre state park in California in 1864. This was followed by "the world's first instance of large-scale wilderness preservation in the public interest." On March 1, 1872, President Ulysses S Grant signed an act designating over 8,000,000 hectares of northwestern Wyoming as Yellowstone National Park.

The establishment of Yellowstone National Park in the United States sparked a global interest in parks. In 1879 Royal National Park was established in New South Wales, Australia, and in 1894 Tongariro National Park was dedicated in New Zealand. Thus, by the turn of the century, the national-parks concept, as we know it today, was underway. ...

With the protection of Banff National Park in 1885, Niagara Falls in 1887, and Ontario's Algonquin Provincial Park in 1893, Canada, perhaps unwittingly, created "a system of parks."

Between 1885 and 1929, Canada established fifteen national parks. [In 1930, the *National Parks Act*, SC 1930, c 33, was passed.] But with the transfer of natural resources in western Canada to the provinces in 1930, the national parks program ground to a halt. Only four parks were established in the next twenty years: Cape Breton Highlands in 1936, Prince Edward Island in 1937, Fundy in 1948, and Terra Nova in 1957. The next thirty years, though, saw the system double. The postwar boom, new cars, and new highways brought a new generation of visitors to North America's parks.

(H Eidsvik, "Canada in a Global Context" in M Hummel, ed, *Endangered Spaces: The Future for Canada's Wilderness* (Toronto: Key Porter Books, 1989) 30.)

Today, there are 48 national parks in Canada (including one national urban park), 6 national marine parks, over 2,000 provincial parks, and a host of other types of conservation areas. Canada's parks protect many of the nation's most spectacular natural features, including the highest mountain (Kluane), the tallest tree (Carmanah Pacific), the largest inland delta (Wood Buffalo), the most northerly point (Ellesmere Island), the most southerly point (Point Pelee), and the strongest tides (Fundy), and many endangered species for which parks are the last refuge. Parks and protected areas are important for recreational, educational, cultural heritage, and ecological reasons.

B. THE IDEA OF WILDERNESS IN NORTH AMERICA

The European settlers brought their attitudes toward nature with them to the new world. Wilderness, at first, was something to be conquered and subdued. The Indigenous peoples of North America, who had lived on, and from, the land for several thousand years had no concept of wilderness, at least in the European sense. The idea of protecting wild places, or of exploiting them, are concepts born in societies that see themselves as separate from, and above, nature. North American Indigenous peoples have evolved a lifestyle based on respect for the land and animals. They took what they needed to live, but never so much as to upset the natural balance. For the Indigenous peoples, natural areas were anything but wild; they were home. It was the cities that were wild.

The creation of the first national parks in the United States sprang largely from the birth of a philosophical belief in the value of wilderness. As the wild frontier was tamed, a romantic reverence for wilderness emerged in the US. Its early origins are found in the mid-1800s in the nature writings of people like Ralph Waldo Emerson ("nature is the symbol of the spirit") and Henry David Thoreau. Their writings later influenced then-president Theodore Roosevelt, who laid the foundations of the US national parks network around the turn of the 20th century.

Roosevelt was also greatly influenced by John Muir, a man who is associated more closely with wilderness thinking than anyone in North America, and perhaps the world. Beginning in the 1890s, after almost losing his sight in an accident, Muir journeyed up and down the west coast of North America from California to Alaska—largely on foot. His articulate writings about the places he visited, and about the value of wilderness, had an almost religious zeal to them and influenced many people. Muir is most famous for his epic struggle to prevent Hetch Hetchy Valley in his beloved Yosemite National Park from being dammed. "Dam Hetch Hetchy," he wrote, "[a]s well dam for water tanks the people's cathedrals and churches, for no holier temple has ever been consecrated by the hand of man" (John Muir, *The Yosemite* (New York: Century, 1912) at 261–262). Although Muir eventually lost the fight, the battle marked the birth of his organization, the Sierra Club, as a potent wilderness advocate.

Although the frontier mentality began to wane in the US around the turn of the 20th century, it remained very much a part of the Canadian psyche. The creation of Canada's first national park sprang less from philosophy and more from a desire for profit. In 1883, with the help of local Indigenous peoples, railway workers discovered the Banff hot springs. The Canadian Pacific Railway (CPR) was quick to realize that the springs and the mountains could provide a popular, and profitable, destination for wealthy tourists. Anxious to enlist riders for the new railway, CPR President William Van Horne wrote to the prime minister, saying "the springs are worth a million dollars." That was enough to stir the fires of preservation in Sir John A Macdonald, who set aside Banff Park because it would provide "large pecuniary advantage to the Dominion." The first *Rocky Mountain Parks Act* (SC 1887, c 32) allowed industrial buildings, mining, and logging in the park, so long as they did not interfere with the tourist trade. Thus, the origins of Canada's national parks lie not in the preservationist zeal of a John Muir, but in the utilitarian desires of the CPR.

For most of the 20th century, Canadians continued to view nature as something to exploit for profit, even within parks. However, there were some strands of wilderness thinking.

C. WHY PARKS?

There are many reasons for creating parks. Seven of the main reasons are set out below. Note that each reason entails a somewhat different vision of what a park is.

1. *Recreation.* Parks offer prized opportunities for outdoor recreation. Different people prefer different types of recreation, ranging from wilderness hiking and canoeing to mountain biking, skiing, and car camping.
2. *Profit.* Tourism is big business. In 2018, expenditures in Canada's parks directly contributed over $4 billion to the Canadian economy.
3. *Education.* Parks provide a living laboratory for the study and appreciation of ecosystems and their component species.
4. *Spiritual value.* Certain places are viewed as sacred by some cultures, particularly Indigenous ones. For others, experiencing spectacular natural locations is of spiritual importance.
5. *Cultural heritage.* Canadian cultural identity has been deeply influenced by wilderness. In the words of Northrop Frye, "The real question is not 'who am I,' but 'where is here'" ("Conclusion" in C Klinck, ed, *Literary History of Canada* (Toronto: University of Toronto Press, 1965) at 346). If we lose wilderness, we lose the ability to understand this aspect of our past and ourselves.
6. *Protecting ecosystems for human needs.* Protecting watersheds ensures the quality and flow of rivers. Intact forests help produce clean air and absorb atmospheric carbon (mitigating climate change). Preserving a wide diversity of species ensures a broad genetic pool for use in future agricultural, medicinal, and scientific research.
7. *Intrinsic preservation.* All life has a right to exist for its own sake. Only by minimizing human intrusion in an area can it be allowed to function naturally.

The first six reasons are based on an *anthropocentric* (human-centred) viewpoint. The first two reasons favour substantial use of parks and extensive development of tourist facilities in some areas. The next four reasons favour limited human alteration of parks. The seventh reason also favours minimal human intrusion into parks but stems from an *ecocentric* viewpoint.

Most parks are created for a mixture of the reasons mentioned above. Federal parks legislation has traditionally enshrined an anthropocentric view of parks but called for a balance between use and preservation. Recent amendments, discussed below, have added an ecocentric mandate as well.

The principal argument *against* the creation of parks is that they "lock up" valuable natural resources. Many national parks are rich in natural resources. As recently as the 1950s, lead, zinc, and silver were mined in the Rocky Mountain national parks. There is a deposit of 500 million tonnes of gypsum in Wood Buffalo National Park. The parks also contain large quantities of high-grade timber. Of course, the extraction of natural resources conflicts with all of the reasons for creating parks listed above. Thus far, because of its vast size and abundant resources, Canada has been able to set aside parks while satisfying the demands for resource extraction. In future years, as our natural resource stocks are depleted, there may be increasing pressure to develop resources inside parks.

D. IS OUR PARK SYSTEM ADEQUATE TO MEET THESE NEEDS?

In designating land for parks, there are a number of important questions to be answered: How much? What size? Where? At what cost?

1. How Much?

The question of how much land to protect as parks is a political, scientific, and ethical question. The Aichi Biodiversity Targets under the United Nations *Convention on Biological Diversity*, 5 June 1992, 1760 UNTS 79, 31 ILM 818 (entered into force 29 December 1993) were agreed to by 194 countries in 2010. Among other things, the Aichi targets call for each country to protect at least 17 percent of its terrestrial area and 10 percent of its marine area by 2020.

As of 2019, only about 20 countries, including New Zealand, Thailand, Slovenia, Venezuela, and Tanzania, have met this target. Canada ranks well down the list, with about 11 percent of its lands and 9 percent of marine areas protected. With over half of its lands in a roadless condition, Canada has a globally unique opportunity to protect large, intact areas. But opportunities for parks in Canada are dwindling, particularly in the south.

2. What Size?

An ecosystem consists of a variety of organisms, existing in an interrelated web. It is difficult to put boundaries on an ecosystem, because many of its constituents—air, rivers, wildlife—will move in and out of any boundary. Still, in establishing parks, it is desirable to include an area sufficient to encompass viable populations of resident animal species. Doing so can be difficult, however. Some animals, such as bears and wolves, require 25 to 50 square kilometres per animal. A park not only must be of sufficient size, but should follow natural boundaries such as mountains or rivers that define the animals' range. A few of Canada's larger parks, such as Wood Buffalo and Kluane, support large, intact ecosystems. However, most are too small or fail to follow natural boundaries and, thus, cannot support a full range of native species.

3. Where?

Canada's landscape is a mosaic of numerous types of topography, vegetative cover, and geological makeup. It is important that protected areas cover a representative mix of the natural regions in the country. Parks Canada lists 39 different natural regions in the country. As of 2018, 30 of those regions contain national parks (although some contain provincial parks), meaning that nine new parks are needed for a fully representative national parks system. A particular problem will be creating parks in areas accessible to Canada's major population centres.

Another challenge is protecting *aquatic* areas. Traditionally, parks have been used to protect *terrestrial* areas. However, in recent years, there has been an increased focus on the establishment of marine parks, recognizing the ecological importance of oceans. The *Canada National Marine Conservation Areas Act*, SC 2002, c 18, enables the creation of a system of marine conservation areas representative of the oceans and Great Lakes. In addition, the *Oceans Act*, SC 1996, c 31, also allows for the establishment of marine-protected areas (by the minister of fisheries and oceans). As of 2019, 14 marine-protected areas have been established, and more are planned. One particular challenge in managing marine parks is that water and many aquatic species move freely across park borders.

4. At What Cost?

Creating new parks can be very expensive. For example, South Moresby National Park, created in 1988, cost the federal government $106 million. Of that amount, $50 million went to the British Columbia government, which owned the land; $26 million was paid to logging companies who held rights to log the land; and the remaining $30 million went to actual park costs.

One expense in creating a park is purchasing the land. Any government can expropriate lands without compensation if it wishes, but, for political reasons, few governments do so. Most "protected areas" legislation in Canada provides for compensation to affected owners. If an act says nothing, there is a presumption at common law that any expropriation of property entails compensation. Since most provinces have significant amounts of undeveloped Crown land, compensating landowners is often not a major expense in creating provincial parks, except near heavily populated areas. However, to create a national park, except in Northwest Territories, Nunavut, and Yukon, the federal government must purchase the land from the provincial Crown or private owners. That is why most of the large national parks in the western provinces were created before the federal government gave up ownership of public lands in 1930.

An even greater expense in creating a park can be compensating all rights holders who have an interest in the Crown land. One very important question is whether a person who holds a licence to mine or log on Crown land must be compensated when that land is set aside as a park.

THE QUEEN IN RIGHT OF BRITISH COLUMBIA V TENER
[1985] 1 SCR 533, 1985 CanLII 76, 17 DLR (4th) 1

[The respondents received a Crown grant in 1937, giving them title to certain sub-surface minerals and entitling them to use surface lands to extract the minerals. In 1973, the land in question was included in a provincial park (Wells Gray), which meant mining was not allowed. The respondents were informed that no further work on their mining claim would be permitted. They sought compensation for the alleged "expropriation."]

ESTEY J.: ...

• • •

... That an interest in minerals is an interest in land is not contested. ... Expropriation or compulsory taking occurs if the Crown or a public authority acquires from the owner an interest in property. ...

• • •

... This kind of legislative and executive action finds its counterpart in many community developments. ... Zoning illustrates the process. Ordinarily, in this country, the United States and the United Kingdom, compensation does not follow zoning either up or down. However, it has been said, at least in some courts of the United States, that a taker may not, through the device of zoning, depress the value of property as a prelude to compulsory taking of the property for a public purpose. ... The same principle was applied in this country as long ago as 1913 by the Court of Appeal of Ontario in *Re Gibson and City of Toronto*, 11 DLR 529 at 536 ...

• • •

These authorities, however, do not deal squarely with the determination of the question as to whether an expropriation has occurred in the circumstances arising in this appeal ... Here, the notice, while inviting some response by the respondents on the question of compensation, neither formally invoked the machinery of compulsory taking nor in precise terms invited a formal claim from the respondents. However, *the longstanding presumption of a right to compensation must be remembered* [emphasis added]. As Lord Atkinson stated in *Attorney-General v. De Keyser's Royal Hotel Ltd.*, [1920] AC 508 at 542, "unless the words of the statute clearly so demand, a statute is not to be construed so as to take away the property of a subject without compensation."

• • •

The respondents and their predecessors in title for many years conducted some kind of development work or operations on these lands. ... Eventually, as we have seen, the authorities advised the respondents in 1982 that no permit would be issued. ... The property rights which were granted to the respondents or their predecessors in title in 1937 were in law thereby reduced. ... The denial of access to these lands occurred under the *Park Act* [SBC 1965, c. 31] and amounts to a recovery by the Crown of a part of the right granted to the respondents in 1937. This acquisition by the Crown constitutes a taking from which compensation must flow. ...

This process I have already distinguished from zoning, the broad legislative assignment of land use to land in the community. It is also to be distinguished from regulation of specific activity on certain land, as [sic] for example, the prohibition of specified manufacturing processes. ... The imposition of zoning regulation and the regulation of activities on lands, fire regulation limits and so on, [sic] add nothing to the value of public property. Here the government wished, for obvious reasons, to preserve the qualities perceived as being desirable for public parks, and saw the mineral operations of the respondents under their 1937 grant as a threat to the park. The notice of 1978 took value from the respondents and added value to the park. ... [It] was an expropriation ... .

NOTES AND QUESTIONS

1. Following this decision, BC rezoned Mr Tener's mineral claim area as a "recreation area" within the park. Thus, mineral activity was permitted, and his compensation claim became moot. Do you agree that companies with licences to extract resources from *public* lands should be compensated for the full market value of the licence, including the future revenue it would have generated, if the land is made a park? (This is the normal rule.)

2. The BC Court of Appeal applied the *Tener* decision in a case stemming from a BC Cabinet decision to stop granting permits to mine in Strathcona Provincial Park on Vancouver Island. In *Cream Silver Mines Ltd v British Columbia*, 1993 CanLII 2878, 99 DLR (4th) 199, 75 BCLR (2d) 324 (CA), the court held that the *Tener* precedent does not apply to a "mining claim," which under BC legislation is personal property (as opposed to a "Crown grant," which is an "interest in land"). In so deciding, the court rejected as "outdated" the presumption of a right to compensation for the taking of any property interest in a park. See also *MacMillan Bloedel Ltd v British Columbia*, 2000 BCCA 422 (a logging company may bring an action for compensation against the government when its contract-based logging rights in an area are cancelled for the establishment of a park).

3. How far can the decision in *Tener* be stretched? Would stringent environmental legislation that severely restricts the use of property amount to a taking? In *Mariner Real Estate Ltd v Nova Scotia (Attorney General)*, 1999 CanLII 7241, 178 NSR (2d) 294, 177 DLR (4th) 696 (CA), several landowners claimed compensation for "de facto expropriation" when the government of Nova Scotia designated their shorefront land as a specially protected beach under the *Beaches Act*, RSNS 1989, c 32, and denied them permits to build single-family homes there. The Court of Appeal reasoned:

[65] Reliance was placed on *Tener* for the proposition that loss of economic value of land is loss of land. In my view, however, there is nothing in ... that case supporting this proposition. The case does stand for the proposition that whether an interest in land has been lost is to be judged by the *effect* of the regulation as opposed to its *form*. ...

• • •

[67] ... It was clear in *Tener* that it was not the loss of the economic value of the minerals that constituted the interest in land taken, but the complete inability to exercise the right of access to, or withdrawal of, the minerals.

The court held that the landowners did not demonstrate a loss of all viable use of the property. While their applications to build traditional homes had been rejected, the ministry had indicated that other environmentally appropriate developments for sand dunes may be acceptable. Therefore, there was no *de facto* expropriation.

E. AN OVERVIEW OF PROTECTED AREAS IN CANADA

As of 2019, approximately 11 percent of Canada's land base falls within some form of protected area. Of this total, federal areas—national parks, national wildlife areas, and migratory bird sanctuaries—account for nearly 5 percent; the remainder (6 percent) consists of provincial and territorial parks, wildlife areas, ecological reserves, and other types of conservation areas. The different types of conservation areas can be distinguished by examining two main factors:

1. *The purpose of the area.* The primary purpose of national and provincial parks is recreation (national parks have also had an ecosystem protection mandate since 1988). The recreational purpose ranges from wilderness parks to roadside rest areas. The purpose of wildlife areas and migratory bird sanctuaries is to protect wildlife and habitat, although recreation is also allowed. The primary purpose of ecological reserves is to protect ecosystems for educational and scientific purposes.

2. *What non-recreational uses are permitted?* National parks do not allow logging, mining, or sport hunting (although some parks allow traditional Indigenous hunting). The same is true of most, but not all, provincial parks. Provincial wilderness areas and ecological reserves generally do not allow logging, mining, or sport hunting. Many wildlife areas and migratory bird sanctuaries allow hunting and "commercial resource utilization."

All told, the national parks are the most protected areas in Canada. They account for about one-third of Canada's protected lands. The remainder of Section I will examine three key issues in the management of protected areas, with particular emphasis on national parks: how competing demands of different recreational users are resolved, how *internal* threats to parks are managed (particularly logging and mining), and how *external* threats are managed.

F. PLAYGROUNDS OR SANCTUARIES? RESOLVING DEMANDS OF COMPETING RECREATIONAL USERS IN PARKS

As noted above, there are a number of different reasons for establishing parks. Some reasons focus on maximizing opportunities for human recreation and enjoyment. Others focus on preserving intact ecosystems where humans are, at best, visitors. This tension is reflected in the *Canada National Parks Act*, SC 2000, c 32 [CNPA]. Section 4(1) of the CNPA sets out the overall mandate for park management:

> 4(1) The national parks of Canada are hereby dedicated to the people of Canada for their benefit, education and enjoyment, subject to this Act and the regulations, and the parks shall be maintained and *made use of* so as to leave them *unimpaired* for the enjoyment of future generations. [Emphasis added.]

Similar wording is found in many provincial parks acts. However, the mandate embodies a fundamental paradox: parks shall be "maintained unimpaired" but are for "use."

1. Parks as Playgrounds

The growing interest in recreation and the environment in recent decades has brought more and more people from around the world into Canada's parks. In 1947, there were roughly

500,000 visitors to the national parks. In 2018, there were nearly 16 million—over 4 million to Banff National Park alone. These visitors have brought with them an influx of tourist dollars that has helped to finance the budget of Parks Canada. They also have brought steadily increasing demands on the parks' limited resources. Overuse is now a significant problem in some parks.

More visitors in parks means more infrastructure used by more people. One major problem is roads. Roads fragment wildlife habitat. They also bring more cars into parks; this means more air pollution and more roadkill of animals (122 large animals—for example, deer, elk, and bear—are killed each year, on average, on highways in Jasper National Park).

More visitors has meant greater development of townsites, complete with boutiques, restaurants, motels, sewage, and garbage. It also has meant increased demand for recreational facilities, such as ski hills and golf courses, which eat into pristine habitat. For example, most of the montane (valley bottom) environment in Banff and Jasper, which comprises only 5 percent of these parks and is very fragile, is now covered with towns, tourist accommodations, airports, roads, and recreational facilities.

In the Rocky Mountain national parks, the proliferation of recreational facilities had gotten so bad that, in 1988, Parliament amended the *National Parks Act*, RSC 1985, c N-14 (which was repealed by the CNPA in 2000), to prohibit any new commercial ski areas. However, existing ski areas were allowed to develop within their lease boundaries. In 1992, a major expansion proposal by Sunshine Village ski area in Banff National Park led to a lengthy legal battle between developers and environmentalists. Sunshine Village Corporation (SVC) wanted to increase the capacity of its ski area by over 50 percent and sought approval to build new runs, lifts, a hotel, and parking facilities. The proposed parking area was particularly problematic; it would be built in a narrow valley that is an important movement corridor for bears and wolves. The company obtained approval to begin clearing ski runs while the rest of the expansion proposal was still undergoing environmental assessment. Environmentalists promptly took Parks Canada to court, arguing that the agency was required to assess the cumulative effects of the whole proposal before deciding whether to approve any particular part. SVC countersued, claiming that Parks Canada was required to approve the entire proposal, without environmental assessment, because the environment minister had given it "preliminary approval." In the end, after four years of court hearings, the Federal Court of Appeal ruled that Parks Canada was required to assess the cumulative impacts of the overall proposal, and a public review panel was appointed to do so. SVC subsequently abandoned its long-range development proposal, although the development of Goat's Eye Mountain and the expansion of other improvements did proceed. See *Sunshine Village Corp v Canada (Superintendent of Banff National Park)*, [1995] 1 FC 420, 1994 CanLII 3525, *(sub nom Canadian Parks and Wilderness Society v Banff National Park (Superintendent))* 84 FTR 273 (TD), aff'd 1996 CanLII 11890, 202 NR 132 (FCA).

The *Sunshine* case was the first legal challenge to excessive recreational development in a national park, and it marked a turning point in the struggle between recreational use and ecological protection in Canada's national parks. Since *Sunshine*, there have been several more cases about recreational development in national parks. See, for example, *Young v Canada (Attorney General)*, 1999 CanLII 8624, 174 FTR 100 (TD) (the court upheld the decision of Parks Canada to end river rafting on Jasper's Maligne River because of impacts on harlequin duck nesting areas); *Bow Valley Naturalists Society v Canada (Minister of Canadian Heritage)*, [2001] 2 FC 461, 2001 CanLII 22029 (CA) (an environmental assessment of a new Lake Louise convention centre was not required to consider cumulative impacts from secondary development); *Canadian Parks and Wilderness Society v Maligne Tours Ltd*, 2016 FC 148 (Parks Canada was authorized to give "*conceptual* approval" to build commercial cabins at Jasper's Maligne Lake, even though they were not in the park management plan); *Bowen v Canada (Attorney General)*, [1998] 2 FC 395, 1997 CanLII 6383 (TD) (closing the airstrip in Banff National Park requires an environmental assessment).

2. Parks as Wilderness

For many people, national parks represent one of the few remaining opportunities to experience solitude in a pristine wilderness setting. For them, hiking or canoeing is more than just a recreational outing; it is an opportunity to experience Canada in a way that the settlers and their native predecessors experienced it. Such experiences can contribute to mental and physical well-being and promote an appreciation of one's cultural heritage. In 1944, following a wilderness canoe voyage, a young Pierre Trudeau wrote: "I know a man whose school could never teach him patriotism, but who acquired that virtue when he felt in his bones the vastness of his land, and the greatness of those who founded it" ("Exhaustion and Fulfilment: The Aesthetic in a Canoe," in Borden Spears, ed, *Wilderness Canada* (Toronto and Vancouver: Clarke, Irwin, 1970) 4.).

The US passed the world's first *Wilderness Act* in 1964. The Act (in 16 USC § 1131 (1964)) sets out a powerful and eloquent definition of "wilderness":

A wilderness, in contrast with those areas where man and his own works dominate the landscape, is hereby recognized as an area where the earth and its community of life are untrammeled by man, where man himself is a visitor who does not remain. An area of wilderness is further defined to mean ... land retaining its primeval character and influence, without permanent improvements or human habitation, which is protected and managed so as to preserve its natural conditions ... .

Since the Act's passage, more than 4 percent of the US lands have been protected as wilderness.

Canada does not have a *Wilderness Act per se*. Some provinces have created ecological reserves and wilderness areas, but these account for less than 0.5 percent of Canada's lands. The 1988 amendments to the CNPA introduced the first vestige of federal wilderness legislation in Canada, stating:

14(1) The Governor in Council may, by regulation, declare any area of a park that exists in a natural state or that is capable of returning to a natural state to be a wilderness area.

(2) The Minister may not authorize any activity to be carried on in a wilderness area that is likely to impair the wilderness character of the area.

This provision gives substantial protection to wilderness. However, so far, only 8 of 48 national parks have had areas designated as wilderness areas, including the four Rocky Mountain national parks.

3. Zoning: The Solution?

The principal response to the overuse of parks has been zoning. Section 11(1) of the CNPA requires the preparation of a management plan for each park after public consultation. Management plans must address park zoning. There are five different zones:

1. *Zone I—Special preservation* (no motorized access or man-made facilities permitted);
2. *Zone II—Wilderness* (only primitive visitor facilities and no motorized access permitted);
3. *Zone III—Natural environment* (limited facilities and motorized access permitted);
4. *Zone IV—Outdoor recreation* (recreational facilities and motorized access permitted); and
5. *Zone V—Park services* (includes towns and visitor facilities).

The majority of national park area is either in Zone I or Zone II. In Banff, for example, 4 percent of the park is zoned as special preservation and 93 percent as wilderness.

Over 90 percent of park visitors never get more than one kilometre off the road system, venturing no further than well-maintained roadside trails or campgrounds.

For a stirring comment on commercialization and overuse of parks, see Edward Abbey, "Polemic: Industrial Tourism and the National Parks" in *Desert Solitaire: A Season in the Wilderness* (New York: McGraw-Hill, 1968).

4. Maintaining "Ecological Integrity" as the First Priority

Beginning in the early 1990s, there was growing concern about the declining health of Canada's national parks. In Banff, for example, a host of major developments as well as massive visitor increases were taking a toll on the fragile ecology of Canada's oldest park. Already one species had gone extinct, and the long-term survival of others was at risk. In 1998, the minister appointed a blue-ribbon panel to look at conserving ecological integrity in Canada's national parks. The panel concluded that national parks are under stress, and Parks Canada must make protecting ecological integrity the first priority in managing national parks.

As a result of the report, the CNPA was amended to add a strong requirement to make ecological integrity the first priority in all aspects of park management. This new provision of was the subject of a legal challenge shortly thereafter.

CANADIAN PARKS AND WILDERNESS SOCIETY V CANADA (MINISTER OF CANADIAN HERITAGE)
2003 FCA 197, [2003] 4 FC 672

[The applicant challenged a decision of the minister of Canadian heritage to approve the construction and operation of a winter road, 118 kilometres in length, through Wood Buffalo National Park. The road was being built to provide a faster north–south transportation route for Fort Smith and other communities outside the park. The park management plan stated, and Parks Canada acknowledged, that the road was not required for park management purposes.]

EVANS JA:

A. INTRODUCTION

[1] Wood Buffalo National Park is the biggest national park in Canada and one of the world's largest. ... It ... remains home to the largest herd of free-roaming bison in the world. The Park also contains the last known nesting area of the endangered whooping crane, ... and vast undisturbed boreal forests. In recognition of its ecological importance, Wood Buffalo National Park was declared a UNESCO [United Nations Educational, Scientific and Cultural Organization] world heritage site in 1987.

• • •

E. ISSUES AND ANALYSIS

[The court had to deal with several issues, including whether "the Minister's approval of the road [was] in breach of the statutory requirement that 'ecological integrity' shall be the 'first priority'" in "all aspects of park management" (at para 65).]

[66] The duty in question is contained in subsection 8(2) of the CNPA ... .

8. ...

(2) Maintenance or restoration of ecological integrity, through the protection of natural resources and natural processes, shall be the first priority of the Minister when considering all aspects of the management of parks.

• • •

Failure to consider a relevant consideration

• • •

[84] ... I am not persuaded that the Minister committed a reviewable error when she failed to refer specifically to the need to ensure that the maintenance of ecological integrity was the first priority when exercising her power to approve the road under subsection 8(1).

[85] That a decision-maker does not expressly mention a relevant consideration in the reasons for decision does not necessarily mean that it was not in fact considered. ...

• • •

Was the Minister's decision patently unreasonable on the material before her?

[92] Counsel for CPAWS [Canadian Parks and Wilderness Society] submits that the decision to approve the road is patently unreasonable in view of the Minister's duty to afford the first priority to ecological integrity and to ensure that the Park is "made use of so as to leave it unimpaired for the enjoyment of future generations" as required by subsection 4(1) of the CNPA.

• • •

(I) PARK PURPOSES

[94] CPAWS submits that national parks are created for the "benefit, education and enjoyment" of the people of Canada (subsection 4(1) of the CNPA) and that the satisfaction of local and regional transportation needs is irrelevant to the attainment of these statutory objects. Hence, since the road proposed for Wood Buffalo National Park is intended to provide improved road transportation for people living in and adjacent to the Park, it does not further the purposes that subsection 4(1) declares that national parks serve. There was thus no competing priority against which the Minister could legitimately balance the restoration and maintenance of ecological integrity.

[95] ... I am not persuaded that [this] is correct. In my opinion, subsection 4(1) does not provide a comprehensive statement of the purposes for which the Minister may exercise her powers of management of national parks ... [S]ubsection 4(1) is not worded as a statutory objects or purposes clause: it merely states for what purposes parks are created. It is not necessary that every action taken by the Minister advances one or more of the purposes for which parks were established, namely, "the benefit, education and enjoyment" of the people of Canada.

• • •

[98] Accordingly, in principle the Minister could approve the road proposal, even though it was not required for the operation of the Park or for the benefit, education and enjoyment of the people of Canada as a whole ... [and] it does not advance any of the reasons for which national parks are created as set out in subsection 4(1).

• • •

(II) DAMAGE TO THE PARK'S ECOLOGICAL INTEGRITY

• • •

[10] CPAWS' argument is that the material before the Minister identified a variety of environmental harms that the construction of the road might cause and that, given her duty under subsection 8(2), her approval of the road was unreasonable. ...

[102] The weakness of this part of CPAWS' case is indicated by the fact that its memorandum of fact and law does not specify in what respects the ecological integrity of the Park would be degraded if the road were built. ...

• • •

[106] In conclusion, even though the Minister did not specifically state that she had applied her mind to the concept of ecological integrity itself and to her duty to afford it the first priority, the material before her, and the analysis of it in the reasons for decision, amply demonstrate that the Minister's approval of the road was not unreasonable ... . She cannot be said to have been dismissive of ecological integrity, nor to have treated the evidence pertaining to it in a summary manner.

NOTES AND QUESTIONS

1. Do you agree with the reasoning of Evans JA that (a) the minister should be presumed to have considered ecological integrity despite never mentioning it in her reasons, and (b) by considering "adverse environmental effects" under the *Canadian Environmental Assessment Act*, SC 1992, c 37 (now the *Impact Assessment Act*, SC 2019, c 28, s 1), the minister also satisfied her duty to give first priority to "ecological integrity" under the CNPA? Are the two the same?

2. The judge noted that the applicant had not specified how the park's ecological integrity would be degraded if the road were built. How do you think that affected his decision? It is often said that "bad facts make bad law."

3. The winter road through Wood Buffalo National Park was not constructed, in part, because a local First Nation had successfully challenged its approval on the basis of failure to consult on trapping and other rights. The Supreme Court of Canada, in *Mikisew Cree First Nation v Canada (Minister of Canadian Heritage)*, 2005 SCC 69, [2005] 3 SCR 388, reasoned:

> 44 ... The Draft Environmental Assessment Report acknowledged the road could potentially result in a diminution in quantity of the Mikisew harvest of wildlife, as fewer furbearers ... will be caught in their traps ... [and] the more lucrative or rare species of furbearers may decline in population. Other potential impacts include fragmentation of wildlife habitat, disruption of migration patterns, loss of vegetation, increased poaching because of easier motor vehicle access to the area and increased wildlife mortality due to motor vehicle collisions. [I]t is apparent that the proposed road will adversely affect the existing Mikisew hunting and trapping rights, and therefore ... "trigger" ... the duty to consult ... .

> • • •

> 64 ... The Crown was required to provide notice to the Mikisew and to engage directly with them (and not, as seems to have been the case here, as an afterthought to a general public consultation with Park users). ... The Crown was required to solicit and to listen carefully to the Mikisew concerns, and to attempt to minimize adverse impacts on the Mikisew hunting, fishing and trapping rights.

4. How should the balance between Aboriginal rights to hunt and trap and the conservation goals of parks be struck, keeping in mind s 35 of the *Canadian Charter of Rights and
Freedoms*, Part I of the *Constitution Act, 1982*, being Schedule B to the *Canada Act 1982* (UK),
1982, c 11?

G. THREATS TO PARKS

Overuse is far from the only threat to the integrity of parks. The 11 percent of Canada's lands
within protected areas is subject to severe encroachments, both from within and without.

1. Internal Threats

a. National Parks

Section 4(1) of the CNPA dictates that national parks be maintained "unimpaired for the enjoyment of future generations." Despite these lofty words, some parks are anything but
unimpaired.

One problem is *pollution*. Sewage from townsites and ski areas in Banff and Jasper national
parks has significantly degraded water quality in the once-pristine Bow and Athabasca rivers.
Dump sites for waste from towns and visitor facilities in parks attract bears and scar the park
landscape. A number of parks are bisected by highways, and roadkills (as well as railroad kills)
are a significant threat to park wildlife. Also, park highways are used by trucks carrying dangerous cargo. An accident could cause a spill of toxic substances within a park. See s 32 of the
CNPA, directed at the discharge of harmful substances in a park.

Another potential problem is *resource extraction*—including logging, mining, and oil drilling. Many parks are rich in natural resources. In the parks' early years, resource extraction was
sanctioned as long as it did not interfere with tourism. In the 1920s, the federal government
avoided many resource conflicts by simply removing resource-rich areas from parks.

Resource extraction is now illegal in national parks, and has been since 1930 (one exception is "traditional renewable resource harvesting" by Indigenous peoples—which the CNPA
specifically authorizes in some parks (s 17)). However, the prohibition against resource extraction has frequently been honoured in its breach.

Throughout the 1930s, 1940s, and 1950s, mining of silver, lead, and zinc continued in
Glacier, Yoho, and Kootenay national parks. During the same era, commercial logging was
taking place in Prince Albert, Riding Mountain, Wood Buffalo, and the four Rocky Mountain
national parks. Wood Buffalo and Riding Mountain even had sawmills in the parks! In 1964,
Parks Canada stopped issuing new logging and mining permits, and, by 1969, it had bought up
most of the existing rights. Still, logging rights remain in Banff and Terra Nova and Wood Buffalo national parks. For more information, see L Bella, *Parks for Profit* (Montreal: Harvest
House, 1987).

Over the years, these incursions into parks had provoked public outcry, but never *litigation*
(as has been used frequently to protect parks in the US). One reason was that, until 1986, only
persons whose private property or economic interests were affected had standing to bring a
judicial review action. This ruled out action over parks, which, by definition, were public property. The decision in *Finlay v Canada (Minister of Finance)*, [1986] 2 SCR 607, 1986 CanLII 6
extended standing to public interest groups. In 1992, for the first time ever, a lawsuit challenging development activity within a national park was launched. Newly formed Ecojustice went
to court, on behalf of the Canadian Parks and Wilderness Society, to strike down a federal
licence permitting logging in Wood Buffalo National Park. Before trial, the federal government
conceded that the licence was illegal, and the Federal Court issued a consent judgment,
declaring the licence and the implementing order in council "invalid and unauthorized by the

provisions of the *National Parks Act*" (in particular, s 4). See *Canadian Parks and Wilderness Society v Superintendent of Wood Buffalo National Park*, [1992] FCJ No 553 (QL) (TD). Future cases will be needed to determine exactly what other development activities violate s 4. Would construction of a new paved highway through a park violate s 4? A new golf course? Is cattle grazing in Grasslands National Park unlawful?

b. Provincial Parks

Resource extraction poses a greater threat in *provincial* protected areas, which account for almost 50 percent of Canada's conservation lands. In most provinces, wildlife areas are legally open to resource extraction. Of even greater concern are provincial parks—areas that one might expect to be protected from resource extraction. Most provinces' parks legislation has a dedication clause similar to the one in s 4 of the CNPA. Ontario's *Provincial Parks and Conservation Reserves Act, 2006*, SO 2006, c 12, s 6, reads:

> 6. Ontario's provincial parks ... are dedicated to the people of Ontario and visitors for their inspiration, education, health, recreational enjoyment and other benefits with the intention that these areas shall be managed to maintain their ecological integrity and to leave them unimpaired for future generations.

What is the main difference between this provision and s 4 of the CNPA? Similar dedications—but without the "unimpaired" requirement—can be found in parks legislation in New Brunswick (*Parks Act*, RSNB 2011, c 202, s 3), Saskatchewan (*Parks Act*, SS 1986, c P-1.1, s 3(1)), Nova Scotia (*Provincial Parks Act*, RSNS 1989, c 367, s 2(2)), and BC (*Park Act*, RSBC 1996, c 344, s 5(3)).

Despite these dedication provisions, most provincial parks laws do not prohibit logging, mining, or other forms of resource extraction. That is not to say that resource extraction is actively occurring in provincial parks; in most provinces, it is presently not allowed as a matter of *policy*. But policies are not enforceable and can be changed. Moreover, resource extraction *is* actively occurring in a number of provincial parks. For example, Ontario's Algonquin Provincial Park, one of the most popular parks in Canada, is being logged extensively, and logging in Manitoba's Duck Mountain Provincial Park has been upheld as lawful (*Western Canada Wilderness Committee v Manitoba*, 2013 MBCA 11). Several mines have operated in Strathcona Provincial Park—BC's oldest park—for decades, and oil drilling is occurring in Alberta's Dinosaur Provincial Park, which is a UN World Heritage Site.

Quebec appears to be one of the few provinces that excludes resource extraction in all provincial parks (*Parks Act*, CQLR c P-9, s 7). However, most of Quebec's protected lands are in wildlife areas, where resource extraction is allowed. Check the provincial parks legislation in your area. Does it allow resource extraction? In what parks is such extraction occurring?

2. External Threats

The greatest threat to parks comes from activities outside their borders. No park is a self-contained ecosystem. All have air and water that flow in and out as well as species that range beyond park borders. What goes on outside a park can have effects inside it. This is known as the "island effect," because the park becomes an island of protection amidst a sea of development.

Examples are not hard to find. Vast expanses of clear-cut forest surround Pacific Rim National Park—right up to its border. In fact, all of BC's national parks as well as the four Rocky Mountain national parks are bordered by logging operations. Not only is such logging a visual eyesore, but it can damage a park's ecology by affecting its water quality and soil temperature and stability and by degrading the habitat of animals that range beyond the park.

Water and air pollution also moves freely into parks. Many of the lakes in Ontario's Killarney Provincial Park were virtually dead in the 1980s due to acid rain caused by the nearby INCO plant in Sudbury, until tougher sulphur dioxide laws were passed. Municipalities, pulp mills, and other industries upstream from parks discharge toxic pollutants into waters that flow into park rivers and lakes (as is happening in Wood Buffalo National Park). Dams and water diversions have significantly affected the aquatic ecosystems of Wood Buffalo and Grasslands national parks.

If our parks are to remain unimpaired islands amidst an increasingly developed landscape, solutions to the external threats problem must be found. One future solution is to create parks large enough to contain relatively complete ecosystems. In the meantime, the most effective solution is for park managers to coordinate with private and government landowners around parks. Thus far, efforts to do so have met with only limited success, since adjacent owners have no incentive to restrict development in order to protect nearby parks. This problem is further exacerbated for national parks, because it is generally provinces that are in charge of land management and pollution control around their borders. Thus, the problem becomes one not only of coordinating between departments, but of coordinating between different governments, often from opposing political parties.

In the US, this problem has been addressed, to some extent, by law. The federal *Clean Air Act* and *Clean Water Act* impose stringent limits on emissions that affect national parks and wilderness areas (see 42 USC §§ 7470(2), 7472, 7473(b), 7475(d)(2), 7491). Also, the *Wilderness Act* has been interpreted to require protection of adequate water flows in wilderness areas (*Sierra Club v Block*, 622 F Supp 842 (D Col 1985). In Canada, unfortunately, federal environmental and wildlife laws make no special provision for activities that affect parks.

3. The Public Trust Doctrine

Another legal approach that has been used in the US to address external threats to parks is the public trust doctrine. The origins of this doctrine lie in Roman, and later English, common law. The public had a right of access to all navigable waters for purposes such as fishing and navigation, and the sovereign had a duty to manage all navigable waters so as to uphold this right (*Gann v Free Fishers of Whitstable* (1865), 11 HL Cas 192, 11 ER 1305). The Canadian courts have adopted this common law duty, but they have neither expanded its scope nor explicitly labelled it as a trust obligation (*Rhodes v Perusse*, 41 SCR 264, 1908 CanLII 47). US courts, however, have done both.

In 1892, the US Supreme Court clearly stated that the government's duty to preserve public access to waters was a trust duty. In so doing, the court struck down the Illinois legislature's attempt to convey a large area of submerged land along the shore of Lake Michigan to a private railway (*Illinois Central Railway Co v Illinois*, 146 US 387 (1892)). Subsequent US cases have gone even further and extended the public trust obligation to apply to public lands, particularly parks. For example, a Massachusetts court struck down a statute that authorized construction of a private ski resort in a state park (*Gould v Greylock Reservation Commission*, 215 NE (2d) 114 (Mass 1966)).

The US public trust doctrine is not an outright prohibition against government alienation of interests in public lands and waters. To do so, in effect, would be to give to the courts the policy-making role of elected legislatures. Rather, the doctrine has evolved to mean as follows:

> When a state holds a resource which is available for the free use of the general public, a court will look with considerable skepticism upon any government conduct which is calculated either to reallocate that resource to more restricted uses or to subject public uses to the self interest of private parties.

(Joseph L Sax, "The Public Trust Doctrine in Natural Resources Law: Effective Judicial Intervention" (1970) 68 Mich L Rev 471 at 484.)

In 2004, the Supreme Court of Canada, in *British Columbia v Canadian Forest Products Ltd*,
2004 SCC 38, [2004] 2 SCR 74 [*Canfor*], opened the door to potential adoption of the public
trust doctrine in Canada. The issue was whether the BC government could sue a forestry company for ecological damages caused to Crown forests. After tracing the history of the public trust
doctrine in the US and its origins in European and Roman law, the court (at para 76) found that

> [s]ince the time of [Henry] de Bracton [who wrote a treatise on English law in the 13th cen-
> tury] ... [t]his notion of the Crown as holder of inalienable "public rights" in the environment
> and certain common resources was accompanied by the procedural right of the Attorney
> General to sue for their protection representing the Crown as *parens patriae*.

The court (at para 81) recognized that this finding raised questions about "the existence or
non-existence of enforceable *fiduciary duties owed to the public* by the Crown in that regard"
[emphasis added], but concluded (at para 82) "[t]his is not a proper appeal ... to embark on a
consideration of these difficult issues."

Since *Canfor*, the issue of a public trust obligation has come up in several lower court deci-
sions, but it has yet to be adopted by the Canadian judiciary. See *PEI v Canada (Fisheries &*
Oceans), 2006 PESCAD 27, *(sub nom PEI v Can (AG))* 263 Nfld & PEIR 4, 798 APR 4; and *Burns*
Bog Conservation Society v Canada, 2014 FCA 170, 464 NR 187.

The public trust concept has been explicitly incorporated by statute in a number of US states
and in several Canadian provinces and territories (see Chapter 20). For more information on the
public trust doctrine in Canada and the US, see Mary Christina Wood, *Nature's Trust: Environ-*
mental Law for a New Ecological Age (New York: Cambridge University Press, 2014); Jerry
DeMarco, Marcia Valiante & Marie-Ann Bowden, "Opening the Door for Common Law Environmental Protection in Canada: The Decision in British Columbia v Canadian Forest Products Ltd"
(2005) 15 J Envtl L & Prac 233; and Anna Lund, "Canadian Approaches to America's Public Trust
Doctrine: Classic Trusts, Fiduciary Duties & Substantive Review" (2012) 23 J Envtl L & Prac 135.

The common law public trust doctrine has provided the intellectual roots for US courts to
find a statutory public trust duty flowing from parks legislation and affecting the management
of lands in and around national parks.

SIERRA CLUB V DEPARTMENT OF INTERIOR
376 F Supp 90 (ND Cal 1974) [footnotes omitted]

[Redwood National Park was created in 1968. The park sheltered some of the last
remaining stands of California's magnificent 100-metre-high redwood trees—some
of which had been growing for nearly 2,000 years. Logging on the steep-sloped
lands (both private and federal) surrounding the park was seriously affecting soil
stability and water quality within the park. The Sierra Club filed an action alleging
that the secretary of the interior was violating his statutory trust obligation by failing
to take action to protect the park's ecological resources.]

SWEIGERT, District Judge:

• • •

The *National Park System Act*, 16 U.S.C.A. Sec. 1, provides for the creation of the
National Park Service in the Department of the Interior which Service shall:

regulate the use of Federal areas known as national parks ... to conserve the scenery and the natural and historic objects and the wildlife therein and to provide for the enjoyment of the same in such manner and by such means as will leave them *unimpaired for the enjoyment of future generations* [emphasis added].

In addition to these general *fiduciary obligations* [emphasis added] ...of the Secretary of the Interior, the Secretary has been invested with certain specific powers and obligations in connection with the unique situation of the Redwood National Park. ...

• • •

Title 16 U.S.C. Sec. 79c(e) provides:

In order to afford as full protection as is reasonably possible to the timber, soil, and streams within the boundaries of the park, the Secretary is authorized ... to acquire interests in land from, and to enter into contracts and cooperative agreements with, the owners of land on the periphery of the park and on watershed tributary to streams within the park designed to assure that the consequences of forestry management, timbering, land use, and soil conservation practices conducted thereon ... will not adversely affect the timber, soil, and streams within the park as aforesaid.

• • •

In *Rockbridge v. Lincoln*, 449 F.2d 567 (9th Cir. 1971) our Circuit ...held that, in view of the trust relationship of the Secretary toward the Indians... such discretion as was vested in the Secretary was not an unbridled discretion. ...

In view of the analogous trust responsibility of the Secretary of the Interior with respect to public lands as stated in *Knight* v. *United Land, supra*, ... we consider *Rockbridge, supra*, to be strongly persuasive to the point that a case for judicial relief has been made out by plaintiff.

• • •

We are of the opinion that the terms of the statute ... impose a legal duty on the Secretary to utilize the specific powers given to him whenever reasonably necessary for the protection of the park and that any discretion vested in the Secretary ... is subordinate to his paramount legal duty imposed, not only under his *trust obligation* but by the statute itself, to protect the park. [Emphasis added.]

NOTES AND QUESTIONS

1. In a second decision, the court determined that the secretary had violated his statutory and public trust obligations (*Sierra Club v Department of Interior*, 398 F Supp 284 (ND Cal 1975)). The secretary had entered into cooperative agreements with several logging companies, as contemplated by the *Redwood National Park Act*, 16 USC § 79a *et seq*, but the court found (at 293, 293) that the agreements were "so general and so full of qualifications as to render them practically meaningless and unenforceable" and were "inadequate to prevent or reasonably minimize damage to the resources of the Park resulting from timber harvesting operations." The court ordered the secretary to come up with a plan of action by a certain date, and the court would judge its adequacy. Does this remedy strike an adequate balance between the court's duty to review the legality of agency action and its duty not to take over the role of government?

2. In 1978, following a third court case, Congress expanded Redwood National Park by purchasing the lands in dispute.

In Canada, the issue of whether a public trust obligation existed over lands in and around a park was also litigated in the 1970s, with a very different result.

GREEN V THE QUEEN IN RIGHT OF THE PROVINCE OF ONTARIO
1972 CanLII 538, [1973] 2 OR 396, 34 DLR (3d) 20 (H Ct J)

The statement of claim ... sets out s. 2 of the *Provincial Parks Act* which states:

> 2. All provincial parks are dedicated to the people of the Province of Ontario and others who may use them for their healthful enjoyment and education, and the provincial parks shall be maintained for the benefit of future generations in accordance with this Act and the regulations.

and on the basis of s. 2 alleges that it imposes a trust upon the Province of Ontario with regard to Sandbanks Provincial Park, to maintain that park in keeping with the "spirit" of s. 2 and that by permitting the use of the adjoining lands [for sand excavation by a cement company]... were in breach of the trust implicit in s. 2 set out above.

Notwithstanding the philosophical and noble intentions (my expression) of the Legislature to express in [s 2 of the *Provincial Parks Act*, RSO 1970, c 371] an ideological concept, no statutory trust has been created. It becomes necessary to break down the wording thereof: "All provincial parks are dedicated to the people of the Province of Ontario and others who may use them ... ." This simply makes it clear that all persons ... are entitled to make use of the parks ... ."... [A]nd the provincial parks shall be maintained for the benefit of future generations in accordance with this Act and the regulations" implies that the Province of Ontario is required to physically maintain the parks so dedicated. ...

• • •

... [T]he Province of Ontario cannot be held to be a trustee. Section 3(2) cannot be construed as *compelling* the Province to hold these lands or for that matter any park lands, [sic] for any certain period of time or forever for the purposes that are alleged by the respondent to be read into s. 2 of the *Provincial Parks Act*.

[The action was dismissed with costs.]

NOTES AND QUESTIONS

1. The judge found that the plaintiff lacked standing because he had no "special interest above that of the general public." Would he be denied standing today?

2. The judge applied strict trust law to reach his finding (which the US court in the first *Sierra Club* case did not do). He then (at 407) accused the plaintiffs of bringing an "ill-founded actions for the sake of using the Courts as a vehicle for expounding philosophy." Compare the two judgments. Do differences in the facts or legislation explain the widely different decisions? If not, what does?

3. Ontario has now strengthened the wording of the dedication section in the *Provincial Parks and Conservation Reserves Act*, s 6 (see above). Also, the Act now requires approval of the legislature to reduce the size of a park by more than 1 percent—it cannot simply be done by Cabinet order. Do these changes affect the judge's trust law analysis?

4. Shortly after the *Green* decision, the province announced that it would expropriate the lease of Lake Ontario Cement Ltd, although it claimed that the litigation played no role in its decision.

5. A recent Federal Court of Appeal decision also took a conventional trust law approach in rejecting a public trust claim (*Burns Bog Conservation Society*).

6. In the first *Sierra Club* case, the public trust obligation was supported by analogy to the trust obligation toward "Indians." In Canada, the courts also have found a "fiduciary duty" to Indigenous peoples (*Guerin v R*, [1984] 2 SCR 335, 13 DLR (4th) 321). Compare s 18(1) of the *Indian Act*, RSC 1985, c I-5, with s 4(1) of the CNPA.

7. A 2001 case considered the issue of the Crown's jurisdiction to regulate activity *outside* the boundaries of a park. A tourist operator set up a float camp just outside Gwaii Haanas National Park in BC. Parks Canada determined that the camp interfered with the wilderness experience within the park and that it also was inconsistent with plans to make the adjacent aquatic area a marine park. Parks Canada refused to issue the operator a quota to use the park for its kayaking and diving tours. The operator went to court, challenging the authority of Parks Canada to make decisions based on activities occurring outside a park. The Federal Court, in *Moresby Explorers Ltd v Canada (Attorney General)*, 2001 FCT 780, [2001] 4 FC 591, agreed, reasoning (at para 108):

> [108] ... [T]here are legitimate conservation and ecological issues arising from unregu-lated float camp operation [*sic*] in remote areas which abut onto park lands. The mandate conferred on the Minister and the Superintendent to preserve the ecological integrity of the park lands gives them a legitimate interest in the conduct of operations in areas which impact on the park lands. But a legitimate interest is not the same as a right to prohibit that which is otherwise lawful in an area outside the park's jurisdiction by means of conditions attached to a park business licence. ... In my view, the mandate conferred by the *National Parks Act* does not extend to regulating behaviour outside park boundaries through the device of business licences on the ground of conservation.

The judge did not explain *why* the CNPA does not authorize Parks Canada to address activities that are outside a park and detrimental to the park. Do you agree with the decision?

8. For more discussion of the issues surrounding Canada's parks, see Monte Hummel, ed, *Endangered Spaces: The Future for Canada's Wilderness* (Toronto: Key Porter Books, 1989); Parks Canada, *Canada's Conservation Vision: A Report of the National Advisory Panel* (23 March 2018), online (pdf): <https://static1.squarespace.com/static/57e007452e69cf9a7af0a033/t/5b23dce1562fa7bac7ea095a/1529076973600/NAP_REPORT_EN_June+5_ACC.pdf>; and CPAWS, *Canada's Nature Emergency: Scaling up Solutions for Land and Freshwater* (2019), online (pdf): *CPAWS* <https://cpaws.org/wp-content/uploads/2019/07/CPAWS_ParksReport2019_fnl_web2.pdf>.

II. ENDANGERED SPECIES

To keep every cog and wheel is the first precaution of intelligent tinkering.

Aldo Leopold, *A Sand County Almanac*
(New York: Oxford University Press, 1949)

A. DEFINING THE PROBLEM

1. The Extent of the Problem

Species extinction has been a natural fact of life on Earth for billions of years. Over 90 percent of the species that have inhabited the Earth at one time are now extinct. Thus, extinction *per se* is not a problem. What is a problem is the alarming *rate of extinction* in recent decades.

Although no one knows for certain, scientists estimate that, before the last few millennia, an average of two to three species of plants and animals went extinct every year worldwide. Natural processes were able to replace these species, and then some. Currently, conservative estimates indicate that we are losing two to three species *per day* worldwide, but the rate may be more like two to three species *per hour*. It is simply impossible to know for sure, since only 1.2 million out of an estimated 9 million species have been discovered.

Canada, because of its northern latitude, has fewer species than tropical countries. Having fewer species means that the loss of a small number of them will have more drastic effects on Canada's ecosystems than it would on more diverse tropical ecosystems. In Canada, there are currently 430 plant and animal species officially listed as endangered or threatened (by comparison, in the US, there are over 1,660). These include well-known species such as the beluga whale and wood bison and lesser-known ones such as Furbish's lousewort. Even these alarming numbers vastly understate the problem. Lack of firm data means that many species suspected of being endangered have not yet been listed. Moreover, we may be driving countless species that we have not yet discovered to extinction.

One thing that all scientists can agree on is that the rate of extinction is rising rapidly. Today's endangered species are a prophecy of wide-scale extinctions in the future if current practices are not reversed soon.

2. Why Save Species?

There are many reasons for saving species, some anthropocentric and some ecocentric:

- *Ecosystem benefits.* Wild plants and animals play an important role in maintaining the planet's ecological functions. Plants clean the air and preserve the carbon balance. Microorganisms break down pollutants in water and on land, and they renourish the soil. In short, all life is a complex, interrelated web. Humans are dependent upon other species for our survival. Just how many strands of the web we can cut before the web starts to collapse, we do not know.
- *Food.* Species of plants and animals make up virtually all the food we eat. We use less than 4 percent of known plant species for food. If we are to produce enough food to meet the needs of a rapidly growing population, we will need to explore the potential of many more species. Moreover, in many places around the world, including Canada, wild plants and animals still provide a major food source for Indigenous peoples.
- *Medicinal uses.* Nearly half of the medicine prescribed in North America comes from natural species. Yet only a small percentage of the Earth's species have been screened to determine their medicinal value. For example, BC's Pacific yew tree was long regarded as a weed and cut indiscriminately until it was found to contain taxol, which has become one of the most important drugs in fighting cancer.
- *Recreational and aesthetic benefits.* Wildlife viewing is very popular—over 60 percent of Canadians enjoy it. In fact, bird watching is now the world's most popular hobby. Wildlife plays an important role in Canadians' national identity. Wild animals adorn our currency, our artwork, and even our flags. They provide a sense of fascination and awe, reminding us of our "wild" roots.
- *Economic benefits.* Protecting species makes good sense ecologically and economically. In 2012, Canadians spent an estimated $41.3 billion on nature and wildlife-related activities.

- *Ethical reasons.* Many people believe that all species have an inherent right to exist. They find it arrogant for human beings, who have occupied the planet for only a tiny fraction of its history, to wipe out many other species simply to meet their own insatiable needs. This ethic has been best expressed by Leopold (1949):

The first ethics dealt with the relation between individuals; the Mosaic Decalogue is an example. Later accretions dealt with the relations between the individual and society. The Golden Rule tries to integrate the individual into society; democracy to integrate social organization to the individual.

There is no ethic yet dealing with man's relation to land and the plants and animals which grow upon it. Land, like Odysseus's slave-girls, is still property. The land relation is still strictly economic, entailing privileges but not obligations. The extension of ethics to this third element in human environment is, if I read the evidence correctly, an evolutionary possibility and an ecological necessity. It is the third step in a sequence. ...

All ethics so far evolved rest upon a single premise: that the individual is a member of a community of interdependent parts. ... The land ethic simply enlarges the boundaries of the community to include soils, waters, plants, and animals, or collectively, the land.

For a more detailed discussion, see Mattia Fosci & Tom West, "In Whose Interest? Instrumental and Intrinsic Value in Biodiversity Law" in Michael Bowman, Peter Davies & Edward Goodwin, eds, *Research Handbook on Biodiversity and Law* (Cheltenham, UK; Northampton, Mass: Edward Elgar, 2016). See also Chapters 1 and 2 of this book.

3. Threats to Species

Human interference is the cause of most extinctions. The current rate of extinction is at least 1,000 times higher than the natural rate. The explosion of the human population in recent decades has pushed human settlements into most corners of the planet, displacing many other resident species. Our increasing demand for resources has further accelerated the problem. Human consumption now captures over 40 percent of the Earth's net primary productivity (living matter produced by the sun's photosynthetic energy)—the basis of life on Earth.

Some of the main threats facing species are:

- *Habitat loss.* The single most important cause of extinction is destruction of habitat that species need for their survival. Over 80 percent of species decline in Canada can be traced to habitat loss. Seventy-five percent of Canada's original prairie has been paved over or plowed, including 99 percent of tall-grass prairie. Southern Ontario—the most densely populated region in Canada—has lost more than 90 percent of its original Carolinian forests and wetlands, giving it the nation's highest concentration of endangered species.
- *Direct human exploitation.* Hunting and harvesting of species is another major cause of extinction. Historically, many species, such as the passenger pigeon, which once numbered in the billions and could blacken the sky for days, were hunted to extinction. Today, many of the world's endangered species, including elephants and rhinoceroses, are still hunted (legally and illegally). In Canada, this is less of a problem, but some threatened species, such as the grizzly bear, are open for hunting, and others are subject to poaching.
- *Pollution.* Pollution of the air and water threatens numerous species. The poisoning of the Great Lakes and acidification of many lakes in eastern Canada has reduced stocks of fish and other organisms. Pollution of rivers and coastal areas is placing stress on aquatic species. For example, beluga whales inhabiting the mouth of the St Lawrence River absorb so much toxic pollution that when they die and wash up on shore, they sometimes must be disposed of as hazardous waste.
- *Climate change.* Another growing threat is climate change, which is predicted to significantly alter the planet's natural regions, resulting in a substantial displacement of species.

It already has caused a thickening of the ice sheet covering Canada's Arctic islands, resulting in the near-extinction of the Peary caribou. And it is the main reason why most polar bear populations are declining.

This is not to say that all human-induced change must stop. To live, like all species, humans must affect other organisms. Species can tolerate some change, and most can adapt, given enough time. What must stop is the current rate and extent of human intervention.

For a comprehensive global review of threats to biodiversity and the drivers, see Eduardo S Brondizio et al (eds), *Global Assessment Report on Biodiversity and Ecosystem Services* (2019), online: *IPBES* <https://www.ipbes.net/global-assessment-report-biodiversity-ecosys-tem-services>. For a Canadian assessment, see *Living Planet Report Canada: A National Look at Wildlife Loss* (2017), online: *WWF-Canada* <http://www.wwf.ca/about_us/lprc/>.

4. Endangered Species Legislation

Near the turn of the century, Canadian governments took measures to help save the beaver from excessive trapping and to protect habitat for the rapidly disappearing bison. The signing of the *Migratory Birds Convention*, [1916] CTS 465, with the US was designed to protect migratory birds from overhunting and other threats. These isolated efforts typified the approach to species protection for most of the past century. It was not until the 1970s that North American governments began to pass legislation to address the problem of overall species extinction directly.

B. US LEGISLATION

The US was the first country to pass legislation protecting endangered species. The US *Endangered Species Act* (ESA) was passed in 1966 and significantly strengthened in 1973 (16 USC § 1531 *et seq*). The current Act has three main steps:

1. listing of all endangered and threatened species;
2. designation and protection of critical habitat for all listed species; and
3. prohibition against "takings" of any listed species.

In addition, there are at least two other important provisions: the US Fish and Wildlife Service must develop a recovery plan for each listed species, and all federal agencies must "insure that actions authorized, funded or carried out by them do not jeopardize the continued existence of an endangered species" (ESA, s 7).

One major strength of the US legislation is that its mandatory wording allows citizens to go to court, if necessary, to compel agencies to carry out their species protection duties. The importance of these citizen enforcement powers was demonstrated in the *Spotted Owl* litigation, which dealt with the Act's first two steps—listing and critical habitat designation.

NORTHERN SPOTTED OWL (STRIX OCCIDENTALS CAURINA) V HODEL
716 F Supp 479 (WD Wash 1988)

[The US Fish and Wildlife Service's ("Service") expert review of the spotted owl's status concluded "continued old growth harvesting is likely to lead to the extinction of the subspecies in the foreseeable future which argues strongly for listing ... as threatened or endangered ... ." Peer reviewers agreed. Three days later, the Service concluded that listing was "not warranted at that time". Environmental groups challenged the decision in court. District Judge Zilly concluded the following:]

The Service's documents ... lack any expert analysis supporting its conclusion. Rather, the expert opinion is entirely to the contrary. ...

• • •

The Court will reject conclusory assertions of agency "expertise" where the agency spurns unrebutted expert opinions without itself offering a credible alternative explanation. ... Here, the Service disregarded all the expert opinion on population viability, including that of its own expert, that the owl is facing extinction, and instead merely asserted its expertise in support of its conclusions. ...

[T]he decision not to list at this time the northern spotted owl as endangered or threatened under the *Endangered Species Act* was arbitrary and capricious and contrary to law.

In June 1990, 19 months after the court's decision, the Fish and Wildlife Service listed the spotted owl as a "threatened" species. However, the owl was not out of the woods yet. A second case focused on the failure of the Fish and Wildlife Service to designate the owl's critical habitat.

NORTHERN SPOTTED OWL V LUJAN
758 F Supp 621 (WD Wash 1991) [footnotes omitted]

ZILLY, District Judge:

• • •

Plaintiffs move this Court to order the federal defendants to designate "critical habitat" for the northern spotted owl. As defined under the ESA, "critical habitat" refers to geographic areas which are essential to the conservation of the spotted owl and which may require special management considerations or protection. ...

• • •

The [Secretary of the Interior], through the Service, claims that critical habitat for the spotted owl was not "determinable" when, in June 1989, the Service proposed to list the owl as threatened ... [and] that, under these circumstances, they are entitled to a twelve-month extension of time ...

• • •

The language employed in Section 4(a)(3) ... evidence[s] a clear design by Congress that designation of critical habitat coincide with the species listing determination. ... [I]t reflects the studied and deliberate judgment of Congress that destruction of habitat was the most significant cause of species endangerment. ...

• • •

This Court rejects as incongruous the federal defendants' argument that Section 4(b)(6)(C) authorizes an automatic extension of time merely upon a finding that critical habitat is not presently "determinable," even where no effort has been made to secure the information necessary to make the designation. To relieve the Secretary of any affirmative information gathering responsibilities would effectively nullify Congress' charge that the species listing and habitat designation occur concurrently, "to the maximum extent ... determinable." 16 U.S.C. § 1533(a)(3).

• • •

The Service's actions in June 1990 merit special mention. In its final rule the Service stated that the northern spotted owl is "overwhelmingly associated" with mature and old-growth forests. ... The Service further stated that, at present rates of timber harvesting, much of the remaining spotted owl habitat will be gone within 20 to 30 years. ... Despite such dire assessments, the Service declined to designate critical habitat in its final rule ... . Whatever the precise contours of the Service's obligations under the ESA, clearly the law does not approve such conduct.

[The court ordered the Service to publish its proposed critical habitat plan within 90 days and to designate critical habitat as soon as possible thereafter.]

NOTES

1. The lead plaintiff in each case is the spotted owl itself. This is not because owls, or trees, have standing under US law. US courts have developed a principle of "standing for one means standing for all" to avoid frivolous challenges to the standing of some plaintiffs where at least one plaintiff clearly has standing. This principle allowed the spotted owl to be listed as the lead plaintiff, followed by other plaintiffs with standing.

2. *Northern Spotted Owl v Lujan* focused on the requirement to designate critical habitat within one year of listing. Compare this to the Canadian court decision in *Environmental Defence Canada*, below, addressing a similar requirement in Canada's *Species at Risk Act*, SC 2002, c 29 [SARA].

3. The *Spotted Owl* cases involved the first two steps under the US ESA. The third step is the prohibition against "taking" an endangered species. In 1979, the US Federal Court in *Palila v Hawaii Department of Land and Natural Resources*, 471 F Supp 985 (D Hawaii 1979), aff'd 639 F (2d) 495 (9th Cir 1981) ruled that significant habitat destruction constitutes "taking." In that case, the State of Hawaii challenged the constitutional jurisdiction of a federal statute (the ESA) to dictate the management of state lands. The court determined that protection of endangered species was a matter of sufficient "national concern" to invoke the federal commerce power and that the federal treaty-making power also supported the Act, including its application to state and private lands. Would the result have been the same under Canada's constitution?

4. The prohibition on "taking" became quite controversial when it resulted in the regulation of logging of old growth forests on *private and state* lands in Washington and Oregon, which were home to the spotted owl. A lawsuit by a coalition of timber-dependent communities challenged the validity of the regulation defining "take," arguing that the term should cover only direct physical harm to animals, not habitat destruction. The case reached the US Supreme Court.

BABBITT V SWEET HOME CHAPTER OF COMMUNITIES FOR A GREAT OREGON
515 US 687, 115 S Ct 2407 (1995) [footnotes omitted]

STEVENS J:

... Section 9 of the [ESA] makes it unlawful for any person to "take" any endangered or threatened species. ...

• • •

Section 3(19) of the Act defines the statutory term "take" [as meaning] "to harass, *harm*, pursue, hunt, shoot, wound, kill, trap, capture, or collect ... ." [Emphasis added.]

...

The ... regulations that implement the statute ... define the statutory term "harm":

"*Harm* ... means an act which actually kills or injures wildlife. [Emphasis in original.] Such act may include *significant habitat modification or degradation* where it actually kills or injures wildlife by significantly impairing essential behavioral patterns, including breeding, feeding, or sheltering." [Emphasis added.] 50 CFR § 17.3 (1994).

• • •

Respondents [assert] that Congress did not intend the word "take" in § 9 to include habitat modification, as the [Secretary of the Interior's] "harm" regulation provides.

...

• • •

The text of the Act provides three reasons for concluding that the Secretary's interpretation is reasonable. First, an ordinary understanding of the word "harm" supports it. The dictionary definition of the verb form of "harm" is "to cause hurt or damage to: injure." ... In the context of the ESA, that definition naturally encompasses habitat modification that results in actual injury or death to members of an endangered or threatened species.

• • •

Second, the broad purpose of the ESA supports the Secretary's decision to extend protection against activities that cause the precise harms Congress enacted the statute to avoid. ... As stated in § 2 of the Act, among its central purposes is "to provide a means whereby the ecosystems upon which endangered species and threatened species depend may be conserved ... ."

NOTES

1. Critics of the US Act argued that the law was too iron clad in its prohibition against any harm to an endangered species, regardless of a project's benefits. The issue was highlighted in 1978, when the US Supreme Court blocked construction of the Tellico dam in Tennessee because it would destroy the habitat of a tiny, endangered fish—the snail darter (*Tennessee Valley Authority v Hill*, 437 US 153 (1978)). As a result of the controversy, a limited exemption procedure was inserted into the Act. A seven-member committee of cabinet ministers and senior officials (known as the "God Committee"), after holding hearings, may grant an exemption for a project if it finds that (a) there are no feasible and prudent alternatives to the project, (b) the benefits of the project clearly outweigh the benefits of alternative courses of action that would conserve the species or its critical habitat, and (c) the action is in the public interest (*Endangered Species Act*, 16 USC § 1536(h)(1) (1973)).

The committee has been convened on only three occasions. In its first case, the committee denied an exemption for the Tellico Dam (although the project was later exempted by legislation). Later, the committee decided to allow logging in 40 percent of spotted owl critical habitat.

2. For further information, see J Peyton Doub, *The Endangered Species Act: History, Implementation, Successes, and Controversies* (Boca Raton: CRC Press, 2013); and Zygmunt JB Plater, "Endangered Species Act Lessons over 30 Years, and the Legacy of the Snail Darter, a Small Fish in a Pork Barrel" (2004) 34 Envtl L 289.

C. CANADIAN LEGISLATION AND PROGRAMS

1. The Federal Endangered Species Program

In the early 1970s, following passage of the US ESA, two Canadian provinces (Ontario and New Brunswick) passed their own (weak) legislation. The federal government did not. In the late 1970s, however, Canada established an unofficial committee to identify species at risk. The Committee on the Status of Endangered Wildlife in Canada (COSEWIC) consists of representatives of wildlife departments of the federal, territorial, and provincial governments as well as three independent scientists. COSEWIC assesses species suspected of being at risk, then assigns a designation to each species. Possible designations include the following:

- *Extinct:* a species formerly indigenous to Canada that no longer exists anywhere.
- *Extirpated:* a species no longer known to exist in the wild in Canada but existing elsewhere.
- *Endangered:* a species threatened with imminent extirpation throughout all or significant portions of its Canadian range.
- *Threatened:* a species likely to become endangered if the factors affecting its vulnerability are not reversed.
- *Special concern:* a species that is particularly at risk because of low or declining numbers, because it occurs at the fringe of its range, or because of some other reason.

As of 2019, there are 817 species on COSEWIC's list, and 545 are listed as threatened or endangered. The list is growing at a rate of about 20-25 new species per year, and even these figures understate the extent of the problem. Due to limited resources and staff, COSEWIC has been unable to review many Canadian species suspected of being at risk.

NOTES AND QUESTIONS

1. The complete COSEWIC list of species at risk can be found at "A to Z Species Index" (last modified 29 November 2011), online: *Government of Canada* <https://wildlife-species.canada.ca/species-risk-registry/sar/index/default_e.cfm>.

2. Find four species at risk in your province. What are the reasons for their decline? Do any of them have approved recovery plans?

2. Federal Legislation

Otto von Bismarck said, "There are two things you do not want to see made: legislation and sausages." These words aptly describe the evolution of Canada's federal endangered species legislation.

In 1992, at the Rio Earth Summit, Canada was the first western nation to sign, and later ratify, the *Convention on Biological Diversity*. Article 8 provides:

Each Contracting Party shall, as far as possible and as appropriate:

(k) Develop ... necessary *legislation* and/or other regulatory provisions for the protection of threatened species and populations. [Emphasis added.]

The federal government initially took the position that this provision did not require Canada to pass endangered species legislation. Then, following a high-profile public campaign by conservationists, the government announced its commitment to an endangered species law. Between 1996 and 2000, two different endangered species bills were introduced and went through extensive committee hearings, but both died on the order paper when elections were called. Finally, SARA was passed by Parliament in December 2002.

The development of this law attracted a great deal of attention from the public, media, and industry, due in part to controversy about the US Act and its perceived impacts on development. When you read the statute, you will note that in some places, its drafting was quite complex. This is because the initial Bill was significantly revised and strengthened by Parliament's Environment Committee following extensive hearings (this was very unusual at the time). Then, when the Bill went for final debate in Parliament, the government sought to reverse most of the committee's key changes. This led to intense negotiations that produced compromise (and even more complex) wording. For more detail about the Bill's history, see Stewart Elgie, "The Politics of Extinction: The Birth of Canada's Species at Risk Act" in Debora L VanNijnatten & Robert Boardman, eds, *Canadian Environmental Policy and Politics: Prospects for Leadership and Innovation*, 3rd ed (Don Mills, Ont: Oxford University Press, 2009).

Read SARA. Focus on the main sections about listing (ss 15, 22, 27, 29), species protection (ss 32-34, 80), recovery plans (ss 37-38, 41-42, 65), critical habitat protection (ss 58, 61), permits (ss 73, 77-78), and the relevant definitions (s 2).

NOTES AND QUESTIONS

1. Almost all scientists and environmental groups wanted species listing decisions to be made by COSEWIC, whereas the government wanted this decision left to Cabinet's full discretion. During final debate on the Bill, a compromise was reached. Under s 27 of SARA, how is the ultimate listing decision made? How does this differ from the US ESA? How does SARA's approach distinguish the roles of science and politics (a key issue in environmental law generally)?

2. Have most of COSEWIC's listing recommendations been followed? Look at SARA registry and find a species that was not listed. What do you think of the reasons given? For more information on non-listing under SARA, see C Scott Findlay et al, "Species Listing Under Canada's Species at Risk Act" (2009) 23:6 Conserv Biol 1609.

3. The Bill automatically prohibits the destruction of a listed species' "residence" (s 33). What is a residence? How does it differ from "habitat"?

4. Habitat protection is the key to saving endangered species. The first step is to identify critical habitat. How and when is that done in SARA? Much like in the US (see the *Northern Spotted Owl v Lujan* case, above), in Canada, the Canadian government regularly failed to identify critical habitat in SARA's early years. Environmentalists brought a series of test cases challenging this practice.

The first case, *Alberta Wilderness Association v Canada (Minister of Environment)*, 2009 FC 710, involved the sage grouse. The evidence indicated that the location of many of the species' breeding sites ("leks") and nesting sites in the prairies were well known and studied. But Environment Canada concluded that more information was needed. The Federal Court (at para 25) ruled that the environment minister's complete failure to identify any critical habitat violated SARA:

> There is no discretion vested in the Minister in identifying critical habitat under the SARA. Subsection 41(1)(c) requires that the Minister identify in a recovery strategy document as much critical habitat as it is possible to identify at that time, even if all of it cannot be identified, and to do so based on the best information then available. I note that this requirement reflects the precautionary principle [see s 38 of SARA] that "where there are threats of serious or irreversible damage, lack of full scientific certainty should not be used as a reason for postponing measures to prevent environmental degradation" ... .

A second case involved the Nooksack Dace, an endangered minnow found south of Vancouver.

ENVIRONMENTAL DEFENCE CANADA V CANADA (FISHERIES AND OCEANS)
2009 FC 878

[The recovery team's scientists examined all four streams where the dace lived, and it identified the remaining suitable habitat in those streams "with a reasonable degree of certainty." The Department of Fisheries and Oceans (DFO) then directed "that critical habitat should be removed from all recovery strategies" (para 16) because (1) the critical habitat "had not yet undergone scientific peer review" (para 16), (2) further policy guidance and consultation was required, and (3) "[w]e would like to proceed cautiously with the identification of critical habitat ... " (para 16). The environmental applicants sought judicial review of that decision.

After referencing the recent decision in *Alberta Wilderness Association*, discussed above, the court concluded that DFO's decision to remove critical habitat from recovery strategies was contrary to "the mandatory requirements of s. 41(1)(c) of *SARA*," and "fundamentally inconsistent with the precautionary principle as codified in *SARA*."

The second issue was what level of *specificity* is required in identifying critical habitat under SARA. The final recovery strategy identified the streams inhabited by the dace and also the "general habitat features" it needed, but it did "not make specific geospatial recommendations"—that is, it did not identify the specific habitat features the dace required in those areas.]

CAMPBELL J:

[45] ... [T]his is the primary question in dispute: what are the constituents that must be included in the identification of a species' critical habitat? The answer to the question lies in the correct interpretation of the definition of "habitat" ... in s. 2 of *SARA* ... :

"habitat" means

(b) in respect of aquatic species, spawning grounds and nursery, rearing, food supply, migration and any *other areas* on which aquatic species depend directly or indirectly in order to carry out their life processes, or areas where aquatic species formerly occurred and have the potential to be reintroduced; [emphasis added] ... .

[46] The [environmental] Applicants maintain that the constituents of the habitat, and accordingly the critical habitat, of a specific species are *an identifiable location and the attributes of that location* that meet the criteria of the statutory definition of both terms. [Emphasis added.] ... The bone of contention that fuelled the present Application was the Minister's removal of the location constituent from the Final Recovery Strategy.

To be habitat under the SARA definition, [the Applicant argues,] an area must contain features useful to a species. ... In the case of the Nooksack Dace, while the dace is not located up in the trees of the riparian buffer zone, it depends on this biological component of habitat to survive and to recover. ...

• • •

[53] ...

[T]he Minister's construction of critical habitat as merely a location, that does not contain any physical or biological features that a species relies on directly or indirectly for survival or recovery, renders s. 41(1)(c) absurd and defeats the Act's purposes.

For example, ... it would be impossible to prohibit the destruction of any part of a species' critical habitat—like trees, water, or food—if those parts went unidentified [s. 58(1)]. ...

Except perhaps by nuclear Armageddon, one cannot destroy a place in its entirety. Nor can one destroy a set of geospatial co-ordinates. Rather, the destruction of critical habitat involves destruction of the *components* of that habitat. ...

• • •

[66] ... [T]he Applicants are wholly successful in the present Application.

NOTES AND QUESTIONS

1. Before these two cases, as of 2009, only about 20 percent of species had their critical habitat identified (mostly in protected areas). Following these cases, the rate has risen to over 50 percent. However, there is still much room for improvement. See Sarah C Bird & Karen E Hodges, "Critical Habitat Designation for Canadian Listed Species: Slow, Biased, and Incomplete" (2017) 71 Envtl Sci & Policy 1.

2. Once habitat is identified, the next step is its protection. In the original SARA Bill, critical habitat protection was discretionary ("may"). Parliament's Environment Committee voted to make it mandatory ("shall"). The end result in the final law was a negotiated compromise on the wording. Is critical habitat protection mandatory under s 58, for "federal" species? The following case addressed that question.

CANADA (FISHERIES AND OCEANS) V DAVID SUZUKI FOUNDATION
2012 FCA 40

[The southern and northern killer whale populations off BC's west coast were listed as endangered and threatened, respectively, under SARA. A recovery strategy was released in 2008. It identified the main threats to the whales and their habitat. The DFO then issued a protection statement under s 58(5)(b) of SARA (see below). It identified the whale's critical habitat as including only the "geophysical attributes"—that is, a specific physical area.

The critical habitat in the protection statement did *not* include the biological and "ecosystem features" of that habitat or the threats to those features, such as "acoustic degradation [for example, military seismic activity], chemical and biological contamination and diminished prey availability [for example, salmon]"—even though the recovery strategy had identified those as the major threats to the species. These threats would not be protected under SARA but, rather, "managed" through "a variety of legislative and policy tools" such as whale watching guidelines, wild salmon policy, and military sonar protocols.

Several environmental groups filed a judicial review application, arguing that the protection statement did not meet SARA's requirements. Shortly after that lawsuit was filed, DFO reversed itself and issued a "protection order" under s 58(4) of SARA (see below), legally protecting the whale's critical habitat—which was still defined as including just the "geophysical attributes."

The Federal Court's decision first dealt with the issue of what constitutes protection under SARA:

[299] The legislative history of section 58, as cited by the Applicants, illustrates that Parliamentarians recognized that critical habitat protection under SARA must be mandatory and not discretionary. Parliament did not intend to allow ministers to "choose" whether to protect critical habitat.

• • •

[300] The Protection Statement in this application cites the following non-statutory instruments: ... whale-watching guidelines; ... sensitive benthic areas policy; wild salmon policy; ... and military sonar protocols. These are policies, not laws that legally protect critical habitat from destruction.

[301] ... [I]t is trite law that ministerial policy does not, and cannot, bind the minister.

The court then addressed DFO's identification of critical habitat. Following the recent decision in *Environmental Defence*, discussed above, it ruled (at para 163): "the Protection Order was and is incorrect and unlawful because, in limiting its application to geophysical areas, the Respondents failed to respond to a duty assigned to them by statute ... ."

The Federal Court found that both the critical habitat protection statement and protection order did not comply with SARA. DFO appealed, but only on one main issue.]

DID THE MINISTER ERR BY RELYING ON THE PROVISIONS OF THE FISHERIES ACT ... IN MAKING THE KILLER WHALES PROTECTION STATEMENT?

• • •

[106] The Minister concedes that the protection of the critical habitat of endangered and threatened aquatic species under the SARA is not discretionary. However, the Minister submits that Parliament intended that he be allowed some flexibility as to how to provide that compulsory protection. ...

• • •

[108] ... The Minister specifically identifies provisions of the *Fisheries Act* [RSC 1985, c F-14] as appropriate alternatives to a protection order. ...

[109] The difficulty I have with the Minister's position is that it is not compatible with the provisions of the SARA, which clearly require compulsory "legal protection" for all identified critical habitat of listed endangered or threatened aquatic species. If I were to accept the Minister's position, the compulsory *non-discretionary critical habitat protection scheme* under the SARA would be effectively replaced by the *discretionary management scheme* of the *Fisheries Act*. That is not what the SARA provides for. [Double emphasis in original.]

• • •

[111] Section 58 of the SARA adds that [species] protection must be achieved through legally enforceable measures. ...

58.(1) Subject to this section, no person shall destroy any part of the critical habitat of any listed endangered species or of any listed threatened species ...

• • •

(5) Within 180 days after the recovery strategy or action plan that identified the critical habitat is included in the public registry, the competent minister *must*, [...] with respect to all of the critical habitat or any portion of the critical habitat [...]

(a) make the order referred to in subsection (4) if the critical habitat or any portion of the critical habitat *is not legally protected by provisions in, or measures under, this or any other Act of Parliament*, including agreements under section 11; or

(b) if the competent minister does not make the order, he or she must include in the public registry a statement setting out how the critical habitat or portions of it, as the case may be, are *legally protected*.

[Emphasis in original] [Ellipses in square brackets in original.]

• • •

[114] ... Parliament's intent was to avoid interference with and destruction of critical habitat. We are far removed from the concept of critical habitat management advanced by the Minister. Moreover, the juxtaposition of the word "legally" ... with the word "protected" ... to form the expression "legally protected" ... leaves little ambiguity as to the intent of Parliament: critical habitat must be preserved through legally enforceable measures.

• • •

[120] Sections 74 and 77 of the SARA also support the view that the provisions in, or measures under, an Act of Parliament should achieve the same objective as a protection order if they are to be accepted as a substitute to such an order.

[121] Section 74 of the SARA restricts the authority of a "competent minister"—including the appellant Minister in this case—from entering into an agreement, issuing a permit or licence or making an order under another Act of Parliament—such as the *Fisheries Act*—authorizing a person to engage in an activity "affecting" the critical habitat of a listed wildlife species unless ...

[122] ... the competent minister is of the opinion that all reasonable alternatives have been considered and the best solution has been adopted, measures have been taken to minimize the impact of the activity, and the activity will not jeopardize the survival or recovery of the species: paragraph 74(a) and subsection 73(3) of the SARA.

• • •

[126] I will now turn to the *Fisheries Act* to ascertain if the provisions of that statute may be relied upon by the Minister for the purposes of section 58 of the SARA.

• • •

[128] [Section 35 of the *Fisheries Act*] reads as follows:

35.(1) No person shall carry on any work or undertaking that results in the harmful alteration, disruption or destruction of fish habitat.

(2) No person contravenes subsection (1) by causing the alteration, disruption or destruction of fish habitat by any means or under any conditions authorized by the Minister or under regulations made by the Governor in Council under this Act.

• • •

[130] ... There is no dispute that the protection offered fish habitat under subsection 35(1) may be waived at the discretion of the Minister acting under subsection 35(2). Consequently, this provision cannot ensure that the critical habitat of endangered or threatened aquatic species is "legally protected" under the meaning of section 58 of the SARA.

[131] The Minister—through his counsel—states that he intends not to use his discretion under subsection 35(2) of the *Fisheries Act* to authorize the destruction of critical habitat. However, he does not explain how his intent can be legally enforced should he change his mind in the future for some presumably good reason; nor does he explain how his current intent would bind his successors. Intent not to use discretion is not legally enforceable. A mere intent does not ensure that critical habitat is "legally protected" under the meaning of section 58 of the SARA.

NOTES AND QUESTIONS

1. Before the killer whale case, no species had received habitat protection under SARA (outside of protected areas). Since that case, the government has begun applying s 58 to protect habitat, though still selectively.

2. SARA provides different degrees of protection for (so-called) "federal" and "non-federal" species. What are the main differences in the types of protection afforded these two categories (see ss 58 and 61)? Why do you think the drafters of the Act chose to treat aquatic species, migratory birds, and species on federal lands as "federal," and all other species as "non-federal" (that is, primarily a provincial responsibility)? Is this bifurcated approach required for constitutional reasons? See *Groupe Maison Candiac Inc v Canada (Attorney General)*, 2018 FC 643, which found that SARA's habitat protection provisions fall within federal constitutional authority, under the criminal law power, even when applied to provincial or private lands. Do you agree with this decision? What other constitutional powers could be the basis for SARA?

3. Section 58(5.1) of SARA treats migratory birds differently from other "federal" species in terms of habitat protection. What are the main differences? Why do you think this was done? Read the *Migratory Birds Convention Act, 1994*, SC 1994, c 22; does it apply to habitat?

4. The majority of SARA's listed species do not fall within s 58. Their habitat protection falls under s 61, the "safety net." Is the application of s 61 mandatory or discretionary? Section 61 has never been used, despite the fact that the majority of listed species do not receive "effective protection" under provincial law. See S Wojciechowski et al, "SARA's Safety Net Provisions and the Effectiveness of Species at Risk Protection on Non-Federal Lands" (2011) 22 JELP 203.

5. The US ESA (and most US environmental laws) specifically permits citizens to bring a civil enforcement action against anyone who violates the Act. SARA does not provide for "citizen suits"; they were included in an earlier version of the Bill but were removed because of the objections of industry and landowner groups.

3. Provincial Legislation

In 1996, the federal government and all provinces and territories signed the *National Accord for the Protection of Species at Risk* (3 October 2014, online (pdf): *Government of Canada* <https://www.registrelep-sararegistry.gc.ca/6B319869-9388-44D1-A8A4-33A2F01CEF10/Accord-eng.pdf>. It commits each jurisdiction to pass endangered species legislation containing 15 specific requirements (such as habitat protection and recovery plans). In 2018, building on the accord, federal, provincial, and territorial governments agreed to the *Pan-Canadian Approach to Transforming Species at Risk Conservation in Canada* (Gatineau, Qc: Environment and Climate Change Canada, 2018), online: *Government of Canada* <https://www.canada.ca/en/services/environment/wildlife-plants-species/species-risk/pan-canadian-approach/species-at-risk-conservation.html>, identifying priority species, spaces, and threats for joint action.

Only six of ten provinces have passed specific endangered species legislation (Ontario, New Brunswick, Quebec, Manitoba, Nova Scotia, and Newfoundland and Labrador). None has yet come close to fulfilling all of the requirements of the accord.

a. Listing

Each province takes one of three different approaches to listing. Two of them (Manitoba and Quebec) leave listing up to the *complete discretion* of Cabinet. In these two provinces, less than half of the species recommended by COSEWIC are legally listed. Three provinces (Nova Scotia, Ontario, and New Brunswick) take a *science-based* listing approach: all species listed by COSEWIC (or their scientific committee) *must* be listed under their laws. Newfoundland and Labrador takes a middle-ground approach, like SARA: there is a time limit to make a listing decision, and a duty to give reasons if the scientific committee's advice is not followed. And like SARA, it has listed about 90 percent of COSEWIC-recommended species. These different outcomes show why there was such debate under SARA about whether COSEWIC or Cabinet should make listing decisions.

b. Habitat

Three of the six provincial Acts include an automatic prohibition against destroying the habitat of a listed endangered species. In Manitoba, for example, *The Endangered Species and Eco-systems Act*, CCSM c E111, provides:

> 10(1) No person shall
>
> • • •
>
> (b) destroy, disturb or interfere with the habitat of an endangered species, a threat-ened species or an extirpated species that has been reintroduced ... .

This strong prohibition is somewhat undermined by a provision allowing the Minister to exempt any development "if the Minister is satisfied that (a) protection and preservation of the species and its habitat is assured; or (b) appropriate measures ... will be established ... to reduce ... the impact of the development upon the species and its habitat" (s 12(1)). Quebec's *Act respecting threatened or vulnerable species*, CQLR c E-12.01, also contains a fairly broad exemption provision (s 17). By contrast, Ontario's *Endangered Species Act, 2007*, SO 2007, c 6, provides rigorous conditions for issuing an exemption permit (these conditions are similar to those found in SARA)—with the additional requirement to pay a fee to a conservation fund to offset the habitat destruction. In the other three provinces (Nova Scotia, New Brunswick, and Newfoundland and Labrador), habitat protection is left up to the discretion of the minister or Cabinet.

Three of the four provinces without endangered species laws have added provisions to their wildlife laws (all except BC). These acts typically leave listing and habitat protection up to the discretion of Cabinet. See, for example, *The Wildlife Act, 1998*, SS 1998, c W-13.12, in Saskatchewan.

The spotted owl provides a graphic illustration of the relative strength of the Canadian and US endangered species laws. Efforts to protect the owl are controversial because doing so involves setting aside large tracts of coastal old-growth forests, a valuable commodity to timber companies. In the US, as a result of litigation, the owl was listed as threatened in 1990, and vast areas of its critical habitat were identified and protected. In Canada, the owl was listed by COSEWIC as endangered in 1986. Despite this listing, there has been no final designation of its critical habitat, and none of its habitat has been protected (outside of parks); there is simply reduced logging in a small part of it. The owl is now close to extinction in BC.

Under the US system, it was politically decided that preserving species is of paramount importance. Once science indicates that a species is endangered, it must be listed, and its habitat must be protected. Exceptions can be made, but only in rare cases after a very thor-ough, rigorous process. Under the Canadian system, no firm political commitment has been made to protect species. Scientists indicate if a species is endangered, but it is left to politicians to decide whether to list a species and protect its habitat.

For further information, see Robin S Waples et al, "A Tale of Two Acts: Endangered Species Listing Practices in Canada and the United States" (2013) 63:9 BioScience 723.

D. OTHER APPROACHES

Many people have criticized the "endangered species" approach to protecting species. These criticisms come from a number of angles.

Some have argued that the goal of saving every species is impossible. Recovery efforts are expensive—recovering all of Canada's listed species could cost over $100 million per year. Others point out that this is less than the cost of ten miles of new highway. If we decide that we cannot save every species, we face difficult decisions. Which ones do we sacrifice? On what basis? Politicians' natural inclination is to save large mammals and "warm and fuzzy" species because they evoke the most emotional response in people. But scientists point out that cuteness is not an accurate measure of ecological value. No one has yet come up with a satisfactory solution to the problem of deciding which species to save.

Others have recommended that rather than trying to save individual species, we should focus on saving endangered ecosystems, which would also save its resident species. The problem with this approach is how to identify an endangered ecosystem. One of the best ways to identify an ecosystem, and to measure its health, is to examine the species that depend on it. Thus, we are back to protecting species again.

Some maintain that we should focus on protecting biological diversity. This argument raises the questions: How much biological diversity should we save? Which species can we let go? By conserving "hot spot" areas of greatest biological diversity, we can put our limited species preservation dollars to their best use. Overall, a preventive rather than a critical care approach seems most promising.

For more information, see An Cliquet & Kris Decleer, "Halting and Restoring Species Loss: Incorporating the Concepts of Extinction Debt, Ecological Trap and Dark Diversity into Conservation and Restoration Law" (2017) 26:2 Griffith L Rev 178; Eric Freyfogle, "Conservation Biology and Law: Only a Start" (2006) 20:3 Conserv Biol 679.

FURTHER READINGS

Benidickson, Jamie, "Protecting Areas and Endangered Species" in Jamie Benidickson, *Environmental Law*, 5th ed (Toronto: Irwin Law, 2019) ch 14.

Living Planet Report Canada: A National Look at Wildlife Loss (2017), online: *WWF-Canada* <http://www.wwf.ca/about_us/lprc/>.

Morgera, Elisa & Jona Razzaque, eds, *Biodiversity and Nature Protection Law*, Elgar Encyclopedia of Environmental Law, vol III (Cheltenham, UK; Northampton, Mass: Edward Elgar, 2017).

Olive, Andrea, *Land, Stewardship, and Legitimacy: Endangered Species Policy in Canada and the United States* (Toronto: University of Toronto Press, 2014).

CHAPTER TWENTY-TWO

MUNICIPAL LAW AND ENVIRONMENT

Arlene Kwasniak

I. INTRODUCTION

Municipalities, urban and rural, dot landscapes throughout Canada, each with its own regulatory regime. Typically, municipalities have a range of powers to regulate activities and projects that can impact their environment. They have powers over local development, businesses, transportation and roads, land use planning and zoning, waste, composting, recycling, landfills, infrastructure projects (including their own), and energy use and demands, to identify a few.

This chapter looks at the role of municipalities in regulating and managing environment and environmental quality, jointly called "environmental values." "Municipality" includes the range of local governments that provincial or territorial legislation may establish. The Alberta *Municipal Government Act*, for example, defines "municipality" as including a city, village, town, summer village, and municipal district.[1]

This chapter begins with an examination of sources of and limitations on municipal authority (sometimes in this chapter called "powers") and follows that with a discussion of conflict between municipal laws and federal or provincial legislation. Next it looks at municipal land use planning, development controls, and restrictions on private land use. The final section contemplates the role of municipalities where municipal actions can adversely affect or impact Indigenous rights or interests. A case study and questions follow each section.

II. MUNICIPAL AUTHORITY: SOURCES, SCOPE, AND LIMITATIONS

A. THE CANADIAN CONSTITUTION AND MUNICIPAL LEGISLATION

The Canadian Constitution divides legislative powers between the federal and provincial governments. There is no constitutional head of power for municipalities. Municipal powers are derived from provincial legislation, since provinces have legislative jurisdiction over municipal institutions.[2] Hence, to determine municipal authority, one must look at the provincial or territorial legislation that creates or empowers a municipality (in this chapter called "municipal legislation") and court interpretation of the municipal legislation. In contrast to municipal legislation, municipalities themselves develop their own legislation, usually in the form of by-laws or resolutions.

Every province and territory ("province" for convenience in this chapter) has municipal legislation that creates and governs municipalities. The statutes have various names, for example, *Municipal Government Act*, *Municipal Act*, *Municipalities Act*, *Municipal Affairs Act*, *Cities and Towns* or *Cities and Towns and Villages Act*, and *Local Government Act*. Some provinces consolidate municipal authorities in one statute, and some spread authorities over two or more statutes. For example, there may be a statute on municipal governance, on municipal planning and development, on municipal assessment and taxation, on municipal expropriation, or on some combination of these.

Laws that create and govern municipalities usually apply to all types of municipalities, although specific authorities may vary depending on a municipality's size or nature. For example, s 16 of the Alberta MGA establishes that *cities* own roads, while the *Crown* owns roads in other types of municipalities. There are also differences between *charter* municipalities and *mainstream* municipalities. A few large urban Canadian municipalities enjoy special status as charter cities. A charter city is governed by stand-alone legislation that modifies the main municipal legislation and that provides charter cities greater autonomy and additional powers. To ascertain a charter city's authority, one must examine the city's charter legislation in addition to reviewing the main municipal legislation.[3]

1   RSA 2000, c M-26, s (1)(s) [MGA].
2   *Constitution Act, 1867* (UK), 30 & 31 Vict, c 3, s 92(8).
3   Section III.E of this chapter provides examples of provisions from Calgary's and Edmonton's charter legislation in the context of a case study.

B. COURT INTERPRETATION OF MUNICIPAL LEGISLATION

1. Dillon's Rule: Acceptance and Retreat

A discussion of the interpretation of municipal legislation invariably begins with "Dillon's Rule," which interpreted municipal powers narrowly and strictly. The rule derives from the 1800s Iowa judge John Dillon, who stated:

> It is a general and undisputed proposition of law that *a municipal corporation possesses and can exercise the following powers, and no others*: First, those granted in *express words*; second, those *necessarily or fairly implied* in or *incident* to the powers expressly granted; third, those *essential* to the accomplishment of the declared objects and purposes of the corporation,—not simply convenient, but indispensable. Any fair, reasonable, substantial doubt concerning the existence of power is resolved by the courts against the corporation, and the power is denied.[4]

Although Dillon's Rule has been adopted in Canada, over the years, its influence has declined.[5] The courts' move away from a strict application of Dillon's Rule was partly due to a change in drafting style. Municipal legislation evolved from setting out a list of specific (also called "express") powers to a combination of general powers and specific powers. Where an authority is specific, courts tend toward a "Dillon's Rule" type of interpretation. But where a power is couched in general terms, courts apply a more liberal interpretation. As put by the Supreme Court of Canada, "[t]his shift in legislative drafting reflects the true nature of modern municipalities which require greater flexibility in fulfilling their statutory purposes."[6]

2. General and Specific Authorities

The Prince Edward Island *Municipal Government Act*[7] offers an example of a general (sometimes called "omnibus" or "general welfare") source of authority:

General jurisdiction to pass bylaws and provide services

180. A council may pass bylaws and provide services for municipal purposes respecting

(a) the safety, health and welfare of people and the protection of persons and property ... .

"Safety," "health," "welfare," and "protection of property" are all general terms and give a PEI municipality broad powers to pass a range of by-laws falling within them. However, as we will see, general powers are not limitless.

Municipal legislation also contains specific authorities, applying to specific matters, for example, taxation of private property and subdivision and development of private land. Specific authorities are typically couched in precise and limited terms, thus inviting a more strict court interpretation. For example, the Alberta MGA grants authority to municipalities to require a person to be issued a development permit to carry out a "development." The MGA defines "development" narrowly, thus limiting municipal powers in this regard.

Permit

683. Except as otherwise provided in a land use bylaw, a person may not commence any development unless the person has been issued a development permit in respect of it pursuant to the land use bylaw.

---

4   *Commentaries on the Law of Municipal Corporations*, 5th ed (Boston: Little, Brown, 1911) at para 237.
5   See Ron Levi & Mariana Valverde, "Freedom of the City: Canadian Cities and the Quest for Governmental Status" (2006) 44 Osgoode Hall LJ 409.
6   *United Taxi Drivers' Fellowship of Southern Alberta v Calgary (City)*, 2004 SCC 19 at para 6, [2004] 1 SCR 485.
7   RSPEI 1988, c M-12.1.

Definitions

616. In this Part,

• • •

(b) "development" means

(i) an excavation or stockpile and the creation of either of them,

(ii) a building or an addition to or replacement or repair of a building and the construction or placing of any of them on, in, over or under land,

(iii) a change of use of land or a building or an act done in relation to land or a building that results in or is likely to result in a change in the use of the land or building, or

(iv) a change in the intensity of use of land or a building or an act done in relation to land or a building that results in or is likely to result in a change in the intensity of use of the land or building ... .

The Supreme Court discussed limitations on general welfare provisions in *114957 Canada Ltée (Spraytech, Société d'arrosage) v Hudson (Town)*.[8] In this case, the plaintiff, Spraytech, a landscaping company, challenged the validity of Town By-Law 270, which restricted the cosmetic use of pesticides (to kill dandelions). The plaintiff argued that *The Cities and Towns Act*[9] did not authorize the by-law, and, thus, it was *ultra vires* and inoperative. The court found that the by-law was authorized and valid under the following general welfare provision of the Act:

410. The council may make by-laws:

(1) To secure peace, order, good government, health and general welfare in the territory of the municipality ... .[10]

When reading the following case excerpt, note the limitation that applies when municipal legislation contains both a specific power and a general power relevant to a challenged by-law.

114957 CANADA LTÉE (SPRAYTECH, SOCIÉTÉ D'ARROSAGE) V HUDSON (TOWN)
2001 SCC 40, [2001] 2 SCR 241

L'HEUREUX-DUBÉ J (Gonthier, Bastarache, and Arbour JJ concurring):

• • •

18 In *R. v. Sharma*, [1993] 1 S.C.R. 650, at p. 668, this Court recognized "the principle that, as statutory bodies, municipalities 'may exercise only those powers expressly conferred by statute, those powers necessarily or fairly implied by the expressed power in the statute, and those indispensable powers essential and not merely convenient to the effectuation of the purposes of the corporation' (Makuch, *Canadian Municipal and Planning Law* (1983), at p. 115)." Included in this authority are "general welfare" powers, conferred by provisions in provincial enabling legislation, on which municipalities can draw. ...

19 Section 410 *C.T.A. [Cities and Towns Act]* is an example of such a general welfare provision and supplements the specific grants of power in s. 412. More open-ended or "omnibus" provisions such as s. 410 allow municipalities to respond expeditiously to new challenges facing local communities, without requiring amendment of the provincial enabling legislation. There are analogous provisions in other provinces' and territories' municipal enabling legislation ...

8 2001 SCC 40, [2001] 2 SCR 241.

9 CQLR c C-19.

10 SQ 2005, c 6, s 194, repealed.

20 While enabling provisions that allow municipalities to regulate for the "general welfare" within their territory authorize the enactment of by-laws genuinely aimed at furthering goals such as public health and safety, it is important to keep in mind that such open-ended provisions do not confer an unlimited power. ...

21 Within this framework, I turn now to the specifics of the appeal. As a preliminary matter, I agree with the courts below that By-law 270 was not enacted under s. 412(32) *C.T.A.* This provision authorizes councils to "make by-laws: To regulate or prohibit the storage and use of gun-powder, dry pitch, resin, coal oil, benzine, naphtha, gasoline, turpentine, gun-cotton, nitro-glycerine, and *other combustible, explosive, corrosive, toxic or radioactive or other materials that are harmful to public health or safety*, in the territory of the municipality or within 1 km therefrom" (emphasis added). ... As a result, since there is no specific provision in the provincial enabling legislation referring to pesticides, the by-law must fall within the purview of s. 410(1) *C.T.A.* The party challenging a by-law's validity bears the burden of proving that it is *ultra vires*: see *Kuchma v. Rural Municipality of Tache*, [1945] S.C.R. 234, at p. 239, and *Montréal (City of) v. Arcade Amusements Inc.*, [1985] 1 S.C.R. 368, at p. 395.

22 The conclusion that By-law 270 does not fall within the purview of s. 412(32) *C.T.A.* distinguishes this appeal from *R. v. Greenbaum*, [1993] 1 S.C.R. 674. In that case, various express provisions of the provincial enabling legislation at issue covered the regulation of Toronto sidewalks. The appellant was therefore trying to expand the ambit of these specific authorizations by recourse to the "omnibus" provision in Ontario's *Municipal Act* [RSO 1990, c M.45]. ... Since the *C.T.A.* contains no such specific provisions concerning pesticides (nor a clause limiting its purview to matters not specifically provided for in the Act)[,] the "general welfare" provision of the *C.T.A.*, s. 410(1), is not limited in this fashion.

• • •

LEBEL J (Iacobucci and Major JJ concurring):

• • •

52 In the case of a specific grant of power, its limits must be found in the provision itself. Non-included powers may not be supplemented through the use of the general residuary clauses often found in municipal laws (*R. v. Greenbaum*, [1993] 1 S.C.R. 674).

53 The case at bar raises a different issue: absent a specific grant of power, does a general welfare provision like s. 410(1) authorize By-law 270? A provision like s. 410(1) must be given some meaning. It reflects the reality that the legislature and its drafters cannot foresee every particular situation. It appears to be sound legislative and administrative policy, under such provisions, to grant local governments a residual authority to deal with the unforeseen or changing circumstances, and to address emerging or changing issues concerning the welfare of the local community living within their territory. Nevertheless, such a provision cannot be construed as an open and unlimited grant of provincial powers. It is not enough that a particular issue has become a pressing concern in the opinion of a local community. This concern must relate to problems that engage the community as a local entity, not a member of the broader polity. It must be closely related to the immediate interests of the community within the territorial limits *defined* by the legislature in a matter where local governments may usefully intervene. ...

54 In the present case, the subject matter of the by-law lies within the ambit of normal local government activities. It concerns the use and protection of the local environment within the community. The regulation targets problems of use of land and property, and addresses neighbourhood concerns that have always been within the realm of local government activity. Thus, the by-law was properly authorized by s. 410(1).

3. Municipal Purposes

In addition to being authorized by municipal legislation, a municipal by-law or resolution must fall within municipal purposes. Here is an example of the municipal purposes provision in Saskatchewan's *The Municipalities Act*:

> 3(2) Having regard to the principles mentioned in subsection (1), the purposes of this Act are the following:
>
> (a) to provide the legal structure and framework within which municipalities must govern themselves and make the decisions that they consider appropriate and in the best interests of their residents;
>
> (b) to provide municipalities with the powers, duties and functions necessary to fulfil their purposes;
>
> (c) to provide municipalities with the flexibility to respond to the existing and future needs of their residents in creative and innovative ways;
>
> (d) to ensure that, in achieving these objectives, municipalities are accountable to the people who elect them and are responsible for encouraging and enabling public partici-pation in the governance process.[11]

Although purpose clauses may appear broad, they are not unlimited, as demonstrated by the Supreme Court in *Shell Canada Products Ltd v Vancouver (City)*.[12] During the time of the apartheid regime in South Africa, the City passed resolutions "first, not to do business with Shell Canada and Royal Dutch/Shell as long as Shell continues to do business in South Africa; and second, to declare the City a 'Shell Free' zone until such time as Shell should disinvest from South Africa."[13] The Supreme Court considered whether the resolutions were within municipal purposes as set out in the *Vancouver Charter*.[14]

SHELL CANADA PRODUCTS LTD V VANCOUVER (CITY)
[1994] 1 SCR 231, 1994 CanLII 115

SOPINKA J (La Forest, Cory, Iacobucci, and Major JJ concurring):

• • •

Generally, a municipal authority is authorized to act only for municipal purposes. ... The "purposes of the corporation" or "municipal purposes" are determined by reference to not only those that are expressly stated but those that are compatible with the purpose and objects of the enabling statute. ...

In most cases, as here, the problem arises with respect to the exercise of a power that is not expressly conferred but is sought to be implied on the basis of a general grant of power. It is in these cases that the purposes of the enabling statute assume great importance. ...

I must, therefore, determine whether the Resolutions were passed for a municipal purpose. Their purpose is amply defined in the preambles and the operative parts of the Resolutions. The explicit purpose is to influence Shell to divest in South Africa by expressing moral outrage against the apartheid regime and to join the alleged international boycott of its subsidiaries and products until Shell "completely with-draws from South Africa". There is no mention as to how the good government, health or welfare of the City or its citizens is affected or promoted thereby.

---

11 SS 2005, c M-36.1.
12 [1994] 1 SCR 231, 1994 CanLII 115 [*Shell Canada* cited to SCR].
13 *Ibid* at 237.
14 SBC 1953, c 55.

Specifically, there is no mention of any objective of improving relations among its citizens. In view of the detailed recital of the purposes of the Resolutions, no such implicit purpose can be read in. The fourth recital hints at the existence of a broader program to control with whom the City does business. It refers to doing business with South Africa as one of the criteria to be employed. There is, however, no evidence that such a program exists and, indeed, its existence is contradicted by the fact that the City continued to purchase from Chevron. I therefore agree with the trial judge that the respondent was seeking to use its powers to do business "to affect matters in another part of the world" (pp. 348-49), a purpose which is directed at matters outside the territorial limits of the City.

Is this in relation to a municipal purpose? Clearly there is no express power in the *Vancouver Charter* authorizing the Resolutions and if they are valid the respondent must rely on such powers being implied. This requires a consideration of the relevant provisions of the *Vancouver Charter* on the basis of the principles outlined above. So far as the purpose of the *Vancouver Charter* is concerned it is perhaps best expressed in s. 189, which provides that "Council may provide for the good rule and government of the city." In this regard its purpose does not differ from the purpose generally of municipal legislation which, as stated above, is to promote the health, welfare, safety or good government of the municipality. This places a territorial limit on Council's jurisdiction. No doubt Council can have regard for matters beyond its boundaries in exercising its powers but in so doing any action taken must have as its purpose benefit to the citizens of the City. ...

• • •

In summary on this point, applying the principles enunciated above, I have concluded, as did the trial judge, that the purpose of the Resolutions is to affect matters beyond the boundaries of the City without any identifiable benefit to its inhabitants. This is a purpose that is neither expressly nor impliedly authorized by the *Vancouver Charter* and is unrelated to the carrying into effect of the intent and purpose of the *Vancouver Charter*.

III. CONFLICT WITH PROVINCIAL OR FEDERAL LEGISLATION

A. THE CONFLICT QUESTION

A municipality may regulate as authorized by provincial legislation. But what if a province or the federal government has legislated in the same area as a municipality? Does this affect the operation of the municipal regulation? This section discusses three tests that courts have developed to address this question: impossibility of dual compliance, frustration of purpose, and express legislative test.[15]

---

15 This chapter does not discuss how interjurisdictional immunity (IJI) may be relevant to a conflict between a municipal by-law and the fact of federal jurisdiction in the area. See Chapter 10 for a discussion of IJI. See also A89360 National Energy Board—Letter—Trans Mountain Pipeline ULC—Trans Mountain Expansion Project—Notice of Constitutional Question MH-081-2017—Reasons for Decision (18 January 2018), online (downloadable pdf): *National Energy Board* <https://apps.neb-one.gc.ca/REGDOCS/File/Download/3436250>. In the decision (at 3), the National Energy Board found that IJI applied and that, accordingly, Trans Mountain could proceed with its terminal work without the City of Burnaby issuing preliminary plan approvals otherwise required under a zoning by-law, or tree cutting permits otherwise required under a tree by-law.

B. IMPOSSIBILITY OF DUAL COMPLIANCE

The first test—the impossibility of dual compliance—was a focus of *Spraytech*, discussed above. Recall that the plaintiff, Spraytech, challenged the validity of a Town by-law that restricted the cosmetic use of pesticides. In addition to arguing that By-law 270 was not authorized by the Act, Spraytech argued that there was an operational conflict with provincial and federal legislation and that paramountcy rendered the by-law inoperative. (See Chapter 10 for a discussion of paramountcy.) The following excerpt relates how the court dealt with the alleged operational conflict.

114957 CANADA LTÉE (SPRAYTECH, SOCIÉTÉ D'ARROSAGE) V HUDSON (TOWN)
2001 SCC 40, [2001] 2 SCR 241

L'HEUREUX-DUBÉ J:

• • •

38 Some courts have already made use of the *Multiple Access* [*Multiple Access Ltd v McCutcheon*, [1982] 2 SCR 161, 1982 CanLII 55] test to examine alleged provincial–municipal conflicts. For example, in *British Columbia Lottery Corp. v. Vancouver (City)* (1999), [*sic*] 1999 BCCA 18, 169 D.L.R. (4th) 141, at pp. 147-48, the British Columbia Court of Appeal stated that cases pre-dating *Multiple Access*, including the Ontario Court of Appeal decision in *Mississauga*, … [*Attorney General for Ontario v City of Mississauga*, 1981 CanLII 1860, 15 MPLR 212 (Ont CA)], "must be read in the light of [that] decision." … The court summarized the applicable standard as follows: "A true and outright conflict can only be said to arise when one enactment compels what the other forbids." See also … *Huot v. St-Jérôme (Ville de)*, J.E. 93-1052 (Sup. Ct.), at p. 19: [TRANSLATION] "A finding that a municipal by-law is inconsistent with a provincial statute (or a provincial statute with a federal statute) requires, first, that they both deal with similar subject matters and, second, that obeying one necessarily means disobeying the other."

39 As a general principle, the mere existence of provincial (or federal) legislation in a given field does not oust municipal prerogatives to regulate the subject matter. … In this case, there is no barrier to dual compliance with By-law 270 and the *Pesticides Act* [CQLR c P-9.3], nor any plausible evidence that the legislature intended to preclude municipal regulation of pesticide use. The *Pesticides Act* establishes a permit and licensing system for vendors and commercial applicators of pesticides and thus complements the federal legislation's focus on the products themselves. Along with By-law 270, these laws establish a tri-level regulatory regime.

• • •

LEBEL J:

• • •

46 … As L'Heureux-Dubé J. points out, the applicable test to determine whether an operational conflict arises is set out in *Multiple Access Ltd. v. McCutcheon*, [1982] 2 S.C.R. 161, at pp. 187 and 189. There must be an actual conflict, in the sense that compliance with one set of rules would require a breach of the other. … The basic test remains the impossibility of dual compliance. From this perspective, the alleged conflict with federal legislation simply does not exist. The federal Act and its regulations merely authorize the importation, manufacturing, sale and distribution of the products in Canada. They do not purport to state where, when and how pesticides could or should be used. They do not grant a blanket authority to pesticides'

manufacturers or distributors to spread them on every spot of greenery within Canada. This matter is left to other legislative and regulatory schemes. Nor does a conflict exist with the provincial *Pesticides Act*, and I agree with L'Heureux-Dubé J.'s analysis on this particular point. The operational conflict argument thus fails.

C. FRUSTRATION OF PURPOSE

The Supreme Court decision *Rothmans, Benson & Hedges Inc v Saskatchewan*[16] concerned a federal law and a provincial law. The issue was whether a section of the Saskatchewan *Tobacco Control Act*[17] was inoperative because of a conflict with a section of the federal *Tobacco Act*.[18] The Saskatchewan law regulated the retail display of tobacco products; that is, it prohibited displaying tobacco products where young persons may be present. The federal *Tobacco Act* expressly permitted tobacco products to be displayed for retail. The applicant argued that the federal and provincial laws conflicted, and federal paramountcy required the court to declare the provincial law inoperative to the extent of the conflict.

The court found no conflict because there was no impossibility of dual compliance. One could comply with both laws by complying with the provincial law. The federal law was permissive, not mandatory. However, the court added a test to determine if a legislative provision is conflicting and inoperative: if the provincial law frustrates the purpose of a federal law, the federal law will prevail.[19]

ROTHMANS, BENSON & HEDGES INC V SASKATCHEWAN
2005 SCC 13, [2005] 1 SCR 188

12 However, subsequent cases indicate that impossibility of dual compliance is not the sole mark of inconsistency. Provincial legislation that displaces or frustrates Parliament's legislative purpose is also inconsistent for the purposes of the doctrine. ...

13 This concern about frustration of Parliament's legislative purpose may find its roots in *McCutcheon* [*Multiple Access Ltd v McCutcheon*, [1982] 2 SCR 161], in which Dickson J. stated, at p. 190:

... [T]here is no true repugnancy in the case of merely duplicative provisions since it does not matter which statute is applied; *the legislative purpose of Parliament will be fulfilled regardless of which statute is invoked by a remedy-seeker; application of the provincial law does not displace the legislative purpose of Parliament.* [Emphasis added.]

14 In my view, the overarching principle to be derived from *McCutcheon* and later cases is that a provincial enactment must not frustrate the purpose of a federal enactment, whether by making it impossible to comply with the latter or by some other means. In this way, impossibility of dual compliance is sufficient but not the only test for inconsistency.

15 It follows that in determining whether s. 6 of *The Tobacco Control Act* is sufficiently inconsistent with s. 30 of the *Tobacco Act* so as to be rendered inoperative through the paramountcy doctrine, two questions arise. First, can a person simultaneously comply with s. 6 of *The Tobacco Control Act* and s. 30 of the *Tobacco Act*?

---

16 2005 SCC 13, [2005] 1 SCR 188.

17 SS 2001, c T-14.1.

18 SC 1997, c 13.

19 *Rothmans, Benson & Hedges*, *supra* note 16 at para 25.

Second, does s. 6 of *The Tobacco Control Act* frustrate Parliament's purpose in enacting s. 30 of the *Tobacco Act*?

• • •

25 Section 6 of The *Tobacco Control Act* does not frustrate the legislative purpose underlying s. 30 of the *Tobacco Act*. Both the general purpose of the *Tobacco Act* (to address a national public health problem) and the specific purpose of s. 30 (to circumscribe the *Tobacco Act*'s general prohibition on promotion of tobacco products set out in s. 19) remain fulfilled. Indeed, s. 6 of The *Tobacco Control Act* appears to further at least two of the stated purposes of the *Tobacco Act*, namely, "to protect young persons and others from inducements to use tobacco products" (s. 4(b)) and "to protect the health of young persons by restricting access to tobacco products" (s. 4(c)).

D. EXPRESS LEGISLATIVE TEST

The express legislative test overrides the impossibility of the dual compliance test. The express legislative test applies where legislation prescribes the consequences of overlapping municipal law and provincial law. *Peacock v Norfolk (County)*[20] provides an illustration. An Ontario municipal by-law prohibited siting intensive livestock operations within certain land-use zones. However the province had approved the plaintiff's operations within the zones under provincial legislation. The application of the express legislative test by the Ontario Superior Court of Justice resulted in the plaintiff being able to carry on the operations, notwithstanding the municipal prohibition.[21]

PEACOCK V NORFOLK (COUNTY)
2004 CanLII 66340, 73 OR (3d) 200 (Sup Ct J)

[50] In the case at bar, the provincial legislation in fact specifies a different test [from the impossibility of dual compliance]. Section 61(1) of the Nutrient Management Act, 2002, S.O. 2002, c. 4 states:

61(1) A regulation supersedes a by-law of a municipality or a provision in that by-law if the by-law or provision addresses the same subject-matter as the regulation.

(2) A by-law or a provision of a by-law that is superseded under subsection (1) is inoperative while the regulation is in force.

[51] The appropriate test is therefore whether the by-law "addresses the same subject matter as the regulation."

[52] It is also clear on the evidence before this court that the Nutrient Management Act, 2002 and O. Reg. 267/03 constitute a comprehensive scheme to regulate management of nutrients, including handling and storage of same. Where a municipality passes a by-law which in whole or part is in conflict with such a provincial scheme, the by-law is inoperative (see Superior Propane Inc. v. York (City), ... [1995 CanLII 415, 23 OR (3d) 161 (CA)], and Nutrient Management Act, 2002, s. 61(1) and (2), supra).

---

20 2004 CanLII 66340, 73 OR (3d) 200 (Sup Ct J), aff'd 2006 CanLII 21752, 81 OR (3d) 530 (CA), leave to appeal to SCC refused, 2007 CanLII 6820.

21 For more on frustration and the impossibility of dual compliance, see Chapter 10's discussion of *Orphan Well Association v Grant Thornton Ltd*, 2019 SCC 5.

E. CASE STUDY AND QUESTIONS: MUNICIPALITIES AND CLIMATE CHANGE

Although atmospheric carbon dioxide (CO_2) is the most prominent of greenhouse gases (GHGs), others also are significant. This case study[22] concerns landfill gas (LFG). As put by the United States Environmental Protection Agency:

> Landfill gas (LFG) is a natural byproduct of the decomposition of organic material in landfills. LFG is composed of roughly 50 percent methane (the primary component of natural gas), 50 percent carbon dioxide (CO_2) and a small amount of non-methane organic compounds. Methane is a potent greenhouse gas 28 to 36 times more effective than CO_2 at trapping heat in the atmosphere over a 100-year period ... .[23]

According to Environment and Climate Change Canada, "Emissions from Canadian landfills account for 20% of national methane emissions."[24] Clearly, effective climate change mitigation requires reducing and managing landfill gas.[25]

This case study considers municipal jurisdiction in such mitigation.[26] The case study concerns a fictional Alberta municipality, "Greensboro," that passed a by-law prohibiting LFG emissions over specified amounts (the "LFG By-law"). A developer of a proposed private landfill contests the validity of the by-law, claiming that it is beyond municipal authority and conflicts with provincial legislation.

These excerpts from the Alberta MGA are relevant:

- The following municipal purposes (s 3) are relevant:

    (a) to provide good government,
    (a.1) to foster the well-being of the environment,

    • • •

    (c) to develop and maintain safe and viable communities ... .

- The following provisions from general jurisdiction to pass by-laws (in part 2, division 1, s 7) are relevant:

    7. A council may pass bylaws for municipal purposes respecting the following matters:
       (a) the safety, health and welfare of people and the protection of people and property;

       • • •

       (c) nuisances, including unsightly property;

       • • •

       (e) businesses, business activities and persons engaged in business ... .

22 Parts of this case study are drawn from Arlene J Kwasniak "Municipalities and the Regulation and Management of GHGs" (Paper delivered at the Symposium on Environment in the Courtroom: Enforcing Canadian GHG Emissions Laws, Université Laval, Quebec City, 25-26 October 2018), online (pdf): *Canadian Institute of Resources Law* <https://cirl.ca/files/cirl/municipalities-and-the-regulation-and-management-of-ghgs.docx1_.pdf>.

23 EPA, Landfill Methane Outreach Program (LMOP), "Basic Information About Landfill Gas" (last visited 10 June 2019), online: *EPA* <https://www.epa.gov/lmop/basic-information-about-landfill-gas>.

24 Environment and Climate Change Canada, "Solid Waste and Greenhouse Gases" (last modified 11 August 2017), online: *Government of Canada* <http://www.ec.gc.ca/gdd-mw/default.asp?lang=En&n=6f92e701-1&wbdisable=true>.

25 Management approaches include capture and combustion or utilizing landfill gas for "various energy purposes." See Environment and Climate Change Canada, *ibid*. See also "Reducing Greenhouse Gas Emissions at Landfills" (last visited 10 June 2019), online: *Metro Vancouver* <http://www.metrovancouver.org/services/liquid-waste/innovation-wasterwater-reuse/biosolids/reducing-greenhouse-gas-landfills/Pages/default.aspx>.

26 For a United States perspective on municipalities and climate change, see Cynthia Rosenzweig, "All Climate Is Local: How Mayors Fight Global Warming" *Scientific American* 305:3 (September 2011) 70.

- The following powers under general by-laws are relevant:

    8. Without restricting section 7, a council may in a bylaw passed under this Division
       (a) regulate or prohibit;

                    • • •

       (c) provide for a system of licences, permits or approvals, including any or all of the following:

                    • • •

          (iii) prohibiting any development, activity, industry, business or thing until a licence, permit or approval has been granted;

                    • • •

          (v) setting out the conditions that must be met before a licence, permit or approval is granted or renewed, the nature of the conditions and who may impose them ... .

- Sections 616 and 683 are relevant. They are specific authorities and are set out in Section II.B.2 of this chapter.
- A land use by-law may do the following:

    640(1) A land use bylaw may prohibit or regulate and control the use and development of land and buildings in a municipality.

- The relationship to provincial law is as follows:

    13. If there is a conflict or inconsistency between a bylaw and this or another enactment, the bylaw is of no effect to the extent of the conflict or inconsistency.

Assume that no provincial law prohibits LFG emissions over a certain amount. However, the province has legislation imposing a carbon levy and legislation that regulates CO_2 emissions over specified amounts. Assume that Alberta legislation has the potential to regulate LFG emissions, but such emissions have not yet been added to the list of regulated GHGs. Assume no existing federal legislation is relevant.

QUESTIONS

1. Is the LFG By-law within municipal purposes?
2. Is the by-law authorized by the MGA? If so, by what sections? Are these general or specific provisions? How would courts interpret such sections? What is the relationship between them?
3. Does the by-law conflict with provincial law? (Confine your discussion to the sections of the MGA set out in this case study.)
4. Would your answers to any of the previous questions change in light of the fact that Alberta gives charter cities (Edmonton and Calgary (E&C)) specific authorization under their charters[27] to regulate GHG mitigation? Section 4(2)(a)(i) of both the E&C charters adds to the general jurisdiction to pass by-laws (MGA, s 7) respecting

    (h.1) the well-being of the environment, including bylaws providing for the creation, implementation and management of programs respecting any or all of the following:

                    • • •

    (ii) climate change adaptation and greenhouse gas emission reduction ... .

Part 16.1 of both the E&C charters also requires the cities to establish climate change mitigation and adaptation plans.

---

27 *City of Edmonton Charter,* 2018 Regulation, Alta Reg 39/2018 and *City of Calgary Charter,* 2018 Regulation, Alta Reg 40/2018.

IV. LAND USE PLANNING, DEVELOPMENT CONTROLS, AND PROPERTY RIGHTS

A. PLANNING, DEVELOPMENT, ZONING, AND SUBDIVISION

Municipalities primarily exercise their authorities over private land use through their planning, development, zoning, and subdivision powers. How they exercise these powers will have impacts on the environment, for better or worse. This section briefly discusses each power.

1. Planning

Municipalities engage in planning to set out goals, objectives, and actions in target areas, and to better ensure rationality and consistency throughout its activities. Municipal legislation may set out purposes for planning. For example, the Ontario *Planning Act*[28] provides:

> 1.1 The purposes of this Act are,
>
> (a) to promote sustainable economic development in a healthy natural environment within the policy and by the means provided under this Act;
>
> (b) to provide for a land use planning system led by provincial policy;
>
> (c) to integrate matters of provincial interest in provincial and municipal planning decisions;
>
> (d) to provide for planning processes that are fair by making them open, accessible, timely and efficient;
>
> (e) to encourage co-operation and co-ordination among various interests;
>
> (f) to recognize the decision-making authority and accountability of municipal councils in planning.

Municipal legislation may require or permit a range of statutory plans, may prescribe the relation among plans (which plan takes precedence over others), and may set out the legal status of plans (must they be conformed with, or are they merely advisory?). A specific plan can be statutorily based, meaning its role and components are established in municipal legislation, or non-statutory, meaning it sets out municipal policy direction but is not explicitly anticipated in legislation.[29] All plans must fall within municipal purposes.

The Ontario "official plan" offers an example of a statutory plan.[30] Among other requirements, the official plan must contain the "goals, objectives and policies established primarily to manage and direct physical change and the effects on the social, economic, built and natural environment of the municipality or part of it, or an area that is without municipal organization."[31] An example of a non-statutory plan is the Calgary *Wetland Conservation Plan*, which "provide[s] policies and procedures for the protection of [Calgary's] priority wetlands."[32]

A municipality's autonomy with respect to planning depends on the presence or absence of legislative constraints. Provincial legislation may, for example, impose the precedence of provincial laws, policies, or plans over municipal plans and other municipal authorities.

---

28 RSO 1990, c P.13.

29 Case law has established that absent words to the contrary, municipalities have authority to establish non-statutory plans. See, for example, *Dalhousie Station Ltd v Calgary (City)*, 1991 CanLII 5936, 83 Alta LR (2d) 228 (QB).

30 *Planning Act*, ss 14.7-23.

31 *Planning Act*, s 16(1)(a).

32 (14 May 2004) at 37, online (pdf): *Calgary* <http://www.calgary.ca/CSPS/Parks/Documents/Planning -and-Operations/Natural-Areas-and-Wetlands/wetland_conservation_plan.pdf>.

2. Development and Zoning

Municipalities typically have power to regulate when a person may legally carry out a "development," as defined or characterized by the legislation. Through their zoning (sometimes called "districting") powers, municipalities prescribe (for example, through by-law) how land may be developed within the physical boundaries of a land-use zone (district). Typical zones include residential, industrial, commercial, and agricultural zones as well as parks and green or open spaces. One land-use zone may permit intense industrial development, which could negatively affect environmental values, while another may be structured to enhance environmental values by, for example, maintaining green spaces. Although legislation varies throughout Canada, within each zone there will usually be permitted uses and discretionary uses.

3. Subdivision: Reserves, Dedications, Covenants, Conservation Easements

A landowner may wish to divide a parcel of land into smaller titled parcels that may be transferred separately. Subject to legislative exceptions, a landowner requires subdivision approval as stipulated in municipal legislation (for example, from a regional board or a municipality). Depending on the municipal legislation, the subdivision authority may have the right to "dedications" of portions of the land. The dedicated land is "reserved" from the parcel to be subdivided for purposes such as roads, schools, and parkland or because the reserved land is undevelopable or environmentally sensitive. As well, municipal legislation may provide that the land to be subdivided may be subject to covenants or other enforceable restrictions, to prevent development on, for example, lands subject to flooding or other hazardous lands. Depending on the prevailing legislation (which need not be the main municipal legislation), a municipality may also be able to negotiate a conservation easement with a landowner to preserve environmental values within the subdivision process. A conservation easement is a statutorily created interest in land that is constituted through a voluntary legal agreement into which a landowner and persons qualified by the legislation may enter to protect the natural (and other stipulated) values of all or a part of a parcel by restricting development. Negotiation of a conservation easement may be useful when municipal legislation does not authorize dedications or covenants for the kinds of purposes sought by the municipality. A properly registered conservation easement runs with the land (that is, remains with the land, notwithstanding transfers of ownership), and development restrictions are enforceable in accordance with the legislation and terms of the conservation easement agreement.[33]

B. PROPERTY RIGHTS—TAKINGS

Under Canadian law, if a government appropriates an interest in land without the owner's consent, and the statute under which the appropriation occurred either explicitly or implicitly gives the owner the right to compensation, the government must compensate the owner. Appropriations take different forms. A government may take a physical interest in land through an out-and-out expropriation, for example, a strip of land to expand a highway. By contrast, a government might not directly expropriate land but, rather, impose substantial regulation on land use so that the landowner cannot develop as hoped. In some circumstances, this can amount to a regulatory taking (also called a "*de facto* taking" or "constructive expropriation"). The takings issue is critical when one considers how far municipalities may go in regulating uses of land in order to protect environmental values.

33 See, for example, Arlene J Kwasniak, "Conservation Easements: Pluses and Pitfalls, Generally and for Municipalities" (2009) 46:3 Alta L Rev 651 [Kwasniak, "Conservation Easements"].

US courts recognize regulatory takings on the basis of constitutionally protected property rights under the Fifth and Fourteenth Amendments to the US *Bill of Rights*. The Fifth Amendment reads: "No person shall be ... deprived of life, liberty, or property, without due process of law; nor shall private property be taken for public use, without just compensation." The Fourteenth Amendment states: "[N]or shall any State deprive any person of life, liberty, or property, without due process of law." There is a myriad of US regulatory takings cases where a landowner alleges that a municipality has taken property where the municipality denies the landowner's development application because of the prevailing regulatory development restrictions.

A critical difference between Canada and the US is that property rights are not enshrined in the Canadian Constitution or in the *Canadian Charter of Rights and Freedoms*.[34] Although there is considerable Canadian case law on out-and-out expropriations, there is a much smaller body of jurisprudence dealing with regulatory takings. Nevertheless, as the following case excerpt shows, the Supreme Court has developed fairly strict and formidable rules for findings of regulatory takings.

The 2006 Supreme Court decision *Canadian Pacific Railway Co v Vancouver (City)*[35] is a leading case on regulatory takings. The decision concerns the Canadian Pacific Railway's (CPR) proposal to the City that CPR be permitted to develop a discontinued railway corridor (the "Arbutus Corridor") for residential and commercial purposes, or, alternatively, that the City expropriate the corridor for fair value. The City was not quick to act on the CPR proposal, and CPR accused the City of trying to keep the land intact by delay. Eventually the City made it clear that it would not expropriate or otherwise buy the corridor. Instead, the City "adopted the *Arbutus Corridor Official Development Plan By-law*, [City of Vancouver] By-law No. 8249, 25 July 2000 ('ODP By-law'),"[36] which did not accommodate the uses desired by CPR.

CANADIAN PACIFIC RAILWAY CO V VANCOUVER (CITY)
2006 SCC 5, [2006] 1 SCR 227

McLACHLIN CJ:

1. INTRODUCTION

• • •

5 The City's powers are derived from the *Vancouver Charter*, S.B.C. 1953, c. 55, an Act of the Legislature of British Columbia, which serves the same purpose as a "municipal act" but applies only to the city of Vancouver (see Appendix A). Development plans under s. 561 of the *Vancouver Charter* are essentially statements of intention which do not directly affect land owners' property rights. However, once development plans are adopted as "official" ("ODPs") under s. 562, they preclude development contrary to the plans: s. 563.

6 Building on earlier planning documents, the intent of the ODP By-law was "to provide a context for the future of the [corridor]". More particularly, s. 1.2 stated: "The Arbutus Corridor has been used for many years for a rail line and this plan accommodates this use, but also provides for a variety of other uses."

7 The by-law outlined the uses to which the corridor could be put (s. 2.1):

---

34 Part I of the *Constitution Act, 1982*, being Schedule B to the *Canada Act 1982* (UK), 1982, c 11.
35 2006 SCC 5, [2006] 1 SCR 227.
36 *Ibid* at para 4.

This plan designates all of the land in the Arbutus Corridor for use only as a public thoroughfare for the purpose only of:

(a) transportation, including without limitations:

(i) rail;

(ii) transit; and

(iii) cyclist paths

but excluding:

(iv) motor vehicles except on City streets crossing the Arbutus Corridor; and

(v) any grade-separated rapid transit system elevated, in whole or in part, above the surface of the ground, of which one type is the rapid transit system known as "SkyTrain" currently in use in the Lower Mainland;

(b) greenways, including without limitation:

(i) pedestrian paths, including without limitation urban walks, environmental demonstration trails, heritage walks and nature trails; and

(ii) cyclist paths.

8 The effect of the by-law was to freeze the redevelopment potential of the corridor and to confine CPR to uneconomic uses of the land. CPR regards this effect as unfair and unreasonable. It does not allege that the City acted in bad faith. However, it argues: (1) that the by-law is *ultra vires* the City and should be struck down; (2) that the City is obligated to compensate CPR for the land; and (3) that the by-law suffers from procedural irregularities and should be struck down on that account.

9 The chambers judge held the by-law to be *ultra vires* the City, declined a declaration that the City must compensate CPR and found it unnecessary to consider the procedural issues ((2002), 33 M.P.L.R. (3d) 214). The British Columbia Court of Appeal rejected all three arguments and allowed the City's appeal ((2004), 26 B.C.L.R. (4th) 220). CPR now appeals to this Court. Despite considerable sympathy for CPR's position, I conclude that under the *Vancouver Charter*, the City was entitled to refuse compensation and to pass the by-law, and that the courts have no option but to uphold it. I would therefore dismiss the appeal.

• • •

[The court found that the by-law was within statutory powers of the City.]

3.2 COMPENSATION

27 CPR argues there is a presumption that the Legislature intended any taking of property to be compensated. It argues that the ODP By-law, by limiting its use, constitutes an effective taking of its land. It cannot use the land for any economically viable purpose. ...

• • •

29 CPR argues that at common law, a government act that deprives a landowner of all reasonable use of its land constitutes a *de facto* taking and imposes an obligation on the government to compensate the landowner.

30 For a *de facto* taking requiring compensation at common law, two requirements must be met: (1) an acquisition of a beneficial interest in the property or flowing from it, and (2) removal of all reasonable uses of the property (see *Mariner Real Estate Ltd. v. Nova Scotia (Attorney General)* (1999), 177 D.L.R. (4th) 696 (N.S.C.A.), at p. 716; *Manitoba Fisheries Ltd. v. The Queen*, [1979] 1 S.C.R. 101; and *The Queen in Right of British Columbia v. Tener*, [1985] 1 S.C.R. 533).

31 In my view, neither requirement of this test is made out here.

32 First, CPR has not succeeded in showing that the City has acquired a beneficial interest related to the land. To satisfy this branch of the test, it is not necessary to establish a forced transfer of property. Acquisition of beneficial interest related to the property suffices. ...

33 CPR argues that, by passing the ODP By-law, the City acquired a *de facto* park, relying on the observation of Southin J.A. that "the bylaw in issue now can have no purpose but to enable the inhabitants to use the corridor for walking and cycling, which some do (trespassers all), without paying for that use" (para. 117). Southin J.A. went on to say: "The shareholders of ... CPR ought not to be expected to make a charitable gift to the inhabitants" (para. 118). Yet, as Southin J.A. acknowledged, those who now casually use the corridor are trespassers. The City has gained nothing more than some assurance that the land will be used or developed in accordance with its vision, without even precluding the historical or current use of the land. This is not the sort of benefit that can be construed as a "tak[ing]."

34 Second, the by-law does not remove all reasonable uses of the property. This requirement must be assessed "not only in relation to the land's potential highest and best use, but having regard to the nature of the land and the range of reasonable uses to which it has actually been put": see *Mariner Real Estate*, at p. 717. The by-law does not prevent CPR from using its land to operate a railway, the only use to which the land has ever been put during the history of the City. ... The by-law acknowledges the special nature of the land as the only such intact corridor existing in Vancouver, and expands upon the only use the land has known in recent history.

35 CPR also argues that the British Columbia *Expropriation Act*, R.S.B.C. 1996, c. 125, requires the City to compensate CPR (Appendix B). ... Section 2(1) of the Act provides that "[i]f an expropriating authority proposes to expropriate land, th[e] Act applies to the expropriation, and, if there is an inconsistency between any of the provisions of th[e] Act and any other enactment respecting the expropriation, the provisions of [the *Expropriation Act*] apply." The *Expropriation Act* requires compensation for land expropriated, while the *Vancouver Charter* states the City is not obliged to compensate for adverse effects to land caused by an ODP. CPR argues that this constitutes an inconsistency and that, under s. 2 of the *Expropriation Act*, the requirement of compensation in that Act must prevail.

36 This argument rests on the premise that there is an inconsistency between the *Expropriation Act* and the *Vancouver Charter* as applied to the facts in this case. It assumes that the land is "expropriate[d]" or "taken" and that the two statutes impose different obligations in this event—compensation in one case, no compensation in the other. In fact, however, the provisions of the *Vancouver Charter* prevent a conflict from ever arising. Section 569 of the *Vancouver Charter* provides that property affected by a by-law "shall be deemed as against the city not to have been taken." The *Expropriation Act* applies only where there has been a "tak[ing]" or "expropriat[ion]." Since by statute there is no taking or expropriation here, there is no inconsistency with the *Expropriation Act* and s. 2(1) cannot apply.

• • •

4. CONCLUSION

63 While one may sympathize with CPR's position, none of its arguments withstand scrutiny. The City did not exceed the powers granted to it by the *Vancouver Charter*. Neither the *Vancouver Charter* nor principles of common law require it to compensate CPR for the ODP By-law's effects on its land.

C. CASE STUDY AND QUESTIONS: SOURCE WATER PROTECTION BY-LAW

This case study concerns Springton, a fictional British Columbia municipality. Assume that the city's powers are the same as those of Vancouver discussed in *Canadian Pacific Railway*, above. Accordingly, development plans under the municipal legislation, once adopted as official, preclude development contrary to the plan. The Springton Source Water Protection Plan (SSWPP) has been adopted as an official plan. Natural springs are a major source of drinking water for Springton. Springs form when natural pressure forces shallow groundwater above the surface of the land. To maintain the water source for drinking water, the SSWPP prohibits Springton from permitting development in a spring protection zone (SPZ) if it would adversely interfere with natural spring processes or impair water quality. The SSWPP does, however, permit reasonable use of spring water and groundwater, provided the owner complies with the requirements of the *Water Sustainability Act*,[37] an Act that applies to all water appropriators in the province. Pursuant to the SSWPP, an SPZ has been identified, and a Spring Protection by-law passed. The by-law set out permitted and discretionary uses as follows:

1. The permitted uses for land located in the SPZ are
    (a) greenways, including, without limitation:
        (i) pedestrian paths, including urban walks, environmental demonstration trails, heritage walks, and nature trails, and
        (ii) cyclist paths;
    (b) scientific study, including ecology and hydrology.
2. The discretionary use for land in the SPZ is no-till farming without the use of pesticides or herbicides, provided that such use does not involve any new permanent buildings.

The developer/owner of the land, Builditup Co, has applied to subdivide and develop the land to construct several multibuilding commercial/residential complexes. The relevant municipal decision-maker denied the application because such use was neither permitted nor discretionary in the SSWPP or Spring Protection by-law. Builditup does not contest the validity of the SSWPP or by-law, but it claims that the refusal constitutes a regulatory taking, requiring compensation. You may assume that the BC *Expropriation Act* described in para 35 of the *Canadian Pacific Railway* case, above, applies, and also assume that the municipal legislation provides that the City is not obliged to compensate for adverse effects to landowners caused by the SSWPP or by-law.

When answering the questions below, keep in mind *Lynch v St John's (City)*,[38] a 2016 Newfoundland and Labrador case. The NL Court of Appeal found that there was a regulatory taking on the basis that the imposition of a municipal policy met the criteria in para 30 of the *Canadian Pacific Railway* decision. The policy required watershed land to be kept "unused in its natural state"[39] "to avoid the City having an impure and polluted water supply for City residents and others who depend upon the City for clean water."[40] The court found that the policy removed all reasonable uses of the property and that the City acquired a beneficial interest in the nature of a *profit à prendre* or a restrictive covenant (both being property interests) by taking "away the Lynches' right to appropriate the groundwater on their land" and thereby conferring on the City "a beneficial interest in the Lynch property, consisting of the right to a continuous flow of uncontaminated groundwater downstream to the City's water facilities."[41] The court found that there was a constructive expropriation, and, in the circumstances, the plaintiffs were entitled to compensation under the NL *Expropriation Act*.[42]

---

37 SBC 2014, c 15.
38 2016 NLCA 35, leave to appeal to SCC refused, 2017 CanLII 4184 [*Lynch* cited to NLCA].
39 *Ibid* at paras 23, 62, 63.
40 *Ibid* at para 14.
41 *Ibid* at para 60.
42 RSNL 1990, c E-19.

QUESTIONS

1. Did Springton's refusal amount to a regulatory taking? What arguments may be made on behalf of Builditup and on behalf of Springton?
2. If there was a taking, is Springton liable to pay Builditup compensation?
3. Adjust the facts so that only some of Builditup's land is within the SPZ; the rest of the parcel is within a land-use zone where Builditup's proposed use is a discretionary use. What approaches might the municipality take to enable a modified development while protecting source water? What further information about reserves and dedications, etc. do you need to address this question? If the available reserves or dedications will not meet Springton's needs, what other tools would you investigate to protect the SPZ?[43]

V. MUNICIPAL ACTION AND INDIGENOUS RIGHTS AND INTERESTS

A. MUNICIPAL ROLE IN CONSULTATION AND ACCOMMODATION

This section assumes that the reader is familiar with Chapter 12. Chapter 12 sets out the source and nature of Indigenous rights and interests and explains key concepts relevant to a situation where government action could permit impacts on them. Concepts include honour of the Crown and duty to consult and accommodate. This section focuses on the role of municipalities in respect of the Crown's duty to consult and accommodate where municipal action might adversely affect or impact constitutionally protected Indigenous rights or interests. That role could fall within a range, as shown below:

1. The *Crown* in respect of the duty to consult *includes* municipalities "so as to bind them to uphold the honour of the Crown in dealing with Aboriginal peoples."[44] Crown action that can adversely affect or impact Indigenous rights or interests, in this sense, includes municipal action. Where municipal consultation is inadequate, the pertinent dominant Crown (provincial, territorial, or federal) must supplement it to fulfill the duty.
2. Municipalities are not the Crown and do not technically have a duty to consult, but they have an obligation (at least moral or political) to carry out the Crown duty to consult when municipal action may adversely affect Indigenous rights or interests. Where municipal consultation is inadequate, the dominant Crown must supplement it to fulfill the duty.
3. Municipalities have no duty or obligation to consult when municipal action may adversely affect Indigenous rights or interests. Any such duty/obligation rests with the Crown.

B. COURT DECISIONS: MUNICIPALITIES AND DUTY TO CONSULT

A 2012 BC Court of Appeal decision supports option 3, above, that municipalities have no duty or obligation to consult. However, two 2017 Supreme Court decisions may support option 1, that the *Crown* can include municipalities with respect to the duty, or at least option 2, that municipalities technically hold no duty to consult but may have an obligation to do so.

---

43 See discussions and case references on this issue in Kwasniak, "Conservation Easements," *supra* note 33 at 12-14. To generalize from the comments therein, depending on the jurisdiction and statutory language, a municipality may use a conservation easement in subdivision and development processes but may not force or impose a conservation easement/covenant because such an interest is voluntary.
44 See Felix Hoehn & Michael Stevens, "Local Governments and the Crown's Duty to Consult" (2018) 55:4 Alta L Rev 971 at 992.

Whether the 2017 decisions lend such support depends on whether their reasoning applies to municipalities.

The petitioner in the 2012 decision *Neskonlith Indian Band v Salmon Arm (City)*[45] argued that the City of Salmon Arm owed a duty to consult prior to its decision to issue an "Environmentally Hazardous Area Development Permit" to a developer of a proposed shopping centre adjacent to the Neskonlith Indian Band (NIB) reserve. The NIB claimed that the area was traditional land and that the permit and development would adversely affect or impact Indigenous rights and interests. The court found that the City did not owe a duty to consult the NIB. In so finding, the court relied on the Supreme Court decisions *Haida Nation v British Columbia (Minister of Forests)*[46] and *Rio Tinto Alcan Inc v Carrier Sekani Tribal Council*.[47] These cases set out the three required elements to meet the threshold for the duty to consult:

> [31] The ... duty to consult arises *"when the Crown has knowledge, real or constructive, of the potential existence of the Aboriginal right or title and contemplates conduct that might adversely affect it"* (para. 35 [of *Haida*]). This test can be broken down into three elements: (1) the Crown's knowledge, actual or constructive, of a potential Aboriginal claim or right; (2) contemplated Crown conduct; and (3) the potential that the contemplated conduct may adversely affect an Aboriginal claim or right. [Emphasis added in *Rio Tinto Alcan*.][48]

As evident in the following excerpt, the stickler in *Neskonlith* was element (2). The contemplated conduct, the issuance of the permit, was that of the municipality.

NESKONLITH INDIAN BAND V SALMON ARM (CITY)
2012 BCCA 379

[61] The argument of the Neskonlith in favour of a municipal duty to consult can be described fairly succinctly. First, they emphasize that the honour of the Crown is a "core constitutional principle" informing all interactions between Aboriginal persons and "government," citing *Haida* at para. 16. The purpose of the duty is to protect Aboriginal rights while furthering the goal of reconciliation. The Supreme Court of Canada has said that the honour of the Crown must be understood "generously" in this context (*Haida* at para. 17) and in the Band's submission, a "generous and purposive application of the honour of the Crown requires consultation whenever government authorizes activities which interfere with Aboriginal rights and title, whether that authorization comes directly from the Province or from local governments exercising delegated provincial authority." Thus, it is said, the honour of the Crown imposes a constraint on the exercise of authority delegated by the Province. If it were otherwise, the Province would be in a position to eliminate or avoid this core principle by delegating the decision to its statutory creature, a local government. Such avoidance would not be consistent with the honour of the Crown.

[62] Counsel for the Neskonlith finds an analogy in various decisions of the Supreme Court of Canada holding that statutory authorities, including municipalities, are subject to the *Charter*. ...

• • •

[64] As for the notion, expressed at para. 53 of *Haida*, that "the honour of the Crown cannot be delegated," the Band notes that that statement was made in

---

45   2012 BCCA 379.
46   2004 SCC 73, [2004] 3 SCR 511.
47   2010 SCC 43, [2010] 2 SCR 650.
48   *Ibid* at para 31.

the context of the argument that a private party, the forestry contractor which held the tree farm license in that case, itself owed a duty to consult to the Haida. Here, however, the "third party" is a local *government*, which is said to have the statutory authority to affect Aboriginal rights and title through the exercise of its authority. While the Neskonlith acknowledge that the Province may have a "residual" obligation to ensure that the honour of the Crown is discharged, they also say that the "constraint" (i.e., the duty to consult founded in the honour of the Crown) attaches "automatically" to any governmental body exercising the authority of the Crown. This, they say, makes practical sense—the local government is in the best position to assess the effect of its decisions on First Nations. ...

[65] ... In the Neskonlith's submission, the duty to consult in this case attaches to the City, not because of the delegation of the duty by a decision-maker, but because the local government *is itself the decision-maker*.

[66] These are all strong arguments. There are, however, even more powerful arguments, both legal and practical, that in my view militate against inferring a duty to consult on the part of municipal governments. ...

[67] In *Rio Tinto*, the Court made an apparent exception to its statement in *Haida*, observing at para. 56:

> The legislature may choose to delegate to a tribunal the Crown's duty to consult. As noted in *Haida Nation*, it is open to governments to set up regulatory schemes to address the procedural requirements of consultation at different stages of the decision-making process with respect to a resource.

Whether the Court intended that *only* "procedural aspects" could be delegated is debatable, but the Court clearly rejected the notion that "every tribunal with jurisdiction to consider questions of law has a constitutional duty to consider whether adequate consultation has taken place and, if not, to itself fulfill the requirement regardless of whether its constituent statute so provides." The Chief Justice stated for the Court:

> ... The *reasoning seems to be that this power flows automatically from the power of the tribunal to consider legal and hence constitutional questions.* Lack of consultation amounts to a constitutional vice that vitiates the tribunal's jurisdiction and, in the case before us, makes it inconsistent with the public interest. In order to perform its duty, it must rectify the vice by itself engaging in the missing consultation.
>
> *This argument cannot be accepted, in my view. A tribunal has only those powers that are expressly or implicitly conferred on it by statute.* In order for a tribunal to have the power to enter into interim resource consultations with a First Nation, pending the final settlement of claims, the tribunal must be expressly or impliedly authorized to do so. *The power to engage in consultation itself, as distinct from the jurisdiction to determine whether a duty to consult exists, cannot be inferred from the mere power to consider questions of law.* Consultation itself is not a question of law; it is a distinct and often complex constitutional process and, in certain circumstances, a right involving facts, law, policy, and compromise. *The tribunal seeking to engage in consultation itself must therefore possess remedial powers necessary to do what it is asked to do in connection with the consultation.* The remedial powers of a tribunal will depend on that tribunal's enabling statute, and will require discerning the legislative intent: *Conway* [R v Conway, 2010 SCC 22, [2010] 1 SCR 765], at para. 82. [At paras. 59-60; emphasis added.]

• • •

[70] By virtue of *Haida* and *Rio Tinto* alone, then, it seems to me this appeal must fail as a matter of law. It is not for this court to create an exception to or modification of the very clear statements the Supreme Court has made. And while it is true that First Nations may experience difficulty in seeking appropriate remedies in the courts in cases like this one, it is also true that as creatures of statute, municipalities do not in general have the authority to consult with and[,] if indicated, accommodate First Nations as a specific group in making the day-to-day operational decisions that are the diet of local governments.

[71] I also suggest that ... municipal governments lack the *practical resources* to consult and accommodate. Such governments (of which there are 191 in British Columbia) range greatly in size and tax-base, and are generally concerned with the regulation of privately-owned land and activities thereon. Crown land and natural resources found thereon remain within the purview of the Province. It is precisely because the Crown asserted sovereignty over lands previously occupied by Aboriginal peoples that the Crown in right of the Province is now held to the duty to consult: see *Haida* at paras. 26, 32 and 59.

[72] Finally, I consider that the "push-down" of the Crown's duty to consult, from the Crown to local governments, such that consultation and accommodation would be thrashed out in the context of the mundane decisions regarding licenses, permits, zoning restrictions and local bylaws, would be completely impractical. These decisions, ranging from the issuance of business licences to the designation of parks, from the zoning of urban areas to the regulation of the keeping of animals, require efficiency and certainty. Daily life would be seriously bogged down if consultation— including the required "strength of claim" assessment—became necessary whenever a right or interest of a First Nation "might be" affected. In the end, I doubt that it would be in the interests of First Nations, the Crown or the ultimate goal of reconciliation for the duty to consult to be ground down into such small particles, obscuring the larger "upstream" objectives described in *Haida*.

The *Neskonlith* decision was criticized on many bases, including the fact that it left no practical remedy for affected Indigenous peoples, it left inconclusive who had the responsibility to exercise the duty to consult, and it concluded that municipalities had no duty even though they may be in the best position to carry out consultation.[49]

At the time of writing, the Supreme Court has not articulated whether municipalities have a legal-based or other duty to consult. However, the Supreme Court has refined the application of the duty in a way that by analogy might apply to municipalities.[50] *Clyde River (Hamlet) v Petroleum Geo-Services Inc*[51] and *Chippewas of the Thames First Nation v Enbridge Pipelines Inc*[52] concerned permitting by the National Energy Board (NEB), a federal tribunal and regulatory agency that regulates pipelines and other energy development falling within federal jurisdiction. Both cases concerned whether the NEB had a duty or obligation to carry out the Crown's duty to consult. The following excerpt from *Clyde River* explains the issues and their resolution. As you read, consider to what extent the discussion might, by analogy, apply to municipalities.

49 See Shin Imai & Ashley Stacey "Municipalities and the Duty to Consult Aboriginal Peoples: A Case Comment on Neskonlith Indian Band v Salmon Arm (City)" (2014) 47 UBC L Rev 293.
50 See Hoehn & Stevens, *supra* note 44.
51 2017 SCC 40, [2017] 1 SCR 1069.
52 2017 SCC 41, [2017] 1 SCR 1099.

CLYDE RIVER (HAMLET) V PETROLEUM GEO-SERVICES INC
2017 SCC 40, [2017] 1 SCR 1069 [footnotes omitted]

KARAKATSANIS AND BROWN JJ:

I. INTRODUCTION

[1] ... In this appeal, and its companion *Chippewas of the Thames First Nation v. Enbridge Pipelines Inc.*, 2017 SCC 41, [2017] 1 S.C.R. 1099, we consider the Crown's duty to consult with Indigenous peoples before an independent regulatory agency authorizes a project which could impact upon their rights. The Court's jurisprudence shows that the substance of the duty does not change when a regulatory agency holds final decision-making authority in respect of a project. While the Crown always owes the duty to consult, regulatory processes can partially or completely fulfill this duty.

• • •

[4] While the Crown may rely on the NEB's process to fulfill its duty to consult, considering the importance of the established treaty rights at stake and the potential impact of the seismic testing on those rights, we agree with the appellants that the consultation and accommodation efforts in this case were inadequate. For the reasons set out below, we would therefore allow the appeal and quash the NEB's authorization.

• • •

III. ANALYSIS

• • •

B. CAN AN NEB APPROVAL PROCESS TRIGGER THE DUTY TO CONSULT?

[25] The duty to consult is triggered when the Crown has actual or constructive knowledge of a potential Aboriginal claim or Aboriginal or treaty rights that might be adversely affected by Crown conduct (*Haida*, at para. 35; *Carrier Sekani*, at para. 31). Crown conduct which would trigger the duty is not restricted to the exercise by or on behalf of the Crown of statutory powers or of the royal prerogative, nor is it limited to decisions that have an immediate impact on lands and resources. The concern is for adverse impacts, however made, upon Aboriginal and treaty rights and, indeed, a goal of consultation is to identify, minimize and address adverse impacts where possible (*Carrier Sekani*, at paras. 45-46).

[26] In this appeal, all parties agreed that the Crown's duty to consult was triggered, although agreement on *just what* Crown conduct triggered the duty has proven elusive. The Federal Court of Appeal saw the trigger in *COGOA's* [*Canada Oil and Gas Operations Act*, RSC 1985, c O-7] requirement for ministerial approval (or waiver of the requirement for approval) of a benefits plan for the testing. In the companion appeal of *Chippewas of the Thames*, the majority of the Federal Court of Appeal concluded that it was not necessary to decide whether the duty to consult was triggered since the Crown was not a party before the NEB, but suggested the only Crown action involved might have been the 1959 enactment of the *NEB Act* (*Chippewas of the Thames First Nation v. Enbridge Pipelines Inc.*, 2015 FCA 222, [2016] 3 F.C.R. 96). In short, the Federal Court of Appeal in both cases was of the view

that only action by a minister of the Crown or a government department, or a Crown corporation, can constitute Crown conduct triggering the duty to consult. And, before this Court in *Chippewas of the Thames*, the Attorney General of Canada argued that the duty was triggered by the NEB's approval of the pipeline project, because it was state action with the potential to affect Aboriginal or treaty rights.

[27] Contrary to the Federal Court of Appeal's conclusions on this point, we agree that the NEB's approval process, in this case, as in *Chippewas of the Thames*, triggered the duty to consult.

[28] It bears reiterating that the duty to consult is owed by the Crown. In one sense, the "Crown" refers to the personification in Her Majesty of the Canadian state in exercising the prerogatives and privileges reserved to it. The Crown also, however, denotes the sovereign in the exercise of her formal legislative role (in assenting, refusing assent to, or reserving legislative or parliamentary bills), and as the head of executive authority (*McAteer v. Canada (Attorney General)*, 2014 ONCA 578, 121 O.R. (3d) 1, at para. 51; P.W. Hogg, P.J. Monahan and W.K. Wright, *Liability of the Crown* (4th ed. 2011), at pp. 11-12; but see *Carrier Sekani*, at para. 44). For this reason, the term "Crown" is commonly used to symbolize and denote executive power. ...

[29] By this understanding, the NEB is not, strictly speaking, "the Crown." Nor is it, strictly speaking, an agent of the Crown, since—as the NEB operates independently of the Crown's ministers—no relationship of control exists between them (Hogg, Monahan and Wright, at p. 465). As a statutory body holding responsibility under s. 5(1)(b) of *COGOA*, however, the NEB acts on behalf of the Crown when making a final decision on a project application. Put plainly, once it is accepted that a regulatory agency exists to exercise executive power as authorized by legislatures, any distinction between its actions and Crown action quickly falls away. In this context, the NEB is the vehicle through which the Crown acts. Hence this Court's interchangeable references in *Carrier Sekani* to "government action" and "Crown conduct" (paras. 42-44). It therefore does not matter whether the final decision maker on a resource project is Cabinet or the NEB. In either case, the decision constitutes Crown action that may trigger the duty to consult. As Rennie J.A. said in dissent at the Federal Court of Appeal in *Chippewas of the Thames*, "[t]he duty, like the honour of the Crown, does not evaporate simply because a final decision has been made by a tribunal established by Parliament, as opposed to Cabinet" (para. 105). The action of the NEB, taken in furtherance of its statutory powers under s. 5(1)(b) of *COGOA* to make final decisions respecting such testing as was proposed here, clearly constitutes Crown action.

C. CAN THE CROWN RELY ON THE NEB'S PROCESS TO FULFILL THE DUTY TO CONSULT?

[30] As we have said, while ultimate responsibility for ensuring the adequacy of consultation remains with the Crown, the Crown may rely on steps undertaken by a regulatory agency to fulfill the duty to consult. Whether, however, the Crown is capable of doing so, in whole or in part, depends on whether the agency's statutory duties and powers enable it to do what the duty requires in the particular circumstances (*Carrier Sekani*, at paras. 55 and 60). In the NEB's case, therefore, the question is whether the NEB is able, to the extent it is being relied on, to provide an appropriate level of consultation and, where necessary, accommodation to the Inuit of Clyde River in respect of the proposed testing.

[The court then reviewed relevant powers of the NEB.]

• • •

[34] In sum, the NEB has (1) the procedural powers necessary to implement consultation; and (2) the remedial powers to, where necessary, accommodate affected Aboriginal claims, or Aboriginal and treaty rights. Its process can therefore be relied on by the Crown to completely or partially fulfill the Crown's duty to consult. Whether the NEB's process did so in this case, we consider below.

[The court considered the NEB's consultation and determined that it was not adequate to fulfill the Crown's duty to consult. By contrast, in *Chippewas of the Thames First Nation*, the court found the NEB consultation to be adequate.[53]]

C. CASE STUDY AND QUESTIONS: MUNICIPALITIES AND ADVERSE EFFECTS OR IMPACTS ON INDIGENOUS RIGHTS AND INTERESTS

This case study concerns Butte, a fictional Manitoba town. Butte owns surplus land (Butte Land) that it wishes to sell. Butte Land is adjacent to a particular First Nation's (FN) reserve. Amusement Inc (AMI) wants to acquire Butte Land and develop an amusement park, including permanent and moveable structures, on it. AMI expects that the park will attract thousands of people annually. For the development, in addition to acquiring Butte Land from Butte, AMI requires municipal zoning changes and development permits. For the purposes of this case study, assume that the proposed project requires no provincial or federal assessment or authorizations.

The FN claims that Butte Land is traditional land to which it has hunting and fishing rights, that the proposed sale and development will impair the FN's rights, and that Butte owes the FN a duty to consult and accommodate. The provincial policy on the duty to consult provides:

The Manitoba government recognizes it has a duty to consult in a meaningful way with First Nations, Métis communities and other Aboriginal communities when any proposed provincial law, regulation, decision or action may infringe upon or adversely affect the exercise of a treaty or Aboriginal right of that First Nation, Métis community or other Aboriginal community.[54]

QUESTIONS

1. Apply the threshold tests from para 31 of *Rio Tinto Alcan* (set out above) to the case study facts. Is there a duty to consult? What needs to be argued or established for Butte to hold either a Crown duty to consult (option 1 in the range of roles of municipalities, discussed in Section V.A. of this chapter) or some other based obligation to carry out the Crown duty (option 2 in the range)? How would the Manitoba provincial policy need to be interpreted if the duty falls in option 1 or in option 2?

2. Review para 29 of the *Clyde River* case, above, and consider to what extent *municipalities* could be substituted for the NEB. Are there relevant differences between municipalities and highly regulated tribunals such as the NEB? Consider that municipalities, compared to statutory tribunals, are a level of government, generally enjoy considerably more autonomy, and have greater accountability and responsibilities. Do such differences affect the answer to the question of whether municipalities owe a duty or have a responsibility to consult?

53 See Nigel Bankes, "Clyde River and Chippewas of the Thames: Some Clarifications Provided but Some Challenges Remain" (4 August 2017), online (pdf): *ABlawg* <http://ablawg.ca/wp-content/uploads/2017/08/Blog_NB_Clyde_River_CTFN.pdf>.

54 Manitoba, Indigenous and Northern Relations, "Interim Provincial Policy for Crown Consultations with First Nations, Métis Communities and Other Aboriginal Communities," Policy Statement (last visited 11 June 2019), online: *Province of Manitoba* <https://www.gov.mb.ca/inr/reconciliation-strategy/duty-to-consult-framework.html>.

3. The *Neskonlith* court claims that there are practical issues related to a municipal duty or responsibility to consult (paras 71 and 72). Consider ways in which these claims and issues might be countered, or addressed.

4. Suppose you are a member of a team that is assisting your provincial government in developing a policy on municipalities and duty to consult. Suppose the team is consulting Indigenous communities regarding what role municipalities should play in Crown consultation. Some responses reflect the view of the plaintiff in *Neskonlith*. However other responses hold that although municipalities have an important role to play with respect to duty to consult and accommodate when municipal action may impact Indigenous rights or interests, in some such circumstances an affected Indigenous community may prefer only to deal with the dominant Crown. Provide direction to your team as to how to proceed in developing policy recommendations in view of these diverse responses.

FURTHER READINGS

Atkins, Judy, Ann Hillyer & Arlene Kwasniak, *Conservation Easements, Covenants and Servitudes in Canada—A Legal Review*, Report No 04-1 (Ottawa: North American Wetlands Conservation Council (Canada), 2004), online (pdf): <http://nawcc.wetlandnetwork.ca/conseasecov04-1.pdf>.

Epstein, Howard, *Land Use Planning* (Toronto: Irwin Law, 2017).

Hoehn, F, *Municipalities and Canadian Law* (Saskatoon: Purich, 1996).

Laux, Frederick A, *Planning Law and Practice in Alberta*, 3rd ed (Edmonton: Juriliber, 2002) (loose-leaf).

Maclean, M Virginia & John R Tomlinson, *A User's Guide to Municipal By-Laws*, 2nd ed (Toronto: LexisNexis, 2008).

Makuch, Stanley, Neil Craik & Signe B Leisk, *Canadian Municipal and Planning Law*, 2nd ed (Toronto: Thomson Carswell, 2004).

Reynolds, L, "Environmental Regulation and Management by Local Public Authorities in Canada" (1993) 3 J Envtl L & Prac 41.

Rogers, Ian & Alison Scott Butler, *Canadian Law of Planning and Zoning*, 2nd ed (Toronto: Carswell, 2005) (loose-leaf).

CHAPTER TWENTY-THREE

ENVIRONMENTAL CONSIDERATIONS IN BUSINESS TRANSACTIONS

Chidinma B Thompson, PhD*

---

* Chidinma B Thompson is a partner at Borden Ladner Gervais LLP. The views expressed in this chapter are solely her own.

This chapter identifies key environmental issues that determine the parties' choices of the core elements of a business transaction, including, *inter alia*, the structure, parties to the agreement, subject matter, price, financing, and timing for completion.

I. TYPES OF BUSINESS TRANSACTIONS

A fundamental question in structuring a business transaction is whether to purchase specific assets to the exclusion of certain liabilities, lease the assets, or purchase all or a majority of the shares of a target company.[1] Historically, environmental issues were given little or no attention in the negotiations for the sale and purchase of businesses and were not specifically addressed in purchase and sale agreements.[2] However, there has been a shift toward environmental stewardship in every sphere and at every level.[3] Over time, environmental liabilities have become one, among many, of the key legal and practical considerations in business transactions.

The heightened environmental awareness has been judicially recognized and was recently endorsed in the dissenting reasons of the Alberta Court of Appeal and of the Supreme Court of Canada in *Orphan Well Association v Grant Thornton Ltd*.[4] A general effect of *Redwater*, a popular name for this decision, is that environmental considerations will rank higher in priority than usual in the purchase and sale of businesses. It has become even more critical to understand the nature and scope of environmental liabilities that exist or may accrue, where those liabilities will reside post-closing of the transaction, and who may be affected by those liabilities, especially in a corporate group context. In an asset transaction, liabilities originate from the vendor. The liabilities that would transfer with the assets to the purchaser are subject to the bargaining powers of the parties as well as to legislative provisions. As discussed further below, transfer of ownership of an asset does not always transfer the associated statutory environmental liabilities. In a share transaction, environmental liabilities of the target company remain with the target company post-closing, but the value of the shares purchased may be affected by such liabilities.

II. OWNERSHIP VERSUS LIABILITY

Ownership of the asset or business being sold does not always equate with ownership of the associated environmental liabilities. In most cases, the owner of the asset is also the owner of the environmental liabilities. However, in some cases that may not be true. This is because most environmental statutes in Canada are based on the "polluter pays" principle, and environmental liability is attached to "person responsible."

1   Jennifer E Babe, *Sale of a Business*, 9th ed (Markham, Ont: LexisNexis, 2012) at 1. Note that leasing of assets and real estate is beyond the scope of this chapter.
2   *Ibid* at 169.
3   Chidinma B Thompson et al, "Redwater Decision" (4 February 2019), online: *Borden Ladner Gervais LLP* <https://blg.com/en/News-And-Publications/Publication_5556> [Thompson, "Redwater Decision"].
4   2017 ABCA 124 at para 107, rev'd 2019 SCC 5 [*Redwater*].

A. LIABILITY OF PERSONS RESPONSIBLE

Most environmental statutes in Canada define "person responsible" very broadly. In Alberta, liability for releases are dealt with under the *Environmental Protection and Enhancement Act*[5] in two ways: part 5, division 1 (releases of substances generally, primarily used by the regulators); and part 5, division 2 (contaminated sites designation). In both cases, persons responsible as defined in the EPEA are liable. Under division 1 of part 5, "person responsible," to whom the regulator may issue an environmental protection, includes

    (i) the owner and a previous owner of the substance or thing,

    (ii) every person who has or has had charge, management or control of the substance or thing, including, without limitation, the manufacture, treatment, sale, handling, use, storage, disposal, transportation, display or method of application of the substance or thing,

    (iii) any successor, assignee, executor, administrator, receiver, receiver–manager or trustee of a person referred to in subclause (i) or (ii), and

    (iv) a person who acts as the principal or agent of a person referred to in subclause (i), (ii) or (iii) ... .[6]

The test is based on the relationship to the substance or the release.

Under division 2 of part 5, "person responsible for the contaminated site" includes

    (i) a person responsible for the substance that is in, on or under the contaminated site,

    (ii) any other person who the [regulator] considers caused or contributed to the release of the substance into the environment,

    (iii) the owner of the contaminated site;

    (iv) any previous owner of the contaminated site who was the owner at any time when the substance was in, on or under the contaminated site;

    (v) a successor, assignee, executor, administrator, receiver, receiver–manager or trustee of a person referred to in any of subclauses (ii) to (iv), and

    (vi) a person who acts as the principal or agent of a person referred to in any of subclauses (ii) to (v) ... .[7]

The test is based on the relationship to the substance, the release, or the property.

The regulator must consider several factors before issuing an environmental protection order for a contaminated site, including

    (b) in the case of an owner or previous owner of the site,

• • •

    (iii) whether the presence of the substance in, on or under the site ought to have been discovered by the owner had the owner exercised due diligence in ascertaining the presence of the substance before the owner became an owner, and whether the owner exercised such due diligence;

    (iv) whether the presence of the substance in, on or under the site was caused solely by the act or omission of another person, other than an employee, agent or person with whom the owner or previous owner has or had a contractual relationship;

    (v) the price the owner paid for the site and the relationship between that price and the fair market value of the site had the substance not been present in, on or under it.[8]

Division 2 offers options otherwise unavailable to potential persons responsible in division 1, including the allocation of responsibility to present and past site owners who may have

---

5   RSA 2000, c E-12 [EPEA].

6   EPEA, s 1(tt).

7   EPEA, s 107(1)(c).

8   EPEA, s 129(2)(b).

contractually assumed liability for the pollution, remedial action plans and agreements with the regulator, and the apportionment of costs of remedial work among responsible parties.[9] In practice, division 2 is rarely used by the regulator.[10] Given the broad definition of "person responsible" in environmental statutes, lenders and insurers of persons responsible are potentially exposed to the environmental liabilities.[11]

In addition to environmental statutes, parties to an oil and gas transaction should also consider the chain of liability in conservation legislation. For example, in Alberta, the *Oil and Gas Conservation Act*[12] governs oil and gas operations and attaches liabilities, such as abandonment obligations, to licensees and working interest owners.[13] Consequently, understanding the extent of environmental obligations of the business or assets to be transferred and the requirements of other potential persons responsible, such as lenders and insurers, are critical for a successful negotiation and closing of the transaction.[14]

B. STATUTORY AND COMMON LAW LIABILITY

The two main sources of environmental liability are statute and common law. Statutory liabilities are those imposed by legislation; they include environmental offences, environmental protection orders, and other regulatory restrictions on operations. Common law environmental liabilities are those arising from judicial decisions on environmental damage or harm.[15] Canadian environmental statutes create a wide range of environmental offences, the breach of which may result in substantial penalties, including profit-stripping elements.[16] These statutes also include civil remedies for the regulators and the government but do not affect or take away statutory and common law civil remedies available to affected third parties.[17] Furthermore, as part of the regulatory due diligence that is conducted prior to the issuance of licences and approvals to businesses for their operations, some regulators consider the frequency of statutory breaches, including environmental breaches, by the applicant business. Consequently, prior environmental offences may result in future denial of regulatory licences and other approvals necessary for operations. Also, environmental statutes give regulators a wide range of powers to carry out environmental audits, inspections, and investigations and to issue a broad range of remedial orders, including cessation of operations.[18] Therefore, these should be investigated during the sale–purchase transaction.

In an asset sale, depending on the definition of "person responsible" in the applicable legislation, the vendor will continue to be liable in the future for statutory environmental damage unless it can establish that it never had any connection with the substance causing the environmental damage or that the environmental contamination did not occur at the time the vendor owned or operated the business.[19] In a share transaction, the purchaser, as a shareholder, would not be exposed to the environmental liabilities of the target corporation,[20] although the purchaser's

---

9 EPEA, s 131.

10 Chidinma B Thompson, "Environmental Issues in Expropriation" (17 December 2018), online (blog): *THE RESOURCE® BLG Energy Law Blog* <https://blog.blg.com/energy/Pages/Post.aspx?PID=401> [Thompson, "Environmental Issues in Expropriation"].

11 Babe, *supra* note 1 at 171.

12 RSA 2000, c O-6 [OGCA].

13 OGCA, ss 27-30.

14 Babe, *supra* note 1 at 171.

15 *Ibid* at 170.

16 *Ibid*.

17 EPEA, ss 216, 217.

18 Babe, *supra* note 1 at 170-71.

19 *Ibid* at 171.

20 *Ibid*.

investment in the corporation would be at risk. Directors and officers, as the directing minds of corporations, have been held personally liable for statutory environmental liabilities of corporations.[21] In Alberta, in addition to charging persons with an offence under the EPEA, the regulator may issue a declaration naming individual directors and officers of licensee corporations for failure to comply with environment-related orders issued at the time they were in control of the corporation.[22] The declaration is for an indefinite period of time, unless there are extenuating circumstances; it inflicts reputational damage; or it takes away the ability of the individuals and their other associated entities to conduct business with the regulator. The declaration may be rescinded by the regulator if the named director or officer repays any cost incurred by the regulator in remedying the environmental issue.

Corporations may have environmental liabilities arising from breach of contract, negligence, trespass, nuisance, misrepresentation, deceit or lack of disclosure, deliberate or intentional acts or omissions, bad faith, etc. A corporation as a former owner of an asset may, in certain circumstances, be liable in negligence to the current owner of the asset in respect of environmental harm caused by the predecessors' negligence.[23] Liability for nuisance would arise if the source of the nuisance originated outside the lands in issue.[24] Directors and officers may be personally liable for common law environmental liabilities of corporations despite the fact that the impugned acts were performed in the course of their duties to the corporation. They may be liable in tort, where their act or conduct is in itself tortious or exhibits an identity or interest separate from that of the corporation, so as to make the act or conduct their own.[25]

C. OTHER SCENARIOS

There are some transactions that may be affected by environmental liability without the fault of any of the parties to the business transaction. One example is the sale of a parcel of land the use of which was granted to a third-party operator by the applicable regulatory authority for a specific activity that caused environmental damage on the land. Another such scenario is a parcel of land contaminated by offsite migration of substances or a redeveloped brownfield. These scenarios bring different dynamics into the transaction, including the potential assignment of choses in action to pursue the liable third party. Choses in action for environmental liability have been given little or no attention in business transactions. In the new era of prioritizing environmental obligations in all spheres, and the potential monetary reserves that may be created by businesses for environmental contingencies, choses in action for environmental liability require more attention in the future negotiation and documentation of business transactions.

---

21 EPEA, s 232; *Environmental Protection Act*, RSO 1990, c E.19, s 194; Alberta Energy Regulator, Bulletin 2016-10, "Obligations of Licensees When in Insolvency or When Otherwise Ceasing Operations" (8 April 2016); *Legal Oil and Gas Ltd v Alberta (Minister of Environment)*, 2000 ABQB 388 at paras 45-46; *Sarg Oils Ltd v Environmental Appeal Board*, 2007 ABCA 215 at para 8; *Northstar Aerospace Inc (Re)*, 2013 ONCA 600, 8 CBR (6th) 154; *Regional Water Services Ltd and Jeff Colvin v Director, Southern Region, Operations Division, Alberta Environment and Sustainable Resource Development* (17 April 2014), Appeal No 12-014-R1 (AEAB), online (pdf): *Environmental Appeals Board* <http://www.eab.gov.ab.ca/dec/12-014-R1.pdf>.

22 OGCA, s 106.

23 David Estrin, *Business Guide to Environmental Law*, vol 1 (Scarborough, Ont: Carswell, 1992) (looseleaf, updated 2017) at para 1.3.1.2.2; *Heighington v Ontario*, 1987 CanLII 5417, 41 DLR (4th) 208 (Ont H Ct J), aff'd 1989 CanLII 4314, 61 DLR (4th) 190 (Ont CA).

24 *1317424 Ontario Inc v Chrysler Canada Inc*, 2015 ONCA 104; Estrin, *supra* note 23 at para 1.3.1.2.3.

25 *United Canadian Malt Ltd v Outboard Marine Corp of Canada Ltd*, 2000 CanLII 22365 at paras 9-17, 48 OR (3d) 352 (Sup Ct J); *Midwest Properties Ltd v Thordarson*, 2015 ONCA 819 at paras 113-16.

III. SOME COMMON TYPES OF ASSET TRANSACTIONS

The parties should consider the particular industry of the business or assets in a transaction. The context of each transaction is important to take into account, given the role of industry norms, custom, and usage, as well as the factual matrix, in interpreting the purchase and sale contract in the event of a dispute. Examples of industries where environmental liability would be most relevant in the transactions are real estate (residential, commercial, leasing, and expropriation) and oil and gas. The nature of each transaction and the level of sophistication of the parties determine the type of contract the parties use in documenting the terms of their agreement. The parties may use pro forma contracts or get their legal professionals to draft the agreement.

Expropriation is a variation of a real estate transaction, in that the transaction is not consensual because the parties involved are the expropriating authority and the owner. However, some statutes, such as the Alberta *Expropriation Act*, provide for expropriation by consent.[26] In such cases, the transaction defaults to a regular real estate transaction, except for the compensation, which is determined by the applicable board or tribunal. Environmental liabilities complicate the compensation for the expropriated asset, especially when the vendor is a faultless third party and not the person responsible for the statutory environmental liability. Compensation in expropriation is based on the market value of the expropriated land. The value in turn is "the amount the land might be expected to realize if sold in the open market by a willing seller to a willing buyer," plus provable damages.[27] The determination of market value accounts for everything that is present in the site, except for the legislated exclusions. While the "polluter pays" principle has been largely ignored in the valuation of expropriated assets, case law suggests that the law is not blind to the causation of the contamination in the expropriation context. Given that liability for contamination does not run with the land (that is, does not remain with the land itself regardless of change in ownership) in Alberta but resides with the person responsible, the allocation of environmental liability in an asset transaction involving expropriation may consider, as part of the valuation, the chose in action that a faultless vendor may have to recover from a person responsible and deal with it appropriately in the negotiations and the agreement.[28]

The purchase and sale of oil and gas assets is a complex transaction.[29] The industry operations are divided into upstream, midstream, and downstream. Therefore, the assets or business in a given sale will conform to the nature of the vendor's operations. Upstream assets include the rights to the minerals in the ground; the tangible assets associated with production, processing, and transport; and the miscellaneous interests such as contracts and other intangible rights. Midstream and downstream assets do not include *in situ* mineral rights.

IV. DOCUMENTING THE TRANSACTION

It is critical that the parties enter into clear contractual arrangements to address environmental issues that are known or contingent or that may be identified during the transaction.[30] As discussed above, parties may draft and negotiate their own agreements[31] or use pro forma or "standard form" contracts with boilerplate, modified boilerplate, or elective alternate clauses.

---

26 *Expropriation Act*, RSA 2000, c E-13, s 30.

27 *Expropriation Act*, ss 41-42.

28 Thompson, "Environmental Issues in Expropriation," *supra* note 10.

29 Michael A Marion et al, "Sober Second Thoughts: Litigating Purchase and Sale Agreements in the Energy Industry" (2018) 56:2 Alta L Rev 447.

30 Babe, *supra* note 1 at 174.

31 For sample purchase and sale agreements and environmental clauses, see Babe, *ibid* at 386-444.

The use of standard form contracts has its own dangers. The principles of contractual interpretation for standard form contracts are slightly different from those discussed below. The Supreme Court has described standard form contracts as generally not having relevant surrounding circumstances relating to their negotiation because there is in no real sense any negotiation of their terms.[32] The Alberta Court of Appeal has held that any attempt to identify the intention of the parties or to inject the circumstances surrounding the formation of the "standard form" contract into the analysis is nothing but a legal fiction; essentially, it is the intention of the committee that drafted it that prevails.[33] Parties should, therefore, exercise caution in choosing how to document their transactions.

Many industry associations have developed agreements for their industry members to use in business transactions. Real estate associations and oil and gas associations have such agreements, which they continue to update as issues arise and courts interpret them. An example is the residential real estate purchase contract that was developed by the Alberta Real Estate Association and interpreted by the Alberta Court of Appeal in *Vozniak*. The oil and gas industry has attempted to standardize agreements to govern the construction and operation of various assets, as well as their transfer and assignment. Examples of such agreements are the Canadian Association of Petroleum Landmen (CAPL) Operating Procedure, Property Transfer Procedure, and Assignment Procedure. There are also standard agreements specifically for joint ventures. These agreements include the Petroleum Joint Venture Association (PJVA) agreements and the Association of International Petroleum Negotiators (AIPN) agreements, which have specific clauses on disposition and environmental matters. These agreements contain alternative provisions, as well as election provisions that allow parties to modify the terms of a transaction to fit their particular needs. Industry association agreements contain specific industry terms, norms, and practices. Professionals who are familiar with the particular industry and agreements should be engaged when parties choose them for documenting the transaction.

V. CONTRACTUAL INTERPRETATION PRINCIPLES

Notwithstanding the careful attention paid at the drafting stage of agreements, interpreting clauses of an agreement can be complicated.[34] As a starting point, the purpose of contractual interpretation is to ascertain the "objective intent" of the parties. The objective intent is what a reasonable person would have objectively understood from the words of the agreement in the factual matrix in which the agreement was made.[35] The words used must be given their "ordinary and grammatical meaning, consistent with the surrounding circumstances known to the parties at the time of formation of the contract."[36] As stated in "Sober Second Thoughts," "[i]t is not just what the parties knew at the time, but also 'what the parties using those words against the relevant background would reasonably have been understood to mean.'"[37] Therefore,

> the ordinary and technical usage of a particular word is not necessarily determinative of a word's meaning because "[t]he meaning of words is a matter of dictionaries and grammars;

32 *Ledcor Construction Ltd v Northbridge Indemnity Insurance Co*, 2016 SCC 37 at paras 28, 31-32, 106.
33 *Vallieres v Vozniak*, 2014 ABCA 290 at para 13; *Stewart Estate v TAQA North Ltd*, 2015 ABCA 357 at paras 273-83.
34 For a comprehensive overview of the principles of contractual interpretation, which is beyond the scope of this chapter, see Marion et al, *supra* note 29 at 448-57.
35 *Sattva Capital Corp v Creston Moly Corp*, 2014 SCC 53 at para 49, [2014] 2 SCR 633; *IFP Technologies (Canada) Inc v EnCana Midstream and Marketing*, 2017 ABCA 157 at para 79.
36 *Sattva, supra* note 35 at para 47.
37 Marion et al, *supra* note 29 at 449, citing *Sattva, supra* note 35 at para 48.

the meaning of the document is what the parties using those words against the relevant background would reasonably have been understood to mean."[38]

The authors further add, "[c]ourts will adopt the meaning of words that parties have defined themselves in agreements." This is the case "even if the express definition conflicts with the ordinary or technical usage of the word." Nevertheless, "the words of the contract, and the entire contract itself, must be read in context."[39] The scope of the background context or factual matrix is broad, and "the surrounding circumstances can include 'absolutely anything which would have affected the way in which the language of the document would have been understood by a reasonable [person].'"[40] They can include "(1) the genesis, aim or purpose of the contract; (2) the nature of the relationship created by the contract; and (3) the nature or custom of the market or industry in which the contract was executed."[41] Even so, "the factual matrix cannot overwhelm or contradict the words in the contract, add new terms to the contract, or create an ambiguity that otherwise does not exist."[42]

It should be noted that "even where the literal meaning of words is apparent, they will not be relied upon where to do so would 'bring about an unrealistic result or a result which would not be contemplated in the commercial atmosphere' in which the contract was entered into."[43] Nevertheless, "while commercial common sense can be a factor in interpretation, it cannot supersede the actual language used in a contract."[44] Courts will generally try to hold parties to their bargains and will assume that parties are aware of and intended the natural legal consequences of the terms to which they agreed.[45] The rule of *contra proferentum* will generally "not apply where there are sophisticated commercial entities involved in a transaction."[46]

In the transactional context, the evidence that will likely support arguments for the interpretation of purchase and sale agreement includes

the agreement itself; documents referenced in the agreement; ancillary or related agreements or documents (for example, letters of intent, memorandums of understanding, or technical reports); evidence of negotiations generally;[47] ... evidence from individuals actually involved in the negotiation of the transaction (including their memories of events, emails, or other records); previous drafts of the agreement; and evidence of how the parties conducted themselves before and ... after the transaction was closed.[48]

---

38 *Ibid.*

39 Marion et al, *supra* note 29 at 449, citing *Lake Louise Limited Partnership v Canad Corp of Manitoba Ltd*, 2014 MBCA 61 at para 144, leave to appeal to SCC refused, 2015 CanLII 14729; *NOV Enerflow ULC v Enerflow Industries Inc*, 2015 ABQB 759 at para 17; *IFP Technologies*, *supra* note 35 at para 83; *Sattva*, *supra* note 35 at para 58.

40 Marion et al, *supra* note 29 at 451, citing *IFP Technologies*, *supra* note 35 at para 83; *Sattva*, *supra* note 35 at para 58.

41 Marion et al, *supra* note 29 at 451, citing *IFP Technologies*, *supra* note 35 at para 83.

42 Marion et al, *supra* note 29 at 451, citing *IFP Technologies*, *supra* note 35 at para 124.

43 Marion et al, *supra* note 29 at 449, citing *Consolidated Bathurst Export Ltd v Mutual Boiler & Machinery Insurance Co*, [1980] 1 SCR 888 at 901, 1979 CanLII 10.

44 Marion et al, *supra* note 29 at 449, citing *Valard Construction Ltd v Bird Construction Co*, 2016 ABCA 249 at para 184.

45 Marion et al, *supra* note 29 at 448 and 450, citing *Guarantee Co of North America v Gordon Capital Corp*, [1999] 3 SCR 423 at para 46, 1999 CanLII 664; *Eli Lilly & Co v Novapharm Ltd*, [1998] 2 SCR 129 at para 56, 1998 CanLII 791.

46 Marion et al, *supra* note 29 at 450, n 14, citing *Royal Bank of Canada v Swartout*, 2011 ABCA 362 at para 48.

47 Only to the extent it is used to explain the genesis and aim of the contract. See Marion et al, *supra* note 29 at 453, citing *IFP Technologies*, *supra* note 35 at para 85.

48 Marion et al, *supra* note 29 at 451, also noting at 452, however, that "[e]vidence as to the conduct of the parties after the transaction is generally not relevant to the interpretation of the agreement, unless the

However, there are limitations on the use of such evidence as part of establishing the factual matrix, given that their admission and weight are arguable, and there are complications posed by privilege in communications with counsel during negotiations.[49]

The relevance of the factual matrix in interpreting "standard form" contracts is limited because the parties do not really negotiate terms.[50] The Supreme Court held that when interpreting a "standard form" contract, one should consider factors such as the purpose of the contract, the nature of the relationship that it creates, and the market or industry in which it operates. However, those considerations are generally not "inherently fact specific" but will usually be the same for everyone who may be a party to a particular "standard form" contract.[51]

VI. KEY ISSUES IN THE TRANSACTIONS

With the legal principles covered, below are key environmental topics and contractual provisions to which the vendor and purchaser should pay particular attention.

A. DISCLOSURE, DUE DILIGENCE, AND CAVEAT EMPTOR

The same level of due diligence should be conducted regardless of whether the transaction is shares or assets. In an asset transaction, the parties must determine by way of full disclosure and appropriate due diligence whether there are environmental liabilities that should be excluded from the transaction. In a share transaction, information on all environmental liabilities of the target business should also be available by way of full disclosure and appropriate due diligence, given that the new owner's investment will be assuming them.[52]

Due diligence should be conducted as early as possible. The environmental requirements of all interested parties must be understood early; these include the requirements of lenders, insurers, and regulators.[53] Parties should engage environmental services professionals who are familiar with and will provide the particular legal, policy, and practical context for the transaction.[54] For example, in the Alberta oil and gas industry, wells and facilities that have reclamation certificates are not transferrable. Therefore, such assets must remain with the vendor in an asset deal. Also, as discussed below, the regulator will refuse consent for the transfer of assets where the vendor and the purchaser do not meet the conditions for holding the licence. It is, therefore, very important to understand the applicable environmental laws, standards, and policies governing the business.[55]

The vendor should anticipate that the purchaser will ask for environmental records.[56] Such records, where available, should be included in the data room by the vendor as part of the vendor's disclosure. If data room is not used in the transaction, the vendor should organize the

---

contract is held to be ambiguous." See *Weyerhaeuser Co v Ontario (Attorney General)*, 2017 ONCA 1007 at para 116.

49 Marion et al, *supra* note 29 at 451-54.
50 *Ledcor, supra* note 32 at paras 28, 31-32.
51 *Ibid.*
52 Babe, *supra* note 1 at 90.
53 *Ibid* at 170.
54 *Ibid.*
55 *Ibid.*
56 For checklists for an environmental audit, see Babe, *ibid* at 273-83, and Estrin, *supra* note 23 at para 1.8, appendix A, "Environmental Risk Assessment Questionnaire," and appendix B, "Checklist of Public Agency Records and Other Sources of Environmental Information."

production of environmental records to the purchaser.[57] In real estate transactions, the principle of *caveat emptor*, that is, "let the buyer beware," applies, and the vendor has no common law obligation to disclose a patent defect concerning the physical attributes and conditions of real property that, although known to the vendor, can be discovered on inspection by a reasonably careful purchaser.[58]

Caveat emptor has been described by the courts as a caution to purchasers of assets to ensure that they are getting what they think they have paid for.[59] However, the vendor has a legal obligation to disclose any known latent defect that renders the property unfit or dangerous or poses a likelihood of danger.[60] Failure of the vendor to voluntarily disclose a latent defect, or misrepresentation by the vendor with respect to latent defects, will entitle the purchaser to rescission of the contract and damages or to damages for fraud and/or deceit. However, if the vendor is not aware of contamination and has no reason to know of such, the vendor will not be liable.[61] Other exceptions to *caveat emptor* include "(1) fraud; (2) a mutual mistake; (3) a contractual condition; [and] (4) a warranty collateral to the contract which survives closing."[62]

Regardless of common law, the vendor may have statutory disclosure obligations, such as PCB waste storage sites and underground storage tanks.[63] Without complete knowledge of all the potential statutory obligations to disclose, it is in the interest of the vendor to disclose as much information concerning the environmental status of the asset or business as possible. The information disclosed may even assist the vendor in establishing a stronger bargaining position for a better sale price.[64] Evidence of the environmental status of the asset or business at the time of sale will also assist the vendor in any subsequent claims by the purchaser, third parties, or the regulator with respect to environmental liability.[65]

Although an honest vendor is the most timesaving and cost-effective source of information, the vendor may be ignorant of many of the potential environmental problems.[66] The purchaser must conduct suitable due diligence to understand what it is purchasing. The purchaser should conduct searches and obtain environmental information and records from public authorities such as the departments of the environment, municipalities, other applicable regulators and appeal boards, courts, and land title registries.[67] The purchaser should obtain the specific right from the vendor to obtain copies of documents in the files of relevant government ministries and agencies at the federal, provincial, and municipal levels, subject in the usual case to a requirement of confidentiality.[68] Alberta Environment and Parks provides the Environmental Site Assessment Repository (ESAR), an online searchable database that contains scientific and technical information about the province's assessed and reclaimed sites. All environmental site assessment reports conducted at any location in Alberta and filed with the regulator can be obtained from ESAR. Reclamation certificates, applications, and reports for upstream oil and gas well sites up to 2014, gravel pits, and other private lands can also be found on ESAR.[69]

---

57 Babe, *supra* note 1 at 90.
58 *Ibid* at 172; Estrin, *supra* note 23 at para 1.3.2.2.1.
59 *Quicksilver Resources Canada Inc (Re)*, 2018 ABQB 653 at para 1.
60 Babe, *supra* note 1 at 172.
61 Estrin, *supra* note 23 at para 1.3.2.2.1; *Antorisa Investments v Petro Canada Ltd* (1996), 29 CELR (NS) 52 (Ont Gen Div).
62 Marion et al, *supra* note 29 at 464, note 118, citing *Motkoski Holdings Ltd v Yellowhead (County)*, 2010 ABCA 72 at para 112.
63 Babe, *supra* note 1 at 172.
64 *Ibid* at 173.
65 *Ibid*.
66 Estrin, *supra* note 23 at para 1.8.2.1.
67 Babe, *supra* note 1 at 173.
68 Estrin, *supra* note 23 at para 1.8.2.1.
69 (Last visited 23 June 2019), online: *Government of Alberta* <https://www.alberta.ca/environmental -site-assessment-repository.aspx?utm_source=redirector>.

Depending on the nature of the business involved, site visit and physical inspection are necessary for the purchaser and may reveal details and issues that may not have been captured in the records. The purchaser should insist on full and uninhibited access to the property. This includes the right of an appropriately qualified, independent third-party assessment or technical analysis appropriate to the circumstances. The purchaser should also insist on having full access to the vendor's business records and approval to conduct interviews with officers, directors, and employees of the vendor.[70]

Where environmental records are not available, or the environmental status of the assets or business is unknown, the vendor or purchaser, or any of the potential persons responsible (for example, the lender) may request an independent environmental site assessment (ESA) to be conducted by a qualified environmental consultant who has liability insurance, which can be a source of comfort in the event that the assessment fails to disclose environmental liabilities.[71] The ESA process is often implemented in phases. Phase 1 involves an evaluation of historical and current land use by review of records, site visit, and interviews.[72] Phase 2 is intrusive in order to obtain quantitative analytical information regarding the nature and extent of any contaminants and site conditions. It involves delineation of areas of potential concern, data collection, sampling, analysis, and quantification.[73] Phase 3 analyzes the extent and nature of the environmental problems and develops a remediation plan, including calculation of remediation costs.[74]

Where an ESA is required, the issues to be addressed by the vendor and the purchaser include (1) whether the ESA should be a joint assessment and, if so, selection of the consultant, definition of the scope of the assessment, terms of payment, and remediation standards/level; (2) access and timing for completion; (3) the result—whether and how recommendations are to be received, work schedule/plan, and cost-sharing; (4) reporting of the results of the ESA to the regulators—who and when; (5) confidentiality and/or privilege protection for data obtained, sensitive records, and resulting reports;[75] (6) insurance and responsibility for any damage or resulting injury and site restoration;[76] (7) allocation of the liability for remediation and costs between the parties on a percentage basis or reduction in purchase price to account for the environmental risk if assumed by the purchaser; and (8) procurement of a remediation certificate from the regulator or any other form of regulatory closure to current remediation standard (post-remediation) and which party bears the responsibility.

Where the vendor refuses to participate, the purchaser should consider undertaking the environmental audit without the vendor's financial participation.[77]

It is possible for the vendor to use the "as is, where is" clause to capture all environmental liabilities.[78] This is similar to the concept of "white map sale" employed by the oil and gas industry, discussed further below. Pursuant to the "as is, where is" clause, the purchaser may be acknowledging that (1) the past use of the property is either known or irrelevant to the purchaser; (2) the purchaser has conducted or had the opportunity to conduct a thorough environmental investigation; (3) the purchaser waives its rights to rescind the agreement on the basis of discovery of environmental conditions adverse to the asset; and (4) the purchaser

70 Estrin, *supra* note 23 at para 1.8.2.1.
71 *Ibid* at paras 1.8.1.2, 1.8.3.
72 Government of Alberta, Alberta Environment and Parks, *Alberta Environmental Site Assessment Standard* (Edmonton, 2016) at 3, online (pdf): <https://open.alberta.ca/dataset/3acc7cff-8c50-44e8-8a33-f4b710d9859a/resource/579321b7-5b66-4022-9796-31b1ad094635/download/environmentsiteassessstandard-mar01-2016.pdf>; Babe, *supra* note 1 at 173.
73 *Ibid*.
74 Estrin, *supra* note 23 at para 1.8.3.1.
75 Babe, *supra* note 1 at 173-74.
76 *Ibid* at 174.
77 Estrin, *supra* note 23 at para 1.8.3.1.
78 Babe, *supra* note 1 at 174.

accepts all liability, including that for any necessary remedial work arising from environ-mental conditions of the property.[79] A purchaser may not accept such a clause unless there is a significant reduction in the purchase price or it is a sale by a trustee or receiver in insolvency proceedings.[80]

Given statutory environmental liabilities of former owners, and the fact that the vendor can-not effectively contract out of them, it may be more advantageous for the vendor to determine the environmental status of the asset, and, if contamination exists, either eliminate it prior to sale or quantify the level of contamination at a specific point in time.[81]

B. DEFINITION OF TERMS

The parties should use an elaborate definition section to clearly define terms used in the agreement.[82] Courts have interpreted words commonly used in particular industry agree-ments, especially those used in the oil and gas industry, including "working interest,"[83] "assets," and "indemnified losses."[84] The scope of the definition of some of the terms has been deter-minative of who is responsible for environmental liabilities in many cases.

1. Assets

Precise definition of the assets in a transaction is critical, since disputes as to whether certain liabilities were either purchased or associated with the assets purchased often arise. While "assets" in the oil and gas context is broadly defined as "petroleum and natural gas rights," "tangibles," and "miscellaneous interests," certain environmental liabilities arising therefrom have been the subject of dispute requiring judicial interpretation of the purchase and sale contract.[85] In both *Talisman* and *Anadarko*, environmental liabilities in the form of a sulphur stockpile leaching into ground-water and an abandoned oilfield battery, respectively, were held to be neither tangibles nor miscellaneous interests and, therefore, not part of the "assets" purchased. The value of "seeking a more precise description of the assets conveyed" has also been emphasized in *Quicksilver Resources*.[86] However, regard should also be had to the concept of "white mapping," which is used in the oil and gas industry when companies choose to divest all of their assets in a given geographical area. In a white map sale, any asset with its associated environmental liabilities in a particular area on a map, which is attached as a schedule to the purchase and sale agreement, will form part of the assets conveyed unless expressly excluded by the parties.[87]

2. Environmental Liabilities

Parties should be vigilant of the scope of the definition of "environmental liabilities" or "abandon-ment and reclamation obligations" in their agreements, and, in particular, whether the liabilities captured are only those occurring *after* the closing date, or whether they include pre-existing and contingent liabilities. There are different conventions in particular industries and in particular

---

79 Estrin, *supra* note 23 at para 1.8.1.2.

80 Babe, *supra* note 1 at 174.

81 Estrin, *supra* note 23 at para 1.8.1.2.

82 Babe, *supra* note 1 at 174.

83 Marion et al, *supra* note 29 at 450, citing *IFP Technologies, supra* note 35 at para 98.

84 Marion et al, *supra* note 29 at 450, citing *NOV Enerflow, supra* note 39 at para 20.

85 *Talisman Energy Inc v Esprit Exploration Ltd*, 2013 ABQB 132; *Anadarko Canada Corporation v Can-adian Natural Resources Limited*, 2006 ABQB 590; and *ConocoPhillips Canada Resources Corp and Shell Canada Limited*, 2019 ABQB 727.

86 *Supra* note 59 at para 27.

87 *Canlin Resources Partnership v Husky Oil Operations Limited*, 2018 ABQB 24 at para 24.

jurisdictions. For example, in the oil and gas industry in Canada, the purchaser by convention assumes environmental liabilities whenever they occur or accrue and also represents that it has no notice of formal environmental proceedings.[88] The purchaser also gives the vendor an environmental indemnity against all damages arising from environmental liabilities pertaining to the assets, whenever they occurred or accrued, except where the vendor has breached its environmental representation. However, courts have interpreted these indemnities narrowly in that they relate only to the assets acquired.[89] This convention is not used in United States jurisdictions where vendors and purchasers split the cost of environmental liabilities accruing before and after closing pursuant to the concept of "my watch/your watch."[90]

C. NOVATION OR ASSIGNMENT

Contracts relating to the assets being purchased have to be transferred to the purchaser through assignment or novation. While it is beyond the scope of this chapter to discuss the legal differences between assignment and novation, it is noteworthy that novation substitutes the purchaser (the continuing party) for the vendor (the substituted). The essence of novation is that the purchaser discharges the vendor from all liability thereafter.[91] With respect to assignment, common law has long recognized that the vendor can assign only the contractual benefits of the contract to the purchaser while remaining liable for the performance of the obligations under the contract being assigned.[92]

In business transactions, the purchaser will want the full assignment of choses in action and all rights, title, and estate, including the right of subrogation for any insurance claims the vendor may have had, pertaining to the asset in the event of third-party claims. The purchaser also requires the assignment of the choses to be able to sue and obtain damages for prior trespass, nuisance, and other common law causes of action. However, the parties cannot deem environmental liabilities to be transferred to the purchaser by assignment or novation if those liabilities do not pertain to the assets sold. In *Talisman*, the court rejected that the sulphur stockpile was transferred to the purchaser through the assignment and novation of other contracts that related to the assets purchased.[93]

D. CONDITIONS AND COVENANTS

The transfer of the risk and title to assets occurs at the closing date, which is different from the date of signing the purchase and sale agreement.[94] In the period between the signing date and the closing date, "the vendor and the purchaser have conditions to satisfy and covenants to perform (or negative covenants not to undertake) before [c]losing can occur."[95] In addition to those, the parties must be aware of the duties owing between them to finalize a transaction,

---

88 See clause 1.01 for the definitions of "Abandonment and Reclamation Obligations," "Environmental Liabilities," and "Permitted Encumbrances" and clauses 2.04(B) and 13.04 in "2017 CAPL Property Transfer Procedure" (2017), online (pdf): *Canadian Association of Petroleum Landmen* <https://landman.ca/wp/wp-content/uploads/2017/12/2017-CAPL-PTP-Unannotated-Text-Final-Clean.pdf> (offline as of November 2019).

89 *Talisman*, *supra* note 85 at para 120.

90 Oil & Gas M&A Portal, "Purchase Agreements (Upstream Deals)" (last visited 23 June 2019), online (pdf): *Latham & Watkins LLP* <https://www.lw.com/admin/Upload/Documents/OilAndGasMandA/Oil_and_Gas_Concepts/Oil_and_Gas_Concepts_Upstream_to_Diligence_Considerations.pdf>.

91 *National Trust Co v Mead*, [1990] 2 SCR 410 at paras 34-40, 1990 CanLII 73, [1990] SCJ No 76 (QL).

92 *Ibid* at para 35.

93 *Talisman*, *supra* note 85 at paras 118-122.

94 Marion et al, *supra* note 29 at 454.

95 *Ibid*.

including the duty to act honestly in performance of the contract.[96] The duty of honest performance of the contract does not abrogate the purchaser's duty to conduct prior due diligence, since the vendor's duty of honest performance does not extend to negotiation and any pre-contractual relationship between the parties.[97]

The purchaser will want to obtain a series of covenants from the vendor, including covenants to provide notice and continuous disclosure of any breach of the representations or warranties, to allow for access and inspection of the assets or business during a specified period of time, and a general "assurances covenant" to do all acts or provide all documentation reasonably requested by the purchaser before or after the closing of the transaction.[98]

Conditions (condition precedent) are more important than representations and warranties in that they must be met prior to the closing of the transaction. The purchaser will want to seek broad conditions, while the vendor will want them narrowed or limited by time and materiality thresholds. It is important that the parties have specific conditions and covenants as to the issues arising from ESA results in the purchase and sale agreement. These conditions could include the purchaser's option to terminate or to require rectification of the environmental issue or an agreement as to the sharing of cleanup costs, which may be negotiated on a percentage basis.[99]

The purchaser will want to include the following conditions: (1) all representations and warranties will be deemed to be true at the time of closing, as if made at such time; (2) the vendor is deemed to accept all representations made by its directors, officers, employees, and agents; (3) the vendor has performed and complied with all of the covenants and terms of the agreement as required prior to closing; (4) no material change has occurred to the property or to legislation regulating such property prior to closing; [100] (5) the environmental issue will be rectified by the vendor or remediation, and details including the allocation of management and financial responsibilities of the vendor and purchaser will be mutually agreed upon in the event of any pre-closing or post-closing discovery of latent environmental issues; and (6) the exercise of rights of inspection do not affect or withdraw any covenant, warranty, or representation made within the text of the agreement.[101]

Upon failure of the vendor to comply with the conditions, the agreement should generally provide the purchaser with (1) a right to rescind the agreement and be released from any liabilities under it, (2) the right to rescind and bring an action in damages and/or for abatement of the purchase price, and (3) the right to waive compliance with conditions on terms to be agreed upon by the parties.[102]

E. FINANCING THE TRANSACTION AND THE LENDER'S ENVIRONMENTAL REQUIREMENTS

A business transaction may be financed by equity (investors) or loan (lenders). While the sale of assets in the insolvency proceedings is beyond the scope of this chapter, the principles of

---

96   *Ibid* at 455-56, citing *Bhasin v Hrynew*, 2014 SCC 71 at paras 73, 75.

97   Marion et al, *supra* note 29 at 457, citing *Styles v Alberta Investment Management Corporation*, 2017 ABCA 1 at para 51; *Empire Communities Ltd v HMQ*, 2015 ONSC 4355.

98   Estrin, *supra* note 23 at para 1.8.4.2.

99   Babe, *supra* note 1 at 173-74; Estrin, *ibid* at paras 1.8.3.1, 1.8.4.3.

100 *Brent Petroleum Industries Ltd v Caine Enterprises Ltd*, 1984 CanLII 1340 at paras 46-48, 59 AR 78 (QB); *Marathon Canada Limited v Enron Canada Corp*, 2009 ABCA 31; *Mull v Dynacare Inc*, 1998 CanLII 14814, 44 BLR (2d) 211 (Ont Gen Div); *Stetson Oil & Gas Ltd v Stifel Nicolaus Canada Inc*, 2013 ONSC 1300.

101 Estrin, *supra* note 23 at para 1.8.4.7.

102 *Ibid*.

law arising from judicial treatment of environmental liabilities in insolvency proceedings tend to influence the conditions for financing business transactions.[103]

Recently in Canada, environmental remediation has become a paramount public interest, ranking above secured creditors' interests in the administration of a bankrupt's estate. In *Redwater*, the core issue was whether there was a conflict between Alberta's oil and gas environmental scheme and s 14.06 of the federal *Bankruptcy and Insolvency Act*,[104] which pertains to disclaiming environmental liabilities by a trustee in bankruptcy (trustee) or receiver in a receivership. In issue in this case were two powers of the regulator designed to ensure that companies holding the regulator's licences (licensees) satisfy their end-of-life obligations: (1) the regulator's power to order a licensee to abandon and reclaim licensed assets and associated statutory powers to enforce such orders; and (2) the regulator's power to impose conditions upon a licensee's transfer of the licences.

A majority of the Supreme Court held that s 14.06(4) of the BIA is concerned with the personal liability of the trustee and does not empower the trustee to walk away from or disclaim the environmental liabilities of the bankrupt estate it is administering. The majority found that the regulator was not asserting any claims provable in the bankruptcy by its abandonment orders and that the priority scheme in the BIA is not upended. Furthermore, the regulator's refusal to approve licence transfers unless and until the obligations to maintain the licence have been satisfied does not give the regulator a monetary claim provable in the bankruptcy of the licensee. The majority concluded that Alberta's oil and gas environmental regime can coexist with and apply alongside the BIA.[105]

It is anticipated that funding of the purchase of assets or the continuation of the operations may trigger broader inquiries into environmental liabilities and more stringent measures, such as requiring specific environmental protection expenditures, for securing the investment/loan.[106] The lender/investor will likely be more thorough in due diligence and investigation of potential environmental liabilities before investing and will likely ensure that some of the funds invested are allocated toward environmental compliance.[107] Some lenders may compel borrowers to implement responsible environmental practices and an annual environmental update.[108] It is incumbent on the purchaser to understand the lender's or investor's conditions and have a strategy for meeting them in advance of closing.

F. ASSUMPTION AND TRANSFERABILITY OF LIABILITY

Environmental-related statutes often require approvals, permits, or licences for certain activities that cause adverse environmental effects. Transferability of these approvals, permits, and licences is always a concern.[109] Most of the statutes expressly permit transfer of these licences and approvals, but with the consent of the applicable regulator. Some of the approvals and their authorizing statutes are silent on transfer. An example in Alberta is the approval of the Natural Resources Conservation Board (NRCB) pursuant to the *Natural Resources Conservation Board Act*.[110] The question remains whether such an approval is transferable. The NRCB confirmed that its legislated mandate is primarily limited to a one-time granting of approval,

---

103 *Ibid* at para 9.1, citing Canadian Bankers Association, "Sustainable Capital: The Effect of Environmental Liability in Canada on Borrowers, Lenders and Investors" (November 1991).

104 RSC 1985, c B-3 [BIA].

105 For an analysis of the decision and summary of the reasons, see Thompson, "Redwater Decision," *supra* note 3.

106 Estrin, *supra* note 23 at para 9.1.

107 *Ibid*.

108 *Ibid* at paras 9.1, 1.8.3.5.

109 Babe, *supra* note 1 at 171-72.

110 RSA 2000, c N-3.

and it delegates ongoing regulation and enforcement of the conditions of its approval to a provincial department, most commonly Alberta Environment and Parks. The NRCB also confirmed that its approvals are binding on successors.[111] There is a view that the terms and conditions of such an approval run with the project, that is, remain with the project, regardless of change in ownership, and because the approval survives any change in ownership, it need not be transferred. It has been suggested that the purchaser should notify the applicable authority or its delegate of the change in ownership, but this notification may trigger a review and update of the approval's conditions by the authority.[112]

1. Dealing with the Regulator's Consent for Transfer

In the oil and gas context, a licence or approval of certain assets requires the regulator's consent for their transfer to a purchaser. Alberta, British Columbia, and Saskatchewan have environmental liability management regimes that require each oil and gas licensee to maintain a certain rating. Alberta's liability regime is directly relevant to the regulator's consent to transfer licences of assets in a sale transaction. The purchase and sale agreement does not transfer licences for the assets unless approved by the regulator.[113] The vendor and purchaser will want to ensure that licences can be transferred as part of assets. The conveyance of all the assets, when transferability of the associated licences is uncertain, may render the vendor incapable of holding the licences.

Licensees in Alberta are required to maintain, on a corporate basis, a Liability Management Rating (LMR) ratio of 2.0. LMR is a licensee's deemed assets versus its deemed liabilities. In any given month, if the licensee's LMR is less than 2.0 (that is, the deemed liabilities exceeds its deemed assets), the licensee must post a security deposit with the regulator in an amount that represents the difference between its deemed assets and deemed liabilities, or the licensee must perform abandonment and reclamation obligations to bring the liabilities down. In order to transfer licences, both the vendor and the purchaser must have an LMR of 2.0 after the transfer.[114] If any required security deposit is not posted, the licence transfer application will be closed, and the vendor will have to demonstrate that it retained the mineral rights to entitle it to hold the licence.[115] If a vendor has transferred the mineral rights to a purchaser, the regulator may issue closure and abandonment orders.[116] In such a situation, while the vendor remains environmentally liable as the licensee of record, the purchaser owns the assets but does not have the licences to operate.

It is critical, therefore, that the parties include in their representations and warranties that each of the vendor and purchaser does not have an LMR of less than 2.0 and will not have an LMR of less than 2.0 following closing and that each of the vendor and purchaser is not aware of any fact or circumstance that would prevent, adversely affect, or delay the transfer of any licence.[117]

---

111 Natural Resources Conservation Board, Board Decision NR 2009-01—Alberta Sulphur Terminals Ltd—Sulphur Forming and Shipping Facility near Bruderheim (July 2009) at 8, 117, online (pdf): *NRCB* <https://www.nrcb.ca/download_document/2/191/5336/sulphur-decision-report>.
112 Babe, *supra* note 1 at 172.
113 OGCA, s 24.
114 Alberta Energy Regulator, Directive 006, "Licensee Liability Rating (LLR) Program and Licence Transfer Process" (17 February 2016) at 12. Bulletin 2016-16, *Licensee Eligibility—Alberta Energy Regulator Measures to Limit Environmental Impacts Pending Regulatory Changes to Address the Redwater Decision* (20 June 2016) and Bulletin 2016-21, *Revision and Clarification on Alberta Energy Regulator's Measures to Limit Environmental Impacts Pending Regulatory Changes to Address the Redwater Decision* (8 July 2016) increased the LMR to 2.0.
115 OGCA, s 16.
116 OGCA, s 27.
117 Chidinma B Thompson et al, "Licensee Liability Ratings and Stakeholder Exposure in Insolvency: Risk Management for Lenders, Principals and the Regulator," BLG Seminar (20 April 2016) at 27, *THE*

In any event, if the consequences of breach of such representations and warranties are not sufficient; the purchaser is better off conducting its own due diligence.[118] The parties may also hold the licences and associated assets in escrow if transferability of licences is uncertain. Thus, if the licences are unable to transfer, the purchaser will have the option of posting the required security deposit or terminating the transaction.[119]

2. Dealing with Statutory and Common law Liability

The purchaser's recovery after closing is limited to indemnity claims against representations and warranties of the vendor. In an asset sale, the vendor remains the person responsible under legislation and will want to obtain indemnity from the purchaser in the purchase and sale contract. However, previous owners up the chain of statutory environmental liability may not have privity for recourse to the contractual indemnity provided by the purchaser.[120] Other means of securing performance of contractual environmental obligations are discussed below.

It has been considered whether there is a corporate group liability for environmental contamination. In *Yaiguaje v Chevron Corporation*,[121] the plaintiffs sought to enforce their Ecuadorian judgment of approximately US$18 billion against Chevron Corporation (Chevron, a Delaware entity), Chevron Canada Limited (Chevron Canada, a seventh-level indirect subsidiary of Chevron), and Chevron Canada Finance Limited (CCFL) for the environmental liabilities of Chevron's predecessors in Ecuador from 1964 to 1992. One of the issues was whether Chevron Canada's corporate veil should be pierced so that its shares and assets would be available to satisfy the Ecuadorian judgment against Chevron. The Ontario Superior Court of Justice, affirmed by the Court of Appeal, dismissed the claim against Chevron Canada. The court reasoned that Chevron Canada was not the judgment debtor under the Ecuadorian judgment, and its shares and assets were not exigible to satisfy the Ecuadorian judgment against Chevron. Pursuant to the principle of corporate separateness, the assets of the corporation are owned exclusively by the corporation, not the shareholders of the corporation.

The court held that while the "group enterprise" or "single business entity" theory exists in Canadian law, it applies only as a carefully limited exception: where a corporate entity (1) is completely dominated and controlled and (2) is being used as a shield for fraudulent or improper conduct.

The first element, complete control, requires more than ownership; there must be complete domination. However, the subsidiary does not in fact function independently, nor is the subsidiary a "puppet" of the parent.

The second element relates to conduct akin to fraud that would otherwise unjustly deprive claimants of their rights. The group enterprise exception has been further clarified by Canadian courts to the effect that even where complete domination is present, the corporate veil would not be pierced in the absence of wrongdoing akin to fraud in the establishment or use of the corporation. The court concluded that there is no independent "just and equitable" exception to the principle of corporate separateness in Canada.

G. REPRESENTATIONS AND WARRANTIES

Representations and warranties are relied upon by the parties as key sources of information in connection with transactions. The level of detail required and the nature of the rights that

---

RESOURCE® BLG Energy Law Blog, online (blog): *Borden Ladner Gervais LLP* <https://blog.blg.com/energy/Pages/Post.aspx?PID=196>.

118 *Ibid* at 27.
119 *Ibid* at 28.
120 *Ibid* at 30.
121 2017 ONSC 135, rev'd on cost award, 2018 ONCA 472, leave to appeal to SCC refused, 2019 CanLII 25908.

can flow if they are inaccurate depend on each particular transaction.[122] The purchaser will always want to negotiate broad representations and warranties that cover specific risks so that the vendor retains as much liability as possible. The purchaser will request that the vendor make representations and warranties as to the condition of the assets or business, as well as to compliance with all environmental legislation and regulations: that no orders, directives, or notices applicable to the property or the business other than those already disclosed exist; and that no civil or criminal proceedings with respect to the environmental status of the assets or business are pending or anticipated.[123] The purchaser will wish to ensure that the agreement expressly states that (1) the representations and warranties are true, both at the time of the agreement and at the time of closing; (2) they survive the completion of the transaction and continue for a specified period of time after closing; and (3) the truth of the representations and warranties constitutes a condition of the agreement, the breach of which may result in an action for rescission or damages (or both) by the purchaser, the rectification by the vendor of the environmental problems warranted against, or abatement of the purchase price.[124]

The purchaser, even if conducting its own investigations, will rely on these provisions.[125] It has been disputed whether a party is required to prove reliance on a representation and warranty in order to recover damages for a breach. In other words, "[i]f a purchaser knows that a representation and warranty given by the vendor is untrue at [c]losing, but closes anyway, the issue becomes whether that knowledge precludes [the purchaser] from successfully recovering damages for that breach."[126] While reliance is not a necessary element to prove a breach of contract, it is a necessary element of a claim for misrepresentation in tort (as "a representee who knows the truth is not deceived").[127] Parties attempt to address this issue expressly in their contract through the use of sandbagging clauses.[128] The purchaser will want to include a sandbagging clause stating that "knowledge of the purchaser of any breach of a warranty or representation prior to [c]losing does not impact any right to indemnification or other remedy post-[c]losing."[129] The vendor will want to include an anti-sandbagging clause stating that "the purchaser waives any right to claim for a breach of a representation or warranty if it had knowledge of the breach prior to [c]losing."[130] The parties should consider the negative impact of an

---

122 Babe, *supra* note 1 at 174.

123 Estrin, *supra* note 23 at para 1.8.4.1.

124 *Ibid.*

125 *Ibid.*

126 Marion et al, *supra* note 29 at 469.

127 *Ibid*, citing *French Family Funeral Home Limited v William Player, Joanne Harpell and Bruce Holtom, and 1564714 Ontario Ltd and 1872864 Ontario Inc*, 2015 ONSC 182 at paras 57, 61.

128 Marion et al, *supra* note 29 at 469-70, citing *Eagle Resources Ltd v MacDonald*, 2001 ABCA 264, 96 Alta LR (3d) 3.

129 Marion et al, *supra* note 29 at 469.

130 *Ibid*, citing Paul AD Mingay, Colin Cameron-Vendrig & Andrew Bunston, "Good Tactics or Bad Faith: The Divisive Issue of Sandbagging in M&A" (19 January 2017), online: *Borden Ladner Gervais LLP* <http://blg.com/en/News-And-Publications/Publication_4799>; Stikeman Elliott, "Sandbagging Clauses in Acquisition Agreements: A Little Knowledge Can Be a Dangerous Thing" (29 October 2012), online: *Stikeman Elliott LLP* <https://www.stikeman.com/en-ca/kh/canadian-ma-law/sandbagging-clauses-in-acquisition-agreements-a-little-knowledge-can-be-a-dangerous-thing>; Sara Josselyn, "Seller Beware: Sandbagging in Canadian Private M&A" (8 August 2017), *Deal Law Wire*, online (blog): *Deal Law Wire* <https://www.deallawwire.com/2017/08/08/seller-beware-sandbagging-in-canadian-private-ma/>; Benjamin Layton et al, "Sandbagging in Good Faith: How Bhasin v Hrynew Can Impact Indemnification for Known Breaches" (28 November 2016), *Canadian M&A Perspectives*, online (blog): *McCarthy Tetreault LLP* <https://www.mccarthy.ca/en/insights/blogs/canadian-ma-perspectives/sandbagging-good-faith-how-bhasin-v-hrynew-can-impact-indemnification-known-breaches>.

anti-sandbagging clause on the purchaser. For example, if the vendor provides volumes of records as part of the purchaser's due diligence process, information received by any employee of the purchaser could constitute "knowledge of the defect" and preclude any claim for a breach of a representation and warranty.[131]

The vendor will want to resist or limit providing any representations and warranties that would impose post-closing liability for environmental matters. The vendor will want to insert as many exceptions as possible. For example, the vendor will want to have the purchaser acknowledge that any environmental reports provided by the vendor are for information purposes only and that the vendor makes no representation or warranty as to the accuracy, completeness, or comprehensiveness of the reports and/or audits.[132]

The vendor will want to include materiality clauses and qualifications, such as "to the knowledge of the vendor"[133] or "not in material default," in the agreement. If a vendor is not prepared to make inquiries of its officers, directors, employees, consultants, agents, and any other person who may have knowledge of the environmental status of a property and the structures located thereon, then all representations should be limited to the best of the vendor's knowledge without having made due inquiry.[134] Courts in Canada have held that a warranty or representation "starkly qualified" by the words "to the best of the Seller's knowledge and belief" did not warrant the absolute truth of the statement.[135] The statement being so qualified can be untrue only if the contrary to what is stated is the truth.[136] Accordingly, where the defendant honestly believed in the truth of the statements he made and relied on the information he had before him, there is no breach of warranty if there is no duty of further inquiry.[137] The vendor may also request that the purchaser exclude specific matters already known or disclosed from the scope of any representation or warranty within the agreement.[138]

H. INDEMNITY, HOLDBACK, OR PRICE ADJUSTMENT

Indemnity ensures a party's recourse against the other party for specified damages or losses that arise as a consequence of the ownership of the property. This also applies to claims from third parties and government agencies.[139] The starting principle is that indemnity is only as good as the party giving it, and in the event of insolvency of the giving party, it may be worth little or nothing. Indemnity clauses need to be clearly drafted, given their complexities involving conditions precedent to the right to indemnification, such as exclusions, minimum and maximum claim amount, limitation on time periods, threshold of deductible claim amount, cost sharing arrangement, notification requirements, participation, settlement, or defence of third-party claims and procedures.[140]

---

131 Marion et al, *supra* note 29 at 470.

132 Estrin, *supra* note 23 at paras 1.8.1.3, 1.8.4.1.

133 Babe, *supra* note 1 at 174.

134 Estrin, *supra* note 23 at para 1.8.1.3.

135 *Melko v Lloyd Estate*, 2002 CanLII 13191 at paras 46-52, 30 BLR (3d) 37 (Ont Sup Ct J); *Gladu v Robineau Estate*, 2017 ONSC 37 at paras 289-91; *Armstrong v London Life Insurance Co* (1999), 103 OTC 192, 27 RPR (3d) 243 at paras 39-48 (Sup Ct J).

136 *Vokey v Edwards*, 1999 CarswellOnt 1440, [1999] OJ No 1706 (QL) at paras 59-64 (Sup Ct J); *Vaz-Oxlade v Volkenstein*, 2000 CanLII 4111 at para 2, 135 OAC 140, 35 RPR (3d) 165 (CA).

137 *John Levy Holdings Inc v Cameron & Johnstone Ltd*, 26 RPR (2d) 130, 1992 CarswellOnt 602 at paras 59-66, 35 ACWS (3d) 134 (Ont Gen Div), aff'd 1993 CarswellOnt 5613, [1993] OJ No 3183 (QL), 39 ACWS (3d) 533 (CA).

138 Estrin, *supra* note 23 at para 1.8.4.1.

139 *Ibid* at para 1.8.4.4; Marion et al, *supra* note 29 at 467-68, citing *CIT Financial Ltd v Canadian Imperial Bank of Commerce*, 2017 ONSC 38 at para 52.

140 Babe, *supra* note 1 at 175; Estrin, *supra* note 23 at para 1.8.4.4.

The "[p]arties can expand or limit the scope of liability that would ordinarily exist at common law through express language."[141] As stated in "Sober Second Thoughts,"

> [i]ndemnities can be drafted in a number of ways, including using a fault-based structure (whereby one party agrees to indemnify the other for losses suffered by the other as a result of a breach of a representation, warranty, or other contractual term) or a no-fault-based structure (whereby one party agrees to indemnify the other on the occurrence of a certain type of loss).[142]

The purchaser will want to negotiate specific environmental indemnities. An overly broad indemnity could impose on the vendor liability that goes on forever, except to the extent that it is limited by statutory limitations.[143] The vendor will want to (1) resist providing any indemnities and rights of action that would impose post-closing environmental liabilities; (2) insist that potential liability is to be capped at a specified dollar amount; (3) limit the scope of the indemnity to only onsite or offsite contamination; (4) or require proof as to the type or cause of potential contamination and/or limit the term of the indemnity.[144] The vendor will also want to have the purchaser indemnify it against all damages suffered as a result of any environmental matters whenever occurring or accruing.[145]

The parties should carefully consider the types and nature of the loss covered by the indemnity and whether the indemnity only covers damages incurred by third parties. As "Sober Second Thoughts" points out, "While indemnities often only cover third-party claims," there is no general principle for this, and "a contractual interpretation exercise is required to determine whether the indemnity extends to losses suffered by an indemnitee directly."[146] If parties intend that an indemnity should not apply to third-party claims, they must do so through clear and express language.[147]

The purchaser will want to negotiate price adjustment, holdback, or the creation of a contingency fund from a portion of the price where environmental costs are known or anticipated. There may be a myriad of problems in enforcing an indemnity even if the vendor provides it. The purchaser may gain the best possible knowledge of the expected environmental issues and deal with the cost implications in the purchase price.[148] Where there is full knowledge of the risk, the preferred approach to effective negotiation of environmental issues is an allocation of those risks with appropriate compensation in the pricing of the transaction for the party fixed with the risk.[149]

I. LIMITATION OF LIABILITY AND EXCLUSION CLAUSES

Clauses limiting or excluding liability present a further bone of contention in business transactions. Such clauses place a cap on the amount either party can recover for a breach of the

---

141 Marion et al, *supra* note 29 at 467, citing Nick Kangles et al, "Risk Allocation Provisions in Energy Industry Agreements: Are We Getting It Right?" (2011) 49:2 Alta L Rev 339 at 349.

142 *Ibid*.

143 Marion et al, *supra* note 29 at 467-68, citing Scott R Miller & Kevin S MacFarlane, "Environmental Risk Allocation in the Asset Rationalization Process" (1992) 30:1 Alta L Rev 94; *TransCanada Pipelines Ltd v Potter Station Power Ltd Partnership*, 2002 CanLII 49642 at paras 35-36, 22 BLR (3d) 210 (Ont Sup Ct J).

144 Estrin, *supra* note 23 at para 1.8.1.3.

145 *Anardako, supra* note 85; *Talisman, supra* note 85.

146 Marion et al, *supra* note 29 at 468, citing *Potter, supra* note 143 at paras 35-36; *Weyerhaeuser, supra* note 48 at paras 101, 208.

147 Marion et al, *supra* note 29 at 468, citing *Potter, supra* note 143 and *Herron v Chase Manufacturing Inc*, 2003 ABCA 219 at paras 34, 36.

148 Estrin, *supra* note 23 at para 1.8.1.3.

149 *Ibid* at para 1.8.1.3.6.3.

agreement or limit the possibility or extent of recovery for particular losses.[150] These clauses may be in various forms and may preclude or limit things such as pre-contractual representations, consequential damages, recovery for specific liabilities, or time and survival periods.[151]

However, such clauses require express and clear language to be enforceable.[152] Where the parties are sophisticated, with independent legal advice, and there is equality or similarity in bargaining powers, it may be difficult to establish unenforceability of such clauses on grounds of unconscionability or public policy unless there is some evidence of fraud or deceit.[153] The principles of contractual interpretation discussed above will apply in an analysis to determine whether limitation and exclusion clauses are enforceable, and any ambiguity is generally resolved against the party seeking to rely on them.[154]

Careful attention should also be paid to the scope of the limitations in such clauses. Some clauses limit liability only to contractual breaches, whereas others might extend to tortious claims, and there is no requirement to expressly list the torts excluded.[155] The Supreme Court has provided guidance and examples of clauses "from prior cases which it deemed to be sufficiently clear and precise enough to warrant enforcement."[156] Furthermore, the scope of the limitation of liability clauses can have a much broader impact, not just for recovery of damages. In *IFP Technologies*, the Alberta Court of Appeal considered the effect of a clause that capped damages at $16 million on (1) the continued ownership of the assets in dispute; (2) entitlement to net revenue from primary production from the assets; and (3) recovery of significant legal costs incurred.[157] Finally, regardless of how express and clear the terms are, parties cannot avoid the duty of honest performance of the contract through the use of limitation of liability clauses.[158]

J. LIMITATION PERIODS

There is a potential to confuse the various applicable limitation periods in business transactions. This is because there are statutory limitation periods and contractual limitation periods.

1. Statutory Limitation Periods

Parties should be mindful to review the various statutes and regulations governing the particular business for applicable limitation periods at the outset in order to better negotiate their contractual limitation periods. This is because certain statutory limitation periods cannot be shortened by agreement. For our context, the two statutory limitation periods are ruled by

---

150 Marion et al, *supra* note 29 at 475.

151 *Ibid.*

152 *Tercon Contractors Ltd v British Columbia (Transportation and Highways)*, 2010 SCC 4 at paras 73, 122-23, [2010] 1 SCR 69.

153 Marion et al, *supra* note 29 at 476, citing *Horizon Resource Management Ltd v Blaze Energy Ltd*, 2011 ABQB 658 at para 1021; *John Deere Financial Inc v 1232291 Ontario Inc (Northern Haul Contracting)*, 2016 ONCA 838 at para 46; and *Curtis Chandler v Karl Hollett*, 2017 ONSC 2969 at para 55.

154 Marion et al, *supra* note 29 at 476, citing *Spartek Systems Inc v Brown*, 2014 ABQB 526 at para 274.

155 Marion et al, *supra* note 29 at 476, citing *ITO-Int'l Terminal Operators v Miida Electronics Inc*, [1986] 1 SCR 752 at 799, 1986 CanLII 91.

156 Marion et al, *supra* note 29 at 476, citing *Tercon*, *supra* note 152 at para 73; *Hunter Engineering Co v Syncrude Canada Ltd*, [1989] 1 SCR 426 at 450, 1989 CanLII 129; *Guarantee*, *supra* note 45 at para 5; and *Fraser Jewellers (1982) Ltd v Dominion Electric Protection Co*, 1997 CanLII 4452, 34 OR (3d) 1 at 4 (CA).

157 Marion et al, *supra* note 29 at 477.

158 *Ibid* at 455, citing *Bhasin*, *supra* note 96 at para 75.

(1) the general limitation statutes such as the *Limitations Act*;[159] and (2) environmental statutes such as the Alberta EPEA.

The Alberta *Limitations Act*, as an example, provides immunity from a claim,[160] with certain specified exceptions, if the claimant does not seek a remedial order within the earlier of (1) two years after the date on which the claimant first knew, or ought to have known, that the injury for which a remedial order was being sought had occurred, was attributable to conduct of the defendant, and warrants bringing a proceeding; or (2) ten years after the claim arose.[161] The first part deals with discoverability of the injury. The second part is the ultimate limitation period beyond which no claim can be recovered regardless of the fact that it was not discoverable.

The concept of discoverability in the *Limitations Act* generally relates to facts rather than law.[162] There is a three-part test "based on a reasonable awareness of the injury, attribution of the injury to the defendant, and a claim warranting a proceeding for a remedial order."[163] The test is described as a "restrictive subjective/objective approach" that asks the question, "[I]n light of his or her own circumstances and interests, at what point could the plaintiff reasonably have brought an action?" Thus, while the test is objective, in that it employs the "ought to have known" standard, it is applied having regard to a claimant's personal circumstances.[164] Furthermore, the immunity is linked with the discoverability of the injury, not the discoverability of a cause of action for an injury. In addition, separate limitation periods may apply to different injuries arising from the same event.[165] For claims involving breaches of contract, the same three-part test for discoverability applies.[166] The nature and terms of the contract will be relevant in assessing the subjective/objective facts.

The Alberta EPEA provides another typology of statutory limitation periods. This statute does not provide a specific limitation period but grants courts the power to extend the general statutory limitation period in cases of environmental contamination.[167] An application for extension of the limitation period may be made before or after the expiry of the limitation period, and the judge should consider the following factors, where information is available: (1) timing—when the alleged adverse effect occurred; (2) due diligence—whether the alleged adverse effect ought to have been discovered by the claimant had the claimant exercised due diligence and whether the claimant exercised such due diligence; (3) prejudice—whether extending the limitation period would prejudice the proposed defendant's ability to maintain a defence on the merits; and (4) any other criteria the court considers to be relevant.[168]

Section 218 was added to the EPEA in 1998 as a sensible solution "for some harmful effects may not be evident for several years."[169] The provision has not been used much in Alberta, given the challenges in its application.[170] The courts initially struggled with whether these factors

---

159 RSA 2000, c L-12.
160 "Claim" is defined as "a matter giving rise to a civil proceeding in which a claimant seeks a remedial order," and "injury" is defined as "(i) personal injury, (ii) property damage, (iii) economic loss, (iv) non-performance of an obligation, or (v) in the absence of any of the above, the breach of a duty": *Limitations Act*, ss 1(a), (e).
161 *Limitations Act*, s 3; *Gayton v Lacasse*, 2010 ABCA 123 at para 17.
162 *Amack v Wishewan*, 2015 ABCA 147.
163 *Weir-Jones Technical Services Incorporated v Purolator Courier Ltd*, 2019 ABCA 49 at para 50.
164 *Gayton*, *supra* note 161 at para 20.
165 *Ibid* at para 18.
166 *Weir-Jones*, *supra* note 163 at para 52.
167 EPEA, s 218(1).
168 EPEA, ss 218(2) and (3).
169 Alberta, Legislative Assembly, "Monday, April 6, 1998, Evening," *Alberta Hansard*, 24-2 (6 April 1998) at 1385 (Debby Carlson).
170 The cases that have considered s 218 are *Jager Industries Inc v Canadian Occidental Petroleum Ltd*, 2001 ABQB 182; *Wainwright Equipment Rentals Ltd v Imperial Oil Limited*, 2003 ABQB 898; *Floate v Gas Plus Inc*, 2015 ABQB 725; *Lakeview Village Professional Centre Corporation v Suncor Energy Inc*,

should be a preliminary or conclusive determination, considering the state of the action and the status of the evidentiary record. The court determined that to justify moving to trial under s 218, the applicant must meet the threshold of a good arguable case on the s 218 factors following a two-step approach: (1) "Is there sufficient evidence on the s 218 factors to grant an extension of the limitation period?" (2) If evidence is insufficient or if an issue for trial could be determined prematurely, "has the claimant shown a good arguable case for an extension?" If the claimant has done so, "the claimant is entitled to an extension of the limitation period subject to a final determination of the issue at trial."[171]

The summary judgment process created complications for the established test for s 218. In an application for extension of limitation period to bring an action for contamination where the respondent also brought a cross-application for summary judgment, the court held that while the s 218 preliminary test may be appropriate where there is a stand-alone application, the parties are required to put their "best foot forward" where there is a cross-application for summary dismissal.[172]

In business transactions involving environmental claims, parties in Alberta and other jurisdictions with similar extension provisions in their environmental statutes should be mindful of extended statutory limitation periods. Extra thought should be put into allocation of environmental risks, indemnities, and other forms of securing performance, given that these statutes look back to former owners who may have no privity with an applicant for extension.

2. Contractual Limitation Periods

Given that environmental issues and associated liabilities may not be discovered until many years after an initial ESA has been done,[173] the length of time during which representations and warranties can be relied upon (survival period) or a claim can be brought pursuant to an indemnity, as well as provisions for notice of any breach, are often thorny items that parties are at liberty to negotiate.[174] Purchasers may require a period of two years or more post-closing to make further environmental investigations and make claims if necessary.[175] The vendor will want to obtain a clause in the agreement stipulating that the vendor's representations and warranties terminate on closing or in a shorter period of time.[176]

The contractual limitation period and the applicable statutory limitation period may sometimes conflict. Pursuant to s 7(2) of the Alberta *Limitations Act*, "[a]n agreement that purports to provide for the reduction of a limitation period provided by this Act is not valid."[177] Since the survival period of the representations and warranties in the agreement may be less than two years, such clauses could potentially be inconsistent with the *Limitations Act* and be deemed invalid.[178] The potential conflict has been interpreted in different ways.

It has been held that the contractual survival period was valid, given that it was simply a clause that puts limits on the warranties provided under the agreement and did not address limitation period to commence an action.[179] It has also been held that the only way to reconcile such a conflict is to determine the last day on which the *Limitations Act* allows the

2016 ABQB 288; and *Brookfield Residential (Alberta) LP (Carma Developers LP) v Imperial Oil Limited*, 2017 ABQB 218, aff'd in 2019 ABCA 35 [*Brookfield* cited to ABQB].
171 *Lakeview, supra* note 170 at para 19.
172 *Brookfield, supra* note 170 at para 49.
173 *Lakeview, supra* note 170.
174 Estrin, *supra* note 23 at para 1.8.4.1.
175 Babe, *supra* note 1 at 173.
176 Estrin, *supra* note 23 at para 1.8.1.3.
177 Marion et al, *supra* note 29 at 471-72.
178 *Ibid* at 472, citing *NOV Enerflow, supra* note 39.
179 Marion et al, *supra* note 29 at 472, citing *Edmonton (City) v Transalta Energy Marketing Corporation*, 2008 ABQB 426 at para 83.

claimant to sue and whether the contract chose a date earlier or later than that allowed by the *Limitations Act*; if earlier, the contract is invalid, and, if later, the contract is valid.[180] Another court concluded that the timely notice requirement, which was a mutually agreed-upon contractual condition precedent for a right of indemnity, is acceptable in the context of commercial agreements between sophisticated parties, and, once given, it triggers the accrual of the cause of action as well as the statutory limitation period.[181]

A court made a distinction in respect of a shorter contractual survival period that does not preclude a claim (although the claim would be unsuccessful) and a shorter contractual survival period that purports to preclude access to the courts.[182] The safer option for parties in a business transaction is to choose a survival period consistent with the applicable statutory limitation period where there is potential that such a conflict may arise.

K. SECURING PERFORMANCE OF CONTRACTUAL ENVIRONMENTAL OBLIGATIONS

The purchaser will want to secure the vendor's performance of agreed-upon environmental obligations relating to environmental issues by other financial security arrangements in the event of default.[183] This may be especially necessary where one or both parties are newly incorporated or "special purpose" legal entities. Such financial arrangements include extended payment terms, escrow arrangements, third-party guarantees, letters of credit, performance bonds, and pollution insurance.[184] The vendor will want to resist such an arrangement. A reasonable compromise can be a limitation period on the release of security or a trigger event such as the completion of excavations or the completion of all subsurface construction for the remediation work.[185]

VII. CONCLUSION

This chapter has focused on key environmental topics that significantly influence business transactions, guiding legal principles, and practical strategies to navigate such environmental issues.

QUESTIONS FOR DISCUSSION

1. You are counsel to the vendor of a reclaimed brownfield previously used for oil and gas development. Consider how you would handle the following:

   a. disclosure of patent and latent environmental liabilities to the purchaser;
   b. the types of clauses allocating environmental risks and liabilities between the parties to include in the purchase and sale agreement;
   c. the terms that will protect the vendor from future environmental exposure post-closing.

---

180 Marion et al, *supra* note 29 at 472-73, citing *Shaver v Co-operators General Insurance Company*, 2011 ABCA 367 at para 36.
181 Marion et al, *supra* note 29 at 473, citing *NFC Acquisition LP v Centennial 2000 Inc*, 2011 ONCA 43 at para 4.
182 Marion et al, *supra* note 29 at 473, citing *NOV Enerflow*, *supra* note 39 at paras 47, 60-61.
183 Babe, *supra* note 1 at 175.
184 *Ibid*.
185 Estrin, *supra* note 23 at para 1.8.4.6.

2. You are counsel to the purchaser of a business by a share purchase. The closing date is three months from the execution of the share purchase and sale agreement. Consider the approach you would adopt toward the following:

    a. environmental due diligence of the target company;

    b. key considerations to ensure that there is value in what is being purchased;

    c. the types of clauses protecting the purchaser to include in the purchase and sale agreement.

3. You were counsel to the purchaser of a hog farm business 11 years ago. The purchaser recently discovered that the brand-new processing plant he had purchased with the hog business from the previous owner was, unknown to the parties, leaking substances into the ground before and at the time of the transaction and continues to leak substances. The purchaser needs to understand how he may be able to recover from the previous owner. Assume the following:

    a. the purchaser conducted reasonable due diligence but no detailed environmental audit;

    b. the vendor made full disclosure to the "best of its knowledge and belief," including "risks" associated with processing plants.

FURTHER READINGS

Babe, Jennifer E, *Sale of a Business*, 9th ed (Markham, Ont: LexisNexis, 2012).

Estrin, David, *Business Guide to Environmental Law*, vol 1 (Scarborough, Ont: Carswell, 1992) (loose-leaf).

Hilton, James S, et al, *Due Diligence Techniques and Procedures* (Toronto: Federated Press, 1999).

Marion, Michael A, et al, "Sober Second Thoughts: Litigating Purchase and Sale Agreements in the Energy Industry" (2018) 56:2 Alta L Rev 447.

CHAPTER TWENTY-FOUR

THE FUTURE OF ENVIRONMENTAL LAW

Marcia Valiante

I. INTRODUCTION

Modern environmental law in Canada began to evolve more than 40 years ago as governments were called on to respond to serious air and water pollution "crises" threatening public health and environmental quality. In responding to public concern, Canadian governments adopted legislation and took on the administrative role of regulators of industry, constructing increasingly complex "command and control" standards and administrative machinery to ensure compliance. This was followed by a second generation of laws taking a more proactive approach, through the adoption of environmental assessment and planning legislation, public participation rights, and pollution prevention. In the 1990s, Canadian institutions experimented with alternative dispute resolution, economic instruments, voluntary initiatives, and other approaches. Enormous efforts and financial resources have been expended across multiple sectors of Canadian society in implementing these rules. The result has been a marked improvement in air and water quality in many areas, conservation of species and spaces, as well as a shift of environmental awareness into mainstream political discourse. Yet, even as environmental security is recognized by central institutions as a "fundamental value in Canadian society" and a matter of "superordinate importance" (*R v Hydro-Québec*, [1997] 3 SCR 213 at paras 85, 123, 125, 1997 CanLII 318, 217 NR 241), it is clear that evermore complex and challenging threats to health and the environment continue to emerge. Thus, despite much progress, we are nowhere near the end of the demand for environmental law.

Other chapters of this book examine specific reform proposals intended to make Canadian environmental law more responsive, more equitable, and more effective. The purpose of this chapter is to explore at a more general level the continued relevance of the underlying conceptual basis and design of environmental law and to consider future directions.

The nature of Canadian environmental law reflects the dominant ethical, political, cultural, and economic beliefs and the mainstream values of our society with respect to the Earth, other species, future generations, and the place of humans in relation to nature. Because these values influence one's perception of both the problems and the appropriate solutions, they will continue to influence the shape of environmental law and policy; as they change, whether slowly or abruptly, so too will the legal response. Environmental law is also informed by discoveries in ecological science. Over time, the focus of environmental law has expanded beyond a primarily anthropocentric concern for human health and interests (such as aesthetics and recreation) to incorporate a growing ecological focus on biodiversity, ecosystem integrity, and other species. Whether this shift is sufficient to enable us to meet future environmental problems is explored in this chapter.

II. WHERE ARE WE NOW? CRITIQUES OF THE CURRENT STATE OF CANADIAN ENVIRONMENTAL LAW

Identifying the current state of environmental law and understanding its successes and failures is essential to charting a course for a better future. One assessment of what has been accomplished since the early 1970s, and what remains to be done, is set out in the following extract, describing a discussion among environmental lawyers as to whether the early goals of environmental law have been achieved.

D PAUL EMOND, "'ARE WE THERE YET?': REFLECTIONS ON THE SUCCESS OF THE ENVIRONMENTAL LAW MOVEMENT IN ONTARIO"
(2008) 46 Osgoode Hall LJ 219 at 238-39 [footnotes omitted]

As to whether we are there yet, there are two "theres." [sic] One is the "there" that environmental lawyers sought in terms of new and improved environmental protection and conservation laws; the second is the "there" or the result that environmental lawyers had imagined they could achieve in terms of a better, cleaner, more sustainable environment—the substantive improvements to the environment that would flow from the laws that were enacted. We have made some progress on the first goal, as many at the round table were quick to point out. As for the second, the problems of pollution and environmental degradation have proven to be far more complex than was first imagined, and hence more difficult to fix. In fact, it may be fair to say that the legal tools promoted by the environmental lawyers in the 70s and 80s were simply not up to the task that lay ahead. Perhaps we could not have imagined in the late 60s and early 70s "the worrisome effects of growing populations, increasing consumption, and invasive technologies." Nor could we have imagined the scale or complexity of the problems. Looking back, the pollution from a pulp and paper plant seemed relatively straight forward [sic], especially when compared with the problems of ozone layer depletion, global climate change, biodiversity loss, hydrological system disruption, trace chemical contamination, and now, zoonoses (transfer of disease from animals to humans). What laws are going to solve these problems?

• • •

As for the early demands for better environmental legislation, we are at least partly there. The list of what has been accomplished is impressive. Under all environmental protection acts pollution is a crime ... . Command and control instruments are in place ... . Environmental assessment and planning legislation has been in place across Canada for more than thirty years (although not as long at the federal level) and has required the public sector, at least, to make environmental assessment and planning a part of its decision-making process. And some provinces have environmental bill of rights legislation, even if it is not quite what was envisioned by the early environmental law advocates. Finally, ... a more recent focus on toxins has led to an impressive array of federal and provincial controls.

So we are almost "there," or at least we could be there with some relatively modest improvements to the laws. The problem is that having achieved much of what was aspired to, the environmental problems persist. ...

• • •

... Global warming, the growing loss of biodiversity, the reluctance to embrace sustainable practices, and the resulting (and growing) carbon footprint of individuals and communities on the planet all suggest that we are not there yet.

Predicting how environmental law will develop in the future is fraught with too much uncertainty to be particularly useful, especially in the long term. Up until now, Canadian environmental law has undergone several waves of changes in response to new scientific understandings, new challenges, and shifting economic, political, and legal trends. Going forward, regulatory responses similar to those used in the past will likely be applied incrementally to certain new challenges—for example, to control the adverse impacts of new technologies and processes such as artificial intelligence and biotechnology or to address new material threats such as nanomaterials, microplastics, or pharmaceuticals in aquatic systems. Yet, increasingly, there are many who recognize that more complex challenges such as climate change cannot be met with the same type of responses as were used in the past; rather, a more radical change in Canadian (and global) society—culturally, economically, politically, and spiritually—may be the only effective road forward.

The rest of this section explores some critiques of Canadian environmental law and considers some of the reasons for the current state of (or lack of) progress.

STEPAN WOOD, GEORGIA TANNER & BENJAMIN J RICHARDSON, "WHAT EVER HAPPENED TO CANADIAN ENVIRONMENTAL LAW?"
(2010) 37 Ecology LQ 981 at 993-95, 1006-7, 1038-40 [footnotes omitted]

The extraordinary growth in [Canada's] environmental laws in the 1970s marked a period of exuberant confidence in the ability of states to solve environmental problems through enlightened regulation. Later, Canada's increasingly mangled environmental regulations reflected the effects of neoliberal deregulation, fiscal restraint, and corporate influence. The sustainability discourse has also been influential in Canadian law-making, though it too has not resolved the contradictions in environmental governance nor reversed [sic] Canada's environmental decline.

• • •

There was a time when there was a much greater public faith in the transformative capacity of politics to solve environmental problems. The late 1960s and early 1970s were heady days for environmental law advocacy in Canada and some other countries. Through legislative reform, lobbying, and other strategies, environmentalists believed that they could use the organs of the state as a means to solve the mounting pollution, resource depletion, and other environmental problems of industrial capitalism. ...

Many of the basic features of environmental law that we know today are traceable to innovations in this period. Milestones such as environmental impact assessment legislation, endangered species protection laws, and specialist environmental agencies and courts were among the flurry of reforms in an era where many were optimistic about the ability of the state to solve environmental challenges. ...

• • •

The combination of factors that enabled environmental awareness and institutional reforms to flourish in Canada during the 1970s and 1980s had collapsed by the early 1990s. While the trend was not unique to Canada, the decline there was particularly steep. According to a 1995 review of Canada's environmental performance by the Organisation for Economic Co-operation and Development (OECD), the country faced three main challenges: "difficulties in translating the concept [of sustainable development] into practical changes in economic decisions and practices and in economic signals; consumption and production patterns, which are often intensive in their use of natural resources; and increased concerns regarding the economy, employment and public deficits, which tend to reduce the prominence of environmental matters." Because of these and other circumstances, Canada's record on many environmental indicators deteriorated both absolutely and relatively to its peers.

• • •

... While virtually all countries are experiencing sharp environmental decline and are struggling to design or implement effective legislative and policy responses, Canada's record is among the worst. Its performance is all the more disappointing given that at one time it was widely admired for its progressiveness in dealing with environmental issues. The depth of decline in Canada would be more obvious were it not for the country's relatively small population and abundant natural resources. But its per capita "eco-footprint" is a high seven hectares per person, placing it seventh among all nations. This is both unsustainable and inequitable.

Although an extensive literature has mapped the weaknesses of environmental law generally, to understand fully Canada's circumstances requires additional analysis of the interplay of specific domestic political, economic, and legal issues. Federal–provincial relations, the political influence of neo-liberalism, the economic primacy of extractive industries, and an electoral system that can be unresponsive to public environmental concerns are all salient factors that have hindered environmental law reform in Canada. ...

• • •

... Sustainability in Canada, as elsewhere, will likely only arise if people are prepared to choose fundamentally different goals for their society, including a fundamentally different economic model in which maintenance of ecological integrity is a precondition to all development. Environmental law is a means to an end, not an end in itself.

NOTES AND QUESTIONS

1. Do you agree that Canada is a laggard and has fallen behind in environmental protection? What examples have you seen from your readings throughout this book? What factors have contributed to this? Can these factors be overcome? How?
2. What are the priority issues for environmental law reform today?

Canada's inconsistent record on securing environmental protection and integrating sustainability is also discussed in the following extract, which reflects specifically on the legacy of the significant changes in federal environmental laws made by the Conservative government of then–Prime Minister Stephen Harper after 2011. However, the author does not contend that it is only one government alone that has demonstrated ambivalence toward environmental goals; this can also be seen at the provincial level, as control of provincial governments have see-sawed back and forth between political parties with widely differing ideologies. (The result in some cases has been the quick repeal of one regime's progress on environmental law by the next government taking power.) As you read the following excerpt, consider also whether "ambivalence" toward environmental goals is more deeply embedded in contemporary Canadian culture.

DEBORA L VANNIJNATTEN, "INTRODUCTION"
in *Canadian Environmental Policy and Politics: The Challenges of Austerity and Ambivalence*, 4th ed (Don Mills, Ont: Oxford University Press, 2016) at xvii, xviii, xx [endnotes omitted]

[E]vidence of ambivalence in our environmental policy architecture is seen ... in attempts to graft more environmentally friendly policy tools onto regimes fundamentally favouring extractive and other economic activities. ... So deeply entrenched is this ambivalence in our environmental policy regime, [sic] that even the most well-intended government ... will face immense difficulties [sic] trying to overcome this tendency.

The problem ... is that when "austerity" hits and budgets/programs get cut, environmental policies are not rooted firmly enough to survive, and they get stripped away or are left untended/unenforced/unimplemented.

• • •

The link between the existing and increasing ambivalence in the Canadian environmental policy regime and the resilience of that regime is most worrying. It is no secret that those working in the environmental policy sphere are, for the most part, interested in building and maintaining a policy and program regime that is, to the greatest extent possible, "bullet-proof" in the face of political, economic, and social change. What we want is a regime that puts in place a framework for environmental protection and sustainability that can withstand the winds of change—changes in government and leadership, economic highs and lows, alterations in societal trends. This we do not have. The mixed impulses in our regime provide a few foundation blocks, but the architecture is clearly not able to withstand the political damage that has been done. The increasing extent of ambivalence in the regime coupled with the austerity legacy will have long-lasting consequences for our ability to respond to current and future environmental challenges.

• • •

One of the clearest weaknesses in our environmental policy architecture is an inability to integrate and co-ordinate—across issues, functions, and instruments ... [q]uite aside from our failure to co-ordinate efforts across federal, provincial, and local jurisdictions ... At the most basic levels, we fail to integrate sustainable development into government planning and programming. We fail to think broadly about policy instrument choice, in terms of how different combinations of instruments can achieve our goals. We fail to think about how incentive structures might be strategically inserted into programs, in more holistic ways. Without a more integrative policy perspective, we are unable to understand the complexities of environmental problems, to co-ordinate our efforts in such a way that we can deliver cobenefits in terms of addressing more than one environmental problem, or to assess adequately where we are succeeding or failing with our chosen policy instruments.

Several authors have identified specific characteristics of the Canadian system as reasons for a lack of progress in advancing environmental goals. For example, David Boyd identifies a number of structural obstacles to progress, including "the continued predominance of economic interests over environmental protection, international trade liberalization, unresolved constitutional problems, the lack of separation of powers between the legislative and executive branches of government, the extraordinary concentration of power in the prime minister's and premiers' offices, and barriers to an effective role for the courts" (*Unnatural Law: Rethinking Canadian Environmental Law and Policy* (Vancouver: UBC Press, 2003) at 251). Another critique is offered in the following extract, which focuses on "regulatory capture" of governments by economically powerful private interests as the root cause of the weaknesses in Canadian environmental law and a significant obstacle to our ability to solve complex environmental problems.

JASON MACLEAN, "STRIKING AT THE ROOT PROBLEM OF CANADIAN ENVIRONMENTAL LAW: IDENTIFYING AND ESCAPING REGULATORY CAPTURE"
(2016) 29 J Envtl L & Prac 111 at 113, 121, 125, 128 [footnotes omitted]

Systemic corruption—regulatory capture and its corollary, irresponsible government—is the root problem of Canadian environmental law. ...

Systemic corruption blocks principled reforms and fuels unprincipled reforms in Canadian environmental law—it is at the root of every identifiable systemic weakness infecting Canadian environmental law today, both federally and provincially. ...

• • •

... Canadian environmental law scholars tend to misdiagnose, underestimate, and/or defer the analysis of regulatory capture ... . Far too often, we analyze environmental laws and regulations at face value, failing to peer beneath their official forms and surfaces to adequately account for the actual origins. ... We find ourselves caught in a kind of Catch-22 dilemma, where the political barriers necessitating law reform render proposed reforms politically impossible to implement.

• • •

A comprehensive identification and mapping of the regulatory capture of Canadian environmental laws is plainly beyond the scope of this ... paper. ... Important and instructive examples, however, can readily be identified. There is perhaps no more important and instructive instance in Canada than that of the oil and gas industry's corrosive and cultural capture of federal and provincial legislation regarding greenhouse gas emissions and climate change. ...

• • •

Government regulation is not merely a fact of modern life; in a great many instances regulation is necessary to protect the public and to stave off catastrophe. Regulations, when designed properly and not compromised by special interests, not only promote the public interest, but can also promote innovation. Thus do Carpenter and Moss [Daniel Carpenter & David A Moss, eds, *Preventing Regulatory Capture: Special Interest Influence and How to Limit It* (New York: Cambridge University Press, 2014)] argue that "[t]he critical question is whether capture, where it exists, can be mitigated or prevented."

• • •

... [T]he core problem beyond the specific issue of the government's resource industry dependence is how to counterbalance the structural power of capital in the political process. This core problem is all the more pressing given that capital's power has been greatly reinforced by trade liberalization and the weakening of the traditional counterbalancing organization of labour. What is thus urgently needed, and what enhanced academic public policy engagement could help bring about, is a broad, popular political movement capable of redirecting government legislation and regulation away from the private interests of industry to the public interest of citizens in order to close the democratic deficit in Canadian environmental law and policy.

NOTES AND QUESTIONS

1. Do you agree with these assessments regarding systemic obstacles to further progress on environmental issues? Are there other factors that may be relevant?

2. What strategies would be effective to address or overcome the "ambivalence" of Canadian economic and political elites or to avoid "regulatory capture"?

3. For a wide-ranging discussion of obstacles and opportunities for the future of environmental law in the United States, see Inara Scott et al, "Environmental Law. Disrupted" (2019) 49 Envtl L Rep 10038.

III. WHERE ARE WE GOING? FUTURE DIRECTIONS FOR CANADIAN ENVIRONMENTAL LAW

Once we understand the limits of Canadian environmental law within the existing political and economic structures, the next step is to explore how to reconstruct a principled system for responding to critical environmental problems. Assuming that Canadian society and lawmakers can be galvanized to take action to address future environmental issues, most commentators counsel that deep changes are required. As a starting point, it is useful to consider whether the current objectives or goals of environmental law continue to be relevant, appropriate, and effective.

Early goals of environmental law were often expressed as the "conservation," "protection," or "preservation" of "the environment" generally or individual physical components or species. As discussed throughout this book, other fundamental principles of environmental law have emerged. These principles include the precautionary principle, "polluter pays" principle, environmental justice, and intergenerational equity.

In the 1990s, "sustainability" emerged as a core, integrative objective of environmental law following the work of the Brundtland commission (World Commission on Environment and Development, *Our Common Future* (Oxford: Oxford University Press, 1987)) in the lead-up to the 1992 United Nations Conference on Environment and Development in Rio de Janeiro. "Sustainable development," usually expressed as "development that meets the needs of the present without compromising the ability of future generations to meet their own needs" (at 43), was meant to incorporate and integrate environmental, social, and economic goals. This object-ive was adopted in numerous international instruments and national (including Canadian) laws, and by public and private institutions.

There are by now decades of debate in the literature over the meaning and implications of sustainability and sustainable development, including a debate over whether the goal should be a "strong" form of sustainability requiring fundamental changes in society or a "weak" form requiring less radical solutions. There is growing awareness that the achievement of sustain-ability may be elusive and that the goal has been co-opted by dominant economic interests. Some people question whether sustainability should continue to be the central principle and call for a rethinking of the ethical foundations and objectives of environmental law.

A summary discussion of the core elements of sustainability and concerns with the failure of its adoption into law to bring about fundamental change is set out in the following excerpt.

BENJAMIN J RICHARDSON & STEPAN WOOD, "ENVIRONMENTAL LAW FOR SUSTAINABILITY"
in Benjamin Richardson, ed, *Environmental Law for Sustainability: A Reader* (Oxford: Hart, 2006) 1 at 14-17 [footnotes omitted]

So far, the sustainability discourse has coalesced into a set of fairly general normative principles, rather than a precise formula for environmental policy ... . The *integration principle* suggests that development decisions should take into account their environmental sequelae. ... The principle of *equity* has two major components. *Intergenerational equity* requires that the present generation ensure that the health and productivity of the biosphere is maintained or enhanced for the benefit of posterity. ... *Intragenerational equity*, on the other hand, addresses justice between contemporary communities and nations. Protection of human rights and enhanced opportunities for public participation ... provide one means to promote intragenera-tional equity. Legal protections for [I]ndigenous peoples' lands and environmental resources ... is another way by which environmental law is becoming more sensitive to cultural and social justice issues. Finally, addressing inequities between the global "North" and "South" is an indispensable requirement of intragenerational equity, yet one of the most intractable problems in environmental affairs ... .

The sustainability principle that has attracted the greatest fervour is the *pre-cautionary principle*, gaining recognition in EU and international law. ...

Yet, while governments have generally been prompt to create a new layer of insti-tutions, real progress in transforming their economies has lagged considerably.

[S]ustainability presents formidable policy and legal problems for governments. The likelihood of absolute ecological limits to human activity, the existence of irreversible environmental impacts and concomitant sense of policy urgency, and the systemic problem sources located in patterns of production and consumption are some of the challenges that demand greater innovations in policy instruments and management institutions. More radical possibilities of reform have yet to be seriously advanced. These could include an emphasis on the promotion of ethical change ... to unseat the dominant anthropocentric and instrumental policies of environmental management. Alternatively, we could reform the underlying mech-anisms of capital allocation that shape growth and investment. ...

Without a new wave of institutional reforms along these lines, it is doubtful that the current menu of environmental law instruments and policies will steer society away from its still largely negative trajectory. Is there hope of radical change for the better soon? Not necessarily. The sustainability discourse is in danger of being—indeed many would say it already has been—co-opted and tamed by interests opposed to fundamental economic and social policy change for the sake of the health and survival of the planet. It is dangerous to assume that human society will "inevitably" progress towards more effective systems of environmental law. Crucial to the achievement of sustainable development is the need for institutional frameworks that can assist people to transcend the tension between short-term, individual self-interest and broader, long-term social welfare. ... [T]he core task is to reorient social and economic systems "as if the future mattered."

NOTES AND QUESTIONS

1. An important discussion of the meaning and role of sustainability in environmental law, and an argument for strong, "ecological" sustainability, is found in Klaus Bosselmann, *The Principle of Sustainability: Transforming Law and Governance*, 2nd ed (London; New York: Routledge, 2017). Bosselmann (at 120) asserts that the building blocks of ecological sustainability include a concept of justice that requires a focus on intragenerational, intergenerational, and inter-species justice, noting that the "inclusion of an elaborate concept of interspecies issues is certainly crucial for a theory on ecological justice as distinct from mere social justice." (See also K Bosselmann, "Ecological Justice and Law" in Richardson & Wood, *Environmental Law for Sustainability*.)

2. At the international level, the UN General Assembly endorsed the outcome document (*The Future We Want*, UN General Assembly Resolution 88/288 of 27 July 2012, 66th Sess, UN Doc A/RES/66/288, Annex (11 September 2012), online: *UN* <https://www.un.org/ga/search/view_doc.asp?symbol=A/RES/66/288&Lang=E>) from the Rio+20 conference in 2012 (UN Conference on Sustainable Development), reaffirming the global community's commitment to sustainable development:

> 4. We recognize that poverty eradication, changing unsustainable [sic] and promoting sustainable patterns of consumption and production and protecting and managing the natural resource base of economic and social development are the overarching objectives of and essential requirements for sustainable development. We also reaffirm the need to achieve sustainable development by promoting sustained, inclusive and equitable economic growth, creating greater opportunities for all, reducing inequalities, raising basic standards of living, fostering equitable social development and inclusion, and promoting the integrated and sustainable management of natural resources and ecosystems that supports, inter alia, economic, social and human development while facilitating ecosystem conservation, regeneration and restoration and resilience in the face of new and emerging challenges.

3. One key future direction to achieve sustainable development as promoted in the outcome document is for national governments to work toward shifting to a "green economy":

> 56. We affirm that there are different approaches, visions, models and tools available to each country, in accordance with its national circumstances and priorities, to achieve sustainable development in its three dimensions which is our overarching goal. In this regard, we consider green economy in the context of sustainable development and poverty eradication as one of the important tools available for achieving sustainable development and that it could provide options for policymaking but should not be a rigid set of rules. We emphasize that it should contribute to eradicating poverty as well as sustained economic growth, enhancing social inclusion, improving human welfare and creating opportunities for employment and decent work for all, while maintaining the healthy functioning of the Earth's ecosystems.

57. We affirm that policies for green economy in the context of sustainable development and poverty eradication should be guided by and in accordance with all the Rio Principles [*Rio Declaration on Environment and Development*, UNGA UN Doc No A/CONF.151/26/Rev.1 (Vol 1), annex I (1992), online (pdf): *Sustainable Development Goals* <https://sustainable development.un.org/content/documents/1709riodeclarationeng.pdf>], *Agenda 21* [United Nations Conference on Environment & Development, Rio de Janeiro, Brazil, 3-14 June 1992), online (pdf): United Nations Sustainable Development <https://sustainabledevelopment.un.org/content/documents/Agenda21.pdf>] and the Johannesburg Plan of Implementation [*Plan of Implementation of the World Summit on Sustainable Development* (2002), online (pdf): *UNDESA* <https://www.un.org/esa/sustdev/documents/WSSD_POI_PD/English/WSSD_PlanImpl.pdf>] and contribute towards achieving relevant internationally agreed development goals, including the Millennium Development Goals [(2000), online: *UN* <https://www.un.org/millenniumgoals/>].

58. We affirm that green economy policies in the context of sustainable development and poverty eradication should:

(a) Be consistent with international law;

(b) Respect each country's national sovereignty over their natural resources, taking into account its national circumstances, objectives, responsibilities, priorities and policy space with regard to the three dimensions of sustainable development;

(c) Be supported by an enabling environment and well-functioning institutions at all levels, with a leading role for governments and with the participation of all relevant stakeholders, including civil society;

(d) Promote sustained and inclusive economic growth, foster innovation and provide opportunities, benefits and empowerment for all and respect for all human rights;

(e) Take into account the needs of developing countries, particularly those in special situations;

(f) Strengthen international cooperation, including the provision of financial resources, capacity-building and technology transfer to developing countries;

(g) Effectively avoid unwarranted conditionalities on official development assistance and finance;

(h) Not constitute a means of arbitrary or unjustifiable discrimination or a disguised restriction on international trade, avoid unilateral actions to deal with environmental challenges outside the jurisdiction of the importing country and ensure that environmental measures addressing transboundary or global environmental problems, as far as possible, are based on international consensus;

(i) Contribute to closing technology gaps between developed and developing countries and reduce the technological dependence of developing countries, using all appropriate measures;

(j) Enhance the welfare of [I]ndigenous peoples and their communities, other local and traditional communities and ethnic minorities, recognizing and supporting their identity, culture and interests, and avoid endangering their cultural heritage, practices and traditional knowledge, preserving and respecting non-market approaches that contribute to the eradication of poverty;

(k) Enhance the welfare of women, children, youth, persons with disabilities, smallholder and subsistence farmers, fisherfolk and those working in small and medium-sized enterprises, and improve the livelihoods and empowerment of the poor and vulnerable groups, in particular in developing countries;

(l) Mobilize the full potential and ensure the equal contribution of both women and men;

(m) Promote productive activities in developing countries that contribute to the eradication of poverty;

(n) Address the concern about inequalities and promote social inclusion, including social protection floors;

(o) Promote sustainable consumption and production patterns;

(p) Continue efforts to strive for inclusive, equitable development approaches to overcome poverty and inequality.

4. What steps have been taken toward a green economy in Canada? What effective steps could be taken at the federal, provincial, and local levels to induce such a shift?

Despite continuing and widespread support for the goal of sustainable development in Canadian and global environmental law and policy, the following article critiques our understanding of the concept, particularly in light of the contemporary framing of the human impact on the environment; this framing is known as the "Anthropocene."

LOUIS J KOTZÉ, "RETHINKING GLOBAL ENVIRONMENTAL LAW AND GOVERNANCE IN THE ANTHROPOCENE"
(2014) 32:2 J Energy & Nat'l Res L 121 at 136-37 [footnotes omitted]

[W]e could expect the Anthropocene manifestly to alter society's view of sustainability (or sustainable development) in the context of the human–environment interface. Sustainability has been at the centre of the environmental law, policy and governance architecture for the greater part of the 20th century, and in many ways it has been and continues to function as the guiding principle for all socio-legal and political interventions and reforms that seek to govern the human–environment interface. A generous interpretation of the concept suggests that sustainability does not aim for a "singular 'steady state,' but rather the best possible dynamic for dwelling in the world taking into account the needs of economy, society and environment." Herein, however, lies the greatest political fallacy of sustainability, namely its disingenuousness and its complacent promise of sufficient resources in a time of global ecological crisis and resource scarcity, which it promotes through deep socially entrenched rhetoric and (corporate and state) practices. The earth can possibly sustain a small number of people in some parts of the world for a short span of time, but it cannot extend this sustenance to an ever-growing population all over the world until the proverbial end of time. Another fallacy of sustainability is that it is based on false assumptions. One of these is that it accepts as correct the fact that humans are capable of assuming how much ecological capital is needed to satisfy socio-economic demands of present and, more worryingly, future generations. Another is that sustainability assumes that the earth and its systems are in a steady state and are generally stable. The very nature of the Anthropocene, however, suggests that the earth and its systems are highly unpredictable, uncertain and erratic. In doing so, the Anthropocene exposes sustainable development for the fraud that it is, including its naive fallacies and inappropriateness in times of unpredictable socio-ecological upheaval.

The Anthropocene instead demands from society acting through its social institutions, [sic] not to continue to be "blinded by ideological palliatives such as 'sustainable development' that help us rationalize our continuing encroachments upon the planet." What would be necessary is a paradigm shift in either discarding or reimagining sustainability as the orthodox and hitherto failing fulcrum of global environmental law and governance. A new vision of sustainability in the Anthropocene, or a possible substitute, is needed, which could arguably have a profound effect on our perceptions and design of global environmental law and governance. At the same time a re-envisioned and redesigned global environmental law and governance effort may be able better to achieve the objectives of a "different" (possibly a strong as opposed to a weak) sustainability paradigm.

The next extract also questions, from an ecological perspective, the relevance and effectiveness of continuing to rely on the principle of sustainability as the central objective of environmental action. The authors argue that a new objective is required to meet the challenges of the future.

ROBIN KUNDIS CRAIG & MELINDA HARM BENSON, "REPLACING SUSTAINABILITY"
(2013) 46 Akron L Rev 841 at 844, 846-49, 850, 858-60, 862, 865-66
[footnotes omitted]

This Article argues that, from a policy perspective, we must face the impossibility of even defining—let alone pursuing—a goal of "sustainability" in a world characterized by such extreme complexity, radical uncertainty, and discomfiting loss of stationarity. Instead, we need new policy directions and orientations that provide the necessary capacity to deal with these "wicked problems" in a meaningful and equitable way. The realities of current and emerging SES [socioecological system] dynamics warrant a new set of tools and approaches to governance of those systems.

• • •

As a governance measure, at least in theory, sustainability leads to laws and policies that limit human activity in and consumption of the natural environment to levels that can be continued on a long-term basis with minimal harm to either side of the equation. ...

Nevertheless, linguistically and politically, sustainability goals depend on a conservation assumption of ecological stationarity. ... Thus, ... sustainability is about human efforts to maintain continuity and to keep things—natural resources—in the same state of being as when management started or with reference to this baseline. ...

Similar assumptions that human effort can keep SESs in desirable states of productivity inhere in almost all sustainability goals. More specifically, first, sustainability assumes that humans can figure out how much human use of an ecosystem or natural resource can be maintained indefinitely without untoward consequences—despite complex and multiscalar ecological system dynamics and despite natural variability in temperature, precipitation, species population levels, species migrations, and other variables that affect any given ecosystem on a seasonal, yearly, or longer basis. ...

Second, sustainability assumes that baseline environmental conditions ... will remain more or less the same, within natural variability envelopes, over long periods of time. ...

Sustainability, therefore, is a conservative concept that assumes a lack of baseline environmental change and minimal ecological complexity. ... These assumptions imply that management of human uses of the environment lies largely within human control ... . While this is, of course, an overly simplistic *ecological* description—as ecologists and biologists have known for years—it remains a fairly accurate description of how the *laws and policies* governing natural resources management have operated. ... The concept of discontinuous regime change, and the idea that there might not be a way back to "optimality," however defined, are not part of current legal regimes.

• • •

... "[O]ne of the assumptions that pervades these laws is that anthropogenic change is unnatural and degrading, but also non-transformative and hence (generally) reversible. This assumption sets up the most basic paradigms of environmental and natural resource regulation and management: preservation and restoration." ...

• • •

[C]limate change is creating a world of non-stationarity—a world where baseline conditions in the natural world can no longer be assumed. ...

Thus, climate change is creating an increasingly uncomfortable world of unpredictability. Nevertheless, this is our new reality, and it poses non-hypothetical challenges for our reigning sustainability paradigm for law, ecosystem governance, and environmental policy. ... The implications for natural resources law and policy are clear: natural resources law and policy in a climate change era can no longer be preservationist or restorationist. ...

As a consequence, governance models for the climate change era must treat with considerable skepticism—and be willing in many places to outright reject—all traditional paradigms that are based on assumptions of stationarity. These paradigms include not only preservation and restoration but also sustainability. Finding a successor to the sustainability paradigm is critical.

The rejection of sustainability will likely be met with considerable resistance. This resistance is understandable because sustainability goals certainly can and have fostered less destructive relationships than unbridled consumerism between particular groups of humans and the ecosystems upon which they depend. ... In addition, sustainability goals added a much-needed temporal perspective to environmental law and natural resources management. ...

This Article is not arguing that sustainability is a *bad idea*, [sic] it is arguing that it is just an increasingly futile one at anything but the largest and most general of scales. ...

• • •

... While it is always important to remember that there will be no panacea—"one size fits all" solution to environmental problems—particularly in the realm of natural resources management, we must begin to formulate ecological governance goals by some metric other than sustainability.

The concept of resilience, and the theory of resilience thinking offers a new and potentially more productive orientation than sustainability to the environmental challenges ahead. ...

• • •

... In putting an awareness of continual change at its core, resilience thinking contrasts sharply with the restoration-, preservation-, and optimization-based paradigms that currently dominate environmental law and natural resource management. ...

The difference in emphasis may at times be subtle, but it is enough of a difference that true adoption of resilience thinking would force several changes in natural resource management. For example, resilience thinking should force managers to act in terms of entire systems, not specific and favored ecosystem goods and services

.... Thus, resilience theory recognizes that a management focus that seeks to stabilize a selected set of ecosystem services tends instead to actually increase system vulnerability to shocks and perturbations.

In addition, ... it promotes a more flexible and responsive approach to natural resource management, including but not limited to adaptive management. ... As a result, resilience thinking allows environmental law and policy to forge a new, more realistic relationship with science as a method for providing information—one that is capable of designing interesting and informative questions rather than expecting definitive answers.

Ensuring ecological and social resilience is often linked with expanded reliance on adaptive governance as an approach to environmental law. Tony Arnold has described the growing use of adaptive governance techniques as a "fourth generation of environmental law" ("Fourth Generation Environmental Law: Integrationist and Multimodal" (2011) 35 Wm & Mary Envtl L & Pol'y Rev 771). In the following article, he discusses the need to focus on resilience and the opportunities for, and limitations on, the adoption of adaptive governance, in the context of US environmental law.

CRAIG ANTHONY ARNOLD, "ENVIRONMENTAL LAW, EPISODE IV: A NEW HOPE: CAN ENVIRONMENTAL LAW ADAPT FOR RESILIENT COMMUNITIES AND ECOSYSTEMS"
(2015) 21:1 J Envtl & Sustainability L 1 at 6-7, 9, 11, 12-13, 37-39
[footnotes omitted]

A fourth generation of environmental law appears to be emerging. In some respects, this new generation is a reaction to and rejection of the prior generations' assumptions that the environment is a static good to preserve, commodify, or sustain. Based in [sic] the science of resilience and panarchy, the fourth generation recognizes natural environments and human environments as highly dynamic, shaped by complex and nonlinear interconnections among ecological systems, social systems, and institutions. It aims to enhance or support the resilience of both ecosystems and human communities by focusing on the interconnections among ecosystems, social systems, and institutions (systems of systems). However, the fourth generation embraces prior generations by using their tools and instruments (e.g., regulation, incentives, adaptive management, participatory processes), as well as other tools and instruments in a multimodal—or toolbox—approach. It is also characterized by emergent and evolving polycentric governance systems that are loosely linked through networks and feedback, including many different kinds of federal–state partnerships, multi-stakeholder collaborative processes, litigation and regulation as stimuli to negotiated problem-solving, community-based activism, and others. In the fourth generation, law is meant to stimulate and support adaptive governance, although often law actually serves as a barrier to adaptive governance.

• • •

One of the primary lessons to learn from the four generations of environmental law is that environmental law evolves relatively rapidly, with new structures and frameworks (or generations) emerging in response to the inadequacies of existing structures and frameworks and to the needs created by new problems or changing conditions. Changes in environmental law institutions—the rules, norms, and cognitive–cultural beliefs that shape and structure human interactions regarding the environment—are influenced by the pace and magnitude of change in ecosystems, society, and other institutions. They are also influenced by the complex and multidimensional nature of environmental problems, and how those problems are framed by people and groups in society.

• • •

Fourth-generation environmental law is concerned not only with resilience in general but also with the concept of social–ecological resilience. The resilience of social systems and the resilience of ecological systems are interconnected in complex, dynamic, and nonlinear relationships. The resilience of human communities and social institutions depends on the resilience of natural communities and ecosystems, and vice-versa [sic]. Interconnected systems affect one another across types of systems ... .

• • •

Given the feedbacks between social systems and ecosystems, fourth-generation environmental law seeks to strengthen the resilience of both ecosystems and human communities by strengthening their adaptive capacity. A resilient system has enough flexibility, redundancy, and learning capacity to adapt to disturbances and surprises without collapsing or flipping into a fundamentally different system.

However, resilience is not always a normatively desirable goal. Science does not dictate maintaining the resilience of any particular systems, because systems can function in more than one state and disturbances will inevitably force at least some changes to systems. Normatively, we do not want to enhance or even maintain the resilience of some systems, such as brutal dictatorships, patterns of injustice, landscapes or waterscapes dominated by aggressive invasive species (e.g., kudzu, Asian carp), or environmentally harmful consumer behaviors. Moreover, rigid legal systems can preserve their status quo by resisting change while simultaneously undermining the resilience and functions of ecosystems and other institutions.

Nonetheless, society values the resilience of many ecosystems and human communities. We desire that democracy, just laws, native ecosystems, and local economies thrive and be resilient to disturbances. Waters teeming with aquatic life are preferable to turbid or eutrophic waters. Increasingly, social–ecological resilience is replacing sustainability as the primary desired policy goal of environmental law and related fields of law and policy.

• • •

Despite its promise, fourth-generation environmental law may prove to be quite disappointing for several reasons. First, it might simply be an additive phenomenon and not truly transformational. This would mean that it would help to improve systemic resilience and adaptive capacity in incremental or small-scale ways but not be adequate to facilitate the navigation of communities and ecosystems through changes, disturbances, and instabilities.

Second, fourth-generation environmental law might under-protect both ecosystems and human communities because it lacks sufficiently clear, mandatory standards for decisions and actions. Flexibility and adaptive capacity without any rules, standards, or accountability mechanisms to constrain this flexibility could facilitate behaviors and policies that favor uncontrolled exploitation of and harm to the environment for short-term gain.

Third, complexity is complex. Fourth-generation environmental law might contemplate the complexity of interconnected social–ecological systems, but this acknowledgement is not adequate by itself to build resilient institutions and produce adaptive responses to this complexity. The environmental problems that American society faces now, and will face in the future, will be difficult to solve or manage, regardless of which generation of environmental law is being used.

Finally, one of the most persistent and frustrating limitations of adaptive management, planning, law, and governance is the failure to translate the theory of feedback loops into the reality of feedback loops. In most examples there is very little creation of formal, mandatory processes of monitoring, assessment, learning, and adaptation of decisions based on lessons learned from monitoring and assessment. This is just another type of standardless flexibility: governance experimentation without rigorous methods and processes for assessing the outcomes of the experiments and making changes to governance decisions based on those outcomes.

Each of these reasons why fourth-generation environmental law might be disappointing and inadequate has a corresponding reason why fourth-generation environmental law is promising and could be helpful. First, environmental law and governance are evolutionary by nature. What might appear to be merely incremental and small-scaled changes in systemic capacity could turn out to be significant, even transformational, over time.

Second, fourth-generation environmental law's use of resilience science allows for the development and application of rigorous standards that are better matched to social–ecological complexity and dynamism than rigid rules and standards aiming to sustain or preserve environments in their existing state or restore them exactly to some pre-disturbance state. ...

Third, social–ecological complexity is a reality that cannot be "solved" or simplified by social engineering. Thus, environmental law frameworks and features that acknowledge and are built around social–ecological complexity are more promising than those that either ignore or challenge this reality. Fourth-generation environmental law is an attempt to deal with social–ecological complexity.

Finally, fourth-generation environmental law is characterized by informal and emergent feedback loops through iterative governance processes and community learning.

NOTES AND QUESTIONS

1. Do you agree that the complex nature of environmental problems facing Canada and the global community makes sustainability, as the central goal of environmental laws and policies, a "failing fulcrum" and increasingly futile? What are some examples of Canadian environmental laws that take a preservationist or restorationist approach and are based on an assumption of stationarity?

2. What are some of the implications of changing from a focus on sustainability to a focus on resilience? Would such a change necessarily incorporate the concept of equity—either between communities today or for future generations?

3. Conceptualizing our current epoch as the "Anthropocene" to frame governance has generated significant critique. Some of the key problems with the concept are reviewed in Charles Stubblefield, "Managing the Planet: The Anthropocene, Good Stewardship, and the Empty Promise of a Solution to Ecological Crisis" (2018) 8:2 Societies 1. He notes (at 6):

[B]oth the term Anthropocene and the discourse that commonly surrounds it are, as has been widely noted, highly problematic ... obscuring as much as it reveals, reifying the same Cartesian dualism separating humanity from nature that it professes to transcend, misinterpreting and misrepresenting historical change, variability, and conflict, and agglomerating and homogenizing humanity as uniformly and innately at odds with and destructive toward its natural surroundings and the other beings that reside within them.

4. A shift in environmental law toward adaptive governance is also contested. Some of the serious limits to adopting adaptive governance as the primary future direction of environmental law are reviewed in Eric Biber, "Adaptive Management and the Future of Environmental Law" (2013) 46 Akron L Rev 933.

5. What changes would have to be made to the existing framework of Canadian environmental laws to recognize resilience as a core value and to incorporate a "more adaptive management," planning, or governance approach?

There is by no means a consensus that resilience should become a central objective of environmental policy and law, displacing sustainability. Some of the criticisms are outlined in the following extract.

KATRINA BROWN, "GLOBAL ENVIRONMENTAL CHANGE I: A SOCIAL TURN FOR RESILIENCE?"
(2014) 38:1 Progress in Human Geography 107 at 109 and 114

Yet resilience ideas ... have generated a chorus of disapproval from different sources. ... First, there is the failure to recognize resilience as socially contingent, rarely addressing the question of "resilience for whom?"; second, its mainstream usage is conservative, focused on the persistence of a "system"; third, it focuses on a system which is disturbed by external or exogenous forces, so it underplays the internal, endogenous and social dynamics of the system. ...

A common criticism is that resilience fails to take account of politics and power relations. ... First, in considering resilience as an end or an outcome of action, much literature on SES [social ecological systems] assumes there is consensus on the "desired state" or that a desired state even exists. Second, resilience as a process overlooks conflicts over resources and the importance of power asymmetries. Thus, in focusing on management of ecosystem services for human well-being and development, resilience studies to date have not adequately considered whose needs are being met and the politics of their distribution and management. ...

• • •

... While resilience ideas and applications are disputed and critiqued, I suggest that its multiple meanings and interpretations can—and should—result in rich scholarship and discussion. In many ways, resilience is similar to sustainability, in that the very malleability and plasticity of the term itself means that it can act as a boundary object or bridging concept, but may also be co-opted by different interests. However, the creative alternatives to which resilience has contributed are significant and surprising, opening important debates and space for discussion about uncertain futures.

Critical scholarship, including Indigenous scholarship and socio-historical and post-colonial studies, is central to the re-envisioning of environmental law and policy. (Refer to Chapter 12 of this book.)

The call for deep reform in line with "green legal theory" is outlined in the following excerpt.

MICHAEL M'GONIGLE & LOUISE TAKEDA,
"THE LIBERAL LIMITS OF ENVIRONMENTAL LAW:
A GREEN LEGAL CRITIQUE"
(2013) 30 Pace Envtl L Rev 1005 at 1112-15 [footnotes omitted]

Despite the depth of the present critique, the development of a green legal theory [GLT] toward which this critique points ultimately is not directed to a rejection of environmental law but its transformation within a larger framework of theoretical understanding and strategic action. As we have acknowledged from the start, GLT is certainly not seeking to replace the role of environmental law as *resistance*, although it would definitely question its role *as reformer*. Given a new understanding of the limitations of environmental law's capacity for prospective action, a corollary need exists to open a new, critical, and theoretically-informed [*sic*] landscape beyond intra-systemic "reform" and toward larger "re-forms." Still addressing the real world of the present but opening up the discourse, GLT should help to unveil a "new narrative" of our past, a more informed context for environmental action in our present, new imaginaries of possible futures and, above all, new strategies for getting there. In the process, the *practice* of environmental law would evolve into a *praxis*, that is, a practice that is theoretically informed and committed to manifesting where that theory leads.

Neither can this discussion be dismissed as environmental lawyers "being realistic" while green legal theorists engage in mere speculation. As we have argued, social practice without an explicit theoretical frame is blind, and easily leads to outcomes that contradict its own avowed goals as environmental law now does with its promulgation of carbon taxes, ecosystem pricing, green energy, and so on. Action without the right frame is akin to an American in London in a hurry to cross the road, looking left as he steps off the curb, not having taken the time to learn the new frame that demands that one must look in the other direction because cars there are on the "wrong" side of the road. The result is mission failure. At the same time, social theory without a practical commitment easily becomes detached and self-indulgent. Having said that, however, the yawning gap that exists in critical legal theory provides sufficient justification on its own for GLT in its general green(*ing*) function to address all aspects of the modern legal order, not just environmental law. GLT has immense practical value, for example, in helping to understand why democracy is necessarily imperiled and how we might begin to address new "constitutive" arrangements that could actively constitute new economic and political imaginaries. At more immediate levels of action, it would situate environmental reforms (for example, for the industrial sectors discussed in the opening pages of this article) within an agenda of the broader, post-industrial re-formation. In this task, it would also help identify principles not for legal law reform but for what might be seen as the re-formation of culturally constitutive logics. Merely by way of illustration, such principles might include: radical demand reduction (as compared with incremental eco-efficiency); displacement of capital dependence (as compared with capital growth); substantive project assessments (as compared with price-based assessments) and so on. As guiding principles for responding to climate change, their goal would not be to internalize or create new rights that legitimate the problematic context, but to re-form that context. Thus, green legal re-form would explicitly work not for energy efficiency for a new generation of hybrid cars but to escape the "social economy" of automobility.

In his recent book about climate change [*The Politics of Climate Change* (Cambridge; Malden, Mass: Polity, 2009)], Anthony Giddens complained that "we have no politics of climate change" because the politics being applied to this global threat remain rooted in a world now past, a world still stuck in a set of naturalized economic and political realities that lead people to believe that a deal to resolve climate change will "be reached as soon as the nations of the world see reason." Such a world would, of course, turn to environmental law to enshrine this reason—but this world is now past. If there is no politics, there is certainly no law of climate change, just a law of symptoms. This paper has begun to hint at the vast new conceptual, analytical, and practical spaces that need to be opened up, spaces that would allow environmental lawyers to make common cause with the wide new array of constituencies and knowledges pointing the way to the needed "legal" reformations. Humanity is at a turning point, but we fail to embrace its possibilities. Instead, in the well-worn phrase of American cultural theorist, Frederic Jameson, "it is easier to imagine the end of the world than the end of capitalism." Like Giddens, Mitchell [Timothy Mitchell, "Carbon Democracy" (2009) 38 Econ & Soc'y 399] comments that "the democratic machineries that emerged to govern the age of carbon energy seem to be unable to address the processes that may end it." At the liberal limits of environmental law, the time is upon us to move beyond a bounded heritage so that we might let loose new imaginaries without which our shared goals will fade from the world.

Some authors and practitioners have focused on the need to move from environmental law to "ecological law," sometimes expressed as "Earth jurisprudence." The core principle behind this shift is to move from a system that is human-centred to one that is ecocentric, focusing on justice across human communities as well as justice for other species and future generations, and supporting the integrity of natural systems.

An ecocentric approach to law has been discussed by many authors. One of the leading scholars in this area is Cormac Cullinan. In *Wild Law: A Manifesto for Earth Justice* (Devon, UK: Green Books, 2003), Cullinan charts the need for a new philosophy of governance and law—an "Earth jurisprudence"—to be able to transcend the limits of existing systems that facilitate and legitimize the exploitation and destruction of Earth by humans. In his view, these existing systems are based on false premises, in particular the "core falsehood" that "we humans are separate from our environment and that we can flourish even as the health of the Earth deteriorates" (at 45). He notes that human laws must operate within the framework of principles that govern the universe and must be designed to "promote human behaviour that contributes to the health and integrity not only of human society, but also of the wider ecological communities and of Earth itself" (at 90). See also Peter Burdon, "Wild Law: The Philosophy of Earth Jurisprudence" (2010) 35:2 Alternative LJ 62 and "A Theory of Earth Jurisprudence" (2012) 37 Australian J of Leg Philosophy 28; and Jamie Murray, "Earth Jurisprudence, Wild Law, Emergent Law: The Emerging Field of Ecology and Law—Part 1" (2014) 35:3 Liverpool L Rev 215 and "Earth Jurisprudence, Wild Law, Emergent Law: The Emerging Field of Ecology and Law—Part 2" (2015) 36:2 Liverpool L Rev 105.

The rationale for "ecological law" as the necessary approach to the future of environmental law, as well as its basic elements, is set out in the following manifesto, which has been adopted by leading environmental law practitioners.

OSLO MANIFESTO FOR ECOLOGICAL LAW AND GOVERNANCE
(Adopted at the International Union for Conservation of Nature
[IUCN] World Commission on Environmental Law [WCEL] Ethics
Specialist Group Workshop, IUCN Academy of Environmental Law
Colloquium, University of Oslo, 21 June 2016), online: *Ecological
Law and Governance Association* <https://www.elga.world/
oslo-manifesto/>

FROM ENVIRONMENTAL LAW TO ECOLOGICAL LAW: A CALL FOR RE-FRAMING LAW AND GOVERNANCE

1. Environmental law is at a crossroads. As a legal discipline, environmental law has always aimed at protecting the natural environment and ecological systems. Yet, in fifty years of its history environmental law has failed to halt ecological degradation and continues to fall short of its objectives. The Earth's ecological systems deteriorate at an accelerating rate with no signs of regaining their integrity and sustainability.

2. There are many reasons for the growing ecological crisis. Among them are the dynamics of economic growth, population development and overconsumption, aptly described as the "Great Acceleration." However, there are also reasons peculiar to the philosophy, ontology and methodology underpinning environmental law.

3. Environmental law is rooted in modern Western law with its origins in religious anthropocentrism, Cartesian dualism, philosophical individualism and ethical utilitarianism. In our ecological age, this worldview is out-dated [sic] and counterproductive, yet it continues to dominate the way environmental laws are conceived and interpreted. Most notably, nature is perceived as "the other" overlooking ecological interdependencies and human–nature interrelations.

4. Among the flaws of environmental law are its anthropocentric, fragmented and reductionist characteristics. It is not only blind to ecological interdependencies, but also politically weak as it competes with other, more powerful areas of law such as individualized property and corporate rights. As a consequence, the legal system has become imbalanced and unable to secure the physical and biological conditions, upon which all human and other life depends.

5. To overcome the flaws of environmental law, mere reform is not enough. We do not need more laws, but different laws from which no area of the legal system is exempted. The ecological approach to law is based on ecocentrism, holism, and intra-/intergenerational and interspecies justice. From this perspective, or worldview, the law will recognise ecological interdependencies and no longer favour humans over nature and individual rights over collective responsibilities. Essentially, ecological law internalizes the natural living conditions of human existence and makes them the basis of all law, including constitutions, human rights, property rights, corporate rights and state sovereignty.

6. The difference between environmental law and ecological law is not merely a matter of degree, but fundamental. The former allows human activities and aspirations to determine whether or not the integrity of ecological systems should be protected. The latter requires human activities and aspirations to be determined by the need to protect the integrity of ecological systems. Ecological integrity becomes a precondition for human aspirations and a fundamental principle of law. In other words, ecological law reverses the principle of human dominance over nature, which the current iteration of environmental law tends to reinforce, to a principle of human responsibility for nature. This reversed logic is arguably the key challenge of the Anthropocene.

7. The transformation from environmental law to ecological law will not occur without people committed to the change. For environmental law scholars such commitment includes critical self-reflection, imagination, courage and a willingness to become truly eco-literate. ...

8. The approach of ecological law is, however, not new. Its foundational values and principles have guided ancient cultures and [I]ndigenous peoples in all parts of the world and are also part of the pre-industrial history of Western civilisation. ...

9. The values and principles of ecological law are expressed in ecocentric jurisprudence (e.g. rights of nature, "Mother Earth" rights, Earth jurisprudence, ecofeminism, ecological legal theory, "environmental law methodology") and are also present in constitutional and international theory ...

10. This makes it possible to identify ecological approaches to law with a view to create [*sic*] a unifying framework for promoting effective law and governance. As we face disintegrating ecological and socio-economic systems and in light of greater, but still incomplete understanding of how ecosystems function and maintain their resilience, now is the time for creating an alternative.

As noted in the Oslo Manifesto, one way of operationalizing this concept is through the recognition of legal rights for nature, as discussed in the following excerpt. (Refer also to Chapter 20 of this book.)

DAVID R BOYD, THE RIGHTS OF NATURE: A LEGAL REVOLUTION THAT COULD SAVE THE WORLD
(Toronto: ECW Press, 2017) at 230-31

To move from exploiting nature to respecting nature requires a massive transformation of law, education, economics, philosophy, religion, and culture. The shift is underway but will take years, probably decades, to be implemented. And yet it is a scientific fact that all living things share common ancestors, and all depend on air, water, earth, and sunlight to survive. Humans must acknowledge that we are related to millions of other amazing species. We must increase our understanding of and appreciation for their intelligence, abilities, and communities.

Rights for nature impose responsibilities on humans to modify our behaviour in ways that will re-establish a mutually beneficial relationship. Recognizing and respecting nature's rights does not put an end to all human activities, but requires eliminating or modifying those which inflict suffering on animals, threaten the survival of species, or undermine the ecological systems that all life depends on. The precise meaning and effects of recognizing the rights of nature will be worked out through community conversations, scholarly dialogue, public and political debates, negotiation, and, where necessary, litigation, just as all novel legal concepts evolve.

It should be obvious that nature's rights cannot be reconciled with endless economic growth, consumerism, unconstrained globalization, or laissez-faire capitalism. We cannot continue to prioritize property rights and corporate rights, burn fossil fuels at current rates, or perpetuate today's linear economy that treats nature as a commodity rather than a community. ...

Perhaps the most critical missing piece of the puzzle is an informed public willing and able to close the gap between their actions and their professed love of animals, endangered species, and nature. ...

Many questions remain regarding the impact of recognizing nature's rights. Yet there is a widespread and growing sense that treating nature as a mere warehouse of resources for our use, and a repository for our pollution and garbage, is fundamentally wrong.

NOTES AND QUESTIONS

1. Do you agree that environmental law requires a fundamental transformation to achieve its goals? What steps could and should be taken to bring about a fundamental shift in the theory and practice of environmental law? Are "critical self-reflection, imagination, courage and a willingness to become truly eco-literate" sufficient to meet this challenge? How can resistance to such a shift be overcome?

2. What are some examples of the recognition of rights for nature? How can rights for nature be adopted within a Canadian context?

3. What should the objectives of environmental law be in the future? What is the "alternative" future for Canadian environmental law?

4. Some scholars have suggested that the "ecocentric" approach to environmental law is as problematic as the anthropocentric one, in that both equally

[fail] to capture ... the highly complex, non-linear, and irreducibly genealogical field of discourse and practice that environmental law is. ...

Anthropocentrism ... refers to a particular subset of humanity that historically has colonized, exploited and plundered both other human communities and the non-human world ...

[E]cocentrism's legal trajectory remains thickly embedded *within* modernity, at least to the extent that ecocentrism is often associated with the ethical and legal framework of *rights* (eg [*sic*] "rights of nature"—but of *what* "nature"'?). A rights-based strategy risks locking the framework of legal analysis within a cultural and legal horizon premised on a subject–object grammar and maintains an inevitable linkage with *human* rights and their anthropocentric frame of reference.

(Vita De Lucia, "Beyond Anthropocentrism and Ecocentrism: A Biopolitical Reading of Environmental Law" (2017) 8:2 J of Human Rights & the Envt 181 at 189-90 [footnotes omitted].)

IV. RECENT LEGISLATION

With the *Greenhouse Gas Pollution Pricing Act*, SC 2018, c 12, s 186, the Canadian federal government adopted a national carbon pollution pricing system for the first time. The mechanisms under the first two parts of the Act apply to fuels and to industrial emissions. Using economic measures to advance environmental policy, the Act represents a new approach for the federal government, which has long been criticized for lagging behind other jurisdictions in the use of economic instruments. Some provinces have challenged the federal government's constitutional authority to adopt the Act. While court decisions to date have upheld the constitutionality of the Act, there will remain some uncertainty until the issue is finally determined. If ultimately upheld, the Act would clarify the federal government's authority to use similar instruments to advance other environmental policies.

Another recently enacted Act, the *Impact Assessment Act*, SC 2019, c 28, s 1, came into force in August 2019, replacing the federal environmental assessment regime. Although the process will continue to apply primarily to individual projects, the minister of the environment has the authority to require regional assessments and strategic assessments of policy, creating potential opportunities for developing more integrated and holistic approaches to policy.

For impact assessments of projects, the new Act has among its purposes those of fostering sustainability; protecting the components of the environment as well as health, social, and economic conditions; integrating science and Indigenous knowledge into decision-making; and encouraging innovation. The mandate of all authorities under the Act is to exercise their powers in a manner that fosters sustainability, respects the government's commitments with respect to the rights of Indigenous peoples, and applies the precautionary principle. As set out in s 22 of the Act, an assessment must identify and take into account a broad range of factors in determining whether a project is in the public interest, including "the intersection of sex and gender with other identity factors" in order to assess the potential disproportionate impact on women and groups defined by factors such as age, socio-economic status, ethnicity, and disability. The tailored impact statement guidelines issued by the Impact Assessment Agency of Canada provide detail on the range of "valued components" that must be identified and the principles that must be applied in considering the impacts, both positive and negative, on these components, including the interconnectedness and interdependence of human–ecological systems and the well-being of present and future generations.

Certainly, the new legislation has the potential to open up federal environmental decisions to broader, more integrated considerations. There continues to be an emphasis on sustainability as a key objective of federal policy, and individual and community well-being are central decision-making criteria. A more ecocentric focus is not precluded and may well emerge under the new mandate.